THE LAST CENTURY OF SEA POWER

THE LAST CENTURY OF SEA POWER

Volume Two: From Washington to Tokyo, 1922–1945

H. P. Willmott

INDIANA UNIVERSITY PRESS

BLOOMINGTON AND INDIANAPOLIS

This book is a publication of

Indiana University Press
Office of Scholarly Publishing
Herman B Wells Library 350
1320 E. 10th Street
Bloomington, IN 47405 USA

www.iupress.indiana.edu

♾ The paper used in this publication meets the minimum requirements of the American National Standard for Information Sciences—Permanence of Paper for Printed Library Materials, ANSI Z39.48-1992.

Manufactured in the United States of America

The Library of Congress has catalogued the first volume in this series as follows:

Willmott, H. P.
The last century of sea power : from Port Arthur to Chanak, 1894–1922 / H.P. Willmott.
p. cm.
Includes bibliographical references and index.
ISBN 978-0-253-35214-9 (cloth : alk. paper) 1. Naval history, Modern—19th century. 2. Naval history, Modern—20th century. I. Title.
D362.W68 2008
359'.0309041—dc22
2008015018

2 3 4 5 15 14

Dedicated to FY1645
and in praise of
Dissent, Uncertainty, and Tolerance

O lente lente currite equis nocti
and
to the memory of Everton, Sherry, Kondor,
Jamie, Suki, Lancaster, and Junior

CONTENTS

CHAPTER APPENDIXES

MAPS AND A DIAGRAM

TABLES

ACKNOWLEDGMENTS

In the first volume of *The Last Century of Sea Power* there was a preface that set out the terms of reference of this work, specifically the various considerations that over time established the basis of this work. This preface is not the place to repeat such matters and hence what was in the first volume a preface and acknowledgement in this volume should be no more than the acknowledgement section.

I would specifically acknowledge and offer my sincere and unreserved gratitude for all the help and advice I received from Ola Bøe Hansen, Hasegawa Rei, Paul Latawski, Captain Francesco Loriga, and Tohmatsu Haruo and from Jennie Wraight and Iain Mackenzie, and from Anthony Clayton, Sarandis Papadopoulos, and Steven Weingartner, and with these individuals I would add those persons who were always at my side that went beyond the call of friendship, namely Michael and Sara Barrett, Bernard Cole, Michael Coles, Gerard Roncolato, William Spencer and Andrea Johnson and family, John Andreas and Tine Olsen, Jack and Gee Sweetman, and Spencer C. and Beverly Tucker. To all of these people I would simply state my thanks and appreciation for help and camaraderie that are beyond my poor powers to acknowledge properly.

I would also acknowledge the support and encouragement provided by various colleagues and friends in a period of very considerable personal and professional misfortune and without whose quiet companionship what was bad might well have been nigh-impossible. Among those I would acknowledge my debt of gratitude to Tim Bean, Patrick Birks, Nigel and Martine de Lee, Paul Harris, Cliff Krieger, Jim Mattis, Lars Neilsen, George Raach, Kyle Sinisi, Frederick Snow, Patrick and Jennifer Speelman, David Vance, John Votaw, and David White, and with this acknowledgement I would state my hope that this book is some small token of my appreciation and esteem.

I also wish to acknowledge my debt to those without whose patience, tact, and literary ability this book would probably have gone the way of many of the ships cited in these pages. Specifically I would wish to acknowledge my debts to Robert Sloan and Brian Herrmann of Indiana University Press, to Keith Chaffer for his professionalism and imaginative work upon the maps, and to the library personnel who professionally and personally have helped me at every stage of proceedings, Ken Franklin, Andrew Orgill, and John Pearce: I trust they will accept this poor acknowledgement of their support and efforts.

There remains one group that always appears in my acknowledgements section and for one reason: they have been the means of ensuring continuing sanity. I would acknowledge my debt to and love for my beloved woofers. Would that Everton, Sherry, Kondor, Jamie, Suki, Lancaster, and Junior be at peace and together, and in terms of my present debt and love for Mishka, Cassie, and Ozzie, and for Yanya, I would merely express my hope that much time will pass before they join their predecessors and chase together across the celestial fields.

H. P. Willmott
Englefield Green
Surrey
United Kingdom
4 October 2009

THE LAST CENTURY OF SEA POWER

PART 1

NAVAL RACES AND WARS

CHAPTER ONE

INTRODUCTION: WASHINGTON, LONDON, AND TWO VERY SEPARATE WARS, 1921–1941

Arms races are not the cause of rivalries and wars but rather the reflection of conflicting ambition and intent, though inevitably they compound and add to these differences. The First World War was not the product of Anglo-German naval rivalry, though this was one of the major factors that determined Britain's taking position in the ranks of Germany's enemies, and most certainly it was a major factor in producing the growing sense of instability within Europe in the decade prior to 1914. But if the naval race was indeed one of the factors that made for war in 1914—although it should be noted that the most dangerous phase of this rivalry would seem to have passed by 1914—then there is the obvious problem of explaining the war in 1939–1941, in that the greater part of the inter-war period, between 1921 and 1936, was marked by a very deliberate policy of naval limitation on the part of the great powers. Admittedly the arrangements that were set in place in various treaties had lapsed by 1937, and a naval race had begun that most certainly was crucially important in terms of Japanese calculations in 1940 and 1941 and indeed was critical in the decision to initiate war in the Pacific. In summer 1941, as the Japanese naval command was obliged to consider the consequences of its own actions and the full implications of the U.S. Congress having passed the Two-Ocean Naval Expansion Act in July 1940, the Imperial Navy, the Kaigun, was caught in a go-now-or-never dilemma, and it, like its sister service, simply could not admit the futility and pointlessness of past endeavors and sacrifices. But, of course, not a few of these endeavors and sacrifices had been military and Asian and most definitely were not naval and Pacific.

* * *

The obvious problem that attends any attempt to set out the course of naval history in the twentieth century is the place that the Second World War has come to occupy in popular perception. We as societies look to the two world wars, and specifically the Second World War, as the yardsticks against which other conflicts are measured, but that is exactly the wrong way to consider these conflicts. Perhaps the more relevant way of considering the twentieth century, warfare, and the two world wars is to start from the premise that these wars were so very different in so many ways from wars that came before and since that they should be regarded as exceptions and discounted from consideration as a basis of comparison other than with and against each other. But such matters really are of small account when set alongside what should be the proper consideration of the Second World War, and on two very different counts.

The first is that really there was no such thing as the Second World War. What is regarded as the Second World War was two partially overlapping conflicts that were largely separate from one another, though their common outcome and the fact that after 1941 certain powers were involved in both wars represent points where the two conflicts joined as one. The first of these two conflicts originated in eastern Asia, between China and Japan, and dates if not from September 1931—which is the date when the Japanese official histories begin their nation's story—then certainly from July 1937 with the Lukouchiao, or Marco Polo Bridge, Incident and the start of Japan's "special undeclared war" against her continental neighbor. The second conflict is the European conflict that began in September 1939. Neither of these two conflicts, however, represented a war: both were a series of campaigns that only came together in the course of 1941, for very different reasons and under very different circumstances. Of course such a perspective can be challenged, and rightly so on the obvious grounds: these were wars in terms of national commitments and in terms of both the nature and conduct of these conflicts. But what was in place until 1941 was a series of campaigns, some successive and others concurrent, that were joined in fearful array in the course of 1941.

For example, in eastern Asia after July 1937 a series of campaigns saw the Japanese conquest of much of northern and central China. Then, with the nationalist regime at Chungking refusing to enter negotiations that would confirm Japan in her position of primacy, two strategic bombing campaigns in 1939 and 1940 likewise failed to force the Chinese leadership to the conference table and to acceptance of defeat and acknowledgement of Japanese primacy and leadership in east Asia.[1] But thereafter, what had been a single conflict came to embrace five very different parts that were separated from one another to a surprising degree: the continuing conflict within China; a conflict throughout southeast Asia; a conflict in the western Pacific that was primarily concerned with fleet action and landing operations and that in its final stages embraced the bombardment of the home islands by carrier aircraft and warships and involved a strategic bombing offensive; a conflict in the western Pacific that was directed against Japanese shipping; and in the final stages, the campaign in Manchuria and northern China that followed from the Soviet Union's entry into the war against Japan. To these military aspects of what was the Japanese war may be added two other conflicts: first, the political conflict throughout east and southeast Asia that was the product of the Japanese aim of creating a new order throughout these areas and that necessarily involved the attempt to mobilize the will and moral force of the peoples of east and southeast Asia to support the Japanese cause, and second, an economic dimension to the national efforts that obviously extended beyond the campaign against Japanese shipping.

In a sense, the situation within Europe was much simpler, or at least can be defined in simpler terms: between September 1939 and May 1941 Germany fought and won a series of campaigns against individual enemies, each of which was, in terms of demographic and economic resources, geographical position, and military power, much inferior to Germany. As long as Hitler was able to dictate the terms of reference of these conflicts, German success was so great that by the end of May 1941 the German domination of the continental mainland made the German national position all but unchallengeable, at least by the only state that remained at war with Germany. There was in military terms one element of continuity, and that was the war at sea, but with respect to the terms of reference supplied by Hitler, the events of September 1939–April 1941 did not represent the real war, which was the *Volksgemainschaft*. The struggle to achieve racial purity was more important than campaigns per se, though obviously they were related, because Aryan supremacy could not be achieved except by conquest of inferior peoples. In that sense struggle and campaigns were the two sides of a single coin, but in the European conflict's first phases, when Germany was able to fight as it would, what it fought was a series of campaigns largely separated from one another, rather than a war.

This second matter is perhaps a more delicate one, involving national perspective, and specifically American and British national mythology in terms of these countries' part in the fight, and hence contribution to victory. In terms of the British, the problem can be defined very simply: if, as Prime Minister Winston Churchill (1874–1965) stated, 1940 really represented Britain's finest hour, then what came next has to be anti-climatic, and one would suggest that there has been a deliberate sheltering behind the events of the Second World War to ensure continuing national importance and proper status. But in looking at the British military contribution to victory one confronts a troublesome point: between February 1941 and May 1943, in the course of the North African campaign, first the British and then (after November 1942) the British and Americans accounted for fourteen German dead a day: at such a rate, to have inflicted the total number of military dead that Germany incurred between 1 September 1939 and 12 May 1945 would have taken the British military 588 years. Perhaps that is an overstatement—it may be that it would have only taken 587 years—but the basic point is that while Britain was important in certain aspects of this anti-German struggle, most notably in providing continuity between 1939 and 1941, in the role of democratic beacon at a time when representative government was all but extinguished throughout Europe,[2] and in terms of a military commitment that was primarily naval, air, and positional, the British military contribution to Allied victory in terms of conquest and the inflicting of telling commitment and losses on Germany was minimal. Lest the point be doubted, the British naval dimension in Germany's defeat was basically irrelevant: Germany was not defeated because it lost the war at sea.

The same basic point may be made about the American dimension. There is no disputing the simple fact that the most important single national contribution to victory over Japan was that of the United States. In terms of the German war, however, the American contribution helped complete the Allied victory, but it was only a contribution and not cause: it was not until the summer of 1944 that the United States was able to deploy armies in the field in northwest Europe, and by that time the issue of victory and defeat had been resolved, and on the Eastern Front. American air power and support for allies possessed more than *en passant* importance, but in Germany's final defeat a whole number of matters came together, and perhaps the most important single factor was one very seldom afforded much in the way of serious consideration. The nature of the German regime and system precluded the consolidation of victories and the winning of endorsement and support across a continent; the result was that despite access to economic resources and industrial infrastructure not markedly inferior to that of the United States, Germany was out-produced by Britain until 1942 and thereafter was condemned to economic, industrial, and financial defeat as American production was added to the scales. But if there were important political and economic aspects of Germany's defeat, in the final analysis that defeat had to be registered on the battlefield, and the most important single national contribution to victory over Germany was that of the Soviet Union, and at a horrendous price. Many statistics can be quoted, but perhaps two possess suitable poignancy: the total American dead in the Second World War was less than the number of Soviet second lieutenants who were killed, and of every hundred Soviet males aged eighteen in 1941 just three remained alive at war's end.

The problem that the Second World War presents in terms of this second volume of *The Last Century of Sea Power* can be defined very simply: how to separate the story of two conflicts without following well-worn paths. The answer should be to tell the story not of the successful application of victorious sea power but of the lessening effectiveness of defeated sea power, the separation between the German and Japanese wars then becoming self-evident; but more interesting would be, in the case of the European war, to look at the naval matters neglected over the years. But first the inter-war period.

CHAPTER TWO

WASHINGTON AND LONDON

Allies are not necessarily friends, and victory, or defeat, inevitably weakens the links that made for alliances and coalitions: the conflicting interests held in check by common need invariably reassert themselves, often with greater force than previously was the case. the First World War saw the passing of four empires, three of them multi-national empires, and the triumph of what in July 1919 were the five leading naval powers in the world, but those five powers' wartime cooperation and common cause did not survive such episodes as the "Naval Battle of Paris" and the negotiations that produced the treaties that closed the First World War.

* * *

The period between the end of the war and the Washington conference and treaties, between November 1918 and February 1922, was a strange one in regard to naval power, and primarily for one reason. The war resulted in the elimination of three major navies, those of Germany, Russia, and Austria-Hungary, yet it ended with no fewer than three naval races, if not already ongoing then most certainly in the making: between Britain and the United States, between Japan and the United States, and, somewhat muted, between France and Italy. Leaving aside the latter, which never assumed importance or gained momentum in the twenties, the key development was the emergence of the United States as the greatest power in the world and its declared intention to secure for itself "a navy second to none." To realize such an ambition the U.S. Congress authorized, in the act of 29 August 1916, the construction of no fewer than 162 warships, including 10 battleships, 6 battlecruisers, 10 cruisers, 50 destroyers, and 67 submarines. All of these warships were to be built between 1916 and 1919, and were in addition to a 1915 program that had made provision for 6 battleships, the general intention being that the United States would provide for itself no fewer than 60 battleships and battlecruisers by 1925. In framing its program the U.S. Navy, quite deliberately, had set aside the situation created by general war in Europe in favor of what it considered the "worst-case" possibility that might emerge after this war. What it planned for was the need to guard against either a German-Japanese or an Anglo-Japanese alliance that would be capable of threatening the United States in two oceans and preventing any expansion of American overseas trade. The total of 60 capital ships that were to be acquired by 1925 matched the total that Britain and Japan together might be able to deploy in a war against the United States. The least that could be said about such logic was that it grasped at the exceedingly unlikely in order to justify the manifestly unnecessary.

The program did not survive American involvement in the First World War, when more immediate needs took precedence, but with the end of the war the "second to none" logic reasserted itself, and on two separate counts: internationalism, or at least a Wilsonian version of internationalism tailored to American requirements, and status pointed to a resurrection of the July 1915 program and August 1916 provisions.[1] The crucial point here is that status was not related to any direct or immediate security need. What the United States sought was confirmation of greatness, and in this respect Britain found itself in an unenviable position with war's end. For well over a hundred years Britain's status as a great power, and indeed status as the world's greatest industrial, trading, financial, and naval power, was synonymous with its assured naval superiority over potential enemies. Quite clearly Britain was unwilling to cede pride of place to any nation, not least in the aftermath of the defeat of the second-ranked navy in the world. But British intent to maintain its superiority faced three facts of life. First, Britain—like France and Italy—was morally and physically exhausted as a result of war, and most certainly psychologically spent by its efforts in a way that the United States was not. The total number of American battlefield dead in the First World War was fewer than the number of British missing at Ypres, and in the immediate aftermath of the November 1918 armistice, there could be no question of British pursuit of a course of action that might involve any major war or military undertaking. Second, Britain could not consider any course of action that might involve collision with the one power that had represented its greatest market and source of earnings, that dominated the Caribbean, and that was its greatest creditor. Third, with the end of the war Britain, in effect, had to pick up the bill for having been the first naval power to build dreadnoughts. The British margin of superiority in numbers of capital ships over the German Navy in the First World War and then the United States after the war was primarily vested, depending on perspective, in either aging, first-generation dreadnoughts or battlecruisers, and certainly both were obsolescent. Britain at war's end had ten battleships and four battlecruisers that were armed with 12-in. main armament, were some ten years old, and were hopelessly outclassed in terms of size, armament, protection, and speed by the capital ships that were now in service: for example, the 18.4-knot *Dreadnought,* when it entered service in 1907, was accorded a standard displacement of 17,900 tons and a deep-load displacement of 21,845 tons, whereas the 31.9-knot *Hood,* when it entered service in 1920, recorded comparable figures of 41,200 and 45,200 tons respectively. Simply to maintain existing numbers thus presented Britain with massive problems in terms of both building and cost.

The situation in which Japan found itself in 1918–1920 was even more complicated and difficult. Where one starts an examination of that situation is fraught with difficulty, but the United States' purchase of the Philippines in 1898, which placed it cheek by jowl with Japan in the western Pacific, and the Russo-Japanese War, which in effect left Japan with no potential naval enemy in the western Pacific against which it could measure itself except the United States, were factors. Sufficient for our purpose, however, would be the Imperial Defense Policy statement of April 1907, which defined Russia as Japan's most likely military opponent in eastern Asia but underwrote two sets of demands on the part of the Imperial Japanese Navy (the *Nippon Teikoku Kaigun*). In effect it sanctioned the *taikan kyohoshugi* doctrine, which stressed the importance of acquiring big ships with big guns, in the form of a construction program for eight 20,000-ton dreadnoughts and eight 18,000-ton battlecruisers. The justification for such a program was identified as the U.S. Navy. Both quite deliberately and mendaciously, the latter had been selected as, if not the only possible enemy, then the only potential enemy that could justify programs of the size that the Kaigun sought, and the sequel was perhaps predictable: the April 1907 statement and the Eight-Eight formula form the basis on which Japan started building dreadnoughts and battlecruisers and found itself by the end of World War I in a construction race with the United States.

This had come about partly because of the *taikan kyohoshugi* provision, which meant that successive classes of Japanese capital ships showed massive qualitative improvement; indeed, it is possible to argue that the *Kongo*, *Fuso*, and *Nagato* classes were in their turn the most powerful capital ships in the world. The problem was that by 1916 the Diet refused to authorize more than one battleship and two battlecruisers, at the very time when the United States was vociferously claiming the right to build a fleet "second to none." The implications of American numbers for Japan need no elaboration; suffice it to note that had the U.S. programs been fully implemented, the Kaigun would have been rendered irrelevant. As it was, in 1917 the Kaigun secured authorization for the construction of sixty-three warships, three battleships included, and in 1918 two more battlecruisers were approved. In other words, on the back of the unprecedented prosperity that World War I brought to Japan, the Kaigun secured endorsement in 1917 of what was an Eight-Six program, and in the following year of its full Eight-Eight program. Nonetheless, between 1910 and 1918 fifteen American battleships entered service compared to six Japanese dreadnoughts and four battlecruisers, the Japanese battleship total having to be adjusted downward to take account of the loss of the *Kawachi*, which was destroyed by the explosion of its magazine when in Tokuyama Bay on 12 July 1918. What made the situation even worse for Japan was that even if the early American dreadnoughts were discounted from consideration, Japan's position really did not change much, because in 1918 the United States had another five dreadnoughts under construction, compared to just two being built in Japanese yards. Thus the situation in which Japan found herself was potentially disastrous. Japan had been out-built 3:2 by the United States, and even allowing for the quality of its capital ships, there was no escaping the fact that Japan simply could not match either the immediate 1916 program or the general American intention with its 1925 perspective.

Such a situation was potentially disastrous for both Japan and the United States, but Japan's reaction to the situation in which it found itself was all but willfully perverse. Despite having somehow taken on board the Eight-Eight formula, by 1918 Japan risked being overwhelmed by a United States that, without really trying, had comfortably outstripped it in terms of the number of capital ships built over the last decade. That, of course, was not how most Japanese naval officers saw things. In June 1918 the Japanese government undertook the first revision of its Imperial Defense Policy since 1907. Russia, then in the grip of revolution, remained the enemy on the mainland, and in effect the United States retained its position as the country against which naval provision had to be made. To deal with the American naval challenge, the Kaigun proposed that Japan should accept the Eight-Eight formula over an eight-year period, with the commitment to the building of three capital ships every year.

By this time Kaigun doctrinal orthodoxy had embraced the conclusion that massed battle fleets and extended battle lines were unviable, that in effect no battle formation should consist of more than a couple of divisions numbering more than eight dreadnoughts or battlecruisers. Thus the Kaigun was feeling its way to the idea whereby in eight years it would come into possession of three fleets each with eight capital ships. At the time that the U.S. Navy was thinking in terms of battleships and battlecruisers of unprecedented size and armament, the Kaigun was drafting plans and recasting its designs in order to provide two high-speed battleships (the *Tosa* and *Kaga*) capable of 26.5 knots and armed with ten 16-in. guns in five twin turrets, followed by two more fast battleships (the *Akagi* and *Amagi*) that, on a full-load displacement of 47,000 tons, were to have the same ten 16-in. guns, slightly thinner armor, and, with an almost 50 percent increase in power, a speed of 30 knots. These two ships were authorized in 1919 and laid down in 1920, while their sister ships *Atago* and *Takao* were authorized in 1920 and laid down in 1921. They were deliberately conceived as direct counters to the British *Hood*, then nearing completion, and the American *Saratoga*-class battlecruisers.

These six ships, however, were not the sum of Kaigun aspirations and planning at this time. With various designs being cast and recast and initial appropriations voted, there were two more classes for which plans and designs were being prepared. The first, planned for the 1921 program, was a four-strong class of slightly improved *Tosas*; the second, planned for the 1922 program, was a four-strong class of battleships nearly one hundred feet longer than the members of the *Tosa* class and afforded thicker armor, the same speed, and eight 18-in. guns. All had been assigned their respective shipyards, with the Kure and Yokosuka navy yards and Kawasaki at Kobe and Mitsubishi at Nagasaki each assigned one unit from each class.

* * *

Overall the Japanese situation is cause for a certain wonderment: the fact that Japan was out-built by a potentially decisive margin between 1906 and 1916 seems only to have deepened a commitment to a failed Eight-Eight formula, which, both despite and because of its inadequacies, thereafter was expanded. But at this stage of proceedings there emerged onto center stage a number of other considerations that together were to spell a halt to any naval race and that were to result, in part, in the Washington conference, November 1921–February 1922, and in the naval limitation treaty of 6 February 1922.

* * *

Three of these other considerations were of specific and primary importance. First, there was throughout the world a post-war reaction to any prospect of an arms race. The pre-war Anglo-German naval race was widely regarded as having been a major cause of war in 1914; even if this was somewhat simplistic or mistaken—and arms races are primarily the symptom rather than the illness—there was no mistaking the force of this particular argument in terms of public belief in many allied countries: there was a determination to avoid a new naval race just as there was a general confidence and hope vested in the League of Nations as the means of ensuring peace.

Second, and a point to which reference has been made obliquely with respect to Britain's position, the cost of an individual battleship had more than tripled in little more than a decade; nonetheless, the price, around £7,500,000 or $34,500,000 each, was not altogether excessive.[2] But, of course, the point was not the cost of an individual capital ship: naval construction programs necessarily had to involve many capital ships and their attendant cruisers, destroyers, and auxiliary support shipping, plus, given the growth of size of ships in recent years, major capital programs for expanded slips and docks. By 1921 Britain, Japan, and the United States were committed to programs that would have involved costs of £252,000,000/U.S.$1,152,000,000 for just the required number of capital ships, and herein perspective is provided by a number of related matters. The United States had emerged from the war as industrially and financially the world's greatest power, with the second largest merchant fleet in the world, but the American national debt had risen from about a billion dollars in 1914 to nearly $27 billion in 1919, and in 1918 almost seven dollars in ten of all state spending was financed by borrowing. The political and naval leadership of the United States might insist on the acquisition of "a navy second to none," but such matters as financial orthodoxy, reduced state spending, and general economy pointed in a somewhat different direction. Britain's position was similar and merely reinforces the point: the First World War saw a fifteen-fold increase in state expenditure in Britain. The projected expenditure estimates for 1918–1919 (£3,146,475,568) provided for six votes—spending on the army (£974,033,762), munitions (£562,227,196), the navy (£356,044,688), shipping (£285,466,121), the financing of debt (£281,344,867),[3] and the provision of loans to allies and dominions (£264,575,684)—that were each greater than the sum of state spending in 1913–1914 (£194,994,468), and the loans, munitions, and shipping expenditure had never existed prior to the outbreak of war. By 1919 the British government was in the process of trying to reduce expenditure to a more modest £1,231,076,000 for 1920–1921, a reduction of three-fifths of state spending from the 1918–1919 level, with debt and the armed forces in 1920–1921 accounting for 49.88 percent of all state spending. The desire to return to prewar days carried with it a return not simply to the laissez-faire state but to financial orthodoxy and the lowest possible level of government spending commensurate with real needs—and extra dreadnoughts did not fall into this category.

The third matter is perhaps the most difficult to define and evaluate because it presents perspectives that were not generally held. There were within the major navies schools of thought that questioned the course of confrontation and possible conflict on which their countries and services seemed to be embarked in the aftermath of war. Within Britain there was a general disbelief that the country could set itself on a course that might lead to war with the United States, while in Japan the twenties was the time of "constitutionalism at home, imperialism abroad"; the latter was primarily peaceful and stressed cooperation between powers, not exclusiveness.[4] This period saw the emergence, first as navy minister and subsequently as prime minister, of Admiral Kato Tomosaburo (1861–1923), who was the very embodiment of the belief that the only eventuality that could be worse for Japan than an unrestricted naval construction race with the United States would be war against that country. To Kato an unrestricted naval race could only result in the remorseless and irreversible erosion of Japan's position relative to the United States, and Japan had to seek security through peaceful cooperation and diplomatic arrangements rather than through international rivalry and conquest. The Kaigun itself saw its role as deterrent and, in the event of war, defensive, but individuals such as Kato saw Japan's best interest served not by confrontation and conflict with the United States but by arrangements that limited American construction relative to Japan and that provided the basis of future American recognition and acceptance of Japan's regional naval position.

In the United States there was a large and vehement anti-British lobby that at various times in the twenties proved very important, at least negatively: it could forestall Anglo-American cooperation and agreement. There were many officers within the U.S. Navy of such persuasion, but equally there were many who had been party to wartime cooperation and who were well aware of the pre-war period of collaboration and support between the British and American navies in China and the western and southwest Pacific. There was also those in the U.S. Navy who saw internationalism in racist terms: the United States and Britain, being primarily Anglo-Saxon states and peoples, should not find themselves on opposite sides of the fence. But if this pointed in the direction of détente if not entente between these nations and peoples, then there was the obvious problem. Britain remained allied to one country, Japan, that clearly did not meet requirements, and Japan presented one very specific difficulty for the United States: Japan's acquisition of German possessions in the Pacific north of the Equator placed it astride American lines of communication between the West Coast and the Philippines, or expressed another way, across the U.S. Navy's line of advance from Hawaii to the western Pacific.

But the crucial development in terms of naval matters lay in the public repudiation in the November 1918 election of President Woodrow Wilson (1856–1924) and internationalism and then the refusal of a Republican-controlled Congress to ratify the treaty of Versailles and with it U.S. membership of the League of Nations. The basic point was that a "second to none" navy and an unprecedented U.S. overseas commitment went hand in hand, and once the American public turned its collective back on internationalism, the "second to none" navy was left, metaphorically, if not on the rocks then certainly aground. The November 1920 election resulted in major Republican victories, with Senator Warren Harding (1865–1923) elected with a record 60.32 percent of the poll: if the victory itself was predictable, its margin was not.[5] The election was very deliberately fought, on both sides, over the Wilsonian legacy; with "the return to normalcy" and an overwhelming electoral repudiation of Wilson, the Democrats, and internationalism, the "navy second to none" was very literally dead in the water.

But December 1920 saw the British government adopt a one-power standard, and in that development lay the basis of future limitation. Adopted by the Imperial Conference of June 1921, where Canada advised Britain to end the Japanese alliance and Australia advised Britain to renew it, the espousal of the one-power standard went alongside public indication that the British government intended to call a conference on Pacific and Far Eastern affairs (7 July). At the same time, within the Harding administration a proposal for a naval limitation conference involving Britain, France, Italy, and Japan was under consideration, and with the British government's announcement the two parts came together with the American proposal for a conference that would embrace both subjects, naval limitation and the affairs of east Asia and the Pacific (11 July).

* * *

The Washington conference, attended by nine countries,[6] opened on 12 November 1921 and resulted in the conclusion of seven treaties, of which four were specifically relevant to naval matters, namely, the four-power treaty of 13 December 1921, the nine-power and Sino-Japanese treaties of 4 February 1922, and the naval limitation treaty of 6 February. These treaties were accompanied by the ending of the Anglo-Japanese alliance.

The four-power treaty was an agreement between Britain, France, Japan, and the United States to respect one another's possessions and rights in the Far East and to consult with one another in the event of crisis. As their common date suggests, the nine-power and Sino-Japanese treaties were linked. Under the terms of the first the territorial integrity of China was acknowledged by all parties, certain rights that had been exacted over the years were restored, the promise of restoration to China of various financial provisions that were the prerogative of certain powers was given, and the Open Door policy, so beloved by the United States not least because as the world's greatest industrial power it stood to benefit most, was confirmed. The Sino-Japanese treaty made provision for the Japanese surrender of various rights that it had exacted in Shantung province, that is, captured German concessions that should have been returned to China with the end of the First World War.

The naval limitation treaty limited the size of the battle forces of five major navies by aggregate tonnage and size of individual units. With capital ships limited to a maximum displacement of 35,000 tons and not allowed to carry a main armament larger than the 16-in. gun, Britain was afforded 580,450 tons of capital ships, the United States 500,650 tons, Japan 301,320 tons, France 221,170 tons, and Italy 182,800 tons. There was to be no new construction for ten years, and the replacement of capital ships within twenty years of completion was prohibited, but reconstruction in order to provide for increased defense against air and submarine attack was permitted within the limit of maximum increased dimension of 3,000 tons. With certain provisions to take account of various special circumstances, such as British retention of the *Hood* and the right to build two battleships to balance Japan's right to retain the *Mutsu*, the various scrapping arrangements provided for Britain and the United States ultimately retaining 500,000 tons of capital ships, Japan 300,000 tons, and France and Italy 175,000 tons. Similar arrangements were crafted with reference to aircraft carriers, which were allocated on the basis of 135,000 tons for Britain and the United States, 81,000 tons for Japan, and 60,000 tons for France and Italy, the maximum size of a carrier being 27,000 tons with provision for all powers being allowed to build two of 33,000 tons subject to aggregate totals remaining within overall quota allowances. Because aircraft carriers, on account of their newness, were deemed experimental warships, they could be replaced at any time, again subject to aggregate totals remaining within overall quota allowances. There were, however, no provisions limiting the aggregate tonnage totals, numbers, and displacement of cruisers, destroyers, and submarines. There was agreement between the Americans and British on a 10,000-ton displacement and 8-in. gun main armament for cruisers, but not on the crucial question of replacements: the American position was that cruisers should be afforded a seventeen-year life expectancy, but the British, after a hard-working war, needed to replace units on a shorter time scale. Likewise, there was general agreement that destroyers should not exceed 1,500-ton displacement, with destroyer leaders afforded an additional 500 tons, but there was no other agreement about overall numbers and aggregate tonnage, and no agreement about submarines, in terms of their being either banned or limited by size and numbers. These matters, however, were to be left to future conferences; at the Geneva conference in 1927 the cruisers issue again, for a number of reasons, would defy resolution.

* * *

The overall result of the Washington limitation arrangement can be summarized very briefly: Britain scrapped and the others did not build. That is not wholly accurate, but the general sense is correct, and the advantage conferred to Britain under these arrangements can be gauged by the fact that Britain scrapped seventeen capital ships and canceled contracts on four 48,000-ton battlecruisers, whereas the United States scrapped four dreadnoughts and cancelled contracts on eleven capital ships with another two units—the intended battlecruisers *Lexington* and *Saratoga*—converted to aircraft carriers. Inevitably the fact that Britain was obliged to scrap so many capital ships was cause for denunciation on the part of many of its naval officers and the naval lobby, but the fact was that at war's end the British, having lost five capital ships during the war, had forty dreadnoughts and battlecruisers,[7] plus one more battleship under construction. Of these, ten dreadnoughts and two battlecruisers were laid down before or in 1909 and were armed with 12-in. guns, and all had ceased to be with front-line formations by the time of the Washington conference; indeed, two, the *Dreadnought* and *Bellerophon*, had been sold and scrapped, and another three, the *Téméraire, Neptune*, and *Hercules*, had been stricken even before the opening of the Washington conference. The remaining five battleships (the *Superb, Collingwood, St. Vincent, Colossus*, and *Agincourt*) and two battlecruisers (the *Indomitable* and *Inflexible*) had been reduced to training or other secondary-tertiary duties; with the exception of the *Colossus*, which remained in service until 1923 as a training ship, all were stricken and sold in 1922.[8] In real terms the scrapping of these ships represented no real loss, and much the same can be said about the 13.5-in. gunned battleships and battlecruisers, which had been laid down between 1909 and 1911, that were either stricken, sold and scrapped, or paid off and passed into the reserve pending disposal prior to the London conference of 21 January–22 April 1930. Five dreadnoughts—the *Conqueror, Orion*, and *Thunderer* and the *Ajax* and *King George V*—and the battlecruisers *Lion* and *Princess Royal* had disappeared from the lists by December 1926, while the battleship *Monarch* had been sunk as a target ship in January 1925: the *Centurion* remained in service as a target ship and after a somewhat checkered career was expended as a breakwater off the Normandy beachhead in June 1944. The remaining 13.5-in. gunned battleships, the four members of the *Iron Duke* class, served with the Atlantic Fleet until 1929 and the battlecruiser *Tiger* served until 1931, when they were paid off; the *Iron Duke* alone remained in service first as a training ship and then as a depot ship. The passing of these units from the scene had been foreshadowed under the terms of the Washington treaty and on account of their advancing years, but the scrapping was ordered under the terms of the subsequent London treaty.[9] Kato commented that the Washington treaty was "the gift of the gods" in terms of Japan being extricated from the self-imposed impossibilities presented by the Eight-Eight program,[10] but the comment applied, *mutatis mutandis*, equally to Britain. Scrapping the capital ships was the price exacted for avoiding a naval race with the United States that Britain could only lose, and the British warships that were scrapped simply did not begin to compare with the 34,500-ton *Washington*, six 43,900-ton *South Dakota*-class battleships, and four 44,200-ton *Lexington*-class battlecruisers that were abandoned on the slips. But, of course, Kato's comment could also be applied to the United States.

* * *

The Washington naval limitation treaty was not comprehensive, but as the first of its kind it represented a remarkable achievement in terms of leading powers deliberately and voluntarily accepting measures of moderation and control as the means of avoiding future confrontation and conflict. Of course, the treaty and the others concluded at Washington at this time were necessarily flawed in one obvious and vital respect. There was no means of compulsory consultation and arbitration about the position of the powers, individually and collectively, relative to China, and there was no means whereby Japan was tied into some form of economic system that made for long-term cooperation with the other powers, and specifically the United States. In effect, Japan was left to fend for itself without recourse to the wider international community, and if this presented no real problem at this time, within ten years the situation would change massively, and to the detriment of peace and restraint. But such measures and such cooperation were not how things were done at that time.

Washington could not settle everything, and arrangements for cruisers, destroyers, and submarines were left for future deliberation, but it made two provisions not noted thus far. In terms of preparing naval bases, Britain, Japan, and the United States undertook measures of restraint: the British undertook not to fortify any base north of Singapore, the Americans west of Pearl Harbor and Dutch Harbor, and the Japanese outside the home islands, that is, in the mandated islands that had come their way via the League of Nations. Japan was thus left in the position of marked potential advantage in the western Pacific that had aroused American concerns before the conference, and this position became very real in the inter-war period, specifically regarding developments affecting the range and operational capacity of submarines and shore-based aircraft. The arrangement even at this time left Japan as the power in the western Pacific, but the Sino-Japanese treaty did something more. The treaty with China provided Japan with the basis for forging a new arrangement with that country. Japan retained many rights and concessions inside China, most obviously in southern Manchuria, but the treaty of February 1922 nonetheless represented something different. There was a basic equality between China and Japan in its spirit, and there was a return to China of what was properly China's; if Japan was obliged to be the first country to make such an arrangement, then it was genuinely the case of its being the first, not the only, country to make such concessions. There was, for the first time since 1894, a basis for China and Japan to go forward together in certain areas and on a new footing. In this respect the episode of March 1927, in which Britain and the United States sought to involve Japan in mounting punitive operations against Kuomintang forces at Nanking, was significant: Japan refused to join the other two powers, and was not involved in any military operations against Chinese forces, whether Kuomintang or otherwise, at this time. But things were to change very quickly thereafter.

* * *

The final aspect of the 1921 naval arrangements relates to a matter that over the years seems to have been largely forgotten, if indeed it was ever much known in the first place. The naval treaty's provisions whereby France and Italy, in light of their lack of building in recent years given their military commitments in the First World War, were afforded certain dispensations in terms of new construction is well known: France, for example, was allowed to lay down two battleships in 1927 and 1929 as replacement for the aging *Danton*-class units and was also allowed to build a third battleship as replacement for the *France*, which was lost in Quiberon Bay on 26 August 1922. Neither country availed itself of that provision. The main reason for this was that in the straitened circumstances of the twenties both France and Italy, given their vying with one another for primacy in the Mediterranean, hesitated to undertake major capital ship building programs; the focus of their immediate attention—and for that matter that of the other three powers as well—was upon cruisers. But in May 1925 the French government placed before the national assembly a program that would have included two *croiseurs de combat* with standard displacement of 17,500 tons—deliberately calculated to provide for two that would total 35,000 tons—with a main armament of eight 12-in./305-mm guns in two offset quadruple turrets and a top speed of 35 knots: designed primarily to defend shipping against attack by Washington heavy cruisers, the armor to be afforded these battlecruisers was to be sufficient to counter 8-in. shells[11] The bill was lost, but these two ships, never built but clearly the forerunners of the *Dunkerque* and *Strasbourg*, do provide a neat juxtaposition to both the 15,900/16,200-ton *panzerschiffe Lützow, Admiral Scheer*, and *Admiral Graf Spee* of 1929–1931, with their six 11-in./280-mm guns and 27 knots, and the 18,200-ton heavy cruisers *Admiral Hipper, Blücher*, and *Prinz Eugen*, with their eight 8-in./203-mm main armament and 32 knots.

* * *

The subsequent Geneva naval limitation conference, involving just Britain, Japan, and the United States after France and Italy declined to attend, met between 20 June and 4 August 1927, and its course and outcome are sufficiently well known to permit reference to only three matters. First, the origins of this conference lay in the failure of the Washington agreements to complete the process of limitation and the resultant concentration by the powers upon cruisers—tonnage, armament, numbers, and aggregate tonnage—with the result that by 1926–1927 there appeared a very real danger of a naval race, regarding not capital ships and carriers but cruisers, a race that would be politically and financially costly to all involved. Second, the conference failed to come to any agreement on the crucial question of cruisers, and for one reason. The United States was primarily concerned with battle and sought to standardize cruisers in terms of 10,000-ton units armed with 8-in./203-mm guns, and it sought to curb numbers—specifically British numbers—as the means of ensuring itself against major building obligations. The British were primarily concerned with the security of overseas territories and trade defense, and the focus of their attention was the 7,000-ton light cruiser complete with a 6-in./152-mm main armament, and on numbers. The American insistence on aggregate limitation of between 250,000 and 300,000 tons for Britain and the United States ran directly counter to the British calculation that what was needed to ensure imperial security was twenty-five cruisers for the fleet (i.e., 10,000-ton heavy cruisers) and forty-five for trade defense (i.e., 7,000-ton light cruisers). There was no basis of agreement between the two positions: the Americans from the outset made clear a point-blank refusal even to consider a 400,000-ton limitation, whereas the initial British position embraced 562,000 tons more or less as the sine qua non. There were British proposals to expressly limit the numbers of heavy cruisers that could be acquired, but with the Americans' display of reluctance even to consider the light cruiser per se, and specifically a 6,000-ton light cruiser, even Japanese attempts to fashion some form of compromise proved unavailing, and the conference ended with no agreement. Indeed, there never was any basis of agreement: the British sought to ensure that all three powers spread their attention across both heavy and light cruisers, whereas the Americans were simply not interested in anything but heavy cruisers, and the Americans again were simply not interested in a diversity that would confirm Britain in its existing position of a massive advantage of numbers that would entail major U.S. construction programs merely to register parity. The whole process of negotiation was, naturally, somewhat acerbic.

Third, one of the lesser known aspects of the Geneva impasse was the fact that over the next two years (and related in part to the Kellogg-Briand process that saw the signing of that treaty on 27 August 1928) the Americans and British involved themselves in direct and very deliberate negotiations in an attempt to ensure that future negotiations would not end in futility. In 1929 an agreement was reached whereby the two countries accepted a limit of fifty cruisers and aggregates of 339,000 tons, but there was no agreement on the maximum number of heavy cruisers that would be permitted under these totals, though that was not the immediate point of relevance. What was relevant were two matters, the first being that in December 1927 a bill was placed before the House of Representatives that provided for seventy-one warships; it was greeted with such lack of enthusiasm by both society in general and the Congress that in February 1928 a "fifteen cruiser bill" was introduced. Such modesty in terms of ambition nonetheless carried obvious implications for Britain, but the element of restraint explicit in such a proposal, given previous claims, carried even more obvious implications for the United States. The second point was that after March 1929 in Washington and June 1929 in London new administrations were very receptive to restraint and limitation, and the agreement that was reached between the Americans and British at this time pointed to the very real prospect of future agreement in the next major limitation conference, which was to be held in London the following year.

* * *

The London conference and treaty together form the acme of the inter-war naval limitation, for one very obvious reason: subsequently there were two, not one, limitation conferences—Geneva in 1932 and a second London in 1935—but in real terms these achieved nothing, and London 1930 in one very obvious sense was to be the end of the line. This conference saw genuine compromise, as well as three strong governments that in a little more than a year were no more, and it saw genuine concessions made to Japan. There was, however, widespread opposition within that country to the final treaty, with two markers: Kaigun acceptance of a treaty that really did provide it with all that it could have wished and sought, but acceptance only on condition that this would be the last such limitation treaty, and the shooting of Prime Minister Hamaguchi Osachi (1870–1931) by a nationalist fanatic in November 1930.[12] The very strange fact that within the Japanese body politic there emerged this opposition to a treaty that so closely accorded with Kaigun aspiration is matched only by one equally strange fact. The terms of this treaty prohibited replacement construction and laying down of new ships until 1937, provided for another conference in 1935, stated that refusal to be bound by renewed limitation had to be announced one year in advance of that conference, and marked the formal end of existing limitation arrangements as 31 December 1936. Japan gave notice of such intent and in 1935 left the second London conference, but with Japan having spent years working on the design of new battleships, the very odd fact was that Britain and the United States both laid down battleships before Japan—the *King George V* and *Prince of Wales* were both laid down on 1 January 1937, the *North Carolina* on 27 October 1937, and the *Yamato* on 4 November—and both laid down more battleships than did Japan: between January 1937 and August 1939 the British laid down five battleships and one battlecruiser, the Americans four battleships, and the Japanese the *Yamato* and *Musashi*.[13] Given that the Kaigun calculation was to end limitation in order to build and build rapidly, such a state of affairs is surprising.

The main terms of the London treaty can be defined very simply: with provision for the scrapping or decommissioning of various units, the famous 5:5:3 ratio was applied to capital ships, with Britain and the United States afforded fifteen units and Japan nine. The existing restriction on carriers was maintained, but regarding cruisers, destroyers, and submarines change took the form of adoption of a 10:10:7 ratio for cruisers, destroyers, and all forms of auxiliary warships and support shipping, with parity afforded with respect to submarines. The legacy of the 1929 Anglo-American agreement over cruisers manifested itself in arrangements that provided 339,000 tons for Britain, 323,500 tons for the United States, and 208,850 tons for Japan, with the maximum numbers of heavy cruisers set at eighteen for the United States, fifteen for Great Britain, and twelve for Japan. At American insistence the maximum displacement for a light cruiser was set at 10,000 tons, a figure determined by distances across the Pacific, but the American concession in terms of the 10:10:7 arrangement was tacit: in heavy cruiser numbers Japan was still set at 5:5:3, but the United States, having come down from the previous demand for twenty-one heavy cruisers, undertook not to build to full numbers and thereby allow Japan to have the 10:10:7 ratio across the cruiser and destroyer board. This, in terms of Japanese calculations, was massively important, in part because Japanese public expectation had been focused upon the 70 percent ratio since Geneva and 1927 as symbolic proof of great power status and in part because of Kaigun operational and tactical doctrine. The conventional wisdom of the day set down relative effectiveness in terms of the difference of the squares of relative strength, the logic being that the weaker side, fighting defensively, could conduct a successful campaign on condition it was maintained at a strength at least the half of the enemy's. Thus by Kaigun calculations, the 5:3 ratio placed Japan in a potentially disastrous 25:9 position—outmatched almost 3:1—but the 10:7 ratio placed Japan in the 100:49 position. This, alongside the parallel calculation that an American force advancing into the western Pacific would lose one tenth of its effectiveness for every thousand miles it advanced, thus provided the basis of Kaigun optimism about the conduct of a defensive campaign and a "decisive battle" in the general area of the Marianas and the western Pacific.

* * *

Such were the arrangements crafted at London in 1930, and what followed was basically irrelevant. The Geneva talks in 1932 formed part of a general disarmament endeavor that was sponsored by the League of Nations, involved the Soviet Union and the United States, but foundered with Germany's departure from the League and renunciation of the Versailles armament provisions. The 1935 London conference, in the wake of Japan's departure, resulted in a largely meaningless agreement between Britain, France, and the United States and closed a limitation process that had one very curious feature. The whole process had begun in the early twenties, when in real terms the focus of American attention was Japan, but given the "second to none" formula the point of comparison had to be Britain, and therefore despite the fact that there was no real issue of significant importance that divided the two countries, Britain was "the enemy," as it were, while Japan was assigned a *sotto voce* role. On the other side of the fence Japan and its navy measured themselves against the United States and the U.S. Navy, but again not directly and in public; if the U.S. Navy was discounted from consideration, however, then Japan had nothing against which its navy might be measured. The raison d'être of the two navies at the heart of the naval race problem in the twenties could be secured only in a process in which both desisted in making direct comparison, yet at the end of the day one basic point remained: the Japanese Navy sought an end to limitation, but with the end of limitation its relative position worsened, and Japan in 1936–1939 found itself in exactly the same position relative to the United States that it had held before 1921—comprehensively out-built—even before the 1940 program that was put together when for the first time the United States was confronted by the prospect of German victory and predominance in Europe.

* * *

France and Italy refused to be parties to the 1927 and 1930 arrangements and indeed in this period were measuring themselves against one another, the French laying down the modestly proportioned battlecruisers *Dunkerque* on Christmas Eve 1932 and *Strasbourg* on 25 November 1934, the latter less than a month after the Italians laid down the *Littorio* and *Vittorio Veneto*, which at this time in terms of displacement ceded pride of place only to the *Hood:* within a year the French had moved to a position alongside their neighbor with their laying down of the battleship *Richelieu.*[14] This Franco-Italian rivalry in the Mediterranean in the inter-war period, however, invites the comment made about the Falklands war in 1982—a fight between two bald men about a comb—while the whole inter-war period for Britain would seem to have been unfortunate by any criteria. The disparity between what the Royal Navy was in the inter-war period and what it had to become between 1939 and 1945 is most striking, though obviously there was no enemy, and certainly no German enemy, for most of the inter-war period, and most definitely for most of the inter-war period there was no enemy committed to a submarine *guerre de course.* The payoff, clearly, was in the first two years of war, between September 1939 and June 1941, when Germany, with a U-boat service smaller than in 1917–1918, inflicted greater losses on British, Allied, and neutral shipping and suffered far fewer losses in the process; indeed, had it not been for Dutch and Norwegian shipping, and American indulgence, Britain would have been finished, such was the ineffectiveness of its navy. The fact that in the inter-war period fewer than one British admiral in fifty had risen to flag rank via anti-submarine duty really was at the core of British difficulties that provide comment on the state of the inter-war British Navy in the form of the *Royal Oak* affair. What may be defined as the intellectual high-water mark of the British Navy in the inter-war period, the *Royal Oak* irrelevance invokes the imagery of the (apocryphal) story of the incident in which a British naval officer was almost trampled to death by a horse while two other British naval officers who tried to come to his assistance were also badly injured: in the event, all were saved when the manager of the store came out the shop and unplugged the horse.[15] In the inter-war period a mindless commitment to torpedo attacks by destroyer formations and to keeping correct station on the flagship was the be-all and end-all, at the expense of such matters as objective assessment of air power, provision of adequate anti-aircraft armament, and trade defense, as well as other mundane matters such as the Ethiopian crisis, the Spanish Civil War, and the outbreak of Japan's "special undeclared war" in China.

APPENDIX 2.1.

THE BRITISH NAVY'S LAST HURRAH: THE CORONATION REVIEW OF 20 MAY 1937

THE FLEET REVIEW arguably dates back to the fourteenth century, to Edward III (1327–1377), who in June 1346 inspected the fleet prior to the sailing of an expeditionary force to France and to a campaign that culminated with the battle of Crécy-en-Ponthieu and the subsequent English capture of Calais. Over the next five hundred years reviews followed at irregular intervals, and while some were inspections for war (e.g., in 1415 and 1778), the majority of reviews were staged for three basic purposes—to celebrate victory either in battle or in a war (e.g., the reviews in February 1693, June 1794, and 1814), as a token of courtesy[1] and to impress visiting monarchs with the display of British strength and power (e.g., the review of March 1700 and the visit of Tsar Peter) and, to move one step beyond this second purpose, to intimidate and to overawe (e.g., the review of October 1844 on the occasion of the visit to Britain of the Russian emperor and kings of France and Prussia, and the 1889 review and the visit of the German emperor). In the course of the reign of Victoria (1837–1901) there were no fewer than seventeen reviews, with these purposes vying with one another and with one other consideration, namely, the display of national strength with reference to public access and accountability that were part of the widening democratic process.[2]

Perhaps this latter consideration was never more obvious than in the short reign of Edward VII (1901–1910), when, in addition to the coronation review of August 1902, there were four reviews that presented the dreadnought battleship and the battlecruiser to the public; more importantly, these reviews were part of the process of redeployment and concentration of forces in home waters to meet a potential German enemy. The reign of George V (1910–1936) saw three more reviews prior to the outbreak of war, a celebratory review off Southend in 1919, a review in 1924, and then the silver jubilee review on 16 July 1935. At this latter review no foreign warships were present. It had become the custom that invited foreign countries might send a single warship to reviews, and prior to 1914 various countries had copied the British practice and instituted their own (more modest) reviews, but after 1918 the re-ordering of Europe, and with the thirties the impositions of financial stringency, meant that reviews were very few: the eleven-year gap between 1924 and 1935 represented the longest period between British reviews since 1842.

The coronation review of May 1937 represented the largest and most cosmopolitan gathering of warships since the coronation review of June 1911, and in historical terms it was the last parade of the Royal Navy as the world's greatest and most prestigious navy. Paradoxically there were to be more British warships present at the next coronation review, on 15 June 1953, than at the review in May 1937, but at the later review more than a third of the British warships were frigates and minesweepers, and by that time the British navy had been reduced to secondary status, as had the battleship. In 1937 no fewer than fourteen battleships and battlecruisers were present; in 1953 there was just the *Vanguard*. Four British fleet and three light carriers were also present, plus single Australian and Canadian light carriers, compared to the four British carriers that were off Portsmouth in May 1937.

Between 1911 and 1937 four European empires passed from the scene, but ten republics nonetheless provided single representatives at the 1937 review, as did seven monarchies, two dominions, and India; in 1953 Britain played host to representatives of sixteen foreign and five commonwealth navies. As it was, in 1937 Japanese and American and French and German warships were kept apart, but German and Soviet ships were placed next to one another. If a certain symbolism is sought then the reader need look no further than the fact that when the Japanese heavy cruiser *Ashigara* sailed from Spithead, it set course for Kiel and German reception, leaving a former ally and going to a future one.

Just one ship—the Greek cruiser *Giorgios Averoff*—was at both the 1911 and 1937 reviews: its place in the 1953 review was taken by the destroyer *Navarinon*, present at the 1937 review as the British destroyer *Echo*. Only one foreign warship, the Portuguese sloop *Bartolomeu Dias*, was present, unchanged, at both the 1937 and 1953 reviews. Of the 145 British warships and submarines in the 1953 review only the heavy cruiser *Devonshire*, the sloop *Fleetwood*, and the netlayer *Protector* had been present at the 1937 review.

The greater part of British attention to the foreign presence at the 1937 review was directed toward the month-old *Dunkerque* and the formidably aggressive *Ashigara*, but this preoccupation has served to obscure related matters. A Japanese prince and princess were among the official guests and were photographed being received in the battleship *Queen Elizabeth*. On 18 May the band from the *Ashigara* became the first foreign naval band ever to play in Hyde Park. On the same day a party of Soviet sailors from the *Marat* visited (of all places) the Tower of London, while a German field marshal was at Bovington inspecting British tanks of 1918.

The review separated disasters. It came some two weeks after the German airship *Hindenburg* crashed at the Lakehurst Naval Air Station, New Jersey, and a little more than a week before Neville Chamberlain became prime minister. More importantly, at the time of the review England beat Sweden and Finland in away football matches, while the Somerset cricketer Harold Gimblett scored forty-two runs off eight balls[3] and Herbert Sutcliffe became the highest-scoring cricketer in Yorkshire history. Just to keep things in proper perspective.

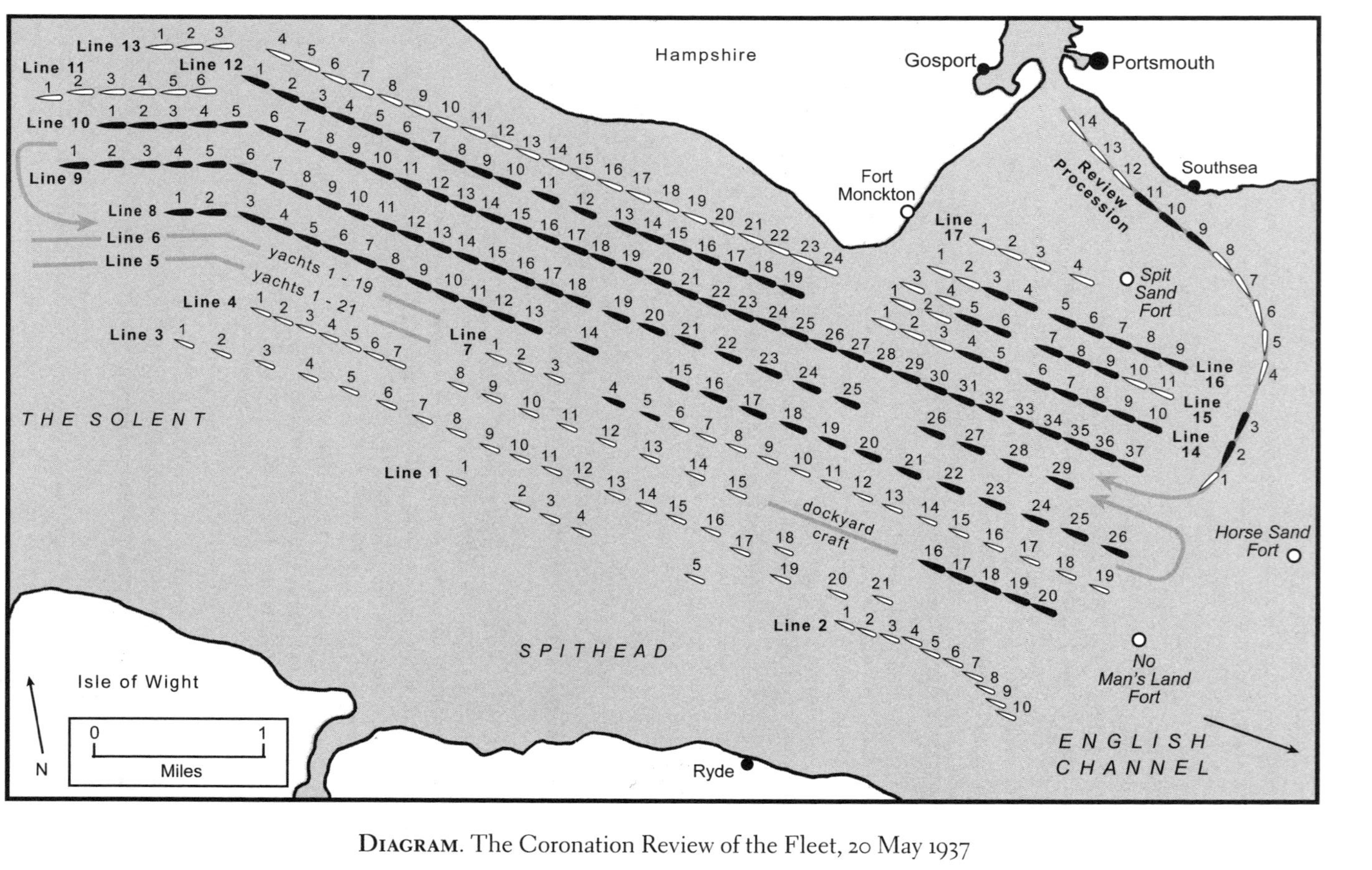

Diagram. The Coronation Review of the Fleet, 20 May 1937

THE CORONATION REVIEW: DETAILED KEY

[a] denotes units with the Home Fleet
[b] denotes units with the Mediterranean Fleet
[c] denotes units with the Reserve Fleet and other units
† denotes units sunk during the Second World War

Merchantmen displacements are given in gross registered tons as per the Lloyd's Lists. The tonnages of warships and submarines are given as per deep-load displacement other than for the Scandinavian armored ships, standard displacements being given for these three warships.

Line 1: 1. The 1,023-ton (1911) steam twin-screw schooner *Jeannette.* 2. The 149-ton (1930) Southern Railways car ferry *Hilsea.* 3. The 169-ton (1886) Channel Island ferry *Joy-Bell III.* 4. The *Westward,* which was either a 323-ton (1910) gaff schooner or (more likely) a 2,001-ton (1920) twin-screw four-masted schooner. 5. The 3,791-ton (1929) Coast Lines (Belfast-Liverpool) ferry *Ulster Prince.*†

Line 2: 1. The 412-ton (1924) Southern Railways (Portsmouth-Ryde) paddle steamer ferry *Shanklin.* 2. The 553-ton (1922) P. & A. Campbell (south coast) paddle steamer ferry *Glen Gower.* 3. The 524-ton (1914) P. & A. Campbell (Bristol Channel) paddle steamer ferry *Glen Usk.* 4. The 519-ton (1905) P. & A. Campbell (south coast) paddle steamer ferry *Brighton Queen.*† 5. The 520-ton (1905) P. & A. Campbell (Ilfracombe-Swansea) paddle steamer ferry *Devonia.*† 6. The 537-ton (1899) P. & A. Campbell (south coast) paddle steamer ferry *Waverley.*† 7. The 482-ton (1906) New Medway Steam Packet Co. (Rochester-Southend) paddle steamer ferry *Royal Daffodil.* 8. The 798-ton (1916) New Medway Steam Packet Co. (diverse routes/pleasure steamer) paddle steamer *Queen of Kent.* 9. The 793-ton (1909) General Steam Navigation Co. (London-Southend/Clacton) paddle steamer ferry *Golden Eagle.* 10. The 229-ton (1884) Cosens and Co. pleasure steamer/paddle steamer *Victoria.*

Line 3: 1. The 8,009-ton (1935) motor tanker *Anadara.*† 2. The 8,406-ton (1936) BP tanker *British Fame.*† 3. The 13,245-ton (1923) liner *Voltaire.*† 4. The 16,738-ton (1925) P&O liner *Ranchi.* 5. The 16,556-ton (1922) P&O liner *Moldavia.* 6. The 15,363-ton (1913) Royal Mail Line *Atlantis.* 7. The 45,647-ton (1914) Cunard liner *Aquitania.* 8. The 16,243-ton (1922) Cunard R.M.S. *Lancastria.*† 9. The 2,974-ton (1936) Gas, Light and Coke Co. merchantman *Mr. Therm.* 10. The 1,546-ton (1931) Stevenson Clarke Co. merchantman *Flathouse.* 11. The 1,091-ton (1936) County Borough of Brighton local coaster *Henry Moon.*† 12. The 921-ton (1909) Northern Lighthouses vessel *Pharos.* 13. The 106-ton (1916) harbor tug *Rector.*† 14. The 634-ton (1937) F. T. Everard coaster *Suavity.*† 15. The 618-ton (1904) Irish Lights vessel *Alexandra.* 16. The 10,697-ton (1921) City Line passenger ship *City of Simla.*† 17. The 3,285-ton (1921) Yeoward Line passenger ship *Aquila.* 18. The 1,548-ton (1932) General Steam Navigation Co. (London-Southend/Margate/Ramsgate) pleasure steamer/paddle steamer *Royal Eagle.* 19. The 4,227-ton (1929) London and North East Railway (Harwich-Hook of Holland) ferry *Vienna.* 20. The 4,413-ton (1930) London and North East Railways (Harwich-Hook of Holland) ferry *Amsterdam.*† 21. The 1,552-ton (1933) Southern Railway (Guernsey/Jersey-French ports) ferry *Brittany.*

Line 4: 1. The 175-ton (1930) yacht *Taransay.* 2. The 100-ton (1911) 19-m (Belgian?) yacht *Mariquita.* 3. The 66-ton (1932) two-masted motor schooner *Vera Mary.* 4. The 41-ton (1914) auxiliary ketch *Best Friend.*† 5. The 455-ton (1905) steam yacht *Zaza.* 6.

The 483-ton (1903) steam sloop *Lady Vagrant*. 7. The 275-ton (1899) schooner *Lucinda*. 8. The 15,501-ton (1927) Star Line/Leyland liner *Arandora Star*.† 9. The 15,248-ton (1925) P&O liner *Comorin*.† 10. The 20,097-ton (1929) Orient liner *Orontes*. 11. The 20,033-ton (1925) Orient liner *Otranto*. 12. The 9,081-ton (1912) British India Steam Navigation (London-Calcutta) liner *Neuralia*.† 13. The 9,557-ton (1917) Bibby Line liner *Lancashire*. 14. The 12,555-ton (1936) British India Steam Navigation liner/troop ship *Dilwara*. 15. The 16,402-ton (1922) Canadian Pacific liner *Montrose*.† 16. The 953-ton (1917) *Hunt*-class minesweeper *Tedworth*.[c] 17. The 995-ton (1919) *Hunt*-class survey ship *Flinders*.[c] 18. The 1,244-ton (1917) *R*-class destroyer *Skate*.[c] 19. The 1,051-ton (1917) Later *M*-class destroyer *Tyrant*.[c] 20. The 1,225-ton (1919) S-class destroyer *Sardonyx*.[c]

Line 5: 1. The 102-ton (1930) ketch *Maria Catharina*. 2. The 614-ton (1901) steam yacht *Rosabelle*.† 3. The 21-ton (1882) motor cutter *Vanda*. 4. The 254-ton (1925) motor ketch *Sylvia*.† 5. The 68-ton (1898) motor ketch *Rubicon*. 6. The 361-ton (1902) steam schooner *Osprey*.† 7. The 214-ton (1874) motor brigantine *Lady of Avenel*. 8. The 147-ton (1937) motor ketch *Thendara*. 9. The 670-ton (1919) steam schooner *Foinaven*. 10. The 581-ton (1931) motor schooner *Evadne*. 11. The 447-ton (1882) steam schooner *Boadicea*. 12. The 751-ton (1924) motor schooner *Princess*.† 13. The 326-ton (1913) steam schooner *Anglia*. 14. The 367-ton (1883) steam schooner *Melisande*. 15. The 140-ton (1875) motor schooner *Tamesis*. 16. The 555-ton (1922) motor schooner *Sona*.† 17. The 10-ton (1900) motor cutter *Laura*. 18. The 439-ton (1897) steam schooner *Schievan*. 19. The 909-ton (1929) motor schooner *Migrante*. 20. The 886-ton (1911) steam schooner *Conqueror*. 21. The 384-ton (1919) steam ketch *Ocean Rover*.

Line 6: 1. The 18-ton (1936) motor yacht *Esmeralda*. 2. The 88-ton (1930) motor ketch *Silver Cloud*. 3. The 118-ton (1923) twin-screw schooner *Mandolin*. 4. The 223-ton (1926) steam yacht *Atlantis*.† 5. The 103-ton (1899) motor ketch *Moyana*. 6. The 275-ton (1902) twin-screw schooner *Ombra*. 7. The 735-ton (1888) steam yacht *Star of India*. 8. The 659-ton (1929) motor yacht *Sunbeam II*. 9. The 186-ton (1920) motor ketch *Lulworth*. 10. The 550-ton (1927) motor yacht *Radiant*. 11. The 164-ton (1928) Bermuda cutter *Astra*. 12. The 36-ton (1882) Royal Naval Sailing Association motor yawl *Amaryllis*. 13. The 568-ton (1905) steam yacht *Venetia*. 14. The 227-ton (1903) motor ketch *Diane*. 15. The 1,421-ton (1912) twin-screw schooner *Sapphire*. 16. The 161-ton (1887) twin-screw schooner *Amphitrite*. 17. The *Medusa* which was either a 627-ton (1906) steam schooner or (more likely) a 32-ton (1929) motor yacht, House of Lords owner. 18. The 709-ton (1929) motor schooner *Rhodora*.† 19. The 161-ton (1931) motor yawl *Altair*.

Line 7: 1. The Estonian 850-ton (1937) submarine *Kalev*.† 2. The Polish 1,920-ton (1929) *Wicher*-class destroyer *Burza*. 3. The Turkish 1,650-ton (1931) class-name destroyer *Kocatepe*. 4. The 651-ton (1906) naval (Chatham-Sheerness) ferry *Nimble*.[c] 5. The 7,080-ton (1914) depot ship *Pegasus*.[c4] 6. The Romanian 1,850-ton (1929) *Regele Ferdinand*-class destroyer *Regina Maria*. 7. The Portuguese 2,440-ton (1934) *Albuquerque*-class sloop *Bartolomeu Dias*. 8. The Cuban 2,055-ton (1911) sloop *Cuba*. 9. The Finnish 4,000-ton (1930) armored ship *Väinämöinen*. 10. The Danish 4,100-ton (1918) armored ship *Niels Iuel*. 11. The Swedish 7,900-ton (1917) armored ship *Drottning Victoria*. 12. The Japanese 14,980-ton (1928) *Myoko*-class heavy cruiser *Ashigara*.† 13. The Dutch 8,339-ton (1921) *Sumatra*-class light cruiser *Java*.† 14. The Greek 9,956-ton (1910) light cruiser *Giorgios Averoff*. 15. The German 16,154-ton (1934) *Deutschland*-class armored ship *Admiral Graf Spee*.† 16. The Soviet 26,170-ton (1911) *Gangut*-class battleship *Marat*.† 17. The Argentinian 31,000-ton (1911) *Rivadavia*-class battleship *Moreno*. 18. The French 35,200-ton (1935) class-name battleship *Dunkerque*.† 19. The U.S. 31,924-ton (1912) *Texas*-class battleship *New York*.

Line 8 (with ships that were to leave to the east): 1. The 1,890-ton (1936) *H*-class destroyer *Hereward*.[a]† 2. The 1,940-ton (1934) *F*-class destroyer *Foresight*.[a]† 3. The 1,940-ton (1934) *F*-class destroyer *Fame*.[a] 4. The 1,940-ton (1934) *E*-class destroyer *Encounter*.[a]† 5. The 1,940-ton (1934) *E*-class destroyer *Electra*.[a]† 6. The 1,940-ton (1934) *E*-class destroyer *Eclipse*.[a]† 7. The 1,940-ton (1934) *E*-class destroyer *Echo*.[a] 8. The 1,940-ton (1934) *E*-class destroyer *Esk*.[a]† 9. The 1,940-ton (1934) *E*-class destroyer *Express*.[a] 10. The 1,940-ton (1934) *E*-class destroyer *Escort*.[a]† 11. The 1,940-ton (1934) *E*-class destroyer *Escapade*.[a] 12. The 2,049-ton (1934) *E*-class destroyer *Exmouth*.[a]† 13. The 5,300-ton (1918) *Carlisle*-class light cruiser *Cairo*.[a]† 14. The 5,276-ton (1917) *Ceres*-class light cruiser *Curlew*.[c]† 15. The 5,276-ton (1917) *Ceres*-class light cruiser *Coventry*.[c]† 16. The 5,300-ton (1918) *Carlisle*-class light cruiser *Colombo*.[c] 17. The 5,300-ton (1918) class-name light cruiser *Carlisle*.[c] 18. The 5,276-ton (1917) *Ceres*-class light cruiser *Cardiff*.[c] 19. The 5,276-ton (1917) *Ceres*-class light cruiser *Curacao*.[c]† 20. The 6,030-ton (1918) *D*-class light cruiser *Dunedin*.[c]† 21. The 33,500-ton (1915) *Royal Sovereign*-class battleship *Resolution*.[a] 22. The 33,500-ton (1915) *Royal Sovereign*-class battleship *Revenge*.[a] 23. The 33,500-ton (1916) *Royal Sovereign*-class battleship *Ramillies*.[a] 24. The 33,500-ton (1915) class-name battleship *Royal Sovereign*.[a] 25. The 35,500-ton (1925) *Nelson*-class battleship *Rodney*.[a] 26. The 35,500-ton (1925) class-name battleship *Nelson*.[a]

Line 9 (with ships that were to leave to the west): 1. The 12,300-ton (1917) fleet oiler *Brambleleaf*.† 2. The 1,508-ton (1919) Modified W-class destroyer *Wild Swan*.[c]† 3. The 1,490-ton (1917) W-class destroyer *Winchelsea*.[c] 4. The 1,508-ton (1919) Modified W-class destroyer *Whitshed*.[c] 5. The 1,508-ton (1919) Modified W-class destroyer *Verity*.[c] 6. The 1,812-ton (1926) destroyer *Amazon*.[c] 7. The 1,815-ton (1930) A-class destroyer *Acheron*.[c]† 8. The 1,490-ton (1918) W-class destroyer *Wrestler*.[c] 9. The 1,490-ton (1918) W-class destroyer *Winchester*.[c] 10. The 1,815-ton (1930) *B*-class destroyer *Beagle*.[a] 11. The 1,815-ton (1930) *B*-class destroyer *Brazen*.[a]† 12. The 1,815-ton (1930) *B*-class destroyer *Brilliant*.[a] 13. The 1,815-ton (1930) *B*-class destroyer *Blanche*.[a]† 14. The 1,815-ton (1930) *B*-class destroyer *Bulldog*.[a] 15. The 1,815-ton (1930) *B*-class destroyer *Boadicea*.[a]† 16. The 1,815-ton (1930) *B*-class destroyer *Boreas*.[a] 17. The 1,815-ton (1930) *B*-class destroyer *Basilisk*.[a]† 18. The 1,942-ton (1931) destroyer leader *Kempenfelt*.[a] 19. The 13,700-ton (1919) light carrier *Hermes*.[b]† 20. The 11,350-ton (1936) Southampton-class light cruiser *Newcastle*.[a] 21. The 11,350-ton (1936) class-name light cruiser *Southampton*.[a]† 22. The 27,165-ton (1916) aircraft carrier *Furious*.[a] 23. The 27,560-ton (1916) class-name aircraft carrier *Courageous*.[a]† 24. The 27,560-ton (1916) *Courageous*-class aircraft carrier *Glorious*.[b]† 25. The 37,490-ton (1916) *Renown*-class battlecruiser *Repulse*.[b]† 26. The 41,200-ton (1918) battlecruiser *Hood*.[b]† 27. The 21,250-ton (1912) gunnery training ship *Iron Duke*. 28. The 36,600-ton (1914) *Queen Elizabeth*-class battleship *Barham*.[b]† 29. The 35,500-ton (1913) class-name battleship *Queen Elizabeth*.[b]†

Line 10 (with ships that were to leave to the east). 1. The 1,508-ton (1919) Modified W-class destroyer *Wanderer*.[c] 2. The 1,508-ton (1919) Modified W-class destroyer *Wren*.[c]† 3. The 1,530-ton (1919) Modified W-class destroyer *Wishart*.[c] 4. The 1,512-ton (1917) V-class destroyer *Viscount*.[c] 5. The 1,523-ton (1918) V-class destroyer *Vidette*.[c] 6. The 1,490-ton (1918) W-class destroyer *Wolfhound*.[c] 7. The 1,523-ton (1917) V-class destroyer *Vanquisher*.[c] 8. The 1,490-ton (1918) W-class destroyer *Walpole*.[c] 9. The 1,512-ton (1918) W-class destroyer *Woolston*.[c] 10. The 2,000-ton *Shakespeare*-class (1920) destroyer leader *Broke*.[c]† 11. The 504-ton (1919) *H*. 21-class submarine H. 49.[a]† 12. The 504-ton (1918) *H*. 21-class submarine H. 33.[a] 13. The 1,150-ton (1919) *L*. 50-class submarine L. 54.[a] 14. The 1,089-ton (1919) *L*. 9-class submarine L. 26.[a] 15. The 1,870-ton

Australian (1926) O-class submarine *Oxley.*[a] 16. The 1,831-ton (1926) O-class submarine *Oberon.*[a] 17. The 504-ton (1919) *H.* 21-class submarine H. 50.[a] 18. The 504-ton (1918) *H.* 21-class submarine H. 34.[a] 19. The 504-ton (1918) *H.* 21-class submarine H. 32.[a] 20. The 1,089-ton (1919) *L.* 9-class submarine L. 27.[a] 21. The 960-ton (1936) *S*-class submarine *Spearfish.*[a]† 22. The 927-ton (1932) *S*-class submarine *Sturgeon.*[a] 23. The 5,270-ton (1915) depot ship *Titania.*[a] 24. The 1,890-ton (1935) *G*-class destroyer *Griffin.*[b] 25. The 1,890-ton (1935) G-class destroyer *Grenade.*[b]† 26. The 1,890-ton (1935) G-class destroyer *Glowworm.*[b]† 27. The 1,890-ton (1935) G-class destroyer *Greyhound.*[b]† 28. The 1,890-ton (1935) G-class destroyer *Gallant.*[b]† 29. The 1,890-ton (1935) G-class destroyer *Grafton.*[b]† 30. The 1,890-ton (1935) G-class destroyer *Gipsy.*[b]† 31. The 1,890-ton (1935) G-class destroyer *Garland.*[b] 32. The 2,030-ton (1935) destroyer leader *Grenville.*[b]† 33. The 12,300-ton (1920) *Hawkins*-class heavy cruiser/cadet training ship *Frobisher.*[a] 34. The 9,280-ton New Zealand (1931) class-name light cruiser *Leander.*[c] 35. The 13,315-ton (1927) *London*-class heavy cruiser *Devonshire.*[b] 36. The 13,315-ton (1928) *London*-class heavy cruiser *Shropshire.*[b] 37. The 13,315-ton (1927) name-ship heavy cruiser *London.*[b]

Line 11: 1. The 1,224-ton (1926) four-masted twin-screw schooner *Flying Cloud.* 2. The 762-ton (1911) yacht *Sayonara.* 3. The 984-ton (1914) Southampton Steam Ship Co. twin-screw passenger ferry *Greetings.* 4. The 509-ton (1930) Alexandra Towing Co. Southampton tug/tender *Romsey.* 5. The 700-ton (1913) Alexandra Towing Co. Southampton tug/passenger ferry *Flying Kestrel.* 6. The 264-ton (1927) Southern Railways (Lymington-Yarmouth) paddle steamer ferry *Freshwater.*

Line 12 (with ships that were to leave to the west): 1. The 1,510-ton (1933) *Grimsby*-class sloop *Fleetwood.*[a] 2. The 2,860-ton (1932) netlayer *Guardian.*[a] 3. The 927-ton (1932) *S*-class submarine *Seahorse.*[a]† 4. The 927-ton (1933) *S*-class submarine *Starfish.*[a]† 5. The 927-ton (1933) *S*-class submarine *Swordfish.*[a]† 6. The 2,157-ton (1935) *Porpoise*-class submarine *Narwhal.*[a]† 7. The 2,053-ton (1932) class-name submarine *Porpoise.*[a]† 8. The 5,805-ton (1907) depot ship *Lucia.*[a] 9. The 2,900-ton (1936) netlayer *Protector.*[b] 10. The 8,750-ton (1934) depot ship *Woolwich.*[b] 11. The 11,300-ton (1905) repair ship *Cyclops.*[b] 12. The 2,157-ton (1936) *Porpoise*-class submarine *Grampus.*[b]† 13. The 2,157-ton (1936) *Porpoise*-class submarine *Rorqual.*[b] 14. The 2,753-ton (1934) *Thames*-class submarine *Clyde.*[b] 15. The 2,753-ton (1934) *Thames*-class submarine *Severn.*[b] 16. The 2,680-ton (1932) class-name submarine *Thames.*[b]† 17. The 1,942-ton (1931) C-class destroyer *Comet.*[b] 18. The 1,225-ton (1919) S-class destroyer *Stronghold.*[a]† 19. The 1,942-ton (1931) C-class destroyer *Crusader.*[a]†

Line 13: 1. The 288-ton (1893) Southampton, Isle of Wight, and South of England Royal Mail Steam Packet Co. ferry *Vulcan.* 2. The 684-ton (1930) Southampton, Isle of Wight, and South of England Royal Mail Steam Packet Co. tug/tender *Calshot.* 3. The 1,922-ton (1930) Fishguard-Rosslare Railway Co. ferry *St. Patrick.*† 4. The 2,294-ton (1924) Southern Railway (Southampton-St. Malo) ferry *Dinard.* 5. The 2,143-ton (1929) Southern Railway (Southampton-Channel Islands) ferry *Isle of Jersey.* 6. The 1,774-ton (1913) London, Brighton, and South Coast Railway (Newhaven-Dieppe) ferry *Paris.*† 7. The 2,288-ton (1928) Southern Railway (Newhaven-Dieppe) ferry *Worthing.* 8. The 2,912-ton (1929) Southern Railway (Dover-Calais) ferry *Canterbury.* 9. The 2,391-ton (1933) Southern Railway (Newhaven-Dieppe) ferry *Brighton.*† 10. The 2,211-ton (1931) Southern Railway (Southampton-Channel Islands) ferry *Isle of Sark.* 11. The 2,291-ton (1924) Southern Railway (Southampton-Channel Islands/Brittany) ferry *St. Briac.*† 12. The 2,143-ton (1930) Southern Railway (Southampton-Channel Islands) ferry *Isle of Guernsey.* 13. The 206-ton (1880) twin-screw schooner *Oceana.* 14. The 138-ton (1930) yacht *Caleta.* 15. The 59-ton (1922) schooner *Michabo.* 16. The 2,386-ton (1918) Southern Railways (Folkestone-Boulogne) ferry *Maid of Orleans.*† 17. The 576-ton (1898) Trinity House ship *Vestal.* 18. The 699-ton (1927) three-masted sailing ship *Creole.* 19. The 821-ton (1933) motor schooner *Trenora.* 20. The 828-ton (1920) steam yacht *Cutty Sark.* 21. The 90-ton (1907) Bermudan schooner *Joyette.* 22. The 112-ton (1904) steam yacht *Medea.* 23. The 68-ton (1925) motor schooner *Seaward.* 24. The 32-ton (1909) motor schooner *Hoshi.*

Line 14 (with ships that were to leave to the east): 1. The 271-ton (1935) Directorate of Fisheries research vessel/diesel trawler *Mary White.* 2. The 324-ton (1917) Directorate of Fisheries research vessel *George Bligh.* 3. The 290-ton (1901) Scottish Fisheries research/fisheries protection vessel *Minna.* 4. The 1,640-ton (1930) class-name sloop *Hastings.*[c] 5. The 1,350-ton (1916) *Flower*-class sloop *Lupin.*[c] 6. The 1,890-ton (1936) *I*-class destroyer *Icarus.*[b] 7. The 1,815-ton (1929) destroyer *Antelope.*[b] 8. The 2,012-ton (1929) destroyer leader *Codrington.*[b]† 9. The 6,715-ton (1933) *Arethusa*-class light cruiser *Galatea.*[b]† 10. The 1,510-ton (1936) *Grimsby*-class sloop *Aberdeen.*[b]

Line 15: 1. The 127-ton (1928) steam drifter *D'Arcy Cooper.*† 2. The 448-ton (1935) steam trawler *Stormflower.* 3. The 90-ton (1915) steam drifter *Ocean Pioneer.* 4. The 275-ton (1919) Milford Steam Trawling Co. trawler *Milford Countess.* 5. The 745-ton (1936) *Kingfisher*-class patrol sloop *Kittiwake.*[c] 6. The 745-ton (1936) *Kingfisher*-class patrol sloop *Puffin.*[c] 7. The 1,815-ton Canadian (1930) A-class destroyer *Saguenay.*[c] 8. The 1,815-ton Canadian (1930) A-class destroyer *Skeena.*[c]† 9. The 1,680-ton Indian (1934) sloop *Indus.*[c]† 10. The 579-ton (1937) Mersey Dock and Harbour Board pilot vessel *William M. Clarke.* 11. The 342-ton (1932) Trinity House pilot vessel *Brook.*

Line 16: 1. The Lowestoft smack *Telesia.* 2. The 745-ton (1936) *Kingfisher*-class patrol sloop *Mallard.*[c] 3. The 1,330-ton (1934) *Halcyon*-class minesweeper *Harrier.*[c] 4. The 1,330-ton (1934) *Halcyon*-class minesweeper *Skipjack.*[c]† 5. The 1,330-ton (1934) *Halcyon*-class minesweeper *Hussar.*[c]† 6. The 1,330-ton (1936) *Halcyon*-class minesweeper *Niger.*[c]† 7. The 1,330-ton (1935) *Halcyon*-class minesweeper *Speedwell.*[c] 8. The 1,330-ton (1936) *Halcyon*-class minesweeper *Salamander.*[c] 9. The 1,330-ton (1933) class-name minesweeper *Halcyon.*[c]

Line 17: 1. The 342-ton (1928) Southern Railways (Isle of Wight) paddle steamer ferry *Merstone.* 2. The 381-ton (1911) London, Brighton, and South Coast Railway (Isle of Wight) paddle steamer ferry *Duchess of Norfolk.* 3. The 684-ton (1934) Southern Railways (Isle of Wight) paddle steamer ferry *Sandown.* 4. The 825-ton (1930) Southern Railway (Isle of Wight) paddle steamer ferry *Southsea.*†

Review procession: 1. The 793-ton (1910) Trinity House yacht *Patricia.* 2. The 4,700-ton (1899) royal yacht *Victoria and Albert.* 3. The 1,650-ton (1934) Admiralty yacht *Enchantress.* 4. The 23,500-ton (1935) P&O R.M.S. *Strathmore.* 5. The 13,241-ton (1921) Lamport and Holt cruise liner *Vandyke.*† 6. The 16,755-ton (1928) New Zealand Shipping Co. R.M.S. *Rangitiki.* 7. The 18,724-ton (1927) Cunard R.M.S. *Laurentic.*† 8. The 16,280-ton (1920) Donaldson Atlantic liner *Cameronia.* 9. The 995-ton (1919) *Hunt*-class minesweeper *Alresford.* 10. The 995-ton (1918) *Hunt*-class minesweeper *Saltburn.* 11. The 995-ton (1919) *Hunt*-class survey ship *Kellett.* 12. The 792-ton (1916) New Medway Steam Packet Co. paddle steamer ferry *Queen of Thanet.* 13. The 825-ton (1930) Southern Railway (Isle of Wight) paddle steamer ferry *Whippingham.* 14. The 342-ton (1928) Southern Railway (Isle of Wight) paddle steamer ferry *Portsdown.*†

E&OE

THE CORONATION REVIEW: ALPHABETICAL LIST OF SHIPS

The sloop *Aberdeen:* 14.10. The destroyer *Acheron:* 9.7. The German armored ship *Admiral Graf Spee:* 7.15. The *Alexandra:* 3.15. The minesweeper *Alresford:* rp.9. The yawl *Altair:* 6.19. The yawl *Amaryllis:* 6.12. The destroyer *Amazon:* 9.6. The schooner *Amphitrite:* 6.16. The ferry *Amsterdam:* 3.20. The tanker *Anadara:* 3.1. The schooner *Anglia:* 5.13. The destroyer *Antelope:* 14.7. The passenger ship *Aquila:* 3.17. The liner *Aquitania:* 3.7. The liner *Arandora Star:* 4.8. The Japanese heavy cruiser *Ashigara:* 7.12. The cutter *Astra:* 6.11. The R.M.S. *Atlantis:* 3.6. The yacht *Atlantis:* 6.4.

The battleship *Barham:* 9.28. The Portuguese sloop *Bartolomeu Dias:* 7.7. The destroyer *Basilisk:* 9.17. The *B*-class destroyer *Beagle:* 9.10. The ketch *Best Friend:* 4.4. The destroyer *Blanche:* 9.13. The destroyer *Boadicea:* 9.15. The schooner *Boadicea:* 5.11. The destroyer *Boreas:* 9.16. The oiler *Brambleleaf:* 9.1. The destroyer *Brazen:* 9.11. The ferry *Brighton:* 13.9. The paddle steamer *Brighton Queen:* 2.4. The destroyer *Brilliant:* 9.12. The tanker *British Fame:* 3.2. The *Brittany:* 3.21. The destroyer leader *Broke:* 10.10. The pilot vessel *Brook:* 15.11. The destroyer *Bulldog:* 9.14. The Polish destroyer *Burza:* 7.2.

The light cruiser *Cairo:* 8.13. The yacht *Caleta:* 13.14. The tug *Calshot:* 13.2. The ship *Cameronia:* rp.8. The ferry *Canterbury:* 13.8. The light cruiser *Cardiff:* 8.18. The light cruiser *Carlisle:* 8.17. The passenger ship *City of Simla:* 3.16. The submarine *Clyde:* 12.14. The destroyer leader *Codrington:* 14.8. The light cruiser *Colombo:* 8.16. The destroyer *Comet:* 12.17. The liner *Comorin:* 4.9. The schooner *Conqueror:* 5.20. The aircraft carrier *Courageous:* 9.23. The light cruiser *Coventry:* 8.15. The sailing ship *Creole:* 13.18. The destroyer *Crusader:* 12.19. The Cuban (1911) sloop *Cuba:* 7.8. The light cruiser *Curacao:* 8.19. The light cruiser *Curlew:* 8.14. The yacht *Cutty Sark:* 13.20. The repair ship *Cyclops:* 12.11.

The drifter *D'Arcy Cooper:* 15.1. The paddle steamer *Devonia:* 2.5. The heavy cruiser *Devonshire:* 10.35. The ketch *Diane:* 6.14. The liner *Dilwara:* 4.14. The ferry *Dinard:* 13.4. The Swedish armored ship *Drottning Victoria:* 7.11. The paddle steamer *Duchess of Norfolk:* 17.2. The light cruiser *Dunedin:* 8.20. The French battleship *Dunkerque:* 7.18.

The destroyer *Echo:* 8.7. The destroyer *Eclipse:* 8.6. The destroyer *Electra:* 8.5. The yacht *Enchantress:* rp.3. The destroyer *Encounter:* 8.4. The destroyer *Escapade:* 8.11. The destroyer *Escort:* 8.10. The destroyer *Esk:* 8.8. The yacht *Esmeralda:* 6.1. The schooner *Evadne:* 5.10. The destroyer *Exmouth:* 8.12. The destroyer *Express:* 8.9.

The destroyer *Fame:* 8.3. The merchantman *Flathouse:* 3.10. The sloop *Fleetwood:* 12.1. The survey ship *Flinders:* 4.17. The cutter *Flying Cloud:* 11.1. The ferry *Flying Kestrel:* 11.5. The schooner *Foinaven:* 5.9. The destroyer *Foresight:* 8.2. The paddle steamer *Freshwater:* 11.6. The heavy cruiser *Frobisher:* 10.33. The aircraft carrier *Furious:* 9.22.

The light cruiser *Galatea:* 14.9. The destroyer *Gallant:* 10.28. The destroyer *Garland:* 10.31. The research vessel *George Bligh:* 14.2. The Greek light cruiser *Giorgios Averoff:* 7.14. The destroyer *Gipsy:* 10.30. The paddle steamer *Glen Gower:* 2.2. The paddle steamer *Glen Usk:* 2.3. The aircraft carrier *Glorious:* 9.24. The paddle steamer *Golden Eagle:* 2.9. The destroyer *Glowworm:* 10.26. The destroyer *Grafton:* 10.29. The submarine *Grampus:* 12.12. The ferry *Greetings:* 11.3. The destroyer *Grenade:* 10.25. The destroyer leader *Grenville:* 10.32. The destroyer *Greyhound:* 10.27. The destroyer *Griffin:* 10.24. The netlayer *Guardian:* 12.2.

The submarine H. 32: 10.19. The submarine H. 33: 10.12. The submarine H. 34: 10.18. The submarine H. 49: 10.11. The submarine H. 50: 10.17. The minesweeper *Halcyon:* 16.9.

The minesweeper *Harrier:* 16.3. The sloop *Hastings:* 14.4. The coaster *Henry Moon:* 3.11. The destroyer *Hereward:* 8.1. The light carrier *Hermes:* 9.19. The ferry *Hilsea:* 1.2. The battlecruiser *Hood:* 9.26. The schooner *Hoshi:* 13.24. The minesweeper *Hussar:* 16.5.

The destroyer *Icarus:* 14.6. The sloop *Indus:* 15.9. The gunnery training ship *Iron Duke:* 9.27. The ferry *Isle of Guernsey:* 13.12. The ferry *Isle of Jersey:* 13.5. The ferry *Isle of Sark:* 13.10.

The Dutch *Sumatra*-class light cruiser *Java:* 7.13. The schooner *Jeannette:* 1.1. The ferry *Joybelle III:* 1.3. The schooner *Joyette:* 13.21.

The Estonian submarine *Kalev:* 7.1. The survey ship *Kellett:* rp.11. The destroyer leader *Kempenfelt:* 9.18. The sloop *Kittiwake:* 15.5. The Turkish destroyer *Kocatepe:* 7.3.

The submarine L. 26: 10.14. The submarine L. 27: 10.20. The submarine L. 54: 10.13. The brigantine *Lady of Avenel:* 5.7. The yacht *Lady Vagrant:* 4.6. The liner *Lancashire:* 4.13. The R.M.S. *Lancastria:* 3.8. The cutter *Laura:* 5.17. The R.M.S. *Laurentic:* rp.7. The light cruiser *Leander:* 10.34. The heavy cruiser *London:* 10.37. The depot ship *Lucia:* 12.8. The schooner *Lucinda:* 4.7. The ketch *Lulworth:* 6.9. The sloop *Lupin:* 14.5.

The ferry *Maid of Orleans:* 13.16. The sloop *Mallard:* 16.2. The schooner *Mandolin:* 6.3. The Soviet battleship *Marat:* 7.16. The ketch *Maria Catharina:* 5.1. The yacht *Mariquita:* 4.2. The trawler *Mary White:* 14.1. The yacht *Medea:* 13.22. The schooner *Medusa:* 6.17. The schooner *Melisande:* 5.14. The paddle steamer *Merstone:* 17.1. The schooner *Michabo:* 13.15. The schooner *Migrante:* 5.19. The trawler *Milford Countess:* 15.4. The research vessel *Minna:* 14.3. The merchantman *Mr. Therm:* 3.9. The liner *Moldavia:* 3.5. The liner *Montrose:* 4.15. The Argentinian battleship *Moreno:* 7.17. The yacht *Moyana:* 6.5.

The submarine *Narwhal:* 12.6. The battleship *Nelson:* 8.26. The liner *Neuralia:* 4.12. The light cruiser *Newcastle:* 9.20. The U. S. battleship *New York:* 7.19. The Danish armored ship *Niels Iuel:* 7.10. The minesweeper *Niger:* 16.6. The ferry *Nimble:* 7.4.

The submarine *Oberon:* 10.16. The schooner *Oceana:* 13.13. The trawler *Ocean Pioneer:* 15.3. The ketch *Ocean Rover:* 5.21. The schooner *Ombra:* 6.6. The liner *Orontes:* 4.10. 5. 6. The *Osprey:* 5.6. The liner *Otranto:* 4.11. The submarine *Oxley:* 10.15.

The ferry *Paris:* 13.6. The yacht *Patricia:* rp.1. The depot ship *Pegasus:* 7.5. The lighthouse vessel *Pharos:* 3.12. The submarine *Porpoise:* 12.7. The paddle steamer *Portsdown:* rp.14. The schooner *Princess:* 5.12. The netlayer *Protector:* 12.9. The sloop *Puffin:* 15.6.

The battleship *Queen Elizabeth:* 9.29. The paddle steamer *Queen of Kent:* 2.8. The paddle steamer *Queen of Thanet:* rp.12.

The yacht *Radiant:* 6.10. The battleship *Ramillies:* 8.23. The liner *Ranchi:* 3.4. The R.M.S. *Rangitiki:* rp.6. The tug *Rector:* 3.13. The Romanian destroyer *Regina Maria:* 7.6. The battlecruiser *Repulse:* 9.25.The battleship *Resolution:* 8.21. The battleship *Revenge:* 8.22. The schooner *Rhodora:* 6.18. The battleship *Rodney:* 8.25. The tug *Romsey:* 11.4. The submarine *Rorqual:* 12.13. The yacht *Rosabelle:* 5.2. The paddle steamer *Royal Daffodil:* 2.7. The paddle steamer *Royal Eagle:* 3.18. The battleship *Royal Sovereign:* 8.24. The ketch *Rubicon:* 5.5.

The destroyer *Saguenay:* 15.7. The ferry *St. Briac:* 13.11. The ferry *St. Patrick:* 13.3. The minesweeper *Salamander:* 16.8. The minesweeper *Saltburn:* rp.10. The paddle steamer *Sandown:* 17.3. The schooner *Sapphire:* 6.15. The destroyer *Sardonyx:* 4.20. The yacht *Sayonara:* 11.2. The schooner *Schievan:* 5.18. The submarine *Seahorse:* 12.3. The schooner *Seaward:* 13.23. The submarine *Severn:* 12.15. The paddle steamer *Shanklin:* 2.1. The heavy cruiser *Shropshire:* 10.36. The ketch *Silver Cloud:* 6.2. The destroyer *Skate:* 4.18. The destroyer *Skeena:* 15.8. The minesweeper *Skipjack:* 16.4. The schooner *Sona:* 5.16. The light cruiser *Southampton:* 9.21. The paddle steamer *Southsea:* 17.4. The submarine

Spearfish: 10.21. The minesweeper *Speedwell*: 16.7. The submarine *Starfish*: 12.4. The yacht *Star of India*: 6.7. The trawler *Stormflower*: 15.2. The R.M.S. *Strathmore*: rp.4. The destroyer *Stronghold*: 12.18. The submarine *Sturgeon*: 10.22. The coaster *Suavity*: 3.14. The yacht *Sunbeam II*: 6.8. The submarine *Swordfish*: 12.5. The ketch *Sylvia*: 5.4.

The schooner *Tamesis*: 5.15. The yacht *Taransay*: 4.1. The minesweeper *Tedworth*: 4.16. The smack *Telesia*: 16.1. The submarine *Thames*: 12.16. The ketch *Thendara*: 5.8. The depot ship *Titania*: 10.23. The schooner *Trenora*: 13.19. The destroyer *Tyrant*: 4.19.

The ferry *Ulster Prince*: 1.5.

The Finnish armored ship *Väinämöinen*: 7.9. The cutter *Vanda*: 5.3. The liner *Vandyke*: rp.5. The destroyer *Vanquisher*: 10.7. The yacht *Venetia*: 6.13. The schooner *Vera Mary*: 4.3. The destroyer *Verity*: 9.5. The Trinity House ship *Vestal*: 13.17. The paddle steamer *Victoria*: 2.10. The royal yacht *Victoria and Albert*: rp.2. The destroyer *Vidette*: 10.5. The ferry *Vienna*: 3.19. The destroyer *Viscount*: 10.4. The liner *Voltaire*: 3.3. The ferry *Vulcan*: 13.1.

The destroyer *Walpole*: 10.8. The destroyer *Wanderer*: 10. 1. The paddle steamer *Waverley*: 2.6. The schooner *Westward*: 1.4. The paddle steamer *Whippingham*: rp.13. The destroyer *Whitshed*: 9.4. The destroyer *Wild Swan*: 9.2. The pilot vessel *William M. Clarke*: 15.10. The destroyer *Winchelsea*: 9.3. The destroyer *Winchester*: 9.9. The destroyer *Wishart*: 10.3. The destroyer *Wolfhound*: 10.6. The destroyer *Woolston*: 10.9. The depot ship *Woolwich*: 12.10. The ferry *Worthing*: 13.7. The destroyer *Wren*: 10.2. The destroyer *Wrestler*: 9.8.

The yacht *Zaza*: 4.5.

THE CORONATION REVIEW: SUMMARY, SOURCES, AND POSTSCRIPTS

Present at the coronation review of 20 May 1937 was a total of 101 warships, 22 submarines, and 11 other units drawn from the Home, Mediterranean, and Reserve Fleets, plus the royal and the admiralty yachts, two minesweepers, and one survey ship that were in the review procession: also present were two Canadian, one New Zealand, and one Indian warships, plus three fisheries protection/research vessels.

Representing seventeen foreign countries were single ships from the Argentinian, Cuban, Danish, Dutch, Estonian, Finnish, French, German, Greek, Japanese, Polish, Portuguese, Romanian, Soviet, Swedish, Turkish, and the U.S. navies. No Italian warship was present at the review, and, with reference to European states with coastlines, there were no warships from Albania, Belgium, Bulgaria, Latvia, Lithuania, Norway, or Yugoslavia, nor, perhaps very predictably, from the Irish Free State.

Allocated berths but not present at the review were five warships, namely the 2,175-ton Spanish (1933) *Churruca*-class destroyer *Ciscar* and, from the Home Fleet, the 33,500-ton (1914) *Royal Sovereign*-class battleship *Royal Oak*, the 2,022-ton (1934) destroyer leader *Faulknor*, and the 1,940-ton (1934) *F*-class destroyers *Foxhound* and *Fearless*. Presumably the aftermath of the Guernica raid (26 April) and the start of the Nationalist offensive that was to result in the fall of Bilbao on 18 June account for the absence of the *Ciscar*. The four British warships were absent because, independently, they had been sent to Saint-Jean-de-Luz and the Bilbao area in order to escort shipping in the area. The *Royal Oak* had sailed from Devonport on 24 April and returned to Portsmouth on 4 June. The *Faulknor* sailed from Portsmouth on 17 April and arrived at Saint-Jean-de-Luz, via La Pallice, two days later, and the *Foxhound* sailed from Portland on 8 May; they returned to Portsmouth on 11

TABLE APPENDIX 2.1

	Home Fleet	Mediterranean Fleet	Reserve Fleet	Other Units*	Total
Capital ships	6	4	-	-	10
Fleet carriers	2	1	-	-	3
Light carrier	-	1	-	-	1
Heavy cruisers	-	3	-	-	3
Light cruisers	3	1	7	1‡	12
Destroyer leaders	1	2	1	-	4
Destroyers	22	11	20	2‡	55
Submarines	17	5	-	-	22
Sloops	1	1	5	1‡	8
Minesweepers	-	-	8	2	10
Netlayers	1	1	-	-	2
Depot/Repair ships	2	2	1	-	5
Survey Ships	-	-	1	1	2
Training ship	1	-	1	-	2
Oiler	-	-	1	-	1
Yachts	-	-	-	2	2
Other (passenger ferry)	-	-	1	-	1
Total	56	32	46	9	143

* The review procession and imperial (‡) naval units only.

June. In the time that they were at Saint-Jean-de-Luz, at La Pallice, and off Bilbao they were in contact with the Spanish Nationalist battleship *Espana* and light cruiser *Almirante Cervera* and the German submarine U. 26, various French warships that included the battleship *Bretagne* and light cruiser *Émile Bertin*, the U.S. destroyers *Hatfield* and *Kane*, a considerable number of merchantmen and auxiliaries, and one ship, the *Habana*, which appears to have run a shuttle-service for refugees. It was escorted to Bilbao by the *Fearless* (and very briefly by the *Royal Oak*) on 16 May, then was escorted initially by the destroyer *Forester*, and then to the Needles off the Isle of Wight by the *Fearless*, the British destroyer then proceeding to Portland while the *Habana* (packed with children) made its way to Southampton, which it reached on 23 May. On 6 June the *Fearless* was again escorting the *Habana*, this time to Bilbao.[5]

* * *

Of the naval units present at the review, a total of forty-four warships, eight submarines, the fleet oiler, and the single Canadian and Indian units were lost to all causes, including constructive total losses, as were six of the foreign warships, in the course of the Second World War. The *Ciscar* was sunk in Gijón harbor by Nationalist aircraft on 21 October 1937 but after the Nationalist capture of the port it was raised (in March 1938), refitted, and returned to service, being involved in operations in the last phase of the war.

* * *

The other ships in attendance at the review numbered sixteen liners, thirty-six ferries, two tankers, four small merchantmen, five fishing vessels, seven harbor and light vessels, and sixty-two yachts, ketches, schooners, and associated craft. A number of vessels have defied identification, and it needs be noted that with reference to the yachts and auxiliaries their details, drawn from the Lloyd's Lists of 1936–1937, 1937–1938, 1938–1939, and 1939–1940, in many cases represent best guesses, ownership by members of the houses of parliament or individuals important in industry and the city, home port, and size being the criteria used as the basis of submission in these tables. The *Westward*, for example, would seem to have been a schooner, but which of two could not be determined, while the *Medusa*'s credentials as a 627-ton schooner seem credible but for the fact that a 32-ton motor yacht of the same name was both local and owned by an earl.

Two ships, namely, the 1,599-ton (1936) Fulham Borough Council ship *Fulham* and the 14,204-ton (1922) Australian passenger-cargo liner *Esperance Bay*, had been afforded berths but apparently were not present, and their places would seem to have been taken by two ships that were not assigned berths on the original chart. Moreover, on certain program lists, but not on any of the charts, there seems to have been provision for the 10,100-ton (1902) naval hospital ship *Maine*, the 6,618-ton (1937) Charente Steam Ship Co. liner *Inkosi*, the 16,418-ton (1921) Canadian Pacific Railways liner *Montcalm*, the 9,648-ton Bibby Line liner *Somersetshire* and the 1,850-ton (1923) Eastern Telegraph cable vessel *Mirror*, but none of these appear to have been present on the day.

Of the units given here as present at the review seven liners, eleven ferries, both tankers, two merchantmen, one harbor tug, and one drifter were sunk in the course of the Second World War: in addition, two of the liners and one of the ferries in the review procession were also lost. Two yachts, two ketches, and three schooners were also sunk. In need be noted, however, that the available record in reference to the fate of these yachts (as opposed to the warships and merchantmen) is necessarily gaps held apart by the occasional detail, and the total of seven must be regarded accordingly.

* * *

The flagship of Trinity House[6] is the only ship allowed to precede the royal yacht when the ruling sovereign is in it and in home waters, and with Trinity House exercising this right the *Patricia* led the *Victoria and Albert* (which left Portsmouth at 1505) and the Admiralty yacht *Enchantress*. These were followed by five liners, two minesweepers, one survey ship, and three paddle steamers. The five liners embarked guests of the British government: the *Alresford* had on board guests of the Board of Admiralty, the *Saltburn* guests of the admiral commanding the Home Fleet, the *Kellett* guests from Portsmouth and Gosport, and the three ferries various naval staff personnel.[7] After the inspection, which lasted between 1530 and 1710, the royal yacht took up position astern of the battleship *Queen Elizabeth*; the *Patricia* took up its position astern of *Victoria and Albert*. The *Enchantress* and the three naval units took up position astern of the *London*, while seven of the other eight ships took up assigned positions in the general area between Horse Sand Fort and No Man's Land Fort. The one remaining unit, the *Rangitiki*, does not seem to have been afforded a berth and presumably did not remain in company. There was a fly-past of Royal Air Force flying boats and aircraft after 1730, and for two hours, beginning at 2200, the fleet was illuminated with different flare, rocket, and searchlight displays.

On the following day, between 1000 and 1415, King George VI personally inspected the three fleet flagships, the *Nelson* (Home Fleet), *Queen Elizabeth* (Mediterranean Fleet), and *Dunedin* (Reserve Fleet), and the *Southampton*, after which he returned to the *Victoria and Albert* and then left for Portsmouth. At that stage the review was over, though many of the British warships remained off Spithead over the following days, and over the next two days selected battlecruisers, carriers, and light cruisers were open to the public, as had been some of their number on 15, 16, and 17 May.

* * *

SOURCES

The obvious source for a diagrammatic representation of the review is P. Ransome-Wallis, *The Royal Navy Reviews 1935–1977*, and the *Coronation Fleet Review Brochure. Souvenir Programme*, which was published by the Admiralty Portsmouth Naval Week Committee and was on sale to the public for the princely sum of six pennies (2.5 pence). The charts of these two publications are clearly derived from *Revue of the Fleet by His Majesty the King at Spithead on 20 May 1937. List of Ships*. This publication has one chart, dated 1 May 1937, but with a note that stated provision for amendments to 6 May, and this chart quite clearly is the one used in the *Brochure*, in various other programs of individual ships, and in the newspapers. This map, in color, followed the *Admiralty Notice to Mariners* of 9 April 1937 that set out the areas that were to be reserved for warships and the review, and these areas, and indeed the lines, corresponded to those of the 1935 Silver Jubilee review.

The representations of the Admiralty publication and *The Royal Navy Reviews 1935–1977* indicate intent rather than what were in position on the day, a state of affairs that is understandable in reference to the programs of 1937 but not to the Ransome-Wallis 1982 publication. *The Daily Telegraph* in its diagram of 20 May included most of these units, albeit with a number of changes: the *Ciscar* and *Royal Oak* were assigned their places in their respective lines but with a footnote in which the absence of these ships was recorded.

The main source for the representation given here has been *The Times* chart of 21 May 1937 purporting to show where ships were at the time of the inspection and *The Daily Mail* report of the same date and its supplement of 22 May 1937. There are a host of differences between *The Times* diagram and the others, for example, the order of the four *Royal Sovereign*-class battleships and the absence of three Home Fleet destroyers.

The newspapers carried photographs of ships, of biplanes over the assembled company, and of the fleet illuminated at night.

What needs be noted, however, is that in the Caird Library within the National Maritime Museum there are a number of brochures relating to this review. There are in this collection railway programs—a 9s.6d./47.5p. day-trip from Waterloo station in

London to Portsmouth, a 10s./50p. round trip from the Tower of London arriving back at 0200 on 21 May, and, more comfortably middle-class, a 32s.6d./£1.62.5p. round-trip from Victoria station that included provision for seeing the royal procession from the ferry *Paris*—that really do belong to a bygone age, and there are a number of other programs, issued by various ships, that most certainly serve only to confuse.

The most obvious areas of disparity in terms of records exist with respect to units stated in these other programs to be present at the review. The 316-ton (1924) *Medway Queen*, a New Medway Steam Packet Company paddle steamer ferry, is one example of a ship which was supposedly present at the review but which does not seem to have been entered on any lists as having been present in any line. But certain of these other programs provide lists of some diversity. Among liners stated to be present were the 22,209-ton (1926) Royal Mail Line ship *Alcantara*, the 8,762-ton (1924) City Line liner *City of Venice*, the 9,213-ton British India Steam Navigation liner *Nevassa*, the 19,627-ton (1929) P&O liner *Viceroy of India*, the 20,445-ton (1930) Union Castle liner *Warwick Castle*, and two other liners, the *Homeric* and *Pura*, the details of which have proved elusive. Reference was also made to the presence of the 10,825-ton (1925) liner *Indrapoera*, but this would seem unlikely given the fact that it was a Dutch Rotterdamsche Lloyd liner, and there was also reference to the presence of the 52,266-ton (1912) liner *Berengaria:* one wonders if its not having been included on official lists and charts had anything to do with the twin facts that it would have been the largest vessel at the review and, sotto voce, it was a German ship taken as a prize and retained in British service but was not a British ship per se.[8] In addition, in various brochures there are some seven fishing vessels, eight yachts, and one merchantmen cited as present at the review, but not on any official lists.[9] As always in such matters, the list and all its entries are submitted alongside E. & O. E.

* * *

POSTSCRIPTS

1. Any consideration of what was present off Portsmouth on 20 May 1937 may well invoke the question of what was not, and the answer in capital ship terms is that two, the *Valiant* and *Renown*, were in shipyard hands and the remaining two, the *Malaya* at Devonport and the *Warspite* at Portsmouth, were not in commission; the carrier *Argus*, for some reason or another, was absent.[10] The number of cruisers that were not present at the review seems surprisingly high, even allowing for the fact that a number were in dockyard hands, in reserve, or on distant stations; little more than one in three British cruisers were at the review.[11] Interestingly there was a report in *The Times* that the carrier *Eagle*, the heavy cruisers *Cumberland* and *Suffolk*, the minelayer *Adventure*, the destroyers *Dainty*, *Decoy*, *Defender*, and *Diana*, and the sloop *Falmouth* were expected to arrive on this day at Wei-hai-wei, where they would join the light cruiser *Danae*, the destroyer leader *Duncan*, and the destroyers *Delight* and *Duchess*, but it seems that this was public-relations gimmickry—just to round off the day—rather than accurate reporting; the *Eagle* sailed from Singapore on 1 May and arrived at Hong Kong on 6 May but did not sail, with the *Dainty* for company, for Wei-Hai-Wei until 28 May; it reached Wei-hai-Wei on 3 June after effecting a rendezvous with the light cruisers *Capetown* and *Danae* and the destroyer *Westcott* on the previous day.[12]

2. The closing of this section could not be considered complete without reference to one ship, the 112-ton (1904) steam yacht *Medea* (13.22). It is one of only two vessels still

in existence that served in both of the twentieth century's world wars, in the French Navy in 1917–1918 and then in the British Navy after 1939.

3. And, of course, it was the 1937 review that inadvertently played host to one celebrated, or perhaps more accurately infamous, episode, well established in British folk lore: the B.B.C. live radio broadcast of proceedings by a reporter who, evidently, had been celebrating both too early and a little too liberally.

NOTES

1. It should be noted that there was a distinction between the review of the fleet and fleet reviews. The review of the fleet would involve a number of fleets, but courtesy and decorum, such as that displayed to the king and queen of Afghanistan, involved only the Atlantic Fleet. Interestingly, the official program for this visit, on 3 April 1928, was written in English and in an Afghan script, but whether the latter was Dari or Pashto is unknown to this author.

2. The first review for a specifically royal occasion was the 1820 coronation review, and this was followed by Queen Victoria's golden and diamond jubilee reviews in 1887 and 1897 respectively. This custom ended in 2002 with the decision that what would have been a golden jubilee review would not be held because of costs, not that Britain had a fleet to review.

3. The highest number of runs ever scored in an over at this time was thirty-four, made in 1911 by Ted Alletson: this record stood until 1968, when Garfield Sobers became the first (and to date only) person ever to score the maximum possible thirty-six runs in an over. It should be noted, however, that Alletson's runs came off eight balls, the over having two illegal no-balls, those of Sobers off the standard six-ball over; Gimblett's runs, obviously, were not scored off a single over.

4. It should be noted that the *Pegasus* was given in the official souvenir brochure as an aircraft carrier, which does seem to be somewhat dated. Its exact status is somewhat elusive, but it was not an aircraft carrier in 1937.

5. The *Fearless* returned to Devonport on 11 June; the *Forester*, which had sailed from Portsmouth on 17 April, arrived back at Portsmouth on 11 June. Other British units involved in these operations included the capital ships *Hood* (before the review) and *Resolution* (both before and after the review), the heavy cruiser *Shropshire*, the destroyer leader *Kempenfelt*, the destroyers *Blanche*, *Boreas*, *Firedrake*, *Fortune*, and *Fury*, and two oilers, the 5,620-ton (1917) *Montenol* and the 11,660-ton (1919) *Wave Nawab*. Sources: logs for April–July 1937 of the *Royal Oak* (ADM 53.105585–105588), the *Faulknor* (103158–103161), *Fearless* (103179–103182), *Forester* (103350–103353) and the *Foxhound* (103421–103424).

6. Trinity House, established by royal charter in 1514, is the corporation responsible for the provision and maintenance of maritime navigation aids—including buoys, lighthouses, and lightships, and the marking of shipping lanes—in British waters.

7. Interestingly, in the official program the *Alresford*, *Saltburn*, *Kellett*, and *Tedworth* (which had embarked the guests of the Admiral Superintendent Portsmouth) were designated as tenders.

In addition to these it would seem that the *Nimble* was host to certain invited but retired naval officers and that three small units not cited in any official listing also discharged hospitality obligations. These were the 134-ton (1914) London-based twin-screw tug *Aid* and the *Pelter* (details unknown), which respectively embarked certain Gosport and Portsmouth personnel while the 274-ton (1906) Mersey Towing Company ferry *Bison* had on board various personnel from the major armaments firms.

8. The same point, *mutatis mutandis*, might apply to the *Homeric*. This ship may have been the 34,351-ton (1913) liner, which was a German prize, but it, a former White Star and then Cunard liner, had been laid up apparently in September 1936 and then sold later that year for scrap. It would seem, however, that it was not scrapped until 1938, and it may be that it was laid up locally and brought back in order to embark sightseers for the review. This would seem unlikely not least because it was sold to Thomas W. Ward and Co. for scrapping, presumably at Inverkeithing, and therefore probably was not laid up at (an expensive) Southampton or in this immediate vicinity, but there seems no other *Homeric* to which the reference may apply.

9. The fishing vessels named in these various programs as being present were the 277-ton (1918) Ritchie and Davies (Milford Haven) steam trawler *Arthur Cavanagh*, the 448-ton (1933) Kingston Steam Trawling Co. trawler *Kingston Cairngorm*, the 125-ton (1930) Bloomfield Company's Fleetwood-based steam trawlers *Ocean Lux* and *Ocean Vim*, the 433-ton (1934) Boston Deep Sea Fishing & Ice Co. Fleetwood-based trawler *Phyllis Rosalie*,† and the *Boy Leslie* and *Eta* (details elusive); the yachts were the 87-ton (1929) motor ketch *Candida*, the 140-ton (1902) motor schooner *Cetonia*, the 436-ton (1896) motor barque *Fantôme II*, the 20-ton (1894) cutter *Shamrock* (from the Clyde), the 113-ton (1933) cutter *Velsheda*, and the 315-ton (1929) motor schooner *Viva II*, and the *Atlantic* and *Yankee* (details elusive); the remaining vessel was the 1,036-ton (1929) merchantman *Discovery II*, which was a Kelper, being owned by the government of the Falkland Islands.

10. The *Malaya* was re-commissioned, with full crew, on 25 May, when it took something like four-fifths of the crew of the *Revenge*, and it would seem that the *Revenge* had been fully commissioned in part because it had taken something like the same number from the *Malaya*—see log of the *Malaya* for May 1937 (ADM 53.104.386)—but this is somewhat difficult to reconcile with the statement that the *Revenge* completed a refit in March 1937 and was re-commissioned on 1 June; presumably it "borrowed" personnel from the *Malaya* just for the review.

The *Warspite* had experienced a number of problems after reconstruction, but it does seem somewhat strange that it could not have been persuaded to make the journey from Portsmouth to Spithead for the review.

11. Absent from the review (and arranged by class and alphabetically) were the heavy cruisers *Effingham* and *Hawkins*; the *Berwick*, *Cornwall*, *Cumberland*, *Kent*, and *Suffolk*; the *Sussex*; the *Dorsetshire* and *Norfolk*; and the *Exeter* and *York*; and the light cruisers *Caledon*, *Calypso*, and *Caradoc*; the *Ceres*; the *Calcutta* and *Capetown*; the *Danæ*, *Dauntless*, *Delhi*, *Dragon*, and *Durban*; the *Despatch* and *Diomede*; the *Emerald* and *Enterprise*; the *Achilles*, *Ajax*, *Neptune*, and *Orion*; and the *Arethusa* and *Penelope*.

12. Source: The logs of the *Eagle* for May and June 1937 (ADM 53.102691 and 102692 respectively). But perhaps what is more interesting than the dates of arrival is the fact that after the French warship *Lamotte Picquet* visited the British formation at Wei-hai-wei on 17 July there was a gathering of warships at Tsingtao on 22 July. Among the units there were the Japanese light cruisers *Tatsuta* and *Tenryu* and destroyers *Asagao*, *Fuyo*, and *Karukaya*; the U.S. heavy cruiser *Augusta*, gunboat *Isabel*, minesweeper *Finch*, submarine tender *Canopus*, four submarines, and submarine rescue vessel *Pigeon*; and three Chinese gunboats, the 870-ton *Yung Hsiang* and the 740-ton *Chu Hu* and *Chu Yu*. What is interesting about this gathering was that it took place after the Lukouchiao/Marco Polo Bridge Incident of 7 July but before the onset of major conflict in northern China; the *Yung Hsiang* and *Chu Hu* were both scuttled at Tsingtao in August, and the *Chu Yu* was sunk by Japanese aircraft on the Yangtse on 2 October.

The *Eagle* left Wei-hai-wei on 7 October 1937 for Taku, below Tientsin, arriving the next day; it sailed from Taku on 10 October and arrived at Hong Kong four days later. By spring 1938 the Japanese occupied Wei-hai-wei and the Shantung peninsula, but after 1930 the main British holdings (on a ten-year lease) were not at Wei-hai-wei but on Liu-kung Island, just off the port, and British warships returned in some number to Liu-kung in spring 1938; the *Eagle* sailed from Hong Kong on 4 June and arrived off Wei-hai-wei on the eighth.

It would seem that the Liukungtao base was progressively scaled down after the outbreak of war in Europe, but in September 1938 the Munich crisis provided warning of what lay ahead. The *Eagle* sailed from Wei-hai-wei on 4 September 1938 and arrived at Hong Kong on the 8th, and sailed four days later for Singapore, arriving on 17 September. On 13 October the carrier sailed from Singapore, arriving back at Hong Kong on the 19th. On 20 September 1938 the British garrison at Shanghai was withdrawn to Hong Kong, but it was returned on 8 October; the battalion was finally withdrawn from Shanghai on 28 August 1940 and transported to Singapore.

The *Eagle* was at Singapore in early May 1939 and sailed for Hong Kong on the 19th, arriving six days later: it sailed from Hong Kong on 29 May and arrived at Wei-hai-wei on 2 June. It seems that the last occasion when a British carrier sailed from the Wei-hai-wei/Liu-kung base was on 26 July, when, in the company of the destroyer *Darling*, the *Eagle* sailed for Hong Kong, arriving on 31 July.

Sources: primarily drawn from the *Eagle*'s logs for July 1937 (ADM 53.102693), for October 1937 (ADM 53.102696) and June 1938 (ADM 53.102704) and for September–October 1938 (ADM 53.102707–102708) and May–July 1939 (ADM 53.108437–108439).

CHAPTER THREE

ETHIOPIA AND SPAIN

What is called the inter-war period actually had many wars and crises, the most obvious being the conflicts that were continuations of the First World War, namely the Russian Civil War, Intervention, the Soviet-Polish War (April 1920–March 1921), and the war that saw the emergence of a new, nationalist Turkey at the expense of Greek dreams of aggrandizement in Anatolia (June 1919–October 1922). To these should be added the series of Chinese civil wars that lasted throughout the twenties and the (very short and minor) wars between China and, first, Japan in Shantung (May 1927–May 1929) and, second, the Soviet Union in Manchuria (October 1929–January 1930). But in terms of popular perception the story of the inter-war period is told largely around the naval limitation treaties, the Ethiopian war, the Spanish Civil War, and the drift to war that is identified, correctly, with one man, Adolf Hitler (1889–1945). The Manchurian campaign (September 1931–March 1932), subsequent Japanese operations north of the Great Wall, and then Japan's "special undeclared war" after July 1937 have been treated as little more than appendices to a text that remains largely dominated by European events.

The inter-war period within Europe witnessed a whole series of (largely forgotten) episodes that range from Hungary's war with Czechoslovakia and Romania in 1919,[1] via the Corfu Incident of August 1923[2] and the Bulgarian-Greek border clashes of October 1925 and January–February 1931,[3] to Albania's all but incessant troubles and turmoil between 1924–1926 and 1937[4] and the various disturbances and coups that afflicted many countries as Europe tried to deal with frontiers and democratic systems that were new.[5] The most important of these various problems in the decade after the end of the First World War was the Franco-Belgian occupation of the Ruhr (January 1923–August 1925), but after this episode was finally resolved with the Locarno Treaty (October 1925) a certain peace, an uneasy peace perhaps, imposed itself upon Europe. Notwithstanding the onset of the Great Depression, for a decade after Locarno there was no major source of potential or immediate conflict within Europe (E&OE).

The first of the major European crises of the thirties unfolded with respect to Ethiopia and Italian ambitions in east Africa, and the second was the Spanish Civil War (July 1936–March 1939); each of these crises definitely possessed a naval dimension. The first of these came hand in hand with a number of related matters that ranged from the installation of Hitler as chancellor in Germany in January 1933 and the subsequent establishment of dictatorship in that country to the conclusion of the Franco-Soviet treaty of alliance of 2 May 1935, the Anglo-German naval treaty of 18 June 1935, and, given the distraction of Britain and France with reference to matters Italian, Mediterranean, and Ethiopian, the German reoccupation of the Rhineland on 7 March 1936. Put at its most simplest, the Ethiopian crisis in general and the Hoare-Laval Pact of December 1935 in particular marked the death of the League of Nations. If the 1935 naval treaty marked the first repudiation of the Versailles treaty and settlement, the British conduct in these various episodes, and subsequently in the first months of the Spanish Civil War, was craven, the pact of December 1935 being a wretched abnegation of responsibility and propriety on the part of Britain and France. If anything, British behavior during the early months of the Spanish war, when Britain faced the problem of one of the very few remaining democracies in Europe being confronted by a fascist military uprising, was even worse: the basic hostility of the Conservative government and senior naval officers toward the Republican government, their clear favoring of the fascist cause, and their consistent refusal to face the challenge presented by very deliberate German and Italian aggression represented a base betrayal of trust and honor.

* * *

Part of the problem in setting out such a perspective lies in the fact that British accounts of these proceedings have read the record of 1940 backward, representing the German threat—which was very real by 1940—as being in place at this time. What has been largely washed from the historical record by so many commentators is the fact that the German military superiority of 1940 was very late in arriving on the scene, and in fact was not in place until the spring of that year, and then only on account of the one matter that is never given proper consideration. German military advantage in 1940 was numerical and was particularly marked in the air; the cutting edge, however, had been provided by the Polish campaign, September–October 1939, which gave one massive advantage in terms of knowledge and experience—how to organize and handle armored divisions in the field—that was of inestimable consequence and to which the French had no answer. Lest the point be doubted: one comparison may serve as example: had the Germans attempted an attack in the west in October or November 1939, as Hitler originally wished, there is no reason to presume that this attack would have been successful; but by spring 1940 the German military knew how to concentrate armor *en echelon* across very narrow sectors, and with armor concentrated rather than dispersed in infantry-support role the Germans possessed superiority of numbers, concentration, and technique over the French. These advantages certainly did not exist in 1935, and there would seem to be little justification for the view that British compliance with Italian aggression against Ethiopia could be justified on the grounds that if Britain alienated Italy, that country "would be a potential enemy astride England's [*sic*] main line of imperial communication at a time when she was already under threat from two existing potential enemies at opposite ends of the line [Germany and Japan]. If—worse—Italy were to fight in a future war as an ally of Germany or Japan, or both, the British would be forced to abandon the Mediterranean for the first time since 1798."[6]

But Britain was not "already under threat from two existing potential enemies"—whatever "two existing potential enemies" might mean—in December 1935, and the real point seems to have been missed, or to have been deliberately misrepresented: Italy did associate with Germany (and Japan) in 1940, but Britain, despite the defeat of France, was not "forced to abandon the Mediterranean for the first time since 1798." Reading a very selective record backward, and with due alteration of detail to fit a predetermined argument, does not make good a series of British actions, or perhaps more accurately inactions, that was abject and contemptible, though perhaps one codicil need be noted. At this time, in the mid-thirties, Italy stood at what turned out to be the peak of its prestige and standing, and it commanded a status that subsequent events mocked. Italy possessed a stable, prestigious, anti-communist regime and the third largest military in the world, and it had a record in terms of Schneider Trophies and the Blue Ribbon, automobiles and aircraft, airships and increased industrial production, that was enviable; at this time, in the mid-thirties, the various weaknesses had not manifested themselves. If this in some way explains Anglo-French behavior, then it may also be noted that the Barnett argument does embrace an irony. Assuming for the sake of argument that the thesis is correct, then von Tirpitz's infamous Risk Theory worked,[7] albeit not quite in the manner and at the time that was intended. And if it had worked to some important purpose for Italy in the mid-thirties then there is little doubt that Britain, in shifting blame and responsibility, would have availed itself of the obvious scapegoats in terms of failure to provide proper support, primarily France and by extension the United States.

* * *

The Ethiopian problem can be given two points of departure in terms of origins, either the tangled and very lengthy process by which Italy established its presence in Massawa and inaugurated the Colonia Eritrea in January 1890 and which was bracketed by the wars of 1887 and 1896 or the border disputes of December 1934 affecting Ethiopia and Italian Somaliland. Thereafter a very minor dispute slowly assumed, as a result of deliberate Italian choice, major significance until the start of the campaign on 23 October with the full-scale Italian invasion of Ethiopia. The naval dimension came from the September 1935 major deployment of British naval units to the Mediterranean, which was clearly intended to provide Italy with reason to pause. The press statement that the British deployment was not intended as an act hostile to Italy was par for the course,[8] and seems to count for little alongside the fact that at this very time the British warned the Italians that they had a total of 144 warships in the Mediterranean.[9] It is difficult to understand the basis of this claim, which would mean that half the whole of the British Navy, and probably something like two-thirds to three-quarters of ships in commission, was in the Mediterranean. The basic point, nonetheless, was that the British and French were well placed in terms of combined strength and advantage of geographical position, specifically between Italy and east Africa, and could close down Italian options. But after Italy's actions were condemned by the League of Nations on 7 October the British reaction was decidedly muted, with the British foreign secretary, Sir Samuel Hoare (1880–1959), ruling out both military action against Italy and the closing of the Suez Canal to Italian warships and shipping. Hoare also displayed a certain antipathy regarding the imposition of sanctions on Italy.[10] In one sense this was crucially important, because this attitude, in effect, closed down the Balkan connection: Greece, Romania, and Yugoslavia committed themselves to the imposition of sanctions on Italy, and if the attitude of Greece and Yugoslavia was understandable in light of their suspicions of Italian intent in the Balkans, the fact was that all three countries were major trading partners of Italy, and three-fifths of Romania's oil exports were to Italy. But the pact agreed between Hoare and the French foreign minister, Pierre Laval (1883–1945), was tantamount to a cynical betrayal of a small nation that was the victim of aggression, involving as it did an almost total acquiescence in Italian demands that, in effect, would have resulted in the demise of Ethiopia as an independent state. In very large measure the immediate responsibility for this pact lay with a France that was determined that relations with Italy, very recently repaired after years of festering rivalry and muted antagonism, were not to be jeopardized by so esoteric a cause as Ethiopia, and in part the attitude of the British government was shaped by the requirements of a general election (14 November 1935) in which the opposition was impaled on the conflicting claims of its contending anti-war and collective-security factions.[11] But for whatever reasons, there was no concerted move to oppose Italian aggression, and sanctions were lifted by the League of Nations on 4 July 1936. Britain and France ended sanctions on 15 and 19 June, respectively,[12] but this was three months after Anglo-French consultation with the Italians that in effect gave the latter a free hand and a month after the Balkan League countries declared themselves free to handle their relations with Germany and Italy without reference to the provisions of the Covenant of the League of Nations.[13]

* * *

The Ethiopian episode killed the League of Nations. The Manchurian episode had gravely damaged the League, which obviously had been found wanting, but Manchuria, China, and Japan very literally were, to borrow a phrase, "far away countries of which we know nothing"[14] and could be quietly dismissed from proceedings; the Ethiopian crisis was very different. It directly involved the two leading European powers, and it involved their deliberate appeasement of a third power and their complicity in aggression: like Czechoslovakia in September 1938, Ethiopia was obliged to pay the price for Britain and France avoiding war.

The reverse of this argument, however, is that Britain and France should have gone to war in order to preserve a general peace, and this in turn raises the obvious question of the balance of naval forces in the Mediterranean and the likely outcome of a conflict had events unfolded to that end. Very simply, in September 1935, in terms of capital ship and cruiser numbers, the British and French formations in the western Mediterranean and the British formations in the eastern Mediterranean were each more than the equal of an Italian Navy that had no capital ships and just one seaplane carrier in service, and if in terms of destroyer and submarine numbers the Italian Navy had been able to secure advantage in the central and eastern Mediterranean, this would have been of small account and certainly not of any real strategic significance.[15] Both Italy on the one hand and Britain and France on the other had difficult defensive obligations: in the case of Italy a long, exposed western coast, the islands, and the lines of communication to Tripolitania and Cyrenaica, along with the small matter of Britain's possession of Gibraltar and the Suez Canal, which placed Britain astride Italy's lines of communication with the world beyond the Mediterranean. For the French the defensive commitment was similar in terms of the coast of the metropolitan homeland and the links with the Maghreb, and for the British there was real difficulty in terms of Malta and the line of communication linking Gibraltar, Malta, Alexandria, and Port Said. Overall, however, the balance of geographical position, commitments, and defensive obligations and overall numbers favored the British and French and would have told against the Italian advantage of concentration. Thus it is somewhat difficult to believe that the outcome of a conflict would not have been very predictable: Italy (and it bears repetition that at this stage it had no capital ships in commission) simply did not have capacity to defeat what historically had been the two greatest European naval powers, while what were on paper Italy's greatest advantages, central position and single nation, would have been no more than that—paper advantages. Supporting evidence for this conclusion exists in two matters, the first being events in the Mediterranean theater between June 1940 and March 1941, which point in an obvious direction: it would be wholly unrealistic to suppose that in 1935–1936 the Italian Navy would have registered a degree of effectiveness and success that eluded it in 1940–1941, when its advantages were significantly greater than they had been five years earlier. That is a comment on the Barnett absurdity, and also upon the British political and naval leadership in the mid-thirties that was responsible for a lack of effective response to Italian aggression and that most definitely had predictable repercussions with reference to the countries of eastern and southeast Europe.

The second matter supporting the thesis of Italian defeat in 1935, had matters come to force of arms, is more relevant in terms of naval power per se; it relates directly to Britain's ability to draw from outside the theater in order to ensure massive superiority of numbers and to the status and the movement of certain cruisers. A point that seems to have escaped historical attention is that the Silver Jubilee review at Spithead on 16 July 1935 placed Britain in a position relative to Italy not dissimilar to the position that Britain had held relative to Germany in August 1914, that is, with most of the fleet, including the reserve, fully manned, and at a degree of readiness that made for immediate and rapid deployment. Admittedly the units that could have been made available and that were in reserve in September—the heavy cruisers *Effingham*, *Hawkins*, and *Vindictive* and the light cruisers *Caledon*, *Calypso*, *Caradoc*, *Cardiff*, *Ceres*, and *Dauntless*—were beginning to age, but most definitely retained a certain usefulness at this stage of proceedings.

But in terms of the movement of units to and within theater, the British situation is not without a certain interest. Perhaps the most obvious of the movements related to those within the Mediterranean and from British home waters, and on the latter score the aircraft carrier *Courageous*, well to the north of Cape Ortegal on 1 September, was at Alexandria on the 7th, while the battleship *Barham* sailed from Devonport on 3 September and arrived at Alexandria on the 14th, and thereafter made its way to Port Said. The battlecruisers *Hood* and *Renown* sailed from Portland on 14 September and arrived at Gibraltar three days later, while the last hours of September saw the *Queen Elizabeth* off Cape Trafalgar as it sought to join the other two capital ships.[16] In theater the

Table 3.1. Comparative Naval Strengths with Reference to the Situation in the Mediterranean September 1935

	Capital ships	Heavy cruisers	Light cruisers	Aircraft/seaplane carriers
British Home Fleet:	*Nelson* *Rodney*		*Cairo*	*Furious*
at Portland	*Royal Sovereign*			
at Portsmouth	*Ramillies*	*Suffolk*	*Curacao* *Neptune*	
at Devonport			*Leander*	
in the Azores			*Achilles*	
en route to Gibraltar	*Queen Elizabeth*			
French Navy at Brest:	*Bretagne* *Provence*		*Duguay Trouin* *Emile Bertin* *Jeanne d'Arc*	
British Navy at Gibraltar:	*Hood* *Renown*		*Orion*	
French Navy in Western Mediterranean		*Algérie* *Dupleix* *Duquesne* *Foch* *Suffren* *Tourville*	*Pluton* *Strasbourg*	*Commandant Teste*
Italian Navy:		*Bolzano* *Fiume* *Gorizia* *Pola* *Trento* *Trieste* *Zara*	*Albercio da Barbiano* *Amberto di Giussano* *Armando Diaz* *Bartolomeo Colleoni* *Emanuele Filiberto Duca D'Aosta* *Giovanni dalle Bande Nere* *Luigi Cadorna* *Muzio Attendolo* *Raimondo Montecuccoli*	*Giuseppe Miraglia*

	Capital ships	Heavy cruisers	Light cruisers	Aircraft/seaplane carriers
at Massawa			*Bari* *Taranto*	
British Navy:	*Resolution*	*Devonshire*	*Despatch*	*Courageous*
at Alexandria:	*Revenge* *Valiant*	*Exeter* *London* *Shropshire* *Australia*		*Glorious*
at Port Said	*Barham*			
at Haifa			*Ajax* *Arethusa* *Delhi* *Durban*	
at Aden		*Norfolk*	*Emerald* *Colombo*	
en route to Aden		*Berwick* *Sussex*	*Dunedin*	
at Simon's Town			*Carlisle*	
French Navy in Indo-China:			*Lamotte-Picquet* *Primaguet*	
British Navy:				
at Wei-hai-wei		*Dorsetshire* *Kent*		
at Kobe			*Capetown*	
at Singapore		*Cornwall*		*Hermes*
at Auckland NZ			*Diomede*	
in the Caymans			*Danae*	
at Bermuda		*York*	*Dragon*	

battle and cruiser formations that had been at Malta sailed after 29 August for bases in the eastern Mediterranean; among the warships that made their way to bases beyond the immediate range of Italian aircraft were the battleships *Resolution* and *Valiant*, the aircraft carrier *Glorious*, and the heavy cruisers *Devonshire* and *London*.

Further afield, the light cruiser *Ajax* was at Barbados on 1 September 1935. On 16 September it was at Gibraltar, and ten days later it arrived at Haifa, there joining three other light cruisers on station. Its place on the West Indies station had been filled by the *Danae*, which on 26 September arrived at Kingston, Jamaica, after having sailed from Santa Barbara on the third day of the month and from San Diego the next day. On the last day of the month the heavy cruiser *York*, having been at Bar Harbor, Newport, and Philadelphia in turn, arrived at Bermuda, where it joined the light cruiser *Dragon*, which had arrived there on 6 September fresh from the reserve at Sheerness. In the meantime the heavy cruiser *Exeter*, which on 1 September was making its way south from Valparaíso in Chile, passed around Cape Horn on the afternoon of the following day and then made for the Falkland Islands. Sailing from Port Stanley on 5 September it arrived at Gibraltar on the 20th and, after pausing for breath there and at Malta, arrived at Alexandria on the last day of September: in one month it had journeyed across 91 degrees of latitude and 105 degrees of longitude.

Half a world away, movements were no less interesting. The heavy cruiser *Norfolk* sailed from Colombo and the light cruiser *Emerald* from Port Victoria in the Seychelles on 7 September; the latter arrived at Aden three days later, while the *Norfolk* arrived the following day. The light cruiser *Dunedin*, which had been on the New Zealand station on 1 September, was making its way to Aden on the last day of the month, but perhaps the most interesting of all the movements were those that related to the warships on the China station and to the heavy cruiser *Sussex*. With reference to the former, Wei-hai-wei had been returned to China on 1 October 1930, but on 1 September 1935 deployed on station were the aircraft carrier *Hermes* and heavy cruisers *Berwick*, *Cornwall*, *Dorsetshire*, and *Kent*, while the light cruiser *Capetown* was at Hong Kong. By the last day of the month, with the *Capetown* at Kobe, just two heavy cruisers remained at Wei-hai-wei. The *Cornwall* and *Hermes* were at Singapore, having arrived on the 12th and 19th respectively, while the *Berwick* on 30 September was three days from Aden; on 7 October it arrived at Alexandria. The point may seem of little relevance, but given the fact that the withdrawal of major British warships from Wei-hai-wei was not subsequently reversed, in real terms September 1935 marked the start of the final phase of a British naval presence in northern China that reached back the best part of a century.[17]

The heavy cruiser *Sussex*'s claim to special attention rests not just on the distance it traveled in a single calendar month—across 27 degrees of latitude and (in sixteen days) 85 degrees of longitude—but on places the names of which were so little known at the time but which were to become somewhat familiar within seven years, and then to be quickly and quietly forgotten. On 1 September it sailed between Upstart Bay and Fantome Island, which bracket Townsville in northeast Queensland, and on 6 September was off Faisi in the Shortland group, off southern Bougainville, in the upper Solomons. On 15 September the *Sussex* was off Tulagi, the administrative center of the Solomons, and on 19 September it was at Darwin, where, of course, the highest form of life is the kangaroo that lives in trees. Sailing four days later, on the last day of the month it passed through the Maldives on its way to Aden, which it reached on 4 October: it arrived at Port Said four days later and was at Alexandria on the 10th, where it joined hands with the *Berwick* and *Exeter*, a hitherto scattered Pacific trinity regathered.[18] And at this time there were still three heavy and seven light cruisers in reserve, not to mention one cruiser in the South Atlantic, another on the New Zealand station, three in the western Atlantic and Caribbean, and others, such as the *Neptune*, in home waters. [19]

* * *

The final part of Britain's abandonment of Ethiopia and the League of Nations and acquiescence in Italian aggrandizement came on 10 July 1936 with the governmental announcement of intention to withdraw non–Mediterranean Fleet formations and units from the Mediterranean.[20] For the better part of nine months the Mediterranean had played host to units from the Mediterranean and Home Fleets, and quite obviously there was a need to re-deploy formations and units, but within a week the intention was reversed with the announcement that certain formations and units were to remain in theater and that the Mediterranean Fleet was to consist of three *Queen Elizabeth*–class battleships with the *Hood* and *Repulse* to come, the *Glorious*, four heavy, five light, and two AA cruisers, thirty-eight destroyers, and eight submarines, plus six sloops, ten anti-submarine patrol vessels, and nineteen minesweepers, to make a formation with "well over a hundred" units, though in fact that total is ninety-eight.[21] Interestingly, this second announcement came on the same day as the military uprising in Spanish Morocco that marked the start of the Spanish Civil War and a British commitment in the western Mediterranean that was neither intended nor sought.

* * *

Civil wars are not won and lost by navies, but in this war sea power was important in deciding the outcome of the conflict even though actions between the warships of the two sides were few and the overall result of operations was primarily negative. But in the Spanish Civil War sea power manifested itself in

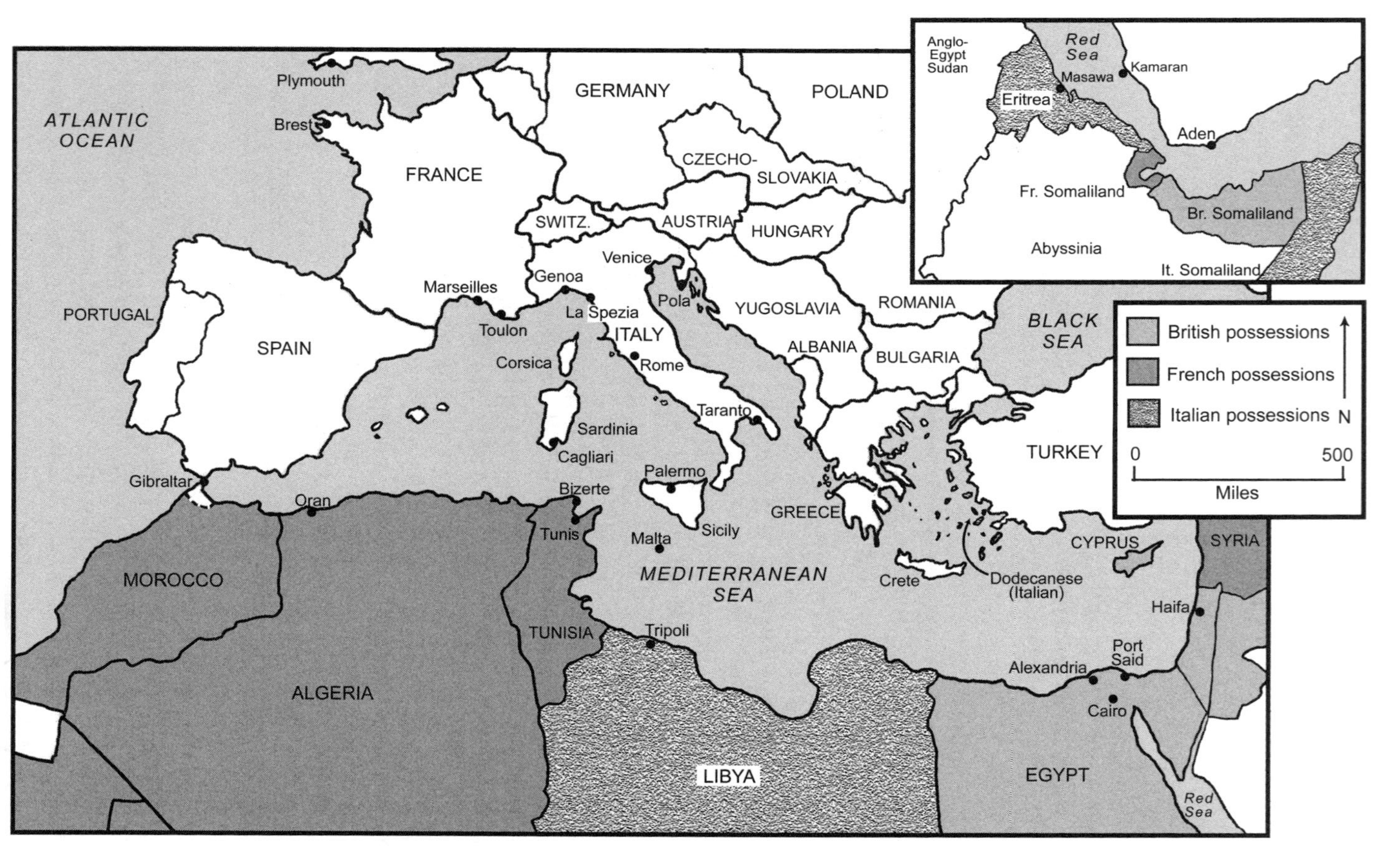

Map 1. The Mediterranean and the Red Sea: 30 September 1935

three ways. First, at the outset of war the fascist military was able to move its formations to the mainland and to establish these in the south and the north of the country primarily because the naval units that remained loyal to the legal government of the Republic were unable to prevent such movement. As the old saying has it, "The mighty 'ifs' accumulate," but it is possible to argue either one of two, or indeed both, cases about the origins and first days of this war. On the one hand, it is possible to argue that had the uprisings worked as planned, the military might have been able either to successfully topple the government without a civil war or to secure such overwhelming advantage that conflict would have been relatively minor. On the other hand, had the government immediately sanctioned a general mobilization of the people, then the various military rebel groups scattered in various parts of Spain would almost certainly have been overwhelmed.[22] But whichever argument is embraced, it is difficult to resist the view that had the navy remained loyal to the elected government, the fascist military formations and units in the overseas possessions would have had real difficulty in establishing themselves in peninsular Spain.

The second manifestation of sea power lay in the fact that in the first days of the uprising the fascist military secured not merely Spanish Morocco and the Canary Islands but in the south Sevilla, Córdoba, and Granada and in the north Pamplona on 18 July, Burgos, Valladolid, and Salamanca on 19 July, and Oviedo and Zaragoza on 20 July, as well as on the latter day Cádiz and, crucially, La Coruña and Vigo and the naval base at El Ferrol.[23] Without the latter, naval units loyal to the government were obliged to sail either to Bilbao or to the Mediterranean. Given that the series of uprisings had divided government-held Spain into two parts and that the fascist capture of Pamplona and Irún (4 September) in effect sealed off the northern enclave, most of the loyal Republican naval units were moved south, with one major result: the Nationalist rebels had secure sea-borne lines of communications westward across the North Atlantic and northward, and specifically to Nazi Germany.[24] Moreover, the combination of Cádiz and Spanish Morocco placed the Nationalists astride Republican lines of communication across the North Atlantic and hence the sources of oil on which the Spanish Navy had drawn over the previous decades. In terms of position and strategic advantage, in addition to their possession of Cádiz and Spanish Morocco the Nationalists seized Palma, on Mallorca, on 18 July and then, in September, secured Ibiza, and with their capture of Mallorca and Ibiza they established themselves astride the Republican routes eastward from Barcelona, Valencia, Cartagena, and Málaga. Nationalist cruisers were based at Mallorca after February 1937, but the real presence in the islands was Italian, specifically the Italian Air Force: Mallorca and Ibiza were under Italian control, an arrangement which the Italian authorities wanted to be permanent.[25]

The third manifestation of sea power was German and Italian support for the Nationalists in the form of the dispatch of air and military forces, the provision of supplies, and the conduct of naval operations, which drew the inevitable response: the Republican bombing of the Italian auxiliary cruiser *Barletta* at Palma on 24 May 1937 and the *panzerschiffe Deutschland* at Ibiza five days later.[26] The crucial point, however, was that German and Italian involvement in the war dates from its first days, with a total of 12,000 Nationalist troops being airlifted to Spain by German and Italian aircraft in the first two months—and 1,500 in the critical days between 28 July and 5 August 1936—while the *Deutschland* and its sister ship *Admiral Scheer* were involved in the convoying of troopships across the strait from Morocco.[27]

The better known aspect of German and Italian naval participation in the Spanish Civil War are the German bombardment of Almería on 31 May 1937 in retaliation for the bombing of the *Deutschland* and the series of Italian submarine attacks on shipping in spring-summer 1937 as part of the concerted attempt to cut Republican links with the outside world. It has been suggested that Nationalist, German, and Italian warships and submarines sank a total of forty-four merchantmen, seized as prizes another twenty-three ships, and impounded the cargoes of another ninety-eight ships in the course of the war, and their actions, in conjunction with the insipid British and French response to clear breaches of international law, was to a degree successful. Soviet supplies continued to reach Republican ports until December 1938, but by increasingly diverse routing usually with penultimate ports of call in French North Africa. Whatever reached the Republic, however, was little in comparison with the total of 180 German and 290 Italian merchantmen that made their way to ports in Nationalist hands, and they did so very often disguised, ignoring international requirements and conventions, and refusing to respond to challenge by warships supposedly enforcing a policy of non-intervention.[28] A contemptible British government thus publicly argued that it had no evidence of intervention and was unwilling to hold Italy directly responsible for the sinkings of merchantmen in the Mediterranean by its submarines. At every step British inaction, and even a willingness to accede to Nationalist claims of belligerent rights at sea, formed part of the Chamberlain policy of appeasement, "the whetting of the appetite of the insatiable," *à propos* Munich in September 1938, some six months before the end of the Spanish Civil War. At every stage there was a British compliance with German and Italian operations, even to the extent that an increasingly scornful Nationalist government in spring 1938 sanctioned the bombing of no fewer than twenty-two British merchantmen in the Mediterranean, eleven of which were sunk. With no action other than the submission of bills to the Nationalist regime—bills that were never paid—the British connivance with the fascist trio helped ensure that the war was fought between very unbalanced sides: Nationalists who had access to adequate supplies and Republicans beset by increasingly severe shortages of weapons, ammunition, and food. The price of such connivance was the demise of what in 1936 had been one of the very few democracies on mainland Europe.

* * *

The initial government response to the various military uprisings was to send warships south, specifically to Spanish Morocco, in the hope that naval forces would be able to suppress the revolt, but more immediately to prevent any movement of troops from the Canaries to the mainland. One of the destroyers thus involved, the *Churruca*, became involved in the first movement of some two hundred Moorish regular troops to the mainland, to Cádiz,[29] before it experienced something that happened in various Spanish warships. Many naval officers had been involved in the planning of the uprising, but in the battleship *Jaime Primero* and light cruisers *Libertad* and *Miguel de Cervantes*, which were ordered south, in the three destroyers sent to Melilla, and on all the warships that were at Cartagena there were lower deck risings that resulted in the imprisonment of those officers who were not killed. In the *Jaime Primero* all officers were killed, and it has been calculated that overall of the officers in ships that declared themselves for the Republic—as did the *Churruca* after it had delivered troops to the mainland—98 percent were killed or were subsequently executed at Cartagena.[30] Whatever the numbers, as a result of these developments the initial move of Nationalist troops across the strait was checked by the presence of Republican warships that made their way to Tangier and Gibraltar, but in the longer term the results did not necessarily work to Republican advantage. The Nationalist uprisings in the north meant that El Ferrol and the warships at the base were secured for the rebel cause. In the south Republican warships, hampered by uncertainty about fuel supply and most definitely anxious not to become involved in action with German and Italian warships, were based at Málaga; they played a decreasingly active role, seemingly the result, at least in part, of their being "officered-by-committee," committees that were ever more faction-riven. This is somewhat strange, because in perhaps the only two formation actions of any note the Republican formations and units most definitely were not worsted by their enemy. In the action off Cape Cherchell, west of Algiers, on 7 September 1937 the Nationalist heavy cruiser *Baleares* encountered a convoy escorted by the light cruisers *Libertad* and *Méndez Núñez*, and a number of destroyers, and was quite extensively but not seriously damaged as a result.[31] In the second action, fought on the night of 5–6 March 1938 off Cape Palos east of Cartagena, the *Baleares*, its sister ship *Canarias*, and light cruiser *Almirante Cervera*, operating as a covering force for a convoy from Italy and having been in the company of three destroyers and two minelayers that had returned to Palma with nightfall, by chance encountered a Republican formation that consisted of the *Libertad* and *Méndez Núñez* and the destroyers *Almirante Artequera, Sánchez Barcáiztegui,* and *Lepanto.* In a somewhat confused action in which ranges came down to less than three miles without the cruisers being able to hit one another, the Republican destroyers were able to close the range, with the result that torpedoes, believed to have been fired by the *Lepanto,* hit the *Baleares* and detonated its forward magazine, resulting in its immediate sinking. Some 372 of its crew were rescued by the British destroyers *Boreas* and *Kempenfelt,* which transferred these survivors to the *Canarias.*[32]

The Republican success in this action was, in terms of morale and standing, perhaps the most important registered by the Republican navy; the sinking of the battleship *España* off Cape Penas, near Santander, on 30 April 1937 to a mine was the only other Nationalist loss of real significance. But in strategic terms the Republican success, the sinking of one heavy cruiser, was of no real importance, and on several counts. Whether real or impending, the Nationalist conquest of the northern provinces freed warships from El Ferrol for service in the Mediterranean, and as early as September 1936 this change manifested itself first in the exchange in the Strait of Gibraltar between the Nationalist light cruisers *Almirante Cervera* and *Canarias* and the Republican destroyers *Almirante Juan Ferrándiz* and *Gravina* in which the *Ferrándiz* was sunk, and then in the incident in which the *Canarias* sank a Soviet merchantman off Oran on 12 December.[33] Increasingly from this time the Republican navy was second to its enemy in the western Mediterranean, while by spring 1938 Italy had given the Nationalists submarines and were to give them the old ex-German light cruiser *Taranto* later in 1938. By this time, moreover, the Nationalists had made ready the old light cruiser and thrice-named *Navarra* (formerly first the *Reina Victoria Eugenia* and then the *República*) for service, and in spring 1938 it replaced the *Baleares* in the cruiser formation. But the Cape Palos action came at the same time as the battleship *Jaime Primero* was very badly damaged at Cartagena by a German air attack; infinitely more serious for the Republic, this action came at the same time as the Nationalist offensive on the Ebro, which over the next four months cleared the area between the Ebro and the Palancia and, by reaching the sea on 14 April, divided the Republic into two parts. Then on 17 June the *Jaime Primero* was heavily damaged by a magazine explosion and major fire while undergoing repair at Cartagena and was in effect written off. It was scuttled just prior to the Nationalist capture of the port, but despite being re-floated was deemed beyond economical repair and was scrapped after July 1939.[34]

In the last two years of the war various Republican warships conducted bombardments and had brushes with enemy warships and Italian submarines,[35] but increasingly the real and immediate problem facing the Republican warships was the enemy command of the air, which in the war's second and third years was all but overwhelming. Nationalist aircraft accounted for the seaplane tender *Dédalo,* which was laid up at Sagunto,[36] on 18 July 1937;

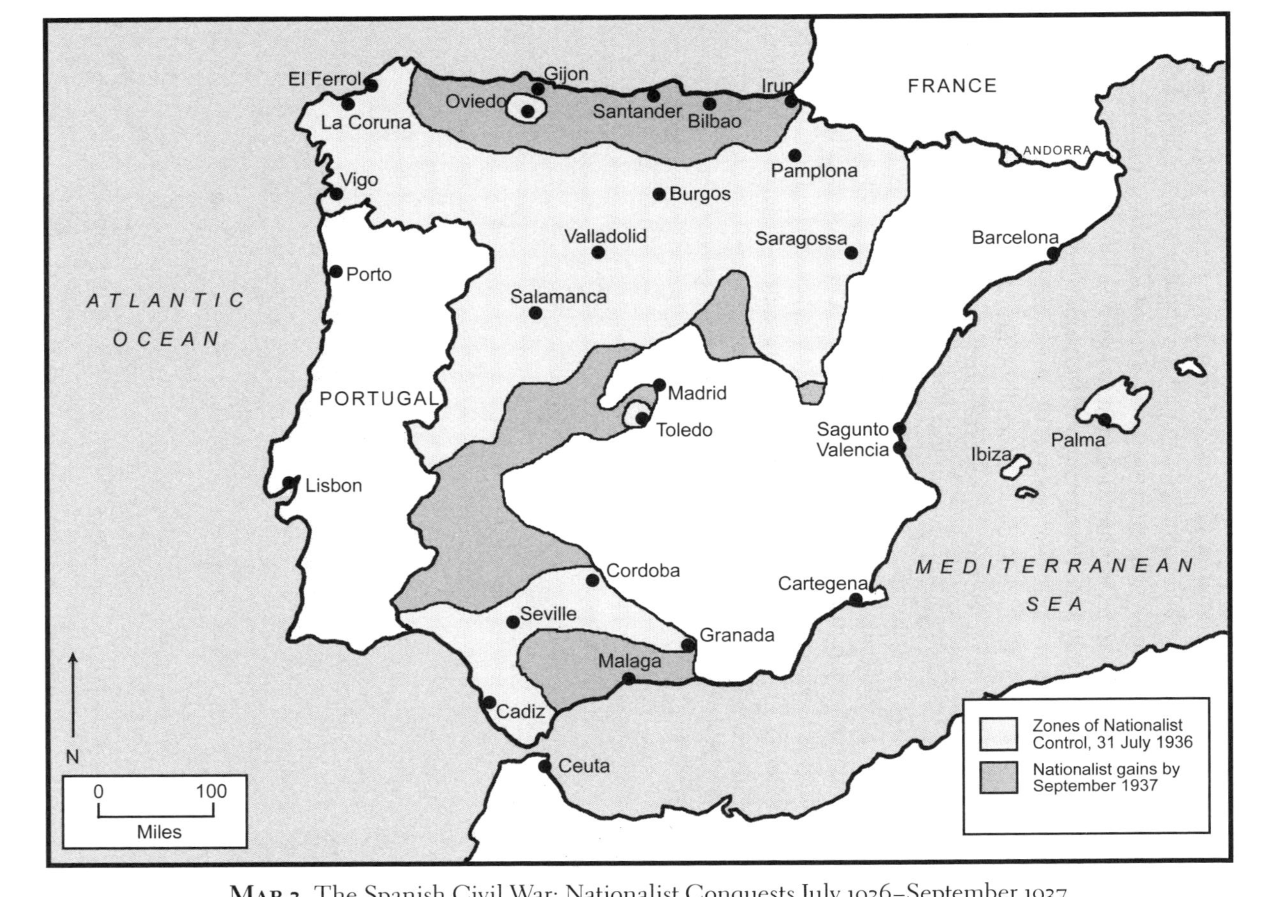

Map 2. The Spanish Civil War: Nationalist Conquests July 1936–September 1937

the submarine C. 6 (scuttled after having been badly damaged) on 20 October 1937 and the destroyer *Císcar* the following day, both units being lost off Gijón in the final act in the northern provinces;[37] the gunboat *Laya* at Valencia on 15 June 1938; and the submarine C. 1/*Isaac Peral* at Barcelona on 9 October. The modesty of such numbers was a reflection of the smallness of the Republican fleet and the fact that by the war's third year it faced increasing difficulties in terms of refit and repair, ammunition, and manpower; the needs of the army in the field obviously took precedence, and the resources of the Republic simply could not cover naval requirements. At war's end in March 1939 the Republican warships that could escape (including the *Libertad, Méndez Núnez,* and *Miguel de Cervantes*) sailed for Bizerte prior to their being surrendered to the Nationalists—and, a little known fact, the U.S. formation in theater, consisting of the light cruiser *Trenton* and destroyers *Badger* and *Jacob Jones,* sailed for Villefranche, in southern France, where it remained until 20 September, the French declaration of war necessitating a move to Lisbon. With the German victory in northwest Europe in May–June 1940, the formation, Squadron 40-T, was withdrawn from European waters, arriving at Norfolk, Virginia, on 25 July; it was disbanded on 22 October.

APPENDIX 3.1.

BRITISH, FRENCH, AND ITALIAN WARSHIPS AND 30 SEPTEMBER 1935

UNITS HAVE BEEN NAMED in alphabetical order and not by class, pennant number, or date of completion/entry into service.

The whereabouts of the French battleships, cruisers, and seaplane carrier *Commandant Teste* on 30 September 1935 represent the conclusions of the author and Anthony Clayton after extensive consultation of secondary sources; the author's request of 17 January 2008 for assistance in this matter, which was directed to the Service Historique de la Défense, was refused in the letter of 21 January on the part of Capitaine de vaisseau Serge Thébaut, Chef du Départment Marine.

The deployment of the Italian battleships, cruisers, and seaplane carrier *Giuseppe Miraglia* on 30 September 1935 was provided in the letters of 7 February and 30 June 2008 from Captain Francesco Loriga, head of the Ufficio Storico della Marina Militare. These letters set out the formation record in detail and were received with unreserved gratitude by the author.

The deployment of Italian warships on 30 September 1935 was as follows:

The battleships *Conte di Cavour* and *Giulio Cesare* were being rebuilt at Trieste and Genoa respectively; the *Andrea Doria*, at La Spezia, and *Caio Duilio*, at Taranto, had been decommissioned in readiness for their entering dockyard and being rebuilt.

With the 1st Cruiser Squadron, based at Taranto, were the 1st Cruiser Division, which was at La Maddalena island off northeast Sardinia with the heavy cruisers *Fiume*, *Gorizia*, *Pola*, and *Zara*, and the 3rd Cruiser Division, which was at Taranto with the heavy cruisers *Bolzano*, *Trento*, and *Trieste*.

With the 2nd Cruiser Squadron, based at La Spezia, were the 2nd Cruiser Division, which was dividing its time between Palermo and Messina in Sicily with the light cruiser and flagship *Giovanni dalle Bande Nere* and its sister ship *Bartholomeo Colleoni*, the 4th Cruiser Division, which was at Cagliari in southeast Sardinia with the light cruisers *Alberto di Giussano* and *Armando Diaz*, the 5th Cruiser Division, which was at Taranto with the light cruisers *Alberico da Barbiano* and *Luigi Cadorna*, and the newly raised 6th Cruiser Squadron, which was at La Spezia with the light cruisers *Emanuele Filiberto Duca D'Aosta*, which had been completed on 13 July, and *Raimondo Montecuccoli*, which had been completed on 30 June.

Also assigned to the 6th Cruiser Division was the light cruiser *Muzio Attendolo*, which had been completed on 7 August 1935 but which was not in company, being at Taranto. The light cruiser *Eugenio di Savoia* was at Genoa fitting out and was not in service. On 16 February 1936 the 7th Cruiser Squadron was formed with these two units, the *Muzio Attendolo* and the *Eugenio di Savoia*, under command.

The armored cruisers *San Giorgio* and *San Marco*, of 1908 vintage, were no longer in service as cruisers; the former was at Pola in service as a training ship, and the latter was at La Spezia in service as a trials ship.

The ex-protected cruiser/gunboat (1912) *Campania* was at sea on 30 September 1935 with cadets from the naval academy; the protected cruiser (1914) *Libia* was in dry dock awaiting being laid up pending disposal.

There were also five former enemy light cruisers under Italian colors at this time. The *Ancona* (ex-German *Graudenz*) and *Venezia* (ex-Austro-Hungarian *Saida*) were in dry dock at Taranto and La Spezia respectively, awaiting being laid up prior to disposal. The *Brindisi* (ex-Austro-Hungarian *Helgoland*) was in dry dock at Ancona and was in service as an accommodation/barracks ship. In the Red Sea with the local East Africa command were the *Bari* (ex-German *Pillau*) and *Taranto* (ex-German *Strassburg*). Also at Massawa on 30 September 1935 were the destroyers (1925) *Francesco Nullo*, (1919) *Palestro*, (1923) *Pantera*, and (1923) *Tigre*; the torpedo-boat (1916) *Audace*; and the submarines *Luigi Settembrini*, *Narvalo*, *Ruggiero Settimo*, and *Tricheco*.

At Rhodes, in the Dodecanese, on 30 September 1935, were four units, the (1914) *Alessandro Poerio*, (1916) *Aquila*, (1919) *Falco*, and (1914) *Guglielmo Pepe*, which at different times during their service were classified as torpedo vessels, scout cruisers, and destroyers; the 1926-vintage destroyers *Bettino Ricasoli* and *Giovanni Nicotera* and the *Cesare Battisti* and *Nazario Sauro*; and the torpedo-boats MAS 212 and 418.

The whereabouts of British battleships, cruisers, and aircraft carriers on 30 September 1935 were established on the basis of the ships' logs for September 1935. These, in the ADM 53 series, were as follows: the battleships *Barham* 94938, *Hood* 97660, *Nelson* 98367, *Queen Elizabeth* 98659, *Ramillies* 98684, *Renown* 82485, *Resolution* 98741, *Revenge* 98810, *Rodney* 98879, *Royal Sovereign* 98926, and *Valiant* 99983; the heavy cruisers *Berwick* 95085, *Cornwall* 95740, *Devonshire* 96251, *Exeter* 96836, *Kent* 97890, *London* 98056, *Norfolk* 98423, *Shropshire* 99489, *Suffolk* 99656 (to 4 October when she was paid off into reserve), and *York* 100681; the light cruisers *Achilles* 94559, *Ajax* 94627, *Arethusa* 94868, *Caledon* 95425, *Capetown* 95475, *Carlisle* 95499, *Colombo* 95699, *Curacao* 95877, *Danae* 95975, *Dauntless* 96040, *Delhi* 96150, *Despatch* 96227, *Dragon* 96502, *Durban* 96511, *Emerald* 96640, *Leander* 97985, and *Orion* 98447; with no logs for September 1935 available, the whereabouts of the *Cairo* 95403 and *Neptune* 98391 are given as per 1 October 1935. After 17 October the *Neptune* was at Gibraltar, and it should be noted that on 30 September the *Achilles* was at Ponta Delgada, San Miguel, in the Azores and not in home waters. In the case of the heavy cruisers *Berwick* and *Sussex*, their October 1935 logs were consulted, 95085 and 99669 respectively.

It would seem that the logs of certain ships have not been kept, namely, the heavy cruiser *Frobisher*, which between 1932 and 1939 was a cadet training ship, and the light cruisers *Calcutta* (also a training ship, at Chatham, at this time), *Caradoc*, *Cardiff*, *Ceres*, *Curlew*, *Diomede*, *Dunedin*, and *Enterprise*. The whereabouts of these ships were checked against *Service Histories of Royal Navy Warships in World War 2*, of which http://www.naval-history.net/xGM-Chrono-06CL-Calcutta.htm is but one example.

Excluded from the lists are ships undergoing reconstruction or major refit, namely the capital ships *Malaya* at Devonport between 20 October 1934 and 30 October 1936 (80325 and 98179), *Repulse* at Portsmouth between 31 March 1933 and 21 January 1936 (82584 and 98721), *Royal Oak* at Devonport between 24 May 1934 and 21 August 1936 (83394 and 98913), and *Warspite* at Portsmouth between 15 December 1933 and 24 February 1937 (91766 and 106823); the aircraft carrier *Eagle* at Devonport between May 1935 and 21 January 1936 (96536 and 102657); and the light cruiser *Coventry* at Portsmouth between 25 July and 18 December 1935 (95780 and 95781); the heavy cruiser *Cumberland* was at Chatham between 12 March 1933 and 13 May 1936 (95861 and 95862), was recommissioned on the latter date but was paid off a second time, and was passed back to the dockyard thirteen days later, on 26 May.

The dates and location of the ships in reserve (apart from reviews) are as follows: the heavy cruisers *Hawkins* at Portsmouth between 25 April 1935 and 18 August 1936 and the *Vindictive* at Chatham prior to 17 August 1937; after being in reserve both were taken in hand and converted in order to serve as training ships, becoming operational in 1938; the light cruisers *Caradoc* at Sheerness between 17 November 1934 and 12 August 1938, a period that includes time in dock prior to recommissioning as training ship; the *Caledon* at Devonport between 31 July 1931 and July 1938, when she was towed to Chatham for refit (she was commissioned in December 1934 for carrying personnel to Malta); the *Calypso* at Devonport between 21 February 1935 and 31 July 1939; the *Ceres* at Chatham between October 1932 and May 1935 and at Devonport between May 1935 and August 1939; and the *Dauntless* at Portsmouth between March 1935 and August 1939. In addition, the light cruiser *Curlew* was in reserve at Sheerness between 1933 and 1938.

Also in the reserve were two more cruisers, the light cruiser *Cardiff*, which was at Chatham between 14 July 1933 and July 1938, and the heavy cruiser *Effingham*, which was at Portsmouth after May 1932. Technically both were in commission, the *Cardiff* as the reserve fleet flagship and the *Effingham* as a flagship in the reserve fleet; in real terms, however, both were decommissioned.

In addition, at this time the light cruiser *Enterprise* was employed as tender to the stone frigate *Pembroke* at Chatham, but it was back in service in January 1936.

Finally, there were two more units, namely the heavy cruiser *Frobisher*, which was a training ship and at Rosyth between 20 September and 20 October, and the light cruiser *Diomede*, which was at Auckland, New Zealand between 23 August and 2 October 1935.

The whereabouts of the *Curlew*, *Diomede*, and *Frobisher* were checked against the Admiralty Movement Books by Iain Mackenzie of the Admiralty Library and sent to the author by e-mail on 14 January 2008.

CHAPTER FOUR

JAPAN AND ITS "SPECIAL UNDECLARED WAR"

THE PERIOD BETWEEN the two world wars saw a series of conflicts, and the importance of naval power in some of these wars is seldom acknowledged. The Allied intervention in the Russian civil wars and involvement in the Greek-Turkish conflict were based on naval power, but, arguably, in the inter-war period in only one conflict did a navy play a major, indeed significant, role and possess more than *en passant* importance. The Sino-Japanese conflict, which began in July 1937, saw the major involvement of the Imperial Japanese Navy in two areas of operations with immediate and long-term relevance: a series of coastal operations and landings in southern China, most obviously the occupation of Canton in 1938 and Hainan Island in 1939, and involvement in air operations, and specifically in the strategic bombing campaigns staged in 1939 and 1940.[1]

* * *

The inter-war period was one that saw Japanese forces, and specifically the Imperial Japanese Army, the *Nippon Teikoku Rikugun*, involved in a series of conflicts that began with intervention in the Russian civil wars in which Rikugun forces reached as far west as Novosibirsk.[2] The main focus of Japanese military attention, however, was China, with its interminable civil wars, power struggles, and secessionist problems, and specifically was directed to Manchuria, Inner Mongolia, and northern China after September 1931. In the course of a three-month campaign the local Japanese garrison force, the Kwantung Army, overran three of Manchuria's four provinces and paved the way for a double development.

First, having secured Liaoning, Kirin, and Heilingkiang provinces by 18 November though the process of pacification continued into March 1932, the Japanese were able to overrun the remaining province, Jehol, in January–March 1933, and then to undertake a series of local operations over the next four years that in effect eliminated potential opposition north of the Great Wall and secured for the Kwantung Army positions from which to advance into Inner Mongolia. By a combination of force, intimidation, blandishments, inducements, and flattery, the Japanese military was able to neutralize Chinese and Kuomintang influence in Inner Mongolia and Shansi, Hopei, and Shantung provinces. The ease with which these provinces were overrun in 1937, with the start of the China war, indicates the extent of Japanese success in these areas after the Manchurian episode.

Second, the Manchurian Incident marked the start of the process whereby parliamentary democracy within Japan was wrought asunder, primarily by a military that within five or six years had established itself with the real power of decision. More than the activity of the military, of course, was at work—the debilitating effects of the Depression and the discrediting of political liberalism as a consequence were obvious factors, as was a state and societal ethic that reached back over a number of decades—but the process that is often labeled "government by assassination" had reduced civilian authority to a position of *minor inter pares* relative to the two armed services by the time that Prince Konoye Fumimaro (1891–1945) became prime minister for the first time on 4 June 1937.[3]

* * *

In the process of the military securing control of the Japanese body politic, the Rikugun was dominant: the Manchurian Incident was initiated, deliberately and over a lengthy period of preparation, by the local command, without reference to Tokyo and correctly confident in the belief that the government would not be able to repudiate its actions. Thereafter the principle of *Gekokujo*—the deliberate manipulation of senior command by junior officers— went hand-in-hand with major involvement in coups, attempted coups, and assassinations. But the war that began in July 1937 in the wake of the Marco Polo Bridge/Lukouchiao Incident was different from what had gone previously, on three counts.

First, in a whole series of incidents since 1931 the Japanese military in China had contented itself with local bullying and gains that, over time, were nonetheless quite substantial, and in the immediate aftermath of the Lukouchiao Incident the Japanese military command both in Tokyo and in theater expected such gains. But this belief was very quickly revealed to be flawed, in part because there was within the Japanese military a belief that Japan had to embark upon conquest throughout eastern Asia in order to secure resources, markets, and areas of colonization essential to Japan's well-being and great-power status. In part, moreover, there was within the Japanese military a belief that evidence—specifically, the Sian Incident of 12–25 December 1936—suggested that the Chinese were seeking to end their civil wars in order to present a united front to Japanese expansionism, and that this pointed to Japan's need for preventive action, the undertaking of major operations in an attempt to forestall such a possibility.

A second factor in making what could have been a mere local affair into full-scale warwas that in the summer of 1937 the Kaigun was wholly unprepared to allow an escalation of events that would serve only to ensure the superiority of its sister service within the Japanese political system and in terms of budgetary priorities. The China Incident in very large measure stemmed from ill-advised, and most certainly ill-considered, Kaigun actions in Shanghai in August 1937—in the Kaigun's "areas of responsibility and interest," unlike all the actions to date in the north. The navy's unplanned actions brought it within measurable distance of disastrous defeat: it was saved only by the intervention of the Rikugun and the dispatch of military divisions to Shanghai that very slowly turned round the situation, albeit at the cost of a major, long-term, commitment to war.[4]

The third count, however, was perhaps the most surprising of all: in the conduct of operations the Kaigun came to play a role wholly disproportionate to its commitment in theater, on two separate scores. The Kaigun air arm came to dominate the conduct of Japanese air operations because (as a general rule) its aircraft were bigger and had larger payloads and great ranges than their Rikugun counterparts. This was particularly important in 1939 and 1940, when the Japanese were obliged to undertake major strategic bombing offensives, across the depth of unconquered Chinese territory, in an attempt to force the enemy to come to terms. The army air arm was wholly outclassed by its naval counterpart, and indeed, even in close support operations for ground forces Kaigun aircraft and personnel were generally considered by senior Rikugun commanders to be much superior to those of the army's own air arm. In addition, while the major Japanese effort by definition had to be undertaken by the Rikugun north of and in the Yangtse valley, the Kaigun undertook a whole series of operations to the south. As early as 5 September 1937 the Japanese government proclaimed the blockade of the entire Chinese coastline with the exception of Tsingtao, Hong Kong, Macao, and Canton; on 10 January 1938 the first, and on 21 October the last, of these four ports were secured by amphibious assault.[5] February 1939 saw the occupation of Hainan Island, and November the landings in the area of Pakhoi, which resulted, with the advance to and capture of Nanning on the 24th, in perhaps the most significant Japanese gains of the year.[6] There were no other major undertakings until March–April 1941, when a series of landings were conducted along the whole of the coast from just south of Hangchow Bay via Foochow, opposite Formosa, to southern Kwantung province.

* * *

The start of the China war found both the Japanese services unready to conduct operations, and in terms of air operations, having no real knowledge and understanding of what a war would involve. In effect Japan was the first power in nearly two decades to confront the problem of how to conduct an air campaign, and its experience of air operations in the First World War, Intervention, and various Chinese episodes really had provided it with little or no practical basis for understanding the nature and conduct of air operations: not even the *Kaigun* operations in the Shanghai Incident, 29 January–February 1932, which saw the first use of carriers and carrier aircraft in battle, provided much in the way of forewarning and preparation.[7] There is, of course, a certain irony in such a situation: the first person to commit to paper the idea of the strategic bombing offensive—directed against a civilian population and moral resolve—had been a Japanese naval officer, Nakajima Chikuhei (1884–1949). Leaving aside isolated operations such as the Guernica raid (25 April 1937) and Italian operations in Ethiopia, the China war was to witness the first strategic bombing offensives in the form of systemic area bombing by major formations, and it saw naval aircraft operate across a continental interior at ranges that were unprecedented. It was also the first war in which, to slightly amend a famous comment, the bomber was not assured of getting through.

* * *

At the time of the Lukouchiao Incident the Imperial Navy had three carriers—the *Hosho*, the *Kaga*, and the *Ryujo*, with some eighty aircraft—and two shore-based air groups in the home islands. Apart from the Mitsubishi G3M Nell medium bomber in service with the latter groups, the Kaigun in mid-1937 was in the process of change, this being the time when the monoplane was coming into service in all the air forces of all the major powers. This was a very slow and uneven process: indeed, one of the little-known facts about American use of monoplanes was that even as late as 1941 the fleet carrier *Yorktown* embarked biplanes. But in 1937–1939, if the G3M Nell did cause amazement in western military circles on account of its range, the Japanese air services had no appreciation of the fact that bombers had to be provided with fighter escort, and there was a general belief (which defies understanding) that significant results could be registered by air formations no larger than three bombers. The result was that the initial experience of battle came as a salutary and very considerable shock to the Kaigun and its air arm: in its first three days of operations (14–16 August) the 1st Combined Air Group lost half of its G3M Nells, and there was seemingly no answer to the Curtiss P-36 Hawk fighters of the Chinese Air Force. In large measure such losses, which continued through the second half of August 1937 and which were less than those incurred by carrier aircraft, stemmed from the fact that the Kaigun had largely discounted the possibility of bombers being escorted, though the fact was that Japanese naval aircraft did not have the range to escort bombers even if the need had been recognized.[8]

The situation was redeemed for the Japanese by the coming together of three matters that were related, at least in part. First, in mid-1937 the Kaigun air arm was in the process of fundamental change, most obviously in terms of expansion of numbers, but also of aircraft type, and the most important single aircraft was the Mitsubishi A5M Claude carrier-based fighter. This fixed-undercarriage monoplane flew for the first time in February 1935; while it possessed speed and rate of climb well in excess of both design requirement and contemporaneous biplanes,[9] it did not enter service as the Navy's first-line carrier fighter until autumn 1936. It did not appear in Chinese skies until September 1937, but then its effect was immediate in terms of ending the superiority of Chinese fighters over Japanese bombers.[10] The skies over Shanghai were cleared of Chinese fighters within a matter of days at the beginning of September, and when the Japanese concentrated their efforts against Nanking, the initial action of 19 September saw such losses inflicted by the A5M Claudes that on the following day Chinese fighters refused to give battle and by 22 September had cleared the area, the Japanese being able to send G3M Nells against the Chinese capital in early October.[11]

The second factor that made for Japanese success in the conduct of battle was the fact that both at Shanghai and in later action, naval aircraft were put ashore on airstrips, and by very careful co-ordination of timing the Japanese were able to put fighters into the air in support of bombers and across distances that hitherto were beyond them. But these material changes went alongside the third factor: major changes in terms of doctrine and organization, though this was a somewhat uneven process. The crucial point was that in 1937 the Japanese Navy possessed some of the highest-quality personnel in the world, aircrew intensively trained over extended periods, and with the A5M Claude the fighter arm had an aircraft that more or less matched the quality of its personnel. But over the following months fighter formations were organized in mass, and their collective performance ceased to be the sum of individual endeavors. The old warrior ethic, with emphasis placed on individual combat, became a thing of the past as numbers were gathered to fight systemically for air supremacy. With fighters and bombers unused to working together, and with training, establishment, and operational formations different, the Japanese ability to operate *en masse* was initially limited, Within a matter of months, however, there was set in place both a standardization of formations and major increases in the scale of operations, with provision for the use of unprecedented numbers of fighters both in independent operations in the fight for supremacy over targets and in the escort role.[12]

Inevitably, of course, there were problems, and four presented themselves almost from the outset. Japanese aircraft lacked radios, which made close cooperation between individual aircraft very difficult indeed and obviously precluded effective command and control from the ground once formations were in the air. Moreover, at the outset of operations Japanese aircraft lacked oxygen; indeed, the majority of Claude fighters that saw service in China had open cockpits. The effect on air crew, specifically in missions into a mountainous interior and at increasing altitude, was decidedly unfortunate, as was an intensity of initial operations that made no allowance for the limited number of aircrew that were available for operations at this time. The result was the very rapid exhaustion of bomber crews, and in this respect, and indeed in terms of its overall conduct of operations, the Kaigun air arm pioneered problems. It was really the first air service to undertake a sustained campaign and strategic bombing effort, and was the first air service to learn the limitations of the bomber and bomber operations that would be encountered by the Luftwaffe in 1940 and the British and U.S. bomber arms over the next three years. Herein was the fourth of the four problems: Japanese aircraft were impressive in terms of speed, range, and payload but were decidedly weak structurally and in terms of damage control. The G3M Nell was not untypical, in that it lacked protective armour and an adequate defensive armament and its fuel tanks were unprotected. The Mitsubishi G4M Betty, for example, was deliberately conceived as a land-based torpedo-bomber, with a range of 2,300 miles/3,700-km. that would enable it to mount successive attacks on an American formation advancing into the western Pacific, but this was achieved at a cost of defensive measures sufficient to earn the bomber the sobriquet "The Honorable One-Shot Lighter" from aircrews. And, of course, the latter refused to carry parachutes on operations.[13]

* * *

The A5M Claude was but one of the new generation of monoplanes that came into service in and after 1937 but the aircraft that one always associates with Japanese offensive operations in the first phases of the Pacific war either were ordered before the start of or during the China war but made their operational debut during that conflict. The Aichi D3A Val fixed-undercarriage dive-bomber and the Nakajima B5N Kate torpedo-bomber were both ordered before the start of the China war. The first of the dive-bombers was built in December 1937 but after considerable teething problems did not enter service, with the carriers *Akagi* and *Kaga*, until 1940. The B5N Kate first flew in January 1937; while the first variant saw extensive service in China, its need for escort and its clear vulnerability to the Soviet fighters with which the Chinese air force came to be supplied meant that in early 1940 a new variant was ordered. The B5N2 variant entered service in December 1941 and was the carrier-based torpedo- and medium-altitude bomber that was present at Pearl Harbor; it remained in front-line service until early 1944. The G4M Betty, the design specification of which was issued in September 1937, first flew on 23 October 1939 and entered service in April 1941. It first saw action in China in June, and it was these aircraft that conducted the first day's attacks on U.S. air bases on Luzon and that sank the British capital ships *Repulse* and *Prince of Wales* in the South China Sea on 10 December 1941.

Perhaps inevitably, however, the focus of attention with respect to Japanese aircraft is the Mitsubishi A6M Zero. The first flight of an A6M1 Zero was on 1 April 1939, but its first combat mission was not until 19 August 1940, when twelve of its number escorted a fifty-bomber raid on Chungking. It was thus employed for one very definite reason: just as the A5M Claude had found employment because the fighters then in service lacked the range to escort bombers and reach deep into the enemy heartland, the A6M Zero entered into operational service, before trials had been fully completed and training manuals issued, because the Claude could not escort bombers across the distances that the latter were obliged to cover in what had become, over the previous year, a very different war from what had been fought between July 1937 and October 1939.[14] The Chinese government's refusal to come to terms, to accept defeat and Japan's special position within China, left the Japanese military, confronted by an increasingly difficult numbers-to-space problem, with very little alternative but to undertake a strategic bombing campaign aimed at destroying Chinese morale and will to resist. The operational debut of the A6M Zero came at the same time as the Japanese government, recognizing that any form of arrangement with the Chinese nationalist government in Chungking was impossible, moved to install a quisling regime, headed by the Kuomintang defector Wang Ching-wei, as the legitimate government of China.[15]

* * *

The strategic bombing campaign took the form of three successive efforts, Operation 100 between 3–4 May and 7 October 1939, Operation 101 between 18 May and 4 September 1940, and Operation 102 between 27 July and 31 August 1941. This last endeavor was cut short, almost before it had begun, because of the need to withdraw aircraft from China in readiness for operations in the central Pacific and southeast Asia by year's end, though in fact even in early 1939 the number of naval aircraft in China had been reduced to about 150 of all types. After that time the greater part of Kaigun air strength was based either in the home islands or on Formosa and was committed to individual operations on the basis of availability and need; by the end of 1940 just two Kaigun formations—about forty aircraft—remained in China, and no carriers remained on the China station.

The small Kaigun numbers, combined with the fact that in Operation 101 there were 182 raids involving just 3,715 sorties, or an average of 21 aircraft per mission,[16] point unmistakably to one conclusion: this specific undertaking, and indeed the three offensives together, was undertaken with insufficient numbers to have any real chance of success. When one considers the American and British numbers committed to the strategic bombing campaign against Germany in 1943 and 1944, and the fact that this offensive singularly failed, it would seem to suggest that Japanese under-investment was indeed a major factor, and perhaps *the* major factor, in the failure of this strategic bombing offensive. But Chungking was subject to some 268 raids between 1939 and 1944 and was more or less leveled in the process, the Chinese government and civil population either taking to, or burrowing ever deeper into, the surrounding hills in an attempt to ensure personal safety. Such devastation, registered in spite of the paucity of Japanese aircraft numbers, seems to suggest that much more was at work in frustrating Japanese intent. What was at work was an irreducible force of Chinese nationalism that ruled out any form of compromise or arrangement with the Japanese; this was based on a Sino-centric perspective and was a very deliberate calculation that Japan would ultimately involve itself in war with other powers, specifically the United States, and that it would be defeated. In such a situation China would be freed, and without the necessity of its undertaking any major, destructive effort on its own behalf—and this was of particular importance to the Chinese nationalist government at Chungking, which sought to husband resources in readiness for a resumption of the real war, against the communists. The Japanese, without any real appreciation of the force of any Asian nationalism other than their own, could never recognize the reality that precluded Chinese acceptance of a Japanese arrangement.

These three offensives are notable for three episodes. First, on 4 December 1940, as part of an attempt to sever the line of supply through Singkiang by which Soviet supplies reached the Chinese, a force of Japanese medium bombers attacked Lanchow in the course of an operation at a range of some 750 miles, which was without precedent. Interestingly, Soviet support for the Chungking regime and its supply of equipment, most notably aircraft, was eventually to be countered not by the use of force but the non-aggression treaty of April 1941 and thereafter by the Soviet commitment in its war of survival with Nazi Germany.

Second, the main Japanese effort was directed against the cities that remained under Chungking's authority, and Chungking itself was some 470 miles from the forward Japanese bases around the Wuhan cities; even with forward strips around Ichang, the Chinese capital remained beyond the range of the A5M Claude. This fact, and increased losses among unescorted bombers, made the entry of the A6M Zero into service so important. The problems of 1937 that had been met with the entry of the A5M Claude into service repeated themselves, *mutatis mutandis*, in 1939–1940, and while the losses of 1939–1940 were not on the scale of those of 1937, the A6M Zero was in 1940 exactly what the A5M Claude had been three years previously.

The third episode of note was the raid on 30 August 1941, by twenty-seven Rikugun bombers, on a villa on the outskirts of Chungking where Chiang Kai-shek was known to be holding staff talks. Neither Chiang nor any of the staff officers were killed or wounded, and in the aftermath of this abortive raid the army air commander recommended an end to the strategic air campaign. In fact, this raid was the last in the Operation 102 undertaking, but its significance lies elsewhere: this little-known episode was the first deliberate use of aircraft in an attempt to kill a head of state.[17]

* * *

In terms of amphibious endeavor the Japanese had perhaps set the pace in the twenties, but by the thirties the interest had waned somewhat, and seemingly on three related counts: cost, the relatively small number of formations and units that could be manned and trained for such operations, and the China commitment, which, by definition, was military and not amphibious. To these may be added a fourth count: while Japanese calculations in the mid-twenties with reference to the United States had embraced the idea of landings on Guam and in the Philippines,[18] the fact that the old enemy Russia, now in the form of the Soviet Union, was back in the frame naturally had the effect of refocusing Japanese military attention to the west and not seaward. As it was, the Japanese had worked out the basis of doctrine, specifically in terms of pre-dawn landings with specialist naval troops, with purpose-built landing craft, and, most important of all, in areas where the enemy was not expected to be. Crucial in Japanese calculations was an acceptance of distance from immediate objective as the price exacted for landings in areas where the enemy was not present and could not interfere in the initial, vulnerable, phase of landing operations. But regarding the China war and its first forty-two months, the opportunity and need for amphibious operations was most modest—destroyer, gunboat, and landing operations on the middle Yangtse in 1938 and the Shanghai landings excepted.[19]

With reference to Shanghai, the operations of November 1937, at Chuankungtung (by the 6th and 18th Infantry Divisions) on the 5th and at Fupukow (by the 16th Infantry Division) on the 13th,[20] in effect completed the victory that had been won in and in front of Shanghai over the previous three months, and in any case ceded pride of place to the main movement of Japanese formations, which was direct to Shanghai. Chinese formations had begun to evacuate Shanghai on 11 November, that is, two days before the landings on the south bank of the lower Yangtse. The significance of the landings at Chuankungtung can be gauged by the fact that 10th Army formations (which included the 114th Infantry Division after it had been landed in Hangchow Bay, after and separate from 6th and 18th Infantry Divisions' landing) reached into the area of Tsingpu and Paihokang, roughly halfway between Shanghai and Soochow,[21] as early as 9 November; thereafter, with the main effort directed via Tachien, Wuhsing and Changhing, the 10th Army formations reached the Yangtse at Tangtu, above Nanking, on 11 December, five days after the Chinese government had abandoned its capital but two days before the city fell.[22] Japanese forces did cross Lake Tai, as well as working their way around the lake both to the north and to the south, but perhaps more significant was the fact that as early as 28 October, before the main operations in front of Shanghai, Japanese naval units secured Kinmen Island. Given this island's location opposite Formosa and roughly halfway between Swatow and Foochow, and the fact that this was a solely Kaigun endeavor that seems to have escaped western attention, this action would certain seem to have given notice of the scope of the Imperial Navy's ambition and intent.[23]

Given the advance of Japanese formations to the Tsinan-Weihsien line by the end of the year,[24] the local Chinese command was not prepared to seriously oppose any Japanese moves into the Shantung peninsula, though the abandonment of Shantung without serious and sustained resistance resulted in the execution of the province's military governor by the Chinese government. In fact the Japanese had refrained from blockading or attacking Tsingtao, but after popular disturbances in mid-December 1937 that resulted in the destruction of Japanese-owned cotton mills in the port, the Kaigun made ready to conduct a landing on the Shantung peninsula even as the local Chinese authorities in Tsingtao blew up the port's most important buildings. After having been informed by the British heavy cruiser *Dorsetshire* that Tsingtao was undefended,[25] Japanese warships entered the port on 10 January 1938 and put landing parties ashore, the city and its base being secured by the following day.[26]

Thereafter there was no serious amphibious undertaking until 10 May, when a Japanese force from Kinmen came ashore on eastern Amoy. That town, like Tsingtao, was secured the day after the landing, with the Japanese then moving to secure another tiny island in the channel and, for a day or so, a foothold on the mainland at Kaoyu; the whole episode, and the clearing of Amoy island of all Chinese fortresses and forces, was over by 13 May.[27] The operation that secured Canton was altogether a more substantial affair, directed against the last major port remaining to China, and took Japanese forces, and specifically the Kaigun, deep into southern China.

The Canton landings are of interest specifically in contrast to landings in Europe in 1943–1944. The initial Japanese landings took place on 12 October 1938 inside Bias Bay, east of Hong Kong, and were conducted at night by separated units of the 18th Infantry Division that were re-formed with daylight. Thereafter, with some 35,000 troops having been landed and supported by a naval force that included the carriers *Kaga*, *Ryujo*, and *Soryu*, the heavy cruiser *Myoko*, and no fewer than eight light cruisers and various destroyer formations,[28] Japanese formations moved to the north of Hong Kong on the direct route toward Canton, which had been extensively damaged over previous months by aircraft from the carrier *Kaga*.[29] Against minimal opposition the city was taken on 21 October. Quite separately, on 24 October the 5th Infantry Division moved against the Bocca Tigris fortresses at the mouth of the Pearl river; the Japanese plan involved the use of warship gunfire and naval aircraft to neutralize Chinese artillery, with landing craft thus freed to put troops ashore in flanking positions, from which they could advance and take the Chinese fortresses and their guns from the rear. Resistance again was minimal, and the whole of the Chinese defensive positions covering the Pearl were cleared by the end of the month.[30] The point of contrast with subsequent European landings lies in the fact that two separated efforts, which were not mutually supporting, and the dispersal of units that conducted the landings, could be attempted only against an enemy known to be limited in terms of both numbers and capability. That was a luxury that was not available to the Americans and British in their landings on continental Europe after September 1943.[31] Moreover, lest the point be missed, depending upon definition either the landings at Tsingtao in January 1938 or those at Canton represent the first employment of a carrier, with aircraft as opposed to seaplanes, during a landing operation. The British had employed the seaplane carrier as a transport for aircraft in the Somaliland operations in 1919–1920 and had also employed destroyers when transporting a company of troops by air from Sudan to Cyprus in 1930; but although various cruisers had been involved in the restoration of order during the Moplah Rising in various Indian cities in 1921–1922 and in Trinidad in 1937, it seems that in the inter-war period no British imperial peace-keeping operation involved a carrier and its aircraft.[32] The Tsingtao operation seems to have been the first major landing operation to involve an aircraft carrier, though whether this operation involved an assault landing is not altogether clear; most certainly the scale of the Canton operation, with three carriers with a total capacity of 209 aircraft, was without precedent.

After Canton, and with one very important exception, there were no major Japanese amphibious undertakings for the best part of thirty months; then what followed was first a series of operations astride and on the Luichow peninsula in the first days of March 1941, and then a number of landings in Chekiang and Fukien provinces in April, the finale being a landing that secured Kiatze in

Kwantung province on 1 May. The first of these involved no fewer than seven landings in front of Hoppo, Pakhoi, Luichow, Shuitung, Tinpak, Yeungkong, and Towshan.[33] On 24 March Japanese forces were landed at Swabue,[34] some forty miles up the coast from Hong Kong; then the better part of a month elapsed before no fewer than five landings were conducted on 19–20 April, which resulted in the Japanese occupation of Chinghai, Ninpo, Shipu, Haimen, and Wenchow in Chekiang province.[35] A landing in front of Foochow, in Fukien province, was undertaken on 21 Apri1[36] before attention switched back to Chekiang, with landings on 23 April in Sungmen and Chaikiao bays.[37] The switch of attention back to Kwantung province with the landing in front of Kiatze is perhaps somewhat surprising given its distance from these last Japanese undertakings.[38]

At least with respect to the March 1941 operations, it seems that the Japanese had no intention to hold certain ports on a permanent basis. With no more than single battalions drawn from three different divisions assigned to the March operations, quite clearly they were operating short-term, and indeed Pakhoi, Shuitung, Tinpak, and Yeungkong were abandoned as early as 10 March. The Japanese intention was to destroy local base facilities in what were local ports handling much of what remained of China's overseas trade; apparently Chinese forces reoccupied these heavily damaged towns as early as 13 March, and it was the non-permanent nature of occupation that was the significant aspect of the operation that was the one post-Canton exception. This was the landings by a reinforced 5th Infantry Division in front of Pakhoi and the occupation of the town on 15 November 1939, which led to an Japanese advance over a distance of more than a hundred miles and the capture of Nanning on 24 November.[39] Quite clearly the Japanese move was provoked by the fact that the railway linking Nanning and Hanoi was to come into service in January 1940, but a double set of events conspired and led to the Japanese to abandon Nanning on 29 October 1940. The operation in the south presented the Japanese with what was, long-term, an impossible numbers-to-space problem. After February–March 1940, by which time Japanese forces had advanced almost to Wuchi and to Chien-chiang (respectively some thirty miles north and one hundred miles northeast of Nanning),[40] the Japanese faced a very slowly mounting pressure across southwest Kwangsi province as increasing numbers of Chinese formations moved into theater. By autumn 1940, however, the Japanese need for Nanning was no more: the Maginot Line had been the front line of defense of Indo-China, and on 22 September the French were obliged to accept the Japanese demand for occupation rights in northern Indo-China; thus the Japanese could close down the Chinese lines of supply at source. The Japanese therefore abandoned Nanning, at least until 25 November 1944, when the city was occupied for a second time in the final stages of the Ichi-Go offensive; it was then lost, for a second time, on 27 May 1945, when the March–October 1940 situation repeated itself with the thinning of Japanese forces in this area in readiness for dispatch to the north, to Manchuria, in order to meet the anticipated Soviet threat.

* * *

The Kaigun effort in China ended, as did all Japanese endeavors, in failure, though in terms of the outcome of the Second World War the Japanese failure in China embraced a dimension very seldom acknowledged in western histories. Token of this failure is the fact that the *Soryokusen Kankyujo*/Institute of Total War Studies report presented to the Japanese cabinet on 27 August 1941 indicated that Japanese resources, demographic and economic, could not sustain the burden of the China war should that conflict be continued for another five or ten years.[41] The fact of the matter was not simply that Japan had inflicted upon itself a war that could not be won by military, or concluded by "other," means but that this war produced a logic of its own that ultimately led Japan along a strategic pathway that consisted of operational paving stones that bore the names of Chinese cities and ports and that brought Japan to the impasse of July 1941 and thence to the war that Kato, at the time of Washington, had deemed to be the very worst eventuality that Japan could possibly face.

Overall it is very difficult to determine the importance and the influence of the China war upon the Kaigun, other than in two dimensions. The first is somewhat nebulous in that undoubtedly the China war created a general confidence. Navies, admittedly, are endowed with a "can-do" ethic, and most certainly the Kaigun's performance, and specifically that of the air arm, added an extra layer or two to its self-belief and its self-assurance in facing the future. The point, of course, is that it is possible to argue that such a self-justifying ethic was wholly misplaced, that the Kaigun drew exactly the wrong lessons from China, and that whatever conclusions could be drawn from the China war had little or no relevance in terms of a Pacific war and an American enemy. But certainly in one matter the experience that the Kaigun derived from the China war resulted in one fundamental change that by December 1941 placed it streets ahead of its potential American and British enemies.[42]

* * *

In the period during and immediately after the First World War, the emphasis of Japanese naval doctrine was upon dispersal. In terms of planning for a war with the United States in the western Pacific, the Kaigun was to put together something that was by any standard extraordinary and wholly mystifying: it produced a battle plan that in turn came to be a plan of campaign and then, by some baffling process somewhat akin to transubstantiation, became a national war plan, the penultimate phase of which, by a process of strategic employment, was the fighting of a battle.

In essence this policy envisaged the waging of a defensive campaign in the western Pacific. In the period immediately after the First World War, the Kaigun envisaged the U.S. Pacific Fleet advancing from its base in the central Pacific in order to give battle in the general area of the Bonins and Honshu. With the passing of the twenties this defensive policy was succeeded by what was called the "Strategy of Interceptive Operations," which differed from previous policy in two respects. The area of operations was extended to include the Marianas and the Carolines, and doctrine and procurement harmonized in what can be described only as either the Pacific war's counterpart of the Schlieffen Plan or the Japanese naval equivalent of a de Dondi creation, a majestic clockwork of wheels-within-wheels that represented the medieval European view of the universe: ingenious, beautifully crafted, hopelessly wrong.

The defensive battle would be opened off Hawaii by submarines, and three types were built in order to fight an attritional battle as the U.S. Pacific Fleet advanced into the western Pacific. Scouting submarines, equipped with seaplanes, would find the American fleet, which would then be subjected to night surface attacks by cruiser-submarines brought to interception by command-submarines. These cruiser-submarines were endowed with a very high surface speed of 24 knots, the Japanese calculations being that such a speed would allow these submarines to outpace an American fleet advancing at economical cruising speed and thereby mount successive attacks to the limit of their torpedo capacity during the approach-to-contact phase.

These operations would be supported, as the American fleet arrived in the western Pacific, by shore-based aircraft, and to this end the Japanese developed, in the G4M Betty medium bomber, an aircraft that in its own time possessed a speed and range superior to any other medium bomber in service in the world. This advantage of range would enable the Japanese aircraft to reach American formations well beyond the range of American carrier aircraft, and this ability to mount successive attacks would ensure enemy losses.

Thereafter Japanese carriers, operating in independent divisions separately and forward from the battle line, would locate the advancing American fleet and immobilize its carriers through dive-bombing attacks that were to smash the enemy flight-decks. With the American fleet thus blinded, it would be engaged by midget submarines laid across its line of advance, and at the same time it would be engaged by light forces. With the fast battleship and heavy cruiser squadrons sweeping aside the enemy screening forces, massed light cruiser and destroyer flotillas, built around massive torpedo armaments, would attack the head of the American line in a series of night attacks.

In overall terms the Japanese expected that these operations would cost the American fleet perhaps 30 percent of its strength and, more importantly, its cohesion, and at that point action would be joined by the battle force. Between the wars the Imperial Navy undertook the most comprehensive reconstruction of its existing capital ships of any navy, stressing the importance of possession of superior speed, weight of broadside, and range over potential enemies: the counter to American numerical superiority was qualitative superiority of both ships and men. The Kaigun anticipated that the battle line would engage its counterpart in a conventional line of battle engagement with such advantages that the Japanese fleets would inflict a crushing defeat—a Mahanian defeat—upon the American enemy.

The idea of a decisive Mahanian battle was thoroughly in accord with mainstream naval thinking of the time, though very oddly in Japanese naval thinking, and more often in practice, the idea of fighting a battle to the finish seldom figured very highly. The repulse of the enemy, the frustration of his plans, plus the preservation of one's own main strength intact, were more important than annihilation. It was an inconsistency that was never resolved because unless the enemy—the American fleet—was annihilated there was no way in which the Japanese could guarantee the security of their conquests and empire. But in one respect this accorded with one other aspect of Japanese naval calculations.

The Imperial Navy believed that the Pacific was too vast for any navy to command, and it never believed that it could defeat the U.S. Navy comprehensively. What it aimed to do was to fight a limited war in which the American will to resist was eroded until the United States, tiring of the struggle, came to accept the reality of Japanese conquests. The logic of these beliefs eluded the Imperial Navy. The Japanese never recognized that theirs was not the power to determine the terms of reference of the Pacific war and that this war could not be limited in the same way as the wars against China and Russia around the turn of the century had been limited. This miscalculation was to be the basis of the defeat that became reality in 1945: the Japanese failed to appreciate that the alternative to victory in a limited war was not defeat in a limited war but defeat in a total war. This inescapable logic somehow managed to elude the Japanese high command: if these views were correct and no power could hope to command the Pacific, then it followed that the U.S. Navy might come into possession of command of the seas that washed Japan.

This inevitable conclusion followed from the argument that command of the sea could be divided by area or time. The idea of sea denial with which the Kaigun clothed itself admitted that the Japanese Navy might lose command of certain sea areas. But in logical terms the Kaigun could not chose those areas. The test of the Imperial Navy's logic was its recognition that it could lose control of the very waters that it regarded as its own. But this was a point lost upon a Kaigun that either could not or would not admit this reality. Its blindness on this fundamental point resulted in a supreme irony: a navy that fretted at the perceived ignominy of the Washington treaties was to suffer the ignominy of total defeat in home waters and extinction as a service.

The Japanese Navy aimed to fight a defensive campaign behind a perimeter that was extended to include the Marshalls in 1941, and then into the southwest Pacific in 1942, without any commensurate increase of resources that would enable the Kaigun to fight a protracted campaign against an enemy that, by definition, would be superior at the point of contact and would make its effort at a time, in a place, and with a strength that was its to decide. By no rational standard does the strategy with which the Kaigun equipped itself stand careful scrutiny: the navy that with its attack on Pearl Harbor initiated the naval equivalent of *blitzkrieg* in fact planned to conduct the subsequent war behind the Pacific and naval equivalent of the Maginot Line.

* * *

But the point of the China war lay in the fact that in the course of its operations the Imperial Navy learnt the value and importance of mass. Over the previous twenty years it had embraced the idea of dispersal, and indeed the old Eight-Eight formula had envisaged the building of three fleets, each with eight capital ships, as the maximum size compatible with effective handling in battle. The plan of campaign had envisaged the use of carriers independently deployed, and this independent employment was crafted primarily as the means of ensuring a degree of security that might well be compromised by an enemy that might enjoy the advantage of first strike; dispersal might result in single losses, but not concentrated losses. But the China war brought the Kaigun to the realization that meaningful offensive success could be registered only by concentrated air formations. Only numbers offered any real prospect of successful strike operations, but over time came the realization that a concentration of carriers to ensure a concentration of offensive power also provided for a concentration of defensive power. Increased numbers of cruisers and destroyers, of anti-aircraft capability and fighters for combat air patrol and defensive duties, would also be possible, and together these would possess a strength in depth that dispersal could not begin to match.[43]

The least that might be said about such calculation was that it failed to account for the one eventuality in which everything that could go wrong did go wrong, and it was precisely this situation that was to result in the overwhelming defeat off Midway Islands on 4 June 1942. But the fact was that the Pacific war did see the triumph of mass, American mass; it also saw one set of massive changes that accompanied the concentration of carrier numbers to the extent that by June 1944, at the battle of the Philippine Sea, one American task force, with one battle and four carrier groups, more than matched the Japanese carrier force at Pearl Harbor.[44] But one year later, by which time American and British carriers were operating in overwhelming numbers off the Japanese home islands, a massive change in terms of the composition of individual air groups was in place. At the battle of the Coral Sea in May 1942 the carrier groups of the *Lexington* and *Yorktown* consisted of four squadrons, only one of which was a fighter formation. The *Lexington*'s group numbered seventy-one aircraft, of which twenty-two were fighters; the *Yorktown*'s group numbered seventy-two aircraft, of which twenty-one were fighters.[45] By 1945 the five American task groups that sailed from Ulithi on 10 February mustered eleven fleet and five light carriers. As a basic rule of thumb, the fleet carriers each embarked about a hundred aircraft, of which at least seventy were fighters, while the light carriers embarked about thirty-two aircraft, of which twenty-four or twenty-five were fighters.[46] Perhaps somewhat strangely, the increased offensive power of carriers at the strategic level went hand in hand with increased defensive power of their air groups at the operational and tactical levels. In this respect the situation that prevailed between 1941 and 1944 was one of transition, but certainly for the Japanese their parallel transition, at least in its initial stages with its concentration of numbers, had been shaped in large measure by the experience of a war in China after July 1937.

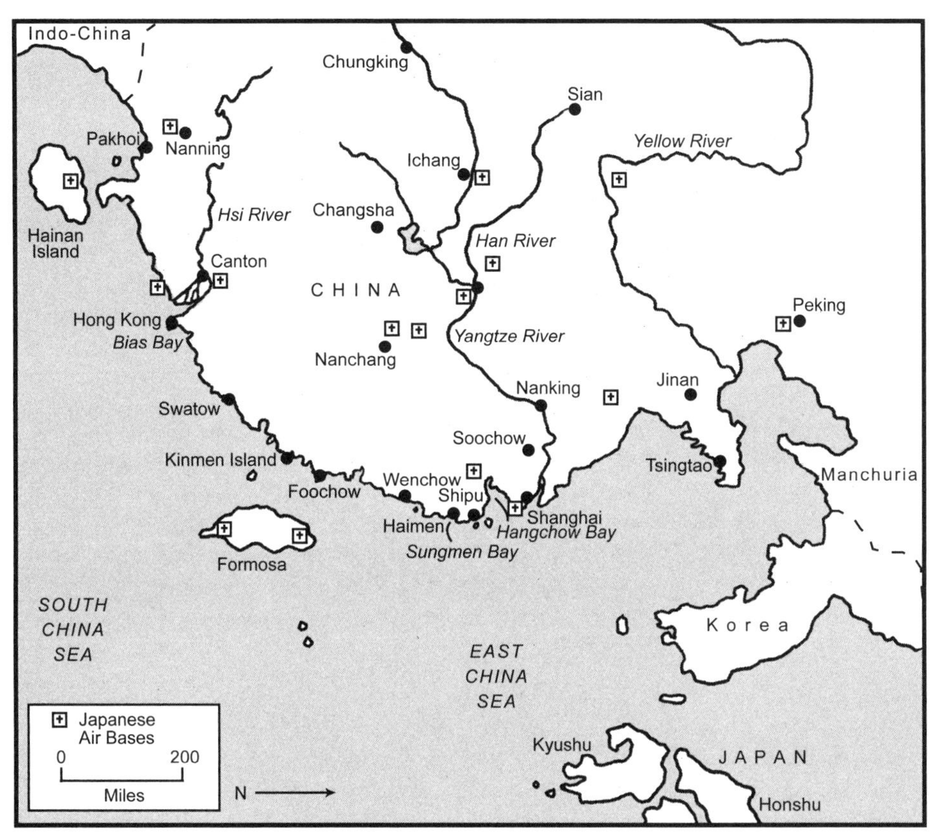

Map 3. Japan's "Special Undeclared War": The China Theater, 1937–1941

PART 2

INTRODUCTION TO THE SECOND WORLD WAR

CHAPTER FIVE

NAVIES, SEA POWER, AND TWO OR MORE WARS

Over the years the story of the war at sea during the Second World War with reference to Germany and Italy has been told mainly in terms of the defeat of the U-boat campaign against shipping. Certainly two, perhaps three, themes have been at the basis of British accounts of the defeat of the German campaign against Allied and neutral shipping. The first has been the British claim for the credit of that defeat, and the second was the abysmally poor showing of the U.S. Navy in the first six months after the American entry into the war. A third point is the assertion of the singular importance of May 1943 in the German defeat.

Most certainly the very bad performance of the U.S. Navy in the first six months of 1942 cannot be gainsaid, not least because of the utter inadequacy of provisions despite the United States' having had some seventeen months' notice of the coming of war to the western North Atlantic. There is no disputing the significance of events in the course of May 1943, but the argument that this was the month of the U-boats' defeat is entirely fatuous. The U-boats were defeated in April–May 1945. The victory that was won in May 1943 had to be secured repeatedly over the following two years, and while the events of May 1943 possess special significance, it is as part of a process of mounting losses that really began in February 1943. Moreover, the events of May 1943 must also be seen in association with those of July–August and October–November 1943, when the U-boats, reorganized, re-equipped and committed afresh to the campaign in the North Atlantic following their previous reverses, incurred defeats that were no less significant than that of May 1943. And while May 1943 was significant in terms of U-boat losses, which were more than double the worst previous month of the war and were the second-heaviest single-month losses in the entire war, August 1943 had special significance, and for a reason that seems to have eluded most historians: it was the first month in the war when the number of U-boats lost exceeded the number of merchantmen sunk by the U-boats.

The defeat of the U-boats was the result of a number of factors coming together over a prolonged period of time. If the British claims to victory are to be afforded due consideration, however, then note needs be made of British culpability in the period between June 1940 and August 1942, and this has very seldom been given much historical examination. The fact is that the British record in these twenty-six months stands in very sharp contrast to events in the last year of the First World War. As was noted in the companion volume of this account, in 1917 a total of seventy-three and in 1918 a total of ninety-one U-boats were lost to all causes, yet in 1940 the U-boats lost to all causes numbered just twenty-four and in 1941 only thirty-five. In 1942 the number reached eighty-seven, but the fact of the matter is that in 1940 and 1941, and on the basis of numbers that initially were less than that available to the German high command in February 1917, the German offensive against shipping was significantly successful, and at minimal cost in the face of what was a singularly ineffectual conduct of the defense on the part of the British Navy.

This latter point may not recommend itself to the naval circle within the United Kingdom, but what seems to have defied proper presentation, examination, and explanation is that in the period prior to August 1942 a German submarine force that began the war with little more than a third of the number of boats with which it had begun the unrestricted campaign in February 1917 inflicted losses, and commanded a rate of exchange, that would have been crippling, and that might well have forced Britain to surrender but for the fact that losses were covered by the Norwegian and Dutch shipping that acceded to the Allied cause after April 1940. How the U-boat service commanded such success, how such a situation could have come about, defies ready understanding. Certainly the defeat of France, and the resultant German acquisition of bases on the Atlantic coast, was a very important factor in German success between June 1940 and June 1942, as was the fact that Britain, which had no submarine threat with which to contend before 1937–1938 and which thereafter had concentrated upon containing a German submarine threat within the North Sea, lacked oceanic escorts; indeed, it was not until summer 1940, after the fall of France, that the first work on frigate design was undertaken. Clearly British increased effectiveness after mid-1942 was tied to numbers and types of escorts that were coming on line in significant numbers by this time, and for the first time, but it was also tied to the provision of long-range land-based aircraft that could patrol sea areas and support convoys, again

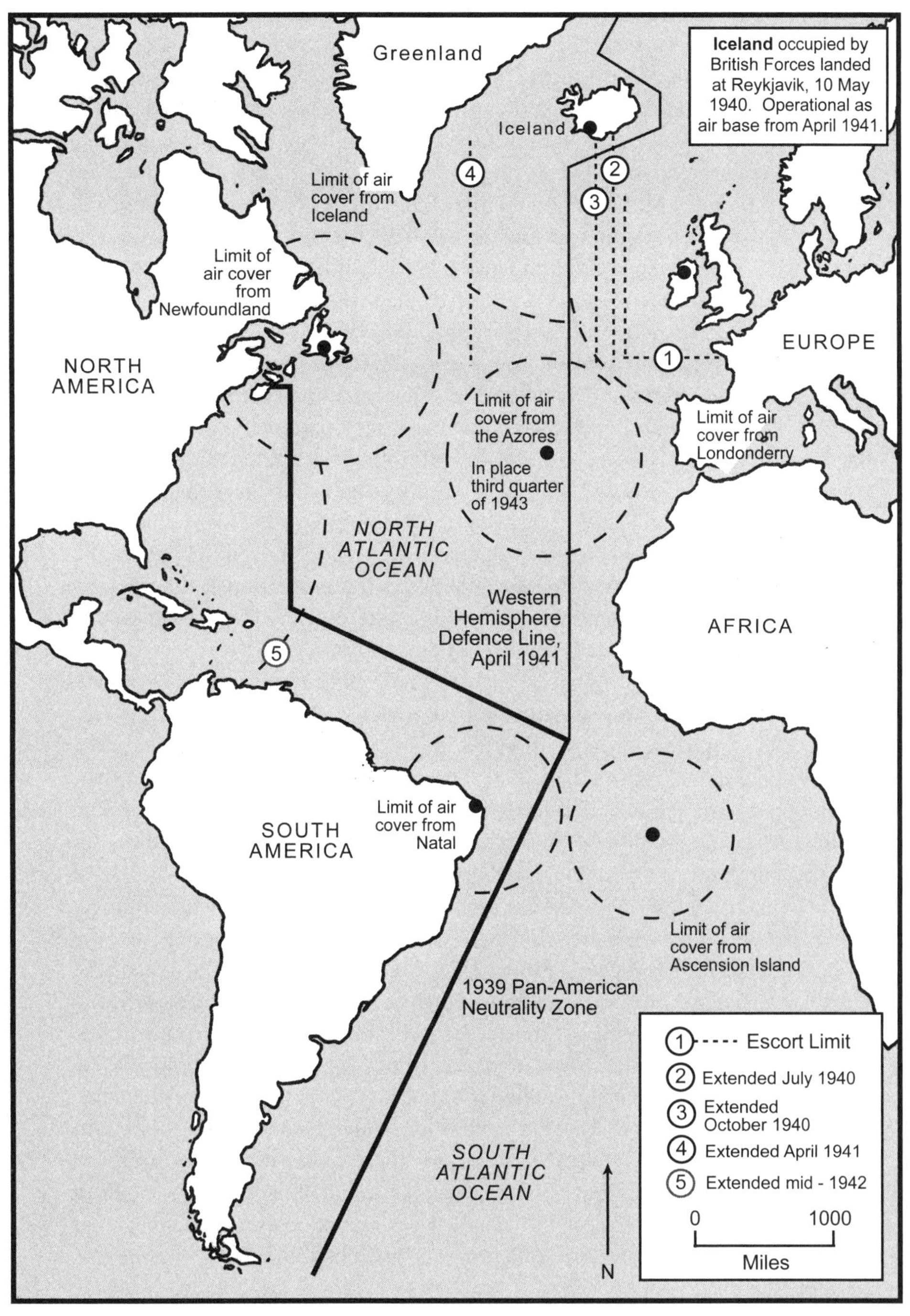

Map 4. North Atlantic Theater: Escort and Air Cover Areas of Operation

the numbers needed being available for the first time. In the end warships and land-based aircraft accounted for very nearly the same number of U-boats, the difference between the two being that the escorts provided merchantmen with protection into port in a way that aircraft, obviously, could not.

One interesting point about the German campaign against shipping is not so much these events, which have attracted their fair share of attention, but the returns of April and May 1941 and the post-June 1942 exchange rate. On the first score, the month of April 1941 was the most costly single month of the war to date, with a total of 195 merchantmen of 687,901 tons lost. But while submarines sank 43 merchantmen of 249,375 tons, land-based aircraft accounted for no fewer than 116 merchantmen of 323,454 tons, and while the following month saw a reversal of toll at least in terms of tonnage, the spring of 1941 was really the only time in the war when there was a balanced German effort against shipping. The contrast is most marked in the sense that after September 1942 the German effort amounted to a U-boat campaign and little else: after September 1942 only in March, July, and December 1943 did German aircraft sink more than ten merchantmen in any month. This lack of balance in terms of the German effort is all the more striking given the fact that June 1942 really marked the peak of the U-boat campaign. That statement can be disputed, and obviously the shipping losses of March 1943 were of special significance because the greater part of these losses were sustained by merchantmen in convoy, but the fact is that the merchantmen/U-boats exchange rate declined with every successive month after June 1942. The peak of returns for German submarines was between February and October 1941, in which period U-boats, which numbered just 32 operational units in April 1941, sank 333 merchantmen at the cost of 20 of their number, an exchange rate of 16.65:1 overall. June 1942 represented the peak of Allied and neutral shipping losses, with no fewer than 173 merchantmen of 834,196 tons lost, and it was the month that saw the greatest returns on the part of the U-boats, with 144 merchantmen of 700,235 tons sunk. But thereafter the returns declined in terms of both the merchantmen/U-boat exchange rate and the returns per U-boat overall and per operational U-boat. The latter fluctuated after April 1941, but on a rough rule of thumb after October 1942 the return per operational U-boat was never more than 0.48, and even in January 1943, before the debacle of May 1943, the return had touched 0.17. The returns also may be expressed in a different but more telling way: in October 1942 it took more than two operational U-boats to sink one merchantmen, and in January 1943 it took six. In twenty of the war's last twenty-four months the number of U-boats sunk was greater than the number of merchantmen sunk by U-boats, and the nadir of German fortunes was in October 1944, when with 401 boats, of which 141 were operational, U-boats accounted for just one merchantmen—and at a cost of twelve of their number.

The bare figures suggest the obvious, that the U-boat service was assigned a

TABLE 5.1. U-BOAT NUMBERS, U-BOAT AND SHIPPING LOSSES, AND THE SHIPPING: U-BOAT EXCHANGE RATES, SEPTEMBER 1939 TO MAY 1945

	Number of U-boats in service and operational	Number of U-boats lost in month and overall	Number of merchantmen sunk by U-boats in month & overall	Exchange rate merchantmen lost:operational U-boats	Exchange rate merchantmen: U-boats lost in month & overall
September 1939	57 49	2 - 2	41 - 41	0.84	21.50 21.50
October 1939	- -	5 - 7	27 - 68	-	5.40 9.71
November 1939	- -	1 - 8	21 - 89	-	21.00 11.13
December 1939	- -	1 - 9	25 - 114	-	25.00 12.67
January 1940	56 32	1 - 10	40 - 154	1.25	40.00 15.40
February 1940	- -	6 - 16	45 - 199	-	7.50 12.44
March 1940	- -	2 - 18	23 - 222	-	11.50 12.33
Phase returns		18	222		12.33
April 1940	52 46	5 - 23	7 - 229	0.15	1.40 9.96
May 1940	- -	1 - 24	13 - 242	-	13.00 10.08
June 1940	- -	1 - 25	58 - 300	-	58.00 12.00
Phase returns		7	78		11.14
July 1940	51 28	2 - 27	38 - 338	1.36	19.00 12.52
August 1940	- -	2 - 29	56 - 394	-	28.00 13.59
September 1940	- -	1 - 31	59 - 453	-	59.00 14.61
October 1940	64 27	1 - 32	63 - 516	2.33	63.00 16.13
November 1940	- -	3 - 34	32 - 48	-	10.67 16.12
December 1940	- -	- 34	37 - 585	-	- 17.21
January 1941	89 22	- 34	21 - 606	0.95	- 17.82
February 1941	- -	- 34	39 - 645	-	- 18.97
March 1941	- -	5 - 9	41 - 686	-	8.20 17.59
April 1941	113 32	2 - 41	43 - 729	1.34	21.59 17.78
May 1941	- -	1 - 42	58 - 787	-	58.00 18.74
Phase returns		17	487		28.65
June 1941	- -	4 - 46	61 - 848	-	15.25 18.43
July 1941	158 65	1 - 47	22 - 870	0.34	22.00 18.51
August 1941	- -	3 - 50	23 - 893	-	7.67 17.86
September 1941	- -	2 - 52	953 - 46	-	26.50 18.19
October 1941	198 80	2 - 54	32 - 978	0.40	16.00 18.11
November 1941	- -	5 - 59	13 - 991	-	2.60 16.80

	Number of U-boats in service and operational	Number of U-boats lost in month and overall	Number of merchantmen sunk by U-boats in month & overall	Exchange rate merchantmen lost:operational U-boats	Exchange rate merchantmen: U-boats lost in month & overall
December 1941	- -	10 - 69	26 - 1017	-	2.60 14.74
Phase returns		27	230		8.52
January 1942	249 91	3 - 72	62 - 1079	0.68	20.67 14.99
February 1942	- -	2 - 74	85 - 1164	-	42.50 15.72
March 1942	- -	6 - 80	95 - 1259	-	15.83 15.74
April 1942	285 121	3 - 83	74 - 1333	0.61	24.67 16.06
May 1942	- -	4 - 87	125 - 1458	-	31.25 16.76
June 1942	- -	3 - 90	144 - 1602	-	48.00 17.80
Phase returns		21	585		27.86
July 1942	331 140	11 - 101	96 - 1698	0.69	8.73 16.81
August 1942	- -	10 - 111	108 - 1806	-	10.80 16.27
September 1942	- -	11 - 122	98 - 1904	-	8.91 15.61
October 1942	365 196	16 - 138	94 - 1998	0.48	5.88 14.48
November 1942	- -	13 - 151	119 - 2117	-	9.15 14.02
December 1942	- -	5 - 156	60 - 2177	-	12.00 13.96
January 1943	393 212	6 - 162	37 - 2214	0.17	6.17 13.67
February 1943	- -	19 - 181	63 - 2277	-	3.32 12.58
March 1943	- -	16 - 197	108 - 2385	-	6.75 12.11
April 1943	425 240	15 - 212	56 - 2441	0.23	3.73 11.51
May 1943	- -	41 - 253	50 - 2491	-	1.22 9.85
Phase returns		163	889		5.45
June 1943	- -	17 - 270	20 - 2511	-	1.18 9.30
July 1943	415 207	37 - 307	46 - 2557	0.22	1.24 8.33
August 1943	- -	25 - 332	16 - 2573	-	0.64 7.75
September 1943	- -	10 - 342	20 - 2593	-	2.00 7.58
October 1943	412 175	26 - 368	20 - 2613	0.11	0.77 7.10
November 1943	- -	19 - 387	14 - 2627	-	0.74 6.78
December 1943	- -	8 - 395	13 - 2640	-	1.63 6.68
January 1944	436 168	15 - 410	13 - 2653	0.08	0.87 6.47
February 1944	- -	20 - 430	18 - 2671	-	0.90 6.21

	Number of U-boats in service and operational	Number of U-boats lost in month and overall	Number of merchantmen sunk by U-boats in month & overall	Exchange rate merchantmen lost:operational U-boats	Exchange rate merchantmen: U-boats lost in month & overall
March 1944	- -	25 - 455	23 - 2694	-	0.92 5.92
April 1944	444 166	21 - 475	9 - 2703	0.05	0.45 5.69
May 1944	- -	23 - 499	4 - 2707	-	0.17 5.42
Phase returns		246	218		0.88
June 1944	- -	25 - 524	11 - 2718	-	0.44 5.19
July 1944	434 188	23 - 547	12 - 2730	0.06	0.52 4.99
August 1944	- -	36 - 583	18 - 2748	-	0.50 4.71
September 1944	- -	22 - 605	7 - 2755	-	0.32 4.55
October 1944	401 141	12 - 617	1 - 2756	0.01	0.08 4.47
November 1944	- -	9 - 626	7 - 2763	-	0.78 4.41
December 1944	- -	16 - 642	9 - 2772	-	0.56 4.32
January 1945	425 144	14 - 656	11 - 2783	0.08	0.79 4.24
February 1945	- -	22 - 678	15 - 2798	-	0.68 4.13
March 1945	- -	30 - 708	13 - 1281	-	0.45 3.97
April 1945	429 166	62 - 770	13 - 2814	0.08	0.21 3.65
May 1945	- -	29 - 799	3 - 2827	-	0.10 3.54
Phase returns		300	120		0.40

Note: The numbers of U-boats in service and operational and the numbers of merchantmen sunk by U-boats have been taken from S. W. Roskill, *The War at Sea*, vol. 1: *The Defensive*, Appendix Q, "German U-boat strength, 1939–41," p. 614, and Appendix R, Table I, "British, Allied and Neutral Merchant Ship Losses and Causes," p. 615; vol. 2: *The Period of Balance*, Appendix K, "German U-boat Strength January 1942–May 1943," p. 475, and Appendix O, Table I, "British, Allied and Neutral Merchant Ship Losses and Causes from Enemy Action January 1942–May 1943," p. 485; vol. 3: *The Offensive*, Part 1, "1st June 1943–31st May 1944," Appendix C, "German U-boat Strength July 1943–April 1944," p. 364, and Appendix K, Table I, "British, Allied and Neutral Merchant Shipping Losses from Enemy Action, and Causes—1st June, 1943–31st May, 1944," p. 388; and vol. 3: *The Offensive*, Part 2, "1st June 1944–15th August 1945," Appendix X, "German U-Boat Strength July, 1944–April, 1945," p. 456, and Appendix Z, Table I, "British, Allied and Neutral Merchant Shipping Losses from Enemy Action, 1st June, 1944–15th August, 1945," p. 477. All other figures and calculations are those of the author.

stern chase and was certainly two and perhaps three years behind schedule in terms of numbers of operational U-boats needed to prosecute the campaign against shipping to a successful conclusion. But the fact remains that while some 21,540,952 tons of Allied and neutral shipping were sunk during the Second World War to all forms of enemy action and other causes, the real cause of defeat lay in the fact that this was only two-thirds of the shipping built in U.S. shipyards between 7 December 1941 and 15 August 1945. Therein lay at least part of the reason for outcome of the campaign against shipping: the simple fact that all forms of German, Italian, and Japanese action, human error, and natural and unknown causes could not begin to equal what American yards were able to produce.

Thus this introduction has put in place the four elements that were at work in ensuring Allied victory at sea: the curbing of the U-boat offensive as a result of losses that were primarily the result of a comprehensive convoy system being put in place during the first four years of war; the acquisition of shipping from previously neutral countries that was crucially important in ensuring British survival at a time of maximum weakness and vulnerability; the ability of the United States to make good all losses; and the fact that on the German side the campaign against shipping came to be primarily the responsibility of just one branch of the Kriegsmarine, which was always operating some two or three years "late" (i.e., the numbers that it had in 1943–1944 were the numbers that it needed in 1940–1942 in order to prosecute the campaign against shipping to a successful conclusion). The chapters that together form the third part of this second volume of *The Last Century of Sea Power* will consider these and other matters, but this second part will continue with consideration of matters that genuinely have commanded but little historical attention, or at least little Anglo-American attention. For example, the general story of the defeat of the U-boat campaign against shipping has been recounted many times and in many ways but always to one end, and the same comment can be made, *mutatis mutandis*, with reference to the American drives across the Pacific. But how much attention is ever afforded overall submarine losses in the war, or the curious if little-known fact that in this war Italy lost more submarines than did the United States—and for that matter so did Britain, the Soviet Union, and, very surprisingly, France? A total of 1,291 submarines were enrolled on the list marked *finis* in the course of the Second World War, and perhaps rather surprisingly the share of overall sinkings by warships relative to land-based patrol and escort aircraft was markedly greater than was the case with the German U-boats. Just what conclusion may be drawn is another matter. That Germany, Italy, and Japan individually and collectively were markedly ineffective in the conduct of aircraft operations against enemy submarines invites one obvious deduction. The point is so obvious that one wonders why no one seems to have noticed: take away the German losses of 1945, and that year's toll of submarines really does consist of gaps held apart by the occasional loss, and seven in ten of these remaining losses were Japanese.

The issue of Italy's submarine losses leads to a related matter: the attention afforded that country's performance, and specifically its naval performance, in the war. Roskill's official history summarized Italian losses on just three pages.[1] But Italian losses were quite considerable; indeed Italian cruiser, destroyer, submarine, and minesweeper losses, and not just submarine losses, were greater than those incurred by the United States—not that such losses prevented Italy's being relegated from the rank of great power to the status of battlefield. The Italian national effort in the Second World War was riddled by too many weaknesses, across the board, for the naval dimension to be singled out for special attention. The fact, however, that Sicily and peninsular Italian came to be subjected to three major amphibious landings is evidence of the Italian failing at sea, and the ambiguity of Italy's role, in terms of switching sides, meant that Italy was one of just two of all the combat nations of the Second World War that had warships deliberately sunk by both sides,[2] and perhaps overall Italy had more enemies than any other country. The Italian naval performance was indeed unfortunate, doubly so because in elegance of profile Italy produced what were probably the most handsome of the world's warships, or at least more than its fair share of the most pleasing to the eye.

We now come to the question, were there more aircraft carriers sunk in the Second World War than battleships, or were there more battleships sunk than aircraft carriers? Given the fact that the Second World War was (with only minimal overstatement) a carrier war, the answer may seem to be obvious, but the argument can turn the other way: given the fact that this was a carrier war, the battleship presented itself as a most numerous victim. The one point that emerges, *en passant*, is the possibly surprising fact that Japan lost more aircraft carriers than Britain and the United States combined. The British lost four fleet, one light, and three escort carriers, while the Americans lost the same number of fleet and light carriers but three more escort carriers, the British and American total therefore being nineteen fleet, light, and escort carriers; the Japanese lost eleven fleet, five light, and six escort carriers. The total of forty-one carriers lost in the course of the war to a variety of causes stands alongside the very surprising total of thirty-seven battleships and battlecruisers that suffered similar fates. In the interest of accuracy and balance, however, it should be noted that this latter total is somewhat inflated by a number of units that were scuttled, only to be raised and sunk a second time, and in two cases, raised a second and sunk a third time.[3] The point about the capital ship losses is that the story of the Second World War at sea is seldom told by reference to such numbers, not least because only six of the capital ships—the *Hood*, *Bismarck*, *Scharnhorst*, *Kirishima*, *Fuso*, and *Yamashiro*—were sunk in action with enemy counterparts.

* * *

The main purpose of this introduction, however, is to make the obvious point that in seeking to set out perspectives somewhat different from those that have held sway over the last six decades, one must first define what has entered the lists as "conventional wisdom" (if indeed the second of those two words can be used in any matter involving naval officers). But one would suggest that there have been two lines of historical representation, one involving Britain and the other the United States, that have done a disservice in terms of the understanding of events. On the British side, and as noted elsewhere, if Churchill was correct and 1940 represented Britain's finest hour, then everything that followed has been anti-climatic, and one would suggest that British historical representation of the Second World War has been shaped, at least in part, as the means of disguising that fact. On the American side the representation of the war at sea has come to take second place behind that in such Internet sites as the Hundred Greatest Americans, with "Eisenhower, the Man Who Won the Second World War." Such a representation is preposterous and grotesque; the Second World War was not won by an individual, and most certainly the European war was not won by an individual or by the United States. To put matters at its simplest, the Allied campaign in northwest Europe between June 1944 and May 1945 resulted in some 128,000 German military dead, the equivalent of a British or American corps at that time. The whole Normandy venture was put into effect after the decision of the war had been reached, and at the very best what the Americans and British put together, which saw these powers committing armies to the European battlefield for the first time, helped complete the enemy's defeat, but most certainly was not the cause of it. The total military dead in northwest Europe in the last year of the war represented something like 3 percent of the total German dead, military and civilian, in the Second World War; even if one concedes that individual Germans would surrender in northwest Europe and that therefore the losses incurred by Germany on this front were greater, perhaps appreciably greater, than may appear prima facie, the fact remains that the issue of victory and defeat had been resolved before June 1944. Had Normandy miscarried, the outcome of the war, and indeed even the timing of Germany's defeat, would not have been affected very much: few German troops in northwest Europe could have been released for service on the Eastern Front, and indeed most of the German troops in France and the Low Countries were in formations that were "second team," deemed by the German high command as not capable of operating in the main theater of operations in the east.

The European war was decided on the Eastern Front, at a cost that was horrendous and that Britain and the United States were spared. On average, every day of its Great Patriotic War cost the Soviet Union 19,014 dead—a Pearl Harbor every 182 minutes for 1,420 days—and in every week between June 1941 and May 1945 the Soviet Union lost the equivalent of the total American dead in the Japanese war. The Soviet Union bought the victory of the United Nations with blood. The United States bought the victory of the United Nations in terms of money and output; the value of all the aid given to its allies was the sum equivalent to that needed for it to raise 2,000 infantry or 555 armored divisions. In terms of battle perhaps the United States' main contribution was in the air, in terms of the defeat of the *Luftwaffe* and its being drawn from over the battlefield.

Britain's contribution was somewhat different; its contribution to the victory of the United Nations was three-fold: (one) continuity of war and hence the denial of victory to Germany in 1940–1941, (two) provision of a haven for the defeated flotsam of Europe, and (three) the example of parliamentary democracy at a time when the latter had been extinguished on the European mainland. Militarily the major British achievement was indeed at sea, but, as noted elsewhere, Germany was not defeated in the Second World War because it lost the war at sea, and defeat at sea was not a major factor in Germany's overall defeat in the Second World War.

* * *

In terms of navies and sea power, the Second World War was of crucial importance in that ownership of the Trident changed in the course of this conflict. For the first time in perhaps two hundred years possession of supremacy at sea changed hands, and rather strangely the change was between allies. For two centuries Britain had possessed a superiority at sea that became increasingly pronounced in the course of the eighteenth century as a result of French distraction and the passing of the Netherlands and Spain from the first rank. Contrary to common interpretation, victory did not provide Britain with supremacy at sea, but the reverse: British victories were the product of an increasing British superiority in terms of warship numbers, training and capability, and geographical position. That superiority lasted into the Second World War, and on one count that had nothing to do with numbers: with the United States possessed of a navy the equal of Britain's after and, as a direct result of, the Washington treaties, British naval superiority after 1921 was moral and historical.

The U.S. Navy entered into its inheritance in the course of this war, and it did so as the war at sea became four-dimensional in terms of naval air operations, submarine operations, operations on the part of fleet and escort formations, and amphibious operations. For the better part of three hundred years battle at sea had been one-dimensional, with warships built around their guns and battles fought at short range. Mines, torpedoes, the submarine, and aircraft had been developed and adopted by navies before the First World War, but heavier-than-air flying machines in that war had been in their infancy and of limited capability and effectiveness, while there was little scope for amphibious operations in the main theaters of operation. The Second World War saw the naval aircraft and the amphibious option come of age, and the U.S. Navy was at the forefront of these developments just as it was in such matters as radars and radio. The U.S. Navy was also the one naval power that successfully put in place a *guerre de course*, and indeed in so doing the United States became the only power ever to have prosecuted a war against enemy commerce to the point of that enemy's defeat. All these matters, however, were secondary to the one point so easily overlooked: the basis of U.S. naval success lay in national power, a strength and stamina in depth that was the product of American industrial and financial power, but the basis of the American way of war in this conflict was not so much naval power as sea power. In the Second World War the United States assumed genuine global status, an ability to reach around the world in a manner that had been denied it hitherto, and the United States gained this position at the very time when Britain and France, despite possessions across the world, were confronted with the reality that global presence was not the same as global power. The United States was able to reach across the Pacific and across the North and South Atlantic Oceans, but the American ability to do so, and to do so with military and air formations, rested upon a lift capability that was unprecedented. In the final analysis, American military formations and air forces depended upon sea power for the movement of personnel, equipment, stores, and fuel. Evidence of this dependence was provided in an exchange in spring 1945 when, in response to a complaint against the naval commander in the Pacific, Admiral Chester W. Nimitz (1885–1966), on the part of General Curtis E. LeMay (1906–1990), to the effect that the naval demand that Army Air Force formations be held in support of naval forces off Okinawa represented effort wasted, the Chief of Naval Operations, Fleet Admiral Ernest J. King (1878–1956), suggested that the navy withdraw its formations and leave the army and army air formations on Okinawa without support, to look to their own resources for supply, a response that marked the end of the exchange.[4] Mixing metaphors, sea power was the bedrock of all forms of American military operations in the Second World War; the U.S. Navy in 1945 came complete with its own military in the form of marine formations that were the equivalent of two corps and with its own air force in the form of carrier formations that, along with four British fleet carriers, was responsible for putting 1,747 aircraft over the Inland Sea, its bays, its harbors, and its islands in the great raid of 24 July 1945.[5] But, of course, the American drives across the Pacific during the war against Japan represented joint offensives in which there was a degree of interdependence and cooperation between services. Indeed, these offensives—with land-based air power neutralizing an objective, carrier formations isolating the same objective, and amphibious force landing and securing this objective, with the result that land-based air formations came forward to begin the process afresh—can be presented as the first genuine joint, three-service, operations, but, as its name indicates, the Army Air Force was not an independent service at this time.

* * *

Discussion of sea power and of lift leads to two other matters that are seldom afforded much in the way of detailed historical analysis and representation. The first of these is that during this war not merely did the United States become the greatest naval power in the world but it also came into possession of the world's greatest merchant fleet. The second is the other side of the coin: Britain's displacement in terms of size of merchant fleet and its position as greatest maritime power.

On the American side, between 1939 and 1945 the yards supervised by the U.S. Maritime Commission built a total of 5,777 ships at a cost of some $13 billion, with the result that, given the slenderness of American shipping losses in the war as a whole, the United States, which built 32,056,140 tons of shipping between 1942 and 1945, ended hostilities with something like 40,000,000 tons of shipping, that is, almost twice as much shipping as Britain had possessed in 1939 when it remained the greatest maritime power in the world, and by a margin. The American achievement was registered during the transformation of the United States from a North Atlantic state with a continental interior to a country that occupied a continent and reached across the oceans that washed its shores, the three west coast states being hosts to a population increase of more than a third—from 9,800,000 to 13,100,000—between 1940 and 1945 and to a process of industrialization, specifically related to shipbuilding that had briefly been set in place during the First World War. Across the continental interior of the United States there was migration and a pattern of industrialization that saw such unlikely developments as the production of tanks in Arizona, aircraft in Nebraska, Kansas, and Oklahoma, warships in Minnesota and Wisconsin and landing craft in inland Illinois. With output doubling between 1939 and 1943, and the United States building almost double the number of aircraft of all other combatant nations combined, the massive increase of industry was accompanied not just by major increases in state spending, taxation, and the raising of loans but by a major increase of imports and, perhaps surprisingly, of exports, while the resultant balance-of-payments surplus of some $34 billions inevitably made the country the greatest credit nation in the world.[6] In terms of navies and shipping, two statistics illustrate the impact of these various developments, most obviously the application of mass-production and assembly-line techniques, plus prefabrication, on what had hitherto been a largely undeveloped west coast: the Kaiser yard in Oregon launched its fiftieth escort carrier one year and one day after it launched its first, and its seventy-fifth Liberty Ship was handed complete to Maritime Commission representatives on 26 September 1942, thirteen days after having been laid down.[7] What is no less remarkable about such construction, indeed the whole of the wartime United States warship and merchant shipping construction programs, is that it was undertaken by an industry that in the lean years of the inter-war period had been reduced to little more than the "Big Five"—Newport News Shipbuilding and Dry Dock Company; the Federal Shipbuilding and Dry Dock Company of Kearney, New Jersey; the New York Shipbuilding Company of Camden, New Jersey; the Sun Shipbuilding and Dry Dock Company of Chester, Pennsylvania; and the Bethlehem Steel Company on the Fore River at Quincy, Massachusetts—while such yards as Cramp of Philadelphia, once all but synonymous with U.S naval aspirations, had been abandoned. It was not until 1940 that there was the first major expansion of construction capacity in the form of new companies, four on the west coast and three in the Gulf, and their performances in this year were decidedly modest, giving no indication of what was to come over the next four years.[8] In no small measure, however, this massive expansion of production was facilitated less by additional companies and yards coming into production than by standardization of types of ships that were built. Whereas the British did not standardize their new construction but left individual yards to furnish their own designs, which were then repeated, the Americans standardized nationwide with obvious effect, most notably in terms of long-term orders for parts.[9]

The American displacement of Britain in size of the merchant fleet had been foreshadowed during the First World War, which had destroyed a British financial primacy that had been under sentence for some two decades, since the time in the last decade of the nineteenth century when the United States overtook Britain in industrial production. The Second World War saw the merchant fleet under British control shrink massively as a result of the losses that were incurred, but two other aspects of shipping operations pointed in the direction of major change. In the course of hostilities about three-fifths of British shipping came to be requisitioned, and it is very easy to lose sight of commitments in place that led to such inordinate demand. By late 1944 there were commitments involving military and air formations in northwest Europe, in Italy and Greece, in India and Burma. There were garrisoning obligations in east Africa, throughout the Middle East, and in southern Iran, and there were the preparations in hand in the Indian and Pacific Oceans pending the arrival of British naval formations in these theaters. The last of these, specifically the obligations regarding Australia and the preparations for the arrival of the British Pacific Fleet on station, proved something of a nightmare, on a number of counts. In the course of 1944 the British high command became aware that national resources would not extend to simultaneous efforts in southeast Asia and the Pacific. With a minimum lead-time of nine months needed to set base facilities in place,[10] the lengthening of the war in Europe into 1945 and the date for the final landings on the Japanese home islands obviously coming forward into 1945 and 1946 found the British high command—which at the Octagon conference in Quebec in September 1944 undertook to send a fleet consisting of four fleet and two light fleet carriers, two battleships, eight cruisers, twenty-four destroyers, and sixty escorts to the Pacific by the end of the year[11]—caught as the sands of time exhausted themselves, not least because the demands of the northwest Europe theater would increase, not decrease, with the end of hostilities.

The need to maintain forces of occupation and to repatriate servicemen and ex-prisoners and, crucially, dominion and imperial personnel placed Britain in an impossible position, and this was at a time when it faced another challenge. Total British imports, including oil, had amounted to almost 60 million tons in 1938, but by 1944 total British import needs were assessed at 28 million tons. On the basis of the shipping that was available to Britain, however, only some 24 million tons of imports were likely to enter the country in both 1944 and 1945. A deficit of 4 million tons in one year could be managed—with some difficulty, but it could be managed—but an 8 million–ton deficit over two years presented real problems: stocks, and specifically food stocks, could cover a seven-week deficit in one year but not a three-month deficit in two.[12]

The second matter relating to shipping was the changing pattern of trade that came as a consequence of war. Just as in the First World War the Allied problems of available shipping space were eased by the exchange of sources between Britain, which had imported grain from Australia, and Italy, which had done likewise from North America, so the Second World War saw major changes in terms of British trade and shipping commitments. These may be summarized succinctly: with trade within Europe obviously at an end, the North Atlantic routes, from Canada and the United States, largely supplanted all other routes, and specifically imperial and Australasian, as the following figures in tables 5.2 and 5.3 indicate.

The Great Depression had produced real problems for empires in terms of the decline of the imperial powers' capacity to trade and to finance development, and even basic education programs, in colonies and territories; the war only compounded problems, especially after the defeat of France in 1940, when quite clearly trade with, and the products and needs of, African colonial territories assumed at very best tertiary status. In the 1934–1938 trading totals Australia and New Zealand accounted for 2,459,000 tons and India, with Burma and Ceylon, for 929,000 tons, but in 1944 these totals were 556,000 and 375,000 tons, which represent falls of some 77 and 60 percent respectively. With European sources having fallen from consideration, the importance of North America, and what in relative terms was short-haul trade, was obvious: Canada and the United States, which had accounted for 2,843,000 tons of these imports in the 1934–1938 period, in 1944 provided 4,652,000 tons of

TABLE 5.2. MAIN SOURCES OF FOOD IMPORTS INTO BRITAIN DURING THE SECOND WORLD WAR

	Average tonnage of imports between 1934 and 1938	Sources of supply	# share	Tonnage of imports in 1944	Sources of Supply	# share	1944 tonnage as percentage of 1934–1938 average
Wheat and flour	5,451,000	Canada	20	3,615,000	Canada	83	66.32
		Australia	24		Argentina	12	
		Argentina	15				
Other grains, rice, and pulses	1,403,000	Canada	20	137,000	United States	58	9.96
		Europe (excluding USSR)	18		Argentina and Brazil	31	
		U.S. and South America	17				
		Iraq and Iran	12				
		Soviet Union	12				
Animal feeding stuffs	5,137,000	Argentina	57	216,000	Argentina	72	4.20
		India and Burma	11		Iceland	14	
					United States	10	
Meat (including canned meats, bacon, and ham)	1,546,000	Argentina	31	1,796,000	Argentina	32	116.17
		Australia and New Zealand	31		United States	24	
		Denmark	12		Canada	20	
					Australia and New Zealand	16	
Oilseed and nuts, vegetable oil, and animal fats	1,917,000	Egypt and Sudan	22	1,975,000	British West Africa	36	103.03
		India, Burma, and Ceylon	19		India, Burma, and Ceylon	19	
		British West Africa	16		Argentina	16	
		Argentina and Brazil	11		French West and Equatorial Africa	11	

Whale oil	88,000	Netherlands	47	N/A	N/A	N/A	0.00
		Norway	17				
Sugar	2,168,000	Cuba and Dominican Republic	37	1,155,000	Cuba and Dominican Republic	77	53.27
		Australia	15		Mauritius, South Africa, British West Indies, and British Guiana	16	
		Mauritius	11				
		British West Indies and British Guiana	11				
Dairy produce	935,000	Europe (including USSR)	46	685,000	Canada and United States	59	73.26
		Australia and New Zealand	37		Australia and New Zealand	34	
Fruit and vegetables	2,639,000	Europe (including Canary Is.)	41	649,000	United States	28	24.59
		Brazil, British West Indies, and Palestine	20		Europe (including Canary Is.)	27	
		United States	12		Iraq, Palestine, and Turkey	14	
					South Africa	13	
					Australia and Canada	11	
Volume of all items	**22,830,000 tons**			10,365,000 tons			45.40

Source: W. K. Hancock, ed., *History of the Second World War: The United Kingdom Civil Series.* R. J. Hammond, *Food,* vol. 1: *The Growth of Policy,* p. 395, table 6, "Main Sources of Imports of Principal Groups of Food and Feeding-Stuffs (a) 1934–38 (b) 1944."

Table 5.3. Imports of Food and Animal Feeding-Stuffs into Britain in the Course of the Second World War

	Average level of imports 1934–1938		1940		1941		1942		1943		1944		1945		
	tonnage	%	tonnage	%	tonnage	%	tonnage	%	tonnage	%	tonnage	%	tonnage	%	%
Wheat	5,031	22.37	5,754	114.37	5,393	107.20	3,487	69.31	3,256	64.72	2,824	56.13	3,552	70.60	32.36
Wheatmeal and flour	420	1.87	577	137.38	708	168.57	374	89.05	718	170.95	791	188.33	543	129.29	4.95
Rice, other grains, and pulses	1,403	6.24	1,077	76.76	514	35.64	163	11.62	257	18.32	137	9.76	340	24.23	3.10
Maize and maize meal	3,395	15.09	2,192	64.57	702	20.68	135	3.98	66	1.94	118	3.48	510	15.02	4.64
Oilcake	595	2.65	417	70.08	204	34.29	55	9.24	-	-	68	11.43	190	31.93	1.73
Other animal feeding stuffs	1,147	5.10	648	56.50	120	10.46	19	1.66	12	1.05	30	2.62	10	0.87	0.09
Meats	1,096	4.87	1,128	102.92	1,073	97.90	1,047	95.53	1,051	95.89	1,182	107.85	832	75.91	7.58
Bacon and ham	387	1.72	241	62.27	281	72.61	362	93.54	387	100.00	408	105.43	244	63.05	2.22
Canned meats	63	0.28	122	193.65	226	358.73	249	395.24	246	390.47	206	326.98	97	153.97	0.88
Oilseeds and nuts	1,522	6.77	1,630	107.10	1,506	98.95	1,361	89.42	1,621	106.50	1,468	96.45	1,055	69.32	9.61
Oils and fats	395	1.76	366	92.66	439	111.14	539	136.46	542	137.22	507	128.35	304	76.96	2.77
Unrefined whale oil	88	0.39	82	93.18	31	35.23	42	47.72	14	15.91	-	.	39	44.31	0.36
Sugar	2,168	9.64	1,526	70.39	1,652	76.20	768	35.42	1,425	65.73	1,155	53.27	1,066	49.17	9.71

Dairy produce:															
Butter	480	2.13	264	55.00	218	45.42	134	27.92	152	31.67	153	31.88	190	39.58	1.73
Cheese	142	0.63	156	109.86	203	142.96	315	221.83	207	145.77	252	177.46	191	134.51	1.74
Processed milk	104	0.46	87	83.65	167	160.58	261	250.96	223	214.42	177	170.19	96	92.31	0.87
Eggs	159	0.71	99	62.26	59	37.11	23	14.47	15	9.43	23	14.47	48	30.19	0.44
Other dairy produce	50	0.22	42	84.00	48	96.00	65	130.00	74	148.00	80	160.00	37	74.00	0.34
Dried fruit	175	0.78	128	73.14	210	120.00	198	113.14	181	103.43	253	144.57	155	88.57	1.41
Fresh fruit	1,502	6.68	839	55.86	115	7.66	131	8.72	58	3.86	213	14.69	398	27.44	3.66
Canned and preserved fruit, pulp, and juices	257	1.14	202	78.60	112	43.58	114	44.36	72	28.02	125	48.64	87	33.85	0.79
Vegetables	705	3.13	392	55.60	105	14.89	67	9.50	23	3.26	58	8.23	79	11.21	0.72
Tea, coffee, and cocoa	346	1.54	370	106.94	371	107.22	344	92.77	422	121.97	381	110.12	321	92.77	2.92
Other foods	861	3.83	847	93.37	609	70.73	584	67.83	591	68.64	546	63.41	591	68.64	5.38
Total	22,491	-	19,186	85.31	15,066	66.99	10,837	48.18	11,613	51.63	11,155	49.60	10,975	48.88	

Volume expressed in terms of thousands of tons.

In this table, the percentage figures for 1940, 1941, 1942, 1943, 1944 and the first percentage figure for 1945 relate to that year's level of imports relative to the 1934–1938 average, which is taken as 100 for each and every commodity: the percentage figure for the 1934–1938 average and second 1945 percentage figure relate to the individual commodity relative to overall level of imports for that period and year respectively.

The returns for imported whale oil do not include returns on the part of British whaling ships.

Table 5.4. Domestic Production of Certain Crops in Britain in the Course of the Second World War

	Average level of production 1936–1938	1939		1940		1941		1942		1943		1944		1945	
		tonnage	%	tonnage	%	tonnage	%	tonnage	%	tonnage	%	tonnage	%	tonnage	%
Wheat	1,651	1,645	99.64	1,641	99.39	2,018	122.23	2,567	155.48	3,447	208.78	3,138	190.07	2,176	131.80
Barley	765	892	116.60	1,104	144.31	1,144	149.54	1,446	189.02	1,645	215.03	1,752	229.02	2,108	275.56
Oats	1,940	2,003	103.25	2,892	149.07	3,247	167.37	3,553	183.14	3,064	157.94	2,953	152.22	3,245	167.27
Potatoes	4,873	5,218	107.08	6,405	131.44	8,004	164.25	9,393	192.76	9,822	201.56	9,096	186.66	9,791	200.92
Sugar	2,741	3,529	128.75	3,176	115.87	3,226	117.69	3,923	143.12	3,760	137.18	3,267	119.19	3,886	141.77
Vegetables	2,371	2,403	101.35	2,617	110.38	2,884	121.64	3,693	155.76	3,144	132.60	3,423	144.37	3,240	136.65
Total	14,341	15,690	109.41	17,835	124.36	20,523	143.11	24,575	171.36	24,882	173.50	23,629	164.77	24,446	170.46

Volume expressed in terms of thousands of tons.

With reference to table 5.3, the percentage figures for 1940, 1941, 1942, 1943, and 1944 and the first percentage figure for 1945 relate to that year's level of imports relative to the 1934–1938 average, which is taken as 100 for each and every commodity; the percentage figure for the 1934–1938 average and the second 1945 percentage figure relate to the individual commodity relative to overall level of imports for that period and year respectively.

The returns for imported whale oil do not include returns on the part of British whaling ships.

With reference to this table, all percentage figures relate to that year's level of production relative to the 1936–1938 figure, which is taken as 100 for each and every commodity.

These returns are cited as output excluding that of holdings of one acre or less in Great Britain and one-quarter of an acre or less in Northern Ireland.

Source: W. K. Hancock, ed., *History of the Second World War: The United Kingdom Civil Series.* R. J. Hammond, *Food*, vol. 1: *The Growth of Policy*, pp. 392–393, table 2, "Imports of Food and Animal Feeding-Stuffs into the United Kingdom," and table 3, "Estimated Production of Principle Crops in the United Kingdom." It should be noted that the figures given in table 5.2, drawn from Board of Trade data, differ from those in 5.4, drawn from Ministry of Food returns.

British imports in these commodities, and in relative terms this represented a growth from 12.45 to 44.88 percent—with Argentina adding 1,030,000 tons and the Caribbean another 982,000 tons of 1944 imports, or 9.94 and 9.47 percent respectively. Put at its simplest, while there was a major decline in the volume of British imports, the relative contribution of North America and the Caribbean increased more than four-fold between 1934–1938 and 1944.[13]

By definition, however, there were matters that defeated changes of source and shipping; the sort of problem that emerged in the course of the war may be illustrated by reference to one commodity, timber. Before the war British timber imports were drawn primarily from the Baltic, but with the outbreak of war a major increase in British needs—for military accommodation, for stores, and for government building generally—coincided with the closing of the Baltic trade, and that meant that Britain really had but one possible source to make good its deficiencies. But Canada in effect meant British Columbia, and certainly the British did not have long-haul shipping to make good its timber needs when the needs for iron ore and wheat had to take precedence in using available shipping space. These problems of timber supply and the definition of import and shipping priorities presented themselves for the first time in the first quarter of 1940, but by the very nature of things kept re-presenting themselves over the next five years, and always with the same result.[14]

* * *

This introductory piece must end here, leaving the reader free to consider what was not one war but two, and two that were largely separate from one another. At sea both wars separately played hosts to a number of different conflicts: in the European context the war at sea in the North Atlantic was very different from the war in the Mediterranean. In the Pacific there were also two very different wars, but it is the conflicts that made up the war at sea in the European context that now invite attention.

APPENDIX 5.1.

SUBMARINE LOSSES IN THE SECOND WORLD WAR

Agency of destruction	1939	1940	1941	1942	1943	1944	1945	Total	As % of national losses	As % of total losses
Sinkings by warships										
of American submarines	na	na	-	2	6.50	6	5.50	20	38.46	1.55
British submarines	-	13.50	5	8	7.50	1	-	35	38.89	2.71
Dutch submarines	na	-	2	-	-	-	-	2	25.00	0.15
French submarines	-	3	-	4.50	-	-	-	7.50	13.39	0.58
German submarines	5	12	25	36	69.50	80	48	275.50	34.48	21.34
Italian submarines	na	11	10.50	9.50	10.50	na	na	41.50	48.82	3.21
Japanese submarines	na	na	-	8.50	20	34	12.50	75	58.59	5.81
Soviet submarines	na	na	2	5	6.50	3	1	17.50	26.12	1.36
TOTAL	5	39.50	44.50	73.50	120.50	124	67	474	-	36.72
as % of overall losses	0.39	3.06	3.45	5.69	9.33	9.60	5.19	-	-	-
Sinkings by ship-based aircraft										
of American submarines	na	na	-	-	-	-	-	-	-	-
British submarines	-	-	-	-	-	-	-	-	-	-
Dutch submarines	na	-	-	-	-	-	-	-	-	-
French submarines	-	-	-	1.50	-	-	-	1.50	2.68	0.12
German submarines	-	1	0.50	1.50	25.50	23.75	1	53.25	6.66	4.14
Italian submarines	na	1	-	-	-	na	na	1	1.18	0.08
Japanese submarines	na	na	1	1	2	4.50	4.50	13	10.16	1.01
Soviet submarines	na	na	-	-	-	-	-	-	-	-
TOTAL	-	2	1.50	4	27.50	28.25	5.50	68.75	-	5.33
as % of overall losses	-	0.15	0.12	0.31	2.13	2.19	0.43	-	-	-

Agency of destruction	1939	1940	1941	1942	1943	1944	1945	Total	As % of national losses	As % of total losses
Sinkings by land-based aircraft of										
American submarines	na	na	-	-	2.50	2	2.50	7	13.46	0.54
British submarines	-	0.50	-	4	0.50	-	1	6	6.67	0.46
Dutch submarines	na	-	-	-	-	-	-	-	-	-
French submarines	-	-	-	5	-	-	-	5	62.50	0.39
German submarines	-	2	3.50	38.50	121	56.75	43	264.75	33.14	20.51
Italian submarines	na	3	1.50	3.50	6.50	na	na	14.50	17.06	1.12
Japanese submarines	na	na	-	2.50	-	-	1	3.50	2.73	0.27
Soviet submarines	na	na	-	1	2	-	-	3	4.48	0.23
TOTAL	-	5.50	5	54.50	132.50	58.75	47.50	303.75	-	23.53
as % of overall losses	-	0.43	0.39	4.33	10.26	4.55	3.68	-	-	-
Destroyed in bombing raids										
American submarines	na	na	1	-	-	-	-	-	1.92	0.08
British submarines	-	-	-	-	-	-	-	-	-	-
Dutch submarines	na	-	1	-	-	-	-	-	12.50	0.08
French submarines	-	-	-	-	-	-	-	-	-	-
German submarines	-	-	-	-	2	25	42	-	8.64	5.34
Italian submarines	na	-	-	1	1	na	na	-	2.35	0.15
Japanese submarines	na	na	-	-	-	-	-	-	-	-
Soviet submarines	na	na	1	1	-	-	-	-	2.98	0.15
TOTAL	-	-	3	2	3	25	42	75	-	5.81
as % of overall losses	-	-	0.23	0.15	0.23	1.94	3.25	-	-	-

Agency of destruction	1939	1940	1941	1942	1943	1944	1945	Total	As % of national losses	As % of total losses
Sinkings by submarines										
of American submarines	na	na	-	-	1	-	-	1	1.92	0.08
British submarines	-	4	-	-	1	-	-	5	5.56	0.39
Dutch submarines	na	-	-	1	-	-	-	1	12.50	0.08
French submarines	-	-	1	-	-	-	-	1	1.79	0.08
German submarines	1	2	2	2	6	7	3	23	2.88	1.78
Italian submarines	na	2	4	7	5	na	na	18	21.18	1.39
Japanese submarines	na	na	-	5	2	6	6	19	14.84	1.47
Soviet submarines	na	na	-	3	-	-	-	3	4.48	0.23
TOTAL	1	8	7	18	15	13	9	71	-	5.50
as % of overall losses	0.08	0.62	0.54	1.39	1.16	1.01	0.70	-	-	-
Sinkings by mines										
of American submarines	na	na	-	-	2	2	-	4	7.69	0.31
British submarines	-	7	3	4	2	1	-	17	18.89	1.32
Dutch submarines	na	-	-	-	-	-	-	-	-	-
French submarines	-	1	-	-	-	-	-	1	1.79	0.08
German submarines	3	2	-	3	1	14.50	10	33.50	4.19	2.59
Italian submarines	na	-	-	-	-	na	na	-	-	-
Japanese submarines	na	na	-	1	1	-	1	3	2.34	0.23
Soviet submarines	na	na	13	6	3.50	-	-	22.50	33.58	1.74
TOTAL	3	10	16	14	9.50	17.50	11	81	-	6.27
as % of overall losses	0.23	0.77	1.24	1.08	0.74	1.36	0.85	-	-	-

Agency of destruction	1939	1940	1941	1942	1943	1944	1945	Total	As % of national losses	As % of total losses
Losses to accidental causes										
of American submarines	na	na	-	1	1	4	-	6	11.54	0.46
British submarines	1	1	1	4	-	2	-	19	10	0.70
Dutch submarines	na	-	1	-	-	-	-	1	12.50	0.08
French submarines	-	2	-	1	-	-	-	1	1.79	0.08
German submarines	-	2	3	4	8	13	3	33	4.13	2.56
Italian submarines	na	2	-	-	1	na	na	3	3.53	0.23
Japanese submarines	na	na	1	-	1	1.50	-	3.50	2.73	0.27
Soviet submarines	na	na	-	2	-	2	-	4	5.97	0.31
TOTAL	1	7	6	12	11	22.50	3	62.50	-	4.84
as % of overall losses	0.08	0.54	0.46	0.93	0.85	1.74	0.23	-	-	-
Losses to marine causes										
of American submarines	na	na	-	3	1	1	-	5	9.62	0.39
British submarines	-	-	-	-	-	2	-	2	2.22	0.15
Dutch submarines	na	-	-	-	-	-	1	1	12.50	0.08
French submarines	-	-	-	-	-	-	-	-	-	-
German submarines	-	-	-	-	2	6	2	10	1.25	0.77
Italian submarines	na	-	-	-	-	na	na	-	-	-
Japanese submarines	na	na	1	-	1	-	-	2	1.56	0.15
Soviet submarines	na	na	-	-	-	-	-	-	-	-
TOTAL	-	-	1	3	4	9	3	20	-	1.55
as % of overall losses	-	-	0.08	0.23	0.31	0.70	0.23	-	-	-

Agency of destruction	1939	1940	1941	1942	1943	1944	1945	Total	As % of national losses	As % of total losses
Losses to unknown causes										
of American submarines	na	na	-	1	3	3	-	7	13.46	0.54
British submarines	-	3	3	3	4	3	-	16	17.78	1.24
Dutch submarines	na	-	-	-	-	-	-	-	-	-
French submarines	-	-	-	1	-	-	-	1	1.79	0.08
German submarines	-	3	1	2	1	8	5	20	2.50	1.55
Italian submarines	na	1	2	1	1	na	na	5	5.88	0.39
Japanese submarines	na	na	-	2	4	2	1	9	7.03	0.70
Soviet submarines	na	na	2	5	3	1	-	11	16.42	0.85
TOTAL	-	7	8	15	16	17	6	69	-	5.34
as % of overall losses	-	0.54	0.62	1.16	1.24	1.32	0.46	-	-	-
Losses to all other causes										
of American submarines	na	na	-	-	-	1	-	1	1.92	0.08
British submarines	-	-	-	-	-	-	-	-	-	-
Dutch submarines	na	-	1	1	-	-	-	2	25.00	0.15
French submarines	-	4	-	32	-	-	-	36	64.29	2.79
German submarines	-	-	-	-	1	14	2	17	2.13	1.32
Italian submarines	na	-	-	-	-	na	na	-	-	-
Japanese submarines	na	na	-	-	-	-	-	-	-	-
Soviet submarines	na	na	4	-	-	-	-	4	5.97	0.31
other submarines	-	1	-	-	5	-	-	6	-	0.47
TOTAL	-	5	5	33	6	15	2	66	-	5.11
as % of overall losses	-	0.39	0.39	2.56	0.46	1.16	0.15	-	-	-

Total number of										
American submarines lost	na	na	1	7	17	19	8	52	-	4.03
as % of overall national losses	-	-	1.92	13.46	32.69	36.54	15.38			
British submarines lost	1	29	12	23	15	9	1	90	-	6.97
as % of overall national losses	1.11	32.22	13.33	25.56	16.67	10.00	1.11			
Dutch submarines lost	na	-	5	2	-	-	1	8	-	0.62
as % of overall national losses	-	-	62.50	25.00	-	-	12.50			
French submarines lost	-	10	1	45	-	-	-	56	-	4.34
as % of overall national losses	-	17.86	1.79	80.36	-	-	-			
German submarines lost	9	24	35	87	237	248	159	799	-	61.89
as % of overall national losses	1.13	3.00	4.38	10.89	29.66	31.04	19.90			
Italian submarines lost	na	20	18	22	25	na	na	85	-	6.58
as % of overall national losses	-	23.53	21.18	25.88	29.41	-	-			
Japanese submarines lost	na	na	3	20	31	48	26	128	-	9.91
as % of overall national losses	-	-	2.34	15.63	24.22	37.50	20.31			
Soviet submarines lost	na	na	22	23	15	6	1	67	-	5.20
as % of overall national losses	-	-	32.84	34.33	22.39	8.96	1.49			
Other submarines lost	-	1	-	-	5	-	-	6	-	0.46
Total number of submarines lost	10	84	97	229	345	330	196	1291	-	-
as % of overall losses	0.77	6.51	7.51	17.74	26.72	25.56	15.18	-	-	-

The total of six units listed under the "other" label includes one Norwegian, two ex-Yugoslavian, and three Danish submarines that were scuttled; the ex-Yugoslavian units, held by the Royal Italian Navy, were scuttled in 1943 at the time of Italy's surrender.

The totals do not include five French boats that passed into Italian possession with the Axis occupation of Tunisia, the uncertain status of at least four of these boats precluding their inclusion in these lists.

APPENDIX 5.2.

FLEET, LIGHT, AND ESCORT CARRIERS SUNK DURING THE SECOND WORLD WAR

CERTAIN OF THE ENTRIES provided herein do not meet the requirements of definition in terms of "sinking," but the ships listed herein were most definitely lost in the sense that they were left in condition that precluded future employment; for example, the *Shimane Maru* is included in the list because her back was broken as a result of attack by carrier aircraft. This caveat notwithstanding, the units that were lost were as follows:

The British units that were lost were the fleet carrier *Courageous* on 17 September 1939 to attack by the submarine U. 29; the fleet carrier *Glorious* on 8 June 1940 in an action with enemy warships; the fleet carrier *Ark Royal* and escort carrier *Audacity* to attacks by the submarine U. 81 on 14 November and the submarine U. 751 on 21 December 1941 respectively; the light carrier *Hermes* on 9 April 1942 to attack by carrier aircraft; the fleet carrier *Eagle* and escort carrier *Avenger* to attacks by the submarine U. 73 on 11 August 1942 and the submarine U. 155 on 15 November 1942 respectively; and the escort carrier *Dasher* on 27 March 1943 as a result of internal fire and explosion.

To this total of eight units could be added two more escort carriers, the *Nabob* and *Thane*, neither of which were repaired and returned to service after having been torpedoed by the submarine U. 354 on 28 August 1944 and the submarine U. 482 on 15 January 1945 respectively; they were classified as constructive total losses.

The American units that were lost were the fleet carrier *Lexington* on 8 May 1942 to carrier aircraft; the fleet carrier *Yorktown* on 7 June 1942 to a combination of attacks by carrier aircraft and submarine I. 168; the fleet carrier *Wasp* on 15 September 1942 to an attack by the submarine I. 19; the fleet carrier *Hornet* to attack by carrier aircraft; the escort carriers *Liscome Bay* and *Block Island* to attacks by the Japanese submarine I. 175 on 24 November 1943 and by the German submarine U. 549 on 29 May 1944 respectively; the light carrier *Princeton* on 24 October 1944 to attack by a land-based aircraft; the escort carrier *Gambier Bay* in an action with enemy warships on 25 October 1944; and the escort carriers *St. Lo*, *Ommaney Bay*, and the *Bismarck Sea* as a result of *kamikaze* attacks on 25 October 1944, 4 January 1945, and 21 February 1945 respectively.

The Japanese units that were lost were the light carrier *Shoho* on 6 May 1942, the fleet carriers *Kaga* and *Soryu* on 4 June 1942, and the *Akagi* and *Hiryu* on the following day, and the light carrier *Ryujo* on 24 August 1942, all to attack by carrier aircraft; the escort carrier *Chuyo* to attack by the submarine *Sailfish* on 4 December 1943; the fleet carriers *Shokaku* and *Taiho* to attacks by the submarines *Cavalla* and *Albacore* respectively on 19 June 1944 and the *Hiyo* to attack by carrier aircraft on the following day; the escort carriers *Taiyo* and *Unyo* to attacks by the submarine *Rasher* on 18 August 1944 and the submarine *Barb* on 16 September 1944 respectively; the fleet carrier *Zuikaku* and the light carriers *Chitose*, *Chiyoda*, and *Zuiho* to attack by carrier aircraft on 25 October 1944; the escort carrier *Shinyo* and the fleet carriers *Shinano* and *Unryu* all to submarine attack, by the *Spadefish* on 17 November, the *Archerfish* on 29 November, and the *Redfish* on 19 December 1944 respectively; and the *Amagi* and the escort carriers *Kaiyo* and *Shimane Maru* on 24 July 1945, all to attack by carrier aircraft though none, technically, was sunk: the *Amagi* settled, the *Kaiyo* capsized, and the fate of the *Shimane Maru* has already been noted. All Japanese losses were to American carrier aircraft and submarines other than the *Shimane Maru*: British carrier aircraft were the source of its discomfiture.

APPENDIX 5.3.

THE CAPITAL SHIPS LOST IN THE SECOND WORLD WAR

CERTAIN OF THE ENTRIES provided herein do not meet the requirements of definition in terms of "sinking"; a number settled, with the result that they were salved, and a number were deliberately scuttled and not sunk as a result of enemy action. Moreover, certain of these units were returned to service but not as capital ships, and technically their being listed for a second or third time is not wholly accurate, but they are given here in the ruggedly confident manner that asserts that they were still capital ships. These caveats notwithstanding, the list of capital ships "that ceased to be" (if, in some cases, only temporarily) is as follows:

14 October 1939, the British battleship *Royal Oak* inside the Scapa Flow anchorage by the German submarine U. 47;

3 July 1940, the French battleships *Bretagne* and *Provence** at Mers El Kébir in surface action with British warships;*

11 November 1940, the Italian battleship *Conte di Cavour** in Taranto harbor by carrier aircraft;

24 May 1941, the British battleship *Hood* in the Denmark Strait in action with German warships;

27 May 1941, the German battleship *Bismarck* in the North Atlantic in action with British warships;

23 September 1941, the Soviet battleship *Marat** at Kronstadt by German land-based aircraft;

25 November 1941, the British battleship *Barham* in the eastern Mediterranean by the German submarine U. 331;

7 December 1941, the U.S. battleships *Arizona*, *California*,* *Oklahoma*,* and *West Virginia** at Pearl Harbor by Japanese carrier aircraft;

10 December 1941, the British capital ships *Prince of Wales* and *Repulse*, in the South China Sea by Japanese land-based aircraft;

19 December 1941, the British battleships *Queen Elizabeth** and *Valiant** in Alexandria harbor to Italian charioteer attack;

13 November 1942, the Japanese battleship *Hiei* off Guadalcanal, scuttled after a night action with U.S. light forces and after daytime attacks by land- and carrier-based aircraft;

15 November 1942, the Japanese battleship *Kirishima* off Guadalcanal in action with the U.S. battleship *Washington;*

27 November 1942, the French battleships *Dunkerque, Provence,** and *Strasbourg* scuttled in Toulon harbor to avoid capture;

8 June 1943, the Japanese battleship *Mutsu* in Hiroshima Bay by explosion of magazine;

9 September 1943, the Italian battleship *Roma* west of Bonifacio Strait by German land-based aircraft;

10 September 1943, the Italian battleship *Conte di Cavour** scuttled in Trieste harbor to avoid capture;

26 December 1943, the German battleship *Scharnhorst* in the Arctic off the North Cape in action with British warships;

18 August 1944, the French battleship *Strasbourg,* in German ownership, at Toulon by American land-based aircraft;

In August 1944, the French battleship *Provence* scuttled as blockship in Toulon harbor by German forces;

24 October 1944, the Japanese battleship (1942) *Musashi* in the Visayan Sea by U.S. carrier aircraft;

25 October 1944, the Japanese battleships *Fuso* and *Yamashiro* in the Surigao Strait in action with allied warships;

12 November 1944, the German battleship *Tirpitz* at Tromsø by British land-based aircraft;

21 November 1944, the Japanese battleship *Kongo* northwest of Formosa by the U.S. submarine *Sealion;*

15 February 1945, the Italian battleship *Conte di Cavour,* in German ownership, at Trieste by U.S. land-based aircraft;

27 March 1945, the German battleship *Gneisenau* scuttled as blockship at Gotenhafen;

7 April 1945, the Japanese battleship *Yamato* southwest of Kyushu by U.S. carrier aircraft;

24 July 1945, the Japanese battleship *Hyuga* in Kure harbour by U.S. carrier aircraft;

28 July 1945, the Japanese battleships *Haruna* and *Ise* off Kure by U.S. carrier aircraft.

In addition, the *Centurion* and *Courbet* were scuttled as breakwaters in June 1944 off the Normandy beaches, but neither had been in service as a battleship for some time; it is possible to argue, on the same premise, that the *Gneisenau* should not be included on this list and that units such as the *Cavour* and *Provence* likewise should be excluded because they were not returned to duties as battleships after initial loss.

The ships marked with asterisks were those that settled and were salved in the course of the Second World War, and of these only one, the *Oklahoma,* was salved but not returned to service. It was stripped and treated as a constructive total loss and after the war was sold for scrap; it foundered en route to the breaker's yard on 17 May 1947.

PART 3

THE SECOND WORLD WAR: THE EUROPEAN THEATER

CHAPTER SIX

BRITAIN AND THE DEFEAT OF THE U-BOAT *GUERRE DE COURSE*

STATES AND THEIR ARMED FORCES must fight wars as they must rather than as they would, but at a distance of some eight decades from events it is very difficult to discern what the inter-war British Navy intended, hoped, or anticipated would be the type of war it would be called upon to fight. What seems clear is that for most of the inter-war period the navy never expected to have to fight another U-boat *guerre de course*, and there are at least three obvious indications of this belief. First, for much of the inter-war period British destroyers were not equipped with depth-charges. The first destroyers built after the war with asdic (to Americans, sonar) were ordered in 1923–1924,[1] and very few escorts were built in a period of difficult financial circumstances. Second, in the entire inter-war period something like one in fifty appointments to flag rank were officers versed in anti-submarine operations, and in 1935 just 11 of 1,029 lieutenants and 16 of 972 lieutenant-commanders in the British navy were anti-submarine specialists.[2] Third, the one detailed study of convoy and the experience of the First World War, undertaken in 1917–1918 by Commander Rollo Appleyard, was classified, with the result that in the inter-war period his study was all but inaccessible to its intended readership, and in 1939 the Admiralty ordered that all copies of his report be destroyed.[3]

* * *

The war at sea in the European part of the Second World War can be divided in many ways, but one approach is division into eight constituent parts.The first four were the periods September 1939 to March 1940, which is generally known as the Phoney War but which was anything but that for the Poles; April to June 1940, in which time Germany fought a series of campaigns that brought successive victories over and the occupation of Denmark and Norway, the Netherlands, Belgium, and Luxembourg, and northern and western France; July 1940 to May 1941, which is the first period of very considerable German success in the conduct of the war against shipping, in large measure because of marked British weakness and vulnerability on account of threatened invasion; and June to December 1941, which saw the German invasion of and seeming victory over the Soviet Union, but which ran in tandem with a checking—an exercise of deliberate restraint in the conduct—of the U-boat campaign in the North Atlantic, primarily because of the increased forward American stance in theater. These four periods were not so much four parts of a war as, on the German side, four campaigns that really represented an attempt to avoid a war, or at least a general war. But with the German failure in front of Moscow and declaration of war on the United States in the wake of the Japanese attack on the U.S. Pacific Fleet at its Pearl Harbor base, this war was reality, and what followed at sea were four more parts. First was the period December 1941 to June 1942, in which time of major American and British distraction and weakness, there was major U-boat success. These declined quite markedly in the second period, between July 1942 and April 1943, when Britain for the first time came into possession of adequate numbers of escorts and was able to concentrate patrols and searches in the eastern North Atlantic. At the same time the American measures on the eastern seaboard more or less ended the vulnerability of shipping in the western North Atlantic and Caribbean and forced the U-boats back to the east, and to losses that for the first time assumed significant proportions: U-boat losses were in double figures for eight of the ten months between July 1942 and April 1943, before the disastrous month of May 1943. Thereafter the phase of Allied success divides into two, between June 1943 and May 1944 and between June 1944 and May 1945. The natural dividing line between the two is the invasion of northwest Europe, which, over the next three months, resulted in the German loss of most of its U-boat bases in France, and with them immediate and ready access to the North Atlantic. This, however, did not amount to anything of real strategic significance: between June 1943 and May 1944 the U-boats accounted for just 216 merchantmen, while losses in the North Atlantic in this period—76 merchantmen of 442,684 tons—were less than the 87 ships of 533,049 tons lost in the Indian Ocean,[4] and the latter could not provide the German submarine effort with

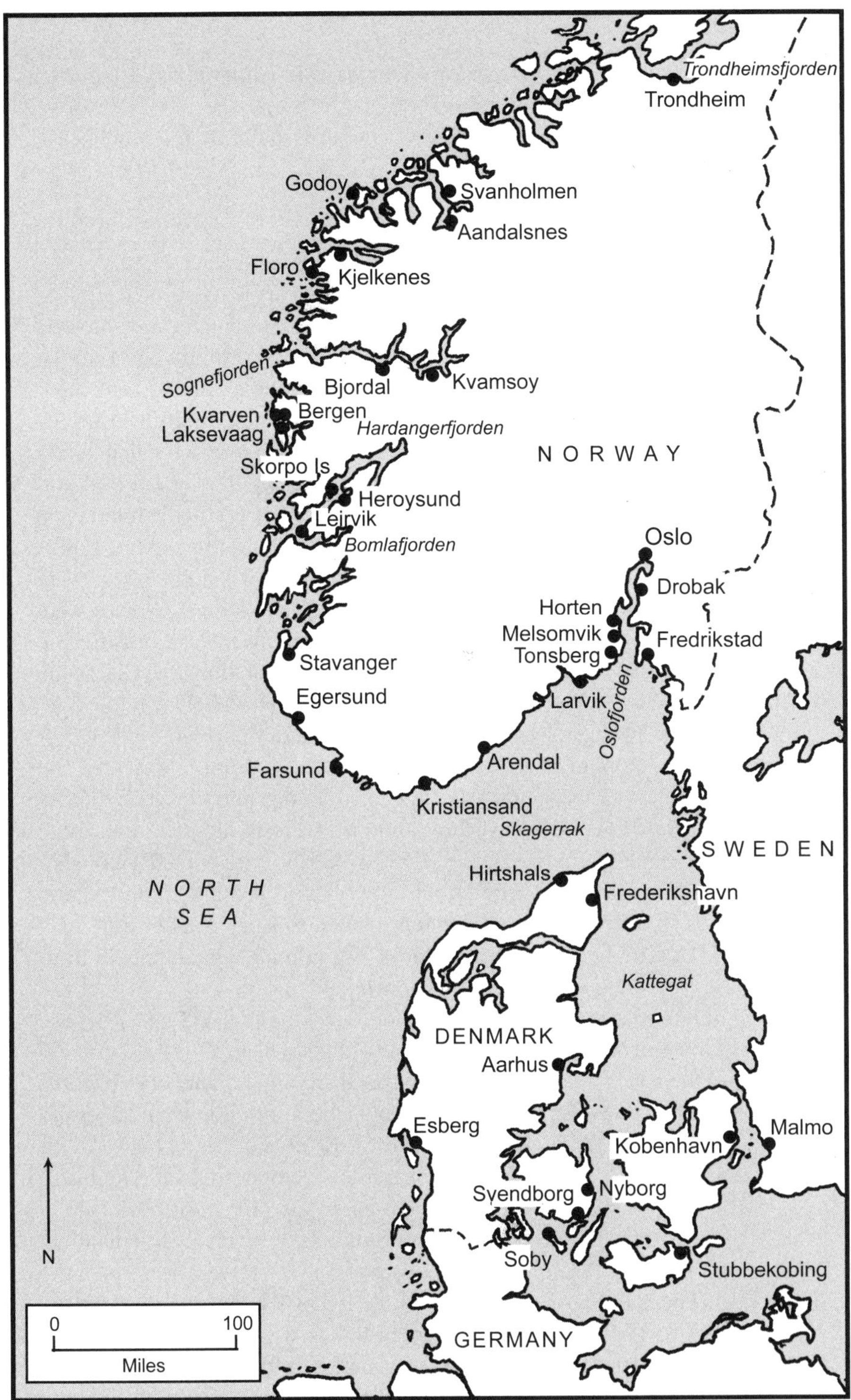

Map 5. The Denmark and Southern Norway Theaters, 1940

a measure of compensation for the decline of returns in the all-important North Atlantic theater in the wake of May 1943.

* * *

The pattern of the war at sea prior to December 1941 is most interesting in two respects. The relationship between defeats in campaigns and shipping losses is very clear with respect to northwest Europe and June 1940, Yugoslavia and Greece and April 1941, and the start of the Pacific war and December 1941: the fact that these three months recorded the largest monthly losses between September 1939 and December 1941 cannot be mere coincidence, but points, unmistakably, to unprecedented vulnerability of naval forces and shipping when committed to lost campaigns. But what is equally interesting is the slenderness of losses in this first twenty-eight months of war. Losses prior to April 1940 and the German invasions of Denmark and Norway were certainly very modest, most obviously in March 1940, when U-boats were being withdrawn from the campaign against shipping in readiness for the Norwegian invasion. But—and contrary to the representation of events as the first of the U-boats' "happy time"—the losses in the period between July 1940 and March 1941 averaged less than 400,000 tons a month, which was just over two-fifths of all shipping losses in April 1917, which month represented the peak of losses in the First World War. The losses in this period, which did rise quite considerably over the next three months, were in fact less than those recorded in eight of the first nine months of the unrestricted campaign against shipping that began in February 1917. One is at a loss to understand how successive British histories have represented this period after June 1940 as a period of dire danger, at least in terms of shipping. The danger of invasion in this period is obvious, though on reflection one imagines that the British counter to any German invasion force seeking to negotiate either the Strait of Dover or the English Channel would have been the *Hood*, the *Renown*, and the *Repulse* committed at full speed among the rows of transports, and to an end that needs little in the way of elaboration. But when losses did mount, in spring 1941, the main agency of loss was not the U-boats—their sinkings in May 1941 were at their highest since October 1940, although still below the level of that month—but shore-based aircraft, most obviously in the Mediterranean theater of operations. Sinkings by warships in effect had reached their peak in March 1941; the losses of April 1942 were very much the exception. Those losses, of course, were inflicted by Japanese warships in the Indian Ocean and not by either German or Italian warships in the European context—and in any case losses to warships were, with the exception of the PQ.17 debacle in June 1942, very much a thing of the past after the loss of the *Bismarck* in the North Atlantic in May 1941.

The representation of this period, between the fall of France and the invasion of the Soviet Union, as one of major German success is not really confirmed by even the most cursory examination of data, and it is very difficult to resist the conclusion that past British representation of this period of the war is highly inaccurate, perhaps deliberately so in order to deflect attention from the manifest ineffectiveness of the British navy at this time. Between 1 December 1940 and 28 February 1941 not one U-boat was lost to any cause whatsoever; in the whole period between July 1940 and May 1941 just sixteen boats were sunk, and of these two were lost to causes that remain unknown to this day and one was sunk in an accident in the Elbe. The fact that five were sunk in March 1941, four to convoy escorts, points very clearly to the utter inadequacy of British arrangements and performance in the period as a whole. Expressed in slightly different terms, in November 1940 the German U-boat service lost three of its number and in March 1941 five, and in all of the other months between July 1940 and May 1941 it lost units in trios: no submarines in each of three months, one submarine in each of three months, and two submarines in each of three months, and two submarines sunk in April 1917 was the nadir of British returns after February 1917; therefore, the worst returns recorded by British forces between February 1917 and November 1918 was equal, or more than equal, to the returns of nine months between July 1940 and May 1941.

* * *

But if there has been deliberate misrepresentation in order to deflect attention from what was undoubtedly a less than impressive British naval performance in this period when the war in Europe was a series of campaigns rather than a war, then, in the interest of impartiality and objectivity, certain matters need be considered under the label of pleas of mitigation. The first and most obvious of these is that for most of the inter-war period the British navy did not have to consider a war against an enemy with a submarine force that would direct its attention against shipping. Certainly British arrangements in terms of escorts and land-based aircraft were not what was needed to fight the war in which Britain found itself, especially after June 1940. Britain in 1939 had three air groups committed to naval and maritime operations, but only one of these covered southwest approaches, and two were stationed in order to conduct operations over the North Sea. The standard escort was the corvette, built for short-range operations and all but wholly unfit for oceanic, and certainly transatlantic, operations.

To these basic problems presented by what had been a North Sea commitment that envisaged a return to the situation that had prevailed in 1918 were added three other problems of major significance. The first was that the Norwegian campaign and the campaign in northwest Europe that left the British navy with significant losses—four destroyers in April, seven in May, and another seven in

June—but also with damaged units and the disruption of destroyer formations, which was not properly remedied until spring 1942—though this matter related primarily to the Home Fleet and not to the defense of shipping. The second factor was the fact that until the latter part of autumn 1940 the greater part of British naval forces had to be held in defense of the home islands, and the third factor was the massive geo-strategic change wrought by the fall of France and the German occupation of the Channel and Biscay ports. The German conquest of France in effect placed the U-boats on an equal footing with British escorts in terms of access to the North Atlantic. British shipping was forced to abandon the southwest approaches because of the proximity of German air bases, while the Channel ports and London in effect were abandoned in terms of handling of shipping. Tobermory and the Kyle of Lochalsh assumed an importance and significance that did not outlast hostilities, while the importance of Glasgow and Liverpool as ports handling the imports of the nation was massively enhanced.[5]

* * *

The period between April 1940 and May 1941 saw Germany establish a primacy within Europe that Britain could not dispute: in this period Germany fought not a war but a series of campaigns in which it brought advantages of position, timing, and concentration to add to its advantages of numbers and industrial resources against enemies each inferior to itself. Britain, through its refusal to treat, denied Germany victory, but by the spring of 1941 it had been reduced to a state that bordered upon impotent irrelevance: it might be able to take control of Iraq, of Syria and Lebanon and *Africa Orientale Italiana*, but these were of little if any strategic relevance when set alongside a lack of allies, a patent inability to clear North Africa in the face of minimal German presence, and Britain's continuing vulnerability at sea. The immediate danger to the home islands had eased with the coming of the winter of 1940–1941, but with the spring, and as a result of the German invasion of the Soviet Union, there was to be no return to the situation of previous months. These lines are not the place to examine in any detail this campaign, except to note two points: first, an examination of the map in May 1941 would suggest that any German attempt to conquer the Soviet Union was doomed to failure, yet an examination of the map in August 1941 would suggest that there was no way in which the German campaign could fail; second, the fact that it did fail despite German possession of the initiative and massive advantages of timing and concentration suggests that the German plan of campaign was flawed, the German conduct of operations was flawed, or both. As it was, one wonders about German intent on two separate scores. First, Germany could have defeated the Soviet Union but failed because Germany sought to destroy it and to enslave its peoples, and second, Germany could have defeated the Soviet Union had it planned for a two-year campaign and not attempted to destroy the Soviet Union in a single campaign, and one the start of which was delayed until late June because of the state of the ground following one of the wettest winters in a hundred years.

The German attack on the Soviet Union had little immediate relevance in terms of the conduct of the war at sea, and Soviet ability to survive the 1941 and 1942 campaigns owed little, if anything, to supporting operations on the part of aid supplied by Britain and then Britain and the United States. What was sent to the Soviet Union was very important indeed, but selectively so: the military items sent were of limited usefulness. The most important items were food, to the value of $1.3 billion, some 2,670,000 tons of petrol (which does beggar belief), and 842,000 tons of chemicals, to which should be added 49,000 tons of leather and 5 million pairs of boots. In addition 1,981 locomotives, 11,155 railway wagons, and 540,000 tons of rail were sent to the Soviet Union, and to these have to be added the items of real military value—375,883 four-wheel-drive trucks, 51,503 jeeps, 35,170 motorcycles, and a million miles of field telephone cable—that in effect put seven Soviet armies on wheels in 1944 and that massively contributed to Soviet offensive capability.[6] But what is interesting, and little known, about this aid was that of a total of 17,499,861 tons of cargo shipped to the Soviet Union, 47.11 percent was shipped across the North Pacific, 23.77 percent through the Gulf and Iran, and 22.65 percent through the White Sea ports.[7] The Arctic convoys thus were third of three, and the main efforts to the White Sea ports were made in 1942 and 1944, but certainly the 1942 effort does command attention on two very different counts. The volume of goods that arrived at the White Sea ports would have been in the order of 3,900,000 tons or so, and British monthly import levels were below that level in thirty-five months between July 1941 and April 1945; the 1942 effort must be seen against a major reduction, indeed precipitous decline, in British import levels. Moreover, the British effort in this year must be seen against the background provided by the misfortunes that overwhelmed PQ.17 in June–July. This was the one convoy that the Admiralty managed to get wrong and with a vengeance, but it really was the exception and proved to be the darkest hour immediately before the dawn. The next convoy, PQ.18 in September, was grim—thirteen from forty lost compared to twenty-three of thirty-six in the predecessor—but thereafter just five merchantmen were lost by the Arctic convoys during the remainder of the war, and that provides comment on the declining numbers and effectiveness of German surface formations, submarines, and aircraft based in Finnmark and neighboring areas.[8]

* * *

What are undoubtedly the most interesting phases of the war at sea were the periods between January and June 1942 and between July 1942 and May 1943, and

TABLE 6.1. CONVOYS AND SHIPS SAILING FOR AND ARRIVING IN WHITE SEA PORTS, 1941–1945

	Number of convoys	Number of ships in convoy	Percentage of sailings in given year	Number of ships that arrived	Percentage of arrivals in given year	Percentage arrivals: sailings by year
1941	8	64	7.89	62	8.61	96.88
1942	13	256	31.57	185	25.69	72.27
1943	6	112	13.81	105	15.56	93.75
1944	9	284	35.02	275	38.19	96.83
1945	4	95	11.71	93	12.92	97.89
Totals	40	811	-	720	-	88.78

on account of both comparison and contrast. Perhaps common to both periods is the basic point that the German effort was based upon a denial of sea control to enemies, and that purpose necessarily was flawed, for an obvious reason: in two world wars, not one, Germany sought not to secure control of the sea for itself but to deny control to its enemies, and that intention was inherently unsound. In the First World War the German creation of a fleet for the purposes laid down in the risk theory and without regard to that fleet's disadvantage to its perceived enemy in terms of numbers, geographical position, and history, left it with a desire—or at least a stated desire—to do battle that was but the least tactical response to its strategic futility. The Second World War came some five years too early for the Kriegsmarine, which lacked the numbers and balance that it might have acquired had the 1944 schedule been realized, though by that time what would have happened in terms of the U.S. Navy and an emergent German threat seems obvious. But the point is that the fifteen months between January 1942 and March 1943 represent the period of greatest German effectiveness, but this German effort was one that failed.

The first six months of 1942 was a major change from the previous six months, with sinkings by U-boats in this latter period increasing by almost 250 percent, from an average of 147,186 tons per month over seven months between June and December 1941 to 513,489 tons per month over the next six months, with the May figures reaching over 600,000 tons and the June figures over 700,000 tons, or 23,342 tons a day. Of course the point about U-boat returns in the last seven months of 1941 was that an increasing American assertiveness in the North Atlantic—which claimed some four-fifths of the ocean as belonging to the western hemisphere[9]—forced the German leadership to rein in the U-boats, to reduce operations in the North Atlantic, and to direct submarines into the Mediterranean, where there was little chance of dispute with the United States. The result was that in November 1941 U-boat returns, at thirteen ships of 62,196 tons, were the lowest for two years, and were but a fifth of the June 1941 sinkings.

With the Japanese attack on the U.S. Pacific Fleet at Pearl Harbor and the German and Italian declarations of war on the United States, restraint was ended, and Operation Drumbeat was initiated with the first sailing of a U-boat from its French base on 23 December. The result was a major rise of sinkings, with one April blip, over the next six months. It was the U.S. introduction of a comprehensive convoy system on the East Coast and in the Caribbean in summer 1942 that marked the end of this period of major success—just 13 boats were lost between 1 January and 30 June 1942 in the North Atlantic, while 588 merchantmen of 2,993,915 tons were sunk in the North Atlantic and British waters—and the first monthly losses in double figures: in both July and August 1942 the U-boat service lost as many boats as it had lost in the previous six months.[10]

But the normal portrayal of events during Operation Drumbeat—the major losses in the western North Atlantic and off the eastern seaboard in the wake of the U.S. entry into the war and then the decline of losses after June 1942—is somewhat simplistic. Losses in the period between July and November 1942 were some three times those that had been incurred in the first six months of the year, and indeed the average monthly returns registered by the submarines increased in this second phase. The real curb upon their activities came on account of an atrocious winter rather than British counter-measures.

In the first six months of 1942 total losses, inflated somewhat by the March 1942 figures, which represent a mass of shipping in the Indies simply written off, were in the order of 989 merchantmen of 4,147,406 tons, while submarines accounted for 585 merchantmen of 3,080,934 tons—and these figures represent monthly averages of 164.83 merchantmen of 691,234 tons (overall) and 97.5 merchantmen of 513,489 tons (submarines). In the next five months, total losses, inflated somewhat by the November 1942 figures that were in some measure the result of declining numbers of escorts committed to the defense of trade, given the Operation Torch commitment, were in the order of 600 merchantmen of 3,292,160 tons, while submarines accounted for 515 merchantmen of 2,854,465 tons for the period July–November 1945. These figures represent monthly averages of 120 merchantmen of 658,432 tons (overall) and 103 merchantmen of 570,893 tons (submarines).

But the real point of difference lay in the fact that by the time that the U-boat offensive off the eastern seaboard of the United States was abandoned, the British had acquired numbers of escorts that permitted a comprehensive convoy system throughout the Atlantic and could raise groups for the hunting of U-boats and the support of threatened convoys in mid-Atlantic.[11] Given the disruption of the previous months, however, what should have been elements of advantage could not be put in place immediately. For their part the U-boats by this time had acquired numbers sufficient to mount patrol lines across the

North Atlantic and, of course, had acquired technique in terms of the summoning of numbers to attack convoys. But crucially, by this time radar provided the escorts with the ability to "sight" surfaced boats at night, and long-range land-based aircraft were becoming available in numbers for the first time, and with immediate consequences.

In the first sixteen months of the war, land-based patrol and escort aircraft had shared with warships in the destruction of two U-boats, and one U-boat was sunk in the Shillig Roads by a Blenheim strike aircraft. In 1941 land-based aircraft accounted for three boats and shared with warships in the destruction of a fourth; in the first six months of 1942 land-based aircraft accounted for six U-boats, one of which was sunk in the eastern Mediterranean. Then in the next six months land-based aircraft sank thirty U-boats and shared with warships in the destruction of another five. The overall total of 38.5 "kills" in this single year represented a seven-fold increase over the first twenty-eight months of war—in July 1942 alone land-based aircraft sank more submarines than between September 1939 and December 1941—and this total was significant in that for the first time in a calendar year, the number of U-boats sunk by aircraft was greater than the number of U-boats sunk by warships.

* * *

Such was the context of, and the prelude to, the events of March and May 1943, the neat juxtaposition created by unprecedented losses on each side. In March U-boats exacted a toll of 108 merchantmen of 627,377 tons, which has elicited the comment that "the Germans never came so near to disrupting communications between the New World and the Old as in the first twenty days of March 1943," and for one reason: some two-thirds of the 95 merchantmen sunk in these first twenty days of March 1943 were sunk while in convoy. For the first time the Admiralty was confronted by the prospect that it would "not be able to continue [to regard] convoy as an effective system of defence." In fact, the Admiralty did not regard convoy as *an* effective system of defense; the Admiralty saw convoy as the *only* effective system of defense, and had convoy failed at this point it is very hard to see how the British could have continued the war at sea. As it was, the turn-around came, as Roskill has noted, with astonishing rapidity.[12] In fact, the change came even in the last eleven days of March, when losses fell considerably,[13] but inevitably the change is associated with the month of May 1943.

In that month the U-boats lost forty-one of their number, and this remained the highest total in any calendar month until April 1945, when all the aspects of defeat came together with a toll of sixty-two U-boats. The scale of the defeat of May 1943 has served to obscure the scale of losses over the following months, and the fact is that in the remainder of the war U-boat losses were in single figures in just two months and were between ten and nineteen in another seven months. In no fewer than fifteen months U-boat losses were in excess of twenty, and what seems to have escaped general notice is that there was one one-month period when losses were greater than the total of forty-one boats sunk in May 1943, but the total of forty-three in thirty-one days straddles two calendar months, between 12 July and 11 August 1943. The relevance of this latter fact, as noted elsewhere, lies in the fact that the battle at sea does not result in establishing lines of possession. A victor in one action does not hold ground or ridge or river line in the manner the victor in a battle on land does. The battle at sea has parameters set by time and distance, and battles have to be fought and victories have to be won repeatedly over the same stretches of water; hence the special relevance of July–August and October–November 1943 in terms of their supplementing the victory of May 1943.

Any examination of this period as a whole, from spring 1943 onward, seems to point in the direction of two conclusions that have not been afforded much in the way of detailed historical consideration. The first is the massive decline in importance of the North Atlantic in terms of sinkings by U-boats. It is generally known that U-boat attentions were directed toward the Indian Ocean in the wake of the defeats of mid-1943. While shipping losses in the North Atlantic totaled seventy-six merchantmen of 442,684 tons between June 1943 and May 1944—which were totals U-boats exceeded in no fewer than ten single months of the war—shipping losses in the Indian Ocean were indeed greater, but the greatest toll of shipping was not exacted in the Indian Ocean: the very strange fact is that the theater in which the heaviest single losses were sustained was the one theater where the Allies had "won," and before June 1943, namely the Mediterranean. Inevitably the exercise of general control attracts less attention than the battle for control, and the Allies had to take losses as the price for the taking of war to the Italian homeland, but the Mediterranean theater—at least in naval terms—has been afforded little attention in terms of post–September 1943 events.

The second of the two conclusions relates to the relative decline in terms of sinkings of U-boats by warships in comparison to sinkings by land-based aircraft. It is perhaps little appreciated, but the U-boat losses in spring 1943 were closely balanced between warships and land-based aircraft. In this period between March and June 1943, warships accounted for 30.50 submarines compared to the 44 credited to land-based aircraft, a clear margin between the two agencies of destruction but, one would suggest, perhaps closer than generally realized, especially given the attention paid to the May 1943 returns and an assumption that the greater part of destruction was registered on the part of Bay of Biscay air patrols. But in the following four months what had been a 2:3 ratio was transformed: between July and October 1943 warships accounted for 17 U-boats compared to the 54 sunk by land-based aircraft—a 1:3 ratio. More-

Table 6.2. U-boat Losses, the North Atlantic Theater of Operations, and Losses by Date and Cause, 1 March 1943–30 June 1944

March 1943	1	2	3	4	5	6	7	8	9	10	11	12	13	14	15	16	17	18	19	20	21	22	23	24	25	26	27	28	29	30	31	TOTAL
Total U-boat losses	-	-	-	2	1	-	1	1	-	-	1	1	1	-	-	-	-	-	1	1	-	2	-	-	1	-	1	1	-	1	-	16
Sunk by warships	-	-	-	1	-	-	-	-	-	-	1	1	1	-	-	-	-	-	-	-	-	-	-	-	-	-	-	-	-	-	-	4
Sunk by land-based aircraft	-	-	-	1	1	-	1	1	-	-	-	-	-	-	-	-	-	-	-	1	-	2	-	-	1	-	1	1	-	-	-	10
Sunk by carrier aircraft	-	-	-	-	-	-	-	-	-	-	-	-	-	-	-	-	-	-	-	-	-	-	-	-	-	-	-	-	-	-	-	-
Sunk by all other causes	-	-	-	-	-	-	-	-	-	-	-	-	-	-	-	-	-	-	1	-	-	-	-	-	-	-	-	-	-	1	-	2
Sunk in the North Atlantic	-	-	-	1	1	-	1	1	-	-	1	1	1	-	-	-	-	-	-	1	-	2	-	-	1	-	1	-	-	-	-	12
Total merchantman losses	1	1	4	2	6	4	4	4	8	7	3	-	11	-	3	6	16	4	6	4	1	1	1	-	1	8	2	7	4	4	-	120
Sunk in the North Atlantic	-	1	-	1	2	3	2	2	7	6	2	-	8	-	1	4	15	4	3	-	1	-	-	-	-	-	-	5	4	2	-	84

April 1943	1	2	3	4	5	6	7	8	9	10	11	12	13	14	15	16	17	18	19	20	21	22	23	24	25	26	27	28	29	30	TOTAL
Total U-boat losses	-	1	-	-	1	2	1	-	-	1	-	-	-	1	-	-	1	-	-	-	-	-	3	1	1	-	1	-	-	1	15
Sunk by warships	-	1	-	-	-	1	-	-	-	-	-	-	-	-	-	-	1	-	-	-	-	-	1	-	1	-	-	-	-	-	5
Sunk by land-based aircraft	-	-	-	-	1	1	-	-	-	1	-	-	-	-	-	-	-	-	-	-	-	-	1	1	-	-	1	-	-	1	7
Sunk by carrier aircraft	-	-	-	-	-	-	-	-	-	-	-	-	-	-	-	-	-	-	-	-	-	-	-	-	-	-	-	-	-	-	-
Sunk by all other causes	-	-	-	-	-	-	1	-	-	-	-	-	-	1	-	-	-	-	-	-	-	-	1	-	-	-	-	-	-	-	3
Sunk in the North Atlantic	-	1	-	-	1	2	-	-	-	1	-	-	-	1	-	-	1	-	-	-	-	-	2	1	1	-	1	-	-	1	13
Total merchantman losses	1	5	1	1	7	6	-	1	1	-	8	3	1	2	-	-	3	3	-	2	4	1	-	3	-	-	2	-	3	5	64
Sunk in the North Atlantic	1	3	1	1	6	1	-	1	1	-	6	3	-	1	-	-	2	1	-	-	3	1	-	2	-	-	-	-	2	4	44

May 1943	1	2	3	4	5	6	7	8	9	10	11	12	13	14	15	16	17	18	19	20	21	22	23	24	25	26	27	28	29	30	31	TOTAL
Total U-boat losses	-	1	2	2	2	3	3	-	-	-	1	2	1	2	3	2	2	-	4	1	1	1	1	-	2	1	-	2	-	-	2	41
Sunk by warships	-	-	-	-	2	3	-	-	-	-	½	1½	½	-	1	1	1	-	3	1	-	-	-	-	1	1	-	-	-	-	-	16½
Sunk by land-based aircraft	-	1	-	1	-	-	3	-	-	-	½	-	½	2	2	1	1	-	1	-	-	-	-	-	1	-	-	2	-	-	2	18
Sunk by carrier aircraft	-	-	-	-	-	-	-	-	-	-	-	½	-	-	-	-	-	-	-	-	-	1	1	-	-	-	-	-	-	-	-	2½
Sunk by all other causes	-	-	2	1	-	-	-	-	-	-	-	-	-	-	-	-	-	-	-	-	1	-	-	-	-	-	-	-	-	-	-	4
Sunk in the North Atlantic	-	1	2	2	2	3	3	-	-	-	1	2	1	2	3	1	2	-	4	1	-	1	1	-	1	1	-	1	-	-	2	37
Total merchantman losses	6	-	-	1	13	1	3	2	2	-	4	3	3	-	2	1	3	1	2	2	-	1	1	1	-	-	1	3	2	1	1	58
Sunk in the North Atlantic	4	-	-	1	13	-	2	1	1	-	2	3	2	-	2	-	1	-	1	1	-	1	-	1	-	-	-	-	-	1	1	35

June 1943	1	2	3	4	5	6	7	8	9	10	11	12	13	14	15	16	17	18	19	20	21	22	23	24	25	26	27	28	29	30	TOTAL
Total U-boat losses	2	2	-	2	1	-	-	-	-	-	1	1	-	2	-	1	-	-	-	1	-	-	-	4	-	-	-	-	-	-	17
Sunk by warships	1	1	-	-	-	-	-	-	-	-	-	-	-	1	-	-	-	-	-	-	-	-	-	2	-	-	-	-	-	-	5
Sunk by land-based aircraft	1	1	-	1	-	-	-	-	-	-	1	-	-	1	-	1	-	-	-	1	-	-	-	2	-	-	-	-	-	-	9
Sunk by carrier aircraft	-	-	-	-	1	-	-	-	-	-	-	1	-	-	-	-	-	-	-	-	-	-	-	-	-	-	-	-	-	-	2
Sunk by all other causes	-	-	-	1	-	-	-	-	-	-	-	-	-	-	-	-	-	-	-	-	-	-	-	-	-	-	-	-	-	-	1
Sunk in the North Atlantic	2	2	-	2	1	-	-	-	-	-	1	1	-	2	-	-	-	-	-	1	-	-	-	4	-	-	-	-	-	-	16
Total merchantman losses	1	-	3	-	1	1	-	-	-	1	-	1	-	-	3	-	2	-	1	-	2	-	4	1	1	3	2	2	-	-	29
Sunk in the North Atlantic	-	-	1	-	-	-	-	-	-	1	-	-	-	-	-	-	-	-	-	-	-	-	2	-	-	1	-	-	-	-	5

July 1943	1	2	3	4	5	6	7	8	9	10	11	12	13	14	15	16	17	18	19	20	21	22	23	24	25	26	27	28	29	30	31	TOTAL
Total U-boat losses	-	-	2	-	1	1	2	-	2	-	-	3	2	1	3	1	-	-	1	1	1	-	3	2	-	1	-	2	1	6	1	37
Sunk by warships	-	-	-	-	-	-	-	-	-	-	-	2	-	-	1	-	-	-	-	-	-	-	-	-	-	-	-	-	-	2	-	5
Sunk by land-based aircraft	-	-	2	-	1	1	2	-	2	-	-	1	1	-	1	-	-	-	1	1	1	-	1	1	-	1	-	2	1	3	1	24
Sunk by carrier aircraft	-	-	-	-	-	-	-	-	-	-	-	-	1	1	1	1	-	-	-	-	-	-	2	-	-	-	-	-	-	1	-	7
Sunk by all other causes	-	-	-	-	-	-	-	-	-	-	-	-	-	-	-	-	-	-	-	-	-	-	-	1	-	-	-	-	-	-	-	1
Sunk in the North Atlantic	-	-	2	-	1	1	2	-	1	-	-	1	2	1	3	1	-	-	-	1	-	-	2	1	-	1	-	2	1	4	-	27
Total merchantman losses	2	2	3	5	2	4	4	3	3	3	4	4	1	1	4	4	-	1	1	1	1	1	2	2	1	1	1	1	1	-	-	61
Sunk in the North Atlantic	-	1	1	-	1	1	-	3	3	1	2	-	-	1	1	-	-	1	1	-	-	-	-	-	-	1	-	1	-	-	-	19

August 1943	1	2	3	4	5	6	7	8	9	10	11	12	13	14	15	16	17	18	19	20	21	22	23	24	25	26	27	28	29	30	31	TOTAL
Total U-boat losses	2	2	2	1	-	2	1	-	1	-	3	-	-	-	-	-	-	1	-	1	1	1	-	3	1	-	1	-	-	2	-	25
Sunk by warships	-	-	-	-	-	-	-	-	-	-	½	-	-	-	-	-	-	-	-	-	-	1	-	-	1	-	-	-	-	1	-	3½
Sunk by land-based aircraft	2	2	1	1	-	1	-	-	-	-	1½	-	-	-	-	-	-	1	-	1	-	-	-	1	-	-	-	-	-	-	-	11½
Sunk by carrier aircraft	-	-	-	-	-	-	1	-	1	-	1	-	-	-	-	-	-	-	-	-	-	-	-	2	-	-	1	-	-	-	-	6
Sunk by all other causes	-	-	1	-	-	1	-	-	-	-	-	-	-	-	-	-	-	-	-	-	1	-	-	-	-	-	-	-	-	1	-	4
Sunk in the North Atlantic	2	2	2	1	-	1	1	-	1	-	2	-	-	-	-	-	-	1	-	-	-	-	-	3	1	-	1	-	-	1	-	19
Total merchantman losses	2	1	1	2	2	2	3	-	1	-	2	-	1	1	1	1	1	-	-	1	2	-	-	1	2	1	-	-	-	1	-	25
Sunk in the North Atlantic	-	-	1	-	-	-	1	-	-	-	-	-	-	-	1	-	-	-	-	-	-	-	-	-	-	-	-	-	-	-	-	3

September 1943	1	2	3	4	5	6	7	8	9	10	11	12	13	14	15	16	17	18	19	20	21	22	23	24	25	26	27	28	29	30	TOTAL
Total U-boat losses	-	-	-	-	-	-	2	1	-	-	1	-	-	-	-	-	-	-	1	2	-	1	-	-	-	-	2	-	-	-	10
Sunk by warships	-	-	-	-	-	-	-	-	-	-	½	-	-	-	-	-	-	-	-	-	-	1	-	-	-	-	-	-	-	-	1½
Sunk by land-based aircraft	-	-	-	-	-	-	2	-	-	-	½	-	-	-	-	-	-	-	1	1	-	-	-	-	-	-	2	-	-	-	6½
Sunk by carrier aircraft	-	-	-	-	-	-	-	-	-	-	-	-	-	-	-	-	-	-	-	-	-	-	-	-	-	-	-	-	-	-	-
Sunk by all other causes	-	-	-	-	-	-	-	1	-	-	-	-	-	-	-	-	-	-	-	1	-	-	-	-	-	-	-	-	-	-	2
Sunk in the North Atlantic	-	-	-	-	-	-	2	-	-	-	-	-	-	-	-	-	-	-	1	1	-	1	-	-	-	-	1	-	-	-	6
Total merchantman losses	-	-	-	-	-	-	2	-	1	-	-	-	2	1	-	-	-	-	-	5	2	2	5	1	-	3	-	-	1	2	29
Sunk in the North Atlantic	-	-	-	-	-	-	-	-	-	-	-	-	1	-	-	-	-	-	-	2	-	-	4	-	-	-	-	-	-	-	8

October 1943	1	2	3	4	5	6	7	8	9	10	11	12	13	14	15	16	17	18	19	20	21	22	23	24	25	26	27	28	29	30	31	TOTAL
Total U-boat losses	-	-	-	4	1	-	-	3	-	-	-	-	1	-	-	4	3	-	-	1	-	-	1	1	-	1	-	1	1	1	3	26
Sunk by warships	-	-	-	-	1	-	-	-	-	-	-	-	-	-	-	-	2	-	-	-	-	-	1	-	-	-	-	-	1	-	2	7
Sunk by land-based aircraft	-	-	-	2	-	-	-	3	-	-	-	-	-	-	-	4	1	-	-	-	-	-	-	1	-	1	-	-	-	-	-	12
Sunk by carrier aircraft	-	-	-	2	-	-	-	-	-	-	-	-	1	-	-	-	-	-	-	1	-	-	-	-	-	-	-	1	-	-	1	6
Sunk by all other causes	-	-	-	-	-	-	-	-	-	-	-	-	-	-	-	-	-	-	-	-	-	-	-	-	-	-	-	-	-	1	-	1
Sunk in the North Atlantic	-	-	-	4	1	-	-	3	-	-	-	-	1	-	-	3	3	-	-	1	-	-	1	1	-	1	-	1	1	-	3	24
Total merchantman losses	4	1	-	3	4	-	-	-	1	1	1	-	-	-	1	1	-	-	2	-	2	1	2	3	-	-	1	-	-	-	1	29
Sunk in the North Atlantic	-	-	-	-	4	-	-	-	1	-	-	-	-	-	-	1	-	-	2	-	-	1	-	1	-	-	-	-	-	-	1	12

November 1943	1	2	3	4	5	6	7	8	9	10	11	12	13	14	15	16	17	18	19	20	21	22	23	24	25	26	27	28	29	30	TOTAL
Total U-boat losses	2	-	-	-	1	2	-	-	1	1	-	1	-	-	-	1	-	1	1	2	1	-	1	-	2	-	-	1	1	-	19
Sunk by warships	1½	-	-	-	-	2	-	-	-	-	-	-	-	-	-	-	-	-	-	1	1	-	1	-	1	-	-	-	-	-	7½
Sunk by land-based aircraft	½	-	-	-	1	-	-	-	1	1	-	1	-	-	-	1	-	-	1	-	-	-	-	-	1	-	-	1	-	-	8½
Sunk by carrier aircraft	-	-	-	-	-	-	-	-	-	-	-	-	-	-	-	-	-	-	-	-	-	-	-	-	-	-	-	-	1	-	1
Sunk by all other causes	-	-	-	-	-	-	-	-	-	-	-	-	-	-	-	-	-	1	-	1	-	-	-	-	-	-	-	-	-	-	2
Sunk in the North Atlantic	2	-	-	-	-	2	-	-	1	1	-	1	-	-	-	1	-	-	1	1	1	-	1	-	1	-	-	1	1	-	15
Total merchantman losses	-	4	-	1	-	3	-	-	-	1	6	1	1	-	-	1	-	3	-	1	1	-	1	1	1	2	1	-	2	-	29
Sunk in the North Atlantic	-	-	-	1	-	-	-	-	-	-	4	-	1	-	-	-	-	-	-	-	1	-	1	1	-	1	-	-	1	-	13

December 1943	1	2	3	4	5	6	7	8	9	10	11	12	13	14	15	16	17	18	19	20	21	22	23	24	25	26	27	28	29	30	31	TOTAL
Total U-boat losses	-	-	-	-	-	-	-	-	-	-	-	1	3	-	-	1	-	-	-	1	1	-	-	1	-	-	-	-	-	-	-	8
Sunk by warships	-	-	-	-	-	-	-	-	-	-	-	½	1	-	-	1	-	-	-	-	-	-	-	1	-	-	-	-	-	-	-	3½
Sunk by land-based aircraft	-	-	-	-	-	-	-	-	-	-	-	-	1	-	-	-	-	-	-	-	-	-	-	-	-	-	-	-	-	-	-	1
Sunk by carrier aircraft	-	-	-	-	-	-	-	-	-	-	-	½	-	-	-	-	-	-	-	1	-	-	-	-	-	-	-	-	-	-	-	1½
Sunk by all other causes	-	-	-	-	-	-	-	-	-	-	-	-	1	-	-	-	-	-	-	-	1	-	-	-	-	-	-	-	-	-	-	2
Sunk in the North Atlantic	-	-	-	-	-	-	-	-	-	-	-	1	1	-	-	-	-	-	-	1	1	-	-	1	-	-	-	-	-	-	-	5
Total merchantman losses	-	16	1	1	-	-	-	1	1	-	-	-	1	2	-	2	1	-	1	-	2	-	1	-	1	-	-	1	-	-	-	31
Sunk in the North Atlantic	-	-	1	1	-	-	-	1	1	-	-	-	-	-	-	1	1	-	1	-	1	-	-	-	1	-	-	-	-	-	-	8

January 1944	1	2	3	4	5	6	7	8	9	10	11	12	13	14	15	16	17	18	19	20	21	22	23	24	25	26	27	28	29	30	31	TOTAL
Total U-boat losses	-	-	-	-	-	-	-	2	1	-	-	-	1	-	1	1	1	-	1	1	-	-	-	-	-	-	-	2	-	2	1	15
Sunk by warships	-	-	-	-	-	-	-	1	-	-	-	-	-	-	-	-	1	-	1	-	-	-	-	-	-	-	-	-	-	1	1	5
Sunk by land-based aircraft	-	-	-	-	-	-	-	1	-	-	-	-	1	-	-	-	-	-	-	-	-	-	-	-	-	-	-	2	-	1	-	5
Sunk by carrier aircraft	-	-	-	-	-	-	-	-	-	-	-	-	-	-	-	1	-	-	-	-	-	-	-	-	-	-	-	-	-	-	-	1
Sunk by all other causes	-	-	-	-	-	-	-	-	1	-	-	-	-	-	1	-	-	-	-	1	-	-	-	-	-	-	-	-	-	-	-	4
Sunk in the North Atlantic	-	-	-	-	-	-	-	2	-	-	-	-	1	-	1	1	1	-	1	1	-	-	-	-	-	-	-	2	-	1	1	13
Total merchantman losses	-	1	2	-	1	4	-	-	-	2	-	-	-	-	-	1	-	-	-	1	-	-	-	-	5	2	-	-	2	-	2	26
Sunk in the North Atlantic	-	-	-	-	1	3	-	-	-	-	-	-	-	-	-	-	-	-	-	-	-	-	-	-	3	-	-	-	-	-	2	13

February 1944	1	2	3	4	5	6	7	8	9	10	11	12	13	14	15	16	17	18	19	20	21	22	23	24	25	26	27	28	29	TOTAL
Total U-boat losses	-	-	-	1	-	1	-	1	2	2	2	-	-	2	-	-	-	2	2	-	-	-	-	3	2	-	-	-	-	20
Sunk by warships	-	-	-	-	-	-	-	1	2	-	1	-	-	-	-	-	-	1	2	-	-	-	-	2½	1	-	-	-	-	9½
Sunk by land-based aircraft	-	-	-	-	-	1	-	-	-	1	1	-	-	-	-	-	-	-	-	-	-	-	-	½	1	-	-	-	-	4½
Sunk by carrier aircraft	-	-	-	-	-	-	-	-	-	1	-	-	-	-	-	-	-	-	-	-	-	-	-	-	-	-	-	-	-	1
Sunk by all other causes	-	-	-	1	-	-	-	-	-	-	-	-	-	2	-	-	-	1	-	-	-	-	-	-	-	-	-	-	-	4
Sunk in the North Atlantic	-	-	-	-	-	-	-	1	2	2	2	-	-	-	-	-	-	1	2	-	-	-	-	2	1	-	-	-	-	13
Total merchantman losses	2	3	1	-	-	-	-	-	1	1	1	1	-	-	3	-	-	-	-	-	-	3	2	1	-	2	1	-	2	23
Sunk in the North Atlantic	-	-	-	-	-	-	-	-	-	1	-	-	-	-	-	-	-	-	-	-	-	-	-	1	-	1	-	-	-	5

March 1944	1	2	3	4	5	6	7	8	9	10	11	12	13	14	15	16	17	18	19	20	21	22	23	24	25	26	27	28	29	30	31	TOTAL
Total U-boat losses	3	-	-	1	1	2	-	-	-	4	3	-	1	2	-	-	3	-	1	-	-	-	-	-	1	-	-	-	2	-	-	25
Sunk by warships	3	-	-	-	-	1	-	-	-	3	-	-	⅓	1	-	-	½	-	-	-	-	-	-	-	-	-	-	-	2	-	-	10
Sunk by land-based aircraft	-	-	-	-	-	-	-	-	-	1	1	-	⅓	½	-	-	-	-	-	-	-	-	-	-	1	-	-	-	-	-	-	3
Sunk by carrier aircraft	-	-	-	1	1	1	-	-	-	-	-	-	⅓	½	-	-	½	-	1	-	-	-	-	-	-	-	-	-	-	-	-	5⅓
Sunk by all other causes	-	-	-	-	-	-	-	-	-	-	2	-	-	-	-	-	2	-	-	-	-	-	-	-	-	-	-	-	-	-	-	5
Sunk in the North Atlantic	3	-	-	-	-	1	-	-	-	2	-	-	1	2	-	-	1	-	1	-	-	-	-	-	1	-	-	-	-	-	-	13
Total merchantman losses	1	-	2	1	1	3	2	-	3	1	-	-	2	-	1	1	2	2	1	2	1	1	-	-	-	1	1	-	1	2	-	25
Sunk in the North Atlantic	1	-	-	1	1	-	1	-	-	-	-	-	-	-	-	-	-	1	-	1	-	1	-	-	-	-	-	-	-	-	-	7

April 1944	1	2	3	4	5	6	7	8	9	10	11	12	13	14	15	16	17	18	19	20	21	22	23	24	25	26	27	28	29	30	TOTAL
Total U-boat losses	1	1	1	-	-	2	1	2	1	1	1	-	-	1	-	1	2	-	1	-	-	1	-	-	-	1	1	-	1	-	21
Sunk by warships	½	1	-	-	-	1	1	1	½	-	-	-	-	1	-	1	1	-	-	-	-	1	-	-	-	1	-	-	-	-	10
Sunk by land-based aircraft	-	-	-	-	-	-	-	-	-	-	-	-	-	-	-	-	1	-	-	-	-	-	-	-	-	-	-	1	-	-	2
Sunk by carrier aircraft	½	-	1	-	-	-	-	-	½	1	-	-	-	-	-	-	-	-	-	-	-	-	-	-	-	-	-	-	-	-	3
Sunk by all other causes	-	-	-	-	-	1	-	1	-	-	1	-	-	-	-	-	-	-	1	-	-	-	-	-	-	-	1	-	1	-	6
Sunk in the North Atlantic	-	-	-	-	-	1	1	1	1	1	-	-	-	1	-	1	2	-	-	-	-	1	-	-	-	1	-	1	-	-	12
Total merchantman losses	1	-	-	-	-	2	-	1	-	-	1	-	-	-	-	3	-	-	4	3	-	1	-	1	-	1	-	-	-	1	13
Sunk in the North Atlantic	-	-	-	-	-	2	-	-	-	-	-	-	-	-	-	1	-	-	-	-	-	1	-	1	-	1	-	-	-	1	6

May 1944	1	2	3	4	5	6	7	8	9	10	11	12	13	14	15	16	17	18	19	20	21	22	23	24	25	26	27	28	29	30	31	TOTAL
Total U-boat losses	1	2	1	2	1	2	-	-	-	-	-	-	-	1	1	1	1	1	2	-	1	-	-	2	1	-	1	-	1	1	-	23
Sunk by warships	-	-	-	1	1	1	-	-	-	-	-	-	-	-	½	-	½	-	½	-	1	-	-	-	-	-	-	-	1	1	-	7½
Sunk by land-based aircraft	-	-	1	1	-	-	-	-	-	-	-	-	-	-	½	1	½	1	½	-	-	-	-	2	1	-	1	-	-	-	-	9½
Sunk by carrier aircraft	1	2	-	-	-	1	-	-	-	-	-	-	-	-	-	-	-	-	-	-	-	-	-	-	-	-	-	-	-	-	-	4
Sunk by all other causes	-	-	-	-	-	-	-	-	-	-	-	-	-	1	-	-	-	-	1	-	-	-	-	-	-	-	-	-	-	-	-	2
Sunk in the North Atlantic	-	-	-	1	1	2	-	-	-	-	-	-	-	-	1	-	-	1	-	-	-	-	-	-	-	-	-	-	1	-	-	6
Total merchantman losses	1	-	-	-	-	1	-	-	-	-	2	-	1	-	-	-	-	-	1	1	-	-	-	-	-	-	-	-	-	-	1	5
Sunk in the North Atlantic	-	-	-	-	-	-	-	-	-	-	-	-	-	-	-	-	-	-	-	1	-	-	-	-	-	-	-	-	-	-	-	-

June 1944	1	2	3	4	5	6	7	8	9	10	11	12	13	14	15	16	17	18	19	20	21	22	23	24	25	26	27	28	29	30	TOTAL
Total U-boat losses	-	-	1	1	-	-	2	2	1	1	2	-	1	-	2	1	1	2	-	-	-	-	-	2	2	2	-	-	1	1	25
Sunk by warships	-	-	-	½	-	-	-	-	-	-	1	-	-	-	-	-	-	1	-	-	-	-	-	½	2	1	-	-	½	-	6½
Sunk by land-based aircraft	-	-	1	-	-	-	2	2	1	1	1	-	1	-	-	-	1	1	-	-	-	-	-	1½	-	1	-	-	½	1	15
Sunk by carrier aircraft	-	-	-	½	-	-	-	-	-	-	-	-	-	-	1	-	-	-	-	-	-	-	-	-	-	-	-	-	-	-	1½
Sunk by all other causes	-	-	-	-	-	-	-	-	-	-	-	-	-	-	1	1	-	-	-	-	-	-	-	-	-	-	-	-	-	-	2
Sunk in the North Atlantic	-	-	-	1	-	-	2	2	1	1	1	-	1	-	-	-	-	2	-	-	-	-	-	2	-	1	-	-	1	1	16
Total merchantman losses	-	-	-	-	2	1	1	2	-	4	-	-	1	1	-	2	-	1	3	-	-	1	-	3	-	-	-	3	5	1	26
Sunk in the North Atlantic	-	-	-	-	1	1	-	2	-	4	-	-	-	1	-	1	-	1	1	-	-	-	-	3	-	-	-	2	4	1	21

over, the sinkings of July and August 1943 were notable not simply in terms of disparity of returns between warships and land-based aircraft (at 8.50 to 35.50, greater than 1:4) but on account of their being the first months when there were appreciable returns on the part of escort carrier aircraft; indeed, in this second period, between July and October 1943, aircraft from the escort carrier groups accounted for more U-boats than did warships—19 to 17.[14]

* * *

As a direct result of the losses in the first three weeks of May 1943, and specifically as a result of a series of unprecedented losses in the conduct of attacks on convoys, U-boat operations were curtailed on 24 May 1943—two years to the day since the sinking of the *Hood* in the Denmark Strait. At the time the reverses and losses of the month were attributed to an Allied advantage in radars, specifically in terms of the inability of German search receivers to detect the transmissions of new Allied radars and to the effectiveness of Allied air patrols over the Bay of Biscay. The U-boat command expected that the battle in the North Atlantic could be resumed with the introduction of new weapons and appropriate training that would confound the Allied initiative. The first acoustic torpedoes had been developed as early as 1936, but in the first four years of war their employment was deemed unnecessary, with the result that in spring 1943 very few T5 torpedoes were on hand. The Kriegsmarine hoped that these torpedoes, and with them a counter to the convoy's escorts, might be available in sufficient numbers to enter service in the autumn, and that the counter to Allied land-based aircraft was a considerably increased anti-aircraft armament. In fact, this latter process had been initiated six months earlier, in November 1942, as the response to the U-boats having taken their first (appreciable) losses to land-base aircraft.[15] The response, however, was not standardized, but generally took the form of a enlarged platform on the conning tower that could house first one and then two twin 20-mm guns, while an added platform abaft the conning tower provided for either a single 37-mm gun or quadruple 20-mm guns. Moreover, even as early as May 1943 there was the removal of the standard gun, either 88-mm for the Type VII or 105-mm for the Type IX, but both useless in terms of the battle in the central North Atlantic, and replacement by more anti-aircraft guns, which for the first time provided the U-boat with all-round fire; what had been hitherto the standard armament, at the rear of and abaft the conning tower, had not been able to fire forward. But this process of re-arming the boats was necessarily took time, and the two twin 20-mm gun arrangement for the conning tower was not in place until August 1943.[16]

The provision of a considerably enhanced AA armament went hand in hand with a complementary arrangement, the sailing of U-boats in small groups in tight formation in order to concentrate their defensive firepower. The Allied counter to this was the obvious one: once the sighting had been made, the gathering of as many aircraft as possible in order to mount simultaneous attacks that would divide the U-boats' attention and fire. But in reality these various measures could not provide an answer to the current U-boats' problems; indeed, there was no answer, because much more than radars, search receivers, and anti-aircraft guns (or the lack of adequate numbers of anti-aircraft guns) was involved in producing the situation that came into place in May 1943. It is possible to identify four elements that, coming together at this time, provided the Allies with the initiative. The first was that by 1943 the British naval command had acquired experience and technique in tracking U-boats, diverting convoys, and directing support groups to where they were needed, and through signals intelligence—an ability to read German signals real time—had an advantage of incalculable importance. The second was that by spring 1943 there were escort and aircraft numbers sufficient to cover the North Atlantic and to provide convoys with unprecedented levels of cover: support groups and escort carrier groups were available in numbers for the first time. And lest the point be missed, a crucial factor in producing this situation was the emergence in strength of a Canadian Navy that in 1935 numbered just four destroyers. It took time for the Canadian Navy to acquire numbers of ships and to work up units and formations, and the latter task proved very difficult, but by 1943 the Canadian Navy most definitely had acquired a certain status and capability, and over the last two years of the war provided all but half the convoy escorts crossing the North Atlantic. At war's end Canada's was the third largest navy in the world.[17]

Third, by this time various technological matters were in place, most obviously centimetric radar for escorts and airborne radar, but also new depth-charges and other weapons such as the Hedgehog and Squid for escorts and rockets for aircraft. Certain items, such as airborne radar, had first been used in late 1941, but by the nature of things the general use of airborne radar took time to be slotted into place, and with reference to centimetric radar a very real advantage was to come the Allied way for a wholly unanticipated reason. The German scientific and research establishment was of the view that the centimetric radar could not be produced, and when for the first time German search receivers could not detect Allied transmissions, the obvious reason for such a state of affairs for the moment eluded the German operational and scientific staffs.

The fourth element in the Allied victory was the fact that the operational U-boat of May 1943 was the second- or third-generation boat but showed very little basic change over its 1918 predecessor. What was needed was a new submarine per se; the events of May 1943 pointed in the direction of the obsolescence of the Type VIIC submarine that was the standard boat in service and that, numbering 659, was the most numerous class of submarine ever built. The German problem was that while such a submarine *de novo*—the Walter boat with hydrogen peroxide fuel—had been first proposed in 1942, and the first Walter boat had been launched on 28 September and commissioned into service on 16 November, in summer 1943 the entry of such submarines into service in real numbers was still perhaps three years into the future.[18] In 1943 the Kriegsmarine had to accept two make-shifts in an attempt to counter the declining effectiveness and increasing vulnerability of the U-boats. The first was the employment of the Schnorkel, which would allow a boat to use its diesel engines underwater, the need for conventional boats to spend time on the surface in order to recharge batteries being a major handicap in a situation in which they faced aircraft, both carrier and land-based, operating in the immediate vicinity of convoys. The second was the introduction of the Type XXI, which was a large ocean-going boat that was to replace the Types VIIC and XI, and the Type XXIII, which was a small coastal submarine and which might be produced in sufficient numbers to compensate for limited operational capacity. These two new boats were electro-boats, and leaving aside the Walter boat and all that it implied for the future, the Type XXI, streamlined and with batteries of considerably greater capacity than those of its predecessors, was to represent massive change.

Yet the basic problems confronting the Kriegsmarine with reference to the Type XXI were obvious: final details of design and construction were not settled until 18 June 1943, and approval was not forthcoming until 8 July 1943—in the middle of the battle of Kursk-Orel. But with a planned delivery of some thirty-three boats a month beginning in autumn 1944,[19] such a schedule left U-boat service with a wait for the Types VIIC and IX of some eighteen months and, given all the problems of introducing a new system, not to mention Allied depredations in terms of bombing raids, with no guarantee that boats would be operational before spring or summer 1945. This was only one of many related problems: three-shift working in shipyards, prefabrication of parts, the requirements of extra personnel and of more steel (by more than half) presented a host of problems, not least that presented by the manufacture of more than two hundred Walter engines before the first had been tested at sea. This was an effort that would result in the ending of Type VII construction, but was intended only as an interim program, the anticipation being that the Walter boats would not be available in real numbers until 1946.[20] The first Type XXI was delivered in June 1944, and by the end 1944 eighty, and by the end of April 1945 a total of 119, Type XXI submarines had been delivered into service,[21] but such numbers could not represent the difference between victory and defeat. As it was, intelligence sources provided the British naval command with knowledge of the German programs from which it drew one conclusion: that sometime in 1945 command of the sea would be lost—but that Germany's defeat would have been completed beforehand. So the Admiralty did get something right.

Table 6.3. Major Characteristics of the Type XXI and Other U-boats

		Type VIIC	Type IXC/40	Type XXI	Type XXIII	Type XVIIB
Number built		659	97	118	62	3
First laid down:		?	6 December 1938	3 April 1944	?	1 December 1942
First commissioning		?	16 December 1939	27 June 1944	?	16 November 1943
Dimensions:	length	219.42	251.01	250.81	113.40	135.54-ft.
	beam	20.27	22.11	26.16	9.88	14.72-ft.
	draught	15.50	15.37	20.67	11.97	14.06-ft.
Displacement:	surface	770	1,120	1,620	235	312 tons.
	submerged	1,070	1,540	2,100	275	280 tons.
Maximum speed:	surface	17.7	18.2	15.6	9.7	8.8 knots.
	submerged	7.6	7.3	17.2	12.5	26 knots.
Cruising speed:	surface	10	10	10	6 knots.	?
	submerged	4	4	10	10 knots.	?
Range at cruising speed:	surface	8,500	13,450	15,500 @ 10 5,100 @ 15.6	4,450 @ 6 2,600 @ 8	3,000 n.m @ 8 knots
	submerged	80	63	30 @ 15 110 @ 10	35 @ 10 200 @ 4	125 n.m. @ 25 knots.

	Type VIIC	Type IXC/40	Type XXI	Type XXIII	Type XVIIB
			365 @ 5		
Maximum diving depth	817.50	654	817.50	490.50	
Torpedo tubes	five	six	six	two	two 21-in/533-mm.
Maximum number of torpedoes carried:	14	22	24	two	
Complement (maximum)	4 & 56	4 & 44	5 & 52	2 & 12	three officers & sixteen men.

The Type XVIIB was an experimental Walter boat.

Sources: Robert Hutchinson, Submarines: War beneath the Waves from 1776 to the Present Day.

Eberhard Möller and Werner Brack, The Encyclopedia of U-boats: From 1904 to the Present, pp. 73–93, 99–101, 109, 110–113, 113–115.

Eberhard Rössler, The U-boat: The Evolution and Technical History of German Submarines.

Jak P. Mallmann Showell, The German Navy in World War II: A Reference Guide to the Kriegsmarine, 1935–1945, p. 138.

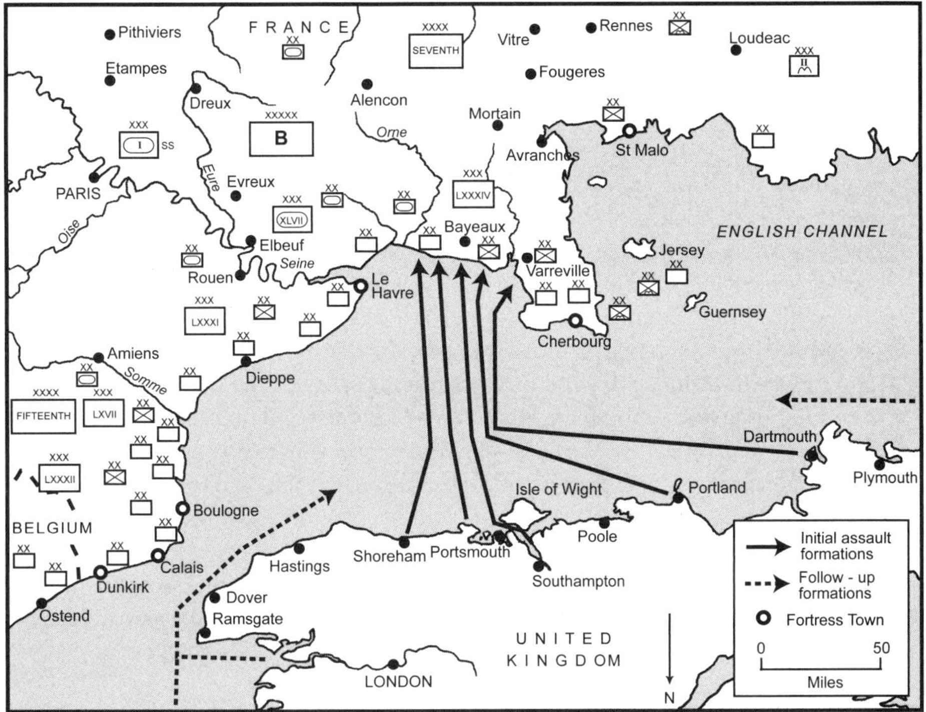

Map 6. Cross Channel Invasion Routes

* * *

The story of the last eighteen months of the war at sea is one of the contraction of German capability, and between April 1944 and May 1945 the total Allied and neutral shipping losses exceeded 100,000 tons in only five months, the peak of 134,913 tons in December 1944 being the lowest December total of the war. But if the Allied invasion and campaign in France forced the U-boats to abandon their French bases with obvious strategic implications, perhaps two matters might draw this chapter to its close.

The first matter is a very personal prejudice that has found expression elsewhere: an understanding of total war, and specifically of its reach, is perhaps helped by reference to one small incident on 5 October 1944. On that date, and in the wake of the German decision to close down the U-boat base at Penang and to end operations in the Indian Ocean, the U. 168 was sunk in the Java Sea by the Dutch submarine *Zwaardvisch*, which was operating from an Australian base under American orders: a war across the world, in one incident.[22]

The second is more contentious, and relates to two of the three actions between British and German capital ships that were fought to a finish. The first is the strange process whereby the *Hood* was sunk as a result of most impressive shooting on the part of the *Bismarck,* and the *Bismarck* was crippled as a result of a lucky torpedo hit, though in making this point one raises another. Underwater damage may be something of a lottery, though it is somewhat odd to note that the British fleet carrier *Ark Royal* was sunk as a result of a solitary torpedo hit, whereas at the battle of Tassafaronga (30 November–1 December 1942) the U.S. heavy cruisers *Minneapolis, New Orleans, Northampton,* and *Pensacola* respectively took two, one, one, and two hits from Japanese Long Lance torpedoes, but only the *Northampton* was sunk. The second is the action off the North Cape, in the Arctic, on 26 December 1943, in which the *Scharnhorst* was caught and sunk by a British formation that included the battleship *Duke of York.* What is interesting about this action is that the British battleship allowed the range to close to 12,000 yards before opening fire at 1650 on a German warship taken completely by surprise. By 1740 the range was between 17,000 and 20,000 yards, and the *Scharnhorst* was pulling clear of the British formation, but by 1820 it had been slowed and was subsequently closed and sunk. In other words, initially at a range of 12,000 yards and then for ninety minutes the *Duke of York* could not hold and slow its enemy, still less sink the German battleship. One is left to wonder why this was the case and what, for example, the U.S. battleship *Washington* would have made of this episode, had it been asked.[23]

APPENDIX 6.1.

ALLIED AND NEUTRAL SHIPPING LOSSES BY CAUSE AND BY PERIODS OF OPERATIONS BETWEEN 3 SEPTEMBER 1939 AND 15 AUGUST 1945

		Submarines	Aircraft	Mines	Warships	Raiders	E-boats	All other causes	----- TOTAL ----
September	1939	41: 153,879	- -	8: 29,537	1: 5,051	- -	- -	3: 6,378	53: 194,845
October	1939	27: 134,807	- -	11: 29,490	8: 32,058	- -	- -	- -	46: 196,355
November	1939	21: 51,589	- -	27: 120,958	2: 1,722	- -	- -	- -	50: 174,269
December	1939	25: 80,881	10: 2,949	33: 82,712	4: 22,506	- -	- -	1: 875	73: 189,923
January	1940	40: 111,263	11: 23,693	21: 77,116	- -	- -	- -	1: 2,434	73: 214,506
February	1940	45: 169,566	2: 853	15: 54,740	1: 1,761	- -	- -	- -	63: 226,920
March	1940	23: 62,781	7: 8,694	14: 35,501	- -	- -	- -	1: 33	45: 107,009
Period total		222: 764,766	30: 36,169	129: 430,054	16: 63,098	- -	- -	6: 9,720	403: 1,303,827
Monthly average		31.71 109,252	4.29 5,167	18.43 61,436	2.29 9,014	- -	- -	0.86 1,389	57.57 186,261
% share		55.09% 58.66%	7.44% 2.77%	32.01% 32.98%	3.97% 4.84%	- -	- -	1.49% 0.75%	- -
April	1940	7: 32,467	7: 13,409	11: 19,799	- -	1: 5,207	1: 151	31: 87,185	58: 158,218
May	1940	13: 55,580	48: 158,348	20: 47,716	- -	1: 6,199	1: 694	18: 19,924	101: 288,461
June	1940	58: 284,113	22: 105,193	22: 86,076	2: 25,506	4: 29,225	3: 6,856	29: 48,527	140: 585,496
Period total		78: 372,160	77: 276,950	53: 153,591	2: 25,506	6: 40,631	5: 7,701	78: 155,636	299: 1,032,175
Monthly average		26.00 124,053	25.67 92,317	17.67 51,197	0.67 8,502	2.00 13,544	1.67 2,567	26.00 51,879	99.67 344,058
% share		26.09% 36.06%	25.75% 26.83%	17.73% 14.88%	0.67% 2.47%	2.01% 3.94%	1.67% 0.75%	26.09% 15.08%	- -
July	1940	38: 195,825	33: 70,193	14: 35,598	- -	11: 67,494	6: 13,302	3: 4,501	105: 386,913
August	1940	56: 267,618	15: 53,283	5: 11,433	- -	11: 61,767	2: 1,583	3: 1,545	92: 397,229
September	1940	59: 295,335	15: 56,328	7: 8,269	- -	8: 65,386	7: 14,951	4: 8,352	100: 448,621
October	1940	63: 352,407	6: 8,752	24: 32,548	- -	4: 30,529	1: 1,595	5: 17,144	103: 442,985
November	1940	32: 146,613	18: 66,438	24: 46,762	11: 48,748	9: 74,923	- -	3: 2,231	97: 385,715
December	1940	37: 212,590	8: 14,890	24: 54,331	3: 20,971	5: 25,904	2: 8,853	3: 12,029	82: 349,568
January	1941	21: 126,782	20: 78,597	10: 17,107	3: 18,738	20: 78,484	- -	2: 532	76: 320,240
February	1941	39: 196,783	27: 89,305	10: 16,507	17: 79,086	1: 7,031	3: 2,979	5: 11,702	102: 403,393
March	1941	41: 243,020	41: 113,314	19: 23,585	17: 89,838	4: 28,707	9: 20,361	8: 10,881	139: 529,706
April	1941	43: 249,375	116: 323,454	6: 24,888	- -	6: 43,640	3: 4,299	21: 42,245	195: 687,901
May	1941	58: 325,492	65: 146,302	9: 23,194	- -	3: 15,002	- -	4: 1,052	139: 511,042
Period total		487: 2,611,840	364: 1,020,856	152: 294,222	51: 257,381	82: 498,877	33: 67,923	61: 112,214	1,230: 4,863,313
Monthly average		44.27 237,440	33.09 92,805	13.82 26,747	4.64 23,398	7.45 45,352	3.00 6,175	5.55 10,201	111.82 442,119
% share		39.59% 53.70%	29.59% 20.99%	12.36% 6.05%	4.15% 5.29%	6.67% 10.26%	2.68% 1.40%	4.96% 2.31%	- -

		Submarines	Aircraft	Mines	Warships	Raiders	E-boats	All other causes	----- TOTAL ----
June	1941	61: 310,143	25: 61,414	10: 15,326	- -	4: 17,759	- -	9: 27,383	109: 432,025
July	1941	22: 94,209	11: 9,275	7: 8,583	- -	1: 5,792	- -	2: 3,116	43: 120,975
August	1941	23: 80,310	9: 23,862	3: 1,400	- -	3: 21,378	2: 3,519	1: 230	41: 130,699
September	1941	53: 202,820	12: 40,812	9: 14,948	1: 7,500	2: 8,734	3: 6,676	4: 4,452	84: 285,942
October	1941	32: 156,554	10: 35,222	4: 19,737	- -	- -	2: 3,305	3: 3,471	51: 218,289
November	1941	13: 62,196	10: 23,015	5: 1,714	- -	- -	7: 17,715	- -	35: 104,640
December	1941	26: 124,070	25: 72,850	19: 63,853	2: 6,661	- -	- -	213: 316,272	285: 583,706
Period total		230: 1,030,302	102: 266,450	57: 125,561	3: 14,161	10: 53,663	14: 31,215	232: 354,924	648: 1,876,276
Monthly average		32.86 147,186	14.57 38,064	8.14 17,937	0.43 2,023	1.43 7,666	2.00 4,459	33.14 50,703	92.57 268,039
% share		35.49% 54.91%	15.74% 14.20%	8.80% 6.69%	0.46% 0.75%	1.54% 2.86%	2.16% 1.66%	35.80% 18.92%	- -
January	1942	62: 327,357	15: 57,086	11: 10,079	1: 3,275	- -	- -	17: 22,110	106: 419,907
February	1942	85: 476,451	28: 133,746	2: 7,242	- -	- -	- -	39: 62,193	154: 679,632
March	1942	95: 537,980	15: 55,706	5: 16,862	8: 16,072	2: 8,591	1: 951	147: 198,002	273: 834,164
April	1942	74: 431,664	17: 82,924	9: 15,002	20: 100,001	5: 31,187	- -	7: 13,679	132: 674,457
May	1942	125: 607,247	14: 59,014	6: 18,795	- -	3: 19,363	- -	3: 631	151: 705,050
June	1942	144: 700,235	11: 54,769	8: 19,936	- -	7: 48,474	- -	3: 10,782	173: 834,196
Period total		585: 3,080,934	100: 443,245	41: 87,916	29: 119,348	17: 107,615	1: 951	216: 307,397	989: 4,147,406
Monthly average		97.50 513,489	16.67 73,874	6.83 14,653	4.83 19,891	2.83 17,936	0.17 159	36.00 51,233	164.83 693,234
% share		59.15% 74.29%	10.11% 10.69%	4.15% 2.12%	2.93% 2.88	1.72% 2.59%	0.10% 0.02%	21.84% 7.41%	- -
July	1942	96: 476,065	18: 74,313	2: 8,905	- -	6: 42,166	5: 12,192	1: 4,472	128: 618,113
August	1942	108: 544,410	6: 60,532	- -	- -	2: 12,946	4: 37,570	3: 5,675	123: 661,133
September	1942	98: 485,413	12: 57,526	- -	1: 3,188	3: 21,200	- -	- -	114: 567,327
October	1942	94: 619,417	1: 5,683	3: 5,157	- -	- -	3: 7,576	- -	101: 637,833
November	1942	119: 729,160	6: 53,868	1: 992	1: 7,925	1: 5,882	4: 5,371	2: 4,556	134: 807,754
December	1942	60: 330,816	3: 4,853	4: 1,618	- -	1: 4,816	6: 7,496	1: 1,532	75: 351,131
January	1943	37: 203,128	5: 25,503	5: 18,745	- -	1: 7,040	- -	2: 6,943	50: 261,359
February	1943	63: 359,328	1: 75	7: 34,153	- -	- -	1: 4,858	1: 4,648	73: 403,062
March	1943	108: 627,377	10: 65,128	2: 884	- -	- -	- -	- -	120: 693,389
April	1943	56: 327,943	2: 3,034	5: 11,961	- -	- -	1: 1,742	- -	64: 344,680
May	1943	50: 264,852	5: 20,942	1: 1,568	- -	- -	- -	2: 12,066	58: 299,428
Period total		889: 4,967,909	69: 371,457	30: 83,983	2: 11,113	14: 94,050	24: 76,805	12: 39,892	1,040: 5,645,209
Monthly average		80.82 451,628	6.27 33,769	2.73 7,635	0.18 1,010	1.27 8,550	2.18 6,982	1.09 3,627	94.55 513,201
% share		85.48% 88.00	6.63% 6.58%	2.88% 1.49%	0.19% 0.20%	1.35% 1.67%	2.31% 1.36%	1.15% 0.71%	- -

		Submarines	Aircraft	Mines	Warships	Raiders	E-boats	All other causes	----- TOTAL ----
June	1943	20: 95,753	3: 6,083	3: 4,334	- -	2: 17,655	- -	- -	28: 123,825
July	1943	46: 252,145	13: 106,005	1: 72	- -	1: 7,176	- -	- -	61: 365,398
August	1943	16: 86,579	5: 14,133	1: 19	- -	- -	- -	3: 19,070	25: 119,801
September	1943	20: 118,841	4: 22,905	3: 4,396	- -	1: 9,977	- -	1: 300	29: 156,419
October	1943	20: 97,407	4: 22,680	5: 19,774	- -	- -	- -	- -	29: 139,861
November	1943	14: 66,585	7: 62,452	3: 6,666	- -	- -	4: 8,538	1: 150	29: 144,391
December	1943	13: 86,967	17: 75,471	1: 6,086	- -	- -	- -	- -	31: 168,524
January	1944	13: 92,278	4: 24,237	1: 7,176	- -	- -	5: 6,420	3: 524	26: 130,635
February	1944	18: 92,923	3: 21,616	- -	- -	- -	1: 2,085	1: 231	23: 116,855
March	1944	23: 142,944	- -	1: 7,176	1: 7,840	- -	- -	- -	25: 157,960
April	1944	9: 62,585	3: 19,755	- -	- -	- -	1: 468	- -	13: 82,372
May	1944	4: 24,424	1: 2,873	- -	- -	- -	- -	- -	5: 27,297
Period total		216: 1,218,995	64: 378,210	19: 55,699	1: 7,840	4: 34,808	11: 17,511	9: 20,275	324: 1,733,338
Monthly average		18.00 101,583	5.33 31,518	1.58 4,642	0.08 653	0.33 2,901	0.92 1,459	0.75 1,690	27.00 144,445
% share		66.67% 70.33%	19.75% 21.82%	5.86% 3.21%	0.31% 0.45%	1.23% 2.01%	3.40% 1.01%	2.78% 1.17%	- -
June	1944	11: 57,875	2: 9,008	6: 24,654	- -	- -	3: 1,812	4: 10,735	26: 104,084
July	1944	12: 63,351	- -	3: 8,114	- -	- -	1: 7,219	1: 72	17: 78,756
August	1944	18: 98,729	- -	3: 7,194	- -	- -	1: 7,176	1: 5,205	23: 118,304
September	1944	7: 43,368	- -	1: 1,437	- -	- -	- -	- -	8: 44,805
October	1944	1: 7,176	- -	3: 4,492	- -	- -	- -	- -	4: 11,668
November	1944	7: 29,592	1: 7,247	- -	- -	- -	1: 1,141	- -	9: 37,980
December	1944	9: 58,518	5: 35,920	10: 35,612	- -	- -	- -	2: 4,863	26: 134,913
January	1945	11: 56,988	1: 7,176	5: 16,368	- -	- -	1: 2,365	2: 1,806	20: 84,703
February	1945	15: 65,233	1: 7,177	6: 18,076	- -	- -	2: 3,889	2: 941	26: 95,316
March	1945	13: 65,077	- -	7: 36,064	- -	- -	2: 3,968	5: 6,095	27: 111,204
April	1945	13: 72,957	3: 22,822	6: 8,733	- -	- -	- -	- -	22: 104,512
May	1945	3: 10,022	1: 7,176	- -	- -	- -	- -	- -	4: 17,198
June	1945	1: 11,439	- -	1: 7,176	- -	- -	- -	- -	2: 18,615
July	1945	- -	- -	2: 7,210	- -	- -	- -	1: 27	3: 7,237
August	1945	- -	- -	1: 36	- -	- -	- -	- -	1: 36
Period total		121: 640,325	14: 96,526	54: 175,166	- -	- -	11: 27,570	18: 29,744	218: 969,331
Monthly average		10.54 55,777	1.22 8,408	4.70 15,258	- -	- -	0.96 2,402	1.57 2,591	18.99 84,436
% share		55.50% 66.06%	6.42% 9.96%	24.77% 18.07%	- -	- -	5.05% 2.84%	8.26% 3.07%	- -

Source: S. W. Roskill, *The War at Sea*, vol. 1: *The Defensive*, appendix R, table I, "British, Allied and Neutral Merchant Ship Losses and Causes," p. 615; vol. 2: *The Period of Balance*, appendix O, table I, "British, Allied and Neutral Merchant Ship Losses and Causes from Enemy Action January 1942–May 1943," p. 485; vol. 3: *The Offensive*, part 1, *1st June 1943–31st May 1944*, appendix K, table I, "British, Allied and Neutral Merchant Shipping Losses from Enemy Action, and Causes--1st June, 1943–31st May, 1944," p. 388; and vol. 3: *The Offensive*, part 2, *1st June 1944–15th August 1945*, appendix Z, table I, "British, Allied and Neutral Merchant Shipping Losses from Enemy Action, 1st June, 1944-15th August, 1945," p. 477.

Note: It should be noted that in Roskill's second volume there is a discrepancy of 12,000 tons in the returns of April 1942 under the "unknown and other causes" label: it seems that this total should read 13,679 tons, which is the figure provided here in this table.

It should also be noted that Roskill has certain entries with no known dates, and these have been assigned arbitrary homes in this table, namely:

the two ships of 2,229 tons lost sometime in 1942 have been included in the December 1942 returns

the two ships of 1,806 tons lost during 1945 have been included in the January 1945 returns

These months have been selected on the basis that there were no other sinkings under the appropriate heading in these months, though by definition the months assigned must be wrong.

APPENDIX 6.2.

ALLIED AND NEUTRAL SHIPPING LOSSES BY THEATER AND PERIODS OF OPERATION BETWEEN 3 SEPTEMBER 1939 AND 15 AUGUST 1945

			British waters	North Atlantic	Mediterranean	South Atlantic	Indian Ocean	Pacific Ocean	---- Total ----
	September	1939	33: 84,965	19: 104,829	- -	1: 5,051	- -	- -	53: 194,845
	October	1939	24: 63,368	18: 110,619	- -	4: 22,368	- -	- -	46: 196,355
	November	1939	43: 155,668	6: 17,895	- -	- -	1: 706	- -	50: 174,269
	December	1939	66: 152,107	4: 15,852	- -	3: 21,964	- -	- -	73: 189,923
	January	1940	64: 178,536	9: 35,970	- -	- -	- -	- -	73: 214,506
	February	1940	46: 152,161	17: 74,759	- -	- -	- -	- -	63: 226,920
	March	1940	43: 95,794	2: 11,215	- -	- -	- -	- -	45: 107,009
	Period total		319: 882,599	75: 371,139	- -	8: 49,383	1: 706	- -	403: 1,303,827
	Monthly average		45.57 126,086	10.71 54,448	- -	1.14 7,055	0.14 101	- -	57.57 186,261
	% share		79.16% 67.69%	18.61% 28.47%	- -	1.99% 3.79%	0.25% 0.05%	- -	- -
	April	1940	54: 133,648	4: 24,570	- -	- -	- -	- -	58: 158,218
	May	1940	90: 230,607	9: 49,087	1: 2,568	1: 6,199	- -	- -	101: 288,461
	June	1940	77: 208,924	53: 296,529	6: 45,402	- -	2: 15,445	2: 19,196	140: 585,496
	Period total		221: 573,179	66: 370,186	7: 47,970	1: 6,199	2: 15,445	2: 19,196	299: 1,032,175
	Monthly average		73.67 191,060	22.00 123,395	2.33 15,990	0.33 2,067	0.67 5,148	0.67 6,399	99.67 344,058
	% share		73.91% 55.53%	22.07% 35.86	2.34% 4.65	0.33% 0.60	0.67% 1.50	0.67% 1.86%	- -
	July	1940	67: 192,331	28: 141,474	2: 6,564	6: 31,269	2: 15,275	- -	105: 386,913
	August	1940	45: 162,956	39: 190,048	1: 1,044	- -	5: 31,001	2: 12,180	92: 397,229
	September	1940	39: 131,150	52: 254,553	2: 5,708	1: 17,801	6: 39,409	- -	100: 448,621
	October	1940	43: 131,620	56: 286,644	1: 2,897	- -	2: 14,621	1: 7,203	103: 442,985
	November	1940	48: 92,713	38: 201,341	- -	- -	7: 57,665	4: 33,996	97: 385,715
	December	1940	34: 83,308	42: 239,304	- -	- -	- -	6: 26,956	82: 349,568
	January	1941	15: 36,975	42: 214,382	- -	17: 58,585	2: 10,298	- -	76: 320,240
	February	1941	26: 51,381	69: 317,378	2: 8,343	- -	5: 26,291	- -	102: 403,393
	March	1941	73: 152,862	63: 364,689	2: 11,868	- -	- -	1: 287	139: 529,706
	April	1941	40: 99,031	45: 260,451	105: 292,518	3: 21,807	2: 14,094	- -	195: 687,901
179>	May	1941	99: 100,655	58: 324,550	19: 70,835	2: 11,339	1: 3,663	- -	139: 511,042
1270>	Period total		529: 1,234,982	532: 2,794,814	134: 399,777	29: 140,801	32: 212,317	14: 80,622	1,230: 4,863,313
	Monthly average		00.00 112,271	00.00 254,074	00.00 36,343	00.00 12,800	00.00 19,302	00.00 7,329	111.82 442,119
	% share		00.00% 25.39%	00.00% 57.47%	00.00% 8.22%	00.00% 2.90%	00.00% 4.37%	00.00% 1.66%	- -

		British waters	North Atlantic	Mediterranean	South Atlantic	Indian Ocean	Pacific Ocean	---- Total ----
June	1941	34: 86,381	68: 318,740	3: 9,145	2: 10,134	2: 7,625	- -	109: 432,025
July	1941	18: 15,265	23: 97,813	2: 7,897	- -	- -	- -	43: 120,975
August	1941	11: 19,791	25: 83,661	2: 5,869	- -	- -	3: 21,378	41: 130,699
September	1941	13: 54,779	51: 184,546	4: 15,951	2: 15,526	3: 10,347	1: 4,793	84: 285,942
October	1941	12: 35,996	32: 154,593	6: 22,403	1: 5,297	- -	- -	51: 218,289
November	1941	20: 30,332	10: 50,215	4: 19,140	1: 4,953	- -	- -	35: 104,640
December	1941	19: 56,845	10: 50,682	9: 37,394	1: 6,275	5: 837	241: 431,673	285: 583,706
Period losses		127: 299,389	219: 940,250	30: 117,799	7: 42,185	10: 18,809	245: 457,844	648: 1,876,276
								638>
Monthly average		00.00 42,770	00.00 134,321	00.00 16,828	00.00 6,026	00.00 2,687	00.00 65,406	92.57 268,039
% share		00.00% 15.96%	00.00% 50.11%	00.00% 6.29%	00.00% 2.25%	00.00% 1.00%	00.00% 24.40%	- -
January	1942	14: 19,341	48: 276,795	1: 6,655	- -	13: 46,062	30: 71,054	106: 419,907
February	1942	5: 11,098	73: 429,891	4: 19,245	- -	18: 38,151	54: 181,247	154: 679,632
March	1942	8: 15,147	95: 534,064	4: 19,516	3: 13,125	65: 68,539	98: 183,773	273: 834,164
April	1942	14: 54,589	66: 391,044	6: 12,804	8: 48,177	31: 153,930	7: 13,913	132: 674,457
May	1942	14: 59,396	120: 576,350	6: 21,215	2: 9,081	4: 22,049	5: 16,959	151: 705,050
June	1942	5: 2,655	124: 623,545	16: 59,971	4: 26,287	18: 90,322	6: 31,416	173: 834,196
Period losses		60: 162,226	526: 2,831,689	37: 139,406	17: 96,670	149: 419,053	200: 498,362	989: 4,147,406
Monthly average		10.00 27,038	87.67 471,948	6.17 23,234	2.83 16,112	24.83 69,842	33.33 83,060	164.83 693,234
% share		6.07% 3.91%	53.19% 68.28%	3.74% 3.36%	1.72% 2.33%	15.07% 10.10%	20.22% 12.02%	- -
July	1942	9: 22,557	98: 486,965	3: 5,885	3: 23,972	9: 47,012	6: 31,722	128: 618,113
August	1942	- -	96: 508,426	13: 110,423	10: 35,494	1: 5,237	3: 1,553	123: 661,133
September	1942	1: 1,892	95: 473,585	4: 813	7: 57,797	6: 30,052	1: 3,188	114: 567,327
October	1942	6: 12,733	62: 399,715	- -	20: 148,142	11: 63,552	2: 13,691	101: 637,833
November	1942	5: 6,363	83: 508,707	13: 102,951	10: 58,662	23: 131,071	- -	134: 807,754
December	1942	10: 9,114	46: 262,135	3: 5,649	8: 43,496	6: 28,508	2: 2,229	75: 351,131
January	1943	4: 15,819	27: 172,691	14: 47,506	3: 16,116	- -	2: 9,227	50: 261,359
February	1943	2: 4,925	46: 288,625	14: 52,718	4: 21,656	3: 15,787	4: 19,351	73: 403,062
March	1943	2: 884	82: 476,349	16: 86,230	8: 61,462	10: 62,303	2: 6,161	120: 693,389
April	1943	5: 9,926	39: 235,478	6: 13,972	1: 7,129	6: 43,007	7: 35,168	64: 344,680
May	1943	1: 1,568	34: 163,507	6: 32,300	6: 40,523	6: 28,058	5: 33,472	58: 299,428
Period losses		45: 85,781	708: 3,976,183	92: 458,447	80: 514,449	81: 454,587	34: 155,762	1,040: 5,645,209
Monthly average		4.09 7,798	64.36 361,471	8.36 41,677	7.27 85,742	7.36 75,765	3.09 26,960	94.55 513,201
% share		4.33% 1.52%	68.08% 70.43%	8.85% 8.12%	7.69% 9.11%	7.79% 8.05%	3.27% 2.76%	- -

		British waters	North Atlantic	Mediterranean	South Atlantic	Indian Ocean	Pacific Ocean	---- Total ----
June	1943	1: 149	4: 18,379	7: 24,533	3: 11,587	12: 67,929	1: 1,248	28: 123,825
July	1943	1: 72	18: 123,327	14: 80,307	11: 64,478	17: 97,214	- -	61: 365,398
August	1943	1: 19	2: 10,186	11: 43,351	2: 15,368	7: 46,401	2: 4,476	25: 119,801
September	1943	- -	8: 43,775	11: 52,426	3: 10,770	6: 39,471	1: 9,977	29: 156,419
October	1943	- -	12: 56,422	9: 45,767	1: 4,663	6: 25,833	1: 7,176	29: 139,861
November	1943	7: 13,036	6: 23,077	10: 67,846	1: 4,573	4: 29,148	1: 6,711	29: 144,391
December	1943	1: 6,086	7: 47,785	18: 83,480	- -	5: 31,173	- -	31: 168,524
January	1944	8: 6,944	5: 36,065	5: 31,413	- -	8: 56,213	- -	26: 130,635
February	1944	3: 4,051	2: 12,577	8: 36,058	- -	10: 64,169	- -	23: 116,855
March	1944	- -	7: 36,867	5: 40,900	1: 4,695	12: 75,498	- -	25: 157,960
April	1944	1: 468	5: 34,227	5: 34,141	2: 13,539	- -	- -	13: 82,372
May	1944	- -	- -	2: 10,020	3: 17,277	- -	- -	5: 27,297
Period losses		23: 30,825	76: 442,684	105: 550,242	27: 146,950	87: 533,049	6: 29,588	324: 1,733,338
Monthly average		1.92 2,569	6.33 36,890	8.75 45,854	2.25 12,246	7.25 44,421	0.50 2,466	27.00 144,445
% share		7.10% 1.78%	23.46% 25.54%	32.41% 31.74%	8.33% 8.48%	26.85% 30.75	1.85% 1.71%	- -
June	1944	19: 75,166	2: 4,294	1: 2,037	1: 3,268	3: 19,319	- -	26: 104,084
July	1944	8: 19,038	2: 15,480	- -	2: 14,062	5: 30,176	- -	17: 78,756
August	1944	12: 54,834	1: 5,685	1: 53	- -	9: 57,732	- -	23: 118,304
September	1944	3: 21,163	3: 16,535	1: 1,437	- -	1: 5,670	- -	8: 44,805
October	1944	2: 1,722	- -	1: 2,770	- -	- -	1: 7,176	4: 11,668
November	1944	3: 8,880	3: 7,828	- -	- -	2: 14,025	1: 7,247	9: 37,980
December	1944	18: 85,639	1: 5,458	1: 716	- -	- -	6: 43,100	26: 134,913
January	1945	12: 46,553	5: 29,168	- -	- -	2: 1,806	1: 7,176	20: 84,703
February	1945	19: 48,551	5: 32,452	- -	1: 7,136	1: 7,176	- -	26: 95,316
March	1945	23: 83,864	3: 23,684	- -	1: 3,656	- -	- -	27: 111,204
April	1945	14: 49,619	5: 32,071	- -	- -	- -	3: 22,822	22: 104,512
May	1945	2: 4,669	1: 5,353	- -	- -	- -	1: 7,176	4: 17,198
June	1945	- -	- -	1: 7,176	- -	- -	1: 11,439	2: 18,615
July	1945	2: 39	- -	1: 7,198	- -	- -	- -	3: 7,237
August	1945	1: 36	- -	- -	- -	- -	- -	1: 36
Period losses		138: 499,773	31: 178,009	7: 21,387	5: 28,122	23: 135,904	14: 106,136	218: 969,331
Monthly average		12.02 43,534	2.70 15,506	0.61 1,863	0.44 2,450	2.00 11,838	1.22 9,245	18.99 84,436
% share		63.30% 51.56%	14.22% 18.36%	3.21% 2.21%	2.29% 2.90%	10.55% 14.02%	6.42% 10.95%	- -

APPENDIX 6.3.

BRITISH FLEET UNITS, ESCORTS, AND FLEET MINESWEEPERS LOST, BY THEATER AND YEAR, IN THE SECOND WORLD WAR

	1939	1940	1941	1942	1943	1944	1945	Total
Capital ships:								
British home waters	1	-	-	-	-	-	-	1
North Atlantic	-	-	1	-	-	-	-	1
Mediterranean	-	-	3	-	-	-	-	3
Indian Ocean	-	-	-	-	-	-	-	-
Pacific Ocean	-	-	2	-	-	-	-	2
	1	-	6	-	-	-	-	7
Fleet and light carriers:								
British home waters	1	1	-	-	-	-	-	2
North Atlantic	-	-	-	-	-	-	-	-
Mediterranean	-	-	1	1	-	-	-	2
Indian Ocean	-	-	-	1	-	-	-	1
Pacific Ocean	-	-	-	-	-	-	-	-
	1	1	1	2	-	-	-	5
Escort carriers:								
British home waters	-	-	-	-	1	-	-	1
North Atlantic	-	-	1	1	-	-	-	2
Mediterranean	-	-	-	-	-	-	-	-
Indian Ocean	-	-	-	-	-	-	-	-
Pacific Ocean	-	-	-	-	-	-	-	-
	-	-	1	1	1	-	-	3
Heavy cruisers:								
British home waters	-	1	-	-	-	-	-	1
North Atlantic	-	-	-	-	-	-	-	-
Mediterranean	-	-	1	-	-	-	-	1
Indian Ocean	-	-	-	2	-	-	-	2
Pacific Ocean	-	-	-	2	-	-	-	2
	-	1	1	4	-	-	-	6
Light cruisers:								
British home waters	-	-	-	2	-	2	-	4
North Atlantic	-	2	1	1	-	-	-	4
Mediterranean	-	-	7	5	2	2	-	16
South Atlantic	-	-	-	-	-	-	-	-
Indian Ocean	-	-	1	-	-	-	-	1
Pacific Ocean	-	-	-	1	-	-	-	1
	-	2	9	9	2	4	-	26

	1939	1940	1941	1942	1943	1944	1945	Total
Destroyers:								
British home waters	3	29	-	6	1	12	2	53
North Atlantic	-	5	5	6	3	1	-	20
Mediterranean	-	4	16	22	8	3	-	53
South Atlantic	-	-	-	-	-	-	-	-
Indian Ocean	-	-	-	2	-	-	-	2
Pacific Ocean	-	-	1	6	-	-	-	7
	3	38	22	42	12	16	2	135
Submarines:								
British home waters	1	19	1	1	2	3	-	27
North Atlantic	-	-	2	4	1	1	-	8
Mediterranean	-	10	9	18	12	3	-	52
Indian Ocean	-	-	-	-	-	2	1	3
Pacific Ocean	-	-	-	-	-	-	-	-
	1	29	12	23	15	9	1	90
Corvettes:								
British home waters	-	1	1	-	-	5	4	11
North Atlantic	-	-	6	6	1	3	-	16
Mediterranean	-	-	1	3	4	-	-	7
Indian Ocean	-	1	-	2	-	-	-	3
Pacific Ocean	-	-	-	-	-	-	-	-
	-	2	8	11	5	8	4	38
Sloops:								
British home waters	-	1	-	-	-	1	1	3
North Atlantic	-	2	-	-	1	-	-	3
Mediterranean	-	-	3	1	-	1	-	5
Indian Ocean	-	-	-	2	-	-	-	2
Pacific Ocean	-	-	-	-	-	-	-	-
	-	3	3	3	1	2	1	13
Escort destroyers:								
British home waters	-	1	1	2	1	1	-	6
North Atlantic	-	-	-	-	2	-	-	2
Mediterranean	-	-	-	6	3	2	-	11
Indian Ocean	-	-	-	-	-	-	-	-
Pacific Ocean	-	-	-	-	-	-	-	-
	-	1	1	8	6	3	-	19

	1939	1940	1941	1942	1943	1944	1945	Total
Frigates:								
British home waters	-	-	-	-	-	6	1	7
North Atlantic	-	-	-	-	1	3	-	4
Mediterranean	-	-	-	-	-	-	-	-
Indian Ocean	-	-	-	-	-	-	-	-
Pacific Ocean	-	-	-	-	-	-	-	-
	-	-	-	-	1	9	1	11
Fleet minesweepers:								
British home waters	-	4	-	4	-	7	2	17
North Atlantic	-	-	-	1	1	1	2	5
Mediterranean	-	-	4	3	6	-	1	14
Indian Ocean	-	-	-	1	1	-	-	2
Pacific Ocean	-	-	-	-	-	1	-	1
	-	4	4	9	8	9	5	39

Definitions:

British home waters includes the Channel, the North and Norwegian Seas, and the Arctic; the North Atlantic includes the Caribbean; and the Pacific includes the South China Sea and all areas north of the line of the Malay Barrier.

Dominion and Indian warships that were lost are included as British.

Allied warships operating under British direction that were lost are also listed as British. The lists thus include Dutch, French, Greek, Norwegian, and Polish warships that were lost, plus one Italian submarine lost in 1944.

APPENDIX 6.4.

GERMAN NAVAL LOSSES IN THE SECOND WORLD WAR

NOTED ELSEWHERE IN these pages is the argument that British naval victories in the eighteenth and early nineteenth centuries were the products of an existing and growing British supremacy at sea in terms of national resources and geographical position and superiority of numbers. Any consideration of German naval losses in the Second World War would seem to be, *mutatis mutandis*, of reverse pedigree, the product rather than the cause of defeat. Other than the U-boat arm, which did grow into a considerable numerical strength, the German navy was never possessed of more than modest size: at the outbreak of war on 1 September 1939 it mustered the capital ships *Gneisenau* and *Scharnhorst*, the armored ships *Admiral Graf Spee*, *Admiral Scheer*, and *Deutschland*, the heavy cruiser *Admiral Hipper*, and the light cruisers *Emden*, the *Karlsruhe*, *Köln*, and *Königsberg*, and the *Leipzig* and *Nürnberg*, plus the pre-dreadnoughts *Schleswig-Holstein* and *Schlesien*, the latter being in service as a training ship though it did take part in the bombardment of Polish positions on the Hela peninsula in mid-September 1939. By the end of April 1940 three of these units, namely the *Admiral Graf Spee*, the *Königsberg*, and the *Karlsruhe*, had been lost and a fourth, the *Leipzig*, had incurred such damage that it never returned to operational service. Losses thereafter had to be, and by definition were, few and far between.

But any consideration of losses of destroyers, escorts, torpedo-boats, and minecraft clearly points to the significance of April 1940 and the Norwegian campaign. At the outbreak of war, and in addition to twelve torpedo-boats of the *Möwe* class, the German navy possessed just twenty-one destroyers: the losses incurred in the two battles of Narvik all but represented half of its destroyers. But what is so striking about German losses is how few units were lost before 1944, and the fact was that by 1944 the decision of the war had been reached and Germany had been condemned to certain defeat. The final form of that defeat remained to be decided, but the decision of victory and defeat had been reached, and basically without reference to the war at sea. Germany was not defeated because it lost the war at sea, and the greater part of German naval losses came as a result of defeat, specifically as the manifestation of Allied superiority: German naval losses were not important in terms of the cause of national and service defeat.

Obviously these losses represented an element of defeat, these losses helped complete the process of defeat, but the losses were not those incurred in the course of the battle for supremacy: they were incurred after that battle had been lost, and lost more or less by default because the German Navy never possessed the means to secure supremacy; the best that the U-boat arm might achieve was the denial of supremacy to the enemy. The decision of the war had been reached, if not in December 1941 or in the course of 1942, most obviously in November 1942, then in 1943, and the Italian surrender in September 1943 was a de facto acknowledgment that the war's outcome had been resolved. It was after that time, and specifically in the war's last year, that the greater part of German losses were incurred, primarily as a result of Allied air operations and military offensives that cleared Germany of its earlier conquests and carried the tide of war to the German heartland. The point applies to warships and the U-boat arm alike, one of the obvious—if seldom properly acknowledged—points being how few German warships were sunk by Allied warships; the U-boat losses were somewhat different, with Allied aircraft and warships more or less evenly balanced in terms of their contribution to German losses in the war's last two years. As always in such matters it was the combination of many things coming together that produced the overall result, and in the case of Germany's naval defeat these were many years in the making. Lack of numbers and balance and an absence of coherent planning and procurement in the period before, and then in, the first years of war, when Germany might indeed have secured victory at sea had it possessed the numbers that were available once the war had been lost, were major factors. But the basic point remains beyond dispute: the greater part of German naval losses came as a direct result of defeat.

German major naval units in service in the Second World War (with dates commissioned):

- the capital ships *Gneisenau* (21 May 1938) and *Scharnhorst* (7 January 1939), and the *Bismarck* (28 April 1940) and *Tirpitz* (21 February 1941);
- the armored ships *Deutschland* (1 April 1933), *Admiral Scheer* (12 November 1934), and *Admiral Graf Spee* (6 January 1936);
- the heavy cruisers *Admiral Hipper* (29 April 1939), *Blücher* (20 September 1939), and *Prinz Eugen* (1 August 1940);
- the light cruisers *Emden* (15 October 25), the *Karlsruhe* (20 August 1927), *Königsberg* (17 April 1929), and *Köln* (15 January 1930), and the *Leipzig* (8 October 1931) and *Nürnberg* (2 November 1935).

GERMAN U-BOAT LOSSES IN THE SECOND WORLD WAR

1939

14 September:	U. 39:	British destroyers *Faulknor, Firedrake*, and *Foxhound*: sea patrol: 58°32'North 11°49'West: off the Hebrides.
20 September:	U. 27:	British destroyers *Faulknor, Fearless, Forester*, and *Fortune*: sea patrol: 58°35'North 09°02'West: off the Hebrides.
8 October:	U. 12:	Mine laid by warship: Straits of Dover.
13 October:	U. 40:	Mine laid by warship: Straits of Dover.

13 October:	U. 42:	British destroyers *Ilex* and *Imogen:* sea escorts: 49°12'North 16°00'West: southwest of Ireland.
14 October:	U. 45:	British destroyers *Icarus, Inglefield, Intrepid,* and *Ivanhoe:* sea patrol: 50°58'North 12°07'West: off southern Ireland.
15 October:	U. 16:	Mine laid by warship: 51°09'North 01°28'East: in the Straits of Dover.
29 November:	U. 35:	British destroyers *Icarus, Kashmir,* and *Kingston:* sea escorts: 60°53'North 02°28'West: east of the Shetland Islands.
4 December:	U. 36:	British submarine *Salmon:* 57°00'North 05°10'East: in the Heligoland Bight.
1940		
30 January:	U. 55:	British destroyer *Whitshed* and sloop *Fowey* and French destroyer *Valmy,* and Sunderland of 228 Squadron RAF: sea escort and land-based air patrol: 48°37'North 07°10'East: west of the English Channel.
1 February:	U. 15:	Lost as a result of a collision with the torpedo-boat *Iltis* in the North Sea.
5 February:	U. 41:	British destroyer *Antelope:* sea escort: 49°21'North 10°04'West: off southern Ireland.
12 February:	U. 33:	British minesweeper *Gleaner:* sea patrol: 55°25'North 05°07' West: in the Clyde estuary.
22 February:	U. 54:	Unknown cause: in all probability mined in the North Sea.
23 February:	U. 53:	British destroyer *Gurkha:* on passage: 58°50'North 02°28'West: south of the Faeroe Islands.
25 February:	U. 63:	British destroyers *Escort, Imogen,* and *Inglefield:* sea escort: 58°40'North 00°10'West: in the North Sea east of Wick.
11 March:	U. 31:	Blenheim of 82 Squadron RAF: land-based air strike: in the Shillig Roads. The boat was raised and recommissioned into service.
20 March:	U. 44:	British destroyers *Faulknor, Firedrake,* and *Fortune:* 63°27'North 00°36'East: north of the Shetland Islands.
23 March:	U. 22:	Mine: in the Skagerrak.
8 April:	U. 1:	Mine: off Heligoland.
10 April:	U. 50:	British destroyer *Hero:* sea escort: 61°59'North 00°14'West: off the Shetland Islands.
13 April:	U. 64:	Walrus from the battleship *Warspite:* 68°29'North 17°30'East: at second battle of Narvik.
15 April:	U. 49:	British destroyers *Brazen* and *Fearless:* sea escort: 68°53'North 16°59'East: off Vaagsfjorden, beyond Narvik.
31 May:	U. 13:	British minesweeper *Weston:* sea escort: 52°27'North 02°02'East: off Lowestoft.
22 June:	U. 122:	Unknown cause: in the North Sea.
1 July:	U. 26:	British corvette *Gladiolus* and aircraft of 10 Squadron RAAF: sea- and land-based air escort: 48°03'North 11°30'West: southwest of Ireland.
1 July:	U. 102:	British destroyer *Vansittart:* sea escort: 48°33'North 10°26'West: southwest of Ireland.

3 August:	U. 25:	Mine laid by British warship: 54°00'North 05°00'East: northwest of Heligoland.
20 August:	U. 51:	British submarine *Cachelot:* 47°06'North 04°51'West: west of St. Nazaire.
3 September:	U. 57:	Lost as a result of a collision with the steamer *Rona:* at Brunsbüttel in the Elbe at the entrance to the Kiel canal.
30 October:	U. 32:	British destroyers *Harvester* and *Highlander:* sea escorts: 55°37'North 12°20'West: northwest of Malin Head.
2 November:	U. 31:	British destroyer *Antelope:* sea escort: 56°26'North 10°18'West: northwest of Malin Head.
c.27 November:	U. 104:	Lost to cause or causes unknown: south of Rockall.
1941		
7 March:	U. 70:	British corvettes *Arbutus* and *Camellia:* sea escort: 60°15'North 14°00'West: north of Rockall.
8 March:	U. 47:	British destroyer *Wolverine:* sea escort: 60°47'North 19°13'West: south of Iceland.
17 March:	U. 99:	British destroyers *Vanoc* and *Walker:* sea escort: 61°00'North 12°00'West: southwest of Faeroe Islands.
17 March:	U. 100:	British destroyer *Walker:* sea escort: 61°00'North 12°00'West: southwest of Faeroe Islands.
23 March:	U. 551:	British trawler *Visenda:* sea escort: 62°37'North 16°47'West: in the Iceland-Faeroes Gap.
5 April:	U. 76:	British destroyer *Wolverine* and sloop *Scarborough:* sea escort: 58°35'North 20°20'West: in the central North Atlantic.
28 April:	U. 65:	British corvette *Gladiolus:* sea escort: 60°04'North 15°45'West: north of Rockall.
9 May:	U. 110:	British escort destroyers *Aubrietia, Broadway,* and *Bulldog:* sea escort: 60°31'North 33°10'West: west of Cape Farewell, Greenland.
2 June:	U. 147:	British destroyer *Wanderer* and corvette *Periwinkle:* sea escort: 56°38'North 10°24'West: in the eastern North Atlantic.
18 June:	U. 138:	British destroyers *Faulknor, Fearless, Forester, Foresight,* and *Foxhound:* sea patrol: 36°04'North 07°09'West: west of Straits of Gibraltar.
27 June:	U. 556:	British corvettes *Celandine, Gladiolus,* and *Nastersium:* sea escort: 60°24'North 20°00'West: south of Iceland.
29 June:	U. 651:	British destroyers *Malcolm* and *Scimitar,* corvettes *Arabis* and *Violet,* and minesweeper *Speedwell:* sea escort: 59°52'North 18°36'West: northwest of Rockall.
28 July:	U. 144:	Soviet submarine *Shch-307:* presumably in the Gulf of Finland.
3 August:	U. 401:	British destroyers *St. Albans* and *Wanderer* and corvette *Hydrangea:* sea escorts: 59°27'North 19°50'West: northwest of Rockall.
25 August:	U. 452:	British trawler *Vascama* and Catalina of 209 Squadron RAF: sea escort and land-based air patrol: 61°30'North 15°30'West: south of Iceland.

27 August: U. 570: Surrendered after attack by Hudson of 269 Squadron RAF and captured by a combination of destroyers and trawlers: 62°15'North 18°35'West: south of Iceland.

10 September: U. 501: Canadian corvettes *Chambly* and *Moosejaw:* sea escort: 62°50'North 37°50'West: off southeast Greenland.

11 September: U. 207: British destroyers *Leamington* and *Veteran:* sea escort; 63°59'North 34°48'West: in the western Denmark Strait.

4 October: U. 111: British trawler *Lady Shirley:* sea escort: 27°15'North 20°27'West: off Madeira.

19 October: U. 204: British sloop *Rochester* and corvette *Mallow:* sea patrol: 35°46'North 06°02'West: west of the Straits of Gibraltar.

11 November: U. 580: Lost as a result of a collision with the freighter *Angelburg* in the Baltic.

15 November: U. 583: Lost as a result of a collision with U. 153 off Danzig.

16 November: U. 433: British corvette *Marigold:* on passage: 36°13'North 04°42'West: east of Gibraltar.

28 November: U. 95: Dutch submarine *O.21:* 36°24'North 03°20'West: southeast of Malaga.

30 November: U. 206: Whitley of 502 Squadron RAF: land-based (Bay of Biscay) air patrol: 46°55'North 07°16'West: southwest of Brest.

11 December: U. 208: British corvette *Bluebell:* sea escort: 36°40'North 09°20'West: south of Cape St. Vincent.

15 December: U. 127: Australian destroyer *Nestor:* sea patrol: 36°28'North 09°12'West: south of Cape St. Vincent.

16 December: U. 557: Lost as a result of a collision with the Italian torpedo boat *Orione:* 35°33'North 23°14'East: off northwest Crete.

17 December: U. 131: Scuttled after being damaged by gunfire from escort destroyers *Blankney, Exmoor,* and *Stanley,* sloop *Stork,* and corvette *Penstemon* from convoy screen after being attacked by Martlet from escort carrier *Audacity:* carrier air and sea escort: 34°12'North 13°35'West: northwest of Madeira.

18 December: U. 434: British escort destroyers *Blankney* and *Stanley:* sea escort: 36°15'North 15°48'West: northeast of Madeira.

19 December: U. 574: British sloop *Stork:* sea escort: 38°12'North 17°23'West: north of the Azores.

21 December: U. 451: Swordfish of 812 Squadron FAA: land-based air patrol: 35°55'North 06°08'West: west of the Straits of Gibraltar.

21 December: U. 567: British sloop *Deptford* and Canadian corvette *Sampshire*: sea escort: 44°02'North 20°10'West: in the eastern North Atlantic.

23 December: U. 79: British destroyers *Hasty* and *Hotspur:* sea escort: 32°15'North 25°19'East: northeast of Sidi Barrani.

28 December: U. 75: British destroyer *Kipling:* sea escort: 31°30'North 26°40'East: northwest of Sidi Barrani.

1942

9 January: U. 577: Sunderland of 230 Squadron RAF: land-based air patrol: 32°22'North 26°54'East: northeast of Sidi Barrani.

12 January: U. 374: British submarine *Unbeaten:* 37°50'North 16°00'East: south of Cape Spartivento, toe of Italy.
15 January: U. 93: British destroyer *Hesperus:* sea escort: 36°40'North 15°52'West: north of Madeira.
2 February: U. 581: British destroyer *Westcott:* sea escort: 39°00'North 30°00'West: in the central North Atlantic.
6 February: U. 82: British sloop *Rochester* and sloop *Tamarisk:* sea escort: 44°10'North 23°52'West: in the eastern North Atlantic.
1 March: U. 656: Hudson of VP-82 USN: land-based air escort: 46°15'North 53°15'West: off Newfoundland.
14 March: U. 133: Accidental detonation of own mine: 38°00'North 24°00'East: in the central Aegean.
15 March: U. 503: Hudson of VP-82 USN: land-based air escort: 45°40'North 48°50'West: southeast of Newfoundland.
24 March: U. 655: British minesweeper *Sharpshooter:* sea escort: 73°00'North 21°00'East: west of Novaya Zemlya.
27 March: U. 587: British destroyers *Aldenham, Grove, Leamington,* and *Volunteer:* sea escort: 47°41'North 21°39'West: in the eastern North Atlantic.
29 March: U. 585: Lost in a German minefield in the Arctic.
14 April: U. 85: U.S. destroyer *Roper:* on passage: 35°55'North 75°13'West: off Cape Hatteras, North Carolina.
14 April: U. 252: British sloop *Stork* and corvette *Vetch:* sea escort: 47°00'North 18°14'West: in the eastern North Atlantic.
-- April: U. 702: Unknown cause: probably lost in Iceland-Faeroes Gap.
1 May: U. 573: Hudson of 233 Squadron RAF: land-based air patrol: 37°00'North 01°00'East: north of Cape Ténès, western Algeria. The U. 573 was so badly damaged in the course of this attack that it was forced into Cartagena, where it was paid off and sold to Spain.
2 May: U. 74: British destroyers *Wishart* and *Wrestler* and Catalina of 202 Squadron RAF: sea- and land-based air patrol: 37°32'North 00°10'East: southeast of Cartagena, Spain.
9 May: U. 352: Grounded and subjected to attack by U.S.C.G. cutter *Icarus,* surfaced and scuttled: marine cause and sea patrol: 34°12'North 76°35'West: south of Cape Hatteras, North Carolina.
28 May: U. 568: British destroyers *Eridge, Hero,* and *Hurworth:* sea patrol: 32°42'North 24°53'East: off Sollum, Egypt.
2 June: U. 652: Blenheim of 203 Squadron RAF and Swordfish of 815 Squadron FAA, and scuttled on the 2nd: land-based air patrol: 31°55'North 25°13'East: Off Sollum, Egypt.
13 June: U. 157: U.S.C.G. cutter *Thetis:* sea patrol: 24°13'North 82°03'West: off Key West, Florida.
30 June: U. 158: Mariner of VP-74 USN: land-based air escort: 32°50'North 67°02'West: off Bermuda.
3 July: U. 215: Free French *Le Tigre:* sea escort: 41°48'North 66°38'West: east of Nantucket Island, Massachusetts.

5 July: U. 502: Wellington of 172 Squadron RAF: land-based (Bay of Biscay) air patrol: 46°10'North 06°40'West: west of La Rochelle.

7 July: U. 701: Hudson of 396 Bombardment Squadron USAAF: land-based air patrol: 34°50'North 74°55'West: off Cape Hatteras, North Carolina.

11 July: U. 136: British frigate *Spey* and sloop *Pelican* and Free French destroyer *Leopard:* sea escort: 33°30'North 22°52'West: northwest of the Azores.

13 July: U. 153: U.S. destroyer *Lansdowne:* sea patrol: 09°56'North 81°29'West: off the Panama Canal.

15 July: U. 576: Aircraft of VS-9 USN and American freighter *Unicoi:* land-based air escort and escorted merchantman: 34°51'North 75°22'West: south of Cape Hatteras, North Carolina.

17 July: U. 751: Lancaster of 61 Squadron and Whitley of 502 Squadron RAF: land-based (Bay of Biscay) air patrol: 45°14'North 12°22'West: west of the Gironde estuary.

24 July: U. 90: Canadian destroyer *St. Croix:* sea escort: 48°12'North 40°56'West: in the central North Atlantic.

31 July: U. 213: British sloops *Erne, Rochester,* and *Sandwich:* sea escort: 36°45'North 22°50'West: northwest of the Azores.

31 July: U. 588: Canadian destroyers *Skeena* and *Wetaskiwin:* sea escort: 49°59'North 36°36'West: in the central North Atlantic.

31 July: U. 754: Hudson of 113 Squadron RCAF: land-based air patrol: 43°02'North 64°52'West: off southwest Nova Scotia.

1 August: U. 166: J4F Widgeon of 212 Squadron U.S.C.G.: land-based air escort: 28°37'North 90°45'West: off the Mississippi estuary.

3 August: U. 335: British submarine *Saracen:* 62°48'North 00°12'West: off the Shetlands.

4 August: U. 372: British destroyers *Croome, Sikh, Tetcott,* and *Zulu* and Wellington of 203 Squadron RAF: sea- and land-based air patrol: 32°00'North 34°00'East: west of Haifa, Palestine.

6 August: U. 612: Lost as a result of a collision with U. 444 in the Baltic.

6 August: U. 210: Canadian destroyer *Assiniboine:* sea escort: 54°25'North 39°37'West: in the central North Atlantic.

8 August: U. 379: British corvette *Dianthus:* sea escort: 57°11'North 30°57'West: in the central North Atlantic.

10 August: U. 578: Wellington of 311 (Czech) Squadron RAF: land-based (Bay of Biscay) air patrol: 45°59'North 07°44'West: west of Rochefort.

20 August: U. 464: Catalina of VP-73 USN: land-based air escort: 61°25'North 14°40'West: southeast of Iceland.

22 August: U. 654: Aircraft of 45 Bombardment Squadron USAAF: land-based air patrol: 12°00'North 78°56'West: off the Panama Canal.

27 August: U. 94: Canadian corvette *Oakville* and Catalina of VP-92 USN: sea- and land-based air escort: 17°40'North 74°30'West: in the Windward Passage.

1 September: U. 756: Canadian corvette *Morden:* 57°41'North 31°30'West: in the central North Atlantic.

2 September:	U. 222:	Lost as a result of a collision with U. 626: 54°25'North 19°50'East: in the Gulf of Danzig.
3 September:	U. 162:	British destroyers *Pathfinder*, *Quentin*, and *Vimy:* sea escorts: 12°21'North 59°29'West: off Barbados.
3 September:	U. 705:	Whitley of 77 Squadron RAF: land-based (Bay of Biscay) air patrol: in the Bay of Biscay.
9 September:	U. 446:	Mine: off Danzig.
12 September:	U. 88:	British destroyer *Onslow:* sea escort: 75°04'North 04°49'East: southwest of Spitzbergen.
14 September:	U. 589:	British destroyer *Faulknor:* sea escort: 70°40'North 20°32'East: off Bear Island in the Arctic Ocean.
15 September:	U. 261:	Whitley of 58 Squadron RAF: land-based air patrol: 59°49'North 09°28'West: northwest of Butt of Lewis.
16 September:	U. 457:	British destroyer *Impulsive:* sea escort: 75°05'North 43°15'East: off Novaya Zemlya in the Arctic.
23 September:	U. 253:	Mine: 67°00'North 23°00'East: off southwest Iceland.
27 September:	U. 165:	Unknown cause, possibly a mine: off Belle-Ile in the Bay of Biscay.
2 October:	U. 512:	B-18A Bolo of 99 Bombardment Squadron USAAF: land-based air patrol: 06°50'North 52°25'West: north of Cayenne, French Guiana.
5 October:	U. 582:	Catalina of VP-73 USN: land-based air escort: 58°41'North 22°58'West: south of Iceland.
8 October:	U. 179:	British destroyer *Active:* sea escort: 33°28'South 17°05'East: off Cape Town.
9 October:	U. 171:	Mine: 47°30'North 03°30'West: off Lorient.
12 October:	U. 597:	Liberator of 120 Squadron RAF: land-based air escort: 56°50'North 28°05'West: in the central North Atlantic.
15 October:	U. 619:	Hudson of 269 Squadron RAF: land-based air escort: 53°42'North 35°56'West: in the central North Atlantic.
15 October:	U. 661:	British destroyer *Viscount:* sea escort: 53°58'North 33°43'West: in the central North Atlantic.
16 October:	U. 353:	British destroyer *Fame:* sea escort: 53°54'North 29°30'West: in the central North Atlantic.
20 October:	U. 216:	Liberator of 224 Squadron RAF: land-based (Bay of Biscay) air patrol: 48°21'North 19°25'West: in the eastern North Atlantic.
22 October:	U. 412:	Wellington of 179 Squadron RAF: land-based air patrol: 63°55'North 00°24'East: north of the Shetland Islands.
24 October:	U. 599:	Liberator of 224 Squadron RAF: land-based (Bay of Biscay) air patrol: 46°07'North 17°40'West: northwest of Cape Finisterre.
27 October:	U. 627:	Fortress of 206 Squadron RAF: land-based air escort: 59°14'North 22°49'West: south of Iceland.
30 October:	U. 520:	B-18A Digby of 10 Squadron RCAF: land-based air escort: 47°47'North 49°50'West: in the central North Atlantic.
30 October:	U. 559:	British destroyers *Dulverton*, *Hero*, *Hurworth*, *Pakenham*, and *Petard* and Wellesley of 47 Squadron RAF: sea- and

		land-based air patrol: 32°30'North 33°00'West: south of Cyprus.
30 October:	U. 658:	Hudson of 145 Squadron RCAF: land-based air escort: 50°32'North 46°32'West: southeast of St. John's, Newfoundland.
-- October:	U. 116:	Unknown cause: in the North Atlantic.
5 November:	U. 132:	Destroyed by force of explosion of the ammunition ship *Hatimura* which it had torpedoed: 55°38'North 39°52'West: southeast of Cape Farewell, southern Greenland.
5 November:	U. 408:	Catalina of VP-84 USN: land-based air patrol: 67°40'North 18°32'West: in the eastern Denmark Strait.
12 November:	U. 272:	Lost as a result of a collision: off Hela in the Baltic.
12 November:	U. 660:	British corvettes *Lotus* and *Starwort:* sea escort: 36°07'North 01°00'West: off Oran.
13 November:	U. 411:	Hudson of 500 Squadron RAF: land-based air patrol: 36°00'North 09°35'West: southwest of Straits of Gibraltar.
14 November:	U. 595:	Hudsons of 500 and 608 Squadrons RAF: land-based air patrol: beached 36°38'North 00°30'East: west of Cape Ténès, western Algeria.
14 November:	U. 605:	Hudson of 233 Squadron RAF: air escort: 36°20'North 01°01'West: north of Algiers.
15 November:	U. 259:	Hudson of 500 Squadron RAF: land-based air patrol: 37°20'North 03°05'East: north of Algiers.
16 November:	U. 173:	U.S. destroyers *Quick, Swanson,* and *Woolsey:* sea escort: 34°40'North 07°35'West: off Rabat, Morocco.
17 November:	U. 331:	Albacore of 820 Squadron from fleet carrier *Formidable* and Hudsons of 500 Squadron RAF: carrier air and land-based air patrol: 37°00'North 02°24'East: northeast of Algiers.
19 November:	U. 98:	Hudson of 608 Squadron RAF: land-based air escort: 35°38'North 11°48'West: southwest of Cape St. Vincent.
20 November:	U. 184:	Norwegian corvette *Potentilla:* sea escort: 49°25'North 45°25'West: in the central North Atlantic.
21 November:	U. 517:	Albacore of 817 Squadron from British fleet carrier *Victorious:* carrier air patrol: 46°16'North 17°09'West: in the eastern North Atlantic.
8 December:	U. 254:	Lost as a result of collision with U. 221 in the North Atlantic.
10 December:	U. 611:	Liberator of 120 Squadron RAF: land-based air escort: 57°25'North 35°19'West: southeast of Cape Farewell, southern Greenland.
15 December:	U. 626:	U.S.C.G. cutter *Ingham:* sea escort: 56°46'North 27°12'West: in the central North Atlantic.
26 December:	U. 357:	British destroyers *Hesperus* and *Vanessa:* sea escorts: 57°10'North 15°40'West: southwest of Rockall.
27 December:	U. 356:	Canadian destroyer *St. Laurent* and corvettes *Battleford, Chilliwack,* and *Napanee:* sea escort: 45°30'North 25°40'West: in the central North Atlantic.

1943

6 January: U. 164: Catalina of VP-83 USN: land-based air escort: 01°58'South 39°23'West: off Ceara, northeast Brazil.

13 January: U. 224: Canadian corvette *Ville de Quebec:* sea escort: 36°28'North 00°49'East: off Cape Ténès, western Algeria.

13 January: U. 507: Catalina of VP-83 USN: land-based air escort: 01°38'South 39°52'West: off Ceara, northeast Brazil.

15 January: U. 337: Fortress of 206 Squadron RAF: land-based air escort: 57°40'North 27°10'West: in the central North Atlantic.

21 January: U. 301: British submarine *Sahib:* 41°27'North 07°04'East: west of Corsica.

-- January: U. 553: Unknown cause: in the North Atlantic.

3 February: U. 265: Fortress of 220 Squadron RAF: land-based air escort: 56°35'North 22°49'West: in the eastern North Atlantic.

3 February: U. 187: British destroyer *Vimy* and escort destroyer *Beverley:* sea escort: 50°12'North 36°34'West: in the central North Atlantic.

7 February: U. 609: Free French corvette *Lobelia:* sea escort: 55°17'North 26°38'West: in the central North Atlantic.

7 February: U. 624: Fortress of 220 Squadron RAF: sea escort and/or land-based air escort: 55°42'North 26°17'West: in the central North Atlantic.

10 February: U. 519: Liberator of 2 Anti-submarine Squadron USAAF: land-based (Bay of Biscay) air patrol: 47°05'North 18°34'West: in the eastern North Atlantic.

12 February: U. 442: Hudson of 48 Squadron RAF: land-based air escort: 37°32'North 11°56'West: southwest of Cape St. Vincent.

14 February: U. 620: Catalina of 202 Squadron RAF: land-based air escort: 39°27'North 11°34'West: west of Lisbon.

15 February: U. 529: Cause of loss unknown and given as east of Newfoundland but possibly Liberator of 120 Squadron RAF: land-based air escort: 55°45'North 31°09'West: in the central North Atlantic.

17 February: U. 69: British destroyer *Fame:* sea escort: 50°36'North 41°07'West: in the central North Atlantic.

17 February: U. 201: British destroyer *Viscount:* sea escort: 50°50'North 40°50'West: in the central North Atlantic.

17 February: U. 205: British destroyer *Paladin* and Bisley of 15 SAAF: sea- and land-based air escort: 32°56'North 22°01'West: northwest of Derna, Libya.

19 February: U. 562: British destroyers *Hursley* and *Isis* and Wellington of 38 Squadron RAF: sea- and land-based air escort: 32°57'North 20°54'West: northeast of Benghazi, Libya.

19 February: U. 268: Wellington from 172 Squadron RAF: land-based (Bay of Biscay) air patrol: 47°03'North 05°56'West: west of St. Nazaire.

21 February: U. 623: Liberator of 120 Squadron RAF: land-based air escort: 47°00'North 33°00'West: in the central North Atlantic.

21 February: U. 225: Liberator of 120 Squadron RAF: land-based air escort: 51°25'North 27°28'West: in the central North Atlantic.

22 February: U. 606: Polish destroyer *Burza*, British corvette *Chilliwack* and U.S.C.G. cutter *Campbell:* sea escort: 47°44'North 33°43'West: in the central North Atlantic.
23 February: U. 443: British escort destroyers *Bicester, Lamerton,* and *Wheatland:* sea patrol: 36°55'North 02°25'East: off Algiers.
23 February: U. 522: British sloop *Totland:* sea escort: 31°27'North 26°22'West: west of the Azores.
24 February: U. 649: Lost as a result of a collision with U. 232 in the Gulf of Danzig.
4 March: U. 83: Hudson of 500 Squadron RAF: land-based air patrol: 37°10'North 00°05'East: southeast of Cartagena, Spain.
4 March: U. 87: Canadian destroyer *St. Croix* and corvette *Shediac:* sea escort: 41°36'North 13°31'West: west of Porto.
7 March: U. 633: Fortress of 220 Squadron RAF: land-based air escort: 57°14'North 26°30'West: south of Iceland.
8 March: U. 156: Catalina of VP-53 USN: land-based air patrol: 12°38'North 54°39'West: east of Barbados.
11 March: U. 432: British corvette *Aconite:* sea escort: 51°35'North 28°20'West: in the central North Atlantic.
11 March: U. 444: British destroyer *Harvester* and corvette *Aconite:* sea escort: 51°14'North 29°18'West: in the central North Atlantic.
12 March: U. 130: U.S. destroyer *Champlin:* sea escort: 37°10'North 40°21'West: in the central North Atlantic.
19 March: U. 5: Lost as a result of a diving accident: 54°25'North 19°50'East: off Pillau in the Baltic.
20 March: U. 384: Fortress of 206 Squadron RAF: land-based air escort: 54°18'North 26°15'West: in the central North Atlantic.
22 March: U. 524: Liberator of 1 Anti-submarine Squadron USAAF: land-based air patrol: 30°15'North 18°13'West: off the Canaries.
22 March: U. 665: Wellington of 172 Squadron RAF: land-based (Bay of Biscay) air patrol: 46°47'North 09°58'West: southwest of Brest.
25 March: U. 469: Fortress of 206 Squadron RAF: land-based air escort: 62°12'North 16°40'West: south of Iceland.
27 March: U. 169: Fortress of 206 Squadron RAF: land-based air patrol: 60°54'North 15°25'West: northwest of Rockall.
28 March: U. 77: Hudsons of 48 and 233 Squadrons RAF: land-based air patrol: 37°42'North 00°10'East: between Capes Palos and Ténès.
30 March: U. 416: Mine laid by Soviet submarine *L-3:* in the Baltic. Raised, re-commissioned, and sunk a second time in December 1944.
-- March: U. 163: Unknown cause: in the Bay of Biscay.
2 April: U. 124: British sloop *Black Swan* and corvette *Stonecrop:* sea escort: 41°02'North 15°39'West: west of Porto.
5 April: U. 167: Scuttled on the 6th after attack by Hudsons of 233 Squadron RAF: land-based air escort: 27°47'North 15°00'West: off the Canaries.
5 April: U. 635: Liberator of 120 Squadron RAF: land-based air escort: 58°20'North 31°52'West: in the central North Atlantic.

6 April: U. 632: Liberator of 86 Squadron RAF: land-based air escort: 58°02'North 28°42'West: in the central North Atlantic.
7 April: U. 644: British submarine *Tuna:* 69°38'North 05°40'West: southeast of Jan Mayen Island in the Arctic Ocean.
10 April: U. 376: Wellington of 172 Squadron RAF: land-based (Bay of Biscay) air patrol: 46°48'North 09°00'West: southwest of Brest.
14 April: U. 526: Mine: 47°30'North 03°45'West: off Belle-Ile, in the Bay of Biscay.
17 April: U. 175: U.S.C.G. cutter *Spencer:* sea escort: 48°50'North 21°20'West: in the eastern North Atlantic.
23 April: U. 602: Unknown cause: off Algiers.
23 April: U. 189: Liberator of 120 Squadron RAF: land-based air escort: 59°51'North 34°43'West: in the central North Atlantic.
23 April: U. 191: British destroyer *Hesperus:* sea escort: 56°45'North 34°25'West: in the central North Atlantic.
24 April: U. 710: Fortress of 206 Squadron RAF: land-based air escort: 61°25'North 19°48'West: south of Iceland.
25 April: U. 203: British destroyer *Pathfinder:* sea escort: 55°05'North 42°25'West: in the central North Atlantic.
27 April: U. 174: Ventura of VP-125 USN: land-based air escort: 43°45'North 56°18'West: southeast of Canso, Nova Scotia.
29 April: U. 332: Liberator of 224 Squadron RCAF: land-based (Bay of Biscay) air patrol: 45°08'North 09°33'West: west of Bordeaux.
30 April: U. 227: Hampden of 455 Squadron RAF: land-based air patrol: 64°05'North 06°40'West: north of the Faeroe Islands.
2 May: U. 465: Sunderland of 461 Squadron RAF: land-based (Bay of Biscay) air patrol: 44°48'North 08°58'West: west of Bordeaux.
4 May: U. 439: Lost as a result of a collision with U. 659: 43°32'North 13°20'West: west of Vigo, northwest Spain.
4 May: U. 659: Lost as a result of a collision with U. 439: 43°32'North 13°20'West: west of Vigo, northwest Spain.
4 May: U. 630: Canso of 5 Squadron RCAF: air patrol: 56°38'North 42°32'West: southeast of Cape Farewell, Greenland.
5 May: U. 192: British corvette *Pink:* sea escort: 54°56'North 43°44'West: in the central North Atlantic.
5 May: U. 638: British corvette *Loosestrife:* sea escort: 53°06'North 45°02'West: in the central North Atlantic.
6 May: U. 125: Sunk as a result of being rammed by British destroyer *Oribi* and gunfire from corvette *Snowflake:* sea escort: 52°13'North 44°50'West: in the central North Atlantic.
6 May: U. 438: British sloop *Pelican:* sea escort: 52°00'North 45°10'West: in the central North Atlantic.
6 May: U. 531: British destroyer *Vidette:* sea escort: 52°31'North 44°50'West: in the central North Atlantic.
7 May: U. 109: Liberator of 86 Squadron RAF: land-based air escort: 47°22'North 22°40'West: northwest of Cape Ortegal.
7 May: U. 447: Hudsons of 233 Squadron RAF: land-based air patrol: 35°50'North 11°55'West: south of the Gettysburg Bank.

7 May: U. 663: Halifax of 58 Squadron RAF: land-based (Bay of Biscay) air patrol: 46°33'North 11°12'West: southwest of Brest.

11 May: U. 528: British sloop *Fleetwood* and corvette *Mignonette* and Halifax of 58 Squadron RAF: sea- and land-based air escort: 46°55'North 14°44'West: in the eastern North Atlantic.

12 May: U. 89: Aircraft of 811 Squadron FAA from the British escort carrier *Biter* and escort destroyer *Broadway,* and frigate *Lagan:* carrier air and sea escort: 46°30'North 25°40'West: in the central North Atlantic.

12 May: U. 186: British destroyer *Hesperus:* sea escort: 41°54'North 31°49'West: in the central North Atlantic.

13 May: U. 456: Liberator of 86 Squadron RAF: land-based air escort: 46°40'North 26°20'West: in the eastern North Atlantic.

14 May: U. 657: Catalina of VP-84 USN: land-based air escort: 60°10'North 31°52'West: in the central North Atlantic.

15 May: U. 266: Halifax of 58 Squadron RAF: land-based air escort: 47°28'North 10°20'West: in the central North Atlantic.

15 May: U. 753: British frigate *Lagan* and Canadian corvette *Drumheller* and Sunderland of 423 Squadron RCAF: sea- and land-based air escort: 48°37'North 22°39'West: in the eastern North Atlantic.

15 May: U. 463: Halifax of 58 Squadron RAF: land-based (Bay of Biscay) air patrol: 45°28'North 10°20'West: west of the Gironde estuary.

15 May: U. 176: Cuban chaser C.S.13 and aircraft from VP-62 USN: sea- and land-based air escort: 23°21'North 80°18'West: in the Florida Strait.

16 May: U. 128: Scuttled itself on the approach of warships after damaged in attack by Mariners of VP-72 USN: land-based air escort: 10°00'South 35°35'West: east of Recife, northeast Brazil.

16 May: U. 182: U.S. destroyer *Mackenzie:* sea escort: 33°55'North 20°35'West: northwest of the Azores.

17 May: U. 640: British frigate *Swale:* sea escort: 58°54'North 42°33'West: in the central North Atlantic.

17 May: U. 646: Hudson of 269 Squadron RAF: land-based air patrol: 62°10'North 14°30'West: south of Iceland.

19 May: U. 209: British frigate *Jed* and sloop *Sennen:* sea escort: 54°54'North 34°19'West: in the central North Atlantic.

19 May: U. 273: Hudson of 269 Squadron RAF: land-based air escort: 59°25'North 24°33'West: south of Iceland.

19 May: U. 381: British destroyer *Duncan* and corvette *Snowflake:* sea escort: 54°41'North 34°45'West: in the central North Atlantic.

19 May: U. 954: British frigate *Jed* and sloop *Sennen:* sea escort: in the central North Atlantic.

20 May: U. 258: Liberator of 120 Squadron RAF: land-based air escort: 55°18'North 27°49'West: in the central North Atlantic.

21 May: U. 303: British submarine *Sickle:* 43°10'North 05°55'East: off Toulon.

22 May: U. 569: Avengers of VC-9 from the U.S. escort carrier *Bogue*: carrier air escort: 50°40'North 35°21'West: in the central North Atlantic.
23 May: U. 752: Swordfish of 819 Squadron FAA from the British escort carrier *Archer*: carrier air escort: 51°40'North 29°49'West: in the central North Atlantic.
25 May: U. 414: British corvette *Vetch:* sea escort: 36°31'North 00°40'East: east of Cape Caxine, western Algeria.
25 May: U. 467: Catalina of VP-84 USN: land-based air escort: 62°25'North 14°52'West: east of the Faeroe Islands.
26 May: U. 436: British frigate *Test* and Indian corvette *Hyderabad:* sea escort: 43°49'North 15°56'West: west of Cape Finisterre.
28 May: U. 304: Liberator of 120 Squadron RAF: land-based air escort: 54°50'North 37°20'West: in the central North Atlantic.
28 May: U. 755: Hudson of 608 Squadron RAF: land-based air patrol: 39°58'North 01°41'West: off Algiers.
31 May: U. 440: Sunderland of 201 Squadron RAF: land-based (Bay of Biscay) air patrol: 45°38'North 13°04'West: west of the Gironde estuary.
31 May: U. 563: Halifax of 58 Squadron and Sunderlands of 228 Squadron RAF and 10 Squadron RAAF: land-based air patrol: 46°35'North 10°40'West: southwest of Brest.
1 June: U. 202: British sloop *Starling:* sea escort: 56°12'North 39°52'West: in the central North Atlantic.
1 June: U. 418: Beaufighter of 236 Squadron RAF: land-based (Bay of Biscay) air patrol: 47°05'North 08°55'West: southwest of Brest.
2 June: U. 105: Potez flying boat of 141 Squadron French Air Force: land-based air escort: 14°15'North 17°35'West: off Dakar.
2 June: U. 521: U.S. chaser *PC565*: sea escort: 37°43'North 73°16'West: east of Chesapeake Bay.
4 June: U. 308: British submarine *Truculent:* 64°28'North 03°09'West: off the Faeroe Islands.
4 June: U. 594: Hudson of 48 Squadron RAF: land-based air patrol: 35°55'North 09°25'West: southwest of Cape St. Vincent.
5 June: U. 217: Avenger and Wildcat of VC-9 from the U.S. escort carrier *Bogue:* carrier air escort: 30°18'North 42°50'West in the central North Atlantic.
11 June: U. 417: Fortress of 48 Squadron RAF: land-based air patrol: 63°20'North 10°30'West: in the Iceland-Faeroes Gap.
12 June: U. 118: Avenger and Wildcats of VC-9 from the U.S. escort carrier *Bogue:* carrier air escort: 30°49'North 33°49'West: southwest of the Azores.
14 June: U. 334: British frigate *Jed* and sloop *Pelican:* sea escort: 58°16'North 28°20'West: southwest of Iceland.
14 June: U. 564: Whitney of 10 OTU RAF: land-based (Bay of Biscay) air patrol: 44°17'North 10°25'West: northwest of La Coruña.
16 June: U. 97: Hudson of 459 Squadron RAAF: land-based air patrol: 33°00'North 34°00'East: west of Haifa, Palestine.

20 June: U. 388: Catalina of VP-84 USN: land-based air escort: 57°36'North 31°20'West: southwest of Iceland.
24 June: U. 119: British sloop *Starling:* sea patrol: 45°00'North 11°59'West: northwest of La Coruña.
24 June: U. 194: Liberator of 120 Squadron RAF: land-based air escort: 58°15'North 25°25'West: south of Iceland.
24 June: U. 200: Catalina of VP-84 USN: land-based air escort: 59°00'North 26°18'West: south of Iceland.
24 June: U. 449: British sloops *Kite, Wild Goose, Woodpecker,* and *Wren:* sea patrol: 45°11'North 11°59'West: northwest of Cape Ortegal.
3 July: U. 126: Wellington of 172 Squadron RAF: land-based (Bay of Biscay) air patrol: 46°02'North 11°23'West: northwest of La Coruna.
3 July: U. 628: Liberator of 224 Squadron RAF: land-based (Bay of Biscay) air patrol: 44°11'North 08°45'West: north of Cape Ortegal.
5 July: U. 535: Liberator of 53 Squadron RAF: land-based (Bay of Biscay) air patrol: 43°38'North 09°13'West: off La Coruna.
7 July: U. 951: Liberator of 1 Anti-submarine Squadron USAAF: land-based air patrol: 37°40'North 15°30'West: north of Madeira.
8 July: U. 232: Liberator of 2 Anti-submarine Squadron USAAF: land-based air patrol: 40°37'North 13°41'West: northeast of the Azores.
8 July: U. 514: Liberator of 224 Squadron RAF: land-based (Bay of Biscay) air patrol: 43°37'North 08°59'West: off Cape Ortegal.
9 July: U. 435: Wellington of 179 Squadron RAF: land-based air patrol: 39°48'North 14°22'West: northeast of the Azores.
9 July: U. 590: Catalina of VP-94 USN: land-based air escort: 03°22'North 48°38'West: off the Amazon estuary.
12 July: U. 409: British destroyer *Inconstant:* sea escort: 37°12'North 04°00'East: north of Cape Tedlès, central Algeria.
12 July: U. 506: Liberator of 1 Anti-submarine Squadron USAAF: land-based (Bay of Biscay) air patrol: 42°30'North 16°30'West: in the eastern North Atlantic.
12 July: U. 561: British motor torpedo boat *MTB81:* sea patrol: 38°16'North 15°39'East: in the Strait of Messina.
13 July: U. 487: Avengers and Wildcats of VC-13 from U.S. escort carrier *Core:* carrier air escort: 27°15'North 34°18'West: west of the Canaries.
13 July: U. 607: Sunderland of 228 Squadron RAF: land-based (Bay of Biscay) air patrol: 45°02'North 09°14'West: west of Bordeaux.
14 July: U. 160: Avengers of VC-29 from U.S. escort carrier *Santee:* carrier air escort: 33°54'North 27°13'West: south of the Azores.
15 July: U. 135: British sloop *Rochester* and corvettes *Balsam* and *Mignonette:* sea escort: 28°20'North 13°17'West: off the eastern Canaries.
15 July: U. 159: Mariner of VP-32 USN: land-based air escort: 15°58'North 73°44'West: off the Windward Passage.
15 July: U. 509: Avengers of VC-29 from U.S. escort carrier *Santee:* carrier air escort:34°02'North 26°02'West: south of the Azores.

16 July: U. 67: Avengers of VC-13 from U.S. escort carrier *Core:* carrier air escort: 30°05'North 44°17'West: in the central North Atlantic.

19 July: U. 513: Mariner of VP-74 USN: land-based air escort: 27°17'South 47°32'West: east of Santa Catarina Island, southern Brazil.

20 July: U. 558: Liberator of 19 Squadron USAAF: land-based (Bay of Biscay) air patrol: 45°10'North 09°42'West: west of the Gironde estuary.

21 July: U. 662: Mariner of VP-94 USN: land-based air escort: 03°56'North 48°46'West: off the Amazon estuary.

23 July: U. 527: Avenger of VC-9 from the U.S. escort carrier *Bogue*: carrier air escort: 35°25'North 27°56'West: south of the Azores.

23 July: U. 598: Liberator of VP-107 USN: land-based air patrol: 04°05'South 33°23'West: northeast of Natal, Brazil.

23 July: U. 613: U.S. destroyer *Badger:* sea escort from escort carrier group: 35°32'North 28°36'West: south of the Azores.

24 July: U. 459: Wellingtons of 172 and 547 Squadrons RAF: land-based (Bay of Biscay) air patrol: 45°53'North 10°38'West: west of the Gironde estuary.

24 July: U. 622: Fortresses of the 8th Air Force: USAAF strategic bombing raid: 63°27'North 10°23'West: at Trondheim.

26 July: U. 759: Mariner of VP-32 USN: land-based air patrol: 18°06'North 75°00'West: off the Windward Passage.

28 July: U. 359: Mariner of VP-32 USN: land-based air patrol: 15°57'North 68°30'West: south of Mona Passage, Caribbean.

28 July: U. 404: Liberators of 224 Squadron RAF and 4 Squadron USAAF: land-based (Bay of Biscay) air patrol: 45°53'North 09°25'West: west of the Gironde estuary.

29 July: U. 614: Wellington of 172 Squadron RAF: land-based (Bay of Biscay) air patrol: 46°42'North 11°03'West: west of Ile d'Yeu.

30 July: U. 43: Avenger of VC-29 from U.S. escort carrier *Santee*: carrier air escort: 34°57'North 35°11'West: southwest of the Azores.

30 July: U. 375: U.S. chaser *PC624*: sea patrol: 36°40'North 12°28'East: southeast of Pantelleria.

30 July: U. 461: Sunderland of 461 Squadron RAF: land-based (Bay of Biscay) air patrol: 45°42'North 11°00'West: west of the Gironde estuary.

30 July: U. 462: Halifax of 502 Squadron RAF: land-based (Bay of Biscay) air patrol: 45°08'North 10°57'West: west of the Gironde estuary.

30 July: U. 504: British sloops *Kite, Wild Goose, Woodpecker,* and *Wren:* sea patrol: 45°33'North 10°47'West: west of the Gironde estuary.

30 July: U. 591: Liberators of 127 Bombardment Squadron USAAF: land-based air escort: 08°36'South 34°34'West: off Recife, northeast Brazil.

31 July: U. 199: Mariners of VP-74 USN and Brazilian aircraft: land-based air escort: 23°54'South 42°54'West: southern of Rio de Janeiro.

1 August: U. 383: Sunderland of 228 Squadron RAF: land-based (Bay of Biscay) air patrol: 47°24'North 12°10'West: west of St. Nazaire.

1 August: U. 454: Sunderland of 10 Squadron RAAF: land-based (Bay of Biscay) air patrol: 45°36'North 10°23'West: west of the Gironde estuary.

2 August: U. 106: Sunderlands of 228 and 461 Squadrons RAAF: land-based (Bay of Biscay) air patrol: 46°35'North 11°55'West: west of La Rochelle.

2 August: U. 706: Hampden of 415 Squadron RCAF and Liberator of 4 Squadron USAAF: land-based (Bay of Biscay) air patrol: 46°15'North 10°23'West: west of La Rochelle.

3 August: U. 572: Mariner of VP-205 USN: land-based air patrol: 11°33'North 54°05'West: east of Trinidad, Caribbean.

3 August: U. 647: Unknown cause, possibly mined in the Iceland-Faeroes Gap.

4 August: U. 489: Sunderland of 423 Squadron RCAF: land-based air patrol: 61°11'North 14°38'West: west of the Faeroe Islands.

5 August: U. 34: Lost as a result of a collision with the tender *Lech*: west of Memel in the Baltic. Raised but decommissioned.

7 August: U. 117: Avengers and Wildcats of VC-1 from U.S. escort carrier *Card:* carrier air escort: 39°32'North 38°21'West: in the central North Atlantic.

7 August: U. 615: Aircraft of VP-204, VP-205 USN, VPB-130 USN, and 10 Squadron USAAF: land-based air patrol: scuttled on the approach of the U.S. destroyer *Walker* in 12°38'North 64°15'West: northwest of Trinidad.

9 August: U. 664: Avengers and Wildcats of VC-1 from U.S. escort carrier *Card:* carrier air escort: 40°12'North 37°29'West: in the central North Atlantic.

11 August: U. 468: Hudson of 200 Squadron RAF: land-based air patrol: 12°20'North 20°07'West: off Dakar.

11 August: U. 525: Avenger of VC-1 from U.S. escort carrier *Card:* carrier air escort: 41°29'North 38°55'West: in the central North Atlantic.

11 August: U. 604: Scuttled after being damaged in a series of attacks on 30 July by Ventura of VB-129 USN, on 3 August by Liberator(s) from VP-107 USN and on 4 August by the U.S. destroyer *Moffett:* sea- and land-based air escort: 05°00'South 20°00'West: northwest of Ascension Island.

18 August: U. 403: Hudson of 200 Squadron RAF and Wellington of 697 Squadron French Air Force: land-based air escort: 14°11'North 17°40'West: off Dakar.

20 August: U. 197: Catalinas of 259 and 265 Squadrons RAF: land-based air patrol: 28°40'South 42°36'West: off Madagascar.

21 August: U. 670: Lost as a result of a collision with the target ship *Bolkoburg* in the Bay of Danzig.

22 August: U. 458: British destroyer *Easton* and Greek destroyer *Pindos:* sea escort: 36°25'North 12°39'East: southwest of Pantelleria.

24 August: U. 84: Avenger of VC-13 from U.S. escort carrier *Core:* carrier

		air escort: 27°09'North 37°03'West: in the central North Atlantic.
24 August:	U. 134:	Wellington of 179 Squadron RAF: land-based (Bay of Biscay) air patrol: 42°07'North 09°30'West: off Vigo, northwest Spain.
24 August:	U. 185:	Avenger and Wildcats of VC-13 from U.S. escort carrier *Core:* carrier air escort: 27°00'North 37°06'West: southwest of the Azores.
25 August:	U. 523:	British destroyer *Wanderer* and corvette *Wallflower:* sea escort: 42°03'North 18°02'West: west of Cape Finisterre.
27 August:	U. 847:	Avenger and Wildcats of VC-1 from U.S. escort carrier *Card:* carrier air escort: 28°19'North 37°58'West: southwest of the Azores.
30 August:	U. 634:	British sloop *Stork* and corvette *Stonecrop:* sea escort: 40°13'North 19°24'West: west of Porto.
30 August:	U. 639:	Soviet submarine *S-101:* off Novaya Zemlya in the Arctic.
7 September:	U. 669:	Wellington of 407 Squadron RCAF: land-based (Bay of Biscay) air patrol: 45°36'North 10°13'West: west of the Gironde estuary.
8 September:	U. 760:	Interned, depending on source, either at Vigo on 8 September or at El Ferrol the following day, after having been damaged by an aircraft of 103 Squadron USAAF: land-based air patrol: whereabouts unclear.
8 September:	U. 983:	Lost as a result of collision with U. 988: off Leba in the Baltic.
11 September:	U. 617:	British corvette *Hyacinth*, trawler *Haarlem* and Australian minesweeper *Woolongong* and Wellingtons of 179 Squadron RAF: sea- and land-based air patrol: beached and abandoned: 35°38'North 03°27'West: on the Moroccan Mediterranean coast.
19 September:	U. 341:	Liberator of 10 Squadron RCAF: land-based air escort: 58°40'North 25°30'West: in the central North Atlantic.
20 September:	U. 338:	Liberator of 120 Squadron RAF: land-based air escort: 57°40'North 29°48'West: in the central North Atlantic.
20 September:	U. 346:	Lost as a result of diving accident: 54°25'North 19°50'East: off Hela in the Baltic.
22 September:	U. 229:	British destroyer *Keppel:* sea escort: 54°36'North 36°25'West: in the central North Atlantic.
27 September:	U. 161:	Mariner of VP-74 USN: land-based air patrol: 12°30'South 35°35'West: off Bahia, northeast Brazil.
27 September:	U. 221:	Halifax of 58 Squadron RAF: land-based (Bay of Biscay) air patrol: 47°00'North 18°00'West: in the eastern North Atlantic.
4 October:	U. 279:	Liberator of 120 Squadron RAF: land-based air patrol: 60°51'North 28°26'West: southwest of Ireland.
4 October:	U. 336:	Ventura of VB-128 USN: land-based air patrol: 60°40'North 26°30'West: southwest of Iceland.
4 October:	U. 422:	Avenger of VC-9 from U.S. escort carrier *Card:* carrier air escort: 43°18'North 28°58'West: north of the Azores.

4 October: U. 460: Avenger and Wildcats of VC-9 from U.S. escort carrier *Card:* carrier air escort: 43°13'North 28°58'West: north of the Azores.

5 October: U. 389: Hudson of 269 Squadron RAF: land-based air escort: 62°43'North 27°17'West: southwest of Iceland.

8 October: U. 419: Liberator of 86 Squadron RAF: land-based air escort: 56°31'North 27°05'West: in the central North Atlantic.

8 October: U. 610: Sunderland of 423 Squadron RCAF: land-based air escort: 55°45'North 24°33'West: in the eastern North Atlantic.

8 October: U. 643: Liberators of 86 and 120 Squadrons RAF: land-based air escort: 56°14'North 26°55'West: in the central North Atlantic.

13 October: U. 402: Avenger of VC-9 from U.S. escort carrier *Card:* carrier air escort: 48°56'North 29°41'West: in the central North Atlantic.

16 October: U. 470: Liberators of 59 and 120 Squadrons RAF: land-based air escort: 58°20'North 29°20'West: in the central North Atlantic.

16 October: U. 533: Bisleys of 244 Squadron RAF: land-based air patrol: 25°28'North 56°50'East: in the Gulf of Oman.

16 October: U. 844: Liberators of 59 and 86 Squadrons RAF: land-based air escort: 58°30'North 27°16'West: in the central North Atlantic.

16 October: U. 964: Liberator of 86 Squadron RAF: land-based air escort: 57°27'North 28°17'West: in the central North Atlantic.

17 October: U. 540: Liberators of 59 and 120 Squadrons RAF: land-based air escort: 58°38'North 31°56'West: in the central North Atlantic.

17 October: U. 631: British corvette *Sunflower:* sea escort: 58°13'North 32°29'West: in the central North Atlantic.

17 October: U. 841: British escort destroyer *Byard:* sea escort: 59°57'North 30°06'West: in the central North Atlantic.

20 October: U. 378: Avenger and Wildcat of VC-13 from U.S. escort carrier *Core:* carrier air escort: 47°40'North 28°27'West: in the central North Atlantic.

23 October: U. 274: British destroyers *Duncan* and *Vidette:* sea escort: 57°14'North 27°50'West: in the central North Atlantic.

24 October: U. 566: Wellington of 179 Squadron RAF: land-based air patrol: 41°12'North 09°31'West: off Porto.

26 October: U. 420: Liberator of 10 Squadron RCAF: land-based air escort: 50°04'North 41°01'West: in the central North Atlantic.

28 October: U. 220: Avenger and Wildcat of VC-1 from U.S. escort carrier *Block Island:* carrier air patrol: 48°53'North 33°30'West: in the central North Atlantic.

29 October: U. 282: British destroyers *Duncan* and *Vidette* and corvette *Sunflower:* sea escort: 55°28'North 31°57'West: in the central North Atlantic.

30 October: U. 431: British submarine *Ultimatum:* 43°04'North 05°57'East: off Toulon.

31 October: U. 306: British destroyer *Whitehall* and corvette *Geranium:* sea escort: 46°19'North 20°44'West: in the eastern North Atlantic.

31 October: U. 584: Avengers of VC-9 from U.S. escort carrier *Card:* carrier air patrol: 49°14'North 31°55'West: in the central North Atlantic.
31 October: U. 732: British destroyer *Douglas* and trawlers *Imperialist* and *Loch Osaig:* sea patrol: 35°54'North 05°52'West: in western Straits of Gibraltar.
1 November: U. 340: Scuttled after being damaged by attacks by British destroyers *Active* and *Witherington* and sloop *Fleetwood* and Wellington of 179 Squadron RAF: sea- and land-based air patrol: 36°33'North 06°37'West: off Cape Trafalgar.
1 November: U. 405: Sunk by and sank U.S. destroyer *Borie:* sea patrol from escort carrier group: 49°00'North 31°14'West: in the central North Atlantic.
5 November: U. 848: Liberators of VB-107 USN and 1 Composite Air Squadron USAAF: land-based air patrol: 10°09'South 18°00'West: southwest of Ascension Island.
6 November: U. 226: British sloops *Kite, Starling,* and *Woodcock:* sea escort: 44°49'North 41°13'West: in the central North Atlantic.
6 November: U. 842: British sloops *Starling* and *Wild Goose:* sea escort: 43°42'North 42°08'West: in the central North Atlantic.
9 November: U. 707: Fortress of 220 Squadron RAF: land-based air escort: 40°31'North 20°17'West: west of Porto.
10 November: U. 966: Beached and scuttled after attack by Liberator of 311 (Czech) Squadron RAF, Wellington of 612 Squadron RAF, and Liberators of VPB-103 and VPB-110 USN: land-based (Bay of Biscay) air patrol: 44°00'North 08°30'West: off De Santafata Bay, north of Spain.
12 November: U. 508: Liberator of VPB-103 USN: land-based (Bay of Biscay) air patrol: 46°00'North 07°30'West: west of La Rochelle.
16 November: U. 280: Liberator of 86 Squadron RAF: land-based air escort: 49°11'North 27°32'West: in the central North Atlantic.
18 November: U. 718: Lost as a result of a collision with U. 476: off Bornholm Island in the Baltic.
19 November: U. 211: Wellington of 179 Squadron RAF: land-based air escort: 40°15'North 19°18'West: west of Porto.
20 November: U. 536: British frigate *Nene* and Canadian corvettes *Calgary* and *Snowberry:* sea escorts: 43°50'North 19°39'West: west of Vigo, northwest Spain.
20 November: U. 768: Lost as a result of a collision in the Gulf of Danzig.
21 November: U. 538: British sloop *Crane* and escort destroyer *Foley:* sea escort: 45°40'North 19°35'West: in the eastern North Atlantic.
23 November: U. 648: British escort destroyer *Blackwood:* sea escort: 42°40'North 20°37'West: west of Porto.
25 November: U. 600: British escort destroyers *Bazely* and *Blackwood:* sea patrol: 41°45'North 22°30'West: west of Porto.
25 November: U. 849: Liberator of VP-107 USN: land-based air patrol: 06°30'South 5°40'West: east of Ascension Island.
28 November: U. 542: Wellington of 179 Squadron RAF: land-based air escort: 39°03'North 16°25'West: west of Lisbon.

29 November: U. 86: Avengers and Wildcats of VC-19 from U.S. escort carrier *Bogue:* carrier air escort: 39°33'North 19°01'West: northeast of the Azores.

12 December: U. 172: Avengers and Wildcats of VC-19 from U.S. escort carrier *Bogue* and destroyers *Badger, Clemson, Du Pont,* and *Osmond Ingram:* carrier air and sea escort: 26°19'North 29°58'West: northeast of the Azores.

13 December: U. 345: Heavily damaged as a result of an 8th Air Force attack on Kiel: stricken on 23 December but neither repaired nor scrapped.

13 December: U. 391: Liberator of 53 Squadron RAF: land-based (Bay of Biscay) air patrol: 45°45'North 09°38'West: west of the Gironde estuary.

13 December: U. 593: British escort destroyer *Calpe* and U.S. destroyer *Wainwright:* sea escort: 37°38'North 05°58'West: northeast of Bougie.

16 December: U. 73: U.S. destroyers *Trippe* and *Woolsey:* sea escort: 36°07'North 00°50'West: off Oran.

20 December: U. 850: Avengers and Wildcats of VC-19 from U.S. escort carrier *Bogue:* carrier air escort: 32°54'North 37°01'West: southwest of the Azores.

21 December: U. 284: Damaged and flooded by heavy seas on the 16th and scuttled: 55°04'North 30°23'West: in the central North Atlantic.

24 December: U. 645: U.S. destroyer *Schenck:* sea patrol from escort carrier group: 45°20'North 21°40'West: in the central North Atlantic.

1944

8 January: U. 426: Sunderland of 10 Squadron RAAF: land-based (Bay of Biscay) air patrol: 46°47'North 10°42'West: southwest of Brest.

8 January: U. 757: British escort destroyer *Bayntun* and Canadian corvette *Camrose:* sea escort: 50°33'North 18°03'West: in the eastern North Atlantic.

9 January: U. 81: Allied bombing raid: 44°52'North 13°52'East: at Pola, northeast Italy.

13 January: U. 231: Wellingtons of 172 Squadron RAF: land-based air escort: 44°15'North 20°38'West: in the eastern North Atlantic.

15 January: U. 377: Sunk by own homing torpedo in action with escorts of the *Santee* carrier group: accidental loss: in the North Atlantic.

16 January: U. 544: Avengers of VC-13 from the U.S. escort carrier *Guadalcanal:* carrier air patrol: 40°30'North 37°20'West: in the central North Atlantic.

17 January: U. 305: British destroyer *Wanderer* and frigate *Glenarm:* sea escort: 49°39'North 20°10'West: in the eastern North Atlantic.

19 January: U. 641: British corvette *Violet:* sea escort: 50°25'North 18°49'West: off southwest Ireland.

20 January: U. 263: Probable cause of loss a mine laid by RAF aircraft: 46°10'North 01°14'West: off La Rochelle.

28 January: U. 271: Liberator of VP-103 USN: land-based air escort: 53°15'North 15°52'West: west of Ireland.

28 January: U. 571: Sunderland of 461 Squadron RAF: land-based air escort: 52°42'North 14°27'West: west of Ireland.
30 January: U. 314: British destroyers *Meteor* and *Whitehall:* sea escort: 73°41'North 24°30'East: southeast of Bear Island in the Arctic Ocean.
30 January: U. 364: Wellington of 172 Squadron RAF: land-based (Bay of Biscay) air patrol: 45°25'North 05°15'West: west of Bordeaux.
31 January: U. 592: British sloops *Starling* and *Wild Goose:* sea patrol: 50°20'North 17°29'West: in the eastern North Atlantic.
-- January: U. 972: Unknown cause: in the North Atlantic.
4 February: U. 854: Mine laid by RAF aircraft: 53°55'North 14°17'West: off Swinemünde in the Baltic.
6 February: U. 177: Liberator of VB-107 USAAF: land-based air patrol: 10°35'North 23°15'West: off Ascension Island.
8 February: U. 762: British sloops *Starling* and *Woodpecker:* sea escort: 49°02'North 16°58'West: southwest of Ireland.
9 February: U. 238: British sloops *Kite, Magpie, Starling,* and *Wild Goose:* sea escort: 49°44'North 16°07'West: southwest of Ireland.
9 February: U. 734: British sloops *Kite, Magpie, Starling* and *Wild Goose:* sea escort: 49°43'North 16°23'West: southwest of Ireland.
10 February: U. 545: Wellington of 612 Squadron RAF: land-based air escort: 58°17'North 13°22'West: northeast of Rockall.
10 February: U. 666: Swordfish of 842 Squadron FAA from British escort carrier *Fencer:* carrier air escort: 53°56'North 17°16'West: west of Ireland.
11 February: U. 283: Wellington of 407 Squadron RAF: land-based air escort: 60°45'North 12°50'West: southeast of the Faeroe Islands.
11 February: U. 424: British sloops *Wild Goose* and *Woodpecker:* sea escort: 50°00'North 18°14'West: in the eastern North Atlantic.
14 February: U. 738: Lost as a result of a collision with a steamer: 54°31'North 18°33'East: in the Gulf of Danzig.
14 February: U.IT. 23: British submarine *Tally Ho!:* 05°45'North 99°52'East: off Penang, Malaya.
18 February: U. 406: British frigate *Spey:* sea escort: 48°32'North 23°36'West: in the eastern North Atlantic.
18 February: U. 7: Marine accident: 54°25'North 19°50'East: in the Gulf of Danzig.
19 February: U. 264: British sloops *Starling* and *Woodpecker:* sea escort: 48°31'North 22°05'West: in the eastern North Atlantic.
19 February: U. 386: British frigate *Spey:* sea escort: 48°51'North 22°41'West: in the eastern North Atlantic.
24 February: U. 257: British frigate *Nene* and Canadian frigate *Waskesiu:* sea escort: 47°19'North 26°00'West: in the eastern North Atlantic.
24 February: U. 713: British destroyer *Keppel:* sea escort: 69°27'North 04°53'East: northwest of Lofoten Islands.
24 February: U. 761: British destroyers *Anthony* and *Wishart* and Catalinas of 202 Squadron RAF and VP-63 USN and Ventura of VPB-

127 USN: British warships and both British and U.S. land-based air patrol: 35°55'North 05°45'West: in the Straits of Gibraltar.

25 February: U. 91: British escort destroyers *Affleck, Gore,* and *Gould:* sea escort: 49°45'North 26°20'West: in the central North Atlantic.

25 February: U. 601: Catalina of 210 Squadron RAF: land-based air escort: 70°26'North 12°40'West.

1 March: U. 358: British escort destroyers *Affleck, Garlies, Gore,* and *Gould:* sea escort: 45°23'North 23°16'West: in the eastern North Atlantic.

1 March: U. 709: U.S. destroyer escorts *Bostwick, Bronstein,* and *Thomas:* sea patrol from escort carrier group: 49°10'North 26°00'West: in the central North Atlantic.

1 March: U. 603: U.S. destroyer escort *Bronstein:* sea patrol from escort carrier group: 48°55'North 26°10'West: in the central North Atlantic.

4 March: U. 472: Swordfish of 816 Squadron FAA from British escort carrier *Chaser:* scuttled itself on approach of destroyer *Onslaught:* carrier air escort: 73°05'North 26°40'East: north of the North Cape.

5 March: U. 366: Swordfish of 816 Squadron FAA from British escort carrier *Chaser:* carrier air escort: 72°10'North 14°45'East: southwest of Bear Island in the Arctic Ocean.

6 March: U. 744: British destroyer *Icarus* and frigate *Kenilworth Castle* and Canadian destroyer *Chaudiere,* destroyer *Gatineau,* frigate *St. Catherine's* and corvettes *Chilliwack* and *Fennel:* sea escort: 52°01'North 22°37'West: in the eastern North Atlantic.

6 March: U. 973: Swordfish of 816 Squadron FAA from British escort carrier *Chaser:* carrier air escort: 70°04'North 05°48'East: northwest of Lofoten Islands.

10 March: U. 343: British A/S trawler *Mull:* sea patrol: 38°07'North 09°41'East: south of Sardinia.

10 March: U. 450: British escort destroyers *Blankney, Blencartha, Brecon,* and *Exmoor* and U.S. destroyer *Madison:* sea escort: 41°11'North 12°27'East: off Anzio.

10 March: U. 625: Sunderland of 422 Squadron RCAF: land-based air escort: 52°35'North 20°19'West: in the eastern North Atlantic.

10 March: U. 845: British destroyer *Forester* and Canadian destroyer *St. Laurent,* frigate *Swansea,* and corvette *Owen Sound:* sea escort: 48°20'North 20°33'West: in the eastern North Atlantic.

11 March: U. 380: Liberators of the 15th Air Force: USAAF strategic bombing raid: 43°10'North 05°55'East: at Toulon.

11 March: U. 410: Liberators of the 15th Air Force: USAAF strategic bombing raid: 43°10'North 05°55'East: at Toulon.

11 March: U.IT. 22: Catalinas of 262 and 279 Squadrons SAAF: land-based air patrol: 41°28'South 17°40'East: off the Cape of Good Hope.

13 March: U. 575: Canadian frigate *Prince Rupert* and Wellington of 172 Squadron and Fortresses of 206 Squadron RAF and Aveng-

ers of VC-95 USN from U.S. escort carrier *Bogue* and destroyer escorts *Haverfield* and *Hobson:* U.S. carrier air and sea patrol, British sea escort and land-based air escort: 46°18'North 27°34'West: in the central North Atlantic.

14 March: U. 653: Swordfish of 825 Squadron FAA from British escort carrier *Vindex* and British sloops *Starling* and *Wild Goose:* carrier air and sea patrol: 53°46'North 24°35'West: in the eastern North Atlantic.

14 March: U. 392: British destroyer *Vanoc* and escort destroyer *Affleck* and Catalinas of VP-63 USN: sea- and land-based air patrol: 35°55'North 05°41'West: in the Straits of Gibraltar.

17 March: U. 28: Marine accident: raised but decommissioned: off Neustadt in the Baltic.

17 March: U. 801: Avengers and Wildcat of VC-6 from U.S. escort carrier *Block Island* and destroyer escorts *Bronstein* and *Corry:* carrier air and sea patrol: 16°42'North 30°28'West: west of Cape Verde Islands.

17 March: U. 1013: Lost as a result of a collision with U. 286: off Ruegen in the Baltic.

19 March: U. 1059: Avenger and Wildcat of VC-6 from U.S. escort carrier *Block Island:* carrier air patrol: 13°10'North 33°44'West: off Cape Verde Islands.

25 March: U. 976: Mosquito of 248 Squadron RAF: land-based (Bay of Biscay) air patrol: 46°48'North 02°43'West: off La Rochelle.

29 March: U. 223: British destroyers *Blencartha*, *Hambledon*, and *Tumult:* sea patrol: 38°48'North 14°10'East: north of Sicily.

29 March: U. 961: British sloop *Starling:* sea escort: 64°31'North 03°19'West: southeast of Jan Mayen Island.

-- March: U. 851: Unknown cause: in the North Atlantic.

1 April: U. 355: Avenger of 846 Squadron FAA from British escort carrier *Tracker* and British destroyer *Beagle:* carrier air and sea escort: 73°07'North 10°21'East: north of Narvik.

2 April: U. 360: British destroyer *Keppel:* sea escort: 73°28'North 13°04'East: north of Tromsø.

3 April: U. 288: Avenger of 819 Squadron FAA from British escort carrier *Activity* and Avenger and Wildcat of 846 Squadron from the escort carrier *Tracker:* carrier air escort: 73°44'North 27°12'East: north of the North Cape.

6 April: U. 302: British frigate *Swale:* sea escort: 45°05'North 35°11'West: in the central North Atlantic.

6 April: U. 455: Accidental detonation of own mines: 44°04'North 09°51'East: off La Spezia.

7 April: U. 856: U.S. cutter *Champlin* and destroyer escort *Huse:* sea patrol: 40°18'North 62°22'West: southeast Cape Sable, Nova Scotia.

8 April: U. 2: Lost as a result of a collision with the fishing vessel *Heinrich Freese:* off Pillau in the Baltic.

8 April: U. 962: British sloops *Crane* and *Cygnet:* sea patrol: 45°43'North 19°57'West: in the eastern North Atlantic.

9 April: U. 515: Avengers and Wildcats of VC-58 from U.S. escort carrier *Guadalcanal* and destroyer escorts *Chatelain, Flaherty, Pillsbury,* and *Pope:* carrier air and sea patrol: 34°35'North 19°18'West: northwest of Madeira.

10 April: U. 68: Avengers of VC-58 from U.S. escort carrier *Guadalcanal:* carrier air patrol: 33°23'North 18°59'West: west of Madeira.

11 April: U. 108: Fortresses and Liberators of the 8th Air Force: USAAF strategic bombing raid: 53°23'North 14°32'East: at Stettin.

14 April: U. 448: British sloop *Pelican* and Canadian frigate *Swansea:* sea escort: 46°22'North 19°35'West: in the eastern North Atlantic.

16 April: U. 550: U.S. destroyer escorts *Gandy, Joyce,* and *Petersen:* sea escort: 40°09'North 69°44'West: south of Cape Cod, Massachusetts.

17 April: U. 342: Canso of 162 Squadron RCAF: land-based air escort: 60°23'North 29°20'West: southwest of Ireland.

17 April: U. 986: U.S. minesweeper *Swift* and chaser P.C. 619: sea escort: 50°09'North 12°51'West: southwest of Ireland.

19 April: U. 974: Norwegian submarine *Ula:* 59°08'North 05°23'East: southwest of Bergen.

22 April: U. 311: Canadian frigates *Matane* and *Swansea:* sea escort: 50°36'North 18°36'West: in the eastern North Atlantic.

26 April: U. 488: U.S. destroyer escorts *Barber, Frost, Huse,* and *Snowden:* sea escort from escort carrier group: 17°54'North 38°05'West: west of Cape Verde Islands.

27 April: U. 803: Mine laid by RAF aircraft: 53°55'North 14°17'East: off Swinemünde in the Baltic.

28 April: U. 193: Wellington of 612 Squadron RAF: land-based air patrol: 45°38'North 09°43'West: west of the Gironde estuary.

29 April: U. 421: Fortresses and Liberators of the 15th Air Force: USAAF strategic bombing raid: 43°10'North 05°55'East: at Toulon.

1 May: U. 277: Swordfish of 842 Squadron FAA from British escort carrier *Fencer:* carrier air escort: 73°24'North 15°32'East: in the Norwegian Sea southwest of Bear Island in the Arctic Ocean.

2 May: U. 674: Swordfish of 842 Squadron FAA from British escort carrier *Fencer:* carrier air escort: 70°32'North 04°37'East: northwest of Narvik.

2 May: U. 959: Swordfish of 842 Squadron FAA from British escort carrier *Fencer:* carrier air escort: 69°20'North 00°20'West: south of Jan Mayen Island in Arctic Ocean.

3 May: U. 852: Beached and scuttled after attack by Wellingtons of 8 and 621 Squadrons RAF: land-based air patrol: 09°59'North 50°59'East: south of Cape Guardafui, Horn of Africa.

4 May: U. 371: British destroyer *Blankney,* French destroyer *L'Alcyon* and escort destroyer *Senegalais,* and U.S. destroyer escorts *Joseph E. Campbell* and *Pride* and minesweeper *Sustain:* sea escorts: 37°49'North 05°39'East: off the Gulf of Bougie.

4 May: U. 846: Wellington of 407 Squadron RCAF: land-based (Bay of

Biscay) air patrol: 46°04'North 09°20'West: north of Cape Ortegal.

5 May: U. 473: British sloops *Starling, Wild Goose*, and *Wren:* sea escort: 49°29'North 21°22'West: northwest of Palma.

6 May: U. 66: Avenger from U.S. escort carrier *Block Island* and destroyer escort *Buckley:* carrier air and sea patrol: 17°17'North 32°29'West: west of Cape Verde Islands.

6 May: U. 765: Swordfish of 825 Squadron FAA from British escort carrier *Vindex* and escort destroyer *Bligh:* carrier air and sea patrol: 52°30'North 28°28'West: in the central North Atlantic.

14 May: U. 1234: Lost as a result of a collision with the tug *Anton:* off Gdynia in the Baltic. Raised but decommissioned and scuttled 5 May 1945.

15 May: U. 731: British A/S trawler *Blackfly* and sloop *Kilmarnock* and Catalina of VP-63 USN: sea- and land-based air patrol: 35°54'North 05°45'West: in the Straits of Gibraltar.

16 May: U. 240: Sunderland of 330 (Norwegian) Squadron RAF: land-based air patrol: 63°05'North 03°10'East: west of Ålesund.

17 May: U. 616: Wellington of 36 Squadron RAF and U.S. destroyers *Ellyson, Emmons, Gleaves, Hambleton, Hilary P. Jones, Macomb, Nields*, and *Rodman:* sea- and land-based air escort: 36°46'North 00°52'East: off Cape Ténès, northeast of Oran.

18 May: U. 241: Catalina of 210 Squadron RAF: land-based air patrol: 63°36'North 00°42'East: northwest of Shetland Islands.

19 May: U. 960: Wellingtons of 36 Squadron RAF and Ventura of 500 Squadron RAF and U.S. destroyers *Ludlow* and *Niblack:* sea- and land-based air patrol: 37°20'North 01°35'East: north of Oran.

19 May: U. 1015: Lost as a result of a collision with U. 1014: 54°25'North 19°50'East: in the Gulf of Danzig.

21 May: U. 453: British destroyers *Liddlesdale, Tenacious*, and *Termagant:* sea escort: 38°13'North 16°36'East: off Cape Spartivento.

24 May: U. 476: Catalina of 210 Squadron RAF: land-based air patrol: 65°08'North 04°53'East: northeast of Trondheim.

24 May: U. 675: Sunderland of 4 OTU RAF: land-based air patrol: 62°27'North 03°04'East: west of Ålesund, southwest Norway.

25 May: U. 990: Liberator of 59 Squadron RAF: land-based air patrol: 65°05'North 07°28'East: northwest of Trondheim.

27 May: U. 292: Liberator of 59 Squadron RAF: land-based air patrol: 62°37'North 00°57'East: west of Ålesund, southwest Norway.

29 May: U. 549: U.S. destroyer escorts *Eugene E. Elmore* and *Ahrens:* sea patrol from escort carrier group: 31°13'North 23°03'West: southwest of Madeira.

30 May: U. 289: British destroyer *Milne:* sea escort: 73°32'North 00°28'East: in the Norwegian Sea southwest of Bear Island in the Arctic Ocean.

3 June: U. 477: Canso of 162 Squadron RCAF: land-based air patrol: 63°59'North 01°37'East: northwest of Kristiansund.
4 June: U. 505: Captured by U.S. escort carrier *Guadalcanal* and destroyer escorts *Chatelain, Flaherty, Jenks, Pillsbury,* and *Pope:* carrier air and sea patrol: 21°30'North 19°20'West: off Capo Blanco, between the Canaries and Cape Verde Islands.
7 June: U. 955: Sunderland of 201 Squadron RAF: land-based (Bay of Biscay) air patrol: 45°13'North 08°30'West: north of Cape Ortegal.
7 June: U. 970: Sunderland of 228 Squadron RAF: land-based (Bay of Biscay) air patrol: 45°15'North 04°10'West: west of Bordeaux.
8 June: U. 373: Liberator of 224 Squadron RAF: land-based air patrol: 48°10'North 05°03'West: west of Brest.
8 June: U. 629: Liberator of 224 Squadron RAF: land-based air patrol: 48°27'North 05°47'West: west of Brest.
9 June: U. 740: Liberator of 120 Squadron RAF: land-based air patrol: 49°09'North 08°37'West: west of the Scillies.
10 June: U. 821: Liberator of 206 Squadron and Mosquitos of 248 Squadron RAF: land-based air patrol: 48°31'North 05°11'West: off Brest.
11 June: U. 980: Canso of 162 Squadron RCAF: land-based air patrol: 63°07'North 00°26'East: northwest of Bergen.
11 June: U. 490: U.S. destroyer escorts *Frost, Inch,* and *Huse:* sea patrol from escort carrier group: 42°47'North 40°08'West: northwest of the Azores.
13 June: U. 715: Canso of 162 Squadron RCAF: land-based air patrol: 62°45'North 02°59'West: east of the Faeroe Islands.
15 June: U. 860: Avengers and Wildcats of VC-9 from U.S. escort carrier *Solomons:* carrier air patrol: 25°27'South 05°30'West: south of St. Helena.
15 June: U. 987: British submarine *Satyr:* 68°01'North 05°08'East: west of Narvik.
16 June: U. 998: Damaged beyond repair in course of RAF bombing raid: 60°23'North 05°20'East: at Bergen.
17 June: U. 423: Catalina of 333 (Norwegian) Squadron RAF: land-based air patrol: 63°06'North 02°05'East: northwest of Kristiansand.
18 June: U. 441: Wellington of 304 (Polish) Squadron RAF: land-based air patrol: 49°03'North 03°13'West: northeast of Ushant.
18 June: U. 767: British destroyers *Fame, Havelock,* and *Inconstant:* sea patrol: 49°03'North 03°13'West: off north Brittany coast.
24 June: U. 971: British destroyer *Eskimo* and Canadian destroyer *Haida* and Liberator of 311 (Czech) Squadron RAF: sea- and land-based air patrol: 49°01'North 05°35'West: north of Ushant.
24 June: U. 1225: Canso of 162 Squadron RCAF: land-based air patrol: 63°00'North 00°50'West: off the Shetland Islands.
25 June: U. 269: British escort destroyer *Bickerton:* sea patrol: 50°01'North 02°59'West: southeast of Start Point in English Channel.

25 June: U. 1191: British escort destroyers *Affleck* and *Balfour*: sea escort: 50°03'North 02°59'West: southeast of Start Point.

26 June: U. 317: Liberator of 86 Squadron RAF: land-based air patrol: 62°03'North 01°45'East: off southern Norway.

26 June: U. 719: British destroyer *Bulldog:* sea patrol: 55°33'North 11°02'West: off northwest Ireland.

29 June: U. 988: British frigates *Essington*, *Domett*, and *Duckworth* and Liberator of 224 Squadron RAF: sea- and land-based air patrol: 49°37'North 03°41'West: off Lorient.

30 June: U. 478: Liberator of 206 Squadron RAF: land-based air patrol: 63°27'North 03°41'West: off the Shetland Islands.

2 July: U. 543: Avenger of VC-58 from U.S. escort carrier *Wake Island:* carrier air patrol: 25°34'North 21°36'West: southwest of the Canaries.

3 July: U. 154: U.S. destroyer escorts *Frost* and *Inch:* sea patrol from escort carrier group: 34°00'North 19°30'West: northwest of Madeira.

5 July: U. 233: U.S. destroyer escorts *Baker* and *Thomas:* sea patrol from escort carrier group: 42°16'North 59°49'West: off Halifax, Nova Scotia.

5 July: U. 390: British destroyer *Wanderer* and frigate *Tavy:* sea escort: 49°52'North 00°48'West: in Seine Bay.

5 July: U. 586: Fortresses and Liberators of the 15th Air Force: USAAF strategic bombing raid: 43°10'North 05°55'East: at Toulon.

6 July: U. 678: British corvette *Statice* and Canadian destroyers *Ottawa* and *Kootenau:* sea escort: 50°32'North 00°23'West: southwest of Beachy Head in English Channel.

8 July: U. 243: Sunderland of 10 Squadron RAAF: land-based (Bay of Biscay) air patrol: 47°06'North 06°40'West: west of St. Nazaire.

11 July: U. 1222: Sunderland of 201 Squadron RAF: land-based (Bay of Biscay) air patrol: 46°31'North 05°29'West: west of La Rochelle.

14 July: U. 415: Mine laid by RAF aircraft: 48°23'North 04°30'West: in Brest.

15 July: U. 319: Liberator of 206 Squadron RAF: land-based air patrol: 57°40'North 05°00'East: off the Naze, southwest Norway.

17 July: U. 347: Catalina of 210 Squadron RAF: land-based air patrol: 68°35'North 06°00'East: west of the Lofoten Islands.

17 July: U. 361: Liberator of 86 Squadron RAF: land-based air patrol: 68°36'North 08°33'East: west of Narvik.

18 July: U. 672: British escort destroyer *Balfour:* sea patrol: 50°03'North 02°30'West: south of Portland Bill in English Channel.

18 July: U. 742: Catalina of 210 Squadron RAF: land-based air patrol: 68°24'North 09°51'East: west of Narvik.

21 July: U. 212: British escort destroyers *Curzon* and *Ekins:* sea escort: 50°27'North 00°13'West: south of Beachy Head.

24 July: U. 239: RAF strategic bombing raid: 54°20'North 10°08'East: at Kiel.

24 July: U. 1164: RAF strategic bombing raid: 54°20'North 10°08'East: at Kiel.

24 July: U. 2323: RAF strategic bombing raid: 54°20'North 10°08'East: at Kiel.
26 July: U. 214: British frigate *Cooke:* sea patrol: 49°55'North 03°31'West: southeast of Start Point in English Channel.
28 July: U. 1166: Accidental torpedo explosion: 54°28'North 09°50'East: at Eckernförde in the Baltic.
29 July: U. 872: Fortresses of the 8th Air Force: USAAF strategic bombing raid: 53°05'North 08°48'East: at Bremen.
30 July: U. 250: Soviet cutter MO-103: sea patrol: in the Baltic.
31 July: U. 333: British frigate *Loch Killin* and sloop *Starling:* sea patrol: 49°39'North 07°28'West: west of the Isles of Scilly.
4 August: U. 671: British destroyer *Wensleydale* and escort destroyer *Stayner:* sea patrol: 50°23'North 00°06'East: southwest of Beachy Head in English Channel.
6 August: U. 471: Fortresses and Liberators of the 15th Air Force: USAAF strategic bombing raid: 43°10'North 05°55'East: at Toulon.
6 August: U. 642: Fortresses and Liberators of the 15th Air Force: USAAF strategic bombing raid: 43°10'North 05°55'East: at Toulon.
6 August: U. 736: British frigate *Loch Killin* and sloop *Starling:* sea patrol: 47°19'North 04°16'West: in the Bay of Biscay.
6 August: U. 952: Fortresses and Liberators of the 15th Air Force: USAAF strategic bombing raid: 43°10'North 05°55'East: at Toulon.
6 August: U. 969: Fortresses and Liberators of the 15th Air Force: USAAF strategic bombing raid: 43°10'North 05°55'East: at Toulon.
10 August: U. 608: British sloop *Wren* and Liberator of 53 Squadron RAF: sea- and land-based (Bay of Biscay) air patrol: 46°30'North 03°08'West: south of Belle-Ile.
11 August: U. 385: British sloop *Starling* and Sunderland of 461 Squadron RAAF: sea- and land-based (Bay of Biscay) air patrol: 46°16'North 02°45'West: west of La Rochelle.
12 August: U. 198: Indian frigate *Findhorn* and sloop *Godaveri:* sea patrol from escort carrier group: 03°35'South 52°49'East: northwest of the Seychelles.
12 August: U. 270: Sunderland of 461 Squadron RAAF: land-based (Bay of Biscay) air patrol: 46°19'North 02°56'West: west of La Rochelle.
12 August: U. 981: Badly damaged by mine laid by RAF aircraft and destroyed by Halifax of 502 Squadron RAF while trying to return to base: mine and land-based (Bay of Biscay) air patrol: 45°41'North 01°25'West: in the Gironde estuary.
14 August: U. 618: British frigates *Duckworth* and *Essington* and Liberator of 53 Squadron RAF: sea- and land-based air patrol: 47°22'North 04°39'West: west of St. Nazaire.
15 August: U. 741: British corvette *Orchis:* sea escort: 50°02'North 00°35'West: north of Le Havre.
18 August: U. 107: Sunderland of 201 Squadron RAF: land-based (Bay of Biscay) air patrol: 46°46'North 03°39'West: west of La Rochelle.
18 August: U. 621: Canadian destroyers *Chaudiere, Kootenay,* and *Ottawa:* sea patrol: 45°52'North 02°36'West: off La Rochelle.

19 August: U. 123: Scuttled: unseaworthy because of lack of batteries: 47°45'North 03°23'West: at Lorient.
19 August: U. 129: Scuttled: unseaworthy because of lack of batteries: 47°45'North 03°23'West: at Lorient.
19 August: U. 466: Scuttled: 43°10'North 05°55'East: at Toulon.
19 August: U. 967: Scuttled: 43°10'North 05°55'East: at Toulon.
20 August: U. 413: British destroyers *Forester*, *Vidette*, and *Wensleydale*: sea patrol: 50°21'North 00°01'West: north of Le Havre.
20 August: U. 984: Canadian destroyers *Chaudiere*, *Kootenay*, and *Ottawa*: sea patrol: 48°16'North 05°33'West: in the Bay of Biscay.
20 August: U. 1229: Avengers and Wildcats of VC-42 from U.S. escort carrier *Bogue*: carrier air patrol: 42°20'North 51°39'West: on the Newfoundland Rise.
20 August: U. 9: Soviet bombing raid: 44°12'North 28°40'East: at Constanta, Black Sea.
20 August: U. 188: Scuttled: unseaworthy because of lack of batteries: 44°50'North 00°36'West: at Bordeaux.
20 August: U.IT. 21: Scuttled: 44°50'North 00°36'West: at Bordeaux.
21 August: U. 766: Decommissioned and scrapped: under the circumstances tantamount to scuttling: at La Pallice.
21 August: U. 230: Scuttled: outside Toulon.
22 August: U. 180: Mine: 45°00'North 02°00'West: in the Bay of Biscay.
22 August: U. 344: Swordfish of 825 Squadron FAA from British escort carrier *Vindex*: carrier air patrol: 72°49'North 30°41'East: northeast of the North Cape.
24 August: U. 354: Swordfish of 825 Squadron FAA from British escort carrier *Vindex* and the destroyer *Keppel*, frigate *Loch Dunvegan*, and sloops *Mermaid* and *Peacock*: carrier air and sea escort: 74°54'North 15°26'East: northwest of Bear Island in the Arctic Ocean.
24 August: U. 445: British frigate *Louis*: sea patrol: 47°21'North 05°50'West: west of St. Nazaire.
24 August: U. 178: Scuttled: unseaworthy because of lack of batteries: 44°50'North 00°36'West: at Bordeaux.
25 August: U. 667: Mine laid by RAF aircraft: 46°10'North 01°14'West: off La Pallice.
25 August: U. 18: Scuttled: 44°12'North 28°40'East: at Constanta, Black Sea.
25 August: U. 24: Scuttled: 44°12'North 28°40'East: at Constanta, Black Sea.
25 August: U. 1000: Damaged beyond repair by mine laid by RAF aircraft: in the Baltic: subsequently decommissioned at Stettin.
1 September: U. 247: Canadian frigates *St. John* and *Swansea*: sea patrol: 49°54'North 05°49'East: south of Land's End.
2 September: U. 394: Swordfish of 825 Squadron FAA from British escort carrier *Vindex*, destroyers *Keppel* and *Whitehall*, and sloops *Mermaid* and *Peacock*: carrier air and sea escort: 69°47'North 04°41'East: in Norwegian Sea roughly mid-point between Jan Mayen Island and Bodø.
6 September: U. 362: Soviet minesweeper T-116: in the Kara Sea in the Arctic.

6 September:	U. 1054:	Damaged beyond repair in collision with Norwegian motor vessel *Peter Wessel:* off Hela, in the Baltic. Stricken at Kiel on 16 September and decommissioned but not scrapped.
9 September:	U. 743:	British frigates *Helmsdale* and covette *Portchester Castle:* sea escort: 55°45'N 11°41'West: off northwest Ireland.
9 September:	U. 484:	Canadian frigate *Dunver* and corvette *Hespeler:* sea escort: 56°30'North 07°40'West: off the Hebrides.
10 September:	U. 19:	Scuttled with the loss of the Black Sea ports: 41°17'North 31°26'East: off Erekli, Black Sea.
10 September:	U. 20:	Scuttled with the loss of the Black Sea ports: 41°17'North 31°26'East: off Erekli, Black Sea.
10 September:	U. 23:	Scuttled with the loss of the Black Sea ports: 41°17'North 31°26'East: off Erekli, Black Sea.
19 September:	U. 865:	Mine laid by RAF aircraft: 62°20'North 02°30'East: west of Ålesund.
19 September:	U. 867:	Liberator of 224 Squadron RAF: land-based air patrol: 62°15'North 01°50'East: off southwest Norway.
19 September:	U. 407:	British destroyers *Terpsicord* and *Troubridge* and Polish destroyer *Garland:* sea patrol: 36°27'North 24°33'East: north of Crete.
23 September:	U. 859:	British submarine *Trenchant:* 05°46'North 100°04'East: off Penang, Malaya.
24 September:	U. 565:	Liberators of the 15th Air Force: USAAF strategic bombing raid: 38°00'North 23°35'East: at Skaramanga, Greece.
24 September:	U. 596:	Liberators of the 15th Air Force: USAAF strategic bombing raid: 38°00'North 23°35'East: at Skaramanga, Greece.
24 September:	U. 855:	Liberator of 224 Squadron RAF: land-based air patrol: 61°00'North 04°07'East: off southwest Norway.
26 September:	U. 871:	Fortress of 220 Squadron RAF: land-based air patrol: 43°18'North 36°28'West: off the Azores.
29 September:	U. 863:	Liberators of VB-107 USN: land-based air patrol: 10°45'South 25°30'West: southwest of Ascension Island.
30 September:	U. 921:	Swordfish of 813 Squadron FAA from British escort carrier *Campania:* carrier air escort: 72°32'North 12°55'East: northwest of Tromsø.
30 September:	U. 1062:	U.S. destroyer escort *Fessenden:* sea patrol: 11°35'North 34°44'West: off Cape Verde Islands.
-- September:	U. 703:	Mine laid by British warship: off southeast Iceland.
-- September:	U. 925:	Unknown cause: in the Iceland/Faeroes Gap.
4 October:	U. 92:	RAF strategic bombing raid: damaged beyond repair and decommissioned: 60°23'North 05°20'East: at Bergen, Norway.
4 October:	U. 228:	RAF strategic bombing raid: 60°23'North 05°20'East: at Bergen, Norway.
4 October:	U. 437:	RAF strategic bombing raid: damaged beyond repair and decommissioned: 60°23'North 05°20'East: at Bergen, Norway.

4 October: U. 993: RAF strategic bombing raid: 60°23'North 05°20'East: at Bergen, Norway.
5 October: U. 168: Dutch submarine *Zwaadvisch:* 06°20'South 111°28'East: north of Java.
10 October: U. 777: RAF strategic bombing raid: 53°32'North 08°07'East: at Wilhelmshaven.
10 October: U. 2331: Marine cause: raised but decommissioned: off Gdynia in the Baltic.
16 October: U. 1006: Canadian frigate *Annan:* sea patrol: 60°59'North 04°49'West: off the Faeroe Islands.
19 October: U. 957: Damaged beyond repair as a result of a collision with a transport: marine accident: 70°00'North 15°00'East: off the Lofoten Islands. Decommissioned and surrendered at Trondheim in May 1945.
22 October: U. 985: Mine laid by RAF aircraft: off southern Norway.
24 October: U. 673: Lost as a result of a collision with U. 382: 59°20'North 05°33'East: off Stavanger.
28 October: U. 1226: Unknown cause in the North Atlantic, possibly as a result of snorkel malfunction.
1 November: U. 262: Damaged beyond repair and decommissioned as a result of a collision: off Danzig in the Baltic.
4 November: U. 1060: Beached after attack by Firefly of 502 Squadron from British fleet carrier *Implacable* on 27 October and destroyed by Liberators of 311 (Czech) Squadron and Halifaxes of 502 Squadron RAF: carrier aircraft and land-based air patrol: 65°24'North 12°00'East: northwest of Namsos.
9 November: U. 537: U.S. submarine *Flounder:* 07°13'South 115°17'East: off Java.
11 November: U. 771: British submarine *Venturer:* 69°17'N 16°28'East: west of Tromsø.
11 November: U. 1200: British corvettes *Launceston Castle, Kenilworth Castle, Pevensey Castle,* and *Portchester Castle:* sea patrol: 50°24'N 09°10'West: west of the Isles of Scilly.
25 November: U. 322: British frigate *Ascension* and Sunderland of 330 (Norwegian) Squadron RAF: sea- and land-based air patrol: 60°18'N 04°52'West: off the Shetland Islands.
28 November: U. 80: Diving accident: 54°25'N 19°50'East: off Pillau in Gulf of Danzig.
30 November: U. 196: Mined in the Sunda Strait: off western Java.
6 December: U. 297: British frigate *Loch Insh* and escort destroyer *Goodall:* sea patrol: 58°44'North 04°29'West: northeast of Cape Wrath.
9 December: U. 387: British corvette *Bamborough Castle:* sea escort: 69°41'North 33°12'East: off Murmansk.
12 December: U. 416: Lost as a result of a collision with the minesweeper *M.203:* 54°41'North 19°59'East: at Pillau in Gulf of Danzig.
12 December: U. 479: Mine laid by Soviet submarine *Lembit:* in the Gulf of Finland.
13 December: U. 365: Swordfish of 813 Squadron FAA from British escort carrier

		Campania: carrier air escort: 70°43'North 08°08'East: east of Jan Mayen Island.
17 December:	U. 400:	British frigate *Nyasaland:* sea escort: 51°16'North 08°05'West: off Cork, southeast Ireland.
18 December:	U. 1209:	Ran aground: marine accident: in 49°55'North 05°48'East: on the Wolf Rock off the Isles of Scilly.
18 December:	U. 737:	Lost as a result of a collision with the minesweeper depot ship MRS.25: 70°00'North 15°00'East: off Vestfjorden in the Lofoten Islands.
26 December:	U. 2342:	Mine laid by RAF aircraft: 53°55'North 14°17'East: east of Swinemünde.
27 December:	U. 877:	Canadian corvette *St. Thomas:* sea escort: 46°25'North 36°38'West: northwest of the Azores.
28 December:	U. 735:	RAF strategic bombing raid: 59°25'North 10°30'East: at Horten in Oslofjorden.
30 December:	U. 772:	Wellington of 407 Squadron RAF: land-based air escort: 50°05'North 02°31'West: south of Portland Bill.
31 December:	U. 547:	Decommissioned at Stettin and stricken.
31 December:	U. 906:	Fortresses and Liberators of the 8th Air Force: USAAF strategic bombing raid: 53°33'N 10°00'East: at Hamburg.
31 December:	U. 2532:	Fortresses and Liberators of the 8th Air Force: USAAF strategic bombing raid: 53°33'N 10°00'East: at Hamburg.
31 December:	U. 2537:	Fortresses and Liberators of the 8th Air Force: USAAF strategic bombing raid: 53°33'N 10°00'East: at Hamburg.
1945		
9 January:	U. 679:	Soviet cutter MO-124: off Baltic Port (which is in 59°21'North 24°03'East) at entrance to Gulf of Finland.
16 January:	U. 248:	U.S. destroyer escorts *Hayter, Joseph C. Hubbard, Otter,* and *Varian:* sea patrol: 47°43'North 26°37'West: in the central North Atlantic.
16 January:	U. 482:	British frigate *Loch Craggie* and sloops *Amethyst, Hart, Peacock,* and *Starling:* sea patrol: 55°30'North 05°53'West: in the North Channel.
17 January:	U. 2523:	Heavy bombers of the 8th Air Force: USAAF strategic bombing raid: 53°33'North 10°00'East: at Hamburg. The boat was later raised but decommissioned.
17 January:	U. 2530:	Heavy bombers of the 8th Air Force: USAAF strategic bombing raid: 53°33'North 10°00'East: at Hamburg.
17 January:	U. 2534:	Heavy bombers of the 8th Air Force: USAAF strategic bombing raid: 53°33'North 10°00'East: at Hamburg. The boat was later raised and returned to service.
21 January:	U. 1199:	British destroyer *Icarus* and corvette *Mignonette:* sea escort: 49°57'North 05°42'West: off Land's End.
21 January:	U. 763:	Soviet bombing raid: 54°40'North 20°30'East: at Königsberg.
26 January:	U. 1051:	British escort destroyers *Aylmer, Bentinck, Calder,* and

Manners: sea escort: 53°39'North 05°23'West: off Dublin in the Irish Sea.

27 January: U. 1172: British escort destroyers *Bligh*, *Keats*, and *Tyler*: sea escort: 52°24'North 05°42'West: off Wexford in the Irish Sea.

31 January: U. 3520: Mine (laid by RAF aircraft?): 54°27'North 09°26'East: in Kiel Bay.

-- January: U. 382: RAF strategic bombing raid: 53°32'North 08°07'East: at Wilhelmshaven. Raised 20 March and scuttled in Kupfermuehlen Bay on 8 May 1945.

-- January: U. 650: Unknown cause, probably in the Iceland-Faeroes Gap en route for southern Irish Sea.

-- January: U. 1020: Unknown cause: off northeast Scotland.

3 February: U. 1279: British escort destroyers *Bayntun* and *Braithwaite* and frigate *Loch Eck*: sea patrol: 61°21'North 02°00'West: north of the Shetland Islands.

4 February: U. 745: Unknown cause: probably lost on a mine in the Gulf of Finland.

4 February: U. 1014: British frigates *Loch Scavaig*, *Loch Shin*, *Nyasaland*, and *Papua*: sea patrol: 55°17'North 06°44'West: off northern Ireland.

9 February: U. 864: British submarine *Venturer*: 60°46'North 04°35'East: off southwest Norway.

9 February: U. 923: Mine: in Kiel Bay.

14 February: U. 989: British frigates *Loch Dunvegan* and *Loch Eck* and escort destroyers *Bayntun* and *Braithwaite*: sea patrol: 61°36'North 01°35'West: north of the Shetland Islands.

15 February: U. 1053: Accidental loss during trials: 60°22'North 05°10'East: off Bergen, Norway.

16 February: U. 309: Canadian frigate *St. John*: sea patrol: 58°09'North 02°23'West: northeast of Cromarty.

17 February: U. 425: British frigate *Alnwick Castle* and sloop *Lark*: sea escort: 69°39'N 33°50'East: off Murmansk.

17 February: U. 1273: Mine laid by RAF aircraft: 59°30'North 10°30'East: at Horten, in Oslofjorden.

17 February: U. 1278: British escort destroyer *Bayntun* and *Loch Eck*: sea patrol: 61°32'North 01°36'West: off the Shetland Islands.

18 February: U. 2344: Lost as result of collision with U. 2336: off Heiligendamm (which is in 59°09'North 11°50'East) in the Baltic.

19 February: U. 676: Sunk in Soviet minefield in Gulf of Finland or the Baltic.

20 February: U. 1208: British sloops *Amethyst*: sea escort: 51°48'North 07°07'West: off Cork in St. George's Channel.

22 February: U. 300: British minesweepers *Pincher* and *Recruit*: sea escort: 36°29'North 08°20'West: off Cádiz.

24 February: U. 480: British escort destroyers *Duckworth* and *Rowley*: sea escort: 49°55'North 06°08'West: southwest of Land's End.

24 February: U. 927: Warwick of 179 Squadron RAF: land-based air patrol: 49°54'North 04°45'West: southwest of the Lizard.

24 February: U. 3007: Heavy bombers of the 8th Air Force: USAAF strategic bombing raid: 53°05'North 08°48'East: at Bremen.

27 February: U. 1018: British frigate *Loch Fada:* sea escort: 49°56'North 05°20'West: south of the Lizard.

27 February: U. 327: British frigates *Labuan* and *Loch Fada* and sloop *Wild Goose* and Liberator of VPB-112 USN: sea- and land-based air escort: 49°46'North 05°47'West: southwest of the Lizard.

28 February: U. 869: U.S. frigate *Knoxville* and destroyer escorts *Francis M. Robinson* and *Fowler* and French coastal escorts *L'Indiscret* and *Le Resolu:* sea escort: 34°30'North 08°13'West: off Casablanca.

-- February: U. 21: Decommissioned and scrapped: 54°41'North 19°59'East: at Pillau on the Baltic.

2 March: U. 3519: Mine: 54°11'North 12°05'East: outside Warnemünde in the Baltic.

7 March: U. 1302: Canadian frigates *La Hulloise, Strathadam,* and *Thetford Mines:* sea patrol: 52°19'North 05°23'West: off St. David's Head.

9 March: U. 682: RAF strategic bombing raid: 53°33'North 10°00'East: at Hamburg.

10 March: U. 275: Mine: 50°36'North 00°04'East: off Beachy Head in the English Channel.

11 March: U. 681: Badly damaged when run aground in the Isles of Scilly and scuttled after attack by Liberator of VPB-103 USN: marine causes and land-based air patrol: 49°53'North 06°31'West: in the southern Irish Sea.

11 March: U. 2515: Heavy bombers of the 8th Air Force: USAAF strategic bombing raid: 53°33'North 10°00'East: at Hamburg.

12 March: U. 260: Mine: 51°15'North 09°05'West: off Kinsale, Irish Sea.

12 March: U. 683: British frigate *Loch Ruthven* and sloop *Wild Goose:* sea escort. 49°52'North 05°52'West: southwest of Land's End.

14 March: U. 714: South African frigate *Natal:* on passage: 55°57'North 01°57'West: off St. Abbs Head, North Sea.

15 March: U. 367: Mine: 54°25'North 19°50'East: off Hela in the Baltic.

18 March: U. 866: U.S. destroyer escorts *Lowe, Menges, Mosley,* and *Pride:* sea patrol: 43°18'North 61°08'West: off Sable Island, Nova Scotia.

20 March: U. 905: Liberator of 86 Squadron RAF: land-based air patrol: 59°42'North 04°55'West: northwest of the Orkney Islands.

20 March: U. 1003: Canadian frigate *New Glasgow:* sea escort: 55°25'North 06°53'West: off Lough Foyle, Northern Ireland.

26 March: U. 399: Canadian destroyer escort *Duckworth:* sea escort: 49°56'North 05°22'West: off the Lizard.

27 March: U. 722: British escort destroyers *Byron, Fitzroy,* and *Redmill:* sea patrol: 57°09'North 06°55'West: off Dunvegan, Inner Hebrides.

27 March: U. 965: British escort destroyer *Conn:* sea patrol: 58°34'North 05°46'West: off Cape Wrath.

29 March: U. 246: Canadian destroyer escort *Duckworth:* sea escort: 49°58'North 05°25'West: southeast of the Lizard.
29 March: U. 1106: Liberator of 224 Squadron RAF: land-based air patrol: 61°46'North 02°16'West: off the Shetland Islands.
29 March: U. 72: Fortresses of the 8th Air Force: USAAF strategic bombing raid: 53°05'North 08°48'East: at Bremen.
29 March: U. 96: Liberators of the 8th Air Force: USAAF strategic bombing raid: 53°32'North 08°07'East: at Wilhelmshaven.
30 March: U. 429: Liberators of the 8th Air Force: USAAF strategic bombing raid: 53°32'North 08°07'East: at Wilhelmshaven.
30 March: U. 430: Fortresses of the 8th Air Force: USAAF strategic bombing raid: 53°05'North 08°48'East: at Bremen.
30 March: U. 870: Fortresses of the 8th Air Force: USAAF strategic bombing raid: 53°05'North 08°48'East: at Bremen.
30 March: U. 882: Fortresses of the 8th Air Force: USAAF strategic bombing raid: 53°05'North 08°48'East: at Bremen.
30 March: U. 1021: British escort destroyer *Rupert:* sea patrol: 58°19'North 05°31'West: off the Hebrides.
30 March: U. 3508: Liberators of the 8th Air Force: USAAF strategic bombing raid: 53°32'North 08°07'East: at Wilhelmshaven.
-- March: U. 296: Cause of loss unknown: claims of Liberator of 120 Squadron RAF: land-based air patrol: 55°23'North 06°40'West: off the Giant's Causeway, Northern Ireland on 22 March, disputed and apparently incorrect.
1 April: U. 348: RAF strategic bombing raid: 53°33'North 10°00'East: at Hamburg.
1 April: U. 350: RAF strategic bombing raid: 53°33'North 10°00'East: at Hamburg.
1 April: U. 1167: RAF strategic bombing raid: 53°33'North 10°00'East: at Hamburg.
1 April: U. 2340: RAF strategic bombing raid: 53°33'North 10°00'East: at Hamburg.
2 April: U. 321: Wellington of 304 (Polish) Squadron RAF: land-based air patrol: 50°00'North 12°57'West: southwest of Ireland.
3 April: U. 1276: Liberator of 224 Squadron RAF: land-based air patrol: 61°42'North 00°24'West: off the Shetland Islands.
4 April: U. 237: Heavy bombers of the 8th Air Force: USAAF strategic bombing raid: 54°20'North 10°08'East: at Kiel.
4 April: U. 749: Heavy bombers of the 8th Air Force: USAAF strategic bombing raid: 54°20'North 10°08'East: at Kiel.
4 April: U. 1221: Heavy bombers of the 8th Air Force: USAAF strategic bombing raid: 54°20'North 10°08'East: at Kiel.
4 April: U. 2542: Heavy bombers of the 8th Air Force: USAAF strategic bombing raid: 54°20'North 10°08'East: at Kiel.
4 April: U. 3003: Heavy bombers of the 8th Air Force: USAAF strategic bombing raid: 54°20'North 10°08'East: at Kiel.
4 April: U. 3505: Heavy bombers of the 8th Air Force: USAAF strategic bombing raid: 54°20'North 10°08'East: at Kiel.

5 April: U. 242: Mine: 52°03'North 05°53'West: off St. David's Head in St. George's Channel.
5 April: U. 1169: Cause of loss unknown: somewhere in the English Channel.
6 April: U. 1195: British destroyer *Watchman:* sea escort: 50°33'North 00°55'West: off Sandown in the English Channel.
7 April: U. 857: U.S. frigates *Eugene* and *Knoxville* and destroyer escorts *Gustafson* and *Micka:* sea patrol: 42°22'North 69°46'West: off Cape Cod, Massachusetts.
8 April: U. 774: British escort destroyers *Bentinck* and *Calder:* sea patrol: 49°58'North 11°51'West: southwest of Ireland.
8 April: U. 1001: British escort destroyers *Byron* and *Fitzroy:* sea patrol: 49°19'North 10°23'West: southwest of Ireland.
8 April: U. 3512: RAF strategic bombing raid: 53°33'North 10°00'East: at Hamburg.
9 April: U. 747: RAF strategic bombing raid: 53°33'North 10°00'East: at Hamburg.
9 April: U. 677: RAF strategic bombing raid: 53°33'North 10°00'East: at Hamburg.
9 April: U. 804: Mosquitos of 143, 235, and 248 Squadrons RAF: land-based air strike: 57°58'North 11°15'East: in the Skagerrak.
9 April: U. 843: Mosquitos of 235 Squadron RAF: land-based air strike: 57°58'North 11°15'East: in the Skagerrak.
9 April: U. 982: RAF strategic bombing raid: 53°33'North 10°00'East: at Hamburg.
9 April: U. 1065: Mosquitos of 143, 235, and 248 Squadrons RAF: land-based air strike: 57°48'North 11°26'East: in the Skagerrak.
9 April: U. 1131: RAF strategic bombing raid: 53°33'North 10°00'East: at Hamburg.
9 April: U. 2509: RAF strategic bombing raid: 53°33'North 10°00'East: at Hamburg.
9 April: U. 2514: RAF strategic bombing raid: 53°33'North 10°00'East: at Hamburg.
10 April: U. 878: British destroyer *Vanquisher* and corvette *Tintagel Castle:* sea escort: 47°35'North 10°33'West: west of Cape Finisterre.
10 April: U. 1227: RAF strategic bombing raid: 54°20'North 10°08'East: at Kiel.
10 April: U. 2516: RAF strategic bombing raid: 54°20'North 10°08'East: at Kiel.
12 April: U. 486: British submarine *Tapir:* 60°44'North 04°39'East: off Bergen.
12 April: U. 1024: British frigate *Loch Glendhu:* sea escort: 53°39'N 05°03'West: off Holyhead, Irish Sea.
14 April: U. 235: Sunk in error by German torpedo boat T.17: 57°44'North 10°39'East: in the Skagerrak.
14 April: U. 1206: Accidental loss: abandoned after grounding: 57°21'North 01°39'East: northeast of Aberdeen.
15 April: U. 103: RAF strategic bombing raid: 54°20'North 10°08'East: at Kiel.

15 April: U. 285: British escort destroyers *Grindall* and *Keats:* sea patrol: 50°13'North 12°48'West: southwest of Ireland.
15 April: U. 1063: British frigate *Loch Killin:* sea escort: 50°08'North 05°52'West: off Land's End.
15 April: U. 1235: U.S. destroyer escort *Frost* and *Stanton:* sea patrol from escort carrier group: 47°54'North 30°25'West: in the central North Atlantic.
16 April: U. 78: Soviet artillery: 54°41'North 19°59'East: at Pillau on the Baltic.
16 April: U. 880: U.S. destroyer escort *Frost* and *Stanton:* sea patrol from escort carrier group: 47°53'North 30°26'West: in the central North Atlantic.
16 April: U. 1274: British destroyer *Viceroy:* sea escort: 55°36'North 01°24'West: off St. Abbs Head, North Sea.
19 April: U. 251: Mosquitos of 143, 235, 248, and 333 (Norwegian) Squadrons RAF: land-based air strike: 56°37'North 11°51'East: off Gothenburg, Sweden.
19 April: U. 879: U.S. destroyer escorts *Buckley* and *Reuben James:* sea patrol: 42°19'North 06°45'West: off Halifax, Nova Scotia.
21 April: U. 636: British escort destroyers *Bazely, Bentinck,* and *Drury:* sea patrol: 55°50'North 10°31'West: northwest of Ireland.
22 April: U. 518: U.S. destroyer escort *Carter* and *Neal A. Scott:* sea patrol from escort carrier group: 43°26'North 38°23'West: northwest of the Azores.
23 April: U. 183: U.S. submarine *Besugo:* 04°57'South 112°52'East: north of Soerabaja, Java Sea.
23 April: U. 396: Liberator of 86 Squadron RAF: land-based air patrol: 59°29'North 00°22'West: off the Hebrides.
24 April: U. 546: U.S. destroyer escorts *Chatelain, Flaherty, Hubbard, Janssen, Keith, Neunzer, Pillsbury,* and *Varian:* sea escort from escort carrier group: 43°53'North 40°07'West: northwest of the Azores.
25 April: U. 1107: Liberator of VPB-103 USN: land-based air patrol. 48°12'North 05°43'West: southwest of Ushant.
25 April: U. 1197: Decommissioned: stricken at Bremerhaven.
28 April: U. 56: RAF strategic bombing raid: 54°20'North 10°08'East: at Kiel.
28 April: U. 1223: RAF strategic bombing raid: at Wesermünde.
29 April: U. 286: British frigates *Anguilla, Cotton, Loch Insh,* and *Loch Shin:* sea escort: 69°29'North 33°37'East: off Murmansk.
29 April: U. 307: British frigate *Loch Insh:* sea escort: 69°24'North 33°44'East: off Murmansk.
29 April: U. 1017: Liberator of 120 Squadron RAF: land-based air patrol: 56°04'North 11°06'West: off northwest Ireland.
30 April: U. 548: U.S. destroyer escorts *Bostwick, Coffman, Natchez,* and *Thomas:* sea escort: 36°34'North 74°00'East: northeast of Cape Hatteras.
30 April: U. 1055: Catalina of VP-63N: land-based air patrol: 48°00'North 6°30'West: southwest of Ushant.

-- April: U. 325: Unknown cause: in the English Channel or southwest of Ireland.

-- April: U. 326: Unknown cause: in the English Channel or southwest of Ireland.

1 May: The following units were scuttled in German ports in imminent danger of occupation by Allied military formations:

U. 3009: in 53°33'North 08°35'East at Bremerhaven/Wesermunde.

U. 3525: in 54°20'North 10°08'East at Kiel.

U. 3006: in 53°32'North 08°07'East at Wilhelmshaven.

2 May: U. 1007: Cause of loss disputed: sunk either by mine laid by RAF Typhoon of 245 Squadron RAF: 53°54'North 11°28'East: off Wismar.

2 May: U. 2359: Aircraft of 143, 235, 248, 333 (Norwegian) Squadrons RAF and 404 Squadron RCAF: land-based air strike: 57°29'North 11°24'East: in the Kattegat.

2 May: The following U-boats were scuttled in German ports imminently threatened by the advance of Allied military formations:

U. 72: in 53°05'North 08°48'East at Bremen.

U. 120, U. 121: in 53°33'North 08°35'East at Bremerhaven/Wesermünde.

U. 2327, U. 2370, U. 3994, U. 3506, and the damaged U. 2549: in 53°33'North 10°00'East: at Hamburg.

U. 316, U. 2510, U. 2526, U. 2527, U. 2528, U. 2531, U. 3002, U. 3016, U. 3018, U. 3019, U. 3020, U. 3021, U. 3521, U. 3522: in 53°57'North 10°53'East at Travemünde/Neustadt.

U. 612, U. 1308: in 54°12'North 12°05'East at Warnemünde.

U. 717: in 54°47'North 09°27'East at Wasserslebem/Flensburg.

U. 8, U. 14, U. 17, U. 60, U. 61, U. 62, U. 71, U. 137, U. 139, U. 140, U. 141, U. 142, U. 146, U. 148, U. 151, U. 152, U. 552, U. 554, U. 3504: in 53°32'North 08°07'East at Wilhelmshaven.

3 May: U. 1210: Typhoons of 83 and 84 Groups RAF: land-based air strike: in the southern Kattegat.

3 May: U. 3028: Typhoons of 83 and 84 Groups RAF: land-based air strike: in the southern Kattegat.

3 May: U. 3030: Typhoons of 83 and 84 Groups RAF: land-based air strike: in the southern Kattegat.

3 May: U. 3032: Typhoons of 83 and 84 Groups RAF: land-based air strike: in the southern Kattegat.

3 May: U. 2524: Beaufighters of 236 and 254 Squadrons RAF: land-based air strike: In the southern Kattegat.

3 May: The following U-boats were scuttled in German ports in imminent danger of occupation by Allied military formations:

U. 822, U. 828, U. 1232, U. 3001, U. 3509: in 53°33'North 08°35'East at Bremerhaven.

U. 876, U. 2512: in 54°28'North 09°50'East at Eckernförde on the Baltic.

U. 2332, U. 2371, U. 2501, U. 2504, U. 2505, U. 3502: in 53°33'North 10°00'East at Hamburg.

U. 11, U. 52, U. 57, U. 58, U. 59, U. 446, U. 475, U. 560, U. 795, U.

903, U. 922, U. 924, U. 958, U. 1166, U. 1192, U. 1205, U. 1227, U. 2330, U. 2508, U. 2519, U. 2520, U. 2539, U. 2543, U. 2545, U. 2546, U. 2548, U. 2552, U. 3005, U. 3010, U. 3029, U. 3031, U. 3038, U. 3039, U. 3040, U. 3518, U. 3530, U. 4705: in 54°20'North 10°08'East at Kiel.

U. 428, U. 748: in the Kiel canal.

U. 2355: 54°24'North 10°14'East: at Laboe (below Kiel).

U. 323: in 53°30'North 08°29'East at Nordenham.

U. 1170, U. 2533, U. 2535, U. 2536, U. 3011, U. 3012, U. 3013, U. 3023, U. 3025, U. 3026, U. 3027, U. 3037, U. 3501, U. 3511, U. 3513, U. 3516, U. 3517: in 53°11'N 08°37'East at Travemünde.

U. 704: in 54°12'North 12°05'East at Vegesack.

U. 929: in 53°32'North 08°07'East at Warnemünde.

U. 339, U. 708: in 53°32'North 08°07'East: at Wilhelmshaven.

4 May: U. 236: Beaufighters of 236 and 254 Squadrons RAF: land-based air strike: south of the Kattegat.

4 May: U. 393: Damaged and beached as result of attack by Beaufighters of 236 and 254 RAF: land-based air strike: south of the Kattegat.

4 May: U. 711: Aircraft from British escort carriers *Queen*, *Searcher*, and *Trumpeter*: carrier air strike: 68°48'North 16°38'East: off Hardstadt, northern Norway.

4 May: U. 904: Typhoons of 2nd TAF: land-based air strike: either in Kiel Bay or at Eckernförde.

4 May: U. 2338: Beaufighters of 236 and 254 Squadrons RAF: land-based air strike: south of the Kattegat.

4 May: U. 2503: Beaufighters of 236 and 254 Squadrons RAF: land-based air strike: south of the Kattegat.

4 May: U. 2521: Typhoons of 2nd TAF: land-based air strike: southeast of Århus (which is in 56°09'North 10°13'East on eastern Jutland).

4 May: U. 2540: Scuttled off the Flensburg light after being extensively damaged by British land-based aircraft in the southern Kattegat on the previous day.

5 May: U. 534: Liberator of 86 Squadron RAF: land-based air strike: in the Kattegat.

5 May: U. 579: Liberator of 224 Squadron RAF: land-based air strike: south of Kattegat.

5 May: U. 2365: Liberator of 224 Squadron RAF: land-based air strike: in the Kattegat.

5 May: U. 3503: Liberator of 206 Squadron RAF: land-based air strike: in the Kattegat.

5 May: U. 3523: Liberator of 311 (Czech) Squadron RAF: land-based air strike: in the Kattegat.

5 May: The following boats were scuttled with the announcement of the impending surrender of German forces:

U. 2544: at Århus.

U. 1406 and U. 1407: in 53°52'North 08°42'East at Cuxhaven.

U. 733 and U. 1405: in 54°28'North 09°50'East: at Eckernförde.

U. 750, U. 827, and U. 999: in the Flensburger Förde.

U. 267, U. 349, U. 370, U. 397, U. 721, U. 746, U. 794, U. 1056, U. 1101, U. 1162, U. 1168, U. 1193, U. 1204, U. 1207, U. 1306, U. 2333, U. 2339, U. 2343, U. 2346, U. 2347, U. 2349, U. 2357, U. 2358, U. 2360, U. 2362, U. 2364, U. 2366, U. 2368, U. 2369, U. 2507, U. 2517, U. 2522, U. 2525, U. 2541, U. 3015, U. 3022, U. 3044, U. 3510, U. 3524, U. 3526, U. 3529, U. 4703, and U. 4710: in 54°44'North 09°54'East in Geltinger Bay.

U. 351, U. 1234, U. 2354, U. 4701, U. 4702, U. 4704: in 54°53'North 09°58'East at Horup Haff.

U. 29, U. 30, U. 46, U. 290, U. 382, U. 1132, U. 1161, U. 1303, U. 1304: in Kupfermuhlen Bay (which is in 54°50'North 09°25'East on the Flensburger Förde on the Danish border).

U. 1016: in 53°52'North 10°40'East in Lübeck Bay.

U. 2551: at Solituede (which is in 54°49'North 09°30'East near Flensburg).

U. 3033 and U. 3034: in 51°56'North 10°45'East in Wassersleben Bay (which is next to Kupfermuhle on the Flensburger Förde on the Danish border).

U. 38, U. 3501, U. 3527, U. 3528: at Wesermünde.

6 May: U. 853: U.S. destroyer escort *Atherton* and frigate *Moberley*: sea patrol: 41°13'North 71°27'West: off Martha's Vineyard.

6 May: U. 881: U.S. destroyer escort *Farquhar:* sea patrol from escort carrier group: 43°18'North 47°44'West: off the Grand Banks, Newfoundland.

6 May: U. 1008: Liberator of 86 Squadron RAF: land-based air strike: 57°52'North 10°49'West: in the Kattegat.

6 May: U. 2534: Liberator of 86 Squadron RAF: land-based air strike: 57°00'North 11°52'East: in the Kattegat.

7 May: U. 320: Catalina of 210 Squadron RAF: land-based air patrol: 61°32'North 01°53'East: East of Shetland Islands.

-- May: U. 398: Unknown cause: East coast of Scotland.

Boats that were destroyed in strategic bombing raids but that apparently were incomplete and thus not in service:

30 March: U. 329: Previously damaged in raid in September 1944. Fortresses of the 8th Air Force: USAAF strategic bombing raid: 53°05'North 08°48'East: at Bremen.

30 March: U. 884: Fortresses of the 8th Air Force: USAAF strategic bombing raid: 53°05'North 08°48'East: at Bremen.

30 March: U. 886: Fortresses of the 8th Air Force: USAAF strategic bombing raid: 53°05'North 08°48'East: at Bremen.

30 March: U. 3036: Fortresses of the 8th Air Force: USAAF strategic bombing raid: 53°05'North 08°48'East: at Bremen.

9 April: U. 2550: RAF strategic bombing raid: 53°33'North 10°00'East: at Hamburg.

Apparently construction of these boats was abandoned after these raids.

Requisitioned and Captured Boats:

In addition, the German Navy had a one requisitioned and seven captured boats in service that were scuttled at the end of the war. These were:

UA: requisition in 1939 when building for Turkey: scuttled on 2 May in 54°20'North 10°08'East: at Kiel.

UB: the British submarine *Seal*, captured in 1940: scuttled on 2 May in 54°22'North 10°12'East: at Heikendorf (below Kiel).

UD. 1 and UD. 2: the Dutch submarines O-8 and O-12 respectively, captured in 1940: scuttled on 3 May in 54°20'North 10°08'East at Kiel.

UD. 3: the Dutch submarine O-25, captured in 1940: scuttled in May in 54°20'North 10°08'East at Kiel.

UD. 4: the Dutch submarine O-26, captured in 1940: scuttled on 3 May in 54°20'North 10°08'East at Kiel.

U.IT.2 and U.IT.3: the Italian submarines R.11 and R. 12 respectively: captured in 1943: scuttled on 24 April in 44°24'North 08°56'East at Genoa.

Other boats:

U. 2367: Cause of loss disputed. Tarrant, *The Last Year of the Kriegsmarine*, and Kemp, *U-boats Destroyed*, state that this boat was sunk as a result of a collision with another U-boat when under air attack in the Kattegat on 5 May. Rohwer and Hummelchen, *Chronology of the War at Sea*, and Möller and Brack, *The Encyclopedia of U-boats*, state that this boat, in a damaged condition as a result of a collision, was scuttled at Schleimunde. The official British list does not record its loss. The boat is also given as having been raised in 1956 and brought into service with the West German Navy.

UF.2: Allegedly this ex-French boat, *La Favorite*, was commissioned into German service and sunk on 7 July 1944, agency of destruction undefined. Other sources indicate its being scuttled at the end of hostilities, but it is not included in any list provided in R&H as either scuttled or surrendered. For accounting purposes, this boat is considered to have been lost in 1944 to cause(s) unknown.

With the surrender of Germany, requisitioned by and commissioned into the Imperial Japanese Navy were the following boats:

U. 181: renumbered I.501 in July 1945: surrendered at Singapore and scuttled 12 February 1946.

U. 195: renumbered I.506 in July 1945: surrendered at Soerabaja.

U. 219: renumbered I.505 in July 1945: surrendered at Batavia.

U. 862: renumbered I.502 in July 1945: surrendered at Singapore and scuttled 12 February 1946.

10 May: U.IT. 24: the ex-Italian boat *Commandante Cappellini* and used as a transport: with the surrender of Germany, requisitioned by and commissioned into the Imperial Japanese Navy: renumbered I.503 in July 1945: surrendered at Kobe and scuttled 16 April 1946.

? May: U.IT. 25: The ex-Italian boat *Luigi Torelli*, initially seized by the Japanese in September 1943 before being transferred to the Kriegsmarine and used as a transport: with the surrender of Germany, requisitioned by and commissioned into the Imperial Japanese Navy: renumbered I.504 in July 1945: surrendered at Kobe and scuttled on 16 April 1946.

Table Appendix 6.4.1. German Naval Losses in the Second World War

		BB/CC	AC	CA	CL	DD	Esc	Tb	CM	AM	AM(A)	SS
September	1939	-	-	-	-	-	-	-	-	-	-	2
October	1939	-	-	-	-	-	-	-	-	1	-	5
November	1939	-	-	-	-	-	-	-	-	1	-	1
December	1939	-	1	-	-	-	1	-	-	-	-	1
1939	Total	-	1	-	-	-	1	-	-	2	-	9
January	1940	-	-	-	-	-	-	-	-	-	-	2
February	1940	-	-	-	-	2	-	-	-	-	-	5
March	1940	-	-	-	-	-	-	-	-	-	1	3
April	1940	-	-	1	2	10	-	2	-	-	-	4
May	1940	-	-	-	-	-	-	-	-	-	-	1
June	1940	-	-	-	-	-	-	-	-	2	-	1
July	1940	-	-	-	-	-	-	1	-	3	1	2
August	1940	-	-	-	-	-	-	-	-	-	1	2
September	1940	-	-	-	-	-	-	1	-	-	1	1
October	1940	-	-	-	-	-	-	-	-	-	-	1
November	1940	-	-	-	-	-	-	1	-	-	-	2
December	1940	-	-	-	-	-	-	-	-	-	1	-
1940	Total	-	-	1	2	12	-	5	-	5	5	24
January	1941	-	-	-	-	-	-	1	-	-	-	-
February	1941	-	-	-	-	-	-	-	-	-	-	-
March	1941	-	-	-	-	-	-	-	-	-	-	5
April	1941	-	-	-	-	-	-	-	-	-	-	2
May	1941	1	-	-	-	-	-	-	-	-	1	1
June	1941	-	-	-	-	-	-	-	-	-	-	4
July	1941	-	-	-	-	-	-	-	3	2	-	1
August	1941	-	-	-	-	-	-	-	-	-	-	3
September	1941	-	-	-	-	-	-	-	1	-	-	2
October	1941	-	-	-	-	-	-	-	-	1	-	2
November	1941	-	-	-	-	-	-	-	-	1	-	5
December	1941	-	-	-	-	-	-	-	-	2	-	10
1941	Total	1	-	-	-	-	-	1	4	6	1	35
January	1942	-	-	-	-	1	-	-	-	-	-	3
February	1942	-	-	-	-	-	-	-	-	-	1	2
March	1942	-	-	-	-	1	-	-	-	-	1	6
April	1942	-	-	-	-	-	-	-	-	-	-	3
May	1942	-	-	-	-	1	-	-	-	3	2	4
June	1942	-	-	-	-	-	-	-	-	-	2	3

		BB	AC	CA	CL	DD	Esc	Tb	CM	AM	AM(A)	SS
July	1942	-	-	-	-	-	-	-	-	-	2	11
August	1942	-	-	-	-	-	-	-	2	-	2	10
September	1942	-	-	-	-	-	-	-	-	-	3	11
October	1942	-	-	-	-	-	-	-	-	-	1	16
November	1942	-	-	-	-	-	-	-	-	1	1	13
December	1942	-	-	-	-	1	-	-	-	-	3	5
1942	Total	-	-	-	-	4	-	-	2	4	18	87
January	1943	-	-	-	-	-	-	-	-	-	-	6
February	1943	-	-	-	-	-	-	-	-	-	-	19
March	1943	-	-	-	-	-	-	2	1	-	-	16
April	1943	-	-	-	-	-	-	-	-	-	-	15
May	1943	-	-	-	-	1	-	2	-	3	1	41
June	1943	-	-	-	-	-	-	-	-	1	1	17
July	1943	-	-	-	-	-	-	-	-	3	1	37
August	1943	-	-	-	-	-	2	1	-	-	-	25
September	1943	-	-	-	-	-	1	2	1	2	-	10
October	1943	-	-	-	-	-	-	-	4	-	-	26
November	1943	-	-	-	-	-	-	-	-	1	-	19
December	1943	1	-	-	-	3	-	-	-	-	-	8
1943	Total	1	-	-	-	4	3	7	6	10	3	239
January	1944	-	-	-	-	-	-	-	1	1	1	15
February	1944	-	-	-	-	-	1	-	1	1	-	20
March	1944	-	-	-	-	-	-	2	-	1	3	25
April	1944	-	-	-	-	2	-	1	1	2	1	21
May	1944	-	-	-	-	-	-	1	3	4	-	23
June	1944	-	-	-	-	3	1	10	-	7	1	25
July	1944	-	-	-	-	-	-	2	-	6	2	23
August	1944	-	-	-	-	7	7	3	2	28	21	36
September	1944	-	-	-	-	-	-	5	1	6	2	22
October	1944	-	-	-	-	-	-	4	1	3	-	12
November	1944	1	-	-	-	1	-	2	2	3	2	9
December	1944	-	-	-	-	2	-	1	-	2	-	16
1944	Total	1	-	-	-	15	9	31	12	64	33	247
January	1945	-	-	-	-	-	1	-	1	6	1	14
February	1945	-	-	-	-	-	-	5	-	2	2	22
March	1945	1	-	-	-	1	1	3	-	11	-	30
April	1945	-	2	-	1	-	2	5	5	6	1	62
May	1945	-	-	1	1	1	1	3	-	6	1	30
1945	Total	1	2	1	2	2	5	16	6	31	5	158
Overall	Total	4	3	2	4	37	18	60	30	122	65	799

In addition to the total of 30 U-boats cited as losses in May 1945, another 212 were scuttled.

Key:

BB/CC	Capital ships	DD	Destroyers	CM	Minelayers
AC	Armored ships	Esc	Escorts	AM	Minesweepers
CA	Heavy cruisers	Tb	Torpedo-boats	AM(A)	*Sperrbrecher*
CL	Light cruisers			SS	Submarines

Map 7a. Losses of Major German Naval Units, 1939–1941

Map 7.a. German losses of major naval units, 1939–1941.

KEY:

1939

001.	17 December	Armored ship *Admiral Graf Spee*	Outside Montevideo	35°11'North 56°26'West	Scuttled (not shown).

1940

002.	22 February	Destroyer Z. 1/ *Leberecht Maass*	Off Borkum	53°35'North 06°40'East	Mine.
003.	22 February	Destroyer Z. 3/*Max Schlutz*	Off Borkum	53°35'North 06°40'East	Mine.
004.	9 April	Heavy cruiser *Blücher*	In Oslofjorden	59°44'North 10°36'East	Coastal battery.
005.	9 April	Light cruiser *Karlsruhe*	Off Kristiansand	58°04'North 08°04'East	Torpedoed by British submarine and scuttled.
006.	10 April	Light cruiser *Königsberg*	Off Bergen	60°24'North 05°19'East	Carrier aircraft.
007.	10 April	Torpedo-boat *Albatros*	Off Søstren Bolaerne	59°24'North 10°35'East	Ran aground.
008.	11 April	Destroyer Z. 21/ *Wilhelm Heidkamp*	First Narvik	68°25'North 17°24'East	Surface action
009.	11 April	Destroyer Z. 22/ *Anton Schmitt*	First Narvik	68°25'North 17°24'East	Surface action
010.	13 April	Destroyer Z. 2/*Georg Thiele*	Second Narvik	68°24'North 17°35'East	Surface action.
011.	13 April	Destroyer Z. 9/ *Wolfgang Zenker*	Second Narvik	68°25'North 17°55'East	Scuttled after surface action.
012.	13 April	Destroyer Z. 11/ *Bernd von Arnim*	Second Narvik	68°25'North 17°54'East	Scuttled after surface action.
013.	13 April	Destroyer Z. 12/*Erich Giese*	Second Narvik	68°25'North 17°39'East	Surface action.
014.	13 April	Destroyer Z. 13/ *Erich Köllner*	Second Narvik	68°24'North 16°48'East	Surface action.
015.	13 April	Destroyer Z. 17/ *Diether von Röder*	Second Narvik	68°25'North 17°34'East	Scuttled after surface action.
016.	13 April	Destroyer Z. 18/ *Hans Lüdemann*	Second Narvik	68°25'North 17°54'East	Scuttled after surface action.
017.	13 April	Destroyer Z. 19/ *Hermann Künne*	Second Narvik	68°31'North 17°35'East	Scuttled after surface action.
018.	30 April	Torpedo-boat *Leopard*	In the Skagerrak	58°00'North 10°00'East	Collision.
019.	26 July	Torpedo-boat *Luchs*	In the North Sea	60°00'North 04°00'East	British submarine.
020.	18 September	Torpedo-boat T. 3	At Le Havre	49°30'North 00°06'East	British aircraft.
021.	7 November	Torpedo-boat T. 6	Off Aberdeen	57°08'North 01°58'West	Mine.

1941

022.	8 January	Torpedo-boat *Wolf*	Off Dunkirk	51°05'North 02°08'East	Mine.
023.	27 May	Battleship *Bismarck*	In the North Atlantic	48°10'North 16°12'West	Surface action.

Map 7b. Losses of Major German Naval Units, 1942 and 1943

Map 7B. Losses of Major German Naval Units, 1942 and 1943

KEY:

1942					
024.	25 January	Destroyer Z. 8/ *Bruno Heinemann*	Off Dunkirk	51°02'North 02°23'East	Mine.
025.	29 March	Destroyer Z. 26	In the Barents Sea	72°07'North 32°15'East	Surface action
026.	2 May	Destroyer Z. 7/ *Hermann Schoemann*	In the Arctic	73°30'North 35°10'East	Scuttled after surface action.
027.	13 May	Torpedo-boat *Iltis*	Off Boulogne	50°46'North 01°34'East	British MTBs.
028.	13 May	Torpedo-boat *Seeadler*	Off Cap Griz-Nez	50°48'North 01°32'East	British MTBs.
029.	31 December	Destroyer *Freidrich Eckoldt*	In the Barents Sea	77°19'North 30°47'East	Surface action.
1943					
030.	18 March	Torpedo-boat TA. 24	Off northeast Corsica	42°49'North 09°40'East	Surface action.
031.	18 March	Torpedo-boat TA. 29	Off northeast Corsica	43°30'North 09°30'East	Surface action.
032.	7 May	Destroyer ZG. 3	Outside Tunis	36°46'North 10°21'East	Scuttled as blockship.
033.	22 August	Torpedo-boat TA. 12	Near Cape Prasonesi	35°08'North 27°53'East	Surface action.
034.	24 August	Escort SG. 14	South of Capri	40°35'North 14°12'East	U.S. aircraft.
035.	28 August	Escort SG. 10	West of Corsica	42°24'North 09°41'East	British submarine.
036.	11 September	Torpedo-boat TA. 11	Outside Piombino	42°55'North 10°32'East	Italian tanks.
037.	23 September	Escort SG. 2	At Nantes	47°13'North 01°34'West	U.S. aircraft.
038.	25 September	Torpedo-boat TA. 10	At Rhodes	36°25'North 28°14'East	Sank after surface action
039.	13 December	Torpedo-boat T. 15	At Kiel	54°20'North 10°08'East	U.S. aircraft.
040.	26 December	Battleship *Scharnhorst*	Off North Cape	72°16'North 28°41'East	Surface action.
041.	28 December	Destroyer T. 25	In the Bay of Biscay --°-- 'North --°-- 'East	British warships.	
042.	28 December	Destroyer T. 26	In the Bay of Biscay --°-- 'North --°-- 'East	British warships.	
043.	28 December	Destroyer Z. 27	In the Bay of Biscay --°-- 'North --°-- 'East	British warships.	

MAP 7C. Losses of Major German Naval Units, 1944

Map 7.c. German losses of major naval units, 1944

KEY:

1944					
044.	4 February	Escort SG. 18	At Toulon	43°07'North 05°55'East	U.S. aircraft.
045.	8 March	Torpedo-boat TA. 15	At Heraklion	35°28'North 25°07'East	British aircraft.
046.	18 March	Torpedo-boat TA. 36	Off Fiume	45°07'North 14°21'East	Mine.
047.	26 April	Destroyer T. 29	Off Les Sept Iles	48°53'North 03°33'West	British warship.
048.	26 April	Torpedo-boat TA. 23	North of Elba	43°02'North 10°12'East	Mined and scuttled.
049.	29 April	Destroyer T. 27	west of Roscoff	48°39'North 04°21'West	Canadian warship.
050.	23 May	Torpedo-boat *Greif*	Off Ouistreham	49°21'North 00°19'West	British aircraft and collision.
051.	2 June	Escort SG. 11	At Port Vendres	42°30'North 03°07'East	British submarine.
052.	2 June	Torpedo-boat TA. 16	At Heraklion	35°20'North 25°10'East	British aircraft.
053.	9 June	Destroyer Z. 32	Off Roscoff	48°47'North 04°07'West	Surface action
054.	9 June	Destroyer ZH. 1	Off Roscoff	48°47'North 04°07'West	Surface action
055.	9 June	Torpedo-boat TA. 27	At Portoferraio, Elba	42°49'North 10°20'East	U.S. aircraft.
056.	15 June	Torpedo-boat *Möwe*	Off Le Havre	49°30'North 00°07'East	British aircraft.
057.	15 June	Torpedo-boat *Falke*	Off Le Havre	49°30'North 00°07'East	British aircraft.
058.	15 June	Torpedo-boat *Jaguar*	Off Le Havre	49°30'North 00°07'East	British aircraft.
059.	15 June	Torpedo-boat TA. 26	Off La Spezia	43°58'North 09°29'East	U.S. PT-boat.
060.	15 June	Torpedo-boat TA. 30	Off La Spezia	43°58'North 09°29'East	U.S. PT-boat.
061.	20 June	Destroyer T. 31	In Gulf of Finland	60°16'North 28°17'East	Soviet MTBs
062.	21 June	Torpedo-boat TA. 25	Off Viareggio	43°49'North 10°12'East	U.S. PT-boat.
063.	24 June	Torpedo-boat TA. 34	West of Sebenico	43°47'North 15°36'East	Surface action and ran aground.
064.	28 June	Torpedo-boat *Kondor*	In dock at Le Havre	49°30'North 00°06'East	British aircraft.
065.	29 July	Torpedo-boat T. 2	At Bremen	53°05'North 08°48'East	U.S. aircraft.
066.	29 July	Torpedo-boat T. 7	At Bremen	53°05'North 08°48'East	U.S. aircraft.
067.	6 August	Escort SG. 3	At Les Sables d'Olonne	46°30'North 01°47'West	British(?) aircraft.
068.	9 August	Torpedo-boat TA. 19	Off Vathi, Sámos	37°44'North 26°59'East	Greek submarine.
069.	15 August	Escort SG. 21/ *Bernd von Arnim*	Off St. Tropez	43°16'North 06°39'East	Surface action.
070.	17 August	Torpedo-boat TA. 35	Near Pola	44°53'North 13°47'East	Mine.
071.	18 August	Destroyer T. 22	Outside Narva	59°42'North 27°44'East	Mine.
072.	18 August	Destroyer T. 30	Outside Narva	59°43'North 27°44'East	Mine.
073.	18 August	Destroyer T. 32	Outside Narva	59°42'North 27°43'East	Mine.
074.	21 August	Destroyer Z. 23	At La Pallice	46°10'North 01°12'West	British aircraft and scuttled.
075.	22 August	Escort SG. 16	At Marseille	43°18'North 05°22'East	Scuttled.
076.	22 August	Escort SG. 24	At Marseille	43°18'North 05°22'East	Scuttled.
077.	? August	Escort SG. 17	At Marseille	43°18'North 05°22'East	Scuttled.
078.	23 August	Torpedo-boat TA. 9	At Toulon	43°07'North 05°56'East	U.S. aircraft.
079.	24 August	Destroyer T. 24	In the Gironde estuary	45°31'North 01°05'West	British aircraft.
080.	24 August	Destroyer Z. 37	At Bordeaux	44°50'North 00°34'West	Scuttled.
081.	25 August	Destroyer Z. 24	In the Gironde estuary	45°31'North 01°06'West	British aircraft.
082.	28 August	Escort SG. 12/M. 6062	At Marseille	43°18'North 05°22'East	Scuttled.
083.	28 August	Escort SG. 13/M. 6063	At Marseille	43°18'North 05°22'East	Scuttled.
084.	4 September	Torpedo-boat TA. 28	In dock at Genoa	44°23'North 08°51'East	U.S. aircraft.
085.	15 September	Torpedo-boat TA. 14	At Salamina	37°57'North 23°32'East	U.S. aircraft.
086.	17 September	Torpedo-boat T. 18	Off Tallinn	59°22'North 24°03'East	Soviet aircraft.
087.	18 September	Torpedo-boat TA. 17	At Piraeus	37°57'North 23°42'East	British aircraft.
088.	27 September	Torpedo-boat TA. 7	In the Horten dockyard	59°25'North 10°30'East	Sabotage.
089.	7 October	Torpedo-boat TA. 37	Off Salonika	40°36'North 22°46'East	Surface action
090.	12 October	Torpedo-boat TA. 15	At Piraeus	37°57'North 23°42'East	British (?) aircraft.
091.	12 October	Torpedo-boat TA. 38	At Vólos	39°22'North 22°57'East	British carrier aircraft.
092.	16 October	Torpedo-boat TA. 39	Off Cape Dermata, Crete	--°-- 'North --°--'East	Mine.
093.	19 October	Torpedo-boat TA. 18	Off Vólos	39°22'North 22°57'East	Surface action.
094.	1 November	Torpedo-boat TA. 20	Off Pag Island, Zara	37°45'North 26°59'East	Surface action.
095.	5 November	Torpedo-boat TA. 21	At Fiume	45°20'North 14°27'East	U.S. aircraft.
096.	12 November	Battleship *Tirpitz*	At Tromsø	69°36'North 18°59'East	British aircraft.
097.	20 November	Destroyer T. 34	Off Cape Arkona	54°40'North 13°29'East	Soviet mine.
098.	12 December	Destroyer Z. 35	Off Tallinn	59°34'North 24°49'West	Mine.
099.	12 December	Destroyer Z. 36	Off Tallinn	59°37'North 24°51'West	Mine.
100.	18 December	Pre-dreadnought *Schleswig-Holstein*	At Gotenhafen	54°32'North 18°34'East	British aircraft.
101.	18 December	Torpedo-boat T. 10	At Gotenhafen	54°32'North 18°34'East	British aircraft.

Map 7D. Losses of Major German Naval Units, 1945

Map 7.d. German losses of major naval units, 1945.

KEY:

102.	17 February	Torpedo-boat TA. 41	At Trieste	45°39'North 13°47'East	U.S. aircraft.
103.	17 February	Torpedo-boat TA. 44	At Trieste	45°39'North 13°47'East	U.S. aircraft.
104.	20 February	Torpedo-boat TA. 40	At Trieste	45°39'North 13°47'East	U.S. aircraft.
105.	20 February	Torpedo-boat TA. 46	At Fiume	45°20'North 14°27'East	U.S. aircraft.
106.	20 February	Torpedo-boat TA. 48	At Trieste	45°39'North 13°47'East	U.S. aircraft.
107.	6 March	Destroyer Z. 28	At Sassnitz	54°30'North 19°40'West	British aircraft
108.	14 March	Torpedo-boat T. 3	North of Hela	54°39'North 18°47'East	Mine.
109.	14 March	Torpedo-boat T. 5	North of Hela	54°39'North 18°47'East	Mine.
110.	15 March	Battleship *Gneisenau*	At Gotenhafen	54°32'North 18°34'East	Scuttled.
111.	21 March	Torpedo-boat TA. 42	At Venice	45°26'North 12°20'East	British aircraft.
112.	9 April	Armoured ship *Admiral Scheer*	At Kiel	54°20'North 10°08'East	British aircraft.
113.	10 April	Torpedo-boat T. 1	At Kiel	54°20'North 10°08'East	U.S. aircraft.
114.	10 April	Torpedo-boat T. 13	In the Kattegat	--°-- 'North --°-- 'East	British aircraft.
115.	13 April	Torpedo-boat T. 16	At Frederikshavn	57°28'North 10°33'East	British aircraft.
116.	13 April	Torpedo-boat TA. 45	In the Morlacca Channel between Rab and coast	--°-- 'North --°-- 'East	British MTBs.
117.	16 April	Armoured ship *Lützow*	At Swinemünde	53°56'North 14°17'East	British aircraft.
118.	24 April	Torpedo-boat TA. 32	At Genoa	44°24'North 08°56'East	Scuttled.
119.	25 April	Escort SG. 20	At Oneglia	43°53'North 08°03'East	Scuttled.
120.	26 April	Escort SG. 15	Off Genoa	44°24'North 08°56'East	British submarine.
121.	30 April	Light cruiser *Köln*	At Wilhelmshaven	53°32'North 14°18'East	British aircraft.
122.	1 May	Torpedo-boat TA. 43	At Trieste	45°39'North 13°47'East	Scuttled.
123.	3 May	Heavy cruiser *Admiral Hipper*	At Kiel	54°20'North 10°08'East	Scuttled.
124.	3 May	Torpedo-boat T. 8	Off Kiel	54°26'North 10°05'East	British aircraft.
125.	3 May	Torpedo-boat T. 9	Off Kiel	54°26'North 10°05'East	British aircraft.
126.	4 May	Destroyer T. 36			either mined and bombed by Soviet aircraft in the central Baltic or sunk by British aircraft in the Belts.
127.	5 May	Pre-dreadnought *Schlesien*	Off Swinemünde	53°55'North 14°18'East	Mined, bombed, and scuttled.

Notes for map 7c:

1. Certain German units incurred various degrees of damage but were not sunk or lost and were subsequently scuttled, this being most apparent in the war's last weeks. Warships rendered hors de combat as a result of attack, which were not returned to service and which were scuttled have been afforded dates that accord with the Allied attack rather than the dates when the coup de grâce was administered. For example, the torpedo-boat TA. 40 was rendered hors de combat by American bombers in the raid on Trieste of 20 February and was scuttled at Monfalcone on 4 May 1945. The first date is given as date of loss (i.e., the date after which it was never in service) and cause of loss cited accordingly.

2. Excluded from the lists are armed merchant raiders that were lost, namely:

8 May 1941	The 7,766-ton *Pinquin*	North of the Seychelles	British warship.
19 November 1941	The 8,736-ton *Kormoran*	Off western Australia	Australian warship.
22 November 1941	The 7,862-ton *Atlantis*	North of Ascension Island	British warship.
27 September 1942	The 4,778-ton *Stier*	In the South Atlantic	U.S. merchantman.
14 October 1942	The 3,287-ton *Komet*	Off Cherbourg	British MTBs.
30 November 1942	The 3,862-ton *Thor*	At Yokohama	Explosion of tanker Uckermark alongside.
17 October 1943	The 4,740-ton *Michel*	Off Yokohama	U.S. submarine.

3. German units surrendered at war's end:

The heavy cruiser *Prinz Eugen* and the light cruiser *Nürnberg*.
The destroyers T. 23, T. 28, T. 33, and T. 35.
The destroyers Z. 4/*Dietrich Beitzen*, Z. 5/*Paul Jacobi*, Z. 6/*Theodor Riedael*, Z. 10/*Hans Lody*, Z. 14/*Friedrich Ihn*, Z. 15/*Erich Steinbrinck*, and Z. 20/*Karl Galster*.
The destroyers Z. 25, Z. 29, Z. 30, Z. 31, Z. 33, Z, 34, Z. 38, and Z. 39.
The torpedo-boats T. 4, T. 11, T. 12, T. 14, T. 17, T. 19, T. 20, and T. 21.

Table Appendix 6.4.2. German Minelayers, Minesweepers, and *Sperrbrecher* Lost in the Second World War[1]

Date	Vessel	Location	Position	Cause
1939				
1 October	Minesweeper M. 85	Northeast of Heisternest	54°45'North 18°45'East†	Mine laid by Polish submarine.[2]
19 November	Minesweeper M. 132	Off Lister Bank in southwest Norway	58°17'North 06°40'East	Damaged by depth-charges of another minesweeper and beached as total loss.[3]
1940				
20 March	The 8,132-ton *Sperrbrecher* 12	Off Ameland in the Friesian Islands	53°27'North 05°48'East	British aircraft.
6 June	Minesweeper M. 11	Off the Feistenen light vessel	58°53'North 05°36'East	Mine laid by British submarine.[4]
18 June	Minesweeper M. 5	In Ramsøyfjorden	63°30'North 08°12'East	Mine laid by British submarine.[5]
16 July	The 1,025-ton *Sperrbrecher* 71	Off Dragor at entrance to Öre Sund	55°36'North 12°42'East	Mine.
26 July	Minesweeper M. 61	Off the Hook of Holland	51°59'North 04°07'East	Mine laid by British warships.
26 July	Minesweeper M. 89	Off the Hook of Holland	51°59'North 04°07'East	Mine laid by British warships.
26 July	Minesweeper M. 136	Off the Hook of Holland	51°59'North 04°07'East	Mine laid by British warships.
1 August	The 7,512-ton *Sperrbrecher* 12	Off Schiermonnikoog Island	53°50'North 06°15'East	Mine.
22 September	The 4,450-ton *Sperrbrecher* 2	In the harbor entrance at Boulogne	50°43'North 01°37'East	Mine: salved.
1 December	The 764-ton *Sperrbrecher* 38	In the Elbe off Brunsbüttel	53°54'North 09°08'East	Collision: salved.
1941				
25 May	The 1,049-ton *Sperrbrecher* 33	Off Texel	53°09'North 04°43'East	British aircraft.
9 July	The 2,431-ton minelayer *Hansestadt Danzig*	Off southern Öland in the Baltic	56°12'North 16°17'East†	Swedish mine.
9 July	The 2,529-ton minelayer *Preussen*	Off southern Öland in the Baltic	56°12'North 16°17'East†	Swedish mine.
9 July	The 5,504-ton minelayer *Tannenberg*	Off southern Öland in the Baltic	56°12'North 16°17'East†	Swedish mine.
10 July	Minesweeper M. 201	In the Irben Strait, Gulf of Riga	57°48'North 22°12'East	Mine. Salved & returned to service.
11 July	Minesweeper M. 23	At Pernau on the Gulf of Riga	58°28'North 24°30'East	Mine. Salved & returned to service.

25 September	The 2,399-ton minelayer *Königin Luise*	South of Helsinki	60°07'North 24°56'East†	Soviet mine.
23 October	Minesweeper M. 6	South of Lorient	47°18'North 04°20'West†	Mine.
3 November	Minesweeper M. 511	Outside Kolberg harbor	54°10'North 15°35'East	Mine.
2 December	Minesweeper M. 529	Outside Kolberg harbor	54°10'North 15°35'East	Mine.
23 December	Minesweeper M. 557	Off Rügen Island in the Baltic	54°25'North 13°24'East	Mined in storm and foundered.
1942				
20 February	The 1,025-ton *Sperrbrecher* 171	Northwest of Calais	50°57'North 01°52'East	Mine.
27 March	The 482-ton *Sperrbrecher* 147	Off the Hook of Holland	51°59'North 04°07'East	Mine.
9 May	Minesweeper M. 533	Off Boulogne	50°43'North 01°37'East	Collision with warship.
15 May	Minesweeper M. 26	Off Cap de la Hague	49°43'North 01°56'West	British aircraft.
15 May	Minesweeper M. 256	In the harbor at Cherbourg	49°38'North 01°37'West	Sank after action with British aircraft: salved and returned to service.
28 May	The 1,337-ton *Sperrbrecher* 174	Off Dunkirk	51°02'North 02°23'East	Mine.
29 May	The 750-ton *Sperrbrecher* 150	Off Ameland in the Friesian Islands	53°27'North 05°48'East	Allied aircraft.
8 June	The 7,003-ton *Sperrbrecher* 15	Off Scharnhorn near the Elbe light	53°58'North 08°28'East	British aircraft: salved.
23 June	The 560-ton *Sperrbrecher* 183	Off Dunkirk	51°02'North 02°23'East	Mine.
1 July	The 1,392-ton *Sperrbrecher* 191	West of Ochakov on the Black Sea	46°37'North 31°33'East	Mine.
4 July	The 1,078-ton *Sperrbrecher* 61	Off Schiermonnikoog Island	53°50'North 06°15'East	Mine.
7 August	The 1,598-ton *Sperrbrecher* 170	Off Ostend	51°13'North 02°55'East	Mine.
16 August	The 1,136-ton *Sperrbrecher* 60	Off Den Helder	52°58'North 04°46'East	Mine.
25 August	The 3,071-ton minelayer *Ulm*	South of Bear Island in the Arctic	74°31'North 19°01'East	British warships.
27 August	The 2,131-ton minelayer *Cobra*	At Schiedam near Rotterdam	51°55'North 04°25'East	U.S. aircraft.
2 September	The 1,172-ton *Sperrbrecher* 164	Off Schiermonnikoog Island	53°50'North 06°15'East	Mine.
12 September	The 7,019-ton *Sperrbrecher* 14	Off Royan in the Gironde estuary	45°38'North 01°02'West	Mined and *hors de combat*.[6]
14 September	The 499-ton *Sperrbrecher* 142	Off Ostend	51°13'North 02°55'East	Mine.
9 October	The 498-ton *Sperrbrecher* 143	Off Nieuwpoort/Nieuport, Belgium	50°08'North 02°45'East	Mine.

19 November	The 1,078-ton *Sperrbrecher* 169	North of Norderney in the Friesians	53°43'North 07°09'East	Mine.
25 November	Minesweeper M. 101	Off Namsos in central Norway	64°20'North 11°30'East	Collision with merchantman.
12 December	The 1,236-ton *Sperrbrecher* 178	Off Dieppe in the English Channel	50°03'North 01°07'East†	Allied warships.
23 December	The 1,262-ton *Sperrbrecher* 138	Off Borkum Island, southern North Sea	53°35'North 06°40'East	Mine.
28 December	The 544-ton *Sperrbrecher* 149	Off Den Helder	52°58'North 04°46'East	Mine.
1943				
4 March	The 5,154-ton minelayer *Doggerbank*	In the central North Atlantic	29°10'North 34°10'West†	In error by German submarine.
14 May	Minesweeper M. 8	Off the Hook of Holland	52°03'North 03°51'East†	British MTBs.
17 May	Minesweeper M. 414	West of Texel in southern North Sea	53°09'North 04°38'East†	British aircraft.[7]
18 May	Minesweeper M. 345	Off Gravelines in the Dover Strait	51°03'North 02°07'East	British aircraft.
25 May	The 1,288-ton *Sperrbrecher* 173	Off Ameland in the Friesian Islands	53°27'North 05°48'East	Mine.
13 June	Minesweeper M. 483	South of Alderney, Channel Islands	49°43'North 02°12'East	British aircraft.
16 June	The 2,446-ton *Sperrbrecher* 21	In the Gironde estuary	45°31'North 01°05'West	Mine.
8 July	The 1,481-ton *Sperrbrecher* 165	East of the Gedser Odde, Falster Island, Denmark	54°34'North 11°58'East	Mine.
10 July	Minesweeper M. 153	Off the Ile d'Ouessant, Brittany	48°28'North 05°05'West	British warships.
17 July	Minesweeper M. 346	Off Gamvik, Tanafjorden, in Finnmark	71°03'North 28°10'East	Soviet submarine.
23 July	Minesweeper M. 152	In the Gironde estuary	45°30'North 01°00'West	Mine.
21 September	The 3,894-ton minelayer *Brandenburg*	Off Capraia northeast of Corsica	43°03'North 09°51'East	British submarine.
25 September	Minesweeper M. 471	In the roadstead at Den Helder	52°58'North 04°46'East	British aircraft.[8]
27 September	Minesweeper M. 534	Off Fécamp in the English Channel	49°45'North 00°23'East	Allied MTB/MGBs.
6 October	The 2,956-ton minelayer *Pommern*	Off San Remo, northwest Italy	43°47'North 07°51'East†	Mine.
8 October	The 1,108-ton minelayer *Bulgaria*	South of Amorgós in the Aegean	39°46'North 25°54'East	British submarine.

29 October	The 742-ton minelayer *Juminda*	West of Porto San Stefano	42°27'North 11°01'East	British MTBs.
-- October	The 1,071-ton minelayer *Westmark*	In the harbor at La Spezia	44°06'North 09°49'East	Allied aircraft.
4 November	Minesweeper M. 16	In the harbor at Kotka, Finland	60°26'North 26°55'East	Soviet aircraft.[9]
1944				
20 January	The 1,281-ton minelayer *Skagerrak*	Off Egersund in southwest Norway	58°27'North 06°01'East	British aircraft.
28 January	The 996-ton *Sperrbrecher* 137	Off St. Nazaire	47°17'North 02°12'East	Mine.
30 January	Minesweeper M. 451	Off Porkkala in the Gulf of Finland	60°00'North 24°25'East	Ran aground and scuttled.
6 February	Minesweeper M. 156	At L'Aber-Wrach in Brittany	48°35'North 04°36'West	British aircraft.
15 February	The 1,794-ton minelayer *Niedersachsen*	Off Toulon	43°02'North 06°01'East†	British submarine
7 March	The 7,358-ton *Sperrbrecher* 10	North of Norderney in the Friesians	53°43'North 07°09'East	Mine.
14 March	Minesweeper M. 10	Outside Dunkirk	51°02'North 02°23'East	British MTB.
20 March	The 1,029-ton *Sperrbrecher* 163	Off Cuxhaven	53°52'North 08°42'East	Mine.
31 March	The 465-ton *Sperrbrecher* 141	Off Oostende/Ostend	51°13'North 02°55'East	Mine.
10 April	Minesweeper M. 459	In Narva Bay in the Gulf of Finland	59°30'North 27°05'East†	Soviet aircraft
10 April	The 600-ton *Sperrbrecher* 193	At Sulina in Romania	45°07'North 29°40'East	Soviet aircraft.
21 April	The 2,436-ton minelayer *Roland*	In Narva Bay in the Gulf of Finland	59°43'North 22°28'East	Mine.
21 April	Minesweeper M. 553	Off the Brüster Ort headland	54°57'North 20°02'East	Mined: salved.
12 May	The 3,152-ton minelayer *Romania*	Between Odessa and Constanta	44°12'North 28°40'East	Soviet aircraft.
12 May	Minesweeper M. 372	In the harbor at Swinemünde	53°55'North 14°18'East	British aircraft.[10]
14 May	Minesweeper M. 435	Northeast of Ameland	53°34'North 06°04'East†	British aircraft.
19 May	The 606-ton minelayer *Kehrwieder*	In the harbor at La Spezia	44°06'North 09°49'East	U.S. aircraft.
22 May	The 1,071-ton minelayer *Vallelunga*	In the harbor at Genoa	44°24'North 08°56'East	Allied aircraft.

24 May	Minesweeper M. 39	Off Ouistreham, Normandy	49°21'North 00°19'West†	British MTB.
31 May	Minesweeper M. 13	In the Gironde estuary	45°30'North 01°00'West	One of her own mines.
1 June	The 1,747-ton *Sperrbrecher* 181	Off Ålesund in central Norway	62°28'North 06°11'East	British aircraft: run aground.
4 June	Minesweeper M. 37	In Narva Bay in the Gulf of Finland	59°30'North 27°36'East†	Soviet MTB.
14 June	Minesweeper M. 83	North of St. Malo	48°39'North 02°00'West	British warships.[11]
14 June	Minesweeper M. 343	North of St. Malo	48°39'North 02°00'West	Allied warships.[12]
15 June	Minesweeper M. 103	Off Schiermonnikoog Island	53°35'North 06°10'East†	British aircraft.
15 June	Minesweeper M. 402	In the harbor at Boulogne	50°43'North 01°37'East	British aircraft.
15 June	Minesweeper M. 507	In the harbor at Boulogne	50°43'North 01°37'East	British aircraft.
15 June	Minesweeper M. 550	In the harbor at Boulogne	50°43'North 01°37'East	British aircraft.
1 July	The 5,828-ton *Sperrbrecher* 9	In the harbor at La Pallice	46°10'North 01°12'West	Scuttled.
4 July	Minesweeper M. 469	Northwest of Vlieland Island	53°21'North 04°57'East†	British MTB.
8 July	Minesweeper M. 264	West of Heligoland	54°09'North 07°52'East	British aircraft.
20 July	Minesweeper M. 20	Off Narva in the Gulf of Finland	59°22'North 28°01'East	Soviet aircraft.
21 July	Minesweeper M. 307	Between Langeoog and the coast	53°30'North 07°36'West	British aircraft.[13]
21 July	Minesweeper M. 413	In Narva Bay in the Gulf of Finland	59°30'North 28°01'East	Soviet aircraft.
24 July	The 4,006-ton *Sperrbrecher* 25	In the harbor at Kiel	54°20'North 10°08'East	British aircraft
30 July	Minesweeper M. 455	In the harbor at Hamburg	53°33'North 10°00'East	U.S. aircraft. Salved.
4 August	Minesweeper M. 422	In the harbor at St. Malo	48°39'North 02°00'West	British aircraft.
4 August	Minesweeper M. 424	In the harbor at St. Malo	48°39'North 02°00'West	British aircraft.
4 August	The 479-ton *Sperrbrecher* 146	At Pauillac on the Gironde	45°12'North 00°44'West	Allied aircraft.
5 August	Minesweeper M. 271	At Pauillac on the Gironde	45°12'North 00°44'West	British aircraft.
5 August	Minesweeper M. 325	At Pauillac on the Gironde	45°12'North 00°44'East	British aircraft.
6 August	Minesweeper M. 133	In the harbor at St. Malo	48°39'North 02°00'West	Scuttled.[14]
6 August	Minesweeper M. 263	North of the Ile d'Yeu	46°43'North 02°20'West	British warships.
6 August	Minesweeper M. 486	South of the Ile d'Yeu	46°30'North 01°47'West	British warships.
8 August	Minesweeper M. 366	In the harbor at St. Nazaire	47°17'North 02°12'West	British aircraft.[15]

8 August	Minesweeper M. 367	In the harbor at St. Nazaire	47°17'North 02°12'West	British aircraft.
8 August	Minesweeper M. 428	In the harbor at St. Nazaire	47°17'North 02°12'West	British aircraft.
8 August	Minesweeper M. 438	In the harbor at St. Nazaire	47°17'North 02°12'West	British aircraft.
10 August	Minesweeper M. 384	At Nantes on the Loire	47°14'North 01°35'West	Scuttled.
11 August	Minesweeper M. 27	In the Gironde estuary	45°15'North 00°44'West†	Mine.
11 August	Minesweeper M. 84	In dock at Le Havre	49°30'North 00°06'East	Scuttled.
11 August	The 5,487-ton *Sperrbrecher* 16	In the harbor at La Pallice	46°10'North 01°12'West	Allied aircraft.
11 August	The 3,723-ton *Sperrbrecher* 20	In the harbor at Nantes	47°14'North 01°35'West	Scuttled.
12 August	The 984-ton minelayer *Dietrich von Bern*	In the harbor at Genoa	44°24'North 08°56'East	British aircraft.
12 August	Minesweeper M. 370	At Royan at the mouth of the Gironde	45°38'North 01°02'West	British aircraft and run aground.
12 August	Minesweeper M. 468	West of Namsos, central Norway	64°29'North 10°31'East†	Mine.
12 August	The 7,087-ton *Sperrbrecher* 7	Off La Pallice	46°10'North 01°12'West	Allied warships.
12 August	The 997-ton *Sperrbrecher* 134	Off Ile de Groix south of Lorient	47°45'North 03°21'West	British aircraft.
13 August	Minesweeper M. 383	Off Spiekeroog in the Friesians	53°50'North 07°45'East†	British aircraft.
13 August	The 6,128-ton *Sperrbrecher* 6	At Royan at the mouth of the Gironde	45°38'North 01°02'West	Allied aircraft: scuttled.
14 August	Minesweeper M. 206	In the harbor at St. Malo	48°39'North 02°00'West	Scuttled.
14 August	Minesweeper M. 444	In the harbor at Brest	48°23'North 04°30'West	British aircraft.
14 August	The 5,339-ton *Sperrbrecher* 5	At Royan at the mouth of the Gironde	45°38'North 01°02'West	Allied aircraft.
15 August	Minesweeper M. 385	Off Les Sables d'Olonne	46°30'North 01°47'West	British warships.
15 August	The 1,495-ton *Sperrbrecher* 157	In harbor at Les Sables d'Olonne	46°30'North 01°47'West	Allied aircraft
18 August	The 4,820-ton *Sperrbrecher* 37	In the harbor at St. Nazaire	47°17'North 02°12'East	Scuttled.
21 August	Minesweeper M. 292	In the Gironde estuary	45°30'North 01°00'West	British aircraft.
23 August	Minesweeper M. 344	In the harbor at Rochefort	45°57'North 00°58'West	Scuttled.
24 August	The 2,406-ton minelayer *Cyrnos*	In the harbor at Marseille	43°18'North 05°22'East	Scuttled.
24 August	The 3,261-ton *Sperrbrecher* 1	In the harbor at Brest	48°23'North 04°30'West	Allied aircraft.

24 August	The 995-ton *Sperrbrecher* 135	In the harbor at Brest	48°23'North 04°30'West	Allied aircraft.
25 August	Minesweeper M. 262	In the harbor at Bordeaux	44°50'North 00°34'West	Scuttled.
25 August	Minesweeper M. 304	In the harbor at Bordeaux	44°50'North 00°34'West	Scuttled.
25 August	Minesweeper M. 347	Off Schiermonnikoog Island	53°34'North 06°01'East†	British aircraft.
25 August	Minesweeper M. 363	In the harbor at Bordeaux	44°50'North 00°34'West	Scuttled.
25 August	Minesweeper M. 463	In the harbor at Bordeaux	44°50'North 00°34'West	Scuttled.
25 August	The 7,019-ton *Sperrbrecher* 122	In the Gironde or at St. Nazaire	--°--'North --°--'East	Scuttled.
25 August	The 1,297-ton *Sperrbrecher* 162	In the harbor at Brest	48°23'North 04°30'West	Allied aircraft: salved.
25 August	The 1,747-ton *Sperrbrecher* 180	In the harbor at Brest	48°23'North 04°30'West	Allied aircraft.
25 August	The 800-ton *Sperrbrecher* 194	On the Danube at Brăila in Romania	45°17'North 27°58'East	Soviet army artillery.
25 August	The 5,191-ton *Sperrbrecher* 195	At Constanta in Romania	44°12'North 28°40'East	Scuttled.
26 August	Minesweeper M. 266	Outside Kiel	54°20'North 10°08'East	British aircraft: salved.
27 August	The 6,757-ton *Sperrbrecher* 4	In the harbor at Brest	48°23'North 04°30'West	Allied aircraft.
27 August	The 1,543-ton *Sperrbrecher* 153	Off Brest	48°23'North 04°30'West	Mine.
28 August	The 8,417-ton *Sperrbrecher* 8	In the harbor at Brest	48°23'North 04°30'West	Allied aircraft.[16]
29 August	The 1,450-ton *Sperrbrecher* 176	In the Elbe estuary	53°50'North 09°00'East	Allied aircraft.
30 August	The 2,503-ton *Sperrbrecher* 26	In the Elbe estuary	53°50'North 09°00'East	Allied aircraft.
5 September	Minesweeper M. 274	In the Scheldt estuary	51°22'North 03°50'East	Scuttled.
5 September	Minesweeper M. 276	In the Scheldt estuary	51°22'North 03°50'East	Scuttled.
11 September	Minesweeper M. 462	Northeast of Skagen	55°44'North 10°37'East	British aircraft.
12 September	Minesweeper M. 426	Northeast of Skagen	55°44'North 10°37'East	British aircraft.[17]
20 September	Minesweeper M. 132	Off the Egerøy light, Egersund	58°23'North 05°34'East†	British submarine.
22 September	The 1,870-ton minelayer *Drache*	In Vathí harbor, Sámos	37°45'North 26°59'East	British aircraft.
-- September	Minesweeper M. 25	Whereabouts unknown but in a French Atlantic port	--°--'North --°--'West	Scuttled.
-- September	The 1,497-ton *Sperrbrecher* 155	In the harbor at Antwerp	51°13'North 04°25'East	Scuttled.

-- September	The 1,248-ton *Sperrbrecher* 168	In the harbor at St. Nazaire	47°17'North 02°12'East	Presumably scuttled.
11 October	Minesweeper M. 303	In the Kirkenes area	69°41'North 30°02'East	Soviet MTBs.
21 October	Minesweeper M. 31	Off Honningsvaag, North Cape	70°58'North 25°59'East	Soviet MTB.
27 October	Minesweeper M. 433	Northwest of Namsos, central Norway	64°20'North 11°30'East	British carrier aircraft.
30 October	The 2,423-ton minelayer *Zeus*	In the harbor at Salonika	40°38'North 22°58'East	British aircraft and scuttled.
4 November	The 3,162-ton minelayer *Kuckuck*	In the harbor at Fiume	45°20'North 14°27'East	British aircraft.
5 November	The 3,667-ton minelayer *Kiebitz*	In the harbor at Fiume	45°20'North 14°27'East	U.S. aircraft.
11 November	The 1,110-ton *Sperrbrecher* 190	At Svendborg, southern Fyn, Denmark	55°04'North 10°38'East	Sabotage.
12 November	Minesweeper M. 416	Off Egersund in southwest Norway	58°20'North 06°00'East	British warships.
13 November	Minesweeper M. 427	Off Flekkefjord in southwest Norway	58°17'North 06°40'East	British warships.[18]
15 November	The 1,592-ton *Sperrbrecher* 166	At Kobenhavn	55°43'North 12°34'East	Sabotage.
30 November	Minesweeper M. 584	In Ålborg Bay in the Kattegat	56°53'North 10°48'East†	Mine.
23 December	Minesweeper M. 489	Off Mosterhamn in Bømlafjorden, southwest Norway	59°42'North 05°24'East	Norwegian MTBs.
31 December	Minesweeper M. 445	In the harbor at Hamburg	53°33'North 10°00'East	U.S. aircraft.
1945				
3 January	The 2,687-ton minelayer *Elsass*	East of Samsø in the Belt	55°43'North 10°40'East†	Mine.
4 January	The 6,095-ton *Sperrbrecher* 11	Outside Flensburg	54°47'North 09°27'East	Mine.
10 January	Minesweeper M. 322	Off Lepsøya Island, central Norway	62°37'North 06°10'East	Ran aground: subsequently salved.
11 January	Minesweeper M. 273	Off Egersund in southwest Norway	58°20'North 06°01'East†	British warships.
12 January	Minesweeper M. 1	In Nordbyfjorden, near Bergen, in southwest Norway	60°23'North 05°20'East	British aircraft.
17 January	Minesweeper M. 305	Off the Brüster Ort headland	54°57'North 20°02'East	Foundered in storm.
17 January	The 1,350-ton *Sperrbrecher* 120	In the harbor at Hamburg	53°33'North 10°00'East	U.S. aircraft.
26 January	Minesweeper M. 538	Off the Hela peninsula	54°36'North 18°48'East	Ran aground in storm: abandoned.

31 January	Minesweeper M. 382	Off Molde in Ravnefjorden in central Norway	62°44'North 07°08'East	Norwegian MTB.[19]
12 February	Minesweeper M. 381	Off Kristiansand in southwest Norway	58°08'North 08°01'East	British submarine.
17 February	Minesweeper M. 421	Off Kolberg in the Baltic	54°10'North 15°35'East	British mine.
17 February	The 975-ton *Sperrbrecher* 139	Off Lindesnes, southwest Norway	58°06'North 07°17'East	Mine.
2 March	Minesweeper M. 575	In the Öre Sund off Kobenhavn	55°46'North 12°42'East	Capsized and sank.
9 March	Minesweeper M. 412	Outside Granville	48°50'North 01°37'West	Ran aground and scuttled.
11 March	Minesweeper M. 2	In Fedjeforden, southwest Norway	60°45'North 04°47'East	British aircraft.
11 March	Minesweeper M. 266	In the harbor at Kiel	54°20'North 10°08'East	U.S. aircraft.
11 March	Minesweeper M. 804	In the harbor at Kiel	54°20'North 10°08'East	U.S. aircraft.
11 March	Minesweeper M. 805	In the harbor at Kiel	54°20'North 10°08'East	U.S. aircraft.
20 March	Minesweeper M. 15	In the harbor at Kiel	53°33'North 10°00'East	U.S. aircraft.
20 March	Minesweeper M. 18	In the harbor at Kiel	54°20'North 10°08'East	U.S. aircraft or scuttled.
20 March	Minesweeper M. 19	In the harbor at Kiel	54°20'North 10°08'East	U.S. aircraft and run aground.[20]
20 March	Minesweeper M. 522	In the harbor at Kiel	54°20'North 10°08'East	U.S. aircraft.
30 March	Minesweeper M. 329	In the harbor at Wilhelmshaven	53°32'North 08°07'East	U.S. aircraft.
3 April	The 1,860-ton minelayer *Brummer*	In the harbor at Kiel	54°20'North 10°08'East	British aircraft.
3 April	Minesweeper M. 802	In the harbor at Kiel	54°20'North 10°08'East	U.S. aircraft.
9 April	Minesweeper M. 504	In the harbor at Kiel	54°20'North 10°08'East	British aircraft.
11 April	Minesweeper M. 376	Off Hela in the Baltic	54°36'North 18°48'East	Soviet aircraft.
15 April	Minesweeper M. 368	Off Lindesnes in southwest Norway	58°06'North 07°17'East	Collision with U-boat.
19 April	The 1,071-ton minelayer *Westmark*	In the harbor at La Spezia	44°06'North 09°49'East	Scuttled.
19 April	Minesweeper M. 403	Southeast of Anholt in the Kattegat	56°36'North 11°49'East†	British aircraft.[21]
21 April	The 3,047-ton minelayer *Ostmark*	West of Anholt in the Kattegat	56°43'North 11°34'East	British aircraft.

25 April	The 1,141-ton minelayer *Oldenburg*	In the harbor at Genoa	44°24'North 08°56'East	Scuttled.
27 April	The 1,506-ton *Sperrbrecher* 167	Off Heligoland in the Bight	54°09'North 07°52'East	Mine.
30 April	Minesweeper M. 455	In the harbor at Cuxhaven	53°52'North 08°42'East	British aircraft.
-- April	The 735-ton minelayer *Nymphe*	whereabouts unknown	--°--'North --°--'East	Scuttled.
2 May	Minesweeper M. 293	In the Kattegat	57°00'North 11°00'East	British aircraft.
2 May	Minesweeper M. 387	In the harbor at Lübeck	53°52'North 10°40'East	Scuttled.
3 May	Minesweeper M. 14	Off Swinemünde in the Baltic	53°55'North 14°18'East	Mine.
4 May	Minesweeper M. 36	In the Kattegat	57°00'North 11°00'East	British aircraft.
4 May	Minesweeper M. 301	South of Kristiansand in Skagerrak	57°56'North 07°34'East	British aircraft.
7 May	Minesweeper M. 22	In the Kiel canal at Achterwehr	54°19'North 09°58'East†	Scuttled.
-- May	The 4,845-ton *Sperrbrecher* 11	In the Elbe	53°50'North 09°00'East	Allied aircraft: beached.

Not included in these lists and accompanying table are the following:

The 999-ton *Sperrbrecher* 136: given either as mined off St. Nazaire on 20 November 1942 or beached off Memel (55°43'North 21°07'East) on 22 November 1944.

The 800-ton *Sperrbrecher* 192: given as having been abandoned on the Danube in May 1945, which would seem somewhat unlikely.

The 1,724-ton Sperrbrecher 123: given as having been sunk by allied aircraft at Oreglia, which would seem to be an erroneous rendition of Oneglia (43°53'North 08°02'East), in May 1945.

1. Only units of 450 tons or more are included in these lists; included under the auxiliary label are various foreign naval units, acquired by various and diverse means, and requisitioned vessels.

With reference to fleet units and submarine losses elsewhere in this volume the coordinates represent whereabouts of loss: in the case of the units listed here in these tables, other than those marked with the cross (†), the coordinates are those of the point of reference and not the place of sinking, though in the case of ships sunk in harbor the two would be the same (within a minute or so).

2. Various places on the Hela peninsula seem to have carried the label *Heisternest* as part of their name, but Heisternest would seem to be present-day Jastarnia, which is in 54°41'North 18°40'East.

3. Lister Bank (and Lister Deep) would seem to be at the mouth of what is presently called Listafjorden, which lies between Egersund and Lindesnes in southwest Norway. The spelling in the German *Stielers Hand-Atlas* of 1930-1931 was Lister rather than Lista, though what German minesweepers were doing off Lister Deep in November 1939 does defy ready understanding.

4. Feiestein is the name given in various sources to the whereabouts of this loss but does not correspond to any village or settlement in Norway and would seem to be a case of error once made being repeated in various secondary sources. It would seem, from the German *Stielers Hand-Atlas* of 1930-1931, that Feiestein was the Feistenen lightship, which was off the southwest side of the headland on which Stavanger stands, in the general area of Verdalen (58°47'North 05°23'East). Verdalen is next to Bore, where, in August 2008, there is a farm named Feistenen, which one assumes reaches down to the sea and either borrowed or lent its name in reference to a lightship that seemingly no longer exists. Gröner, *German Warships*, vol. 2, p. 123, gives Feiestein [*sic*] in the vicinity of Hellestø, which is on the coast some three or four miles north of Verdalen and Bore.

5. The location of this sinking has been taken from Groner, *German Warships*, vol. 2, p. 123, but accounts do differ, with Kristiansund and the Fro Havet southeast of the Fiskolmnes light (again in or off Ramsøyfjorden) also cited as the whereabouts of loss. Ramsøyfjorden is given alternatively as Ramsø fjorden or Romsö fjorden and separates the islands of Smöla and Hitra, but the Fro Havet is a stretch of water--where Trondheimsfjorden reaches the sea--that heads to the northeast, away from Hitra, and is many miles distant from Ramsøyfjorden. The coordinates given are those used in various sources as the whereabouts of loss but would seem not to square with those of the Fro Havet, though the raising of one point is in order: *Fro Havet* (or *Frohavet* or *Fro-havet*) is the name given in various sources, from the German *Stielers Hand-Atlas* of 1930-1931 to *The Times Atlas* (1985), but the proper name would seem to be *Fra havet*, which in Norwegian means "from the sea."

6. Laid up in Bassens harbor (44°50'North 00°31'West, akin to Bordeaux), the *Sperrbrecher* 14 was scuttled as a blockship on 25 August 1944.

7. The main Dutch islands that reach from Den Helder to Borkum and the Ems in the southern North Sea are (in order from west to east) Texel, Vlieland, Terschelling, Ameland, and Schiermonnikoog.

8. This sinking presents a number of difficulties. Certain sources give the date as 25 September 1943, while Rohwer and Hummelchen, *Chronology of the War at Sea*, p. 305, same day and month but in 1944; Gröner, *German Warships*, vol. 2, p. 129, gives the date of sinking as 25 April 1943. The date given here is arbitrary and occasioned by the fact that an auxiliary warship, the V. 316, was sunk on 25 September 1943 off Den Helder by British aircraft.

9. The ship was rendered *hors de combat*, was towed to Kiel and stricken. She was finally sunk in the course of the air raid of 20 March 1945.

10. Gröner, *German Warships*, vol. 2, p. 127, gives the location of sinking as "the vicinity of Swinemünde" in 54°41'North 12°33'East, but this would seem to be erroneous given that this position is on the wrong side of Rugen Island.

11. Sources seem to differ in reference to the loss of M. 83 and M. 343 even to the extent of Rohwer and Hummelchen, *Chronology of the War at Sea*, p. 283, having the M. 83 sunk on two different days and by different units, while the coordinates given by Gröner, *German Warships*, vol. 2, p. 124, seem to

be erroneous: what is given as 49°44'8"North 01°59'9"West would seem to be north of Cap de la Hague: it would seem that this is an erroneous rendition of 48°44'8"North 01°59'9"West.

12. Also given as having been rendered *hors de combat* in this action but managed to reach St. Malo where she was scuttled at St. Malo on 6 August.

13. Langeoog is a German island in the East Friesian group and is separated from the Jade by Spiekeroog and Wangerooge.

14. There is a certain disparity of information with reference to the loss of the M. 133 on 6 August and M. 206 on 14 August; it may be that the two units have been confused with one another and dates should be exchanged: it may also be that the unit sunk on 6 August was lost to Allied aircraft rather than scuttling.

15. This unit, and the other three given as having been sunk at St. Nazaire on this same day, are given in Gröner, *German Warships*, vol. 2, pp. 127-128, as having been sunk off Noirmoutier, an island roughly halfway between St. Nazaire and the Ile d'Yeu in 47°01'North 02°15'West.

16. *Sperrbrecher* 8 is given as having been sunk in the harbor at Brest by Allied aircraft on 28 August 1944, but certain sources, such as Rohwer and Hummelchen, *Chronology of the War at Sea*, p. 301, give her place of sinking as Bremen and specifically by U.S. aircraft. Bremen was not subjected to attack by American aircraft on 28 August, which means that either the alternative Brest rendition is correct or both are incorrect. Shipping and installations at Bremen were subjected to attack by American aircraft on 30 August, but with no obvious indication of correct date and place this entry has been given the 28 August slot and Brest location on the basis of E.& O.E.

17. Skagen is all but the most northern point of Denmark and stands more or less where the Skagerrak and Kattegat meet. It should be noted, however, that Gröner, *German Warships*, vol. 2, p. 128, gives the whereabouts of this sinking as the entrance of the harbor at Kristiansand.

18. This sinking is generally given as having occurred off Rekkefjord--for example, Gröner, *German Warships*, vol. 2, p. 128 gives the whereabouts of the sinking of M. 427 as "at Rekkefjord" in 58°20'North 06°13'East---but, reference note 4 above and Feiestein and Feistenen, this would seem to be an erroneous rendition of Flekkefjord. The actions of 12-13 November took place in the general area between Egersund and Lista, and Flekkefjord thus presents itself as the place, opposite Lista, off which this second sinking took place; there seems be no Rekkefjord in this area either then or at present time.

19. Gröner, *German Warships*, vol. 2, p. 128, gives the whereabouts of the sinking as 63°06'North 07°32'East, but while this may indeed be accurate, on the previous page the whereabouts of the sinking of M. 381 is given as "at Kristiansand N" in position 63°07'North 07°32'East; the implications would seem not to need elaboration.

20. This unit is alternatively given in some sources as having been sunk in the raid of 9 April 1945.

21. A point of total irrelevance: the British occupied Anholt between 1808 and 1814 during the Napoleonic wars.

CHAPTER SEVEN

WITH FRIENDS LIKE THESE

Anglo-American historiography of the Second World War and the war at sea invariably traces the course and outcome of the two conflicts that together made up the Second World War in terms of the defeat of the German submarine offensive against shipping and the American advance across the southwest and central Pacific to the Japanese home islands. In the European conflict the focus of most historical attention has been on the British Navy, and specifically its escort forces, and the German U-boat service, and in the Pacific upon American carrier and amphibious formations. In a very obvious sense it is right and proper that this should be the case: at sea the European war was largely synonymous with the "Battle of the Atlantic," whatever that phrase might mean, and in the Pacific the war was decided by fleet actions that ran in tandem with landing operations; the Imperial Japanese Navy and even the American submarine offensive against Japanese shipping have never been afforded consideration and recognition commensurate with that afforded American carrier operations.

But the Second World War at sea involved seven major navies, and three of these have received no more Anglo-American attention than has been afforded the fact that in September 1945 the third largest navy in the world was that of Canada. Of the three navies that "make up the numbers," the Soviet Navy has been given historical attention in accord with its contribution to victory. It had virtually no "blue-water" capability and role, and in the Great Patriotic War's first weeks it took such losses that its importance was, at very best, marginal, as the record of operations in the Baltic indicates. It had a very limited role in northern waters, and the Soviet merchant marine was important in the Pacific, specifically in the movement of U.S. lend-lease shipments across the northern ocean, but in terms of Soviet survival and victory in the Second World War the Soviet Navy was largely irrelevant. The second of these three navies, the Royal Italian Navy, suffered the ultimate humiliation—surrender without having been defeated in battle. The third of these three navies, and the navy that was the inter-war counterpart of the Royal Italian navy, was that of France. The author would plead guilty to any charge of Francophilia to which he was subjected, but one does not have to admit to such prejudice to see in the record of the French Navy in the Second World War a poignancy, a melancholy and sad languor that speaks of suffering synonymous with humiliation and destruction, a destruction at the hands not of enemies but of past and future friends and, worst of all, *elle-même*.

* * *

The story of the French Navy in the Second World War has two signposts, those marked Mers El Kébir and Toulon. In truth, though, even the most cursory treatment should properly consider French naval operations in the first ten months of war, when the French naval contribution to the Allied cause was perhaps more substantial than is often realized: the July 1940 episode and its immediate aftermath, the war with Thailand, the nemesis of November 1942, and then what might be defined as a very small "nice-to-have role" in the war's last thirty-three months. The Thai episode is obviously the most esoteric and least known, and indeed it possessed no lasting importance; the French victory in the action off Koh Chang on 17 January 1941 was undone within a matter of days as a result of Japanese intervention, which, with the treaty of 11 March 1941, saw Thailand's acquisition of various gains for which it had begun hostilities and which reversed the territorial losses that it had incurred at French hands in the treaties of 1984, 1904 and 1907. But the 17 January 1941 action is worthy of only *en passant* reference and proved small change in a series of events that were nothing short of disastrous for the French Navy.[1]

* * *

The story of the war's first ten months is invariably portrayed as a successful British clearing of the high seas of German shipping and an allegedly brilliant victory won in the Rio Plata, though in truth this was not so much a British victory as a German defeat: in the action of 13 December 1939 the *panzerschiff Admiral Graf Spee* should have prevailed. The sequel of this action, the British destroyer *Cossack* and the attack on the German supply ship *Altmark* in Jössingfjorden on

16 February 1940 that resulted in the release of prisoners captured by the *Graf Spee*, used to be prominently displayed in British books and magazines, evidence of daring and imagination. But over the years this episode has faded from the forefront of British public attention, along with other matters such as the sinkings of the aircraft carrier *Courageous* by the German submarine U. 29 on 17 September 1939 in the southwest approaches, the battleship *Royal Oak* by the U. 47 on 14 October at Scapa Flow, and the aircraft carrier *Glorious* (and the destroyers *Acasta* and *Ardent*) by the German battleships *Scharnhorst* and *Gneisenau* in the Arctic on 8 June 1940.[2] With reference to the last of these, British reticence has some validity, given the appallingly incompetent conduct of operations that left a fleet carrier within the range of battleship guns, but this was but one part of an episode that does present real problems in terms of explanation and reason. The loss of the three British warships in June 1940 formed the postscript to the Norwegian campaign, and midway through this disastrously inept campaign the person who bore the greatest single culpability for this unfolding calamity was promoted to the rank of prime minister.

These months that represent the war's opening phases, between September 1939 and March 1940 and between April and June 1940, saw the French Navy assume a modest and secondary role but one that was nonetheless necessary and that the British Navy could not discharge. At the outbreak of war France mustered a very respectable total of two modern capital ships, three older battleships, a single aircraft carrier, seven heavy and thirteen light cruisers, thirty *contre-torpilleurs*[3] and another twenty-five of more modest dimensions, and sixty-five submarines, plus escorts, minelayers, minesweepers, gunboats, and various assorted craft. In effect, the navy was divided into four distinct parts: first, a major task force stationed at Brest, second, two task forces in the western Mediterranean; third, local commands in the Channel, Bay of Biscay, southern France, at Bizerte and Oran and at Casablanca and Dakar, and fourth, a number of other commands that, with one exception, may be termed token, showing the flag. The last of these included a warship and three submarines at Beirut, single sloops at Papeete, Tahiti, and Djibouti, and perhaps a surprising large number of units in the Far East, albeit scattered. At or en route for Saigon at war's start were single heavy and light cruisers, four sloops, two gunboats, and (under repair) a submarine, while another three gunboats were at Haiphong. A sloop and a gunboat were at Shanghai, with another sloop at Amoy and single gunboats were at Hong Kong, Hankow,[4] and Chungking, though it would seem that these last three commanded only refugee status.

The local commands, such as those at Brest, Toulon, and Bizerte, mustered destroyers, minesweepers, and submarines, but the main formations were those held at Brest, Oran, and Toulon. In the Mediterranean the French held what was in effect the second team, though clearly its numbers in some way compensated for the fact that the two new battlecruisers and France's only carrier were elsewhere. At Oran the French held their three battleships and eight destroyers and at Toulon six heavy cruisers and nine *contre-torpilleurs*, while a total of no fewer than forty-six submarines were in the Mediterranean theater. But the main force was that gathered at Brest, which consisted of the battlecruisers *Dunkerque* and *Strasbourg*, the aircraft carrier *Béarn*, the light cruisers *Georges Leygues*, *Gloire*, and *Montcalm*, and the *contre-torpilleurs Mogador* and *Volta*, the *Le Malin*, *Le Triomphant*, and *L'Indomptable*, and the *L'Audacieux*, *Le Fantasque*, and *Le Terrible*, and one can take from the record a contribution to the Allied cause every month. For example, in October 1939 two of the eight task groups organized to search the South Atlantic for the *Graf Spee* were French, and a third group in the West Indies employed the *Strasbourg* with the British carrier *Hermes*; in the same month the *Dunkerque*, three cruisers, and eight destroyers were involved in the covering of convoy in the North Atlantic against possible attack by the *panzerschiffe Deutschland*. In November the *Dunkerque* sailed with the *Hood* in the aftermath of the sinking of the *Rawalpindi* to search out the enemy, and the two ships sailed together under French command. In December French submarines sailed with three convoys in the North Atlantic in order to provide some measure of defense against German warships, and to come forward to March 1940, a French submarine formation, with twelve boats, was at Harwich and involved in operations in the southern North Sea.[5] The results registered in terms of contact with the enemy or the capture of German merchantmen seeking the safety of home waters were few, and indeed French warships and submarines did not account for a single U-boat, though the involvement of the *contre-torpilleurs Valmy* in the sinking of the U. 55 on 30 January 1940 in the southwest approaches, given the fact that it was operating with the British destroyer *Whitshed* and sloop *Fowey* and in consort with a Sunderland flying-boat of 228 Squadron R.A.F., does represent a fair element of diversity of contribution.[6] French losses were correspondingly modest. The largest single loss was the training ship–minelayer *La Tour d'Auvergne*, formerly the cruiser-minelayer *Pluton*, and it was lost at Casablanca on 13 September 1939 as a result of the detonation of its own mines. It was not alone in terms of self-destruction: the destroyer *La Railleuse* at Casablanca on 24 March 1940 and the *contre-torpilleur Maillé Brézé* at Greenock on 30 April were both lost as a result of the detonation of their own torpedoes.

The only period of sustained losses, inevitably, was when French ships were caught in northern waters during the campaign that resulted in France being driven from the war; yet the losses in this period are curious in that in terms of fleet units, French losses during the evacuation of Anglo-French forces from Dunkirk were virtually the same as those of the British. The official British naval history gives a total of seventy-two ships of all descriptions sunk by enemy action during Operation Dynamo, and of this total nine were destroyers, one was a gunboat, and five were minesweepers.[7] The French losses in the same series of operations numbered two *contre-torpilleurs* and five destroyers;[8] one sloop was subsequently sunk off Brest by a mine.

Another destroyer, the *Cyclone*, was also lost, but its loss represents cause for separate treatment: it was torpedoed by the motor torpedo-boat S. 24 on 31 May off Dunkirk and lost its bow, but it was able to reach Brest, where it was scuttled on 18 June as German forces closed on the port and on the day after France sued for an armistice. The relevance of its fate lies in the logic [*sic*] that led to the British attack on the French naval forces gathered at Mers El Kébir in the first week of July. The ostensible reason for this British attack was uncertainty about the fate of the French fleet under the terms of the armistice of 25 June. The British, or more accurately, Winston Churchill, in the absence of a French refusal to sail their warships to British or neutral ports, decided on an attack on the main French naval formation at Mers El Kébir in order to ensure that the French warships would not be surrendered to the Germans and Italians. How this calculation squares with two very different sets of events is somewhat difficult to discern. The systematic French scuttling of warships and submarines that could not be sailed from Channel and Bay of Biscay ports in June 1940 does present a question mark regarding Churchill's logic, or lack of logic, while the fact that in November 1942 the French Navy scuttled its ships rather than see them surrendered to the Germans and Italians, and that this came after the British attacks on French military and naval forces at Mers El Kébir, Dakar, Gabon, Syria, Madagascar, and finally northwest Africa, hardly suggests that the French would have surrendered their warships and submarines to the Germans and Italians in 1940—though this, obviously, could not be known at the time. But the point is that Churchill's demand for an attack on the French force at Mers El Kébir was opposed within the British war cabinet, by the First Sea Lord Admiral Sir Dudley Pound (1877–1943), by the Admiralty as a whole, and by the commander in the Mediterranean, Admiral Sir Andrew Cunningham (1883–1963), and there is little doubting that their shared perspective, that the French would not allow their warships to be surrendered to any foreign power, was correct. In addition, because of British access to French signals, before the attack Churchill was aware that French warships were under orders to scuttle or to sail either to Martinique or the United States rather than be surrendered.

But this latter point aside, the British operation nonetheless sits uneasily alongside a number of related points, of which three are significant. First, the British attack on French warships at Mers El Kébir was conducted at the same time as the seizure of French units in British ports, by force but for the most part without bloodshed, and at Alexandria. With reference to the latter, despite the bitterness that the Mers episode generated among French commanding officers, and as result of difficult negotiations that were punctuated by the two sides at one stage squaring off before wiser counsel prevailed, the French were allowed to disarm their ships.[9] Given the outcome in these "other" bases, the evidence of July 1940 hardly suggests that the use of force at Mers El Kébir was a matter on which the British had little if any choice, that there was no real alternative to the use of force against a defeated ally. Second, the fact that a British task group attacked French warships at Mers El Kébir but nowhere else in the western Mediterranean does present a problem of comprehension, because it is difficult to believe that Britain's security rested on the loyalties and whereabouts of just the French ships—and specifically four capital ships—gathered here at a single base in the western Mediterranean. If it was so essential to neutralize French naval forces, then it is hard to see how this might be achieved without any form of action against French formations at Toulon and Bizerte, to see how this might be achieved solely at the expense of the *Dunkerque* and *Strasbourg*, with the *Bretagne* and *Provence*—even the *Bretagne* and *Provence* as rebuilt between 1932 and 1935—being discounted from consideration. Of course the question of available force does present itself, and the fact was that the British did not have the means to simultaneously attack French naval forces at these three major bases in the western and central Mediterranean; but it is nonetheless difficult, if not impossible, to believe that the *Force de Raid* at Mers El Kébir alone presented itself as the basis of Britain's vulnerability, that the *Dunkerque* and *Strasbourg* really represented the margin between Britain's surrender and survival.

Third, the British conduct of this operation presents other challenges to understanding, and for a reason that seems to have attracted little in the way of historical comment. The British task group that conducted this operation consisted of the battlecruiser *Hood*, the battleships *Resolution* and *Valiant*, the aircraft carrier *Ark Royal*, the light cruisers *Arethusa* and *Enterprise*, and eleven destroyers, and the heavy units conducted a bombardment of French warships inside the base, yet the *Strasbourg* and five *contre-torpilleurs* nonetheless managed to get under way, cleared the harbor, and escaped to Toulon.[10] It would seem that opposite the harbor entrance was but a single British destroyer, the *Wrestler*, that in breaking out the *Strasbourg* very briefly had the carrier *Ark Royal* within range of its guns but did not fire, and that the subsequent attack on the French warships by aircraft from the carrier *Ark Royal* was feeble, even by the least exacting of standards. Moreover, the attack of 3 July was followed by a second attack, conducted by twelve Swordfish from the *Ark Royal* on 6 July, that resulted in the sinking of the auxiliary patrol boat *Terre Neuve* and tug *Esterel* that were alongside the *Dunkerque*; perversely, this attack perhaps possessed more lasting value than that of the 3rd. In the first attack the *Bretagne* was hit in a magazine, exploded, and capsized with the loss of 997 of its crew, and the *Provence* and the *Dunkerque* were both hit and beached in order to ensure themselves against loss.[11] The *Dunkerque* was hit by four shells and incurred major damage in one ammunition handling room and in its engine rooms, but in the second attack the exploding depth-charges of the stricken *Terre Neuve* opened a gash more than 40 meters long down its starboard side, and with bulkheads damaged, the battlecruiser settled by the bow and with a starboard list. Re-floated on 8 August—which suggests that the damage was local rather than extensive—the *Dunkerque*, given the limited repair facilities at Mers El Kébir, was not readied to sail until 19 February 1942, and it did so and reached Toulon the following day where, of course, it was scuttled on 27 November.

* * *

The Mers El Kébir episode can be seen in a number of ways, ranging from a demonstration of British ruthlessness and resolve to a shameful act that in terms of self-delusion was for Churchill what the Dardanelles fiasco had been in an earlier conflict. Any objective assessment must correctly note that there seems to be some truth to both of these perspectives, particularly the latter. It may be safely stated, however, that Operation Catapult certainly seems to have been noted in Washington, and it set back the Free French cause by some measure. The point is that within a week British naval formations were involved in actions in both the western and central Mediterranean, but in neither area were they able to force battle on an enemy that declined to be thus drawn. One destroyer on each side was lost, the sinking of the Italian destroyer *Pancaldo* being of *en passant* interest in that it was sunk by a torpedo from a carrier aircraft while in the harbor at Augusta in southeast Sicily.

In terms of the French Navy, the British attacks of July 1940 were followed by Operation Menace, the attack on Dakar, Senegal, between 23 and 25 September 1940 that degenerated to a level indistinguishable from farce. The British battleship *Resolution* was torpedoed by the French submarine *Bévéziers*, whereupon the proposed landing and attack on the French naval units was abandoned; in three days of bombardment by British warships that included two battleships and two heavy cruisers, the stationary *Richelieu* was hit just once, and to no effect.[12] The subsequent British invasion and conquest of Syria (8 June–12 July 1941), which involved a double effort from Palestine and from recently occupied Iraq, saw the sinking by British carrier aircraft of the *contre-torpilleur Chevalier Paul* (16 June), but in the course of a night action another, the *Guépard*, was able to escape and make its way to Salonika; the French submarine *Souffleur* was sunk on 25 June by the British submarine *Parthian* off Djounieh. At the end of the campaign, which saw *Légion Etrangère* and *Tirailleurs Sénégalaise* units on both sides fight one another, French troops were given the option of receiving safe conduct and repatriation or joining the Free French: only some 3,200 of a total garrison of some 35,000 officers and men chose the second course of action.[13]

The Madagascar operation, Operation Ironclad, must be one of the most bizarre operations of the war. It was staged ostensibly to prevent the island being occupied by the Japanese; as an example of strategic percipience its only rival in terms of arrant stupidity and irrelevance must be the sending of Canadian troops to the Falklands at the same time and for the same purpose. Admittedly one Japanese submarine conducted a reconnaissance of Aden on 7 May and seaplanes from another submarine flew over Durban on 20 May, and these ventures formed but the opening phase of four months of operations by submarines and auxiliary raiders in the Indian Ocean that accounted for some twenty-five merchantmen of 120,199 tons. The fact was, however, that the battles in the Coral Sea and off Midway Islands provided evidence of the direction of Japanese strategic attention and intent, which was not on the western side of the Indian Ocean. But even though Japanese commitment elsewhere meant that the British move would not be countered by any major naval force, the British landings at Diégo Suarez on 5 May and the rapid collapse of French resistance in the northern area—Diégo Suarez was captured within three days of the initial landings—proved deceptive.[14] The campaign and the Allied commitment on the island was to last six months and came to an end only in the first week of November,[15] and it was to see six more landings, the first two on 3 June on Nossi-Bé island and in Sahamalaz Bay near Maromandia.[16] The next landing was at Majunga, the main port on the west coast, on 10 September, and after its capture troops were then re-embarked and landed at Tamatave, the main port on the east coast, on the 18th, though by that time what had been a virtually unopposed advance from Majunga was just five days from the capital, Tananarive. After landings at Tuléar and Fort Dauphin in the south of the island on 29 September, the advance southward from Tananarive and over the mountain range was resumed in the rains of the first week of October, and resulted in the taking of Antsirabe, Ambositra, and, on 29 October, Alakamisy.[17] Thereafter the campaign was over, but it was not until 5 November, after British forces had reached Vatoavo in front of Ihosy, that an armistice was concluded.[18] Thus ended a campaign that saw the loss of five French naval units during its first four days,[19] and the torpedoing of the British battleship *Ramillies* and the sinking of the 6,993-ton tanker *British Loyalty* by Japanese midget submarines on the evening of 30 May.[20] Moreover, there is one matter that defies ready understanding: the French submarine *Le Glorieux* and gunboat *D'Iberville* both managed to escaped initially to southern Madagascar and then somehow made their way back to Toulon—and at the scuttling in November the *Le Glorieux* was the one submarine that managed to escape to Oran. Her adventures, and these events, may possess a certain passing interest, but in strategic terms the Madagascar campaign was irrelevant—witness the eleven lines afforded the campaign between 1 June and 5 November 1942 in the official British naval history.[21]

* * *

For the French Navy the clear British failure at Dakar represented a very modest success, and some four months later another was registered in the Gulf of Siam in a little-known episode against an enemy that is never considered in naval terms. The pattern of European and American imperialism, and the decline in the number of fully independent indigenous states outside Europe by this time, has meant that Thailand has attracted a certain attention in terms of musicals and film, but not serious historical consideration, while the idea of its possession of naval capability in 1941 does enter the realm of the unlikely. But in 1941 Thailand had acquired not so much a naval as a coastal capability, with British-, Italian- and Japanese-built naval units. By 1941 one First World War British destroyer had aged almost twenty years in Thai service, and if the thirties had seen the scrapping of some old gunboats and torpedo-boats, these years had also seen the acquisition of two 2,265-ton coastal defense ships, each complete with four 8-in. guns, two 1,400-ton sloops, and three 110-ton torpedo-boats from Japan, and two 368-ton minelayers and nine 318-ton torpedo-boats from Italy, to go alongside the two 886-ton British-built armored gunboats of the previous decade. But also acquired in the thirties from Japan were four 370-ton coastal submarines, and these must represent the only submarines "outside the fold," as it were,[22] at least in terms of Africa and Asia: Thailand also possessed some 140 aircraft, including a number of P. 36/Hawk 75 monoplanes.[23]

The Koh Chang episode was very simple in terms of origin and events: the defeat of France in 1940 bared the British and French empires in southeast Asia, and if Japan stood to be the main beneficiary of French weakness, Thailand was ahead of Japan in terms of timing. By the end of 1940 it had embarked upon a series of small-scale military actions, supported by naval units, that had two objectives: to secure gains that would reverse the losses of bygone years and, no less importantly, to provide the means of ensuring national discipline and popular support for the incumbent military dictatorship. The weaknesses of this policy lay in the assumption of French passivity and compliance and the commitment of forces in detail, and with reference to the latter the French move in January 1941 was very deliberate in that it sought to bring superior numbers against the fragmented and divided force off the scattered islands in the border area.

Just what happened on 17 January 1941 is very elusive: there are few accounts of the battle of Koh Chang, but there is no agreement between them over exactly what happened and what the Thai Navy lost. What is clear is that, preceded by air reconnaissance, a French force that consisted of the light cruiser *Lamotte-Picquet* and four sloops, the 1,969-ton *Dumont d'Urville* and *Amiral Charner* and the much smaller and aging *Tahure* and *Marne*, closed Koh Chang in the knowledge that certain Thai warships were in this area, while others were at Satahib.[24] With the French dividing their formation into three in order to ensure the sweeping of the myriad of islands and passages to the south of the island, the *Lamotte-Picquet* encountered and rapidly dispatched the torpedo-boats *Chandraburi* and *Chonburi* and then, with the heavy sloops joining it, inflicted such damage on the coastal defense ship *Dhonburi* that it was run aground in order to prevent its sinking. An alternative account is that three torpedo-boats, the *Chonburi*, *Songhkli*, and *Trad*, were sunk, and both of the Thai coastal defense ships, the *Dhonburi* and *Sri Ayuthia*, were beached in order to avoid sinking after being roughly handled by the French force. Whatever the numbers and identity of the Thai unfortunates,[25] it would seem that the *Dhonburi*, after being refloated, capsized and sank while under tow, while the *Ayuthia* was repaired in a Japanese yard later that year to await a rather unusual fate, that of being sunk by Thai aircraft during the attempted coup of July 1951 after the prime minister had been kidnapped by a group of naval officers and taken aboard the ship. The prime minister was uninjured, but the whole episode invites an obvious comment that will be resisted.[26]

* * *

The Koh Chang episode was nickel-and-dime stuff. However welcome a victory, it was not one that could provide any element of compensation for the reverses incurred elsewhere, and thus this chapter will not linger here in the Gulf of Siam. Rather, with Syria and Madagascar already considered, this summary of French misfortune will come forward to Torch and to the Anglo-American landings in the Maghreb, briefly and on four main counts.

The first of these is to note the naval formations that were committed to this operation. The main American formation, committed to covering the landings on the Moroccan Atlantic coast, consisted of the battleships *Massachusetts*, *New York*, and *Texas*, the aircraft carrier *Ranger* (which basically was considered by the U.S. Navy to be unfit to serve in the Pacific), the escort carriers *Sangamon*, *Santee*, and *Suwannee*, three heavy and four light cruisers, thirty-eight destroyers, and four submarines, plus minelayers, minesweepers, a tender, transports, and tankers.[27] The British, inside the Mediterranean, committed the monitor *Roberts*, the old (light) carrier *Argus*, the escort carriers *Avenger*, *Biter*, and *Dasher*, five AA ships, twenty-six destroyers, seventeen escorts, and five submarines, plus assorted auxiliaries and transports and landing ships to the landings at Oran and Algiers, and the battleships *Duke of York*, *Nelson*, and *Rodney*, the battlecruiser *Renown*, the fleet carriers *Formidable*, *Furious*, and *Victorious*, three light cruisers, and seventeen destroyers with the covering formation.[28] With such numbers there is paradox. It was by some measure the largest single naval operation conducted to date in the war, and such numbers really were without precedent—the total of five fleet carriers, six escort carriers, and seven capital ships was simply beyond British and now Allied capability prior to this time. But paradox lies in the fact that by 1944 and 1945 such numbers would have represented more than a task group but certainly not a task force: when compared, for example, with the formations committed to the landings in the Marianas in June or Leyte in October 1944 the Torch figures are modest, though a certain care is needed here. The landings on Sicily (July 1943), and at Salerno (September 1943), at Anzio (January 1944), and in the south of France (August 1944), and even at Normandy (June 1944), were not supported on the scale that was slotted into place during 1944 in the Pacific, and in this sense the argument that Torch was of "modest dimensions" can be disputed. In these cases, however, the scale of land-based air support that was available had the effect of lessening the scale of covering forces, specifically of carrier forces, and most definitely there was no concentration of forces that began to equate with what was slotted into place during 1944 and in the Pacific; at Leyte, for example, the Americans had more destroyers than the Japanese had carrier aircraft. But to repeat the point: Torch may have been the largest naval operations, to date but it was the end of modest dimensions in terms of what was to come.[29]

The second is to note that Torch came only after very difficult Anglo-American negotiations. The British argument in favor of Torch was in part strategic and in part administrative, namely, that a cross-Channel operation in 1942 was impossible and Torch represented the best, indeed only, practical proposition open to the western Allies in that year. The American argument in favor of Torch—or more accurately President Franklin D. Roosevelt's decision to endorse it—was political, the need to have American forces committed in numbers in theater—and in its final form the Torch plan included ironic comment on an American military that was so insistent on a cross-Channel operation in 1942 and that expressed dark suspicions of British intentions. If a cross-Channel operation was so important in 1942, if it was so important for the German Army to be brought to battle immediately, then why the American military leaders refused to consider landings in eastern Algeria and Tunisia is incomprehensible, and it needs be noted that the American military had to be ordered by Roosevelt to include Algiers among the landing sites of the operation. The strategic logic that substituted North Africa for France can be understood; the operational logic that substituted Casablanca for Brest is harder to discern. The U.S. military high command wanted to invade France and get to grips with the German Army in 1942, but in the first operation that was planned it proved reluctant to undertake a landing within 550 miles of Italian forces based at Palermo in Sicily. It does seem a little difficult to square Washington's rhetoric with reality.[30]

The third is to note that in this episode there was evidence not of a French willingness to surrender—that would be the wrong word—but certainly a French unwillingness to resist. There had been a certain element of this in Madagascar, and it is not hard to discern two reasons for such a state of affairs. There seems to have been an element of a medieval *baroud d'honneur* about the initial proceedings, but the real reason for a lack of sustained and serious resistance was that after December 1941 it was no longer the British in the ring but the British and the Americans, and with the latter there was the promise of liberation.[31] That reality was still nearly two years down the road, but within a month of the Torch landings the *Détachment d'Armée Française* was in the Allied order of battle, and within weeks divisions, and then within months a corps, were in place.[32] But in setting forth this argument a certain care needs be exercised. The French military seems to have felt that way, but less so the navy, and certainly there was French naval resistance, and losses, that went beyond the *baroud d'honneur.* Indeed, with reference to the latter, French losses during the Torch operation were indeed modest but nonetheless were probably more substantial than is generally recognized—the light cruiser *Primaguet*, the three *contre-torpilleurs*, seven destroyers, and no fewer than fifteen submarines, plus two sloops and a chaser. Most of these warships were sunk off Casablanca by American warships and aircraft, though the largest single group of losses was the five submarines scuttled at Oran on 9 November.

Fourth, and last, is the fact that this landing did see the initial clash of French and Allied naval forces, and the sinking of three British warships by French shore batteries. Suffice it to note two episodes. The first was an exchange between battleships, between the *Massachusetts* and the *Jean Bart*, which was moored to the jetty in the Delandé Dock at Casablanca. The French battleship, which had never been completed and commissioned and was without a full armament, fired on U.S. warships on both 8 and 10 November but paid accordingly. Without a working pump system it suffered progressive flooding that finally resulted in the grounding of the ship by the stern, but the combination of incomplete state, extensive damage, and other American priorities meant that after November 1942 the *Jean Bart* was in service as an accommodation ship. Its completion awaited the post-war period: commissioned into service in April 1950,[33] it was the last of a type of warship that reached back over four hundred years: in its final state it possessed size, speed, and armament that compared very well with the *Iowa* class. The second episode is concerned not with Torch but with a little-known action in the Gabon expedition of November 1940 that resulted in the Free French capture of Libreville, Gabon, and indeed the whole of French Equatorial Africa. This final comment is to note its saddest single incident, the sinking of the Vichy sloop *Bougainville* off Libreville on 9 November. It was sunk by its Free French sister ship, the *Savorgnan de Brazza. Ah, mes pauvres petits enfants:* such things should never be.

* * *

The scuttling of the fleet at Toulon in November 1942 represents the moment of truth for the French fleet in the Second World War, and it seems to have been afforded little in the way of proper consideration in Anglo-American historiography in at least three respects. The first, and somewhat contentiously, is the failure of the French warships at Toulon to make any attempt to escape to North Africa, and to join the Allied cause, in the time between the German invasion of

Vichy France in the aftermath of Anglo-American landings in the Maghreb on 8–9 November and the move against Toulon. The second is the somewhat vexed question of what warships could have attempted to escape to North Africa; the condemnation of French warships' failure to attempt an escape begs the obvious point, that the number of warships that might have attempted to escape was very few indeed, probably less than twenty, plus a handful of submarines.

The third is an equally vexed question of the value to the Allied cause of such warships had they attempted to escape and managed to reach North Africa and welcoming Anglo-American arms. Given the uncertainty with reference to numbers, this latter question presents any number of problems of interpretation and evaluation but does invite two very cautious conclusions. First, probably no more than a single battleship, a cruiser division, and a destroyer flotilla might have escaped, and these, in military terms, would have represented a token contribution to the Allied cause and no more. If this seems somewhat (unintentionally) condescending, the total number of *contre-torpilleurs* and destroyers that were scuttled was about the same number as the destroyers commissioned into service by the U.S. Navy between 1 October and 31 December 1942 and was on a par with the number of escort destroyers commissioned in the each of the last three months of 1943.[34] But, second, certainly such numbers would have represented something significant in terms of French political and diplomatic standing relative to Britain and the United States. One cannot prove the point, but it is very difficult to resist the argument that the symbolic value of a sortie would have been far more important than the number of ships that managed to escape, but that if a reasonable number of ships had managed to escape the political fallout might well have been disproportionate to numbers. Between 1940 and 1942 the Free French naval force commanded a status that arguably was wholly at variance with reference to numbers and capability; had some numbers escaped in November 1942 to join the Allied forces, then the Gaullist hand, at least the Gaullist diplomatic hand, might well have been strengthened, though given the fact that France itself was occupied this could never have been more than a marginal strengthening of the Allied cause. It is perhaps worth noting, if only *en passant*, that after Toulon, as the Americans and British were obliged to deal for the first time with a French naval contribution to the Allied cause, their provision was very minor, being local and coastal. The Americans provided some thirty-two PC-type coastal escorts and fifty-two SC-class submarine chasers, the British some six *River*-class frigates, a number of wooden minesweepers, and thirty motor launches. American escort carriers and destroyers were being produced at this time in numbers that suggest some could have made their way into French service just as the British were afforded escort carrier numbers that they could never have built for themselves, but none were made available to the French—at least not before April 1945.[35] Quite obviously the British and U.S. navies treated the newly recovered French Navy as "nice-to-have" but most definitely not "need-to-have," and the obvious question presents itself: would such treatment, which was not dismissive but which can hardly be deemed generous, have followed in the wake of a major French force having sailed from Toulon and joined the Allied cause?

The immediate point of departure in the Toulon story is the Allied landings in North Africa and the German occupation of Vichy France. The latter represented a clear breach of the 1940 armistice terms, and in a number of warships in Toulon was met by a number of demonstrations by the lower deck in favor of immediate sailing to North Africa and adherence to the Allied, and Gaullist, cause. The least that can be said about these demonstrations is that they really do seem surprising: the anger against the Americans and British for their attack on the Maghreb was there on 9 November, but by the following day this was giving way to the desire to join the Allies in order to fight the real enemy. It needs be noted that these demonstrations—most notably in the battleship *Strasbourg*, heavy cruisers *Colbert* and *Foch*, and the *contre-torpilleur Kersaint*—were suppressed very quickly and in a forthright manner by French naval authorities, and in that fact is evidence of the divisions within the officer corps between Pétainist and Gaullist, and an attendant anti-British virulence, that were very marked indeed, certainly more marked than on the lower deck. The reason for such a state of affairs is somewhat hard to discern. Certainly the series of British operations against French possessions and forces—Mers El Kébir, Dakar, Syria, Madagascar, and finally Torch—had the effect of turning what had always been a rivalry with Britain into tangible hatred, and understandably so. That rivalry, based upon hundreds of years of wars, had been marked by an antipathy that was latent, and most certainly was never allowed to intrude upon deliberations between 1904 and 1940, but it was always there and indeed was there in 1944.[36] But it is clear that the British actions, and specifically Mers El Kébir, brought out this festering rivalry, at least among the senior officers. The divisions between Vichy and Free French, however, were far more virulent. For British and Americans such divisions are well-nigh incomprehensible, for obvious reason: the British and Americans have never had to face such a dilemma as the one that confronted French officers, and indeed all Frenchmen, after 25 June 1940. Suffice it to note two points, one cause and the other effect. In terms of cause, the creation of the Vichy state and de Gaulle's raising of the Cross of Lorraine forced the French military to chose between conflicting soldierly virtues: Pétain represented duty, obedience, service, but de Gaulle something much worse, *l'honneur*.[37] It was to Pétain that the overwhelming part of the military pledged its allegiance, but it was de Gaulle who, by November 1942, was being vindicated by events. In terms of effect, in autumn 1944 Philippe Leclerc de Hauteclocque (1902–1952), one of the very first officers to join de Gaulle back in 1940, refused to allow his division, the 2nd Armored Division from Normandy, to join the 1st French Army in Alsace because it was commanded by an officer who had sided originally with Vichy. De Gaulle himself brought into command French forces such individuals as Alphonse Juin (1888–1967), a St. Cyr graduate from the same year (1912) as himself, and he allowed Jean de Lattre de Tassigny (1889–1952) to command the one army that a redeemed France was able to put into the field. But if certain individuals could indeed rise above such matters, the bitterness and rancor of two years' standing ran very deep indeed within the officer corps and should not be underestimated.

This was certainly the case of Admiral Jean de Laborde (1878–1977), commander of the fleet units at Toulon in November 1942, who had a pronounced hatred of the British that went hand-in-hand with total obedience to Pétain, and with two other matters: an awareness that French warships were not to be surrendered to the armed forces of any country, Axis or Allied, and a refusal to countenance resistance to German and Italian forces that had invaded Vichy France. Within two days these forces had established themselves within ten miles of Toulon, which, as a result of a German promise made after the incursion, was established as a Vichy enclave, with a guarantee that there would be no attempt to seize the French fleet. Inevitably, this promise went alongside the development of a plan to seize the French fleet, a development and plan that, in a curious parallel with July 1940, was opposed by the head of the German Navy, Grossadmiral Erich Raeder (1876–1960), who was convinced that French officers would never allow their ships to be surrendered to any foreign power and who expressed the hope that the Anglo-American landings in northwest Africa might push the Pétainist regime into a state of co-belligerency. The latter would seem to have been wishful thinking, though it should be noted that de Laborde's initial reaction to the Allied landings in North Africa was to ask superior authority for permission to take the fleet to sea in order to fight the Allies:[38] given the disparity of forces that would have been in theater there can be little doubt about the outcome of such a foray.[39] As it was, on 12 November Admiral Jean-François Darlan (1881–1942), the commander of Vichy naval forces but in North Africa at the time of the Allied landings, ordered an end to resistance and made a broadcast by radio urging the fleet units at Toulon to sortie and join the Allies. But this came at the very time when, with distrust of the Gaullists, the British, Darlan, and the Germans present in roughly equal proportions within the Vichy high command, the French naval command put in effect measures that would ensure the scuttling of the fleet should the Germans and Italians attempt to seize it. On 18 November the Germans demanded the dissolution of the French military formations in and around Toulon, and with no real choice in the matter, the Vichy regime complied, with the result that after 19 November there was no defensive force in position between the French fleet and German forces. The latter then set about progressive encroachment and established themselves in positions from which they could quickly secure the headlands, from which they could bring concentrated fire against any French warship that attempted to sail from the harbor. Moreover, given the fact that by this time the Germans were moving air formations forward and that French warships would not have air cover,[40] the fact was that the French opportunity to sail had passed: if the French fleet ever was to have sailed to join the Allies, it would have been obliged to do so between 12 and 16 November.[41]

But at this stage the question of what numbers and type of warships might have been able to make the attempt to join the Allies presents itself. There were some 135 warships, auxiliaries, support ships, store ships, and training ships in Toulon, and these were divided into three groups: the fleet (*Forces de Haute Mer*), the local command (*Forces Navales de la Troisième Region*), and warships that had been disarmed and immobilized under the terms of the 1940 armistice. Many of the latter ships, which included the *Dunkerque*, two cruisers, fourteen destroyers, and a number of auxiliaries, had been damaged, some were in dock, and none had complete crews and thus they could not have attempted to sortie. The units under local command numbered six destroyers, three sloops, and twenty small patrol boats plus the training ships (the old battleship *Provence*, the seaplane carrier *Commandant Teste*, two sloops, five small patrol craft, and two ex-battleship hulks, the *Condorcet* and *Océan*), and one group of six operational submarines: a sortie on the part of most of these warships (submarines excluded) was at best a dubious proposition. That left the fleet units, and these were the battleship *Strasbourg*, five cruisers, and thirteen destroyers, and of these one cruiser was in dock and not fit for sea.

At very best, therefore, any formation that the French might have been able to get to sea would have been small, and the numbers contrast sharply with those that were in service in June 1940 and that represented a major loss to the Allied cause when France was forced to leave the war. By 1943 the numbers that might have made their way across the Mediterranean were largely irrelevant because the British and Americans either had or in the immediately foreseeable future would have numbers enough to meet requirements: these French ships in 1943 would have occupied a position similar to the Italian ships in 1944—very attractive, and most certainly good-looking, but really having no role to play. Moreover, putting even these ships into service and maintaining them would have presented formidable problems; witness what happened to the battleship *Richelieu*, which, at Dakar in November 1942, came aboard the Allied cause and was taken in hand by the New York Navy Yard between February and August 1943. That the yard was able to complete a major overhaul in six months was comment on American industrial management, investment, and technique, but it was a task that was barely removed from a nightmare. With no plans from which to work, obliged to work with measurements and French steel alloys that were not compatible with those in American service, and with the need to realign shafts and engines, the American achievement was impressive by any standard, but two points need be noted. First, the Americans had to re-bore the main guns from 380-mm in order to take British 15-in./381-mm shells, and second, the *Richelieu* was able to have a complete main armament only because two damaged guns were exchanged with those taken from its sister-ship, *Jean Bart*, which was laid up at Casablanca. Herein, perhaps, is an indication of what might well have happened to the four cruisers and thirteen destroyers of *Forces de Haute Mer* had they escaped from Toulon and made it safely across the Mediterranean to join the Allied cause: in all likelihood, some of their number—perhaps a cruiser and possibly a couple of destroyers—would have been written off as constructive total losses and cannibalized in order to provide for those that were in service.

The German attempt to seize French warships in the early hours of 27 November resulted in no major captures. The original scuttling plan had involved the deliberate capsizing of warships, but this was basically abandoned in favor of letting ships settle on even keels in order to facilitate post-war salvage. The days of notice, however, had left the French crews with time to prepare for scuttling and the systematic destruction of turrets, guns, machinery of all types, and range-finding and radio equipment; the resultant destruction of warships was therefore thorough, comprehensive, and deeply impressive. The *Strasbourg*, to all appearances undamaged but all but gutted by internal explosions, sank to a depth of two meters in the harbor mud, while the fires that consumed the *Marseillaise* burned for a week, the *Dupleix* for ten days, and the *Algérie* for twenty days; the *Jean de Vienne* was deliberately moved half in and half out its dock, and in sinking thus blocked it. With the heavy cruisers *Colbert* and *Foch* and light cruiser *La Galissonnière* also destroyed, all the main units were wrecked beyond recall. The only units that were captured and returned to German or Italian service were the destroyer leaders *Lion* and *Tigre*, the destroyer *Trombe*, the torpedo-boats *Baliste* and *La Bayonnaise*, the sloops *La Curieuse* and *Les Eparges*, and the netlayer *Le Gladiateur*, and such numbers represented a very poor return, given German intent.[42] On the other side of the coin, of the six operational submarines at Toulon, five sailed in the face of mines, German aircraft, and fire from German armor and infantry over the harbor. One, the *Vénus*, never managed to leave and was scuttled at the exit from the harbor, and the *Iris* sailed for Barcelona and internment,[43] but the *Casabianca* and *Marsouin* reached Algiers and *Le Glorieux* reached Oran, and service with the Allies. Again, such numbers represented a most disappointing return given Allied intent in terms of "what might have been," while for the French Navy as an institution the day's proceedings most certainly were bittersweet: a certain sense of honor could be embraced in terms of the denial of the fleet to the German enemy, but the sense of loss, of ships and of purpose, was very real indeed, as indeed it was for the *Dunkerque* and *Strasbourg, en larmes pour ses enfants perdus car elles n'existent plus.*[44]

* * *

The postscript to this whole sorry tale was provided, somewhat inadvertently perhaps, by the *Richelieu*. After finishing its refit it was sent on trials and in November 1943 joined the British Home Fleet. But such was the fickleness of Fate that it was not involved in the action off the North Cape, and herein is a matter of historical regret: it was rather unfortunate that such units as the *Dunkerque* and *Strasbourg* never did battle with any of the *panzerschiffe*, or the *Richelieu* with the *Scharnhorst*, not because the French and Germans might have sunk one another, but because one suspects that the French performance would have been better than is generally recognized; certainly qualitatively the French ships were at least the equal of their enemies. But in March 1944, with the British obliged to react to the re-deployment of Japanese carrier and battle formations to Singapore in order to put distance between themselves and American carrier forces, the *Richelieu* and the U.S. carrier *Saratoga* were separately sent to the Indian Ocean to support a British fleet that was hopelessly outnumbered and outclassed in theater. The Japanese had no intention of conducting operations in the Indian Ocean, and the apparent danger very quickly passed; by November, and in the aftermath of the battle of Leyte Gulf, most of what was gathered at Singapore were warships beyond repair and future action. The *Richelieu* remained on station until war's end, but points of real interest about it are two-fold. Its file in the Public Record Office remains closed,[45] but it seems that its contents point to the violent feuds within the ship between Vichy and Free French, the state of certain of the ship's divisions, and a very pronounced anti-British sentiment on the part of the crew as a whole. The latter, however, was tempered by something else: a very great pride in being a French ship in a British fleet, and there was a determination that the ship would be second to none in whatever British formation it found itself. Both the Home and the Eastern/East Indies Fleets reported in the most favorable of terms about the French ship and its performance, and it is clear that its crew took real, if tight-lipped, pride in such achievement. The second matter provides comment on the Pétainist-Gaullist division within the French Navy in general and the *Richelieu* in particular. At war's end the *Richelieu* was at Trincomalee and was involved in the British reoccupation of Singapore before returning to Ceylon and then sailing with a destroyer and two troopships for Indo-China. It anchored off Cape St. Jacques on 3 October while its companions sailed up the Mekong to Saigon. With one break at Singapore, the *Richelieu* remained on station until 29 December,[46] and in the time that it was in Indo-Chinese waters it was visited by Leclerc, the commander of French forces now returning in numbers to Indo-China. He ordered the removal of the portrait of Pétain from the ship's wardroom.

APPENDIX 7.1.

FRENCH WARSHIP AND SUBMARINE LOSSES DURING TORCH

THE FRENCH WARSHIP LOSSES during the Torch operation were as follows:

On 8 November outside or at Casablanca:

The 9,50-ton light cruiser *Primaguet*, heavily damaged by the *Augusta* and *Brooklyn*, beached and written off as a total loss; the 3,410-ton *contre-torpilleur Albatros*, heavily damaged in action with the U.S. heavy cruisers *Augusta*, *Tuscaloosa*, and *Wichita* and by attack by aircraft, and beached but salved in March 1943, and subsequently repaired and returned to service; the 3,410-ton *contre-torpilleur Milan*, heavily damaged in action with American heavy cruiser(s), beached and written off as a total loss; the 2,000-ton destroyer *Boulonnais*, sunk in action with the U.S. light cruiser *Brooklyn;* the 2,000-ton destroyer *Brestois*, heavily damaged in action with the U.S. heavy cruiser *Augusta* and a destroyer but reached her berth, where she sank; and the 2,000-ton destroyer *Fougueux*, sunk in action with U.S. battleship *Massachusetts* and heavy cruiser *Tuscaloosa*. In addition an auxiliary patrol boat, the *Estafette*, was sunk by a combination of gunfire and bombs on this same day.

On 8 November outside Oran:

In an action with the British light cruiser *Aurora* and associated destroyers, the 1,900-ton destroyer *Tornade* and the 879-ton minesweeping sloop *La Surprise* were sunk, and both the 3,41-ton *contre-torpilleur Épervier* and the 1,900-ton destroyer *Tramontane* were beached and subsequently written off as total losses.

In addition, the sloop *Dubourdieu* is given as having been sunk this same day, but place and cause of losses are unknown to the author.

On 9 November at Casablanca:

The 2,000-ton destroyer *Frondeur*, heavily damaged in action with the heavy cruisers *Tuscaloosa* and *Wichita*, but she managed to reach harbor, where she capsized;

At Oran:

The 1,900-ton destroyer *Typhon*, which was scuttled as a block-ship.

French submarine losses during Torch were as follows:

On 8 November at Casablanca:

The 809-ton *Amphitrite*, *La Psyché*, and *Oréade*, all sunk by U.S. carrier aircraft.

On 8 November south of Casablanca:

The 809-ton *Méduse*, damaged by U.S. carrier aircraft and beached near Magazan, present-day El Jadida, some sixty miles south along the coast from Casablanca.

On 8 November north of Oran:

The 2,084-ton *Actéon* and the 798-ton *Argonaute*, sunk by the British destroyers *Westcott* and *Achates* respectively.

On 9 November at Oran:

The 787-ton *Ariane*, 856-ton *Cérès*, 787-ton *Danaé*, 809-ton *Diane*, and 856-ton *Pallas*, all boats being scuttled.

On or about 11 November:

The 809-ton *La Sybille* and the 2,084-ton *Sidi Ferruch*, whereabouts and cause of losses unknown. The *La Sybille* is believed to have been sunk in error by the German submarine I. 173 in this general area, and the *Sidi Ferruch* is believed to have been the submarine sunk by aircraft from the U.S. escort carrier *Suwannee* off Fedhala, some fifteen miles up the coast from Casablanca.

On 13 November:

The 2,084-ton *Le Conquérant*, sunk off Dakhla, in southern Spanish West Africa/Rio del Oro, by two U.S. Catalina flying boats.

On 15 November:

The 2,084-ton *Le Tonnant*, having almost reached Cádiz, scuttled rather than be surrendered.

APPENDIX 7.2.

SCUTTLING OF THE FRENCH FLEET AT TOULON, 27 NOVEMBER 1942

THE COMPILING OF the list of units scuttled at Toulon in November 1942 is fraught with difficulty: no two sources seem to agree about numbers, identities, and spellings, and the two maps that were consulted with reference to position of ships within the Toulon base invariably differ, and quite considerably. For example, one map has a number of units, without names or numbers, as having been scuttled while the other map has a number of named units marked that were not on the first map, but these units do not accord, in numbers and position, with those unnamed units on the first map—and, perhaps predictably, the total number of units marked, named, and numbered on these two maps do not agree with one another, and indeed do not accord with totals given in other sources. Moreover, in seeking to provide a full account of the units that were scuttled there are basic problems of definition with respect to the raising of units and specifically their fate after 27 November 1942, whether this involved their being raised and abandoned during the war or after the war, of their being commissioned or merely entering nominal service with either the German or the Italian navies. Many reference books, and specifically most English-language reference books, simply have ships scuttled on 27 November 1942, without any reference to their subsequently being raised, stricken and scrapped, or returned to service.

To give but three examples of these problems, a consultation of three major sources—*Les Flotte of Combat* (1947), *Conway's All the World's Fighting Ships, 1922–1946*, and Samuel Eliot Morison's *History of United States Naval Operations in World War II*, vol. 2: *Operations in North African Waters, October 1942–June 1943*—seems to indicate that in terms of fleet units a total of three battleships, one seaplane carrier, four heavy and three light cruisers, seventeen *contre-torpilleurs*, eleven destroyers, and three torpedo-boats were scuttled, as were sixteen submarines. In addition, six sloops, three submarine-chasers, four patrol boats, and one netlayer are given as having been scuttled. This would give a total of seventy-two units, plus another four transports, two tankers, and one cable-layer. E. H. Jenkins, *A History of the French Navy: From Its*

Beginnings to the Present Day, page 336, gives a total of seventy-seven units—three battleships, one seaplane carrier, four heavy and three light cruisers, thirty-two destroyers, sixteen submarines, and nineteen other units—scuttled, while Jean Jacques Antier, on pages 132–133 of *La Sabordage de la flotte française à Toulon,* cites as present on the morning of 27 November three battleships, one seaplane carrier, four heavy and three light cruisers, eighteen *contre-torpilleurs,* fifteen destroyers, twenty submarines, six sloops, and three submarine-chasers, for a total of seventy-three units, of which four submarines escaped and either two or three *contre-torpilleurs,* two destroyers, and two submarines are listed as having been captured intact. Antier also gives a total of five *contre-torpilleurs,* seven destroyers, and four sloops having been assigned Italian commissioning numbers. C. Peter Chen, in the file *Scuttling the French Fleet 27 November 1942,* at http://ww2.db.cim/battle spec.php?battle id-210, states that the French "destroyed" three battleships, seven cruisers, fifteen destroyers, thirteen "torpedo boats," six sloops, twelve submarines, nine patrol boats, nineteen auxiliaries, one "school ship," twenty-eight tugs, and four cranes, and that the Germans were able to capture three disarmed destroyers, four damaged submarines, three civilian ships, "two obsolete battleships of little military value," and no fewer than twenty-seven other small vessels. This source also states that one ship, the *Léonor Frésnel,* escaped from Toulon to reach Algiers, and it seems that this is confirmed by a number of other sources. It appears, however, that the *Léonor Frésnel* escaped from Les Salins d'Hyères, some ten miles east of Toulon, which was home to a number of warships and auxiliaries, and not from Toulon itself. Other than four submarines, no unit, whether naval, auxiliary, or civilian, escaped from Toulon.

* * *

French Ships Scuttled at Toulon, at http://www.bobhenneman.info/toulon.htm, provides a list of formations (with admirals) and units (with captains of major units) at Toulon under operational headings, for example, the fleet with the battleship *Strasbourg,* the 1st Cruiser Squadron with the heavy cruisers *Algérie, Dupleix,* and *Colbert,* the 3rd Cruiser Division with the light cruisers *Marseilles* and *Jeanne de Vienne,* and the *3eme Escadre Légère* with the *contre-torpilleur Volta* (flag), the destroyers *Le Siroco, L'Adroit, La Trombe,* and *Le Foudroyant,* the *contre-torpilleurs Kersaint* and *Vauquelin,* the destroyers *Mameluck* and *Casque,* and the *contre-torpilleurs Verdun, Gerfaut,* and *Vautour.* This list is given as it was given in this file, other than the inclusion of type, its being noted that after the *Volta* was included a ship named as the *Le Borbelais,* which has defied identification: the obvious point would seem to be that this was the *Bordelais,* but it is included in the next formation. Given as assigned to the 3rd Naval District are the 1st Torpedo Squadron with two *contre-torpilleurs,* three destroyers, and one torpedo-boat, the 3rd Escort Squadron, which seems to have taken its number from the number of minesweeping sloops under command, and the 1st Patrol Flotilla with one sloop, one patrol boat, and three submarine-chasers plus "fourteen other patrol boats." In addition, the District is credited with six fully operational submarines and no fewer than thirty-eight auxiliaries, civilian ships, and tugs of various descriptions under command. The training establishment is given as six named and five numbered units, the latter not being identified and one of the six named units having already been listed under the patrol label. The remaining ships, which bring the total to 116 units, are those listed as having been disarmed under the provisions of the 1940 armistice agreement—the battleship *Dunkerque*, heavy cruiser *Foch*, and light cruiser *La Galissonnière*, ten *contre-torpilleurs*, two destroyers, and two torpedo-boats, and twelve submarines. The balance of six units, in this last category, would seem to include one submarine, the *Vengeur*, listed twice, one submarine listed under two names, the *Espoir* and the *L'Espoir*, and two submarines, the *Aréthuse* and *Perle*, which seemingly were not at Toulon; the *Perle* is generally listed in reference books as being in service with the Allies and being mistakenly sunk in July 1944, while the *Aréthuse* is not on any other list of units at Toulon, but survived this episode and the war in general in order to be sold and scrapped in 1946. If the *Le Borbelais/Bordelais* is erroneous and double-counted, this file would seem to have listed 111 units.

* * *

Five main sources have been depended on in devising the following list: Antier, *Le sabordage de la flotte française à Toulon*; Hannsjörg Kowark, *Hitler et la flotte française: Toulon 1940–1944*; Franck Lecalve and Jean-Michel Roche, *Liste des Bâtiments de la flotte de guerre française de 1700 à nos jours*; Jean Michael Roche, *Dictionnaire des Bâtiments de la Flotte de guerre française de Colbert à nos jours*; and http//www.mere-1939a.1945.fr/index.php?NIUpage=30. The first two sources carry maps, the latter acknowledging as source the original map of 21 December 1942 that is in the archives of the Service Historique de la Marine at Vincennes; the obvious problem with this map is whether or not it includes units that came into the various basins after 27 November. As noted previously, there are certain differences between the maps, and the following list, based primarily on these two maps in association with the contents of a file, entitled *Position des bâtiments au matin du 27 Novembre 1942* as per http//www/netmarine.net/forces/operatio/sabordage/position.htm, necessarily comes with a warning in the form of the "balance of probability" label. For example, Antier has one submarine-chaser in two different places, in the Old Harbor and at St. Mandrier, whereas the other two sources indicate that Chasseur I was at St. Mandrier; other sources, while agreeing that three chasers were at Toulon, together cite four different ones (Chasseurs I, II, IV, and XXV). One could continue to provide examples of inconsistency, areas of doubt, and even areas of agreement (if only in part), but such a process would certainly prove exhausting long before it was exhaustive, suffice it to note six matters.

First, the following list presents units in a trace from west to east via the various piers, jetties, and docks. Second, displacement figures are given as full-load displacement for fleet units, full-load submerged for submarines, and standard displacement for all other units, and expressed in imperial tons and not metric tonnes. Third, all names and spellings have been taken from *Les Flotte de Combat*, 1947. Fourth, it should be noted that certain Dutch and French companies and personnel were involved in the raising of certain ships—for example, the *Casque* by La sociéte van Wiennen and the *Vautour* by La société Nautilus de Paris—and quite clearly these, and possibly certain Italian companies, worked under German direction; accordingly the raising of units is given only under German and Italian auspices, where known. Fifth, there is a certain area of difficulty in defining a number of the "other" units at Toulon on 27 November that are defined as *arraisonneur-dragueur*, a French term that defies easy translation, not least on account of the fact that Kowark, *Hitler et la flotte fran-*

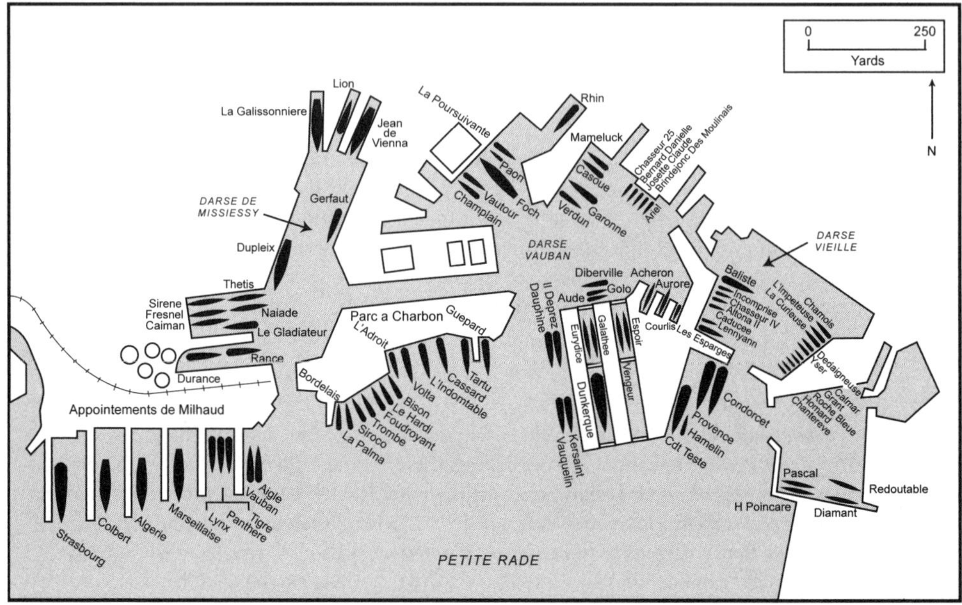

Map 8. Port of Toulon and Berths, 27 November 1942

çaise, pages 81–82, lists sixteen such vessels, ten identified as being at Toulon on 27 November, that were not armed and lacked minesweeping equipment, which does place a question mark against the *dragueur* label. As a consequence these units are cited as auxiliaries and not assigned any other title unless definitively known from other sources, for example, armed trawler status. Sixth and last, all entries must be regarded as subject to the usual E&OE provision.

* * *

The fate of French warships at Toulon on the morning of Friday, 27 November 1942, was as follows:

At St. Mandrier:

The ex-battleship training hulk *Océan:* Captured intact. Damaged by heavy bombers of 15 U.S. Air Force in raid of 7 March 1944; used as a target ship by the Germans and sunk eight days later. Raised on 14 December 1945 and scrapped 1946–1947.

The 180-ton submarine-chaser Chasseur I: Raised on 13 January 1944 by the Germans. Details of subsequent fate not forthcoming, but represented as being in the Missiessy basin on 1 September 1944, state and status not known to the author. Details of subsequent fate not forthcoming.

The auxiliary trawler/drifter *Roche Françoise:* Details of displacement and fate not forthcoming.

Off Lazaret:

The 1,968-ton destroyer *Le Mars*: Settled; hull damaged, machinery and guns wrecked. Raised on 6 March 1944 by the Germans with the aid of the floating dock: deemed beyond repair and grounded off La Seyne. Wreck ceded to Vichy regime in May 1944. Raised in 1947 preparatory to scrapping.

In La Seyne yard:

The 3,251-ton *contre-torpilleur Valmy*: Alongside the *Mogador*. Settled; guns wrecked. Raised between 1 February and 15 March 1943 by the Italians. Commissioned and in nominal service as the F.R. 24, 1–2 July, towed to La Spezia, arriving 6 July. Seized by the Germans at the time of the Italian surrender. Badly damaged in RAF raid on Savona on 20 January 1944. Details of subsequent fate not clear, but it appears that it was scuttled by the Germans at Genoa some time in 1944 and that the wreck was raised in 1945 and subsequently scrapped.

The 4,018-ton *contre-torpilleur Mogador*: Between the *Valmy* and the quay. Settled. Raised between 17 March and 5 April 1943 by the Italians. Moored in the roads with no work done on it: in effect abandoned. In the raid of 29 April 1944 by heavy bombers of 15 U.S. Air Force it was hit by a bomb that penetrated its second funnel, and as a result of damage sustained it slowly settled; the wreck was badly shaken by a series of near-misses in the raid of 4 May. Raised and ceded to the Vichy regime on 22 May 1944 and grounded off La Seyne. Raised in 1949 and subsequently scrapped.

The 2, 577-ton destroyer *Lansquenet*: In dock. Settled: guns wrecked. Raised on 24 April 1943 and towed to La Spezia on 31 August 1943: in nominal service as the F.R. 34. Seized by the Germans at the time of the Italian surrender, it entered German service as the T.A. 34 and was scuttled at Genoa on 24 April 1945. Raised on 19 March 1946 and towed to Toulon. The *Lansquenet* was the subject of various plans to return it to service, and in the course of these it was renamed the *Cyclone*, but the plans came to nothing. Details of subsequent fate not forthcoming.

In the Milhaud berths:

The 34,865-ton battleship *Strasbourg*: Alongside the western (No. 6) pier. Settled upright: hull damaged, machinery and guns wrecked. Raised 17 July 1943 and partially dismantled. Moored in Lazaret Bay and sunk by medium bombers of 12 U.S. Air Force in raid of 18 August 1944. Raised in August 1945 and used as trials ship until 1951. Stricken 22 March 1955 and sold 27 May: scrapped thereafter.

The 12,752-ton heavy cruiser *Colbert*: Alongside the No. 5 pier. Settled upright but extensively damaged by six-day fire and magazine explosion: hull damaged and machinery and guns wrecked. Written off and abandoned. Raised in 1946 and scrapped.

The 13,433-ton heavy cruiser *Algérie*: Alongside the No. 4 pier. Settled upright but burnt throughout its length: hull damaged and machinery and guns wrecked. Raised between 9 April and 19 August 1943 by the Italians. Towed into the inner harbor to be made ready to move to La Seyne yard for major repair. Moved on 1 January 1944 but shipped water and sank. Raised but damaged by heavy bombers of 15 U.S. Air Force in raid of 7 March. Settled, written off, and abandoned. Raised in 1949 and apparently used as trials ship. Stricken in 1955. Sold on 21 December 1956 and scrapped thereafter.

The 8,937-ton *Marseillaise*: Alongside the No. 3 pier. Settled with list of 45° to port and burnt out after twenty-day fire: hull damaged and machinery and guns wrecked. Written off and abandoned. Wreck was further damaged by heavy bombers of 15 U.S. Air Force in raids of 11 March and 29 April 1944. Raised on 8 April 1946 and scrapped thereafter.

The 3,098-ton *contre-torpilleur Lynx:* Between the No. 2 pier and the *Panthère*. Settled: hull damaged, machinery and guns wrecked. Raised on 22 January 1944 by the Germans preparatory to being towed to La Seyne where it sank. Wreck assigned to the Vichy regime in May 1944. Written off and abandoned. Raised in 1948 preparatory to scrapping.

The 3,098-ton *contre-torpilleur Panthère:* Between the *Lynx* and *Tigre*. Alternatively given as having been scuttled and raised on 23 March 1943 by the Italians or, with a skeleton crew that could not ensure its destruction, captured intact. Towed to La Spezia and re-armed, nominally entering Italian service as the F.R. 22. Scuttled with the Italian surrender on 8 September 1943. Details of subsequent fate not forthcoming.

The 3,098-ton *contre-torpilleur Tigre:* Between the *Panthère* and the No. 1 pier. Skeleton crew and captured intact. Towed to La Spezia and re-armed as the F.R. 23, and entered service as a troop transport. Captured by British forces at Taranto in September 1943 and formally returned to French ownership at Bizerte on 28 October: recommissioned on 15 December 1943. Refitted at Casablanca and returned to service in March 1944. Stricken in 1954. Details of subsequent fate not forthcoming.

The 3,251-ton *contre-torpilleur Vauban:* Alongside the No. 1 pier and the *Aigle*. Settled keel uppermost. Raised, at the fifth attempt, in June 1943 and in German possession but suffered further damage by heavy bombers of 15 U.S. Air Force in raid of 24 November 1943. Sunk in raid of 4 February 1944, and wreck incurred further damage in raid of 7 March. Raised on 12 May 1947 preparatory to scrapping.

The 3,190-ton *contre-torpilleur Aigle:* Alongside the *Vauban*. Settled. Raised on 10 July 1943 and sunk by heavy bombers of 15 U.S. Air Force in raid of 24 November 1943. Wreck heavily damaged in raid of 29 April 1944. Not raised, and scrapped *in situ* in 1952.

In the western berths south of the Parc à Charbon headland:

One 1,080-ton floating dock: Alongside the western side of the pier. Apparently scuttled but raised and in service in 1943 and on station in September 1944. Details of subsequent fate not forthcoming.

The 1,968-ton destroyer *Bordelais:* In No. 18 position alongside the eastern side of the pier. Settled keel uppermost: hull damaged, machinery and guns wrecked. In effect written off and abandoned. Ceded to the Vichy regime; an attempt to raise it in May 1944 was abandoned. Partially scrapped, *in situ,* in 1950, and wreck still in place.

The 1,968-ton destroyer *La Palme:* In No. 17 position alongside the *Bordelais* and *Le Siroco*. Settled keel uppermost: hull damaged, machinery and guns wrecked. Raised on 26 December 1943 by the Germans: deemed to be beyond repair and towed to La Seyne, where it sank. Wreck ceded to Vichy regime on 19 May 1944. Raised and scrapped in 1947.

The 2,577-ton destroyer *Le Siroco:* In No. 15 position alongside the *La Palme* and *La Trombe*. Settled with list. Raised on 16 April 1943 by the Italians. Towed to Genoa and, on 10 June, entered nominal service as the F.R. 32. Seized by the Germans at time of the Italian surrender, 9 September 1943. Sunk as blockship at Genoa on 28 October 1944. Subsequently broken up and scrapped *in situ*.

The 1,968-ton destroyer *La Trombe:* In No. 14 position alongside the *Le Siroco* and *Le Foudroyant*. Captured intact and passed into Italian possession on 19 January 1943. Sailed for first time on 6 April 1943 and then for Italy nine days later. Commissioned on 16 April and numbered the F.R. 31 on the following day. Ran aground on 2 May and repaired. Involved, on the Allied side, in the liberation of Corsica in September 1943. Returned to French ownership at Bizerte on 28 October 1943; commissioned on 29

October and renamed *Trombe* on the following day. Involved in Dragoon landings in August 1944 and torpedoed off San Remo on 17 April 1945, apparently by German MTBs. Placed in reserve at Toulon on 3 July 1945. Stricken on 12 December 1946 and partially dismantled after February 1950. Placed on sale on 7 December 1950: details of subsequent fate not forthcoming.

The 1,968-ton destroyer *Le Foudroyant:* In No. 13 position alongside the *La Trombe* and *Le Hardi.* Settled upright. Raised between 16 March and 20 May 1943. First in the Missiessy and then the Castigneau basins, and in nominal Italian service as the F.R. 36. At a Milhaud berth when seized by the Germans at time of the Italian surrender, 9 September 1943. Damaged by heavy bombers of 15 U.S. Air Force in raid of 7 March 1944. Repaired at La Seyne yard. Ceded to Vichy regime on 22 May 1944. Seized by the Germans and scuttled in the main channel on 17 August 1944. Raised in 1951 and scrapped in 1957.

The 2,577-ton destroyer *Le Hardi:* In No. 12 position alongside the *Le Foudroyant* and *Bison.* Settled with list. Raised on 12 June 1943 and in nominal Italian service as the F.R. 37. Left Toulon on 7 September 1943 and seized by the Germans at Savona. Scuttled at Genoa on 24 April 1945. Decision of 23 July 1946 not to attempt to raise the ship; subsequently scuttled *in situ.*

The 2,577-ton destroyer *Bison:* Alongside the *Le Hardi.* Incomplete and not in commission at the time of the scuttling. Settled and subsequently raised: details not forthcoming. Seized by the Germans at time of the Italian surrender, 9 September 1943. Used as a smoke-generator and damaged in raids by Allied bombers at some time in spring 1944: details not forthcoming. Scuttled at Toulon as a blockship on 25 June 1944. Details of subsequent fate not forthcoming.

In the eastern berth, on the Quai Noël, south of the Parc à Charbon headland:

The 1,968-ton destroyer *L'Adroit:* In No. 11 position alongside the *Volta.* Settled upright and burnt throughout its length. Raised between 26 February and 20 April 1943 and beached outside La Seyne. Re-armed and in nominal Italian service as the F.R. 33. Seized by the Germans with the Italian surrender, 9 September 1943. Damaged by heavy bombers of 15th U.S. Air Force in raids of 27 November 1943 and 4 February 1944; after second raid partially aground. Wreck ceded to Vichy regime on 19 May 1944. In September 1945, after five months of work and two failed attempts, finally raised: subsequently scrapped. Details of fate not forthcoming.

The 4,018-ton *contre-torpilleur Volta:* In No. 9 position alongside *L'Adroit* and *L'Indomptable.* Scuttled upright: guns wrecked. Raised between 11 March and 20 May 1943 by the Italians. Towed to La Seyne yard: written off. Damaged by heavy bombers of 15 U.S. Air Force in raid of 24 November 1943: decision to sink as constructive total loss in January 1944. Wreck ceded to Vichy regime in May 1944. Raised and scrapped in 1948.

The 3,454-ton *contre-torpilleur L'Indomptable:* In No. 7 position alongside the *Volta* and *Cassard.* Settled with list to port: hull damaged, machinery and guns wrecked. Hit by single bombs in each of the 15 U.S. Air Force raids of 4 February, 7 March, and 29 April 1944, the latter wrecking the anti-aircraft gun position aft. In effect abandoned. Forward section salvaged in 1946 for the refitting of its sister ship, the *Le Malin.* The remainder of the ship was scrapped, underwater, in 1950.

The 3,190-ton *contre-torpilleur Cassard:* In No. 5 position alongside the *L'Indomptable* and *Tartu.* Settled upright: hull damaged, machinery and guns wrecked. Attempt to raise in late 1943 abandoned and second attempt forestalled by further damage inflicted by heavy bombers of 15 U.S. Air Force in raid of 7 March 1944; written off next month. Scrapped in 1956.

The 3,190-ton *contre-torpilleur Tartu:* In No. 3 position alongside the *Cassard* and the western side of the pier. Capsized to starboard: hull damaged, machinery and guns wrecked. Start of Italian attempt to raise the ship 16 March 1943; abandoned on 11 December. Further damage inflicted in heavy bomber raids of 7 and 11 March and 29 April 1944. Scrapped *in situ* in 1956.

The 3,251-ton *contre-torpilleur Guépard:* Alongside the eastern side of the pier. Settled keel uppermost: hull damaged and guns wrecked. Raised between March and 4 September 1943 by the Italians. Heavily damaged by heavy bombers of 15 U.S. Air Force in raid of 11 March 1944: capsized four days later. Wreck subsequently ceded to Vichy regime. Raised and scrapped in 1947.

In the Missiessy basin:

The 1,055-ton tanker *La Rance:* In the tanker basin. Scuttled. Raised 30 May 1943 by the Germans. Details of subsequent fate not forthcoming.

The 1,055-ton tanker *La Durance:* In the tanker basin. Scuttled. Raised 15 May 1943 by the Germans. Details of subsequent fate not forthcoming.

The 2,293-ton netlayer *Le Gladiateur:* In the submarine basin. Raised in March 1943 by the Germans and entered service in January 1944 as the S.G. 18 in the role of anti-aircraft corvette/minelayer. Capsized after being hit in 15 U.S. Air Force raid of 4 February 1944. Details of subsequent fate not forthcoming.

The 1,415-ton submarine *Caïman:* Alongside the *Frésnel* in the submarine basin. Scuttled; machinery wrecked. Raised between 25 January and 15 February 1943 by the Italians. In the Castigneau basin and sunk by heavy bombers of 15 U.S. Air Force in raid of 11 March 1944. Raised in August 1945. Details of subsequent fate not forthcoming.

The 2,084-ton submarine *Frésnel:* Alongside the Caïman in the submarine basin. Scuttled. Raised on 29 January 1943 by the Germans. Sank on 19 February 1943. Raised 4 May 1943 by the Germans. Taken to La Seyne. Sunk by heavy bombers of 15 U.S. Air Force in raid of 11 March 1944; wreck ceded to Vichy regime thereafter. Raised, foundered, and broken up, *in situ*, in 1946.

The 757-ton submarine *Sirène:* Alongside the jetty in the submarine basin. Scuttled: machinery wrecked. Raised between 16 and 23 March 1943 by the Italians and sank the next day. Raised on 25 April by the Germans. Taken to and moored at La Seyne on 26 January 1944. Sunk by heavy bombers of 15 U.S. Air Force in raid of 29 April 1944. Written off and abandoned. Details of subsequent fate not forthcoming.

The 757-ton submarine *Naïade:* Alongside the *Thétis* in the submarine basin. Scuttled: machinery wrecked. Raised 16 March 1943 by the Germans but then sank. Raised again on 17 July 1943. Sunk by heavy bombers of 15 U.S. Air Force in raid of 24 November 1943. Abandoned. Details of subsequent fate not forthcoming.

The 776-ton submarine *Thétis:* Alongside the jetty and the Naïade in the submarine basin. Scuttled: machinery wrecked. Raised between 7 February and 1 March 1943 by the Italians: written off. Moored in the Missiessy basin in January and off La Seyne on 4 February 1944. Ceded to Vichy regime in April 1944. Damaged by heavy bombers of 15 U.S. Air Force in raid of 6 August 1944 and thereafter sank, but whether as the result of this damage, German scuttling on 15 August, or another cause is unknown. Raised in September 1945 and scrapped.

The 12,752-ton heavy cruiser *Dupleix:* Alongside the western quay. Settled upright and burnt throughout its length: hull damaged, machinery and guns wrecked. Deemed beyond repair by the Germans but had to be raised in order to clear the quay. Raised between 16 April and 3 July 1943 by the Italians. Severely damaged by heavy bombers of 15 U.S. Air Force in raid of 11 March 1944 and sank four days later. Abandoned. Scrapped in 1951.

The 8,937-ton light cruiser *La Galissonnière:* In the No. 3 dock. Settled. Assigned to Italy in December 1942 as the F.R. 12. Raised on 9 March 1943. Seized by Germans at time of the Italian surrender, 9 September 1943. Damaged on 24 November 1943 and sunk on 18 August 1944 by heavy bombers of 15 U.S. Air Force. Raised and scrapped in 1952.

The 3,251-ton *contre-torpilleur Lion:* In No. 2 dock. Skeleton crew and captured with hull intact but guns destroyed. Left the dock on 9 February 1943 and commissioned into Italian service as the F.R. 21 next day. Sailed for La Spezia on 16 April, where it was refitted and re-armed. Scuttled on 9 September 1943 at the time of the Italian surrender. Cited as having been raised by the Germans but sunk in a bombing raid in 1944, but detail of raid and that of subsequent fate not forthcoming.

The 8,937-ton light cruiser *Jean de Vienne:* In the No. 1 dock. Settled upright. Recovered on 18 February 1943 by the Italians after the draining of the dock. Nominally in Italian service as the F.R. 11. Seized by the Germans at time of the Italian surrender, 9 September 1943. Set on fire by heavy bombers of 15 U.S. Air Force in raid of 24 November 1943: extensively damaged and sank. Wreck damaged in raids of 4 February and 11 March 1944: wreck subsequently ceded to Vichy regime. Raised in 1948 preparatory to scrapping.

The 3,190-ton *contre-torpilleur Gerfaut.*

Alongside the eastern quay. Settled with list to starboard: hull damaged, machinery wrecked. Raised between 12 March and 1 June 1943 by the Italians: deemed to be beyond repair. Hulk sunk by heavy bombers of 15 U.S. Air Force in raid of 7 March 1944: written off and abandoned. Raised and scrapped in 1948.

In the Castigneau basin:

The 526-ton refrigerator ship/transport *Champlain:* Between the No. 1 dock and the *Vautour.* Settled. Raised on 18 March 1943 by the Germans. Details of subsequent fate not forthcoming.

The 3,190-ton *contre-torpilleur Vautour:* Between the *Champlain* and *Foch.* Settled with list to port. Raised on 17 July 1943 by the Germans. Sunk by heavy bombers of 15 U.S. Air Force in raid of 4 February 1944. Renewed attempt to raise the ship defeated by the raid of 29 April: the *Vautour* incurred damage to stern and port side and sank. Wreck ceded to Vichy regime on 19 May 1944. Raised and scrapped in 1951.

The 12,752-ton heavy cruiser *Foch:* Between the *Vautour* and *Paon.* Settled upright with guns intact. Deemed to be beyond repair and written off. Raised between 24 February and 16 April 1943 by the Italians and moored first at the Milhaud No. 6 pier and then at la Seyne. Stripped, with AA armament put ashore, and subsequently scrapped.

The 767-ton fleet tug *Paon:* Alongside the *Foch* and *La Poursuivante.* Details of fate not forthcoming, but the fact that it was assigned escort duties in December 1942 indicates that it was not scuttled. Details of subsequent fate not forthcoming.

The 879-ton torpedo-boat *La Poursuivante:* Alongside the *Paon.* Settled keel uppermost: machinery and guns wrecked. Raised 1 July 1943 by the Germans. Moored in basin until 11 September preparatory to removal of screws and then moved to La Seyne. Subsequent decision to cannibalize the ship, specifically in order to refit the *La*

Bayonnaise, but this intention abandoned. Hull recovered after Liberation and lost in 1946 under tow, presumably en route to the breakers.

The 590-ton fleet tug *Six-Fours:* Details of fate not forthcoming.

The *Servaux IV:* Displacement and type unknown and subsequent fate not forthcoming.

The auxiliary minesweeper *Cap Noir:* Settled. Raised on 18 April 1943 by the Germans. Details of subsequent fate not forthcoming.

The auxiliary patrol/mine warfare school boat *La Havraise:* Settled but not wrecked. Raised between 5 March and 24 April 1943 by the Germans. Entered service as the escort U.J. 6078. Sunk by the British submarine *Untiring* in 48°08'North 05°36'East, some ten miles southwest of La Ciotat, on 10 June 1944.

The 451-ton boom vessel *Endurante:* Raised 4 July 1943 by the Germans. Details of subsequent fate not forthcoming.

Unit marked but unnamed: It would seem that this vessel was the auxiliary *La Socoa;* details of displacement and subsequent fate not forthcoming.

The *La Division d'Instruction* accommodation ship *Rhin:* Launched in 1884 as *La Gironde,* the *Rhin* was not scuttled but seized intact by the Germans and remained in service as an accommodation ship at Toulon. Sunk by heavy bombers of 15 U.S. Air Force in raid of 7 March 1944, and wreck further damaged in raid of 29 April. Written off and abandoned. Raised in 1948 preparatory to scrapping.

The 876-ton fleet tug *Laborieux:* Bombed 4 February 1944. Details of fate not forthcoming.

In the Vauban basin and docks:

The 3,251-ton *contre-torpilleur Verdun:* Settled upright with guns intact; hull damaged. 16 January 1943 and start of first attempt to raise the ship; abandoned. Raised on 29 September 1943 by the Germans and moored at La Seyne. Sunk by heavy bombers of 15 U.S. Air Force in raid of 7 March 1944; wreck further damaged in raid of 11 March. Written off and wreck ceded to Vichy regime thereafter. Raised in 1948 and towed to Savona for scrapping.

The 3,533-ton tanker *La Garonne:* Seized intact by the Germans. Refitting of ship halted in September 1943 and on 6 October moored inside the Old Harbor. Ceded to Vichy regime on 30 November 1943 and subsequently moved to the Milhaud No. 2 pier. Sunk by heavy bombers of 15 U.S. Air Force in raid of 7 March 1944. Raised on 21 April and damaged in raid of 29 April. Scuttled by the Germans as a blockship in the main channel on 20 June 1944. Raised 24 October 1944 and stricken 1 February 1946. Details of subsequent fate not forthcoming.

The 2,577-ton destroyer *Casque:* Settled keel uppermost: hull damaged, machinery wrecked. Attempt to raise the destroyer that began on 15 January 1943 was abandoned, and a second attempt was halted after the ship was heavily damaged by heavy bombers of 15 U.S. Air Force in raid of 29 April 1944. Written off. Raised and towed to Port de Bouc in 1948 and subsequently scrapped.

The 2,577-ton destroyer *Mameluck:* Settled: hull damaged. Attempt to raise the ship after 25 January 1943 quickly abandoned. Damaged by heavy bombers of 15 U.S. Air Force in raid of 4 February 1944. March 1944 saw resumption of attempt but while raised was sunk again, presumably in the raid of 29 April. It was then raised and ceded to the Vichy regime on 19 May. Sunk, again, in the raid of 6 August. Finally raised in 1947: stricken on 2 January 1958 and scrapped thereafter.

The 60-ton submarine-chaser Chasseur XXV: Raised on 25 January 1943 by the Germans. Details of subsequent fate not forthcoming.

The auxiliary *Bernard Danielle:* Details of displacement and fate not forthcoming.

The auxiliary/armed trawler *Josette-Claude:* Details of displacement and fate not forthcoming, but the fact it was assigned minesweeping duties in December 1942 indicates that it was not scuttled. Details of subsequent fate not forthcoming.

The auxiliary *Brin de Jonc Moulinais:* Details of displacement and fate not forthcoming, but the fact that it was assigned minesweeping duties in December 1942 indicates that it was not scuttled. Details of subsequent fate not forthcoming.

The auxiliary patrol boat *Ariel:* Not scuttled and assigned local defensedefense duties in December 1942. Sunk in course of an air raid of Toulon in August 1944. Details of subsequent fate not forthcoming.

The 393-ton netlayer *Agissante:* Settled. Raised between 14 December 1942 and 7 January 1943 and towed to La Ciotat for repair and fitting out: commissioned as M.T. 42 in January 1944. Scuttled in Marseilles in August 1944. Raised on 15 May 1945 and refitted 1947–1948 with engines and boilers from the *Mordante.* In service at Oran between 1949 and 1962. Towed to Toulon in 1962 and stricken on 28 February 1963. Scrapped at Toulon in 1964.

Le Sabordage de la flotte française à Toulon presents a total of fifteen unnamed vessels scuttled off the quay and its four piers in the area between the *Agissante* and the *Courlis. Position des bâtiments au matin du 27 novembre 1942* provides a list of ships in the Vauban basin that includes thirteen ships in addition to those cited above. These ships were, in the order given in this file: the 672-ton fleet tug *Cépet,* the 236-ton tug *Coudon,* the 250-ton tug *Carqueiranne,* the 196-ton tug *Zèbre,* the *Servaux VI* (details of displacement and type not forthcoming), the 324-ton tug *Tabarca,* the 122-ton tug *Camilia,* the *Servaux XIV* (details of displacement and type not forthcoming), the 393-ton mooring vessel *La Prudente,* the 157-ton tug *Thésée,* the 265-ton tug *Loup,* the 324-ton tug *Corse,* and the *Héron* (details of displacement and type not forthcoming, though this may be the *Le Héron II,* a 767-ton fleet tug).

The auxiliary *Courlis:* In the No. 1 dock. Details of displacement and subsequent fate not forthcoming.

The 1,170-ton submarine *L'Aurore:* In the No. 2 dock. Settled. Raised on 3 April 1943 by the Germans. Moored in Lazaret Bay and sank. Abandoned. Raised in 1946. Details of subsequent fate not forthcoming.

The 2,084-ton submarine *Achéron:* In the No. 3 dock. First raised on 26 June 1943 by the Germans and sank: raised a second time on 6 July 1943 by the Italians. Decision taken in August 1943 not to repair the boat. Sunk by heavy bombers of 15 U.S. Air Force in raid of 24 November 1943. Raised a third time, with the aid of the floating dock, on 23 February 1944. Moored in Lazaret Bay and sank. Scrapped in 1951.

The 1,821-ton transport *Aude:* Alongside the northeast docks. Settled. Raised on 7 July 1943 by the Germans. Sunk a second time by heavy bombers of 15 U.S. Air Force in raid of 24 November 1943. Sources differ in reference to subsequent fate; it has been suggested that it was raised again on 17 December 1943, but it seems more likely that it was abandoned with this second sinking and its being raised awaited 6 March 1945, after which time it was scrapped.

The 2,118-ton transport *Golo:* Between the *Aude* and *D'Iberville.* Details of subsequent fate not forthcoming.

The 2,553-ton colonial sloop *D'Iberville:* Alongside the *Golo.* Settled: machinery and guns wrecked. An attempt to raise the ship was undertaken at the end of January 1943 and continued until March 1944 without success. Renewed attempt began in early May but apparently the same result. The wreck was demolished, by underwater explosions, in 1956.

The 2,084-ton submarine *L'Espoir*: In the northeast dock with the *Vengeur*. Settled but captured intact. Raised by the Italians but deemed to be of no real military value: decision to clear the basin and thus scrap the boat. Scrapped between March and May 1943.

The 2,084-ton submarine *Vengeur*: In the northeast dock with the *L'Espoir*. Machinery wrecked. Scrapped between March and May 1943, and presumably for the same reasons as the *L'Espoir*.

The 757-ton submarine *Galatée*: In the northwest dock with the *Eurydice*. Settled: machinery wrecked. Raised on 25 June 1943 by the Germans and repaired using equipment stripped from the *L'Espoir* and *Vengeur*. Placed in reserve by the Italians. Seized by the Germans with the Italian surrender and moored in the Missiessy basin in January and off La Seyne in February 1944. Ceded to the Vichy regime and moved into Lazaret Bay in June 1944. Sunk by heavy bombers of 15 U.S. Air Force in raid of 5 July. Details of subsequent fate not forthcoming.

The 787-ton submarine *Eurydice*: In the northwest dock with the *Galatée*. Settled but captured intact. Raised on 26 June 1943 by the Germans after work to ensure the integrity of the hull. Deemed to be of no real military value on 26 January 1944 and moved to La Seyne: subsequently ceded to the Vichy regime. Sunk in an Allied raid of 22 June 1944. Raised in 1945. Details of subsequent fate not forthcoming.

The 34,865-ton battleship *Dunkerque*: In the southwest dock. Dock flooded, machinery and guns wrecked. At the end of 1942, decision to scrap, with the Italians starting to dismantle the superstructure. May 1943 saw the removal of the screws. The forward part of the ship was separated and stripped. Wreck was heavily damaged by two 1,000-lb. bombs from heavy bombers of 15 U.S. Air Force in raid of 4 February 1944 and suffered further damage in raids of 7 March and 29 April; settled on 6 May. Wreck further damaged in raid of 5 July. Ceded to Vichy regime thereafter. Undocked in August 1945 and moored off La Seyne; apparently used for explosive trials. Stricken 15 September 1955 and sold on 30 September 1958; scrapped thereafter.

The 9,895-ton civilian tanker *Henri Desprez*: Alongside the northwest dock and the *Dauphiné*. Not scuttled and seized by Germans. Torpedoed and sunk by British submarine *Unruffled* some seventy miles northeast of Messina on 3 June 1943, so presumably entered German (or possibly Italian) service.

The civilian tanker *Dauphiné*: Alongside the *Henri Desprez*. Details of subsequent fate not forthcoming.

The 3,190-ton *contre-torpilleur Kersaint*: Alongside the southwest dock and the *Vauquelin*. Settled upright: hull damaged. Short-lived Italian attempt to raise the ship abandoned on 10 February 1943; in effect written off. Scrapped in 1950.

The 3,190-ton *contre-torpilleur Vauquelin*: Alongside the *Kersaint*. Settled upright: hull damaged and guns wrecked. Short-lived Italian attempt to raise the ship abandoned on 10 February 1943; in effect written off. Wreck further damaged in Allied air raids in 1944. Scrapped in 1951.

Outside the Old Harbor on the Angle Robert and the east quay of the Vauban docks:

The 11,294-ton seaplane carrier *Commandant Teste*: Alongside the main jetty and the *Hamelin*. Settled with list to port. Raised between 16 March and 15 May 1943. Anti-aircraft armament removed by the Germans. At various moorings and officially announced, on 15 May 1944, that it would be ceded to the Vichy regime. Sunk in the raids of 18 and 19 August 1944. Raised in February 1945 and entered service as a stores ship for equipment for ex-American units in French naval service. Placed in reserve in March 1946. Stricken on 15 May 1950. Scrapped in 1963.

The 622-ton aircraft supply ship/transport *Hamelin:* Alongside the *Commandante Teste* and *Provence.* Settled. Raised on 30 October 1943 by the Germans. Details of subsequent fate not forthcoming.

The 27,990-ton battleship *Provence:* Alongside the *Hamelin* and *Condorcet.* Settled upright. Raised between 25 March and 11 July 1943 by the Italians; eight 75-mm guns removed for local batteries. After August 1943 superstructure dismantled and cut down to level of main deck. October 1943 and main 340-mm guns removed and taken to Ruelle in order to be re-bored; two guns subsequently installed at the Cépet battery. Scuttled by Germans as blockship at Toulon in August 1944. Raised in April 1949 and scrapped thereafter.

The ex-battleship barrack ship *Condorcet:* Alongside the *Provence.* Minor damage as a result of explosion but remained afloat and captured intact: remained in service as an accommodation ship for the crews of barges and other harbor craft. Seriously damaged by heavy bombers of 15 U.S. Air Force in raid of 7 March 1944; listing heavily, it was deliberately sunk on 15 March in order to prevent its capsizing, and written off. Scuttled as a blockship in August 1944. Raised between October and 14 December 1945 after the dismantling of its superstructure and belt. Stricken in 1947. Scrapped in 1959.

In the Old Harbor:

The 644-ton survey sloop *Les Eparges:* Alongside the Angle Robert. Settled. Raised in December 1942, it was commissioned into German service as the S.G. 25 in May 1943 with the intention that it serve as an escort. Badly damaged by fire on 1 March 1944 and intention abandoned. Details of subsequent fate not forthcoming.

The auxiliary patrol boat *Lennyann:* Between the *Les Eparges* and *Caducée.* Details of displacement and fate not forthcoming, but the fact that it was assigned local defense duties in December 1942 indicates that it was not scuttled. Details of subsequent fate not forthcoming.

The auxiliary *Caducée:* Between the *Lennyann* and *Alton II.* Details of displacement and fate not forthcoming, but the fact that it was assigned minesweeping duties in December 1942 indicates that it was not scuttled. Details of subsequent fate not forthcoming.

The auxiliary *Alton II:* Between the *Caducée* and Chasseur IV. Details of displacement and fate not forthcoming, but the fact that it was assigned minesweeping duties in December 1942 indicates that it was not scuttled. Details of subsequent fate not forthcoming.

The 180-ton submarine-chaser Chasseur IV: Alongside the *Alton II.* Raised 10 May 1943 by the Germans. Details of subsequent fate not forthcoming.

Unit marked but unnamed: On the map of 21 December 1942 marked simply as "*incomprise*"; obviously with name unknown, displacement, type, and subsequent fate not forthcoming.

The 879-ton torpedo-boat *Le Baliste:*

At the northern end of the Grand Rang. Raised 15 May 1943 by the Italians and nominally commissioned into Italian service as the F.R. 45 the next day. Seized by the

Germans at the time of the Italian surrender and commissioned into service as the T.A. 12. Sunk by heavy bombers of 15 U.S. Air Force in raid of 24 November 1943. Not raised but scrapped, *in situ*, beginning in December 1943.

The 879-ton minesweeping sloop *Chamois:* Opposite *Le Baliste* and the end of the Petit Rang. Raised by the Germans on 7 March 1943; in nominal Italian service as the F.R. 53 from the next day. Seized by the Germans at the time of the Italian surrender. Sunk by heavy bombers of 15 U.S. Air Force in raid of 24 November 1943. Raised between 7 March and 26 June 1944 and taken to La Seyne, where it was scrapped after the war, details of which are not forthcoming.

The 879-ton minesweeping sloop *L'Impétueuse:*

Between the *Chamois* and *La Curieuse*. Settled: machinery and guns wrecked. Raised 5 May 1943 by the Germans but initially assigned to the Italians as the F.R. 56. Seized by the Germans at the time of the Italian surrender. Damaged by heavy bombers of 15 U.S. Air Force in raid of 24 November 1943. Commissioned as the S.G. 17 and sailed to Marseilles in mid-May; scuttled on 7 August 1944. Raised and scrapped after June 1945.

The 879-ton minesweeping sloop *La Curieuse:* Between the *L'Impétueuse* and *Dédaigneuse*. Settled: hull damaged, guns wrecked. Raised between 10 January and 6 April 1943 by the Germans. Put in mothballs at La Seyne on 27 April and commissioned into the Italian navy and numbered the F.R. 55 over the next two days. Seized by the Germans at the time of the Italian surrender and commissioned as the S.G. 16 in May 1944. Scuttled at Marseilles on 22 August. Raised and scrapped in 1945.

The 265-ton training ship/patrol boat *Dédaigneuse:* Between the *La Curieuse* and *Yser*. Raised on 27 March 1943 by the Germans. Details of subsequent fate not forthcoming.

The 576-ton training ship/sloop *Yser:* Between the *Dédaigneuse* and *Camlar*. Raised on 5 February 1943 by the Germans. Arrived at La Ciotat on 19 June 1943 for refitting preparatory to being commissioned into German service as the S.G. 27. Scuttled off La Ciotat in August 1944. Details of subsequent fate not forthcoming other than "scrapped after 1945."

The 354-ton tug *Calmar:* Between the *Yser* and *Granit*. Details of fate not forthcoming, but the fact that it was assigned escort duties in December 1942 indicates that it was not scuttled. Details of subsequent fate not forthcoming.

The 360-ton minesweeping sloop *Granit:* Between the *Calmar* and *Roche Bleue*. Details of fate not forthcoming.

The auxiliary *Roche Bleue:* Between the *Granit* and *Homard*. Details of fate not forthcoming, but the fact that it was assigned escort duties in December 1942 indicates that it was not scuttled. Details of subsequent fate not forthcoming.

The 324-ton auxiliary *Homard:* Between the *Roche Bleue* and *Chanterève*. Details of fate not forthcoming, but the fact that it was assigned escort duties in December 1942 indicates that it was not scuttled. Details of subsequent fate not forthcoming.

The auxiliary *Chanterève:* Between the *Homard* and the pier. Details of fate not forthcoming, but the fact that it was assigned local defense duties in December 1942 indicates that it was not scuttled. Details of subsequent fate not forthcoming.

Position des bâtiments au matin du 27 novembre 1942 lists the *arraisonneur-dragueur Charcot* in the Old Harbor; details of displacement, whereabouts and subsequent fate not forthcoming.

In the Mourmillon north basin:

The 1856-ton submarine *Iris:* Alongside the *Le Glorieux*. Escaped from Toulon and interned at Barcelona. Returned to France on 29 November 1945. Details of decommissioning and being stricken not forthcoming. Sold 1 February 1950 and scrapped thereafter.

The 2,084-ton submarine *Le Glorieux:* Alongside the *Iris*. Escaped from Toulon and reached Oran via Valencia. In Allied service thereafter. Stricken 27 October 1952 and scrapped thereafter.

The 856-ton submarine *Vénus:* Alongside the *Casabianca*. Incurred some form of damage being before or during its attempt to escape from Toulon and scuttled, machinery wrecked, outside the gate in the Grande Rade. Details of subsequent fate not forthcoming.

The 2,084-ton submarine *Casabianca:* Alongside the *Vénus*. Escaped from Toulon and reached Algiers. Entered Allied service in 1943. Stricken on 12 February 1952 and sold and scrapped in February 1956.

The 925-ton minelayer-submarine *La Diamant:* Alongside the *Marsouin*. Raised between 1 February and 27 March 1943 and run aground in the Vauban basin; deemed beyond repair by the Germans. Moored off La Seyne on 3 February 1944 and ceded to Vichy regime on 22 May 1944; moved to Lazaret. Sank and was raised in February 1945. Details of subsequent fate not forthcoming.

The 1,415-ton submarine *Marsouin:* Alongside the *La Diamant*. Escaped and reached Algiers. Detail of subsequent service and fate not forthcoming. Scrapped after February 1946.

The 2,084-ton submarine *Pascal:* Alongside the jetty astern of the *Redoutable*. Raised between 12 February and 26 May 1943 by the Italians; thereafter moored first in the Missiessy basin and then off La Seyne. Sunk by heavy bombers of 15 U.S. Air Force in raid of 11 March 1944; wreck ceded to Vichy regime. Raised in 1948 preparatory to scrapping.

The 2,084-ton submarine *Redoutable:* Alongside the jetty astern of the *Henri Poincaré*. Settled; machinery wrecked. Raised on 16 May 1943 by the Italians and written off as beyond repair. Stripped and towed to La Seyne. Sunk by heavy bombers of 15 U.S. Air Force in raid of 11 March 1944; wreck ceded to Vichy regime. Raised in 1948 preparatory to scrapping.

The 2,084-ton submarine *Henri Poincaré:* Alongside the jetty. Raised at some time in 1943. Towed to Genoa on night of 2–3 September 1943. Details of subsequent fate not forthcoming.

Duty ship at the gate in the main channel:

The 879-ton torpedo-boat *La Bayonnaise:* Settled in the road. Raised 28 April 1943 by the Italians: in nominal Italian service from the next day. Seized by the Germans at the time of the Italian surrender and renumbered T.A. 13 on the following day. German intention was to refit the ship by cannibalization with reference to the *La Poursuivante*, but came to nothing. Scuttled on 25 August 1944 at Toulon. Raised in 1949 and scrapped thereafter.

* * *

It seems that perhaps as many as ten other named ships were present at Toulon, but not all were scuttled, and their whereabouts, obviously, remain elusive. The first three of these were the 412-ton patrol/fisheries protection vessel *Fauvette II*, the 180-ton submarine-chaser Chasseur II, and the 391-ton cable-layer *Ampère*. The latter is cited as having been captured intact by the Germans and refitted with a view to its serving as an anti-aircraft corvette; assigned the S.G. 24 label, it "was sunk in Marseilles in August 1944 while still being rebuild [*sic*]." Whether this means that it was scuttled or sunk in raids, such as those of 12, 15, 24, 25, 26, or 27 August on the part of 15 U.S. Air Force bombers, is not forthcoming, but one suspects the former.

French Ships Scuttled at Toulon provides a total of eight named units at Toulon that seemingly do not appear on any other list. These are the seaplane support ship/patrol boat *Pétrel* 8; the auxiliary patrol boats *Cap Nord, Clairvoyant,* and *Cyrnos;* two tugs, namely, the 187-ton *Argens* and 265-ton *Marcassin;* and two water carriers, namely, the 419-ton *Gave* and the 483-ton *Vague.* The three patrol boats are cited as not having been scuttled.

As per http//www.german-navy.de/Kriegsmarine/captured/escorts/sg14/ index.html it would seem that 3,230-ton *Cyrnos* was in service as the guardship P. 2 at Marseilles and was seized by the Germans on 7 January 1943, refitted, and taken into service as the S.G. 13 on 1 May 1943. It was badly damaged by an aerial torpedo off Naples on 11 July but was beached, salved, and towed into La Ciotat, arriving on 23 July. It was then refitted as a minelayer and was commissioned as M. 6063. It was sunk at Marseilles in August 1944—and the comments about the *Ampère* are not repeated—but was raised and returned to (French) service in 1948, and was scrapped in 1966. It would seem that it was not at Toulon on 27 November 1942, and that the total of three plus eight is therefore ten.

To repeat the most important single entry in this appendix, E&OE.

* * *

The full roll-call of ships cited above, and arranged by type, class, and alphabetical precedence, and in that order, is as follows:

Battleships: The 27,990-ton *Provence* and the 34,865-ton *Dunkerque* and *Strasbourg.*

Seaplane carrier: The 11,294-ton *Commandant Teste.*

Heavy cruisers: The 12,752-ton *Colbert, Dupleix,* and *Foch* and the 13,433-ton *Algérie.*

Light cruisers: The 8,937-ton *Jean de Vienne, La Galissonnière,* and *Marseilles.*

Contre-torpilleurs: The 3,098-ton *Lynx, Panthère,* and *Tigre,* the 3,251-ton *Guépard, Lion, Valmy, Vauban,* and *Verdun,* the 3,190-ton *Aigle, Gerfaut,* and *Vautour,* the 3,190-ton *Cassard, Kersaint, Tartu,* and *Vauquelin,* the 3,454-ton *L'Indomptable,* and the 4,018-ton *Mogador* and *Volta.*

Destroyers: The 1,968-ton *La Trombe,* the 1,968-ton *L'Adroit, Le Mars,* and *La Palme* (first series), the *Bordelais* (second series), and the *Le Foudroyant* (third series), and the 2,577-ton *Bison, Casque, Lansquenet, Le Hardi, Le Siroco,* and *Mameluck.*

Torpedo-boats: The 879-ton *Le Baliste, La Bayonnaise,* and *La Poursuivante.*

Submarines: The 1,415-ton *Caïman* and *Marsouin,* the 757-ton *Galatée, Naïade,* and *Sirène,* the 787-ton *Eurydice,* the 776-ton *Thétis,* the 2,084-ton *Achéron, Frésnel, Henri Poincaré, Pascal, Redoutable,* and *Vengeur* (first series), the *L'Espoir* and *Le Glorieux* (second series), and the *Casabianca* (third series), the 925-ton *La Diamant,* the 856-ton *Vénus* and *Iris,* and the 1,170-ton *L'Aurore.*

Sloops: The 360-ton minesweeping sloop *Granit,* the 2,600-ton colonial sloop *D'Iberville,* the 644-ton survey sloop *Les Eparges,* the 576-ton sloop/training ship *Yser,* and the 879-ton minesweeping sloops *Chamois, La Curieuse,* and the *L'Impétueuse.*

Patrol boats: The 265-ton *Dédaigneuse,* the 412-ton patrol/fisheries protection boat

Fauvette II, the patrol boat/seaplane support ship *Pétrel 8*, the auxiliary patrol boats *Ariel*, *La Havraise*, and *Lennyann*, and the auxiliary patrol boats *Cap Nord*, *Clairvoyant*, and *Cyrnos*.

Submarine-chasers: The 180-ton Chasseur I, Chasseur II, and the Chasseur IV and the 60-ton Chasseur XXV.

Netlayers: The 393-ton *gabare*/lighter *Agissante* and the 2,293-ton *Le Gladiateur*.

Boom vessel: The 451-ton *Endurante*.

Tankers: The 3,533-ton *La Garonne*, the 1,055-ton *La Durance* and *La Rance*, and two civilian tankers, the *Dauphiné* and the 9,895-ton *Henri Desprez*.

Cable-layer: The 398-ton *Ampère*.

Transports: The 1,821-ton *Aude*, the 526-ton *Champlain*, the 2,118-ton *Golo*, and the 622-ton *Hamelin*.

Water-carriers: The 419-ton *Gave* and the 483-ton *Vague*.

Fleet tugs: The 672-ton *Cépet*, the 876-ton *Laborieux*, the 767-ton *Paon*, and the 590-ton *Six-Fours*.

Tugs: The 187-ton *Argens*, the 360-ton *Calmar*, the 122-ton *Camilia*, the 250-ton *Carqueiranne*, the 324-ton *Corse*, the 236-ton *Coudon*, the 265-ton *Loup* and *Marcassin*, the 324-ton *Tabarka*, the 157-ton *Thésée*, and the 196-ton *Zèbre*.

Mooring vessel: The 393-ton *Prudente*.

Auxiliaries: The *Alton II*, *Bernard Danielle*, *Brin de Jonc Moulinauis*, and *Caducée*, the auxiliary minesweeper *Cap Noir*, the *Chanterève*, the *Charcot*, and the *Courlis*, the 324-ton *Homard*, the armed trawler *Josette-Claude*, the *La Socoa* and the *Roche Bleue*, and the auxiliary patrol boat *Roche Françoise*.

Units unidentified by type: The *Héron*, the *Servaux VI*, and the *Servaux XIV*.

School/accommodation ships: The accommodation ship *Rhin*, the ex-battleship accommodation ship *Condorcet*, and the ex-battleship training hulk *Ocean*.

* * *

A minimum total of five French warships, four minesweepers under construction, and four civilian ships were captured by the Germans at either Toulon or Marseilles and, after completion and/or refitting, were commissioned into service under the *Schnelles Geleitboot* label. The five warships were the *La Curieuse* (S.G. 16), *L'Impétueuse* (S.G. 17), *Le Gladiateur* (S.G. 18), *Ampère* (S.G. 24), and *Les Eparges* (S.G. 25). The civilian ships were three fruit transports, namely the 3,750-ton *Félix-Henri* (S.G. 10) the 4,600-ton *Alice Robert* (S.G. 11), and the 4,700-ton *Djebel Dira* (S.G. 12), plus the *Cyrnos*.

Under construction, and hence never commissioned into the French Navy but captured and completed after November 1942 for the German Navy, were the following 917-ton minesweepers:

The *Matelot Le Blanc*, completed and commissioned as S.G. 14 on 6 May 1943, was sunk by Allied (seemingly British) aircraft south of Capri on 24 August 1943.

The *Rageot de la Touche*, first in service on 3 October 1943 as an escort under the S.G. 15 title and then in May 1944 as the submarine-hunter U.J. 2229; in the latter role the hunter was the hunted, and it was sunk by the British submarine *Universal* on 26 May 1944.

The *Admiral Sénès*, seized by the Germans on 12 or 13 February 1943, was launched as the *Bernd von Arnim* on 19 October 1943 and entered service as the S.G. 21 on 28 March

1944. Most accounts give the S.G. 21 as being scuttled after having been wrecked in an exchange with the U.S. destroyer *Somers* on the night of 15 August 1944 during the approach to the coast of southern France and the Dragoon/Anvil landings—see, for example, J. Rohwer and G. Hummelchen, *Chronology of the War at Sea*, 1939–1945, page 298, and the 15–17 August 1944 Mediterranean entry.

This is different from the account set out in Morison's *History of United States Naval Operations in World War II*, vol. 11: *The Invasion of France and Germany 1944–1945*, page 252, which very definitely names the ships that were sunk as the auxiliary *Escaburt* and its escort, the U.J. 6081, being the former Italian corvette *Camoscio*. It may well be that the Morison account, published in 1957, is erroneous; on the other hand it may be that the S.G. 21 was scuttled at Toulon on or about 21 August. The *Enseigne Ballande*, assigned the S.G. 22 designation, was never completed and commissioned, and was scuttled at Port de Bouc on 20 August 1944.

Also listed are the minesweeper *Commandant Rivière*, which is given as having been sunk while in Italian service on 28 May 1943, and the minesweeper *La Batailleuse*, which is given as having been scuttled at Genoa on 25 April 1945. Given that these were not captured at Bizerte, one assumes that they were captured in French ports, possibly at Toulon but in all probability elsewhere, most obviously Marseilles.

* * *

The author would remind the reader that many pages ago he wrote that trying to provide an account of these proceedings was likely to be exhausting long before it was exhaustive.

With apologies.

CHAPTER EIGHT

ITALY AND THE WAR IN THE MEDITERRANEAN THEATER OF OPERATIONS

The Mediterranean theater has figured large in British accounts of the Second World War, but what can be termed the British representation of this theater, its events and importance, invites ridicule, incredulity, and scorn. Such a statement is not likely to be well-received by British readers, but one fact may be cited to set in place the dubious importance, perhaps more accurately the basic irrelevance, of this theater before November 1942. Between February 1941 and May 1943 the total German dead in North Africa numbered 12,810—less than a single division. On the basis of such a return, fourteen dead a day for twenty-seven months, to have inflicted upon Germany the total military dead of the Second World War would have taken the British Army 588 years. That may be an exaggeration—it might have only taken 587 years—but the fact is that the only army that Britain was able to put into the field between February 1941 and October 1942 was unable to defeat two German armored and associated Italian divisions. The British military performance in North Africa, for all the national self-acclaim, really was beneath contempt.

* * *

Any examination of the Mediterranean campaign must begin with two matters: the strategic geography of the theater that was so important in the shaping of events and outcomes and the record of Italy in this conflict. In terms of the strategic geography of the theater, the crucial importance of Malta was but little appreciated before June 1940. As a base for British naval and air operations across Italian lines of communication to north Africa it was crucial, but its proximity to Sicily and the difficulty of ensuring its proper supply produced a vulnerability that the British, with the French, initially were not prepared to try to remedy; the dual refusal to accept Italian naval primacy in the central Mediterranean and the loss of Malta provided one part of the geographical and strategic context of this campaign.[1] The other part was the crucial importance of the Jabal Akhdar relative to Malta.[2] British possession of Cyrenaica would give the means to provide air support for naval forces and convoys making their way to Malta from Alexandria for a very considerable part of the latter's voyage, indeed almost to Malta itself, whereas if Cyrenaica were in Italian or Axis possession, British shipping would be exposed to attack for the greater part of its passage; in truth, however, holding Cyrenaica and Jabal Akhdar was but one part of Italy's problems. The larger ports in the colony were in the west, specifically Tripoli; the ports to the east, Benghazi, Derna, Tobruk, and Bardia, were very small and, leaving aside their vulnerability to air attack from British bases in Egypt, simply could not handle the shipping needed to sustain major formations in Cyrenaica.[3] But there was no railway from Tripoli into Cyrenaica, and the enforced reliance upon the road for the movement of logistics forward to the front necessarily involved having to provide road transport on a scale that, for a country with such slender industrial resources as Italy, bordered on the prohibitive. This was combined with the fact that at sea Italy was scarcely better provided. What shipping was left to it after its declaration of war on 10 June 1940 was marginal to requirements, and in addition there was the related long-term problem of access to oil and coal.

For the British the problems were very similar, *mutatis mutandis*. The major logistical problem lay in the fact that once the Mediterranean was closed to through shipping, British troops, equipment, and supplies had to make their way around the Cape of Good Hope and thence via the Horn of Africa, the Red Sea, and the Suez Canal to the eastern Mediterranean, which represented a massively expensive commitment in terms of day-tons for shipping. This route around Africa also involved something else, and it is a matter seldom afforded much in the way of historical consideration: until April 1941 the Red Sea represented an active theater of operations. Italian possession of Eritrea and Abyssinia meant that it had naval units on station; indeed when Italy entered the war it had a total of seven destroyers, five motor torpedo-boats, two torpedo-boats, two gunboats, one minelayer, two armed merchant cruisers, one "colonial sloop," and eight submarines on station.

It is one of those very curious aspects of the Second World War how and why Italian forces failed to punch their weight. For example, by November 1940 the

Italians had some twenty-six submarines based at Bordeaux for operations in the North Atlantic; such numbers, given the smallness of the U-boat service at this time, could have had a very real impact on the Battle of the Atlantic, but the Italian contribution to British discomfiture was minimal. In the Red Sea the situation was much the same. The MAS boats were all but immobilized, presumably for want of spare parts, and within a matter of days of the start of hostilities four submarines on station had been lost, though they exacted a price. The British destroyer *Khartoum* had to be beached off Perim island[4] and was lost as a result of an accidental internal explosion in the course of the action that resulted in the destruction of the Italian submarine *Evangelista Toricelli.* On the same day, 23 June, the Italian submarine *Luigi Galvani,* operating near the Gulf of Oman, sank the Indian sloop *Pathan,* but then the *Luigi Galvani* was caught and sunk the following day by the British sloop *Falmouth.*

Thereafter the Red Sea was quiet; the Italian command clearly was waiting on events elsewhere and not prepared to undertake operations that might provoke British retaliatory action that would endanger the considerable amount of German and Italian shipping that had taken refuge in the east African ports, and the British clearly were not in a position to force the issue in this theater. The only episode of any note was the Italian invasion and occupation of British Somaliland and the British evacuation of forces to Aden (July–August).[5] The situation began to change with the gathering of British imperial forces that permitted the invasion of Eritrea and northern Abyssinia by Indian divisions operating from the Sudan on 19–20 January 1941. This initial move was followed on 11 February by the invasion of Italian Somaliland by east, west, and South African formations operating from Kenya and finally, on 25 February, by a British force that was landed at Berbera on 25 February, three days after the occupation of Mogadishu.[6] Thereafter there was a general collapse of Italian resistance except in the north, around Keren, but as this neared its end and British formations closed on Massawa in the last ten days of March, a number of ships attempted to escape.[7] In fact the first such attempt was made as early as 20 February, when the sloop *Eritrea* and auxiliary cruisers *Ramb I* and *Ramb II* sailed from Massawa, the immediate aim being to escape into the Indian Ocean and to prey upon shipping in the Indies. They managed to evade blockading units and once in the Indian Ocean separated, but while the *Ramb I* was caught and sunk off the southern Maldives by the New Zealand light cruiser *Leander* seven days later, the other two units reached Kobe, Japan, via Timor.[8] The next departures, between 1 and 4 March, were of the four remaining submarines—the *Gauleo Ferraras* and *Guglielmo* and the *Archimede* and *Perla*—which were resupplied in the South Atlantic by the German auxiliary cruiser *Atlantis* and fleet tanker *Nordmark* between 29 March and 16–17 April, the boats arriving at Bordeaux between 7 and 20 May. The subsequent attempts to escape from Eritrea, made around the time that the *Ramb II* arrived at Kobe on 23 March, were frustrated by British blockading units. After one abortive sortie by the remaining destroyers directed against Port Sudan (31 March–2 April),[9] the fall of Massawa on 8 April was accompanied by a general scuttling of warships and merchantmen, the latter numbering seventeen ships of 89,870 tons. Another eight ships of 61,890 tons were scuttled off Dalac and in Assab over the next two days, the British light cruiser *Capetown* being torpedoed, but not sunk, by the last remaining MAS boat outside Massawa on 6 April 1941, on which day Addis Ababa was liberated.[10] Apparently a couple of Italian merchantmen, identity not given, did manage to escape from the Red Sea and reached Madagascar. After Keren the main Italian forces withdrew southward to Amba Alagi, where there was a general surrender on 16 May, though isolated resistance continued into November in the Gondar area.[11] Thereafter there appears to have been a very small-scale guerrilla campaign fought by two Italian groups, one fascist, that lasted until September–October 1943, though the main part of this effort ended with the defeat at El Alamein and the Torch landings in October–November 1942.[12]

* * *

The general representation of the Italian performance in the Second World War has been extremely dismissive, indeed contemptuous, of the tanks-with-four-reverse-gears variety, and from the outset it is perhaps important to note one matter and then to seek to set in place various factors that made for Italy's defeat and what must be admitted was a less than impressive performance on the part of its armed forces. The one matter that relates not to the Mediterranean theater and the war at sea, but to the performance of the 8th Italian Army, on the Don in December 1942, provides reason to reconsider the common representation of Italian performance. With two corps in the line, the 8th Italian Army was assigned the role of flank defense for the German 6th Army at Stalingrad. Its defensive positions were some three to four miles deep; its formations, primarily mountain infantry with fifty tanks in support, were armed with nothing larger than the 37-mm anti-tank gun; and it was attacked by Soviet formations that deployed some 1,200 tanks. It took the Soviet formations three days to break through the Italian positions, and in the process these lost 90 percent of their armor.[13] By the end of that third day the 8th Italian Army had ceased to exist; the fact is that the Italians incurred more fatal casualties on the Eastern Front than in North Africa and the Mediterranean theater, though it needs be noted that on other fronts there was a willingness to surrender that was notably lacking on this one. If one seeks examples of the Italian naval willingness to fight, then the example of the torpedo-boat escort *Lupo* in the action of 21 May 1941 with three cruisers and four destroyers and the operations undertaken to support forces in Tunisia and Tripolitania after

November 1942 should suffice. The problem of presenting such examples of Italian tenacity and professionalism is that these are always overshadowed by more numerous illustrations of other matters, such as the assertion that Italy employed 153 submarines between 10 June 1940 and 8 September 1941, but it seems that these accounted for just 18 warships and 132 merchantmen—that is, over thirty-nine months the Italian submarines managed to sink one ship apiece.[14] This claim might be an overstatement, but if it is, then it cannot be by very much, and some form of explanation is needed, but remains elusive.

* * *

In considering the Italian naval performance in the Mediterranean theater, one must look at a combination of five matters, with the possibility of two more lurking in the background, that ensured that this performance was a failing one. The first factor is that the advantage that is so often associated with central position simply was not there; indeed, central position proved a liability. Italy simply did not possess the numbers to permit facing twin obligations, in the western Mediterranean and in the central and eastern Mediterranean, and for virtually the whole length of the war it was obliged to respond to events on the basis of numbers marginal to requirements. This obligation to respond is important enough in its own right to merit inclusion as the second point, but turned around and provided with proper military designation: the Italian lack of the initiative. Even in the first month of war, after Italy entered the war at a time of its own choosing, Italy's enemies secured the initiative, most obviously in the action of 9 July off Calabria (aka the Battle of Punto Stila),[15] which was never fully ceded. In one sense such a situation is explicable in terms of Italian expectation of a short, victorious war won primarily by Germany, with Italy standing to benefit without having to do too much on its own behalf. But the fact is that in 1940 the Royal Italian Navy, which had never—not even in 1866—faced an enemy such as those that it ranged against itself in June 1940, did not embrace a consistently aggressive and forward strategy in the Mediterranean. Put another way, the British in effect held the initiative in the eastern Mediterranean even before the Taranto attack in November 1940[16] and the Cape Matapan action in March 1941,[17] and even after the Crete campaign, and the serious losses sustained by the fleet, the British generally remained assertive and possessed the initiative at sea.

If this was indeed the case—and it is possible to dispute that latter point—then it is very difficult not to see Italian naval (for want of a better word) caution in terms of institutional weakness; this third point is the Italian Navy's lack of carriers and its somewhat tenuous arrangements with a separate and independent air force. The lack of carriers and the eccentricities of land-based air support, plus the presence of British carriers with battle formations—witness Calabria and Cape Matapan—presented operational problems that remained throughout the war, as did two other matters that most certainly provided the British with real advantage. The British advantage in terms of radar, the fourth point, provided the means for such unlikely victories as that won in November 1941, when a formation consisting of two light cruisers and two destroyers from Malta intercepted a convoy making its way to Tripoli from Naples and sank all seven transports and one escorting destroyer. The British formation was able to choose its line of advance and direction of attack, and to move against the convoy, which had its covering force of two heavy cruisers and four destroyers caught "on the wrong side" and unable to intervene effectively, in very large measure because the British ships possessed radar, whereas the Italian ships did not. A parallel advantage, and the fifth point, was an intelligence advantage, the ability to read Luftwaffe signals being a major factor in the November 1941 success because it provided notice of Axis intention and order of battle, and with that came an ability to anticipate and not to react. The Sigsint battle was not all one-sided; the Italian ability to read U.S. military signals between Cairo and Washington provided their German ally in North Africa with full detail of the British Army in theater, which was very significant in terms of the victories that were won between January and July 1942. But definitely the British advantage in terms of Ultra signals was very real at the time of the greatest British weakness in theater.

The last two points that may have been at work are ones that could never be proved and are in a sense personal opinion (one trusts not personal prejudice); both relate to personnel and to questions of numbers and motivation. Italy in 1940 was still very largely agrarian, with only a small industrial base, and in terms of industrial output it was the least of the great powers, with less than 30 percent of Britain's manufacturing output despite overall and working populations that were closely matched.[18] But Italy had to provide quality personnel for industry and trade, for government, for the overseas possessions, for the party, and for the three armed services, and with reference to the last of these the Royal Italian Navy did not hold pole position in reference to manpower requirements: in terms of numbers the army came first, and in terms of scientific and technological qualifications the air force held advantage over the navy. The Italian military ultimately had more than eighty divisions, and the Germans divided them into two, northern and southern, with a definite affinity to just one of the two, on account of the fact that the northern divisions were better officered and included men who were better educated and motivated than "peasant divisions" from the south. This latter point permits the raising of the related—seventh and last—matter: the question of motivation within the Italian Navy. There has long been a school of thought that holds to the view that the Italian Navy was monarchical, properly patriotic, and conservative, but not fascist, but question marks need to be placed against a number of other, related, matters—the desire for war after years of upheaval and conflict; the desire for war against Britain and, specifically, after December

1941 against the United States; the desire for war in association with Germany, and a Germany led by a person who was born a citizen of Italy's historic enemy. Morale does not translate easily in terms of ships but relates primarily to armies and men, but one wonders how far these various matters intruded upon the deliberations of the lower deck, and specifically how the Italian Navy fared in seeking to prosecute a war against the navy that was regarded by all as the foremost in the world.

A concentration on the five *materiél* points serves this argument; personnel matters might fall under the "any other business" label. Certainly the Italian weaknesses of position and numbers were present from the start of hostilities in the Mediterranean, though the figures are deceptive in terms of quality. In June 1940 the British battle squadron at Alexandria consisted of the *Warspite* plus three others: the *Malaya* and the *Ramillies* and *Royal Sovereign* had not been modernized and were most definitely "second team," while the aircraft carrier *Eagle* was of similar ilk.[19] With the departure of France from the war the numbers situation did reverse itself, though not to any marked degree, as British units, mostly either new or modernized, were gathered at Gibraltar and Alexandria. It is notable, for example, that the operations of November 1940 saw the British employment of the carriers *Ark Royal* and *Illustrious*, the battleships *Barham*, *Malaya*, *Valiant*, *Warspite*, and *Ramillies*, and the battlecruiser *Renown*, while the *Eagle* was still on station but with engine defects and was not able to take part in the attack on the Italian fleet at Taranto; off Cape Matapan, four months later, the carrier *Formidable* was present.

With all four of the British light cruisers that were commissioned in 1940 making their way to the Mediterranean within months of entering service, the British, who after May 1941 faced a declining threat from warships in home waters and the North Atlantic and thus had an available reserve to hand, could add to their formations in the Mediterranean in a way that the Italians, with very limited building capacity, could not. But in these opening months one pattern established itself in terms of battle and another in terms of strategic application; on the first score is the interesting fact that Italian warships and aircraft seem to have taken out patents on near-misses. Repeatedly in action the warships fired and the aircraft bombed with very considerable accuracy, but amid the many straddles there were very few hits indeed, and undoubtedly this near-immunity from losses in the opening months of the war rendered the losses that were sustained in April in the waters off mainland Greece and in May off Crete all the more damaging. The obvious point needs be made: the losses of April 1941, primarily in Greek harbors to German aircraft, were indeed massive; certainly nothing that had happened in the theater to date could have prepared the Greeks and British for the losses of that and the next month.[20] Between April 1940 and March 1941 the British lost one heavy and three light cruisers and five destroyers, and a total of seventeen merchantmen

TABLE 8.1. FLEET UNITS IN THE MEDITERRANEAN THEATER 9 JUNE 1940

	Western Mediterranean British	Western Mediterranean French	Central Mediterranean Italian	Eastern Mediterranean British	Eastern Mediterranean French
Battleships	-	4	6	4	1
Aircraft carriers	-	-	-	1	-
Cruisers	-	10	21	9	4
Destroyers	10	37	52	25	3
Submarines	-	36	106	10	-

of 84,396 tons were lost in theater; in April 1941 three destroyers and 105 merchantmen of 292,518 tons were sunk; and in May 1941 losses were about the April 1940–March 1941 aggregate, with two light cruisers, eight destroyers, and nineteen merchantmen of 70,835 tons lost. Of the warships sunk in April and May 1941 all but one were sunk by German aircraft, but it is worth noting that between 5 and 12 May the British were able to fight a through convoy of five transports with tanks and aircraft from Gibraltar to Alexandria in the face of attack by German and Italian warships and aircraft, one transport being lost.

* * *

The arrival of the Germans in theater took three forms: the army divisions committed to Tripolitania and Cyrenaica in February 1941; the Luftwaffe and the Yugoslavian and Greek campaigns with the resultant, if for the most part residual, presence in the eastern Mediterranean; and the submarines committed to this theater in the second half of 1941. Together these gave the theater an importance it had previously lacked, but with one implication that proved disastrous for Axis fortunes. Italy's dependence upon Germany after spring 1941 left the power of decision with the latter, but Hitler's personal program, and specifically Barbarossa and then the widening of the war on the Eastern Front, meant that the Mediterranean was only of *en passant* importance, and with immediate consequence. It is very difficult to resist the thought that had the Germans committed two or three full-strength corps, with liberal transport and supply allowances, the British might well have been driven from Egypt, and perhaps even Palestine, Trans-Jordan, and Syria in the second half of 1941; given the forces that Germany committed to North Africa in November 1942, and to a lost cause, one is left to consider what might have happened had a quarter of such numbers been made available some eighteen months previously. That point being noted, however, the problem of supply remained, and for both sides; but in the case of Italy during 1941, there was the enforced recourse to the ferrying of supplies to North African ports by submarines and warships simply because of shortage of shipping and British operations.

The basic problem in North Africa was not that either side was unable to win battles but that neither could consolidate success: what was at work was the Clausewitzian concept of the declining force of the offensive, and the inability of both sides to move their bases and supplies forward before the inevitable enemy counter-attack reclaimed lost ground. It was not until the end of 1942 that this situation changed, the British advance from El Alamein to the Mareth Line between November 1942 and 16 February 1943 being unprecedented, but in large measure made possible by the Anglo-American landings in Morocco and Algeria. These threatened the entire Axis position in theater, provoked a German effort that represented wasted effort, and provided an eventual Allied victory on a scale that belied the previous importance of the Mediterranean theater and campaigns.

* * *

The German commitment of submarines to the Mediterranean in the second half of 1941 definitely had its impact in terms of British operations; the *Ark Royal* was sunk in the western Mediterranean while off the Egyptian coast the *Barham* on 25 November, earned the unwanted distinction of being the first dreadnought to be sunk by a submarine while at sea with full power of maneuver. Interestingly, in the period between 13 November and 31 December 1941 the British lost the *Ark Royal*, the *Barham*, the light cruisers *Galatea* and *Neptune*, and destroyer *Kandahar* in the Mediterranean, and when the battleships *Queen Elizabeth* and *Valiant*, having sunk to the bottom of Alexandria harbor after attacks by Italian charioteers, are added to the scales, then the American losses at Pearl Harbor on the day that will live in infamy begin to come into perspective—and the British in this same seven-week period astride 7 December also lost the capital ships *Prince of Wales* and *Repulse*, the escort carrier *Audacity*, the light cruisers *Sydney* and *Dunedin*, and destroyers *Thracian* and *Stanley* outside this theater.[21]

The sinking of the fleet flagship and its sister ship inside the Alexandria base on 19 December represents the peak of Italian naval achievement in the war, but what is striking about this particular action, indeed this period in the last two months of 1941, is that it ushered in a period in which the conduct of operations played host to the failure of all parties. Perhaps the most notable failure was the German; in summer the German high command most definitely held the initiative in theater with the advance to the El Alamein position (7 July) and the neutralization of the air and naval forces at Malta. In the month of August 1942 alone shipping losses in theater were about the same as what had been lost between June and December 1941, and not too far short of what had been lost between January and July 1942, and, of course, August 1942 saw Operation Pedestal and the attempt to fight a convoy to Malta from Gibraltar.

Of the thirteen transports and one oiler that were escorted by four light cruisers and eleven destroyers and supported by a covering force that included the battleships *Nelson* and *Rodney*, four carriers, three light cruisers, and thirteen destroyers, just four transports and the oiler reached Malta.[22]

By this time, however, two courses of events had begun that would result in the first part of the Allied victory in theater and Italy's being forced to sue for an armistice. The start of the Japanese war had seen a massive expansion of British defensive commitments, with the enforced dispatch of major naval forces into the Indian Ocean, but after the Ceylon raid of April and then the Japanese check in the Coral Sea in May and defeat off Midway Islands in June, that defensive commitment lessened, with the result that, with German attention re-focused on the Eastern Front and the advance on Stalingrad, a certain balance returned to the eastern Mediterranean. One immediate result was that the Italian high command, faced with the need to get supplies forward to Axis positions deep inside Egypt, deliberately chose to send shipping to Tripoli rather than ports to the east, for an obvious reason—the greater security of the sea routes to and the greater handling capacity of Tripoli compared to points east—and with obvious result. Supplies to the formations at El Alamein had be moved 1,180 miles by road, which, in terms of numbers of vehicles, petrol, loads, and time and distance was impossible: and the formations at El Alamein in effect stood condemned to defeat.

The second matter was the American commitment to the "Germany-first" principle that in effect meant a commitment to the Maghreb in November 1942: in effect, the American commitment to a campaign in North Africa would have closed down Axis operations in Cyrenaica even without the defeat at El Alamein; as it was, the landings on 8 November prepared the way for a campaign in Tunisia that was to last some six months. Moreover, and as noted elsewhere, the landings in North Africa produced one major change in the form of the German-Italian invasion and occupation of Vichy France and the scuttling of the French fleet at Toulon, with the result that very few naval units were able to join the Allies in the campaigns that were to result, in time, in the liberation of their country.[23]

* * *

The following months witnessed a slow gathering of the forces that were to all but sever the lines of communication between Italy and Tunisia and that, in the form of medium and heavy bombers, were to take the war to the major ports of Sardinia, southern Italy, and Sicily.[24] The combination of submarines deployed forward, mines, warships, and, most importantly, air patrols inflicted disastrous losses upon Italian shipping as the Allies took the tide of war to and beyond the Sicilian Channel. Italy reputedly lost a total of 904 ships in the course of its war with the Allies, and it would seem that of this total almost half were sunk in the first five months of 1943, with more than a quarter sunk between 1 June and 9 September 1943. Put another way, if the figures are correct, between 10 June 1940 and 31 December 1942—that is, in a period of thirty months less ten days, Italy lost 219 ships, and that would be to all causes, including the accidental, maritime, and unknown. That indicates, again if the figures are correct, that Italy was losing seven a month; even allowing for the fact that the ships that it lost in this time must have been (in general) much larger than those lost January–May 1943 and 1 June–8 September 1943, the modesty of such numbers suggests an obvious comment on British conduct of operations at sea and specifically against Italian lines of communication to North Africa. Be that as it may, or may not, the losses in the period 1 January–8 September 1943 were as shown in table 8.2.

The blockade could not be total, of course, but in April, as Allied forces cleared southern Tunisia and advanced to the north, fifteen of twenty-six Axis transports that tried to make their way to Tunis were sunk, and only 27,000 tons of supplies could be landed, while in the first thirteen days of May, before the final surrender, eight supply ships and fifteen minor vessels were sunk, but only 2,163 tons of supplies made their way to North Africa. During April some 18,000 troops and 5,000 tons of supplies were flown into Tunisia, but the cost exacted was 117 transport aircraft—and by the end of that month the first headquarters and landing ships had arrived at Aden in readiness for the landings on Sicily.[25]

* * *

The clearing of North Africa in May 1943 had the immediate effect of opening the Mediterranean to through shipping, but the most important consequences were the landings on Sicily on 10 July and the dismissal of the Italian dictator, Benito Mussolini, on 25 July, the latter being seen correctly by the German high command as notice of national defection. That became reality on 3 September, when an armistice was concluded, but the Allied landings in southern Italy on 9 September came the day after German forces in Italy had moved to occupy peninsular Italy and thus ensured that the mainland was to be a battlefield for what remained of the war.[26] Their doing so created a basic dilemma for both sides. For the Allies there was the problem of definition of objective, specifically in terms of conquest and cost. To inflict on the enemy maximum possible cost, the ideal battlefield would be southern Italy, with the German defense thus saddled with the longest possible lines of communication, difficult and vulnerable, and with the Allies possessed of amphibious options, at least on the west coast. The Allies, however, could not embrace a strategy of protracted attrition, but had to seek German defeat, and there was also the problem of a civilian population and its food requirements: put at its crudest, the greater the area liberated, the more mouths to feed. For the Germans the need to keep the enemy at arm's length

Table 8.2. German and Italian Shipping Losses, 1 January–8 September 1943

		Warships	Submarines	Aircraft	Mines	Other causes	Total
Period I.							
1 January-31 May 1943:							
January:	Italian	9: 5,825	16: 19,246	13: 27,223	1: 5,186	33: 42,651	72: 100,131
February:	Italian	- -	18: 42,636	26: 32,223	4: 7,668	12: 808	60: 83,335
March:	Italian	- -	15: 21,976	36: 41,845	3: 2,218	10: 13,847	64: 79,886
April:	Italian	5: 939	17: 35,530	55: 52,668	3: 1,641	24: 6,268	104: 97,886
May:	Italian	1: 3,566	12: 12,469	101: 58,482	- -	30: 20,548	144: 95,065
Total Losses:	Italian	15: 10,330	78: 131,857	231: 212,441	11: 16,713	109: 84,122	444: 455,463
	German	2: 2,173	11: 29,546	28: 57, 700	6: 10,442	15: 11,206	62: 111,067
Overall Losses		17: 12,503	89: 161,403	259: 270,141	17: 27,155	124: 95,328	506: 566,530
Period II.							
1 June-8 September 1943:							
June:	Italian	- -	12: 23,652	19: 31,418	1: 1,413	6: 4,994	38: 61,477
July:	Italian	- -	19: 33,745	24: 25,827	3: 2,436	55: 15,098	101: 77,106
August:	Italian	- -	8: 12,091	27: 32,153	1: 1,416	11: 16,063	47: 61,723
1-8 September:	Italian	- -	5: 881	1: 61	1: 846	48: 11,770	55: 13,558
Total Losses:	Italian	- -	44: 70,369	71: 89,459	6: 6,111	120: 47,925	241: 213,864
	German	- -	9: 39,925	4: 16,637	1: 50	3: 2,077	17: 58,689
Overall Losses		- -	53: 110,294	75: 106,096	7: 6,161	123: 50,002	258: 272,553
Losses between 1 January and 8 September 1943:							
	Italian	15: 10,330	122: 202,226	302: 301,900	17: 22,824	229: 132,047	685: 669,327
	German	2: 2,173	20: 69,471	32 74,337	7 10,492	18: 13,283	79: 169,756
Combined losses:		17: 12,503	142: 271,697	334: 376,237	24: 33,316	247: 145,330	764: 839,083

Source: Roskill, *The War at Sea*, vol. 2, p. 432, and vol. 3, part 1, p. 186. These sources add certain notes, the first that the German tonnage was primarily the result of acquisition of French shipping in November 1942; that of the shipping sunk by aircraft (which one assumes means land-based aircraft) just 41 ships of 111,086 tons were sunk at sea, with 218 (much smaller) ships of 159,053 tons sunk in port, which one assumes means both Italian and North African ports; and that in the January-May 1943 phase 336 of the ships sunk were of less than 500 tons. The second source notes that 78 of the 104 ships sunk by aircraft were sunk in port (tonnages not given) and that 300 of the ships sunk were less than 500 tons. This second source also notes that the Germans employed various tugs, coasters, and Greek caïques as auxiliaries and that the losses incurred by these ships are not included in totals. The German losses are stated to be those incurred in the Mediterranean, those of Italy in all theaters: the latter does present problems of understanding.

was uppermost, but the best and most sensible course of action would have been to cede the southern and central areas and hold in the north, on the shortest possible lines of communication. But one obvious problem presented itself on this particular score: whatever areas were ceded would become home to Allied airfields, and clearly it was in German interest to keep these at the maximum possible distance from the homeland. One basic point about the strategic geography of Italy seems to have been missed, however: the road north up the length of peninsular Italy led nowhere, witness the First World War. British prime minister Churchill tried to argue in favor of a forward effort in Italy that would lead to advances into what had been (pre-1938) Austria and Yugoslavia, but this was arrant nonsense: in 1943 the Allies lacked the numbers that such an undertaking would involve, and the routes forward, to Innsbruck and to Klagenfurt and Graz and to Ljubljana and Zagreb, would represent major and hazardous undertakings.[27] The best for which the Allies could hope was the assumption of a secondary commitment that could be held in place until the major commitment, in northwest Europe, was realized in 1944 and that what might be achieved in Italy would be not Germany's defeat, or even a major German defeat, but a costly long-term obligation that would weaken the enemy.

* * *

In terms of the naval war, Italy's defection from the Axis camp is always associated with the *Warspite* and the scene at Malta "when along the purple street came in trail the Roman Navy to surrender at her feet."[28] This was the second of only two cases in history when a fleet surrendered, and two British battleships, the *Valiant* and *Warspite*, were present at both. Italy's defection is also always associated with the sinking of the battleship *Roma* west of the Bonifacio Strait en route for Malta from La Spezia by two 3,461-lb. radio-controlled glider bombs fired by a Do. 217K-2 bomber.[29] Less well known is the fact that the battleship *Italia* was also damaged and four destroyers were lost, one to a German coastal battery in the Strait, one on a mine, and two as a result of a collision outside Port Mahon.[30]

After Italy's defection and Mussolini's rescue (12 September) and subsequent installation as head of a puppet fascist republic in northern Italy by the Germans, the "Italian naval effort" took three very different forms. First, the German capture of northern and central Italy and the Italian zones of occupation in the Balkans yielded considerable numbers of small vessels, both warships and civilian, and many were afforded commissioned status and local duties in the central and eastern Mediterranean. At regular intervals over the next twenty months there were losses of German, and ex-Italian, warships in theater, and the last British naval action in theater, northwest of Corsica in the Gulf of Genoa on 18 March 1945, saw the destroyers *Lookout* and *Meteor* sink two ex-Italian torpedo-boats, while a third warship escaped.[31] This was the fourth such action involving former Italian and British warships that had resulted in sinkings by the latter, but in truth these actions, after September 1944, were of small account. After June 1944 the Mediterranean theater had little importance; indeed, the last sinking by a German U-boat in the Mediterranean was as early as 18 May 1944, when the U. 453 sank a Liberty ship from a convoy and in turn was sunk three days later.

Second, the convoy that was attacked was working the local Taranto-Augusta route and was provided with Italian escort, and after September 1943 there were in the Mediterranean two separate Italian navies. There was a fascist navy, which was tiny, not trusted by the Germans, and essentially irrelevant, and there was the residual Royal Italian Navy with ships and men that served alongside the Allies. This primarily involved escort and local duties, and their share of losses, of which the destroyer *Euro* and the submarines *Axum* and *Luigi Settembrini* were just three—the first to German aircraft, the second to the Greek coastline, and the third, apparently, to a U.S. destroyer escort in the North Atlantic in a case of mistaken identity.[32] It appears that more than 4,000 Italian naval officers and men were killed after the changing of sides, a total that one assumes must include the 1,254 killed in the *Roma*.

The third matter is the most exotic, and relates to the units, particularly one unit, that were in or en route for the Far East at the time of the Italian defection. Italian submarines had been involved in the little-known episode in which seaplanes flown from Italy down the Red Sea into the Indian Ocean were refueled and then made their way to Singapore and Japan, an odd and very rare case of intercontinental flight initiated in wartime, and there were a number of gunboats and other minor units, plus two merchantmen, in Japanese waters or at Darien. But more importantly, Italian submarines were involved in the ferrying of personnel and scarce commodities, specifically rubber, tin, and quinine from the Far East and technical equipment from Europe, albeit at very high cost and to somewhat erratic schedules. In September 1943 there were four Italian submarines at Singapore and two at Sabang,[33] with three more en route to the Far East. Of these one, the *Ammiraglio Cagni*, forewarned of the surrender, turned back and surrendered itself at Durban in South Africa; likewise, the *Eritrea*, last noted arriving at Kobe from Massawa, managed to escape and make its way to Colombo, Ceylon, where it surrendered to its old foe. But certain boats kept faith with their German ally, and the fate of four has a certain interest. The *Reginaldo Giuliani* was seized by the Japanese at Singapore and transferred to the German Navy as the U.IT.23, while the Germans at Bordeaux seized the *Alpino Bagnolini*, renamed it as the U.IT.22, and sailed it for the Far East. It was sunk by South African Catalina flying-boats off the Cape of Good Hope on 11 March 1944, a little less than a month after the U.IT.23, with a mixed German and Italian crew, had been torpedoed by the British submarine *Tally Ho!* off Penang.

What happened to the remaining two Italian boats in very large measure depends on what account of rubbish on the Internet one happens to read and believe. What is beyond dispute is that with the Italian defection the *Commandante Cappellini* and *Luigi Torelli* were both seized by the Japanese and transferred to the Kriegsmarine, and were commissioned as the U.IT.24 and U. IT.25 respectively. The officers and eight men of the *Torelli* refused to serve alongside the Germans and were imprisoned by the Japanese, but the remainder of the crew chose to remain with their boat in German service until, with the surrender of Germany, it and its sister boat were requisitioned by the Japanese and commissioned into service, the *Cappellini*/U.IT.24 as the I. 503 and the *Torelli*/U.IT.25 as the I. 504. Allegedly the latter, with some twenty Italians who again volunteered to remain with their boat, was employed ferrying cargoes between southeast Asia and the home islands, and it has been claimed that the I. 504 shot down a B-25 Mitchell in home waters. Whether that is true or not, and an Italian involvement in shooting down an American medium bomber over Japanese home waters must border on the bizarre, the presence of Italian sailors in a unit that served in three defeated navies in the Second World War is not unique—witness the *Dubrovnik, Premuda,* and TA-32 and the I. 503—but is somewhat esoteric. With Japan's surrender the *Torelli* was seized by, and thus came under the ownership of, the U.S. Navy, which, perhaps, represents a case of a ski competition, that is, downhill all the way. Along with the *Cappellini,* it was scuttled off Kobe on either 1 or 16 April 1946, depending on source.[34] A consultation with the Japanese records indicates that both boats were in Japanese waters, at Kobe, at the time of Germany's surrender, and it is difficult to see how they could have been employed as transports on the routes to the Southern Resources Area in the very short time between May 1945 and Japan's surrender: if these two boats were thus employed then it seems that they must have been working these routes before Germany's surrender. The two boats were taken into U.S. possession on 30 November and were scuttled on 16 April 1946, off the Kii peninsula and presumably in or off the Kii Strait, after having been used as targets for B-25 bombers on that same day.[35]

Of course, there is a story at the end of this tale, and it relates to an Italian cook on one of these boats who, given constraints of space in the submarine, devised a square pizza. After the war, when in Yokohama, he decided to stay and to open a restaurant, which to this day remains in business, and the square pizza is an item for which it has acquired and retained a certain reputation.[36] In which boat this Italian cook served is not known to this author, but the whole episode seems to suggest an Italian civilizing mission that has never been afforded the attention it deserves.

APPENDIX 8.1.

ITALIAN NAVAL LOSSES, 10 JUNE 1940–8 SEPTEMBER 1943

(A) FLEET AND ESCORT WARSHIPS

1940

28 June	Destroyer *Espero:* off Tobruk: Australian light cruiser *Sydney.*
5 July	Destroyer *Zeffiro:* in Tobruk harbor: aircraft from the British carrier *Eagle.*
10 July	Destroyer *Leone Pancaldo:* in Augusta harbor: aircraft from the British carrier *Eagle:* salved and returned to service in December 1941.
19 July	Light cruiser *Bartolomeo Colleoni:* off Cape Spada, Crete: Australian light cruiser *Sydney* and British destroyers *Hasty, Havock, Hero, Hyperion,* and *Ilex.*
20 July	Destroyers *Nembo* and *Ostro:* in the Gulf of Bomba off Tobruk: aircraft from the *Eagle.*
17 September	Destroyer *Aquilone:* given either as having been mined off Benghazi or, along with the destroyer *Borea,* sunk in Benghazi harbor by aircraft from the British carrier *Illustrious.*
22 September	Escort *Palestro:* in the southern Adriatic: British submarine *Osiris.*
12 October	Escorts *Ariel* and *Airone:* southeast of Sicily: British light cruiser *Ajax.*
13 October	Destroyer *Artigliere:* east of Malta: scuttled after having been disabled in action with British light cruiser *Ajax* the previous day.
22 October	Destroyer *Francesco Nullo:* on Harmi island in the Red Sea: beached after action with British destroyer *Kimberley* on the previous day: destroyed in attacks by three Blenheim medium bombers.
12 November	Battleship *Conte di Cavour:* in Taranto harbor: aircraft from British carrier *Illustrious:* salved but not returned to service.
20 November	Escort *Confienza:* off Brindisi: accidental collision with the warship *Cecchi.*

5 December Escort *Calipso:* off Tolmeita, Cyrenaica: mined.
23 December Escort *Fratelli Cairoli:* off Tolmeita, Cyrenaica: mined.

1941

10 January Escort *Vega:* south of Pantelleria: British light cruiser *Bonaventure* and destroyer *Hereward.*

22 January Coastal defense ship *San Giorgio:* in Tobruk harbor: scuttled with British capture of city.

25 February Light cruiser *Armando Diaz:* in cover formation for convoy between Naples and Tripoli: British submarine *Upright.*

17 March Escort *Andromeda:* off the Albanian coast: British air attack (?).

28 March Heavy cruisers *Fiume, Pola,* and *Zara* and destroyers *Vittorio Alfieri* and *Giosuè Carducci:* off Cape Matapan: action with British warships after the *Pola* had been torpedoed by Swordfish aircraft from the carrier *Formidable.* Escort *Generale Antonio Chinotto:* off Cape Gallo near Palermo: mined.

1 April Destroyer *Leone:* in the Red Sea: ran aground on uncharted rock on previous day and scuttled.

3 April Destroyer *Cesare Battisti:* north of Massawa in the Red Sea: scuttled. Destroyers *Daniele Manin* and *Nazario Sauro:* off Port Sudan in the Red Sea: land-based aircraft (from the British carrier *Eagle*). Destroyers *Pantera* and *Tigre:* off Massawa: scuttled.

4 April Escort *Giovanni Acerbi:* at Massawa: alternatively given as having been sunk by British aircraft on this date or scuttled at the mouth of the harbor as a blockship but date not cited.

8 April Escort *Vincenzo Giordano Orsini:* in Massawa harbor: scuttled with the fall of the city.

16 April Destroyers *Luca Tarigo, Lampo,* and *Baleno:* off Kerkennah Island: surface action (the battle of the *Tarigo* convoy off Sfax) with British destroyers *Janus, Jervis, Mohawk,* and *Nubian.* The *Lampo* was run aground in order to prevent its sinking; it was salved in August and returned to service after May 1942.

24 April Escort *Simone Schiaffino:* off Cape Bon: mined.

3 May Escort *Canopo:* in Tripoli harbor: air raid by British bombers. Escort *Giuseppe la Farina:* off Kerkennah Island: mined, alternative given as sunk 4 May.

20 May Escort *Curtatone:* off Piraeus: mined.

21 May Destroyer *Carlo Mirabello:* off Cape Dukato on Kefallinia island at mouth of Gulf of Corinth: mined.

27 September Escort *Albatros:* off Messina: British submarine *Upright.*

14 October Escort *Pleiada:* off Tripoli: beached after being hit by crashing Italian aircraft: subsequently bombed and foundered. (Rohwer and Hummelchen gives the original date of its being bombed by an Italian aircraft as 31 May.)

20 October Escorts *Altair* and *Aldebaran:* in the Gulf of Athens: mined. (Rohwer and Hummelchen gives the *Aldebaran* sunk off Valona by British naval aircraft on 18 March 1941 and also sunk on this date.)

9 November Destroyer *Fulmine:* southeast of Cape Spartvento in Ionian Sea: in

	the early hours surface action (the battle of the *Duisburg* convoy) with British cruisers *Aurora* and *Penelope* and destroyers *Lance* and *Lively*; the following morning the destroyer *Libeccio*: in the same area: British submarine *Upholder*.
1 December	Destroyer *Alvise da Mosto*: northwest of Tripoli: British cruisers *Aurora* and *Penelope* and destroyer *Lively*.
11 December	Escort *Alcione*: north of Crete: beached and lost after having been torpedoed by submarine *Truant*.
13 December	Light cruisers *Albercio da Barbiano* and *Amberto di Giussano*: off Cape Bon: British destroyers *Legion*, *Maori*, and *Sikh* and the Dutch destroyer *Isaac Sweers*.

1942

23 March	Destroyers *Lanciere* and *Scirocco*: foundered in storm after second battle of Sirte.
1 April	Light cruiser *Giovanni dalle Bande Nere*: off Stromboli in the Tyrrhenian Sea: British submarine *Urge*.
29 May	Destroyer *Emanuele Pessagno*: northwest of Benghazi: British submarine *Turbulent*.
8 June	Destroyer *Antoniotto Usodinare*: off Cape Bon: torpedoed in error by Italian submarine *Alagi*.
15 June	Heavy cruiser *Trento*: in the Ionian Sea: torpedoed by Malta-based Wellington or Beaufort bombers and by submarine *Umbra*.
21 June	Destroyer *Strale*: off Cape Bon: ran aground and wreck torpedoed on 6 August by British submarine *Turbulent*.
22 August	Escort *Generale Antonio Cantore*: northeast of Tobruk: mined.
4 September	Escort *Polluce*: some fifty miles north of Tobruk: air attack.
19 October	Destroyer *Giovanni da Verazzano*: south of Pantelleria: British submarine *Unbending*.
4 November	Escort *Centauro*: in Benghazi harbor: air raid by British bombers.
27 November	Escort *Circe*: off Sicily: after being rammed by a merchantmen.
2 December	Destroyer *Folgore*: off the Skerki Bank off the Sicilian Channel: British light cruisers *Argonaut*, *Aurora*, and *Sirius* and destroyers *Quentin* and (Australian) *Quiberon*. Escort *Lupo*: off Kerkennah Island: British destroyers *Janus*, *Javelin*, *Jervis*, and *Kelvin*.
4 December	Light cruiser *Muzio Attendolo*: in Naples harbor: air raid by U.S. heavy bombers.
17 December	Destroyer *Aviere*: off Bizerte: British submarine *Splendid*.

1943

3 January	Light cruiser *Ulpio Traiano*: in Palermo harbor: rendered *hors de combat* by charioteer attack. (The *Traiano* was fitting out and question is whether it had been commissioned.)
7 January	Destroyer *Bersagliere*: in Palermo harbor: air raid by U.S. heavy bombers.
12 January	Escort *Ardente*: off Sicily: accidental collision with destroyer *Grecale*.
17 January	Destroyer *Bombardiere*: off Marettimo island off western Sicily: British submarine *United*.

31 January Escorts *Cosaro* and *Generale Marcello Perestinari:* north of Bizerte: mined.

3 February Destroyer *Saetta* and escorts *Procellario* and *Uragano:* north of Bizerte: mined.

1 March Escort *Monsone:* in Naples harbor: air raid by U.S. heavy bombers.

2 March Destroyer *Geniere:* at Palermo in drydock: rendered *hors de combat* in air raid by U.S. heavy bombers.

8 March Escort *Ciclone:* north of Cape Bon: mined.

24 March Destroyers *Corraziere Ascari* and *Lanzerotto Malecello:* north of Cape Bon: mined.

1 April Destroyer *Lubiana:* in the Gulf of Tunis: ran aground and abandoned.

10 April Heavy cruiser *Trieste:* at La Maddalena, Sardinia: air raid by U.S. heavy bombers.

16 April Escort *Giocomo Medici:* at Catánia: air raid by U.S. heavy bombers. Escort *Cigno:* southwest of Marsala: British destroyers *Paladin* and *Pakenham.*

19 April Destroyer *Alpino:* in La Spezia harbor: air raid by British bombers.

28 April Escort *Climene:* off Sicily: British submarine *Unshaken.*

30 April Destroyers *Lampo* and *Leone Pencaldo:* off Cape Bon: attacks by U.S. land-based aircraft.

4 May Escort *Perseo:* off Kelibia/Cape Bon: British destroyers *Nubian, Paladin,* and *Petard.*

7 May Escort *Tifone:* in Tunis harbor: (U.S.?) air attack.

25 May Escort *Groppo:* in Messina harbor: air raid by U.S. heavy bombers.

28 May Escorts *Antares* and *Angelo Bassini:* in Livorno harbor: air raid by U.S. heavy bombers.

2 June Escort *Castore:* off Cape Spartivento: the British destroyer *Jervis* and Greek destroyer *Vasilissa Olga.*

28 June Light cruiser *Bari:* in Livorno harbor: air raid by U.S. heavy bombers.

5 August Escort *Gazella:* off Asinara Island off northwest Sardinia: mined. Escort *Pallade:* in Naples harbor: capsized after sustaining damage in air raid by U.S. heavy bombers.

8 August Destroyer *Freccia:* in Genoa harbor: air raid by British bombers.

9 August Destroyer *Vincenzo Gioberti:* off La Spezia: British submarine *Simoom.*

28 August Escort *Lince:* in the Gulf of Taranto: British submarine *Ultor.*

(B) SUBMARINES

1940

15 June Submarine *Macallè:* 19°00'North 38°00'East off the island of Barr Musa Chebir in the Red Sea: ran aground and wrecked.

17 June Submarine *Provana:* off Oran: rammed and sunk by French sloop *La Curieuse.*

19 June Submarine *Galileo Galilei:* 12°48'North 45°12'East off Aden: captured after surface action with British auxiliary *Moonstone.*

20 June	Submarine *Diamante:* 32°42'North 23°49'East some thirty miles from Tobruk: British submarine *Parthian.*
23 June	Submarine *Evangelista Toricelli:* 12°34'North 43°16'East south of Perim Island in the Red Sea: British destroyers *Kandahar* and *Kingston* and sloop *Shoreham* and scuttled.
24 June	Submarine *Luigi Galvani*: 25°55'North 56°55'East in Gulf of Oman: British sloop *Falmouth.*
27 June	Submarine *Console Generale Liuzzi:* 33°46'North 27°27'East west of Crete: British destroyers *Dainty, Defender,* and *Ilex.*
28 June	Submarine *Argonauta:* 35°16'North 20°20'East off southwest Greece: British destroyers *Dainty, Decoy, Defender, Ilex,* and *Voyager.*
29 June	Submarine *Uebi Scebeli:* 35°29'North 20°06'East southwest of Crete: British destroyers *Dainty* and *Ilex* and scuttled: one source gives all five destroyers as per the previous entry, while the official British history gives these two for both.
29 June	Submarine *Rubino:* 39°10'North 18°49'East off Cape Santa Maria di Leuca in the Ionian Sea: Sunderland of 230 Squadron RAF.
22 August	Submarine *Iride:* in the Gulf of Bomba off Tobruk: Swordfish from the carrier *Eagle.*
30 September	Submarine *Gondar:* 31°33'North 28°33'East off Marsa Mutruh: Australian destroyer *Stuart* and Sunderland flying boat.
2 October	Submarine *Berillo:* 33°09'North 26°24'East off Sollum: British destroyers *Havock* and *Hasty* and scuttled.
6 October	Submarine *Gemma:* 36°00'North 28°00'East in the Scarpanto-Rhodes area: torpedoed in error by Italian submarine *Tricheco.*
18 October	Submarine *Durbo:* 35°54'North 04°17'West east of Gibraltar: British destroyers *Firedrake* and *Wrestler* and two London flying boats.
20 October	Submarine *Lafolé:* 36°00'North 03°00'West east of Gibraltar British destroyers *Gallant, Griffin,* and *Hotspur.*
-- October	Submarine *Foca:* cause of loss unknown; missing either as a result of or after its mining of Haifa on 13 October.
8 November	Submarine *Commandante Faà di Bruno:* 45°25'North 01°22'West in the Bay of Biscay: British destroyer *Havelock.*
14 December	Submarine *Naiade:* 32°03'North 25°26'East off Bardia: British destroyers *Hereward* and *Hyperion.*
15 December	Submarine *Capitano Raffaele Tarantin* off the Gironde estuary in the Bay of Biscay: torpedoed by British submarine *Thunderbolt.*

1941

17 January	Submarine *Nani:* 60°15'North 15°27'West off the North Channel: British corvette *Anemone.*
19 January	Submarine *Neghelli:* in the Ionian Sea: British destroyer *Greyhound.*
-- February	Submarine *Marcello:* believed to have been sunk west of the Hebrides by British destroyer *Montgomery* on 22 February.
6 March	Submarine *Anfitrite:* east of Cape Sidero in eastern Crete: British destroyer *Greyhound.*
31 March	Submarine *Pier Capponi:* 38°32'North 15°15'East off northeast Sicily: British submarine *Rorqual.*

27 June Submarine *Glauco:* 35°06'North 12°41'West southwest of Cape St. Vincent: scuttled after action with British destroyer *Wishart.*

27 June Submarine *Salpa:* 32°05'North 26°47'East off Sollum: British submarine *Triumph.*

5 July Submarine *Jantina:* 37°30'North 25°00'East off Mikonos in the southern Aegean: British submarine *Torbay.*

5 July Submarine *Michele Bianchi:* in the Bay of Biscay: British submarine *Tigris.*

2 August Submarine *Tembien:* 36°21'North 12°40'East southwest of Sicily: rammed and sunk by British light cruiser *Hermione.*

8 September Submarine *Maggiore Francesco Baracca:* 40°30'North 21°15'West some 600 miles west of Porto in North Atlantic: rammed and sunk by British destroyer *Croome.*

28 September Submarine *Fisalia:* 32°19'North 34°17'East off Haifa: British corvette *Hyacinth.*

30 September Submarine *Adua:* 37°10'North 00°56'East off Ténès: British destroyers *Gurkha* and *Legion.*

21 September Submarine *Alessandro Malaspina:* in North Atlantic: cause of loss unknown, on or after 7 September. Official British naval history credits the *Vimy* with its destruction on -- September, Italian account presently states that it was sunk on 10 September in 46°23'North 11°22'West by Sunderland of 10 Squadron RAAF.

-- September Submarine *Smeraldo:* last reported position off Sollum: cause of loss unknown, on or after 16 September.

25 October Submarine *Galileo Ferraris:* 37°07'North 14°19'West: after being damaged in attack by a Catalina from 202 Squadron RAF: sunk by British destroyer *Lamerton.*

-- October Submarine *Guglielmo Marconi:* in the North Atlantic: cause of loss unknown, on or after 26–27 October.

11 December Submarine *Ammiraglio Caraccioli:* 32°09'North 25°19'East thirty miles off Bardia: British destroyer *Farndale* and scuttled.

1942

5 January Submarine *Ammiraglio Saint-Bon:* 38°22'North 15°22'East north of Milazzo, Sicily: British submarine *Upholder.*

30 January Submarine *Medusa:* 44°55'North 13°46'East in Gulf of Venice off the Istrian coast: British submarine *Thorn.*

14 March Submarine *Ammiraglio Enrico Millo:* 38°27'North 16°37'East off Calabria: British submarine *Ultimatum.*

17 March Submarine *Guglielmotti:* 37°42'North 15°58'East off Calabria: British submarine *Unbeaten.*

18 March Submarine *Tricheco:* 40°45'North 17°56'East off Brindisi: British submarine *Upholder.*

7 June Submarine *Veniero:* 38°21'North 03°21'East south of Majorca: attack by Catalina from 202 Squadron RAF.

9 June Submarine *Zaffiro:* cause of loss unknown but given as either off the Balearic Islands in attack by Catalina or in 34°20'North 24°09'East by British submarine *Ultimatum* from 202 Squadron RAF.

9 July Submarine *Perla:* 33°50'North 35°19'East off Beirut: captured by British corvette *Hyacinth.*

11 July Submarine *Ondina:* 34°35'North 34°56'East off Syrian coast: South African warships *Protea* and *Southern Maid* and Walrus flying boat.

14 July Submarine *Pietro Calvi:* 30°35'North 25°58'West south of Azores: scuttled after action with British cutter *Lulworth.*

10 August Submarine *Scirè:* 33°00'North 34°00'East off Haifa: British armed trawler *Islay.*

12 August Submarine *Cobalto:* 37°39'North 10°00'East south of Sardinia: rammed and sunk by British destroyer leader *Ithuriel* with the destroyer *Pathfinder.*

12 August Submarine *Dagabur:* 37°18'North 01°55'East off Algiers: rammed and sunk by British destroyer *Wolverine.*

-- August Submarine *Morosini:* supposedly lost in the Bay of Biscay to cause unknown, though one source gives it as sunk in the bay by a British patrol aircraft on 11 August 1842 [*sic*]. But other sources gives it as involved in mining operation as late as July 1943.

14 September Submarine *Alabastro:* 37°28'North 04°34'East off Algiers: attack by Sunderland flying boat of 202 Squadron RAF.

7 November Submarine *Antonio Sciesa:* beached in 32°05'North 23°59'East off Derna as a result of damage sustained in an attack by U.S. land-based aircraft: scuttled presumably as a result of the abandonment of Derna in the wake of the defeat at Alamein, on 12 November.

9 November Submarine *Granito:* 38°34'North 12°00'East off Cape Vito, north-west tip of Sicily: British submarine *Saracen.*

10 November Submarine *Emo:* 36°50'North 02°50'East off Algiers: British armed trawler *Lord Nuffield.*

28 November Submarine *Dessiè:* 37°48'North 02°14'East north of Algiers: British destroyer *Quentin* and Australian destroyer *Quiberon.*

6 December Submarine *Porfido:* 38°10'North 08°35'East northeast of Bone: British submarine *Tigris.*

13 December Submarine *Corallo:* 36°58'North 05°07'East north of Gulf of Bougie, eastern Algeria: rammed by British sloop *Enchantress.*

15 December Submarine *Uarsciek:* 35°08'North 14°22'East south of Malta: British destroyer *Petard* and Greek destroyer *Vasilissa Olga:* captured but sank while under tow.

1943

14 January Submarine *Narvalo:* 34°08'North 16°04'East off Malta: attack by Beaufort medium bomber and British destroyers *Pakenham* and *Hursley.*

19 January Submarine *Tritone:* 37°06'North 05°22'East off Bougie: Canadian corvette *Port Arthur.*

20 January Submarine *Santorre Santarosa:* ran aground in 37°10'North 03°15'East off Tripoli and torpedoed by British MTB 260.

8 February Submarine *Avorio:* 37°10'North 06°42'East off Philippeville, eastern Algeria: Canadian corvette *Regina.*

9 February Submarine *Malachite:* 38°42'North 08°52'East off southern Sardinia: Dutch submarine *Dolfijn.*

17 February Submarine *Asteria:* 37°14'North 04°27'East off Bougie: British destroyers *Bicester, Easton, Lamerton,* and *Wheatland* and scuttled.

23 March Submarine *Delfino:* off Taranto: collision with escorting warship.

15 April Submarine *Archimede:* 03°23'South 30°28'West near Fernando di Noronha Island, off Brazil: Catalina of No. 83 Squadron, USN.

13 May Submarine *Mocenigo:* at Cagliari, Sardinia: U.S. heavy bomber raid.

16 May Submarine *Enrico Tazzoli:* in the Bay of Biscay: British patrol aircraft.

23 May Submarine *Leonardo da Vinci:* 42°16'North 15°40'West northeast of Azores: British destroyer *Active* and frigate *Ness.*

-- May Submarine *Gorgo:* cause of loss unknown.

-- June Submarine *Barbarigo:* in the Bay of Biscay on or after 19 June.

5 July Submarine H. 8: La Spezia harbor: air raid by British bombers.

11 July Submarine *Flutto:* 37°34'North 15°43'East south end of Strait of Messina: surface action with British MTB 640, 651, and 670.

12 July Submarine *Bronzo:* 37°06'North 15°24'East off Siracusa: captured in action involving the British minesweepers *Boston, Cromarty, Poole,* and *Seaham.*

13 July Submarine *Nereide:* 37°25'North 16°07'East off Straits of Messina: British destroyers *Echo* and *Ilex.*

13 July Submarine *Acciaio:* 38°30'North 15°49'East north of Straits of Messina: British submarine *Unruly.*

15 July Submarine *Remo:* 39°19'North 17°30'East in the Gulf of Taranto: British submarine *United.*

18 July Submarine *Romolo:* 37°20'North 16°18'East in western Ionian Sea: British Wellington bomber.

23 July Submarine *Ascianghi:* 37°09'North 14°22'East off Augusta, southeast Sicily: British destroyer leader *Laforey* and destroyer *Eclipse.*

29 July Submarine *Pietro Micca:* 39°48'North 18°43'East off Cape Santa Maria di Leuca in the Otranto Strait: British submarine *Trooper.*

3 August Submarine *Argento:* 36°52'North 12°08'East off Pantelleria: U.S. destroyer *Buck* and scuttled.

7 September Submarine *Velella:* 40°07'North 14°50'East in Gulf of Salerno: British submarine *Shakespeare.*

Ex-French submarines captured at Bizerta in December 1942:

28 February The FR 111: sunk by aircraft off Cape Passaro/Cape Murro di Porco.

31 March The *Calipso* and *Nautilus:* air raid at Bizerte.

6 May The FR 116 and FR 117: scuttled at Bizerte.

These have not been included in totals because it is not clear if and when these boats were commissioned, though the fact that FR 111 was at sea when sunk would suggest that it was in service.

It seems that a number of boats, mostly of advancing years, were stricken at different times:

1941

28 April The *Balilla:* laid up and used as a floating oil depot under the name of GR.247.

15 May The *Domenico Millelire:* laid up and used as a floating oil depot

under the name of GR.248, alternative date of laying up is given as 15 April but this seems erroneous given the 247–248 sequence.

25 October The *Ettore Fieramosca:* alternatively given as laid up on this date apparently as a result of having sustained battle damage that reduced it to *hors de combat* status or stricken on 1 March 1943, the two are not incompatible.

8 November The *Giovanni Bausan:* alternatively given as laid up on this date or on 16 April 1942 (along with two sisters) or on 18 May 1942.

1942

16 April The *Marcantonio Colonna:* alternatively given as laid up on this date or removed from service because of serious damage to its engines on 1 June. The *Des Geneys:* alternatively given as having been laid up on this date or, no cause cited, laid up on 28 May 1943.

1943

2 April The *Enrico Toti:* having been reduced to training duties and then employed as supply transport, stricken on this date and subsequently scrapped.

In addition, the X 2 and X 3 were laid up on 16 October 1940, but it seems that these two coastal boats, having been launched in 1917, had not seen action over the previous four months.

CHAPTER NINE

THE LESSER ALLIED NAVIES AND MERCHANT MARINES IN THE SECOND WORLD WAR

Over the years British and American naval accounts of the Second World War have been very much ethnocentric and have paid very little attention the contribution of others, most notably that of the defeated Allied countries, navies, and merchant marines. While the importance of these countries, such as Poland, Denmark and Norway, the Netherlands, Belgium and France, and Greece and Yugoslavia within Europe and such countries as Brazil and Cuba in the Americas, to the United Nations' victory at sea was minor, on one count it was not without significance. As noted elsewhere, the acceding of the Dutch and Norwegian merchant navies to the Allied cause in 1940 provided Britain with a measure of insurance that it could never have provided for itself. In 1940 and 1941 Britain, Allied, and neutral losses amounted to some 8,300,000 tons of shipping; the Dutch and Norwegians most certainly could not cover such losses, but what they did bring to the British and Allied cause was a certain measure of security against loss. Expressed another way, given its aim of forcing Britain from proceedings by inflicting losses of 750,000 tons a month, the Germany Navy between May 1940 and December 1941 in effect lost probably nine or ten months in its conduct of the war at sea as a direct result of the driving of two major neutral merchant services into the ranks of the enemy. This does not explain the United Nations' victory in 1945, but it goes some way to explain the British avoidance of defeat in 1940–1941; the fact remains, however, that the treatment afforded the losses and contribution of the lesser navies has bordered on the dismissive. To give but one example, Roskill's *The*

War at Sea, volume 2, page 57, notes that in April 1942 German and Italian air raids on Malta accounted for two (unnamed) submarines and the destroyers *Gallant* and *Lance*; volume 3, part 2, pages 441, 443, and 445, provides the names of the destroyers *Lance* and *Kingston*, the submarines P. 36 and *Pandora*, and the minesweeper *Abingdon* as sunk at Malta in this month. The Greek submarine *Glavkos* does not merit a mention in either volume.

One short chapter, most of it concerning individual ships and their fates, will not redress years, decades, of neglect, but with due respect, the situation and losses of the lesser Allied navies were as follows.

POLAND

At the outbreak of war the Polish Navy mustered four destroyers, eight gun- and torpedo-boats, and five submarines, plus, with the river flotillas, no fewer than forty-four coastal and riverine craft of some 1,100 tons or an average of 25 tons per vessel. Given the fact that certain units were over seventy tons, some of these forty-four vessels must have been no more than motor launches, and it would seem that in real terms, in terms of appreciable size and capability, there were sixteen gunboats along with twenty aircraft committed to riverine operations, as opposed to the eighty-five aircraft with the naval formations.

Three of the destroyers—the *Błyskawica*, the *Burza*, and the *Grom*—sailed from Poland on 30 August 1939 for Britain, and thereafter entered Allied service: subsequently two of the submarines escaped from the Baltic, the remaining three boats being interned in Sweden. All the remaining units either were sunk by enemy action or were scuttled, a number of the latter—for example, four of the six-strong *Jaskolka* class of minesweepers—being raised and commissioned into German service.

The major units lost in the course of the September–October 1939 campaign were as follows:

1 September: The 360-ton torpedo-boat/training ship *Mazur* and the 110-ton diving-boat/school-ship *Nurek*: at the Gdynia-Oksywie naval base: German aircraft.

3 September: The 1,920-ton destroyer *Wicher* and the 2,250-ton minelayer *Gryf*: at or outside the Hela naval base: German aircraft. In addition, two gunboats, the 441-ton *Komendant Piłsudski* and 438-ton *General Haller*, also at the Hela base, having been wrecked by German aircraft, were stripped of weapons and abandoned.

4 September: After having been rendered *hors de combat* by German aircraft two days previously, the 538-ton auxiliary gunboats *Gdynie* and *Gdańsk*: in the Gulf of Danzig: scuttled.

After having been rendered *hors de combat* by German aircraft the previous day, the 183-ton minesweeper *Mewa:* at or outside the Hela naval base: scuttled: all four units are also given as having been scuttled at the base on 2 October.
The 365-ton torpedo-boat *Kujawiak:* either at Gdynia/Hela by German aircraft or in the Gulf of Danzig by scuttling.
The 203-ton minesweeper *Rybitwa*, the 183-ton minesweepers *Czajka* and *Zuraw*, and the 711-ton tug *Smok:* at or outside the Hela naval base: scuttled.

10 September: The motor gunboat *Nieuchwytny* and motorboats KM 12 and KM 13: at Brwilno: scuttled. The tugs *Hetman Zolkiewski* and *Lubecki:* at Dobrzyn: scuttled.

11 September: The 8,100-ton ex-French second-class cruiser *D'Entrecasteaux* in service as training school and hulk *Bałtyk:* in the area of Hela naval base: disabled by air attack and captured on 21 September.

14 September: After having been damaged by air attack on 1 September, the 203-ton minesweepers *Czapla* and *Jaskółka:* at Jastarnia: German aircraft, the former (whick was not in service on 1 September) being writtwn off and the latter sunk. The 280-ton auxiliary *Lech:* at Jastarnia: scuttled.

17 September: The 1,650-ton submarine *Sep* and 1,250-ton submarine *Ryś:* at Stavnas, Sweden: interned. The 48-ton rescue tug *Neptun:* at or near Pinsk: attributed to undefined Soviet action.

18 September: The 113-ton river gunboat *Warszawa:* at Mostów Wolaıskich on the Dnepr: scuttled.

19 September: The 90-ton river monitor *Wilno:* at Osobowicze on the Bug/near Pinsk: scuttled.

21 September: The 90-ton river monitor *Krakow:* at Kuzliczyn (between Brest and Pinsk in present-day Belorussia): scuttled.
The tug *Kilinski:* outside Pinsk: scuttled.

27 September: The 1,250-ton submarine *Zbik:* at Stavnas, Sweden: interned.

28 September: The motor gunboat KU 30: at Modlin: scuttled.

1 October: The 113-ton river gunboat *Horodyszcze:* at Mostów Wolaıskich on the Dnepr: scuttled.

1 October: The gunboats *Komendant Piłsudski* and *General Haller:* at the Hela naval base, which was surrendered on 1 October and occupied on the following day: scuttled.

2 October: The 193-ton survey ship *Pomorzanin:* at Jastarnia: scuttled, apparently after having been rendered *hors de combat* by air attack on 15 September.

Details of the fate of other and assorted units are not forthcoming.

Among numbered units it appears that the Polish Navy had nineteen KU-class and twelve other motor gunboats and eight minesweepers/minelayers in service and that of these, KU 16 is given as scuttled on 21 September, three other gunboats are given as having been sunk on various dates and another three sunk in September 1939, and three mine craft are given as having been scuttled on 20 September.

In addition there were a number of named units, apparently mostly with river formations, the fates of which are not forthcoming. Four units each have one set of details, namely the *Admiral Dickman*: scuttled but whereabouts and date not forthcoming; the 110-ton river gunboats *Pińsk* and *Tońun*, on the Dnepr but cause and date not forthcoming; and the river gunboat *Zuchwala*, date of loss given as 19 September but cause and whereabouts not forthcoming. In addition, there are seven other units named in various texts but their details of size, type, whereabouts and cause of loss not given. These were the headquarters ship *Admiral Sierpinek*, the anti-aircraft paddle steamer *General Sikorski*, the hospital ship *General Sosnkowski*, the minelayer/paddle steamer *General Szeptycki*, the anti-aircraft paddle steamer *Hetman Chodkiewicz*, and the *Niedosciagnova* and *Niezwyciezona*. It would seem that most of these units were scuttled to avoid their being captured

In the course of the war the Polish Navy commissioned the light cruisers *Dragon* and *Danae*; the destroyers *Garland*, *Ouragan*, *Nerissa*, and *Myrmidon*; the escort destroyers *Silverton*, *Oakley*, and *Bedale*; the submarines P. 52, S. 25, and *Urchin*; and twelve submarine-chasers. One destroyer and two of the chasers had been French, seized in 1940 by the British: the remainder were drawn directly from the British Navy. Total Polish naval losses of fleet units after re-constitution under British auspices were one light cruiser, two destroyers, one escort destroyer and two submarines. A total of thirty-eight Polish merchantmen were clear of the Baltic at the outbreak of war and thus entered British service, and most accounts indicate that eleven of their number, including three liners, were sunk in the course of the war.

Polish naval losses after October 1939 were as follows:

1940

4 May: The 3,383-ton destroyer *Grom*: in Rombaksfjorden above Narvik: German aircraft.

On or after 25 May: The 1,650-ton submarine *Orzeł*: in the North Sea: unknown cause but probably mined.

1942

2 May: The 1,062-ton submarine *Jastrzab*: in the Norwegian Sea: sunk in error by British escorts.

16 June: The 1,625-ton destroyer escort *Kujawiak*: off Malta: mine.

1943

8 October: The 2,840-ton destroyer *Orkan* (ex-*Myrmidon*): south of Iceland: German submarine U.610.

1944

9 June: The 3,250-ton transport, and seven-times renamed, *Modlin:* off Normandy: constructive total loss as breakwater.

8 July: The 5,730-ton light cruiser *Dragon:* off Normandy: human torpedo: beached as constructive total loss as a blockship off Juno beach.

FRANCE

The French Navy has been afforded its own chapter, and therefore the list of ships lost necessarily repeats the contents of the relevant appendixes; suffice it to note that while France took losses before but most obviously in May–June 1940, the losses of November 1942 do assume obvious significance, and proper proportion, when set alongside a statement of overall losses.

The French losses were as follows:

1939

13 September: The 6,500-ton cruiser-minelayer *La Tour d'Auvergne:* at Casablanca: detonation of its own mines.

20 October: The auxiliary minesweeper *Etoile du Nord:* off Dunkirk: mine.

21 November: The 57-ton auxiliary minesweeper *Sainte-Claire:* in the North Sea: mine.

23 November: The auxiliary minesweeper *Jean-Pierre-Claude:* at Casablanca: accidental explosion.

1940

6 January: The 1,145-ton auxiliary sloop *Barsac:* Onza Island, off Vigo: ran aground.

6 February: The 253-ton auxiliary minesweeper *Vétéran:* off Cap Gris-Nez: collision with British cable ship *Alert.*

7 March: The 286-ton auxiliary minesweeper *Marie-Yette:* in the Gironde: collision with French merchantman *Spramex.*

9 March: The auxiliary patrol boat *Murad:* off Latakia in Syria: ran aground and wrecked.

24 March: The 2,000-ton destroyer *La Railleuse:* at Casablanca: detonation of own torpedo.

27 March: The auxiliary minesweeper *Blei-Mor:* off Flanders: foundered in storm.

12 April: The submarine-chaser Chasseur 107: off Lorient: marine accident.

29 April: The auxiliary minesweeper *Cap Bear:* whereabouts not known: fire.

30 April: The 3,140-ton *contre-torpilleur Maillé Brézé:* at Greenock in the Clyde: detonation of own torpedo.

3 May: The 3,200-ton *contre-torpilleur Bison:* off Namsos: German aircraft.

4 May: The 400-ton armed trawler *La Cancalaise:* off the Dyck light vessel: mine.

8 May: The 776-ton submarine *Doris:* off Dutch coast: German submarine U. 9.

13 May: The 32-ton auxiliary minesweeper *Ville de Bizerte:* off Cape Guardia near Bizerte: mine.

15 May: The 251-ton auxiliary minesweeper *Henri-Guégan* and 184-ton auxiliary minesweeper *Le Duquesne:* in the Scheldt: mines.

19 May: The 175-ton auxiliary minesweeper *Augustin Normand:* off Le Havre: mine.

21 May: The 2,000-ton destroyer *L'Adroit,* the 352-ton auxiliary minesweeper *Le Pierrot,* the 339-ton auxiliary minesweeper *Notre Dame de Lorette,* the 142-ton auxiliary minesweeper *Rien sans Peine,* the 315-ton auxiliary minesweeper *Saint-Benoit* and the 192-ton auxiliary minesweeper *Saint Joachim,* the 137-ton submarine-chaser Chasseur 9, and the 5,482-ton tanker *Le Niger:* at or off Dunkirk: German aircraft. The 285-ton auxiliary minesweeper *Jacques Cœur I:* off Fécamp: German aircraft.

23 May: The 3,050-ton *contre-torpilleur Jaguar:* English Channel: German MTBs. The 1,900-ton destroyer *Orage:* off Boulogne: German aircraft.

24 May: The 3,050-ton *contre-torpilleur Chacal* off Boulogne and the auxiliary minesweeper *Le Matelot* off Dunkirk: German aircraft.

25 May: The 49-ton auxiliary minesweeper *La Jeannine* and the auxiliary minesweepers *La Trombe II* and *Marguerite Rose:* off Dunkirk: German aircraft.

26 May: The auxiliary minesweeper *Dijonnais:* off Dunkirk: German aircraft.

27 May: The 47-ton auxiliary minesweeper *La Majo:* off Dunkirk: German aircraft.

30 May: The 1,900-ton destroyer *Bourrasque:* off Nieuwport: German artillery.

31 May: The 1,900-ton destroyer *Siroco:* off Dunkirk: German MTBs.

1 June: The 2,000-ton destroyer *Foudroyant,* the 309-ton auxiliary minesweeper *Denis Papin,* the 264-ton auxiliary minesweeper *Vénus,* and the 38-ton auxiliary minesweeper *Le Moussaillon:* off Dunkirk: German aircraft.

3 June: The 603-ton patrol boat *Purfina:* off Le Havre: mined. The 348-ton auxiliary minesweeper *Emile Deschamps:* off Foreness: mine.

9 June: The 646-ton auxiliary minesweeper *Madelaine Louise* and the 481-ton auxiliary minelayer *Notre Dame des Dunes:* in the English Channel: German aircraft.

11 June: The 628-ton auxiliary minesweeper *Le Bretonniere:* at Le Havre: scuttled. The 247-ton auxiliary minesweeper *Patrice II:* off Fécamp: German artillery.

12 June: The 1,049-ton auxiliary sloop *Céron:* off St. Valéry: German aircraft.

13 June: The auxiliary patrol boat *Granville:* off St. Valéry: German artillery. The 85-ton auxiliary minesweeper *Marthe Roland Michel* and the harbor defense vessel *Reine des Flots:* off Le Havre: scuttled.

15 June: The 1,441-ton submarine *Morse:* Off Sfax: mine.

18 June: The 1,900-ton destroyer *Cyclone;* the 2,084-ton submarines *Achille, Agosta, Ouessant,* and *Pasteur;* the 310-ton sloop *Etourdi;* the 303-ton auxiliary patrol boat *Mouette;* the 675-ton auxiliary minesweeper *Ingénieur Reibel;* the 208-ton auxiliary minesweeper *Roche Noire;* and the 7,333-ton tanker *Dordogne:* at or outside Brest: scuttled. The 850-ton sloop *Vauquois:* mined off Brest: beached and scuttled. The 453-ton dispatch vessel *Enseigne Henri,* the 261-ton auxiliary minesweeper *Kergroise,* and 150-ton auxiliary minesweeper *Pluvoise:* at Lorient: scuttled. The 137-ton submarine-chaser Chasseur 16: in the Groix roadstead outside Lorient: scuttled. The 301-ton auxiliary minesweeper *Gaulois:* outside St. Malo: scuttled. The auxiliary minesweeper *Jeanne Pascal* and the 74-ton auxiliary minesweeper *Marquita:* at Cherbourg: scuttled. In addition, the 640-ton auxiliary *La Quimperoise* was scuttled at Lorient on or about this date.

21 June: The auxiliary patrol boat *Mercedita:* off Le Verdon, Gironde estuary: scuttled.

22 June: The 895-ton corvette *La Bastiaise:* off Hartlepool, North Sea:

mined on trials. The 9,900-ton tanker *Le Loing:* in the La Pallice roadstead: scuttled. The 1,443-ton torpedo-boat *Le Fler:* off the Ile d'Oleron: ran aground after being bombed.

23 June: The 723-ton auxiliary patrol boat *La Cherbourgeoise:* at Le Verdon, Gironde estuary: scuttled.

25 June: The 48-ton auxiliary patrol boat *Sainte Marguerite:* at Le Verdon, Gironde estuary: scuttled.

In addition, the following units were sunk in June 1940 but dates not forthcoming:

The auxiliary minesweeper *Matelot II* and tug *Tumulte*: off Dunkirk: German aircraft.

The 146-ton auxiliary minesweeper *Christiane Cécile* and the tugs *Barfleur* and *Orme*: at Boulogne: scuttled.

The 160-ton submarine chasers Chasseurs 45 and 46: at Fécamp: scuttled.

The 160-ton submarine chaser Chasseur 44 and the auxiliary minesweeper *Intrépide*: at Le Havre: scuttled.

The auxiliary minesweeper *Cap Carteret*: at Le Havre: seemingly marine accident.

The auxiliary minesweeper *Etienne Rimbert*: off Dieppe: scuttled.

The tug *Goury*: at Cherbourg: scuttled.

The 590-ton fleet tug *Athlète* and 80-ton tender *Pétrel V*: at Brest: scuttled.

Thereafter French losses, between 26 June 1940 and 8 December 1942, were as follows:

1940

3 July: The 27,990-ton battleship *Bretagne:* at Mers El Kébir: British warships.

4 July: The 2,600-ton colonial sloop *Rigault de Genouilly:* off Algiers: British submarine *Pandora.*

6 July: The 780-ton auxiliary patrol boat *Terre Neuve:* at Mers El Kébir: British carrier aircraft.

23 September: The 3,400-ton *contre-torpilleur L'Audacieux:* outside Dakar: British warships: beached and salved. The 2,084-ton submarine *Persée:* off Dakar: British warships.

24 September: The 2,084-ton submarine *Ajax*: off Dakar: British warship.

6 October: The 350-ton auxiliary minesweeper *Poulmic* (under British flag): off Rame Head, Plymouth: mine.

11 October: The 137-ton Free French submarine-chasers Chasseur 6 and Chasseur 7: off the Isle of Wight: German torpedo-boats.

7 November: The 2,084-ton submarine *Poncelet:* off Libreville: British warship.

9 November: The 2,600-ton colonial sloop *Bougainville:* at Libreville: sunk by Free French warship.

14 December: The 895-ton Free French torpedo-boat *Branlebas:* in the English Channel: foundered.

15 December: The 1,441-ton Free French submarine *Narval:* off the Tunisian coast: Italian mine.

19 December: The 2,084-ton submarine *Sfax* and 2,785-ton tanker *Rhône* in central North Atlantic: erroneously by German submarine U. 37.

1941

14 April: The 604-ton Free French sloop *Suippe* and the 457-ton Free French minesweeper *Conquérante:* at Falmouth: German bombing raid.

23 May: The 400-ton auxiliary minesweeper *La Meulière*: off Ajaccio, Corsica: ran aground and wrecked: apparently salved and taken to Toulon but not returned to service.

16 June: The 3,140-ton *contre-torpilleur Chevalier Paul:* off the Syrian coast: British land-based aircraft.

25 June: The 1,441-ton submarine *Souffleur:* off the Syrian coast: British submarine *Parthian.*

1942

9 February: The 900-ton Free French escort *Alysse:* east of Newfoundland: German submarine U. 654.

18 February: The 4,304-ton Free French submarine *Surcouf:* Gulf of Mexico: collision with U.S. merchantman *Thompson Lykes.*

16 April: The 1,150-ton auxiliary patrol boat *Viking:* off the Syrian coast: German submarine U. 81.

5 May: The 4,200-ton auxiliary cruiser *Bougainville* and the 288-ton auxiliary *Edmond René:* at Diégo Suarez: British carrier aircraft. The 2,084-ton submarine *Bévéziers:* off Diégo Suarez: British carrier aircraft. The 2,600-ton sloop *D'Entrecasteaux:* off Diégo Suarez: damaged by British carrier aircraft, beached and abandoned.

7 May: The 2,084-ton submarine *Le Héros:* off northwest Madagascar: British corvette and carrier aircraft.

8 May: The 2,084-ton submarine *Monge:* off northwest Madagascar: British destroyers.

9 June: The 925-ton escort *Mimosa:* with convoy in mid-Atlantic: German submarine U. 124.

13 July: The 137-ton Free French submarine-chaser *Rennes:* in the English Channel: German aircraft.

8 November: The light cruiser *Primaguet,* the *contre-torpilleurs Albatros,* and *Milan,* and the destroyers *Boulonnais, Brestois,* and *Fougueux:* outside or at Casablanca: U.S. warships. The submarines *Amphitrite, La Psyché,* and *Oréade* and the 315-ton survey ship *Estafette:* at Casablanca, and the submarine *Méduse:* at Magazan: U.S. carrier aircraft. The 2,084-ton submarine *Actéon* and the 798-ton submarine *Argonaute:* outside Oran: British destroyers.

9 November: The destroyer *Frondeur:* at Casablanca: U.S. warships. The *contre-torpilleur Epervier;* the destroyers *Tornade, Tramontane,* and *Typhon;* and the minesweeper *La Surprise:* outside or at Oran: British warships. The submarines *Ariane* and *Danaé, Cérès* and *Pallas,* and *Diane:* at Oran: scuttled.

11 November: The submarine *Sidi Ferruch:* off Casablanca: U.S. carrier aircraft. The submarine *La Sybille:* unknown: cause unknown.

13 November: The submarine *Le Conquérant:* off Dakhla, Rio del Oro: U.S. flying boats.

15 November: The submarine *Le Tonnant:* off Cádiz: scuttled.

27 November: The battleships *Provence* and the *Dunkerque* and *Strasbourg;* the seaplane carrier *Commandant Teste;* the heavy cruisers *Algérie* and the *Colbert, Dupleix,* and *Foch;* the light cruisers *Jean de Vienne, La Galissonnière,* and *Marseillaise;* the *contre-torpilleurs Lynx, Panthère,* and *Tigre,* the *Guépard, Lion, Valmy, Vauban,* and *Verdun,* the *Aigle, Gerfaut,* and *Vautour,* the *Cassard, Kersaint, Tartu,* and *Vauquelin,* the *L'Indomptable,* and the *Mogador* and *Volta;* the destroyers *La Trombe,* the *L'Adroit, Le Mars,* and *La Palme,* the *Bordelais,* the *Le Foudroyant,* and the *Bison, Casque, Lansquenet, Le Hardi, Le Siroco,* and *Mameluck;* the torpedo-boats *La Baliste, La Bayonnaise,* and *La Poursuivante;* the colonial sloop *D'Iberville,* the survey sloop *Les Eparges,* the training sloop *Yser,* and the minesweeping sloops *Granit,* and the *Chamois, La Curieuse,* and *L'Impétueuse;* the submarines *Caïman* and *Marsouin,* the *Galatée, Naïade,* and *Sirène,* the *Eurydice,* the *Thétis,* the *Achéron, Frésnel, Henri Poincaré, Pascal, Redoutable,* and *Vengeur,* the *L'Espoir* and *Le Glorieux,* and the *Casabianca,* the *La Diamant,* the *Vénus* and *Iris,* and the *L'Aurore;* and the submarine-chasers Chasseur I, Chasseur II, and the Chasseur

IV and Chasseur XXV: at Toulon: all units scuttled. The *La Garonne:* at Toulon: captured.

8 December: The 3,400-ton *contre-torpilleur L'Audacieux;* the 895-ton torpedo-boats *La Pomone, L'Iphigénie,* and *Bombarde;* 776-ton submarines *Circé* and *Calypso;* the 1,441-ton submarines *Dauphin, Requin, Phoque,* and *Espadon;* the 925-ton submarines *Saphir, Turquoise,* and *Nautilus;* the 895-ton sloops *Commandant Rivière* and *La Batailleuse;* and the 3,150-ton minelayer *Castor:* at Bizerte: captured.

Thereafter French losses were as follows:

1943

26 March: The 1,147-ton auxiliary patrol boat *Sergeant Gouarne:* off Cueta, Morocco: German submarine U. 755.

27 May: The 3,050-ton *contre-torpilleur Léopard:* off Tobruk: ran aground and wrecked.

22 June: The 4,220-ton tanker *Lot:* northwest of Cape Verde Islands: German submarine U. 572.

11 November: The 4,763-ton tanker *Nivôse:* with convoy east of Oran: German aircraft.

26 November: The 442-ton auxiliary patrol boat *Béryl:* off Cape Varella, Indo-China: cause of loss not forthcoming.

28 November: The 285-ton auxiliary minesweeper *Marie Mad:* off Corsica: mine.

21 December: The 180-ton submarine-chaser Chasseur V: in the English Channel: foundered in storm.

29 December: The 2,084-ton submarine *Protée:* off Toulon: German patrol vessel.

1944

26 February: The 413-ton survey ship *Astrolabe:* at Tourane in Indo-China: B-25 Mitchell medium bombers of the 14th Air Force operating from Nanning.

30 April: The 644-ton gunboat *Tahure:* off Cape Varella, Indo-China: U.S. submarine *Flasher.*

9 June: The accommodation ship *Courbet:* at Normandy: constructive total loss.

10 June: The 1,900-ton destroyer *Mistral:* off Quineville: German coastal battery.

8 July: The 925-ton submarine *La Perle:* whereabouts not forthcoming: mistakenly by British aircraft.

16 August: The 9,548-ton training ship *Gueydon:* at Brest: British aircraft.
27 August: The 9,177-ton training ship *Montcalm:* at Brest: British aircraft.
25 October: The 215-ton minesweeper D. 202: at the mouth of the Rhône: mine.

1945

9 January: The 325-ton submarine-chaser *L'Enjoué:* west of Gibraltar: German submarine U. 870.
12 January: The 9,350-ton light cruiser *Lamotte-Picquet* and the 315-ton survey ship *Octant:* Camranh Bay, Indo-China: U.S. carrier aircraft.
31 January: The 463-ton submarine-chaser *L'Ardent:* off Casablanca: ran aground and wrecked.
24 February: The 1,435-ton destroyer *La Combattante:* in the North Sea: mine.
9 March: The 135-ton gunboats *Avalanche* and *Commandant Bourdais:* at My Tho in the Mekong delta and at Haiphong respectively: scuttled. The 732-ton river gunboat *Francis Garnier:* at Kratié on the Mekong: scuttled.
10 March: The 2,600-ton colonial sloop *Amiral Charner,* the 601-ton sloop *Marne,* and the 95-ton gunboat *Mytho:* at My Tho in the Mekong delta: scuttled.
11 March: The 780-ton survey ship *La Pérouse:* at Can Tho in the Mekong delta, Indo-China: scuttled.

DENMARK

Denmark and Germany concluded a non-aggression treaty on 31 March 1939, which just so happened to be the day on which Britain gave its guarantee to Poland. Denmark sought to stand aside from the war that began in September 1939 just as it had in the 1914–1918 conflict, but on 9 April 1940, and as the first part of an offensive that took German forces across the Skagerrak and as far north as Narvik, German forces invaded and occupied Denmark in a matter of hours. The Danish government, recognizing the inevitable, ordered no resistance and remained in office until August 1943. In that time it was obliged to become increasingly tied to Germany, but with two by-products. The British occupied the Faeroe Islands on 16 April and then Iceland on 9 May 1940, and their possession, not least on account of Iceland being garrisoned by American forces after July 1941, was important in the conduct of the anti-submarine campaign in the North Atlantic in terms of land-based air escort and patrols mounted from Iceland. In addition, Danish shipping outside the Baltic joined the Allied cause, and some five thousand Danish sailors ultimately served with the Allies.

The Danish Navy on 9 April 1940 was both small and composed of aging units, with a number of torpedo-boats, some into their fifth decade, serving as minesweepers. Overall it mustered two coast defense ships, six torpedo-boats, ten small submarines, five minelayers, nine minesweepers, and assorted old torpedo-boats, patrol and fishery protection vessels and twenty-four seaplanes. In February 1941 Germany demanded the surrender of twelve units, and while this was reduced to six, the demand was the shape of things to come. On 29 August 1943 the German move to disarm Danish forces resulted in a triple development involving the Danish Navy: a total of twenty-seven Danish warships were scuttled at Copenhagen; the largest ship in the navy, the *Niels Iuel*, for some reason not altogether clear, put to sea, was attacked by German aircraft, was beached but salved by the Germans, and was put into service as a training ship; and a number of units—including one torpedo-boat, *Havkatten*, and three minesweepers—successfully sought the safety of Swedish waters. In effect the Danish Navy ceased to exist on 29 August 1943.

On 9 April the 1940 what was not so much a navy as a collection of patrol boats was deployed as follows:

At Esbjerg in southwest Jutland: The patrol boat *Beskytteren*.

At Hirtshals on the northern cape on the Skaggerak: the 705-ton fisheries patrol vessel *Hejmdal*.

At Frederikshavn on the north cape on the Kattegat: the 3,785-ton coastal defense ship *Oeder Skram* and the 335-ton torpedo-boats *Dragen*, *Hvalen*, and *Laxen*.

At Åarhus in eastern Jutland: the 402-ton submarines *Havfruen*, *Havkalen*, and *Havmanden* and the 463-ton submarine tender *Henrik Garner*.

At Nyborg on eastern Fyn: the 335-ton torpedo-boat *Ørnen*, and at Slipshaven, just outside Nyborg, the 108-ton ex-torpedo-boat guardship *Sælen*.

In the Great Belt were the 335-ton torpedo-boats *Glenten* and *Høgen*, the minelayer *Lossen*, the 304-ton minesweepers *Søløven* and *Søridderen*, the 108-ton ex-torpedo boat *Støren*, and the 1280-ton patrol boat *Ingolf*.

At Svendborg on southeast Fyn the 186-ton minelayer *Sixtus* under repair.

At Søby on the isle of Ærø the 186-ton minelayer *Kvintus*.

At Stubbekøbing on southern Møn two unnamed patrol cutters, and at the Grønsund minefield between Møn and Falster two more unnamed cutters.

At Copenhagen was the 706-ton patrol vessel *Island Falk*, and at the main naval base were the 4,100-ton coastal defense ship *Niels Iuel*, the 381-ton submarines *Daphne* and *Dryaden* and the 369-ton *Flora* and *Rota*, two ex-torpedo boats serving as minesweepers, the 143-ton *Havøren* and the 108-ton *Søhunden*, and the 108-ton ex-torpedo boats serving as guardships, the *Havkatten* and *Makrelen*.

In addition, no longer in commission but at this main base in Copenhagen were the 381-ton submarine *Bellona*; the 235-ton submarines *Galathea*, *Ran*, and *Triton*; four 108-ton ex-torpedo-boats, namely, the guardship *Hvalrossen* and the minesweepers *Narvalen*, *Søulven*, and *Springeren*; and the repair ship *Grøsund*.

In Greenland were two patrol cutters, the 110-ton *Maagen* and the 80-ton *Ternen*.

No Allied warships were Danish or manned by Danish personnel, but the only member of the Special Air Service ever to been awarded the Victoria Cross was a Dane, Major Anders Frederik Emil Victor Schau Lassen, killed in Italy on 9 April 1945.

NORWAY

In the inter-period the Norwegian Navy, like those of the other Scandinavian countries, underwent major reduction and neglect, and this in spite of the merchant shipping losses that had been incurred in the First World War during the German submarine campaign against shipping and the open advocacy of the occupation of Norway in any future war by the influential Vice Admiral Wolfgang Wegener (1875–1956) in *Die Seestrategie des Weltkrieges*, published in 1929. By 1939 the Norwegian Navy possessed four coastal defense ships that were in or approaching their fifth decade, four destroyers that pre-dated the outbreak of the First World War, three modern and no fewer than twenty-six old torpedo-boats, most of which were less than 100-ton displacement, six modern and three older submarines, and a number of old sloops and minelayers.

Most of these ships were lost in 1940 in the course of a three-month campaign that saw significant losses on the part of the Norwegians, obviously, but also on the part of both the British and the Germans. The German losses, most obviously in Oslofjorden and off Narvik, destroyed whatever chance there was of Germany ever acquiring a sizable and balanced navy, while for the British a disastrous campaign culminated with the loss under disgraceful circumstances of the fleet carrier *Glorious* (and the destroyers *Acasta* and *Ardent*) to the German battleships *Gneisenau* and *Scharnhorst* on 8 June 1940. The German occupation of Norway and the losses incurred during this campaign, however, were set in place by the defeat of France and the German occupation of the Netherlands, Belgium, Luxembourg, and northern and western France, 10 May–25 June.

Norwegian units lost in the course of the April–June 1940 campaign were as follows:

8 April: The 107-ton torpedo-boat *Skrei:* off the Færder light house, outside Tjørne, in Oslofjorden: sunk by German torpedo-boat *Albatros*.

9 April: From north to south along the coast:
At Narvik (68°26'North 17°25'East): the 3,645-ton coastal defense ships *Eidsvold* and *Norge:* torpedoed by the German destroyers *Wilhelm Heidkamp* and *Bernd von Arnim* respectively.

The 300-ton fisheries protection vessel *Michael Sars:* surrendered: it was sunk on 13 April during the second battle of Narvik. The 376-ton auxiliary patrol boat *Kelt:* captured by German destroyer *Roeder* off Baroy.

At Trondheim (63°36'North 10°23'East): the 84-ton torpedo-boat *Laks:* in dock: captured (also given as scuttled on 12 April).

At Kvarven, Bergen (60°23'North 05°20'East): the 250-ton gunboat-minelayer *Uller:* captured and put into immediate service and sunk by Norwegian aircraft in Sognefjorden (northward around the coast from Bergen) on 30 May.

At Stavanger (58°58'North 05°45'East): the 597-ton destroyer *Aeger:* German aircraft.

At Egersund (58°27'North 06°01'East): the 92-ton torpedo-boat *Skarv:* captured by German minesweeper M. 1.

At Marvika, Kristiansand (58°08'North 08°01'East): The 84-ton torpedo-boat *Kjell:* captured.

At Falconbridge, Kristiansand: the 545-ton submarine B. 5: captured by German S-boat.

At Horten (59°25'North 10°30'East): the 3,380-ton coastal defense ships *Harald Haarfagre* and *Tordenskjold,* both of which were rebuilt as AA batteries, the 370-ton minesweepers *Otra* and *Rauma,* the 1,596-ton minelayer *Olav Tryggvason,* the 266-ton patrol boat *Senja,* and the 64-ton ex-torpedo boat minesweeper *Hauk:* all units captured and put into German service.

At Karljohansvern, Horten: the 55-ton torpedo-boats *Lom* and *Ørn:* captured.

In Oslofjorden: the 340-ton submarine A. 2: damaged in exchange with German warships at Valø in Oslofjorden and ran aground; salvaged next day and sailed to the Teie naval base (which is directly outside Tønsberg), where it was abandoned and scuttled: wreck captured on 12 April by German forces. The 214-ton auxiliary patrol boat *Pol III:* sunk in surface action with German torpedo-boat *Albatros.*

At Fredrikstad (59°15'North 10°55'East), eastern Oslofjorden: the torpedo-boat *Tor:* scuttled.

10 April: The 365-ton submarine B. 4: at Filtvet, near Drøbak (59°40'North 10°40'East), on east bank of Oslofjorden: captured.

11 April: The 365-ton submarine B. 2: at Fiskaa Verk, some twenty miles southwest of Kristiansand: captured. The 708-ton torpedo-boat *Gyller* and 632-ton torpedo-boat *Odin* at Kristiansand: surrendered. The 38-ton torpedo-boats *Blink, Kvik,* and *Lyn:* at Vigebukta, Kristiansand: captured. The 90-ton torpedo-boat

Brand: at Laksevaag (60°23'North 05°18'East) just outside Bergen: captured. The 64-ton ex-torpedo boat minesweeper *Hvas:* at Stavern near Larvik (59°04'North 10°02'East) on the west bank at the entrance to Oslofjorden: captured.

12 April: The 64-ton ex-torpedo boat minesweepers *Falk* and *Kjæk:* at the Teie base on Oslofjorden: captured.

13 April: The 595-ton minelayer *Frøya:* in Trondheimfjorden: deliberately run aground and wrecked. The 107-ton torpedo-boat *Storm:* ran aground off Stangholmene on the previous day: returned to Godøy (62°28'North 05°59'East), where it capsized.

14 April: The 330-ton minelayers *Glommen* and *Laugen:* at Melsomvik (59°13'North 10°21'East), western Oslofjorden below Horten: surrendered. The 92-ton torpedo-boat *Teist:* at Drange I Herad, northeast of Farsund (58°05'North 06°49'East): scuttled.

16 April: The 340-ton submarines A. 3 and A. 4: at Tønsberg (59°16'North 10°25'East), western Oslofjorden: scuttled.

17 April: The 70-ton torpedo-boats *Grib, Jo,* and *Ravn:* between Lyngør and Arendal (58°27'North 08°56'East): scuttled.

19 April: The 90-ton torpedo-boat *Sael:* beached after action with German torpedo-boats (whereabouts not forthcoming; given as Aabuglo, but there seems to be no such place, and it may be that this was Angulo, a small place northeast of Leirvik, which is 59°47'North 05°30'East on Stord Island, on Bømlafjorden).

20 April: The 220-ton torpedo-boat *Steegg:* at Herøysund (59°55'North 05°48'East) in Hardangerfjorden: in action with German gunnery training ship *Bremse.* The 290-ton gunboat-minelayer *Tyr:* off Skorpo Island (59°57'North 05°50'East) in Hardangerfjorden: beached and abandoned and subsequently captured.

26 April: The 540-ton *Garm:* at Bjordal (61°04'North 05°50'East) on a southern inlet on Sognefjorden: German aircraft. The 220-ton torpedo-boat *Trygg:* at Aandalsnes (62°33'North 07°43'East) at the head of Romdalsfjorden: German aircraft.

2 May: The 67-ton minesweepers *Djerv* and *Dristig:* at Kvamsøy (61°07'North 06°25'East) on Sognefjorden: scuttled.

4 May: The 540-ton destroyer *Troll* and 220-ton torpedo-boat *Snøgg:* at Flørø (61°36'North 05°04'East): abandoned.

5 May: The 107-ton torpedo-boat *Sild:* at Svanholmen in Trænenfjoprden off Molde (62°45'North 07°14'East): scuttled. The 250-ton gunboat-minelayer *Vale* (launched in 1874) and the 290-ton gunboat-minelayer *Gor:* at Kjelkenes near Svelgen (61°47'North 05°18'East), which is on an inlet south of Frøysjøen: abandoned and subsequently captured.

10 June: The 365-ton submarine B. 3: near Alsvaag (68°54'North 15°17'East) in the Vesteraalen group: scuttled after an explosion of its batteries on 8 June, when it was making its way to Britain, forced it to return to Norwegian waters.

Subsequently the Norwegian Navy, in addition to those units that had escaped and made their way to Britain,[1] commissioned into service the British destroyers *Shark* and *Success* and the escort destroyers *Eskdale* and *Glaisdale*; the old flush-deck destroyers *Bath, Lincoln, Mansfield, Newport*, and *St. Albans* that Britain had acquired from the United States in 1940; the corvettes *Acanthus, Buttercup, Eglantine, Montbretia, Potentilla, Rose*, and *Tunsberg*; and the submarines *Uredd, Varne, Variance, Venturer, Viking*, and *Votary*. In addition, four U.S. submarine-chasers and twenty British motor torpedo boats and nine motor launches and, from the United States, four submarine-chasers, were commissioned into Norwegian service.

The losses of the Norwegian Navy after 11 June 1940 were as follows:

1940

26 September: The 20-ton MTB 6: in the English Channel: sprang leak in heavy weather and abandoned.

8 November: The 1,275-ton gunboat *Fridtjof Nansen:* at Redvedbukta, Jan Mayen Island: ran aground and wrecked.

1941

1 July: The 20-ton MTB 5: inside Dover harbor: accidental explosion.

19 August: The 1,090-ton destroyer *Bath:* North Atlantic convoy escort: German submarine U. 204.

24 August: The 258-ton auxiliary minesweeper Kos XVI: off Hull: collision with British destroyer *Wolsey*.

29 November: The 153-ton auxiliary minesweeper *Egeland:* off Gaza: ran aground and wrecked.

1942

12 December: The 1,630-ton corvette *Tunsberg:* off Makkaur, Finnmark: mine.

1943

4 January: The 351-ton ex-whaler and minesweeper *Bodø:* in the North Sea: mine.

27 February: The 250-ton auxiliary minesweeper *Harstad:* in the English Channel: German MTBs.

c. 10 February: The 732-ton submarine *Uredd:* in Fugløyfjorden south of Bodø: mine.

14 March: The 18-ton motor torpedo boat MTB 631: off Flørø: ran aground.

27 July: The 18-ton MTB 345: off Aspoy near Bergen: ran aground.

14 November: The 1,590-ton escort destroyer *Eskdale:* off the Lizard, English Channel: German MTBs.

18 November: The 1,390-ton corvette *Montbretia:* in North Atlantic: German submarine U. 262.

22 November: The 18-ton MTB 626: inside Lerwick harbor: petrol explosion and fire, and was towed out the harbor and scuttled.

1944

15 February: The 76-ton motor launch ML 210: in the English Channel: mine.

6 June: The 2,545-ton destroyer *Svenner* (ex-*Shark*): off Normandy: German MTBs.

26 October: The 1,390-ton corvette *Rose:* in North Atlantic: collision with frigate *Manners.*

1945

10 March: The 425-ton auxiliary minesweeper *Nordhav II:* off Dundee: German submarine U. 714.

7 May: The 278-ton minesweeper YMS 382: in the Irish Sea: German submarine U. 1023. This was the last Allied warship sunk in the European war.

THE NETHERLANDS

The Dutch were to experience not one defeat but two, and both disastrous in terms of nation and navy. The first defeat was that of 1940, between 10 and 15 May, which saw the homeland invaded and thereafter occupied by German forces. The second defeat was that of 1941–1942, when in southeast Asia, the Japanese overran the Dutch East Indies. In both campaigns the Dutch Navy fought but was hopelessly placed and incurred comprehensive defeats.

With the 585-ton minesweeper *Willem van Ewijck* lost off Terschelling in its own minefield on 8 September 1939, the losses of the Dutch Navy in May–June 1940 were as follows:

11 May: The 1,640-ton destroyer *Van Galen:* at Rotterdam: German aircraft. The naval hospital ships *Emergo* and *Luctor:* at Vlessingen: German aircraft.

12 May: The 542-ton gunboat *Friso:* in the IJsselmeer: scuttled after air attack. The 240-ton minelayers *Bulgia* and *Thor:* at Vlessingen: German aircraft.

13 May: The 238-ton minesweeper M. 2: in the North Sea: mine.

14 May: The 343-ton submarine O. 8, the 647-ton submarine O. 11, and the 715-ton submarine O. 12: Den Helder: scuttled. The 1,795-ton gunboat *Johan Maurits van Nassau:* off Callantsoog in North Sea: German aircraft. The 542-ton gunboat *Brinio:* inside the IJsselmeer: German aircraft. The 280-ton gunboat *Hefring:* inside the IJsselmeer: scuttled. The 280-ton gunboat *Tyr:* at Rotterdam: captured. The 280-ton gunboat *Freijr:* whereabouts not forthcoming: scuttled. The 277-ton torpedo-gunboat Z. 3: at Enkhuisen inside the IJsselmeer: scuttled and burnt out. The 180-ton torpedo-gunboat G. 16: at Willemsoord: scuttled. The 48-ton torpedo-gunboat *Christiaan Cornelis:* off Numansdorp: German artillery. The 280-ton minelayer *Braga:* at Pannerden above Nijmegen: scuttled. The 280-ton minelayers *Balder* and *Hadda:* Hook of Holland: scuttled. The 585-ton minesweepers *Abraham van der Hulst* and *Peiter Florisz:* at Enkuizen: scuttled. The 238-ton minesweeper M. 1: whereabouts not forthcoming: captured. The 238-ton minesweepers M. 3 and M. 4: at IJmuiden: scuttled, the former as a blockship.

15 May: The 593-ton minelayer *Hydra:* whereabouts not forthcoming: German aircraft.

17 May: The 3,970-ton ex-cruiser/accommodation ship *Noordbrabank:* whereabouts unknown: fire, but whether deliberate, accidental, or result of enemy action not forthcoming.

In addition: The 280-ton minelayer *Vidar:* at Vlessingen: date of capture not forthcoming.

A total of two light cruisers, one solitary destroyer, nine submarines, two gunboats, one sloop, and six torpedo-boats escaped to Britain to continue resistance after the surrender of the homeland, and over the next five years the British transferred to the Dutch Navy the submarines P. 47, *Sturgeon, Talent,* and *Tarn,* the frigate *Ribble,* the corvette *Carnation,* eighteen motor minesweepers, twelve torpedo-boats, and four motor launches. The Americans transferred the submarine-chaser PC. 468, and thirteen American- and Canadian-built PT boats were also transferred to the Dutch, three being ceded to the British Navy as target boats in 1943.

Between 20 June 1940 and 15 December 1941 the Dutch Navy lost the following:

20 June 1940: The 715-ton submarine O. 13: in the North Sea: mistakenly by Polish submarine *Wilk.*

8 November: The 1,350-ton submarine O. 22: off Lindesnes, southwest Norway: German warships.

22 May 1941: The 800-ton minelayer *Nautilus*: off Grimsby: collision with British merchantman *Murrayfield*.

In addition, on 4 June 1941 the 687-ton minelayer *Van Meerlant*, which had been transferred to Britain and operated under British flag, was lost to a mine in the Thames estuary.

With the start of hostilities in the Pacific and southeast Asia on 7–8 December 1941, the Dutch incurred the following losses:

1941

16 December: The 1,170-ton submarine O. 16: off Singapore: lost in British minefield.

19 December: The 1,536-ton submarine O. 20: in the Gulf of Siam: Japanese destroyer *Uranami*.

24 December: The 1,008-ton submarine K. XVII: off Kota Bharu: Japanese destroyers.

25 December: The 1,008-ton submarine K. XVI: off Kuching: Japanese submarine I. 66.

1942

12 January: The 1,291-ton minelayer *Prins van Orange*: off Tarakan: surface action.

15 February: The 1,640-ton destroyer *Van Ghent*: south of Banka Island: caught on uncharted reef. The 612-ton minelayer *Pro Patria*: in the River Musi(?): scuttled.

17 February: The 1,650-ton destroyer *Van Nes*: in the Banka Strait: Japanese aircraft.

18 February: The 520-ton submarine K. VII and 815-ton submarine K. XII: at Soerabaja: Japanese aircraft, the damaged K. XII being scuttled in early March.

20 February: The 1,640-ton destroyer *Piet Hein*: off Bali: surface action.

27 February: The 7,548-ton light cruiser *De Ruyter*, the 6,670-ton light cruiser *Java*, and the 1,640-ton destroyer *Kortenaer*: action in the Java Sea: Japanese warships.

28 February: The 1,640-ton destroyer *Evertsen*: in the Sunda Strait: surface action.

2 March: The 175-ton minesweeper *Endeh*: in the Java Sea: Japanese destroyer. The 1,650-ton destroyers *Banckert* and *Witte de With*,

the 520-ton submarine K. X, and the 1,008-ton submarine K. XVIII: at Soerabaja: all battle-damaged and scuttled, the destroyers in dock. The 179-ton minesweepers M. A, M. B, M. C, and M. D: at Soerabaja: all damaged by air attack, and scuttling administered the coup de grâce. The minesweeper *Bangkalen*, the 227-ton minesweeper *Soemenep*, and the 120-ton minesweepers *Ardjoeno* and *Kawi*: at Soerabaja: scuttled. The 1,631-ton minelayer *Rigel*, the 175-ton minesweepers *Djember, Djombangh, Djampea*, and *Enggano*, and the 131-ton minesweepers *Alor, Aroe, Bantam, Boeroe, Bogor, Ceram*, and *Cheribon:* at Tandjong Priok: scuttled.

6 March: The 585-ton minesweeper *Pieter de Bitter:* off Soerabaja: scuttled.

7 March: The 1,291-ton minelayer *Gouden Leeuw:* at Soerabaja: scuttled.

8 March: The 982-ton minelayer *Krakatau:* off Madoera: scuttled. The 585-ton minesweeper *Eland Dubois:* in the Madoera Strait: scuttled. The 585-ton minesweeper *Jan van Amstel:* off the Gili Islands in the Lombok Strait: Japanese warship.

In addition the following units are given in various sources as scuttled, but complete details regarding date, displacement, and whereabouts not forthcoming:

2 March: The 680-ton minelayer *Serdang:* off Java: scuttled.

2 March: The 120-ton minesweepers *Gedeh, Lawoe*, and *Salak:* given as scuttled at either Soerabaja or Tandjong Priok.

The 520-ton submarines K. IX and K. XII and the 6,426-ton training ship *Soerabaja* given as scuttled at Soerabaja: no dates but presumably on or about 2 March.

Patrol boats that belonged to the Netherlands East Indies *gouvernementsmarine* and that are listed as lost in 1942 are as follows:

ND: The *Canopus* and *Deneb:* whereabouts not forthcoming: Japanese aircraft.

26 January: The 936-ton *Wega:* whereabouts and cause of loss not forthcoming.

28 February: The 936-ton *Sirius:* scuttled, and the 623-ton *Reiger:* wrecked: whereabouts of these losses not forthcoming.

1 March: The 623-ton *Fazant:* whereabouts not forthcoming: scuttled.

2 March: The 800-ton *Fomalhout* and 592-ton *Merel:* whereabouts not forthcoming: scuttled.
-- March: The 775-ton *Arend* and *Valk:* whereabouts not forthcoming: scuttled.

The following units are listed as having been scuttled, no details forthcoming: the *Albatros, Aldebaren, Bellatrix, Eridanus,* and *Gemma.*

Thereafter the Dutch losses were as follows:

1942
13 November: The 2,228-ton destroyer *Isaac Sweers:* off Algiers: German submarine U. 431.

1943
27 February: The 10,972-ton submarine depot ship *Columbia:* southeast of East London, South Africa: German submarine U. 516.

1944
18 May: The 18-ton motor torpedo boat MTB 203: English Channel: surface action(?).
20 May: The 200-ton minesweeper *Marken:* in the North Sea: mine.
9 June: The 6,670-ton light cruiser *Sumatra:* Normandy: constructive total loss.
12 June: The 200-ton minesweeper *Terschelling:* in the North Sea: mine.

1945
8 July: The 1,536-ton submarine O. 19: in the South China Sea: wrecked.

The survey ships *Eilerts de Haan* and *Hydrograaf* and (NEI) *Tydeman* and *Willebrord Snellius* are not included in these lists.

GREECE

The Greeks found themselves the victims of aggression before the start of the Italian invasion on 28 October 1940, but it was after the German intervention, in April 1941, that Greek national exhaustion was overtaken by losses that reduced the Greek Navy to the single light cruiser *Giorgios Averoff,* six destroyers, and five submarines that took refuge in Alexandria.

The losses incurred by the Greek Navy between 15 August 1940 and 15 May 1941 were as follows:

1940

15 August: The 2,600-ton torpedo-cruiser *Helle:* off Tínos in the northern Cyclades: Italian submarine *Delfino.*

29 December: The 960-ton submarine *Proteus:* off the Albanian coast: Italian escort *Antares.*

1941

4 April: The 241-ton torpedo-boat *Proussa:* off Corfu: Italian aircraft.

Thereafter to German aircraft unless otherwise stated:

11 April: The 2,561-ton hospital ship *Attiki:* in the channel off Cape Doro.

13 April: The 2,050-ton destroyer *Psara:* off Mégara.

20 April: The 1,850-ton destroyer *Vasilevs Georgios:* partially scuttled because the floating dock in which it was being repaired (after being damaged on 13 April) was damaged by German bombing and could not be sunk: destroyer raised and entered German service. The 37-ton torpedo-boats T. 1 and T. 2: in the Salamis navy yard.

21 April: The 1,461-ton hospital ship *Esperos:* at Missolonghi.

22 April: The 2,050-ton destroyer *Hydra,* the 241-ton torpedo-boat *Kios,* and the tanker *Prometheus:* at or off Piraeus, Athens. The 350-ton torpedo-boat *Thyella:* off Kavouri in Vuliagmeni Bay. The 338-ton *Aliakmon:* in the Gulf of Athens. The 1,134-ton hospital ship *Sokratis:* at Antikyra.

23 April: The 12,500-ton ex-battleships and training ship *Kilkis* and accommodation ship *Lemnos:* at the Salamis navy yard. The 120-ton torpedo-boat *Doris:* off Port Rafti. The 120-ton torpedo-boat *Arethousa:* off Salamis. The 460-ton minelayer *Tenedos:* in Saronis Bay in the Gulf of Athens. The 241-ton torpedo-boat *Kios* and the 395-ton minelayer *Paralos:* at Vuliagmeni in the Gulf of Athens. The 380-ton minelayer *Korgialenios:* off Corfu. The 338-ton minesweeper *Nestos:* in the Gulf of Corinth. The 325-ton minesweeper *Strymon:* in the Athens navy yard. The minesweeper *Palaslcas*: at Vólos.

24 April: The 120-ton torpedo-boats *Aigli* and the *Alkioni:* at Fleves/Elevsís in the Gulf of Athens. The 2,068-ton hospital ship *Andros:* in the Gulf of Corinth.
It has been stated that in addition to the ships named herein, forty-three merchant ships were sunk between 20 and 24 April by German aircraft.

25 April: The 241-ton torpedo-boats *Kyzikos* and *Pergamos:* at or off the

Salamis navy yard. The 520-ton survey ship *Pleias:* in the Gulf of Patra.

26 April: The 241-ton torpedo-boat *Kydoniai:* at Monemvasisa in the southern Peloponnese.

28 April: The 325-ton minesweeper *Axios:* at Syros in the Gulf of Athens.

15 May: The 980-ton destroyer *Leon:* in Suda Bay, Crete.

Also given as sunk by German aircraft in April 1941 but with dates, types and displacement, and locations that proved elusive: the *Aias*, *Amfitriti*, *Irakalis*, *Kentavros*, *Kichli*, *Kyklops*, *Navtilos*, *Orion*, *Palaskas*, and *Titan*.

Subsequently the Greek Navy, in addition to those units that had escaped to continue the war from British bases, commissioned into service the destroyers *Echo* and *Salamis*; the escort destroyers *Bolebrooke*, *Border*, *Bramham*, *Hatherleigh*, *Hursley*, and *Modbury*; the corvettes *Coreopsis*, *Hyacinth*, *Peony*, and *Tamarisk*; the submarines *Untiring*, *Upstart*, *Veldt*, and *Vengeful*; eleven BYMS; and one MMS; plus, courtesy of the United States, one submarine-chaser and four LSTs. Overall, by 1944 the Greek Navy had a total of forty-four units in service, and perhaps surprisingly, given that the tide of war had moved from the Mediterranean, by this time the Greek Navy was second in size only to the British Navy in the Mediterranean: the Italian Navy was inoperative, the French Navy in real terms was no more, and the U.S. Navy, other than Dragoon, was elsewhere. It has been suggested that in the war's last year the Greek Navy accounted for four-fifths of all non-British Allied naval operations in the Mediterranean and were primarily directed to the clearing of mines, a task that continued at least until 1956. Little noted are two facts, namely that something like three-fifths of all Greek merchantmen were lost in the course of the war and that in April 1944 a series of mutinies in Greek ships in Alexandria and Bizerte and at Malta foreshadowed the civil war that was to follow two years hence.

Losses in the period after April–May 1941 were as follows:

1942

4 April: The 960-ton submarine *Glavkos:* at Malta: German or Italian strategic bombing raid.

16 November: The 960-ton submarine *Triton:* in the Porthmós Kafiréos between Euboea and Ándros in the Aegean: German patrol craft U.J. 2102.

1943

14 September: The 778-ton submarine *Katsonis:* off Vólos in northern Sporades: German submarine-chaser U.J. 2101.

26 September: The 1,850-ton destroyer *Vasilissa Olga:* at Leros: German aircraft.

22 October: The 1,590-ton escort destroyer *Adrias:* lost bow to a mine but managed to return to Alexandria: constructive total loss.

1944

6 January: The 1,625-ton LST *Lesvos:* given as having been lost after running aground either off Bizerte or "in the eastern Mediterranean."

15 October: The 207-ton minesweeper *Kassos* and 215-ton minesweeper *Kos:* in the Gulf of Athens: mined.

1945

2 May: The 250-ton auxiliary minesweeper *Spercheios:* off Cape Zourba, northeast Hydra, in the Gulf of Athens: mine.

24 October: The 250-ton auxiliary minesweeper *Pinios:* outside Préveza: mine.

YUGOSLAVIA

The story of the Yugoslavian Navy would seem to present a degree of difficulty that is inversely related to size and importance but that accords with one very simple fact: in what was the inter-war Kingdom of Serbs, Croats, and Slovenes there are places that existed under five different states in the course of the twentieth century, and the Yugoslav Navy possessed ships with pedigree not dissimilar. For example, the pre-war Yugoslav Navy possessed a torpedo-boat launched in July 1916 for the Austro-Hungarian Navy, which was captured by the Italians in April 1943, was seized by the Germans in September 1943, and then served with the Croat Navy until sunk in June 1944; one of its sister ships survived in service into the 1960s after it was returned to the Yugoslav Navy.

What is truly surprising about the Yugoslav Navy in 1941 is how few of its small number of ships were either sunk by enemy action or scuttled, the majority being captured, and primarily by the Italians. Once one stops to consider the strategic situation of Yugoslavia, however, such a strange development seems logical: here was a country surrounded on three sides by potential enemies and possessed of a coastline that led only to an Italian strait. Every advantage of position lay in the hands of the enemies of a surrounded Yugoslavia, and under such circumstances it was perhaps both natural and inevitable that capture should indeed have been the fate of most of its naval units.

The losses incurred in 1941 campaign were as follows:

11 or 12 April: The 530-ton river monitors *Morava, Sava,* and the *Vardar:* all scuttled, whereabouts unknown to the author.

12 April: The 530-ton river monitor *Drava*: whereabouts unknown to the author: German aircraft.

17 April: The 1,655-ton destroyer *Zagreb*: at Kotor: scuttled. The 2,350-ton destroyer leader *Dubrovnik* and the (damaged) 1,655-ton destroyer *Beograd*: at Cattaro: and the 1,655-ton destroyer *Ljubljana*: at Sebenico: surrendered to Germans. The 4,500-ton tanker *Perun*: sunk but whereabouts and to what cause not forthcoming.

Given as surrendered to or captured by the Italians during April 1941, dates and places not known:

The 262-ton torpedo-boats T. 1 and T. 3; the 266-ton torpedo-boats T. 5, T. 6, T. 7, and T. 8; the 809-ton submarines *Osvetnik* and *Smeli*, and the 1,164-ton submarine *Hrabri*; the 330-ton minelayers *Galeb, Gavrac, Jastreb, Kobac, Orao*, and *Sokol*; the 130-ton mining tenders *Malinska, Marjan, Meljine, Mljet*, and *Mosor*; and the 2,370-ton gunnery training ship *Dalmacija*.

Also captured by the Italians, date unknown, was the 660-ton gunboat *Beli Orao*: captured in the Boka Kotorska.

The 1,870-ton seaplane tender *Zmaj* is given as having been captured by the Germans at Split on 17 April, being taken into German service thereafter, and sunk by British aircraft at Vathi, Sámos island, in the Aegean on 22 September 1944.

Two Yugoslav torpedo-boats and the submarine *Nebojsa* escaped to Suda Bay, Crete, the former arriving on 22 April and the submarine the following day. The latter then made its way to Alexandria, where it entered Allied service. Perhaps the most interesting of all episodes was the capture by Italian marines of the Yugoslavian steamer *Tomislav* on 22 April. The 5,387-ton steamer was seized at Shanghai, and subsequently entered first Italian and then Japanese service.

After its defeat Yugoslavia was dismembered, with Bulgaria, Germany, Hungary, and Italy all annexing parts of the country and with what remained divided between a client fascist Croatia and a collaborationist, and largely irrelevant, Serbia that was under direct German occupation. After this time there emerged a Croat navy and ultimately, and in addition to a royal and largely Serbian government and armed forces in exile, a Yugoslavian People's Liberation Army that had its own naval and riverine force. The latter had (during late 1943 and after) a number of captured units of more than a hundred tons, but for the most part the units were very small, less than twenty tons, and very modestly armed. The only unit of any size seems to have been the 2,819-ton transport *Dubac*, but it has been suggested that though the communist navy boasted some 302 units, perhaps four-fifths were really in the category of motor launches or river boats and perhaps half could be expected not to be in service at any one time. Their contribution to resistance and eventual liberation was minimal.

Very few Allied units made their way into Yugoslav commission after April 1941, the British corvette *Mallow* and eight former U.S. PT boats seemingly being alone in being transferred in 1944. The Yugoslav Navy apparently sustained no losses after April 1941, but it should be noted that virtually every one of the major units that had been lost through capture in April 1941 was transferred to various navies and was sunk, mostly in 1943–1944, by which time the various advantages of numbers, position, and air power had changed sides.

* * *

Warship losses on the part of the states of Central and South America were decidedly modest. The tide of war did reach these shores, but Brazil was alone among the Latin American countries in sending naval and military forces to the Mediterranean and to Italy. In the New World the war at sea was primarily the responsibility of Canada and the United States, and German operations in the waters of Central and South America were very limited in terms of both submarine numbers and duration.

The warship and auxiliary losses of the Latin American states were as follows:

ARGENTINA

4 October 1941: The 1,375-ton destroyer *Corrientes:* off Tierra del Fuego: collision with heavy cruiser *Almirante Brown.*

BRAZIL

20 July 1944: The 1,737-ton transport *Vital de Oliveira:* southeast of Cape São Tomé: German submarine U. 861.

21 July 1944: The 552-ton minelayer *Camaquan:* foundered 60 miles east of Recife.

In addition, on 4 July 1945 the 3,150-ton light cruiser *Bahia* was sunk by an accidental explosion some seventy miles off Pernambuco while operating as guardship on behalf of American patrol aircraft based in Brazil.

CUBA

4 December 1943: The 5,441-ton transport *Libertad:* in convoy southeast of Cape Hatteras, North Carolina: German submarine U. 129.

MEXICO

Apparently no naval unit was lost, but merchant shipping losses, according to *Conway's All the World's Fighting Ships*, page 414, were "significant." If indeed the official British civil history *Merchant Shipping and the Demands of War*, page 23, appendix 7, was correct in the statement that in 1939 the Mexican merchant fleet consisted of four merchantmen and two tankers of 18,000 tons, it is difficult to resist the notion that any single loss would have been significant: as it is, by the author's reckoning Mexico lost six ships of 29,942 tons in the course of the war, so the losses, greater than the pre-war shipping available to Mexico, must indeed have been significant.

* * *

And that leaves the British dominions and India unaccounted, and also one other navy that was not minor in terms of national standing—but the Soviet Navy's record will await the third volume. Table 9.1 summarizes the state of world shipping in 1939.

BRITISH, IMPERIAL, AND DOMINION SHIPPING AND FOREIGN SHIPPING IN BRITISH SERVICE IN THE SECOND WORLD WAR

The importance of foreign shipping to British survival in the Second World War may be glimpsed by reference to tables 9.2 and 9.3.

Clearly a certain care needs be exercised in the drawing of conclusions from these tables, and most obviously with reference to the exclusion of ships under 1,600 gross tonnage from calculations, but with reference to oceangoing shipping there can be little doubt that the figures provided in *Statistical Digest of the War* do provide the basis of objective consideration.

Definitive statements are difficult to make, but prior to 1939 between a quarter and a third of British imports were carried in foreign bottoms, and one can assume that between 10 and 12 percent of shipping would have been unavailable for service at any given time, being in dockyard undergoing refit or repair or awaiting sale and disposal. Therefore a goodly percentage of the total amount of shipping available to Britain could be expected to have been non-British, but the manner in which the figures are given in *Statistical Digest of the War* is interesting in one respect. The foreign element of shipping is divided into three, and two are included within the "British" total; this does have the result of writing down the "foreign tonnage." For example, the peak of foreign tanker employment was 30 September 1941, when under time-charter to Britain were tankers that in numbers and tonnage were equivalent to half of what Britain had available on 3 September 1939, but when requisitioned foreign shipping is added to the scales the total comes to more than half, and this at a time when the British oiler fleet had been reduced by a quarter since the outbreak of war. When figures are stripped and reduced to British national and foreign ships and dominion shipping is discounted, the foreign tankers accounted for 38.73 percent of the

Table 9.1. World Shipping in 1939

A. THE MERCHANT MARINES OF GREATER THAN 100,000 GROSS REGISTERED TONS:

	Non-tankers	Tankers	Overall total
Britain	2,520: 14,352,000	445: 3,172,000	2,965: 17,524,000
Canada	47: 233,000	12: 96,000	59: 307,000
Other Dominions	170: 667,000	9: 69,000	179: 937,000
British Empire	111: 373,000	4: 30,000	115: 520,000
United States	1,020: 5,670,000	389: 2,836,000	1,409: 8,506,000
Japan	1,007: 4,600,000	47: 430,000	1,054: 5,030,000
Norway	548: 2,100,000	268: 2,109,000	816: 4,209,000
Germany	676: 3,506,000	37: 256,000	713: 3,762,000
Italy	489: 2,680,000	82: 427,000	571: 3,107,000
Netherlands	370: 2,111,000	107: 540,000	477: 2,651,000
France	454: 2,313,000	48: 326,000	502: 2,639,000
Greece	383: 1,638,000	6: 25,000	389: 1,663,000
Soviet Union	277: 927,000	22: 121,000	299: 1,048,000
Sweden	240: 882,000	19: 158,000	259: 1,040,000
Denmark	226: 760,000	13: 106,000	239: 966,000
Spain	198: 752,000	16: 86,000	214: 838,000
Panama	60: 228,000	53: 471,000	113: 699,000
Finland	158: 428,000	1: 6,000	159: 434,000
Brazil	107: 398,000	2: 7,000	109: 405,000
Yugoslavia	86: 365,000	1: 3,000	87: 368,000
Belgium	61: 295,000	9: 67,000	70: 362,000
Argentina	18: 57,000	23: 136,000	41: 193,000
Portugal	38: 175,000	2: 3,000	40: 178,000
Latvia	57: 169,000	- -	57: 169,000
Chile	47: 156,000	- -	47: 156,000
Turkey	47: 147,000	1: 4,000	48: 151,000
China	58: 145,000	- -	58: 145,000
Estonia	44: 103,000	- -	44: 103,000
Poland	22: 102,000	- -	22: 102,000
World total	9,310: 45,413,000	1,622: 11,390,000	10,932: 56,803,000

B. THE BALANCE OF NUMBERS AT SEA:

	Non-tankers	Tankers	Overall total
The European Axis countries*	1,356: 6,742,000	123: 704,000	1,479: 7,446,000
Japan	1,007: 4,600,000	47: 430,000	1,054: 5,030,000
Allied & neutral countries	6,947: 34,071,000	1,452: 10,256,000	8,399: 44,327,000

* Bulgaria, Finland, Germany, Hungary, Italy, and Romania.

Note: The source of these figures is C. B. A. Behrens, *Merchant Shipping and the Demands of War*, p. 23, appendix 3, "Statement of World Tonnage 1939 by Flag Steam and Motor Vessels of 1,600 Tons and Over." The figures were calculated on the basis of the *Lloyd's Register*, and the 1,600-ton limit thus excludes many lake and riverine ships, fishing vessels of all description, and miscellaneous craft such as ferries, pilot vessels, and tugs, as well as tramps and local shipping. The figures therefore have to be afforded a certain tolerance but may be regarded as generally accurate, most obviously in indicative terms: E&OE.

For purposes of comparison, Michael Ellis, *The World War II Data Book*, p. 249, table 50, "Size of the Merchant Fleets of the Major Belligerent Nations and Total World Shipping 1939," lists thirteen entries and one "Whole World" total:

Belgium	200 ships of	408,014 tons
Commonwealth	2,255 ships of	3,110,791 tons
Denmark	705 ships of	1,174,944 tons
France	1,231 ships of	2,933,933 tons
Germany	2,459 ships of	4,482,662 tons
Greece	607 ships of	1,780,666 tons
Italy	1,227 ships of	3,424,804 tons
Japan	1,609 ships of	5,996,607 tons
Netherlands	1,523 ships of	2,969,578 tons
Norway	1,987 ships of	4,833,813 tons
United Kingdom	6,722 ships of	17,891,134 tons
United States	2,347 ships of	8,909,892 tons
Soviet Union	n.a.	n.a.
Whole world	29,763 ships of	68,509,432 tons

The displacement figures must represent GRT; Japanese figures are given as per December 1941 and American figures represent seagoing ships only, i.e., not Great Lakes and riverine shipping.

Table 9.2. The Merchant Shipping Available to Britain in the Second World War

		British Dominions Ships GRT	Britain/British empire Ships GRT	Foreign ships single-voyage charter Ships GRT	Foreign ships requisitioned Ships GRT	Total British tonnage Ships GRT	Foreign ships time-charter Ships GRT	Total shipping available to Britain Ships GRT
1939:								
3 September	non-tankers	217: 900,000	2,303: 13,452,000	- -	- -	2,520: 14,352,000	- -	2,520: 14,352,000
	tankers	21: 165,000	424: 3,007,000	- -	- -	445: 3,172,000	34: 260,000	479: 3,432,000
31 December	non-tankers	245: 957,000	2,257: 13,181,000	1: 5,000	- -	2,503: 14,143,000	21: 121,000	2,524: 14,264,000
	tankers	24: 169,000	425: 3,079,000	- -	- -	449: 3,248,000	34: 260,000	483: 3,508,000
1940:								
31 March	non-tankers	243: 957,000	2,250: 13,263,000	5: 25,000	- -	2,498: 14,242,000	55: 242,000	2,553: 14,484,000
	tankers	25: 171,000	428: 3,021,000	- -	- -	453: 3,192,000	69: 524,000	522: 3,716,000
30 June	non-tankers	291: 1,075,000	2,242: 13,235,000	310: 51,000	54: 198,000	2,597: 14,559,000	309: 1,367,000	2,906: 15,926,000
	tankers	28: 198,000	419: 2,937,000	- -	5: 42,000	452: 3,177,000	177: 1,374,000	629: 4,551,000
30 September	non-tankers	305: 1,124,000	2,170: 12,779,000	7: 34,000	129: 575,000	2,611: 14,512,000	526: 2,398,000	3,137: 16,910,000
	tankers	30: 202,000	399: 2,778,000	- -	13: 98,000	442: 3,078,000	178: 1,385,000	620: 4,463,000
31 December	non-tankers	298: 1,103,000	2,122: 12,425,000	7: 35,000	129: 573,000	2,556: 14,136,000	509: 2,371,000	3,065: 16,507,000
	tankers	31: 203,000	392: 2,727,000	- -	12: 88,000	435: 3,018,000	172: 1,329,000	607: 4,347,000
1941:								
31 March	non-tankers	296: 1,100,000	2,059: 12,093,000	12: 66,000	144: 641,000	2,511: 13,900,000	520: 2,437,000	3,031: 16,337,000
	tankers	30: 201,000	379: 2,615,000	- -	15: 112,000	424: 2,928,000	225: 1,618,000	649: 4,546,000
30 June	non-tankers	296: 1,076,000	1,926: 11,414,000	17: 99,000	143: 634,000	2,382: 13,223,000	561: 2,557,000	2,943: 15,780,000

	tankers	28: 179,000	367: 2,530,000	- -	13: 93,000	408: 2,802,000	216: 1,549,000	624: 4,351,000
30 September	non-tankers	298: 1,090,000	1,898: 11,355,000	20: 112,000	142: 664,000	2,358: 13,221,000	592: 2,704,000	2,950: 15,925,000
	tankers	28: 180,000	386: 2,671,000	- -	13: 93,000	427: 2,944,000	231: 1,683,000	658: 4,627,000
31 December	non-tankers	306: 1,094,000	1,886: 11,400,000	25: 148,000	143: 687,000	2,360: 13,329,000	602: 2,754,000	2,962: 16,083,000
	tankers	28: 180,000	387: 2,688,000	- -	12: 87,000	427: 2,955,000	227: 1,655,000	654: 4,610,000
1942:								
31 March	non-tankers	299: 1,046,000	1,810: 11,114,000	30: 175,000	143: 682,000	2,282: 13,017,000	619: 2,812,000	2,901: 15,829,000
	tankers	25: 147,000	362: 2,528,000	- -	11: 80,000	398: 2,755,000	209: 1,536,000	607: 4,291,000
30 June	non-tankers	296: 1,030,000	1,739: 10,766,000	39: 245,000	140: 668,000	2,214: 12,709,000	609: 2,851,000	2,823: 15,560,000
	tankers	23: 122,000	341: 2,383,000	- -	11: 80,000	375: 2,585,000	200: 1,478,000	575: 4,063,000
30 September	non-tankers	290: 1,006,000	1,681: 10,387,000	55: 351,000	135: 648,000	2,161: 12,392,000	584: 2,655,000	2,745: 15,047,000
	tankers	24: 123,000	334: 2,329,000	- -	11: 80,000	369: 2,532,000	179: 1,377,000	548: 3,909,000
31 December	non-tankers	289: 999,000	1,569: 9,686,000	87: 581,000	120: 556,000	2,065: 11,822,000	542: 2,477,000	2,607: 14,299,000
	tankers	24: 123,000	327: 2,296,000	- -	9: 67,000	360: 2,486,000	175: 1,337,000	535: 3,823,000
1943:								
31 March	non-tankers	273: 958,000	1,529: 9,450,000	115: 742,000	117: 535,000	2,034: 11,685,000	524: 2,427,000	2,558: 14,112,000
	tankers	23: 117,000	321: 2,251,000	- -	9: 68,000	353: 2,436,000	164: 1,244,000	517: 3,680,000
30 June	non-tankers	298: 1,170,000	1,472: 9,103,000	167: 1,002,000	115: 529,000	2,052: 11,804,000	518: 2,403,000	2,570: 14,207,000
	tankers	23: 117,000	320: 2,244,000	- -	9: 68,000	352: 2,429,000	161: 1,222,000	513: 3,651,000
30 September	non-tankers	324: 1,349,000	1,495: 9,299,000	182: 1,067,000	117: 534,000	2,118: 12,249,000	514: 2,382,000	2,632: 14,631,000
	tankers	23: 117,000	323: 2,268,000	- -	9: 68,000	355: 2,453,000	152: 1,141,000	507: 3,594,000
31 December	non-tankers	362: 1,678,000	1,493: 9,323,000	234: 1,436,000	115: 525,000	2,204: 12,962,000	500: 2,310,000	2,704: 15,272,000
	tankers	24: 140,000	330: 2,336,000	- -	9: 68,000	363: 2,544,000	149: 1,123,000	512: 3,667,000

		British Dominions		Britain/British empire		Foreign ships single-voyage charter		Foreign ships requisitioned		Total British tonnage		Foreign ships time-charter		Total shipping available to Britain	
		Ships	GRT	Ships	GRT	Ships	GRT	Ships	GRT	Ships	GRT	Ships	GRT	Ships	GRT
1944:															
31 March	non-tankers	374:	1,766,000	1,501:	9,395,000	282:	1,779,000	115:	538,000	2,272:	13,478,000	499:	2,299,000	2,771:	15,777,000
	tankers	33:	195,000	334:	2,369,000	-	-	9:	68,000	376:	2,632,000	148:	1,119,000	524:	3,751,000
30 June	non-tankers	403:	1,962,000	1,509:	9,487,000	326:	2,073,000	113:	529,000	2,351:	14,051,000	544:	2,631,000	2,895:	16,682,000
	tankers	34:	204,000	336:	2,386,000	-	-	11:	79,000	381:	2,669,000	148:	1,119,000	529:	3,788,000
30 September	non-tankers	428:	2,134,000	1,492:	9,402,000	326:	2,057,000	108:	504,000	2,354:	14,097,000	537:	2,607,000	2,891:	16,704,000
	tankers	37:	197,000	339:	2,415,000	-	-	9:	66,000	385:	2,678,000	148:	1,120,000	533:	3,798,000
31 December	non-tankers	439:	2,267,000	1,508:	9,542,000	325:	2,035,000	103:	486,000	2,375:	14,330,000	532:	2,575,000	2,907:	16,905,000
	tankers	37:	197,000	345:	2,463,000	-	-	8:	60,000	390:	2,720,000	146:	1,101,000	536:	3,821,000
1945:															
31 March	non-tankers	449:	2,337,000	1,506:	9,565,000	321:	2,011,000	99:	474,000	2,375:	14,387,000	526:	2,552,000	2,901:	16,939,000
	tankers	37:	197,000	344:	2,445,000	-	-	9:	68,000	390:	2,710,000	144:	1,085,000	534:	3,795,000
30 June	non-tankers	456:	2,365,000	1,537:	9,746,000	324:	2,017,000	89:	404,000	2,406:	14,532,000	492:	2,375,000	2,898:	16,907,000
	tankers	37:	197,000	352:	2,507,000	-	-	8:	58,000	397:	2,762,000	126:	941,000	523:	3,703,000
30 September	non-tankers	467:	2,428,000	1,579:	9,907,000	337:	2,075,000	57:	265,000	2,440:	14,675,000	333:	1,599,000	2,773:	16,274,000
	tankers	36:	196,000	363:	2,594,000	3:	12,000	5:	39,000	407:	2,836,000	47:	340,000	454:	3,176,000

Table 9.3. The Merchant Shipping Available to Britain during the Second World War Expressed in Relative Terms Reference 3 September 1939

		British dominions	Britain/British empire	Foreign ships single-voyage charter	Foreign ships requisitioned	Total British tonnage	Foreign ships time-charter	Total shipping available to Britain
1939:								
3 September	non-tankers	8.61: 6.27	91.39: 93.73	- -	- -	100.00: 100.00	- -	100.00: 100.00
	tankers	4.38: 4.81	88.52: 87.62	- -	- -	92.90: 92.42	7.10: 7.58	100.00: 100.00
31 December	non-tankers	9.72: 6.67	89.56: 91.84	0.04: 0.03	- -	99.33: 98.54	0.83: 0.84	100.16: 99.39
	tankers	5.01: 4.92	88.72: 89.71	- -	- -	93.73: 94.64	7.10: 7.57	100.84: 102.21
1940:								
31 March	non-tankers	9.64: 6.67	89.29: 92.41	0.20: 0.17	- -	99.13: 99.25	2.18: 1.67	101.31: 100.92
	tankers	5.22: 4.98	89.35: 88.02	- -	- -	94.57: 93.01	14.41: 15.26	108.98: 108.28
30 June	non-tankers	11.55: 7.49	88.97: 92.22	0.40: 0.36	2.14: 1.38	103.06: 101.44	12.26: 9.52	115.32: 110.97
	tankers	5.85: 5.77	87.47: 85.58	- -	1.04 1.22	94.36 92.57	36.95 40.03	131.32: 132.60
30 September	non-tankers	12.10: 7.83	86.11: 89.04	0.28: 0.23	5.12: 4.01	103.61: 101.11	20.87: 16.71	124.48: 117.82
	tankers	6.26: 5.89	83.30: 80.94	- -	2.71 2.86	92.28 89.69	37.16 40.36	129.44: 130.04
31 December	non-tankers	11.83: 7.69	84.21: 86.57	0.28: 0.24	5.12: 3.99	101.43: 98.49	20.20: 16.52	121.62: 115.02
	tankers	6.47: 5.91	81.84: 79.46	- -	2.51: 2.56	90.81: 87.94	35.91 38.72	126.72: 126.66
1941:								
31 March	non-tankers	11.74: 7.66	81.71: 84.26	0.48: 0.46	5.71: 4.47	99.64: 96.86	20.63: 16.98	120.28: 113.83
	tankers	6.26 5.86	79.12: 76.19	- -	3.13 3.26	88.52 85.31	46.97: 47.14	135.49: 132.46
30 June	non-tankers	11.75: 7.49	76.43: 79.53	0.67: 0.69	5.67: 4.42	94.52: 92.13	22.26: 17.82	116.79: 109.95
	tankers	5.85 5.22	76.62 73.72	- -	2.71: 2.71	85.18: 81.64	45.09: 45.13	130.27: 126.78

		British dominions	Britain/British empire	Foreign ships single-voyage charter	Foreign ships requisitioned	Total British tonnage	Foreign ships time-charter	Total shipping available to Britain
30 September	non-tankers	11.83: 7.59	75.32: 79.12	0.79: 0.78	5.63: 4.63	93.57: 92.12	23.49: 18.84	117.06: 110.96
	tankers	5.85: 5.24	80.58: 77.83	- -	2.71: 2.71	89.14: 85.78	48.23: 49.04	137.37: 134.82
31 December	non-tankers	12.41: 7.62	74.84: 79.43	0.99: 1.03	5.67: 4.79	93.65: 92.87	23.89: 19.19	117.54: 112.06
	tankers	5.85: 5.24	80.79: 78.32	- -	2.71: 2.53	89.14: 86.10	47.39: 48.22	136.53: 134.32
1942:								
31 March	non-tankers	11.87: 7.29	71.83: 77.43	1.19: 1.22	5.67: 4.75	90.56: 90.70	24.56: 19.59	115.12: 110.29
	tankers	5.22: 4.28	75.57: 73.66	- -	2.30: 2.33	83.09: 80.27	43.63: 44.75	126.72: 125.03
30 June	non-tankers	11.75: 7.18	69.01: 75.01	1.55: 1.71	5.56: 4.65	87.86: 88.55	24.17: 19.86	112.02: 108.42
	tankers	4.80: 3.55	71.19: 69.43	- -	2.30: 2.33	78.29: 75.32	41.75: 43.07	120.04: 118.39
30 September	non-tankers	11.51: 7.01	66.71: 72.37	2.18: 2.45	5.36: 4.52	85.75: 86.34	23.17: 18.50	108.93: 104.84
	tankers	5.01: 3.58	69.73: 67.86	- -	2.30: 2.33	77.04: 73.78	37.37: 40.12	114.41: 113.90
31 December	non-tankers	11.47: 6.96	62.26: 67.49	3.45: 4.05	4.76: 3.87	81.94: 82.37	21.51: 17.26	103.45: 99.63
	tankers	5.01: 3.58	68.27: 66.90	- -	1.88: 1.95	75.16: 72.44	36.53: 38.96	111.69: 111.39
1943:								
31 March	non-tankers	10.83: 6.68	60.67: 65.84	4.56: 5.17	4.64: 3.73	80.71: 81.42	20.79: 16.91	101.51: 98.33
	tankers	4.80: 3.41	67.01: 65.59	- -	1.88: 1.98	73.69: 70.97	34.24: 36.25	107.93: 107.23
30 June	non-tankers	11.83: 8.15	58.41: 63.43	6.63: 6.98	4.56: 3.69	81.43: 82.25	20.56: 16.74	101.98: 98.99
	tankers	4.80: 3.41	66.80: 65.38	- -	1.88: 1.98	73.49: 70.78	33.61: 35.61	107.10: 106.38
30 September	non-tankers	12.86: 9.40	59.33: 64.79	7.22: 7.43	4.64: 3.72	84.05: 85.35	20.40: 16.60	104.44: 101.94
	tankers	4.80: 3.41	67.43: 66.08	- -	1.88: 1.98	74.11: 71.47	31.73: 32.25	105.85: 104.72
31 December	non-tankers	14.37: 11.69	59.25: 64.96	9.29: 10.01	4.56: 3.66	87.46: 90.31	19.84: 16.10	107.30: 106.41
	tankers	5.01: 4.08	68.90: 68.07	- -	1.88: 1.98	75.78: 74.13	31.11: 32.72	106.89: 106.85

1944:								
31 March	non-tankers	14.84: 12.30	59.56: 65.46	11.19: 12.40	4.56: 3.75	90.16: 93.91	19.80: 16.02	109.96: 109.93
	tankers	6.89: 5.68	69.73: 69.03	- -	1.88: 1.98	78.50: 76.69	30.90: 32.60	109.39: 109.29
30 June	non-tankers	15.99: 13.67	59.88: 66.10	12.94: 14.44	4.48: 3.69	93.29: 97.90	21.59: 18.33	114.88: 116.23
	tankers	7.10: 5.94	70.15: 69.52	- -	2.30: 2.30	79.54: 77.77	30.90: 32.60	110.44: 110.37
30 September	non-tankers	16.98: 14.87	59.21: 65.51	12.94: 14.33	4.29: 3.51	93.41: 98.22	21.31: 18.16	114.72: 116.39
	tankers	7.72: 5.74	70.77: 71.77	- -	1.88: 1.75	80.38: 78.03	30.90: 32.63	111.27: 110.66
31 December	non-tankers	17.42: 15.80	59.84: 66.49	12.90: 14.18	4.09: 3.39	94.25: 99.85	21.11: 17.94	115.36: 117.79
	tankers	7.72: 5.74	72.03: 71.77	- -	1.67: 1.75	81.42: 79.25	30.48: 32.08	111.90: 111.33
1945:								
31 March	non-tankers	17.82: 16.28	59.76: 66.65	12.74: 14.01	3.93: 3.30	94.25: 100.24	20.87: 17.78	115.12: 118.03
	tankers	7.72: 5.74	71.82: 71.24	- -	1.88: 1.98	81.42: 78.96	30.06: 31.61	111.48: 110.58
30 June	non-tankers	18.10: 16.48	60.99: 67.91	12.86: 14.05	3.53: 2.81	95.48: 101.25	19.52: 16.55	115.00: 117.80
	tankers	7.72: 5.74	73.49: 73.05	- -	1.67: 1.69	82.88: 80.48	26.30: 27.42	109.19: 107.90
30 September	non-tankers	18.53: 18.53	62.66: 69.03	13.37: 14.46	2.26: 1.85	96.83: 102.25	13.21: 11.14	110.04: 113.39
	tankers	7.52: 5.71	75.78: 75.58	0.63 0.35	1.04: 1.14	84.97: 82.63	9.81: 9.91	94.78: 92.54

Source: W. K. Hancock, ed., *History of the Second World War: United Kingdom Civil Series: Statistical Digest of the War*, p. 173, table 151, "Merchant Shipping under British Control (i) Vessels of 1,600 Gross Tons and Over: Number," and p. 174, table 152, "Merchant Shipping under British Control (i) Vessels of 1,600 Gross Tons and Over: Gross Tonnage."

In a footnote it is stated, "For the earlier months of the war the information about foreign flag vessels on time-charter is incomplete," so clearly a certain caution needs be exercised in the use of these figures. Moreover, the 1,600-ton limit must exclude many fishing vessels of all descriptions, and miscellaneous craft such as ferries, pilot vessels, and tugs, as well as tramps and local shipping. The figures therefore have to be afforded a certain tolerance but may be regarded as generally accurate, most obviously in indicative terms: E&OE.

The second table represents the figures given in the first table in percentage terms, each of the four figures under the label "Total shipping available to Britain" on 3 September 1939 being given the base of 100: the relative figures have been corrected to two decimal places.

number and 39.94 percent of tonnage available to Britain as the war entered its third year. In terms of dry-cargo merchantmen and other ships, the "foreign contribution" was of similar order. Between September 1940 and September 1943 the number of foreign ships under time-charter was always between 20 and 25 percent of the British-only total at the outbreak of war, and in terms of tonnage after September 1940 was always about one-sixth of the British September 1939 figure. But crucially important though this contribution was, when the foreign ships requisitioned and under single-voyage charter are placed alongside those on time-charter, the totals are perhaps surprising, not least in terms of time. All types of foreign ships contributed a total number that was equivalent to 39.01 percent and by tonnage 36.46 percent of the British September 1939 figures, and did so on 30 June 1944, by which time the number of ships under single-voyage charter had assumed significant proportions and presumably on two counts: the number of American-built ships that were then available and the fact that British chartering at this time was underwritten by the United States with payment in dollars rather than sterling.

Perhaps no less significant is the fact that with reference to the British dominions, ship numbers more than doubled and tonnage almost tripled in the course of the war. If the real increases came in and after 1943 and were not really in place in the years 1940–1942, which were the years of weakness and need, the fact remains that the increases did manifest themselves and quite clearly eased British burdens. By definition some, perhaps most, of these increases of numbers and tonnage were not directly involved with Britain and the North Atlantic, but when such matters as Indian famine relief are considered with reference to Australian grain and shipment, the easing of British obligation was not small. It is worth noting that this particular episode, in 1943–1944, came at a time when in terms of British shipping and tonnage national fortunes were at their nadir; between 30 June 1943 and 31 March 1945 shipping numbers were always less than three-fifths of what had been available at the outbreak of war, while the tonnage figures, very slightly better, were consistently around the two-thirds figure. What the British figures do not reveal, however, is the division of shipping and tonnage between British and the overseas territories, most obviously India, but overall the real significance lies in the weakening of Britain in each successive year between 1939 and 1943. In terms of numbers of ships—both tankers and non-tankers together—but not tonnages, the first year of war, between 3 September 1939 and 30 September 1940, saw a reduction of 5.79 percent, the year between 30 September 1940 and 30 September 1941 a reduction of 11.09 percent, the year between 30 September 1941 and 30 September 1942 a reduction of 11.78 percent, and the year between 30 September 1942 and 30 September 1943 a reduction of 9.78 percent, the overall result being that on the latter date the total number of British and British empire ships, both tankers and non-tankers, was exactly two-thirds of the number that had been on the 3 September 1939 list—1,818 compared to 2,727.

TABLE 9.4. ANNUAL OUTPUT OF SHIPYARDS OF MAJOR POWERS, 1939–1945

	Britain	British Commonwealth	United States	Japan	Italy
1939	629,705	36,142	376,419	320,466	119,757
1940	842,910	18,886	528,697	293,612	35,299
1941	1,185,894	90,595	1,031,974	210,373	96,999
1942	1,270,714	720,172	5,479,766	260,059	153,656
1943	1,136,804	1,002,850	11,448,360	769,085	63,895
1944	919,357	692,405	9,288,156	1,699,203	-
1945	393,515	141,893	5,839,858	599,563	-
Total	6,378,899	2,702,943	33,993,230	4,152,361	469,606

Source: Michael Ellis, *The World War II Database*, p. 280, table 96, "Annual Allied and Axis Production of Merchant Shipping 1939–1945 (Gross Tons)."

And, of course, these reductions came on top of new building, but that is another story.

Even admitting that every source that might be consulted will give different figures, these no doubt possess indicative accuracy, suffice it to note three matters. First, and with reference to the United States, the 1942 and 1943 output was greater than the size of the British merchant fleet in 1939, and it bears repeating that in 1943 and again in 1944 the United States commissioned into service with the U.S. Navy a tonnage of warships greater than that of the Imperial Japanese Navy on 6 December 1941. Second, the British output seems surprisingly low given British ship-building status, most obviously in the first three years of war: very clearly, the output of 1940 and 1941 in no way provided a measure of insurance against defeat. Third, the Japanese figures are interesting in terms of output in 1944 that was considerably greater than Britain at peak of production, though the Japanese figures between 1939 and 1942 point clearly in the direction of Japan's insoluble problems in that it could not build merchantmen and warships at one and the same time.

Finally, with reference to Japanese output in 1941, the sum of its efforts was less than the average output of American yards in any single week of 1943; by the same token, the outputs of the British Commonwealth yards in 1939 and Italian yards in 1940 were only slightly greater than the average output of American yards on any single day of 1943.

* * *

It is fitting that this short piece should end with a statement of the position and losses of these lesser maritime powers, not least because the situation of such countries as Norway and the Netherlands was much more difficult than might appear, prima facie, to a British or American observer.

Not by choice Denmark and Norway and the Netherlands and Belgium found themselves in Allied ranks as a result of German aggression and, as a result of the conquest of the homelands, were committed to liberation and therefore obliged to work with Britain after April–June 1940. In the course of the campaigns that had resulted in the conquest of these four countries, the Germans captured about a quarter of their dry-cargo merchantmen,[2] a state of affairs that presented what survived with a veritable option of difficulties. The Belgian government, despite the monarch remaining in Brussels, established itself in Britain and placed all remaining Belgian shipping under British jurisdiction and control. The Dutch and Norwegian heads of state and governments likewise took up residence in Britain, but their positions proved very different from Belgium's; indeed, they differed from one another: the Dutch possessed an empire in southeast Asia and needed shipping to maintain it, but the Norwegians were not so fortunately placed. The merchant marines of these two countries, prior to April–May 1940, were heavily involved in trade east of Suez, specifically between British dominions and possessions, and with the United States. With the conquest of the homelands, for the Dutch and Norwegian governments the merchant navies alone provided identity and standing with allies; while this meant that the Dutch and Norwegian authorities sought to preserve their merchant marines as proof of national worth, there was one basic problem. The Dutch and Norwegians saw their marines as the means of earning the money that alone would pay their way in the war in which they found themselves, not least in meeting interest payment on national debts, and their merchant fleet would be the means of ensuring relief once the homelands were liberated. To such ends independent charter, at vastly inflated freight rates, presented an obvious enticement, very different indeed from the terms enforced by Britain. This situation was exacerbated by the bankruptcy of Britain by spring 1941, which meant that as the war lengthened there was no point in working for sterling that would be worthless in the post-war world. Moreover, the losses that were incurred in 1940 and 1941 served to compound problems, for obvious reason: Britain could not afford losses, but the defeated countries, dealing with their last remaining assets, could afford losses even less.In addition, ships working in American waters or the East Indies necessarily saw things in very different ways than governments and owners in Britain, and underlying these matters was the constancy of the German threat to owners and families in the home countries.

The British position in 1940 was that the ships of the conquered nations should be available for charter, a seemingly reasonable position but one fraught with difficulty. Not least was the question of which freight rates should be applied and how to ensure equality of treatment between the different merchant services and, crucially, between the different merchant services and that of

Britain.[3] These difficulties were compounded by the position of Denmark and France on this particular score. Because legal governments remained in these two countries, the British requisitioned their ships, and their crews in effect became British at the expense of their own national identity. In large measure, this British action was prompted by the calculation that if Danish and French ships were left with their own flags it could so happen that in neutral ports, and most obviously in the United States, legal action could be initiated, with the result that ships were removed from Allied/British ranks and possibly assigned to Germany with obvious implications. But the British arrangement, however modest and reasonable, presented an obvious problem: the Danish and French were paid at British rates, that is, less than the rates afforded the Dutch and Norwegians, and the resultant resentment was very real.

The British acquired a little over 500,000 tons of Norwegian dry-cargo merchantmen in May 1940 and another 285,000 tons the following month,[4] and between June 1940 and the end of the year some 850,000 tons of Dutch shipping of similar ilk. While these amounts were roughly half of what shipping remained to these two countries—the result being that the other half could work the more lucrative lines—this amount of shipping was more than a little useful at this precarious time.

The importance of the lesser powers and their shipping was very real to Britain in 1940, for two reasons seldom afforded much consideration. The obvious contribution, in terms of balance against the number of ships that were lost, was very important indeed, but the arrival of ships of Belgian, Danish, Dutch, French, and Norwegian origin to the British fold in summer of 1940 came at a time when unprecedented problems of distance manifested themselves. The Italian entry into the war meant that the 3,000 miles between home ports and Suez suddenly quadrupled, while the 6,000 miles to Bombay almost doubled; the closing of the English Channel to shipping meant that the time of passage across the North Atlantic to London was increased by eleven days, almost half—the time for return passage between west coast ports of arrival and London via northern Scotland and the east coast. If this seems of dubious relevance in light of today's shipping patterns, it bears recall that through the inter-war period London was the biggest port in Britain, and the attempt to reduce the volume of shipping using east coast ports during the first two years of war provoked one major problem and in any case had to be rescinded. The west coast ports were obviously limited in terms of handling capacity, but no less important was that the diversion of raw materials that normally would have gone to London and east coast ports to these west coast ports necessarily placed unprecedented strain on the rail system. The German bombing campaign directed against west coast ports had the effect of forcing shipping to use London and other east coast ports to the extent that whereas by spring 1941 east coast imports amounted to about one-sixth of all national imports, in the wake of the German effort this figure rose to over a quarter. The end

Table 9.5. Foreign Shipping under British Control during the Second World War

	In service on 30 April 1940	Lost between 3 September 1939 and 30 April 1940	In service in December 1941	Lost between 30 April 1940 & December 1941	In service in December 1942	Lost in 1942	
	ships GRT	ships GRT	ships GRT	ships GRT	ships GRT	ships GRT	Status
Belgium	- -	- -	34: 158,000	12: 55,000	28: 137,000	12: 59,000	Time-charter
China	1: 2,000	- -	1: 2,000	1: 2,000	- -	- -	Time-charter
Denmark	4: 11,000	- -	43: 162,000	15: 45,000	30: 108,000	13: 54,000	Captured prizes
Egypt	12: 41,000	- -	2: 11,000	5: 22,000	3: 19,000	2: 5,000	Time-charter
Estonia	- -	- -	3: 9,000	- -	3: 9,000	- -	Requisitioned
Finland	- -	- -	4: 13,000	1: 3,000	4: 11,000	3: 10,000	Captured prizes
France	- -	- -	- -	- -	- -	- -	Time-charter
	- -	- -	13: 84,000	1: 3,000	10: 66,000	3: 18,000	Captured prizes
	1: 3,000	- -	46: 333,000	19 89,000	38: 282,000	10: 62,000	Requisitioned
Germany	11: 45,000	- -	10: 65,000	10: 48,000	12: 80,000	2: 11,000	Captured prizes
Greece	36: 160,000	1: 5,000	156: 692,000	58: 252,000	127: 559,000	51: 237,000	Time-charter
Hungary	2: 6,000	- -	- -	2: 6,000	- -	- -	Time-charter
Italy	- -	- -	- -	- -	- -	- -	Time-charter
	- -	- -	18: 97,000	11: 66,000	14: 78,000	6: 32,000	Captured prizes
Latvia	- -	- -	2: 5,000	1: 5,000	1: 2,000	1: 3,000	Requisitioned
Netherlands	- -	1: 2,000	147: 928,000	48: 310,000	139: 798,000	48: 292,000	Time-charter
Norway	13: 38,000	- -	180: 650,000	59: 216,000	162: 971,000	40: 154,000	Time-charter
Panama	- -	- -	20: 86,000	2: 8,000	18: 77,000	4: 13,000	Time-charter
	- -	- -	1: 3,000	1: 3,000	2: 7,000	1: 3,000	Requisitioned
	- -	- -	- -	1: 6,000	- -	- -	Purchased
Poland	3 37,000	1: 4,000	13: 58,000	2: 13,000	16: 79,000	- -	Time-charter
Sweden	- -	- -	40: 156,000	23: 89,000	25: 92,000	16: 59,000	Time-charter
UnitedStates	15: 75,000	- -	73: 428,000	29: 165,000	42: 241,000	31: 187,000	Purchased
Yugoslavia	1: 6,000	- -	34: 149,000	10: 42,000	24: 108,000	14: 58,000	Time-charter
TOTAL	99: 424,000	3: 11,000	840: 4,089,000	311: 1,448,000	698: 3,361,000	257: 1,257,000	Overall losses

	In service in December 1943	Losses in 1943	In service in December 1944	Losses in 1944	In service in June 1945	Losses in first half of 1945		Overall wartime losses
	ships GRT	ships GRT	ships GRT	ships GRT	ships GRT	ships GRT	Status	ships GRT
Belgium	28: 142,000	5: 27,000	24: 121,000	3: 19,000	23: 110,000	2: 12,000	Time-charter	34: 172,000
China	- -	- -	- -	- -	- -	- -	Time-charter	1: 2,000
Denmark	30: 94,000	4: 23,000	30: 94,000	1: 2,000	26: 72,000	4: 23,000	Captured prizes	37: 147,000
Egypt	3: 23,000	- -	3: 13,000	2: 14,000	3: 13,000	- -	Time-charter	9: 41,000
Estonia	3: 9,000	- -	2: 6,000	1: 3,000	2: 6,000	- -	Requisitioned	1: 3,000
Finland	4: 11,000	- -	2: 4,000	2: 7,000	2: 4,000	- -	Captured prizes	6: 20,000
France	15: 87,000	6: 22,000	16: 97,000	3: 15,000	14: 87,000	2: 6,000	Time-charter	11: 43,000
	9: 60,000	1: 6,000	7: 50,000	2: 10,000	5: 35,000	2: 15,000	Captured prizes	9: 52,000
	35: 267,000	3: 18,000	20: 178,000	15: 86,000	16: 157,000	4: 21,000	Requisitioned	51: 276,000
Germany	12: 80,000	- -	11: 72,000	1: 8,000	11: 72,000	- -	Captured prizes	13: 67,000
Greece	108: 488,000	24: 106,000	97: 431,000	6: 29,000	95: 419,000	2: 11,000	Time-charter	142: 640,000
Hungary	- -	- -	- -	- -	- -	- -	Time-charter	2: 6,000
Italy	- -	- -	4: 22,000	- -	4: 21,000	- -	Time-charter	- -
	13: 70,000	2: 11,000	9: 43,000	4: 25,000	8: 40,000	1: 6,000	Captured prizes	24: 140,000
Latvia	1: 2,000	- -	1: 2,000	- -	1: 2,000	- -	Requisitioned	2: 8,000
Netherlands	124: 715,000	23: 146,000	157: 993,000	7: 36,000	133: 870,000	1: 2,000	Time-charter	128: 788,000
Norway	143: 535,000	19: 63,000	153: 558,000	9: 40,000	141: 515,000	4: 13,000	Time-charter	131: 486,000
Panama	18: 77,000	- -	17: 76,000	1: 4,000	17: 76,000	2: 5,000	Time-charter	9: 30,000
	2: 7,000	- -	1: 4,000	1: 4,000	1: 4,000	- -	Requisitioned	3: 10,000
	- -	- -	- -	- -	- -	- -	Purchased	1: 6,000
Poland	19: 94,000	- -	18: 91,000	1: 4,000	18: 91,000	- -	Time-charter	4: 21,000
Sweden	21: 75,000	4: 18,000	21: 75,000	- -	21: 75,000	- -	Time-charter	43: 166,000
United States	31: 178,000	11: 63,000	26: 147,000	5: 32,000	26: 147,000	- -	Purchased	76: 447,000
Yugoslavia	21: 95,000	4: 19,000	22: 96,000	3: 14,000	23: 98,000	- -	Time-charter	31: 133,000
TOTAL	640: 3,095,000	106: 522,000	641: 3,175,000	67: 352,000	590: 2,914,000	24: 114,000	overall losses	768: 3,704,000

The figures have been taken from Behrens, Merchant Shipping and the *Demands of War*, pp. 113–118, appendix 15, "Foreign Dry-Cargo Ships 1,600 g.t. and Over under British Control (Other than United States and Canadian Ships Transferred to the British Flag) in Service and Lost at Various Dates."

of the German bombing campaign enabled the British problems to be resolved, but the one question that presents itself is the obvious one: what might have been the consequence had the German bombing campaign been continued through summer 1941 and directed primarily at a very vulnerable London?[5] As it was, in overall terms the cost of time with reference to days lost to shipping and cargo space as a result of the defeats of 1940 and France's departure from the war has been estimated at a minimum of 30 percent—which meant that whereas merchantmen bringing imports into Britain four times in any year before 1939 were reduced to three, with all that that implied in terms of volume of imports, the business of war, and nutrition, public health, and welfare.[6]

The importance of the shipping of the occupied countries to the British cause, and specifically in 1941, is most obviously related to the size and losses of the British merchant marine, but real significance lay in matters that normally command little in the way of historical attention. By 1941 the military demands on shipping were finally in place in terms of troop, ammunition, and stores ships and the establishment of reception facilities overseas on scales that were unprecedented, and this came at a time when the average two-way voyage across the North Atlantic had reached 122 days. A merchantman making perhaps seven or eight knots would ordinarily need about 20 days to cross the North Atlantic, from a British port to New York on a direct line. With war, however, the days lost gathering for convoy, diversion, zig-zagging, and then the demands of loading and unloading cargos meant that as the war entered its third year what had been in peacetime perhaps eight one-way crossings in a year had been reduced to six, and with the delays imposed by such matters as the closing of the English Channel to shipping, the number was less. This meant that by 1942 the amount of British shipping handling British imports was perhaps no more than two-fifths, possibly a third, of what had been thus employed in 1938; as it was British imports in 1942 were little more than one-half of their total in the first year of war, as shown on table 9.6.

What these figures do not reveal is that in 1941 the level of imports, involving as it did an increase of industrial reserves of 1,400,000 tons—which in fact was probably not much more than three weeks' supply to factories—was achieved only at a cost of major reductions of food imports, most obviously fruit and vegetables, but also animal foodstuffs, with the result that in this single year the pig population of Britain fell by 41 percent and poultry by 17 percent. By the end of 1944 British hospital recovery times, that is the time between operations and discharge, had lengthened considerably, and the population was encountering real problems in terms of eyesight and of vitamin deficiency. While the British problems in these matters were really small-change compared to the situation that prevailed in eastern and southeast Europe and in the Netherlands at this time, and while it was the United States in terms of shipping, building, and supplies that ensured that Britain ultimately

Table 9.6. British Import and Consumption Levels, 1939-1945

	Imports	Import level ref. previous year	Consumption human and industrial	Change in level of reserves
Between September 1939 and September 1940	44,200,000	100	43,300,000	+ 900,000
Between September 1940 and September 1941	31,500,000		29,600,000	+ 1,900,000
In calendar year 1941	30,500,000	69.00	29,100,000	+ 1,400,000
In calendar year 1942	22,900,000	51.81	25,350,000	- 2,450,000
In calendar year 1943	26,400,000	59.73	23,600,000	+ 2,800,000
In calendar year 1944	25,100,000	56.79	27,000,000	- 1,900,000

Note: For purposes of comparison, the September 1939–September 1940 figure is taken to be the figure for calendar year 1940.

Source: The source of these figures is Behrens, *Merchant Shipping and the Demands of War*, p. 201, appendix 31, "Net Consumption of Imported Supplies."

Table 9.7. British, Allied, and Neutral Shipping Losses in the Second World War

SUMMARY TABLE

	Losses to all causes other than captured		Vessels captured		Overall losses	
	ships	tonnage	ships	tonnage	ships	tonnage
British shipping	2,952:	11,337,831	383:	446,749	3,335:	11,784,580
Allied shipping	1,882:	8,454,386	279:	743,336	2,161:	9,197,752
Neutral shipping	577:	1,522,431	91:	226,070	668:	1,748,501
Total shipping losses	5,411:	21,314,648	753:	1,416,185	6,164:	22,730,833

was able to survive, the importance in 1940 and 1941 of the various merchant fleets that came the way of Britain in the wake of national defeats cannot be gainsaid: as a very rough rule of thumb the four million tons of foreign shipping working for or under British direction must be a sum equivalent to half the British shipping working British import requirements.

Admittedly not all this foreign shipping would have been employed on routes that made their way eastward and northward across the North Atlantic. Some of these foreign ships must have been working for British overseas possessions at a time when the withdrawal of British shipping had very serious consequences for these possessions —for example Egyptian imports declined by 67.85 percent between 1936–1938 and 1941. But if the British position in 1942 was as desperate as the figures suggest, and one must assume that in that year Britain must have used some four or five weeks of industrial reserves but was nonetheless on short-time working, then one is left to wonder what might have happened had foreign shipping not been available.

By 1943 and 1944 the United States had acquired a volume of shipping that was sufficient to meet not American and not British but Allied needs. While there were some real problems in the workings of allocations in 1944 and 1945, these were the sort of problems that it was nice to have, and most certainly would not have existed in 1944 and 1945 had not the problems of 1940–1942 been overcome. Therein lies the true significance of 840 foreign ships of 4,089,000 tons in 1941 and 698 foreign ships of 3,361,000 tons in 1942 to Britain in those early years.

APPENDIX 9.1.

ALLIED AND NEUTRAL MERCHANT SHIPPING LOSSES IN THE SECOND WORLD WAR

THE FOLLOWING TABLES set out, by period, Allied and neutral merchant shipping losses in the Second World War by country and by cause. Each table sets out overall losses, losses incurred by Allied states, and losses incurred by neutral states. In addition, the losses incurred by individual states are then listed in two groupings, Allied and neutral.

In terms of agencies of destruction, losses are listed under six headings: to submarines, mines, aircraft whether ship-borne or land-based, raiders, warships, and other and unknown causes. With reference to the raiders and warships labels, the raiders represent both warships and auxiliaries operating on the high seas; the warships represent E-boats, motor torpedo boats, and fleet units operating locally, though some returns in the Arctic do present obvious problems of assignation. As a basic rule, returns registered in the course of a short-term sortie as opposed to longer-term cruise fall under the local category, i.e., warships as opposed to raiders.

Losses incurred by the Faeroe Islands and Iceland are included under the Denmark label and are not listed separately even though Iceland, established as a fully sovereign dominion under the Danish crown under the terms of the 1 December 1918 union but separated from Denmark by the events of April 1940, established itself as an independent republic on 17 June 1944. For the purposes of these lists Denmark, the Faeroes, and Iceland are treated as one, namely Denmark, for the full duration of the war. French losses after June 1940, which come under both Allied and neutral categories and on occasion in the same month, are assigned as per the source and with no attempt to subject these figures to personal and subjective analysis; one assumes that the losses registered as Allied after June 1940 were those incurred by the Gaullist F.N.F.L.

In a number of cases countries are listed with losses under both Allied and neutral headings in the same month, for example, Norway in April 1940, Greece in October 1940, and the United States in December 1941. The difference relates to status and losses before and losses after formal declaration of war and entry into Allied ranks. Certain entries, and specifically those listed under the headings of Palestine, Lebanon, and Syria, present obvious problems in terms of their being mandated territories and not independent states, but presumably the losses that were recorded under these headings related to ships and where they originally had been/were registered, contemporaneous status and other matters notwithstanding. Likewise, one assumes that the entries for Estonia and Latvia after June 1940 related to ships that were in British or Allied service in June 1940, when the Baltic states were annexed by the Soviet Union, their national status remaining unchanged as far as documentation was concerned.

* * *

The figures have been taken from—and this is the full title—*Lloyd's War Losses: The Second World War*, vol. 2: *British, Allied and Neutral Merchant Vessels: Statistics—Vessels Listed at Lloyd's as Missing Or Untraced—Vessels Seriously Damaged by War Causes. British, Allied and Neutral Warships and Naval Craft Lost. Vessels Lost or Damaged by Mines or Underwater Explosions since Cessation of Hostilities.* Published by Lloyd's of London Press in 1991, the list appears to be contemporaneous and therefore needs be treated with a certain caution, for obvious reason: while the lists presumably were those with which Lloyd's and the Admiralty were working at the time, obviously question marks must be placed against the overall accuracy of the statistics. The problem here, however, is that every source is different in terms of totals, individual ships, and agencies of destruction, and there is simply no way in which detail may be checked. To cite but one example, the author first used the Naval Historical Branch, then in Earl's Court, in 1968, and worked in the Branch for some sixteen months in 1999–2000, but over more than three decades was never able to ascertain the whereabouts of the statistics and records used by Roskill in the official naval histories; the only advice that was forthcoming was that they were probably in some file in the Public Record Office, but detail was unknown. As it is, Roskill's figures of sinkings in May and September 1941, as presented in the first volume of the official history, pages 617–618, do not tally, and with respect to the Lloyd's list the sum of monthly figures does not accord with the totals that are given on page 1265, and, of course, there are errors with reference to individual months, perhaps the most notable being December 1941, where the number of ships lost by cause is 119, by country 120, while the total given is 121 (p. 1085). Such errors, however, are of minor consequence and fall within the range of reasonable tolerance; given the confusion and difference that always exist when tonnage figures are at the center of examination, the basic point must be the observation of such tolerance with reference of proportionality and relative standing rather than final, irrefutable, accuracy.

* * *

The Lloyd's figures, as per *Lloyd's War Losses*, vol. 2, p. 1265, cite British, Allied, and neutral shipping losses in the Second World War, September 1939–August 1945, as follows:

These Lloyd's figures should be considered in terms of general accuracy and indicative of losses and trends, though quite clearly losses have been unrecorded with reference to one state, the Soviet Union. Obviously because Soviet shipping did not enter into normal commercial practice, the Lloyd's list would seem to have underrecorded

TABLE APPENDIX 9.1.1.

	Losses to all causes other than captured		Vessels captured		Overall losses	
	ships	tonnage	ships	tonnage	ships	tonnage
British shipping	2,952:	11,337,831	383:	446,749	3,335:	11,784,580
Other Allied shipping	1,882:	8,454,386	279:	743,366	2,161:	9,197,752
Total Allied shipping	4,834:	19,792,217	662:	1,190,115	5,496:	20,982,332
Neutral shipping	577:	1,522,431	91:	226,070	668:	1,748,501
Total shipping losses	5,411:	21,314,648	753:	1,416,185	6,164:	22,730,833

Soviet losses: by the least exacting standard, it is difficult to believe that Soviet losses were just forty-four ships of 166,882 tons sunk or lost to all causes other than captures.

What follows are tables that are drawn primarily from the Lloyd's lists but that are the author's own summary, and they are presented here, in this appendix, along with the observation that they should come with the attached E&OE label.

Table Appendix 9.1.2. Allied and Neutral Shipping Losses in the Second World War

	Submarines	Mines	Aircraft	Raiders	Warships	Other and unknown causes	Total Losses	Seized/ captured
Overall shipping:								
1 September 1939–31 March 1940	186: 716,665	147: 454,387	34: 38,353	12: 73,748	- -	10: 2,829	389: 1,285,982	21: 42,763
1 April 1940–30 June 1940	81: 421,704	69: 179,849	94: 343,239	8: 56,965	4: 7,550	68: 90,724	324: 1,100,031	165: 390,383
1 July 1940–31 May 1941	468: 2,540,846	256: 355,878	473: 1,077,570	127: 653,693	40: 84,808	38: 31,660	1402: 4,744,455	53: 220,882
1 June 1941–30 November 1941	196: 883,782	62: 85,219	99: 212,488	8: 41,548	17: 49,205	13: 21,984	395: 1,294,226	18: 48,302
1 December 1941–30 June 1942	586: 3,061,879	80: 192,243	171 605,819	23: 107,133	27: 81,940	260: 208,049	1147: 4,257,063	411: 491,782
1 July 1942–31 May 1943	888: 4,900,833	63: 179,495	90: 388,809	12: 81,043	31: 86,484	20: 41,007	1104: 5,677,671	14: 31,157
1 June 1943–31 May 1944	233: 1,254,223	31 76,097	76: 408,909	2: 15,555	19: 19,058	9: 23,565	370: 1,797,407	7: 17,636
1 June 1944–8 May 1945	117: 605,545	70: 206,047	24: 129,550	- -	12: 27,623	54: 163,216	277: 1,131,981	15: 28,060
Overall losses	2755: 14,385,477	778: 1,729,215	1061: 3,204,737	192: 1,029,685	150: 356,668	472: 583,034	5408: 21,288,816	704: 1,270,965
in % terms	50.94 67.57	14.39 8.12	19.62 15.05	3.55 4.84	2.77 1.68	8.73 2.74		
Allied shipping:								
1 September 1939–31 March 1940	93: 430,932	79: 256,150	25: 32,694	11: 71,830	- -	6: 2,109	214: 793,715	2: 6,385
1 April 1940–30 June 1940	54: 329,972	54: 144,765	82: 292,963	7: 56,814	4: 7,550	65: 82,367	266: 914,431	133: 327,370
1 July 1940–31 May 1941	399: 2,294,886	242: 338,495	457: 1,031,657	122: 624,924	39: 78,681	37: 30,555	1296: 4,399,198	41: 181,650
1 June 1941–30 November 1941	177: 835,932	51: 60,546	93: 199,140	8: 41,548	17: 49,205	9: 14,296	355: 1,200,667	14: 41,123
1 December 1941–30 June 1942	553: 2,919,390	71: 182,470	164: 587,932	23: 107,133	27: 81,940	260: 208,049	1098: 4,086,914	410: 489,822
1 July 1942–31 May 194	837: 4,777,283	41: 129,827	82: 382,310	12: 81,043	29: 82,507	18: 37,356	1019: 5,490,326	13: 29,957
1 June 1943–31 May 1944	216: 1,236,927	23: 70,514	68: 401,493	2: 15,555	15: 17,286	9: 23,565	333: 1,765,340	6: 16,388
1 June 1944–8 May 1945	112: 604,192	56: 197,343	20: 125,320	- -	11: 27,570	51: 161,369	250: 1,115,794	3: 1,523
Allied losses	2441: 13,429,514	617: 1,380,110	991: 3,053,509	185: 998,847	142: 344,739	455: 559,666	4831: 19,766,385	622: 1,094,218
in % terms	45.14 63.08	11.41 6.48	18.32 14.34	3.42 4.69	2.63 1.62	8.41 2.63	89.33 92.85	

Neutral shipping:								
1 September 1939–31 March 1940	93: 285,733	68: 198,237	9: 5,659	1: 1,918	- -	4: 720	175: 492,267	19: 36,378
1 April 1940–30 June 1940	27: 91,732	15: 35,084	12: 50,276	1: 151	- -	3: 8,357	58: 185,600	32: 63,013
1 July 1940–31 May 1941	69: 245,960	14: 17,383	16: 45,913	5: 28,769	1: 6,127	1: 1,105	106: 345,257	12: 39,232
1 June 1941–30 November 1941	19: 47,850	11: 24,673	6: 13,348	- -	- -	4: 7,688	40: 93,559	4: 7,179
1 December 1941–30 June 1942	33: 142,489	9: 9,773	7: 17,887	- -	- -	- -	49: 170,149	1: 1,960
1 July 1942–31 May 1943	51: 123,550	22: 49,668	8: 6,499	- -	2: 3,977	2: 3,651	85: 187,345	1: 1,200
1 June 1943–31 May 1944	17: 17,296	8: 5,583	8: 7,416	- -	4: 1,772	- -	37: 32,067	1: 1,248
1 June 1944–8 May 1945	5: 1,353	14: 8,704	4: 4,230	- -	1: 53	3: 1,847	27: 16,187	12: 26,537
Neutral losses	314: 955,963	161: 349,105	70: 151,228	7: 30,838	8: 11,919	17: 23,368	577: 1,522,431	82: 176,747
in % terms	5.81 4.49	2.98 1.64	1.29 0.71	0.13 0.14	0.15 0.06	0.31 0.11	10.67 7.15	

Shipping Losses by Country

	Submarines	Mines	Aircraft	Raiders	Warships	Other and unknown causes	Total Losses	Seized/ captured
Allied states:								
Belgium	28: 160,082	15: 6,667	17: 56,971	1: 4,984	1: 70	16: 21,436	78: 250,210	2: 960
Brazil	12: 52,338	- -	- -	- -	- -	1: 300	13: 52,638	- -
Britain	1313: 7,458,372	477: 905,118	625: 1,767,168	136: 728,415	104: 226,222	297: 252,536	2952: 11,337,831	383: 446,749
China	1: 7,176	- -	- -	- -	- -	3: 4,086	4: 11,262	13: 22,918
Colombia	1: 39	- -	- -	- -	- -	- -	1: 39	- -
Cuba	4: 10,134	- -	- -	- -	- -	- -	4: 10,134	- -
Denmark	8: 5,563	5: 2,833	8: 1,535	- -	- -	1: 158	22: 10,089	21: 37,622
Dominican Rep.	4: 3,755	- -	- -	- -	- -	- -	4: 3,755	- -
France	28: 130,111	24: 89,232	27: 89,282	1: 2,488	- -	8: 15,818	88: 326,931	19: 52,065
Greece	86: 372,655	10: 30,540	99: 185,793	8: 37,558	- -	13: 15,998	216: 642,544	27: 56,911
Honduras	10: 24,498	- -	- -	- -	- -	- -	10: 24,498	- -
Italy	- -	- -	4: 12,248	- -	- -	1: ?	5: 12,248	1: 4,200
Latvia	6: 23,595	- -	4: 12,248	- -	- -	1: ?	11: 35,843	- -
Lebanon	4: 302	- -	- -	- -	- -	- -	4: 302	- -
Mexico	6: 29,942	- -	- -	- -	- -	- -	6: 29,942	- -
Netherlands	119: 623,616	23: 31,803	56: 282,642	8: 35,862	13: 26,663	53: 102,693	272: 1,103,279	61: 142,347
Nicaragua	3: 4,850	- -	- -	- -	- -	- -	3: 4,850	- -
Norway	242: 1,203,549	19: 56,438	59: 143,632	21: 122,050	17: 56,999	21: 26,080	379: 1,608,748	54: 231,432
Palestine	11: 1,734	- -	- -	- -	- -	- -	1: 1,734	- -
Panama	73: 407,131	4: 16,300	6: 23,117	1: 10,169	- -	3: 9,236	87: 465,953	2: 2,127
Poland	4: 21,972	- -	4: 16,325	- -	1: 1,971	- -	9: 40,268	- -
Soviet Union	20: 84,777	5: 22,931	11: 32,620	- -	2: 4,500	5: 21,086	43: 165,914	11: 41,702
Syria	9: 406	- -	- -	- -	- -	- -	9: 406	- -
United States	437: 2,755,427	32: 212,579	75: 442,176	8: 53,168	4: 28,314	33: 90,239	589: 3,581,903	28: 55,185
Yugoslavia	12: 47,490	3: 5,669	- -	1: 4,153	- -	- -	16: 57,312	- -

Neutral states:								
Argentina	2: 8,289	- -	- -	- -	- -	- -	2: 8,289	- -
Belgium	1: 2,239	4: 10,449	2: ?	- -	- -	- -	7: 12,688	- -
Brazil	17: 70,528	- -	- -	- -	- -	- -	17: 70,528	- -
Chile	1: 1,858	- -	- -	- -	- -	- -	1: 1,858	- -
Colombia	2: 145	- -	- -	- -	- -	- -	2: 145	- -
Cuba	1: ?	- -	- -	- -	- -	- -	1: ?	- -
Denmark	19: 45,082	6: 16,648	1: 1,353	- -	- -	- -	26: 63,083	- -
Egypt	24: 19,787	1: ?	7: 8,247	1: 8,299	- -	1: 90	34: 36,423	- -
Estonia	6: 10,494	2: 3,329	4: 7,807	- -	- -	1: 300	13: 21,930	9: 12,008
Finland	15: -	7: -	4: -	1: 1,817	- -	4: 720	31: -	26: 47,698
France	- -	2: 3,036	- -	- -	1: 6,127	- -	3: 9,163	2: 2,576
Greece	41: 175,173	8: 33,945	6: 32,195	1: 5,867	- -	- -	56: 247,180	11: 44,791
Hungary	1: 4,295	- -	- -	- -	- -	- -	1: 4,295	- -
Italy	2: 9,551	5: 25,009	1: 3,059	- -	- -	- -	8: 37,619	- -
Japan	- -	2: 16,453	- -	- -	- -	- -	2: 16,453	- -
Latvia	1: 4,434	- -	1: 534	- -	- -	1: 3,077	3: 8,045	5: 9,021
Lithuania	- -	1: 1,566	- -	- -	- -	- -	1: 1,566	- -
Netherlands	8: 52,555	11: 31,342	3: 1,350	1: 151	- -	- -	23: 85,398	- -
Norway	24: 60,790	18: 43,352	2: 2,017	1: 1,918	- -	- -	45: 108,077	- -
Panama	12: 46,889	2: 16,947	4: 11,134	- -	- -	2: 1,849	20: 76,819	1: 2,978
Portugal	7: 15,414	1: 665	2: 1,122	- -	- -	- -	10: 17,201	2: 2,448
Spain	16: 41,402	8: 3,940	4: 1,801	- -	- -	1: 3,561	29: 50,704	- -
Sweden	88: 285,237	73: 103,928	27: 61,274	2: 12,786	5: 5,499	6: 9,966	201: 478,690	20: 29,513
Switzerland	- -	1: 1,437	1: 1,788	- -	- -	- -	2: 3,225	- -
Soviet Union	1: 968	- -	- -	- -	- -	- -	1: 968	- -
Turkey	15: 8,602	3: 3,501	1: 2,485	- -	2: 303	1: 3,805	22: 18,696	- -
Uruguay	2 11,070	- -	- -	- -	- -	- -	2: 11,070	- -
United States	4: 23,799	2: 5,883	1: 5,718	- -	- -	- -	7: 35,400	1: 4,963
Venezuela	1: 2,650	- -	- -	- -	- -	- -	1: 2,650	- -
Yugoslavia	3: 14,670	5: 15,821	- -	- -	- -	- -	8: 30,291	5: 19,761

Table Appendix 9.1.3a Part 1. Allied and Neutral Shipping Losses in the Second World War's First Phase: September 1939–March 1940 and the Initial Phase of Balance

		Submarines	Mines	Aircraft	Raiders	Warships	Other and unknown causes	Total Losses	Seized/ captured
Overall losses									
September	1939	41: 153,627	9: 31,131	2: ?	1: 5,051	- -	1 54	54: 189,863	4: 9,710
October	1939	27: 134,807	12: 34,404	- -	6: 29,330	- -	- -	45: 198,541	6: 18,663
November	1939	18: 65,035	30: 121,585	- -	2: 17,403	- -	3: 1,191	53: 205,214	4: 4,694
December	1939	20: 72,679	41: 89,693	9: 2,739	3: 21,964	- -	2: 1,054	75: 188,129	1: 1,886
January	1940	31: 91,539	23: 89,263	13: 26,179	- -	- -	2: 346	69: 207,327	3: 2,966
February	1940	35: 153,431	13: 50,355	5: 2,034	- -	- -	- -	53: 205,820	2: 3,526
March	1940	14: 45,547	19: 37,956	5: 7,401	- -	- -	2: 184	40: 91,088	1: 1,318
Overall losses		186: 716,665	147: 454,387	34: 38,353	12: 73,748	- -	10: 2,829	389: 1,285,982	21: 42,763
in % terms		47.81 55.73	37.79 35.33	8.74 2.98	3.08 5.73	- -	2.57 0.22		
Allied losses									
September	1939	31: 137,084	4: 15,691	- -	1: 5,051	- -	1: 54	37: 157,880	2: 6,385
October	1939	21: 117,131	3: 6,257	- -	5: 27,412	- -	- -	29: 150,800	- -
November	1939	15: 42,547	17: 46,678	- -	2: 17,403	- -	1: 655	35: 107,283	- -
December	1939	8: 33,618	18: 55,031	8: 1,982	3: 21,964	- -	2: 1,054	39: 113,649	- -
January	1940	4: 13,137	13: 70,273	11: 23,693	- -	- -	2: 346	30: 107,449	- -
February	1940	11: 71,884	10: 41,421	4: 1,405	- -	- -	- -	25: 114,710	- -
March	1940	3: 15,531	14: 20,799	2: 5,614	- -	- -	- -	19: 41,944	- -
Allied losses		93: 430,932	79: 256,150	25: 32,694	11: 71,830	- -	6: 2,109	214: 793,715	2: 6,385
in % terms		23.91 33.51	20.31 19.92	6.43 2.54	2.83 5.59	- -	1.54 0.16	55.01 61.72	
Neutral losses									
September	1939	10: 16,543	5: 15,440	2: ?	- -	- -	- -	17: 31,983	2: 3,325
October	1939	6: 17,676	9: 28,147	- -	1: 1,918	- -	- -	16: 47,741	6: 18,663
November	1939	3: 22,488	13: 74,907	- -	- -	- -	2: 536	18: 97,931	4: 4,694
December	1939	12: 39,061	23: 34,662	1: 757	- -	- -	- -	36: 74,480	1: 1,886
January	1940	27: 78,402	10: 18,990	2: 2,486	- -	- -	- -	39: 99,878	3: 2,966
February	1940	24: 81,547	3: 8,934	1: 629	- -	- -	- -	28: 91,110	2: 3,526
March	1940	11: 30,016	5: 17,157	3: 1,787	- -	- -	2: 184	21: 49,144	1: 1,318
Neutral losses		93: 285,733	68: 198,237	9: 5,659	1: 1,918	- -	4: 720	175: 492,267	19: 36,378
in % terms		23.91 22.22	17.48 15.42	2.31 0.44	0.26 0.15	- -	1.03 0.06	44.99 38.28	

	Submarines	Mines	Aircraft	Raiders	Warships	Other and unknown causes	Total Losses	Seized/captured	Ships	Tonnage
Britain	82: 359,440	71: 231,832	24: 32,519	11: 71,830	- -	5: 2,055	193: 697,676	2: 6,385	49.61	54.25
France	10: 57,198	8: 24,318	1: 175	- -	- -	1: 54	20: 81,745	- -	5.14	6.36
Poland	1: 14,294	- -	- -	- -	- -	- -	1: 14,294	- -	0.26	1.11
Belgium	1: 2,239	4: 10,449	2: ?	- -	- -	- -	7: 12,688	- -	1.80	0.99
Denmark	19: 45,082	6: 16,648	1: 1,353	- -	- -	- -	26: 63,083	- -	6.68	4.91
Estonia	2: 1,609	1: 1,421	- -	- -	- -	- -	3: 3,030	2: 2,076	0.77	0.24
Finland	4: 11,279	4: 5,820	1: 1,133	- -	- -	4: 720	13: 18,952	6 7,114	3.34	1.47
Greece	9: 44,374	5 22,581	- -	- -	- -	- -	14: 66,955	2: 8,940	3.60	5.21
Italy	2: 9,551	5: 25,009	- -	- -	- -	- -	7: 34,560	- -	1.80	2.69
Japan	- -	1: 11,930	- -	- -	- -	- -	1: 11,930	- -	0.26	0.93
Latvia	1: 4,434	- -	- -	- -	- -	- -	1: 4,434	3: 4,879	0.26	0.34
Lithuania	- -	1: 1,566	- -	- -	- -	- -	1: 1,566	- -	0.26	0.12
Netherlands	8: 52,555	9: 30,998	2: 399	- -	- -	- -	19: 83,952	- -	4.88	6.53
Norway	23: 58,672	18: 43,352	2: 2,017	1: 1,918	- -	- -	44: 105,959	- -	11.31	8.24
Panama	- -	- -	1: 757	- -	- -	- -	1: 757	- -	0.26	0.06
Spain	1: 2,140	- -	- -	- -	- -	- -	1: 2,140	- -	0.26	0.17
Sweden	22: 52,830	12: 17,580	- -	- -	- -	- -	34 70,410	5: 7,406	8.74	5.48
Soviet Union	1: 968	- -	- -	- -	- -	- -	1: 968	- -	0.26	0.08
United States	- -	- -	- -	- -	- -	- -	- -	1: 4,963	-	-
Yugoslavia	- -	2: 10,883	- -	- -	- -	- -	2: 10,883	- -	0.51	0.85

Table Appendix 9.1.3b. Part 2. Allied and Neutral Shipping Losses in the Second World War's Second Phase: April–June 1940 and the Period of German Victories in Scandinavia and Northwest Europe

		Submarines	Mines	Aircraft	Raiders	Warships	Other and unknown causes	Total Losses	Seized/ captured
Overall losses									
April	1940	7: 35,212	12: 19,846	12: 22,814	2: 5,358	- -	11: 40,714	44: 123,944	31: 69,983
May	1940	13: 51,106	27: 54,914	53: 168,646	1: 6,199	1: 694	18: 17,298	113: 298,857	39: 64,456
June	1940	61: 335,386	30: 105,089	29: 151,779	5: 45,408	3: 6,856	39: 32,712	167: 677,230	95: 255,944
Overall losses		81: 421,704	69: 179,849	94: 343,239	8: 56,965	4: 7,550	68: 90,724	324: 1,100,031	165: 390,383
in % terms		25.00 38.34	21.30 16.35	29.01 31.20	2.47 5.18	1.23 0.69	20.99 8.25		
Allied losses									
April	1940	5: 24,018	7: 14,564	7: 4,526	1: 5,207	- -	9: 32,657	29: 80,972	12: 35,686
May	1940	9: 36,835	21: 43,320	49: 149,517	1: 6,199	1: 694	17: 16,998	98: 253,563	26: 35,740
June	1940	40: 269,119	26: 86,881	26: 138,920	5: 45,408	3: 6,856	39: 32,712	139: 579,896	95: 255,944
Allied losses		54: 329,972	54: 144,765	82: 292,963	7: 56,814	4: 7,550	65: 82,367	266: 914,431	133: 327,370
in % terms		16.67 30.00	16.67 13.16	25.31 26.63	2.16 5.16	1.23 0.69	20.06 7.49	82.10 83.13	
Neutral losses									
April	1940	2: 11,194	5: 5,282	5: 18,288	1: 151	- -	2: 8,057	15: 42,972	19: 34,297
May	1940	4 14,271	6: 11,594	4: 19,129	- -	- -	1: 300	15: 45,294	13: 28,716
June	1940	21: 66,267	4: 18,208	3: 12,859	- -	- -	- -	28: 97,334	- -
Neutral losses		27: 91,732	15: 35,084	12: 50,276	1: 151	- -	3: 8,357	58: 185,600	32: 63,013
in % terms		8.33 8.34	4.63 3.19	3.70 4.57	0.31 0.01	- -	- 0.76	17.90 16.87	

									Ships	Tonnage
Belgium	2: 13,272	2: 805	7: 37,565	- -	- -	6: 1,969	17: 53,611	1: 150	5.25	4.87
Britain	34: 224,638	35: 82,868	41: 114,203	5: 43,803	4: 7,550	43: 45,881	162: 518,943	59: 105,315	50.00	47.18
Denmark	- -	1: 2,156	- -	- -	- -	- -	1: 2,156	21: 37,622	0.31	0.20
France	3: 12,980	10: 52,161	18: 73,982	- -	- -	6: 15,725	37: 154,848	16: 35,708	11.42	14.07
Netherlands	3: 11,250	5: 5,317	4: 40,889	- -	- -	6: 12,427	18: 69,883	7: 21,748	5.56	6.35
Norway	12: 67,832	1: 1,458	11: 14,882	2: 13,011	- -	4: 6,365	30: 103,548	29: 126,827	9.26	9.41
Poland	- -	- -	1: 11,442	- -	- -	- -	1: 11,442	- -	0.31	1.04
Argentina	1: 3,425	- -	- -	- -	- -	- -	1: 3,425	- -	0.31	0.31
Estonia	1: 1,291	1: 1,908	1: 1,591	- -	- -	1: 300	4: 5,090	5: 6,895	1.23	0.46
Finland	4: 8,033	- -	- -	- -	- -	- -	4: 8,033	8: 14,037	1.23	0.73
Greece	12: 51,726	3: 11,364	4: 21,203	- -	- -	- -	19: 84,293	4: 18,055	5.86	7.66
Italy	- -	- -	1: 3,059	- -	- -	- -	1: 3,059	- -	0.31	0.28
Netherlands	- -	2: 344	1: 951	1: 151	- -	- -	4: 1,446	- -	1.23	0.13
Norway	1: 2,118	- -	- -	- -	- -	- -	1: 2,118	- -	0.31	0.19
Panama	1: 1,885	2: 16,947	1: 5,838	- -	- -	- -	4: 24,670	1: 2,978	1.23	2.24
Spain	2: 216	- -	- -	- -	- -	- -	2: 216	- -	0.62	0.02
Sweden	4: 17,704	7: 4,521	4: 17,634	- -	- -	2: 8,057	17: 47,916	14: 21,048	5.25	4.36
Yugoslavia	1: 5,334	- -	- -	- -	- -	- -	1: 5,334	- -	0.31	0.48

Table Appendix 9.1.3c. Part 3. Allied and Neutral Shipping Losses in the Second World War's Third Phase: July 1940–May 1941 and the Period of Increasing Allied Weakness and Vulnerability

		Submarines	Mines	Aircraft	Raiders	Warships	Other and unknown causes	Total losses	Seized/ captured
Overall losses									
July	1940	38: 193,861	18: 37,621	42: 84,018	10: 58,206	6: 13,302	- -	114: 387,008	9: 44,434
August	1940	58: 297,461	10: 12,555	25: 55,488	11: 61,766	3: 2,587	- -	107: 429,857	3: 4,153
September	1940	52: 263,913	10: 8,396	17: 55,797	7: 61,275	7: 14,951	1: 356	94: 404,688	2: 5,170
October	1940	61: 303,547	38: 38,997	9: 51,285	2: 15,918	1: 1,595	6: 3,029	117: 414,371	4: 18,683
November	1940	33: 173,202	47: 54,984	24: 67,376	15: 119,041	4: 2,574	3: 378	126: 417,555	2: 9,763
December	1940	36: 213,575	31: 56,411	12: 15,285	7: 40,797	3: 9,211	2: 174	91: 335,453	1: 865
January	1941	18: 119,137	22: 40,061	18: 69,924	9: 44,793	- -	1: 73	68: 273,988	15: 47,912
February	1941	30: 150,839	19: 25,144	33: 98,264	17: 79,123	3: 2,979	- -	102: 356,349	2: 12,148
March	1941	37: 219,525	26: 26,024	49: 116,510	39: 100,831	9: 27,637	4: 611	164: 491,138	4: 21,991
April	1941	43: 263,752	16: 30,373	145: 326,441	7: 56,941	4: 9,972	12: 14,763	227: 702,242	6: 28,651
May	1941	62: 342,034	19: 25,312	99: 137,182	3: 15,002	- -	9: 12,276	192: 531,806	5: 27,112
Overall losses		468: 2,540,846	256: 355,878	473: 1,077,570	127: 653,693	40: 84,808	38: 31,660	1402 4,744,455	53: 220,882
in % terms		33.38 53.55	18.26 7.50	33.74 22.71	9.06 13.78	2.85 1.79	2.71 0.67		
Allied losses									
July	1940	26: 149,439	17: 36,170	34: 65,768	10: 58,206	5: 7,175	- -	92: 316,758	5: 29,741
August	1940	41: 242,424	10: 12,555	24: 54,559	10: 59,949	3: 2,587	- -	88: 372,074	1: 434
September	1940	44: 235,179	8: 5,360	16: 50,645	6: 55,408	7: 14,951	1: 356	82: 361,899	1: 4,111
October	1940	49: 256,917	34: 36,377	9: 51,285	2: 15,918	1: 1,595	6: 3,029	101: 365,121	3: 13,060
November	1940	30: 164,712	45: 49,049	23 64,642	15: 119,041	4: 2,574	3: 378	120: 400,396	2: 9,763
December	1940	30: 198,170	31: 56,411	12: 15,285	7: 40,797	3: 9,211	2: 174	85: 320,048	1: 865

January	1941	18: 119,137	21: 38,845	18: 69,924	9: 44,793	- -	1: 73	67: 272,772	15: 47,912
February	1941	29: 147,642	19: 25,144	33: 98,264	17: 79,123	3: 2,979	- -	101: 353,152	2: 12,148
March	1941	33: 199,778	26: 26,024	47: 107,219	38: 95,784	9: 27,637	4: 611	157: 457,053	2: 17,714
April	1941	41: 254,822	14: 27,354	142: 316,884	5: 40,903	4: 9,972	11: 13,658	217: 663,593	4: 18,790
May	1941	58: 326,666	17: 25,206	99: 137,182	3: 15,002	- -	9: 12,276	186: 516,332	5: 27,112
Allied losses		399: 2,294,886	242: 338,495	457: 1,031,657	122: 624,924	39: 78,681	37: 30,555	1296: 4,399,198	41: 181,650
in % terms		28.46 48.37	17.26 7.13	32.60 21.74	8.70 13.17	2.78 1.66	2.64 0.64	92.44	92.72
Neutral losses									
July	1940	12 44,422	1: 1,451	8: 18,250	- -	1: 6,127	- -	22 70,250	4: 14,693
August	1940	17: 55,037	- -	1: 929	1: 1,817	- -	- -	19: 57,783	2: 3,719
September	1940	8: 28,734	2: 3,036	1: 5,152	1: 5,867	- -	- -	12: 42,789	1: 1,059
October	1940	12 46,630	4: 2,620	- -	- -	- -	- -	16: 49,250	1: 5,623
November	1940	3 8,490	2: 5,935	1 2,734	- -	- -	- -	6: 17,159	- -
December	1940	6: 15,405	- -	- -	- -	- -	- -	6: 15,405	- -
January	1941	- -	1: 1,216	- -	- -	- -	- -	1: 1,216	- -
February	1941	1: 3,197	- -	- -	- -	- -	- -	1: 3,197	- -
March	1941	4: 19,747	- -	2: 9,291	1: 5,047	- -	- -	7: 34,085	2: 4,277
April	1941	2 8,930	2: 3,019	3: 9,557	2: 16,038	- -	1: 1,105	10: 38,649	2: 9,861
May	1941	4: 15,368	2: 106	- -	- -	- -	- -	6: 15,474	- -
Neutral losses		69: 245,960	14: 17,383	16: 45,913	5: 28,769	1: 6,127	1: 1,105	106: 345,257	12: 39,232
in % terms		4.92 5.18	1.00 0.37	1.14 0.97	0.36 0.61	0.07 0.13	0.07 0.02	7.56 7.28	

	Submarines	Mines	Aircraft	Raiders	Warships	Other and unknown causes	Total losses	Seized/ captured	Ships	Tonnage
Belgium	10: 58,535	4: 840	4: 10,704	1: 4,984	1: 70	1: 352	21: 75,485	- -	1.50	1.59
Britain	313: 1,909,442	211: 274,651	309: 675,591	96: 486,087	32: 53,526	25: 20,840	986: 3,420,137	12: 68,678	70.33	72.09
Denmark	4: 950	2: 352	4: 948	- -	- -	- -	10: 2,250	- -	0.71	0.05
France	- -	- -	- -	1: 2,488	- -	- -	1: 2,488	- -	0.07	0.05
Greece	12: 50,609	4: 8,969	96: 177,963	5: 24,859	- -	9: 8,703	126: 271,103	8: 23,300	8.99	5.71
Netherlands	18: 91,131	11: 17,011	19: 97,845	5: 25,273	5: 16,761	- -	58: 248,021	1: 9,289	4.14	5.23
Norway	42: 184,219	10: 36,672	23: 65,132	14: 81,233	1: 8,324	2: 660	92: 376,240	20: 80,383	6.56	7.93
Poland	- -	- -	2: 3,474	- -	- -	- -	2 3,474	- -	0.14	0.07
Egypt	1: 3,575	- -	- -	1: 8,299	- -	- -	2: 11,874	- -	0.14	0.25
Estonia	3: 7,594	- -	3: 6,216	- -	- -	- -	6: 13,810	- -	0.43	0.29
Finland	6: 17,234	2: 2,054	2: 7,170	1: 1,817	- -	- -	11: 28,275	- -	0.78	0.60
France	- -	2: 3,036	- -	- -	1: 6,127	- -	3: 9,163	1 616	0.21	0.19
Greece	20: 79,073	- -	2: 10,992	1: 5,867	- -	- -	23 95,932	5: 17,796	1.64	2.02
Hungary	1: 4,295	- -	- -	- -	- -	- -	1: 4,295	- -	0.07	0.09
Latvia	- -	- -	1: 534	- -	- -	- -	1: 534	- -	0.07	0.01
Panama	5: 26,897	- -	2: 4,539	- -	- -	1: 1,105	8: 32,541	- -	0.57	0.69
Portugal	- -	- -	1: 853	- -	- -	- -	1: 853	- -	0.07	0.02
Spain	4: 8,146	2: 106	1: 853	- -	- -	- -	7: 9,105	- -	0.50	0.20
Sweden	26: 84,811	4: 1,366	4: 13,124	2: 12,786	- -	- -	36: 112,087	1: 1,059	2.57	2.36
Turkey	- -	- -	1: 2,485	- -	- -	- -	1: 2,485	- -	0.07	0.05
United States	1: 4,999	1: 5,883	- -	- -	- -	- -	2: 10,882	- -	0.14	0.23
Yugoslavia	2: 9,336	3: 4,938	- -	- -	- -	- -	5: 14,274	5: 19,761	0.36	0.30

Table Appendix 9.1.3D. Part 4. Allied and Neutral Shipping Losses in the Second World War's Fourth Phase: June–November 1941 and a Second Period of Balance in the North Atlantic

		Submarines	Mines	Aircraft	Raiders	Warships	Other and unknown causes	Total losses	Seized/ captured
Overall losses									
June	1941	54: 280,039	14: 19,886	30: 61,920	4: 17,759	2: 12,488	2: 4,245	106: 396,337	12: 32,191
July	1941	22: 99,917	13: 11,422	14: 14,397	1: 5,792	- -	2: 3,099	52: 134,627	- -
August	1941	23: 80,310	5: 1,636	13: 28,455	2: 14,056	2: 3,519	1: 158	46: 128,134	1: 7,322
September	1941	52: 204,469	11: 16,949	14: 41,255	1: 3,941	3: 6,676	- -	81: 273,290	1: 4,793
October	1941	31: 154,298	6: 20,202	14: 38,236	- -	2: 3,305	7: 14,420	60: 230,461	2: 1,452
November	1941	14: 64,749	13: 15,124	14: 28,225	- -	8: 23,217	1: 62	50: 131,377	2: 2,544
Overall losses		196: 883,782	62: 85,219	99: 212,488	8: 41,548	17: 49,205	13: 21,984	395: 1,294,226	18: 48,302
in % terms		49.62 68.29	15.70 6.58	25.06 16.42	2.03 3.21	4.30 3.80	3.29 1.70		
Allied losses									
June	1941	49: 269,223	11: 11,060	28: 58,256	4: 17,759	2: 12,488	1: 440	95: 369,226	8: 25,012
July	1941	21: 98,401	11: 8,884	13: 13,092	1: 5,792	- -	1: 22	47: 126,191	- -
August	1941	22: 78,610	5: 1,636	13: 28,455	2: 14,056	2: 3,519	1: 158	45: 126,434	1: 7,322
September	1941	46: 188,073	11: 16,949	13: 35,537	1: 3,941	3: 6,676	- -	74: 251,176	1: 4,793
October	1941	28: 144,049	6: 20,202	12: 35,575	- -	2: 1,768	6: 13,676	54: 216,807	2: 1,452
November	1941	11: 57,576	7: 1,815	14: 28,225	- -	8: 23,217	- -	40: 110,833	2: 2,544
Allied losses		177: 835,932	51: 60,546	93: 199,140	8: 41,548	17: 49,205	9: 14,296	355: 1,200,667	14: 41,123
in % terms		44.81 64.59	12.91 4.68	23.54 15.39	2.03 3.21	4.30 3.80	2.28 1.10	89.87 92.77	
Neutral losses									
June	1941	5: 10,816	3: 8,826	2: 3,664	- -	- -	1: 3,805	11: 27,111	4: 7,179
July	1941	1: 1,516	2: 2,538	1: 1,305	- -	- -	1: 3,077	5: 8,436	- -
August	1941	1: 1,700	- -	- -	- -	- -	- -	1: 1,700	- -
September	1941	6 16,396	- -	1: 5,718	- -	- -	- -	7: 22,114	- -
October	1941	3: 10,249	- -	2: 2,661	- -	- -	1: 744	6: 13,654	- -
November	1941	3: 7,173	6: 13,309	- -	- -	- -	1: 62	10: 20,544	- -
Neutral losses		19: 47,850	11: 24,673	6: 13,348	- -	- -	4: 7,688	40: 93,559	4: 7,179
in % terms		4.81 3.70	2.78 1.91	1.52 1.03	- -	- -	1.01 0.59	10.13 7.23	

	Submarines	Mines	Aircraft	Raiders	Warships	Other and unknown causes	Total losses	Seized/ captured	Ships	Tonnage
Belgium	1: 7,886	- -	3: 1,378	- -	- -	- -	4 9,264	1: 810	1.01	0.72
Britain	131: 636,888	44: 54,797	72: 155,540	6: 33,454	13: 42,046	4: 462	270: 923,187	1: 642	68.35	71.33
Denmark	1: 1,215	1: 236	1: 92	- -	- -	1: 158	4 1,701	- -	1.01	0.13
Greece	10: 42,141	2: 3,959	2: 6,476	1: 3,941	- -	- -	15: 56,517	2: 2,544	3.80	4.37
Netherlands	10: 57,781	3: 621	4: 12,546	- -	1: 1,984	- -	18: 72,932	1: 7,322	4.56	5.64
Norway	21: 83,556	1: 933	8: 12,523	- -	2: 3,204	1: 25	33: 100,241	1: 4,793	8.35	7.75
Palestine	1: 389	- -	- -	- -	- -	- -	1: 389	- -	0.25	0.03
Poland	- -	- -	- -	- -	1: 1,971	- -	1: 1,971	- -	0.25	0.15
Soviet Union	1: 3,487	- -	3: 10,585	- -	- -	3: 13,651	7: 27,723	8: 25,012	1.77	2.14
Yugoslavia	1: 2,589	- -	- -	1: 4,153	- -	- -	2: 6,742	- -	0.51	0.52
Estonia	- -	- -	- -	- -	- -	- -	- -	2: 3,037	-	-
Finland	1: 3,496	1: 5,417	1: 1,894	- -	- -	- -	3: 10,807	- -	0.76	0.84
Japan	- -	1: 4,523	- -	- -	- -	- -	1: 4,523	- -	0.25	0.35
Latvia	- -	- -	- -	- -	- -	1: 3,077	1: 3,077	2: 4,142	0.25	0.24
Panama	6: 18,107	- -	- -	- -	- -	1: 744	7: 18,851	- -	1.77	1.46
Portugal	3: 6,695	- -	- -	- -	- -	- -	3: 6,695	- -	0.76	0.52
Spain	1: 6,600	3: 3,706	- -	- -	- -	- -	4: 10,306	- -	1.01	0.80
Sweden	5: 7,396	5: 11,027	4: 5,736	- -	- -	1: 62	15: 24,221	- -	3.80	1.87
Turkey	2: 573	- -	- -	- -	- -	1: 3,805	3: 4,378	- -	0.76	0.34
United States	1: 4,983	1: ?	1: 5,718	- -	- -	- -	3: 10,701	- -	0.76	0.83

Table Appendix 9.1.3E. Part 5. Allied and Neutral Shipping Losses in the Second World War's Fifth Phase: December 1941–June 1942 and War across the Globe and the German Initiative

		Submarines	Mines	Aircraft	Raiders	Warships	Other and unknown causes	Total losses	Seized/captured
Overall losses									
December	1941	28: 137,657	17: 49,008	33: 82,908	2: 6,661	- -	40: 38,128	120: 314,362	290 269,924
January	1942	57: 311,963	12: 22,557	20: 53,178	1: 3,275	- -	11: 3,580	101: 394,553	16: 25,786
February	1942	69: 391,105	3: 11,730	38: 148,630	- -	9: 5,083	27: 12,675	146: 569,223	44: 67,355
March	1942	86: 494,209	8: 20,439	20: 75,576	8: 21,184	1: 951	157: 137,798	280 750,157	53: 85,817
April	1942	72: 414,173	13: 19,008	22: 119,204	5: 31,187	17: 75,906	12: 6,675	141: 666,153	2: 6,738
May	1942	130: 617,819	7: 18,937	26: 77,784	1: 4,245	- -	5: 375	169: 719,160	4: 18,393
June	1942	144: 694,953	20: 50,564	12: 48,539	6: 40,581	- -	8: 8,818	190: 843,455	2: 17,769
Overall losses		586: 3,061,879	80: 192,243	171 605,819	23: 107,133	27: 81,940	260: 208,049	1147: 4,257,063	411: 491,782
in % terms		51.09 71.92	6.97 4.52	14.91 14.23	2.01 2.52	2.35 1.92	22.67 4.89		
Allied losses									
December	1941	23: 109,589	17: 49,008	33: 82,908	2: 6,661	- -	40: 38,128	115 286,294	289: 267,964
January	1942	55: 301,244	12: 22,557	20: 53,178	1: 3,275	- -	11: 3,580	99: 383,834	16: 25,786
February	1942	64: 363,695	2: 9,934	38: 148,630	- -	9: 5,083	27: 12,675	140: 540,017	44: 67,355
March	1942	81: 469,012	8: 20,439	18: 75,307	8: 21,184	1: 951	157: 137,798	273: 724,691	53: 85,817
April	1942	69: 406,857	10: 14,357	21: 111,426	5: 31,187	17: 75,906	12: 6,675	134: 646,408	2: 6,738
May	1942	125: 595,583	6: 18,809	24: 71,102	1: 4,245	- -	5: 375	161: 690,114	4: 18,393
June	1942	136: 673,410	16: 47,366	10: 45,381	6: 40,581	- -	8: 8,818	176: 815,556	2: 17,769
Allied losses		553: 2,919,390	71: 182,470	164: 587,932	23: 107,133	27: 81,940	260: 208,049	1098: 4,086,914	410: 489,822
in % terms		48.21 68.58	6.19 4.29	14.30 13.81	2.01 2.52	2.35 1.92	22.67 4.89	95.73 96.00	
Neutral losses									
December	1941	5: 28,068	- -	- -	- -	- -	- -	5: 28,068	1: 1,960
January	1942	2: 10,719	- -	- -	- -	- -	- -	2: 10,719	- -
February	1942	5: 27,410	1: 1,796	- -	- -	- -	- -	6: 29,206	- -
March	1942	5: 25,197	- -	2: 269	- -	- -	- -	7: 25,466	- -
April	1942	3: 7,316	3: 4,651	1: 7,778	- -	- -	- -	7: 19,745	- -
May	1942	5: 22,236	1: 128	2: 6,682	- -	- -	- -	8: 29,046	- -
June	1942	8: 21,543	4: 3,198	2: 3,158	- -	- -	- -	14: 27,899	- -
Neutral losses		33: 142,489	9: 9,773	7: 17,887	- -	- -	- -	49: 170,149	1: 1,960
in % terms		2.88 3.35	0.78 0.23	0.61 0.42	- -	- -	- -	4.27 4.00	

	Submarines	Mines	Aircraft	Raiders	Warships	Other and unknown causes	Total Losses	Seized/ captured	Ships	Tonnage
Belgium	3: 17,107	3: 4,799	2: 107	- -	- -	- -	8: 22,013	- -	0.70	0.52
Britain	190: 1,034,160	50: 109,373	96: 330,530	11: 44,981	13: 34,335	181: 71,629	541: 1,625,008	296: 247,560	47.17	38.17
China	- -	- -	- -	- -	- -	3: 4,086	3: 4,086	11: 20,688	0.26	0.10
Dominican Rep.	3: 3,671	- -	- -	- -	- -	- -	3: 3,671	- -	0.26	0.09
France	2: 10,392	- -	- -	- -	- -	- -	2: 10,392	2: 15,672	0.17	0.24
Greece	15: 65,230	4: 17,612	- -	1: 3,942	- -	1: 48	21: 86,832	16: 31,067	1.83	2.04
Honduras	6: 19,249	- -	- -	- -	- -	- -	6: 19,249	- -	0.52	0.45
Latvia	5: 19,075	- -	- -	- -	- -	- -	5: 19,075	- -	0.44	0.45
Mexico	4: 19,080	- -	- -	- -	- -	- -	4: 19,080	- -	0.35	0.45
Netherlands	32: 132,842	3: 6,084	19: 80,732	3: 10,589	5: 4,614	46: 89,104	108: 323,965	52: 103,988	9.42	7.61
Nicaragua	2: 2,787	- -	- -	- -	- -	- -	2: 2,787	- -	0.17	0.07
Norway	66: 354,992	2: 7,004	13: 40,117	3: 12,107	8: 38,005	5: 9,099	97: 461,324	3: 13,535	8.46	10.84
Palestine	2: 175	- -	- -	- -	- -	- -	2: 175	- -	0.17	0.00
Panama	40: 224,960	1: 4,488	2: 6,571	1: 10,169	- -	3: 9,236	47: 255,424	2: 2,127	4.10	6.00
Poland	1: 2,486	- -	- -	- -	- -	- -	1: 2,486	- -	0.09	0.06
Soviet Union	5: 25,272	- -	6: 17,061	- -	- -	- -	11: 42,333	- -	0.96	0.99
United States	170: 959,576	6: 27,776	26: 112,814	4: 25,345	1: 4,986	21: 24,847	228: 1,155,344	27: 55,185	19.88	27.14
Yugoslavia	7: 28,336	2: 5,334	- -	- -	- -	- -	9: 33,670	- -	0.78	0.79
Argentina	1: 4,864	- -	- -	- -	- -	- -	1: 4,864	- -	0.09	0.11
Brazil	8: 43,555	- -	- -	- -	- -	- -	8: 43,555	- -	0.70	1.02
Chile	1: 1,858	- -	- -	- -	- -	- -	1: 1,858	- -	0.09	0.04
Colombia	1: 35	- -	- -	- -	- -	- -	1: 35	- -	0.09	0.00
Egypt	3: 5,629	1: ?	1: 7,778	- -	- -	- -	5: 13,407	- -	0.44	0.31
France	- -	- -	- -	- -	- -	- -	- -	1: 1,960	-	-
Portugal	2: 7,784	- -	1: 269	- -	- -	- -	3: 8,053	- -	0.26	0.19
Spain	2: 9,675	1: 128	1: ?	- -	- -	- -	4: 9,803	- -	0.35	0.23
Sweden	9: 46,307	6: 9,567	4: 9,840	- -	- -	- -	19: 65,714	- -	1.66	1.54
Turkey	2: 530	1: 78	- -	- -	- -	- -	3: 608	- -	0.26	0.01
Uruguay	1: 5,785	- -	- -	- -	- -	- -	1: 5,785	- -	0.09	0.14
United States	2: 13,817	- -	- -	- -	- -	- -	2: 13,817	- -	0.17	0.32
Venezuela	1: 2,650	- -	- -	- -	- -	- -	1: 2,650	- -	0.09	0.06

Table Appendix 9.1.3f. Part 6. Allied and Neutral Merchant Shipping Losses in the Second World War's Sixth Phase: July 1942–May 1943 and a Third Period of Balance and Subsequent Allied Initiative

		Submarines	Mines	Aircraft	Raiders	Warships	Other and unknown causes	Total losses	Seized/ captured
Overall Losses									
July	1942	101: 468,034	12: 54,842	21: 89,935	4: 29,159	6: 12,506	1: 8,141	145: 662,617	3: 13,921
August	1942	112: 560,243	1: 245	9: 51,171	2: 12,946	5: 42,070	2: 34	131: 666,709	2: 2,370
September	1942	97: 459,826	4: 4,499	13: 57,913	3: 21,200	2: 2,533	1: 341	120: 546,312	4: 2,711
October	1942	91: 596,525	8: 35,938	2: 6,706	- -	5: 8,464	- -	106: 647,633	- -
November	1942	120: 763,509	4: 9,608	7: 63,759	1: 5,882	4: 5,371	- -	136: 848,129	3: 5,424
December	1942	59: 313,285	2: 149	2: 4,156	1: 4,816	6: 7,496	4: 1,326	74: 331,228	- -
January	1942	39: 212,174	8: 27,352	6: 20,270	1: 7,040	- -	8: 14,603	62: 281,439	1: 6,689
February	1943	61: 355,597	7: 26,248	1: 75	- -	1: 4,858	2: 8,209	72: 394,987	- -
March	1943	104: 601,650	7: 1,244	17: 66,415	- -	1: 1,444	- -	129: 670,753	- -
April	1943	55: 309,875	6: 15,049	5: 7,458	- -	1: 1,742	1: 1,162	68: 335,286	1: 42
May	1943	49: 260,115	4: 4,321	7: 20,951	- -	- -	1: 7,191	61: 292,578	- -
Overall losses		888: 4,900,833	63: 179,495	90: 388,809	12: 81,043	31: 86,484	20: 41,007	1104: 5,677,671	14: 31,157
		80.43 86.32	5.71 3.16	8.15 6.85	1.09 1.43	2.81 1.52	1.81 0.72		
Allied losses									
July	1942	90: 439,751	10: 45,937	20: 89,892	4: 29,159	6: 12,506	1: 8,141	131: 625,386	3: 13,921
August	1942	98: 515,293	1: 245	9: 51,171	2: 12,946	5: 42,070	2: 34	117: 621,759	2: 2,370
September	1942	91: 444,190	1: ?	13: 57,913	3: 21,200	1: ?	1: 341	110: 523,644	3: 1,511
October	1942	90: 596,325	6: 30,568	2: 6,706	- -	5: 8,464	- -	103: 642,063	- -
November	1942	120: 763,509	2: 3,368	7: 63,759	1: 5,882	4: 5,371	- -	134: 841,889	3: 5,424

		Submarines	Mines	Aircraft	Raiders	Warships	Other and unknown causes	Total losses	Seized/ captured
December	1942	55: 304,038	2: 149	2: 4,156	1: 4,816	6: 7,496	4: 1,326	70: 321,981	- -
January	1942	37: 208,110	3: 8,593	5: 18,651	1: 7,040	- -	7: 14,513	53: 256,907	1: 6,689
February	1943	58: 351,998	7: 26,248	- -	- -	1: 4,858	1: 4,648	67: 387,752	- -
March	1943	100: 596,468	3: 1,190	17: 66,415	- -	- -	- -	120: 664,073	- -
April	1943	50: 299,119	5: 11,961	1: 2,996	- -	1: 1,742	1: 1,162	58: 316,980	1: 42
May	1943	48: 258,482	1: 1,568	6: 20,651	- -	- -	1: 7,191	56: 287,892	- -
Allied losses		837: 4,777,283	41: 129,827	82: 382,310	12: 81,043	29: 82,507	18: 37,356	1019: 5,490,336	13: 29,957
		75.82 84.14	3.71 2.29	7.43 6.73	1.09 1.43	2.62 1.45	1.63 0.66	92.30 96.70	
Neutral losses									
July	1942	11: 28,283	2: 8,905	1: 43	- -	- -	- -	14: 37,231	- -
August	1942	14: 44,950	- -	- -	- -	- -	- -	14: 44,950	- -
September	1942	6: 15,636	3: 4,499	- -	- -	1: 2,533	- -	10: 22,668	1: 1,200
October	1942	1: 200	2: 5,370	- -	- -	- -	- -	3: 5,570	- -
November	1942	- -	2: 6,240	- -	- -	- -	- -	2: 6,240	- -
December	1942	4: 9,247	- -	- -	- -	- -	- -	4: 9,247	- -
January	1943	2: 4,064	5: 18,759	1: 1,619	- -	- -	1: 90	9: 24,532	- -
February	1943	3: 3,599	- -	1: 75	- -	- -	1: 3,561	5: 7,235	- -
March	1943	4: 5,182	4: 54	- -	- -	1: 1,444	- -	9: 6,680	- -
April	1943	5: 10,756	1: 3,088	4: 4,462	- -	- -	- -	10: 18,306	- -
May	1943	1: 1,633	3: 2,753	1: 300	- -	- -	- -	5: 4,686	- -
Neutral losses		51: 123,550	22: 49,668	8: 6,499	- -	2: 3,977	2: 3,651	85: 187,345	1: 1,200
		4.62 2.18	1.99 0.87	0.72 0.11	- -	0.18 0.07	0.18 0.06	7.70 3.30	

	Submarines	Mines	Aircraft	Raiders	Warships	Other and unknown causes	Total losses	Seized/ captured	Ships	Tonnage
Belgium	10: 50,941	2: 109	- -	- -	- -	1: 4,438	13: 55,488	- -	1.18	0.98
Brazil	7: 28,089	- -	- -	- -	- -	- -	7: 28,089	- -	0.63	0.49
Britain	417: 2,508,957	21: 35,926	44: 251,912	6: 40,420	18: 51,553	6: 9,866	512: 2,898,634	8: 15,144	46.38	51.05
China	- -	- -	- -	- -	- -	- -	- -	2: 2,230	-	-
Cuba	3: 4,693	- -	- -	- -	- -	- -	3: 4,693	- -	0.27	0.08
Denmark	1: 292	1: 89	2: 408	- -	- -	- -	4: 789	- -	0.36	0.01
Dominican Rep.	1: 84	- -	- -	- -	- -	- -	1: 84	- -	0.09	0.00
France	7: 17,309	2: 4,100	6: 1,247	- -	- -	- -	15: 22,656	- -	1.36	0.40
Greece	35: 155,164	- -	1: 1,354	1: 4,816	- -	- -	37: 161,334	- -	3.35	2.84
Honduras	4: 5,249	- -	- -	- -	- -	- -	4: 5,249	- -	0.36	0.09
Latvia	1: 4,520	- -	- -	- -	- -	- -	1: 4,520	- -	0.09	0.08
Lebanon	2: 154	- -	- -	- -	- -	- -	2: 154	- -	0.18	0.00
Mexico	2: 10,862	- -	- -	- -	- -	- -	2: 10,862	- -	0.18	0.19
Netherlands	46: 266,078	- -	7: 19,895	- -	1: 2,836	1: 1,162	55: 289,971	- -	4.98	5.11
Nicaragua	1: 2,063	- -	- -	- -	- -	- -	1: 2,063	- -	0.09	0.04
Norway	73 370,521	1: 750	2: 3,298	1: 7,984	6: 7,466	5: 71	88: 390,090	1: 5,894	7.97	6.87
Palestine	7: 1,038	- -	- -	- -	- -	- -	7: 1,038	- -	0.63	0.02
Panama	26: 162,803	2: 8,875	4: 16,546	- -	- -	- -	32: 188,224	- -	2.90	3.32
Poland	2 5,192	- -	- -	- -	- -	- -	2: 5,192	- -	0.18	0.09
Soviet Union	6: 26,937	5: 22,931	1: 3,124	- -	2: 4,500	2: 7,435	16: 64,927	1: 6,689	1.45	1.14
Syria	5: 243	- -	- -	- -	- -	- -	5: 243	- -	0.45	0.00
United States	177: 1,139,529	7: 57,047	15: 84,526	4: 27,823	2: 16,152	3: 14,384	208: 1,339,461	1: ?	18.84	23.59
Yugoslavia	4: 16,565	- -	- -	- -	- -	- -	4: 16,565	- -	0.36	0.29
Brazil	9: 26,973	- -	- -	- -	- -	- -	9: 26,973	- -	0.82	0.48
Colombia	1: 110	- -	- -	- -	- -	- -	1: 110	- -	0.09	0.00
Cuba	1: ?	- -	- -	- -	- -	- -	1: ?	- -	0.09	-
Egypt	13: 9,936	- -	5: 329	- -	- -	1: 90	19: 10,355	- -	1.72	0.18
Portugal	2: 935	- -	- -	- -	- -	- -	2: 935	1: 1,200	0.18	0.02
Spain	5: 14,498	2: ?	1: 300	- -	- -	1: 3,561	9: 18,359	- -	0.82	0.32
Sweden	17: 62,090	20: 49,668	2: 5,870	- -	2: 3,977	- -	41: 121,605	- -	3.71	2.14
Turkey	2: 3,723	- -	- -	- -	- -	- -	2: 3,723	- -	0.18	0.07
Uruguay	1: 5,285	- -	- -	- -	- -	- -	1: 5,285	- -	0.09	0.09

Table Appendix 9.1.3G. Part 7. Allied and Neutral Merchant Shipping Losses in the Second World War's Seventh Phase: June 1943–May 1944 and the Period of Growing Allied Ascendancy

		Submarines	Mines	Aircraft	Raiders	Warships	Other and unknown causes	Total losses	Seized/ captured
Overall losses									
June	1943	26: 137,561	3: 3,309	2: 5,270	1: 7,715	- -	1: 718	33: 154,573	2: 8,249
July	1943	49: 258,753	3: 2,225	14: 106,071	- -	- -	- -	66: 367,049	- -
August	1943	22: 101,178	1: 19	5: 18,601	- -	3: 452	2: 7,214	33: 127,464	2: 2,037
September	1943	19: 112,480	2: 1,945	5: 32,265	- -	1: 314	1: 300	28: 147,304	1: 4,200
October	1943	20: 97,407	5: 12,850	9: 26,502	- -	1: 235	- -	35: 136,994	1: 3,000
November	1943	12: 54,836	3: 4,160	8: 71,652	- -	5: 8,788	3: 10,017	31: 149,453	1: 150
December	1943	15: 94,358	4: 8,473	16: 74,371	- -	1: 296	- -	36: 177,498	- -
January	1944	12: 77,983	1: 7,176	4: 24,237	- -	5: 6,420	- -	22: 115,816	- -
February	1944	20: 92,370	1: 6,176	3: 21,616	- -	2: 2,085	- -	26: 122,247	- -
March	1944	25: 146,001	3: 21,552	2: 2,152	1: 7,840	- -	- -	31: 177,545	- -
April	1944	8: 56,872	3: 7,756	6: 23,023	- -	1: 468	1: 5,277	19: 93,396	- -
May	1944	5: 24,424	2: 456	2: 3,149	- -	- -	1: 39	10: 28,068	- -
Overall losses		233: 1,254,223	31 76,097	76: 408,909	2: 15,555	19: 19,058	9: 23,565	370: 1,797,407	7: 17,636
in % terms		62.97 69.78	8.38 4.23	20.54 22.75	0.54 0.87	5.14 1.06	2.43 1.31		
Allied losses									
June	1943	25: 135,888	3: 3,309	2: 5,270	1: 7,715	- -	1: 718	32: 152,900	1: 7,001
July	1943	44: 247,408	1: 72	13: 106,005	- -	- -	- -	58: 353,485	- -
August	1943	18: 100,880	1: 19	4: 18,461	- -	1: 338	2: 7,214	26: 126,912	2: 2,037
September	1943	18: 112,400	2: 1,945	4: 30,477	- -	1: 314	1: 300	26: 145,436	1: 4,200
October	1943	20: 97,407	4: 12,185	9: 26,502	- -	1: 235	- -	34: 136,329	1: 3,000
November	1943	11: 54,773	3: 4,160	8: 71,652	- -	4: 8,538	3: 10,017	29: 149,140	1: 150

December	1943	14: 94,326	2: 6,442	16: 74,371	- -	1: 296	- -	33: 175,435	- -
January	1944	11: 77,743	1: 7,176	4: 24,237	- -	4: 5,012	- -	20: 114,168	- -
February	1944	19: 92,321	1: 6,176	3: 21,616	- -	2: 2,085	- -	25: 122,198	- -
March	1944	23: 142,485	3: 21,552	1: 274	1: 7,840	- -	- -	28: 172,151	- -
April	1944	8: 56,872	1: 7,176	3: 19,755	- -	1: 468	1: 5,277	14: 89,548	- -
May	1944	5: 24,424	1: 302	1: 2,873	- -	- -	1: 39	8: 27,638	- -
Allied losses		216: 1,236,927	23: 70,514	68: 401,493	2: 15,555	15: 17,286	9: 23,565	333: 1,765,340	6: 16,388
in % terms		58.38 68.82	6.22 3.92	18.38 22.34	0.54 0.87	4.06 0.96	2.43 1.31	90.00 98.22	
Neutral losses									
June	1943	1: 1,673	- -	- -	- -	- -	- -	1: 1,673	1: 1,248
July	1943	5: 11,345	2: 2,153	1: 66	- -	- -	- -	8: 13,564	- -
August	1943	4: 298	- -	1: 140	- -	2: 114	- -	7: 552	- -
September	1943	1: 80	- -	1: 1,788	- -	- -	- -	2: 1,868	- -
October	1943	- -	1: 665	- -	- -	- -	- -	1: 665	- -
November	1943	1: 63	- -	- -	- -	1: 250	- -	2: 313	- -
December	1943	1: 32	2: 2,031	- -	- -	- -	- -	3: 2,063	- -
January	1944	1: 240	- -	- -	- -	1: 1,408	- -	2: 1,648	- -
February	1944	1 49	- -	- -	- -	- -	- -	1: 49	- -
March	1944	2: 3,516	- -	1: 1,878	- -	- -	- -	3: 5,394	- -
April	1944	- -	2: 580	3: 3,268	- -	- -	- -	5: 3,848	- -
May	1944	- -	1: 154	1: 276	- -	- -	- -	2: 430	- -
Neutral losses		17: 17,296	8: 5,583	8: 7,416	- -	4: 1,772	- -	37: 32,067	1: 1,248
in % terms		4.59 0.96	2.16 0.31	2.16 0.41	- -	1.08 0.10	- -	10.00 1.78	

	Submarines	Mines	Aircraft	Raiders	Warships	Other and unknown causes	Total losses	Seized/ captured	Ships	Tonnage
Belgium	- -	1: 19	1: 7,217	- -	- -	- -	2: 7,236	- -	0.54	0.40
Brazil	5: 24,249	- -	- -	- -	- -	1: 300	6: 24,549	- -	1.62	1.37
Britain	89: 495,637	10: 8,525	36: 197,481	1: 7,840	14: 16,818	4: 15,332	154: 741,633	3: 2,187	41.62	41.26
China	1: 7,176	- -	- -	- -	- -	- -	1: 7,176	- -	0.27	0.40
Colombia	1: 39	- -	- -	- -	- -	- -	1: 39	- -	0.27	0.00
Cuba	1: 5,441	- -	- -	- -	- -	- -	1: 5,441	- -	0.27	0.30
Denmark	- -	- -	1: 87	- -	- -	- -	1: 87	- -	0.27	0.00
France	5: 29,454	2: 8,494	2: 13,878	- -	- -	1: 39	10: 51,865	- -	2.70	2.89
Greece	13: 53,841	- -	- -	- -	- -	- -	13: 53,841	- -	3.51	3.00
Italy	- -	- -	4: 12,248	- -	- -	1: ?	5: 12,248	1: 4,200	1.35	0.68
Lebanon	2: 148	- -	- -	- -	- -	- -	2: 148	- -	0.54	0.01
Netherlands	7: 51,461	- -	3: 30,735	- -	1: 468	- -	11: 82,664	- -	2.97	4.60
Norway	20: 115,559	1: 6,086	2: 7,680	1: 7,715	- -	- -	24: 137,040	- -	6.49	7.62
Palestine	1: 132	- -	- -	- -	- -	- -	1: 132	- -	0.27	0.01
Panama	4: 11,801	1: 2,937	- -	- -	- -	- -	5: 14,738	- -	1.35	0.82
Poland	- -	- -	1: 1,409	- -	- -	- -	1: 1,409	- -	0.27	0.08
Soviet Union	5: 19,595	- -	- -	- -	- -	- -	5: 19,595	2: 10,001	1.35	1.09
Syria	4: 163	- -	- -	- -	- -	- -	4: 163	- -	1.08	0.01
United States	58: 422,231	7: 44,118	18: 130,758	- -	- -	2: 7,894	85: 605,001	- -	22.97	33.66
Yugoslavia	- -	1: 335	- -	- -	- -	- -	1: 335	- -	0.26	0.02
Egypt	7: 647	- -	1: 140	- -	- -	- -	8: 787	- -	2.16	0.04
Portugal	- -	1: 665	- -	- -	- -	- -	1: 665	1: 1,248	0.27	0.04
Spain	- -	- -	1: 648	- -	- -	- -	1: 648	- -	0.27	0.04
Sweden	3: 12,897	6: 2,932	5: 4,840	- -	3: 1,522	- -	17: 22,191	- -	4.59	1.23
Switzerland	- -	- -	1: 1,788	- -	- -	- -	1: 1,788	- -	0.27	0.10
Turkey	7: 3,752	1 1,986	- -	- -	1 250	- -	9: 5,988	- -	2.43	0.33

Table Appendix 9.1.3h. Part 8. Allied and Neutral Merchant Shipping Losses in the Second World War's Eighth and Final Phase: June 1944–May 1945 and the Victory of the Allies

		Submarines	Mines	Aircraft	Raiders	Warships	Other and unknown causes	Total losses	Seized/ captured
Overall losses									
June	1944	7: 34,100	9: 33,476	3: 10,858	- -	3: 1,812	11: 49,813	33: 130,059	- -
July	1944	14: 67,949	11: 16,854	2: 1,855	- -	1: 7,219	5: 13,667	33: 107,544	- -
August	1944	14: 86,499	9: 17,459	2: 8,507	- -	2: 7,229	4: 11,965	31: 131,659	- -
September	1944	7: 43,368	1: 1,437	1: 1,496	- -	- -	1: ?	10: 46,301	12: 26,537
October	1944	1: 7,176	3: 3,971	2: 14,352	- -	- -	2: ?	8: 25,499	- -
November	1944	6: 40,060	2: 7,428	- -	- -	1: 1,141	1: 563	10: 49,192	- -
December	1944	5: 30,673	10: 41,111	6: 43,096	- -	- -	6: 33,591	27: 148,471	- -
January	1945	15: 80,125	7: 23,862	2: 12,211	- -	1: 2,365	1: 1,152	26: 119,715	- -
February	1945	16: 67,159	7: 13,940	1: 7,177	- -	2: 3,889	2: 5,512	28: 97,677	- -
March	1945	16: 67,608	5: 14,560	- -	- -	2: 3,968	13: 36,809	36: 122,945	3: 1,523
April	1945	12: 70,458	2: 8,400	4: 22,822	- -	- -	8: 10,144	26: 111,824	- -
May	1945	4: 10,370	4: 23,549	1: 7,176	- -	- -	- -	9: 41,095	- -
Overall losses		117: 605,545	70: 206,047	24: 129,550	- -	12: 27,623	54: 163,216	277: 1,131,981	15: 28,060
in % terms		42.24 53.49	25.27 18.20	8.66 11.44	- -	4.33 2.44	19.49 14.42		
Allied losses									
June	1944	7: 34,100	7: 31,105	3: 10,858	- -	3: 1,812	11: 49,813	31: 127,688	- -
July	1944	12: 67,798	9: 15,242	1: 418	- -	1: 7,219	5: 13,667	28: 104,344	- -
August	1944	13: 86,499	4: 14,328	1: 7,210	- -	1: 7,176	4: 11,965	23: 127,178	- -
September	1944	7: 43,368	- -	- -	- -	- -	1: ?	8: 43,368	- -
October	1944	1: 7,176	2: 3,925	2: 14,352	- -	- -	2: ?	7: 25,453	- -
November	1944	6: 40,060	2: 7,428	- -	- -	1: 1,141	- -	9: 48,629	- -

		Submarines	Mines	Aircraft	Raiders	Warships	Other and unknown causes	Total losses	Seized/ captured
December	1944	5: 30,673	9: 41,067	6: 43,096	- -	- -	5: 32,547	25: 147,383	- -
January	1945	15: 80,125	6: 23,799	2: 12,211	- -	1: 2,365	1: 1,152	25: 119,652	- -
February	1945	16: 67,159	7: 13,940	1: 7,177	- -	2: 3,889	2: 5,512	28: 97,677	- -
March	1945	15: 66,463	4: 14,560	- -	- -	2: 3,968	12: 36,569	33: 121,560	3: 1,523
April	1945	11: 70,401	2: 8,400	3: 22,822	- -	- -	8: 10,144	24: 111,767	- -
May	1945	4: 10,370	4: 23,549	1: 7,176	- -	- -	- -	9: 41,095	- -
Allied losses		112: 604,192	56: 197,343	20: 125,320	- -	11: 27,570	51: 161,369	250: 1,115,794	3: 1,523
in % terms		40.43 53.37	20.22 17.43	7.22 11.07	- -	3.97 2.44	18.41 14.26	90.25 98.57	
Neutral losses									
June	1944	- -	2: 2,371	- -	- -	- -	- -	2: 2,371	- -
July	1944	2: 151	2: 1,612	1: 1,437	- -	- -	- -	5: 3,200	- -
August	1944	1: ?	5: 3,131	1: 1,297	- -	1: 53	- -	8: 4,481	- -
September	1944	- -	1: 1,437	1: 1,496	- -	- -	- -	2: 2,933	12: 26,537
October	1944	- -	1: 46	- -	- -	- -	- -	1: 46	- -
November	1944	- -	- -	- -	- -	- -	1: 563	1: 563	- -
December	1944	- -	1: 44	- -	- -	- -	1: 1,044	2: 1,088	- -
January	1945	- -	1: 63	- -	- -	- -	- -	1: 63	- -
February	1945	- -	- -	- -	- -	- -	- -	- -	- -
March	1945	1: 1,145	1: ?	- -	- -	- -	1: 240	3: 1,385	- -
April	1945	1: 57	- -	1: ?	- -	- -	- -	2: 57	- -
May	1945	- -	- -	- -	- -	- -	- -	- -	- -
Neutral losses		5: 1,353	14: 8,704	4: 4,230	- -	1: 53	3: 1,847	27: 16,187	12: 26,537
in % terms		1.81 0.12	5.05 1.44	0.37 -	- 0.36	0.00 1.08	0.16 9.75	1.43	

	Submarines	Mines	Aircraft	Raiders	Warships	Other and unknown causes	Total losses	Seized/ captured	Ships	Tonnage
Belgium	2: 12,341	3: 95	- -	- -	- -	8: 14,677	13: 27,113	- -	4.69	2.40
Britain	57 289,210	35: 107,146	3: 9,392	- -	10: 20,394	29: 86,471	134: 512,613	2: 838	48.38	45.28
Denmark	2: 3,106	- -	- -	- -	- -	- -	2: 3,106	- -	0.72	0.27
France	1: 2,778	2: 159	- -	- -	- -	- -	3: 2,937	1: 685	1.08	0.26
Greece	1: 5,670	- -	- -	- -	- -	3: 7,247	4: 12,917	1: ?	1.44	1.14
Netherlands	3: 13,073	1: 2,770	- -	- -	- -	- -	4: 15,843	- -	1.44	1.40
Norway	8: 26,870	3: 3,535	- -	- -	- -	4: 9,860	15: 40,265	- -	5.42	3.56
Panama	3: 7,547	- -	- -	- -	- -	- -	3: 7,567	- -	1.08	0.67
Soviet Union	3: 9,486	- -	1: 1,850	- -	- -	- -	4: 11,336	- -	1.44	1.00
United States	32: 234,091	12: 83,638	16: 114,078	- -	1: 7,176	7: 43,114	68: 482,097	- -	24.55	42.59
Finland	- -	- -	- -	- -	- -	- -	- -	12: 26,547	-	-
Spain	1: 127	- -	- -	- -	- -	- -	1: 127	- -	0.26	0.01
Sweden	2: 1,202	13: 7,267	4: 4,230	- -	- -	3: 1,847	22: 14,546	- -	7.94	1.29
Switzerland	- -	1: 1,437	- -	- -	- -	- -	1: 1,437	- -	0.36	0.13
Turkey	2: 24	1: 1,437	- -	- -	1: 53	- -	4: 1,514	- -	1.44	0.13

Table Appendix 9.1.4. Summary of Allied and Neutral Shipping Losses during the Second World War, 1 September 1939–8 May 1945

Phase I. 1 September 1939–31 March 1940		
Overall losses:	389 ships of 1,285,982 tons.	
Allied losses:	214 ships of 793,715 tons:	55.01% of ships and 61.72% by tonnage.
Neutral losses:	175 ships of 492,267 tons:	44.99% of ships and 38.28% by tonnage.
Average losses per month for seven months:		55.57 ships of 183,711.71 tons.
Average losses per day for 213 days:		1.83 ships of 6,037.47 tons.
Average size of ship sunk:		3,305.87 tons.
Phase II. 1 April–30 June 1940		
Overall losses:	324 ships of 1,100,031 tons.	
Allied losses:	266 ships of 914,431 tons:	82.10% of ships and 83.13% by tonnage.
Neutral losses:	58 ships of 185,600 tons:	17.90% of ships and 16.87% by tonnage.
Average losses per month for three months:		108.00 ships of 366,677.00 tons.
Average losses per day for 91 days:		3.56 ships of 12,088.25 tons.
Average size of ship sunk:		3,395.16 tons.
Phase III. 1 July 1940–31 May 1941		
Overall losses:	1,402 ships of 4,744,455 tons.	
Allied losses:	1,296 ships of 4,399,198 tons:	92.44% of ships and 92.72% by tonnage.
Neutral losses:	106 ships of 345,257 tons:	7.56% of ships and 7.28% by tonnage.
Average losses per month for ten months:		140.20 ships of 474,445.50 tons.
Average losses per day for 304 days:		4.61 ships of 15,606.76 tons.
Average size of ship sunk:		3,384.06 tons.
Phase IV. 1 June–30 November 1941		
Overall losses:	395 ships of 1,294,266 tons.	
Allied losses:	355 ships of 1,200,667 tons:	89.87% of ships and 92.77% by tonnage.
Neutral losses:	40 ships of 93,559 tons:	10.13% of ships and 7.23% by tonnage.
Average losses per month for six months:		65.83 ships of 215,704.33 tons.
Average losses per day for 183 days:		2.16 ships of 7,072.27 tons.
Average size of ship sunk:		3,251.82 tons.
Phase V. 1 December 1941–30 June 1942		
Overall losses:	1,147 ships of 4,257,063 tons.	
Allied losses:	1,098 ships of 4,086,914 tons:	95.73% of ships and 96.00% by tonnage.
Neutral losses:	49 ships of 170,149 tons:	4.27% of ships and 4.00% by tonnage.
Average losses per month for seven months:		163.86 ships of 608,151.85 tons.
Average losses per day for 212 days:		5.41 ships of 20,080.49 tons.
Average size of ship sunk:		3,711.48 tons.

Phase VI. 1 July 1942–31 May 1943

Overall losses:	1,104 ships of 5,677,671 tons.	
Allied losses:	1,019 ships of 5,490,336 tons:	92.30% of ships and 96.70% by tonnage.
Neutral losses:	85 ships of 187,345 tons:	7.70% of ships and 3.30% by tonnage.
Average losses per month for eleven months:		100.36 ships of 516,151.91 tons.
Average losses per day for 335 days:		3.30 ships of 16,948.27 tons.
Average size of ship sunk:		5,142.82 tons.

Phase VII. 1 June 1943–31 May 1944

Overall losses:	370 ships of 1,797,407 tons.	
Allied losses:	333 ships of 1,765,340 tons:	90.00% of ships and 98.22% by tonnage.
Neutral losses:	37 ships of 32,067 tons:	10.00% of ships and 1.78% by tonnage.
Average losses per month for twelve months:		30.83 ships of 149,783.91 tons.
Average losses per day for 366 days:		1.01 ships of 4,910.95 tons.
Average size of ship sunk:		4,857.86 tons.

Phase VIII. 1 June 1944–8 May 1945

Overall losses:	277 ships of 1,131,981 tons.	
Allied losses:	250 ships of 1,115,794 tons:	90.25% of ships and 98.57% by tonnage.
Neutral losses:	27 ships of 16,187 tons:	9.75% of ships and 1.43% by tonnage.
Average losses per month for 11.26 months:		24.60 ships of 100,531.17 tons.
Average losses per day for 342 days:		0.81 ships of 3,309.89 tons.
Average size of ship sunk:		4,086.57 tons.

Total losses in the European war, 1 September 1939–8 May 1945

Overall losses:	5,408 ships of 21,288,816 tons.	
Allied losses:	4,831 ships of 19,766,385 tons:	89.33% of ships and 92.85% by tonnage.
Neutral losses:	577 ships of 1,522,431 tons:	10.67% of ships and 7.15% by tonnage.
Average losses per month for 68.26 months:		79.23 ships of 311,878.34 tons.
Average losses per day for 2,046 days:		2.64 ships of 10,405.09 tons.
Average size of ship sunk:		3,936.54 tons.

PART 4

THE SECOND WORLD WAR: THE PACIFIC THEATER

CHAPTER TEN

THE WAR ACROSS THE PACIFIC: INTRODUCTION AND CONCLUSION

THE WAR AGAINST JAPAN is all but synonymous with an American naval war, and that war with American carrier formations. But the real basis of Japan's defeat was the superior demographic, industrial, and financial resources of the United States, which allowed that country to wage war across an ocean in a manner that defied imagination even in 1941. At the time of the Japanese attack on the U.S. Pacific Fleet at its Pearl Harbor base, the United States possessed just seven fleet carriers—the *Lexington* and *Saratoga*, the *Ranger*, the *Yorktown*, *Enterprise*, and *Hornet*, and the *Wasp*—and the escort carrier *Long Island*. On 15 August 1945 the U.S. Navy had in service or in dockyards undergoing refit, repair, or overhaul a total of twenty fleet carriers, eight light carriers, and no fewer than seventy-one escort carriers, and in addition another four fleet and five escort carriers were to be commissioned before the end of the year. Such were the numbers employed by the United States to take the tide of war to the Japanese home islands, and thus it is all the more important to note that the carrier formations were but one dimension of this American effort; carrier operations goes alongside the submarine campaign against Japan shipping, the various amphibious operations that provided the paving stones in the journey across the western Pacific, and the land-based air offensive, which provided the final comment in this war.

* * *

Conversely, the extent of the Japanese naval defeat is seldom properly appreciated, but can be gauged by the following figures in reference to fleet units. At the start of the Pacific war the Kaigun mustered ten capital ships, ten fleet and light fleet carriers, one escort carrier, eighteen heavy and twenty light cruisers, and 112 destroyers; in the course of the war Japanese yards put into service another two capital ships, six fleet and light fleet carriers, four escort carriers, five light cruisers, and thirty-one destroyers, plus escorts, sweepers, and various amphibious units. At war's end the Imperial Navy had one battleship, one fleet and three light carriers, two heavy and three light cruisers, and fifteen destroyers, and most of these were *hors de combat*.

The comprehensiveness of Japan's defeat at sea can perhaps best be gauged by reference to its destroyers. Japan went to war in December 1941 with destroyers drawn from twelve classes. The elderly *Akikaze* class had originally had fifteen units, but by 1941 three, the *Nadakaze*, the *Shimakaze*, and the *Yakaze*, had been reclassified and were no longer first-line units. There were just two members of the *Aoi* class remaining in service as destroyers at this time, while the *Wakatake* and *Kamikaze* classes respectively mustered eight and nine destroyers. The *Mutsuki, Fubuki, Akatsuki, Hatsuharu, Shiratsuyu,* and *Asashio* classes respectively mustered twelve, nineteen, four, six, ten, and ten units: the eighteen-strong *Kagero* class and the first two members of the *Yugumo* class completed the Japanese order of battle. Of the older units, those with 21-in. torpedo armament, four units of the *Akikaze* class survived the war as did both the *Hasu* and *Kuri* of the *Aoi* class, while one of the *Wakatake* and two of the *Kamikaze* classes likewise saw 15 August 1945. The total of nine of thirty-one of the old destroyers that were basically assigned second-line duties contrasts with the total of one destroyer, the *Uraga*, that was the sole survivor of the *Mutsuki, Fubuki, Akatsuki, Hatsuharu, Shiratsuyu,* and *Asashio* classes, while the *Yukikaze* was the only survivor from the *Kagero* class: both the nameship and the *Akigumo* from the *Yugumo* class were sunk. Other statistics and facts can be paraded to reinforce the point: eleven of Japan's twelve capital ships and all but five of her forty-three cruisers had been lost,[1] as had been no fewer than eleven fleet, five light, and six escort carriers.[2]

* * *

The annihilation of whole classes of destroyers—just two units from the total of eighty-one that were built under and after the 1923 program and in service in December 1941—provides striking evidence of the extent of defeat, but what is very difficult to discern is the relationship between losses and the reality of defeat. The obvious question in any examination of the Pacific war is when Japan reached the point when its defeat was inevitable, when the various elements that made for inevitable defeat were in place. It is difficult to resist the idea that Japan's defeat was assured from the outset, from the time that its carrier aircraft attacked the U.S. Pacific Fleet at its Pearl Harbor base, and perhaps this date, the date that will live in infamy, really does provide all the answers. From that date the United States was prepared to wage total war in order to ensure the complete and utter defeat of Japan and was never prepared to even countenance any lesser objective: armed with such intent, it was to determine events that ultimately saw the realization of its objectives. But, of course, the selection of this date raises as many questions as it seeks to answer, and inevitably historians see the outcome of wars in terms of lost campaigns and campaigns in terms of lost battles; more often than not, the criteria of defeat are losses: for armies, losses of men, and for navies and air forces, losses of ships and aircraft respectively. But in any examination of Japan's defeat in the Pacific war three events and dates possess singular significance, the first being Midway and the losses of 4–6 June 1942. Japan's defeat and the loss of four fleet carriers in this battle is important, but so are the other two: Japanese acceptance of defeat in the southern Solomons in the wake of the losses of 13–14 November 1942, and 19 November 1943, with the first of the American offensives that were to carry the tide of war across the central Pacific. It is indeed possible to see in the landings in the Gilbert and Ellice Islands a certain finality, in that with this offensive the Americans secured the means whereby they were able to neutralize an enemy position, isolate it from outside support, subject it to assault, and then, with land-based air power put ashore, move against the next objective. After November 1943 the Americans, with freedom of choice with reference to target and the forces that would be used to secure it, were able to overwhelm and neutralize their objective and to bring such forces to the theater that the Japanese were denied any means of effective response. Lest the point be doubted, between 24 November 1943, when the escort carrier *Liscome Bay* was torpedoed off the Gilberts by the submarine I-175, and 24 October 1944, when the *Princeton* was lost off the northern Philippines as a result of attack by a land-based aircraft, Japanese shells, torpedoes, and bombs failed to account for a single U.S. Navy fleet unit other than the *Fletcher*-class destroyer *Brownson*, which was lost on 26 December 1943 off Cape Gloucester, New Britain, to air attack. In other words, the whole of the American effort that resulted in the breaking of the outer perimeter defense in the central Pacific, the carrier rampages into the western Pacific that resulted in the shipping massacres at Truk (17–18 February) and Koror (30–31 March), the landings at Hollandia and Aitape that took the wide of war from one end of New Guinea to the other in two months, and that finally led to overwhelming victory in the Philippine Sea (19–20 June), all cost the United States just one destroyer, plus the destroyer escort *Shelton*, which was sunk by the submarine RO. 41 off Morotai on 3 October.[3]

Japanese ineffectiveness throughout 1944 has never attracted much in the way of serious historical attention, and quite clearly the U.S. Navy had good

Table 10.1. Japanese Naval and Shipping Losses by Type and Month, 7 December 1941 to 30 November 1942

	After 07 Dec 41	Jan 42	Feb	Mar	Apr	May	Jun	Jul	Aug	Sep	Oct	to 30 Nov 42	Total
Fleet carriers	-	-	-	-	-	-	4	-	-	-	-	-	4
Light fleet carriers	-	-	-	-	-	1	-	-	1	-	-	-	2
Escort carriers	-	-	-	-	-	-	-	-	-	-	-	-	-
Seaplane carriers	-	-	-	-	-	1	-	-	-	-	-	-	1
Battleships	-	-	-	-	-	-	-	-	-	-	-	2	2
Heavy cruisers	-	-	-	-	-	-	1	-	1	-	1	1	4
Light cruisers	-	-	-	-	-	-	-	-	-	-	1	-	1
Destroyers	2	-	1	-	-	1	1	2	2	1	4	4	18
Submarines	3	4	-	-	-	2	-	-	3	-	2	3	17
Fleet units total	5	4	1	-	-	5	6	2	7	1	8	10	49
Escorts	-	-	-	-	-	-	-	-	-	-	-	-	-
Armed merchant cruisers	-	-	-	1	-	-	-	-	-	-	-	1	2
Gunboats	1	2	3	-	-	2	3	-	1	-	3	1	16
Motor gunboats	-	-	-	-	1	-	-	-	-	-	-	-	1
Minelayers	-	-	-	-	-	1	-	-	-	-	-	-	1
Auxiliary minelayers	-	-	-	1	-	-	-	-	-	-	-	-	1
Minesweepers	3	2	1	1	-	-	-	-	-	-	-	-	7
Coastal minesweepers	-	1	-	1	-	3	-	1	-	-	-	-	6
Submarine-chasers	-	-	1	1	-	-	-	2	-	-	-	-	4
Netlayers	-	-	1	-	-	-	-	-	1	1	1	-	4
Other warships total	4	5	6	5	1	6	3	3	2	1	4	2	42
Destroyer-transports	4	1	-	-	-	-	-	-	-	1	-	-	6
LSD	-	-	-	1	-	-	-	-	-	-	-	-	1
Amphibious units total	4	1	-	1	-	-	-	-	-	1	-	-	7
Naval support ships	1	8	1	8	3	5	1	7	8	5	6	8	61
Army transports	5	3	3	7	3	9	2	2	2	1	6	14	57
Merchantmen	2	6	1	3	2	8	4	4	11	8	16	7	72
Others	2	-	-	-	-	-	-	-	-	-	-	-	2
Total	10	17	5	18	8	22	7	13	21	14	28	29	192

reason not to bring the matter to public attention, but in terms of when defeat became reality the twin events, Guadalcanal and Tarawa, really present problems of comprehension. In the eleven or so months of war that culminated with the Japanese defeats off Guadalcanal in mid-November 1942 and then the decisions that led to the decision to abandon the campaign, Japanese fleet losses were decidedly modest, as shown in table 10.1.

Moreover, the losses after 7 August 1942, with the start of the campaign for Guadalcanal, and 14 November 1942, after which time the Imperial Navy accepted defeat in the southern Solomons, were most certainly modest —the light carrier *Ryujo* in the eastern Solomons action, the battleships *Hiei* and *Kirishima*, the heavy cruisers *Kako*, *Furutaka*, and *Kinugasa*, the light cruiser *Yura*, eleven

TABLE 10.2. JAPANESE NAVAL AND SHIPPING LOSSES BY TYPE AND MONTH, 1 DECEMBER 1942 TO 19 NOVEMBER 1943

	After 01 Dec 42	Jan 43	Feb 43	Mar 43	Apr 43	May 43	Jun 43	Jul 43	Aug 43	Sep 43	Oct 43	to 19 Nov 43	Total
Fleet carriers	-	-	-	-	-	-	-	-	-	-	-	-	-
Light fleet carriers	-	-	-	-	-	-	-	-	-	-	-	-	-
Escort carriers	-	-	-	-	-	-	-	-	-	-	-	-	-
Seaplane carriers	-	-	-	-	-	-	-	1	-	-	-	-	1
Battleships	-	-	-	-	-	-	1	-	-	-	-	-	1
Heavy cruisers	-	-	-	-	-	-	-	-	-	-	-	-	-
Light cruisers	1	-	-	-	-	-	-	1	-	-	-	1	3
Destroyers	2	2	2	6	1	3	-	5	3	-	2	3	29
Submarines	3	1	1	-	1	2	4	4	2	3	1	1	23
Fleet units total	6	3	3	6	2	5	5	11	5	3	3	5	57
Escorts	-	-	-	-	-	-	-	-	-	2	-	-	2
Armed merchant cruisers	-	-	-	-	-	1	-	-	-	-	-	-	1
Gunboats	-	-	-	-	2	5	2	-	-	4	1	-	14
Motor gunboats	-	1	1	1	1	1	1	-	2	-	1	-	9
Minelayers	-	-	1	-	-	-	-	1	-	-	-	-	2
Auxiliary minelayers	-	-	-	-	-	-	1	1	-	1	-	1	4
Minesweepers	-	-	-	-	-	-	-	-	-	1	-	1	2
Coastal minesweepers	1	-	1	-	-	-	-	-	-	1	1	-	4
Submarine-chasers	-	1	-	-	2	-	-	-	3	-	2	4	12
Netlayers	1	-	-	-	-	-	-	1	-	-	-	-	2
Other warships total	2	2	3	1	5	7	4	3	5	9	5	6	52
Destroyer-transports	-	1	-	1	1	-	-	2	-	-	-	-	5
LSD	-	-	-	-	-	-	-	-	-	-	-	-	-
Amphibious units total	-	1	-	1	1	-	-	2	-	-	-	-	5
Naval support ships	6	8	7	9	10	6	8	1	7	10	16	15	103
Army transports	7	14	7	12	10	8	5	6	11	20	21	15	136
Merchantmen	15	8	7	13	12	17	8	15	12	22	12	5	146
Others	1	-	-	-	-	-	-	-	-	-	-	-	1
Total	29	30	21	34	32	31	21	22	30	52	49	35	386

destroyers, and five submarines—and really do not explain defeat per se, even allowing for the abruptness and severity of the losses of 13–14 November, namely the two battleships, the *Kinugasa*, and three destroyers, plus the seven transports of 50,531 tons lost on the 14th and another four transports of 27,152 tons on the following day. Certainly the shipping losses were serious, and no state could afford an open-ended commitment that might involve such losses into the indefinite future, but the real point about defeat at this stage lay in two separate, but related, matters. First, by November 1943 the Japanese had some 750,000 tons of shipping committed to the southwest Pacific either in theater or involved in the ferrying of manpower and material to Truk and other harbors en route to the southern Solomons and eastern New Guinea, and to other bases such as Rabaul. With the ship-

Table 10.3. American Naval Losses by Type and Month, 7 December 1941 to 30 November 1942

	After 07 Dec 41	Jan 42	Feb	Mar	Apr	May	Jun	Jul	Aug	Sep	Oct	to 30 Nov 42	Total
Fleet carriers	-	-	-	-	-	1	1	-	-	1	1	-	4
Light fleet carriers	-	-	-	-	-	-	-	-	-	-	-	-	-
Escort carriers	-	-	-	-	-	-	-	-	-	-	-	-	-
Seaplane carriers	-	-	1	-	-	-	1	-	-	-	-	-	2
Battleships	4	-	-	-	-	-	-	-	-	-	-	-	4
Heavy cruisers	-	-	-	1	-	-	-	-	3	-	-	-	4
Light cruisers	-	-	-	-	-	-	-	-	-	-	-	2	2
Destroyers	3	-	3	4	1	1	1	-	4	-	3	7	27
Submarines	1	2	1	1	-	-	1	1	1	-	-	-	8
Fleet units total	8	2	5	6	1	2	4	1	8	1	4	9	51
Escorts	-	-	-	1	-	-	-	-	-	-	-	-	1
Armed merchant cruisers	-	-	-	-	-	-	-	-	-	-	-	-	-
Gunboats	1	-	-	1	-	3	-	-	-	-	-	-	5
Motor gunboats	-	-	-	-	-	-	-	-	-	-	-	-	-
Minelayers	-	-	-	-	-	-	-	-	-	-	-	-	-
Auxiliary minelayers	-	-	-	-	-	-	-	-	-	-	-	-	-
Minesweepers	2	-	-	-	1	2	-	-	-	-	-	-	5
Coastal minesweepers	-	-	-	-	-	-	-	-	-	-	-	-	-
Submarine-chasers	-	-	-	-	-	-	-	-	-	-	-	-	-
Netlayers	-	-	-	-	-	-	-	-	-	-	-	-	-
Other warships total	3	-	-	2	1	5	-	-	-	-	-	-	11
Destroyer-transports	-	-	-	-	-	-	-	-	1	1	-	-	2
LST	-	-	-	-	-	-	-	-	-	-	-	-	-
Amphibious units total	-	-	-	-	-	-	-	-	1	1	-	-	2

ping committed to import needs cut in order to provide for service requirements and operations in 1941–1942, the national reality was that much of this shipping had to be returned by year's end; certainly at this stage of proceedings neither national nor service means could cover the losses incurred on 14–15 November. Second, the Japanese losses, as with all states and navies in similar situations, were measured not simply in terms of ship numbers, but over time and distance and in terms of organization: formations losing ships to yards for repair and refit point irrevocably in the direction of loss of effectiveness that reaches far beyond mere numbers. By way of a parallel example, and to repeat a point made earlier, it was not until the spring of 1942 that British destroyer formations with the Home Fleet were reconstituted in terms of numbers after the twin Norwegian and northwest Europe campaigns of 1940; the Japanese in the southwest Pacific were similarly placed in terms of formation loss that was not directly tied to numbers loss.

Likewise, the period between 30 November 1942 and 19 November 1943 is not one punctuated by major Japanese losses. The only major loss was the

Table 10.4. American Naval Losses by Type and Month, 1 December 1942 to 19 November 1943

	After 01 Dec 42	Jan 43	Feb	Mar	Apr	May	Jun	Jul	Aug	Sep	Oct	to 19 Nov 43	Total
Fleet carriers	-	-	-	-	-	-	-	-	-	-	-	-	-
Light fleet carriers	-	-	-	-	-	-	-	-	-	-	-	-	-
Escort carriers	-	-	-	-	-	-	-	-	-	-	-	-	-
Seaplane carriers	-	-	-	-	-	-	-	-	-	-	-	-	-
Battleships	-	-	-	-	-	-	-	-	-	-	-	-	-
Heavy cruisers	1	1	-	-	-	-	-	-	-	-	-	-	2
Light cruisers	-	-	-	-	-	-	-	1	-	-	-	-	1
Destroyers	-	1	1	-	1	-	-	3	-	1	5	2	14
Submarines	-	1	1	2	2	-	2	-	1	2	2	2	15
Fleet units total	1	3	2	2	3	-	2	4	1	3	7	4	32
Escorts	-	-	-	-	-	-	-	-	-	-	-	-	-
Armed merchant cruisers	-	-	-	-	-	-	-	-	-	-	-	-	-
Gunboats	1	-	-	-	-	-	-	-	-	-	-	-	1
Motor gunboats	-	-	-	-	-	-	-	-	-	-	-	-	-
Minelayers	-	-	-	-	-	-	-	-	-	-	-	-	-
Auxiliary minelayers	-	-	-	-	-	-	-	-	-	-	-	-	-
Minesweepers	1	-	-	-	-	-	-	1	-	1	-	-	3
Coastal minesweepers	-	-	-	-	-	-	-	-	-	-	-	-	-
Submarine-chasers	-	1	-	1	-	-	3	-	2	-	-	1	8
Netlayers	-	-	-	-	-	-	-	-	-	-	-	-	-
Other warships total	2	1	-	1	-	-	3	1	2	1	-	1	12
Destroyer-transports	-	-	-	-	-	-	-	-	-	-	-	1	1
LST	-	-	-	-	-	-	2	2	2	1	2	-	9
Amphibious units total	-	-	-	-	-	-	2	2	2	1	2	1	10

battleship *Mutsu*, which was destroyed by an internal explosion in Hiroshima Bay, while losses of destroyers and submarines each averaged about one every two weeks. Such losses were very modest, though the losses incurred in the Bismarck Sea action in March 1943 and then in the central Solomons in July provided pointers to the future.

But what is very interesting is not simply the fact that Japanese "other" losses were about the same as the "fleet" losses—and these other losses were to escalate disproportionately as the Americans fought their way into the western Pacific and the Southern Resources Area—but how closely balanced were Japanese and American losses. One is reminded of the comment by the Chief of Naval Operations, Admiral Harold N. Stark, to the pessimistic and realistic Japanese ambassador, Admiral Nomura Kichisaburo:

> While you may have your initial successes due to timing and surprise, the time will come when you too will have your losses, but there will be

> this great difference. You will not only be unable to make up your losses but will grow weaker as time goes on; while on the other hand we will not only make up our losses but will grow stronger as time goes on. It is inevitable that we shall crush you before we are through with you.[4]

Herein was the real point of Japanese losses in the period between Guadalcanal and the Gilberts. The American losses were of a very similar scale than those of Japan, especially when the losses of 7 December—the battleships *Arizona, California, Oklahoma,* and *West Virginia* and the destroyers *Cassin, Downes,* and *Shaw*—are removed from the lists. (See table 10.3.)

The disparity of losses in this opening phase of the war was among second-tier units, not the fleet units, and this phenomenon repeated itself in the second and subsequent phases of the war: the Japanese, with their defensive commitment and in the face of superior enemy formations, suffered increasing losses among their escort and local units, specifically as a result of attack by carrier aircraft. (See table 10.4.)

But the real point—other than what was clearly tantamount to an American exemption from real losses—was new American construction, as shown in table 10.5.[5]

Such tables threaten death by statistics, and certainly it is easy to miss what should be the obvious points of significance amid this collection of tables. While it may be clear (albeit perhaps not at first reading) that between 1 August and 19 November 1943 destroyer escorts were completed at a rate of more than one a day and that a destroyer was being completed throughout the period 1 January–19 November 1943 in little more than sixty hours, the fact is that in this latter period American yards completed more fleet carriers than had been built prior to 1941. That is, the total of seven fleet and eight light fleet carriers really represented some two decades of construction—and by 19 November 1943 the greater part of this particular effort had still to manifest itself. A total of seventeen fleet, nine light fleet, and seventy-six escort carriers entered U.S. service in the course of the Pacific war,[6] and the latter total excludes those transferred to Britain on lend-lease.[7]

It is this American productive capacity that lies at the basis of the author's previous comment that

> the basis of Japan's defeat lay in the fact that the Americans were a pack of cheating bastards. It was not that the *Kaigun*'s intention to fight the U.S. Navy to a draw was flawed. The *Kaigun*'s problem was not that it faced a U.S. Navy but that it faced two U.S. Navies. It fought the first U.S. Navy to a standstill, but the problem was that in the process it exhausted itself as well—and the United States built another navy in the meantime.[8]

Table 10.5. The Commissioning of Warships by the U.S. Navy

	After 07 Dec 41	Jan 42	Feb	Mar	Apr	May	Jun	Jul	Aug	Sep	Oct	to 30 Nov 42	Total
Fleet carriers	-	-	-	-	-	-	-	-	-	-	-	-	-
Light fleet carriers	-	-	-	-	-	-	-	-	-	-	-	-	-
Escort carriers	-	-	-	1	1	-	1	-	3	4	-	1	11
Seaplane tenders	-	-	-	-	-	-	-	-	-	-	-	1	1
Battleships	-	-	-	1	1	1	-	-	1	-	-	-	4
Heavy cruisers	-	-	-	-	-	-	-	-	-	-	-	-	-
Light cruisers	1	1	2	-	-	-	1	1	-	1	1	1	9
Destroyers	2	4	2	3	5	5	9	7	9	9	9	9	73
Submarines	3	3	1	2	2	4	4	4	2	3	4	1	33
Fleet units total	6	8	5	7	9	10	15	12	15	17	14	13	131
Destroyer escorts	-	-	-	-	-	-	-	-	-	-	-	-	-

	after 01 Dec 42	Jan 43	Feb	Mar	Apr	May	Jun	Jul	Aug	Sep	Oct	to 19 Nov 43	Total
Fleet carriers	1	-	1	-	1	1	-	-	1	-	1	-	6
Light fleet carriers	-	1	1	1	-	1	1	1	1	-	-	1	8
Escort carriers	1	-	1	1	3	-	-	1	3	2	4	2	18
Seaplane tenders	-	-	-	-	-	-	-	-	-	-	-	-	-
Battleships	-	-	1	-	-	1	-	-	-	-	-	-	2
Heavy cruisers	-	-	-	-	1	-	1	-	-	-	2	-	4
Light cruisers	-	1	-	1	1	-	1	1	1	-	1	-	7
Destroyers	11	8	12	10	14	12	10	13	12	12	7	7	128
Submarines	3	4	3	3	4	5	4	6	4	5	7	2	50
Fleet units total	16	14	19	16	24	20	17	22	22	19	22	12	173
Destroyer escorts	-	1	2	2	11	15	17	25	32	29	34	20	188

In 1943 alone 6 fleet, 9 light, and 24 escort carriers, 2 battleships, 4 heavy and 7 light cruisers, 128 destroyers, 233 destroyer escorts, and 56 submarines were commissioned by the U.S. Navy, in tonnage terms the equivalent of the whole of the Japanese Navy in 1941—and for good measure the United States repeated the performance, *mutatis mutandis,* in 1944.[9] The U.S. Navy, the prewar navy, met and defeated the Kaigun on the perimeter defense, and by spring 1943 was spent. It was spent not so much because of the heaviness of losses but in terms of balance, time, and the need to secure replacement aircrew and air formation on scales that were previously unthinkable. By war's end the U.S. Navy had some 90,000 trained aircrew and numbered 99 fleet, light, and escort carriers, 1,246 fleet units, 5,250 major combat units, and 67,952 units of all and every size and description with the fleet, amphibious forces, logistics organization, and shore establishments. Herein is the basis of the questioning of American honesty and legitimacy: this navy, overwhelmingly, was a wartime creation.

From the time of Grant, the United States waged war on the basis of demographic, industrial, economic, and financial superiority over all enemies, which meant that the American way of war, for a hundred years, stressed superiority of numbers, concentration of massed firepower, and the seeking of battle as the means of ensuring the defeat of an enemy. This formula lacked subtlety and had little in the way of finesse, but the yardsticks by which it must be measured were effectiveness and success, and it stood the United States in good stead until the nation fundamentally failed to understand the nature of the war it fought and of the enemy it faced in southeast Asia in the 1960s.

But if the American way of war was very basic, one can argue that in terms of subtlety, of elegance and sophistication, there are few examples in warfare in the twentieth century to rival the opening Japanese moves, across nine time zones and 7,000 miles, that brought war to southeast Asia and the Pacific in December 1941. The Japanese put together a plan involving successive attacks by forces operating behind a front secured by land-based air power and then penetrated to the Malay Barrier with an effort that was remarkable in terms of economy of effort and lack of overall superiority of numbers but that commanded massive local superiority over enemies defensively dispersed and unable to cooperate to any real effect. And, of course, the war that Japan thus initiated was a war that it lost. If one wants just one set of statistical facts to represent the basis of Japan's defeat and the American victory in the Pacific, the American industrial stamina that enabled it to build a second, wartime navy, then it is provided in the operations of February 1945: of the total of eleven fleet and five light carriers, plus one hundred capital ships, heavy and light cruisers, and destroyers in the five task groups that conducted the raid on Tokyo in this month as part of the prelude to the landings on Iwo Jima, just the carriers *Enterprise* and *Saratoga* and the heavy cruisers *Indianapolis* and *San Francisco* had been in service on 7 December 1941.[10]

The scale of American construction points attention in two directions: the relationship between victory and supremacy via losses, and, for the United States, the basis of the truism that the-more-you-use-the-less-you-lose. On the first matter one of the major problems of historical interpretation lies in the confusion of victory and supremacy. The most obvious point of confusion lies with interpretation of British history, specifically the assumption that British victories at sea provided the basis of British naval supremacy. In reality British naval supremacy, based upon the British state's advantage relative to all potential rivals in terms of credit and ship-building capacity and Britain's advantages in terms of numbers of warships and geographical position, was the basis of victories, and those victories became increasingly marked in the period between 1688 and 1815 as disparity in numbers and quality widened. In the Pacific the war both in its various phases and overall reflected supremacy and its resultant victories. In the war's opening phase Japanese advantages of numbers, position, and timing were combined in a series of phased offensive operations spread over more than ninety degrees of longitude, that produced a series of victories that were remarkable but for one fact: the relative ease with which they were undone. The American victory in the Pacific was the product of overwhelming advantage of numbers and firepower that were combined in an integrated four-phase pattern—the use of land-based air power to neutralize the objective, the isolation of the objective as a result of massed carrier formations being brought to the theater, the assault landing and securing of the objective, and the movement of land-based air power to the new base area preparatory to a repeat of the process. The American drive across the central Pacific was perhaps the first truly joint offensive, with war's three primary dimensions gathered together, interrelated and interdependent, and the overwhelming superiority of numbers and firepower provided the basis of assured success, and Japanese losses and ineffectiveness. It is worth noting, for example, that in 1944 the Imperial Navy lost five fleet, five light fleet, and three escort carriers—more than either the British or Americans lost in the entire war—and such losses were the product rather than the cause of defeat. The road between victory and defeat, between cause and result, is a two-way not one-way road, and Japanese losses were important not simply in terms of their being the product of defeat; the Japanese losses were part of and contributory to defeat, or at least the final defeat in August 1945, but in the final analysis such losses were the result of a defeat that was already in place: what remained to be settled at this stage was the final form, cost, and date of that defeat.

For the best description of Japan's defeat in the Second World War, specifically with reference to the Greater East Asia conference of September 1943, see Milton's *Paradise Lost*, Book X, written nearly three hundred years before the event.

APPENDIX 10.1.

THE BASIS OF AMERICAN VICTORY IN THE PACIFIC

SET OUT ON THE following pages is a statement of the basis of the American victory in the Pacific, and it is in two forms. The first is two tables of construction, the second its attendant detail.

* * *

With reference to the table it should be noted that totals do not necessarily agree and for obvious reason: not included are ships with either or both dates of being laid down and launched if these were before 7 December 1941; by the same token, dates of being launched and commissioned after 15 August 1945 are not included.

* * *

As a basic rule the names given are those with which the individual ship entered service, applied retrospectively where appropriate. The exceptions to this basic rule are the light carriers that were originally laid down as light cruisers. These have been given with their original—intended—names as light cruisers in reference to dates of being laid down; their dates of launch and commissioning have been given, with changed names, as light carriers.

The escort carriers were converted merchant ships or hulls, but because not all dates when keels were laid down could be ascertained, the laid down returns have been deliberately omitted on the premise of battleship armor: all or nothing.

The asterisks in the heavy cruiser lists relate to the "large cruisers" *Alaska* and *Guam*.

The number of destroyer escorts laid down and launched includes units that were subsequently converted, mostly as transports, and also units that were canceled while under construction. The transport list does not include destroyer escorts completed as APD/high-speed transports.

The tenders list represents the destroyer, submarine, and seaplane tenders only.

Totals do not include units completed and transferred under lend-lease to Allied navies.

The listing of Liberty Ships does not include oilers and ships delivered incomplete, and a certain care need be exercised in any examination of the list because various units were requisitioned by the U.S. Navy and commissioned into service.

The lists do not include shipping in service 7 December 1941, but only units that were taken into the naval service thereafter, the dates having been selected on the basis of when units assumed the status of full commission, i.e., the dates of when some ships were acquired by the U.S. Navy, afforded limited commission, and assigned local duties prior to refitting, conversion, and full commission have been set aside.

* * *

Ships have been listed by type and, with one exception, in alphabetic order and not by pennant numbers.

Table Appendix 10.1.1. U.S. Wartime Construction: Fleet Units, Submarines, and Destroyer Escorts, and Minesweepers and Tenders, Transports, and Oilers Commissioned, and Liberty Ships Completed, between 7 December 1941 and 15 August 1945

		CV	CVL	CVE	BB	CA	CL	DD	Total	SS	DE	PF	AM	Tenders	AK/AKA	AP/ APA	AO	Liberty ships
U.S. warships in the Pacific																		
6 December	1941	3	-	-	8	12	9	80	112	27	-	-	?	-	-	-	-	-
7–31 December	1941	-	-	-	-	-	1	2	3	3	-	-	-	2	-	1	1	2
January	1942	-	-	-	-	-	1	4	5	3	-	-	1	1	-	2	2	3
February	1942	-	-	-	-	-	2	1	3	1	-	-	-	-	-	-	3	12
March	1942	-	-	1	1	-	-	3	5	2	-	-	-	-	2	-	-	16
April	1942	-	-	-	1	-	-	5	6	2	-	-	-	-	1	4	2	26
May	1942	-	-	-	1	-	-	5	6	4	-	-	3	1	2	2	2	43
June	1942	-	-	1	-	-	1	9	11	4	-	-	-	-	1	3	1	51
July	1942	-	-	-	-	-	1	7	8	4	-	-	1	-	-	1	1	52
August	1942	-	-	3	1	-	-	9	13	2	-	-	3	-	-	6	1	57
September	1942	-	-	4	-	-	1	9	14	3	-	-	4	-	1	7	4	68
October	1942	-	-	-	-	-	1	9	10	4	-	-	10	-	1	1	2	65
November	1942	-	-	1	-	-	1	9	11	1	-	-	9	1	1	-	2	69
December	1942	1	-	1	-	-	-	11	13	3	-	-	6	-	3	1	-	82
Total for year:		1	-	11	4	-	8	81	105	33	-	-	37	3	12	27	20	544
January	1943	-	1	-	-	-	1	8	10	4	1	-	1	2	3	-	2	78
February	1943	1	1	1	1	-	-	11	15	3	2	-	5	-	1	-	3	81
March	1943	-	1	1	-	-	1	9	12	4	2	-	2	2	1	1	2	102
April	1943	1	-	3	-	1	-	13	18	4	9	-	7	2	2	3	3	112
May	1943	1	1	-	1	-	-	12	15	5	15	-	2	1	6	-	1	119
June	1943	-	1	-	-	1	-	9	11	4	16	-	2	1	1	4	-	116
July	1943	-	1	1	-	-	1	13	16	6	24	-	3	-	7	3	-	109
August	1943	1	1	3	-	-	1	11	17	4	35	-	2	-	4	4	1	109

September	1943	-	-	1	-	-	-	13	14	5	31	1	1	1	1	4	1	112
October	1943	-	-	4	-	1	-	7	12	7	32	3	2	-	14	6	2	117
November	1943	2	1	4	-	-	-	11	18	5	34	3	3	-	10	5	2	104
December	1943	-	1	5	-	1	3	13	23	5	31	4	5	4	3	3	2	127
Total for year:		6	9	23	2	4	7	130	181	56	232	11	35	13	53	33	19	1,286
January	1944	1	-	4	-	-	1	6	12	5	20	4	5	3	7	4	1	76
February	1944	-	-	4	-	-	-	9	13	5	25	4	6	1	4	5	2	77
March	1944	-	-	5	-	-	-	10	15	7	20	7	5	4	8	3	2	84
April	1944	1	-	5	1	-	-	6	13	8	23	9	6	1	3	7	3	77
May	1944	1	-	5	-	-	1	8	15	7	26	5	8	1	3	6	2	65
June	1944	-	-	6	1	1*	2	8	18	8	17	-	6	2	5	4	1	55
July	1944	-	-	2	-	-	1	7	10	7	17	-	6	2	4	6	1	50
August	1944	1	-	-	-	-	1	3	5	7	10	3	5	4	4	8	1	47
September	1944	1	-	-	-	1*	2	3	7	4	10	8	10	1	9	21	-	42
October	1944	1	-	-	-	1	-	2	4	7	7	7	3	1	9	37	-	46
November	1944	1	-	1	-	-	-	8	10	6	4	6	11	2	13	37	2	45
December	1944	-	-	1	-	-	3	6	10	9	1	3	4	2	11	38	-	42
Total for year		7	-	33	2	3	11	76	132	80	180	56	75	24	80	176	15	706
January	1945	1	-	-	-	1	2	3	7	3	2	3	1	2	12	23	3	30
February	1945	-	-	1	-	1	1	8	11	6	1	4	4	1	11	10	2	30
March	1945	-	-	1	-	-	-	10	11	6	1	1	3	1	10	8	1	24
April	1945	1	-	1	-	1	-	5	8	5	-	-	7	1	20	6	-	10
May	1945	-	-	3	-	-	1	9	13	2	-	-	2	2	12	2	1	9
June	1945	1	-	1	-	-	2	5	9	5	1	-	3	-	8	3	-	11
July	1945	-	-	1	-	2	-	8	11	1	-	-	3	1	9	1	-	6
August	1945	-	-	-	-	-	-	1	1	2	-	-	3	1	2	1	-	3
Total 1 January to 15 August	1945	3	-	8	-	5	6	49	71	30	5	8	26	9	84	54	7	123
Wartime Total		17	9	75	8	12	33	338	492	202	417	75	173	51	229	281	62	2,661

CV	Fleet carriers
CVL	Light fleet carriers
CVE	Escort carriers
DD	Destroyers
BB	Battleships
CA	Heavy cruisers
CL	Light cruisers
SS	Submarines
DE	Destroyer escorts
PF	Frigates
AM	Minesweepers
AK/AKA	Cargo/Attack cargo ships
AP/APA	Transports/Attack transports
AO	Fleet oilers

Notes:

The tenders list represents the destroyer, submarine, and seaplane tenders only.

Totals do not include units completed and transferred under lend-lease to Allied navies.

The asterisks in the heavy cruiser lists relate to the "large cruisers" *Alaska* and *Guam*.

The transport list does not include destroyer escorts completed as APD/high-speed transports.

The listing of Liberty Ships does not include oilers and ships delivered incomplete, and a certain care need be exercised in any examination of the list because various units were requisitioned by the U.S. Navy and commissioned into service.

The lists do not include shipping in service 7 December 1941 but only units that were taken into the naval service thereafter, the dates having been selected on the basis of when units assumed the status of full commission; i.e., the dates of when some ships were acquired by the U.S. Navy, afforded limited commission, and assigned local duties prior to refitting, conversion, and full commission have been set aside.

Table Appendix 10.1.2. American Construction and Dates of Laying Down, Launch, and Commissioning

On 7 December 1941 on station in the Pacific were the following:

U.S. Asiatic Fleet: one heavy and 2 light cruisers, 13 destroyers, and 29 submarines

U.S. Pacific Fleet: 8 battleships, 3 carriers, 12 heavy and 9 light cruisers, 67 destroyers, and 27 submarines

The Japanese fleet: 10 battleships, 10 carriers, 18 heavy and 20 light cruisers, 112 destroyers, and 65 submarines.

In the course of the war the output of U.S. shipyards was as follows:

		Fleet carriers			Light carriers			Escort carriers			Destroyer escorts			Heavy cruisers			Light cruisers			Destroyers			Submarines			Battleships		
		LD	L	C	LD	L	C	LD	L	C	LD	L	C	LD	L	C	LD	L	C	LD	L	C	LD	L	C	LD	L	C
December	1941	-	-	-	-	-	-	-	1	-	-	-	-	1	-	-	1	1	1	7	5	2	-	-	3	-	-	-
January	1942	-	-	-	-	-	-	-	-	-	-	-	-	-	-	-	-	-	1	3	2	4	2	2	3	-	-	-
February	1942	1	-	-	-	-	-	-	-	-	-	1	-	-	-	-	-	1	2	9	10	1	4	3	1	3	-	-
March	1942	1	-	-	-	-	-	-	-	1	-	-	1	-	-	-	2	1	-	8	8	3	4	3	2	2	-	-
April	1942	-	-	-	-	-	-	-	1	-	-	-	1	-	-	-	1	1	-	10	12	5	5	4	2	11	-	-
May	1942	-	-	-	-	-	-	-	3	-	-	-	1	-	-	-	-	1	-	13	13	5	3	3	4	-	-	-
June	1942	-	-	-	-	-	-	-	2	1	-	-	-	-	-	-	-	1	1	9	14	9	5	5	4	-	-	-
July	1942	-	1	-	-	-	-	-	-	-	-	-	-	-	1	-	-	-	1	8	9	7	5	3	4	9	5	-
August	1942	1	-	-	-	1	-	-	2	3	-	1	1	-	1	-	1	1	-	6	14	9	4	4	2	2	2	-
September	1942	-	1	-	-	-	-	-	-	4	-	-	-	-	-	-	-	-	1	5	9	9	6	2	3	11	3	-
October	1942	-	-	-	-	1	-	-	-	-	-	-	-	-	-	-	3	1	1	11	15	9	4	4	4	7	4	-
November	1942	-	-	-	-	-	-	-	-	1	-	-	-	-	-	-	1	-	1	10	6	9	2	4	1	19	3	-
December	1942	2	1	1	-	1	-	-	-	1	-	1	-	-	-	-	3	1	-	9	7	11	7	6	3	17	9	-
1942 Total		4	3	1	-	3	-	-	9	11	-	3	4	-	2	-	11	8	8	101	119	81	51	43	33	81	26	-

		Fleet carriers			Light carriers			Escort carriers			Destroyer escorts			Heavy cruisers			Light cruisers			Destroyers			Submarines			Battleships		
		LD	L	C	LD	L	C	LD	L	C	LD	L	C	LD	L	C	LD	L	C	LD	L	C	LD	L	C	LD	L	C
January	1943	2	1	-	-	1	1	-	-	-	-	-	-	-	-	-	1	-	1	4	5	8	7	4	4	33	18	1
February	1943	2	-	1	-	1	1	-	-	1	-	-	1	4	-	-	2	1	-	6	9	11	4	2	3	30	14	2
March	1943	2	-	-	-	-	1	-	-	1	-	-	-	-	-	-	3	1	1	14	12	9	8	3	4	28	15	2
April	1943	-	1	1	-	1	-	-	2	3	-	-	-	1	1	1	1	-	-	5	8	13	9	6	4	25	29	9
May	1943	1	-	1	-	1	1	-	3	-	-	-	1	-	-	-	-	-	-	4	6	12	5	9	5	22	29	15
June	1943	-	-	-	-	-	1	-	1	-	-	-	-	2	1	1	1	1	-	6	12	9	7	5	4	18	26	16
July	1943	-	-	-	-	-	1	-	2	1	-	-	-	2	-	-	1	1	1	10	12	13	7	6	6	25	24	24
August	1943	-	2	1	-	1	1	-	1	3	-	-	-	-	1	-	1	-	1	13	10	11	7	9	4	33	32	35
September	1943	2	-	-	-	1	-	-	3	1	-	-	-	2	-	-	-	-	-	4	5	13	8	4	5	19	18	31
October	1943	1	1	-	-	-	-	-	3	4	-	-	-	-	-	1	1	-	-	7	10	7	6	9	7	23	35	32
November	1943	-	-	2	-	-	1	-	5	4	-	-	-	-	1	-	-	-	-	6	5	11	8	7	5	45	31	34
December	1943	1	-	-	-	-	1	-	5	5	-	1	-	-	-	1	-	3	3	6	6	13	5	3	5	34	30	31
1943 Total		11	5	6	-	6	9	-	25	23	-	1	2	11	4	4	11	7	7	85	100	130	81	67	56	335	301	232
January	1944	-	1	1	-	-	-	-	4	4	-	1	-	-	-	-	2	2	1	7	6	6	3	9	5	27	28	20
February	1944	1	3	-	-	-	-	-	4	4	-	-	-	-	1	-	2	2	-	9	6	9	9	6	5	10	20	25
March	1944	2	-	-	-	-	-	-	5	5	-	-	-	-	1	-	-	2	-	9	9	10	8	7	7	9	14	20
April	1944	-	1	1	-	-	-	-	5	5	-	-	1	1	-	-	1	1	-	10	7	6	9	5	8	8	9	23
May	1944	1	-	1	-	-	-	-	6	5	-	-	1	1	-	-	1	-	1	10	9	8	7	10	7	9	5	26
June	1944	-	1	-	-	-	-	-	3	6	-	-	-	-	-	1	-	-	2	5	4	8	8	8	8	5	5	17
July	1944	3	-	-	-	-	-	-	1	2	-	-	-	-	1	-	-	-	1	5	5	7	5	6	7	2	4	17
August	1944	1	1	1	-	-	-	-	1	-	-	-	-	1	4	-	-	2	1	7	4	3	3	7	7	3	8	10
September	1944	2	-	1	-	-	-	-	2	-	-	-	-	-	1	1	3	2	2	8	12	3	-	3	4	-	-	10
October	1944	-	-	1	-	-	-	-	1	-	-	-	-	-	2	1	1	-	-	9	7	2	1	6	7	2	-	7
November	1944	-	1	1	-	-	-	-	2	1	-	-	-	-	-	-	1	-	-	6	7	8	1	4	6	-	-	4
December	1944	-	1	-	-	-	-	-	1	1	-	-	-	3	-	-	-	1	3	6	7	6	-	9	9	-	-	1
1944 Total		10	9	7	-	-	-	-	35	33	-	1	2	6	10	3	11	12	11	91	83	76	54	80	80	75	93	180

January	1945	1	-	1	-	-	-	-	1	-	-	-	-	1	-	1	1	-	2	7	6	3	2	5	3	-	-	2
February	1945	-	-	-	-	-	-	-	1	1	-	-	-	-	-	1	1	1	1	3	5	8	-	3	6	-	-	1
March	1945	-	1	-	-	-	-	-	1	1	-	-	-	-	-	-	1	-	-	2	11	10	2	1	6	-	-	1
April	1945	-	1	1	-	-	-	-	1	1	-	-	-	-	1	1	-	2	-	10	6	5	3	2	5	-	-	-
May	1945	-	2	-	-	-	-	-	1	3	-	-	-	1	1	-	1	-	1	6	6	9	-	2	2	-	-	-
June	1945	-	-	1	-	-	-	-	1	1	-	-	-	-	2	-	-	-	2	7	7	5	2	3	5	-	-	1
July	1945	-	2	-	-	-	-	-	1	1	-	-	-	1	-	2	-	1	-	7	9	8	1	3	1	-	-	-
August	1945	-	-	-	-	-	-	-	1	-	-	-	-	-	-	-	-	-	-	2	2	1	-	-	2	-	-	-
Total to 15 August	1945	1	6	3	-	-	-	-	8	8	-	-	-	3	4	5	4	4	6	44	52	49	10	19	30	-	-	5
Overall Total		26	23	17	-	9	9	-	78	75	-	5	8	20	20	12	38	32	33	328	359	338	196	209	202	491	420	417

Key: LD Laid down
L Launched
C Commissioned

Table Appendix 10.1.3

(iii) Listing of Fleet Units, Destroyer Escorts, and Submarines
Reference Dates of Being Laid Down, Launched, and Commissioned,
7 December 1941–15 August 1945

The ships listed as escorts are those that were classified as destroyer escorts (DE)

December 1941	
Escort carrier	Launched: The *Bogue* (15).
Heavy cruisers	Laid down: The large cruiser *Alaska* (17).
Light cruisers	Laid down: The *Dayton* (29).
	Launched: The *Columbia* (17).
	Commissioned: The *Atlanta* (24).
Destroyers	Laid down: The *Bennett* (10), *Fullam* (10), *Beale* (19), *Cony* (24), *Bell* (30), *Stevens* (30), and *Boyle* (31).
	Launched: The *Doran* (10), *Earle* (10), *Beatty* (20), *Tillman* (20), and *Bancroft* (31).
	Commissioned: The *Corry* (18) and *Hambleton* (22).
Submarines	Commissioned: The *Flying Fish* (10), *Silversides* (15), and *Gato* (31).
January 1942	
Light cruiser	Commissioned: The *San Diego* (10).
Destroyers	Laid down: The *Mullany* (15), *Saufley* (27), and *Champlin* (31).
	Launched: The *Caldwell* (15) and *Barton* (31).
	Commissioned: The *Forrest* (13), *Hobson* (22), *Macomb* (26), and *Rodman* (27).
Submarines	Laid down: The *Hoe* (2) and *Sawfish* (20).
	Launched: The *Herring* (15) and *Guardfish* (20).
	Commissioned: The *Greenling* (21), *Trigger* (30), and *Finback* (31).
February 1942	
Battleship	Launched: The *Alabama* (16).
Escort carrier	Laid down: The *Card* (22).
Light cruisers	Launched: The *Montpelier* (12).
	Commissioned: The *Juneau* (14) and *San Juan* (28).
Destroyers	Laid down: The *Bush* (12), *Waller* (12), *Brownson* (15), *Shubrick* (17), *Charrette* (20), *Hudson* (20), *Converse* (23), *Davison* (26), and *Edwards* (26).
	Launched: The *Herndon* (5), *Butler* (12), *Coghlan* (12), *Gherardi* (12), *Meade* (15), *Nicholas* (19), *Duncan* (20), *Guest* (20), *Hutchins* (20), and *Lansdowne* (20).
	Commissioned: The *Fitch* (3).
Escorts	Laid down: The *Andres* (12), *Brennan* (28), and *Doherty* (28).
Submarines	Laid down: The *Jack* (2), *Puffer* (16), *Lapon* (21), and *Tinosa* (21).
	Launched: The *Wahoo* (14), *Albacore* (17), and *Bluefish* (21).
	Commissioned: The *Grouper* (12).
March 1942	
Battleship	Commissioned: The *South Dakota* (20).
Fleet carrier	Laid down: The *Oriskany* (18).
Escort carrier	Commissioned: The *Charger* (3).

Light cruisers	Laid down: The *Vincennes* (7) and *Wilmington* (16).
	Launched: The *Birmingham* (20).
Destroyers	Laid down: The *McKee* (2), *Franks* (8), *Murray* (16), *Eaton* (17) *McCord* (17), *Glennon* (25), *Jeffers* (25), and *Haggard* (27).
	Launched: The *Aulick* (2), *Carmick* (8) *O'Bannon* (14), *Charles Ausburne* (16), *Doyle* (17), *Frazier* (17), *Lardner* (20), and *McCalla* (20).
	Commissioned: The *Aaron Ward* (4), *Buchanan* (21), and *Laffey* (31).
Escorts	Laid down: The *Austin* (14) and *Edgar G. Chase* (14).
Submarines	Laid down: The *Mingo* (21), *Scamp* (6), *Scorpion* (20), and *Devilfish* (31).
	Launched: The *Kingfish* (2), *Amberjack* (6), and *Whale* (14).
	Commissioned: The *Haddock* (14) and *Growler* (20).
April 1942	
Battleship	Commissioned: The *Indiana* (30).
Escort carrier	Launched: The *Nassau* (4).
Light cruisers	Laid down: The *Crown Point* (11).
	Launched: The *Denver* (4).
Destroyers	Laid down: The *Sproston* (1), *Boyd* (2), *Hailey* (11), *Hazlewood* (11), *Foote* (14), *Wickes* (15), *Conner* (16), *Hall* (16), *Bradford* (28), and *Daly* (29). Launched: The *Claxton* (1), *Kendrick* (2), *Endicott* (5), *Chevalier* (11), *Gansevoort* (11), *Dyson* (15), *Bennett* (16), *Fullam* (16), *Shubrick* (18), *Laub* (28), *Murphy* (29), and *McCook* (30).
	Commissioned: The *Farenholt* (2), *Duncan* (16), *Lansdowne* (29), *Bancroft* (30), and *Woodworth* (30).
Escorts	Laid down: The *Decker* (1), *Dobler* (1), *Doneff* (1), *Drury* (1), *Edward C. Daly* (1), *Engstrom* (1), *Gilmore* (1), *Burden R. Hastings* (15), *LeHardy* (15), *Harold C. Thomas* (30), and *Wileman* (30).
Submarines	Laid down: The *Paddle* (1), *Tullibee* (1), *Muskallunge* (7), *Snook* (17), and *Dragonet* (28).
	Launched: The *Barb* (2), *Shad* (15), *Blackfish* (18), and *Peto* (30).
	Commissioned: The *Halibut* (10) and *Grunion* (11).
May 1942	
Battleship	Commissioned: The *Massachusetts* (12).
Escort carriers	Launched: The *Core* (15), *Altahama* (22), and *Barnes* (22).
Light cruiser	Launched: The *Mobile* (15).
Destroyers	Laid down: The *Johnston* (6), *Maddox* (7), *Nelson* (7), *Philip* (7), *Renshaw* (7), *William D. Porter* (7), *Young* (7), *Heermann* (8), *Burns* (9), *Izard* (9), *Isherwood* (12), *Spence* (18), and *Laws* (19).
	Launched: The *Pringle* (2), *Stanly* (2), *Fletcher* (3), *Radford* (3), *Mervine* (3), *Quick* (3), *Harrison* (7), *John Rodgers* (7), *Gillespie* (8), *Parker* (12), *Frankford* (17), *Strong* (17), and *Capps* (31).
	Commissioned: The *Beatty* (7), *Bailey* (11), *Lardner* (13), *McCalla* (27), and *Barton* (29).
Submarines	Laid down: The *Rasher* (4), *Pargo* (21), and *Raton* (29).
	Launched: The *Sunfish* (2), *Gunnel* (17), and *Runner* (30).
	Commissioned: The *Herring* (4), *Guardfish* (8), *Wahoo* (14), and *Kingfish* (20).
June 1942	
Escort carriers	Launched: The *Block Island* (6) and *Breton* (27).
	Commissioned: The *Copahee* (15).
Light cruisers	Launched: The *Santa Fe* (10).
	Commissioned: The *Cleveland* (15).

Destroyers	Laid down: The *Hoel* (4), *Terry* (8), *Nields* (15), *Longshaw* (16), *Ringgold* (25), *Schroeder* (25), *Brown* (27), *Thatcher* (29), and *Morrison* (30).
	Launched: The *Charrette* (3), *Hudson* (3), *Hobby* (4), *Taylor* (7), *Baldwin* (14), *Boyle* (15), *Jenkins* (21), *La Vallette* (21), *Bell* (24), *Stevens* (24), *Champlin* (25), *MacKenzie* (27), *De Haven* (28), and *Harding* (28).
	Commissioned: The *Cowie* (1), *Nicholas* (6), *Tillman* (4), *Caldwell* (10), *Mervine* (17), *Meade* (22), *Knight* (23), *O'Bannon* (26), and *Fletcher* (30).
Escorts	Laid down: The *Jacob Jones* (26) and *Robert E. Peary* (30).
Submarines	Laid down: The *Steelhead* (1), *Bluefish* (5), *Escolar* (10), *Bonefish* (25), and *Balao* (26).
	Launched: The *Gurnard* (1), *Haddo* (21), *Pogy* (23), *Sawfish* (23), and *Tunny* (30).
	Commissioned: The *Albacore* (1), *Whale* (1), *Shad* (12), and *Amberjack* (19).
July 1942	
Fleet carrier	Launched: The *Essex* (31).
Heavy cruiser	Launched: The *Baltimore* (28).
Light cruiser	Commissioned: The *Columbia* (29).
Destroyers	Laid down: The *Bearss* (14), *Trathen* (18), *Pritchett* (20), *John D. Henley* (21), *Sigsbee* (22), *Stevenson* (23), *Stockton* (24), *Ordronaux* (25), and *Kimberley* (27).
	Launched: The *David W. Taylor* (4), *Satterlee* (17), *Conner* (18), *Hall* (18), *Kalk* (18), *Davison* (19), *Edwards* (19), *Saufley* (19), and *Bache* (27).
	Commissioned: The *Quick* (3), *Coghlan* (10), *Chevalier* (20), *Radford* (22), *Murphy* (27), *Frazier* (30), and *Jenkins* (31).
Escorts	Laid down: The *Edsall* (2), *Hammann* (10), *Pope* (14), *Stewart* (15), *Sturtevant* (15), *Pillsbury* (18), *Moore* (20), *Buckley* (21), and *Foss* (23).
	Launched: The *Andres* (24), *Decker* (24), *Dobler* (24) *Doneff* (24), and *Engstrom* (24).
Submarines	Laid down: The *Seahorse* (1), *Ray* (20), *Cod* (21), *Billfish* (23), and *Bowfin* (23).
	Launched: The *Hake* (17), *Scamp* (20), and *Scorpion* (20).
	Commissioned: The *Barb* (8), *Sunfish* (15), *Blackfish* (22), and *Runner* (30).
August 1942	
Battleships:	Launched: The *Iowa* (27).
	Commissioned: The *Alabama* (16).
Fleet carriers	Laid down: The *Kearsarge* (3).
Light carrier	Launched: The *Independence* (22).
Escort carriers	Launched: The *Croatan* (3) and *Prince William* (23).
	Commissioned: The *Nassau* (20), *Santee* (24), and *Sangamon* (25).
Heavy cruiser	Launched: The *Boston* (26).
Light cruisers	Laid down: The *Buffalo* (31).
	Launched: The *Miami* (12).
Destroyers	Laid down: The *Robinson* (12), *Anthony* (17), *Miller* (18), *Wadsworth* (18), *Luce* (24), and *Walker* (31).
	Launched: The *McKee* (2), *Burns* (8), *Izard* (8), *Thompson* (10), *Waller* (15), *Conway* (16), *Cony* (16), *Murray* (16), *Abner Read* (18), *Beale* (24), *Glennon* (26), *Jeffers* (26), *Converse* (30), and *Sproston* (31).
	Commissioned: The *Doran* (4), *Strong* (7), *Saufley* (9), *La Vallette* (12), *Boyle* (15), *Butler* (15), *Gansevoort* (25), *Taylor* (28), and *Parker* (31).
Escorts	Laid down: The *Charles Lawrence* (1) and *Keith* (4).
	Launched: The *Brennan* (22) and *Doherty* (29).
Submarines	Laid down: The *Skate* (1), *Hackleback* (15), *Cabrilla* (18), and *Dorado* (27).
	Launched: The *Pompon* (15), *Snook* (15), *Harder* (19), and *Cero* (24).
	Commissioned: The *Gunnel* (20) and *Sawfish* (26).

September 1942	
Fleet carrier	Launched: The *Lexington* (26).
Escort carriers	Commissioned: The *Altahama* (15), *Chenango* (19), *Suwannee* (24), and *Bogue* (26).
Light cruiser	Commissioned: The *Montpelier* (9).
Destroyers	Laid down: The *Cowell* (7), *Ross* (9), *Owen* (17), *Abbot* (21), and *Charles J. Bader* (24).
	Launched: The *McLanahan* (7), *Welles* (7), *Wickes* (13), *Maddox* (15), *Nelson* (15), *Ammen* (17), *Eaton* (20), *Brownson* (24), and *William D. Porter* (27).
	Commissioned: The *Earle* (1), *Davison* (11), *Champlin* (12), *Kendrick* (12), *Gherardi* (15), *Pringle* (15), *Edwards* (18), *Gillespie* (18), and *De Haven* (21).
Escorts	Laid down: The *Charles R. Greer* (7), *Daniel T. Griffin* (7), *Greiner* (7), *Lovering* (7), *Reuben James* (7), *Sanders* (7), *Sims* (7), *Whitman* (7), *Wyman* (7), *Tomich* (15), and *J. Richard Ward* (30).
	Launched: The *Austin* (25) and *Edgar G. Chase* (26).
Submarines	Laid down: The *Redfin* (3), *Capelin* (14), *Crevalle* (14), *Corvina* (21), *Flasher* (30), and *Lancetfish* (30).
	Launched: The *Hoe* (17) and *Steelhead* (15).
	Commissioned: The *Tunny* (1), *Gurnard* (18), and *Scamp* (18).

October 1942	
Light carrier	Launched: The *Princeton* (18).
Light cruisers	Laid down: The *Flint* (23), *Newark* (26) and *Vicksburg* (26).
	Launched: The *Oakland* (23).
	Commissioned: The *Denver* (15).
Destroyers	Laid down: The *Dashiell* (1), *The Sullivans* (10), *John Hood* (12), *Braine* (12), *Bullard* (16), *Kidd* (16), *Tingey* (22), *Colahan* (24), *Stephen Potter* (27), *Erben* (28), and *Hopewell* (29).
	Launched: The *Nields* (1), *Evans* (4), *Mullany* (10), *Foote* (11), *Young* (11), *Philip* (13), *Renshaw* (13), *Trathen* (22), *Daly* (24), *Isherwood* (24), *Bush* (27), *Spence* (27), *Boyd* (29), *Halford* (29), and *Leutze* (29).
	Commissioned: The *Waller* (1), *Glennon* (8), *Conway* (9), *Stanly* (15), *Kalk* (17), *Laub* (24), *Aulick* (27), *Cony* (30), and *Maddox* (31).
Escorts	Laid down: The *Wintle* (1), *Demsey* (1), *Evarts* (17), *Wyffels* (17), *Levy* (19), *McConnell* (19), and *Duffy* (29).
	Launched: The *Burden R. Hastings* (20), *Edward C. Daly* (21), *LeHardy* (21), and *Gilmore* (22).
Submarines	Laid down: The *Darter* (20), *Robalo* (24), *Cisco* (29), and *Flier* (30).
	Launched: The *Tinosa* (7), *Jack* (16), *Balao* (27), and *Lapon* (27).
	Commissioned: The *Haddo* (9), *Scorpion* (10), *Snook* (24), and *Hake* (30).

November 1942	
Escort carrier	Commissioned: The *Card* (8).
Light cruisers	Laid down: The *Duluth* (9).
	Commissioned: The *Santa Fe* (24).
Destroyers	Laid down: The *Halligan* (9), *Haraden* (9), *Black* (14), *Chauncey* (14), *Thorn* (15), *Turner* (15), *Van Valkenburgh* (15), *Twining* (20), *Hale* (23), and *Picking* (24).
	Launched: The *Ordronaux* (9), *Ringgold* (11), *Schroeder* (11), *John D. Henley* (15), *Hazlewood* (20), and *Terry* (22).
	Commissioned: The *Jeffers* (5), *Bache* (14), *Hutchins* (17), *Hobby* (18), *Converse* (20), *MacKenzie* (21), *Philip* (21), *Charles Ausburne* (24), and *Nelson* (26).

Escorts	Laid down: The *Flaherty* (7), *Otterstetter* (9), *Frederick D. Davis* (11), *Osterhaus* (11), *Parks* (11), *Cannon* (14), *Sloat* (21), *Martin* (26), *Stadtfield* (26), *Donnell* (27), *Griswold* (27), *Steele* (27), *Carlson* (27), *Debas* (27), *Emery* (29), *Acree* (30), *Amick* (30), *Baron* (30), and *Herbert C. Jones* (30).
	Launched: The *Edsall* (1), *Stewart* (22), and *Jacob Jones* (29).
Submarines	Laid down: The *Ling* (2) and *Angler* (9).
	Launched: The *Tullibee* (11), *Billfish* (12), *Puffer* (22), and *Mingo* (30).
	Commissioned: The *Peto* (21).
December 1942	
Battleship	Launched: The *New Jersey* (7).
Fleet carriers	Laid down: The *Franklin* (7) and *Bennington* (15).
	Launched: The *Bunker Hill* (7).
	Commissioned: The *Essex* (31).
Light carrier	Launched: The *Belleau Wood* (6).
Escort carrier	Commissioned: The *Core* (10).
Light cruisers	Laid down: The *Oklahoma City* (8), *Wilkes Barre* (14), and *Tucson* (23).
	Launched: The *Reno* (23).
Destroyers	Laid down: The *Yarnall* (5), *Rowe* (7), *Sigourney* (7), *Clarence K. Bronson* (9), *Porterfield* (12), *Stockham* (19), *Stembel* (21), *Albert W. Grant* (30), and *Bryant* (30).
	Launched: The *Heermann* (5), *Thatcher* (6), *Franks* (7), *Sigsbee* (7), *Bradford* (12), *Hoel* (19), and *Anthony* (20).
	Commissioned: The *Eaton* (4), *Claxton* (8), *Guest* (15), *Stevenson* (15), *McLanahan* (19), *Herndon* (20), *Foote* (22), *Beale* (23), *Carmich* (28), *Dyson* (30), and *Ringgold* (30).
Escorts	Laid down: The *Fogg* (4), *Christopher* (7), *Snowden* (7), *Stanton* (7), *Crouter* (8), *Douglas L. Howard* (8), *Farquhar* (14), *Bull* (15), *Hopping* (15), *J.R.Y. Blakely* (16), *Hill* (21), *Fleming* (24), *Sederstrom* (24), *Tomich* (28), *Marchand* (30), *Swasey* (30), and *Gantner* (31).
	Launched: The *Sturtevant* (3), *Evarts* (7), *Wyffels* (7), *Hammann* (13), *Harold C. Thomas* (18), *Wileman* (19), *Keith* (21), and *Moore* (21).
Submarines	Laid down: The *Bashaw* (4), *Flounder* (5), *Apogon* (9), *Lionfish* (15), *Bluegill* (17), *Aspro* (27), and *Batfish* (27).
	Launched: The *Bowfin* (7), *Muskallunge* (13), *Rasher* (20), *Cabrilla* (24), *Cisco* (24), and *Paddle* (30).
	Commissioned: The *Harder* (2), *Steelhead* (7), and *Hoe* (16).
January 1943	
Fleet carriers	Laid down: The *Shangri La* (15) and *Hancock* (26).
	Launched: The *Yorktown* (21).
Light carriers	Launched: The *Cowpens* (17).
	Commissioned: The *Independence* (14).
Light cruisers	Laid down: The *Atlanta* (25).
	Commissioned: The *Birmingham* (29).
Destroyers	Laid down: The *Wedderburn* (10), *Caperton* (11), *Paul Hamilton* (20), and *Twiggs* (20).
	Launched: The *Howorth* (10), *Killen* (10), *McCord* (10), *Wadsworth* (10), and *Walker* (31).
	Commissioned: The *Schroeder* (1), *Spence* (8), *Stockton* (11), *Nields* (15), *Sigsbee* (23), *Harrison* (25), *Doyle* (27), and *Terry* (27).

Escorts	Laid down: The *Burke* (1), *Scott* (1), *Alger* (2), *Robert E. Peary* (3), *Fessenden* (4), *Fiske* (4), *Seid* (10), *Smartt* (10), *Walter S. Brown* (10), *William C. Miller* (10), *Huse* (11), *Brackett* (12), *Donaldson* (12), *Reynolds* (12), *Mitchell* (12), *Frost* (13), *Atherton* (14), *Thomas* (16), *Blair* (19), *Inch* (19), *Jenks* (19), *Brough* (22), *Durik* (22), *Eisele* (23), *Tisdale* (23), *Chatelain* (25), *Cabana* (27), *Camp* (27), *Dionne* (27), *Hurst* (27), *Neunzer* (29), *Booth* (30), and *Carroll* (30).
	Launched: The *Robert E. Peary* (3), *J. Richard Ward* (6), *Buckley* (9), *Griswold* (9), *Steele* (9), *Carlson* (9), *Bebas* (9), *Pillsbury* (10), *Pope* (12), *Flaherty* (17), *Charles R. Greer* (18), *Herbert C. Jones* (19), *Otterstetter* (19), *Whitman* (19), *Sloat* (21), *Douglas L. Howard* (24), *Frederick C. Davis* (24), and *Crouter* (26).
	Commissioned: The *Brennan* (20).
Submarines	Laid down: The *Gabilan* (5), *Perch* (5), *Manta* (15), *Tang* (15), *Archerfish* (22), *Golet* (27), and *Shark* (28).
	Launched: The *Seahorse* (9), *Capelin* (20), *Pargo* (24), and *Raton* (24).
	Commissioned: The *Jack* (6), *Pogy* (10), *Tinosa* (15), and *Lapon* (23).
February 1943	
Battleship	Commissioned: The *Iowa* (22).
Fleet carriers	Laid down: The *Hancock* (1) and *Bon Homme Richard* (1).
	Commissioned: The *Lexington* (17).
Light carriers	Launched: The *Monterey* (28).
	Commissioned: The *Princeton* (25).
Escort carrier	Commissioned: The *Barnes* (20).
Heavy cruisers	Laid down: The *Bremerton* (1), *Pittsburgh* (3), and *St. Paul* (3), and the large cruiser *Guam* (2).
Light cruisers	Laid down: The *Pasadena* (6) and *Springfield* (13).
	Launched: The *Biloxi* (23).
Destroyers	Laid down: The *Cogswell* (1), *Halsey Powell* (4), *Cotten* (8), *Smalley* (9), *Ingersoll* (18), and *Callaghan* (21).
	Launched: The *Kimberley* (4), *Dashiell* (6), *Haggard* (9), *Abbot* (17), *Brown* (21), *Thorn* (28), *Bullard* (28), *Kidd* (28), and *Turner* (28).
	Commissioned: The *Stevens* (1), *Brownson* (3), *Abner Read* (5), *Renshaw* (5), *Shubrick* (7), *Bennett* (9), *John Rodgers* (9), *Thatcher* (10), *Ordronaux* (13), *Endicott* (25), and *Anthony* (26).
Escorts	Laid down: The *Bostwick* (6), *George W. Ingram* (6), *Howard C. Crow* (6), *Pettit* (6), *Reeves* (7), *Fechteler* (7), *Bangust* (11), *Ira Jeffery* (13), *Poole* (13), *Manning* (15), *Neuendorf* (15), *Bunch* (22), *Coolbaugh* (22), *Cooner* (22), *Darby* (22), *Eldridge* (22), *Enright* (22), *Francis M. Robinson* (22), *J. Douglas Blackwood* (22), *Schmitt* (22), *Solar* (22), *Weber* (22), *Canfield* (23), *Cloues* (23), *Deede* (23), *Elden* (23), *Fair* (24), *Manlove* (24), *Waterman* (24), and *Peterson* (28).
	Launched: The *Reuben James* (6), *Sims* (6), *Farquhar* (13), *Charles Lawrence* (16), *Wintle* (18), *Dempsey* (19), *Snowden* (19), *Stanton* (21), *Seid* (22), *Smartt* (22), *Walter S. Brown* (22), *William C. Miller* (22), *Daniel T. Griffin* (23), and *Hill* (28).
	Commissioned: The *Doherty* (6) and *Austin* (13).
Submarines	Laid down: The *Bream* (5), *Rock* (23), *Burrfish* (24), and *Sealion* (25).
	Launched: The *Crevalle* (22) and *Ray* (28).
	Commissioned: The *Balao* (4), *Mingo* (12), and *Tullibee* (15).
March 1943	
Fleet carriers	Laid down: The *Antietam* (15) and *Lake Champlain* (15).
Light carrier	Commissioned: The *Belleau Wood* (31).
Escort carrier	Commissioned: The *Block Island* (8).
Light cruisers	Laid down: The *Amsterdam* (3), *Little Rock* (6), and *Dayton* (8).
	Launched: The *Astoria* (6).
	Commissioned: The *Mobile* (24).

Destroyers	Laid down: The *Dortch* (2), *Gatling* (3), *Healy* (4), *Uhlmann* (6), *Knapp* (8), *Stoddard* (10), *Hickox* (12), *Cassin Young* (18), *Bennion* (19), *Newcomb* (19), *Remey* (22), *Watts* (26), *Hunt* (31), and *Lewis Hancock* (31).
	Launched: The *Luce* (6), *Braine* (7), *Miller* (7), *Hailey* (9), *Cowell* (18), *Halligan* (19), *Haraden* (19), *Erben* (21), *Owen* (21), *Johnston* (25), *Black* (28), and *Chauncey* (28).
	Commissioned: The *Fullam* (2), *Bell* (4), *Daly* (10), *Ammen* (12), *McCook* (15), *Wadsworth* (16), *Dashiell* (20), *Frankford* (31), and *McKee* (31).
Escorts	Laid down: The *Cates* (1), *Foreman* (1), *Gandy* (1), *Lee Fox* (1), *Amesbury* (8), *Joyce* (8), *Earl K. Olsen* (9), *Slater* (9), *Harveson* (9), *Capel* (11), *Weaver* (13), *Kirkpatrick* (15) *Chase* (16), *Ricketts* (16), *Sellstrom* (16), *Fieberling* (19), *Breeman* (20), *Whitehurst* (21), *Blessman* (22), *Menges* (22), *Hilbert* (23), *Burrows* (24), *Leopold* (24), *Mills* (26), *Ramsden* (26), *Rich* (27), *Bates* (29), and *Joseph E. Campbell* (29).
	Launched: The *J.R.Y. Blakely* (7), *Fessenden* (9), *Cabana* (10), *Dionne* (10), *Hopping* (10), *Donnell* (13), *Fiske* (14), *Swasey* (18), *Fogg* (20), *Marchand* (20), *Frost* (21), *Huse* (23), *Bull* (25), *Levy* (28), and *McConnell* (28).
	Commissioned: The *Edgar G. Chase* (14) and *Andres* (15).
Submarines	Laid down: The *Guavina* (3), *Cavalla* (4), *Tilefish* (10), *Sand Lance* (12), *Picuda* (15), *Pampanito* (15), *Cobia* (17), and *Barbero* (25).
	Launched: The *Skate* (4), *Bonefish* (7), and *Apogon* (10).
	Commissioned: The *Muskallunge* (15), *Pompon* (17), *Paddle* (29), and *Seahorse* (31).

April 1943	
Fleet carriers	Launched: The *Intrepid* (26).
	Commissioned: The *Yorktown* (15).
Light carrier	Launched: The *Cabot* (4).
Escort carriers	Launched: The *Casablanca* (5) and *Liscome Bay* (19).
	Commissioned: The *Prince William* (9), *Breton* (12), and *Croatan* (28).
Heavy cruisers	Laid down: The *Fall River* (12).
	Launched: The *Canberra* (19).
	Commissioned: The *Baltimore* (15).
Light cruiser	Laid down: The *Topeka* (21).
Destroyers	Laid down: The *Benham* (3), *Wadleigh* (5) *Marshall* (19), *Wren* (24), and *Norman Scott* (26).
	Launched: The *Hale* (4), *The Sullivans* (4), *Paul Hamilton* (7), *Twiggs* (7), *Clarence K Bronson* (18), *Laws* (22), *Sigourney* (24), and *Stephen Potter* (28).
	Commissioned: The *Thorn* (1), *Burns* (3), *Walker* (3), *Bullard* (9), *Halford* (10), *Isherwood* (12), *Hudson* (13), *Turner* (16), *Murray* (20), *Abbot* (23), *Kidd* (23), *Mullany* (23), and *Baldwin* (30).
Escorts	Laid down: The *Oswald* (1), *Ebert* (1), *England* (4), *Rhodes* (4), *Fowler* (5), *Newell* (5), *Spangenberg* (5), *Mosley* (6), *Lamons* (10), *Pride* (12), *James E. Craig* (15), *Eichenberger* (15), *Kyne* (16), *Richey* (19), *Lake* (22), *Lyman* (22), *Tatum* (22), *Marts* (26), *Pennewill* (26), *Borum* (28), *Snyder* (28), *Spangler* (28), *Witter* (28), *Savage* (30), and *Vance* (30).
	Launched: The *Reuben James* (1), *Burke* (3), *Scott* (3), *Canfield* (4), *Cloues* (4), *Deede* (4), *Elden* (4), *Inch* (4), *Blair* (6), *Brough* (10), *Foss* (10), *Hurst* (14), *Camp* (16), *Duffy* (16), *Emery* (17), *Gantner* (17), *Osterhaus* (18), *Parks* (18), *Chatelain* (21), *Fechteler* (22), *Reeves* (22), *Laning* (23), *Loy* (23), *Chase* (24), *Sims* (24), *Howard D. Crow* (26), *Barber* (27), *Neunzer* (27), and *Pettit* (28).
	Commissioned: The *Edward C. Daly* (1), *Edsall* (1), *Burden R. Hastings* (15), *Evarts* (15), *Gilmore* (17), *Wyfells* (21), *Griswold* (28), *Jacob Jones* (29), and *Buckley* (30).

Submarines	Laid down: The *Croaker* (1), *Guitarro* (7), *Baya* (8), *Parche* (9), *Barbel* (11), *Moray* (21), *Roncador* (21), *Becuna* (29), and *Bang* (30).
	Launched: The *Cero* (4), *Redfin* (4), *Aspro* (7), *Dragonet* (18), *Escolar* (18), and *Cod* (21).
	Commissioned: The *Skate* (15), *Billfish* (20), *Pargo* (26), and *Puffer* (27).
May 1943	
Battleship	Commissioned: The *New Jersey* (23).
Fleet carriers	Laid down: The *Randolph* (10).
	Commissioned: The *Bunker Hill* (24).
Light carriers	Launched: The *Langley* (22).
	Commissioned: The *Cowpens* (28).
Escort carriers	Launched: The *Anzio* (1), *Corregidor* (12), and *Mission Bay* (25).
Destroyers	Laid down: The *Irwin* (2), *Cushing* (3), *Mertz* (10), and *Barton* (24).
	Launched: The *Hopewell* (2), *Stembel* (8), *Caperton* (22), *Tingey* (28), *Albert W. Grant* (29), and *Bryant* (29).
	Commissioned: The *Boyd* (8), *Bush* (10), *Braine* (11), *Izard* (15), *Charrette* (18), *Sproston* (19), *Black* (21), *Kimberley* (22), *Harding* (25), *Erben* (28), *Trathen* (28), and *Chauncey* (31).
Escorts	Laid down: The *Framont* (1), *Micka* (3), *Reybold* (3), *Hemminger* (8), *Maloy* (10), *Cofer* (12), *Kephart* (12), *Durant* (15), *Lansing* (15), *Rudderow* (15), *Haines* (17), *Herzog* (17), *McAnn* (17), *George* (22), *Lovalace* (22), *Crowley* (24), *Lowe* (24), *Rall* (24), *Falgout* (26), *Calaterra* (28), *Chambers* (28), and *Harmon* (31).
	Launched: The *Weber* (1), *George W. Ingram* (8), *Poole* (8), *Acree* (9), *Baron* (9), *Ricketts* (10), *Sellstrom* (12), *Ira Jeffery* (15), *Peterson* (15), *Stadtfield* (17), *Martin* (18), *Barber* (20), *Greiner* (20), *Cannon* (25), *Harveson* (25), *Ramsden* (24, *Joyce* (26), *Mills* (26), *Amick* (27), *Atherton* (27), *Bunch* (29), *Coolbaugh* (29), *Darby* (29), *Enright* (29), *Francis M. Robinson* (29), *J. Douglas Blackwood* (29), *Schmitt* (29), *Solar* (29), and *Lee Fox* (29).
	Commissioned: The *Decker* (3), *Steele* (4), *Carlson* (10), *Levy* (13), *Bebas* (15), *LeHardy* (15), *Dobler* (17), *Hammann* (17), *Hopping* (21), *Crouter* (25), *McConnell* (28), *Harold C. Thomas* (30), *Charles Lawrence* (31), *Robert E. Peary* (31), and *Stewart* (31).
Submarines	Laid down: The *Hammerhead* (5), *Pintado* (7), *Pilotfish* (15), *Spadefish* (27), and *Pipefish* (31).
	Launched: The *Batfish* (5), *Robalo* (9), *Bergall* (13), *Corvina* (21), *Besugo* (27), *Dorado* (27), *Archerfish* (28), *Devilfish* (30), and *Hackleback* (30).
	Commissioned: The *Bowfin* (1), *Cisco* (10), *Bluefish* (24), *Cabrilla* (24), and *Bonefish* (31).
June 1943	
Light carrier	Commissioned: The *Monterey* (17).
Escort carrier	Launched: The *Guadalcanal* (5).
Heavy cruisers	Laid down: The *Macon* (14) and *Columbus* (28).
	Launched: The *Quincy* (23).
	Commissioned: The *Boston* (30).
Light cruisers	Laid down: The *Portsmouth* (28).
	Launched: The *Houston* (19).
Destroyers	Laid down: The *Monssen* (1), *Jarvis* (7), *Walke* (7), *Preston* (13), *McDermut* (14), *Laffey* (28), and *Blue* (30).
	Launched: The *Picking* (1), *Longshaw* (4), *Cogswell* (5), *Clarence K. Bronson* (11), *Cotten* (12), *Porterfield* (13), *Dortch* (20), *Gatling* (20), *Stockham* (25), *Ingersoll* (28), *Halsey Powell* (30), *McGowan* (30), and *McNair* (30).
	Commissioned: The *Conner* (8), *Bradford* (12), *Hale* (15), *Wickes* (16), *Hazlewood* (18), *Luce* (21), *Capps* (23), and *Sigourney* (29).

Escorts	Laid down: The *Muir* (1), *Neal A. Scott* (1), *Thomason* (5), *Jordan* (5), *Raby* (7), *Runels* (7), *Straub* (7), *Trumpeter* (7), *Liddle* (8) *Newman* (8), *Bright* (9), *Brister* (14), *Thomas J. Gary* (15), *Connolly* (21), *Halloran* (21), *Marsh* (23), *Tills* (23), and *Kretchmer* (28).
	Launched: The *Manning* (1), *Neuendorf* (1), *Wyman* (3), *Amesbury* (5), *Kirkpatrick* (5), *Bangust* (6), *Bates* (6), *Leopold* (12), *Menges* (15), *Fleming* (16), *Lovering* (18), *Sanders* (18), *Blessman* (19), *Christopher* (19), *Joseph E. Campbell* (19), *Waterman* (20), *Booth* (21), *Carroll* (21), *Rich* (22), *Mosley* (26), *Frament* (28), *Tisdale* (28), *Eisele* (29), *Newell* (29), *Rhodes* (29), and *Richey* (30).
	Commissioned: The *Seid* (6), *Wileman* (6), *Pillsbury* (7), *Daniel T. Griffin* (9), *Reeves* (9), *Doneff* (10), *Osterhaus* (12), *Sturtevant* (16), *Smartt* (18), *Engstrom* (21), *Parks* (23), *Charles R. Greer* (25), *Pope* (25), *Walter S. Brown* (25), *Donnell* (26), and *Flaherty* (26).
Submarines	Laid down: The *Sabalo* (5), *Sablefish* (5), *Blackfin* (10), *Piranha* (21), *Caiman* (24), *Trepang* (25), and *Plaice* (28).
	Launched: The *Darter* (6), *Burrfish* (18), *Flasher* (20), *Rock* (20), and *Sand Lance* (25).
	Commissioned: The *Capelin* (4), *Rasher* (8), *Cod* (21), and *Crevalle* (24).

July 1943

Light carrier	Commissioned: The *Cabot* (24).
Escort carriers	Launched: The *Manila Bay* (10) and *Natoma Bay* (20).
	Commissioned: The *Casablanca* (8).
Heavy cruisers	Laid down: The *Chicago* (28) and *Los Angeles* (28).
Light cruisers	Laid down: The *Providence* (27).
	Launched: The *Vincennes* (17).
	Commissioned: The *Oakland* (17).
Destroyers	Laid down: The *Heywood L. Edwards* (4), *Richard P. Leary* (4), *Melvin* (6), *Porter* (6), *Allen M. Sumner* (7), *Putnam* (11), *O'Brien* (12), *Strong* (25), *Meredith* (26), and *Brush* (30).
	Launched: The *Bennion* (4), *Healy* (4), *Hickox* (4), *Morrison* (4), *Newcomb* (4), *Knapp* (10), *Twining* (11), *Bearss* (25), *Remey* (25), *Yarnall* (25), *Uhlmann* (30), and *Pritchett* (31).
	Commissioned: The *Satterlee* (1), *Heermann* (6), *Hall* (7), *William D. Porter* (6), *Brown* (10), *Thompson* (10), *Stembel* (16), *Charles J. Badger* (23), *Cotten* (24), *Hoel* (29), *Caperton* (30), *Franks* (30), and *Young* (31).
Escorts	Laid down: The *Haverfield* (1), *Merrill* (1), *Creamer* (5), *Finnegan* (5), *Gustafson* (5), *Hollis* (5), *Samuel S. Miles* (5), *Hissam* (6), *Holder* (6), *Roberts* (7), *Day* (15), *Swenning* (17), *Willis* (17), *Currier* (21), *McCelland* (21), *Willmarth* (25), *Lloyd* (26), *Koiner* (26), *Otter* (26), *Wiseman* (26), *Loeser* (27) *Greenwood* (29), *O'Reilly* (29), *Riddle* (29), and *Wesson* (29).
	Launched: The *Pride* (3), *Laning* (4), *Lovelace* (4), *Loy* (4), *Weaver* (4), *Fogg* (7), *Alger* (8), *Savage* (15), *Sederstrom* (15), *Spangler* (15), *Vance* (16), *Hilbert* (18), *James E. Craig* (22), *Eichenberger* (22), *Foss* (23), *Gantner* (23), *Falgout* (24), *Cooner* (25), *Eldridge* (25), *Harmon* (25), *Fair* (27) *Lowe* (28), *Manlove* (28), and *Thomas* (31).
	Commissioned: The *Fechteler* (1), *Moore* (1), *William C. Miller* (2), *Fowler* (3), *Spangenberg* (3), *Whitman* (3), *Baron* (5), *J. Richard Ward* (5), *Cabana* (9), *Wintle* (10), *Frederick C. Davis* (14), *Dionne* (16), *Chase* (18), *Acree* (19), *Keith* (19), *Scott* (20), *Herbert C. Jones* (21), *Canfield* (22), *Dempsey* (24), *Schmitt* (24), *Amick* (26), *Tomich* (27), *Deede* (29) and *Douglas L. Howard* (29).
Submarines	Laid down: The *Hardhead* (7), *Blenny* (8), *Pomfret* (14), *Sterlet* (14), *Blower* (15), *Dace* (22) and *Queenfish* (27).
	Launched: The *Angler* (4), *Flier* (11), *Picuda* (12), *Pampanito* (12), *Parche* (24) and *Bashaw* (25).
	Commissioned: The *Cero* (4), *Raton* (13), *Apogon* (16), *Dace* (23), *Ray* (27) and *Aspro* (31).

August 1943	
Fleet carriers	Launched: The *Wasp* (17) and *Hornet* (30).
	Commissioned: The *Intrepid* (16).
Light carriers	Launched: The *Bataan* (1).
	Commissioned: The *Langley* (31).
Escort carriers	Launched: The *St. Lo* (17).
	Commissioned: The *Liscome Bay* (7), *Anzio* (27), and *Corregidor* (31).
Heavy cruiser	Launched: The large cruiser *Alaska* (15).
Light cruisers	Laid down: The *Fargo* (23).
	Commissioned: The *Biloxi* (31).
Destroyers	Laid down: The *Lowry* (1), *Colhoun* (3), *Ingraham* (4), *Moale* (5), *DeHaven* (9), *Hart* (10), *Metcalf* (10), *Shields* (10), *Wiley* (10), *Mansfield* (28), *Cooper* (30), *Taussig* (30), and *Gregory* (31).
	Launched: The *Callaghan* (1), *Hunt* (1), *Lewis* (1), *Wedderburn* (1), *Wadleigh* (7), *Norman Scott* (28), *Robinson* (28), *Marshall* (29), and *Benham* (30).
	Commissioned: The *Dortch* (7), *Welles* (16), *Cogswell* (17), *Gatling* (19), *Halligan* (19), *McCord* (19), *Colahan* (23), *Cowell* (23), *Haggard* (31), *Ingersoll* (31), and *Miller* (31).
Escorts	Laid down: The *Gendreau* (1), *Vammen* (1), *Delbert W. Halsey* (2), *Ely* (2), *Gaynier* (4), *Janssen* (4), *Wilhoite* (4), *Gunason* (9), *Hubbard* (11), *Hayter* (11), *Swearer* (12), *Stern* (12), *Major* (16), *Osmus* (17), *Curtis W. Howard* (18), *Richard M. Rowell* (18), *Richard S. Bull* (18), *Weeden* (18), *Yokes* (22), *Keppler* (23), *Lloyd Thomas* (23), *Milton Lewis* (23), *Strickland* (23), *Sutton* (23), *Gillette* (24), *Price* (24), *Chaffee* (26), *O'Neill* (26), *Bronstein* (26), *William T. Powell* (26), *Varian* (27), *Daniel* (30), *Cockrill* (31), *Edward H. Allen* (31), *Forester* (31), *Stockdale* (31), *John J. Van Buren* (31), and *Tweedy* (31).
	Launched: The *Brackett* (1), *Donaldson* (1), *Lamons* (1), *Mitchell* (1), *Reynolds* (1), *Lansing* (2), *Durant* (3), *Foreman* (5), *Tatum* (7), *Marts* (8), *Pennewill* (8), *Liddle* (9), *Newman* (9), *Borum* (14), *George* (14), *Kyne* (15), *Calcaterra* (16), *Chambers* (17), *Lake* (18), *Maloy* (18), *Lyman* (19), *Greenwood* (21), *Thomas J. Gary* (21), *Micka* (22), *Reybold* (22), *Jordan* (23), *Thomason* (23), *Haines* (26), *Merrill* (29), *Snyder* (29), *Bostwick* (30), and *Haverfield* (30).
	Commissioned: The *Laning* (1), *Elden* (4), *Duffy* (5), *Otterstetter* (6), *Stanton* (7), *Farquhar* (8), *Cloues* (10), *George W. Ingram* (11), *Bull* (12), *Emery* (14), *Ira Jeffery* (15), Hill (16), *J.R.Y. Blakely* (16), *Sloat* (16), *Greiner* (18), *Burke* (20), *Bunch* (21), *Cooner* (21), *Duff* (23), *Snowden* (23), *Brister* (24), *Fessenden* (25), *Fiske* (25), *Stadtfield* (26), *Eldridge* (27), *Finch* (28), *Atherton* (29), *Frost* (30), *Hurst* (30), *Huse* (30), *Lee Fox* (30), *Amesbury* (31), *Harmon* (31), *Kretchmer* (31) and *Swasey* (31).
Submarines	Laid down: The *Spot* (3), *Hawkbill* (7), *Boarfish* (12), *Trumpetfish* (28), *Tusk* (28), *Charr* (26), and *Blueback* (28).
	Launched: The *Golet* (1), *Bluegill* (8), *Ling* (15), *Tang* (17), *Flounder* (22), *Lancetfish* (15), *Guavina* (29), *Bang* (30), and *Pilotfish* (30).
	Commissioned: The *Corvina* (6), *Batfish* (21), *Dorado* (28), and *Redfin* (31).

September 1943	
Fleet carriers	Laid down: The *Boxer* (13) and *Valley Forge* (14)
Light carrier	Launched: The *San Jacinto* (26).
Escort carriers	Launched: The *Tripoli* (2), *Wake Island* (15), and *White Plains* (27).
	Commissioned: The *Guadalcanal* (25).
Heavy cruisers	Laid down: The *Helena* (9) and *Toledo* (13).

Destroyers	Laid down: The *Lyman K. Swenson* (11), *Lindsey* (12), *Little* (13), and *Samuel N. Moore* (30).
	Launched: The *Ross* (10), *Mertz* (11), *Cassin Young* (12), *Cushing* (30), and *Rowe* (30).
	Commissioned: The *Healy* (3), *Hickox* (10), *Knapp* (16), *Haraden* (16), *David W. Taylor* (18), *Owen* (20), *Picking* (21), *Hunt* (22), *Lewis Hancock* (29), *Hailey* (30), *Hopewell* (30), *The Sullivans* (30), and *Remey* (30).
Escorts	Laid down: The *Scroggins* (4), *William C. Cole* (5), *Earl V. Johnson* (7), *Baker* (9), *Coffman* (9), *Hodges* (9), *Kinzer* (9), *Ray O. Hale* (13), *Dennis* (15), *Eversole* (15), *Underhill* (16), *Pavlic* (21), *Eisner* (23), *Garfield Thomas* (23), *John J. Powers* (25), *O'Toole* (25), *Paul G. Baker* (26), *Holton* (28), and *Henry R. Kenyon* (29).
	Launched: The *Breeman* (4), *Raby* (4), *Runels* (4), *Cofer* (6), *Kephart* (6), *Whitehurst* (9), *Hollis* (11), *Jenks* (11), *Loeser* (11), *Hemminger* (12), *Swenning* (13), *Willis* (14), *Trumpeter* (19), *Straub* (19), *Gillette* (25), *Marsh* (25), *Bright* (26), and *England* (26).
	Commissioned: The *Wyman* (1), *Marts* (3), *Martin* (4), *Herzog* (5), *McAnn* (5), *Inch* (8), *Marchand* (8), *Sederstrom* (11), *Bates* (12), *Loy* (12), *Blair* (13), *Pennewill* (15), *Camp* (16), *Lovering* (17), *Brough* (18), *Fleming* (18), *Blessman* (19), *Booth* (19), *Enright* (21), *Chatelain* (22), *Joseph E. Campbell* (23), *Micka* (23), *Pettit* (23), *Greenwood* (25), *Cannon* (26), *Howard D. Crow* (27), *Neunzer* (27), *Peterson* (29), *Poole* (29), *Reybold* (29), and *Joyce* (30).
Submarines	Laid down: The *Icefish* (4), *Razorback* (9), *Redfish* (9), *Ronquil* (9), *Chub* (16), *Brill* (23), *Scabbardfish* (27), and *Jallao* (29).
	Launched: The *Perch* (12), *Pintado* (15), *Gabilan* (19), and *Guitarro* (26).
	Commissioned: The *Archerfish* (4), *Darter* (7), *Burrfish* (14), *Flasher* (25), and *Robalo* (28).

October 1943

Fleet carriers	Laid down: The *Midway* (27).
	Launched: The *Franklin* (14)
Escort carriers	Launched: The *Solomons* (6) *Kalinin Bay* (15), and *Kasaan Bay* (24).
	Commissioned: The *Manila Bay* (5), *Natoma Bay* (14), *St. Lo* (23,) and *Tripoli* (31).
Heavy cruiser	Commissioned: The *Canberra* (14).
Light cruiser	Laid down: The *Huntington* (4).
Destroyers	Laid down: The *Collett* (11), *Charles S. Sperry* (19), *English* (19), *Rooks* (27), *Maddox* (28), *Harry E. Hubbard* (30), and *Gwin* (31).
	Launched: The *Heywood L. Edwards* (6), *Richard P. Leary* (6), *Barton* (10), *McDermut* (17), *Melvin* (17), *John Hood* (25), *Smalley* (27), *Walke* (27), *Monssen* (30), and *Irwin* (31).
	Commissioned: The *Marshall* (16), *Wadleigh* (19), *Stephen Potter* (21), *Halsey Powell* (25), *Paul Hamilton* (25), *Johnston* (27), and *Porterfield* (30).

Escorts	Laid down: The *Manning* (1), *O'Flaherty* (4), *John C. Butler* (5), *Wingfield* (7), *Thornhill* (7), *Howard F. Clark* (8), *Silverstein* (8), *Odum* (10), *George M. Campbell* (14), *John M. Bermingham* (14), *Mason* (14), *Cread* (16), *Crosley* (16), *Damon M. Cummings* (17), *Jack W. Wilke* (18), *Neuendorf* (18), *Cronin* (19), *Delong* (19), *Riley* (20), *Winehart* (21), *Roche* (21), *Brock* (27), and *Register* (27).
	Launched: The *Burrows* (2), *O'Reilly* (2), *Gustafson* (3), *Samuel S. Miles* (3), *Tills* (3), *Janssen* (4), *Koiner* (5), *Wilhoite* (5), *Edward H. Allen* (7), *Tweedy* (7), *Durik* (9), *Cates* (10), *Currier* (14), *Day* (14), *Roberts* (14), *Rudderow* (14), *Underhill* (15), *Gunason* (16), *Riddle* (17), *Wesson* (17), *Witter* (17), *Crowley* (22), *Lloyd* (23), *Major* (23), *Otter* (23), *Rall* (23), *Weeden* (27), *McCelland* (28), *Cockrill* (29), *Henry R. Kenyon* (30), *Price* (30), *Stockdale* (30), *Bowers* (31), *Stern* (31), and *Swearer* (31).
	Commissioned: The *Rich* (1), *Ricketts* (5), *Herzog* (6), *Barber* (10), *Loeser* (10), *Sanders* (10), *McAnn* (11), *Tisdale* (11), *Harveson* (12), *Mills* (12), *Sellstrom* (12), *Coolbaugh* (15), *Trumpeter* (16), *Brackett* (18), *Eisele* (18), *Leopold* (18), *Ramsden* (19), *Foreman* (22), *Christopher* (23), *Fair* (23), *Kirkpatrick* (23), *Carroll* (24), *Rhodes* (25), *Straub* (25), *Menges* (26), *Gillette* (27), *Savage* (29), *Bangust* (30), *Mosley* (30), *Newell* (30), *Richey* (30), and *Spangler* (31).
Submarines	Laid down: The *Segundo* (14), *Bugara* (21), *Bullhead* (21), *Kete* (25), *Sea Cat* (30), and *Springer* (30).
	Launched: The *Pipefish* (12), *Bream* (17), *Shark* (17), *Hammerhead* (24), *Tilefish* (25), *Piranha* (27), *Pomfret* (27), *Sterlet* (27) and *Sealion* (31).
	Commissioned: The *Angler* (1), *Sand Lance* (9), *Tang* (15), *Picuda* (16), *Flier* (18), *Bashaw* (25), and *Rock* (26).
November 1943	
Fleet carriers	Commissioned: The *Wasp* (24) and *Hornet* (29).
Light carrier	Commissioned: The *Bataan* (17).
Escort carriers	Launched: The *Fanshaw Bay* (1) *Kitkun Bay* (8), *Tulagi* (15), *Gambier Bay* (22), and *Nehenta Bay* (28).
	Commissioned: The *Wake Island* (7), *White Plains* (15), *Solomons* (21), and *Kalinin Bay* (27).
Heavy cruiser	Launched: The large cruiser *Guam* (21).
Destroyers	Laid down: The *Lofberg* (4), *Ault* (15), *Waldron* (16), *John W. Thomason* (21), *Hyman* (22), and *Henry A. Wiley* (28).
	Launched: The *McGowan* (14), *McNair* (14), *Stoddard* (19), *Laffey* (21), and *Blue* (28).
	Commissioned: The *Twiggs* (4), *Norman Scott* (5), *Newcomb* (10), *Laws* (18), *McDermut* (19), *Mertz* (19), *Uhlmann* (22), *Albert W. Grant* (24), *Melvin* (24), *Tingey* (25), and *Callaghan* (27).

Escorts	Laid down: The *Edmonds* (1), *Frybarger* (8), *Richard W. Suesens* (1), *Shelton* (1), *Lewis* (3), *Osberg* (3), *Raymond* (3), *Rivin* (3), *Rizzi* (3), *Conklin* (4), *Corbesier* (4), *Ahrens* (5), *Alexander J. Luke* (5), *Barr* (5), *Robert I. Paine* (10), *Leslie L.B. Knox* (7), *Abercombie* (8), *Coates* (8), *Oberrender* (8), *Sheeeman* (8), *Sheehan* (8), *Vandiver* (8), *Wagner* (8), *Jack C. Robinson* (10), *Edwin A. Howard* (15), *John Q. Roberts* (15), *William M. Hobby* (15), *Robert Brazier* (16), *McNulty* (17), *Gilligan* (18), *La Prade* (18), *McCoy Reynolds* (18), *Straus* (18), *Carter* (19), *Jesse Rutherford* (22), *George A. Johnson* (24), *Metivier* (24), *Dale W. Peterson* (25), *Eugene E. Elmond* (27), *Martin H. Ray* (27), *Bassett* (28), *Holt* (28), *Jack Miller* (29), and *Stafford* (29).
	Launched: The *John J. Powers* (2), *O'Toole* (2), *Strickland* (2), *Osmus* (4), *Scroggins* (6), *Varian* (6), *Wiseman* (6), *Howard F. Clark* (8), *Silverstein* (8), *Joseph C. Hubbard* (11), *Hayter* (11), *Forster* (13), *Bronstein* (14), *O'Neill* (14), *Darby* (15), *Daniel* (16), *Richard S. Bull* (16), *John M. Bermingham* (17), *Mason* (17), *Richard M. Rowall* (17), *Roy O. Hale* (20), *Willmarth* (21), *Dale W. Peterson* (22), *Delong* (23), *Earl V. Johnson* (24), *Chaffee* (27), *Holder* (27), *William T. Powell* (27), *Baker* (28), *Coffman* (28), and *Martin H. Ray* (29).
	Commissioned: The *Gustafson* (1), *James E. Craig* (1), *Reynolds* (1), *Vance* (1), *Samuel S. Miles* (4), *Lovelace* (7), *Manlove* (8), *Lansing* (10), *Wesson* (11), *Alger* (12), *Pride* (13), *Darby* (15), *Falgout* (15), *Underhill* (15), *Durant* (16), *Calcaterra* (17), *Eichenberger* (17), *Mitchell* (17), *Riddle* (17), *Whitehurst* (19), *George* (20), *Thomas* (21), *Chambers* (22), *Lowe* (22), *Tatum* (22), *Swearer* (24), *Newman* (26), *Thomas J. Gary* (27), *Merrill* (27), *Haverfield* (29), *Borum* (30), *Brister* (30), *Henry R. Kenyon* (30), and *Waterman* (30).
Submarines	Laid down: The *Sea Dog* (1), *Sea Fox* (2), *Bumper* (4), *Turbot* (13), *Ulua* (13), *Cabezon* (18), *Dentuda* (18), and *Sea Devil* (18).
	Launched: The *Lionfish* (7), *Manta* (7), *Barbel* (14), *Cavalla* (14), *Plaice* (15), *Cobia* (28), and *Queenfish* (30).
	Commissioned: The *Pampanito* (6), *Bluegill* (11), *Parche* (20), *Flounder* (29), and *Golet* (30).

December 1943

Battleship	Launched: The *Wisconsin* (7).
Fleet carrier	Laid down: The *Coral Sea* (1).
Light carrier	Commissioned: The *San Jacinto* (15).
Escort carriers	Launched: The *Hoggatt Bay* (4), *Kadashan Bay* (11), *Marcus Island* (16), *Savo Island* (22), and *Ommaney Bay* (29).
	Commissioned: The *Kasaan Bay* (4), *Fanshaw Bay* (9), *Kitkun Bay* (15), *Tulagi* (21), and *Gambier Bay* (28).
Heavy cruiser	Commissioned: The *Quincy* (15).
Light cruisers	Launched: The *Vicksburg* (14), *Wilkes Barre* (24), and *Pasadena* (28).
	Commissioned: The *Houston* (20), *Miami* (28), and *Reno* (28).
Destroyers	Laid down: The *Haynsworth* (16), *Mannert L. Abele* (9), *Aaron Ward* (12), *Purdy* (22), *Zellars* (24), and *Shea* (28).
	Launched: The *O'Brien* (8), *Preston* (12), *Allen M. Sumner* (15), *Van Valkenburgh* (19), *Meredith* (21), and *Brush* (28).
	Commissioned: The *Twining* (1), *Bryant* (4), *Longshaw* (4), *Evans* (11), *Bennion* (14), *Morrison* (18), *Benham* (20), *McGowan* (20), *Barton* (30), *McNair* (30), *Yarnall* (30), *Cassin Young* (31), and *Watts* (31).

Escorts	Laid down: The *Arthur L. Bristol* (1), *Charles J. Kimmel* (1), *Daniel A. Joy* (1), *Don O. Woods* (1), *Ray K. Edwards* (1), *Ulvert M. Moore* (2), *William Seiverling* (2), *Samuel B. Roberts* (6), *Walter C. Wann* (6), *Lough* (8), *Alfred Wolf* (9), *Groves* (9), *Gentry* (13), *Truxtun* (13), *Upham* (13), *Key* (14), *Russell M. Cox* (14), *Thomas F. Nickel* (15), *Goss* (16), *Kendall C. Campbell* (16), *John B. Gray* (18), *Traw* (19), *Jobb* (20), *Lawrence C. Taylor* (20), *LeRay Wilson* (20), *Peiffer* (21), *Tinsman* (21), *Maurice J. Manuel* (22), *Clarence L. Evans* (23), *Knudson* (23), *Ringness* (23), *Naifeh* (29), *Red Nour* (30), and *Tollberg* (30).
	Launched: The *Eversole* (3), *Dennis* (4), *Bivin* (7), *Lewis* (7), *Osberg* (7), *Rizzi* (7), *Coates* (9), *Hodges* (9), *John C. Butler* (11), *Eisner* (12), *Gandy* (12), *Garfield Thomas* (12), *Gendreau* (12), *Holton* (12), *O'Flaherty* (14), *Edmonds* (17), *Jack W. Wilke* (18), *Shelton* (18), *Eugene E. Elmore* (23), *Hissam* (26), *Oswald A. Powers* (27), *Sheehan* (27), *Vandivier* (27), *Wagner* (27), *Riley* (29), *William C. Cole* (29), *Straus* (30), *Thornhill* (30), *La Prade* (30), and *Wingfield* (30).
	Commissioned: The *Swenning* (1), *Bostwick* (1), *Donaldson* (1), *Stern* (1), *Liddle* (6), *O'Neill* (6), *Raby* (7), *England* (10), *Thomason* (10), *Willis* (10), *Breeman* (12), *Bronstein* (13), *Finch* (13), *Kretchmer* (13), *Maloy* (13), *J. Douglas Blackwood* (15), *Cates* (15), *Edward H. Allen* (16), *Wilhoite* (16), *Jordan* (17), *Janssen* (18), *Burrows* (19), *Baker* (23), *Cockrill* (24), *Coffman* (27), *Koiner* (27), *O'Reilly* (28), *Witter* (29), *Delong* (31), *Stockdale* (31), and *Weaver* (31).
Submarines	Laid down: The *Atule* (2), *Capitaine* (2), *Kraken* (13), *Carbonero* (16), and *Carp* (23).
	Launched: The *Barbero* (12), *Hardhead* (12), and *Croaker* (19).
	Commissioned: The *Bang* (4), *Pilotfish* (16), *Guavina* (23), *Gabilan* (28), and *Tilefish* (28).

January 1944

Battleship	Launched: The *Missouri* (29).
Fleet carriers	Launched: The *Hancock* (24).
	Commissioned: The *Franklin* (31).
Escort carriers	Launched: The *Petrof Bay* (1), *Rudyerd Bay* (12), *Saginaw Bay* (19), and *Sargent Bay* (31).
	Commissioned: The *Nehenta Bay* (3), *Hoggatt Bay* (11), *Kadashan Bay* (18), and *Marcus Island* (26).
Light cruisers	Laid down: The *Newark* (17) and *Tallahassee* (31).
	Launched: The *Duluth* (13) and *Flint* (25).
	Commissioned: The *Vincennes* (21).
Destroyers	Laid down: The *Robert H. Smith* (10), *Massey* (14), *Hank* (17), *John W. Weeks* (17), *J. William Ditter* (25), *Douglas H. Fox* (31), and *Thomas E. Fraser* (31).
	Launched: The *DeHaven* (9), *Ingraham* (16), *Moale* (16), *Taussig* (25), *Mansfield* (29), and *Wren* (29).
	Commissioned: The *Pritchett* (15), *Cushing* (17), *Walke* (21), *Allen M. Sumner* (26), *Heywood L. Edwards* (26), and *Robinson* (31).

Escorts	Laid down: The *Formoe* (3), *Grady* (3), *Melvin R. Nawman* (3), *Oliver Mitchell* (3), *William J. Pattison* (4), *Beverly W. Reid* (5), *Parle* (8), *Kenneth M. Willett* (10), *Robert F. Keller* (12), *Tabberer* (12), *Albert T. Harris* (13), *Charles E. Brannon* (13), *Myers* (15), *Walter B. Cobb* (15), *Earle B. Hall* (19), *Harry L. Corl* (19), *Chester T. O'Brien* (21), *Leland E. Thomas* (21), *Willard Keith* (22), *William C. Lawe* (22), *Lloyd E. Acree* (24), *Jaccard* (25), *Belet* (26), *Julius A. Raven* (26), *Bray* (27), *Douglas A. Munro* (31), and *Dufilho* (31).
	Launched: The *Cronin* (5), *Leslie L.B. Knox* (8), *McNulty* (8), *Rinehart* (9), *Roche* (9), *Jack Miller* (10), *Richard W. Suesens* (11), *Stafford* (11), *George A. Johnson* (12), *Metivier* (12), *Abercrombie* (14), *Halloran* (14), *Charles J. Kimmel* (15), *Connolly* (15), *Daniel A. Joy* (15), *Oberrender* (18), *Walter C. Wann* (19), *Samuel B. Roberts* (20), *Lough* (22), *Robert Brazier* (22), *Thomas F. Nickel* (22), *Edwin A. Howard* (25), *Frybarger* (25), *Peiffer* (26), *LeRay Wilson* (28), *Jesse Rutherford* (29), *Lawrence C. Taylor* (29), and *Tinsman* (29).
	Commissioned: The *Eisner* (1), *Marsh* (1), *Runels* (3), *Kephart* (7), *Raymond* (8), *Strickland* (10), *Price* (12), *Hissam* (13), *Francis M. Robinson* (15), *Holder* (18), *Cofer* (19), *Jenks* (19), *O'Toole* (22), *Coates* (24), *Daniel* (24), *Garfield Thomas* (24), *Hollis* (24), *Forester* (25), *Bowers* (27), and *Wingfield* (28).
Submarines	Laid down: The *Catfish* (6), *Lagarto* (12), and *Spikefish* (29).
	Launched: The *Baya* (2), *Spadefish* (8), *Hawkbill* (9), *Razorback* (27), *Redfish* (27), *Ronquil* (27), *Scabbardfish* (27), *Becuna* (30), and *Kraken* (30).
	Commissioned: The *Guitarro* (1), *Pintado* (1) *Perch* (7) *Pipefish* (22), and *Bream* (24).
February 1944	
Fleet carriers	Laid down: The *Crown Point* (21).
	Launched: The *Ticonderoga* (7), *Shangri La* (24), and *Bennington* (26).
Escort carriers	Launched: The *Shamrock Bay* (4), *Shipley Bay* (12), *Sitkoh Bay* (19), and *Steamer Bay* (26).
	Commissioned: The *Savo Island* (3), *Ommaney Bay* (11), *Petrof Bay* (18), and *Rudyerd Bay* (25).
Heavy cruiser	Launched: The *Pittsburgh* (22).
Light cruisers	Laid down: The *Gaveston* (20) and *New Haven* (28).
	Launched: The *Atlanta* (6) and *Oklahoma City* (20).
Destroyers	Laid down: The *Buck* (1), *Hugh W. Hadley* (6), *Henley* (8), *Shannon* (14), *Wallace L. Lind* (14), *Stormes* (15), *Alfred A. Cunningham* (23), *Borie* (29), and *Robert K. Huntington* (29).
	Launched: The *Lowry* (6), *Cooper* (9), *Lyman K. Swenson* (12), *Jarvis* (14), *Samuel N. Moore* (23), and *English* (27).
	Commissioned: The *John D. Henley* (2), *Laffey* (8), *Stockham* (11), *Irwin* (14), *Monssen* (14), *Ross* (21), *Richard P. Leary* (23), *O'Brien* (25), and *Moale* (28).
Escorts	Laid down: The *Thornhill* (1), *Rinehart* (12), *Kirwin* (14), *Mack* (14), *Ruchamkin* (14), *George E. Davis* (15), *Gosselin* (17), *Roche* (21), *Haas* (23), and *Walsh* (27).
	Launched: The *Melvin R. Nawman* (7), *Oliver Mitchell* (8), *Key* (12), *Traw* (12), *Conklin* (13), *Corbesier* (13), *Earl K. Olsen* (13), *Slater* (13), *Gentry* (15), *Holt* (15), *Tabberer* (18), *Maurice J. Manuel* (19), *Robert F. Keller* (19), *Finnegan* (22), *McCoy Reynolds* (22), *Creamer* (23), *Leland E. Thomas* (28), *Carter* (29), *Chester O'Brien* (29), and *Naifeh* (29).
	Commissioned: The *Currier* (1), *Gunason* (1), *Tweedy* (2), *Roy O. Hale* (3), *Eugene E. Elmore* (4), *Hilbert* (4), *Lake* (5), *Gandy* (7), *Lloyd* (11), *Ahrens* (12), *Major* (12), *Barr* (15), *Solar* (15), *Dale W. Peterson* (17), *Alexander J. Luke* (19), *Lyman* (19), *Weeden* (19), *Otter* (21), *Osmus* (23), *Richard S. Bull* (26), *Robert I. Paine* (26), *Martin H. Ray* (28), *John J. Powers* (29), *Lamons* (29), and *Varian* (29).

Submarines	Laid down: The *Entemedor* (3), *Sea Owl* (7), *Amberjack* (8), *Grampus* (8), *Pickerel* (8), *Grenadier* (8), *Chivo* (21), *Lamprey* (22), and *Sea Poacher* (23).
	Launched: The *Segundo* (5), *Bergall* (16), *Icefish* (20), *Sea Cat* (21), *Besugo* (27), and *Sea Devil* (28).
	Commissioned: The *Piranha* (5), *Plaice* (12), *Shark* (14), *Pomfret* (19), and *Cavalla* (29).

March 1944

Fleet carriers	Laid down: The *Kearsarge* (1) and *Tarawa* (1).
Escort carriers	Launched: The *Cape Esperance* (3), *Takanis Bay* (10), *Thetis Bay* (16), *Makassar Strait* (22), and *Windham Bay* (29).
	Commissioned: The *Saginaw Bay* (2), *Sargent Bay* (9), *Shamrock Bay* (15), *Shipley Bay* (21), and *Sitkoh Bay* (28).
Heavy cruiser	Launched: The *Albany* (6).
Light cruisers	Launched: The *Springfield* (9) and *Dayton* (19).
Destroyers	Laid down: The *Willard Keith* (5), *Harry F. Bauer* (6), *William C. Lawe* (12), *Adams* (20), *John R. Pierce* (24), *Rowan* (25), *Lloyd Thomas* (26), *Gainard* (28), and *Compton* (29).
	Launched: The *Collett* (5), *Lindsey* (5), *Charles S. Sperry* (13), *Porter* (13), *Maddox* (19), *Harry E. Hubbbard* (24), *Ault* (26), *Putnam* (26), and *Waldron* (26).
	Commissioned: The *Leutze* (4), *Wedderburn* (9), *Ingraham* (10), *Rowe* (13), *Meredith* (14), *Blue* (20), *Preston* (20), *Cooper* (27), *DeHaven* (31), and *Smalley* (31).
Escorts	Laid down: The *Begor* (6), *Woodson* (7), *Hunter Marshall* (9), *Cross* (19), *Earheart* (20), *Rolf* (20), *Johnnie Hutchins* (21), *Hanna* (22), and *Cavallaro* (28).
	Launched: The *Doyle C. Barnes* (4), *Jobb* (4), *Kenneth M. Willett* (7), *Ulvert M. Moore* (7), *William Seiverling* (7), *Douglas A. Munroe* (8), *Dufilho* (9), *Jaccard* (18), *Goss* (19), *Kendall C. Campbell* (19), *Haas* (20), *Lloyd E. Acree* (21), *Parle* (25), and *Clarence L. Evans* (28).
	Commissioned: The *Hubbard* (6), *Jack W. Wilkie* (7), *Richard M. Rowell* (9), *Riley* (13), *Willmarth* (13), *Fowler* (15), *Hayter* (16), *Gendreau* (17), *Earl V. Johnson* (18), *Dennis* (20), *Mason* (20), *Eversole* (21), *Leslie L.B. Knox* (22), *Durik* (24), *Crowley* (25), *William T. Powell* (28), *Scroggins* (30), *Corbesier* (31), *John C. Butler* (31), and *McNulty* (31).
Submarines	Laid down: The *Sea Robin* (1), *Stickleback* (1), *Chopper* (2), *Sennet* (8), *Lizardfish* (14), *Piper* (15), *Clamagore* (16), and *Threadfin* (18).
	Launched: The *Atule* (6), *Blackfin* (12), *Jallao* (12), *Trepang* (23), *Sea Dog* (28), *Sea Fox* (28), and *Caiman* (30).
	Commissioned: The *Hammerhead* (1), *Sterlet* (4), *Dragonet* (6), *Sealion* (8), *Spadefish* (9), *Queenfish* (11), and *Cobia* (29).

April 1944

Battleship	Commissioned: The *Wisconsin* (16).
Fleet carriers	Launched: The *Bon Homme Richard* (29).
	Commissioned: The *Hancock* (15).
Escort carriers	Launched: The *Makin Island* (5), *Lunga Point* (11), *Bismarck Sea* (17), *Salamaua* (22), and *Hollandia* (28).
	Commissioned: The *Steamer Bay* (4), *Cape Esperance* (9), *Takanis Bay* (15), *Thetis Bay* (21), and *Makassar Strait* (27).
Heavy cruiser	Laid down: The *Oregon City* (8).
Light cruiser	Laid down: The *Buffalo* (3).
	Launched: The *Amsterdam* (25).

Destroyers — Laid down: The *Lansdale* (2), *Seymour D. Owens* (3), *Gwin* (9), *James C. Owens* (9), *Tolman* (10), *Soley* (18), *Frank E. Evans* (21), *Hoel* (21), *Keppler* (23), and *Drexler* (24).

Launched: The *Charles J. Badger* (3), *Hyman* (8), *Colhoun* (10), *Haynsworth* (15), *Henry A. Wiley* (21), *Mannert L. Abele* (23), and *Strong* (23).

Commissioned: The *Howorth* (3), *Bearss* (12), *Mansfield* (14), *Stoddard* (15), *Brush* (17), and *Watts* (29).

Escorts — Laid down: The *Walter S. Gorka* (3), *Joseph E. Connolly* (6), *Rombach* (10), *Pratt* (11), *Rogers Blood* (12), *Donald W. Wolf* (17), *Francovich* (19), and *Heyliger* (27).

Launched: The *Fieberling* (2), *George E. Davis* (8), *Ely* (10), *Delbert W. Halsey* (11), *Mack* (11), *Bray* (15), *Damon M. Cummings* (18), *Oswald* (25), and *Woodson* (29).

Commissioned: The *Edmonds* (3), *Kyne* (4), *Shelton* (4), *Wiseman* (4), *Straus* (6), *Metivier* (7), *John M. Bermingham* (8), *O'Flaherty* (8), *Rall* (8), *Earl K. Olsen* (10), *Fieberling* (11), *Jack Miller* (13), *George A. Johnson* (15), *Raymond* (15), *Spangenberg* (15), *Stafford* (19), *Charles J. Kimmel* (20), *La Prade* (20), *Conklin* (21), *Tabberer* (23), *Richard W. Suesens* (26), *Daniel A. Joy* (28), and *Samuel B. Roberts* (28).

Submarines — Laid down: The *Loggerhead* (1), *Tench* (1), *Cobbler* (3), *Thornback* (5), *Tigrone* (8), *Cochino* (13), *Tiru* (17), *Corporal* (27), and *Tirante* (28).

Launched: The *Blenny* (9), *Kete* (9), *Blower* (23), *Dace* (25), and *Spikefish* (26).

Commissioned: The *Barbel* (3), *Razorback* (3), *Redfish* (12), *Hardhead* (18), *Croaker* (21), *Ronquil* (22), *Barbero* (29), and *Scabbardfish* (29).

May 1944

Fleet carrier — Laid down: The *Oriskany* (1).

Commissioned: The *Ticonderoga* (8).

Escort carriers — Launched: The *Kwajalein* (4), *Commencement Bay* (4), *Admiralty Islands* (10), *Bouganville* (16), *Mantanikau* (22), and *Attu* (27).

Commissioned: The *Windham Bay* (3), *Makin Island* (9), *Lunga Point* (14), *Bismarck Sea* (20), and *Salamaua* (26).

Heavy cruiser — Laid down: The *Rochester* (29).

Light cruiser — Laid down: The *Cheyenne* (29).

Commissioned: The *Astoria* (17).

Destroyers — Laid down: The *Bristol* (5), *Frank Knox* (8), *Hawkins* (14), *John A. Bole* (20), *Abner Read* (21), *Duncan* (22), *Harlan R. Dickson* (23), *Hugh Purvis* (23), *Southerland* (27), and *Henry W. Tucker* (29).

Launched: The *Colahan* (3), *Aaron Ward* (5), *Purdy* (7), *Gregory* (8), *Shea* (20), *Hank* (21), *John W. Weeks* (21), *Little* (22), and *Robert H. Smith* (25).

Commissioned: The *Lyman K. Swenson* (2), *English* (4), *Killen* (4), *Collett* (16), *Charles S. Sperry* (17), *Taussig* (20), *Wren* (20), and *Ault* (31).

Escorts — Laid down: The *Alvin C. Cockrell* (1), *French* (1), *McGinty* (3), *Cook* (7), *Cecil J. Doyle* (12), *John L. Williamson* (22), *Thaddeus Parker* (23), *Kline* (27), and *Walter X. Young* (27).

Launched: The *Johnnie Hutchins* (2), *Ebert* (11), *Walton* (20), *Vammen* (21) and *Rolf* (23).

Commissioned: The *Abercrombie* (1), *Holton* (1), *Slater* (1), *Lough* (2), *McCoy Reynolds* (2), *Walter C. Wann* (2), *Carter* (3), *Cronin* (5), *Snyder* (5), *Chaffee* (9), *LeRay Wilson* (10), *Oberrander* (11), *Gilligan* (12), *William C. Cole* (12), *Lawrence C. Taylor* (13), *Rudderow* (15), *Melvin R. Nawman* (16), *Frybarger* (18), *Robert Brazier* (18), *Edwin A. Howard* (25), *Howard F. Clark* (25), *Paul G. Baker* (25), *Halloran* (27), *Hodges* (27), *Hemminger* (30), and *Jesse Rutherford* (31).

Submarines	Laid down: The *Macabi* (1), *Cubera* (11), *Wahoo* (15) *Trutta* (22), *Cusk* (25), *Toro* (27), and *Mapiro* (30).
	Launched: The *Blueback* (7), *Sea Owl* (7), *Moray* (14), *Roncador* (14), *Spot* (19), *Sea Poacher* (20), *Boarfish* (21), *Sea Robin* (25), *Charr* (28), and *Lagarto* (28).
	Commissioned: The *Segundo* (9), *Sea Cat* (16), *Hawkbill* (17), *Baya* (20), *Trepang* (220, *Sea Devil* (24), and *Becuna* (27).
June 1944	
Battleship	Commissioned: The *Missouri* (11).
Fleet carrier	Launched: The *Randolph* (28).
Escort carriers	Launched: The *Roi* (2), *Munda* (8), and *Block Island* (10).
	Commissioned: The *Hollandia* (1). *Kwajalein* (7), *Admiralty Islands* (13), *Bouganville* (18), *Mantanikau* (24), and *Attu* (30).
Heavy cruiser	Commissioned: The large cruiser *Alaska* (17).
Light cruisers	Commissioned: The *Pasadena* (8) and *Vicksburg* (12).
Destroyers	Laid down: The *Rogers* (3), *Beatty* (4), *Chevalier* (12), *Perkins* (19), and *Higbee* (26).
	Launched: The *Rooks* (6), *Thomas E. Fraser* (10), *Wallace L. Lind* (14), and *Shannon* (24).
	Commissioned: The *Maddox* (2), *Jarvis* (3), *John Hood* (7), *Waldron* (8), *Hyman* (16), *Haynsworth* (22), *Porter* (24), and *Samuel N. Moore* (24).
Escorts	Laid down: The *Williams* (5), *Presley* (6), *Raymond W. Herndon* (12), *Balduck* (17), and *Scribner* (29).
	Launched: The *Pratt* (1), *Muir* (4), *Neal A. Scott* (4), *Rombach* (6), and *French* (17).
	Commissioned: The *William Seiverling* (1), *Key* (5), *Holt* (9), *Thomas F. Nickel* (9), *Day* (10), *Oswald* (12), *Gentry* (14), *Oliver Mitchell* (14), *Peiffer* (15), *Leland Thomas* (16), *Robert F. Keller* (17), *Traw* (20), *Clarence L. Evans* (25), *Tinsman* (26), *Damon M. Cummings* (29), *Bright* (30), and *Maurice J. Manuel* (30).
Submarines	Laid down: The *Diodon* (1), *Torsk* (7), *Menhaden* (21), *Dogfish* (22), *Quillback* (27), *Argonaut* (28), *Greenfish* (29), and SS 517 unnamed (29).
	Launched: The *Sabalo* (4), *Sablefish* (4), *Sennet* (6), *Chub* (18), *Lamprey* (18), *Brill* (25), *Piper* (26), and *Threadfin* (26).
	Commissioned: The *Escolar* (2), *Sea Dog* (3), *Icefish* (10), *Bergall* (12), *Sea Fox* (13), *Besugo* (19), *Atule* (21), and *Spikefish* (30).
July 1944	
Fleet carriers	Laid down: The *Reprisal* (1), *Coral Sea* (10), and *Saipan* (10).
Escort carriers	Launched: The *Gilbert Islands* (20).
	Commissioned: The *Roi* (6) and *Munda* (8).
Heavy cruiser	Launched: The *Bremerton* (2).
Light cruiser	Commissioned: The *Wilkes Barre* (1).
Destroyers	Laid down: The *Gurke* (1), *Vesole* (3), *Benner* (10), *Fred T. Berry* (16), and *Dennis J. Buckley* (24).
	Launched: The *Borie* (4), *J. William Ditter* (4), *Harry F. Bauer* (9), *Hugh W. Hadley* (16), and *Zellars* (19).
	Commissioned: The *Mannert L. Abele* (4), *Colhoun* (8), *Purdy* (18), *John W. Weeks* (21), *Harry B. Hubbard* (22), *Lowry* (23), and *Gregory* (29).
Escorts	Laid down: The *Alexander Diachenko* (18) and *Burdo* (926).
	Launched: The *Cecil J. Doyle* (1), *Cross* (4), *Hanna* (4), and *Raymond W. Herndon* (15).
	Commissioned: The *Chester O'Brien* (3), *Jobb* (4), *Naifeh* (4), *Connolly* (8), *Douglas A. Munro* (11), *Ebert* (12), *Doyle C. Barnes* (13), *Silverstein* (14), *Ulvert M. Moore* (18), *Kenneth M. Willett* (19), *Dufilho* (21), *Jaccard* (26), *Vamman* (27), *Parle* (29), *Kendall C. Campbell* (31), and *Neal A. Scott* (31).

Submarines	Laid down: The *Halfbeak* (6), *Runner* (10), *Conger* (11), *Cutlass* (22), and *Mero* (22).
	Launched: The *Bugara* (2), *Tench* (7), *Thornback* (7), *Bullhead* (16), *Lizardfish* (16), and *Tigrone* (20).
	Commissioned: The *Blackfin* (4), *Jallao* (8), *Caiman* (17), *Sea Owl* (17), *Blenny* (27), *Kete* (31), and *Sea Poacher* (31).
August 1944	
Fleet carriers	Laid down: The *Philippine Sea* (19).
	Launched: The *Antietam* (20).
	Commissioned: The *Bennington* (6)
Escort carrier	Launched: The *Kula Gulf* (15).
Heavy cruisers	Laid down: The *Northampton* (31).
	Launched: The heavy cruisers *Fall River* (13), *Los Angeles* (20), and *Chicago* (20).
Light cruisers	Launched: The *Topeka* (19) and *Little Rock* (27).
	Commissioned: The *Flint* (31).
Destroyers	Laid down: The *Vogelgesang* (3), *Gearing* (10), *Leary* (11), *Myles C. Fox* (14), *Dyess* (17), *Eugene A. Greene* (17), and *Norris* (29).
	Launched: The *Alfred A. Cunningham* (3), *Lofberg* (12), *Massey* (19), and *Willard Keith* (29).
	Commissioned: The *Van Valkenburgh* (2), *Little* (19), and *Hank* (28).
Escorts	Laid down: The *Harold A. Bass* (3), *Wantuck* (17), and *Kleinsmith* (30).
	Launched: The *McGinty* (5), *Joseph E. Connelly* (6), *Sutton* (6), *Alvin C. Cockrell* (8), *Presley* (19), *Williams* (22), *Thaddeus Parker* (26), and *John L. Williamson* (29).
	Commissioned: The *Lloyd E. Acree* (1), *Haas* (2), *Tills* (8), *George E. Davis* (11), *Mack* (16), *Finnegan* (19), *Woodson* (24), *Goss* (26), *Johnnie Hutchins* (28), and *Muir* (30).
Submarines	Laid down: The *Diablo* (11), *Medregal* (21), and *Requin* (24).
	Launched: The *Springer* (3), *Bumper* (6), *Tirante* (9), *Loggerhead* (13), *Trutta* (18), *Toro* (23), and *Cabezon* (27).
	Commissioned: The *Spot* (3), *Sea Robin* (7), *Blower* (10), *Sennet* (22), *Piper* (23), *Blueback* (28), and *Threadfin* (30).
September 1944	
Fleet carriers	Laid down: The *Valley Forge* (7) and *Wright* (21).
	Commissioned: The *Shangri La* (15).
Escort carriers	Launched: The *Cape Gloucester* (12) and *Salerno Bay* (26).
Heavy cruisers	Launched: The *St. Paul* (16).
	Commissioned: The large cruiser *Guam* (17).
Light cruisers	Laid down: The *Youngstown* (4), *Juneau* (15), and *Manchester* (25).
	Launched: The *Tucson* (3) and *Portsmouth* (20).
	Commissioned: The *Springfield* (9) and *Duluth* (18).
Destroyers	Laid down: The *Steinaker* (1), *Everett F. Larson* (4), *Gyatt* (7), *Bordelon* (9), *McKean* (15), *Goodrich* (18), *Kenneth D. Bailey* (21), and *Furse* (23).
	Launched: The *John R. Pierce* (1), *Drexler* (3), *Soley* (8), *Compton* (17), *Frank Knox* (17), *Gainard* (17), *Hart* (25), *Metcalf* (25) *Shields* (25), *Wiley* (25), *Douglas H. Fox* (30), and *John W. Thomason* (30).
	Commissioned: The *Rooks* (2), *Wallace L. Lind* (9), and *Borie* (21).
Escorts	Commissioned: The *Roberts* (2), *Bray* (4), *Walton* (4), *Lewis* (5), *Rolf* (7), *Grady* (11), *Pratt* (18), *McCelland* (19), *Rombach* (20), and *McGinty* (25).
Submarines	Launched: The *Torsk* (6), *Dentuda* (10), and *Macabi* (19).
	Commissioned: The *Devilfish* (1), *Kraken* (8), *Boarfish* (23), and *Charr* (23).

October 1944	
Fleet carrier	Commissioned: The *Randolph* (9).
Escort carrier	Launched: The *Vella Gulf* (19).
Heavy cruisers	Launched: The *Macon* (15) and *Columbus* (30).
	Commissioned: The *Pittsburgh* (10).
Light cruiser	Laid down: The *Chattanooga* (9).
Destroyers	Laid down: The *McCaffery* (1), *Harold J. Ellison* (3), *Hanson* (7), *Newman K. Perry* (10), *William R. Rush* (19), *Henderson* (27), *Harwood* (29), *Floyd B. Parks* (30), and *Herbert J. Thomas* (30).
	Launched: The *James C. Owens* (1) *Frank E. Evans* (3), *Southerland* (5), *Hawkins* (7), *Duncan* (27), *Bristol* (29), and *Chevalier* (29).
	Commissioned: The *Putnam* (12) and *Zellars* (25).
Escorts	Laid down: The *Weiss* (4) and *Carpellotti* (31).
	Commissioned: The *Formoe* (5), *Alvin C. Cockrell* (7), *French* (9), *Cecil J. Doyle* (16), *Thaddeus Parker* (25), *Bivin* (31), and *John L. Williamson* (31).
Submarines	Laid down: The *Irex* (2).
	Launched: The *Argonaut* (1), *Capitaine* (1), *Quillback* (1), *Carbonero* (15), *Runner* (17), and *Conger* (17).
	Commissioned: The *Tench* (6), *Thornback* (13), *Lagarto* (14), *Springer* (18), *Chub* (21), *Tigrone* (25), and *Brill* (26).

November 1944	
Fleet carriers	Launched: The *Lake Champlain* (2).
	Commissioned: The *Bon Homme Richard* (26).
Escort carriers	Launched: The *Siboney* (9) and *Puget Sound* (30).
	Commissioned: The *Commencement Bay* (27).
Light cruiser	Laid down: The *Spokane* (15).
Destroyers	Laid down: The *Charles R. Ware* (1), *William M. Wood* (2), *Turner* (13), *John R. Craig* (17), *Orleck* (28), and *Cone* (30).
	Launched: The *John A. Bole* (1), *Stormes* (4), *Henry W. Tucker* (8), *Higbee* (12), *Rogers* (20), *Beatty* (30), and *Benner* (30).
	Commissioned: The *Compton* (4), *Hart* (4), *Drexler* (14), *Metcalf* (18), *Alfred A. Cunningham* (23), *Gainard* (23), *Massey* (24), and *Hugh W. Hadley* (25).
Escorts	Commissioned: The *Charles E. Brannon* (1), *Presley* (7), *Williams* (11), and *Albert T. Harris* (29).
Submarines	Laid down: The *Sea Leopard* (7).
	Launched: The *Cutlass* (5), *Mapiro* (9), *Carp* (12), and *Catfish* (19).
	Commissioned: The *Lionfish* (1), *Tirante* (6), *Hackleback* (7), *Bugara* (15), *Trutta* (16), and *Lamprey* (17).

December 1944	
Fleet carrier	Launched: The *Boxer* (14).
Escort carriers	Launched: The *Rendova* (28).
	Commissioned: The *Block Island* (30).
Heavy cruisers	Laid down: The *Cambridge* (16), *Norfolk* (27), and *Scranton* (27).
Light cruisers	Launched: The *Providence* (28).
	Commissioned: The *Atlanta* (3), *Oklahoma City* (22), and *Topeka* (23).
Destroyers	Laid down: The *Charles P. Cecil* (2), *Glennon* (12), *Brinkley Bass* (20), *George K. MacKenzie* (21), and *James E. Kyes* (27).
	Launched: The *Richard B. Anderson* (1), *Robert K. Huntington* (5), *Perkins* (7), *Harlan R. Dickson* (17), *Hugh Purvis* (17), *Dennis J. Buckley* (20), *Rowan* (29), and *Vesole* (29).
	Commissioned: The *Soley* (8), *Frank Knox* (11), *Southerland* (22), *Douglas H. Fox* (26), *Willard Keith* (27), and *John R. Pierce* (30).
Escort	Commissioned: The: *Sutton* (1).

Submarines	Launched: The *Diablo* (1), *Odax* (4), *Amberjack* (12), *Grampus* (12), *Pickerel* (12), *Grenadier* (12), *Medregal* (15), *Entemedor* (17), and *Menhaden* (20).
	Commissioned: The *Bullhead* (4), *Toro* (8), *Bumper* (9), *Torsk* (16), *Manta* (18), *Quillback* (29), *Cabezon* (30), *Dentuda* (30), and *Lizardfish* (30).
January 1945	
Fleet carriers	Laid down: The *Iwo Jima* (29).
	Commissioned: The *Antietam* (28).
Escort carriers	Laid down: The *Bairoko* (25).
Heavy cruisers	Laid down: The *Bridgeport* (18).
	Commissioned: The *Chicago* (10).
Light cruisers	Laid down: The *Worcester* (29).
	Commissioned: The *Dayton* (7) and *Amsterdam* (8).
Destroyers	Laid down: The *Stickell* (5), *Sarsfield* (15), *Stribling* (15), *Hollister* (18), *Meredith* (27), *O'Hare* (27), and *Ernest J. Small* (30).
	Launched: The *Myles C. Fox* (13), *Vogelgesang* (15), *Leary* (20), *Dyess* (26), *Everett F. Larson* (28), and *Fred T. Berry* (28).
	Commissioned: The *Chevalier* (9), *Higbee* (27), and *Stormes* (27).
Escorts	Commissioned: The *Cross* (8) and *Hanna* (27).
Submarines	Laid down: The *Sirago* (3) and *Pomodon* (29).
	Launched: The *Requin* (1), *Stickleback* (1), *Chivo* (14), *Mero* (17) and *Irex* (26).
	Commissioned: The *Argonaut* (15), *Capitaine* (26), and *Moray* (26).
February 1945	
Escort carriers	Launched: The *Badoeng Strait* (15).
	Commissioned: The *Gilbert Islands* (5).
Heavy cruiser	Commissioned: The *St. Paul* (17).
Light cruisers	Laid down: The *Fresno* (12).
	Launched: The *Fargo* (25).
	Commissioned: The *Tucson* (3).
Destroyers	Laid down: The *Brownson* (13), *Power* (26), and *Eversole* (28).
	Launched: The *Steinaker* (13), *Gurke* (15), *Gearing* (18), *Goodrich* (25), and *Norris* (25).
	Commissioned: The *Frank E. Evans* (3), *Shields* (8), *Hawkins* (10), *Benner* (13), *Harlan R. Dickson* (15), *James C. Owens* (17), *Wiley* (22), and *Duncan* (25).
Escort	Commissioned: The *Joseph E. Connolly* (28).
Submarines	Launched: The *Chopper* (4), *Clamagore* (25), and *Odax* (10).
	Commissioned: The *Runner* (6), *Carbonero* (7), *Loggerhead* (9), *Lancetfish* (12), *Conger* (14), and *Carp* (28).
March 1945	
Fleet carrier	Launched: The *Midway* (20).
Escort carriers	Launched: The *Saidor* (17).
	Commissioned: The *Cape Gloucester* (5).
Light cruiser	Laid down: The *Wilmington* (5).
Destroyers	Laid down: The *Wiltsie* (13) and *Noa* (26).
	Launched: The *Bordelon* (3), *Furse* (9), *Buck* (11), *Hanson* (11), *Harold J. Ellison* (14), *Arnold J. Isbell* (14), *Newman K. Perry* (17), *Eugene A. Greene* (18), *Herbert J. Thomas* (25), *Floyd B. Parkes* (31), and *McKean* (31).
	Commissioned: The *Hugh Purvis* (1), *Dennis J. Buckley* (2) *John A. Bole* (3), *Robert K. Huntington* (3), *Strong* (8), *Henry W. Tucker* (12), *Bristol* (17), *Rogers* (26), *Beatty* (31), and *Rowan* (31).
Escort	Commissioned: The *Heylinger* (24).

Submarines	Laid down: The *Corsair* (1) and *Remora* (5).
	Launched: The *Sea Leopard* (2).
	Commissioned: The *Cutlass* (17), *Catfish* (19), *Roncador* (27), *Macabi* (29), *Stickleback* (29), and *Diablo* (31).
April 1945	
Fleet carrier	Launched: The *Coral Sea* (29).
	Commissioned: The *Boxer* (26).
Escort carriers	Launched: The *Sicily* (14).
	Commissioned: The *Vella Gulf* (9).
Heavy cruisers	Launched: The *Helena* (28).
	Commissioned: The *Bremerton* (29).
Light cruisers	Launched: The *Huntington* (8) and *Gaveston* (22).
Destroyers	Laid down: The *Joseph P. Kennedy, Jr.* (2), *Corry* (5), *Fiske* (9), *Fechteler* (12), *McCaffery* (12), *New* (14), *Holder* (23), *Theodore E. Chandler* (23), *Warrington* (23), and *Hamner* (25).
	Launched: The *Henley* (8), *Turner* (8), *Charles R. Ware* (12), *John R. Craig* (14), *Gyatt* (15), and *Charles P. Cecil* (22).
	Commissioned: The *Perkins* (4), *Everett F. Larson* (6), *Vesole* (23), *Goodrich* (24), and *Lofberg* (26).
Submarines	Laid down: The *Sarda* (12), *Spinax* (14), and *Unicorn* (25).
	Launched: The *Cobbler* (1) and *Cochino* (20).
	Commissioned: The *Entemedor* (6), *Medregal* (14), *Chivo* (28), *Requin* (28), and *Mapiro* (30).
May 1945	
Fleet carriers	Launched: The *Kearsarge* (5) and *Tarawa* (12).
Escort carriers	Launched: The *Point Cruz* (18).
	Commissioned: The *Kula Gulf* (12), *Siboney* (14), and *Salerno Bay* (19).
Heavy cruisers	Laid down: The *Des Moines* (28).
	Launched: The *Toledo* (6).
Light cruiser	Commissioned: The *Providence* (15).
Destroyers	Laid down: The *Rupertus* (2), *Damato* (10), *Perry* (14), *Rich* (16), *Baussell* (28), and *Shelton* (31).
	Launched: The *Cone* (10), *Orleck* (12), *Harwood* (22), *Brinkley Bass* (26), *William C. Lawe* (25), and *Henderson* (28).
	Commissioned: The *Gearing* (3), *Leary* (7), *Hanson* (11), *Fred T. Berry* (12), *Gurke* (12), *George K. MacKenzie* (13), *Dyess* (21), *Sarsfield* (27), and *Herbert J. Thomas* (29).
Submarines	Launched: The *Sirago* (11) and *Trumpetfish* (13).
	Commissioned: The *Irex* (14) and *Chopper* (25).
June 1945	
Fleet carriers	Commissioned: The *Lake Champlain* (3).
Escort carriers	Launched: The *Mindoro* (27).
	Commissioned: The *Puget Sound* (18).
Heavy cruisers	Launched: The *Oregon City* (9) and *Albany* (30).
Light cruisers	Commissioned: The *Little Rock* (17) and *Portsmouth* (25).
Destroyers	Laid down: The *Bordelon* (5), *Johnston* (5), *Forrest Royal* (8), *Ozbourn* (16), *Epperson* (20), *Robert H. McCard* (20), and *Samuel B. Roberts* (27).
	Launched: The *Stribling* (8), *Ernest J. Small* (14), *Stickell* (16), *Kenneth D. Bailey* (17), *O'Hare* (22), *Meredith* (28), and *Power* (30).
	Commissioned: The *Eugene A. Greene* (8), *McKean* (9), *Norris* (9), *Turner* (12), and *Charles P. Cecil* (29).

Escort	Commissioned: The *Rizzi* (26).
Submarines	Laid down: The *Volador* (15) and *Walrus* (21).
	Launched: The *Corporal* (10), *Pomodon* (12), and *Cubera* (17).
	Commissioned: The *Ling* (8), *Sea Leopard* (11), *Sabalo* (19), *Menhaden* (22), and *Clamagore* (28).
July 1945	
Fleet carrier	Launched: The *Princeton* (8) and *Saipan* (8).
Escort carriers	Launched: The *Rabaul* (14).
	Commissioned: The *Bairoko* (16).
Heavy cruisers	Laid down: The *Salem* (4).
	Commissioned: The *Fall River* (1) and *Los Angeles* (22).
Light cruiser	Launched: The *Juneau* (15).
Destroyers	Laid down: The *Robert L. Wilson* (2), *Basilone* (7), *Seaman* (10), *Castle* (11), *Witek* (16), *Carpenter* (30), and *Richard E. Kraus* (31).
	Launched: The *Brownson* (7), *Richard B. Anderson* (7), *William R. Rush* (8), *Glennon* (14), *Joseph P. Kennedy, Jr.* (26), *Corry* (28), *William M. Wood* (29), and *Noa* (30).
	Commissioned: The *Gyatt* (2), *Furse* (10), *George K. MacKenzie* (13), *McCaffery* (26), *Newman K. Perry* (26), *Floyd B. Parkes* (31), *Kenneth D. Bailey* (31), and *Sarsfield* (31).
Submarines	Laid down: The *Pompano* (16).
	Launched: The *Remora* (7), *Tusk* (8), and *Cusk* (28).
	Commissioned: The *Odax* (11).
August 1945	
Escort carrier	Launched: The *Palau* (6).
Destroyers	Laid down: The *Woodrow R. Thompson* (1) and *Leonard F. Mason* (6).
	Launched: The *James E. Kyes* (4) and *Arnold J. Isbell* (6).
	Commissioned: The *Henderson* (4).
Submarines	Commissioned: The *Cobbler* (8) and *Sirago* (13).

THE FLEET, LIGHT, AND ESCORT CARRIERS IN U.S. SERVICE IN THE SECOND WORLD WAR

On 15 August 1945 in service or in dockyard, undergoing repair or routine maintenance, were (with their pennant number):

The fleet carriers *Saratoga* (3), *Ranger* (4), *Enterprise* (6), and the *Essex*-class *Essex* (9), *Yorktown* (10), *Intrepid* (11), *Hornet* (12), *Franklin* (13) *Ticonderoga* (14), *Randolph* (15), *Lexington* (16), *Bunker Hill* (17), *Wasp* (18), *Hancock* (19), *Bennington* (20), *Boxer* (21), *Bon Homme Richard* (31), *Antietam* (36), *Shangri-La* (38), and *Lake Champlain* (39);

the *Independence-class* light fleet carriers *Independence* (22), *Belleau Wood* (24), *Cowpens* (25), *Monterey* (26), *Langley* (27), *Cabot* (28), *Bataan* (29), and *San Jacinto* (30);

and, arranged by class and alphabetically and not by numbers, the escort carriers:

the *Long Island* (1);

the *Bogue*-class *Altamaha* (18), *Barnes* (20), *Bogue* (9), *Breton* (23), *Card* (11), *Copahee* (12), *Core* (13), *Croatan* (25), *Nassau* (16), and *Prince William* (31);

the *Sangamon*-class *Chenango* (28), *Sangamon* (26), *Santee* (29), and *Suwannee* (27);

the *Charger* (30);

the *Casablanca*-class *Admiralty Islands* (99), *Anzio* (57), *Attu* (102), *Bougainwille* (100), *Cape Esperance* (88), *Casablanca* (55), *Corregidor* (58), *Fanshaw Bay* (70), *Guadalcanal* (60), *Hoggatt Bay* (75), *Hollandia* (97), *Kadashan Bay* (76), *Kalinin Bay* (68), *Kasaan Bay* (69), *Kitkun Bay* (71), *Kwajalein* (98), *Lunga Point* (94), *Makassar Strait* (91), *Makin Island* (93), *Manila Bay* (61), *Marcus Island* (77), *Matanikau* (101), *Mission Bay* (59), *Munda* (104), *Natoma Bay* (62), *Nehenta Bay* (74), *Petrof Bay* (80), *Roi* (103), *Rudyerd Bay* (81), *Saginaw Bay* (82), *Salamaua* (96), *Sargent Bay* (83), *Savo Island* (78), *Shamrock Bay* (84), *Shipley Bay* (85), *Sitkoh Bay* (86), *Solomons* (67), *Steamer Bay* (87), *Takanis Bay* (89), *Thetis Bay* (90), *Tripoli* (64), *Tulagi* (72), *Wake Island* (65), *White Plains* (66), and *Windham Bay* (92);

and the *Commencement Bay*-class *Bairoko* (115), *Block Island* (106), *Cape Gloucester* (109), *Commencement Bay* (105), *Gilbert Islands* (107), *Kula Gulf* (108), *Salerno Bay* (110), *Siboney* (112), *Puget Sound (113)*, and *Vella Gulf* (111.)

Of the fleet carriers only the first three were in service in December 1941; none of the remaining seventeen came into service before May 1943.

Units lost in the course of the war were the fleet carriers *Lexington* (2), *Yorktown* (5), *Wasp* (7), and *Hornet* (8), the light fleet carrier *Princeton* (23), and the escort carriers *Liscome Bay* (56), *Block Island* (21), *Gambier Bay* (73), *St. Lo* (63), *Ommaney Bay* (79), and *Bismarck Sea* (95); of these only the *Block Island* was not sunk in the Pacific.

* * *

The units that were commissioned between war's end and 31 December 1945 were the fleet carriers *Princeton* (37) and *Tarawa* (40) and the *Midway* (41) and *Franklin D. Roosevelt* (42), and the escort carriers *Badoeng Strait* (116), *Point Cruz* (119), *Rendova* (114), *Saidor* (117), and *Mindoro* (120).

Commissioned into service in 1946 were the fleet carriers *Leyte* (32), *Kearsage* (33), *Valley Forge* (45), and *Philippine Sea* (47), and the escort carriers *Sicily* (118) and *Palau*

(122), while another two escort carriers, the *Rabaul* (121) and *Tinian* (123), were never commissioned.

* * *

Lest this listing be considered excessive, the point is that the American program was in large measure dictated by the calculation that the Japanese war would last into 1947 and that construction was organized accordingly, though by 1944 the schedules for landings on the home islands had come forward into 1946.

APPENDIX 10.2.

U.S. LEND-LEASE PRODUCTION OF ESCORT CARRIERS, FRIGATES, AND SLOOPS THAT SAW SERVICE IN THE BRITISH NAVY

(A) TABULAR REPRESENTATION:

		Escort carriers			Frigates			Sloops		
		LD	L	C	LD	L	C	LD	L	C
December	1941	1	-	-	-	-	-	-	-	-
January	1942	-	1	-	-	-	-	2	-	-
February	1942	1	-	-	1	-	-	-	-	-
March	1942	-	2	1	-	-	-	-	-	-
April	1942	1	2	-	2	-	-	2	-	-
May	1942	1	2	1	-	-	-	-	-	-
June	1942	2	1	-	1	2	-	4	-	-
July	1942	1	2	1	-	-	-	3	-	-
August	1942	2	-	-	-	1	-	1	-	-
September	1942	2	1	-	2	-	-	3	3	-
October	1942	3	2	1	1	-	-	1	3	-
November	1942	2	1	1	1	2	-	2	2	-
December	1942	1	5	1	1	-	-	2	-	-
1942	Total	16	19	6	9	5	-	20	8	-
January	1943	1	-	2	1	1	1	5	6	-
February	1943	2	-	1	1	-	1	2	-	-
March	1943	2	2	-	3	2	2	3	1	-
April	1943	1	1	4	15	2	-	2	2	-
May	1943	2	2	-	10	5	1	3	5	1
June	1943	1	2	1	9	4	2	2	5	1
July	1943	-	2	1	11	15	1	-	1	5
August	1943	-	1	7	14	14	5	-	2	4

		Escort carriers			Frigates			Sloops		
		LD	L	C	LD	L	C	LD	L	C
September	1943	-	2	2	13	14	9	-	2	3
October	1943	-	-	1	11	17	15	-	3	5
November	1943	-	2	4	2	13	17	-	2	6
December	1943	-	-	3	-	7	19	-	-	2
1943	Total	9	14	26	90	94	73	17	29	27
January	1944	-	-	4	-	-	11	-	-	-
February	1944	-	-	1	-	-	7	-	-	-
March	1944	-	-	-	-	-	1	-	-	1
April	1944	-	-	-	-	-	-	-	-	2
May	1944	-	-	-	-	-	1	-	-	1
June	1944	-	-	-	-	-	1	-	-	-
July	1944	-	-	-	-	-	3	-	-	-
August	1944	-	-	-	-	-	2	-	-	1
September	1944	-	-	-	-	-	-	-	-	1
October	1944	-	-	-	-	-	-	-	-	1
November	1944	-	-	-	-	-	-	-	-	-
December	1944	-	-	-	-	-	-	-	-	3
1944	Total	-	-	5	-	-	26	-	-	10
January	1945	-	-	-	-	-	-	-	-	-
February	1945	-	-	-	-	-	-	-	-	-
March	1945	-	-	-	-	-	-	-	-	-
April	1945	-	-	-	-	-	-	-	-	-
May	1945	-	-	-	-	-	-	-	-	-
June	1945	-	-	-	-	-	-	-	-	-
July	1945	-	-	-	-	-	-	-	-	-
August	1945	-	-	-	-	-	-	-	-	-
Overall	Total	25	33	37	99	99	99	37	37	37

Key: LD Laid down
L Launched
C Commissioned or, with reference to sloops, completed or transferred

(B) LISTINGS:

DECEMBER 1941
Laid down: The escort carrier *Striker* (15).

JANUARY 1942
Laid down: The sloops *Strenuous* (1) and *Tourmaline* (1).
Launched: The escort carrier *Chaser* (15).

FEBRUARY 1942
Laid down: The escort carrier *Searcher* (20); the frigate *Drury* (12).

MARCH 1942

Launched: The escort carriers *Stalker* (5) and *Tracker* (7).
Commissioned: The escort carrier *Avenger* (1).

APRIL 1942

Laid down: The escort carrier *Ravager* (11); the frigates *Bayntun* (5) and *Bazely* (5); the sloops *Catherine* (11) and *Cato* (11).
Launched: The escort carriers *Battler* (4) and *Fencer* (4).

MAY 1942

Laid down: The escort carrier *Slinger* (25).
Launched: The escort carriers *Striker* (7) and *Hunter* (22).
Commissioned: The escort carrier *Biter* (4).

JUNE 1942

Laid down: The escort carriers *Atheling* (9) and *Emperor* (23); the frigate *Bentinck* (29); the sloops *Pique* (2), *Chamois* (3), *Steadfast* (8), and *Tattoo* (8).
Launched: The escort carrier *Searcher* (20); the frigates *Bayntun* (27) and *Bazely* (27).

JULY 1942

Laid down: The escort carrier *Ameer* (18); the sloops *Gazelle* (2), *Chance* (12), and *Combatant* (12).
Launched: The escort carriers *Ravager* (16) and *Pursuer* (18).
Commissioned: The escort carrier *Dasher* (1).

AUGUST 1942

Laid down: The escort carriers *Begum* (3) and *Trumpeter* (25); the sloop *Gorgon* (15).
Launched: The frigate *Bentinck* (22).

SEPTEMBER 1942

Laid down: The escort carriers *Empress* (9) and *Khedive* (22); the frigates *Berry* (22) and *Blackwood* (22); the sloops *Cynthia* (7), *Elfreda* (7), and *Grecian* (7).
Launched: The escort carrier *Atheling* (7); the sloops *Catherine* (7), *Cato* (7), and *Strenuous* (7).

OCTOBER 1942

Laid down: The escort carriers *Speaker* (9), *Nabob* (20), and *Premier* (31); the frigate *Byard* (15); the sloop *Kilbirnie* (14).
Launched: The escort carriers *Emperor* (7) and *Ameer* (18); the sloops *Tourmaline* (4), *Pique* (26), and *Chamois* (26).
Commissioned: The escort carrier *Attacker* (10).

November 1942

Laid down: The escort carriers *Shah* (13) and *Patroller* (27); the sloops *Kilbride* (17) and *Fairy* (28).

Launched: The escort carrier *Begum* (11); the frigates *Berry* (23) and *Blackwood* (23); the sloops *Chance* (27) and *Combatant* (27).
Commissioned: The escort carrier *Battler* (15).

DECEMBER 1942
Laid down: The escort carrier *Rajah* (17); the frigates *Burges* (8) and *Calder* (11); the sloops *Kilchattan* (7) and *Kilchrenan* (24).
Launched: The escort carriers *Slinger* (15), *Trumpeter* (15), *Khedive* (27), *Empress* (30), and *Speaker* (30).
Commissioned: The escort carrier *Stalker* (30).

JANUARY 1943
Laid down: The escort carrier *Ranee* (5); the frigate *Duckworth* (16); the sloops *Magic* (15), *Kildary* (16), *Floriziel* (27), *Foam* (27), and *Pylades* (30).
Launched: The frigate *Burges* (26); the sloops *Gazelle* (10), *Steadfast* (17), *Gorgon* (24), *Cynthia* (25), *Elfreda* (25), and *Tattoo* (27).
Commissioned: The escort carrier *Hunter* (11) and *Tracker* (31); the frigate *Bayntun* (20).

FEBRUARY 1943
Laid down: The escort carriers *Trouncer* (5) and *Thane* (23); the frigate *Duff* (22); the sloops *Kildwick* (5) and *Kilham* (26).
Commissioned: The escort carrier *Fencer* (20); the frigate *Bazely* (18).

MARCH 1943
Laid down: The escort carriers *Queen* (12) and *Ruler* (25); the frigates *Capel* (11), *Cooke* (11), and *Essington* (15); the sloops *Kilkenzie* (12) and *Kilhampton* (30).
Launched: The escort carriers *Nabob* (9) and *Premier* (22); the frigates *Byard* (6) and *Calder* (27); the sloop *Grecian* (10).
Commissioned: The frigates *Berry* (15) and *Blackwood* (27).

APRIL 1943
Laid down: The escort carrier *Arbiter* (26); the frigates *Anguilla* (ND), *Antigua* (3), *Affleck* (5), *Bahamas* (7), *Dacres* (7), *Domett* (7), *Foley* (7), *Garlies* (7), *Aylmer* (12), *Balfour* (19), *Gould* (23), *Caicos* (23), *Grindall* (23), *Bentley* (26), and *Ascension* (30); the sloops *Japser* (5), *Kilmalcolm* (12), and *Kilmarnock* (24).
Launched: The escort carrier *Shah* (21); the frigates *Capel* (22) and *Cooke* (22); the sloops *Fairy* (5) and *Foam* (28).
Commissioned: The escort carriers *Searcher* (8), *Chaser*(9), *Ravager* (26), and *Striker* (29).

MAY 1943
Laid down: The escort carriers *Smiter* (10) and *Puncher* (21); the frigates *Bickerton* (3), *Bligh* (10), *Braithwaite* (10), *Barbados* (11), *Bullen* (17), *Gardiner* (20), *Goodall* (20), *Goodson* (20), *Gore* (20), and *Byron* (24); the sloops *Kilmartin* (4), *Kilmelford* (13), and *Kilmington* (24).
Launched: The escort carriers *Patroller* (6) and *Rajah* (18); The frigates *Duck-*

	worth (1), *Dacres* (14), *Foley* (19), *Garlies* (19), and *Duff* (22) : the sloops *Kilbirnie* (2), *Kilbride* (15), *Floriziel* (20), *Magic* (24), and *Kilchattan* (27).
Commissioned:	The frigate *Bentinck* (19).
Completed:	The sloop *Strenuous* (18).

JUNE 1943

Laid down:	The escort carrier *Reaper* (5); the frigates *Conn* (2), *Cotton* (2), *Keats* (5), *Kempthorne* (5), *Cranstoun* (9), *Cubitt* (9), *Curzon* (23), *Dakins* (23), and *Deane* (30); the sloops *Kilmore* (3) and *Frolic* (20).
Launched:	The escort carriers *Ranee* (2) and *Trouncer* (16); the frigates *Gould* (4), *Grindall* (4), *Essington* (19), and *Affleck* (30); the sloops *Kilchrenan* (13), *Frolic* (18), *Jasper* (20), *Kildary* (26), and *Pylades* (27).
Commissioned:	The escort carrier *Pursuer* (14); the frigates *Burges* (2) and *Byard* (18).
Completed:	The sloop *Tourmaline* (7).

JULY 1943

Laid down:	The frigates *Ekins* (5), *Kingsmill* (9), *Lawford* (9), *Louis* (9), *Lawson* (9), *Redmill* (14), *Cayman* (15), *Pasley* (18), *Loring* (18), and *Retalick* (21), and *Dominica* (27).
Launched:	The escort carriers *Thane* (15) and *Queen* (31); the frigates *Gardiner* (8), *Goodall* (8), *Goodson* (8), *Gore* (8), *Aylmer* (10), *Balfour* (10), *Anguilla* (14), *Bentley* (17), *Keats* (17), *Kempthorne* (17), *Bickerton* (24), *Drury* (24), *Antigua* (26), *Bligh* (31), and *Braithwaite* (31); the sloop *Kildwick* (10).
Commissioned:	The escort carrier *Ameer* (20); the frigate *Calder* (15).
Completed:	The sloops *Catherine* (8), *Kilbirnie* (16), *Cato* (28), *Gazelle* (28), and *Kilbride* (31).

AUGUST 1943

Laid down:	The frigates *Riou* (4), *Rutherford* (4), *Labuan* (7), *Cosby* (11), *Hoste* (14), *Moorsom* (14), *Manners* (14), *Mounsey* (14), *Tobago* (17), *Rowley* (18), *Fitzroy* (24), *Rupert* (25), *Stockham* (25), and *Montserrat* (28).
Launched:	The escort carrier *Ruler* (21); the frigates *Ascension* (6), *Bullen* (7), *Kingsmill* (13), *Lawford* (13), *Lawson* (13), *Byron* (14), *Bahamas* (17), *Conn* (21), *Cotton* (21), *Cayman* (22), *Barbados* (27), *Cranstoun* (28), Loring (30), *and Pasley* (30); the sloops *Kilham* (2) and *Kilkenzie* (19).
Commissioned:	The escort carriers *Atheling* (1), *Begum* (3), *Trumpeter* (4), *Emperor* (6), *Slinger* (11), *Empress* (13), and *Khedive* (23); The frigate *Duckworth* (4), *Capel* (16), *Cooke* (16), *Duff* (23), and *Dacres* (28).
Completed:	The sloops *Kilchattan* (16), *Gorgon* (28), *Pique* (30), and *Kilchrenan* (31).

SEPTEMBER 1943

Laid down:	The frigates *Seymour* (1), *Nyasaland* (7), *Papua* (7), *Pitcairn* (14), *Spragge* (15), *St. Helena* (22), *Stayner* (22), *Thornborough* (22), *Torrington* (22), *Inman* (25), *Sarawak* (28), *Seychelles* (28), and *Trollope* (29).
Launched:	The escort carriers *Arbiter* (9) and *Smiter* (27); the frigates *Fitzroy* (1),

	Domett (3), *Caicos* (6), *Louis* (9), *Cubitt* (11), *Dominica* (14), *Curzon* (18), *Labuan* (21), Dakins (18), *Hoste* (24), *Mounsey* (24), *Tobago* (27), *Montserrat* (27), and *Deane* (29); the sloops *Kilhampton* (3) and *Kilmalcolm* (17).
Commissioned:	The escort carriers *Nabob* (7) and *Shah* (27); the frigates *Domett* (3), *Essington* (7), *Foley* (8), *Garlies* (13), *Gould* (18), *Grindall* (23), *Gardiner* (28), *Affleck* (29), and *Aylmer* (30).
Completed:	The sloops *Kildary* (14), *Grecian* (22), and *Kildwick* (27).

OCTOBER 1943

Laid down:	The frigates *Tyler* (6), *Narbrough* (6), *Perim* (7), *Halsted* (10), *Somaliland* (11), *Tortola* (16), *Waldegrave* (16), *Whitaker* (20), *Zanzibar* (20), *Holmes* (27), and *Hargood* (27).
Launched:	The frigates *Ekins* (2), *Redmill* (2), *Nyasaland* (6), *Retalick* (9), *Papua* (10), *Halsted* (14), *Pitcairn* (15), *Spragge* (16), *St. Helena* (20), *Riou* (23), *Rutherford* (23), *Sarawak* (25), *Cosby* (30), *Rowley* (30), *Rupert* (31), *Seychelles* (30), and *Stockham* (31); the sloops *Kilmarnock* (1), *Kilmartin* (13), and *Kilmelford* (23).
Commissioned:	The escort carrier *Patroller* (25); the frigates *Goodall* (4), *Balfour* (7), *Goodson* (9), *Bentley* (13), *Gore* (14), *Anguilla* (15), *Fitzroy* (16), *Bickerton* (17), *Keats* (19), *Bligh* (22), *Kempthorne* (23), *Bullen* (25), *Kingsmill* (29), *Byron* (30), and *Conn* (31).
Completed:	The sloops *Kilham* (9), *Kilkenzie* (20), *Chamois* (22), *Magic* (25), and *Kilhampton* (30).

NOVEMBER 1943

Laid down:	The frigate *Hotham* (5).
Launched:	The escort carriers *Puncher* (8) and *Reaper* (22); the frigates *Seymour* (1), *Inglis* (2), *Inman* (2), *Perim* (5), *Stayner* (6), *Somaliland* (11), *Thornborough* (13), *Tortola* (16), *Trollope* (20), *Tyler* (20), *Zanzibar* (21), *Narbrough* (27), and *Torrington* (27); the sloops *Kilmington* (2) and *Kilmore* (9).
Commissioned:	The escort carriers *Premier* (3), *Ranee* (8), *Thane* (19), and *Speaker* (20); the frigates *Halsted* (3), *Lawford* (3), *Antigua* (4), *Cotton* (8), *Louis* (9), *Braithwaite* (13), *Cranstoun* (13), *Lawson* (15), *Cubitt* (17), *Curzon* (20), *Pasley* (20), *Dakins* (23), *Ascension* (24), *Deane* (26), *Loring* (27), *Ekins* (29), and *Redmill* (30).
Completed:	The sloops *Kilmalcolm* (6), *Chance* (13), *Kilmarnock* (13), *Kilmartin* (20), *Combatant* (22), and *Pylades* (24).

DECEMBER 1943

Laid down:	The frigate *Inglis* (29).
Launched:	The frigates *Waldegrave* (4), *Moorsom* (11), *Whitaker* (12), *Manners* (17), *Holmes* (19), *Hargood* (19), and *Hotham* (22).
Commissioned:	The escort carriers *Queen* (7), *Ruler* (22), and *Arbiter* (31); the frigates *Hoste* (3), *Drury* (4), *Bahamas* (6), *Manners* (6), *Retalick* (8), *Riou* (14), *Moorsom* (16), *Rutherford* (16), *Barbados* (18), *Cosby* (20), *Rowley*

	(22), *Rupert* (24), *Stockham* (28), *Mounsey* (23), *Seymour* (23), *Inglis* (29), *Stayner* (30), *Caicos* (31), and *Thornborough* (31).
Completed:	The sloops *Cynthia* (7) and *Elfreda* (23).

JANUARY 1944

Commissioned:	The escort carriers *Rajah* (17), *Smiter* (20) *Reaper* (21), and *Trouncer* (31); the frigates *Trollope* (10), *Inman* (13), *Spragge* (14), *Tyler* (14), *Torrington* (18), *Cayman* (20), *Narbrough* (21), *Dominica* (25), *Waldegrave* (25), *Whitaker* (28), and *Holmes* (31).

FEBRUARY 1944

Commissioned:	The escort carrier *Puncher* (5); the frigates *Labuan* (5), *Hargood* (7) *Sarawak* (7), *Hotham* (8), *Seychelles* (12), *St. Helena* (19), and *Somaliland* (22).

MARCH 1944

Commissioned:	The frigate *Perim* (16).
Completed:	The sloop *Fairy* (24).

APRIL 1944

Completed:	The sloops *Floriziel* (14) and *Foam* (28).

MAY 1944

Commissioned:	The frigate *Tortola* (15).
Completed:	The sloop *Frolic* (18).

JUNE 1944

Commissioned:	The frigate *Zanzibar* (21).

JULY 1944

Commissioned:	The *Pitcairn* (7), *Papua* (25), and *Nyasaland* (31).

AUGUST 1944

Commissioned:	The frigates *Tobago* (12) and *Montserrat* (31).
Completed:	The sloop *Jasper* (12).

SEPTEMBER 1944

Completed:	The sloop *Steadfast* (29).

OCTOBER 1944

Completed:	The sloop *Tattoo* (26 Oct 44).

NOVEMBER 1944

DECEMBER 1944

Completed:	The sloops *Kilmelford* (8), *Kilmington* (11), and *Kilmore* (24).

APPENDIX 10.3.

THE AMERICAN-BUILT ESCORT CARRIERS IN SERVICE WITH THE BRITISH NAVY IN THE SECOND WORLD WAR

In the course of the Second World War U.S. yards were responsible for the construction of escort carriers for service with the British Navy, and these carriers divided into two main groups. The ships in the first group, by virtue of the fact that they had been ordered and British ownership had been agreed in 1941 before the United States entered the war, were not commissioned into the U.S. Navy before transfer. These ships were the *Archer*, which was transferred to British service on 17 November 1941, and the *Avenger*, *Biter*, and *Dasher*. In addition, the *Charger* was launched 1 March 1941 and commissioned as a British escort carrier before being transferred to the U.S. Navy on 4 October 1941, with the result that she never saw British service. Two of these escort carriers were lost, the *Avenger* being torpedoed by the German submarine U.155 in the western Mediterranean on 15 November 1942 and the *Dasher* as a result of an internal explosion of gasoline off the west coast of Scotland during a training exercise on 27 March 1943.

With reference to the second group of warships, once the United States entered the war the system of ordering, building, and commissioning meant that all units were initially commissioned (if only nominally) into the U.S. Navy and then transferred to Britain. The units transferred to Britain after 7 December 1941 were as follows, arranged by class and then in chronological sequence by date of transfer:

with all units converted at Sun Shipbuilding, Chester, Pennsylvania, the *Archer*-class escort carriers *Avenger* (ex-*Rio Hudson:* 1 March 1942), *Biter* (ex-*Rio Parana:* 3 May 1942), and *Dasher* (ex-*Rio de Janeiro:* 1 July 1942), a total of three units;

the *Attacker*- or *Tracker*-class escort carriers *Attacker* (Western Pipe, San Francisco: ex-*Barnes:* 30 September 1942), *Battler* (Ingalls, Pascagoula, Mississippi: ex-*Altamaha:* 31 October 1942), *Stalker* (Western Pipe, San Francisco: ex-*Hamlin* 21 December 1942), *Trailer* (Ingalls, Pascagoula, Mississippi: ex-*Block Island:* 9 January 1943 and renamed the *Hunter*), *Fencer* (Western Pipe, San Francisco: ex-*Croatan* 1 March 1943), *Chaser* (Ingalls, Pascagoula, Mississippi: ex-*Breton:* 9 April 1943), *Striker* (Western Pipe, San

Francisco: ex-*Prince William* 28 April 1943), and *Pursuer* (Ingalls, Pascagoula, Mississippi: ex-*St. George:* 14 June 1943), a total of eight units;

and with all units built at Seattle-Tacoma, Tacoma, Washington unless otherwise stated, the *Ruler*-class escort carriers *Tracker* (31 January 1943), *Searcher* (7 April 1943), *Ravager* (25 April 1943), *Atheling* (Puget Sound, Bremerton, Washington: ex-*Glacier:* 3 July 1943), *Ameer* (ex-*Baffins* 19 July 1943), *Begum* (ex-*Bolinas* 2 August 1943), *Trumpeter* (Portland, Oregon: ex-*Bastian:* 4 August 1943), *Emperor* (ex-*Pybus* 6 August 1943), *Slinger* (ex-*Chatham:* 11 August 1943), *Empress* (ex-*Carnegie* 12 August 1943), *Khedive* (ex-*Cordova* 25 August 1943), *Nabob* (ex-*Edisto* 7 September 1943), *Shah* (ex-*Jamaica* 27 September 1943), *Patroller* (ex-*Keweemaw:* 22 October 1943), *Premier* (Seattle-Tacoma, Washington: ex-*Estero* 3 November 1943), *Ranee* (ex-*Niantic* 8 November 1943), *Thane* (ex-*Sunset* 19 November 1943), *Speaker* (ex-*Delgada:* 20 November 1943), *Queen* (ex-*St. Andrews* 7 December 1943), *Ruler* (ex-*St. Joseph* 22 December 1943), *Arbiter* (ex-*St. Simon* 31 December 1943), *Rajah* (ex-*Prince* 17 January 1944), *Smiter* (ex-*Vermillion:* 20 January 1944), *Trouncer* (Portland, Oregon: ex-*Perdido:* 31 January 1944), *Puncher* (ex-*Willapa:* 5 February 1944), and *Reaper* (ex-*Winjah:* 18 February 1944), a total of twenty-six units.

Thus there were thirty-seven escort carriers built in the United States for Britain, four ordered prior to the U.S. entry into the war and thirty-three thereafter, with, in addition to the *Charger*, six units built for Britain retained by the United States but subsequently replaced as additional units came on line.

None of these units was lost, though two were written off as constructive total losses, the *Nabob*, which served with the Canadian service in 1943–1944, as a result of being torpedoed by the German submarine U. 354 in northern waters on 22 August 1944, and the *Thane* as a result of being torpedoed by the German submarine U. 482 off the Clyde 15 January 1945. The *Nabob* was returned to the U.S. Navy on 16 March 1945 and the *Thane* on 5 December 1945.

In addition, American yards provided the British with frigates, sloops, minesweepers, and amphibious units, and undertook major repair and refit when necessary and appropriate.

APPENDIX 10.4.

U.S. NAVAL LOSSES IN THE SECOND WORLD WAR

(1) TABULAR REPRESENTATION:

		BB	CV	CVL	CVE	CA	CL	DD	Esc	SS	CM	AM	tpt	PG	LST
December	1941	4	-	-	-	-	-	3	-	1	-	2	-	1	-
January	1942	-	-	-	-	-	-	-	1	2	-	-	-	-	-
February	1942	-	-	-	-	-	-	3	-	1	-	-	-	-	-
March	1942	-	-	-	-	1	-	4	1	1	-	-	-	1	-
April	1942	-	-	-	-	-	-	1	-	-	-	1	-	-	-
May	1942	-	1	-	-	-	-	1	-	-	-	2	-	4	-
June	1942	-	1	-	-	-	-	1	-	1	-	-	-	-	-
July	1942	-	-	-	-	-	-	-	-	1	-	-	-	-	-
August	1942	-	-	-	-	3	-	4	-	1	-	-	2	-	-
September	1942	-	1	-	-	-	-	-	-	-	-	-	2	-	-
October	1942	-	1	-	-	-	-	3	-	-	-	-	-	-	-
November	1942	-	-	-	-	-	2	7	-	-	-	-	6	-	-
December	1942	-	-	-	-	1	-	-	1	-	-	1	-	1	-
January	1943	-	-	-	-	1	-	1	-	1	-	-	-	-	-
February	1943	-	-	-	-	-	-	1	-	1	-	-	-	-	-
March	1943	-	-	-	-	-	-	-	-	2	-	-	-	-	-
April	1943	-	-	-	-	-	-	1	-	2	-	-	-	-	-
May	1943	-	-	-	-	-	-	-	-	-	-	-	-	-	-
June	1943	-	-	-	-	-	-	-	-	2	-	-	1	-	1
July	1943	-	-	-	-	-	1	3	1	-	-	1	-	-	3
August	1943	-	-	-	-	-	-	-	-	-	-	-	1	1	2
September	1943	-	-	-	-	-	-	1	1	3	-	1	-	-	1

		BB	CV	CVL	CVE	CA	CL	DD	Esc	SS	CM	AM	tpt	PG	LST
October	1943	-	-	-	-	-	-	5	1	3	-	-	-	-	2
November	1943	-	-	-	1	-	-	3	-	3	-	-	1	-	-
December	1943	-	-	-	-	-	-	2	1	-	-	-	-	-	-
January	1944	-	-	-	-	-	-	1	-	1	-	1	-	1	1
February	1944	-	-	-	-	-	-	-	-	2	-	-	-	-	2
March	1944	-	-	-	-	-	-	-	1	1	-	-	-	-	-
April	1944	-	-	-	-	-	-	1	1	1	-	-	-	-	2
May	1944	-	-	-	1	-	-	1	2	-	-	-	-	-	5
June	1944	-	-	-	-	-	-	3	1	2	-	2	1	-	5
July	1944	-	-	-	-	-	-	-	-	2	-	1	-	-	-
August	1944	-	-	-	-	-	-	-	1	2	-	-	-	-	2
September	1944	-	-	-	-	-	-	1	2	-	1	1	1	-	-
October	1944	-	-	1	2	-	-	2	3	5	1	-	-	-	1
November	1944	-	-	-	-	-	-	1	-	3	-	-	-	-	1
December	1944	-	-	-	-	-	-	6	-	-	-	-	1	-	7
January	1945	-	-	-	1	-	-	-	-	1	-	3	-	-	-
February	1945	-	-	-	1	-	-	-	-	1	1	-	-	-	1
March	1945	-	-	-	-	-	-	1	-	2	-	1	-	-	-
April	1945	-	-	-	-	-	-	9	1	1	-	2	1	-	2
May	1945	-	-	-	-	-	-	9	1	1	-	2	2	-	-
June	1945	-	-	-	-	-	-	2	-	1	-	1	-	-	-
July	1945	-	-	-	-	1	-	1	1	-	-	-	-	-	-
August	1945	-	-	-	-	-	-	-	-	1	-	-	-	-	-
Total Losses		4	4	1	6	7	3	82	21	52	3	22	19	9	38

Key:

BB: Battleships
CV: Fleet carriers
CVL: Light carriers
CVE: Escort carriers
CA: Heavy cruisers
CL: Light cruisers
DD: Destroyers
Esc: Escorts*
SS: Submarines
CM: Minelayers
AM: Minesweepers
tpt: Transports
PG: Gunboats

Note: * The entries under this label include twelve destroyer escorts and nine Coast Guard cutters.

(2) LISTING:

Losses of Fleet Units; Seaplane Tenders, Destroyer Escorts, Minelayers and Minesweepers, Patrol Vessels, and Gunboats; Coast Guard USCG Cutters; and Submarines

OCTOBER 1941:

31: The 1,215-ton destroyer *Reuben James* torpedoed by German submarine U. 562 in the North Atlantic, roughly in mid-ocean, in 51°59'North 27°05'West.

DECEMBER 1941:

7: The 35,929 battleships *Arizona*, the 33,190-ton battleship *California*, the 31,706-ton battleship *Oklahoma*, the 33,590-ton battleship *West Virginia*, the 1,500-ton destroyers *Cassin* and *Downes*, and the 1,450-ton destroyer *Shaw* to Japanese carrier aircraft at Pearl Harbor, Hawaiian Islands, in 21°22'North 157°58'West. The *California* was salved in March 1942 and rebuilt; operational in May 1944. The *West Virginia* was salved in May 1942 and rebuilt; operational in September 1944. The *Shaw* was salved and repaired and was operational in August 1942. The *Cassin* and *Downes* were salved and rebuilt, the *Downes* being operational in March 1944 and the *Cassin* in April 1944.

8: The 840-ton minesweeper *Penguin* to Japanese land-based aircraft off Orote Point, Guam, which is in 13°27'North 144°37'East. The 370-ton gunboat *Wake*, which was captured by a Japanese detachment at Shanghai, in China, in 31°14'North 121°29'East.

10: The 840-ton minesweeper *Bittern*, scuttled after being rendered *hors de combat* by Japanese land-based aircraft at the Cavite naval yard, Luzon, in the Philippines, which is in 14°29'North 120°54'East. The 1,914-ton oil storage vessel *Robert L. Barnes* captured at Guam after having been bombed by Japanese land-based aircraft and abandoned two days earlier.

25: The 2,340-ton submarine *Sealion* scuttled at the Cavite naval yard, Luzon, after having incurred bomb damage in dock on 10 December.

JANUARY 1942:

21: The 1,090-ton submarine S. 36 abandoned after having run aground in the Makassar Strait off southern Celebes in 04°57'North 118°31'East on the previous day.

23: The 5,723-ton oiler *Neches* torpedoed by Japanese submarine I. 172 west of Pearl Harbor in 21°01'North 160°06'West.

24: The 1,090-ton submarine S. 26 rammed in error by U.S. warship in the Gulf of Panama in 08°13'North 79°21'West.

30: The 2,216-ton USCG cutter *Alexander Hamilton*, having been torpedoed by German submarine U. 132 on the previous day, capsized while under tow off Reykjavik, southwest Iceland, in 64°10'North 22°56'West.

FEBRUARY 1942:

11: The 1,968-ton submarine *Shark* to Japanese warships in the Molucca Sea off northwest Halmahera in 01°45'North 127°15'East.

18: The 1,215-ton destroyer *Truxtun* ran aground in gale in Placentia Bay, southeast Newfoundland, which is in the general area of 47°00'North 54°30'West.

19: The 1,190-ton destroyer *Peary* to Japanese carrier aircraft at Darwin in northern Australia in 12°30'South 130°50'East.

27: The 11,050-ton seaplane tender *Langley* to Japanese land-based aircraft south of Tjilatjap, southern Java, in 08°58'South 109°02'East.

28: The 1,090-ton destroyer *Jacob Jones* torpedoed by German submarine U. 587 off Cape May, New Jersey, in 38°37'North 74°32'West.

MARCH 1942:

1: The 11,420-ton heavy cruiser *Houston* to Japanese warships in action off northwest Java in 05°53'South 106°06'East. The 1,190-ton destroyer *Pope* to Japanese carrier aircraft and warships in the Java Sea in 04°00'South 111°30'East. The 1,190-ton destroyers *Edsall* and *Pillsbury* to Japanese warships in action south of Java in 14°30'South 106°30'East. The 5,723-ton oiler *Pecos* to Japanese carrier-based aircraft south of Christmas Island, in the Indian Ocean, in 14°27'South 106°11'East.

2: The 1,215-ton destroyer *Stewart* scuttled in the Soerabaja dockyard, Java, in 07°14'South 112°44'East.

3: The 1,200-ton gunboat *Asheville* to Japanese warships in action south of Java in 12°33'South 111°35'East. The 2,005-ton submarine *Perch* scuttled after sustaining damage on three successive days in the eastern Java Sea.

15: The 1,130-ton USCG cutter *Acacia* sunk by German submarine U. 161 south of Haiti in the Caribbean.

27: The 3,209-ton Q-ship *Atik* torpedoed by German submarine U. 123 east of Norfolk, Virginia, in general area of 36°00'North 70°00'West.

APRIL 1942:

8: The 5,950-ton oiler *Kanawha* to Japanese land-based aircraft in Tulagi harbor, the Solomons, which is in 09°06'South 160°09'East.

10: The 840-ton minesweeper *Finch*, after being damaged by Japanese land-based aircraft on previous day, sank off Corregidor in Manila Bay in 14°22'North 120°35'East. The 7,750-ton submarine tender *Canopus* scuttled in Mariveles Bay, the Bataan peninsula, Luzon.

26: The 1,215-ton destroyer *Sturtevant* to a mine north of Marquesas Keys, Florida, which is a group in 24°34'North 82°07'East.

MAY 1942:

2: The 602-ton gunboat *Cythera* torpedoed by German submarine U. 402 east of Cape Fear, North Carolina, in general area of 34°00'North 76°00'West. The 560-ton gunboat *Mindanao* scuttled after being damaged by Japanese land-based aircraft off Corregidor in Manila Bay.

4: The 840-ton minesweeper *Tanager* to Japanese artillery and the 1,060-ton submarine rescue vessel *Pigeon* to Japanese land-based aircraft off Corregidor in Manila Bay.

5: The 840-ton minesweeper *Quail* scuttled off Corregidor in Manila Bay.

6: The 560-ton gunboat *Luzon* and 450-ton gunboat *Oahu* scuttled off Corregidor in Manila Bay.

7: The 1,570-ton destroyer *Sims* to Japanese carrier aircraft in the Coral Sea in 15°10'South 158°05'East.

8: The 41,000-ton carrier *Lexington* to Japanese carrier aircraft in the Coral Sea in 15°12'South 155°27'East.

11: The 7,470-ton oiler *Neosho* scuttled after being rendered *hors de combat* by Japanese carrier aircraft in the Coral Sea on 7 May.

JUNE 1942:

6: The 1,620-ton destroyer *Hammann* torpedoed by Japanese submarine I. 168 north of Midway Islands in 30°36'North 176°34'West.

7: The 25,500-ton carrier *Yorktown* sank north of Midway Islands after having been rendered *hors de combat* by carrier aircraft on 4 June and torpedoed by Japanese submarine I. 168 on the previous day. The 950-ton seaplane tender *Gannet* torpedoed by German submarine U. 653 off Bermuda in 35°50'North 65°38'West.

25: The 1,090-ton submarine S. 27 abandoned after having run aground on 19 June and rendered *hors de combat* off St. Makarius Point, Kiska Island, in the Aleutians.

JULY 1942:

ND: On or after 30 July, the 2,424-ton submarine *Grunion* to cause unknown north of Kiska Island in the Aleutians.

AUGUST 1942:

4: The 1,500-ton destroyer *Tucker* lost to a mine in the Segond Channel off Espiritu Santo, in the New Hebrides group in the southwest Pacific, on the previous night.

8: The 16,400-ton transport *George F. Elliot* scuttled after having been rendered *hors de combat* by crashing Japanese land-based aircraft off Guadalcanal in the lower Solomons.

9: The 12,493-ton heavy cruisers *Astoria* in 09°10'South 159°51'East, *Quincy* in 09°05'South 159°54'East, and *Vincennes* in 09°06'South 159°52'East to Japanese warships in action off Savo Island in the lower Solomons. The 1,850-ton destroyer *Jarvis* to Japanese land-based aircraft southeast of Guadalcanal in 09°42'South 158°59'East.

16: The 1,090-ton submarine S. 39 abandoned after having run onto submerged rocks off Rossel Island, which is in 11°21'South 154°09'East in the Louisiade archipelago in the Coral Sea, two days earlier.

22: The 1,630-ton destroyer *Ingraham* as a result of a collision south of Sable Island, Nova Scotia, in 42°34'North 60°05'West.

23: The 1,500-ton destroyer *Blue* scuttled after having been torpedoed in action off Savo Island on the night of 21-22 August.

30: The 1,060-ton destroyer-transport *Colhoun* to Japanese aircraft off Guadalcanal in 09°24'South 160°01'East.

SEPTEMBER 1942:

5: The destroyer-transports *Gregory* (1,191 tons) and *Little* (1,060 tons) to Japanese warships in action off Guadalcanal.

9: September 1942: The 1,827-ton weather ship *Muskeget* torpedoed by German submarine U. 755 east of Boston in the general area of 53°00'North 42°30'West.

15: The 19,116-ton carrier *Wasp* torpedoed by Japanese submarine I. 19 south of Guadalcanal in 12°25'South 164°08'East.

OCTOBER 1942:

12: The 1,620-ton destroyer *Duncan* to Japanese warships in action off Cape Esperance, Guadalcanal, in 09°00'South 159°40'East.

15: The 1,630-ton destroyer *Meredith* to Japanese carrier aircraft off San Cristobal, in the southern Solomons, in the southwest Pacific.

19: The 1,960-ton destroyer *O'Brien*, having been torpedoed by Japanese submarine I. 15 north of Espiritu Santo on 15 September, foundered off Samoa in 13°30'South 171°18'West.

27: The 25,600-ton carrier *Hornet* was sunk by Japanese warships in 08°38'South 166°43'East after having been abandoned as a result of being rendered *hors de combat* by carrier aircraft in the action north of the Santa Cruz group on the previous day.

NOVEMBER 1942:

9: The 9,135-ton transport *Leedstown* by German aircraft off Algiers.

11: The 14,100-ton transport *Joseph Hewes* to German submarine U. 173 off Fedala, Morocco, which is in 33°43'North 07°20'West near Casablanca.

12: The 14,330-ton transport *Edward Rutledge*, the 12,479-ton transport *Hugh L. Scott*, and the 12,568-ton transport *Tasker H. Bliss* to German submarine U. 130 off Fedala, Morocco.

13: The 2,200-ton destroyer *Barton*, the 1,500-ton destroyer *Cushing*, the 1,260-ton destroyer *Laffey*, and the 1,630-ton destroyer *Monssen* to Japanese warships in the first naval battle of Guadalcanal. The 8,340-ton light cruiser *Atlanta* scuttled after rendered *hors de combat* by Japanese warships in the first naval battle of Guadalcanal. The 8,340-ton light cruiser *Juneau* torpedoed by Japanese submarine I. 26 off Guadalcanal in 10°34'South 161°44'East.

14: The 1,726-ton destroyer *Preston* and the 1,960-ton destroyer *Walke* to Japanese warships in the second naval battle of Guadalcanal. The 2,050-ton destroyer *Benham* scuttled after being rendered *hors de combat* by Japanese warships in the second naval battle of Guadalcanal.

25: The 16,175-ton transport *Thomas Stone*, torpedoed by a German submarine U. 205 and abandoned on 7 November, towed to Algiers, where it was bombed by German aircraft on 25 November: constructive total loss: stricken in April 1944.

DECEMBER 1942:

1: The 11,420-ton heavy cruiser *Northampton* to Japanese warships in the action off Cape Tassafaronga, between Guadalcanal and Savo Island, in 09°12'South 159°50'East.

5: The 1,900-ton gunboat *Erie* capsized after having been towed to Willemstad, Curacao, after being torpedoed by German submarine U. 164 on 12 November in 12°04'North 68°57'West.

17: The 225-ton USCG cutter *Natsek* foundered in the Strait of Belle Isle between Labrador and Newfoundland.

29: The 1,215-ton minesweeper *Wasmuth* sunk by detonation of her own depth-charges during a storm in the Aleutian Islands two days earlier.

JANUARY 1943:

10: The 4,080-ton submarine-minelayer *Argonaut* to Japanese aircraft and warships southeast of New Britain in 05°40'South 152°02'East.

12: The 1,726-ton destroyer *Worden* ran aground and was lost on Amchitka Island, in the Aleutians, in 51°28'North 179°05'East.

30: The 11,420-ton heavy cruiser *Chicago* to Japanese land-based aircraft off Rennel Island, south of the Solomons, in 11°25'South 160°56'East.

FEBRUARY 1943:

1: The 2,050-ton destroyer *De Haven* to Japanese land-based aircraft off Cape Esperance, Guadalcanal, in 09°09'South 159°52'East.

16: The 2,424-ton submarine *Amberjack* to Japanese warships south of Rabaul, New Britain, in 05°05'South 152°37'East.

MARCH 1943.

15: The 2,370-ton submarine *Triton* to Japanese warships near the Admiralty Islands in the southwest Pacific.

ND: On or after 4 March, the 2,370-ton submarine *Grampus* to cause unknown but probably sunk by Japanese warships in the Blackett Strait off New Georgia on 5 March.

APRIL 1943:

7: The 2,200-ton destroyer *Aaron Ward* to Japanese land-based aircraft off Togoma Point, Guadalcanal, in 09°10'South 160°12'East.

22: The 2,370-ton submarine *Grenadier*, having been badly damaged by Japanese aircraft, on approach of Japanese warships scuttled in order to avoid capture in 06°30'North 97°40'East off George Town at the entrance to the Strait of Malacca.

ND: On or after 7 April, the 2,005-ton submarine *Pickerel* lost to cause unknown but probably off northern Honshu.

MAY 1943.

23: The 1,333-ton tender *Niagara* scuttled after being rendered *hors de combat* by Japanese aircraft off Guadalcanal.

JUNE 1943:

12: The 695-ton submarine R. 12 foundered on exercise off Key West, Florida, in 24°25'North 81°39'West.

13: The 1,005-ton USCG cutter *Escanaba* as a result of explosion (of her own ammunition?) off Ivigtut, southwest Greenland, in 60°50'North 52°00'West.

30: The 9,600-ton transport *McCawley* sunk in error by U.S. motor torpedo-boats in the Blanche Channel, between Rendova and New Georgia in the middle Solomons, after having been torpedoed by Japanese aircraft earlier that day.

ND: On or after 26 June, the 2,424-ton submarine *Runner* lost to cause unknown but probably in the Kuriles.

JULY 1943:

5: The 2,050-ton destroyer *Strong* to Japanese warships off Bairoko in action in Kula Gulf, in the central Solomons, in 08°05'South 157°15'East.

6: The 12,207-ton light cruiser *Helena* to Japanese warships in action in Kula Gulf in 07°46'South 157°11'East.

10: The 1,630-ton destroyer *Maddox* to German aircraft between Malta and Sicily in 36°52'North 13°56'East.

12: The 890-ton minesweeper *Sentinel* to German aircraft off Licata, southern Sicily.
13: The 1,620-ton destroyer *Gwin* scuttled in 07°41'South 157°27'East after having been rendered *hors de combat* by Japanese warships in surface action off Kolombangara, central Solomons.

AUGUST 1943:
5: The 2,265-ton gunboat *Plymouth* torpedoed by German submarine U. 566 east of Kitty Hawk, North Carolina.
13: The 9,360-ton transport *John Penn* torpedoed and hit by crashing Japanese aircraft off Lunga Point, Guadalcanal.

SEPTEMBER 1943:
9: The 2,370-ton submarine *Grayling* rammed by Japanese merchantman west of Luzon.
10: The 1,850-ton destroyer *Rowan* to German motor torpedo-boats off Salerno in 40°07'North 14°18'East.
17: The 2,005-ton submarine *Pompano* probably lost to Japanese aircraft off the eastern approaches to La Pérouse Strait.
25: The 890-ton minesweeper *Skill* torpedoed by German submarine U. 593 in the Gulf of Solerno, southern Italy, in 40°20'North 14°35'East.
28: The 2,424-ton submarine *Cisco* to Japanese aircraft and warships in the Sulu Sea.
30: The 247-ton USCG cutter *Wilcox* foundered in storm off Cape Hatteras, North Carolina.

OCTOBER 1943:
3: The 1,850-ton destroyer *Henley* torpedoed by Japanese submarine RO. 108 off Finschhafen, northeast New Guinea, in 07°40'South 148°06'East.
7: The 2,050-ton destroyer *Chevalier* to Japanese warship in 07°30'South 156°14'East in action off Vella Lavella in the Solomons. The 1,135-ton submarine S. 44 sunk by Japanese warship in the northern Kuriles.
9: The 1,570-ton destroyer *Buck* torpedoed by German submarine U. 616 off Salerno in 39°57'North 14°28'East.
12: The 1,630-ton destroyer *Bristol* torpedoed by German submarine U. 371 off Algiers in 37°19'North 06°19'East. The 2,424-ton submarine *Wahoo* to Japanese warships in 45°13'North 141°56'East in La Pérouse Strait.
14: The 241-ton USCG cutter *Dow* ran aground in storm and was lost off Mayaguez, Puerto Rico.
26: The 1,850-ton destroyer *Porter* torpedoed by Japanese submarine I. 21 off Santa Cruz in the southwest Pacific.
ND: Between 5 and 14 October, the 2,424-ton submarine *Dorado* probably sunk in error by American aircraft northeast of the Panama Canal in general area of 12°20'North 78°50'West on 12 October.

NOVEMBER 1943:
2: The 2,200-ton destroyer *Borie* sank and was sunk by German submarine U. 405 in the North Atlantic and roughly in mid-ocean in 50°12'North 30°48'West.
6: The 1,630-ton destroyer *Beatty* to German aircraft off Philippeville, Algeria, in 37°10'North 06°00'East.

16: The 2,424-ton submarine *Corvina* to Japanese submarine I. 176 southwest of Truk, in the eastern Carolines in 05°05'North 151°10'East.

17: The 1,060-ton destroyer-transport *McKean* torpedoed by Japanese aircraft off Bougainville in the upper Solomons.

19: The 2,350-ton submarine *Sculpin* to Japanese warship in 10°00'North 152°50'East off Truk.

24: The 10,400-ton escort carrier *Liscome Bay* torpedoed by Japanese submarine I. 175 off Makin, in the Gilbert Islands, in 02°34'North 172°30'East.

29: The 2,300-ton destroyer *Perkins* as a result of a collision off Buna, on the north coast of Papua New Guinea, in 09°39'South 150°04'East.

ND: Between 17 November and 9 December, the 2,424-ton submarine *Capelin* to cause unknown but probably lost in the Celebes Sea off Halmahera in the East Indies.

DECEMBER 1943:

10: The 249-ton USCG cutter *Bodega* ran aground and was lost off the Panama Canal.

24: The 1,090-ton destroyer *Leary* torpedoed by German submarine U. 275 in the eastern North Atlantic in 45°15'North 21°40'West.

26: The 2,050-ton destroyer *Brownson* to Japanese land-based aircraft off Cape Gloucester, New Britain, in 05°20'South 148°25'East.

JANUARY 1944:

3: The 1,630-ton destroyer *Turner* by detonation of her own ammunition off the Ambrose Light, New York.

6: The 1,300-ton gunboat *St. Augustine* as a result of a collision with a tanker off Cape May, New Jersey.

22: The 890-ton minesweeper *Portent* to a mine southeast of Anzio, southern Italy, in 41°24'North 12°44'East.

ND: After 5 January, the 2,424-ton submarine *Scorpion* to cause unknown in the western Pacific, the East China Sea, or the Yellow Sea.

FEBRUARY 1944:

13: The 1,653-ton submarine rescue vessel *Macaw*, after having run aground on 16 January and resisting subsequent salvage efforts, sank inside the Midway atoll in 28°12'North 177°24'East.

26: The 2,370-ton submarine *Grayback* to Japanese carrier aircraft in 25°47'North 128°45'East in the East China Sea. The 1,175-ton netlayer *Ailanthus* ran aground and was lost in Alaskan waters.

29: The 2,370-ton submarine *Trout* to a Japanese warship southeast of Okinawa in 22°40'North 131°45'East.

MARCH 1944:

10: The 1,200-ton destroyer escort *Leopold* torpedoed by German submarine U. 255 southwest of Iceland in 58°44'North 25°50'West.

26: The 2,424-ton submarine *Tullibee* was sunk by her own torpedo north of the Palau Islands in 09°30'North 134°45'East.

APRIL 1944:

11: The 1,200-ton destroyer escort *Holder* to German aircraft northeast of Algiers in 37°03'North 03°58'East.

18: The 2,370-ton submarine *Gudgeon* to Japanese naval aircraft southeast of Iwo Jima in 22°52'North 143°32'East.

20: The 1,620-ton destroyer *Lansdale* to German aircraft off Cape Bengut, Algeria, in 37°03'North 03°51'East.

MAY 1944:

2: The 1,190-ton destroyer *Parrott* rendered *hors de combat* after collision at Boston; stricken.

3: The 1,400-ton destroyer escort *Donnell* torpedoed by German submarine U. 473 southwest of Ireland; constructive total loss.

5: The 1,400-ton destroyer escort *Fechteler* torpedoed by German submarine U. 967 northeast of Oran in 36°07'North 02°40'West.

29: The 15,700-ton escort carrier *Block Island* torpedoed by German submarine U. 549 northwest of the Canary Islands in 31°13'North 23°03'West.

JUNE 1944:

1: The 2,424-ton submarine *Herring* to Japanese artillery off Matsuwa Island in the northern Kuriles in 48°00'North 153°00'East.

5: The 810-ton minesweeper *Osprey* to a mine in the English Channel in 50°12'North 01°20'West.

6: The 1,630-ton destroyer *Corry* to a mine off Utah beach, Normandy, in 49°31'North 01°11'West.

7: The 890-ton minesweeper *Tide* to a mine off Normandy in 49°26'North 01°03'West. The 8,195-ton transport *Susan B. Anthony* to a mine in a swept channel off Normandy.

8: The 1,800-ton destroyer escort *Rich* to a mine off Utah beach, Normandy, in 49°31'North 01°10'West.

9: The 2,200-ton destroyer *Meredith* sunk by German aircraft in Seine Bay in 49°27'North 01°00'West after having been mined on 7 June.

10: The 1,620-ton destroyer *Glennon* mined and sunk by German artillery off Quineville, Normandy, in 49°32'North 01°12'West.

14: The 2,424-ton submarine *Golet* to Japanese naval aircraft and warships east of La Pérouse Strait in 41°04'North 141°31'East.

JULY 1944:

4: The 1,090-ton submarine S. 28 lost to cause unknown during training exercise off Pearl Harbor.

9: The 890-ton minesweeper *Swerve* to a mine southwest of Nettuno, Italy, in 41°31'North 12°28'East.

26: The 2,424-ton submarine *Robalo* to a mine off the west coast of Palawan, southwest Philippines in 08°25'North 117°53'East.

AUGUST 1944:

2: The 1,200-ton destroyer escort *Fiske* torpedoed by German submarine U. 804 north of the Azores in 47°11'North 33°29'West.

13: The 2,424-ton submarine *Flier* to a mine in the Balabac Strait between Palawan and northern Borneo, in 09°00'North 117°15'East.

24: The 2,424-ton submarine *Harder* lost to Japanese warship west of Luzon in 15°50'North 119°43'East.

SEPTEMBER 1944:

12: The destroyer-transport *Noa* lost as a result of a collision while en route to the Palaus.

13: The 1,850-ton destroyer *Warrington* foundered in hurricane off the Bahamas in 27°00'North 73°00'West. The 1,190-ton minesweeper *Perry* to a mine off southeast Angaur, in the Palau Islands, in 06°53'North 134°10'East.

14: The 220-ton USCG cutters *Bedloe* and *Jackson* foundered in hurricane off Cape Hatteras, North Carolina.

25: The 2,870-ton minelayer *Miantonomah* to a mine outside Le Havre in the English Channel.

OCTOBER 1944:

3: The 1,350-ton destroyer escort *Shelton* torpedoed by Japanese submarine RO. 41 off Morotai in 02°33'North 129°18'East. The 2,350-ton submarine *Seawolf* sunk in error by U.S. carrier aircraft and warship off Morotai in 02°32'North 129°18'East.

17: The 1,160-ton minelayer *Montgomery* rendered *hors de combat* by mine in the Ngulu atoll, western Carolines, in 08°30'North 137°30'East: stricken.

24: The 15,100-ton light carrier *Princeton* scuttled in 15°21'North 123°31'East after being rendered *hors de combat* by Japanese land-based aircraft off Luzon in the Philippines. The 2,424-ton submarine *Darter* scuttled after running aground in the Palawan Passage. The 2,424-ton submarine *Shark* to Japanese warships in the Luzon Strait in 20°41'North 119°27'East. The 2,424-ton submarine *Tang* was sunk by her own torpedo off northwest Formosa in 25°06'North 119°31'East.

25: The 10,400-ton escort carrier *Gambier Bay* in 11°31'North 126°12'East, the 2,100-ton destroyer *Hoel* in 11°46'North 126°33'East, the 2,700-ton destroyer *Johnston* in 11°46'North 126°09'East, and the 1,745-ton destroyer escort *Samuel B. Roberts* in 11°40'North 126°20'East to Japanese warships in action off Samar. The 10,400-ton escort carrier *St. Lo* to kamikaze aircraft off Leyte in 11°13'North 126°05'East.

28: The 1,350-ton destroyer escort *Eversole* torpedoed by Japanese submarine I. 45 east of Leyte in 10°18'North 127°37'East.

ND: On or after 17 October, the 2,424-ton submarine *Escolar* to cause unknown, but probably mined in the Yellow Sea.

NOVEMBER 1944:

1: The 2,050-ton destroyer *Abner Read* to kamikaze aircraft off Samar in 10°47'North 125°22'East.

7: The 2,424-ton submarine *Albacore* to a mine off northern Honshu, east of La Pérouse Strait, in 41°49'North 141°11'East.

8: The 2,424-ton submarine *Growler* to Japanese warships off Mindoro.

11: The 2,424-ton submarine *Scamp* to Japanese warship south of Tokyo Bay in 33°38'North 141°00'East.

20: The 7,470-ton oiler *Mississinewa* sunk by a *kaiten* submarine in Ulithi atoll, western Carolines, in 10°00'North 139°40'East.

DECEMBER 1944:

3: The 2,200-ton destroyer *Cooper* to Japanese warship in action in Ormoc Bay, Leyte, in 10°54'North 124°36'East.

7: The 1,450-ton destroyer *Mahan* scuttled in 10°50'North 124°30'East after being rendered *hors de combat* by kamikaze attack in Ormoc Bay, Leyte. The 1,247-ton destroyer-transport *Ward* scuttled after being rendered *hors de combat* by kamikaze aircraft off Ormoc, Leyte.

11: The 1,480-ton destroyer *Reid* to kamikaze aircraft in Ormoc Bay, Leyte, in 09°50'North 124°55'East.

18: The 1,395-ton destroyer *Hull*, the 1,500-ton destroyer *Monaghan*, and the 2,050-ton destroyer *Spence* capsized in typhoon northeast of Samar in general area of 15°00'North 128°00'East.

30: The 3,665-ton station tanker *Porcupine* to kamikaze aircraft in Mangarin Bay, Mindoro, which is in 12°19'South 121°06'East.

JANUARY 1945:

4: The 10,400-ton escort carrier *Ommaney Bay* to kamikaze aircraft south of Mindoro, in the Philippines, in 11°25'North 121°19'East.

6: The 1,190-ton minesweeper *Hovey* to Japanese land-based aircraft in Lingayen Gulf, northwest Luzon, in 16°20'North 120°10'East. The 1,190-ton minesweeper *Long* to kamikaze aircraft in Lingayen Gulf, northwest Luzon, in 16°12'North 120°11'East.

7: The 1,190-ton minesweeper *Palmer* to Japanese land-based aircraft in Lingayen Gulf, northwest Luzon, in 16°20'North 120°10'East.

ND: After 3 January, the 2,340-ton submarine *Swordfish* to cause unknown in the western Pacific, south of the Japanese home islands.

FEBRUARY 1945:

4: The 2,424-ton submarine *Barbel* to Japanese aircraft in the Balabac Strait, between northern Borneo and Palawan, in 07°49'North 116°47'East.

18: The 1,160-ton minelayer *Gamble* rendered *hors de combat* off Iwo Jima by Japanese land-based aircraft: scuttled off Guam on 16 July.

21: The 10,400-ton escort carrier *Bismarck Sea* to kamikaze aircraft northeast of Iwo Jima in 24°36'North 141°48'East.

MARCH 1945:

26: The 2,050-ton destroyer *Halligan* to a mine off southwest Okinawa in 26°10'North 127°30'East.

28: The 890-ton minesweeper *Skylark* to mines off southeast Okinawa in 26°20'North 127°40'East. The 2,424-ton submarine *Trigger* to Japanese aircraft and warships in the northern Ryukyus in 32°16'North 132°05'East.

ND: On or after 20 March, the 2,424-ton submarine *Kete* lost to cause unknown in the central Pacific.

APRIL 1945:

2: The 1,090-ton destroyer-transport *Dickerson* rendered *hors de combat* by kamikaze attack and scuttled off Okinawa two days later.

5: The 1,190-ton seaplane tender *Thornton* beached off Okinawa after double collision: constructive total loss.

6: The 2,050-ton destroyer *Bush* to kamikaze aircraft off Okinawa in 26°16'North 127°48'East. The 2,050-ton destroyer *Colhoun* scuttled in 27°16'North 127°48'East after being rendered *hors de combat* by kamikaze aircraft northwest of Okinawa. The 2,050-ton destroyer *Leutze*, the 1,570-ton destroyer *Morris*, and the 2,050-ton destroyer *Newcombe* all *hors de combat* after kamikaze attack off Okinawa: stricken. The 1,630-ton minesweeper *Emmons* to kamikaze aircraft north of Okinawa in 26°48'North 128°04'East.

12: The 2,200-ton destroyer *Mannert L. Abele* sunk by a *baka* bomb northwest of Okinawa in 27°25'North 126°59'East.

16: The 2,940-ton destroyer *Pringle* to kamikaze aircraft northwest of Okinawa in 27°26'North 126°59'East.

22: The 890-ton minesweeper *Swallow* to kamikaze aircraft west of Okinawa in 26°10'North 127°12'East.

24: The 1,200-ton destroyer escort *Frederick C. Davis* torpedoed by German submarine U. 546 in 43°52'North 40°15'West east of Cape Race, Newfoundland.

27: The 2,050-ton destroyer *Hutchins* damaged by kamikaze aircraft off Okinawa: stricken.

29: The 2,050-ton destroyer *Haggard* damaged by kamikaze aircraft off Okinawa: stricken.

ND: On or after 8 April and before 20 April, the 2,424-ton submarine *Snook* to cause unknown in the general area of Okinawa.

MAY 1945:

3: The 1,191-ton destroyer *Little* in 26°24'North 126°15'East and 2,050-ton destroyer *Luce* in 26°35'North 127°10'East to kamikaze aircraft west of Okinawa. The 2,200-ton minesweeper *Aaron Ward* rendered *hors de combat* as result of attack by kamikaze aircraft off Okinawa: stricken. The 2,424-ton submarine *Lagarto* lost to Japanese warship north of Kota Bharu in the Gulf of Siam in 07°55'North 102°00'East.

4: The 2,050-ton destroyer *Morrison* to kamikaze aircraft northwest of Okinawa in 27°10'North 127°58'East.

9: The 1,745-ton destroyer escort *Oberrender* rendered *hors de combat* as result of attack by kamikaze aircraft off Okinawa: expended as target ship post-war.

11: The 2,050-ton destroyer *Evans* and the 2,220-ton destroyer *Hugh W. Hadley* rendered *hors de combat* as result of attack by kamikaze aircraft off Okinawa: stricken.

18: The 2,050-ton destroyer *Longshaw* ran aground and destroyed by Japanese artillery off southern Okinawa in 26°11'North 127°34'East.

20: The 2,050-ton *Thatcher* damaged by kamikaze aircraft off Okinawa: stricken.

25: The 1,630-ton minesweeper *Butler* rendered *hors de combat* as result of attack by kamikaze aircraft off Okinawa: stricken. The 1,673-ton destroyer-transport *Bates* to kamikaze aircraft off Ie Shima, off northwest Okinawa, which is in 26°43'North 127°47'East. The destroyer-transport *Barry*, rendered *hors de combat* by kamikaze aircraft off Okinawa, stricken and constructive total loss: decommissioned and technically no longer a warship, it was used as a decoy and was sunk by kamikaze aircraft on 21 June.

28: The 2,200-ton destroyer *Drexler* to kamikaze aircraft off Okinawa in 27°06'North 127°38'East.
29: The 1,630-ton destroyer *Shubrick* rendered *hors de combat* as result of attack by kamikaze aircraft off Okinawa; stricken.

JUNE 1945:
6: The 2,270-ton gasoline tanker *Sheepscot* ran aground and capsized off Iwo Jima.
8: The 650-ton minesweeper *Salute* to a mine in Brunei Bay, northern Borneo, in 05°08'North 115°05'East.
10: The 2,050-ton destroyer *William D. Porter* to kamikaze aircraft northwest of Okinawa in 27°06'North 127°38'East.
16: The 2,050-ton destroyer *Twiggs* torpedoed and hit by kamikaze aircraft off Okinawa in 26°08'North 127°35'East.
18: The 2,424-ton submarine *Bonefish* to Japanese warships in 37°18'North 137°55'East off northwest Honshu in the Sea of Japan.

JULY 1945:
24: The 1,400-ton destroyer escort *Underhill* sunk by a *kaiten* submarine northeast of Luzon in 19°20'North 126°42'East.
28: The 2,050-ton destroyer *Callaghan* to kamikaze aircraft southwest of Okinawa in 25°43'North 126°55'East.
29: The 12,775-ton heavy cruiser *Indianapolis* torpedoed by Japanese submarine I. 58 in the Philippine Sea in 12°02'North 134°48'East.

AUGUST 1945:
6: The 2,424-ton submarine *Bullhead* to Japanese army aircraft in 08°20'South 115°42'East off northeast Bali.

In addition to the ships in this listing, three salvage vessels, six general cargo ships, ten fleet tugs, two miscellaneous auxiliaries, thirty-eight LSTs and nine LSMs, eighteen submarine chasers, and twenty-seven assorted small units were lost.

* * *

Certain units have been included under the label "stricken." These were ships that sustained varying degrees of damage but were not sunk and were able, with TLC, to reach base, where they were deemed beyond repair. Some of these units were used for "other" purposes but most were returned, usually under tow, to breakers' yards in the United States. These have been included in this listing on the grounds that even if the war had continued these ships would not have been returned to service, that is, they had been lost.

Conversely: sometimes listed in various sources as having been lost, but not included in this listing, are a number of units that sustained varying degrees of damage but were not repaired because of war's end and considerations of time, cost, and lack of any good reason; comparable damage, in earlier years, would have resulted in repair and return to service. These ships, most of which were able to reach ports under their own power, were not lost in the sense that is generally understood and hence have not been included in this listing.

CHAPTER ELEVEN

THE JAPANESE SITUATION—AND A JAPANESE DIMENSION

"The empire of the eight islands" in fact numbered some three thousand islands, totaling some 149,000 square miles, and extended over nearly thirty degrees of latitude. Alone of these just four islands, Kyushu, Shikoku, Honshu, and Hokkaido, formed the core of the Japanese heartland and possessed real political, demographic, and cultural significance. To the core area were three additions secured as a result of success in war. Formosa and the Pescadores, their 14,000 square miles lying across the sea routes to the southwest of the home islands, had been incorporated into the Empire in 1895. On Sakhalin the occupation of the southern 15,000 square miles of the island provided Japan with its only land border, though on the Asian mainland the 85,000 square miles of Korea had been brought within the Empire in 1910.

Such, formally, was an empire that was equivalent in size to Texas or, in European terms, to Britain, the Low Countries, and Germany combined, though to the Empire's islands and territories must be added Japan's other possessions. On the mainland Japan held the Liaotung peninsula, the Kwantung Leased Territories after 1905, and involvement in the First World War on the side of Germany's enemies had brought it into possession of three island groups in the western Pacific—the Marianas, Carolines, and Marshalls—as mandated territories from the League of Nations. On the mainland Japan after 1931 acquired various Chinese territories which it had constituted under four puppet regimes. The first and most important of these was Manchoutikuo, literally the Empire of the Manchus, in the 460,000 square miles (with some 45 million people) of the four northeast provinces that together made up Manchuria. The second of these regimes was the Mongolian Federated Autonomous Government, which had been formed under Japanese auspices in eastern Inner Mongolia on 22 November 1937. In China itself the Japanese had installed the Central Government of the Republic of China at Nanking in April 1940, but the provinces of Hopei, Shantung, Shansi, and Kaifeng were placed under the nominal control of the North China Advisory Authority, formed as successor to the Provisional Government of the Chinese Republic, which the Rikugun had inaugurated on 14 December 1937.[1]

For a state that had been forced to end centuries of self-exclusion from the outside world a little more than a single lifetime before, the extent of Japanese holdings by 1941 was impressive. No less impressive, however, was the industrial development that had accompanied Japan's overseas expansion, most obviously the pace of that development in the 1930s. This single decade saw Japan's heavy and chemical industries expand four-fold, the overall index of industrial output rise by 173 percent, and the index of national industrial production stand in 1939 at 182.5 relative to 1929. By comparison, the U.S. index of national industrial production in 1939 stood at 98.2 relative to 1929.[2]

This industrial expansion, remarkable in the years of the Great Depression, completed a twenty-five-year period in which Japan achieved an annual real growth rate of 3.9 percent percent compared to the 1.1 percent percent of the United States and 0.7 percent percent of Britain.[3] Moreover, both the short-term and long-term performance witnessed some remarkable individual achievements. Coal and electrical generating output doubled during the 1930s: ingot steel output quadrupled in the course of the decade, at the end of which high-explosive production in Japan exceeded that in the United States. Infant and mainly imitative automobile and aircraft industries came of age in the 1930s, the 500 vehicles of all types and 400 aircraft of 1930 being the predecessors of 48,000 vehicles and 5,000 aircraft produced in 1941.[4] Such respectable achievements by certain sectors of the economy were not confined to Japan itself. In Manchuria, even before the conquest, Japan had developed the port of Darien to the extent that it could handle 11 million tons of goods a year and was second only to Shanghai in the Far East in terms of its volume of trade. Ten years of Japanese rule witnessed the construction of 2,650 miles of railroad to add to the 3,600 miles that had existed in 1931.[5] Coal production in Manchuria rose from 8,950,000 tons in 1931 to 13,800,000 tons in 1936 and iron ore production from 673,000 tons to 1,325,000 tons in the same period. Japanese surveys and prospecting resulted in revision of estimated reserves of iron ore from 400 million to 2,700 million tons and coal from 4,800 million to 20,000 million, and in the discovery of valuable reserves of magnesite, molybdenum, tungsten, and vanadium. On the river Yalu the Japanese built a dam larger than the contemporary and more celebrated Boulder Dam on the Colorado.[6]

These were very real achievements, but the fact remained that Japan's development and expansion in the 1930s, indeed in the five decades before the outbreak of the Pacific war, nevertheless was flawed in several respects and failed to address certain aspects of national weakness that were to be crucial to its defeat in the Pacific war. Five factors command attention; though not all were wholly or directly related to Japan's maritime defeat, nevertheless they need to be considered, the less relevant trapped between the more pertinent lest they escape, in the interests of balance. The first, and most obvious, is the fact that despite the impressive achievements of the 1930s, Japan remained massively inferior to the United States in terms of industrial output and, even more importantly, Japan remained massively inferior to the United States in terms of industrial capacity and potential. Evidence of this inferiority abounds, but may be summarized by two examples. For all the achievement of ingot steel production in the 1930s, the Japanese entered the forties with just 11.37 percent of American output.[7] The very respectable achievement of the Japanese chemical sector in the 1930s was in no small measure dependent upon the import of American technology and was nevertheless beset by problems of poor maintenance of equipment, an inadequate pool of skilled labor, and, by American standards, very low productivity levels,[8] which rendered maintenance of existing levels of production, still less continued future expansion, problematic. In such continuing inferiority lies the basis of the argument that Japan's defeat was assured from the time that its carrier aircraft attacked Battleship Row.

Second, however impressive the Japanese industrial performance of the 1930s was, the achievement fell short of intention as set down under the terms of the Miyazaki plan of August 1936.[9] The Synthetic Oil Industry Law of 1937 set down a seven-year program that was to yield 18,206,000 barrels between 1937 and 1941 and 43,620,000 barrels in its full span, but production amounted to no more than 8.33 percent of planned output before the start of the Pacific war. Moreover, despite an expansion program that gave Japan in 1941 an annual refining capacity of 33 million barrels and a storage capacity of 51 million barrels, Japan remained at least in part dependent upon the United States for a supply of high-octane aviation fuel.[10] What is particularly important about Japan's failure to meet its output targets, however, is not so much individual shortfalls but the implication of an overall inability to achieve the terms of a program that was intended to provide Japan with the industrial basis for total war, the rationale of the Miyazaki plan being Japan's need to be able to withstand the full rigors of a war of two or three years' duration. The fact that Japan failed to secure what it itself had set down as the prerequisite for the waging of war seems, in hindsight, to have but one self-evident conclusion: there was no logical basis for the confidence of the Japanese high command in the third and fourth quarters of 1941 that Japan possessed the industrial wherewithal for war.

Third, the industrialization program of the 1930s warped the balance of the

Japanese economy. In 1930 the heavy industrial sector accounted for 38.29 percent of Japan's total industrial production, with light industry contributing 61.71 percent. By 1942 heavy industry is estimated to have accounted for 72.63 percent and light industry 27.37 percent of industrial output.[11] The decline of light industry, however, was not simply relative. In the summer of 1937 the Japanese high command took the decision to seek the quickest possible solution to the China Incident by the use of maximum force and to proceed with the Miyazaki program of industrialization as planned.[12] But without access to foreign credits the cost of this policy had to be carried by a major reduction of domestic consumption, the imposition of currency and import controls, and the deliberate restriction of export performance that included the prohibition on the raising of new capital by major export firms. By 1939 some of these latter restrictions were eased, and military demands were pared back in an attempt to deal with Japan's worsening balance-of-payments problems, but because of deteriorating terms of trade and higher freight charges as a result of the European war, Japan's overall financial position continued to weaken. Thus textile cloth and cotton imports fell by 65.46 percent and 67.98 percent respectively between 1936 and 1941, wool imports by 60.45 percent between 1937 and 1940,[13] and compared to the 1937 index in 1941 domestic rice and food production stood at 83 and 78.1 respectively and textile consumption at 60.4.[14] By any standard, therefore, the war economy that Japan imposed upon itself between 1937 and 1941 left it with very narrow margins on which to operate, even before the onset of the Pacific war. The fact that in 1941 Japan was forced to consider liquidating company and private holdings overseas in order to finance its current trade would suggest that in all probability it could not have continued trading into 1942—a state of affairs that casts an interesting light upon the significance of the trade embargo placed upon it in July 1941 by the United States, Britain, and the Netherlands in response to its occupation of southern Indo-China. Leaving aside this latter consideration, it is sufficient to note the ironies that flowed from Japan's search for autarky: in the process it exchanged one set of imbalances and dependencies for another, rendered itself more dependent than ever before upon a single sector of the economy, massively depressed the living standards of its people, and increasingly tied its industrial and export performance to a single market.

Consideration of Japan's worsening financial position between 1937 and 1941 touches upon a wider matter, and the fourth aspect of Japanese weakness. The industrialization of the 1930s left unchanged the fact that the Japanese home islands in 1941 remained unable to feed themselves and bereft of the raw materials considered essential to the maintenance of Japan as a great power. The home islands in 1941 had to import some 20 percent of their wheat and rice, two-thirds of their soya needs, and almost all of their sugar requirements. Domestic crude and synthetic oil production could cover only some 15 percent of consumption.

In 1941, after considerable stockpiling, Japan remained dependent upon foreign sources for the import of 24 percent of its bauxite, 59 percent of its copper, 71 percent of its iron ore, 78 percent of its industrial salt, 80 percent of its lead, and all its tin and rubber needs. In short, the acquisition of an empire on the Asian mainland failed to resolve Japan's basic problem of assured access to raw materials; to this fact there was a reverse side which constituted the fifth and final aspect of Japanese weakness and which allows this examination of Japan's position to return to the theme of its maritime defeat. This weakness stemmed from the reality that though not without considerable advantage to Japan, the conquest of a mainland empire imposed upon it certain obligations and problems that were critical in shaping its own development and that were crucial to its ultimate failure in the Second World War. Perhaps the single most important of these, and not directly related to the financial, economic, and maritime aspects of Japan's defeat, was political, and followed from the regional aspect of Japan's imperialist expansion. This expansion had one beneficial effect for Japan in that the rice, sugar, and wheat surpluses of Formosa, Korea, and Manchoutikuo allowed the feeding of the home islands without any loss of scarce hard currency. This, however, was more than offset by the fact that in the areas that Japan brought under its control there was not the diversity of resources that it needed to sustain itself as an industrialized society, and after 1931, as the international horizon darkened, there was very little that Japan could do to raise foreign and local capital with which to develop these areas. Thus capitalization had to be made, in large part, at the expense of Japan's own domestic investment. Between 1931 and 1941 total Japanese investment in Manchoutikuo alone amounted to 4,064 million yen, but even in the period 1932–1936, when levels of Japanese investment were modest, the 1,161.7 million yen thus committed represented 8.4 percent of Japanese domestic fixed capital formation.[15]

Lack of capital and industry in those areas of the mainland that fell under Japan's sway naturally facilitated its economic penetration and control, and for that reason Japan welcomed it. But in the course of the 1930s there came to be a two-way dependency between Japan and these areas as the pattern of Japanese trade showed divergent trends. In general terms, Japan's trade within the Yen Bloc—the Empire, Manchoutikuo, and occupied China—showed increasingly favorable balances, while its trade with the rest of the world showed considerable and growing deficits.

The importance to Japan of the Yen Bloc in general, and of Manchoutikuo in particular, is clearly indicated by the fact that whereas in 1932 Manchuria accounted for one-tenth and the Yen Bloc one-quarter of Japanese exports, by 1939 Manchoutikuo took one-third of all Japanese exports; by 1941 it accepted over half of Japan's exports and the trade between Manchoutikuo and Japan amounted to 34.09 percent of all Japan's foreign transactions. Manchoutikuo, moreover, accounted for the greater part of Japan's trading surplus within the Yen Bloc, and the latter provided her with overall trading surpluses in 1935 and between 1938 and 1940. Thus the importance to Japan of its imperial protégé and its trading association cannot be doubted, but nothing about Japan and its conduct of the Second World War is simple and straightforward; the reality of Japan's trading and financial position was far more serious than the trade statistics would suggest. The trade surpluses with Manchoutikuo and within the Yen Bloc were largely illusory. Manchoutikuo through its trade deficits with Japan was indeed able to fund the latter's import of finished items and raw materials, but on the basis of surpluses earned in barter trade with third parties rather than cash. It is estimated that Japan's real trading surplus with Manchoutikuo in terms of goods, remittances, and services never exceeded 315 million yen in any year.[16] The large paper surpluses were in no small measure the result of a ruthless manipulation of the exchange rate between the Manchoutikuo yuan (and later the north China yuan) and the yen, which lost 71.5 percent of its international value between 1930 and 1940.[17] By tying the yuans to a weak yen, Japan fixed the terms of trade within the Yen Bloc by depressing the price of its imports whilst increasing the value of its exports, and between 1932 and 1937 capital transfers accounted for 67.83 percent of its exports to Manchoutikuo. Capitalization and the sale of capital goods necessary for the industrialization of Manchoutikuo rather than trade thus accounted for the greater part of Japan's trade surpluses, which, given the inconvertibility of the yuans, were for the most part nominal. Nevertheless, the Japanese commitment and the drain upon its investment resources were real enough, as, indeed, by 1941 was the commitment of the greater part of the Japanese merchant marine to Yen Bloc trade.

In 1941, after a decade that witnessed the tonnage under the Japanese flag increase by one-half, some 72.58 percent of available tonnage was committed to trade within the Yen Bloc. Some 15.55 percent of Japanese tonnage was involved with trade with southeast Asia, and the balance, some 11.73 percent of Japan's shipping resources, was involved in outside trade.[18] In real terms, therefore, Japanese tonnage committed to outside trade declined by about two-thirds despite its far from insignificant growth. At the same time the amount of imports entering Japanese ports in foreign bottoms declined from about 46 percent of all imports by tonnage to some 35 percent in 1941.[19] Leaving aside this latter consideration, which was mainly the result of the decline of European shipping in the Far East after the outbreak of war in Europe in 1939 and not the result of either changing Japanese demands and capabilities or of the trade embargo imposed by the Allied powers, in part this concentration of Japanese shipping on lines within the Yen Bloc reflected the inability of the occupied territories to support Japanese forces garrisoned upon them and to exploit their own resources except under Japanese direction. But the fact was that the scope of Japanese shipping activity shrank in the decade that followed the Manchurian Incident, and since not one day passed between September 1931 and September 1945 without the sound of

Japanese gunfire being heard in some part of Manchoutikuo or occupied China, the commitments that were incurred in the decade before the outbreak of the Pacific war could not be reduced in anticipation of that war any more than the shipping thus committed to Yen Bloc trade could necessarily be diverted efficiently to long-haul oceanic trade.

* * *

This aspect of Japanese shipping activity invites consideration of related aspects of Japanese merchant marine development in the 1930s, of which two are of singular importance. First, the mountainous, volcanic topography of the home islands was a major obstacle to the development of an efficient and large-scale overland transportation system. In 1941 Japan—in sharp contrast to Britain, which had some 20,227 miles of railroad to service a population of 45 million and a land area of some 94,000 square miles[20]—had just 12,740 miles of railroad. Despite Japan's great hydroelectric power potential only 52 miles of its railroads were electrified and, of critical importance in terms of capacity and loadings and the type of goods that could be carried, of its total system, 11,395 miles was single track, and most was 3 ft. 6 in. rather than standard gauge;[21] perhaps uniquely, the Japanese rail system was geared to passengers rather than freight. The relative isolation of Japan's urban areas and the fact that the vast majority of Japan's cities and 80 million people found themselves on the tidewater thus ensured a heavy dependence upon coastal shipping for the movement of bulk items, particularly coal, sand, and building materials, and by 1940 some 61.47 percent of all internal trade was conducted by sea. Moreover, an intensive rice agriculture within the home islands (that largely precluded a major meat-producing industry), when combined with the isolation of and difficulty of overland movement within the outlying areas, ensured that virtually every coastal village had its own fishing fleet and building slip for inter-island and coastal trade and for fishing. These slips in the 1930s numbered "several thousand," but even in 1944, after major rationalization, there remained some 2,359 in 548 enterprises, the capacity and efficiency of which merited the official description "limited."[22]

The demands of coastal trade and fishing thus ensured that a major part of Japanese shipping resources and manpower was thus committed. What were historically identified as Japanese-styled ships, known as *kihansen*, met part of these demands, the amazing total of 18,789 such junks in service totaling some 1,197,349 tons.[23] In addition, in 1941 almost half of Japan's modern, western-styled ships, known as *kisen*, were of a miscellaneous type and of less than 1,000 tons, but even though these 1,126 ships of just 437,119 tons accounted for only 7.06 percent of all *kisen* tonnage,[24] they were no less demanding on Japan's overworked repair and maintenance facilities than their 1,324 larger sea-going sisters. The *kihansen*, on the other hand, seldom took up too much dockyard space because it was generally more economical to scrap and build anew than to undertake major maintenance of such ships.

This latter point returns the examination of the Japanese marine to the second of the two considerations earlier identified as being of singular importance in Japanese development. Note has been made that in the 1930s the Japanese merchant marine showed a net increase of some 2 million tons.[25] A decade which saw a major growth of the Japanese economy led by the expansion of the chemical and heavy industries also saw Japanese commercial shipyards between 1936 and 1941 achieve an average annual increase of floor space by 8.2 percent and length of slipways by 8.1 percent. By any standard, particularly those of the Depression, such increases represented a formidable achievement, and, amazingly, by 1937 Japan had double the shipbuilding capacity of the United States.[26] But most of these increases were concentrated in existing yards of somewhat dubious efficiency rather than through the construction of new yards where economies of scale and efficiency of working practices could be registered. Moreover, some 60 percent of the increases were registered in the eleven major commercial yards that undertook naval work and that were responsible for 90 percent of all naval construction outside the naval yards.[27] By tonnage the private sector was responsible for 59 percent of all naval construction between 1936 and 1941, and in the latter year naval deliveries accounted for 41 percent of all tonnage delivered by the commercial yards.

Thus the not inconsiderable increase of working capacity of the Japanese shipbuilding industry in the five years before the outbreak of the Pacific war was not as substantial as it might appear at first. Moreover, this increase was somewhat devalued because it was not attended by a commensurate increase in the capacity and output of the domestic tool-making industry, with the result that Japan became ever more dependent upon American imports, the quality of which Japan could not match. The long-term consequences were unfortunate: wartime re-equipment of guillotine shears, keel-benders, and radial drills all but ceased, and declining quality of tools necessitated reduced speed and feeds of machines, with serious effects upon production.[28] But even in the short term, the increase of shipyard capacity did not allow Japan to escape having to make a choice between maritime and naval construction, because resources could not stretch to both, at least not at a time of financial orthodoxy and conventional working patterns; the increase of shipbuilding capacity was not commensurate with national needs.[29] In the five years in which floor space and slipways were substantially increased, some 1,713,985 tons of merchant shipping entered service, but whereas in 1936 some 442,382 tons of merchant shipping and 55,360 tons of warships were commissioned, by 1941 the figures were roughly in balance: 237,617 tons of merchant shipping and 225,159 tons of warships. As the demands of naval rearmament under the terms of the Third Fleet Replacement Program of 1937 became more onerous, so Japan's ability to add to its merchant marine diminished. Moreover, the increasing demands of naval re-armament affected not only the output of shipping but maintenance and refitting.[30] The decline of the number of fleet units refitting and modernizing, from the fifty-one of 1936 to the one solitary destroyer of 8 December 1941, tells its own story,[31] as eloquent as the fact that in 1941 no new oil drilling was undertaken by the Japanese either in the home islands or in the occupied territories; the price of such naval efficiency was that in December 1941 some 21.6 percent of the merchant marine was laid up for want of routine maintenance and refitting.[32] Three inescapable conclusions might be drawn from these various facts, with immediate implications for the course of the Pacific war: first, that Japan, despite its efforts in the decade before the Pacific war, could not undertake simultaneous maritime and naval construction programs on any scale; second, that by beginning hostilities in the Pacific at the peak of its strength Japan committed itself to major refitting programs, if not in 1942 then certainly in 1943 and 1944; third, that the backlog of merchantmen awaiting refit was both a luxury that Japan could not afford and a liability that was more likely to increase rather than be cleared.

The various shortcomings of Japan's ship-building and repair industries meant that its marine, like its industry as a whole, was, for all its quality, narrowly based, and in no respect more obviously than with respect to its tanker fleet. Two-thirds of Japan's tankers were built after 1930, and nearly 40 percent were capable of speeds of 16 knots or more and on average were more than half as big again as contemporary British and American tankers. But the tanker fleet in 1941 mustered just 49 tankers of 587,000 tons to serve alongside the nine fleet oilers, none of which post-dated 1924, which served with the Kaigun; by way of comparison, in 1939 Britain had 425 tankers of 2,997,000 tons and the United States 389 tankers of 2,836,000 tons.[33] Japan's tanker position reflected its overall shipping position. From the twin facts that some 9,500,000 tons of shipping were needed in 1941 to meet Japan's various needs and that one-third of all import tonnage was carried by foreign-registered shipping two conclusions flow: that the merchant marine under the Japanese flag in 1941 was clearly inadequate to meet national requirements, and that by going to war with those states that provided the bulk of its foreign shipping requirement Japan denied itself access to chartering facilities on the scale needed to make good its carrying deficit.[34] But no less serious for the prosecution of the war was a corresponding lack of escort forces. The latter weakness, however, was the product of the Kaigun's lack of concern with trade protection, which was itself a major factor in Japan's defeat in the Second World War.

* * *

Throughout the inter-war period the Kaigun's priorities were the development of its fleet strength and of a tactically offensive doctrine that would allow it to meet a superior enemy in the western Pacific on the basis of equality. Its building programs were thus geared to the construction of battleships and cruisers that were qualitatively superior to those of potential enemies and of destroyer and submarine forces that could operate offensively in support of the battle line.[35] In common with other major navies, the Kaigun faced the problem of trying to decide the role of carrier forces, and for most of the inter-war period it considered such forces to be subordinate to the battle line: it was not until the last eighteen months before the outbreak of the Pacific war that its attention began to turn to the prospect of using carriers independently and offensively. These priorities, and the resultant neglect of trade defense, have been the subject of much critical comment since the end of the Second World War. In one sense, however, the obsession with battle was unavoidable. The Imperial and U.S. Navies could measure themselves only against the other in the inter-war period. They were mirror images of one another as both prepared for decisive fleet action, and neither paid much attention to the *guerre de course*. But the Kaigun's lack of interest in the *guerre de course* was nevertheless somewhat curious in two respects. Its lack of concern with Japan's potential vulnerability to a campaign against its shipping was not wholly consistent with its anticipation after 1939 that a *guerre de course* would bring about Britain's defeat; often forgotten is that in the First World War the Kaigun had deployed destroyers to the eastern Mediterranean where, in 1917 and 1918, they had played their full part in curbing the U-boat threat by the introduction and extension of the convoy system. Britain's greater vulnerability to blockade because of factors of geographical position and distance, plus the United States' declared intention in the inter-war period to accept restrictions upon submarine operations,[36] may have been the considerations that prompted the conclusion that Japan need not regard trade defense to be a major priority, but the fact remains that in the inter-war period the Kaigun never undertook any systematic examination and analysis of the *guerre de course* waged against Allied shipping in the course of the First World War. At no time was there any study that related the number of operational U-boats to the number of merchantmen which they sank, and there was no analysis of the role of anti-submarine units at the time when they made kills. There was no attempt to examine the loss of time and tonnage imposed by independent routing of merchantmen, nor to examine the implications of the fact that in the First World War the number of ships sailing in convoys and the number of U-boats sunk both increased at much the same rate, the figures of one quarter excepted. In none of these matters did the Kaigun undertake proper professional studies, but lest this criticism be overdrawn, it should be noted that in its neglect the Kaigun in was in good company. These comments about the lack of analytical study of the German submarine offensive against Allied shipping in the First World War were made about the inter-war Royal Navy in its own staff history of the Second World War,[37] and, in fairness, in the inter-war period the Kaigun would have been hard-pressed to gather authoritative data on which to make a systematic study of the German U-boat campaign in the First World War. Nevertheless, despite its experience in the Mediterranean the Kaigun set no great store upon trade defense and showed itself reluctant to accept the principle of convoy, even though convoy had proved itself to be the only effective means of ensuring the safe and timely arrival of shipping in the First World War. What seems to have been its only major staff study of trade protection requirements in the 1930s, conducted jointly by officers from the naval staff and ministry, concluded that there was a need for the Kaigun to maintain a permanent force of 20 small destroyers, 12 *kaibokan*, 15 gunboats, 24 torpedo boats, and 16 submarine-chasers and to have a reserve force of some 152 torpedo boats and *kaibokan* to be assigned to specific escort duties in time of war. Since this report referred to the need to consider 24 *kaibokan* and 160 submarine-chasers as the nucleus of the Japanese commerce protection effort,[38] it would seem that the 87-strong permanent force would be assigned to patrol duties, ill though these had served the Allied cause in the First World War. It can be seen, therefore, that though several factors—most obviously the financial and shipbuilding limitations under which the Kaigun labored throughout the 1930s—were at work in ensuring that Japan went to war without an adequate escort force for the protection of shipping, perception, or its absence, was critical to this situation.

* * *

The consequences of the Kaigun's obsession with battle and somewhat casual attitude toward trade defense were to be three-fold, affecting the numbers, equipment, and organization of those escort and anti-submarine forces that it did raise both before and after the start of the Pacific war. It was not until 1931, and apparently as a direct result of the London Treaty of 22 April 1930 that limited the destroyer fleet to 105,500 tons but placed no restriction upon construction of lower-rated ships,[39] that the Kaigun sought to lay down ships that were to be the predecessors of the standard escorts of the Second World War. Financial considerations prevented the ordering of such ships in both the 1931 First and 1933 Second Fleet Replenishment Programs, but under the former the Kaigun, acknowledging the threat presented by the submarine, ordered the *Okinoshima*, a minelayer-netlayer cruiser that could operate as an escort, and its first two submarine-chasers. Four more chasers, of three different types, followed in the 1933 program, but a total of six chasers built and building in 1937 hardly represented an antidote to the submarine, if only because, on original displacements between 170 and 270 tons, lack of endurance precluded the chasers operating in a genuine oceanic role. In the 1937 Third Fleet Replenishment Program, therefore, the Kaigun secured orders for four units of the *Shimushu*, or Type A, class of escort,[40] but such were its priorities that the design tender was given to Mitsubishi Heavy Industries. None were to be laid down before November 1938, and the lateness of their completion, between June 1940 and March 1941, given the gathering pace of events in the Far East, ensured that these four ships were the only purpose-built escorts in service in December 1941. To their number, however, have to be added thirteen conversions, an improved *Okinoshima* ordered in the 1937 program, and the twelve second-class destroyers of the *Tomozuru* and *Otori* classes built in the 1930s[41] that were to be pressed into service in the escort role. Of the conversions, one, the *Shirataka*, had begun life in 1929 as a minelayer-netlayer and was reconstructed as an escort in 1940. Eleven other conversions, namely the *Shimakaze* and *Nadakaze* of the *Minekaze* class of 1918, eight units from the *Momi* classes of 1919 and 1920, and the *Yugao* from the *Wakatake* class of 1921, were aging destroyers, no longer fit for fleet duties, that were converted to general duties and re-entered service in 1940 and 1941. The last of the conversions, the *Sawakaze* of the *Minekaze* class, was in third-grade reserve—unmanned and in need of major overhaul—until September 1941, when it was re-commissioned and re-rated as an aircraft rescue ship with the Tateyama Air Group; it was to be re-assigned from training duties to serve as an escort with the Yokohama Naval District on 1 March 1942. In addition, between 1937 and the outbreak of the Pacific war the Kaigun accepted into service twenty submarine-chasers—nine from the 1937 program, four from the 1939 Fourth Fleet Replenishment Program, and seven from the 1940 Additional War Program. At the time of the outbreak of war another four units, from the 1940 Most Urgent War Program, were within two to eight weeks of completion, and another twelve, from this same program, were to be completed before the end of 1942. On 8 December 1941, however, none of the fourteen escorts of the *Etorofu*, or Modified Type A, class, ordered in that year's Emergency War Program were within two months of being laid down, and a want of slips precluded the lead ship of another escort class, the *Mikura*, being laid down until October 1942.[42] Excluding nineteen minesweepers and the thirty-four converted submarine-chasers that had been secured from trade and that were in service in December 1941,[43] the total number of oceanic and local escorts in commission at the outbreak of the Pacific war was thirty-two escorts of all types and twenty-six submarine-chasers, with another thirty escorts projected and another sixteen chasers either building or about to be laid down.

Such numbers were wholly inadequate to the task of the defense of shipping, while the inability of Japan's yards to lay down the units of the 1940 and 1941 programs pointed to their over-commitment, even as the Kaigun's concern with main force units found full expression in its projected 1941 Fifth Fleet Replenishment Program. In numbers of warships this program alone was to be greater than the 1937 and 1939 programs combined, and with five capital ships, three fleet carriers, five cruisers, thirty-two destroyers, and forty-six submarines figuring prominently amongst its 360 projected units, this program catered for just five escort cruisers, four escorts, and eighteen submarine-chasers. There was in December 1941, therefore, no real prospect of any easement of the problem of lack of oceanic escorts, but in reality lack of numbers was only one aspect of Japan's future anti-submarine problems. No less serious for the Kaigun was to be the inadequacy of the equipment, though examination of this second consequence of the Kaigun's sins of omission and commission should note initially the role assigned even those escorts that were in service in December 1941. The *Shimushu* class had been ordered for evaluation purposes as patrol and fisheries protection ships and had been designed for work in the Kuriles and northern Pacific. As a result the class was singularly ill-suited for escort work; its members initially embarked but eighteen depth-charges and until late in 1942 were not equipped with any form of underwater detection. Moreover, most of the converted patrol boats were fitted for assault duties in the form of their accommodation for 250 troops and two 46-ft. *Daihatsu* landing craft, and it was in this role that two of their number, the P. 32 and P. 33, were to be lost in the course of the second Wake operation of 23 December 1941. The continuing employment of sister ships in the transport role—for example, of the P. 35 in the Midway operation and of the P. 1 and P. 2 in three operations to Guadalcanal in August 1942—points to an erosion of escort strength that could not be afforded, but also to an over-commitment of the Kaigun as a whole that was even more serious. But—to refocus attention upon equipment—diversion of inadequate numbers merely compounded problems of technical deficiency that encompassed virtually every aspect of Japanese anti-submarine capability.

* * *

The most obvious manifestation of Japanese deficiencies was the lack of any airborne anti-submarine weapon other than the bomb, an absence of any ahead-throwing weapon system with escort forces, and the lack of production of any form of influence mine, these omissions applying not simply to the Japanese position in 1941 but throughout the Pacific war. To these could be added another, what was in effect the Japanese failure of in-service depth-charge development. This failure of the Japanese research program stands in sharp and interesting contrast to that of Britain. In many ways the position of the Kaigun in terms of anti-submarine warfare in 1941 was not unlike that of the Royal Navy in 1939. At the start of their respective wars British and Japanese depth-charges were roughly similar, the escorts of the two navies carried about the same number of these weapons, and both navies had developed active sonars in the 1930s. Thus British escorts, depending on type, in 1939 carried between fifteen and thirty Mark VII depth-charges, which weighed 420

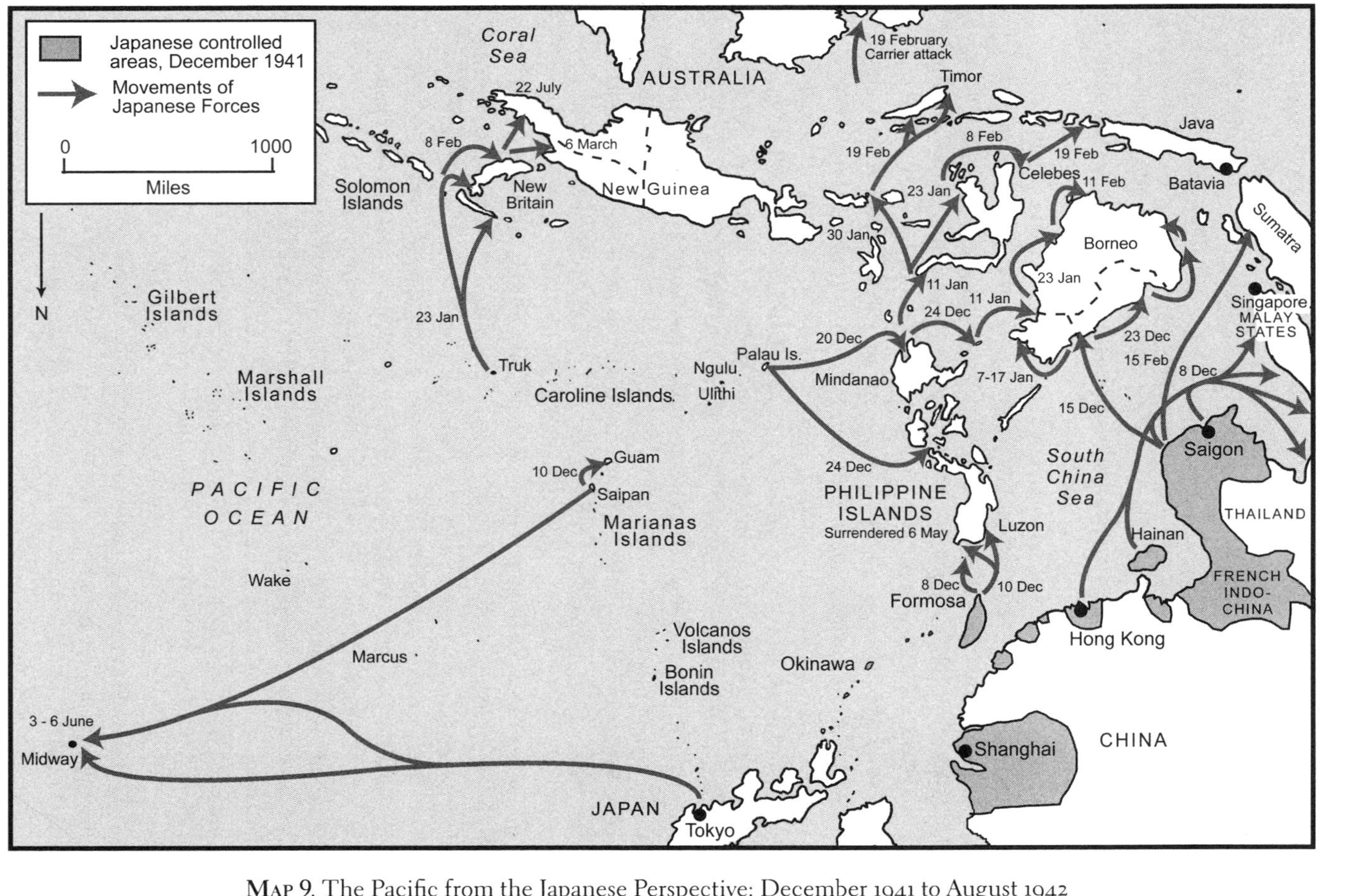

Map 9. The Pacific from the Japanese Perspective: December 1941 to August 1942

lbs., had an explosive charge of 290 lbs., a terminal velocity of 9.9 ft./sec., and a maximum setting of 300 feet. Their Japanese equivalents carried between eighteen and thirty-six Type 95 depth-charges, which weighed 350 lbs., had 220 lbs. of explosive, a terminal velocity of 6 ft./sec., and a maximum setting of 295 feet. Wartime experience saw Japanese depth-charge numbers rise to 120 with the *Ukuru* class, a figure that compared respectably to a British maximum of 160, though the *Hunt* class of escort was limited to 70. But whereas Japanese wartime development resulted in increases of settings to 475 feet and charges of 357 lbs. in the Type 2 Model 1 and Type 2 Model 2 respectively, that of Britain resulted in settings of 900, 1,000, and even 1,450 feet and the introduction of extra-heavy and fast-sinking depth-charges with 2,000 lbs. of explosive and a terminal velocity of 50 ft./sec. in Mark X variants. British research also resulted in the development of the influence depth-charge, though this, like most of the Mark X types, never entered service.[44] It was within the context of this comparative failure of Japanese research and development that the parallel failure of the Kaigun to provide itself with ahead-throwing weapon systems that compared to the Hedgehog and Squid in British service assumed its full significance. By 1944 these latter weapons had replaced the depth-charge as the escorts' primary means of attack, to the extent that by 1945 British depth-charge complements had been reduced to 1939 levels. In the course of the Pacific war, therefore, the Kaigun proved unable to match the pace of British development even in these basic aspects of anti-submarine weaponry.

The Squid proved so important in the last year of the Battle of the Atlantic in large measure because it was the Royal Navy's first fully integrated weapon system, incorporating as it did a three-barrel mortar, the Types 144Q and 147B sonars for depth- and range-finding, and automatic setting and firing mechanisms.[45] Consideration of the Squid leads to examination of Japanese technical capability to address means of detection, and in this endeavor, whether underwater or otherwise, Japanese efforts were woefully inadequate. Already it has been noted that the *Shimushu* and its sisters possessed no means of underwater detection when completed and that it was not until autumn 1942, at a time when the Royal Navy had some 2,100 vessels of all types equipped with sonar,[46] that the class was fitted with hydrophones. The *Mikura* class was the first to be designed and completed with sonar, the Model 93 developed in 1939, and the *Chiburi*, completed in April 1944, was the first Japanese escort to receive the Model 32, developed in 1943.[47] It was not until the autumn of 1944, however, that Japanese escorts began to be fitted with the Type 13 air search radar, though from the outset the *Ukuru* class was designed to carry this and the Type 22 search radar. The contrast with the Royal Navy again is severe. Whereas March 1941 saw the first U-boat kill by a destroyer using radar and also the evaluation trials of Britain's first naval centimetric radar,[48] such important fleet units as Japanese fleet carriers did not receive primary air search radar until the third quarter of 1943.[49]

May 1941 saw the first corvette with radar and the autumn of that same year saw the general use of high-frequency director-finders with British escorts,[50] but Japanese inability to overcome technical problems meant that H/F D/F never went to sea in Japanese warships at any stage of the Pacific war, and low-frequency D/F only in aircraft and seaplane carriers.[51] Moreover, Japanese backwardness compared to its enemies was not confined solely to means of detection; Japanese escorts were equipped with only one radio transmitter, which had to work on both high and low frequencies despite the fact that escorts often were required to work upon both simultaneously, and at no stage of the Pacific war was the Kaigun able to provide its escorts with the high-capacity No. 4 radio transmitter that was essential to long-range operations in distant waters. To complete a rather dismal picture, the Japanese equivalent of T.B.S. (direct talk-between-ships radio) was if not in its infancy then in its early adolescence in spring 1945, when the American landings in the Ryukyu Islands in effect spelled the end of the maritime war in the Pacific.[52]

Such were some of the more obvious Japanese technological failings; others are best considered in the context of autumn 1943, when the Kaigun set about the organization of an escort command. Suffice it here to note two matters: in material terms the Kaigun entered the war as ill-equipped to fight a campaign in defense of trade as had the Royal Italian Navy in 1940, and the absence of an escort command in December 1941 was the third consequence of Japanese neglect of trade defense in the inter-war period.

* * *

The absence in December 1941 of a single authority with responsibility for the use and protection of shipping was but one manifestation of an overall lack of organization and authoritative chain of command that existed at every level of the Japanese war effort and that ensured that Japan was, in terms of ability to wage war, the least organized of the great powers. Inevitably most aspects of administrative weakness reflected those institutionalized within Imperial General Headquarters, wherein government was *minor inter pares*, incapable of formulating and implementing policy in the face of opposition of two armed services each determined to subordinate the national interest to their own separate, and usually conflicting, requirements. This aspect of Japanese weakness, at the very heart of the decision-making process, rightly has attracted much attention. The incoherence of the policy-making process, plus the services' insistence upon trying to determine national priorities with little or no reference to matters outside their own narrow areas of responsibility and interest, was of crucial importance in placing Japan upon the road that led it to war and to defeat. Scarcely less well known is the fact that before the start of the Pacific war the separate interests of the armed services, plus the inability of government to curb service acquisitiveness in terms of merchantmen, resulted in the division of the merchant fleet between the Rikugun, Kaigun, and Communications Ministry, with no organization responsible for the coordination of shipping activity. This examination of Japanese organizational weakness is not concerned with the first of these two matters, nor, apart from *en passant* reference, is it concerned with the process of the second. Its considerations extend to three aspects of Japanese administration, or mal-administration, of shipping resources: the detail and consequences of the three-fold division of the merchant fleet and the lack of any supervisory agency; the lack of an overall organization and doctrine for escort forces; and the lack of any system that involved the use of air power in the defense of trade.

The division of the merchant fleet that allocated 2,100,000 tons of shipping to the Rikugun and 1,500,000 tons to the Kaigun prior to the outbreak of war was unavoidable.[53] Neither the Rikugun for its first-phase obligations nor the Kaigun for its longer-term commitments could prepare for and undertake operations without a substantial requisitioning of merchant vessels, and it is pertinent to note that Britain, which with its empire possessed some 21,200,000 tons of shipping in August 1939, requisitioned some 8,600,000 tons of shipping for military purposes during the Second World War.[54] For Japan the process of requisitioning had begun with the China Incident, but the closeness of Japan to its expanding commitments on the mainland ensured that only a modest total of some 200,000 tons of shipping, much of it riverine, was taken for military purposes between 1937 and 1940. Thereafter, the prospect of trying to counter American re-armament and the needs of mobilization resulted in the Rikugun holding 519 ships of 2,161,500 tons and the Kaigun 482 ships of 1,740,200 tons at the outbreak of the Pacific war.[55]

The service demands imposed upon the national marine a burden that it could not afford, and, indeed, it is tempting to conclude that at least until the end of 1943 the Japanese merchant marine suffered more from the predatory instincts of the Japanese armed forces than from the nation's enemies.[56] In part, some of the service demands represented little real loss. Ten fast passenger-cargo liners had been designed and built in the late 1930s with a view to conversion as aircraft carriers, and their use as fleet units or transports had little significance in terms of cargo-carrying,[57] but overall service demands fell upon the newer and better merchantmen in commission. The great expansion of the Japanese merchant marine in the 1930s was made possible in large part by the "scrap-and-build" policy inaugurated under the Shipping Improvement Program of October 1932, whereby uncompetitive ships, mostly built during and immediately after the First World War, were stricken and replaced by modern, fast units. Under this program state subsidies were granted for construction of ships over 4,000 tons with a minimum speed of 13.5 knots and designed to allow their conversion for military use.[58] It was on such ships that the greater part of service demands fell, and even where such demands did not fall upon larger ships the consequences could be unfortunate. The Kaigun, for example, requisitioned 111 ships to serve as auxiliary minesweepers and 115 ships as auxiliary submarine-chasers during the Pacific war. Most of these were trawlers and whalers, and such reductions from the fishing fleet were in part responsible for the decline of fishing yields from 4,793,421 tons in 1939 to 2,079,216 tons in 1945.[59] But the critical point was that the loss of so much shipping to the services, combined with the loss of other nations' shipping to Japanese trade with the outbreak of war, meant that "the amount of shipping available declined . . . at the moment when [Japan's] commitments and needs increased."[60] As a result of these developments a marine that in 1941 was already inadequate to meet national needs found itself obliged to try to meet the import needs of industry and the civilian population with what remained to it after the armed services had met their requirements. In December 1941 what remained was some 2,228,000 tons of shipping, of which total passenger vessels accounted for some 840,000 tons and 273,000 tons was not in service.[61] Even allowing for pay-back arrangements by which the Rikugun was to reduce its requisitioned shipping to one million tons by and in the eighth month of war,[62] and the Japanese hope that once begun the war could be brought to an end before the weaknesses inherent in Japan's position manifested themselves, how these various circles were to be squared is somewhat hard to discern, as, tacitly, the Rikugun in 1940 and the cabinet office in 1941 admitted. The calculation that requisitioning of shipping on a scale of about 60 percent of what was taken from trade would result in a general 15 percent fall of imports with obvious knock-on effects in terms of manufactured output posed problems that were without solution; these simply were not addressed beyond recourse to exhortations and palliatives, an aspect of Japanese planning that was to become increasingly evident with the passing of time and the worsening of the war situation.[63] But what should have been clear was the need for Japan, given its increased obligations without any commensurate increase of resources, to have exercised the most careful husbandry of its shipping resources, yet it was not until July 1943 that monthly conferences between the services and civilian authorities were initiated. With the Rikugun exercising control of its allocated shipping through headquarters at Ujina, near Hiroshima, and five commands outside the home islands and the Kaigun doing likewise through its transportation offices at Yokosuka and its eight district commands,[64] each of the three parts of the marine was virtually autonomous, with service shipping being in effect beyond the writ of the economic planning agencies. With the separate shipping authorities setting their own sailing schedules and the services usually refusing to meet requests that their ships carry cargoes when returning to Japan, there was "virtually throughout the war the amazing spectacle of ships moving in ballast in opposite directions (at the same time despite) a severe shortage of shipping."[65]

The wastefulness inherent in such lack of coordination of resources was matched by other elements of organizational weakness, though in part the lack of an overseas escort organization was not wholly Japan's fault. That it had no overall command for the defense of shipping was a situation of its own making, but the fact remained that even if it had possessed such an organization in December 1941 its success would have been dependent, at least in part, upon an ability to set up and coordinate the activities of local commands, which could not be established in the Southern Resources Area before the latter was conquered. In this respect, the contrast with the British experience is pertinent. Many factors were at work in ensuring that Britain survived an assault upon its shipping that was longer and more intense than that which broke Japan, but crucial to its survival was the fact that Britain went to war with a single trade defense organization within the Admiralty that had weathered the financial vagaries of the 1930s, a defined doctrine, and a number of local commands distant from the homeland. Britain's problem of survival nevertheless was very real, but its basic task was to provide itself with escort numbers with which to flesh out a system that was intact before the outbreak of hostilities. Britain never had to create a system of integrated local commands in the midst of war: Japan faced exactly this problem, not to develop and expand an existing system but to create one. The only commands that it possessed outside the Empire before the outbreak of the Pacific war were the Port Arthur Naval Guard District and the five that came under the China Area Fleet. Of these three, the special base forces belonging to the Amoy, Hankow, and Tsingtao Areas were deactivated on 15 January 1942, and the Hainan Naval Guard District, though initially it had the *Otori* and *Hayabusha* under command, was primarily responsible for amphibious assault units, not trade defense. The Kaigun in 1941, therefore, had no central or local command infrastructure to serve as the basis of its trade defense effort, and the effects of this lack of organization became apparent once war began, in terms of the local commands that were established throughout the western Pacific and southeast Asia lacking any common system. The local commands possessed very disparate forces that were not trained to work together, lacked common radio nets, and invariably failed to coordinate their efforts in their different sea areas. Inevitably, such shortcomings in the shore-based and seagoing commands extended to the air, and in this matter the disdain afforded trade defense per se led the Kaigun to neglect coordination of sea and air defense and to refuse to commit adequate numbers of first-grade aircraft and personnel to the protection of shipping. At the outbreak of war the Kaigun had just four air groups available for, amongst other things, maritime patrol duties, and it was not until 1943 that it came into the possession of an air group specifically raised for and permanently assigned to escort duties.[66]

* * *

Any examination of the situation in which Japan found itself in 1941, with the approach of hostilities in the Pacific, prompts the conclusion that for all its efforts in the 1930s in terms of industrialization, ship-building, and naval re-armament, Japan found itself committed to waging war on the most slender of administrative margins. Indeed, such was the precariousness of Japan's position that any consideration of its capacity to conduct war on the basis of available shipping resources suggests that it had every reason to avoid a recourse to arms. But, of course, shipping considerations were but one aspect of Japanese calculations in 1941, and of small account when weighed alongside the issues that were at stake in the second half of that year. The achievements of a decade in which Japan climbed the maritime ladder to become the owner of the third-largest merchant marine in the world[67] served to convey a misleading impression of strength and sufficiency,[68] but the reality was that Japan's decision for war was taken despite an awareness of shipping weakness.

As it was, Japan's position was in many ways worse than the bare record suggests. In terms of both light forces and merchant marine, Japan was beset by long-term structural problems of obsolescence and lack of balance that could not be redressed. The experience of the First World War indicated the need for navies to provide themselves with both large, fast, heavily armed, and hence expensive fleet destroyers and large numbers of smaller, cheaper, and specialist escorts because, for the most part, fleet and escort requirements were different and mutually exclusive. In the inter-war period the leading naval powers encountered serious difficulty in trying to reconcile these conflicting demands at a time of financial restraint, and the outbreak of war, whether in 1939 or 1941, found the three major navies desperately short of destroyers and escorts of all types. In one respect the position of Japan in 1941 would seem to have been better than those of Britain in 1939 and United States in 1941: at the respective times of going to war only 10 of Japan's 112 destroyers were more than twenty years old, whereas 80 of Britain's 194 and 71 of the United States' 171 were of First World War vintage. But all but ten of the balance of Britain's destroyers had been launched in the 1930s, and all of the remaining hundred American destroyers had been launched in or after 1934.[69] The newness of the British and American front-line forces contrasts very sharply with a Japanese destroyer force that included sixty-one units that had been completed before 8 December 1931. With twenty-seven of these units between fifteen and twenty years of age, a very significant part of the Japanese destroyer force was obsolescent and could not be expected to continue to discharge front-line duties, and over half of its numbers were into the second half of their careers. Japan, therefore, went to war with an aging destroyer force, the recently completed *Kagero* class and the then-being-built *Yugumo* class being able to do no more than maintain existing numbers and not add to real strength. The British and American positions present peculiar problems of interpretation, but it is difficult to resist the conclusion that with respect to their forces and building programs the Royal and U.S. Navies were placed somewhat differently from the Kaigun.[70]

The age and overall numbers of the Japanese destroyer force suggest how thin-spread would be the net which the Kaigun intended to cast around its conquests, and behind the protection afforded by front-line forces were escorts that were wholly inadequate in terms of numbers, armament, radars, and communications to discharge their responsibilities, lacked any prospect of significant reinforcement for at least eighteen months, and were without any real measure of air support. The merchant marine, by the least exacting of standards, was never more than marginal to national requirements. It was well for Japan, therefore, that the outbreak of war found Japan's enemies ill-prepared to take advantage of these weaknesses.

CHAPTER TWELVE

THE JAPANESE SITUATION—AND AN AMERICAN DIMENSION

In 1940 certain individuals in the higher reaches of the Imperial Japanese Army, the Rikugun, reasoned that there was an overwhelming need to undertake a thorough study of the reality of total war. This was to be undertaken by an organization especially created in October 1940 for the task, the *Soryokusen kenkyujo* (Institute of Total War Studies). Thirty individuals, representing the nation's "brightest and best," and all aged between 31 and 37 years, were drawn from the army, navy, various government ministries and agencies, and prestigious business firms and the press. These people were allocated fictional posts in the government and the service high commands, and were constituted as a shadow cabinet. They were afforded the privilege of unlimited access to the latest information and national statistics, and in summer 1941 completed a massive and detailed report that made lavish use of confidential state papers, which was submitted to the cabinet.

On 27 August 1941, at the initiative of Prime Minister Konoye Fumimaro, the two cabinets held a joint meeting at which the shadow cabinet members made a number of presentations. The real members of the cabinet, including Konoye and War Minister Tojo Hideki (1884–1948), were present and were subjected to the conclusion that the Japanese economy and manpower resources could not sustain the burden of the China war should that conflict continue for another five to ten years; that Japan could never win a war with the United States; and that in a war with the United States Japan's position, in terms of shipping, would become extremely difficult after late 1943, and that by the end of 1944 Japan would have reached the point at which it would no longer be able to wage war effectively. What the report could not predict, of course, was the American development and use of atomic bombs, but it did predict a Soviet entry into war against Japan.

It is difficult to judge to what extent, if at all, note was taken of this report by those with the power of decision in Japan at this time. Tojo ousted Konoye in October 1941, and his government led Japan into war with the United States in December 1941 and into a situation that, by 1944, had borne out the predictions that had been made. Prima facie, therefore, it would seem that the real cabinet paid absolutely no attention to this comprehensive examination of the situation facing the nation.

It is very rare that a state is ever given so detailed an analysis of its own mortality as was the case on this occasion, but perhaps the only safe conclusion to be drawn from this episode is that even the intimation of total and comprehensive defeat may not be enough, in certain cases, to deflect a state from its ordained, self-inflicted, course. But in drawing that conclusion one other point, little noted in Western accounts of these proceedings, need be made: in 1940 and 1941 there was a "weeding out" of middle-ranking officers in the ministries and staffs who were known to be less than enthusiastic about association with Germany and conflict with Britain and the United States. This, apparently, involved both the Rikugun and the Kaigun, and the officers concerned were either retired or shunted into dead-end posts. By the second half of 1941 the process seems to have been more or less complete: officers of proven reliability in these matters filled the key staff positions.

* * *

The Institute's report provides a most convenient start-line in any examination of Japan's subsequent defeat, and for obvious reason: it correctly identified the three main aspects of Japan's military defeat. The Institute's report noted that Japan was saddled with an unwinnable war in China and one that simply could not be sustained over the next decade, and it noted the certainty of defeat in the Pacific and the inevitability of Soviet malevolence. The Institute's members had no means of knowing that the basic ingredients of failure in China were to manifest themselves also throughout southeast Asia: a people that could not recognize the force of nationalism other than its own was wholly unable to bring to its support the conquered peoples of southeast and east Asia. Only individuals associated themselves with the Japanese, whether in China after 1937 or southeast Asia after 1941, and politically various opportunists did come forward. They, however, were never ceded the powers and responsibility that alone could provide them with credibility and authority; the Japanese clearly feared that such capability would be turned against themselves and were never prepared to surrender the power of decision, generally in economic matters and specifically in reference to raw materials, foodstuffs, and rates of exchange, with consequences that were disastrous for local populations.

There was a political dimension to Japan's defeat that reached across east and southeast Asia, and there was an economic dimension to Japan's defeat that in 1941 simply could never have been anticipated: there was simply no way that anyone could have foreseen that the United States would produce almost 100,000 aircraft in 1944. If the Japanese had sunk every warship in the U.S. Pacific Fleet on 7 December 1941 and then not lost a single ship over the following thirty months, the Kaigun would still not have been able to give battle on the basis of equality in the Philippine Sea in June 1944. At peak, in March 1944, when its factories were producing an aircraft every 294 seconds, the United States was able to cover all the aircraft lost on "the day which will live in infamy" in just over fifteen hours. The comparison of American and Japanese aircraft production between 1939 and 1945 is salutary not least because in both 1943 and 1944 the United States produced more aircraft than did Japan between 1939 and 1945.

The total airframe produced in U.S. factories between 1941 and 1945 was more than 1,060,000 tons, while the substantial rise in Japanese airframe per aircraft in 1945 clearly reflected end-run production whereby the number of aircraft and engines that could be completed, and available aviation fuel, were in decline, though airframe production capacity was still more or less at the 1944 level.[1]

But what is really remarkable about the Institute report is the prediction in reference to shipping and Japan's potential position in 1943 and 1944; the percipience of prediction stands in massive and immediate contrast to the Kaigun's deliberations at this very time. In the summer of 1941, as the Kaigun prepared for war, it undertook its first study of the likely effect of a submarine campaign against Japanese shipping. The study was undertaken by a single officer and came to the remarkably reassuring conclusion that in any month Japan might lose some 75,000 tons of shipping, a conclusion for which there would seem to be no possible justification in light of Allied and neutral losses between February 1917 and September 1918 and after June 1940; curiously, though, this study was set in place at the very time when another Kaigun study set out the belief that in any year Japanese yards would be able to produce some 900,000 tons of shipping for the merchant service. Such coincidence invites comment on any number of counts, the first and arguably the least important being that in the previous decade the output of Japanese yards never exceeded even half the total that would be forthcoming in the future, and this at a time when the yards would be committed to no fewer than six major tasks.

With war, Japanese yards would be committed to building fleet units, escorts, and shipping and to undertaking repair and refitting programs for all three types of ship. In other words, with war Japanese yards would find them-

Table 12.1. The United States and Japan: Comparative Populations, Workforces, and Steel, Coal, Electricity, and Aircraft Production

	United States	Japan	Relative Position		
Population:	141,940,000	72,750,000	1.95:1		
Workforce:	52,800,000	34,100,000	1.55:1		
Steel production(1937):	28,800,000	5,800,000	4.97:1	(in tons)	
Coal production(1938):	354,000,000	53,700,000	6.59:1	(in tons)	
Electricity production:	116,600,000	35,000,000	3.33:1	(in mrd Kwh)	
Share of world manufacture:	32.20%	3.50%	9.20:1		
Aircraft manufactured:					
1939	5,856	4,467	1.31:1		
1940	12,804	4,768	2.69:1		
1941	26,277	5,088	4.97:1		
1942	47,836	8,861	5.40:1		
1943	85,898	16,693	5.15:1		
1944	96,318	28,180	3.42:1		
1945	49,761	11,066	4.50:1		
Total	324,750	79,123	4.10:1		
Aero-engines manufactured:					
				engines:	aircraft
1939	n.a.	n.a.	-	-	-
1940	15,513	n.a.	-	1.21	-
1941	58,181	12,151	4.79:1	2.21	2.39
1942	138,089	16,999	8.12:1	2.89	1.92
1943	227,116	28,541	7.96:1	2.64	1.71
1944	256,912	46,526	5.52:1	2.67	1.65
1945	106,350	12,380	8.59:1	2.14	1.12
Total	802,161	116,597	6.75:1	2.52	1.67
Weight (lbs.) of airframe produced:					
				airframe:	aircraft
1939	n.a.	n.a.	- -		-
1940	n.a.	n.a.	- -		-
1941	81,500,000	21,200,000	3.84:1	3,102	4,167
1942	274,900,000	36,500,000	7.53:1	5,747	4,119
1943	650,600,000	65,500,000	9.93:1	7,574	3,924
1944	951,600,000	111,000,000	8.57:1	9,880	3,939
1945	429,900,000	70,000,000	6.14:1	8,639	6,326
Total	2,388,500,000	304,200,000	7.85:1	7,803	4,353

TABLE 12.2. NEW CONSTRUCTION IN JAPANESE YARDS, 1931-1941

Figures Include only Steel Ships over 100 Tons

	Merchant Tonnage	Naval Tonnage	Total Tonnage
1931	92,093	15,050	107,143
1937	442,382**	55,360	497,742
1938	410,644 (- 7.07)	63,589 (+14.86)	474,233 (- 4.72)
1939	343,526 (-16.34)	58,248 (- 8.40)	401,774 (-15.28)
1940	279,816 (-18.55)	94,705 (+62.59)	374,521 (- 6.78)
1941	237,617 (-15.08)	225,159 (+137.75)	462,776 (+23.56)
Total	1,713,985	497,061	2,211,046

Note: The figures in parentheses represent the change from the previous year.

Source: The figures are drawn from Cohen, p. 251. The figures given on this page are the ones used here with post-1937 annual percentage change given in parentheses. Cohen's figures include only steel ships over 100 tons, and it should be noted that on p. 3 Cohen gives different figures for 1937 merchant shipping output (405,195 tons) and for 1941 naval tonnage figure (231,990 tons). There would seem to be no way in which these differences can be reconciled.

selves committed to six separate tasks, when the evidence of the previous decade pointed firmly in the direction of their not being able to undertake probably more than two of these tasks at the same time. When Japan went to war in December 1941 just one fleet unit, a destroyer, was not in service, but the readiness of the fleet had to be balanced against four matters: first, the fleet construction programs of 1939 and 1940 had been lost and there was no way in which these might be completed; second, the escort construction programs were minimal in terms of both numbers and quality; third, the readiness of the fleet had to be set against the major decline of production of merchantmen—the 1941 total was just 53.71 percent of 1937 output—while the merchant service itself, and Japan's import position, were in a state that bordered on the disastrous; fourth, the readiness of the fleet in December 1941 had to be balanced against the fact that not too far distant would be the time when fleet strength would have to be massively reduced in order to release units for routine care and maintenance because readiness at one time had to be bought at such an inevitable price some time in the future.

These matters vie for consideration in terms of their importance, but it is very hard to escape two matters relating to production, shipping, and national needs. In June 1940 Japan started the mobilization of the fleet, a process that, with the requisition of shipping and its preparation to meet military needs, would take some eighteen months. The process, therefore, would be complete about the end of 1941, but what the Kaigun in mid-1940 expected to happen at the end of 1941 is somewhat difficult to discern. Japan could not stay mobilized into the indefinite future, and while there are several reasons for such a state of affairs, the most important single fact was that in 1940,[2] with imports totaling some 49,000,000 tons, Japan needed about 10,000,000 tons of merchant shipping to meet national needs but had no more than 6,250,000 tons under its own flag. With about half of this shipping being requisitioned for the services, how Japan was to survive past the end of 1941 never seems to have been properly addressed, either at the time by the Imperial Navy or by successive generations of historians.

* * *

The story of Japan's defeat in the Pacific has been recounted mostly in terms of fleet action and invasions, but in these chapters it will be told primarily in terms of the virtual annihilation of Japanese shipping, the overwhelming of the trade defense system that the Kaigun sought to put in place in 1943, and the collapse of Japanese import trade,[3] which in effect meant that Japanese industry had entered end-run production by the time of the national surrender in August 1945.

* * *

The consequence of shipping losses was both obvious and immediate in terms of Japan's capacity to wage war. It is a story seldom afforded much in the way of historical attention, and for obvious reason: fleet actions and amphibious landings, with their subsequent campaigns, inevitably had at the time and have retained a higher profile than the campaign against Japanese shipping, and in terms of U.S. national perception and historiography, the campaign against shipping does not sit comfortably alongside American condemnation of German operations in two world wars. Be that as it may, the basic points about the campaign against shipping may perhaps best be presented, and understood, by reference to the division of the war into constituent phases and theaters of operation.

The war between December 1941 and August 1945 basically divides into six phases, the first being the phase of Japanese conquest that was for the most part complete by the end of April 1942. The period thereafter, to October 1943, represents the period of balance, when the Japanese and Americans fought for possession of the initiative. This period consisted of two separate phases, first between May 1942 and February 1943, which was the phase that saw Allied forces secure local victories in eastern New Guinea and the lower Solomons, and then between March and October 1943, which was the phase "when nothing happened." This latter phase saw very little in the way of islands change hands, though there were continuing operations in eastern New Guinea and the central and upper Solomons and in the Aleutians. The fourth phase of the war, between November 1943 and June 1944, opened with the American landing operations in the Gilbert and Ellice Islands and closed with the assault on Saipan and the battle of the Philippine Sea. The fifth phase, between July 1944 and March 1945, was witness to the series of massive American operations that resulted in the re-conquest of the Philippines and the severing of Japanese seaborne lines of communication between the home islands and the Southern Resources Area. The last phase of the war, between April and August 1945, saw American carrier formations operating off the home islands, the Kaigun reduced to the level of an ineffectual coastal defense force, Japanese shipping subjected to a sustained mining offensive (Operation Starvation), and a strategic bombing offensive that had wrecked urban Japan even without the attacks on Hiroshima and Nagasaki. The mining effort was undertaken by aircraft, and indeed in this final phase of the war shore-based aircraft, in the form of this mining effort and direct attacks, accounted for some 264 naval, military, and civilian ships of 500,179 tons, or some 55.58 percent of the ships and 52.99 percent of the tonnage lost by the Japanese in this final phase of the war. This was the only period in the war when the main instrument of destruction of Japanese shipping was shore-based aircraft.

* * *

The war at sea unfolded in six major theaters, the North Pacific theater, Japanese home waters, the East China Sea, the Central Pacific theater, the Southwest Pacific theater, and the Southern Resources Area, along which are the "also-rans," namely the Indian Ocean theater, riverine China, and what must be classified as the other and unknown theaters, the "other" being the provision for the two submarines that were lost in the North Atlantic and the "unknown" for the total of two warships and eighteen naval support, military, and civilian ships lost, whereabouts unknown. But before any examination of Japanese shipping losses can begin three comments, not covered with the accompanying tables, are in order.

First, what is very striking about Japanese losses is the relative slenderness of losses that nonetheless brought Japan to the edge of disastrous defeat by the end of July 1945. It is very easy to lose sight of the fact that Japanese total wartime shipping losses—naval support, military, and civilian shipping losses together—were not that much greater than British losses in both 1941 and 1942; expressed another way, Britain was able to survive despite losses in two single years that were all but the equivalent of Japan's overall shipping losses between December 1941 and August 1945. As was noted in the previous chapter, British, Allied, and neutral shipping losses in the Second World War were in the order of 20 million tons, but Britain and its allies survived such losses and moved

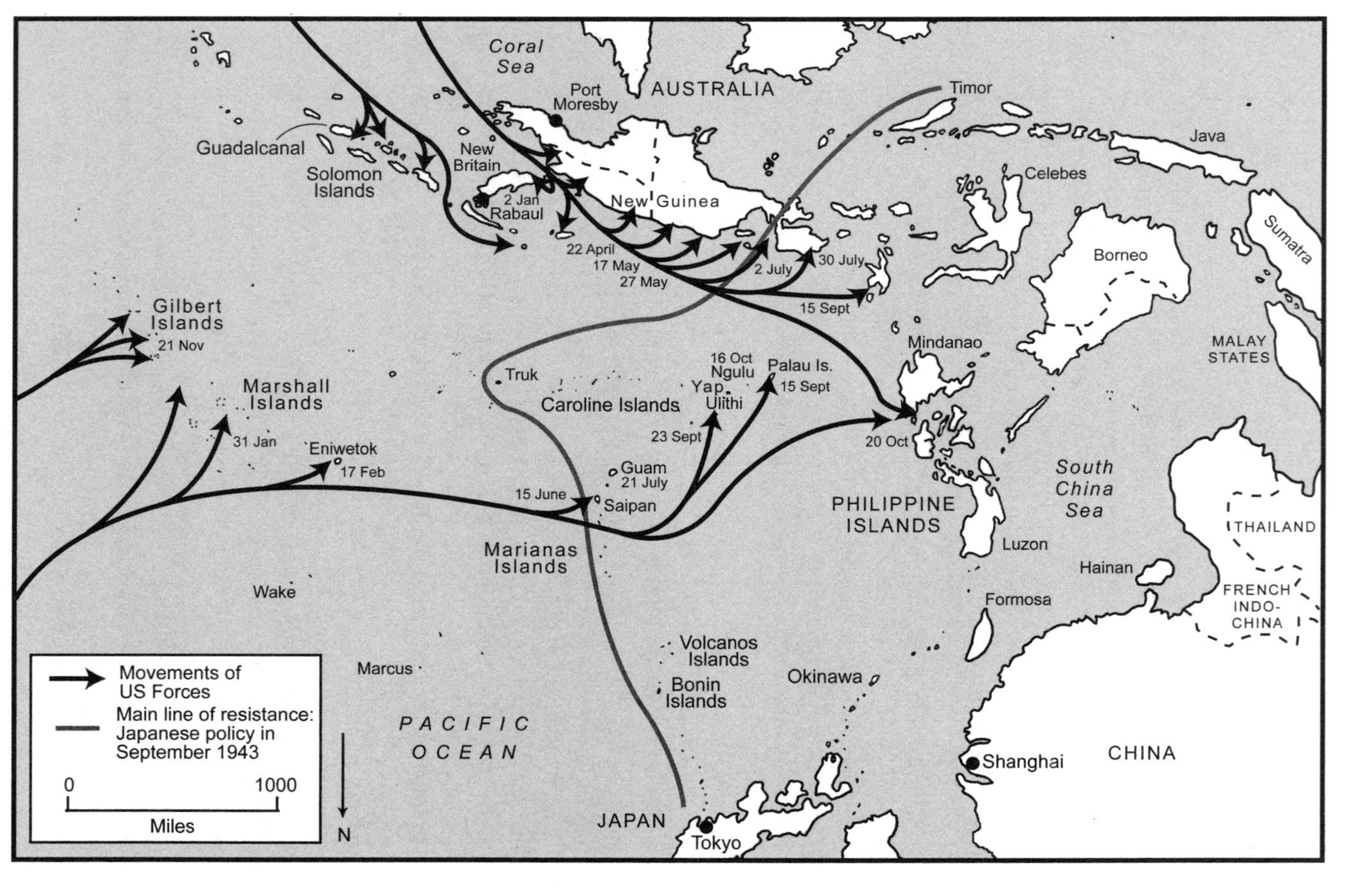

Map 10. The Pacific from the Japanese Perspective: November 1943 to October 1944

forward to victory. The point must be noted that Britain might well have been brought to the point of collapse sometime in 1942 but for the certainties provided by the American and Soviet dimensions, but the fact remains that Japan was defeated in a war in which its shipping losses were about two-fifths of those of its enemies, which were fighting two wars at sea and not one.

Second, the definition of Japanese losses must go alongside the statement of what it had available at the start of Pacific proceedings and what was added in the way of new construction, salving, acquisition through capture, and other means, but these are matters noted elsewhere. To move directly to the third item: any consideration of Japanese losses must go hand in hand with the crucial 75,000-tons calculation of summer 1941, which really provides the basis of examination of Japanese losses, and as such immediately presents one fact: only in seven months between December 1941 and August 1945 were Japanese losses below this figure, and the last of these seven months was September 1942. In seven of the first ten months of the war Japanese shipping losses were within the alleged limits of toleration, but the returns of October and November 1942 were all but triple the losses (by tonnage) of September 1942, and provided indication of what was to come.

What is very interesting is that only in one month of the war, February 1944, did naval shipping, military shipping, and civilian shipping each lose more than 75,000 tons of shipping, and this month really did mark a point of significance. If one looks at the pattern and the rate of Japanese losses, then what is very noticeable is the losses of November 1942 in the southwest Pacific area; while very modest at fifteen ships of 94,597 tons, the latter figure was not far short of almost double the greatest losses in any single theater to date.[4] The losses in the southwest Pacific theater in November 1942 would scarcely seem to represent the margin between victory and defeat, but quite obviously the Imperial Navy could not accept an open-ended commitment in a theater in which in a single forty-eight-hour period it lost the battleship *Kirishima*, the heavy cruiser *Kinugasa*, the destroyer *Ayanami*, and three naval transports of 19,163 tons, plus nine army transports of 61,542 tons. In the two days of 14 and 15 November 1942 the Japanese lost off Guadalcanal a tonnage beyond the "acceptable" national limits of toleration, and in one sense the Japanese decision to accept defeat in the lower Solomons is thoroughly understandable: the losses of 14–15 November represent the equivalent of monthly losses of nigh on 1,250,000 tons, some sixteen times over the 75,000-ton limit; such a rate of losses would have made even the Americans hesitate, albeit only for a moment.

But what is also very interesting about the November 1942 figures is the difference that this month represented from the previous month. In November the total shipping losses were twenty-nine ships of 151,662 tons, whereas in October losses were twenty-eight ships of 154,074 tons, but with the total of

Table 12.3. Japanese Warship and Naval, Military, and Civilian Shipping Losses by Month, 7–8 December 1941 to 15 August 1945

	Warships	Naval shipping	Military shipping	Civilian shipping	Overall shipping losses
1941 December	13: 17,196	1: 2,827	5: 26,745	4: 15,053	10: 44,625
1942 January	10: 15,979	8: 29,660	3: 10,532	6: 28,432	17: 68,624
February	7: 11,041	1: 6,567	3: 17,713	1: 989	5: 25,269
March	6: 24,890	8: 47,481	7: 35,164	3: 16,732	18: 99,377
April	1: 116	3: 10,191	3: 18,714	2: 9,282	8: 38,187
May	11: 38,271	5: 23,035	9: 53,883	8: 31,073	22: 107,991
June	9: 128,895	1: 6,800	2: 12,853	4: 14,853	7: 34,506
July	5: 4,474	7: 29,581	2: 12,765	4: 22,028	13: 64, 374
August	9: 29,787	8: 58,337	2: 12,333	11: 34,226	21: 104,896
September	2: 3,570	5: 29,486	1: 4,070	8: 25,850	14: 59,406
October	12: 35,223	6: 33,546	6: 31,707	16: 88,821	28 154,074
November	12: 99,730	8: 41,998	14: 82,503	7: 27,161	29: 151,662
December	8: 15,043	6: 13,383	7: 22,584	16: 45,913	29: 81,880
1943 January	6: 6,464	8: 39,318	14: 65,696	8: 30,596	30: 135,610
February	6: 8,776	7: 35,317	7: 24,013	7: 25,461	21: 84,791
March	8: 12,774	9: 50,716	12: 48,370	13: 41,441	34: 140,527
April	8: 6,632	10: 84,670	10: 36,325	11: 22,648	31: 143,643
May	12: 25,544	6: 39,769	8: 26,752	17: 54,079	31: 120,600
June	9: 56,391	8: 36,227	5: 13,964	8: 35,834	21: 86,025
July	16: 43,238	1: 2,718	6: 23,668	15: 53,386	22: 79,772
August	0: 14,461	7: 29,108	11: 31,154	12: 46,922	30: 107,184
September	12: 16,187	10: 56,242	20: 64,131	23: 80,423	53: 200,796
October	6: 12,199	16: 83,111	21: 52,581	12: 41,601	49: 177,293
November	20: 27,887	28: 126,424	28: 116,786	11: 56,444	67: 299,654
December	8: 24,218	25: 102,270	8: 25,407	20: 67,778	53: 195,455
1944 January	26: 32,654	32½ 152,887	20: 88,858	18½ 69,505	71: 311,250
February	40: 57,612	51: 279,326	28: 113,110	33: 114,654	112: 507,090
March	28: 20,278	26: 175,754	25: 71,879	14: 38,296	65: 285,929
April	16: 20,673	11: 45,456	19: 63,274	18: 35,253	48: 143,983
May	26: 26,156	22: 93,390	19: 85,310	20: 73,548	61: 252,248
June	32: 125,568	29: 129,338	27: 102,809	20: 63,710	76: 295,857
July	41: 45,512	18: 49,996	18: 101,308	30: 92,200	66 243,504
August	31: 49,870	17: 105,727	18: 55,678	43: 172,251	78 333,656
September	50: 50,337	29: 105,309	37: 153,971	56: 155,390	122: 414,670
October	63: 347,222	27: 139,042	28: 105,274	61: 223,629	116: 467,945
November	64: 224,429	30: 136,797	25: 110,648	43: 165,006	98: 412,451
December	35: 61,520	7: 25,541	12: 50,834	26: 101,302	45: 177,677
1945 January	55: 56,186	19: 78,602	16: 65,227	72: 229,313	107: 373,142
February	31: 21,092	3: 17,962	5: 14,588	32: 85,522	40: 118,072
March	53: 34,144	21: 69,933	21: 56,768	46: 92,825	88: 219,526
April	53: 112,316	10: 43,810	4: 7,692	36: 79,790	50: 131,292
May	30: 44,352	11: 22,474	10: 23,030	100: 163,911	121: 209,415
June	29: 32,654	12: 22,726	9: 23,719	94: 140,912	115: 187,357
July	70: 239,415	8: 31,224	8: 12,450	123: 254,549	139: 298,223
August	30: 33,252	1: 478	2: 16,433	47: 101,412	50: 118,323

TABLE 12.4. JAPANESE LOSSES IN OCTOBER AND NOVEMBER 1942

	Warships	Naval support shipping	Military transports	Civilian merchantmen
October 1942:	12: 35,223	6: 33,546	6: 31,707	16: 88,821
November 1942:	12: 99,730	8: 41,998	14: 82,503	7: 27,161
Expressed in % terms:				
October 1942:	- -	21.43 21.77	21.43 20.58	57.14 57.65
November 1942:	- -	27.59 27.69	48.28 54.40	24.14 17.91

warship tonnage all but tripling between these two months the difference in terms of ownership of losses was very striking, as shown on table 12.4.

Military and civilian losses changed places in these two months, but perhaps more importantly the losses in the southwest Pacific theater in November 1942 stand in sharp contrast to losses of some 40,000 tons of shipping in each of three theaters—Japanese home waters, the East China Sea, and the southwest Pacific—in the previous month, while the change in terms of agency of destruction was perhaps even more interesting. In October 1942 submarines operating from bases in the central Pacific accounted for a total of seventeen naval, military, and civilian ships of 87,019 tons, of which eleven ships of 48,899 tons were sunk in Japanese home waters and five ships of 35,256 tons were sunk in the East China Sea; submarines operating from other bases accounted for six ships of 29,827 tons, of which four ships of 21,468 tons were sunk in the southwest Pacific theater. In November 1942, as the American high command redeployed submarines to the southwest Pacific with what both sides clearly saw as the impending crisis of the campaign, submarines operating from bases in the central Pacific accounted for one merchantman of 1,925 tons in Japanese home waters and one merchantman of 6,567 tons in the East China Sea; submarines operating from other bases accounted for five ships of 23,943, none in the southwest Pacific theater. This interesting if somewhat neglected point represents a repeat of what had happened in mid-1942 with reference to Midway. In May 1942 Japanese losses entered six figures for the first time, but in June were just a third of the previous month's toll: American submarines, operating from bases throughout the Pacific, accounted for just two merchantmen of 7,867 tons, compared to totals of eleven ships of 55,180 tons sunk by submarines based in the central Pacific and seven ships of 36,262 tons sunk by other submarines. Expressed another way, a rate of sinkings by submarines, which was approaching six figures by May 1942 and which was in marked decline after mid-month, was reduced to all but nothing in June 1942; such was the cost of redeployment for battle. This phenomenon repeated itself in October–November 1942 with respect to the southwest Pacific theater.

But what is very revealing about the figures is the way certain theaters were left without even a bit part to play as the Americans carried the tide of war to the

TABLE 12.5. JAPANESE LOSSES OF JULY 1945

	Warships	Naval support shipping	Military transports	Civilian merchantmen
North Pacific:	1: 740	- -	- -	- -
Japanese Home Waters:	59: 219,523	8: 31,224	8: 12,450	120: 251,403
East China Sea:	1: 297	- -	- -	1: 834
Central Pacific:	- -	- -	- -	- -
Southwest Pacific:	- -	- -	- -	- -
Southern Resources Area:	9: 18,855	- -	- -	1: 834
Indian Ocean:	- -	- -	- -	- -
Riverine China:	- -	- -	- -	1: 1,152
Unknown/Other Theaters:	- -	- -	- -	- -
Total:	70: 239,415	8: 31,224	8: 12,450	123: 254,549

home islands. The southwest Pacific is the most obvious and also the first such example. November 1943, in which month American carriers struck at the base at Rabaul as part of the preliminary moves in support of the moves into the Gilbert and Ellice Islands, really marked the end of any substantial operations, and certainly after March 1944 the theater had ceased to count in real terms; between April 1944 and August 1945 just eleven service and civilian ships were sunk in theater, their combined displacement of just 7,372 tons being an adequate comment on the value and significance of this theater in this time. But the same was true of the central Pacific theater after June 1944 when, with the Americans having secured the Marianas, there was no place for Japanese shipping to go either in or across the theater. In the last year of the war Japanese losses in theater amounted to just eighteen ships of 21,471 tons; perhaps what is surprising about this theater in this period is that the number of Japanese warships sunk was likewise modest, though the total of twenty-eight warships did include nineteen submarines in an area well populated by American targets. Likewise, the north Pacific theater was by-passed in 1945, the main American offensive effort in this theater—albeit a modest one—being mounted between May and September 1944, but what is perhaps surprising in terms of tide of war and lack of targets in the bypassed area is the Southern Resources Area. After 31 March 1945 this was a theater of no real account. With the Americans established in the Philippines and thus astride seaborne lines of communication between the home islands and southeast Asia, there was nowhere for Japanese shipping to go, and between 1 July and 15 August the Japanese lost just one 834-ton merchantman at the entrance to the Gulf of Siam, and this in the theater which, arguably, "the war was all about."

The point about Japanese losses in July 1945 can be stated very simply: as a nation Japan had lost all semblance of strategic mobility by this forty-fourth and last full month of the war. It was almost a case of nothing happening outside home waters and the East China Sea—and the lower Yangtse if the one merchantman sunk by land-based aircraft is included in this list. In terms of the warships deemed lost in the Southern Resources Area, the total is exaggerated by inclusion of the 13,400-ton heavy cruiser *Takao*, which, *hors de combat* at the naval base at Singapore, was severely damaged and in effect lost as a result of attack by British midget submarines on 31 July. If it is excluded from the list, then eight warships of 5,455 tons were lost in theater, the average size of 680 tons (with five less than 220 tons) telling its own story.

But perhaps the most important single point to emerge from any careful consideration of Japanese shipping losses relates to something completely different. Overall losses reached the 200,000-ton mark for the first time in September 1943, all but touched the 300,000-ton mark in November 1943, and reached, in tonnage terms, the peak of monthly losses in February 1944, when 507,090 tons of shipping was lost, this latter figure representing 6.76 months of production according to the 75,000-tons-per-month formula. What is very noticeable about these figures is that whereas in September 1943, of the three shipping branches the civilian merchantmen suffered the largest single losses—twenty-three ships of 80,423 tons from a total of fifty-three ships of 200,796 tons—between November 1943 and June 1944, as the Americans fought their way across the central Pacific from the Gilberts to the Marshalls to the Marianas and conducted the pulverizing attacks on Truk and Koror, the burden of losses fell on service shipping, and specifically the naval support shipping, as shown in table 12.6.

In this period as a whole the merchant marine lost a total of 189.5 ships compared to the 250.5 naval support ships and 215 military transports that were sunk, but the point of real difference lay in tonnage lost: the total of 642,212 tons of shipping lost by the merchant fleet compared to the 784,145 tons lost by the military service and the 1,244,198 tons lost by the naval service, that is, some 24.04 percent of losses by displacement compared to 28.93 percent by numbers. It was not the losses incurred by the merchant service in this period that proved crippling, but the losses among the naval support shipping, which obviously had immediate impact in terms of the Kaigun's effectiveness but also in terms of further requisitioning of shipping to cover losses from a merchant marine that simply did not have at hand sufficient shipping to meet these demands. As it was, Kaigun effectiveness was in terminal decline in this period, and two of the little-noted facts of the Pacific war are that Japanese warships failed to account for a single opposite number for more than a year after the U.S. destroyer *Chevalier* was sunk at Vella Lavella on 7 October 1943, while Japanese submarines, which sank just four American destroyers in the whole of the war, accounted for no fleet units after 26 October 1943, the escort carrier *Liscome Bay* (24 November 1943) and the heavy cruiser *Indianapolis* (29 July 1945) excepted.

The significance of losses in this period between September 1943 and June

Table 12.6. Japanese Warship and Naval, Military, and Civilian Shipping Losses, Overall and Specifically in the Central Pacific Theater, to Carrier Aircraft with Warships and to Submarines, in the Period between 1 September 1943 and 30 June 1944

		Losses in the Central Pacific Theater		
	Total losses in all theaters	Overall in theater	To carrier aircraft and warships	To submarines
September 1943				
Warships	12: 16,187	3: 6,763	- -	3: 6,763
Naval shipping	10: 56,242	2: 8,053	- -	2: 8,053
Military shipping	20: 64,131	5: 21,064	- -	3: 18,822
Civilian shipping	23: 80,423	3: 6,585	- -	1: 3,427
Shipping losses:	53: 200,796	10: 35,702	- -	6: 30,302
October 1943				
Warships	6: 12,199	1: 5,935	- -	1: 5,935
Naval shipping	16: 83,111	7: 44,458	- -	4: 36,887
Military shipping	21: 52,581	5: 14,863	- -	4: 14,420
Civilian shipping	12: 42,601	- -	- -	- -
Shipping losses:	49: 178,293	12: 59,321	- -	8: 51,307
November 1943				
Warships	20: 27,887	4: 5,725	- -	- -
Naval shipping	28: 126,424	17: 77,610	- -	13: 67,157
Military shipping	28: 116,786	13: 59,456	- -	12: 57,944
Civilian shipping	11: 56,444	1: 5,874	- -	- -
Shipping losses:	67: 299,654	31: 142,940	- -	25: 125,101
December 1943				
Warships	8: 24,218	3: 4,520	1: 343	2: 4,177
Naval shipping	25: 102,270	17: 66,865	5: 24,190	10: 37,632
Military shipping	8: 25,407	2: 5,740	- -	2: 5,740
Civilian shipping	20: 67,778	3: 14,756	- -	3: 14,756
Shipping losses:	53: 195,455	22: 87,361	5: 24,190	15: 58,128
January 1944				
Warships	26: 32,654	18: 14,035	5: 1,803	6: 10,962
Naval shipping	32½ 152,887	14: 71,513	1: 4,603	9: 57,264
Military shipping	20: 88,858	8: 35,622	- -	6: 29,670
Civilian shipping	18½ 69,505	3: 2,836	- -	1: 784
Shipping losses:	71: 311,250	25: 109,971	1: 4,603	16: 87,718
February 1944				
Warships	40: 57,612	22: 45,150	19: 32,701	3: 12,449
Naval shipping	51: 279,326	38: 218,132	29: 181,566	8: 35,958
Military shipping	28: 113,110	12: 56,185	3: 12,825	7: 42,011
Civilian shipping	33: 114,654	2: 7,075	2: 2,730	1: 5,184
Shipping losses:	112: 507,090	52: 281,392	34: 197,121	16: 83,153

	Total losses in all theaters	Losses in the Central Pacific Theater: Overall in theater	To carrier aircraft and warships	To submarines
March 1944				
Warships	28 20,278	16: 10,680	13: 7,832	2: 2,650
Naval shipping	26: 175,754	18: 124,403	15: 108,517	3: 15,886
Military shipping	25: 71,879	9: 25,482	6: 18,061	3: 7,421
Civilian shipping	14: 38,296	4: 5,899	1: 239	3: 5,660
Shipping losses:	65: 285,929	31: 155,784	22: 126,817	9: 28,967
April 1944				
Warships	16: 20,673	8: 9,746	2: 1,090	2: 5,490
Naval shipping	11: 45,456	5: 27,757	- -	4: 18,410
Military shipping	19: 63,274	3: 21,133	- -	3: 21,133
Civilian shipping	18: 35,253	3: 2,586	- -	1: 2,398
Shipping losses:	48: 143,983	11: 51,476	- -	8: 41,941
May 1944				
Warships	26: 26,156	11: 9,283	6: 3,623	3: 4,929
Naval shipping	22: 93,390	10: 32,271	- -	10: 32,271
Military shipping	19: 85,310	4: 14,984	- -	4: 14,984
Civilian shipping	20: 73,548	1: 3,740	- -	1: 3,740
Shipping losses:	61: 252,857	15: 50,995	- -	15: 50,995
June 1944				
Warships	32: 125,568	19: 100,482	15: 45,037	4: 57,015
Naval shipping	29: 129,338	17: 80,592	12: 56,985	5: 23,607
Military shipping	27: 102,809	5: 24,024	2: 6,682	3: 17,342
Civilian shipping	20: 63,710	2: 9,334	1: 2,245	1: 7,089
Shipping losses:	76: 295,857	24: 113,950	15: 65,912	9: 48,038

TABLE 12.7. JAPANESE LOSSES IN THE PACIFIC TO SUBMARINES BY THEATER, SEPTEMBER 1943–JUNE 1944

			Warships	Naval support shipping	Military transports	Civilian merchantmen
North Pacific:	September	1943	1: 1,368	- -	- -	- -
	October	1943	- -	- -	- -	- -
	November	1943	- -	- -	- -	- -
	December	1943	- -	- -	- -	- -
	January	1944	- -	- -	- -	- -
	February	1944	- -	1: 3,548	- -	- -
	March	1944	- -	1: 4,541	2: 3,867	- -
	April	1944	- -	- -	- -	- -
	May	1944	1: 860	1: 1,053	3: 14,710	1: 1,590
	June	1944	- -	1: 3,124	2: 9,998	2: 4,984
Japanese home waters:	September	1943	- -	2: 4,571	- -	8: 26,939
	October	1943	- -	- -	1: 1,288	3: 12,804
	November	1943	- -	3: 16,317	- -	1: 3,328
	December	1943	1: 17,830	2: 8,274	- -	1: 3,948
	January	1944	2: 5,345	4: 25,282	2: 8,603	2: 6,025
	February	1944	- -	2: 10,009	- -	4: 8,850
	March	1944	3: 6,647	1: 4,667	1: 5,460	- -
	April	1944	1: 1,630	- -	2: 7,665	2: 2,280
	May	1944	- -	2: 7,357	- -	5: 14,276
	June	1944	- -	2: 5,243	2: 8,718	4: 14,166
East China Sea:	September	1943	- -	2: 13,933	1: 2,256	2: 16,316
	October	1943	- -	2: 14,470	1: 5,866	- -
	November	1943	1: 870	- -	- -	1: 6,783
	December	1943	1: 515	- -	1: 3,195	1: 2,627
	January	1944	- -	½ 5,022	2: 13,270	2½ 13,715
	February	1944	- -	1: 10,033	1: 6,989	7: 36,059
	March	1944	- -	- -	- -	1: 5,493
	April	1944	1: 450	- -	- -	2: 5,085
	May	1944	- -	- -	- -	1: 2,201
	June	1944	- -	- -	- -	- -
Central Pacific:	September	1943	3: 6,763	2: 8,053	3 18,822	1: 3,427
	October	1943	1: 5,935	4: 36,887	4: 14,420	- -
	November	1943	- -	13: 67,157	12: 57,944	- -
	December	1943	2: 4,177	10: 37,632	2: 5,740	3: 14,756
	January	1944	6: 10,962	9: 57,264	6: 29,670	1: 784
	February	1944	3: 12,449	8: 35,958	7: 42,011	1: 5,184
	March	1944	2: 2,650	3: 15,886	3: 7,421	3: 5,660
	April	1944	2: 5,490	4: 18,410	3: 21,133	1: 2,398
	May	1944	3: 4,929	10: 32,271	4: 14,984	1: 3,740
	June	1944	12: 73,488	16: 67,192	18: 84,867	11: 46,143

			Warships	Naval support shipping	Military transports	Civilian merchantmen
Southwest Pacific:	September	1943	- -	- -	- -	- -
	October	1943	- -	- -	1: 5,460	- -
	November	1943	- -	- -	1: 11,621	- -
	December	1943	- -	- -	- -	- -
	January	1944	- -	- -	- -	- -
	February	1944	- -	- -	- -	- -
	March	1944	- -	- -	- -	- -
	April	1944	- -	- -	- -	- -
	May	1944	- -	- -	- -	- -
	June	1944	- -	- -	- -	- -
Southern Resources Area:	September	1943	1: 840	1: 8,120	2: 7,407	1: 9,908
	October	1943	- -	- -	4: 17,976	3: 17,512
	November	1943	1: 820	- -	5: 30,974	4: 20,496
	December	1943	1: 820	4: 19,525	- -	2: 18,784
	January	1944	2: 5,456	4: 17,345	2½ 13,822	7½ 33,540
	February	1944	1: 1,215	4: 17,884	8: 38,143	8: 37,021
	March	1944	- -	2: 13,498	1: 5,399	2: 11,188
	April	1944	1: 2,077	- -	6: 23,820	5: 8,045
	May	1944	6: 8,233	7: 50,316	9: 49,059	6: 35,592
	June	1944	7: 13,462	7: 34,088	9: 45,233	4: 19,904

Table 12.8. Japanese Losses, Both Overall and in the Southern Resources Area, to Carrier Aircraft with Warships and to Submarines, in the Period June 1944–March 1945

	Carrier aircraft and warships		Submarines	
	Total sinkings in all theaters	Sinkings in Southern Resources Area		Total sinkings in all theaters
Warships	196½ 470,810	123½ 407,419	68½ 174,225	120½ 362,205
Naval shipping	44½ 172,253	25½ 122,858	56: 333,246	86: 419,811
Military shipping	50: 219,304	35: 161,707	38: 216,760	67: 342,238
Civilian shipping	112½ 327,173	74½ 258,947	87: 442,944	155: 694,623
Shipping losses:	207: 718,730	135: 543,512	181: 992,950	308: 1,456,672

1944 lies in the fact that prior to November 1943 the main burden of the campaign against shipping, and indeed the war per se over the previous year, had been borne by the submarines. U.S. carriers did not sink anything, whether warship or service or merchant ship, after 14–15 November 1942, when their aircraft were involved in the sinking of the heavy cruiser *Kinugasa* and the destruction of transports that had been run ashore on Guadalcanal, and even before that time the carrier aircraft toll of shipping as opposed to warships had been minimal.

November 1943 saw the carrier and the submarine come together, with the main effort made by carrier formations and with the submarines deployed forward in an attempt to counter any enemy formations coming forward and to deal with service shipping seeking to put distance between themselves and American carrier formations. The main successes of carrier formations were registered at Truk in February 1944 and at Koror, in the Palaus, in the following month.

The Truk episode, with carrier aircraft, warships, and submarines accounting for nine Japanese warships of 30,957 tons, twenty-six naval support ships of 169,787 tons, four military transports of 19,679 tons, and two merchantmen of 7,075 tons on just the single day of 17 February, was perhaps the most destructive single day in the history of shipping. In the period between November 1943 and June 1944, the total Japanese losses were in the order of 553 ships of 2,291,345 tons, or an average of 69.13 ships of 286,418 tons per month, nearly four times the 75,000-ton limit. Perhaps rather surprisingly, in this period submarines accounted for more warships, naval support ships, and merchant ships than did carrier aircraft. It is perhaps predictable that submarines should have sunk more merchantmen than did carrier aircraft, but in this phase of the war submarines in the Pacific sank 53 Japanese warships to the 43 sunk by carrier aircraft and 304 naval, military, and civilian ships to the 77½ of carrier aircraft; it was not until the next phase of the war, between July 1944 and March 1945, that carrier and submarine operations were properly complementary in terms of a certain balance of returns.

In this penultimate phase of the war, as the Americans broke into the Southern Resources Area and established themselves across Japanese seaborne lines of communication between the home islands and southeast Asia, there was a certain balance of returns as Japanese merchant shipping losses for the first time exceeded service losses, and indeed for the first time began to come close to equaling the two service losses together, as shown in table 12.8.[5]

Quite clearly the difference of priority in terms of carrier aircraft and enemy warships rather than shipping was present in this phase, but it was even more marked in the final phase of the war, between 1 April and 15 August 1945. Perhaps more noteworthy, however, is the fact that in 1945, with Allied carrier formations established in the western Pacific, submarine operations were reduced to tertiary status at best, as for the first time mines—and with mines

Table 12.9. Japanese Warship and Naval, Military, and Civilian Shipping Losses in the North Pacific Theater, Home Waters, and East China Sea in the War's Last Phase, 1 April–15 August 1945

	Carrier aircraft and warships	Submarines	Land-based aircraft	Mines
April 1945				
Warships	11: 84,248	12: 6,591	3: 3,518	4: 1,536
Naval shipping	- -	6: 14,995	- -	- -
Military shipping	- -	2: 3,127	- -	- -
Civilian shipping	- -	6: 32,528	2: 1,707	9: 9,200
Shipping losses:	- -	14: 50,650	2: 1,707	9: 9,200
May 1945				
Warships	3: 1,790	6: 5,183	- -	7: 15,764
Naval shipping	1: 233	- -	- -	6: 13,684
Military shipping	- -	3: 4,255	2: 2,249	3: 15,439
Civilian shipping	1: 127	8: 13,477	33: 59,396	43: 70,271
Shipping losses:	2: 360	11: 17,732	35: 61,645	52: 99,394
June 1945				
Warships	3: 390	4: 7,832	2: 1,082	5: 4,910
Naval shipping	- -	5: 10,013	- -	4: 3,062
Military shipping	- -	3: 5,368	- -	4: 10,919
Civilian shipping	- -	31: 58,238	1: 3,832	40: 47,552
Shipping losses:	3: 390	39: 73,619	1: 3,832	48: 61,533
July 1945				
Warships	41: 209,343	5: 2,592	4: 2,319	5: 4,278
Naval shipping	8: 31,224	- -	- -	- -
Military shipping	3: 2,534	1: 2,218	3: 6,673	1: 1,025
Civilian shipping	50: 92,960	10: 25,350	17: 43,945	36: 80,469
Shipping losses:	61: 126,718	11: 27,568	20: 50,618	37: 81,494
1–15 August 1945				
Naval shipping	1: 478	- -	- -	- -
Military shipping	- -	- -	1: 6,859	1: 9,574
Civilian shipping	5: 7,196	5: 15,441	18: 45,956	16: 26,275
Shipping losses:	6: 7,674	5: 15,441	19: 52,815	17: 35,849
Total:				
Warships	69: 314,255	31: 26,354	10: 8,529	25: 31,840
Naval shipping	10: 31,935	11: 25,008	- -	10: 16,746
Military shipping	3: 2,534	9: 39,976	6: 15,781	9: 36,957
Civilian shipping	56: 100,283	60: 144,034	71: 154,836	144: 233,767
Shipping losses:	69: 134,752	80: 209,018	77: 170,617	163: 287,469

shore-based aircraft, so long the Cinderella of the Allied effort—emerged to share center stage: the various contributors came together, in this final phase, to share the toll exacted of the enemy, and were not in competition with one another in terms of credit and standing.

But no less noteworthy are the parallel facts that, first, by this stage Japanese service shipping losses were minimal for the very simple reason that the services no longer had any real amounts of shipping in hand and, second, the declining size of merchantmen provided evidence that the merchant marine was dealing with ships that in 1941 would have been considered third-rate or worse. The merchant marine had lost its best shipping to the services in 1940–1941, and throughout the war its lost ships were consistently smaller than their service counterparts; in the war's first phase, until the end of April 1942, the average size of the lost merchantman was 4,406 tons, but by war's end the average size was less than half of that figure. Such were the main aspects of Japan's maritime defeat but for the two matters left to the next chapter.

APPENDIX 12.1.

RAW MATERIALS AND FOOD ENTERING JAPANESE PORTS BETWEEN 1940 AND 1945

	1940	1941	1942	1943	1944	1945	
Coal	7,011,000	6,459,000	6,388,000	5,181,000	2,635,000	548,000	(12.54)
Iron ore	6,073,000	6,309,000	4,700,000	4,298,000	2,153,000	341,000	(9.01)
Iron and steel	621,000	921,000	993,000	997,000	1,097,000	170,000	(43.92)
Scrap iron	2,104,000	246,000	50,000	43,000	21,000	12,000	(0.91)
Bauxite	275,000	150,000	305,000	909,000	376,000	15,500	(9.04)
Lead	100,100	86,530	10,990	24,500	16,810	4,000	(6.41)
Tin	10,500	5,500	3,880	26,800	23,500	3,600	(55.00)
Zinc	23,500	7,900	8,500	10,100	6,100	2,500	(17.07)
Phosphorite, phosphorus	710,400	396,500	342,100	236,700	89,600	23,000	(5.19)
Domomite & magnesite	409,600	506,300	468,700	437,500	287,100	65,900	(25.81)
Raw rubber	27,500	67,600	31,400	42,100	31,500	17,900	(104.42)
Salt	1,728,300	1,438,900	1,499,800	1,425,100	989,700	386,900	(35.91)
Soy bean cake	333,900	337,700	449,500	304,500	384,700	163,400	(78.51)
Soy beans	648,500	572,400	698,800	590,600	728,800	606,900	(150.14)
Rice and paddy	1,694,000	2,232,700	2,629,200	1,135,800	783,200	151,200	(14.29)
Other grains and flours	269,300	267,400	823,300	750,100	506,600	231,400	(137.85)
Total	22,039,600	20,004,430	19,402,090	16,411,880	10,129,600	2,743,200	
Average monthly level of imports	1,836,633	1,667,036	1,616,841	1,367,657	844,133	366,738	
	100	90.77	88.03	74.47	45.97	19.97	

Note: The 1945 percentage figures are calculated on the basis of imports in a period of 7.48 months being corrected to a full 12-month year and then set against the 1940 total, it being noted that the resultant 12-month 1945 figures would represent an overestimation of what Japan could have imported in the period after mid-August 1945 had the war continued until the end of the year. The abandonment of the Yellow Sea routes, and specifically the route from Darien, in June 1945 meant that in real terms Japan lost access to Manchoutikuo products, and especially food imports, after this time.

The 1945 figures given here would probably have been very close to a full year's imports, given the inability of the ports on the Sea of Japan coast to handle any substantial amount of shipping, Japan's shortage of shipping and isolation from overseas areas, and continuing Allied operations, and the percentage figures would have to be correspondingly reduced. For example, the coal import figure of 548,000 tons for 1945 represents 7.82% of the 1940 figure, the corrected 12-month figure being 879,000 tons. But given the closing of the Darien and Tsingtao routes, it is impossible to see how 331,000 tons of coal might have been imported between 15 August and 31 December 1945; whatever might have made its way to Japanese ports in this period had the war continued would have been minimal.

Source: Naval Staff History, *War with Japan*, vol. 5: *The Blockade of Japan*, appendix L, "Japanese Imports of Bulk Commodities 1940–1945," p. 154.

CHAPTER THIRTEEN

THE JAPANESE SITUATION—AND A SECOND JAPANESE DIMENSION

Invariably the story of the Japanese, the Kaigun, and convoy has been told in terms of the creation of the General Escort Command in November 1943 and the subsequent course of events, which saw the devastation of Japanese shipping even before the start of the mining of home waters that was afforded a code-name that really did symbolize intent. Yet this story has been afforded little real consideration, in large measure because the increasing effectiveness of the American campaign against shipping was quite obviously overshadowed by fleet and amphibious operations—Saipan and the Philippine Sea, Leyte Gulf and the Philippines, Iwo Jima and Okinawa—and by the manner in which the war was ended. But in terms of real cause and effect, five matters should be at the forefront of any consideration of Japanese defeat at sea, and this leaves aside the abiding paradox of the U.S. campaign against Japanese shipping: over the last six months of the war the American submarine service was very largely redundant, for the simple reason that the high seas had been scourged of Japanese shipping and there was very little left to sink.

The first and most obvious matter is the formation of the General Escort Command. This organization was established because of the increasing seriousness of losses, yet when it was activated on 15 November 1943 it had just two formations under command, the 1st and 2nd Surface Escort Divisions, the former with nine destroyers, two torpedo-boats, eight escorts, and three auxiliaries and the latter with three destroyers, two torpedo-boats, four escorts, and a single auxiliary under command. The fact that the 2nd Surface Escort Division was placed under the authority of General Escort Command by the 4th Fleet and was based with its headquarters at Truk comments on its role and contribution to trade defense. The real point, however, about the creation of this Command and the formations and units assigned to it is that the new organization was created from what was available, which was already inadequate to meet Japanese needs; it was not until the third quarter of 1944 that the General Escort Command came into possession of long-ranged escorts in numbers that began to meet requirements.[1]

A total of 112 frigates were brought into service between 1 April 1944 and 31 March 1945.[2] By that time, the second matter was in the process of unfolding: even in December 1943, with General Escort Command less than two months old, the first of its convoy routes was abandoned. The American landings in the Gilbert and Ellice Islands in November 1943 clearly pointed to a subsequent move into the Marshalls, as did the parallel Allied moves into the northern Solomons with reference to Rabaul. The Americans chose to bypass Rabaul, but in December 1943 the Japanese abandoned the convoy routes between Truk and the Marshalls and between Truk and Rabaul, a realistic move but for the fact that the fleet remained based at Truk; shipping remained unnecessarily at the atoll and was thus exposed to unprecedented losses in the U.S. carrier raid of 17–18 February 1944. But the point of real relevance is that by June 1944 the Japanese had been forced to abandon virtually all convoy routes east of the Philippines because of American operations and the threat presented by land-based aircraft. The direct route between the home islands and the Palaus had been abandoned in March 1944, the month of the U.S. carrier raid on Koror, and while July 1944 saw a reorganization of this convoy route via Manila as opposed to Formosa, the following month, August 1944, saw this route to the Palaus, and the routes from the west from Davao on Mindanao and Balikpapan on Borneo, abandoned.

The tide of American conquest into and across the western Pacific thus had the immediate effect of denying the Japanese access to direct routes between the home islands and the south, a crucial disadvantage in terms of lost time in length of voyages; This was to pale, however, alongside the resultant disadvantage of position as Japanese shipping was obliged to use the Formosa and Luzon Straits at a time when the U.S. Navy came into possession of unprecedented numbers in terms of submarines, carrier aircraft and their operations, and land-based aircraft. The American moves into the Philippines brought with them airfields from which subsequent moves within the Philippines might be supported and, more generally, shipping to the west of the archipelago could be attacked, with results that need little in the way of elaboration.

This, coming after the circumstances of General Escort Command and the loss of all routes to the east of the Philippines, constitutes the third matter: from September to October 1944 the Japanese convoy system labored under conditions of hopeless inferiority in position and numbers, not to mention that it, along with all local warships and shipping, had been stripped of the protection that should have been available from the fleet. The battle of Leyte Gulf in effect reduced the Japanese fleet to little more than coast guard status, though it is possible to argue that it had been reduced to such status and limited capability even without battle; the fleet's sortie at Leyte was the search for "a fitting place to die" and "the chance to bloom as flowers of death."[3] But the point was that a convoy system operated across oceans in the depth of a defensive system provided by outlying bases and the carrier and battle formations, and once the latter, whether individually or together, were set at nought then the lesser formations were hopelessly exposed, with an inevitable result: between September 1944 and March 1945 the General Escort Command was reduced to a state of impotent irrelevance as a result of the coming together of the various American advantages of position and numbers and the basic inadequacies—of numbers, of equipment and organization—of the Japanese shipping defense system.

The shortcomings of the Japanese convoy system at the time the General Escort Command was established—its lack of numbers of escort, the lack of trained formations, and the general material deficiencies of equipment—resulted in the fourth matter: the order that all merchantman be provided with convoy escort had the effect of imposing shipping delays that simply were not countered by adequate levels of protection. Indeed, it is possible to argue that the institution of convoy in November 1943 imposed unseemly delays on the movement of shipping and had the effect of concentrating vulnerability, a gathering of targets for U.S. submarines, without any commensurate advantage. The Japanese were spared, however, the worst consequences on this particular score at this time: the major losses after November 1943 were incurred by service shipping as the Americans broke into and through the outer defensive zone, and it was not until the third quarter of 1944, in fact in August, that merchant shipping losses assumed disastrous proportions.[4] Herein one touches base with the fifth and final matter: the Japanese inability to cover losses.

Reference has already been made to the fact that Japan simply could not built fleet, escort, and merchant shipping, and engage in routine maintenance and refitting as well as undertaking major repair, at the same time. This basic weakness was not overcome in the course of the war, and thus the Japanese building effort was dissipated across the three very different requirements, with the result that no single effort began to match requirement; at the same time the concentration of resources upon building meant a remorseless increase in shipping laid up for lack of maintenance. The Japanese situation is shown in table 13.1.

The figures seem to be misleading; with some 5,500,000 tons of liners and merchant shipping, plus 587,000 tons of oilers, nominally available on 7 December 1941, the fact that the Kaigun was assigned 160,000 tons of oilers and 1,500,000 tons of other shipping and the Rikugun 13,500 tons of oilers and 2 million tons of other shipping must mean that the greater part of shipping not in service on 31 March 1942 had to be shipping assigned to civilian authority. The total of three-

Table 13.1. Japanese Shipping, by Tonnage, in Terms of Size, Additions, Losses, and Not in Service, 1 January 1942–15 August 1945

	Total available	Captures and salvaged	Built	Total additions	Lost	Balance for year	Nominally available	Not in service	% not in service
On 31 March 1942	6,150,000						5,375,000	775,000	12.61
In 1942		566,000	266,000	832,000	1,065,000	- 233,000			
On 31 December 1942	5,942,000								
On 31 March 1943	5,733,000						4,833,000	900,000	15.70
In 1943		109,000	769,000	878,000	1,821,000	- 943,000			
On 31 December 1943	4,999,000								
On 31 March 1944	4,352,000						3,527,000	825,000	18.96
In 1944		36,000	1,699,000	1,735,000	3,892,000	- 2,157,000			
On 31 December 1944	2,842,000								
On 31 March 1945	2,465,000						1,659,000	806,000	32.69
In 1945		6,000	559,000	565,000	1,782,000	- 1,217,000			
On 15 August 1945	1,625,000						948,000	677,000	41.66
Overall totals		717,000	3,293,000	4,010,000	8,560,000	- 4,550,000			

Note: It should be noted that the figures given here are different from those given in other tables that were calculated by the author, but the various differences are minor in terms of general argument and conclusions. This comment is intended also to cover seeming discrepancies in this table--for example, the tonnage available on 31 March 1942 plus all wartime captures and salvages and new construction comes to 10,160,000 tons, whereas the sum of losses and what was available on 15 August 1945 comes to 10,185,000 tons--but such seeming discrepancies, and there are ones for every year, are explicable in terms of use of different dates. Moreover, the author would note that the Naval Staff History, on p. 121 and in that page's one footnote, gives four different tonnage figures in reference to the start of Operation Starvation in March 1945, along with service shipping totals. The detail, therefore, must be considered negotiable, but basic conclusions are clear.

Source: Naval Staff History, *War with Japan*, vol. 5: *The Blockade of Japan*, pp. 71 and 94, tables 7 (no title) and 9 ("Merchant Shipping Sunk, Captured, Built and Remaining Available"), the former taken from the U.S. Strategic Bombing Survey report, *Japanese Merchant Shipbuilding*, p. 18, and the latter unacknowledged but seeming from the same source. This table reverses the 15 August 1945 available and not in service totals, but on p. 133 gives figures that indicate the previous error.

quarters of a million tons of shipping not in service on this day represents little more than 30 percent of the 2,476,500 tons of civilian shipping that was nominally available on the basis of service requisitions, because it was not until April 1942 that the return of requisitioned shipping—by the army but not the navy—began. Be that as it may, the basic point is simplicity itself: a merchant marine that was basically unable to meet national requirements even before the outbreak of war was wholly inadequate to meet the increased responsibilities of war, while new construction was insufficient to cover losses that by war's end—and indeed perhaps two years previously—had assumed disastrous proportions. With the losses of 1944 alone being the equivalent of two-fifths of the pre-war merchant fleet and more than four times the 75,000-tons-per-month limit, while oiler losses amounted to the whole oiler fleet that had been available on 1 January,[5] Japanese shipping losses in the war as a whole amounted to 84.25 percent of all tonnage available, captured, salvaged, and built; at the end of the war just 6.66 percent of this tonnage remained in service. It was a small token of the desperation of Japan's position by 1945 that whereas in previous years there had been an appreciable conversion of merchantmen to oilers, in 1945 the position was reversed.[6] With such returns, the decline of Japanese imports, both overall but specifically in 1944 and 1945, begins to come into perspective, even though by the war's last six months the only shipping routes open to Japan were in the East China and Yellow Seas and in the end no more than the Sea of Japan; the shortness of these sea passages obviously was more than offset by the American sending of submarines into the Sea of Japan and the impact of mining of home waters.

* * *

In any consideration of the campaign against Japanese shipping certain matters command attention, and the most obvious is the formal decision, taken on 15 March 1945, by the Japanese high command to abandon the South China Sea, which was tantamount to recognition of national defeat. In fact Japanese shipping in the south had been ordered northward as early as December 1944 as a result of two considerations: the realization that shipping in the south amounted to shipping lost and the need to get as much shipping as possible working the shorter northern routes in order to provide some form of compensation for the loss of imports from the Southern Resources Area. Given that the whole rationale for the Japanese decision of war in 1941 lay in this region's crucial importance to Japan, the tacit abandonment of the Southern Resources Area, and specifically the future loss of oil imports, pointed to inevitable defeat; throughout the war oil imports were never more than half the national average between 1931 and 1941, and reserves within Japan that had amounted to 20 million barrels in December 1941 had been reduced to just 200,000 barrels in March 1945.[7]

For Japan the basic problem was not so much the threat from submarines but

Table 13.2. Japanese Losses in the Southern Resources Area, 1 November 1943–31 March 1945

	November 1943	December 1943	January 1944	February 1944	March 1944	April 1944	May 1944	June 1944	July 1944	August 1944
Central Pacific submarines	- -	1: 820	- -	1: 1,215	- -	- -	2: 1,962	1: 940	1: 2,198	4: 8,004
	- -	- -	1: 2,205	1: 10,526	2: 13,498	- -	1: 10,090	2: 5,000	1: 4,471	1: 2,110
	- -	- -	1: 4,092	4: 13,772	1: 5,399	2: 8,991	3: 19,705	1: 7,006	5: 36,631	1: 9,589
	1: 3,177	2: 18,784	2: 8,226	7: 30,821	2: 11,188	2: 5,530	5: 30,542	- -	3: 17,982	5: 28,252
Other submarines	1: 820	- -	2: 5,456	- -	1: 560	1: 2,077	4: 6,271	6: 12,522	8: 16,249	11: 25,690
	- -	4: 19,525	3: 15,140	1: 7,358	1: 10,536	- -	6: 40,226	5: 29,088	4: 20,639	7: 74,573
	5: 30,974	- -	1.5: 9,730	4: 24,371	4: 15,614	4: 14,829	6: 29,354	8: 38,227	7: 40,055	3: 13,136
	3: 17,319	- -	5.5: 25,314	1: 6,200	1: 5,174	3: 2,515	1: 5,050	4: 19,904	6: 25,927	9: 44,612
Carrier- based aircraft	- -	- -	- -	- -	- -	- -	3: 1,235	- -	- -	- -
	- -	- -	- -	- -	- -	- -	1: 993	- -	- -	- -
	- -	- -	- -	- -	1: 575	- -	- -	- -	- -	- -
	- -	- -	- -	- -	- -	- -	- -	- -	- -	- -
Land-based aircraft	1: 525	- -	1: 128	1: 2,531	- -	- -	- -	1: 950	1: 215	- -
	- -	- -	2: 3,714	- -	- -	2: 9,649	- -	- -	2: 5,551	1: 6,659
	2: 1,256	2: 8,303	1: 2,790	1: 377	- -	1: 7,190	1: 3,192	- -	1: 519	7: 7,659
	3: 15,593	3: 8,894	- -	2: 5,104	- -	1: 5,255	1: 2,745	- -	- -	2: 1,345
Warships	- -	- -	- -	- -	- -	- -	- -	- -	- -	- -
	- -	- -	- -	- -	- -	- -	- -	- -	- -	- -
	- -	- -	- -	- -	- -	- -	- -	- -	- -	- -
	- -	- -	- -	- -	- -	- -	- -	- -	- -	- -

Mines	- -	- -	- -	- -	- -	1: 2,090	- -	- -	- -	- -
	- -	- -	- -	- -	- -	- -	- -	- -	- -	- -
	- -	- -	1: 2,197	- -	- -	- -	- -	- -	- -	- -
	- -	- -	1: 1,311	- -	1: 5,457	- -	- -	- -	1: 3,098	1: 1,018
Natural causes	- -	- -	- -	- -	- -	- -	- -	1: 1,685	1: 2,288	- -
	- -	- -	1: 5,135	- -	- -	- -	- -	- -	- -	- -
	- -	- -	- -	- -	- -	- -	- -	- -	1: 2,893	- -
	- -	1: 658	- -	- -	- -	- -	- -	1: 2,670	- -	1: 6,000
Unknown causes	- -	- -	- -	- -	- -	- -	- -	- -	- -	- -
	- -	- -	- -	- -	- -	- -	- -	1: 5,141	- -	- -
	1: 2,841	- -	- -	- -	- -	- -	- -	1: 3,028	- -	1: 238
	- -	- -	- -	- -	- -	1: 450	2: 3,339	1: 5,135	1: 853	4: 19,241
Other causes	- -	- -	- -	- -	- -	- -	- -	- -	- -	- -
	- -	- -	- -	- -	- -	- -	- -	- -	- -	- -
	- -	- -	- -	- -	- -	- -	- -	- -	- -	- -
	- -	- -	- -	- -	- -	- -	- -	- -	- -	- -
Warships	2: 1,345	1: 820	3: 5,584	2: 3,746	1: 560	2: 4,167	9: 1,365	9: 16,097	11: 20,950	15: 33,694
Naval shipping	- -	4: 19,525	7: 26,194	2: 17,884	3: 24,034	2: 9,649	8: 51,309	8: 39,229	7: 30,661	9: 83,342
Military shipping	8: 35,071	2: 8,303	4.5: 18,809	9: 38,520	6: 21,588	7: 31,010	10: 52,251	10: 48,261	14: 80,098	12: 30,622
Merchantmen	7: 36,089	6: 28,336	8.5: 34,851	10: 42,125	4: 21,819	7: 13,750	9: 41,676	6: 27,709	11: 47,860	22: 100,468
Overall shipping	15: 71,160	12: 56,164	20: 79,854	21: 98,529	13: 67,541	16: 54,409	27: 145,236	24: 115,199	32: 158,619	43: 214,432

	September 1944	October 1944	November 1944	December 1944	January 1945	February 1945	March 1945	Overall losses in this period	Overall losses in % terms	Losses in the East China Sea
Central Pacific submarines	3: 20,790	1.5 3,295	3: 2,813	5: 4,750	- -	2: 1,050	- -	24.50: 47,837	8.81 7.23	16: 66,300
	6: 32,790	5: 32,283	7.5 42,577	- -	1.5 9,215	- -	- -	29: 164,015	21.32 22.13	9.50: 49,287
	3: 17,071	2: 12,840	1: 5,271	1: 5,463	- -	- -	- -	25: 145,830	14.41 19.24	17: 68,487
	6: 36,234	12: 67,930	2: 8,466	3.5 20,848	1.5 10,413	- -	- -	54: 298,393	18.85 26.83	34.50: 168,971
Other submarines	3: 7,557	3: 29,130	6: 20,066	5: 18,745	4: 4,285	5: 4,580	4: 5,023	64: 159,031	23.02 24.04	- -
	2: 5,447	7: 31,678	6: 34,094	3: 19,886	2: 10,954	- -	3: 13,279	54: 332,423	39.71 44.85	- -
	1: 6,374	10: 47,712	2: 7,614	1: 9,486	- -	- -	1: 5,518	57.50: 292,994	33.14 38.65	- -
	4: 9,894	10: 59,100	8: 36,433	4: 26,573	- -	8: 41,816	5: 8,464	72.50: 334,295	25.31 30.06	1: 2,345
Carrier-based aircraft	19: 10,887	26: 191,451	26: 54,932	3: 2,110	26: 32,247	- -	3: 390	106: 293,252	38.13 44.32	22: 10,999
	13: 56,677	2: 10,244	2: 8,027	- -	8.5 47,910	- -	- -	26.50: 123,851	19.48 16.71	9: 24,082
	18: 80,409	4: 16,402	7: 28,066	- -	6: 36,830	- -	- -	35: 161,707	20.17 21.33	12: 37,256
	21: 61,434	5: 10,791	10: 44,514	1.5 10,259	37: 131,949	- -	- -	74.50: 258,947	26.00 23.28	30: 60,367
Land-based aircraft	2: 986	0.5 2,585	6: 3,949	8.5 8,703	5: 3,738	3: 1,790	12: 5,832	42: 31,932	15.11 4.83	2: 1,220
	2: 4,160	1: 6,584	4.5: 26,994	- -	1: 1,514	1: 15,450	3: 5,205	19.50: 85,480	14.34 11.53	3: 6,377
	5: 12,118	2: 2,979	5: 27,349	7: 33,038	1: 889	2: 1,498	2: 511	41: 110,243	23.63 14.54	1: 6,385
	1: 119	9: 16,244	1: 7,542	3: 4,127	2.5 7,111	1: 834	7: 14,476	36.50: 89,469	12.74 8.04	4: 4,812
Warships	- -	12: 107,074	2: 1,620	2.5 3,616	3: 2,132	1: 960	- -	20.50: 115,402	7.37 17.44	- -
	- -	- -	- -	- -	- -	- -	- -	- -	- -	- -
	- -	- -	- -	- -	- -	- -	- -	- -	- -	- -
	- -	- -	- -	- -	- -	- -	- -	- -	- -	- -
Mines	- -	- -	- -	- -	1: 340	1: 745	- -	3: 3,175	1.08 0.48	- -
	- -	- -	1: 1,320	- -	- -	1: 1,339	1: 20,000	3: 22,659	2.21 3.06	- -
	- -	1: 2,700	- -	- -	1: 9,574	- -	- -	3: 14,471	1.73 1.91	1: 3,120
	3: 10,073	4: 10,794	- -	- -	2: 7,798	2: 12,903	1: 5,135	16: 57,587	5.58 5.18	2: 10,703

Natural causes	1: 130	1: 130	1: 950	- -	- -	- -	- -	5: 5,183	1.80	0.78	1: 950
	- -	- -	- -	- -	- -	- -	- -	1: 5,135	0.74	0.69	1: 6,530
	- -	- -	- -	- -	- -	- -	- -	1: 2,893	0.58	0.38	1: 495
	1: 834	1: 2,854	1: 3,710	3: 8,962	- -	- -	- -	9: 25,688	3.14	2.31	1: 5,342
Natural causes	6: 2,432	1: 2,198	2: 376	1: 103	- -	- -	- -	10: 5,109	3.60	0.77	2: 440
	- -	- -	1: 277	1: 2,204	- -	- -	- -	3: 7,622	2.21	1.03	1: 223
	1: 6,382	1: 2,158	3: 7,456	2: 2,547	- -	- -	1: 5,239	11: 29,889	6.34	3.94	2.50: 8,676
	3: 3,483	1: 834	1: 834	5: 4,189	1: 834	4: 8,643	- -	24: 47,835	8.38	4.30	2.50: 6,219
Unknown causes	- -	- -	1: 195	- -	2: 486	- -	- -	3: 681	1.08	0.10	- -
	- -	- -	- -	- -	- -	- -	- -	- -	-	-	- -
	- -	- -	- -	- -	- -	- -	- -	- -	-	-	- -
	- -	- -	- -	- -	- -	- -	- -	- -	-	-	- -
Warships	34: 42,782	45: 338,193	47: 84,901	25: 38,027	41: 43,228	12: 9,125	19: 11,245	278: 661,602	-	-	43: 79,909
Naval shipping	23: 98,324	15: 80,789	22: 113,289	4: 22,090	13: 69,593	2: 16,789	7: 38,464	136: 741,185	22.82	28.38	23.50: 86,499
Military shipping	28: 122,354	20: 84,791	18: 75,756	11: 50,534	8: 47,293	2: 1,498	4: 11,268	173.50 758,027	29.11	29.03	34.50: 124,419
Merchantmen	39: 122,151	42: 168,547	23: 101,499	20: 74,958	44: 158,105	15: 64,196	13: 28,075	286.50 1,112,214	48.07	42.59	75: 258,759
Overall shipping	90: 342,829	77: 334,127	63: 290,544	35: 147,582	65: 274,991	19: 82,483	24: 77,807	596: 2,611,426	-	-	133 469,677
						Losses per month:	Warships	16.35 38,918			9.60: 17,837
							Naval shipping	8.00 43,599			5.25: 19,308
							Military shipping	10.21 44,590			7.70: 27,772
							Merchantmen	16.85 65,424			16.74: 57,759
							Shipping overall	35.06 153,613			29.69: 104,839

from U.S. land-based aircraft. In December 1944 the General Escort Command had fifty-five long-range escorts available for the convoying of shipping from the south, and by March 1945 this total had risen to seventy-five, but with the Americans established in the Philippines there was no way that the Japanese could counter the scale and intensity of attacks on the part of U.S. aircraft on Luzon. The Japanese by this time had but one escort carrier and were obliged to use light carriers in the escort role, but the Japanese lacked aircraft numbers and quality aircrew in bases in China and on Formosa that could provide effective cover for oil convoys; in the first quarter of 1945 the Japanese were obliged to resort to two expediencies in an attempt to get oilers to the north. Japanese shipping made increased use of Chinese coastal waters and did not sail in hours of darkness in an attempt to counter the submarine threat, but this did not alter the fact that the voyage north then had to be resumed in hours of daylight. To meet the American air threat, the Japanese resorted to convoys of just three oilers, each heavily armed with anti-aircraft guns. Such measures were of little avail, and after the battleships *Hyuga* and *Ise* returned to Japanese waters in February 1945[8] the lack of oil imports meant that by summer Japan was gripped by increasingly serious shortages of aviation fuel and oil for shipping still working the Manchoutikuo trade. Such was Japan's desperate state with reference to oil that by June 1945, and in spite of the increasingly serious shortage of basic foods for a malnourished population, sweet potatoes and apples were being used to produce aircraft fuel and sugar and vegetables were being used as lubricants.

In effect, the route between Japan and the southern islands was closed to the Japanese even before Okinawa was subjected to assault, and while the final factor in Japan's decision to abandon this route was the American air supremacy over the Luzon and Formosa Straits, it was the combination of the attrition that had been registered by U.S. submarines in the southern seas, the immediacy of American carrier operations in the South China Sea in January 1945, the constancy of short-range strikes by U.S. aircraft in the restricted waters of the straits, and the need to concentrate shipping in the north that together made for the Japanese decision. What is perhaps the most surprising of these four is the losses that were sustained as a result of the operations of American submarines, in light of the twin facts that in 1943 the Americans were sorely pressed to keep eight submarines on station in southern waters at any one time and that in 1944 the priority afforded fleet and amphibious operations meant that the submarines really were not able to undertake serious large-scale and sustained operation against merchantman until the second half of the year.

These figures are interesting on a number of counts, not least the fact that even allowing for a "quiet time," between November 1943 and April 1944, losses per month in the whole of this period, between the formation of General Escort Command and the abandonment of convoys to and from the south, were twice the 75,000-ton limit, while the scale of Japanese losses in the East China Sea in this same period was substantial. The figures provide some sense of proportion with reference to the foray on the part of the U.S. carrier formation into the South China Sea during January 1945, the sinkings of service and merchant shipping that carrier aircraft registered in this episode being roughly twice the total recorded by any single agency of destruction over the previous fourteen months but corrective need be applied lest the figures lend themselves to misinterpretation. The sinkings registered by submarines operating from bases other than in the central Pacific were very considerably greater than those by submarines operating from bases in the central Pacific, but the sinkings of shipping (warships excluded) in the Southern Resources Area on the part of these "other" submarines consisted 80.35 percent of the ships and 85.14 percent of the tonnage of all their sinkings; the corresponding figures were 27.97 and 33.78 percent of the sinkings by the central Pacific submarines. The much wider commitment of the submarines operating from central Pacific bases compared to other submarines, most of which were operating from Australian bases with "direct" access to the Southern Resources Area, accounts for the marked differences of returns in terms of proportion, but the statistics present at least two other interesting points. The first is that the losses that Japan incurred and that brought it to the reality of defeat were really not that much greater than the Allies incurred in 1942, and were less than those incurred between September 1939 and December 1941. The second is the minimal cost incurred by the Americans in terms of submarine losses. All but incomprehensible are such assertions as that the Japanese establishment of General Escort Command and introduction of convoy "soon took effect. Already in the spring of 1944 (the commander of submarines based on Australia) was beginning to worry about the increasing tempo of Japanese anti-submarine measures that were costing a disturbing number of boats,"[9] because in the first five months of 1944 a total of just five U.S. submarines were lost. The number of American boats lost were one that was scuttled in 1941, seven in 1942, seventeen in 1943, nineteen in 1944, and eight in 1945, the overall total thus being fifty-two submarines lost to all causes in the course of the war. Of the 1942 losses one boat was lost as a result of an accident in the Caribbean, three were lost as a result of running aground, and one was lost to cause unknown; of the 1943 losses two were lost in the Caribbean and seven to causes unknown; of the 1944 losses two torpedoed themselves and not one another, one was lost during a training exercise, another was sunk by an American warship off the Philippines, and six were lost to causes unknown; and of the 1945 losses four were lost to cause unknown; when the *Pickerel* was lost in April 1943 it was the first boat operating from Pearl Harbor to have been lost in sixteen months.[10] All forms of Japanese action are known to have accounted for just twenty-four U.S. submarines,[11] and even if this total must be increased in terms of operational losses and "probable cause of loss," the fact remains that the total American submarine losses in the war as a whole was not that much greater than the losses sustained by the U-boat arm in May 1943. Just what in spring 1944 constituted losses of disturbing proportions is far from obvious, but what is very obvious is the very marked ineffectiveness of all forms of Japanese anti-submarine operations—one U.S. submarine a month—and the minimal cost of victory for the United States. Japan in the Second World War could have been defeated either by a campaign involving fleet and amphibious operations that did not account for a single merchantman or by a campaign against shipping that did not account for a single warship, but the war, being a total war, was witness to both campaigns and Japan's defeat registered on both counts; it is possible to then draw the obvious conclusion: the fifth most powerful state in the world was defeated at a cost of forty-eight submarines.[12] This argument cannot be substantiated, but it would seem to be endowed with at least some element of accuracy and relevance and most certainly is more than a clever comment of no real value: the basic point is that Japan was defeated both in a remarkably short time and at very low cost, at least in terms of the Pacific war and the United States though not in terms of east and southeast Asia.

* * *

Three observations should be made here about the campaign against Japanese shipping. The first is to question U.S. conduct in terms of freedom of the seas, which had been so important to it in 1917 and 1941: quite clearly its embrace of this principle was exclusive and denied enemies. This point, which may be a cheap shot, seems to be at the heart of the second point, namely, what was undoubtedly a somewhat indifferent conduct of the campaign against shipping, though not necessarily along the lines of one comment:

> [T]he main reason for the submarine failure of 1942 was not simply mechanical, physical or psychological. [*sic*] [There] was, to put it simply, a failure of imagination [at] the highest levels [of the U.S. naval command that] failed to set up a broad, unified strategy for Pacific submarines aimed at a single specific goal: interdicting Japanese shipping services in the most efficient and telling manner. The lessons of the German U-boat campaigns against Britain in World Wars I and II—the latter in progress almost on Washington's doorstep—had apparently not yet sunk home. The military and maritime theories of Clausewicz [*sic*] and Mahan were ignored. The U.S. submarine force was divided and shunted about willy-nilly on missions for which it was not suited, and the bulk of Japanese shipping sailed unmolested in Empire waters and through the bottleneck in Luzon Strait.[13]

Such blunt criticism of the American naval command's conduct of operations in the Second World War is somewhat unusual. It invites two comments: that it is difficult to discern to which theories of Clausewitz and Mahan this writer refers that were applicable to the conduct of a war against commerce in the Pacific in 1942, and that certainly in the first seven months of the war relatively little Japanese shipping used Luzon Strait, for the very simple reason that the resumption of Japan's trade with the Southern Resources Area had to await the latter's conquest. But even leaving aside the obvious point that if any lesson was to be drawn from the German campaign against Allied shipping in the First World War, it was the difficulty of defeating a maritime nation by a *guerre de course*, such sweeping and powerful criticism is, by any standard, much overdrawn, and on two main counts.

First, and less relevantly, though it cannot be denied that concentration of U.S. submarine operations in the Formosa Strait and East China Sea would certainly have resulted in more sinkings of Japanese ships both in these sea areas and in overall terms, the difference between what was sunk under the American policy and what might have been sunk under ideal conditions hardly means that failure to so direct U.S. submarine efforts to the western Pacific represented the main reason for the alleged failure of this effort overall. If every U.S. Pacific Fleet boat had been directed to the East China Sea and the Formosa Strait, if each of these boats had sunk one Japanese merchantman per mission, and trading off the effect of the Midway deployment against a lower tempo of operations thereafter as a result, then perhaps thirty more Japanese ships would have been sunk by U.S. submarines than was the case between December 1941 and May 1942. Assuming the return of October 1942 to be the return that might have been expected in any given month, then the difference between reality and ideal amounted to perhaps three figures. Such losses would indeed have been serious, but even if those boats that found their way to Australia are added to the lists, the argument is hardly overwhelming. Second, and of infinitely greater importance, neither any service nor any single branch of a service can enjoy an independence that permits it to conduct operations without reference to an overall national requirement. In the first thirteen months of the Pacific war that American national requirement was, within the limits set down in consultation with allies that stressed the primary importance of the European war, to check the tide of Japanese conquest. In the first phase of the Pacific war the U.S. Navy found itself obliged to fight where it was rather than where it would, and if and when, in the months that followed its victories in the Coral Sea and off Midway, it found itself involved in a campaign of its own choice in the southwest Pacific, then its submarines had to conform to that fact of life. The contribution of the U.S. submarine force to the victories that were recorded off Midway and in the Solomons was slight: its returns never justified the effort that it made in either theater. The odds against the submarine force achieving significant results in making its efforts in both theaters were considerable, and known to be so, but it would have availed the U.S. war effort little in moral and immediate practical terms if Midway and the Solomons campaign had been lost whilst the submarine force directed its attentions elsewhere. This particular argument, however, can be countered with the general one that opened this work, and it is the contradiction of interpretation therein that makes the recounting of this war and the relative assessment of the elements that made up Japanese defeat so difficult: had the U.S. submarine force been directed to the western Pacific in strength throughout the first two phases of the war and had it exacted perhaps three times the toll than was the actual case, then in the long term any victory that the Japanese won in the central and southwest Pacific would have availed them nothing. Perhaps the only conclusion that may be drawn with any certainty from these tangled matters is the difficulty that attends the formulation of policy. One suspects that in the writing of history there is a tendency to assume a certain ease in terms of the definition of policy at the highest level of command, a simplicity in terms of the definition of aim and means, which is seldom, if ever, the case.

* * *

Before the outbreak of hostilities the U.S. Navy's main interest in submarine warfare was with fleet operations. Like the Imperial Navy, it saw the main tasks of submarines as scouting and attacks on enemy task forces, and, indeed, given the declared inter-war policy of the United States not to engage in unrestricted submarine warfare against shipping, the submarines could have no other tasks. Naturally, in setting about these tasks, the submarine's target priorities were major fleet units: attacks upon large merchantmen, such as fleet oilers, did not figure highly in American calculations, and such targets were allocated a single torpedo. A single-torpedo allowance was, by definition, a wholly inadequate provision to set against human errors of estimation of size, speed, and course of a target needed for computed settings and against the limitations of the torpedo itself, and certainly was insufficient investment for attacks on large, well-built merchantmen. Moreover, inter-war exercises against friendly forces and the development of aircraft and sonar had instilled into American submarine forces a very considerable caution, and for good reason.

The result, however, was a doctrine that called for submarines to remain submerged during daylight hours in waters where enemy air activity was likely and for the most sparing use of the periscope, and that allowed for attacks, at depth, on the basis of sound location, the reduction of accuracy of such attacks being accepted as the price to be paid for the increased chances of survival of the submarine.[14] Before the outbreak of war, and despite what was happening in the Battle of the Atlantic, the U.S. Navy gave very little consideration either to the requirements of a campaign against Japanese shipping or to alternative forms of attack, most obviously night surface attack and the use of wolf-pack tactics. The scale of protection afforded their merchantmen by the Japanese in fact did away with the need for the latter before the end of

1943; with respect to the former, American submarines, only twenty-nine of which had carried out a night firing practice before the war,[15] proved fast learners. The first night surface attack was conducted by the *Pollack* on 5 January 1942, and the first such successful attack was recorded by the same submarine on the 9th.[16] In the opening phase of the war, however, the majority of submarine commanders, some of whom found their careers blighted as a result, chose to follow established orthodoxy and to conduct submerged night attacks—with night periscopes that were inadequate to the task—after having tracked and moved ahead of the target on the surface. When combined with the deficiencies of their torpedoes, the use of such tactics produced suitably unfortunate results.

In terms of the war in which its submarines found themselves involved after 7 December 1941, therefore, the American campaign against Japanese shipping was flawed in matters of numbers, equipment, and doctrine. It was not until the third quarter of 1943 that most weaknesses were remedied, the completion of the process being marked by the trackless Mark XVIII torpedo entering service in October.[17] But matters of doctrine, and the lack of a systematic study of what a campaign against Japanese shipping would involve, compounded weakness of submarine numbers in limiting the campaign against shipping in one aspect of the conduct of operations. Discounting the returns of May 1942, when preparations for the defense of Midway distorted American deployment figures, before October 1942 monthly submarine sailings from Pearl Harbor entered doubled figures only in April and in July. There were ten sailings of fleet boats in each of the last three months of 1942 and in February and March 1943, but it was not until June 1943 that the number of monthly sailings from Pearl Harbor exceeded twenty, and it was not until September 1943 that the number of submarines at Pearl Harbor allowed monthly sailings to be sustained at that level. In the first two years of war, therefore, the number of Pearl Harbor sailings was hardly sufficient to sustain a serious campaign against Japanese shipping, and American weakness, in terms of numbers and timing, was at its most acute in this opening phase of hostilities. Moreover, in 1942 doctrine, in the form of the dispatch of boats to the Marianas, Marshalls, and Carolines, reduced by almost one-half the number of boats that could be committed to the East China Sea and Japanese home waters. Excluding the seventeen war patrols mounted in defense of the Hawaiian Islands in May and June 1942,[18] Pearl Harbor in 1942 was witness to ninety-six submarine sailings, of which twenty-one were directed to the central Pacific island groups and twenty-four to Australia via the same. The number of war patrols in Empire waters in 1942 totaled thirty-one, of which twenty were in the second half of the year, whilst eighteen war patrols were mounted in the East China Sea, eleven in the first half of 1942.

Statistical analysis, ordeal by data, could be used to sustain any number of arguments, most of them somewhat dubious, concerning American submarine performance in this first phase of war; the most reasonable and pertinent conclusion that might be drawn would be that the figures could be used to show the slowness with which the campaign against Japanese shipping gathered momentum. An equally reasonable and pertinent conclusion would be that Japanese losses, with seventeen of the thirty-seven warships and thirty-one of the fifty-eight auxiliaries and merchantmen sunk in first-phase operations lost in the Southern Resources Area, reflected Japanese military commitments, or, conversely, that sinkings by the Allies were reactive and tactical rather than deliberate and strategic. But despite the fact that definitive judgment is difficult given that sinkings in this opening phase of hostilities were so few, two further conclusions, both reluctant and tentative, present themselves. First, there seems to be a direct correlation between submarine sailings and merchantmen sinkings: the rate of sinking by fleet boats from the U.S. Pacific Fleet followed, with a delay of a month to represent length of passage to war stations, the sailings of the previous month. In the first phase of the war, between December 1941 and April 1942, the U.S. Pacific Fleet committed just over half of its thirty-four war patrols to the East China Sea (ten) and Japanese home waters (eight). In January 1942, when six boats sailed from Pearl Harbor, the *I. 173*, one auxiliary, and two Japanese merchantmen were sunk by Pacific Fleet submarines. In February, when seven boats sailed, sinkings by Pacific Fleet boats totaled one merchantmen and two converted warships. In March, when sailings fell to their lowest point, with just four boats dispatched, three Japanese auxiliaries and two merchantmen were destroyed. In April sinkings followed the decline of March sailings, with boats from the Pacific Fleet accounting for just two merchantmen, but in May, after double-figure sailings from Pearl Harbor in April, sinkings by Pacific Fleet submarines also entered double figures for the first time in the war. The significance of the relationship between sinkings and sailings lies in the fact that Japanese losses in May were not related to the withdrawal of forces in readiness for operations in the central and northern Pacific. It was not a case, as happened in November 1942 in the North Atlantic, when Allied shipping losses reached grievous proportions as a direct result of the withdrawal of escorts in September and October in readiness for the invasion of French North Africa, of losses being directly related to the scale of escort provided. The lack of escorted Japanese shipping at this stage of the war meant that the withdrawal of Japanese naval forces for the Midway and Aleutian ventures did not affect losses one way or another. Though it cannot be denied that in May 1942, with the end of first-phase operations, there were more, and less well-protected, Japanese auxiliaries and merchantmen at sea than hitherto, Japanese losses appear to be related directly to the number of American boats at sea rather than the scale of protection afforded. And that basic point seems to apply not just in the war's opening phase but over its whole duration.

* * *

Quite clearly the American submarine offensive was flawed on a number of counts in the first and second years of the Pacific war, but its various defects were not strategically of major importance and were in any case resolved once the United States had acquired for itself time in which to seek to fight the war in which it found itself on its terms of reference. And in this matter the contrast with Japan is obvious: the U.S. Navy managed to get not a few things wrong but nonetheless came through more or less intact and possessed of choice in terms of how the war in the Pacific was to be conducted, but the conduct of the defense of shipping was but one of a whole number of matters on which the Imperial Navy erred and never had the opportunity to rectify its various sins of omission and commission. Of all the other matters, provision of adequate anti-mine defensive measures proved very important in the war's last six months, because it was in this period that the Americans conducted a mining of Japanese home waters that, combined with such episodes as the submarine foray into the Sea of Japan in June 1945,[19] was so important in what amounted to a collapse of Japanese trade by summer 1945.

* * *

A mining campaign was first discussed within the American high command as early as 1942, and for obvious reason: the mines that would be used would be those of the U.S. Navy, whereas the most effective means of delivery—with a load of a dozen 1,000-lb. mines—would be Army Air Force heavy bombers, and specifically the B-29 Superfortress then under development. The main impetus for the mining campaign was provided by a U.S. Navy that saw the close blockade of the Japanese home island as the means to complete the defeat of Japan without a series of invasions of, and what threatened to be a difficult campaign on, the home islands; in this matter it was supported by the A.A.F., for the same reason but on condition that its own strategic bombing campaign was not materially affected by the diversion of its bombers to this task. In the event something like 5.7 percent of its heavy bomber missions were involved in Operation Starvation.

Four points must be addressed here. First, the immediate impetus for Operation Starvation was directly related to amphibious operations in the sense that the U.S. Navy sought to close the Shimonoseki passage at the time of the landings on Okinawa, and for obvious reason: if the strait was closed then any Japanese fleet sortie would have to come through either the Kii or the Bungo Channel, and these were under effective American surveillance, whereas the strait was not.[20]

Second, Operation Starvation was not the first mining undertaking on the part of the Allies, and over the previous three years there had been extensive

TABLE 13.3. MERCHANT SHIPPING TONNAGE USING THE SHIMONOSEKI STRAIT, 1 MARCH–14 AUGUST 1945

	Tonnage	Tonnage as % of April returns	Change from previous month	Merchant ships lost to mines
March 1945	796,200	92.01	-	-
April 1945	865,300	100	+ 8.68	11
May 1945	512,600	59.24	- 40.76	36
June 1945	208,500	24.10	- 59.68	42
July 1945	165,300	19.10	- 20.75	37
1–14 August 1945	30,900	7.91	- 58.61	2

Note: The 1–14 August percentage figures have been calculated on the basis of a full calendar (31-day) month.

Source: Naval Staff History, *War with Japan*, vol. 5, p. 126. This source also gives the May 1945 tonnage as 486,500 tons (p. 128).

mining of the outer zone. The first mine-laying operation by Allied aircraft was in February 1942, though this was minor and of no real consequence; it was not until February 1943 that there was the first serious air-laid mining, the first mine-laying by American submarines having been undertaken in the previous October. The mining in the outer zone was ended in May 1945, by which time aircraft had laid a total of 9,254 mines and thirty-three operations by submarines had laid more than 4,000 mines, a total of 140 harbors having been mined. These efforts were notable for the fact that nearly half of the mines laid by aircraft were in the India-Burma theater, which included the Gulf of Siam, and between January and March 1945, before the start of Operation Starvation, American bombers closed the approaches to Singapore, Saigon, and Camranh Bay by the use of magnetic mines.[21] No less interesting was the mining of the Palaus undertaken ahead of the carrier strike on shipping on 30 March 1944, the American intention being to trap shipping at Koror; American carrier aircraft accounted for thirteen minor warships and 128,817 tons of service and merchant shipping. Mines did not account for a single ship until 9 April, but the mining of Koror, which remained closed for twenty days after the American operation, was clearly one important factor in the subsequent Japanese decision to abandon the harbor as a base and to hold the fleet at Tawi Tawi in the Sulu archipelago.[22]

Third, Operation Starvation saw an undertaking that in nineteen weeks laid almost as many mines as had been laid by aircraft and submarines in the previous twenty-nine months, a total of forty harbors being deliberately selected for appropriate attention. The major point of difference, however, lay in the fact that with Operation Starvation the Americans were able to concentrate much of their attention on the Shimonoseki Strait, which Japanese shipping was obliged to negotiate, and the harbors on the Inland Sea. Something like 1,750,000 tons of shipping entered various Japanese ports in March 1945, and a goodly proportion of this must have been recorded as a result of shipping entering more than one port, but the basic point is that the American effort resulted in what must have been a disastrous decline of shipping obliged to use a strait that in places was less than 400 yards wide. (See table 13.3.)

Such was the extent of the disruption and losses caused by the American mining effort that by June 1945, which was the first month in which the two services released requisitioned shipping to trade after the formation of a single shipping authority in April, the Japanese had abandoned sailings direct from Manchoutikuo and the Yellow Sea and had chosen to concentrate shipping in the ports of east-coast Korea, with goods from Manchoutikuo sent forward by rail. The problem herein was that with the mining of the strait the diversion of shipping to the ports on the Sea of Japan was of little use because these ports were small, with limited handling capacity, and the rail lines between these ports and the main areas of population on the east coast were few, of limited utility, and, by war's end, three-quarters destroyed as a result of bombing.

Fourth, a certain care is needed in assessing effectiveness because this campaign lends itself to presentation as the cap on the submarine and air campaigns against Japanese shipping, the climax of the naval war against Japan. Undoubtedly this was indeed the case, not so much because of the fact that in the course of this operation the American mines accounted for more than twice the number of ships that had been sunk by mines to date,[23] but because for the Japanese the mining campaign undoubtedly "administered a knock-out blow to their already seriously weakened merchant marine."[24] But the real point is that the naval effort and Operation Starvation sat alongside a strategic bombing campaign that resulted in 43.46 percent of sixty-three major Japanese cities being laid waste and almost the same amount of Japan's industrial capacity had been destroyed; more than 22 million people had been killed, injured, or rendered homeless, the high—or low—point of this particular effort being the Tokyo fire raid of 9–10 March 1945, which left 124,711 killed and 1,008,005 homeless.[25] The use of atomic weapons against Hiroshima and Nagasaki, and the raids on eight other Japanese cities between 6 and 14 August, were probably surplus to requirements, but Operation Starvation and the climax of a naval war must be seen alongside the other parts of an effort on the part of the United Nations, not one single nation, that came together at this time.

* * *

In very large measure the effectiveness of Operation Starvation stemmed from a combination of four major factors, of which the peculiar vulnerability of shipping in the strait and Inland Sea has been noted. But equally important was the fact that mine warfare had never been a Kaigun priority before the war, and the relatively slow pace of Allied mining in 1942 and 1943 meant that by 1944 the Imperial Navy was ill-placed to undertake any major counter-mining effort; it was wholly unprepared for the commitment in home waters that was to be imposed upon it after March 1945,[26] and this was compounded by the third factor, the diversity of the American effort. The Americans did not use contact mines in the course of this operation, but no fewer than five different other types of mine—primarily magnetic, acoustic, and pressure mines—and by use of various combinations, including dead periods, ultimately employed two hundred different combinations, which made effective minesweeping all but impossible and continued to provide problems even after Japan's surrender. But—the fourth and last point—while the Japanese were unable to cope with the threat presented by the very diversity of mine types employed by the Americans, it was the scale of mining operations rather than the different types of mine that were used that overwhelmed the Japanese defensive system,[27] with the result that Japanese shipping, already by March 1945 reduced to a level insufficient to meet requirements placed upon it, was very rapidly reduced to a level below that needed not simply to continue the war but to maintain society and industry.[28]

* * *

Operation Starvation began on the night of 27–28 March when ninety-seven B-29 Superfortresses laid 629 mines in the Shimonoseki Strait, the whole of the subsequent effort being made by 20th Air Force heavy bombers, operating from Tinian, other than the mining in June of the waters of southwest Korea by PB4Y Privateer patrol aircraft based on Okinawa.[29] A second such operation was conducted on the night of 30–31 March and was followed by the mining of Kure and Hiroshima in the first three nights of April. The scale of the subsequent mining effort to 2 May was decidedly modest, the first two operations roughly accounting for two-thirds of all sorties and half the mines laid between 27 March and 2 May, but the American operations found the Japanese unprepared and in no position to put together an effective defense of shipping. Indeed, such was the congestion in ports as a result of American mining that the Japanese were obliged to order shipping through the uncleared strait, evidently lottery tickets having been issued to ships and crews. In the next phase, in the first half of May, the mining of the strait was continued, ports on the Inland Sea were mined, and also mined were Nagoya and Yokosuka, Yokohama and Tokyo; but thereafter, with pressure mines becoming available for the first time, the Americans deliberately opted for small-scale mining operations conducted as frequently as possible rather than large-scale but infrequent operations. In July, and as a result of observation of Japanese shipping movements, the Americans basically stopped the mining of ports in favor of addi-

TABLE 13.4. SHIPPING IN KOBE AND OSAKA, MAY–AUGUST 1945

	Kobe				Osaka			
	Arrivals		Sailings		Arrivals		Sailings	
May 1945	60	–	54	–	109	–	77	–
June 1945	21	35.00	11	20.37	29	26.61	20	25.97
July 1945	15	25.00	16	29.63	53	48.62	41	53.25
August 1945	9	15.00	10	18.52	12	11.01	10	12.99

tional mining of the straits, and for a reason that in retrospect is obvious: there was no point in mining the ports if Japanese shipping could not negotiate the straits. The effect of these second- and third-phase operations (May–June) was immediate: the straits were closed between 14 and 17 May, and shipping using the strait was reduced by two-fifths in May compared to the previous month. In the long term, the decline in the amount of shipping using such ports as neighboring Kobe and Osaka told its own story, as shown in table 13.4.

In fact the strait was closed on five days in May, with less than 10,000 tons of shipping using the strait on another ten days; in June the figures were five and thirteen, in July twelve and thirteen, and in August eight and seven—and Japan was at war for just the first fifteen days of this month.[30]

* * *

The comprehensiveness of Japan's defeat in this final phase of the war can be gauged by the figures relating to the strait, but also by a number of related matters—Japan's moving escorts to minesweeping duties, the collapse of imports in these last months,[31] and the ineffectiveness of Japanese defensive measures in terms of the Japanese inability to counter the heavy bombers that conducted the mining, to keep abreast of American developments and changes, and to clear channels for shipping. Such a list is far from complete; suffice it to note one matter that is seldom properly considered. The mining campaign represented the closing of the circle in that eighteen of the twenty-one largest Japanese repair yards were on the Inland Sea; the mining of these waters had the effect of curtailing their operations, with the result that all repairs had to be undertaken by the yards at Nagasaki in Kyushu, at Toyama on the Sea of Japan, at Hakodate and Muroran on Hokkaido, and at Darien on the Yellow Sea. Given the fact that even at peak activity over the last three years Japanese yards had not been able to make significant reduction of the tonnage not in commission, the yards that remained could do no better; there were Japanese plans to place repair ahead of new construction, but this remained intention only.

* * *

Operation Starvation was the process that completed Japan's defeat at sea. It came as the end piece in a process that had seen first, a submarine campaign against shipping that slowly assumed momentum and significance, specifically after late 1943; second, a campaign across the central Pacific after November 1943 that saw carrier aircraft conduct a series of devastating raids on shipping; and third, a persistent, low-grade attrition inflicted by land-based aircraft. But Operation Starvation should not really be seen in isolation because it was accompanied by submarine operations in the Sea of Japan, by the allied carrier operations of July–August 1945, and by a series of attacks on shipping by land-based aircraft that assumed significant proportions, and ironically so. May 1945 saw the peak of sinkings by land-based aircraft in terms of numbers of merchantmen, with a total of thirty-nine service ships and merchantmen of 64,021 tons sunk, and of this total thirty-two merchantmen of 57,118 tons were sunk off Tsingtao, in Korean waters, or in the Korean Strait by Privateers and PV-1 Ventura from Okinawa—and such reputable returns were pushed into second place, as mines accounted for fifty-two service ships and merchantmen of 99,394 tons.

* * *

Consistently through these chapters dealing with Japan and its naval defeat in the Second World War events have been portrayed in other than single-causation terms, the repudiation of accounts that represent the story of the war in terms of a turning point or decisive battle. Wars of many years' duration invariably are complex; they very seldom, if ever, have a single battle in which Victory switches its favors, where the assured triumph of one side becomes the assured victory of the other. Japan's defeat at sea had a number of different strands that finally came together between March and August 1945, but that defeat nonetheless does present problems of gainful representation. Victories and defeats across a sea or an ocean are rare indeed; in fact, victories and defeats in war by naval power are very few: the Eastern Empire's defeat of the Vandal kingdom in 533–534 and the Norman invasion and conquest of England in 1066 were both based on sea power, as was the Spanish conquest of the Aztec and Inca empires in the sixteenth century. But Japan was defeated across thousands of miles of ocean, and it was defeated in a war in which its navy was revealed as a one-shot affair, with failure the fate of all operations after December 1942. What is very striking about the Imperial Navy is that for more than two decades it prepared itself to fight a battle that it came to identify as a campaign and then a war, and in so doing it ultimately came to be a navy that could fight only one battle and could win only the one battle that it intended to fight. Unfortunately for the Kaigun, the battles that it was called upon to fight were not the ones for which it had prepared, and in this process its enemy, the U.S. Navy, secured overwhelming advantage on account of radar and radio, not to mention signals intelligence and related matters. This enemy proved to have a strength in depth that became increasingly marked with the passing of time; the growing disparity between the Imperial and U.S. Navies reflected relative national positions and accounted for the outcome of a conflict in which the Kaigun, having begun the war with a strike of unprecedented imagination, was outfought in the air, on the sea, and under the sea in the course of a conflict by the end of which, in real terms, it had ceased to exist. States so mismatched in terms of resources and size as Japan and the United States seldom fight one another, and even less frequently do they fight wars initiated by the weaker state. The Second World War, however, was just such a war, and it provides ample evidence of the validity of the eleventh principle of war and the truth of the Clausewitzian dictum:

> The first, the grandest, the most decisive act of judgement which the Statesman and General exercises is rightly to understand (the nature of) the War in which he engages, not to take it for something, or wish to make of it something, which (it is not and) it is impossible for it to be.

All nations have fought the wrong war at the wrong time, but for Japan to have conjured into existence an enemy coalition that consisted of the most populous country in the world, the greatest empires in the world, the greatest industrial, financial, and naval power in the world, and the greatest military power in the world was a formidable achievement, however unintended, as was, for Japan, its final outcome.

APPENDIX 13.1.

THE TABLES: DEFINITIONS, INCONSISTENCIES, AND RATIONALIZATIONS

WITH THIS CHAPTER are included a number of tables that have been some twenty years in the preparation. The basic information was drawn from the JANAC papers, with amendments, and most obviously the tables and their detail lend themselves to criticism in reference to inaccuracy of figures and mendacity of presentation.

The author would accept correction in terms of tonnage detail and that the definition of theaters used here cannot be regarded as definitive and final, but asks that certain points be noted. The list of Japanese warships and naval, military, and civilian ships lost between 7–8 December 1941 and 15 August 1945 was compiled on British A4 paper and landscape, and occupied, with basically one line per entry, a total of eighty-eight pages, ships of less than 100 tons not having been included in totals. Individual tonnages may be wrong, and regularly one has been obliged to make corrections, but within certain limits the general accuracy of figures would be defended. In terms of theaters, the following lines of demarcation were adopted:

the North Pacific theater, the area to the north of a line from the La Pérouse Strait along the north coast of Hokkaido and thence eastward below the most southern of the Kurile Islands and thence due east;

Japanese home waters, from the North Pacific area south to latitude 30° North to the line of the Ryukyu Islands, around the southern tip of Kyushu to latitude 32° North and thence west to the Chinese coast north of Shanghai;

the East China Sea, from the line (slightly east) of the Ryukyu Islands south to the Tropic of Cancer and west via mid-Formosa to the Chinese coast;

the Central Pacific theater, the area bound in the north by latitude 30° North and in the south by the equator, and in the west by the line of the East China Sea theater to longitude 125° East as far south as latitude 15° North, east to 130° East and then due south to the equator;

the Southwest Pacific theater, bound in the north by the equator to a position due north of Manokwari and thence south to the coast of New Guinea and thence from the Vogelkop via northern and eastern New Guinea and via the Torres Strait to the Australian coast;

the Southern Resources Area, the theater bound in the north by the East China Sea area, in the east by the Southwest Pacific and Central Pacific areas, and to the south the Malay Barrier and thence back to Singapore;

the Indian Ocean, the Indian Ocean area;

Riverine China, inland Chinese waters;

and Unknown and other theaters, the Atlantic theaters and with reference to ships of which the whereabouts of loss is not known.

The last set of problems confounding any attempt to put together tables of losses is the definition of "loss." The definition of "sinking" necessarily involves decks under water, but one would suggest that, for example, the *Kaiyo* in July 1945 was sunk though it had capsized, was on the bottom, and was half out the water; likewise, one would include, for purposes of comparison, the U.S. battleship *California* and the British battleships *Queen Elizabeth* and *Valiant* as sunk for the very simple reason that they were on the bottom, though that fact made their salvage possible and worthwhile. But the use of the terms "lost" or "losses" presents any number of problems. For example, there is an obvious question of whether one should include such ships as the *Shimane Maru*, which had her back broken by carrier aircraft while it was in Takamatsu harbor, Shikoku, on 24 July 1945. The lateness of her being damaged naturally precluded her being repaired and returned to service in the period of hostilities, but the fact was that her damage was so serious that her only subsequent move was to the breakers, and it is recorded as lost. But with other ships the situation was more complicated. For example, the oiler *Mirii Maru* was torpedoed by the U.S. submarine *Bang* on 29 June 1944 and thereafter was laid up in Takao harbor, Formosa, where it was finally destroyed by carrier aircraft on 15 January 1945; likewise the heavy cruiser *Takao* was torpedoed and severely damaged by the U.S. submarine *Darter* on 23 October 1944 and was laid up at Singapore, where it was subjected to sabotage attack by British midget submarines on 31 July 1945. Now in both these cases, the *Mirii Maru* and *Takao*, there is very good reason to mark these as lost with their initial dates, but, of course, if they were lost on these original dates then there was no reason why they should have been subjected to further attacks. Therefore these two ships have been entered as have been lost on the second occasion, and the earlier agency of inconvenience has not been credited with share of destruction, but one suspects that other and various, indeed perhaps a fair number of, inconsistencies have been incorporated in lists and tables.

The author does not claim that the totals given in these various tables possess elements of finality that brook no argument, but the tables have been compiled on the basis of the definitions given in the preceding paragraphs, and such definitions seem to be reasoned and reasonable, and most certainly can serve as terms of reference to the matters brought under consideration in this chapter.

APPENDIX 13.2.

TABULAR REPRESENTATION OF OVERALL JAPANESE WARSHIP, NAVAL, MILITARY, AND CIVILIAN SHIPPING LOSSES: 7/8 DECEMBER 1941–15 AUGUST 1945

Agency of Destruction		Northern Pacific theater	Japanese home waters	East China Sea	Central Pacific theater	Southwest Pacific theater	Southern Resources Area	Indian Ocean theater	Riverine China	Other and unknown theaters	Totals	As % of respective overall losses	
Central Pacific submarines	Warships	10: 9,516	76: 198,677	19: 71,880	40: 129,620	3: 5,965	25.5 50,741	- -	- -	- -	173.5 466,399	16.84	20.15
	Naval shipping	9: 25,338	47: 173,911	18.5 124,735	85: 426,641	6: 24,804	29: 164,015	- -	- -	- -	193.5 939,444	32.99	34.23
	Military shipping	13: 49,720	29: 116,839	29: 130,135	42: 196,690	3: 12,963	28: 161,478	- -	- -	- -	144: 667,825	25.53	30.51
	Merchant shipping	14: 35,371	190: 592,472	58.5 300,481	18: 63,851	- -	58: 322,361	- -	- -	- -	338.5 1,314,536	28.75	39.01
Other submarines	Warships	- -	2: 5,345	- -	11: 26,372	7: 22,968	93: 206,338	14: 18,597	- -	- -	127: 279,620	12.33	12.08
	Naval shipping	- -	1: 6,925	- -	21: 98,065	8: 46,591	74: 460,954	6: 11,489	- -	- -	110 624,024	18.76	22.73
	Military shipping	- -	- -	- -	23: 113,055	14: 49,866	88.5 433,268	12: 55,051	- -	- -	137.5 651,240	24.38	29.75
	Merchant shipping	- -	1: 5,244	1: 2,345	- -	- -	99.5 417,637	4: 7,672	- -	- -	105.5 432,898	8.96	12.85
Carrier-based aircraft	Warships	- -	57: 229,101	35: 96,077	89: 208,083	10.75 44,732	108: 303,982	- -	- -	1: 2,095	280.75 884,070	27.26	38.19
	Naval shipping	- -	10: 33,919	10: 24,315	69.5 399,129	2: 7,980	26.5 123,851	2: 3,552	- -	- -	120: 592,746	20.46	21.60
	Military shipping	- -	4: 13,139	12: 37,256	13 47,304	2 12,931	35 161,707	1 778	- -	- -	67: 273,115	11.88	12.48
	Merchant shipping	- -	59: 103,940	32: 61,328	4: 4,905	- -	74.5 258,947	- -	- -	1: 245	170.5 429,365	14.48	12.74
Shore-based aircraft	Warships	3.5 2,875	7: 4,850	5: 4,738	17: 6,299	50.25 77,756	54: 36,565	3: 948	3: 1,054	- -	142.75 135,085	13.86	5.84
	Naval shipping	2.5 18,276	- -	3: 6,377	10: 24,084	39: 168,316	25.5 103,902	2: 5,968	1: 776	1: 1,805	84: 329,504	14.32	12.01
	Military shipping	2: 7,214	4: 13,532	2: 7,283	3: 6,237	70: 191,592	47: 118,926	8: 27,172	3: 1,340	1: 499	140: 373,795	24.82	17.08
	Merchant shipping	8: 28,429	69: 145,205	7: 8,808	8: 5,829	16: 41,526	48.5 118,643	3: 8,052	16: 26,369	- -	175.5 382,861	14.90	11.36
Warships	Warships	7.5 9,127	5: 3,216	1: 960	51: 73,107	46.5 130,877	23.5 126,132	8: 28,563	- -	1: 1,144	143.5 373,126	13.93	16.12
	Naval shipping	0.5 4,286	- -	- -	1.5 5,565	1: 812	3: 17,759	2: 1,898	- -	- -	8: 30,320	1.36	1.10
	Military shipping	1: 3,121	- -	- -	2: 3,858	- -	1: 9,192	1: 335	- -	- -	5: 16,506	0.89	0.75
	Merchant shipping	1: 4,960	1: 2,300	- -	- -	1: 475	1: 5,175	1: 1,591	- -	- -	5: 14,501	0.42	0.43
Mines	Warships	1: 222	27: 32,290	- -	1: 648	5: 9,361	11: 10,091	6: 1,309	1: 625	- -	52: 54,546	5.05	2.36
	Naval shipping	- -	12: 18,614	- -	2: 11,774	3: 10,472	7: 32,445	1: 1,400	2: 2,474	- -	27: 77,179	4.60	2.81
	Military shipping	- -	12: 47,771	1: 3,120	1: 549	1: 2,913	6: 19,256	2: 10,702	2: 4,220	- -	25: 88,531	4.43	4.04
	Merchant shipping	1: unknown	148: 251,565	3: 17,596	- -	- -	23: 74,429	5: 6,940	14: 27,656	- -	194: 378,186	16.48	11.22
Natural causes	Warships	4: 4,401	13: 45,455	4: 1,594	7: 6,643	2.5 3,545	5: 5,183	- -	- -	1: 238	36.5 67,059	3.54	2.90
	Naval shipping	3: 7,376	9: 29,136	3: 32,017	3: 5,918	- -	3: 25,157	- -	1: 600	- -	22: 100,204	3.75	3.65
	Military shipping	- -	2: 2,910	2: 3,673	- -	- -	2: 4,764	- -	- -	- -	6: 11,347	1.06	0.52
	Merchant shipping	- -	62: 132,815	5: 25,044	- -	1: 543	12: 32,265	- -	1: 5,822	2: 8,667	83: 205,156	7.05	6.09

Unknown causes	Warships	1: 2,434	27: 10,765	3: 709	10: 7,757	7: 6,578	14: 5,863	1: 872	- -	1: 389	64: 35,367	6.21	1.53
	Naval shipping	- -	8: 15,679	1: 223	2: 3,365	1: 394	4: 21,672	2: 1,062	- -	3: 7,742	21: 50,137	3.58	1.83
	Military shipping	- -	3: 5,946	4.5 18,441	5: 4,994	6: 3,765	13: 41,015	2: 10,468	- -	2: 3,533	35.5 88,162	6.29	4.03
	Merchant shipping	2: 5,303	50: 99,466	2.5 6,219	7: 15,536	5: 6,006	29: 59,181	2: 2,498	- -	8: 18,291	105.5 212,500	8.96	6.31
Other causes	Warships	- -	- -	1: 540	3: 3,393	- -	6: 15,463	- -	- -	- -	10: 19,396	0.97	0.84
	Naval shipping	- -	- -	- -	- -	- -	- -	1: 984	- -	- -	1: 984	0.17	0.04
	Military shipping	- -	- -	- -	- -	2: 13,576	2: 4,976	- -	- -	- -	4: 18,552	0.71	0.85
	Merchant shipping	- -	- -	- -	- -	- -	- -	- -	- -	- -	- -	-	-
	Warships	27: 28,575	214: 529,699	68: 176,498	209: 461,922	132: 301,782	340: 760,358	32: 50,289	4: 1,679	4: 3,866	1030: 2,314,668	as % of overall shipping losses	
		2.62 1.23	20.78 22.88	6.60 7.63	20.29 19.96	12.82 13.04	33.01 32.85	3.11 2.17	0.39 0.07	0.39% 0.17			
	Naval shipping	15: 55,276	86: 278,184	35.5 187,667	194: 974,541	60: 259,369	172: 949,744	16: 26,353	4: 3,850	4: 9,547	586½ 2,744,542	25.19	33.05
		2.56 2.01	14.66 10.14	6.05 6.84	33.08 35.51	10.23 9.45	29.33 34.60	2.73 0.96	0.68 0.14	0.68 0.35			
	Military shipping	16: 60,055	54: 200,137	50.5 199,908	89: 372,687	98: 287,606	222.5 954,582	26: 104,506	5: 5,560	3: 4,032	564: 2,189,073	24.23	26.36
		2.84 2.74	9.57 9.14	8.95 9.13	15.78 17.02	17.38 13.14	39.45 43.61	4.61 4.77	0.89 0.25	0.53 0.18			
	Merchant shipping	26: 74,063	580: 1,333,007	109: 421,821	37: 90,121	23: 48,550	345½ 1,288,638	15: 26,753	31: 59,847	11: 27,203	1177½ 3,370,003	50.58	40.58
		2.21 2.20	49.27 39.56	9.26 12.52	3.14 2.67	1.95 1.44	29.34 38.24	1.27 0.79	2.63 1.78	0.93 0.81			
	Total shipping losses	57: 189,394	720: 1,811,328	195: 809,396	320: 1,437,349	181: 595,525	740: 3,192,975	57: 157,612	40: 69,257	18: 40,782	2328: 8,303,618		
		2.49 2.28	30.93 21.81	8.38 9.75	13.75 17.31	7.77 7.17	31.79 38.45	2.49 1.90	1.72 0.83	0.77 0.49			

	Losses per day over a 1,348-day period:	**per month over a 44.29-month period:**
Warships:	0.76 units of 1,717 tons	23.26 units of 52,262 tons
Naval shipping:	0.44 ships of 2,036 tons	13.24 ships of 61,968 tons
Military shipping:	0.42 ships of 1,624 tons	12.73 ships of 49,426 tons
Civilian shipping:	0.87 ships of 2,500 tons	26.59 ships of 76,089 tons
Overall shipping:	1.73 ships of 6,160 tons	52.56 ships of 187,483 tons

Average size of lost ships:

Warships:	2,247 tons
Naval support ships:	4,680 tons
Military ships:	3,881 tons
Merchantmen:	2,862 tons

APPENDIX 13.3.

TABULAR REPRESENTATION OF JAPANESE WARSHIP, NAVAL, MILITARY, AND MERCHANT SHIPPING LOSSES BY PHASES DURING THE SECOND WORLD WAR:

Phase I: 7/8 December 1941–30 April 1942.

Phase II: 1 May 1942–28 February 1943.

Phase III: 1 March–31 October 1943.

Phase IV: 1 November 1943–30 June 1944.

Phase V: 1 July 1944–31 March 1945.

Phase VI: 1 April–15 August 1945.

Tabular Representation of Overall Japanese Warship, Naval, Military, and Merchant Shipping Losses: Phase I. 7/8 December 1941–30 April 1942

Agency of Destruction		Northern Pacific theater	Japanese home waters	East China Sea	Central Pacific theater	Southwest Pacific theater	Southern Resources Area	Indian Ocean theater	Riverine China	Other and unknown theaters	Total	As % of losses in this phase	
Central Pacific submarines	Warships	- -	1: 1,498	1: 2,719	1: 1,400	- -	- -	- -	- -	- -	3: 5,617	8.11	8.11
	Naval shipping	- -	2: 3,570	- -	2: 11,923	- -	- -	- -	- -	- -	4: 15,493	19.05	16.02
	Military shipping	- -	2: 5,727	1: 1,434	- -	- -	- -	- -	- -	- -	3: 7,161	14.29	6.58
	Merchant shipping	- -	4: 19,371	- -	- -	- -	- -	- -	- -	- -	4: 19,371	25.00	27.48
Other submarines	Warships	- -	- -	- -	- -	- -	4: 11,176	- -	- -	- -	4: 11,176	10.81	16.15
	Naval shipping	- -	- -	- -	- -	- -	3: 23,279	- -	- -	- -	3: 23,279	14.29	24.07
	Military shipping	- -	- -	- -	- -	- -	10: 55,605	2: 11,719	- -	- -	12: 67,324	57.14	61.84
	Merchant shipping	- -	- -	- -	- -	- -	2: 8,468	- -	- -	- -	2: 8,468	12.50	12.01
Carrier-based aircraft	Warships	- -	1: 116	- -	4: 5,561	3: 15,730	- -	- -	- -	- -	8: 21,407	21.62	30.93
	Naval shipping	- -	- -	- -	1: 6,567	- -	- -	- -	- -	- -	1: 6,567	4.76	6.79
	Military shipping	- -	- -	- -	- -	1: 6,143	- -	- -	- -	- -	1: 6,143	4.76	5.64
	Merchant shipping	- -	- -	- -	- -	- -	- -	- -	- -	- -	- -	-	-
Shore-based aircraft	Warships	- -	- -	- -	1: 1,772	- -	4: 2,283	- -	- -	- -	5: 4,055	13.51	5.86
	Naval shipping	- -	- -	- -	- -	1: 8,524	3: 13,693	- -	- -	- -	4: 22,217	19.05	22.97
	Military shipping	- -	- -	- -	- -	- -	- -	- -	- -	- -	- -	-	-
	Merchant shipping	- -	- -	- -	- -	- -	2: 5,372	- -	- -	- -	2: 5,372	12.50	7.62
Warships	Warships	- -	- -	- -	- -	- -	3: 10,730	1: 1,142	- -	- -	4: 11,872	10.81	17.15
	Naval shipping	- -	- -	- -	- -	- -	3: 17,759	- -	- -	- -	3: 17,759	14.29	18.36
	Military shipping	- -	- -	- -	- -	- -	1: 9,192	- -	- -	- -	1: 9,192	4.76	8.44
	Merchant shipping	- -	- -	- -	- -	- -	1: 5,175	- -	- -	- -	1: 5,175	6.25	7.34
Mines	Warships	- -	- -	- -	- -	- -	4: 3,569	- -	- -	- -	4: 3,569	10.81	5.16
	Naval shipping	- -	- -	- -	- -	- -	2: 7,047	- -	- -	- -	2: 7,047	9.52	7.29
	Military shipping	- -	2: 10,712	- -	- -	- -	1: 1,548	- -	- -	- -	3: 12,260	14.29	11.26
	Merchant shipping	- -	- -	- -	- -	- -	- -	- -	- -	- -	- -	-	-
Natural causes	Warships	1: 2,577	- -	- -	2: 1,976	- -	- -	- -	- -	- -	3: 4,553	8.11	6.58
	Naval shipping	- -	- -	- -	1: 1,273	- -	1: 472	- -	- -	- -	2: 1,745	9.52	1.80
	Military shipping	- -	- -	- -	- -	- -	- -	- -	- -	- -	- -	-	-
	Merchant shipping	- -	2: 6,112	1: 2,963	- -	- -	1: 2,728	- -	1: 5,822	- -	5: 17,625	31.25	25.00

Unknown causes	Warships	- -	- -	- -	1: 2,198	- -	- -	- -	- -	- -	1: 2,198	2.70	3.18
	Naval shipping	- -	1: 2,225	- -	- -	1: 394	- -	- -	- -	- -	2: 2,619	9.52	2.71
	Military shipping	- -	- -	1: 6,788	- -	- -	- -	- -	- -	- -	1: 6,788	4.76	6.24
	Merchant shipping	- -	1: 6,526	- -	- -	- -	1: 7,951	- -	- -	- -	2: 14,477	12.50	20.54
Other causes	Warships	- -	- -	- -	3: 3,393	- -	2: 1,382	- -	- -	- -	5: 4,775	13.51	6.90
	Naval shipping	- -	- -	- -	- -	- -	- -	- -	- -	- -	- -	-	-
	Military shipping	- -	- -	- -	- -	- -	- -	- -	- -	- -	- -	-	-
	Merchant shipping	- -	- -	- -	- -	- -	- -	- -	- -	- -	- -	-	-
Total losses by theater and as % of total losses in Phase I	Warships	1: 2,577	2: 1,614	1: 2,719	12: 16,300	3: 15,730	17: 29,140	1: 1,142	- -	- -	37: 69,222		
	as % of phase losses	2.70 3.72	5.41 2.33	2.70 3.93	32.43 23.55	8.11 22.72	45.95 42.10	2.70 1.65	- -	- -			
	Naval shipping	- -	3: 5,795	- -	4: 19,763	2: 8,918	12: 62,250	- -	- -	- -	21: 96,726		
	as % of phase losses	- -	14.29 5.99	- -	19.05 20.43	9.52 9.22	57.14 64.36	- -	- -	- -			
	Military shipping	- -	4: 16,439	2: 8,222	- -	1: 6,143	12: 66,345	2: 11,719	- -	- -	21: 108,868		
	as % of phase losses	- -	19.05 15.10	9.52 7.55	- -	4.76 5.64	57.14 60.94	9.52 10.76					
	Merchant shipping	- -	7: 32,009	1: 2,963	- -	- -	7: 29,694	- -	1: 5,822	- -	16: 70,488		
	as % of phase losses	- -	43.75 45.41	6.25 4.20	- -	43.75 42.13	6.25 8.26						
	Total shipping losses	- -	14: 54,243	3: 11,185	4: 19,763	3: 15,061	31: 158,289	2: 11,719	1: 5,822	- -	58: 276,082		
	as % of phase losses	- -	24.13 19.65	5.17 4.05	6.90 7.16	5.17 5.46	53.45 57.33	3.45 4.24	1.72 2.11	- -	- -		
Losses as % of overall losses	Warships	0.10 0.11	0.19 0.07	0.10 0.12	0.39 0.70	0.29 0.68	1.65 1.26	0.10 0.05	- -	- -	3.59 2.99		
	Naval shipping	- -	0.51 0.21	- -	0.68 0.72	0.34 0.32	2.05 2.27	- -	- -	- -	3.58 3.52		
	Military shipping	- -	0.71 0.75	0.35 0.38	- -	0.18 0.28	2.13 3.03	0.35 0.54	- -	- -	3.72 4.97		
	Merchant shipping	- -	0.59 0.94	0.08 0.09	- -	- -	0.59 0.88	- -	0.09 0.17	- -	1.36 2.09		

Phase I losses:	**Losses per day over a 155-day period:**	**Losses per month over a period of 4.81 months:**
Warships:	0.24 unit of 447 tons	7.69 units of 14,391 tons
Naval shipping:	0.13 ship of 624 tons	4.37 ships of 20,109 tons
Military shipping:	0.13 ship of 702 tons	4.37 ships of 22,634 tons
Merchant shipping:	0.10 ship of 455 tons	3.33 ships of 14,653 tons
Overall losses:	0.37 ship of 1,781 tons	12.06 ships of 57,398 tons

Average size of lost ships:

Warships:	1,871 tons
Naval support ships:	4,606 tons
Military ships:	5,184 tons
Merchantmen:	4,406 tons

Tabular Representation of overall Japanese Warship, Naval, Military, and Merchant Shipping Losses: Phase II. 1 May 1942–28 February 1943

Agency of Destruction		Northern Pacific theater	Japanese home waters	East China Sea	Central Pacific theater	Southwest Pacific theater	Southern Resources Area	Indian Ocean theater	Riverine China	Other and unknown theaters	Total	As % of losses in this phase
Central Pacific submarines	Warships	4: 4,247	6: 19,208	- -	5: 8,849	3: 5,965	1: 2,904	- -	- -	- -	19: 41,173	23.46 11.12
	Naval shipping	1: 2,864	3: 24,453	2: 16,694	10: 55,286	4: 13,168	- -	- -	- -	- -	20: 112,465	32.79 36.19
	Military shipping	- -	2: 10,448	7: 44,847	1: 7,983	2: 9,860	- -	- -	- -	- -	12: 73,138	19.05 22.68
	Merchant shipping	- -	25: 98,852	10: 49,258	2: 7,889	- -	1: 5,306	- -	- -	- -	38: 161,305	42.70 46.62
Other submarines	Warships	- -	- -	- -	2: 3,397	6: 21,568	3: 4,733	- -	- -	- -	11: 29,698	13.58 8.02
	Naval shipping	- -	- -	- -	2: 11,016	6: 29,884	8: 46,778	- -	- -	- -	16: 87,678	26.23 28.21
	Military shipping	- -	- -	- -	5: 24,989	8: 32,935	7: 28,451	2: 19,364	- -	- -	22: 105,739	34.92 32.80
	Merchant shipping	- -	- -	- -	- -	- -	11: 37,885	- -	- -	- -	11: 37,885	12.36 10.95
Carrier-based aircraft	Warships	- -	- -	- -	5: 121,787	5.75 26,277	1: 10,600	- -	- -	- -	11.75 158,664	14.51 42.85
	Naval shipping	- -	- -	- -	- -	- -	- -	- -	- -	- -	- -	- -
	Military shipping	- -	- -	- -	- -	1: 6,788	- -	- -	- -	- -	1: 6,788	1.59 2.11
	Merchant shipping	- -	- -	- -	- -	- -	- -	- -	- -	- -	- -	- -
Shore-based aircraft	Warships	1.5 2,584	- -	- -	- -	10.75 31,705	- -	- -	- -	- -	12.25 34,289	15.12 9.26
	Naval shipping	2.5 18,276	- -	- -	- -	14: 65,435	1: 678	- -	- -	- -	17.5 84,389	28.69 27.15
	Military shipping	1: 5,863	- -	- -	- -	13: 74,475	2: 5,851	3: 13,702	- -	- -	19: 99,891	30.16 30.98
	Merchant shipping	3: 16,738	- -	- -	- -	9: 35,905	- -	- -	- -	- -	12: 52,643	13.48 15.22
Warships	Warships	0.5 494	- -	- -	1: 3,311	16.5 83,600	- -	1: 10,438	- -	- -	19: 97,843	23.46 26.42
	Naval shipping	0.5 4,286	- -	- -	- -	- -	- -	- -	- -	- -	0.5 4,286	0.82 1.37
	Military shipping	1: 3,121	- -	- -	- -	- -	- -	1: 335	- -	- -	2: 3,456	3.17 1.07
	Merchant shipping	- -	- -	- -	- -	- -	- -	- -	- -	- -	- -	- -
Mines	Warships	- -	- -	- -	- -	1: 2,077	2: 2,486	1: 341	- -	- -	4: 4,904	4.94 1.32
	Naval shipping	- -	- -	- -	- -	- -	1: 1,932	- -	- -	- -	1: 1,932	1.64 0.62
	Military shipping	- -	- -	- -	- -	- -	1: 892	1: 4,821	- -	- -	2: 5,713	3.17 1.77
	Merchant shipping	- -	2: 9,179	- -	- -	- -	3: 11,037	- -	- -	- -	5: 20,216	5.62 5.84
Natural causes	Warships	1: 998	- -	- -	- -	- -	- -	- -	- -	- -	1: 998	1.23 0.27
	Naval shipping	1: 5,950	1: 3,111	1: 7,938	- -	- -	- -	- -	- -	- -	3: 16,999	4.92 5.47
	Military shipping	- -	- -	- -	- -	- -	- -	- -	- -	- -	- -	- -
	Merchant shipping	- -	9: 31,155	3: 16,739	- -	- -	1: 3,350	- -	- -	- -	13: 51,244	14.61 14.81

Unknown causes	Warships	- -	- -	- -	- -	2: 2,382	1: 302	- -	- -	- -	3: 2,684	3.70	0.72
	Naval shipping	- -	1: 1,990	- -	- -	- -	- -	2: 1,062	- -	- -	3: 3,052	4.92	0.98
	Military shipping	- -	- -	1: 2,977	- -	- -	1: 5,307	1: 5,822	- -	- -	3: 14,106	4.76	4.38
	Merchant shipping	- -	5: 16,100	- -	- -	1: 3,393	1: 867	1: 165	- -	2: 2,164	10: 22,689	11.24	6.56
Other causes	Warships	- -	- -	- -	- -	- -	- -	- -	- -	- -	- -	-	-
	Naval shipping	- -	- -	- -	- -	- -	- -	- -	- -	- -	- -	-	-
	Military shipping	- -	- -	- -	- -	2: 13,576	- -	- -	- -	- -	2: 13,575	3.17	4.21
	Merchant shipping	- -	- -	- -	- -	- -	- -	- -	- -	- -	- -	-	-
Total losses by theater and as % of total losses in Phase II	Warships	7: 8,323	6: 19,208	- -	13: 137,344	45: 173,574	8: 21,025	2: 10,779	- -	- -	81: 370,253		
	as % of phase losses	8.64 2.25	7.41 5.18	- -	16.05 37.09	55.56 46.88	9.88 5.68	2.47 2.91	- -	- -			
	Naval shipping	5: 31,376	5: 29,554	3: 24,632	12: 66,302	24: 108,487	10: 49,388	2: 1,062	- -	- -	61: 310,801		
	as % of phase losses	8.19 10.10	8.19 9.51	4.92 7.93	19.67 21.33	39.34 34.91	16.39 15.89	3.26 0.34					
	Military shipping	2: 8,984	2: 10,448	8: 47,824	6: 32,972	26: 137,634	11: 40,501	8: 44,044	- -	- -	63: 322,407		
	as % of phase losses	3.17 2.79	3.17 3.24	12.70 14.83	9.52 10.23	41.27 42.69	17.46 12.56	12.70 13.66					
	Merchant shipping	3: 16,738	41: 155,286	13: 65,997	2: 7,889	10: 39,298	17: 58,445	1: 165	- -	2: 2,164	89: 345,982		
	as % of phase losses	3.37 4.84	46.07 44.88	14.61 19.08	2.25 2.28	11.24 11.36	19.10 16.89	1.12 0.01	2.25 0.63				
	Total shipping losses	10: 57,098	48: 195,288	24: 138,453	20: 107,163	60: 285,419	38: 148,334	11: 45,271	- -	2: 2,164	213: 979,190		
	as % of phase losses	4.69 5.83	22.54 19.94	11.27 14.14	9.39 10.94	28.17 29.15	17.84 15.15	5.16 4.62	- -	0.94 0.22			
Losses as % of overall losses	Warships	0.68 0.36	0.58 0.83	- -	1.26 5.93	4.37 7.50	0.78 0.91	0.19 0.47	- -	- -	7.86 16.00		
	Naval shipping	0.85 1.14	0.85 1.08	0.51 0.90	2.05 2.42	4.09 3.95	1.71 1.80	0.34 0.04	- -	- -	10.40 11.32		
	Military shipping	0.35 0.41	0.35 0.48	1.42 2.18	1.06 1.51	4.61 6.29	1.95 1.85	1.42 2.01	- -	- -	11.17 14.73		
	Merchant shipping	0.25 0.50	3.48 4.61	1.10 1.96	0.17 0.23	0.85 1.17	1.44 1.73	0.08 0.01	- -	0.17 0.06	7.56 10.27		

Phase II losses:	**Losses per day over a 304-day period:**	**Losses per month over a ten-month period:**	**Average size of lost ships:**
Warships:	0.27 unit of 1,218 tons	8.10 units of 37,025 tons	Warships: 4,571 tons
Naval shipping:	0.20 ship of 1,022 tons	6.10 ships of 31,080 tons	Naval support ships: 5,095 tons
Military shipping:	0.21 ship of 1,061 tons	6.30 ships of 32,241 tons	Military ships: 5,118 tons
Merchant shipping:	0.29 ship of 1,138 tons	8.90 ships of 34,598 tons	Merchantmen: 3,887 tons
Overall losses:	0.70 ship of 3,221 tons	21.30 ships of 97,919 tons	

Tabular Representation of overall Japanese Warship, Naval, Military, and Merchant Shipping Losses: Phase III. 1 March–31 October 1943

Agency of Destruction		Northern Pacific theater	Japanese home waters	East China Sea	Central Pacific theater	Southwest Pacific theater	Southern Resources Area	Indian Ocean theater	Riverine China	Other and unknown theaters	Total	As % of losses in this phase
Central Pacific submarines	Warships	1: 1,360	6: 8,941	1: 935	9: 31,218	- -	- -	- -	- -	- -	17: 42,454	20.98 22.62
	Naval shipping	- -	6: 23,693	7: 58,754	16: 110,685	2: 11,636	- -	- -	- -	- -	31: 204,768	46.27 53.53
	Military shipping	- -	2: 4,808	4: 15,367	8: 33,878	1: 3,103	3: 15,648	- -	- -	- -	18: 72,804	19.35 24.78
	Merchant shipping	4: 14,214	44: 152,608	13: 71,003	4: 14,435	- -	3: 18,662	- -	- -	- -	68: 270,922	62.39 71.99
Other submarines	Warships	- -	- -	- -	3: 9,432	1: 1,400	3: 3,293	1: 2,103	- -	- -	8: 16,228	9.88 8.66
	Naval shipping	- -	- -	- -	6: 33,453	1: 5,086	6: 44,830	1: 3,967	- -	- -	14: 87,336	20.90 22.83
	Military shipping	- -	- -	- -	8: 37,792	4: 11,692	14: 56,218	1: 6,925	- -	- -	27: 112,627	29.03 38.33
	Merchant shipping	- -	- -	- -	- -	- -	4: 22,846	- -	- -	- -	4: 22,846	3.66 6.07
Carrier-based aircraft	Warships	- -	- -	- -	- -	- -	- -	- -	- -	- -	- -	- -
	Naval shipping	- -	- -	- -	- -	- -	- -	- -	- -	- -	- -	- -
	Military shipping	- -	- -	- -	- -	- -	- -	- -	- -	- -	- -	- -
	Merchant shipping	- -	- -	- -	- -	- -	- -	- -	- -	- -	- -	- -
Shore-based aircraft	Warships	- -	- -	- -	- -	15.5 34,328	2: 490	1: 355	- -	- -	18.5 35,173	22.84 18.77
	Naval shipping	- -	- -	- -	1: 1,200	8: 28,518	1: 3,200	1: 4,468	1: 776	- -	12: 38,162	17.91 9.98
	Military shipping	- -	- -	- -	1: 285	26: 56,461	2: 1,736	4: 13,076	1: 130	- -	34: 71,688	36.56 24.40
	Merchant shipping	1: 3,110	- -	- -	- -	5: 2,867	2: 2,830	2: 4,872	2: 4,692	- -	12: 18,371	11.01 4.88
Warships	Warships	3: 6,613	- -	- -	- -	19: 31,120	- -	- -	- -	- -	22: 37,733	27.16 20.13
	Naval shipping	- -	- -	- -	- -	- -	- -	- -	- -	- -	- -	- -
	Military shipping	- -	- -	- -	1: 3,019	- -	- -	- -	- -	- -	1: 3,019	1.08 1.03
	Merchant shipping	- -	- -	- -	- -	- -	- -	- -	- -	- -	- -	- -
Mines	Warships	- -	- -	- -	- -	4: 7,284	2: 861	- -	- -	- -	6: 8,145	7.41 4.36
	Naval shipping	- -	- -	- -	- -	1: 6,417	1: 807	- -	- -	- -	2: 7,224	2.98 1.89
	Military shipping	- -	- -	- -	- -	1: 2,913	- -	1: 5,881	- -	- -	2: 8,794	2.15 2.99
	Merchant shipping	- -	- -	1: 6,893	- -	- -	1: 1,972	- -	- -	- -	2: 8,865	1.83 2.36
Natural causes	Warships	- -	2: 40,760	1: 217	- -	2.5 3,545	- -	- -	- -	- -	5.5 44,522	6.79 23.76
	Naval shipping	- -	2: 5,312	1: 17,549	2: 4,645	- -	- -	- -	- -	- -	5: 27,506	7.46 7.19
	Military shipping	- -	1: 2,240	1: 3,178	- -	- -	1: 1,871	- -	- -	- -	3: 7,289	3.23 2.48
	Merchant shipping	- -	11: 29,060	- -	- -	1: 543	- -	- -	- -	- -	12: 29,603	11.01 7.87

Unknown causes	Warships	1: 2,434	1: 148	- -	- -	- -	1: 192	- -	- -	1: 389	4: 3,163	4.94	1.69
	Naval shipping	- -	- -	- -	1: 2,926	- -	1: 14,050	- -	- -	1: 589	3: 17,565	4.48	4.59
	Military shipping	- -	2: 5,059	- -	2: 2,400	1: 543	- -	1: 4,646	- -	- -	6: 12,648	6.45	4.30
	Merchant shipping	1: 3,366	7: 17,810	- -	1: 3,158	- -	1: 164	- -	- -	1: 1,229	11: 25,727	10.09	6.84
Other causes	Warships	- -	- -	- -	- -	- -	- -	- -	- -	- -	- -	-	-
	Naval shipping	- -	- -	- -	- -	- -	- -	- -	- -	- -	- -	-	-
	Military shipping	- -	- -	- -	- -	- -	2: 4,976	- -	- -	- -	2: 4,976	2.15	1.69
	Merchant shipping	- -	- -	- -	- -	- -	- -	- -	- -	- -	- -	-	-
Total losses by theater and as % of total losses in Phase III	Warships	5: 10,407	9: 49,849	2: 1,152	12: 40,650	42: 77,677	8: 4,836	2: 2,458	- -	1: 389	81: 187,418		
	as % of phase losses	6.17 5.55	11.11 26.60	2.47 0.61	14.81 21.69	51.85 41.45	9.88 2.58	2.47 1.31	- -	1.23 0.21			
	Naval shipping	- -	8: 29,005	8: 76,303	26: 152,909	12: 51,657	9: 62,887	2: 8,435	1: 776	1: 589	67: 382,561		
	as % of phase losses	- -	11.94 7.58	11.94 19.95	38.81 39.97	17.91 13.50	13.43 16.44	2.99 2.20	1.49 0.20	1.49 0.15			
	Military shipping	- -	5: 12,107	5: 18,545	20: 77,374	33: 74,712	22: 80,449	7: 30,528	1: 130	- -	93: 293,845		
	as % of phase losses	- -	5.38 4.12	5.38 6.31	21.51 26.33	35.48 25.43	23.66 27.38	7.53 10.39	1.08 0.04	- -			
	Merchant shipping	6: 20,690	62: 199,478	14: 77,896	5: 17,593	6: 3,410	11: 46,474	2: 4,872	2: 4,692	1: 1,229	109: 376,334		
	as % of phase losses	5.50 5.50	56.88 53.00	12.84 20.70	4.59 4.67	5.50 0.91	10.09 12.35	1.83 1.29	1.83 1.25	0.92 0.33			
	Total shipping losses	6: 20,690	75: 240,590	27: 172,744	51: 247,876	51: 129,779	42: 189,810	11: 43,835	4: 5,598	2: 1,818	269: 1,052,740		
	as % of phase losses	2.23 1.97	27.88 22.85	10.03 16.41	18.96 23.55	18.96 12.33	15.61 18.03	4.09 4.15	1.49 0.53	0.74 0.17			
Losses as % of overall losses	Warships	0.48 0.45	0.87 2.15	0.19 0.05	1.17 1.76	4.08 3.36	0.78 0.21	0.19 0.11	- -	0.10 0.02	7.86 8.10		
	Naval shipping	- -	1.36 1.06	1.36 2.78	4.43 5.57	2.05 1.88	1.53 2.29	0.34 0.31	0.17 0.03	0.17 0.02	11.42 13.94		
	Military shipping	- -	0.89 0.55	0.89 0.85	3.55 3.53	5.85 3.41	3.90 3.68	1.24 1.39	0.18 0.01	- -	16.49 13.42		
	Merchant shipping	0.51 0.61	5.27 5.92	1.19 2.31	0.42 0.52	0.51 0.10	0.93 1.38	0.17 0.14	0.17 0.15	0.08 0.04	9.26 11.17		

Phase III losses:	**Losses per day over a 245-day period:**	**Losses per month over an eight-month period:**	**Average size of lost ships:**
Warships	0.33 unit of 765 tons	10.13 units of 23,427 tons	Warships: 2,314 tons
Naval shipping:	0.27 ship of 1,561 tons	8.38 ships of 47,820 tons	Naval support ships: 5,710 tons
Military shipping:	0.27 ship of 1,199 tons	11.63 ships of 36,731 tons	Military ships: 3,160 tons
Merchant shipping:	0.44 ship of 1,536 tons	13.63 ships of 47,042 tons	Merchantmen: 3,453 tons
Overall losses:	1.10 ship of 4,297 tons	33.63 ships of 131,593 tons	

Tabular Representation of overall Japanese Warship, Naval, Military, and Merchant Shipping Losses: Phase IV. 1 November 1943–30 June 1944

Agency of Destruction		Northern Pacific theater	Japanese home waters	East China Sea	Central Pacific theater	Southwest Pacific theater	Southern Resources Area	Indian Ocean theater	Riverine China	Other and unknown theaters	Total	As % of losses in this phase	
Central Pacific submarines	Warships	1: 860	5: 26,107	3: 1,835	16: 84,129	- -	5: 4,937	- -	- -	- -	30: 117,868	15.31	35.18
	Naval shipping	4: 12,266	15: 70,313	1.5 15,055	50: 236,700	- -	7: 41,319	- -	- -	- -	77.5 375,653	34.52	34.00
	Military shipping	7: 28,575	7: 30,446	4: 23,454	30: 145,971	- -	12: 58,965	- -	- -	- -	60: 287,411	34.48	43.07
	Merchant shipping	3: 6,574	19: 57,273	15.5 71,963	11: 39,611	- -	21: 108,268	- -	- -	- -	69.5 283,689	44.98	54.64
Other submarines	Warships	- -	2: 5,345	- -	6: 13,543	- -	15: 27,706	6: 13,193	- -	- -	29: 59,787	14.80	17.84
	Naval shipping	- -	1: 6,925	- -	12: 51,485	1: 11,621	20: 121,873	4: 5,604	- -	- -	38: 197,508	16.93	17.88
	Military shipping	- -	- -	- -	10: 50,274	2: 5,239	32.5 163,099	4: 9,703	- -	- -	48.5 228,315	27.87	34.21
	Merchant shipping	- -	- -	- -	- -	- -	18.5 81,476	1: 2,658	- -	- -	19.5 84,134	12.62	16.20
Carrier-based aircraft	Warships	- -	- -	- -	37: 59,344	2: 2,725	3: 1,235	- -	- -	1: 2,095	43: 65,399	21.94	19.52
	Naval shipping	- -	- -	- -	60.5 370,296	2: 7,980	1: 993	1: 2,722	- -	- -	64.5 381,991	28.73	34.57
	Military shipping	- -	- -	- -	11: 37,568	- -	- -	1: 778	- -	- -	12: 38,346	6.90	5.75
	Merchant shipping	- -	- -	- -	3: 4,375	- -	- -	- -	- -	- -	3: 4,375	1.94	0.84
Shore-based aircraft	Warships	- -	- -	- -	10: 2,123	21: 11,372	4: 4,134	- -	- -	- -	35: 17,629	17.86	5.26
	Naval shipping	- -	- -	1: 3,202	9: 22,884	15: 65,297	4: 13,363	- -	- -	1: 1,805	30: 106,551	13.36	9.64
	Military shipping	- -	- -	1: 6,385	2: 5,952	28: 59,279	9: 23,683	- -	- -	1: 499	41: 95,798	23.56	14.36
	Merchant shipping	- -	- -	2: 3,448	3: 2,222	2: 2,754	10: 37,591	1: 3,180	5: 7,775	- -	23: 56,970	14.89	10.97
Warships	Warships	1: 1,630	- -	- -	26: 36,378	11: 16,157	- -	2: 2,723	- -	1: 1,144	41: 58,032	20.92	17.32
	Naval shipping	- -	- -	- -	1.5 5,565	1: 812	- -	- -	- -	- -	2.5 6,377	1.11	0.58
	Military shipping	- -	- -	- -	1: 839	- -	- -	- -	- -	- -	1: 839	0.57	0.13
	Merchant shipping	1: 4,960	- -	- -	- -	1: 475	- -	- -	- -	- -	2: 5,435	1.29	1.05
Mines	Warships	1: 222	- -	- -	- -	- -	1: 2,090	- -	- -	- -	2: 2,312	1.02	0.69
	Naval shipping	- -	- -	- -	2: 11,774	2: 4,055	- -	1: 1,400	- -	- -	5: 17,229	2.23	1.56
	Military shipping	- -	- -	- -	- -	- -	1: 2,197	- -	- -	- -	1: 2,197	0.57	0.33
	Merchant shipping	- -	1: 875	1: 5,307	- -	- -	2: 6,768	1: 554	- -	- -	5: 13,504	3.24	2.60
Natural causes	Warships	1: 720	1: 2,198	- -	3: 2,032	- -	1: 1,685	- -	- -	- -	6: 6,635	3.06	1.98
	Naval shipping	1: 657	2: 7,058	- -	- -	- -	1: 5,135	- -	- -	- -	4: 12,850	1.78	1.16
	Military shipping	- -	1: 670	- -	- -	- -	- -	- -	- -	- -	1: 670	0.57	0.10
	Merchant shipping	- -	16: 26,547	1: 5,342	- -	- -	2: 3,328	- -	- -	1: 6,932	20: 42,149	12.94	8.12

Unknown causes	Warships	- -	3: 1,039	1: 318	3: 2,076	3: 3,951	- -	- -	- -	- -	10: 7,384	5.10	2.20
	Naval shipping	- -	- -	- -	1: 439	- -	1: 5,141	- -	- -	1: 1,086	3: 6,666	1.34	0.60
	Military shipping	- -	- -	0.5 2,644	2: 2,022	5: 3,222	2: 5,869	- -	- -	- -	9.5 13,757	5.46	2.06
	Merchant shipping	- -	4: 10,081	0.5 2,644	2: 5,874	1: 521	4: 8,924	- -	- -	1: 887	12.5 28,931	8.09	5.57
Other causes	Warships	- -	- -	- -	- -	- -	- -	- -	- -	- -	- -	-	-
	Naval shipping	- -	- -	- -	- -	- -	- -	- -	- -	- -	- -	-	-
	Military shipping	- -	- -	- -	- -	- -	- -	- -	- -	- -	- -	-	-
	Merchant shipping	- -	- -	- -	- -	- -	- -	- -	- -	- -	- -	-	-
Total losses by theater and as % of total losses in Phase IV	Warships	4: 3,432	11: 34,689	4: 2,153	101: 199,625	37: 34,205	29: 41,787	8: 15,916	- -	2: 3,239	196: 335,046		
	as % of phase losses	2.04 1.02	5.61 10.35	2.04 0.64	51.53 59.58	18.88 10.21	14.80 12.47	4.08 4.75	- -	1.02 0.97			
	Naval shipping	5: 12,923	18: 84,296	2.5 18,257	136: 699,143	21: 89,765	34: 187,824	6: 9,726	- -	2: 2,891	224.5 1,104,825		
	as % of phase losses	2.23 1.17	8.02 7.63	1.11 1.65	60.58 63.28	9.35 8.12	15.14 17.00	2.67 0.88	- -	0.89 0.26			
	Military shipping	7: 28,575	8: 31,116	5.5 32,483	56: 242,626	35: 67,740	56.5 253,813	5: 10,481	- -	1: 499	174: 667,333		
	as % of phase losses	4.02 4.28	4.60 4.66	3.16 4.86	32.18 36.36	20.11 10.15	32.47 38.03	2.87 1.57	- -	0.57 0.07			
	Merchant shipping	4: 11,534	40: 94,776	20: 88,704	19: 52,082	4: 3,750	57.5 246,355	3: 6,392	5: 7,775	2: 7,819	154.5 519,187		
	as % of phase losses	2.59 0.00	25.89 0.00	12.94 0.00	12.30 0.00	2.59 0.72	37.22 47.45	1.94 1.23	3.24 1.50	1.29 1.51			
	Total shipping losses	16: 20,690	66: 210,188	28: 139,444	211: 994,851	60: 161,255	148: 687,992	14: 26,599	5: 7,775	5: 11,209	553: 2,291,345		
	as % of phase losses	2.89 0.90	11.93 9.17	5.06 6.06	38.16 43.37	10.85 7.04	26.76 30.03	2.53 1.16	0.90 0.34	0.90 0.49			
Losses as % of overall losses	Warships	0.39 0.15	1.07 1.50	0.39 0.09	9.81 8.62	3.59 1.48	2.82 1.81	0.78 0.69	- -	0.19 0.14	19.03 14.47		
	Naval shipping	0.85 0.47	3.07 3.07	0.43 0.67	23.19 25.47	3.58 3.27	5.80 6.84	1.02 0.35	- -	0.34 0.11	38.28 40.25		
	Military shipping	1.24 1.31	1.42 1.42	0.98 1.48	9.93 11.08	6.20 3.09	10.02 11.59	0.89 0.48	- -	0.18 0.02	30.85 30.48		
	Merchant shipping	0.34 0.34	3.40 2.81	1.70 2.63	1.61 1.55	0.34 0.11	4.88 7.31	0.25 0.19	0.42 0.23	0.17 0.23	13.12 15.41		

Phase IV losses:	**Losses per day over a 243-day period:**	**Losses per month over an eight-month period:**	**Average size of lost ships:**
Warships	0.81 unit of 1,379 tons	24.50 units of 41,881 tons	Warships: 1,709 tons
Naval shipping:	0.99 ship of 4,547 tons	28.06 ships of 138,103 tons	Naval support ships: 4,921 tons
Military shipping:	0.72 ship of 2,746 tons	21.75 ships of 83,417 tons	Military ships: 3,835 tons
Merchant shipping:	0.64 ship of 2,137 tons	19.31 ships of 64,898 tons	Merchantmen: 3,360 tons
Overall losses:	2.28 ship of 9,429 tons	68.75 ships of 286,418 tons	

Tabular Representation of overall Japanese Warship, Naval, Military, and Merchant Shipping Losses: Phase V. 1 July 1944–31 March 1945

Agency of Destruction		Northern Pacific theater	Japanese home waters	East China Sea	Central Pacific theater	Southwest Pacific theater	Southern Resources Area	Indian Ocean theater	Riverine China	Other and unknown theaters	Total	As % of losses in this phase	
Central Pacific submarines	Warships	2: 2,198	29: 118,253	13: 64,465	8: 3,064	- -	19.5 42,900	- -	- -	- -	71.5 230,880	16.90	25.92
	Naval shipping	4: 10,208	10: 27,967	8: 34,232	7: 12,047	- -	22: 122,696	- -	- -	- -	51: 207,150	29.82	28.42
	Military shipping	3: 16,890	10: 54,697	13: 45,033	3: 8,858	- -	13: 86,865	- -	- -	- -	42: 212,343	23.33	29.72
	Merchant shipping	4: 7,947	42: 137,219	19: 97,008	1: 1,916	- -	33: 190,125	- -	- -	- -	99 434,215	24.21	32.96
Other submarines	Warships	- -	- -	- -	- -	- -	49: 131,325	7: 3,301	- -	- -	56: 134,626	13.24	15.11
	Naval shipping	- -	- -	- -	1: 2,111	- -	34: 210,550	1: 1,918	- -	- -	36: 214,579	21.05	29.44
	Military shipping	- -	- -	- -	- -	- -	25: 129,895	3: 7,340	- -	- -	28: 137,235	15.56	19.21
	Merchant shipping	- -	1: 5,244	1: 2,345	- -	- -	54: 252,819	3: 5,014	- -	- -	59: 265,422	14.43	20.15
Carrier-based aircraft	Warships	- -	4: 1,158	22: 10,999	20.5 16,903	- -	103: 292,017	- -	- -	- -	149.5 321,077	35.34	36.05
	Naval shipping	- -	1: 2,217	9: 24,082	8: 22,266	- -	25.5 122,858	1: 830	- -	- -	44.5 172,253	26.02	23.63
	Military shipping	- -	1: 10,605	12: 37,256	2: 9,736	- -	35: 161,707	- -	- -	- -	50: 219,304	27.78	30.70
	Merchant shipping	- -	6: 7,084	30: 60,367	1: 530	- -	74.5 258,947	- -	- -	1: 245	112.5 327,173	27.51	24.83
Shore-based aircraft	Warships	1: 130	- -	2: 1,220	4: 699	3: 351	38: 27,798	- -	3: 1,054	- -	51: 31,252	12.06	3.51
	Naval shipping	- -	- -	2: 3,175	- -	1: 542	15.5 72,117	1: 1,500	- -	- -	19.5 77,334	11.40	10.61
	Military shipping	- -	- -	- -	- -	2: 764	32: 86,560	1: 394	2: 1,210	- -	37: 88,928	20.56	12.45
	Merchant shipping	2: 348	3: 2,598	2: 1,364	4: 2,732	- -	26.5 51,878	- -	8: 12,750	- -	45.5 71,670	11.12	5.44
Warships	Warships	- -	5: 3,216	- -	21.5 31,115	- -	20.5 115,402	2: 840	- -	- -	49: 150,573	11.58	16.90
	Naval shipping	- -	- -	- -	- -	- -	- -	1: 398	- -	- -	1: 398	0.58	0.05
	Military shipping	- -	- -	- -	- -	- -	- -	- -	- -	- -	- -	-	-
	Merchant shipping	- -	- -	- -	- -	- -	- -	- -	- -	- -	- -	-	-
Mines	Warships	- -	2: 450	- -	1: 648	- -	2: 1,085	5: 968	1: 625	- -	11: 3,776	2.60	0.42
	Naval shipping	- -	2: 1,868	- -	- -	- -	3: 22,659	- -	1: 1,674	- -	6: 26,201	3.51	3.59
	Military shipping	- -	1: 111	1: 3,120	1: 549	- -	2: 12,274	- -	1: 2,000	- -	6: 18,054	3.33	2.53
	Merchant shipping	- -	2 7,744	1: 5,396	- -	- -	14: 50,819	4: 6,386	9: 19,761	- -	30: 90,106	7.33	6.84
Natural causes	Warships	- -	1: 130	1: 950	2: 2,635	- -	4: 3,498	- -	- -	- -	8: 7,213	1.89	0.81
	Naval shipping	1: 769	1: 2,728	1: 6,530	- -	- -	- -	- -	1: 600	- -	4: 10,627	2.34	1.46
	Military shipping	- -	- -	1: 495	- -	- -	1: 2,893	- -	- -	- -	2: 3,388	1.11	0.47
	Merchant shipping	- -	10: 14,719	- -	- -	- -	7: 22,360	- -	- -	1: 1,735	18: 38,814	4.40	2.95

Unknown causes	Warships	- -	4: 831	1: 122	6: 3,483	2: 245	10: 5,109	1: 872	- -	- -	24: 10,662	5.67	1.20
	Naval shipping	- -	4: 10,620	1: 223	- -	- -	2: 2,481	- -	- -	1: 6,067	8: 19,391	4.68	2.66
	Military shipping	- -	1: 887	2: 6,032	1: 572	- -	9: 24,020	- -	- -	2: 3,533	15: 35,044	8.33	4.91
	Merchant shipping	1: 1,937	12: 22,895	2: 3,575	4: 6,504	2: 2,092	20: 38,911	1: 2,333	- -	3: 11,791	45: 90,038	11.00	6.83
Other causes	Warships	- -	- -	- -	- -	- -	3: 681	- -	- -	- -	3: 681	0.71	0.08
	Naval shipping	- -	- -	- -	- -	- -	- -	1: 984	- -	- -	1: 984	0.58	0.13
	Military shipping	- -	- -	- -	- -	- -	- -	- -	- -	- -	- -		
	Merchant shipping	- -	- -	- -	- -	- -	- -	- -	- -	- -	- -		
Total losses by theater and as % of total losses in Phase V	Warships	3: 2,328	45: 124,038	39: 77,756	63: 58,547	5: 596	249: 619,815	15: 5,981	4: 1,679	- -	423: 890,740		
	as % of phase losses	0.71 0.26	10.64 13.93	9.22 8.73	14.89 6.57	1.18 0.07	58.87 69.58	3.55 0.67	0.95 0.19	- -			
	Naval shipping	5: 10,977	18: 45,400	21: 68,242	16: 36,424	1: 542	102: 553,361	5: 5,630	2: 2,274	1: 6,067	171: 728,917		
	as % of phase losses	2.92 1.51	10.53 6.23	12.28 9.36	9.36 5.00	0.58 0.07	59.65 75.92	2.92 0.77	1.17 0.31	0.58 0.83			
	Military shipping	3: 16,890	13: 66,300	29: 91,936	7: 19,715	2: 764	117: 504,214	4: 7,734	3: 3,210	2: 3,533	180: 714,296		
	as % of phase losses	1.67 2.36	7.22 9.28	16.11 12.87	3.89 2.76	1.11 0.11	65.00 70.59	2.22 1.08	1.67 0.45	1.11 0.49			
	Merchant shipping	7: 10,232	76: 197,503	55: 170,055	10: 11,682	2: 2,092	229: 865,859	8: 13,733	17: 32,511	5: 13,771	409: 1,317,438		
	as % of phase losses	1.71 0.78	18.58 14.99	13.45 12.91	2.44 0.89	0.49 00.16	55.99 65.72	1.96 1.04	4.16 2.47	1.22 1.05			
	Total shipping losses	15: 38,099	107: 309,203	105: 330,233	33: 67,821	5: 3,398	448: 1,923,434	17: 27,097	22: 37,995	8: 23,371	760: 2,760,651		
	as % of phase losses	1.97 1.38	14.08 11.20	13.82 11.96	4.34 2.46	00.65 00.12	58.95 69.67	2.24 00.98	2.89 1.38	1.05 0.85			
Losses as % of overall losses	Warships	0.29 0.10	4.37 5.36	3.79 3.36	6.12 2.53	0.49 0.03	24.17 26.78	1.46 0.26	0.39 0.07	- -	41.06 38.48		
	Naval shipping	0.85 0.40	3.07 1.65	3.58 2.49	2.73 1.33	0.17 0.02	17.39 20.16	0.85 0.21	0.34 0.08	0.17 0.22	29.16 26.56		
	Military shipping	0.53 0.77	2.30 3.03	5.14 4.20	1.24 0.90	0.35 0.03	20.74 23.03	0.71 0.35	0.53 0.15	0.35 0.16	31.91 32.63		
	Merchant shipping	0.59 0.30	6.45 5.86	4.67 5.05	0.85 0.35	0.17 0.06	19.45 25.69	0.68 0.41	1.44 0.96	0.42 0.41	34.73 39.09		

Phase V Losses:	**Losses per day over a 274-day period:**	**Losses per month over a nine-month period:**	**Average size of lost ships:**
Warships:	1.54 units of 3,251 tons	47.00 units of 98,971 tons	Warships: 2,106 tons
Naval shipping:	0.62 ship of 2,660 tons	19.00 ships of 80,991 tons	Naval support ships: 4,262 tons
Military shipping:	0.66 ship of 2,607 tons	20.00 ships of 79,366 tons	Military ships: 3,968 tons
Merchant shipping:	1.49 ships of 4,808 tons	45.44 ships of 146,382 tons	Merchantmen: 3,221 tons
Overall losses:	2.77 ships of 10,075 tons	84.44 ships of 328,961 tons	

Tabular Representation of overall Japanese Warship, Naval, Military, and Merchant Shipping Losses: Phase VI. 1 April–15 August 1945

Agency of Destruction		Northern Pacific theater	Japanese home waters	East China Sea	Central Pacific theater	Southwest Pacific theater	Southern Resources Area	Indian Ocean theater	Riverine China	Other and unknown theaters	Total	As % of losses in this phase	
Central Pacific submarines	Warships	2: 851	29: 24,670	1: 1,926	1: 960	- -	- -	- -	- -	- -	33: 28,407	15.57	6.15
	Naval shipping	- -	10: 23,915	- -	- -	- -	- -	- -	- -	- -	10: 23,915	23.81	19.81
	Military shipping	3: 4,255	6: 10,713	- -	- -	- -	- -	- -	- -	- -	9: 14,968	27.27	18.18
	Merchant shipping	3: 6,636	56: 127,149	1: 11,249	- -	- -	- -	- -	- -	- -	60: 145,034	15.00	19.58
Other submarines	Warships	- -	- -	- -	- -	- -	19: 28,105	- -	- -	- -	19: 28,105	8.96	6.08
	Naval shipping	- -	- -	- -	- -	- -	3: 13,644	- -	- -	- -	3: 13,644	7.14	11.30
	Military shipping	- -	- -	- -	- -	- -	- -	- -	- -	- -	- -	-	-
	Merchant shipping	- -	- -	- -	- -	- -	10: 14,143	- -	- -	- -	10: 14,143	2.50	1.91
Carrier-based aircraft	Warships	- -	52: 227,827	13: 85,078	2.5 4,488	- -	1: 130	- -	- -	- -	68.5 317,523	32.31	68.73
	Naval shipping	- -	9: 31,702	1: 233	- -	- -	- -	- -	- -	- -	10: 31,935	23.81	26.46
	Military shipping	- -	3: 2,534	- -	- -	- -	- -	- -	- -	- -	3: 2,534	9.09	3.08
	Merchant shipping	- -	53: 96,856	2: 961	- -	- -	- -	- -	- -	- -	55: 97,817	13.75	13.21
Shore-based aircraft	Warships	1: 161	7: 4,850	3: 3,518	2: 1,705	- -	6: 1,860	2: 593	- -	- -	21: 12,687	9.91	2.75
	Naval shipping	- -	- -	- -	- -	- -	1: 851	- -	- -	- -	1: 851	2.38	0.70
	Military shipping	1: 1,351	4: 13,532	1: 898	- -	1: 613	2: 1,096	- -	- -	- -	9: 17,490	27.27	21.25
	Merchant shipping	2: 8,233	66: 142,607	3: 3,996	1: 875	- -	8: 20,972	- -	1: 1,152	- -	81: 177,835	20.25	24.01
Warships	Warships	3: 390	- -	1: 960	2.5 2,303	- -	- -	2: 13,420	- -	- -	8.5 17,073	4.01	3.70
	Naval shipping	- -	- -	- -	- -	- -	- -	1: 1,500	- -	- -	1: 1,500	2.38	1.24
	Military shipping	- -	- -	- -	- -	- -	- -	- -	- -	- -	- -	-	-
	Merchant shipping	- -	1: 2,300	- -	- -	- -	- -	1: 1,591	- -	- -	2: 3,891	0.50	0.53
Mines	Warships	- -	25: 31,840	- -	- -	- -	- -	- -	- -	- -	25: 31,840	11.79	6.89
	Naval shipping	- -	10: 16,746	- -	- -	- -	- -	- -	1: 800	- -	11: 17,546	26.19	14.54
	Military shipping	- -	9: 36,948	- -	- -	- -	1: 2,345	- -	1: 2,220	- -	11: 41,513	33.33	50.43
	Merchant shipping	1: unknown	143: 233,767	- -	- -	- -	3: 3,833	- -	5: 7,895	- -	152: 245,495	38.00	33.15
Natural causes	Warships	1: 106	9: 2,367	2: 427	- -	- -	- -	- -	- -	1: 238	13: 3,138	6.13	0.68
	Naval shipping	- -	3: 10,927	- -	- -	- -	1: 19,550	- -	- -	- -	4: 30,477	9.52	25.25
	Military shipping	- -	- -	- -	- -	- -	- -	- -	- -	- -	- -	-	-
	Merchant shipping	- -	14: 25,222	- -	- -	- -	1: 499	- -	- -	- -	15: 25,721	3.75	3.47

Unknown causes	Warships	- -	19: 8,747	1: 269	- -	- -	2: 260	- -	- -	- -	22: 9,276	10.38	2.01
	Naval shipping	- -	2: 844	- -	- -	- -	- -	- -	- -	- -	2: 844	4.76	0.70
	Military shipping	- -	- -	- -	- -	- -	1: 5,819	- -	- -	- -	1: 5,819	3.03	7.07
	Merchant shipping	- -	21: 26,054	- -	- -	1: unknown	2: 2,364	- -	- -	1: 2,220	25: 30,638	6.25	4.14
Other causes	Warships	- -	- -	1: 540	- -	- -	1: 13,400	- -	- -	- -	2: 13,940	0.94	3.02
	Naval shipping	- -	- -	- -	- -	- -	- -	- -	- -	- -	- -	-	-
	Military shipping	- -	- -	- -	- -	- -	- -	- -	- -	- -	- -	-	-
	Merchant shipping	- -	- -	- -	- -	- -	- -	- -	- -	- -	- -	-	-
Total losses by theater and as % of total losses in Phase VI	Warships	7: 1,508	141: 300,301	22: 92,718	8: 9,456	- -	29: 43,755	4: 14,013	- -	1: 238	212: 461,989		
	as % of phase losses	3.30 0.33	66.51 65.00	10.38 20.07	3.77 2.05	- -	13.68 9.47	1.89 3.03	- -	0.47 0.05			
	Naval shipping	- -	34: 84,134	1: 233	- -	- -	5: 34,045	1: 1,500	1: 800	- -	42: 120,712		
	as % of phase losses	- -	80.95 69.70	2.38 0.19	- -	- -	11.90 28.20	2.38 1.24	2.38 0.66	- -			
	Military shipping	4: 5,606	22: 63,727	1: 898	- -	1: 613	4: 9,260	- -	1: 2,220	- -	33: 82,324		
	as % of phase losses	12.12 6.81	66.67 77.41	3.03 1.09	- -	3.03 0.74	12.12 11.25	- -	3.03 2.70	- -			
	Merchant shipping	6: 14,869	354: 653,955	6: 16,206	1: 875	1: unknown	24: 41,811	1: 1,591	6: 9,047	1: 2,220	400: 740,574		
	as % of phase losses	1.50 2.01	88.50 88.30	1.50 2.19	0.25 0.12	0.25 -	6.00 5.65	0.25 0.21	1.50 1.22	0.25 0.30			
	Total shipping losses	10: 20,475	410: 801,816	8: 17,337	1: 875	2: 613	33: 85,116	2: 3,091	8: 12,067	1: 2,220	475: 943,610		
	as % of phase losses	2.11 2.17	86.32 84.97	1.68 1.84	0.21 0.09	0.42 0.06	6.95 9.02	0.42 0.33	1.68 1.28	0.21 0.24			
Losses as % of overall losses	Warships	0.68 0.07	13.68 12.97	2.14 4.01	0.78 0.41	- -	2.82 1.89	0.39 0.61	- -	0.10 0.01	20.58 19.96		
	Naval shipping	- -	5.79 3.06	0.17 0.01	- -	- -	0.85 1.24	0.17 0.05	0.17 0.03	- -	7.16 4.40		
	Military shipping	0.71 0.26	3.90 2.91	0.18 0.04	- -	0.18 0.03	0.71 0.42	- -	0.18 0.10	- -	5.85 3.76		
	Merchant shipping	0.51 0.44	30.06 19.41	0.51 0.48	0.08 0.03	0.08 -	2.04 1.24	0.08 0.05	0.51 0.27	0.08 0.07	33.97 21.98		

Phase VI Losses:	**Losses per day over a 137-day period:**	**Losses per month over a period of 4.48 months:**	**Average size of lost ships:**
Warships:	1.55 units of 3,372 tons	47.32 units of 103,123 tons	Warships: 2,178 tons
Naval shipping:	0.62 ship of 881 tons	9.38 ships of 26,945 tons	Naval support ships: 2,880 tons
Military shipping:	0.66 ship of 601 tons	7.37 ships of 18,376 tons	Military ships: 2,495 tons
Merchant shipping:	1.49 ships of 5,406 tons	89.29 ships of 165,307 tons	Merchantmen: 1,851 tons
Overall losses:	2.77 ships of 6,889 tons	106.03 ships of 210,681 tons	

CHAPTER FOURTEEN

THE JAPANESE SITUATION—AND ANOTHER, AND FINAL, DIMENSION

In the preceding chapters the Japanese situation in terms of shipping, trade, and production has been subjected to examination, for one reason: for more than six decades the American public perception of the Pacific war has been focused primarily upon fleet and amphibious operations; what has been provided here is not a correction to such perspective but an addition, the presentation of matters seldom afforded much in the way of consideration but gathered here to provide balance and perspective. By definition, these short chapters cannot be comprehensive and must serve only as introduction to matters often given little historical consideration. This final chapter is concerned with battles and individuals, for the same reasons and with the same intent.

Excluding the attack by Japanese carrier aircraft on the U.S. Pacific Fleet at Pearl Harbor on 7 December 1941 and the attacks by Allied carrier aircraft on a variety of targets in Japanese waters in the war's last month (though perhaps the irony should be noted that the last survivor of the Pearl Harbor operation, the heavy cruiser *Tone*, was sunk at its mooring off Kure by U.S. carrier aircraft on 24 July 1945), during the war in the Pacific there were no fewer than eighteen actions involving warship formations on both sides.[1] Of course, there also were actions involving aircraft and warships from opposing sides, the best known of these actions being those in the Bismarck Sea in March 1943 and when the battleship *Yamato* was sunk southwest of Kyushu in April 1945. Of all these actions perhaps the one that possessed greatest historical symbolism was the action off Cape St. George, which was the last action between warship formations other than in the Surigao Strait in October 1944, but the greater part of historical attention over the lifetime that has elapsed since these actions were fought has been directed to the action fought off Midway Islands and Leyte Gulf. The other four major carrier actions—Coral Sea, Eastern Solomons, Santa Cruz, and Philippine Sea—have generally been afforded *en passant* consideration: the Coral Sea was but the prelude to Midway, and the Eastern Solomons and Santa Cruz were not battles on which Americans dwell because neither resulted in victory. The second-tier status of the battle of the Philippine Sea is perhaps surprising given the fact that in terms of fleet and light carriers of the two sides this was the largest carrier battle of the war, larger even than Leyte, though the latter had many more warships than Philippine Sea and with escort carriers added to the list is the larger of the two battles in terms of carrier numbers.

Three of these battles are the subjects of consideration in this chapter, the first being the action fought off Midway Islands in June 1942: it is the one action subjected to repeated presentation as "the decisive battle" or "the turning point." As noted in the previous chapter, there are very few wars in which the assured victory of one side changed allegiance as a result of one single battle, and in this case if Japan's defeat was inevitable then there could not be a "decisive battle" or a "turning point." Any proper consideration of events would suggest that the initiative changed hands as a result of a series of actions over some seven months, between May and December 1942, and that it was the combination of all the actions, plus other related developments such as Japanese shipping losses in the southwest Pacific, that together resulted in the American securing of the strategic initiative. A certain caution, however, is needed in this matter: the Americans fought for and won the initiative in a process in which they took their defeats and losses as well as inflicting the same upon their enemy, but it was not until November 1943 that they were in possession of the means to exploit their advantage. Between January and mid-November 1943 the front-line in the Pacific, if there could be such a thing, barely moved. A number of islands changed hands in this period, but these were of small account, of no real strategic significance; the Americans secured the initiative in a process that for the moment made for exhaustion and the major disruption of formations and that meant that they had to await the arrival in service of the first of the *Essex*-class fleet carriers. Midway was only one battle in the process that saw the initiative wrested from the Japanese, but perhaps its most intriguing single feature lay in the fact that in large measure the battle was fought wrongly by the Americans; virtually everything that had been written about how a battle was to be fought went by the wayside, and the American victory was mainly the result of this fact. A series of uncoordinated attacks, piecemeal and small, wreaked havoc precisely because of their nature, the complete negation of the principles of war. In any staff college examination of this battle the series of attacks that accounted for three of the four

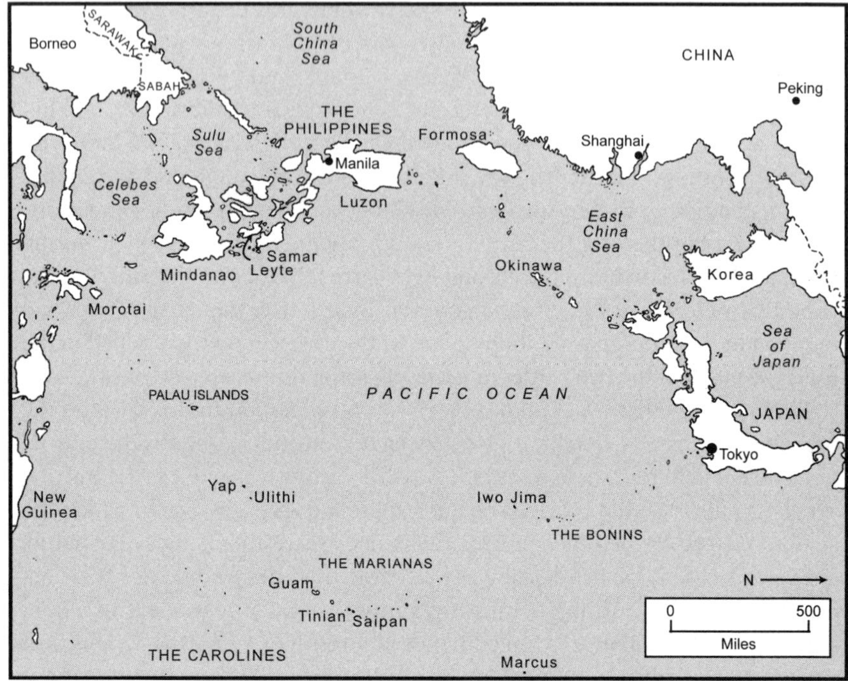

Map 11. The Pacific from U.S. Perspective: October 1944 and March 1945

Japanese carriers would draw the immediate conclusion that the conduct of these attacks was precisely the way battles should not be fought, yet here was the paradox that the way in which these attacks were conducted—along with the Japanese lack of radar—was the very factor that made for success.

The Philippine Sea is a battle that led to much ill-judged criticism at the time within the U.S. military hierarchy in particular and press in general, the general line of criticism being that the Japanese had escaped when overwhelming victory lay within the American grasp. The fact was that in this battle the Japanese suffered such devastating losses among their carrier air groups that these were never reconstituted in the course of the war. That, along with the fact that three fleet carriers were sunk, albeit only one by carrier aircraft, was the basis of what was a very real and overwhelming victory.

Leyte Gulf was the largest single naval battle of war and indeed the largest single naval battle in modern history, but its continuing relevance lies in two matters. It was a very unusual battle in that it extended over some five days and it was fought after the issue of victory and defeat in the war had been decided. But it was a battle that reflected the American way of war in the sense that it was fought on the basis of mass and superiority of numbers. Historical attention naturally has tended to focus upon the carrier and battle groups in this

TABLE 14.1. LOSSES INCURRED BY JAPANESE UNITS INVOLVED IN THE BATTLE OF LEYTE GULF

	Original numbers	The Battle of Leyte Gulf October						Total Lost	A	B	C
		23	24	25	26	27	28				
Battleships	9	-	1	2	-	-	-	3	1	4	1
Fleet carriers	1	-	-	1	-	-	-	1	-	-	-
Light carriers	3	-	-	3	-	-	-	3	-	-	-
Heavy cruisers	14	2	-	4	-	-	-	6	2	4	2
Light cruisers	7	-	-	1	3	-	-	4	-	3	-
Destroyers	31	-	1	5	3	2	-	11	10	8	2
Escorts	4	-	-	-	-	-	-	-	-	1	3
Total	69	2	2	16	6	2	-	28	13	20	8
Submarines	14	-	-	-	-	1	2	3	3	7	1
Escorts	12	-	-	-	-	-	-	-	-	7	5
Oilers	10	-	-	-	-	1	1	2	4	4	-

Key:

A: Sunk in the follow-up phase, 28 October–30 November 1944
B: Sunk between 1 December 1944 and 14 August 1945
C: Remaining at the surrender

battle, but on the American side there were no fewer than nineteen major task groups employed in the various actions that go under the collective name of Leyte Gulf, and these formations between them numbered 9 fleet, 8 light fleet, and 29 escort carriers, 12 battleships, 12 heavy and 16 light cruisers, 178 destroyers, 40 destroyer escorts, and 10 frigates. The relationship between supremacy and victory cannot be gainsaid, but supremacy does not alter the fact that victories nonetheless have to be fought for and won.[2]

What is very interesting about Leyte Gulf, other than the paradox that not one of the actions that was fought under this title was fought in Leyte Gulf, is that it proved a battle of annihilation if not in the literal sense—as was the case with Tsushima, where just three units survived to make their way to Vladivostok—and had two dimensions, the first in the period of the battle itself and then in the immediate follow-up phase. What is seldom considered about this battle is that the Japanese committed what in effect was the whole of their fleet, a total of just sixty-nine warships, plus thirteen escorts and fourteen submarines, but of their fleet units no fewer than twenty-eight were sunk in the period of the battle and another thirteen were sunk in the follow-up phase as American forces reached into and across the Philippines. (See table 14.1.)

These figures clearly point to overwhelming American victory and the reduction of the Kaigun to no more than an ineffective coastal defense force, but the sheer scale of this American victory has tended to overshadow two matters that complemented it. In terms of continuing Japanese warship and shipping losses, the month of November 1944 really represented a second victory for the U.S. Navy that stood comparison with the October victory. Just as there had been what amounted to a massacre of small and auxiliary warships primarily directed to local duties between 1 September and 21 October, before the intervention of the fleet brought not protection but some form of slight and short-lived relief from American attack, so after the battle of 23–27 October there was what amounted to a second massacre of local warships—a total of thirty-one escorts, minelayers and minesweepers, amphibious units, and minor units—as a direct result of these units have been shorn of protection against carrier aircraft attack while the submarines, released from fleet duties in the immediate vicinity of the Philippines, reached beyond these waters. In this period, between 29 October and 30 November, the Japanese lost no fewer than sixty-seven warships of 227,001 tons, and such totals form the basis of the statement that in terms of continuing Japanese warships losses, November represented a second victory for the U.S. Navy that stood comparison with the one won in October. The tables in this chapter tell their own story.

The tables indicate a most marked increase in the tempo of warship sinkings as the Americans reached into and across the Philippines after the battle, though perhaps it should be noted that the most notable victims in the period between 29 October and 30 November 1944 were exacted from the other theaters as submarines reached out beyond Philippine waters: the 17,500-ton escort carrier *Shinyo* torpedoed and sunk by the *Spadefish* northeast of Shanghai on 17 November, the 32,156-ton battleship *Kongo* by the *Sealion* off northwest Formosa in the early hours of 21 November, and, most famously of all, the 64,800-ton fleet carrier *Shinano* by the *Archerfish* south of central Honshu on 29 November. Of course Allied submarines were in these same areas before Leyte, but after the battle they returned in numbers to these waters and exacted their toll of Japanese warships and shipping.

The shipping losses of the corresponding periods basically repeat the same story, though the sheer scale of Japanese shipping losses in this final period (29 October–30 November) would seem to confirm the validity of the statement that in terms of these shipping losses November represented a second victory for the U.S. Navy that stood comparison with the one won in October. In terms of shipping losses, November 1944 represented one of the most costly single months of the entire war, with losses that were exceeded only in February 1944, September 1944, and, very interestingly, October 1944, and with reference to the last of these there is the small matter of an aside that seems to have commanded no historical attention. The shipping losses for these periods are shown in table 14.3.

The obvious significance of these losses is that even in the month of August, which really was merely the prelude to the overture, Japanese shipping losses

TABLE 14.2. TABULAR REPRESENTATION OF JAPANESE WARSHIP LOSSES BETWEEN 1 AUGUST AND 30 NOVEMBER 1944 BY PHASES AND GENERAL AREA

	In the Philippines	Elsewhere in Southern Resources Area	In all other theaters	In all theaters
1–31 August 1944				
Battleships	- -	- -	- -	- -
Fleet carriers	- -	- -	- -	- -
Light carriers	- -	- -	- -	- -
Escort carriers	1: 17,830	- -	- -	1: 17,830
Heavy cruisers	- -	- -	- -	- -
Light cruisers	1: 5,078	- -	1: 5,078	2: 10,156
Destroyers	2: 2,600	- -	2: 2,947	4: 5,547
Submarines	- -	- -	- -	- -
Escorts	4: 3,760	- -	- -	4: 3,760
Minelayers	1: 1,345	- -	- -	1: 1,345
Coastal minelayers	- -	- -	- -	- -
Minesweepers	- -	1: 648	- -	1: 648
Coastal m/sweepers	- -	1: 281	2: 565	3: 846
Gunboats	- -	- -	1: 1,289	1: 1,289
Motor gunboats	- -	- -	2: 351	2: 351
Submarine-chasers	2: 494	- -	4: 1,046	6: 1,540
Netlayers	- -	1: 708	- -	1: 708
Destroyer-transports	- -	- -	2: 3,000	2: 3,000
LSM	1: 950	- -	2: 1,900	3: 2,850
Total	12: 32,057	3: 1,637	16: 16,176	31: 49,870
1–30 September 1944				
Battleships	- -	- -	- -	- -
Fleet carriers	- -	- -	- -	- -
Light carriers	- -	- -	- -	- -
Escort carriers	- -	1: 17,830	- -	1: 17,830
Heavy cruisers	- -	- -	- -	- -
Light cruisers	- -	- -	- -	- -
Destroyers	- -	1: 2,090	- -	1 2,090
Submarines	- -	- -	2: 2,400	2: 2,400
Escorts	2: 1,585	1: 870	2 3,040	5: 5,495
Minelayers	2: 2,743	- -	- -	2: 2,743
Coastal minelayers	- -	- -	- -	- -
Minesweepers	- -	- -	- -	- -
Coastal m/sweepers	2: 415	- -	4: 936	6: 1,351
Gunboats	2: 6,053	- -	- -	2: 6,053
Motor gunboats	4: 666	- -	4: 659	8: 1,325
Submarine-chasers	12: 3,130	- -	4: 520	16: 3,650
Netlayers	2: 1,261	1: 599	- -	3: 1,860

	In the Philippines	Elsewhere in Southern Resources Area	In all other theaters	In all theaters
Destroyer-transports	3: 4,590	- -	- -	3: 4,590
LSM	1: 950	- -	- -	1: 950
Total	30: 21,393	4: 21,389	16: 7,555	50: 50,337
1–21 October 1944				
Battleships	- -	- -	- -	- -
Fleet carriers	- -	- -	- -	- -
Light carriers	- -	- -	- -	- -
Escort carriers	- -	- -	- -	- -
Heavy cruisers	- -	- -	- -	- -
Light cruisers	- -	- -	- -	- -
Destroyers	- -	- -	- -	- -
Submarines	- -	- -	1: 1,630	1: 1,630
Escorts	2: 1,585	- -	1: 1,080	3: 2,665
Minelayers	1: 720	1: 2,330	1: 720	3: 3,770
Coastal minelayers	- -	- -	- -	- -
Minesweepers	- -	- -	- -	- -
Coastal m/sweepers	1: 215	- -	4: 1,111	5: 1,326
Gunboats	- -	- -	- -	- -
Motor gunboats	- -	- -	2: 257	2: 257
Submarine-chasers	1: 130	2: 260	3: 530	6: 920
Netlayers	- -	- -	- -	- -
Destroyer-transports	- -	- -	- -	- -
LSM	- -	1 950	2: 1,900	3: 2,850
Total	5: 2,650	4: 3,540	14: 7,228	23: 13,418
22–28 October 1944				
Battleships	3: 136,523	- -	- -	3: 136,523
Fleet carriers	1: 25,675	- -	- -	1: 25,675
Light carriers	3: 33,642	- -	- -	3: 33,642
Escort carriers	- -	- -	- -	- -
Heavy cruisers	6: 76,021	- -	- -	6: 76,021
Light cruisers	4: 23,335	- -	- -	4: 23,335
Destroyers	11: 23,471	- -	- -	11: 23,471
Submarines	3: 6,522	- -	- -	3: 6,522
Escorts	- -	- -	- -	- -
Minelayers	- -	- -	- -	- -
Coastal minelayers	- -	- -	- -	- -
Minesweepers	- -	- -	- -	- -
Coastal m/sweepers	- -	- -	- -	- -
Gunboats	- -	- -	1: 2,933	1: 2,933
Motor gunboats	- -	- -	- -	- -
Submarine-chasers	1: 130	- -	1: 130	2: 260
Netlayers	- -	- -	- -	- -
Destroyer-transports	- -	- -	- -	- -
LSM	2: 1,900	- -	1: 950	3: 2,850
Total	34: 327,219	- -	3: 4,013	37: 331,232

	In the Philippines	Elsewhere in Southern Resources Area	In all other theaters	In all theaters
29 October–30 November 1944				
Battleships	- -	- -	1: 32,156	1: 32,156
Fleet carriers	- -	- -	1: 64,800	1: 64,800
Light carriers	- -	- -	- -	- -
Escort carriers	- -	- -	1: 17,500	1: 17,500
Heavy cruisers	2: 27,200	- -	- -	2: 27,200
Light cruisers	2: 7,578	- -	- -	2: 7,578
Destroyers	9: 18,730	1: 2,701	1: 2,033	11: 23,464
Submarines	3: 6,658	- -	2: 3,638	5: 10,296
Escorts	6: 5,270	1: 840	- -	7: 6,110
Minelayers	- -	- -	- -	- -
Coastal minelayers	- -	- -	1: 215	1: 215
Minesweepers	1: 648	2: 1,226	2: 1,268	5: 3,142
Coastal m/sweepers	1: 195	- -	- -	1: 195
Gunboats	- -	- -	1: 2,131	1: 2,131
Motor gunboats	1: 246	- -	4: 1,172	5: 1,418
Submarine-chasers	9: 2,670	- -	- -	9: 2,670
Destroyer-transports	2: 3,000	- -	- -	2: 3,000
LSD	1: 5,350	- -	1: 9,433	2: 14,783
LSM	10: 9,471	- -	- -	10: 9,471
Total	47: 87,016	4: 4,767	16: 135,218	67: 227,001

were more than four times the "acceptable" limit of 75,000 tons a month, and thereafter the situation worsened, with the losses of the final period, albeit a few days over a month, all but six times that level. But what is perhaps surprising about these figures is that the peak of shipping losses was in the period 22–28 October. One would expect that any casual perusal of the figures would point in the direction of the fleet and submarine efforts, being directed against enemy main forces, diminishing in terms of the losses incurred by naval support, military, and merchant shipping; however, in this period, 22–28 October, what must have been *en passant* efforts on the part of submarines and carrier aircraft registered a rate of loss—more than 20,000 tons a day—that was greater than at any time in the overall period between 1 August and 30 November, while the overall shipping losses incurred by the Japanese in October 1944 were exceeded only in February 1944. (See table 14.4.)

Even allowing for the inevitable distortion that the returns of a very short and select period may have, clearly two matters were at work in producing losses of this order in the crucial phase of battle. Japanese naval support shipping had to come forward in order to stand by, and thus were exposed to the threat presented by submarines deployed forward of the immediate battle area specifically to meet this eventuality, while merchantmen at some stage had to try to sail and

Table 14.3. Japanese Shipping Losses between 1 August and 30 November 1944 by Classification, Phases, and General Area

	Japanese shipping losses to all causes			
	In the Philippines	Elsewhere in Southern Resources Area	In all other theaters	In all theaters
1–31 August 1944				
Naval shipping	9: 83,342	- -	8: 22,385	17: 105,727
Military transports	3: 14,540	9: 16,082	6: 25,056	18: 55,678
Merchantmen	15: 78,737	7: 21,731	21: 71,783	43: 172,251
Total losses	27: 176,619	16: 37,813	35: 119,224	78: 333,656
1–30 September				
Naval shipping	19: 76,040	4: 22,284	6: 6,985	29: 105,309
Military transports	26: 113,986	2: 8,468	9: 31,517	37: 153,971
Merchantmen	30: 85,678	9: 36,473	17: 33,239	56: 155,390
Total losses	75: 275,704	15: 67,225	32: 71,741	122: 414,670
1–21 October				
Naval shipping	5: 31,491	5: 22,563	5: 19,378	15: 73,432
Military transports	12: 55,408	4: 13,800	5: 16,082	21: 85,290
Merchantmen	10: 54,256	14: 45,080	14: 37,070	38: 136,406
Total losses	27: 141,155	23: 81,443	24: 72,530	74: 295,128
22–28 October				
Naval shipping	4: 23,876	- -	4: 22,510	8: 46,386
Military transports	3: 11,016	1: 989	3: 4,401	7: 16,406
Merchantmen	10: 48,731	4: 8,609	6: 23,332	20: 80,672
Total losses	17: 83,623	5: 9,598	13: 50,243	35: 143,464
29 October–30 November				
Naval shipping	12: 52,262	12: 65,804	9: 31,888	33: 149,954
Military transports	17: 85,951	2: 2,474	7: 34,892	26: 123,317
Merchantmen	19: 70,113	7: 37,937	20: 63,507	46: 171,557
Total losses	48: 208,326	21: 106,215	36: 130,287	105: 444,828
For whole period 1 August–30 November				
Naval shipping	49: 267,011	21: 110,651	32: 103,146	102: 480,808
Military transports	61: 280,901	18: 41,813	30: 111,948	109: 434,662
Merchantmen	84: 339,734	41: 147,611	78: 228,931	203: 716,276
Total losses	194: 887,646	80: 300,075	140: 444,025	414: 1,631,746

TABLE 14.4. DAILY RATE OF LOSS INCURRED BY JAPANESE SHIPPING BETWEEN 1 AUGUST AND 30 NOVEMBER 1944 BY CLASSIFICATION AND PHASES

	Naval Shipping		Military transports		Merchantmen		Overall shipping losses	
	ships	tonnage	ships	tonnage	ships	tonnage	ships	tonnage
1–31 August	0.55	3,411	0.58	1,796	1.39	5,556	2.52	10,763
1–30 September	2.50	9,190	0.50	2,241	1.07	2,391	4.07	13,822
1–21 October	1.29	6,722	1.10	3,878	1.14	3,454	3.52	14,054
22–28 October	2.43	11,946	0.71	1,371	1.86	7,178	5.00	20,495
29 October–30 November	1.45	6,313	0.64	3,219	1.09	3,948	3.18	13,480
Overall	1.59	7,257	0.65	2,460	1.15	3,640	3.39	13,356

thus ran the same risk as the naval support ships, with the additional factor that the scale of escort available was obviously reduced as a result of the fleet and naval support ship commitments. Even allowing for the fact that two-fifths of Japanese losses in this week were outside the area of battle, the scale of shipping losses in this seven-day period, almost half as much again as the next highest rate of losses (1–21 October), is surprising given the American "other" commitments at this time. But no less surprising is the scale of Japanese shipping losses in October and November. The losses of these two months have been pushed to one side by the battle of Leyte Gulf, but nonetheless they are significant not simply because of the scale but because these losses really represented the last quality shipping that was available to Japan. There were good-quality ships remaining in Japanese service but these were few, and by virtue of American depredations, becoming fewer very rapidly; in terms of numbers of ships available to Japan these months represent losses that were disastrous: what had been available from the outset had never been sufficient to meet national needs, but what remained after November 1944 bordered on the negligible. The losses in October and November 1944 were incurred by what was already a massively depleted maritime fleet. After November 1944 Japanese losses declined for the simple reason that there was with every passing month ever less to be lost, most obviously in service shipping; indeed, after November 1944—the last month when service losses were greater than those incurred by the merchant marine[3]—Japanese shipping losses exceeded 250,000 in a month only in January 1945, which month was marked by the American carrier sortie in the South China Sea, and in July 1945, by which time the combination of extensive mining in Operation Starvation and carrier operations against the home islands came together. (See table 14.5.)

Perhaps the most interesting and significant of these statistics is the difference in terms of the losses of the first quarter of 1944, when in tonnage terms the merchant marine incurred just 20.15 percent of losses and the main American efforts were directed against service shipping, and the period between 1

TABLE 14.5. JAPANESE SHIPPING LOSSES BY CLASSIFICATION AND MONTH BETWEEN 1 JANUARY 1944 AND 15 AUGUST 1945

		Naval Shipping Losses	Military Shipping Losses	Merchant Shipping Losses	Overall Shipping Losses
January	1944	32.50: 152,887	20: 88,858	18.50: 69,505	71: 311,250
February	1944	51: 279,326	28: 113,110	33: 114,654	112: 507,090
March	1944	26: 175,754	25: 71,879	14: 38,296	65: 285,929
April	1944	11: 45,456	19: 63,274	18: 35,253	48: 143,983
May	1944	22: 93,390	19: 85,310	20: 73,548	61: 252,248
June	1944	29: 129,338	27: 102,809	20: 63,710	76: 295,857
July	1944	18: 49,996	18: 101,308	30: 92,200	66 243,504
August	1944	17: 105,727	18: 55,678	43: 172,251	78: 333,656
September	1944	29: 105,309	37: 153,971	56: 155,390	122: 414,670
October	1944	27: 139,042	28: 105,274	61: 223,629	116: 467,945
November	1944	30: 136,797	25: 110,648	43: 165,006	98: 412,451
December	1944	7: 25,541	12: 50,834	26: 101,302	45: 177,677
January	1945	19: 78,602	16: 65,227	72: 229,313	107: 373,142
February	1945	3: 17,962	5: 14,588	32: 85,522	40: 118,072
March	1945	21: 69,933	21: 56,768	46: 92,825	88: 219,526
April	1945	10: 43,810	4: 7,692	36: 79,790	50: 131,292
May	1945	11: 22,474	10: 23,030	100: 163,911	121: 209,415
June	1945	12: 22,726	9: 23,719	94: 140,912	115: 187,357
July	1945	8: 31,224	8: 12,450	123: 254,549	139: 298,223
1-15 August	1945	1: 478	2: 16,433	47: 101,412	50: 118,323
Total losses:		384½: 1,725,772	351: 1,322,860	932½ 2,452,978	1,668: 5,501,610
in % terms:		23.05 31.37	21.04 24.04	55.91 44.59	- -

Note: The figures in this table should have E&OE written after them. There are a number of entries, and not just the ones that are unknown, about which certain doubts must be entertained. For example, the hospital ship *Hikawa Maru #2* and the various questions that surround its fate: it has been listed under naval shipping losses for October 1944, but it would seem that it survived the war and was scuttled before the final surrender.

These figures should be regarded with a certain caution, but undoubtedly they are generally accurate and most definitely illustrate the movement of totals downward as the amount of shipping available to the Japanese diminished.

May and 15 August 1945, when merchant shipping incurred 81.25 percent of all losses. When these figures are related to where Japanese losses were incurred—and after March 1945 the vast majority of losses were in home waters and the East China Sea—the extent of Japan's maritime defeat is clear.

And to repeat a point made previously there was just one merchantman lost in the Southern Resources Area between 1 July and 15 August.[4]

TABLE 14.6. JAPANESE SERVICE AND MERCHANT SHIPPING LOSSES AND SELECTED THEATERS OF OPERATIONS, 1 JANUARY 1944–15 AUGUST 1945

	Japanese home waters*	East China Sea	Central Pacific	Southern Resources Area	Overall Japanese losses (again)
1944					
January	9: 46,164	6: 37,295	25: 109,971	20: 79,854	71: 311,250
February	13: 36,124	13: 70,023	52: 281,392	21: 98,529	112: 507,090
March	12: 24,947	1: 5,493	31: 155,784	13: 67,541	65: 285,929
April	9: 25,825	2: 5,085	11: 51,476	16: 54,409	48: 143,983
May	12: 38,986	1: 2,201	15: 50,995	27: 145,236	61: 252,248
June	16: 51,667	2: 6,742	24: 113,950	24: 115,199	76: 295,857
July	21: 57,950	1: 1,922	8: 23,090	32: 158,619	66: 243,504
August	10: 27,574	11: 55,010	8: 24,135	43: 214,432	78: 333,656
September	14: 38,663	5: 12,143	4: 4,373	90: 342,829	122: 414,670
October	9: 34,339	22: 75,326	3: 3,189	77: 334,127	116: 476,945
November	22: 93,161	6: 20,553	2: 1,388	63: 290,544	98: 412,451
1945					
December	2: 7,221	3: 17,101	1: 2,111	35: 147,582	45: 177,677
January	14: 31,728	16: 75,333	3: 1,663	65: 274,991	107: 373,142
February	14: 28,930	2: 1,364	2: 1,075	19: 82,483	40: 118,072
March	16: 29,945	39: 97,493	2: 6,797	24: 77,807	88: 219,526
April	29: 66,793	2: 12,083	- -	14: 44,272	50: 131,292
May	104: 189,110	4: 3,536	- -	10: 13,740	121: 209,415
June	104: 155,514	- -	- -	7: 26,419	115: 187,357
July	136: 295,403	1: 834	- -	1: 834	139: 298,223
1–15 August	48: 116,564	1: 884	1: 875	- -	50: 118,323

Note: * For the purposes of this table and this table only, Japanese home waters include the northern islands.

* * *

For some four decades after the Second World War Western accounts of the Pacific war, and by that one means American accounts, were told primarily in terms of individuals, with MacArthur probably commanding most attention. There were numerous biographies, and the senior naval commanders—such as Admirals King, Nimitz, Halsey, Spruance, and Mitscher—were all afforded treatment that ranged from the overgenerous to the servile. In terms of the opposition, only one Japanese commander was ever afforded much in the way of historians' consideration, fleet commander Yamamoto Isoroku (1884–1943), and the best that can be said about treatment of him is that it seems to have been at best very selective, and at worst highly mendacious and misleading. Some consideration of Yamamoto's record, along with a short examination of the records of three American commanders plus examination of two other matters, forms the concluding part of the chapter and this part of this second volume.

* * *

The first two of the American commanders were admirals whose careers were in effect ended in 1942, and as such they inadvertently provided confirmation of the wisdom of a comment attributed to Nimitz:

> I do believe that we are going to have a major war, with Japan and Germany, and that the war is going to start by a very serious surprise attack and defeat of U.S. armed forces, and there is going to be a major revulsion . . . against all those in command at sea, and they're all going to be thrown out, though it won't be their fault necessarily. And I wish to be in a position of sufficient prominence so that I will then be considered as one to be sent to sea.[5]

Leaving aside one's suspicion that this comment stretches credibility, not least on account of the prediction of "a very serious surprise attack," the two American commanders who were not so fortunate as Nimitz are Frank Jack Fletcher (1885–1973) and Robert Lee Ghormley (1883–1958). Slightly wounded in the battle of the Eastern Solomons in August 1942, Fletcher after "the outbreak of the Pacific war . . . commanded in three major battles. Since April three carriers under his command had been torpedoed, and two of them, the *Lexington* and *Yorktown*, had gone down. With such a record, it was generally agreed that he must be extraordinarily unlucky or extraordinarily inept."[6] The fact of the matter was that Fletcher commanded American forces in the first three carrier battles that were ever fought and was never on the losing side; the comments here are remarkable in the assumption of American invulnerability: there is simply no acknowledgement that in the military profession an individual may make a great number of decisions, each and every one correct, and still be killed because the enemy has the same rights. Herein is a point that is particularly relevant at the present time, because the fact is that no state can carry out attacks on other states and enjoy automatic immunity from counterattack itself, yet here, and at the present time, is an assumption of assured success and victory with no real cost. It was not in Fletcher's power, indeed it was not in the power of any individual, to ensure the U.S. Navy against loss as it did battle with the enemy, yet Fletcher was moved into the backwater of the North Pacific, to Dutch Harbor and the Aleutians,[7] and was left there, and left there with Nimitz's full knowledge and obvious approval.

Certainly the treatment afforded Fletcher stands in very marked contrast to that afforded Marc Andrew Mitscher (1887–1947), who, if various stories are to be believed, deliberately falsified his ship's battle report for Midway and to whom Raymond Ames Spruance (1886–1969) did not speak for over a year as a result. The real point about Fletcher is the dismissive treatment afforded him over the years; it is only in the last year that redress has become possible in the form of

John B. Lundstrom's masterly *Black Shoe Carrier Admiral: Frank Jack Fletcher at Coral Sea, Midway, and Guadalcanal.* Reference to the last of these battles leads to similar comment about Ghormley. Appointed commander in the south Pacific in June 1942, he was responsible for the landing on Guadalcanal in August but was dismissed from his post in October as the crisis in the southwest Pacific deepened. It has been suggested that his medical—in fact dental—condition in some measure explains his alleged ineffectiveness, but one is at a loss to understand what his successor did after 15 October that resulted in the campaign being won within the next month. One is tempted to suggest that virtually everything that was to bring victory was in place by 15 October when Nimitz made the decision to dismiss Ghormley, and one is less than convinced that the victories that were won in the first and second naval battles off Guadalcanal can be attributed directly to his successor. As it was, his successor was William Frederick Halsey Jr. (1882–1959), and here the record is decidedly difficult, because it would seem that he was afforded indulgence denied Fletcher and Ghormley and was never held to account despite manifest errors of judgment with reference to the 1945 typhoons and to his conduct at the battle of Leyte Gulf.

Regarding the latter, Halsey's professional reputation is linked to the "World Wonders" controversy, and specifically to Halsey's representation of the incident in his autobiography,[8] which has received uncritical acceptance over the years. Halsey wrote that Nimitz's signal

> drove all other thoughts out of my mind. I can close my eyes and see it today:
>
> From: CINCPAC.
> To: COM THIRD FLEET.
>
> THE WHOLE WORLD WANTS TO KNOW WHERE IS TASK FORCE 34.
>
> I was as stunned as if I had been struck in the face. The paper rattled in my hands, I snatched off my cap, threw it on the deck and shouted something that I am ashamed to remember. Mick Carney (the chief of staff) rushed over and grabbed my arm: "Stop it! What the hell's the matter with you? Pull yourself together!"
>
> I gave him the dispatch and turned my back. I was so mad I couldn't talk. It was utterly impossible for me to believe that Chester Nimitz would send me such an insult. He hadn't, of course, but I did not know the truth for several weeks. It requires an explanation of Navy procedure. To increase the difficulty of breaking our codes, most despatches are padded with gibberish. The decoding officers almost always recognise it as such and delete it from the transcription, but CINCPAC's encoder was either drowsy or smart-alecky, and his padding—"The whole world wants to know"—sounded so infernally plausible that my decoders read it as a

> valid part of the message. Chester blew up when I told him about it; he tracked down the little squirt and chewed him to bits, but it was too late then: the damage had been done.

It is this version of events that has imposed itself on accounts of the battle, but two points need be noted. First, the signal passed to Halsey, not the version given here, very clearly had "The World Wonders" after the designator, and therefore should have been recognized by Halsey as not having been part of the message. Admittedly, the process of filter-up filter-out might well have meant that Halsey was not familiar with signals procedures and therefore did not realize the significance of the RR designator when he read the signal; that seems more than likely and indeed it makes sense of his being so distraught at the supposed insult. But the most authoritative biography of Halsey wrote of this episode:

> Halsey, speechless, handed the dispatch to his chief of staff and turned away. A check with the *New Jersey*'s (signals personnel) identified the final words of the despatch as padding.[9]

In other words, within a minute or two of having received this dispatch and having indulged himself in his tantrum, Halsey must have been aware of the truth, that Nimitz most definitely had not sent him a studied, very deliberate insult. Even allowing for the aftermath of misplaced indignation, and the fact that for the immediate moment Halsey probably did need a few minutes to calm himself, the point is that in his account of this episode Halsey seems to have been very discerning, and not just in the wording of a signal. It is very hard to resist the conclusion that in setting out this version of events Halsey, if he did not lie and lie very deliberately, was very selective with the truth, and definitely sought to cloud issues and to conceal the true sequence of events. This version of events in Halsey's autobiography seems to be mendacious and wholly self-serving, and one suspects for obvious reason—to deflect attention from his own ill-considered decisions, which could have had very unfortunate consequences and for which he was never held to account.[10] Quite possibly, however, over time Halsey came to believe in the truth of his account.

* * *

Certainly, if for a very different reason, Yamamoto was never to be held account for a series of decisions that do lend themselves to detailed and careful historical scrutiny. It is one of the very curious features of the historiography of the Pacific war that there seems to have been no critical examination of Yamamoto's role and responsibilities as fleet commander in operations. There was the wholly inadequate provision for the operations that resulted in the battle of the Coral Sea and a local check in the southwest Pacific; the planning for and conduct of operations off Midway, which, one would suggest, ranged on Yamamoto's part from the abysmal to worse; the tardy and piecemeal reaction to the American landing on Guadalcanal that condemned the Japanese to the pursuit of objectives always just beyond their reach, whereas a commitment in strength from the outset might well have resulted in victory in this theater; the conduct of the air offensive in the southwest Pacific in April 1943 that embraced claims that were frankly preposterous, that should never have been entertained for a moment, and that certainly were never corrected, and seemingly never even disputed, by Yamamoto.

The acclaim generally afforded Yamamoto in the histories of the Pacific war that have appeared over the last six decades is very difficult to square with Yamamoto's role as commander of the Combined Fleet after 1939, and there is a second matter in similar vein. Yamamoto's reputation as a pioneer of carrier aviation seems rather puzzling, not least on account of a lack of sea time between 1929 and 1939. He did command a carrier division, but did so solely for the period between October 1933 and May 1934, which hardly constituted sufficient time to learn the practical aspects of this new dimension of naval warfare, still less to demonstrate competence, flair, and powers of innovation. Before 1939 he appears to have been outpaced, and outpaced by a margin and a half, in carrier aviation matters by the likes of such individuals as Vice Admiral Inoue Shigeyoshi (1889–1975); if his time in the Aeronautics Department saw the development of the Mitsubishi A6M Zero-sen, there seems to be little evidence to support the view that Yamamoto was in some way personally responsible for, and should be credited with, the development of what was undoubtedly the foremost naval fighter in the world in 1940–1941.

Even the most casual consideration of Yamamoto's record is difficult to reconcile with the admiral's historical reputation, probably primarily as the result of two sets of circumstances. First, Yamamoto was killed—in fact he was murdered when the plane in which he was traveling was deliberately shot down because he was known to be in it—before the real defeats began to materialize. Therefore he could be exonerated from responsibility for the series of comprehensive defeats after November 1943. Second, the treatment afforded Yamamoto and the Kaigun was politically acceptable, and indeed desirable, in the situation after 1945 as Japan moved alongside the United States. Responsibility for the war and for defeat in that war was placed firmly on the Rikugun; in the two decades after war's end there were a series of biographies in which the Kaigun emerged with credit, especially in comparison to the Rikugun, and specifically in terms of their very different treatment of recruits: the Imperial Army had a fiercesome reputation for brutality toward its own soldiers, on the battlefield, and toward conquered civilian populations. But it was the Imperial Navy, not the Imperial Army, that opposed naval limitation treaties in the 1930s, which resulted in the end of such arrangement after 1937; it was the Kaigun, not the Rikugun, that demanded war in 1941; and it was the Kaigun, and specifically Yamamoto, that demanded that war in 1941 should begin with the Pearl Harbor operation.

But if the sequence of events and a certain portrayal of them are somewhat difficult to reconcile, two other matters arise. The first of these two is the very last matter raised in the preceding paragraph, the attack on the Day of Infamy, and specifically the aspect of the Japanese failure to attack the base facilities at Pearl Harbor. This was a point of criticism made by American admirals, most notably Husband Edward Kimmel (1882–1968) and Nimitz, after the war, and it was a point of criticism written into the third volume of the U.S. Navy's official history published in 1948.[11] This criticism has become firmly embedded in public perception, and indeed it is one of the defining moments in the film *Tora! Tora! Tora!* that contributed so massively to the process whereby it became so well established in popular mythology.[12] But the one episode in the film to which this idea owes its strength is the scene on the admiral's bridge in the *Akagi* when the commander of the strike aircraft, Commander Fuchida Mitsuo (1902–1976), confronts the formation commander, Vice Admiral Nagumo Chuichi (1886–1944), with the demand for a follow-up strike. As Fuchida stated, as he flew back to the *Akagi* he "mentally earmarked for destruction the fuel-tank farms, the vast repair and maintenance facilities, and perhaps a ship or two bypassed that morning," but it does defy belief that had Nagumo been confronted with such a demand he would have authorized a follow-up strike that placed shore-based facilities ahead of warships on the list of priorities. There is, however, no independent evidence to suggest that Fuchida had ever considered such targets before the attack, and we are called upon to believe that Fuchida came to a realization that anticipated post-war criticism of the Japanese failure to attack these facilities and that he actually proposed a course of action that would have forestalled it. Moreover, Fuchida's account, and his claim to have foreseen the opportunity to attack the base facilities, does not sit easily alongside the fact that this account was given for the first time on 11 December 1963, in an interview with Gordon W. Prange (1910–1980), the historical adviser in the making of the film. Prange seems to have accepted Fuchida's account uncritically, and we are thus left to believe an account of proceedings given twenty-two years after the event, when for eighteen of those years Fuchida had possessed ample opportunity to inform the world of his insight. What is interesting is that Fuchida made no reference to his grasp of opportunity when subjected to post-war interrogation on 10 October 1945 for the historical study of the Pacific war undertaken under the terms of the U.S. strategic bombing survey during the first months of the American occupation of the home islands.

Perhaps even more relevantly, the post-war account of proceedings provided by Nagumo's chief of staff, Vice Admiral Kusaka Ryunosuke (1892–1971), in *The Pearl Harbor Papers: Inside the Japanese Plans,* makes absolutely no reference to any incident on the bridge of the *Akagi* and Fuchida's demanding a second strike against base facilities. The chief planner of the attack, Commander Genda Minoru (1904–1989), in his own memoirs penned at the end of the sixties, categorically denied that any such incident took place. Genda stated:

> According to Dr. Prange's book *Tora, Tora, Tora* and others, a fierce argument took place on the bridge of the *Akagi* (after the recovery of second-wave aircraft) as regards the proposal for a second strike [i.e., a third wave].
>
> This is not true. The author had been on the bridge for some eight hours before the start of operations and remained there over the following four days. . . . Such a proposal was never made.
>
> I of course did not make such a proposal myself. The day before the attack I suggested to [Nagumo] that a second strike would be necessary should the first strike fall short. . . . That is all I did but . . . Nagumo seemed to have no plan to implement a second strike. Later Kusaka told me that even before the start of the operation he and Nagumo had decided not to carry out a second strike.[13]

There is no doubt that Fuchida was guilty of deliberate lying, of blatant and shameless self-advertisement, in a calculated and false representation of an episode that never took place. His being branded a liar by Genda, of all persons, was reason why, in the aftermath of this episode, Fuchida emigrated to the United States; in Japanese terms, he was dead in the water and the only place for him, along with conversion to Christianity, was an uncritical American society. But this whole episode does raise two related issues.

The first of these is the question of if and when such a strike could have been conducted. Certainly there were sufficient torpedoes—some sixty presumably, with the *Akagi*, *Kaga*, *Hiryu*, and *Soryu*—but the Japanese carrier formation appears to have had no more Type 5 heavy bombs other than those used by Kates in the first-wave attack, and for sustained operations against either major warships or base facilities the smaller 250-kg. bombs lacked real destructive power. But the real question is when such a strike could have been conducted, because by the time that all aircraft from the first strike had been recovered, plans formulated, and aircrew briefed, it would not have been much before 1500 that aircraft could have left their carriers. Allowing four hours for an attack—and that does represent a duration that might be considered too short for a process that had to stretch from the launch of the first to the recovery of the last aircraft as well as the flights to and from Pearl Harbor and the attack itself—then one arrives at 1900, but sunset on 7 December 1941 was at 1712, with civilian twilight, which is the last time when the horizon would have been discernible, at 1734; nautical twilight, with the last traces of daylight in the western skies, was at 1805. No second strike could have been completed, and aircraft recovered, on 7 December 1941 without the lottery of night landings, and it is inconceivable that any Japanese commander, at the very start of a war, would expose his aircraft and personnel to the very strong possibility of loss. But if no strike was possible on 7 December, no strike would have been possible on the following day for one very simple reason: the destroyers needed refueling, and the oilers were one day's steaming distance to the north of the carrier formation. The Japanese force had to turn back and did not complete refueling until 9 December, and then, if a follow-up strike was to be conducted, it would have been obliged to turn back in order to close upon Pearl Harbor. Therefore it would not have been in a position to carry out a second strike until 10 December, and that is perhaps being somewhat liberal: given anticipation of American search operations, the Japanese force may well have been obliged to move to the east and to have conducted any strike operation at some time other than in the early hours, when the American could be expected to be at their most alert. By any reasoned standard, it would seem that a second strike could not have been conducted before 11 December.[14]

What such a strike may have achieved is quite another matter, and perhaps one conclusion may be floated from the outset: it is difficult to believe that a Japanese second-strike against base facilities, and specifically the oil farms, could have been more damaging than the wrecking in 1916 of the Ploesti oilfields, which the Germans were able to restore without undue difficulty. Moreover, given the enormous American capacity to produce machine tools for domestic and Allied needs, the speed with which the Americans were able to build air and naval bases in the course of their drive across the Pacific, and the sheer difficulty involved in seeking to destroy power stations as per the Second World War and the bombing of Germany, one suspects that reconstruction of facilities at Pearl Harbor destroyed by the Japanese in a follow-up strike would not have proved a protracted affair.

With reference to oil farms and storage, work had begun on building underground storage for some 5,400,000 barrels of fuel oil and 600,000 barrels of diesel oil in December 1940; the first vault was completed on 28 September 1942, and the whole project, with tanks 250 feet high and 100 feet wide inside Red Hill, was completed on 20 July 1943. A follow-up attack would therefore have found the greater part of fuel above ground, but one assumes fire suppression systems must have been in place. But even if these were not available and the Japanese had been able to destroy the petrol, oil, and lubricants that were stored at Pearl Harbor, the fact was that there was very substantial reserves in California; in addition, over the previous two months Britain had returned to the United States fifty oilers that had been provided under lend-lease that summer, and some twenty of these could have provided storage for the equivalent of about half of the oil on Oahu on 7 December 1941.[15] Given the loss of four battleships and the damage inflicted on two more, the U.S. Navy's oil requirements in the Pacific were correspondingly reduced, and one is left with the conclusion that the deployment of oilers to Pearl Harbor in a storage role could have met all American needs in the first two years of war; the real oil needs came after November 1943 when the U.S. Navy employed task forces as opposed to task groups.

Overall, even if there had been a demand for a follow-up strike one would not have been possible for several days, would have been conducted in the face of an alert defense, and is unlikely to have inflicted telling, strategic damage: it seems, prima facie, that the only way that the Japanese might have registered significant damage was if they had conducted a major landing operation—the *koryaku* as opposed to the *kogeki* or strike—that resulted in their occupation of the island and destruction of the base. How this could have been done, given the demands of operations in southeast Asia, and how a force put ashore on Oahu could have been sustained across half an ocean, does defy ready understanding.

This touches, however, on the second of "the two other matters" that, several pages ago, were to close this chapter. This, perhaps the most surprising of all the matters that relate to the historical treatment of the Pacific war, is the fact that in the last ten years or so there has emerged in Japan a generation of university students with no ties to the Imperial services. We are now with the third generation of post–1945 students, and the fierce conformity that once seemed to rule Japan appears to have passed. Such national icons as Togo and Yamamoto are now subjected to critical examination unthinkable even in the 1960s and 1970s, and herein perhaps is cause for what, for historians, should be cautious hope. Japan as a nation has had very great problems in coming to terms and settling its accounts with other countries in east and southeast Asia with reference to the Second World War; certainly the manner in which the war ended in many ways enabled Japan to escape the worst consequences of its actions. Hiroshima and Nagasaki made it the victim of the piece, the lack of any campaign on the home islands meant that there was no fundamental re-examination of the national "self" as there had to be in Germany after 1945, and thereafter the force of change throughout the general area in many ways "let Japan off the hook," specifically with respect to the coming to terms with China and post-1937 events. Certainly many of the histories that appeared in the two decades or so after the end of the war seem to have been very selective and definitely minimized Japan's various sins of commission and omission. It may be, however, that at the present time we stand on the brink of new scholarship and new histories, more objective and discerning, and with no specific line of argument, nationalist or otherwise, than have been available to date.

PART 5

DEALING WITH REAL ENEMIES

CHAPTER FIFTEEN

FINIS: THE BRITISH HOME FLEET, 15 AUGUST 1945

On 31 August 1939 the British Navy was by some margin the greatest navy in the world, and by virtue of a history and tradition that reached back hundreds of years. In terms of size it had ceded equality of status to the U.S. Navy at the Washington conference, but throughout the inter-war period it remained, in terms of standing, prestige, and reputation, the leading navy in the world, and a mark of its standing was the fact that throughout this time British warships occupied pride of position on the Bund at Shanghai.

When British warships returned to Shanghai with the end of the Japanese war they found their position already occupied by American warships.

* * *

The Second World War saw the position of naval leadership taken by the U.S. Navy in what was a somewhat unusual process. Ownership of the Trident passed from predecessor to successor without their fighting one another for possession, and perhaps the only parallel, which may be deemed not exact, would be the British acquisition of naval primacy in an eighteenth century, which saw Dutch decline and French defeat (E&OE). But whatever historical examples are drawn for reasons of comparison, the point herein is that in August 1945 the British Navy had ceded pride of place to its American counterpart, yet it remained, by what seemed at that time a very real and comfortable margin, the second greatest navy in the world; with one exception, all the other major navies had been defeated and suffered major losses that had reduced them to the status of the "also-ran." The exception was the Royal Italian Navy, but the end of war pointed in the direction of its incurring major reduction in terms of reparation, even though with the end of the European war and the return of many of its warships to home ports in August 1945 the Italian Navy probably remained the largest single navy in the Mediterranean. The German and Japanese navies in effect ceased to exist with the end of their respective wars, though for some years German and Japanese warships remained in service under Allied operational control with respect to reparation and minesweeping duties. The losses incurred by the French and Soviet navies had reduced both to little more than auxiliary status, in the case of the French relative to the U.S. and British and in the case of the Soviet to its military counterpart. And, too easily forgotten but mentioned previously, the third-largest navy in the world at this time was that of Canada.

* * *

The Pink List was the register of British warships kept by the Admiralty and was updated every few days. It provided the last recorded whereabouts of all warships, submarines, amphibious units, and auxiliaries, including transports, that were under British operational control. It included British and Indian units and those of the Royal Australian, Canadian, and New Zealand Navies and the South African Navy.

On British A4 paper and with a Courier 8 font, and with units listed consecutively and given details of displacement, class, whereabouts, and fate, but not assigned individual lines, *The Pink List* for 15 August 1945 is more than fifty-six pages in length.

In August 1945 the focus of British naval attention was the Pacific, at least in terms of the fleet and future amphibious commitments. Greater numbers, specifically in terms of amphibious shipping, were gathered in the Indian Ocean, but this theater was clearly second to the Pacific. Probably third in the British pecking order was the Mediterranean theater and on account of profile rather than numbers; with reference to fleet unit numbers, the British navy in August 1945 may well have been the third largest in the Mediterranean, and only marginally larger than the Greek Navy, which, given the situation in theater in 1940–1943, seems to border on the extraordinary and the bizarre.

In British home waters were gathered the greatest numbers of warships, with submarines, minesweepers, and the units required for training purposes prominent in the lists. But with the greatest number of warships being those decommissioned and placed in reserve, and many earmarked for disposal and scrapping, the operational strength of the Home Fleet on 15 August 1945, some thirteen weeks after the end of the war in Europe, consisted of:

The 1st Battle Squadron: The 33,950-ton *Nelson*-class battleship [1925] *Rodney* (flagship at Rosyth).

The 10th Cruiser Squadron: The 5,720-ton *Dido*-class light cruiser [1942] *Bellona* (arrived at Rotterdam on 15 August), the 9,100-ton *Southampton*-class light cruiser [1936] *Birmingham* (in the Clyde), the 4,850-ton (Polish) *D*-class light cruiser ex-*Danae* [1918] *Conrad* (at Oslo), and the 5,450-ton [1939] class-name light cruiser *Dido* (at Rosyth).

Non-operational unit: The 5,770-ton *Dido*-class light cruiser [1939] *Diadem* (at Portsmouth: to be ready on 22 August).

The 2nd Destroyer Flotilla, attached to Home Fleet pending redeployment to the East Indies Fleet: The 1,710-ton Z-class destroyers [1943] *Zambesi* (at Kristiansand in Norway), [1944] *Zebra* (at Rosyth), and [1944] *Zodiac* (en route to Flensburg in Schleswig-Holstein on the Baltic).

The 17th Destroyer Flotilla: The 1,550-ton O-class destroyer leader [1941] *Onslow* (arrived at Rotterdam on 15 August), the 1,710-ton C-class destroyer [1944] *Comet* (at Wilhelmshaven), the 1,335-ton (Polish) G-class destroyer [1935] *Garland*, the 1,540-ton O-class destroyers [1942] *Obedient*, [1942] *Opportune* (all at Rosyth), [1941] *Oribi* (in the Clyde), and [1942] *Orwell* (at Rosyth), the 1,690-ton (Polish) destroyer ex-*Nerissa* [1940] *Piorun* (sailed from Copenhagen on 15 August), and the 1,710-ton (Norwegian) destroyer [1943] *Stord* (at Bergen).

Non-operational Units: The 2,144-ton (Polish) *Grom*-class destroyer [1936] *Błyskawica* (at Tobermory working up) and the 1,540-ton O-class destroyers [1942] *Obdurate* (at Plymouth: to be available on 29 August) and [1941] *Offa* (at Devonport: to be available on 23 August).[1]

* * *

Therefore the total in service with the Home Fleet was one battleship, four light cruisers, and twelve destroyers, three of which had been detailed for service in the Far East, and three were with foreign crews, two Polish and one Norwegian.[2] In addition, one light cruiser and three destroyers were in dockyard hands and non-operational; also assigned to the fleet was one warship that was responsible for controlled minefields and three fleet tugs, one of which was non-operational.

* * *

At a distance of a lifetime from events, and a lifetime that has seen the British Navy decline massively in status and numbers of warships and in a manner reminiscent of the Dutch Navy in the eighteen and nineteenth centuries, the reduction of the British Navy to little more than a handful of operational warships in home waters in little more than three months after the end of European war may seem "par for the course," and not a major cause of surprise or comment.[3] But the reduction of what was the world's second largest navy to such numbers nonetheless invites certain observations. The reduction of the fleet to just sixteen units was most obviously the product of four major matters coming together at war's end. First, age and the state of so many British warships at the end of a six-year war precluded major overhaul and continued employment; for example, the battleship *Rodney* might well be the fleet flagship, but it had been laid down on 28 September 1922, launched on 17 December 1925, and had entered service in August 1927. It was, depending on definition, in or about to enter its third decade of life by war's end, and in the course of that war it had steamed 156,000 miles and had not been in dock since the refit of December 1941–May 1942. One would suggest that such a record was not untypical of major British units, and for many British capital ships, carriers, and cruisers, war's end pointed to decommissioning, disposal, and scrapping, and with almost indecent haste.

Second, the end of the Japanese war in August 1945 could not have been more fortunate in terms of timing for Britain because of one seldom-acknowledged fact. On account of the massive fall in birthrate in the latter part of the 1920s, the intake for the armed forces in 1946 was going to be smaller than that required by the Royal Navy, and numerically the demands of that service were smaller than those of each of the other two services. One of the reasons why Britain very deliberately chose to send a fleet to the Pacific was that such a commitment would be in manpower terms smaller than that required for one or two corps, with air support. Other factors were involved, most obviously standing with the United States and the desire to recover possessions lost under disgraceful circumstances in 1941–1942, but the manpower problem was perhaps the most important single factor shaping British decisions in 1944–1945 when the question of the future national commitment beset the deliberations of the British high command.[4]

Third, war's end brought home one very simple and salient fact, to which reference has already been made: Britain was bankrupt. In fact Britain had been bankrupt since 1941, and it had only been American largesse, in the form first of a flagrant breach of neutrality and then of the generosity of an ally, that had provided the means whereby Britain remained in the war. But with war's end the basic problem of straitened circumstances, indeed desperate circumstances, had to be addressed, and these had to be addressed by a newly elected government committed to programs that involved massive social change in terms of employment, social security, health care, education, and housing, which was to result, over the next twenty years, in the emergence of a society in which its children, for the first time, did not know primary poverty. But that was two decades down the road, and in 1945 it was the reality of national impoverishment in terms of credit, overseas investment, and foreign trade that was "on the table," as it were.

The fourth matter is related to the third: the awkward fact that navies always do worse than armies with the end of war. Navies, by definition, are costly, and immediate and major savings can be exacted as a result of cuts of navies that are not so easily registered with reference to armies. Historically, therefore, the major reductions of the British Navy in place with the end of the European war had along pedigree, but in 1945 there was the additional matter that Britain was faced with long-term commitments in Germany and Italy and in Trieste, and there were also the military commitments in Palestine and in Greece that reached indefinitely into the future. These various obligations—and that of Trieste lasted until 25 October 1954, after Italy and Yugoslavia had finally resolved their conflicting claims—by their very nature were primarily military, with troops on the ground. This fact provided added rationale in terms of the military relative to the naval, but two more related matters affected the relative status of the services.

After previous wars the issue had been one between army and navy, but after August 1945 the issue was three-way, with an independent air force, along its claims on strategic capability, added to the script; in effect with war's end the navy was third in the pecking order within the British defense establishment. Moreover, with the end of the European war the British Navy in home waters and the North Atlantic consisted primarily of warships that were in any case redundant in terms of need; anti-submarine capability was at a discount. Minesweepers were assured of a future, and indeed a full ten years later minesweepers were still working European waters, to some, but slowly decreasing, effect; but with the end of the German war there was no enemy and no anti-submarine requirement, and the hundreds of destroyers and escorts that had seen extensive service over the previous six years were bereft of their raison d'être, as one small point appears to confirm.

Any consultation of the lists of British destroyers, frigates, sloops, and corvettes in any of the standard reference works indicates that pre-war units, irrespective of type, were mostly gone by 1950, while the destroyers of the wartime O, P, Q, R, and S classes had been passed to allies and associates, and it was really only the later classes, from 1942 and 1943 onward, that were to remain in service into the 1960s. Corvettes were largely gone by 1950—literally page after page with individual entries of "scrapped-at-some-God-forsaken-place" in 1947, 1948, or 1949—and the position of sloops was little different, though those allocated minesweeping duties tended to survive into the latter part of the 1950s. Frigates were perhaps somewhat more diverse in terms of fate, the second half of the 1950s being the time when most of those that had survived passed finally from the scene. The basic point with reference to British naval needs at this time, at war's end, is simple: the need was high-profile, showing the flag, with carriers and cruisers, but only in terms of numbers consistent with overall budgetary priorities and straitened national circumstances; in fact, however, this process in effect predated the end of the European war and by some margin.

In the last year of the European war, after June 1944, the older British warships that reached back to the previous conflict were being passed into reserve, while units that were damaged by enemy action, mines, or accident for the most part were not afforded repair and returned to service. The demands of routine maintenance, repair, and refit clearly were enough to ensure that dockyards were fully employed, and obviously any lengthy and costly commitment in terms of the repair of a single ship could be set aside, for obvious reason: American yards could produce a replacement more quickly.

At first sight such a development may seem somewhat surprising, because the submarine offensive still remained to be fought, and fought to the war's last hours. Numbers, even of destroyers, escorts, and patrol vessels that had been launched in 1917, 1918, or 1919, remained important, but in this last year of war there were for the Allies numbers sufficient to ensure victory, at this stage at the least demanding cost. Perhaps a token of this situation was the fact that of the fifty flush-deck destroyers that Britain had acquired from the United States in 1940, at immense cost in terms of leased bases in the western hemisphere and hyperbole, just two—the *Lancaster* and *Ludlow*—remained in operational service on 8 May 1945.

Of "the fifty ships that saved the world," no fewer than forty had been either placed in reserve or assigned secondary duties as training and target ships between 1 January 1942 and 8 May 1945, and of these nine had been assigned and transferred to the Soviet Union in 1944, eight into service, and one, the *Lincoln*, for cannibalization for the others. Other than a certain iconic worth, the value of these ships even in 1940, 1941, and 1942 was (at very best) decidedly modest, and the fact that increasing numbers were assigned to local and training duties off Newfoundland and Nova Scotia was evidence of minimal usefulness at this stage of proceedings. By 1943 and 1944, when totals of seventeen and fourteen were removed from active service, they were showing their age, most definitely with reference to the numbers that were then becoming available and that, twenty years younger, represented massive improvement over their predecessors. By 1944 the qualitative improvement of the new ships entering service, their numbers, and Britain's increasing manpower problems in providing crews pointed to older ships, whether British or American, being placed in reserve.[5]

But, of course, such matters were but one aspect of problems to which states at war have no objection: they are the sort of problems that are "nice-to-have." If, however, the worst aspects of problems were avoided in the last year of war, the problems nonetheless had to be confronted with war's end, and with war's end emerged the real enemies—the age and infirmity of warships most certainly, but more importantly national priorities and requirements and hence budgetary provision, and these related back to politicians, parties, and party-politics now that national leadership was no more (or words to that effect). The U.S. Navy, of course, was similarly placed but for the fact that in addition to all these problems it faced revolting admirals. But that is another story.[6]

* * *

O quam cito transit gloria mundi.

APPENDIX 15.1.

THE ORGANIZATION AND DEPLOYMENT OF BRITISH AND ALLIED WARSHIPS UNDER BRITISH OPERATIONAL CONTROL AND IN BRITISH HOME WATERS, 15 AUGUST 1945

THE FOLLOWING LIST relates to major units only and does not include minor units, such as harbor launches and the like, and amphibious units other than major landing ships. Ships are given in italics, stone frigates in ordinary type.

The Admiralty records are by no means complete and are not necessarily standardized.

For example, many units are given dates of when ships were handed over to the breakers, and it would seem that in various accounts this has become all but synonymous with their being sold on that date: some units, however, have both dates, and, of course, the date that the sale was entered in the records was not necessarily the date of sale. In this account, the date of sale is given as the date entered in the records as the date of sale. In setting out the fate of warships use has been made of the term "scrapped after." This was when the unit arrived at the breakers and not necessarily when the scrapping process began. ND means no date is available.

It should be noted, however, that the records of at least sixty-three warships are not complete and that it seems that at least two of the units that appeared in the *Pink List* of 15 August 1945 had been sold and were no longer British and warships: they have nonetheless (and as a matter of courtesy) been included in this list.

Category A reserve status was for ships "all-but-immediately" available. Category B reserve status was for ships that could be returned to service within a four-month period, and Category C reserve status was for ships one step from being stricken and placed on the disposal list, usually for scrapping, and indeed many warships were earmarked for the disposal list and for scrapping prior to being laid up in Category C reserve. By 1948 these categories had been subdivided, but these new designations have not been given.

Plymouth and Devonport are considered as one under the name Plymouth. Likewise, Londonderry and Lisahally are listed under the name Londonderry.

As usual, E&OE.

THE HOME FLEET

1st Battle Squadron:

The 33,950-ton *Nelson*-class battleship [1925] *Rodney* (flagship at Rosyth; paid off on 30 November 1945 at Portsmouth and placed in reserve at Rosyth; sold in February 1948 and scrapped at Inverkeithing after 28 March 1948).

10th Cruiser Squadron:

The 5,720-ton *Dido*-class light cruiser [1942] *Bellona* (arrived at Rotterdam on 15 August. With the New Zealand Navy between 1946 and 1959; scrapped at Briton Ferry, in south Wales, after 5 February 1959); the 9,100-ton *Southampton*-class light cruiser [1936] *Birmingham* (in the Clyde. Remained in service until December 1959; stricken in March 1960 and scrapped at Inverkeithing after 7 September 1960); the 4,850-ton (Polish) *D*-class light cruiser ex-*Danae* [1918] *Conrad* (at Oslo. Returned to British Navy on 28 September 1946; sold on 22 January 1948 and scrapped at Barrow after 27 March 1948); and the 5,450-ton class-name light cruiser [1939] *Dido* (arrived at Rosyth on 7 August. Placed in reserve in October 1947; scrapped at Barrow after 16 July 1958).

Non-operational: The 5,770-ton *Dido*-class light cruiser [1939] *Diadem* (arrived at Portsmouth on 11 July; to be ready on 22 August. In service until 1950; sold to Pakistan in 1956 and transferred on 5 July 1957).

2nd Destroyer Flotilla, attached to Home Fleet pending redeployment to the Far East:

The 1,710-ton Z-class destroyers [1943] *Zambesi* (at Kristiansand. Reserve and training duties after 1946; scrapped at Briton Ferry, in south Wales, after 12 February 1959); [1944] ex-*Wakeful Zebra* (arrived at Rosyth on 3 August. Scrapped at Newport after 12 February 1959); and the [1944] *Zodiac* (en route to Flensburg and arrived on 16 August. Sold to Israel on 15 July 1955).

17th Destroyer Flotilla:

The 1,550-ton O-class destroyer leader ex-*Pakenham* [1941] *Onslow* (D.17: arrived at Rotterdam on 15 August; reduced to care and maintenance status after 14 January 1946 pending deployment to the Mediterranean. Placed in reserve in April 1947. Transferred to Pakistani Navy on 30 September 1949: remained in service until 1987, when assigned duty as accommodation ship); the 1,710-ton *C*-class destroyer [1944] *Comet* (arrived at Wilhelmshaven on 9 August; assigned for service in the Far East. Scrapped in 1962); the 1,335-ton (Polish) G-class destroyer [1935] *Garland* (arrived at Copenhagen on 29 July but probably at Rosyth on 15 August. Returned to British service in July 1946. Sold to the Netherlands on 14 November 1947); the 1,540-ton O-class destroyers [1942] *Obedient* (arrived at Rosyth on 14 August. Scrapped at Blyth after 19 October 1962); [1942] *Opportune* (arrived at Rosyth on 10 August. Scrapped at Milford Haven after 25 November 1955); ex-*Observer* [1941] *Oribi* (arrived in the Clyde on 23 July. Paid off in January 1946 and transferred to Turkey on 18 June 1946); [1942] *Orwell* (arrived at Rosyth on 14 August. Scrapped at Newport after 28 June 1965); the 1,690-ton (Polish) destroyer ex-*Nerissa* [1940] *Piorun* (sailed from Copenhagen on 15 August. Returned to British service in August 1946 as the *Noble*. Scrapped at Dunston, Gateshead, after 2 December 1955); and the 1,710-ton (Norwegian) destroyer ex-*Success* [1943] *Stord* (at Bergen. Sold to Norway in 1946).

Non-operational Units: The 2,144-ton (Polish) *Grom*-class destroyer [1936] *Blyskawica* (at Tobermory working up. Returned to Poland in 1947) and the 1,540-ton O-class

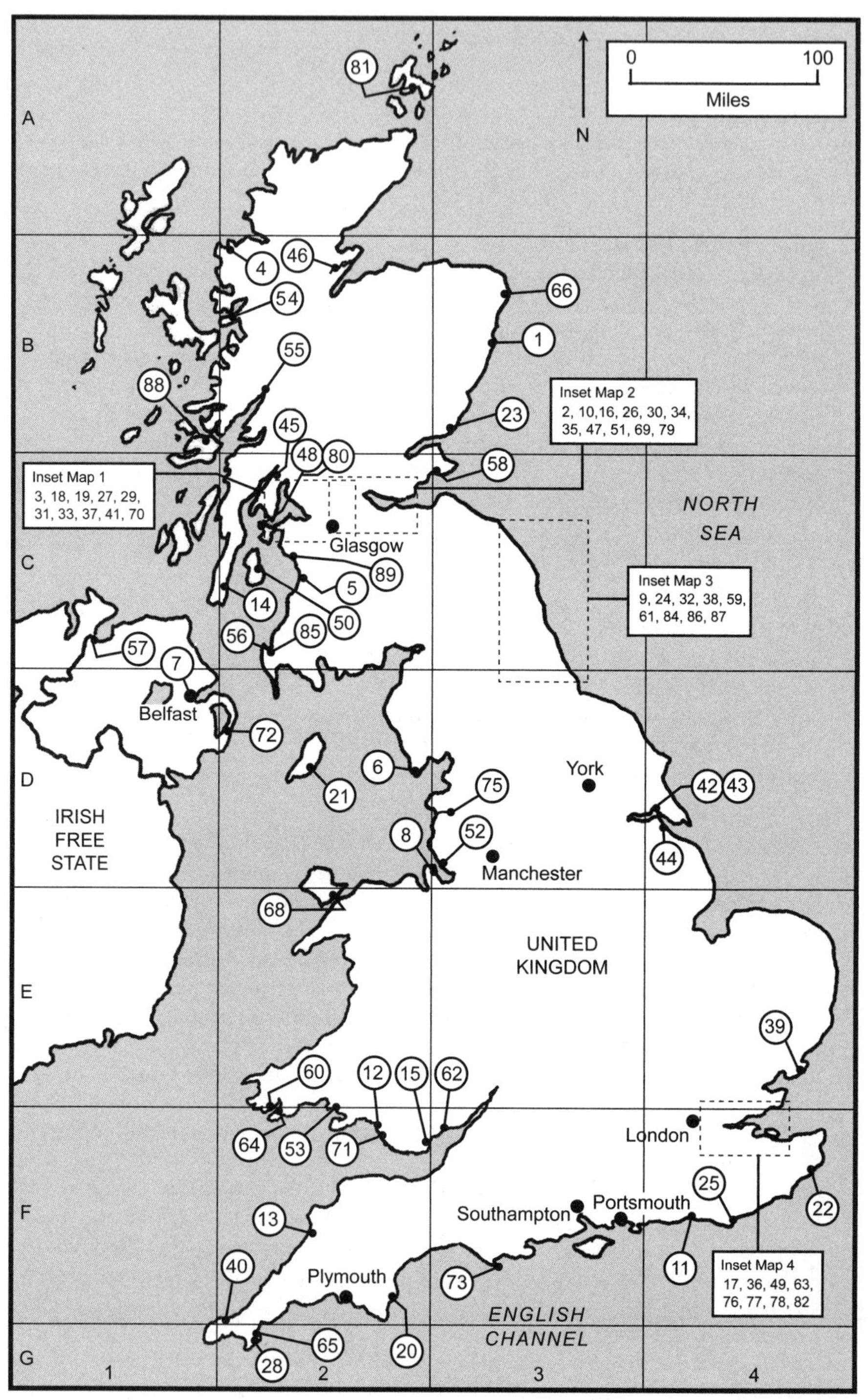

Map 12. Naval Bases and Yards in the United Kingdom, 1939

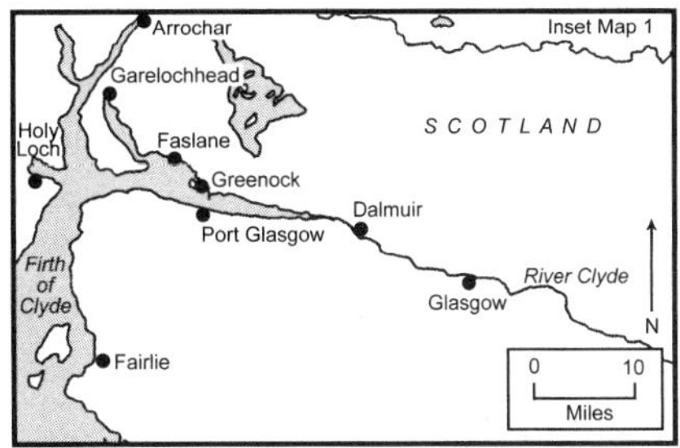

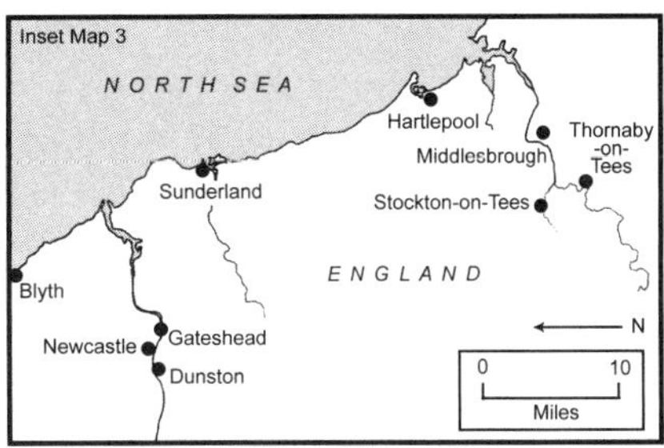

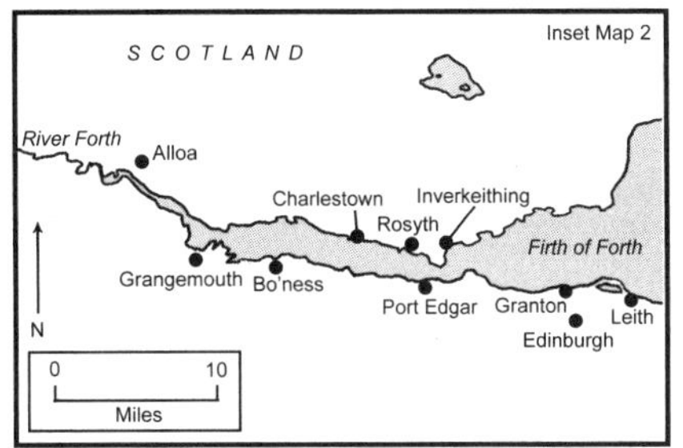

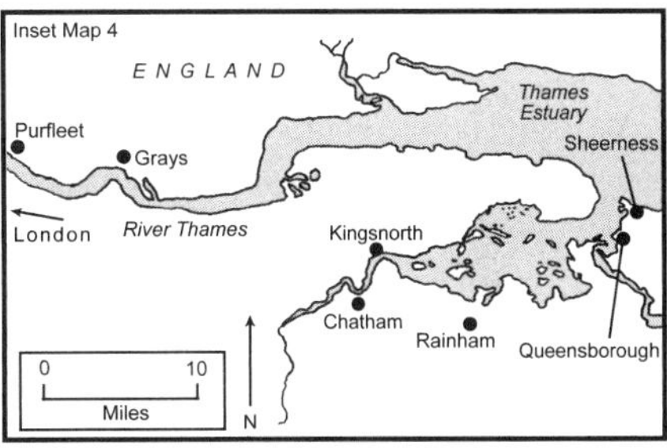

Map 12 Index

1	Aberdeen	B.3
2	Alloa	Inset Map 2
3	Arrochar	Inset Map 1
4	Aultbea	B.2
5	Ayr	C.2
6	Barrow-in-Furness	D.2
7	Belfast	D.1
8	Birkenhead	D.3
9	Blyth	Inset Map 3
10	Bo'ness	Inset Map 2
11	Briton Ferry	F.2
12	Brighton	F.4
13	Bude	F.2
14	Campbeltown	C.2
15	Cardiff	F.2
16	Charlestown	Inset Map 2
17	Chatham	Inset Map 4
18	The Clyde	Inset Map 1
19	Dalmuir	Inset Map 1
20	Dartmouth	F.2
21	Douglas	D.2
22	Dover	F.4
23	Dundee	B.3
24	Dunston	Inset Map 3
25	Eastbourne	F.4
26	Edinburgh	Inset Map 2
27	Fairlie	Inset Map 1
28	Falmouth	G.2
29	Faslane	Inset Map 1
30	The Forth.	Inset Map 2
31	Garelochhead	Inset Map 1
32	Gateshead	Inset Map 3
33	Glasgow	Inset Map 1
34	Grangemouth	Inset Map 2
35	Granton	Inset Map 2
36	Grays	Inset Map 4
37	Greenock	Inset Map 1
38	Hartlepool	Inset Map 3
39	Harwich	E.4
40	Hayle	F.2
41	Holy Loch	Inset Map 1
42	Hull	D.4
43	The Humber	D.4
44	Immingham	D.4
45	Inveraray	C.2
46	Invergordon	Inset Map 4
47	Inverkeithing	Inset Map 2
48	Kames Bay	C.2
49	Kingsnorth	Inset Map 4
50	Lamlash	C.2
51	Leith	Inset Map 2
52	Liverpool	D.3
53	Llanelly	E.2
54	Loch Alsh	B.2
55	Loch Linnhe	B.2
56	Loch Ryan	C.2
57	Londonderry	C.1
58	Methil	C.3
59	Middlesborough	Inset Map 3
60	Milford Haven	E.2
61	Newcastle	Inset Map 3
62	Newport	F.3
63	The Nore	Inset Map 4
64	Pembroke Dock	F.2.
65	Penryn	G.2
66	Peterhead	B.3
67	Plymouth	F.2
68	Port Dinorwic	E.2
69	Port Edgar	Inset Map 2
70	Port Glasgow	Inset Map 1
71	Port Talbot	F.2
72	Portaferry	D.2
73	Portland	F.3
74	Portsmouth	F.3
75	Preston	D.3.
76	Purfleet	Inset Map 4
77	Queensborough	Inset Map 4
78	Rainham	Inset Map 4
79	Rosyth	Inset Map 2
80	Rothesay	C.2
81	Scapa Flow	A.2
82	Sheerness	Inset map 4
83	Southampton	F.3
84	Stockton-on-Tees	Inset Map 3
85	Stranraer	C.2
86	Sunderland	Inset Map 3
87	Thornby-on-Tees	Inset Map 3
88	Tobermory	B.1
89	Troon	C.2

destroyers [1942] *Obdurate* (arrived at Plymouth on 9 August; to be available on 29 August. Trials ship between 1959 and 1964 before being sold and scrapped at Inverkeithing after 30 November 1964) and [1941] *Offa* (arrived at Plymouth on 28 July; to be available on 23 August. At Sheerness after 6 March 1946. Transferred to Pakistani Navy on 3 November 1949: scrapped in 1959).

Controlled Minelayer:

The 346-ton *M*-class [1943] *Miner 8* (arrived at Aultbea on 28 July. Remained in service as the *Mindful* into the sixties).

Fleet Tugs:

The 840-ton *Brigand*-class [1937] *Buccaneer* (arrived at Portland on 14 August; lost in 1946) and [1940] *Freebooter* (at Portland).

Non-operational Unit: The 840-ton *Brigand*-class [1938] *Bandit* (arrived on the Humber on 2 July and undergoing refit; to complete on 30 August).

SUBMARINE COMMAND

3rd Submarine Flotilla:

Depot Ships and Tenders, all at the Holy Loch: The 8,950-ton *Maidstone*-class depot ship [1938] *Forth* (S/M.3. In service [and renamed *Defiance* in 1972] until 1978. Sold in 1985 and scrapped at Kingsnorth, below Chatham on the Medway, after 25 July 1985); the 3,549-ton requisitioned ex-*Ville de Beyrouth*, ex-*Chenals* base and accommodation ship [1911] *Al Rawdah* (returned to owners in 1945); and the 172-ton tender [1936] *Dwarf* (sold on 8 March 1962).

Escorts, all at the Holy Loch: The 1,045-ton class-name sloop [1930] *Hastings* (in the Clyde. Paid off in the Holy Loch on 16 February 1946 and sold on 2 April 1946: scrapped at Troon after 10 April 1946); the 1,370-ton *I*-class destroyer [1936] *Icarus* (arrived in the Clyde on 7 August: paid off in July 1946. Sold on 29 October 1946 and subsequently scrapped at Troon); and the 1,010-ton *Castle*-class corvette [1943] *Morpeth Castle* (at Londonderry, Loch Ryan, and the Holy Loch on 15 August. Scrapped at Llanelly after 9 August 1960).

Non-operational Units: The 1,360-ton *B*-class destroyer [1930] *Brilliant* (arrived at Loch Ryan on 4 August and then on the Clyde undergoing boiler cleaning. Paid off in November 1945 and used as trials ship: placed in Category C reserve on 29 April 1946. Sold on 18 August 1947 and scrapped at Troon after April 1948) and the 525-ton (Dutch) minesweeper [1937] *Jan Van Gelder* (arrived on the Clyde on 25 March and undergoing repair).

Operational and Training Units: The 1,120-ton A-class submarine [1945] *Astute* (arrived at Barrow on 7 August while still on trials. Sold on 2 September 1970 and scrapped at Dunston, Gateshead, after October 1970); the 715-ton *S*-class submarines [1945] *Saga* (arrived in the Clyde on 7 August. Sold on 11 October 1948 to Portugal); [1945] *Springer* (arrived in the Clyde on 1 August. Sold to Israel on 9 October 1958); the 1,090-ton *T*-class submarines ex-*Tasman* [1945] *Talent* (at Arrochar. In the Clyde on 20 August and sailed for Ceylon on 5 October 1945. Wrecked on 15 December 1954 when dock collapsed; raised and rebuilt in 1955. Placed in reserve in 1966. Sold on 6 January 1970 and scrapped at Troon after 1 February 1970); [1943] *Tally Ho!* (arrived in the Clyde on 13 August: sailed for Colombo on 27 October 1945. Scrapped at Briton Ferry, in south Wales, after 10 February 1967); [1943] *Tireless* (arrived in the Clyde on 24 July: sailed on 7 September for Singapore. Paid off in August 1963. Sold on 20 September

1968 and subsequently scrapped at Newport); [1942] *Truculent* (arrived in the Clyde on 24 July. Sunk on 12 January 1950 off the Nore after collision with Swedish merchantman: raised on 14 March 1950. Sold in May 1950 and subsequently scrapped at Grays, near Tilbury); and the [1943] *Truncheon* (arrived in the Clyde on 24 July. To 4th Submarine Flotilla on 1 September and to Singapore after 4 October 1945. Transferred to Israel in 1968).

Non-operational Units: The 1,090-ton A-class submarine [1944] *Amphion* (arrived at Barrow on 18 July and undergoing repair; to complete on 1 September. Sold on 24 June 1971 and scrapped at Inverkeithing after 6 July 1971); the 1,090-ton *T*-class submarines [1943] *Tantalus* (undergoing refit at Dundee; to complete on 10 December. Scrapped at Milford Haven after November 1950); [1942] *Templar* (undergoing refit at Troon after 29 January; to complete on 8 September. Was to be cannibalized in August 1950 but employed as moored target vessel after February 1953. Sunk as target boat in 1954: raised on 4 December 1958. For disposal on 18 March 1959. Scrapped at Troon after 20 July 1959); and the 547-ton V-class submarine [1945] *Venturer* (undergoing refit at Grangemouth after 28 May: undecided. Sold to Norway in 1946).

5th Submarine Flotilla:

Depot Ships and Tenders, at Portsmouth: The Dolphin (S/M.5) and the 5,250-ton class-name [1915] *Titania* (arrived at Portsmouth on 26 July and paid off on 14 September 1945: employed as accommodation ship. Scrapped at Faslane after September 1949) and the 82-ton drifter ex-*Present Help* [1911] *Varbel* (returned to owners in 1945).

Submarine Training Units: The 715-ton S-class submarine [1943] *Sturdy* (at Portsmouth: sold in July 1957 and scrapped at Dunston, Gateshead, after 9 May 1958); the 1,090-ton *T*-class submarines [1943] *Tradewind* (arrived at Portsmouth on 16 July: sailed for refit at Chatham or Sheerness on 5 September. Allocated experimental duties after 11 September 1945: subsequently immobilized and beached as hulk at Fareham Creek near Portsmouth, date unknown. Placed on disposal list, date unknown. Scrapped at Charlestown after 14 December 1955); and the [1940] *Tuna* (arrived at Rotterdam on 15 August. Sold on 19 December 1945 and scrapped at Briton Ferry, in south Wales, after 24 June 1946).

Non-operational Units: The 683-ton submarine [1940] *P. 614* (undergoing refit at Barrow; to complete in November. Having been requisitioned, transferred to Turkish Navy on 17 January 1946); the 715-ton *S*-class submarines [1943] *Sirdar* (arrived at Sheerness on 21 June and undergoing refit after 26 June; to complete on 10 December. Sank in dry dock at Sheerness on 1 February 1953: salved and returned to service. Scrapped at Bo'ness, on the Forth, after 4 May 1965); [1943] *Spiteful* (undergoing repairs at Troon; to complete on 8 September. In French service between January 1952 and November 1958, scrapped at Faslane after 15 July 1963); [1943] *Stoic* (undergoing refit at Portsmouth after 12 March; to complete in August but in fact not completed in 1945. Sold in July 1950 and subsequently scrapped at Dalmuir, below Glasgow); [1943] *Strongbow* (damaged off Malaya on 13 January 1945. Arrived at the Nore on 3 July for docking and examination; deemed beyond economical repair and placed in reserve at Falmouth after 31 October. For disposal on 28 November: scrapped at Preston after April 1946); the 1,090-ton *T*-class submarines [1943] *Tantivy* (arrived at Sheerness on 20 April and undergoing refit; to complete on 25 August. Sunk in the Cromarty Firth as target ship in 1951); [1943] *Telemachus* (undergoing refit at Plymouth after July; to complete in January 1946. Scrapped at Charlestown after 28 August 1961); the 545-ton *U*-

class submarines [1943] *Unswerving* (arrived at Sheerness on 16 May and undergoing refit; to complete on 22 August. Scrapped at Newport after 10 July 1949); and the [1943] *Uther* (arrived at Tilbury to undergo refit on 14 August; to complete on 22 September. Placed in reserve in the Gareloch after 15 November. Sold in February 1950 and scrapped at Hayle in Cornwall after April 1950).

6th Submarine Flotilla, all units at Blyth unless otherwise stated:

Depot Ship: The 84-ton drifter ex-*Rotha* [1937] *Elfin* (paid off at Lowestoft on 14 September 1945: fate unknown).

Submarine Training Units: The 715-ton *S*-class submarine [1942] *Surf* (arrived at Blyth on 27 June. Sold on 28 October 1949 and scrapped at Faslane after July 1950); the 1,090-ton *T*-class submarines [1942] *Tactician* (arrived at Blyth on 11 June. Scrapped at Newport after 6 December 1963) and [1941] *Trespasser* (arrived at Blyth on 27 June. Scrapped at Dunston, Gateshead, after 26 September 1961); and the 545-ton *U*-class submarine [1941] *Ultimatum* (arrived at Blyth, date unknown; sailed on 24 August. Sold on 23 December 1949 and scrapped at Port Glasgow after February 1950).

Non-operational Units: The 715-ton *S*-class submarine [1943] *Spirit* (undergoing refit at Blyth; to complete January 1946. Scrapped at Grays, near Tilbury, after 4 July 1950) and the 545-ton *U*-class submarine [1941] *Unbending* (undergoing refit at Blyth; to complete 21 September. Placed in Category C reserve in the Gareloch on 3 December 1945. Sold on 23 December 1949 and scrapped at Dunston, Gateshead, after May 1950).

Reserve Group: The 1,350-ton *O*-class submarine [1926] *Otway* (arrived at Blyth on 6 March 1945. Sold on 24 August 1945 and subsequently scrapped at Inverkeithing); the 1,090-ton *T*-class submarines [1939] *Taku* (mined on 13 April 1944; deemed *hors de combat* and proceeded to Falmouth and reserve, arriving on 8 November. Sold in November 1946 and subsequently scrapped at Llanelly); [1938] *Tribune* (arrived at Blyth on 23 December 1944. Entered dock on 8 July and to complete in October: to be berthed in reserve at Falmouth. Sold in July 1947 and scrapped at Milford Haven after November 1947); and the [1941] *Trusty* (arrived at Blyth on 2 July. Sold in January 1947 and subsequently scrapped at Milford Haven).

7th Submarine Flotilla:

The 11,300-ton ex-*Indrabarah* depot ship [1905] *Cyclops* (S/M.7 at Rothesay. Relieved by the *Maidstone* on 17 September 1946 and paid off at Faslane on 18 December 1946: for disposal after 8 January 1947. Scrapped at Newport after 29 June 1947); the 574-ton yacht [1930] *Kilma* (at Rothesay; subsequent fate unknown); the 935-ton accommodation ship *Alecto* (arrived at Stranraer and paid off into reserve in Loch Ryan. Sold on 7 July 1949 and subsequently scrapped at Llanelly); the 1,060-ton *Falmouth*-class target vessel [1932] *Milford* (arrived at Rothesay on 23 May. Sold on 3 June 1949 and scrapped at Hayle in Cornwall); and the 222-ton trawler ex-*Elfin* [1933] *Nettle* (at Rothesay as a torpedo recovery vessel: placed on disposal list in 1957).

Submarine Training: The 715-ton *S*-class submarine [1942] *Sportsman* (at Campbeltown, and at Rothesay on 18 August. Arrived at Harwich on 19 December 1845 and placed in Category B reserve next day. In French service after 1951 and lost 23 September 1952); the 1,090-ton *T*-class submarine [1939] *Truant* (arrived at Rothesay on 25 July. Sold on 19 December 1945 and wrecked en route to breakers in December 1946); and the 545-ton *U*-class submarine [1941] *Una* (arrived at Rothesay on 13 July; placed in reserve on 1 December 1945. Sold on 11 April 1949 and subsequently scrapped at Llanelly).

Anti-Submarine Training: The 715-ton S-class submarines [1942] *Satyr* (arrived at Campbeltown on 15 August. In French service between February 1952 and August 1961; returned to Britain and scrapped at Charlestown after April 1962); [1943] *Sceptre* (arrived at Rothesay on 29 June; placed in Category A reserve on 22 July 1947. For disposal on 31 October 1947, trials ships on 12 December and placed in Category C reserve in Upper Loch Linnhie on 23 February 1948. Sold c. 23 August 1949 and scrapped at Dunston, Gateshead, after 9 September 1949); [1941] *Seraph* (arrived at Larne on 14 July. Placed in reserve, undated, and whereabouts not forthcoming; returned to service as target vessel after 28 February 1953 and refit, completed on 1 April 1953. Approved for scrapping 1 March 1963. Placed in reserve on 25 October 1965. Sold on 9 December and scrapped at Briton Ferry, in south Wales, after 20 December 1965); the 545-ton *U*- and *V*-class submarines [1941] *Upshot* (at Plymouth; arrived at the Holy Loch and placed in Category B reserve on 19 December 1945. Scrapped at Preston after 22 November 1949); [1944] *Vagabond* (arrived in the Clyde on 7 June Arrived at the Holy Loch and placed in Category B reserve on 19 December 1945; arrived at Londonderry on 11 February 1946. Scrapped at Newport after 20 January 1950); [1943] *Varangian* (arrived at Rothesay on 5 August. Employed as target ship after September 1946. Approved for scrapping on 18 December 1947; placed in Category C reserve in February 1948 and laid up at Londonderry. Sold in June 1949 and subsequently scrapped at Dunston, Gateshead,); [1944] *Varne* (arrived at Tobermory on 10 July. In reserve at Londonderry after 11 February 1946. Trials vessel after September 1946. Laid up in Loch Alsh in 1948. Scrapped after August 1958); [1944] *Virulent* (at Campbeltown, date unknown. In Greek service between May 1946 and October 1958. Ran aground in November 1958 off northern Spain when being towed home for scrapping; sold in 1961 and scrapped *in situ*); [1944] *Volatile* (arrived at Douglas, Isle of Man, on 12 August. In Greek service between May 1946 and October 1958. Returned to Britain and scrapped at Dunston, Gateshead, after 23 December 1958); [1944] *Votary* (based at Rothesay and at sea, date unknown. In reserve at Arrochar after 31 January 1946. Transferred to Norwegian Navy in July 1946); and the [1943] *Vulpine* (based at Rothesay and at sea, date unknown. In Danish service between September 1947 and 1958. Returned to Britain and scrapped at Faslane after 29 April 1959).

Non-operational Units: The 569-ton *R*-class submarine [1919] P. 511 (having been nominally returned to U.S. Navy on 20 December 1944, laid up at Kames Bay, Kyles of Bute. Foundered on 21 November 1947 and subsequently raised; scrapped after February 1948) and the 854-ton *S*-class submarine [1922] P. 555 (placed in reserve at Rothesay in May 1944 and nominally returned to U.S. Navy on 20 December 1944; sunk as test boat off Portland on 25 August 1947).

9th Submarine Flotilla:

The 6,000-ton requisitioned depot ship ex-*Carmania II* [unkn] *Ambrose* (at Dundee; paid off on 1 March 1946) and the 531-ton trawler [1936] *Loch Monteith* (arrived at Dundee on 26 July; paid off in the Clyde on 12 November 1945).

Operational and Training Units: The 1,090-ton (Dutch) submarine ex-*Taurus* [1942] *Dolfijn* (at Rotterdam. Returned to British service and then again in Dutch service, in the torpedo school, between 1947 and 1952. Sold in May 1952 and scrapped in the Netherlands after May 1952); the 545-ton (Polish) *U*-class submarine [1942] *Dzik* (at

Dundee on 1 August. Returned to British service on 25 July 1946. Transferred to Danish Navy in July 1947. Returned to British service in October 1957; scrapped at Faslane after April 1958); the 546-ton (Dutch) *O. 12*-class submarine [1931] O. 15 (arrived at Dundee on 25 July. Scrapped in 1946); the 888-ton (Dutch) *O. 21*-class submarine [1941] O. 27 (arrived at Dundee on 26 July, being a Dutch boat captured in 1940 and returned with Germany's surrender); the 545-ton (Polish) *U*-class submarine ex-*Urchin* [1940] *Sokół* (docked at Dundee on 27 May. Returned to British service on 3 August 1946; placed in Category C reserve at Londonderry on 23 February 1948: for disposal after April 1949 and scrapped after December 1949); the 670-ton (Dutch) *S*-class ex-*Sturgeon* [1932] *Zeehond* (arrived at Rotterdam on 9 August. Returned to British service on 14 September 1945; scrapped at Granton after January 1946); and the 1,090-ton (Dutch) *T*-class ex-*Talent* [1944] *Zwaardvisch* (arrived at the Hook of Holland on 10 August; sailed for the Tyne and repairs on 25 August. Paid off on 11 December 1962; sold on 12 July 1963 and subsequently scrapped).

Non-operational Units: The 546-ton (Dutch) *O. 12*-class submarine [1931] O. 14 (at Dundee) and the 980-ton (Polish) class-name submarine [1929] *Wilk* (placed in reserve at Plymouth on 2 May 1942. Returned, under tow, to Poland in March 1951).

Surrendered U-boats in British service:

The 749-ton Type VIIc submarines U. 776 (at Kirkwall); U. 1023 (in Loch Ryan); U. 1105 and U. 1171 (both at Londonderry); the 230-ton Type XXIII submarine U. 2326 (at the Holy Loch); and the 1,595-ton Type XXI U. 3017 (at Barrow).

ROSYTH COMMAND

Base and Depot Ship:

The 6,600-ton ex-*Ambrose* [1903] *Cochrane* (C-in-C Rosyth, flagship after 3 November 1940. Sold in August 1946 and scrapped at Inverkeithing after 13 November 1946).

Destroyer Depot Ship:

The 11,500-ton ex-*Manipur* [1905] *Sandhurst* (in the Clyde after 26 August 1942. For disposal and sold in January 1946; scrapped at Dalmuir after 27 April 1946).

Accommodation Ship:

The 1,100-ton W-class destroyer [1918] *Winchester* (arrived at Rosyth on 10 August 1944 and paid off. Sold on 5 March 1946 and subsequently scrapped at Inverkeithing).

Minesweeping Forces:

The Vernon Minesweeping Trials Ships: The 1,140-ton W-class destroyer [1919] *Witch* (arrived at Rosyth on 18 July. Sold on 12 July 1946 and subsequently scrapped at Granton) and non-operational, the 905-ton S-class destroyer [1918] *Sabre* (arrived in the Humber on 27 July. Sold in November 1945 and subsequently scrapped at Grangemouth).

9th Minesweeping Flotilla, administered from Portsmouth and based at Granton:

The 590/672-ton *Bangor*-class sloops [1941] *Sidmouth* (docked at Granton on 1 July for work reference sale to Norway c. 2 October 1945; not forthcoming. Sold on 18 January 1950 and subsequently scrapped at Charlestown); [1940] *Bangor* (at Granton; remained in service until July 1946. Sold to Norway in 1946); [1940] *Blackpool* (arrived at Granton on 1 July. To transfer to Norway and at Kristiansand on 25 October 1945; thereafter in service until July 1946 and then sold into Norwegian service); [1940] *Boston* (arrived at Granton on 6 July 1945. Sold on 1 January 1948 and subsequently scrapped at Charlestown); [1941] *Qualicum* (at sea, having sailed from Harwich on 13 August. Loaned to Norwegian Navy after 6 September and sailed to Kristiansand, arriving 25 October 1945. Sold on 9 February 1949 and subsequently scrapped at Charlestown); (Dutch) [1940] *Romney* (arrived at Granton on 1 July. Was to be transferred to Norway and at Kristiansand on 25 October but remained in service until July 1946. Sold on 18 January 1950 and subsequently scrapped at Granton); and the [1941] *Tenby* (arrived on the Tyne on 1 July. Sold on 1 January 1948 and subsequently scrapped at Dunston, Gateshead).

Attached Danlayers: The 545-ton *Isles*-class trawlers [1944] *Hannaray* (arrived at Granton on 12 July 1945. Sold in 1947) and [1945] *Tahay* (at Granton, having sailed from Kristiansand on 29 June).

40th Minesweeping Flotilla, administered from Rosyth and based at Aberdeen:

The 890-ton *Catherine*-class sloops [1942] *Catherine* (arrived at Aberdeen on 5 July 1945. Returned to U.S. Navy in 1946); [1942] *Gazelle* (arrived at Aberdeen on 8 June 1945. Returned to U.S. Navy in December 1946); and the [1943] *Pique* (at Aberdeen awaiting refit; returned to U.S. Navy in 1946).

Non-operational Units: The 890-ton *Catherine*-class sloops [1943] *Elfreda* (arrived at Rotterdam on 9 August and undergoing refit; arrived in the Humber on 30 November. Returned to U.S. Navy on 30 June 1947); [1943] *Gorgon* (arrived at Rotterdam on 9 August and undergoing refit: undecided. Returned to U.S. Navy on 12 November 1946); [1941] *Grecian* (arrived at Sheerness on 14 July and undergoing refit after 17 July; to complete middle/late September. Returned to U.S. Navy in 1947); and the [1943] *Tattoo* (arrived at Rotterdam on 9 August and undergoing refit: undecided. Returned to U.S. Navy in 1947).

Attached Danlayers: The 890-ton *Catherine*-class sloop [1942] *Chance* (arrived at Aberdeen on 19 June 1945. Returned to U.S. Navy in 1946) and the 545-ton *Isles*-class trawler [1945] *Ronay* (arrived at Aberdeen on 17 June. Placed in Category A reserve on 6 April 1948. Listed for disposal in June 1962. First sold on 26 September 1966 but purchaser defaulted; sold a second time on 13 March 1967 and subsequently scrapped).

42nd Minesweeping Flotilla, administered from the Humber:

The 890-ton *Catherine*-class sloops [1942] *Combatant* (arrived at Aberdeen on 19 July 1945. Returned to U.S. Navy on 15 December 1946); [1943] *Foam* (arrived at Aberdeen on 3 August. Returned to U.S. Navy on 13 November 1946); [1943] *Jasper* (at sea; returned to Aberdeen on 21 August. Returned to U.S. Navy on 24 December 1946); and the [1943] *Steadfast* (arrived at Aberdeen on 27 July. Returned to U.S. Navy on 24 December 1946).

Non-operational Units: The 890-ton *Catherine*-class sloops [1943] *Cynthia* (sailed from Harwich on 11 August and to undergo refit at Ghent, Belgium,: undecided. Returned to U.S. Navy on 20 January 1947); [1943] *Fairy* (arrived at Granton on 13 August. Returned to U.S. Navy on 13 December 1946), [1943] *Florizel* (after 29 March 1945 undergoing repairs at Flushing, the Netherlands, and to complete on 3 October. Returned to U.S. Navy in December 1946); and the [1943] *Frolic* (after 29 March undergoing repairs at Flushing, the Netherlands, and to complete on 3 October. Returned to U.S. Navy in 1947).

Attached Danlayers: The 545-ton *Isles*-class trawler [1944] *Hermetray* (arrived at Harwich on 10 August. Sold in 1947) and the 890-ton *Catherine*-class sloop [1942] *Tourmaline* (en route for Granton, reached on 18 August. Returned to U.S. Navy in 1947).

Unallocated Fleet Minesweepers:

The 850-ton *Algerine*-class sloops ex-Canadian *Orangeville* [1944] *Marmion* (sailed from Ponta Delgada, in the Azores, on 15 August, arriving at Plymouth three days later. Scrapped at Dunston, Gateshead, after August 1958); [1944] *Marvel* (arrived at Granton on 3 August. Scrapped at Charlestown after 7 May 1958); [1944] *Myrmidon* (at Halifax, Nova Scotia, and completed on 7 July 1945. Scrapped at Briton Ferry, in south Wales, after 2 December 1958); [1944] *Mystic* (in Canadian waters and at Halifax, Nova Scotia, on 31 August; scheduled to return to Portsmouth and be laid up at Granton. Scrapped at Llanelly after 3 May 1958); and the [1944] *Rosamund* (at Collingwood, Ontario, on trials, and arrived at Ponta Delgada, in the Azores, on 15 September 1945. Transferred to South African Navy in September 1947).

Netlayer:

The 682-ton requisitioned auxiliary [1940] *Ringwood* (arrived at London on 2 August and paid off; returned to owners in 1945).

Local Escort Forces:

Rosyth: The 1,300-ton *Captain*-class frigates [1943] *Cubitt* (arrived off the Nore on 2 August. Returned to U.S. Navy in 1946); [1943] *Hargood* (arrived at Harwich on 15 August having been in dock at Chatham after 28 July. Returned to U.S. Navy on 31 May 1946); and the 1,435-ton *Loch*-class frigate [1944] *Loch Shin* (sailed from Rosyth for the Clyde on 15 August; paid off in July 1947. Sold to New Zealand Navy on 13 September 1948).

Greenock: The 1,300-ton *Captain*-class frigates [1943] *Cosby* (arrived at Plymouth on 13 August. Returned to U.S. Navy in March 1946); [1943] *Deane* (arrived at Campbeltown on 15 August. Returned to U.S. Navy in March 1946); and the 1,435-ton *Loch*-class frigate [1945] *Loch Tralaig* (arrived in the Clyde on 2 August and completed that month; it remained in service until 1954. Scrapped at Bo'ness after August 1963).

Air/Sea Rescue Duties:

The 1,010-ton *Castle*-class corvettes [1943] *Amberley Castle* (arrived in the Clyde on 6 August and sailed on 19 August. Employed as weather ship after September 1960; scrapped at Troon in 1982); [1943] *Berkeley Castle* (arrived in the Clyde on 21 July. Scrapped at Grays, near Tilbury, after February 1956); [1943] *Dumbarton Castle* (at sea and returned to the Clyde on 22 August. Placed in reserve after 1947. Sold on 16 November 1960 and scrapped at Dunston, Gateshead, after March 1961); and the [1943] *Leeds Castle* (arrived in the Clyde on 5 August. Scrapped at Grays, near Tilbury, after 5 May 1958).

Anti-Submarine Training Flotilla:

Based at Campbeltown: The 1,375-ton *E*-class destroyer [1934] *Escapade* (arrived at Campbeltown on 15 August. For disposal after 18 February 1946. Laid up at Plymouth after 26 November 1946; also used as tender. Sold on 16 February 1947 and scrapped at Grangemouth after 3 August 1947); the 925-ton *Flower*-class corvettes [1941] *Borage* (arrived at Greenock on 12 August. Sold to Irish Free State in 1946); [1941] *Clover* (arrived at Campbeltown on 11 July; placed in reserve in 1946. Sold on 17 May 1947 into commercial service); the 1,010-ton *Castle*-class corvettes [1943] *Flint Castle* (arrived at Bremerhaven on 30 July. Scrapped at Faslane after July 1958), [1944] *Oakham Castle* (arrived at Rosyth on 12 August. Transferred to Air Ministry as weather ship in August 1957); the 1,010-ton *Castle*-class corvette [1943] *Oxford Castle* (arrived at Rosyth on 20

June and at Leith under repair: undecided. Scrapped Briton Ferry, in south Wales, after 6 September 1960); the 925-ton *Flower*-class corvette [1941] *Oxlip* (arrived at Campbeltown on 10 August; paid off and stricken in 1946. Sold to Irish Free State in December 1946); and the 834-ton yacht [1938] *Shemara* (after 30 July at Campbeltown; returned to owners in 1946).

Based at Maydown, outside Londonderry: The 1,350-ton *F*-class destroyer [1934] *Fame* (arrived at Rosyth after refit on 13 August; assigned training duties. Placed in reserve in 1947. Assigned for scrapping on 27 November 1947; cancelled on 6 January 1948 and placed in Category C reserve on 20 January. Agreement that it be sold to Dominican Republic on 28 January 1948. After refit, transferred to the Dominican Republic in February 1949); the 1,340-ton *H*-class destroyer [1936] *Hotspur* (arrived at Rosyth on 3 July. Sold to Dominican Republic on 23 November 1948); the 1,435-ton *Loch*-class frigates [1943] *Loch Dunvegan* (arrived at Rosyth on 25 July. Placed in reserve after January 1953. Scrapped at Briton Ferry, in south Wales, after 24 August 1960); and the [1943] *Loch Fada* (sailed from Methil on 11 August for Hamburg. Remained in service until November 1967. Sold on 21 May 1970 and subsequently scrapped at Faslane).

Experimental Units: The 510-ton sloop [1935] *Kingfisher* (arrived at Fairlie on 11 August; to be paid off into Category C reserve at Faslane. Used as trials ship before being laid up in reserve at Harwich on 2 May 1946: for disposal on 21 April 1947. Sold on 17 May 1947 and subsequently scrapped at Stockton-on-Tees) and, assigned but non-operational, the 1,370-ton *River*-class frigate [1943] *Helmsdale* (arrived at Milford Haven on 21 July and undergoing conversion; to complete in late November. Scrapped at Faslane after 7 November 1957).

Headquarters Ship:

The Faraway (at Greenock).

Light Fleet Carrier:

The 13,190-ton *Colossus*-class [1944] *Ocean* (at Liverpool. Placed in reserve after December 1956. Stricken and sold in 1960; scrapped at Faslane after 6 May 1962).

Escort Carriers:

The 11,420-ton *Ruler*-class [1943] *Patroller* (arrived in the Clyde on 13 August; in Indian Ocean in December 1945. Returned to U.S. Navy on 11 December 1946); [1943] *Premier* (arrived in the Clyde for cleaning this day; to complete 20 August. Returned to U.S. Navy on 12 April 1946); and the [1943] *Queen* (arrived in the Clyde on 10 August. Returned to U.S. Navy after 31 October 1946).

Non-operational Units: The 11,420-ton *Ruler*-class [1943] *Ranee* (arrived in the Clyde on 4 June and undergoing refit; to go to sea on 30 August and to proceed to the Indian Ocean. Returned to U.S. Navy on 21 November 1946); [1943] *Trouncer* (at Belfast between 6 March and 28 August; status uncertain, with conversion option that was declined. Returned to U.S. Navy on 3 March 1946); the 14,050-ton *Vindex*-class [1943] *Nairana* (undergoing refit at Greenock after April 1945; to complete 20 August and to serve as aircraft transport to Australia. In service with Dutch Navy between 1946 and 1948. Returned to Britain and sold into commercial service); the 11,420-ton *Ruler*-class [1943] *Rajah* (arrived in the Clyde on 5 August for conversion to troopship; to go to sea in late September. Returned to U.S. Navy on 13 December 1946); and the [1942] *Tracker* (in the Clyde; to go to sea late October. Returned to U.S. Navy on 29 November 1945).

Deck Landing Training Units:

The 11,420-ton *Attacker*-class escort carrier [1942] *Battler* (arrived in the Clyde on 15 August. Employed as troopship and returned to U.S. Navy on 12 February 1946), and the 11,420-ton *Ruler*-class escort carriers [1943] *Puncher* (arrived in the Clyde on 11 August. Returned to U.S. Navy on 16 January 1946) and [1942] *Ravager* (having been damaged in a collision, under repair on the Clyde after 1 March 1945; briefly returned to training duties in November before being prepared for decommissioning. Returned to U.S. Navy on 27 February 1946).

Aircraft Transport:

The 11,420-ton *Ruler*-class escort carrier [1942] *Atheling* (sailed Cristobal, Panama Canal Zone, en route for Jacksonville, Florida. Employed as troopship until November 1946; returned to U.S. Navy on 13 December 1946).

Controlled Minelayers:

The 727-ton requisitioned base ship [1937] *Manchester City* (arrived in the Clyde on 10 July and was paid off after 28 July. Returned to owners in 1946); the 545-ton *Isles*-class trawler [1943] *Blackbird* (arrived at Aberdeen on 27 July. Arrived at Rosyth on 8 September and placed in Category C reserve on 21 September. Sold in 1949); the 498-ton class-name [1938] *Linnet* (arrived at Sheerness on 28 July. Scrapped after May 1964); the 348-ton *M*-class [1939] *Miner 2* (at Port Edgar, Rosyth; arrived at Harwich on 16 November and passed into reserve); [1940] *Miner 4* (arrived at Hopetown, near Port Edgar, on 14 July); and the 498-ton *Linnet*-class trawler [1938] *Ringdove* (arrived at Scapa Flow on 23 June. Sold to Pakistan as pilot vessel on 8 September 1950).

Escort Carrier (Trials):

The 17,392-ton requisitioned merchantman [1938] *Pretoria Castle* (arrived at Belfast on 31 July; placed in Category B reserve on 31 December 1945. Sold back to original owners on 26 January 1946; paid off, returned and taken in hand for refit on 21 March 1946).

Training Cruisers:

The 4,850-ton *D*-class light cruisers [1918] *Dauntless* (arrived at Rosyth on 19 July to be paid off into Category C reserve, unallocated. Sold on 13 March 1946 and scrapped at Inverkeithing after April 1946); [1919] *Diomede* (arrived at Rosyth on 19 July to be paid off into Category C reserve; unallocated. Placed in Category C reserve in October 1945 and laid up at Falmouth in November 1945. Sold on 5 April 1946 and scrapped at Dalmuir after 13 May 1946); and the 9,860-ton improved *Birmingham*-class heavy cruiser [1920] *Frobisher* (undergoing repairs at Portsmouth: undecided. Placed in reserve on 2 June 1947. Sold on 26 March 1949 and scrapped at Newport after 11 May 1949).

Aircraft Target Ships:

The 1,350-ton A-class destroyer [1934] *Anthony* (arrived at Douglas, Isle of Man, on 12 August. Approved for scrapping on 8 March 1946 and placed in Category C reserve at Invergordon on 27 March 1946; employed as target ship and returned to reserve on 21 July 1946. Sold on 18 August 1947 and scrapped at Troon after May 1948); the 1,050-ton Type II *Hunt*-class escort destroyers [1940] *Blencathra* (damaged in the Humber as a result of collision with the *Willowdale* on this day, 15 August; thereafter undergoing repairs and in service between October 1945 and June 1948. Subsequently in reserve; stricken in October 1956 and scrapped at Barrow after 2 January 1957); [1940] *Brocklesby* (arrived at Dartmouth on 10 June; placed in reserve in May 1946. Returned to service after 1951; paid off in June 1963. Sold on 21 October 1968 and scrapped at Faslane after 28 October 1968); the 907-ton Type I *Hunt*-class escort destroyer [1940] *Fernie* (arrived at Sheerness on 10 August. Placed in reserve in 1947. Scrapped at Port Glasgow after 7 November 1956); the 1,340-ton requisitioned destroyers [1939] *Havelock* (arrived at Rosyth on 13 June 1945. Placed in reserve on 2 August 1946. Sold on 31 October 1946 and subsequently scrapped at Inverkeithing); ex-*Juruena* ex-*Hearty* [1939] *Hesperus* (at Rosyth, having sailed from Lamlash on 9 July. Placed in reserve in May 1946. Sold on 26 November 1946 and scrapped at Grangemouth after May 1947), [1939] *Highlander* (arrived at Portsmouth on 29 July. Approved for scrapping on 18 February 1946 and placed in Category C reserve in 21 March 1946. Sold on 27 May 1946 and scrapped at Charlestown after May 1947); the 907-ton Type I *Hunt*-class escort destroyers [1940] *Meynell* (arrived at Sheerness on 10 August; to proceed to eastern Mediterranean. Placed in reserve in 1947. Sold to Ecuador on 18 October 1954 and entered service in August 1955; stricken in May 1978); [1940] *Pytchley* (arrived at Plymouth on 7 August; placed in reserve in August 1946. Scrapped at Llanelly after 1 December 1956); [1940] *Quantock* (arrived at Greenock on 14 August; placed in reserve in December 1945. Sold to Ecuador on 18 October 1954 and entered service on 16 August 1955; sold in 1978); [1940] *Southdown* (arrived at Sheerness on 15 August; placed in reserve in May 1946. Scrapped at Barrow after 1 November 1956); and the 1,300-ton *Captain*-class frigates [1943] *Aylmer* (arrived in the Clyde at Govan on 11 August. Returned to U.S. Navy on 5 November 1945); [1943] *Balfour* (arrived at Rosyth on 3 August. Returned to U.S. Navy on 25 October 1945); [1943] *Bligh* (arrived at Lamlash on 17 July. Returned to U.S. Navy on 12 November 1945); [1943] *Byron* (sailed from Rosyth on 5 August; at Dundee, date unknown. On 24 November 1945 at Boston, Massachusetts, paid off and returned to U.S. Navy); [1943] *Conn* (at Invergordon. Returned to U.S. Navy on 26 November 1945); the 1,085-ton *Captain*-class frigate [1943] *Moorsom* (arrived at Lamlash on 14 August. Arrived at West Hartlepool on 26 September and placed in Category B reserve on 5 October. Returned to U.S. Navy after 16 October 1945); the 1,300-ton *Captain*-class frigates [1943] *Retalick* (arrived at Rosyth on 11 June. Returned to U.S. Navy on 25 October 1945); [1943] *Rutherford* (arrived in the Clyde on 4 August preparatory to docking. Returned to U.S. Navy in 25 October 1945); and the [1943] *Stayner* (arrived at Rosyth on 3 August. Returned to U.S. Navy on 24 November 1945).

Radar Trails Ship:

The 2,461-ton (French) ex-icebreaker, ex-minelayer [1915] *Pollux* (arrived at Plymouth on 29 June; paid off at Rosyth on 10 December. Returned to French Navy on 29 July 1946).

Miscellaneous Duties:

The 672-ton *Bangor*-class sloop [1940] *Blyth* (arrived at Tobermory 15 August. Sold for commercial use on 25 May 1948. Did not enter service; scrapped after November 1952).

To Reduce To Reserve
Battleship:

The 32,700-ton class-name [1913] *Queen Elizabeth* (arrived at Rosyth on 15 August; employed temporarily as accommodation ship and then returned to operational service before being placed in Category B reserve at Portsmouth after March 1946. Placed in Category C reserve on 15 May 1948 and sold four days later; scrapped at Dalmuir after 22 June 1948 with hull subsequently scrapped at Troon).

Destroyers:

The 1,173-ton [1926] *Ambuscade* (arrived at Campbeltown on 4 July and to berth at Barrow in Category C reserve. Sold on 23 November 1946 and subsequently scrapped at Troon) and the 1,350-ton *F*-class [1934] *Forester* (arrived at Rosyth on 29 June. Arrived at Dartmouth on 7 September and placed in Category B reserve on 2 November 1945. Sold on 22 January 1946 and scrapped at Rosyth after June 1947).

Escorts:

The 1,085-ton *Captain*-class frigate [1943] *Dacres* (arrived in the Clyde on 14 August. To berth in Loch Ryan; unallocated. Returned to U.S. Navy in January 1946); the 1,435-ton *Loch*-class frigate [1943] *Loch Killin* (arrived at Rosyth on 2 July; arrived at Dartmouth on 22 September and placed in Category B reserve on 6 November 1945. For disposal after 12 April 1960 and scrapped at Newport after 24 August 1960); and the 1,300-ton *Captain*-class frigate [1943] *Torrington* (at Rosyth on 24 July. Placed in Category B reserve and employed as accommodation ship at Londonderry after 13 October 1945. Returned to U.S. Navy on 11 June 1946).

Non-operational Units: The 1,300-ton *Captain*-class frigate [1943] *Redmill* (after having been torpedoed on 27 April 1945, arrived at Londonderry two days later; *hors de combat*. Arrived at Barrow on 2 November; placed in Category B reserve on 7 December. Returned to U.S. Navy on 20 January 1947); the 1,010-ton *Castle*-class corvettes [1944] *Hedingham Castle* (arrived at Sheerness on 15 August; unallocated but assigned Category C reserve status. Sold in October 1947 and scrapped at Granton after April 1958); and the [1943] *Tintagel Castle* (arrived at Rosyth on 29 July. Assigned air-sea rescue duties in November, effective January 1946. Scrapped at Troon after June 1958).

Awaiting Disposal:

The 5,000-ton fighter direction ship [1940] *Stuart Prince* (paid off at Lamlash, date unknown) and the 1,629-ton yacht [1937] *Philante* (arrived in the Clyde on 8 June; subsequently paid off at Southampton on 8 September. Sold in 1947).

NORE COMMAND

Base and Depot Ships:

The Badger (at Harwich), Beaver (at Hull), Beaver II (at Immingham), Pembroke I (at Chatham), Pembroke II (at Eastchurch), Pembroke IV (at Chatham) and the Wildfire (at Sheerness).

Royal Navy Training Establishment:

The Duke (at Great Malvern).

Accommodation Ships, previously at Chatham:

The 14,000-ton fleet carrier [1917] *Argus* (arrived at Sheerness on 18 October 1944 and placed in Category C reserve on 6 December 1944. For disposal after 15 November 1946; sold on 5 December 1946 and scrapped at Inverkeithing after May 1947); the 7,200-ton monitor [1916] *Erebus* (arrived at Sheerness on 3 July and placed in Category C reserve, date unknown. Scrapped at Inverkeithing after 29 January 1947); and the ex-training ship *Arethusa* [unkn] *Pekin* (arrived at Greenock on 4 June).

Allied Depot Ship:

The (Dutch) Oranje Nassau (at London).

21st Destroyer Flotilla:

The 907-ton Type I *Hunt*-class escort destroyers [1939] *Eglington* (arrived at and sailed from Rotterdam on 15 August. Scrapped at Blyth after 28 May 1956); [1940] *Garth* (sailed from Sheerness on 15 August and arrived at Rotterdam next day. Placed in reserve in December 1945 for use as accommodation ship; in Category B reserve at Harwich until paid off 6 July 1948. Approved for scrapping on 11 March 1958. Passed to breakers on 25 August 1958; scrapping at Barrow completed 18 November 1959); [1939] *Hambleton* (arrived at Rosyth on 8 August. Placed in reserve in December 1945. Scrapped at Dunston, Gateshead, after September 1957); [1940] *Holderness* (arrived at Sheerness 15 August; placed in reserve in 1946. Scrapped at Preston after 20 November 1956), the 1,050-ton (Polish) Type II *Hunt*-class escort destroyer ex-*Silverton* [1940] *Krakowiak* (arrived in the Humber on 11 August. Returned to British service on 25 August 1945. Sold on 3 March 1948 and scrapped at Grays, near Tilbury, after March 1949); the 907-ton Type I *Hunt*-class escort destroyer [1940] *Mendip* (sailed from Hamburg for Rosyth on 15 August; placed in reserve in January 1946. Sold to China on 28 January 1948 and reverted to Britain on 29 May 1949 with collapse of Kuomintang regime. Sold to Egypt on 9 November 1949 and in service until captured on 31 October 1956; thereafter in Israeli service until scrapped in 1972); and the 1,050-ton (Polish) Type II *Hunt*-class escort destroyer ex-*Bedale* [1941] *Slazak* (at Sheerness. Returned to British service on 27 July 1946. Transferred on loan to India on 27 November 1952 and entered Indian service on 27 April 1953; sold to India in April 1959. Stricken in April 1979 and subsequently sold and scrapped).

1st Minesweeping Flotilla, administered from the Nore and based at Harwich:

The 815/835-ton *Halycon*-class sloops [1934] *Harrier* (S.O. Arrived at Harwich on 14 August 1945 and placed in Category C reserve on 29 July 1946. Sold on 6 June 1950 and subsequently scrapped at Dunston, Gateshead,); [1937] *Gleaner* (arrived at Harwich on 14 August. Sold on 20 April 1950 and subsequently scrapped at Preston); [1933] *Halcyon* (arrived at Harwich on 14 August. Sold on 19 April 1950 and subsequently scrapped at Milford Haven); [1937] *Hazard* (arrived at Harwich on 14 August. Laid up after June 1946. Sold on 22 April 1949 and subsequently scrapped at Grays, near Tilbury); [1937] *Jason* (arrived at Harwich on 27 July 1945. Sold on 3 September 1946 into commercial service. Scrapped at Grays, near Tilbury, in 1950); [1940] *Speedwell* (arrived at Harwich on 14 August. Sold on 5 December 1946); and the [1938] *Speedy* (arrived at Harwich on 14 August. Sold on 5 November 1946).

Attached Danlayers: The 545-ton *Isles*-class trawlers [1943] *Bryher* (arrived at Harwich on 14 August. Sold in 1947) and [1944] *Fuday* (arrived at Harwich on 14 August. Sold in 1946).

10th Minesweeping Flotilla, administered from Rosyth:

The 850-ton *Algerine*-class sloop ex-Canadian *Coppercliff* [1944] *Felicity* (arrived at Harwich on 10 August. Sold in 1947).

Non-operational Units: The 850-ton *Algerine*-class sloops ex-Canadian *Arnprior* [1943] *Courier* (arrived at London on 16 June and undergoing refit at London; to complete 31 August, and Far East service thereafter. Scrapped at Llanelly after 25 March 1959); [1944] *Hare* (arrived at Cardiff on 8 July and undergoing refit; to complete 5 September. Saw service off Singapore, the East Indies and at Hong Kong between October 1945 and September 1946; thereafter in reserve. Sold to Nigeria in 1959; returned to British service in 1962. Scrapped at Faslane after 6 November 1962); [1944] *Liberty* (undergoing refit at

Antwerp: undecided. Saw service off Singapore, the East Indies and at Hong Kong between October 1945 and July 1946. Sold to Belgium and transferred on 29 November 1949; hulk in 1959. Sold and scrapped at Bruges in 1970); [1944] *Michael* (arrived at Granton on 5 August and undergoing repair; to complete 19 August. Scrapped at Bo'ness, on the Forth, after 15 November 1956); [1944] *Minstrel* (arrived at Granton on 5 August and undergoing repair preparatory for service in the Far East; arrived at Singapore on 21 January 1946. Sold to Thailand in April 1947); [1944] *Wave* (arrived at Milford Haven on 26 June and undergoing repair; to complete 15 September and to sail to the Far East. Scrapped at Dunston, Gateshead, after 4 April 1962); and the [1944] *Welcome* (arrived at Liverpool on 19 June and undergoing refit; to complete 31 August and to sail to the Far East. Scrapped at Dunston, Gateshead, after 3 May 1962).

Attached Danlayers: The 545-ton *Isles*-class trawlers [1944] *Shillay* (undergoing repairs at Port Dinorwic, on the Menai Strait, after 29 June; to complete 18 September and to proceed to the Pacific) and [1945] *Trodday* (undergoing refit at Belfast; scheduled to sail for the Pacific in late September).

11th Minesweeping Flotilla, administered from Rosyth:

The 850-ton *Algerine*-class sloop [1944] *Jaseur* (S.O. in the Clyde awaiting a delayed docking preparatory to sailing for the Far East; diverted to Liverpool. Scrapped at Blyth after 26 February 1956).

Non-operational Units: The 850-ton *Algerine*-class sloops ex-Canadian *Tillsonburg* [1944] *Flying Fish* (arrived at Antwerp on 28 July and undergoing repair; to complete 26 September. At Portsmouth on 5 November 1945 before sailing for the Far East. Transferred on loan to Ceylonese Navy on 7 October 1949 and sold to Ceylon on 24 May 1967; scrapped after April 1975); ex-Canadian *Humberstone* [1944] *Golden Fleece* (arrived at Antwerp on 29 July and undergoing repairs; to complete 26 September. Saw service off Singapore, the East Indies and at Hong Kong between November 1945 and October 1946. Sold on 8 June 1960 and scrapped at Llanelly after 8 August 1960); [1944] *Laertes* (arrived at Antwerp on 29 July and undergoing repair; to complete on 26 September in readiness for service in Far East. Scrapped at Barrow after 21 April 1959); ex-Canadian *Petrolia* [1944] *Lioness* (arrived at Aberdeen on 25 July and undergoing repair; to complete early October preparatory to service in the Far East. Scrapped at Rosyth after 15 November 1956); ex-Canadian *Hespeler* [1943] *Lysander* (arrived at Harwich on 12 August and undergoing repair; to complete 24 August. Scrapped at Blyth after 23 November 1957); [1944] *Maenad* (arrived at Harwich on 11 August awaiting delayed refit at Sheerness preparatory to service in the Far East; docked on 20 August. Scrapped at Grays, near Tilbury, after 18 December 1957); and the [1944] *Magicienne* (sailed from Tobermoray on 15 August for repair at Sheerness; scheduled for service in the Far East and docked on 20 August. Placed in Category B reserve at Singapore on 15 March 1947. Placed on disposal list in 1955 and towed to Newport during March 1956; scrapping completed by 5 July 1956).

Attached Danlayers: The 545-ton *Isles*-class trawlers [1945] *Orsay* (undergoing repairs at Ayr; to proceed to Singapore) and [1945] *Vallay* (undergoing refit at Aberdeen after 26 July; to complete 3 September. Sailed for Ceylon on 30 September).

15th Minesweeping Flotilla, administered from the Nore and all units in the Humber:

The 672-ton *Bangor*-class sloop [1941] *Fraserburgh* (S.O. At sea; returned to the Humber on 25 August. Sold on 1 January 1948 and scrapped at Thornaby-on-Tees after March 1948); the 656-ton *Bangor*-class sloops [1941] *Ardrossan* (arrived in the Humber on 6 August. Sold on 1 January 1948 and scrapped at Thornaby-on-Tees after 19 August 1948); [1941] *Bootle* (at sea; returned to the Humber on 19 August. Arrived at Rosyth on 19 January and placed in Category C reserve on 2 February 1946. Sold on 1 January 1948 and scrapped at Charlestown after June 1949); [1941] *Dunbar* (at sea; returned to the Humber on 25 August. sold on 1 January 1948 and subsequently scrapped at Southampton); ex-*Sunderland* [1941] *Lyme Regis* (at sea and returned to the Humber on 19 August. Sold on 24 August 1948 and subsequently scrapped at Sunderland); [1942] *Poole* (arrived in the Humber on 13 August. Sold on 1 January 1948 and subsequently scrapped at Pembroke Dock); and the [1941] *Whitehaven* (arrived in the Humber on 6 August; placed in Category C reserve in 1946. Scrapped at Briton Ferry, in south Wales, after August 1948).

Attached Danlayers: The 545-ton *Isles*-class trawlers [1943] *Calvay* (at sea; returned to the Humber on 19 August. Sold in 1948); [1943] *Farne* (at sea and returned to the Humber on 19 August. Sold in 1946); and the 530-ton *Tree*-class trawler [1939] *Walnut* (arrived in the Humber on 13 August; placed in Category C reserve in December 1945. Sold in 1948).

16th Minesweeping Flotilla, administered from Rosyth and based at Harwich:

The 672-ton *Bangor*-class sloop [1941] *Tadoussac* (S.O. Either at Harwich, where it arrived on 9 August, or at sea. Sold on 18 October 1946); the 656-ton *Bangor*-class sloops [1940] *Beaumaris* (arrived at Harwich on 9 August. Sold on 1 January 1948 and subsequently scrapped at Milford Haven); [1942] *Dornoch* (at sea; returned to Harwich on 18 August. To be placed in Category B reserve. Sold on 1 January 1948 and subsequently scrapped); [1942] *Ilfracombe* (at sea, and returned to Harwich on 19 August; placed in reserve on 2 February 1946. Sold on 1 January 1948 and subsequently scrapped at Dunston, Gateshead,); [1942] *Rye* (sailed from Rosyth for Harwich on 15 August. Placed in Category C reserve on 15 June 1946. Returned to service as target vessel after 24 June 1948. Sold on 24 August 1948 and subsequently scrapped at Purfleet on lower Thames); and the 672-ton *Bangor*-class sloop [1941] *Shippigan* (at sea and returned to Harwich on 19 August. To Swansea and Category C reserve on 2 February 1946. Sold on 1 January 1948 and scrapped at Charlestown after June 1949).

Non-operational Unit: The 672-ton *Bangor*-class sloop [1941] *Parrsborough* (arrived at Tilbury on 30 June and undergoing refit; to complete 29 August. Sold on 1 January 1948 and subsequently scrapped at Pembroke Dock).

Attached Danlayers: The 530-ton *Tree*-class trawler [1939] *Bay* (arrived at Harwich on 1 August. Sold in 1947) and the 545-ton *Isles*-class trawler [1945] *Tocogay* (at sea; returned to Harwich on 19 August. Placed in Category A reserve on 13 April 1950. Sold in July 1959).

18th Minesweeping Flotilla, administered from the Nore and all units at Harwich:

The 850-ton *Algerine*-class sloops [1934] *Ready* (S.O. Arrived at Harwich on 17 July. Placed in reserve in 1948. Sold on 4 July 1951 to Belgium; sold on 7 March 1961 and scrapped at Bruges after August 1961); [1944] *Cheerful* (arrived at Harwich on 17 July 1945; placed in reserve in October 1947. Intermittent service thereafter; scrapped at Queensborough, Kent, after September 1963); [1942] *Cockatrice* (arrived at Harwich on 12 August. Placed in reserve in February 1948; scrapped at Inverkeithing after 29 August 1963); [1942] *Hound* (arrived at Harwich on 12 August. Scrapped at Troon after 1 September 1962); [1944] *Mandate* (arrived at Harwich on 13 August. Placed in Category B reserve on 20 February 1948. Sold in July 1957 and scrapped at Rosyth after December 1957); [1942] *Onyx* (arrived at Harwich on 12 August. Placed in reserve in August 1947. Scrapped at Inverkeithing after 5 April 1967); [1943] *Rattlesnake* (arrived at Harwich on 8 August. Sold in November 1957 and scrapped at Grangemouth after October 1959); and the [1944] *Tanganyika* (arrived at Harwich on 8 August. Scrapped at Inverkeithing after 2 September 1963).

Non-operational Unit: The 850-ton *Algerine*-class sloop [1942] *Orestes* (undergoing repairs at Sheerness after 6 July; to complete mid-September. Scrapped at Troon after March 1963).

Attached Danlayers: The 545-ton *Isles*-class trawlers ex-*Gilsay* [1944] *Harris* (arrived at Harwich on 14 August. Sold in 1947) and [1944] *Sursay* (arrived at Harwich on 12 August).

Cruisers:

The 9,100-ton *Fiji*-class light cruiser [1939] *Kenya* (at Chatham; to complete March 1946. Paid off in September 1958; scrapped at Faslane after 29 October 1962) and the 9,800-ton *Kent*-class heavy cruiser [1926] *Suffolk* (at Liverpool and committed as troopship; placed in reserve in July 1946. Sold on 28 March 1948 and scrapped at Newport between June 1948 and January 1949).

Corvette:

The 925-ton *Flower*-class [1940] *Petunia* (undergoing refit on the Humber after 8 August; to complete 16 October in readiness for loan to China. Transferred to Chinese Navy in January 1946; lost as a result of collision on 20 March 1947).

Minesweepers:

Non-operational Units: The 850-ton *Algerine*-class sloops [1942] *Hydra* (mined off Ostend on 10 November 1944 and arrived, under tow, at Sheerness the next day; constructive total loss and paid off at Chatham on 24 January 1945. Sold on 5 February 1945 and scrapped at Grays, near Tilbury, after November 1945) and ex-Canadian *Huntsville* [1944] *Prompt* (mined off Ostend on 9 May arrived in the Humber *hors de combat* on 22 May 1945; awaiting tow to Sheerness, passing to reserve status and breaking up. Scrapped at Rainham, Kent, after January 1947).

Controlled Minelayer:

The 346-ton *M*-class [1939] *Miner 3* (arrived at Dover on 17 July).

PORTSMOUTH COMMAND

Base and Depot Ships:

The Evolution (at London), the 6,400-ton ex-monitor [1915] *Marshal Soult* (at Portsmouth. Sold in July 1946; scrapped at Troon after November 1946); the 1,540-ton salvaged destroyer [1941] *Porcupine* (*hors de combat* and in two sections ref. accommodation at Portsmouth; sold on 6 May 1946 and scrapped, forward section at Plymouth and aft section at Southampton, in 1947); Shrapnel (at Southampton); Vernon (at Brighton); and Victory I, Victory II (both at Newbury), Victory III (at Wantage) and Victory IV (at Petersfield).

Accommodation Ships, at Portsmouth:

The 4,190-ton light cruiser [1917] *Ceres* (placed in reserve in November 1944, and arrived at Portsmouth in January 1945 for service as an accommodation ship. Sold on 5 April 1946 and scrapped at Blyth after 12 July 1946); the 4,850-ton *D*-class light cruiser [1919] *Despatch* (placed in reserve in December 1944, and arrived at Portsmouth in February 1945 for service as an accommodation ship. Sold on 5 April 1946 and scrapped at Troon after August 1946); and the 1,175-ton *Flower*-class sloop [1916] *Lupin* (used as target ship before being placed on disposal list on 8 March 1946. Sold on 22 March 1946; foundered en route to the breakers but raised and subsequently scrapped); the 32,700-ton *Queen Elizabeth*-class battleship [1915] *Malaya* (placed in reserve at Faslane in October 1944 and returned to service on 15 May 1945 as accommodation ship *Vernon II*. Sold on 20 February 1948 and scrapped at Faslane after 12 April 1948); the 29,150-ton *Royal Sovereign*-class battleship [1916] *Ramillies* (placed in reserve on 31 January 1945 and returned to service in April 1945 as accommodation ship *Vernon III*. Sold on 20 February 1948 and scrapped at Cairnryan after 23 April 1948); and the 4,700-ton royal yacht [1899] *Victoria and Albert* (scrapped at Faslane after December 1954).

Schools and Training Establishments

Training Establishment (Implacable and Foudroyant):

The Implacable and Foudroyant with the decommissioned units of these names attached at Portsmouth, the former being the 74-gun ex-French *Duguay Trouin*, which had been launched in 1800 and which was to be scuttled in the Channel in 1949.

Navigation School:

The Dryad (at Southwick) and the 1,105-ton *Shoreham*-class sloop [1931] *Rochester* (arrived at Liverpool on 12 July; remained in service until September 1949. Sold in January 1951 and subsequently scrapped at Dunston, Gateshead,).

Signal School:

The Mercury (at Portsmouth) and the 710-ton *Hunt*-class sloop [1918] *Saltburn* (ran aground on 26 October 1945 and paid off, as constructive total loss, on 20 November 1945. Placed on disposal list on 23 October 1946 and sold 16 November. Wrecked en route to the breakers at Bude, Cornwall; raised and subsequently scrapped in 1948).

Gunnery School:

The Excellent and the drifter [1910] *Ben and Lucy* employed on target-towing duties (at Portsmouth; returned to owners in 1945).

Torpedo School:

The Marlborough (at Eastbourne)

Radar School:

The Collingwood (at Fareham).

Formations and Units

50th Minesweeping Flotilla, administered from Portsmouth:

The 672-ton *Bangor*-class sloops [1940] *Bude* (arrived at Portsmouth on 13 August en route for Cardiff; sold to Egypt in 1946); [1940] *Eastbourne* (sailed from Portsmouth on 15 August for Cardiff; assigned fisheries duty in November. Sold on 28 September 1948 and subsequently scrapped at Dunston, Gateshead); [1941] *Stornoway* (arrived at Portsmouth on 7 August; arrived at Falmouth on 6 November and placed in Category C reserve on 10 November. Sold into Egyptian commercial service on 11 September 1946); and the [1940] *Wedgeport* (sailed from Portsmouth on 15 August for Cardiff. Arrived in the Fal on 2 November and placed in Category C reserve on 10 November. Sold to Egypt on 11 September 1946).

Non-operational Units: The 672-ton *Bangor*-class sloops ex-*Mignan* [1941] *Fort York* (arrived at Portsmouth on 25 May and undergoing repair; to complete 31 August. Sold to Portugal on 26 September 1950; scrapped in 1975) and [1940] *Seaham* (arrived at Portsmouth on 18 June and undergoing repair; to complete mid-August. Sold to Rangoon port authority on 11 August 1947).

Escort Force:
The 907-ton Type I *Hunt*-class escort destroyers [1940] *Cattistock* (arrived at Sheerness on 3 August; placed in reserve on 26 March 1946. Scrapped at Newport after 2 July 1957), [1940] *Cotswold* (arrived at Rotterdam on 12 August. Placed in Category B reserve at Portsmouth during October 1945. Scrapped at Grays, near Tilbury, after 11 September 1957); [1940] *Cottesmore* (arrived at Portsmouth on 7 August. Arrived at Plymouth on 4 December and placed in Category B reserve in February 1946. Sold to Egypt on 17 September 1950); and the 1,300-ton *Captain*-class frigate [1943] *Riou* (undergoing repairs at Portsmouth: undecided. Returned to U.S. Navy on 28 February 1946).

Cruisers:
The 9,100-ton *Southampton*-class light cruiser [1936] *Glasgow* (at Portsmouth. Sailed 22 August for Colombo, Ceylon, and on station until 1948. Paid off in November 1956; scrapped at Blyth after 8 July 1958); the 8,000-ton *Fiji*-class light cruiser [1940] *Jamaica* (at Plymouth. Sailed 22 August for Colombo, Ceylon, and on station until 1947. Paid off on 20 November 1957; scrapped at Dalmuir after 20 December 1960; hull scrapped at Troon, completed in August 1962); the 9,400-ton *Southampton*-class light cruiser [1937] *Liverpool* (after refit and trails, at Rosyth in care and maintenance after September 1944; at Plymouth awaiting full complement and refit. To Mediterranean Fleet in October 1945. Paid off in April 1952. Stricken in 1957 and scrapped at Bo'ness after 2 July 1958); the 5,450-ton *Dido*-class light cruiser [1940] *Scylla* (mined off Normandy beachhead on 23 June 1944 and *hors de combat* at Chatham: undecided and total constructive loss. Refitted and placed in Category C reserve on 4 February 1948 and then served as target ship between February 1948 and February 1950. Sold on 12 April 1950 and scrapped at Barrow after May 1950); and the 9,100-ton light cruiser *Southampton*-class [1936] *Sheffield* (at Portsmouth; to complete December. In service between 1926 and 1958. Placed in reserve in January 1959 and paid off in September 1964; scrapped at Faslane after 18 September 1967).

Cruisers committed as troopships: The 9,750-ton *Kent*-class heavy cruiser [1926] *Berwick* (en route for Sydney; placed in reserve at Portsmouth on 6 June 1946. Sold on 15 June 1948 and scrapped at Blyth after 12 July 1948) and the 7,580-ton *E*-class light cruiser [1936] *Enterprise* (arrived at Colombo 13 August en route for Britain; subsequent trooping to Ceylon and South Africa. Sold on 11 April 1946 and subsequently scrapped at Newport).

Frigates, undergoing conversion to generating stations for service in the Far East:
The 1,300-ton *Captain*-class frigates [1943] *Hotham* (arrived at Portsmouth on 5 April and undergoing repair; to complete 31 August. To Singapore and employment as power generator in dockyard in November 1945. Returned to U.S. Navy on 11 June 1946); [1943] *Rowley* (arrived at Belfast on 3 August. Returned to U.S. Navy on 12 November 1945); [1943] *Spragge* (undergoing repairs at Portsmouth; to complete 31 August in readiness for service in the Far East. Returned to U.S. Navy on 28 February 1946); [1943] *Stockham* (arrived at Portsmouth on 21 July and undergoing conversion to serve as power generator at Singapore; to complete late September. Returned to U.S. Navy on 15 February 1946); and the [1943] *Tyler* (arrived at Liverpool on 11 August; returned to U.S. Navy on 12 November 1945).

Controlled Minelayers:

The 346-ton *M*-class [1939] *Miner 1* (arrived at Newhaven on 15 January 1945; to be reduced to Category C reserve) and [1944] *Miner 7* (arrived at Arrochar, at the head of Loch Long, on 26 May. Remained in service as the *Steady* until the sixties).

Minelayer:

The 805-ton [1937] *Plover* (arrived at Portsmouth on 5 May. Sold on 26 February 1969 and subsequently scrapped at Inverkeithing).

Boom Carriers:

The 4,918-ton requisitioned ex-*Port Alfred,* ex-*Beldagny,* ex-*Foss Beck* [1930] *Fossbeck* (arrived at Methil on 19 May; returned to owners in 1946).

Non-operational Unit: The 4,990-ton requisitioned [1935] *Kirriemoor* (undergoing refit at Antwerp; to complete late August; returned to owners in 1946).

Netlayer:

The 1,445-ton requisitioned auxiliary [1933] *Brittany* (undergoing refit at Alloa after 7 June; to complete on 25 August. Paid off on 17 October1945 and subsequently returned to owners).

Fleet Tug:

The 860-ton *Saint*-class [1919] *St. Martin* (at Portsmouth; sold in 1947).

Gunnery Firing Ships:

The 1,540-ton *O*-class destroyer ex-*Pathfinder* [1941] *Onslaught* (arrived at Portsmouth on 31 July. Target ship between 1946 and 1949. Sold to Pakistan on 24 January 1950 and transferred on 3 March 1951; stricken in 1977 but was serving as accommodation ship 1987–1988) and the 1,710-ton *S*-class destroyer [1942] *Savage* (arrived at Portsmouth on 26 July and employed as gunnery firing ship after 26 November. Placed in Category B reserve on 22 January 1948. Returned to service on 1 May 1950 and in various roles; placed in reserve after August 1956. For disposal after March 1958; sold in 1963 and scrapped at Newport).

In reserve at Portsmouth

Submarines:

Group A: The 545-ton *U*- and *V*-class submarines ex-*Ullswater* [1940] *Uproar* (arrived at Portsmouth on 25 June. Arrived at Londonderry and placed in reserve on 31 August: for disposal on 28 November. Sold on 13 February 1946 and scrapped at Inverkeithing after December 1946); [1944] *Urtica* (arrived at Portsmouth on 25 June. Employed as trials vessel before being placed in Category C reserve at Londonderry on 23 February 1948. Sold on 23 December 1949 and scrapped at Milford Haven after March 1950); [1943] *Viking* (arrived at Portsmouth on 2 July; subsequently sailed to Troon in readiness for docking in reserve at Londonderry. Transferred to Norwegian Navy in 1946); and the ex-*Untamed* [1942] *Vitality* (foundered on trials, paid off and approved for scrapping on 30 May 1943. Arrived at Portsmouth on 1 August 1945: for disposal on 28 November. Sold on 13 February 1946 and scrapped at Troon after March 1946), and the 30/34-ton midget submarines [1944–1945] XE. 7 (scrapped in 1952), XE. 8 and XE. 9 (expended as targets in 1954), and XE. 12 scrapped in 1953.

Group B: The 545-ton *U*-class submarines [1942] *Universal* (arrived at Portsmouth on 9 July: for disposal. Sold in February 1946 and scrapped at Milford Haven after June

1946); [1942] *Unshaken* (arrived at Portsmouth on 18 May: for disposal. Scrapped at Ardrossan after 13 February 1946); and the [1942] *Unsparing* (arrived at Portsmouth on 9 July: for disposal. Sold on 14 February 1946 and subsequently scrapped at Inverkeithing).

Group C: The 545-ton *U*- and *V*-class submarines [1942] *Ultor* (arrived at Portsmouth on 8 August for disposal; Scrapped at Briton Ferry, in south Wales, after January 1946); [1942] *Unrivalled* (arrived at Portsmouth on 27 July: for disposal. Scrapped at Briton Ferry, in south Wales, after 22 January 1946); [1942] *Unruly* (arrived at Portsmouth on 24 July: for disposal. Scrapped at Inverkeithing after 2 February 1946); and the [1943] *Vampire* (arrived at Portsmouth on 16 June. Scrapped at Dunston, Gateshead, after March 1950).

Group D: The 1,520-ton *Porpoise*-class submarine [1936] *Rorqual* (arrived at Gibraltar on 18 July en route to Britain. Sold on 19 December 1945 and scrapped at Newport after 17 March 1946); the 670-ton *S*-class submarines [1941] *Safari* (arrived at Portsmouth on 9 July; foundered on 7–8 January 1946 en route to breakers); [1941] *Shakespeare* (damaged in operations in the Indian Ocean in February 1945; arrived at Falmouth on 30 June but deemed beyond economical repair. Sold on 14 July 1946 and subsequently scrapped at Briton Ferry, south Wales); and the 545-ton *U*-class submarine [1941] *Umbra* (paid off at Falmouth after 28 June 1945 and for disposal on 28 November; sold on 9 July 1946 and subsequently scrapped at Blyth).

Paid off and awaiting disposal at Portsmouth
The 854-ton U.S. *S*-class submarine [1922] P. 556 (nominally returned to U.S. Navy on 26 January 1946) and the 27/30-ton midget submarines, built in 1944, *X. 20*, *X. 21*, *X. 24*, *X. 25*, *XT. 1*, and *XT. 2*.

PLYMOUTH COMMAND

Base and Depot Ships:

The Colombo, Defiance, Drake I, Drake II and Drake IV, (all at Plymouth); Eaglet (at Liverpool), Foliot I (at Plymouth); and the 1,120-ton Modified *W*-class destroyer [1919] *Vansittart* (at Avonmouth in Category C reserve and in service as accommodation ship. Approved for scrapping on 1 February 1946. Sold on 25 February 1946 and scrapped at Newport after 5 May 1946).

Destroyer Depot Ship:

The 16,600-ton requisitioned [1922] *Philoctetes* (arrived at Plymouth on 5 July: to be accommodation ship at Whitehaven. Scrapped at Newport after November 1948).

Stokers' Training Establishment:

The Impérieuse with the 29,150-ton *Royal Sovereign*-class battleships [1916] *Resolution* (at Portsmouth; sold on 5 May 1948 and scrapped at Faslane after 13 May 1948) and the [1915] *Revenge* (at Portsmouth; sold in July 1948 and scrapped at Inverkeithing after 9 September 1948).

Coding School:

The Cabbala (at Lowton, near Warrington).

Training Establishment:

The Valkyrie (at Douglas).

Torpedo School:
The Defiance (at Plymouth).

Tenders, all at Plymouth:
The 96-ton requisitioned drifter (Belgian) [1930] *Confiance* (returned to owners in 1945); the 355-ton ex-minesweeper *Melpomene* [1915] *Menelaus* (laid up but employed as tender after 30 July 1945. Paid off and for disposal on 16 December 1947 and scrapped at Llanelly after February 1948); and the 225-ton *Elfin*-class tender [1933] *Redwing* (approved for disposal in January 1956 and sold on 27 November 1956).

3rd Minesweeping Flotilla:
The 850-ton *Algerine*-class sloops [1945] *Bramble* (arrived at Liverpool on 14 August; placed in reserve in February 1948. Returned to service in April 1951; placed in reserve in February 1958. Scrapped at Dunston, Gateshead, after August 1961); [1944] *Mameluke* (arrived at Granton on 9 July for repairs; placed in reserve in December 1947. Sold on 27 April 1950 and subsequently scrapped at Thornaby-on-Tees); ex-Canadian *Kincardine* [1944] *Mariner* (arrived at Granton on 20 July. Sold to Burma on 18 April 1958; stricken in 1982); and the [1945] *Romola* (arrived at Granton on 31 July. Scrapped at Plymouth after 19 November 1957).

Attached Danlayers: The 545-ton *Isles*-class trawlers [1945] *Vacesay* (listed at Granton but temporarily assigned to 40th Minesweeping Flotilla at Aberdeen where it arrived on 22 June) and [1944] *Wiay* (listed at Granton but in the Liverpool-Holyhead area).

31st Minesweeping Flotilla, administered from and based at Portsmouth:
The 672-ton *Bangor*-class (Canadian) sloops [1942] *Blairmore* (arrived at Portland on 9 August. Sold on 3 April 1946. Repurchased in July 1951. Sold to Turkey on 29 March 1958), (Canadian) [1941] *Canso* (arrived at Portland on 9 August; placed in Category B reserve at Sheerness on 24 September 1945. Sold on 1 January 1948 and subsequently scrapped at Sunderland); (Canadian) [1941] *Caraquet* (arrived at Portland on 9 August; placed in Category B reserve at Sheerness on 12 September 1945. Sold to Portugal on 29 June 1946 and in service as survey ship); (Canadian) [1940] *Cowichan* (arrived at Portland on 9 August; placed in Category C reserve at Sydney, Nova Scotia, on 28 September. Sold in 1946); (Canadian) [1941] *Fort William* (arrived at Portland on 9 August. Sold to Turkey on 29 November 1957; scrapped in 1970); (Canadian) [1940] *Malpeque* (arrived at Portland on 9 August. Sold in February 1959); [1942] *Milltown* (sailed from Portland to Portsmouth on 15 August. Sold in February 1959); (Canadian) [1941] *Thunder* (arrived at Portland on 9 August. Sold and scrapped in 1947); and the (Canadian) [1941] *Wasaga* (arrived at Plymouth on 7 August. Sold in 1946 and scrapped in 1947).

Non-operational Units: The 672-ton *Bangor*-class sloops (Canadian) [1941] *Georgian* (arrived at Leith on 24 April and under repair after 27 April. Scrapped in 1946); (Canadian) [1942] *Kenora* (arrived at Plymouth on 2 August and undergoing repairs; to complete 25 August. Sold to Turkey on 29 November 1957); and the (Canadian) [1941] *Minas* (arrived at Portsmouth on 15 July and undergoing repair; to complete 20 August. Sailed from Portsmouth for Halifax, Nova Scotia, via the Azores on 4 September. Placed in reserve on 6 October 1945: for disposal 19 February 1946. Sold for scrapping in July 1948 but not scrapped and subject to refit in February 1952 preparatory to returning to service after 25 March 1952. Placed in reserve on 10 February 1958 and scrapped at Seattle after 29 August 1959).

Attached Danlayers: The 672-ton *Bangor*-class sloops (Canadian) [1941] *Bayfield* (arrived at Portland on 9 August; arrived at Sheerness on 12 September and placed in Category C reserve on 24 September. Sold on 1 January 1948 and subsequently scrapped at Dunston, Gateshead,) and the 530-ton *Tree*-class trawler [1940] *Olive* (at Granton having been placed in care and maintenance, pending conversion as danlayer, on 24 December 1944; apparently not effective until 11 August 1946. Sold on or about 5 May 1948 into Swedish commercial service; transferred on 1 June 1948).

Escort Force:

The 1,300-ton *Captain*-class frigates [1943] *Curzon* (arrived off the Nore on 12 August. Returned to U.S. Navy in 1946); [1943] *Holmes* (arrived at Plymouth on 27 July. Returned to U.S. Navy on 3 December 1945); [1943] *Rupert* (arrived at Portsmouth on 22 July. Returned to U.S. Navy in March 1946); and the [1943] *Seymour* (arrived at Rosyth on 9 August. Returned to U.S. Navy in January 1946).

Non-operational Unit: The 1,300-ton *Captain*-class frigate [1943] *Narbrough* (arrived at Plymouth on 1 August and undergoing repair; to complete 20 August. Returned to U.S. Navy on 4 February 1946).

Air/Sea Rescue Duties:

The 1,010-ton *Castle*-class corvettes [1943] *Carisbrooke Castle* (arrived at Plymouth on 13 August. Scrapped at Faslane, in the Gareloch, after 14 June 1958) and [1943] *Rushen Castle* (arrived at Plymouth on 6 August. Served as weather ship after 1960. Sold on 7 July 1977 for service as salvage vessel. Stricken and scrapped in 1982); and the 886-ton requisitioned auxiliary anti-aircraft yacht ex-*Emerald*, ex-*Marynthia* [1911] *Conqueror* (arrived at Plymouth on 6 June; returned to owners on 18 December 1945).

Battleship:

The 32,700-ton *Queen Elizabeth*-class [1914] *Valiant* (undergoing refit at Plymouth; to complete in December. Repairs halted incomplete and entered service as accommodation hulk at Plymouth. Sold on 19 March 1948 and subsequently scrapped at Cairnryan after 16 August 1948 with hull scrapped at Troon after 10 March 1950).

Cruisers committed as troopships:

The 9,850-ton *London*-class heavy cruiser [1927] *Devonshire* (sailed from Fremantle 12 August en route for Britain; converted to training ship in 1947. Sold on 16 June 1954 and scrapped at Newport after 12 December 1954) and the 8,000-ton *Fiji*-class light cruiser [1939] *Mauritius* (undergoing refit at Birkenhead; to complete 30 September. In reserve between 1952 and 1965, scrapped at Inverkeithing after 27 March 1965).

Destroyer:

The 1,360-ton destroyer [1940] *Inconstant* (arrived at Plymouth on 7 August; having been requisitioned, was awaiting transfer to Turkish Navy, which was completed at Istanbul on 9 March 1946).

Controlled Minelayer:

The 346-ton *M*-class [1940] *Miner 5* (arrived at Portsmouth on 14 August).

LANDING SHIPS: HOME WATERS

C.O. Accommodation Ships:

The 1,190-ton *Town*-class ex-USS *McLanahan* destroyer [1918] *Bradford* (paid off at Liverpool in May 1943; employed as accommodation ship/tender at Plymouth. Sold on 19 June 1946 and scrapped at Troon after August 1946) and the 6,900-ton ex-seaplane carrier [1914] *Pegasus* (arrived at Belfast on 8 November 1944; to reduce to Category C reserve, berth unallocated. Sold on 18 October 1946 into commercial service; scrapped at Grays, near Tilbury, after 14 April 1950).

Shuttle-Service Landing Ships, all requisitioned L.S.I.(H):

The 4,178-ton [1939] *Invicta* (arrived at Ostend on 10 August); the 3,250-ton [1936] *Royal Ulsterman* (at Rotterdam. Arrived at Belfast on 22 November and placed in reserve on 20 December 1945; allegedly returned to owners in 1945); and the 3,791-ton [1929] *Ulster Monarch* (arrived at Rotterdam on 14 August. Returned to owners in 1945).

L.S.I.(S):

The 2,950-ton requisitioned [1930] *Princess Josephine Charlotte* (operating between Dover and Ostend; paid off on 1 October and subsequently returned to owners in 1945).

Fighter Direction Ship:

The 1,625-ton converted L.S.T.(2) F.D.T. 217 (undergoing refit at London; to complete 11 October. Returned to U.S. Navy in 1946).

L.S.D:

The 4,230-ton ex-*Battleaxe* [1943] *Eastway* (undergoing refit on the Tyne after 4 May; to complete 26 September. Returned to U.S. Navy in May 1947); ex-*Cutlass* [1943] *Northway* (sailed from Liverpool on 13 August for Port Said and service with the East Indies Fleet. Returned to U.S. Navy in December 1946); and the ex-*Dagger* [1943] *Oceanway* (arrived at Portsmouth on 14 August. Returned to U.S. Navy in 1947).

L.S.G:

The 16,750-ton [1941] *Derwentdale* (undergoing repairs on the Tyne; to complete in August. Remained in service until 19 May 1959 when placed in reserve at Rosyth. Sold into commercial service in December 1959).

L.S.H.(L):

The 9,890-ton ex-*Hydra*, ex-*Kenya* [1930] *Keren* (arrived at Cardiff on 5 February 1945 and thence to Newport and refit and conversion; to complete 1 November. Returned to owners in 1948).

L.S.H.(S):

The 1,370-ton *River*-class frigates [1943] *Chelmer* (arrived at Rotterdam on 4 August, and undergoing conversion: undecided. Arrived at Harwich on 13 October Placed in Category B reserve on 10 November 1945. Scrapped at Charlestown after August 1957); (ex-Canadian) [1943] *Ettrick* (at Southampton undergoing conversion after 28 May; to complete 30 September. Scrapped at Grays, near Tilbury, after June 1953); [1943] *Exe* (arrived at Rotterdam on 4 August and undergoing conversion: undecided. Arrived at Plymouth on 18 September and placed in Category B reserve on 8 November 1945. Sold on 20 May 1956 and scrapped at Preston after September 1956); and the [1943] *Meon* (undergoing repair and conversion at Southampton after 19 April; to complete 20 September. Arrived at Harwich on 21 December and placed in Category C reserve on 25 January 1946. Scrapped at Blyth after 14 May 1966).

L.S.I.(L):

The 11,650-ton C1–S-AY1 type ex-*Empire Lamont* [1943] *Lamont* (arrived at London on 12 July and undergoing refit; to complete 31 December. Returned to U.S. Navy in

1946); ex-*Cape St. Vincent* [1943] *Empire Arquebus* (undergoing conversion at Liverpool and to complete 20 September: undecided. Sold in November 1946 into commercial service); ex-*Cape Berkley* [1943] *Empire Battleaxe* (undergoing conversion at Falmouth: undecided. Returned to U.S. Navy in 1947); ex-*Cape St. Roque* [1943] *Empire Mace* (undergoing conversion at Liverpool: undecided. Sold in November 1946); ex-*Empire Halberd* [1943] *Silvio* (undergoing repairs at London after 15 July; to complete 15 October. Was to be employed as troopship but paid off on 8 November 1945; to shipping ministry on 20 February 1946. Returned to U.S. Navy in June 1948); ex-*Cape Pine* [1943] *Empire Lance* (undergoing conversion at Antwerp: undecided. Returned to U.S. Navy in 1946); and the ex-*Cape Turner* [1943] *Empire Rapier* (undergoing conversion at Rotterdam: undecided. Returned to U.S. Navy in 1946).

L.S.I.(M):

The 6,890-ton requisitioned ex-armed merchant cruiser [1930] *Prince Henry* (undergoing refit at London after 26 April; to complete end October. Sold in 1946).

L.S.I.(S):

The 3,219-ton requisitioned Belgian ferry [1933] *Prince Baudouin* (decommissioned after 19 April and thereafter to Antwerp and refit. Returned to owners on 13 October 1945).

L.S.S:

The 2,680-ton requisitioned train ferry [1917] *Princess Iris* (seemingly at Avonmouth. Sold in 1946).

L.S.T.(1):

The 3,616-ton [1942] *Bruiser* (at Inveraray in care and maintenance; placed in Category C reserve in the Gareloch on 28 February 1946. For disposal on 28 August 1946; sold 16 November 1946 and entered commercial service in 1947).

Special Service Vessels:

The 527-ton requisitioned auxiliary [1930] *Alice* (at Troon; returned to owners in 1945) and the 1,245-ton civilian accommodation ship [1924] *Troubador* (at Lamlash; arrived at Falmouth on 19 January 1946. Paid off at Greenock in September 1946. Sold in 1947).

Other Unit:

The 223-ton requisitioned ex-minesweeping yacht [1926] *Thalaba* (at Bursledon, Southampton, after having been laid up on 8 August 1942. Returned to owners in 1946).

THE RESERVE FLEET

ROSYTH AREA

At Rosyth

Light Cruiser:

The 7,550-ton *E*-class [1920] *Emerald* (in Category B reserve; placed in Category C reserve in December 1945. Target ship in 1947 and sunk in Kames Bay, Kyles of Bute, on 24 October 1947. Raised on 9 June 1948; sold on 23 June 1948 and subsequently scrapped at Troon).

Escort Carrier:

The 11,420-ton *Ruler*-class [1943] *Nabob* (torpedoed on 22 August 1944 in northern waters and *hors de combat*; arrived at Rosyth on 9 September and placed in Category

C reserve on 8 January 1945. Nominally returned to U.S. Navy; sold on 26 October 1946 and sailed for the Netherlands, and ostensibly scrapping, in September 1947. Resold into commercial use in 1951).

Destroyer:

The 1,090-ton V-class [1917] *Verdun* (arrived at Rosyth on 24 May and placed in Category C reserve after 17 June pending disposal. Sold on 22 September and scrapped at Inverkeithing after 5 March 1946).

Forth area, all units Category C reserve unless otherwise stated

Destroyer:

The 1,352-ton [1926] *Amazon* (in service as target ship after December 1943; at Rosyth and placed in reserve. Scrapped at Troon after 6 October 1948).

Escorts:

The 1,190-ton *Town*-class destroyer ex-USS *Hunt* [1920] *Broadway* (arrived at Rosyth on 22 May 1944 and placed in Category B reserve. Sold on 18 February 1947 and scrapped at Charlestown after March 1948); the 1,530-ton *Scott*-class long-range escort [1918] *Campbell* (arrived at Rosyth on 23 June and placed in reserve on 5 July: for disposal. Sold on 18 February 1947 and scrapped at Rosyth after June 1948); the 1,090-ton *Town*-class destroyer ex-USS *Aaron Ward* [1919] *Castleton* (arrived at Rosyth on 17 August 1944 and placed in reserve at Grangemouth on 13 March 1945. Placed on disposal list on 4 March 1947; scrapped at Bo'ness after September 1948); the 1,060-ton *Town*-class destroyer ex-USS *Abbot* [1918] *Charlestown* (after collision off Harwich with minesweeper *Florizel* on 10 December 1944 *hors de combat* and paid off at Grangemouth on 15 January 1945. Placed on disposal list on 4 March 1947 and scrapped at Sunderland after December 1948); the 1,020-ton *Town*-class destroyer ex-USS *Conner* [1917] *Leeds* (placed in reserve at Harwich after 10 April 1945, preparatory to scrapping. Sold on 4 March 1947 and scrapped at Grays, near Tilbury, after January 1949); the 1,530-ton *Scott*-class long-range escort [1918] *Mackay* (at Bergen on 9 June and placed in reserve on 21 July: for disposal on 22 September. Placed on sale list on 18 February 1947; sold in 1948 and scrapped at Charlestown after June 1949); the 1,090-ton V-class escort destroyers [1917] *Valorous* (in the Firth of Forth and placed in reserve on 25 June; on disposal list in March 1946. Placed on disposal list on 4 March 1947 and scrapped at Thornaby-on-Tees after May 1948), [1918] *Vanity* (in the Firth of Forth and placed in reserve on 3 June. Approved for scrapping on 8 March 1946: for disposal on 4 March 1947. Handed over to breakers in May 1948 and subsequently scrapped at Grangemouth); the 1,090-ton V-class long-range escort [1917] *Vanquisher* (arrived in the Firth of Forth and placed in reserve on 7 June. Approved for scrapping on 8 March 1946 and for disposal after March 1947. Sold and scrapped at Charleston after June 1948); the 1,090-ton V-class escort destroyer [1917] *Vega* (arrived at Rosyth and placed in reserve on 28 June. Approved for disposal on 8 March 1947 and scrapped at Dunston, Gateshead, after May 1948); the 1,090-ton V-class long-range escort [1917] *Velox* (placed in reserve on 31 July, apparently at Rosyth. Sold on 18 February 1947 and scrapped at Charlestown after November 1947); the 1,120-ton Modified V-class long-range escort ex-*Venom* [1918] *Venomous* (in the Firth of Forth and placed in reserve, date unknown. Placed on disposal list on 4 March 1947 and scrapped at Charlestown after July 1947); the 1,090-ton V-class long-range escorts [1917] *Versatile* (arrived at Rosyth on 3 June and placed in reserve on 8 June. Sold on 7 May 1947 and scrapped at Granton after 10 September 1948); [1917] *Vesper* (arrived at Rosyth on 29 May and subsequently placed in reserve. Placed on disposal list on 4 March 1947 and scrapped at Inverkeithing after 14 March 1949); the 1,120-ton Modified V-class escort destroyer [1917] *Viceroy* (arrived at Rosyth on 15 June to be placed in reserve. Sold on 17 May 1947 and scrapped at Granton after 10 September 1948), the 1,090-ton V-class long-range escorts [1918] *Vidette* (arrived at Rosyth on 5 June to be placed in reserve after 9 June. Placed on disposal list on 4 March 1947; sold on 3 April 1947 and subsequently scrapped at Grangemouth); [1917] *Vivacious* (sailed from Bergen on 7 June. Placed in reserve at Grangemouth on 3 August. Placed on disposal list on 4 March. Sold on 17 May 1947 and scrapped at Charlestown after 10 September 1948); the 1,090-ton V-class escort destroyer [1918] *Vivien* (arrived at Rosyth on 20 June to be placed in reserve pending disposal. Sold on 18 February 1947 and subsequently scrapped at Charlestown); the 1,120-ton Modified W-class long-range escort [1919] *Volunteer* (arrived at Rosyth on 19 June to be placed in reserve. Placed on disposal list on 4 March 1947. Sold in December 1947 and scrapped at Granton after April 1948); the 1,100-ton W-class escort destroyer [1918] *Westminster* (arrived at Rosyth on 10 June and placed in reserve. Placed on disposal list on 4 March 1947; scrapped at Rosyth after August 1948); the 1,140-ton Modified W-class short-range escort [1919] *Whitshed* (arrived at Rosyth on 29 June: for disposal. Sold on 18 February 1947 and scrapped at Dunston, Gateshead, after April 1948), the 1,120-ton W-class short-range escort [1918] *Windsor* (arrived at Rosyth on 2 June and placed in reserve. Placed on disposal list on 4 March 1947 and scrapped at Charlestown after May 1949); the 1,140-ton Modified W-class short-range escort [1919] *Wivern* (arrived at Rosyth on 19 June and placed in Category B reserve: for disposal. Sold on 18 February 1947 and scrapped at Rosyth after October 1948); the 1,120-ton W-class escort destroyers [1918] *Wolfhound* (arrived at Rosyth on 24 June: for disposal. Sold on 18 February 1947 and subsequently scrapped at Granton); [1918] *Wolsey* (arrived at Rosyth on 16 June and placed in reserve. Placed on disposal list on 4 March 1947 and subsequently scrapped at Sunderland); and the [1918] *Woolston* (arrived at Rosyth on 25 June: for disposal. Sold on 18 February 1947 and subsequently scrapped at Grangemouth).

Sloops:

The 990-ton *Grimsby*-class [1933] *Leith* (arrived at Rosyth on 9 June 1945 and placed in reserve. Sold on 25 November 1946 into commercial service. Bought by Denmark in 1949 and served as survey ship; sold and scrapped in 1955) and the 1,060-ton *Falmouth*-class ex-*Weston-Super-Mare* [1932] *Weston* (arrived at Rosyth on 9 June and placed in reserve on 12 June 1945. Assigned for scrapping on 22 May 1947 and passed to breakers on 19 July 1947; re-assigned on 21 February 1948 and subsequently scrapped at Gelliswick Bay below Milford Haven).

Corvettes:

The 925-ton *Flower*-class [1940] *Bittersweet* (arrived at Rosyth on 19 June and placed in reserve on 26 June. Scrapped at Charlestown after 25 August 1949); [1940] *Burdock* (arrived at Grangemouth on 28 May and placed in reserve on 8 June with provision for disposal. Used as target ship and returned to reserve at Rosyth on 21 July 1946. Laid up at Portsmouth on 15 July 1947 and scrapped at Hayle, Cornwall, after February 1948); [1940] *Campanula* (arrived at Grangemouth on 28 May and placed in reserve on 11 June 1945. Scrapped at Dunston, Gateshead, after 21 August 1947), [1940] *Clematis* (arrived at Rosyth on 23 June and subsequently placed in reserve. Scrapped at Dunston, Gateshead, after September 1949); [1940] *Convolvulus* (arrived at Grangemouth on 28 May and placed in reserve on 6 June. Sold on 21 August 1947 and subsequently scrapped at Newport); [1940] *Gentian* (arrived at Rosyth on 8 June 1945 and placed in reserve. Scrapped at Purfleet, on lower Thames, after August 1947), [1940] *Gloxinia* (arrived at Rosyth on 6 June and placed in reserve on 8 June. Scrapped at Purfleet, on lower Thames, after 15 July 1947); [1941] *Loosestrife* (arrived at Rosyth on 22 June and placed in reserve on 25 June. Sold on 4 October 1946); [1940] *Mayflower* (arrived at Rosyth on 21 May and placed in reserve on 31 May 1945. Scrapped at Charlestown in 1950); [1941] *Myosotis* (arrived at Methil on 28 July; sailed on 3 August and subsequently placed in reserve in the Forth. Sold in February 1946 and entered commercial service in September 1946); and the [1940] *Snowberry* (arrived at Rosyth on 6 June and placed in reserve two days later. Scrapped at Thornaby-on-Tees after August 1947).

Aircraft Target Ships:

The 1,190-ton *Town*-class destroyer ex-USS *Welborn C. Wood* [1920] *Chesterfield* (placed in reserve at Grangemouth on 15 January 1945. Placed on disposal list on 4 March 1947 and scrapped at Dunston, Gateshead after 3 December 1948); the 1,090-ton *Town*-class ex-USS *Philip* [1918] *Lancaster* (arrived and paid off at Rosyth on 30 June 1945. Scrapped at Blyth after May 1947); the 1,060-ton *Town*-class destroyers ex-USS *Ringgold* [1918] *Newark* (arrived at Rosyth on 4 July preparatory to scrapping. Sold on 18 February 1947 and subsequently scrapped at Bo'ness); ex-USS *Sigourney* [1917] *Newport* (in dock at Rosyth after 29 October 1944; arrived at Invergordon on 30 December 1944 and placed in reserve in January 1945 preparatory to scrapping: for disposal on 22 September. Sold on 18 February 1947 and subsequently scrapped at Granton); the 1,190-ton *Town*-class destroyer ex-USS *Meade* [1919] *Ramsey* (arrived at Rosyth on 14 June and placed in reserve on 30 June 1945. Sold on 18 February 1947 and scrapped at Bo'ness after July 1947); and the 1,090-ton V-class long-range escort [1918] *Vanessa* (arrived at Kirkwall, in the Orkneys, on 10 August; placed in reserve in the Forth on 30 September. For disposal after 3 March 1947. Sold in September 1948 and subsequently scrapped at Charlestown).

At Londonderry, all units in Category C reserve unless otherwise stated

Base Ship:

The 1,175-ton *Flower*-class sloop [1915] *Foxglove* (*hors de combat* after being heavily damaged by German aircraft on 9 July 1940 in the English Channel; constructive total loss and used as an accommodation ship. Sold on 7 September 1946 and subsequently scrapped at Troon).

Frigates:

The 1,318-ton *Colony*-class [1943] *Anguilla* (arrived at Londonderry on 18 June; returned to U.S. Navy in May 1946), [1943] *Antigua* (arrived at Londonderry on 18 June. Sailed for St. John's 13 February 1946 and returned to U.S. Navy in May 1946); [1943] *Ascension* (arrived at Greenock on 14 June and placed in Category B reserve on 9 August. Returned to U.S. Navy on 31 May 1946), [1943] *Bahamas* (arrived at and placed in Category B reserve at Londonderry on 13 August. Returned to U.S. Navy on 11 June 1946); [1943] *Dominica* (arrived at Londonderry on 18 June; placed in reserve on 13 August. Returned to U.S. Navy on 23 April 1946); [1943] *Labuan* (arrived at Londonderry on 17 June and placed in Category B reserve. Returned to U.S. Navy on 2 May 1946), [1943] *Montserrat* (arrived at Londonderry on 7 June and placed in Category B reserve on 8 August. Returned to U.S. Navy in June 1946); [1943] *Nyasaland* (arrived at Londonderry on 6 May and placed in reserve on 13 July. Returned to U.S. Navy in April 1946); [1943] *Perim* (arrived in the Clyde on 1 June and placed in Category B reserve on 21 July. Returned to U.S. Navy on 22 May 1946); and the [1943] *Somaliland* (arrived at Londonderry on 23 May and placed in Category B reserve on 10 August. Returned to U.S. Navy on 31 May 1946).

Corvettes:

The 925-ton *Flower*-class [1940] *Abelia* (arrived at Londonderry on 23 June and placed in reserve on 29 June; approved for scrapping 8 March 1946. Sold on 16 November 1947 and entered commercial service on 27 March 1947); [1940] *Aubrietia* (arrived at Londonderry on 10 June and placed in reserve on 14 June. Approved for scrapping on 8 March 1946 and for disposal on 21 July; sold on 16 November 1946 and entered Norwegian commercial service on 29 July 1948); [1940] *Camellia* (arrived at Londonderry on 23 June and placed in reserve on 29 June 1945. Sold on 9 August 1946), [1940] *Celandine* (arrived at Londonderry on 25 June and placed in reserve on 29 June 1945. Scrapped after October 1948); [1940] *Columbine* (arrived at Londonderry on 23 June and placed in reserve on 29 June 1945. Sold on 9 August 1946); [1940] *Cyclamen* (arrived at Londonderry on 12 July and placed in reserve on 23 July 1945: for disposal on 8 March 1946 and listed 21 July. Sold on 22 March 1947 and entered commercial service in 1948); ex-*Daffodil* [1940] *Dianella* (arrived at Londonderry on 12 June and placed in reserve. Scrapped at Portaferry, County Down, after 24 June 1947); [1940] *Fennel* (arrived at Londonderry on 10 June and placed in reserve on 12 June 1945. Sold on 9 August 1946); ex-*Nettle* [1941] *Hyderabad* (arrived at Londonderry and placed in reserve on 20 July 1945. Sold on 1 January 1948 and scrapped at Portaferry, Count Down, after October 1948); [1940] *Lavender* (arrived at Londonderry on 24 June and placed in reserve on 29 June 1945. Sold on 9 August 1946); ex-*Phlox* [1942] *Lotus* (arrived at Londonderry and placed in reserve on 26 June. Sold in 1947), [1941] *Mignonette* (arrived at Londonderry and placed in reserve on 20 July. Sold into Greek commercial service in 1946); [1941] *Pennywort* (arrived at Londonderry on 14 June and placed in reserve on 29 June. Sold in 1947 and scrapped at Troon after January 1949); [1940] *Pimpernel* (arrived at Londonderry on 25 June and placed in reserve on 29 June. Sold on 8 February 1948 and scrapped at Portaferry, County Down, after October 1948); [1941] *Poppy* (arrived at Londonderry on 27 June and paid off into reserve on 29 June. Sold in 1946); [1940] *Primrose* (arrived at Londonderry on 26 June and placed in reserve on 29 June 1945. Sold on 9 August 1946); [1941] *Starwort* (arrived at Londonderry on 13 June and placed in reserve on 29 June. Sold in August 1946); [1941] *Sweetbriar* (arrived at Londonderry on 24 June and placed in reserve on 29 June. Sold on 29 July 1946 and entered Norwegian whaling service in 1949); and the [1940] *Wallflower* (arrived at Londonderry and placed in reserve on 24 June. Sold on 29 July 1946 and entered Norwegian whaling service in 1949).

At Gareloch

Heavy Cruiser:

The 9,850-ton class-name [1926] *Kent* (arrived at Gareloch on 5 January 1945 and placed in Category B reserve on 16 February. Sold on 22 January 1948 and scrapped at Troon after March 1948).

Escort Carrier:

The 11,420-ton *Ruler*-class [1943] *Thane* (*hors de combat* after being torpedoed on 15 January 1945; arrived on the Clyde next day and placed in reserve. Nominally returned to U.S. Navy on 5 December 1945; scrapped at Faslane after April 1947).

Escort Destroyer:

The 1,087-ton Type III *Hunt*-class [1942] *Goathland* (mined on 24 July 1944 in Seine Bay; written off as constructive total loss at Portsmouth. Arrived at Greenock on 11 February 1945 and placed in reserve on 28 May. Sale confirmed on 8 August 1945 and scrapped at Troon after February 1946).

At the Kyle of Lochalsh

Aircraft Carrier:

The 22,450-ton class-name [1916] *Furious* (in reserve after September 1944. Sold on 23 January 1948 and scrapped at Dalmuir after March 1948 and subsequently at Troon).

NORE AREA

At Hull

Frigates:

The 1,085-ton *Captain*-class [1942] *Berry* (arrived in the Humber on 31 May and placed in Category B reserve. Returned to U.S. Navy on 15 February 1946); [1943] *Cooke* (arrived in the Humber on 31 May and placed in Category B reserve on 29 June. Returned to U.S. Navy on 8 March 1946); [1943] *Domett* (arrived in the Humber and placed in Category C reserve on 3 June. Returned to U.S. Navy on 8 March 1946); [1943] *Gardiner* (arrived in the Humber on 29 June; placed in Category B reserve on 31 July. Returned to U.S. Navy on 12 February 1946); [1943] *Inglis* (arrived in the Humber on 25 May and placed in Category B reserve on 29 June. Returned to U.S. Navy on 20 March 1946); [1943] *Inman* (arrived in the Humber on 29 June and placed in Category B reserve on 31 July. Returned to U.S. Navy on 1 March 1946); [1943] *Keats* (arrived in the Humber on 24 June and placed in Category C reserve on 31 July. Returned to U.S. Navy on 27 February 1946); [1943] *Lawson* (arrived in the Humber on 25 May. Returned to U.S. Navy on 20 March 1946); [1943] *Louis* (arrived in the Humber on 31 May. Returned to U.S. Navy on 20 March 1946); and the [1943] *Mounsey* (arrived in the Humber on 25 May and placed in Category C reserve on 29 June. Returned to U.S. Navy on 25 February 1946).

In the Tyne, all units in Category C reserve

Destroyer and escort destroyers:

The 1,350-ton A-class destroyer [1929] *Antelope* (returned from Gibraltar in August 1944 as beyond economical repair; paid off on 3 October 1944. Arrived on the Tyne on 21 August 1945; sold in January 1946 and scrapped at Blyth after 26 January 1946); the 1,530-ton *Scott*-class long-range escort [1918] *Montrose* (seriously damaged in collision off Normandy on 20 July; towed to Immingham dock, arriving 27 July, and constructive total loss. Laid up at North Shields in reserve after 2 November 1944; arrived at Dundee on 17 July 1945. Sold on 31 January 1946 and subsequently scrapped at Blyth); and the 1,100-ton W-class escort destroyer [1919] *Wanderer* (arrived in the Tyne on 27 October 1944 and placed in reserve two days later. Paid off in June 1945. Sold on 31 January 1946 and subsequently scrapped at Blyth).

Corvettes:

The 925-ton *Flower*-class [1941] *Aster* (in reserve at Hartlepool after September 1944. Sold on 29 May 1946 and subsequently scrapped at Bo'ness) and [1941] *Potentilla* (arrived on the Tees and placed in Category B reserve on 1 November 1944; to be reduced to Category C reserve at West Hartlepool. Sold on 13 March 1946 and subsequently scrapped at Dunston, Gateshead,).

At Harwich
Frigates, all units Category B reserve:

The 1,318-ton *Colony*-class [1943] *Caicos* (arrived at Harwich on 30 May. Returned to U.S. Navy on 12 December 1945); the 1,300-ton *Captain*-class [1943] *Cranstoun* (arrived at Harwich on 26 May; placed in reserve at Plymouth on 9 November. Returned to U.S. Navy on 3 December 1945); the 1,085-ton *Captain*-class [1943] *Hoste* (arrived at Harwich and placed in reserve on 2 June. Returned to U.S. Navy on 22 August 1945); and the 1,300-ton *Captain*-class [1943] *Waldegrave* (arrived at Harwich on 17 June; returned to U.S. Navy on 3 December 1945).

Corvettes, all units in Category C reserve:

The 925-ton *Flower*-class [1940] *Anemone* (arrived at Harwich on 12 July and placed in reserve on 21 July; after 25 July in service as accommodation ship. Sold in November 1949 and entered Norwegian commercial service in October 1950); [1941] *Armeria* (arrived at Harwich on 3 June; to be placed in reserve and for disposal. Sold in 1947 and entered commercial service in 1948); [1941] *Coltsfoot* (arrived at Harwich on 26 June and subsequently placed in reserve. Sold in 1947); ex-*Dart* [1941] *Godetia* (arrived at Harwich on 10 June and placed in first Category B and then Category C reserve. Sold on 22 May 1947 and subsequently scrapped at Grays, near Tilbury); the 580-ton *Kingfisher*-class [1939] *Guillemot* (arrived at Harwich and placed in reserve on 30 May 1945. Sold on 6 June 1950 and subsequently scrapped at Grays, near Tilbury); the 925-ton *Flower*-class [1940] *Heather* (arrived at Harwich on 23 May and subsequently placed in reserve. Sold on 22 May 1947 and subsequently scrapped at Grays, near Tilbury); [1940] *Kingcup* (arrived at Harwich on 21 May and placed in reserve. Sold on 31 July 1946); the 530-ton *Kingfisher*-class [1936] *Kittiwake* (arrived at Harwich on 18 May and placed in reserve on 29 May. Sold in 1946); the 510-ton *Kingfisher*-class [1936] *Mallard* (arrived at Harwich on 29 May and placed in reserve. Sold on 21 April 1947 and subsequently scrapped at Dunston, Gateshead,); [1936] *Puffin* (arrived at Harwich on 13 May and placed in reserve next day. Sold on 16 January 1947 and scrapped at Grays, near Tilbury, after 22 April 1947); the 580-ton *Kingfisher*-class [1939] *Shearwater* (arrived at Harwich on 31 May and placed in reserve. Sold on 21 April 1947 and subsequently scrapped at Stockton-on-Tees); the 530-ton *Kingfisher*-class [1937] *Sheldrake* (arrived at Harwich on 28 may and placed in reserve. Sold on 12 August 1946); the 980-ton Modified *Flower*-class ex-USS *Vim* [1939] *Statice* (arrived at Harwich on 10 June and placed in reserve on 26 June 1945. Returned to U.S. Navy on 21 June 1946); the 925-ton *Flower*-class [1940] *Sunflower* (arrived at Harwich on 11 June and placed in reserve on 26 June. Scrapped at Hayle, Cornwall, after August 1947); and the 530-ton *Kingfisher*-class [1938] *Widgeon* (arrived at Harwich on 19 May and placed in reserve; subsequently arrived at Methil, date unknown. Sold on 21 April 1947 and scrapped at Dunston, Gateshead, after September 1947).

At Hartlepool
Escort Destroyers:

The 1,087-ton Type III *Hunt*-class [1942] *Rockwood* (extensively damaged by air attack in the Aegean on 11 November 1943 but returned to Britain under its own power. Berthed in the Tees after 7 April 1944 and paid off on 7 June 1944. For disposal after July 1945; sold in February 1946 and scrapped at Dunston, Gateshead, after August 1946) and [1942] *Wensleydale* (damaged in collision in November 1944 and written off; arrived on the Tees on 26 January 1945; placed in Category C reserve on 17 October and for disposal on 8 November. Sold on 15 February 1946 and scrapped at Blyth after 25 February 1947).

Sloop:
The 1,045-ton *Hastings*-class [1930] *Scarborough* (Flagship Officer Commanding Reserve Fleet. Laid up in Category B reserve in January 1945. Sold on 3 June 1949 and scrapped at Stockton-on-Tees after 3 July 1949).

Frigates, all units in Category B reserve:
The 1,085-ton *Captain*-class [1943] *Gore* (arrived on the Tees on 2 June and placed in reserve on 28 June 1945. Returned to U.S. Navy on 2 May 1946); [1943] *Loring* (arrived on the Tees on 23 May and placed in reserve on 28 June. Nominally returned to U.S. Navy on 7 January 1947: for disposal and sold to be scrapped in Greece); and the 1,300-ton *Captain*-class [1943] *Thornborough* (arrived on the Tees on 21 June; placed in reserve and to await repairs. Nominally returned to U.S. Navy on 30 January 1947: for disposal and sold to be scrapped in Greece).

Controlled Minelayer:
The 545-ton *Isles*-class trawler [1944] *Stonechat* (placed in Category A reserve on 21 December 1944 after having been completed the previous month. Refitted and laid up at Plymouth after December 1952. Listed for disposal in 1962. First sold on 26 September 1966 but purchaser defaulted; sold a second time on 13 March 1967 and subsequently scrapped).

Minesweepers, all units in Category B reserve:
The 590-ton *Bangor*-class sloops [1940] *Bridlington* (arrived on the Tees on 19 June and placed in reserve. Transferred to Air Ministry in 1946 presumably for service as weather ship; scrapped at Plymouth after February 1960); [1940] *Bridport* (arrived on the Tees on 19 June and placed in reserve. Transferred to Air Ministry in 1946 presumably for service as weather ship; scrapped at Plymouth after May 1959); the 656-ton *Bangor*-class sloop [1941] *Brixham* (arrived on the Tees on 9 January 1945 and laid up in April 1945; sold on 7 July 1948 and subsequently scrapped at Dunston, Gateshead,); the 890-ton *Catherine*-class [1942] *Chamois* (mined on 21 July 1944 in Seine Bay; deemed constructive total loss at Portsmouth. Arrived at Aberdeen on 31 August and placed in reserve on 3 October 1944. Nominally returned to U.S. Navy on 10 December 1946. Sold in 1948 and scrapped at Southampton after September 1950); the 656-ton *Bangor*-class sloops [1940] *Polruan* (laid up in April 1945; scrapped at Sunderland after June 1950); [1940] *Rhyl* (arrived at Harwich on 29 January 1945. Sold on 28 September 1948 and subsequently scrapped at Dunston, Gateshead,); [1941] *Rothesay* (arrived at Hartlepool on 9 January 1945 and placed in reserve on 13 February; thereafter detailed for training duties in West Africa. Scrapped at Milford Haven after April 1950); the 815-ton *Halcyon*-class [1936] *Salamander*n (heavily damaged off Normandy by British aircraft on 18 August 1944; *hors de combat* and laid up at Plymouth after 21 February 1945 and for disposal. Sold on 15 December 1946 and scrapped at Blyth after 7 May 1947); and the 890-ton *Catherine*-class [1942] *Strenuous* (placed in reserve on 10 February 1944. Nominally returned to U.S. Navy on 10 December 1946. Laid up until April 1956; sold and scrapped in German yard after July 1956).

Allied Units in reserve:
The 1,540-ton (Polish) *Wicher*-class destroyer [1929] *Burza* (placed in reserve on 9 May 1944 and at Hartlepool after 7 April 1945. Returned to Poland in July 1951); the

1,087-ton Type III *Hunt*-class escort destroyer [1942] *Glaisdale* (arrived in the Humber on 27 June and awaiting tow to Hartlepool and reserve status. Placed in reserve after September 1944. Sold on 1 June 1946 to Norway and entered Norwegian service in February 1947; sold and scrapped after 1962); the 610-ton ex-French *Pomone*-class torpedo-boat [1935] *La Melpomene* (docked at West Hartlepool after 31 April 1945 preparatory to return to France; in Category B reserve; left under tow for Cherbourg on 14 September 1945); and the 1,727-ton ex-French *Simoun*-class destroyer [1924] *Ouragan* (in reserve; returned to France in 1946 and scrapped in 1949).

At Sheerness, all units in Category B reserve
Frigates:

The 1,370-ton *River*-class [1943] *Annan* (arrived at Sheerness on 5 June; to be placed in reserve. Sold to Denmark on 27 November 1945); the 1,435-ton *Loch*-class [1944] *Loch Achanalt* (arrived at Sheerness and placed in reserve on 5 June. Sale to New Zealand Navy agreed on 11 March 1948; formally transferred on 13 September 1948. Stricken in October 1965 and scrapped in Hong Kong after January 1966); [1944] *Loch Alvie* (arrived at Sheerness on 27 May and placed in reserve on 11 June 1945. In service in Persian Gulf between 1953 and 1963; paid off in November 1963. Sold on 18 January 1965 in Singapore and scrapped after September 1965); [1944] *Loch Morlich* (sale to New Zealand Navy agreed on 11 March 1948; formally transferred on 19 April 1949. Sold on 15 December 1961 and subsequently scrapped at Hong Kong); the 1,370-ton *River*-class [1943] *Monnow* (arrived at Sheerness on 27 May and placed in reserve on 11 June. Sold to Denmark and transferred at Copenhagen on 1 November 1945. Scrapped at Odense in 1960); [1942] *Nene* (arrived at Sheerness on 27 May and placed in reserve on 11 June 1945; subsequently in reserve at Harwich and Barrow. Scrapped at Briton Ferry, in south Wales, after 21 July 1955); and the ex-*Duddon* [1943] *Ribble* (arrived at Sheerness on 22 May and placed in reserve on 11 June. Scrapped at Blyth after 9 July 1957).

Corvettes:

The 1,010-ton *Castle*-class [1944] *Allington Castle* (at Dover; no date of arrival. Subsequently involved in fisheries protection duties. Scrapped at Sunderland after 20 December 1958); [1944] *Alnwick Castle* (arrived at Sheerness on 24 May and placed in reserve; subsequently employed on air-sea rescue duties. Scrapped at Dunston, Gateshead, after December 1951); [1944] *Bamborough Castle* (arrived at Sheerness on 24 May. Subsequently involved in fisheries protection duties. Scrapped at Llanelly after 22 May 1959); and the [1944] *Farnham Castle* (arrived at the Nore on 24 May and paid off into reserve at Sheerness. Scrapped at Dunston, Gateshead, after 31 October 1960).

Anti-Submarine Vessels:

The 795-ton *Kil*-class patrol sloops [1943] *Kilbirnie* (arrived at Sheerness on 18 June; Placed in reserve on 12 July 1945. Returned to U.S. Navy in December 1946); [1943] *Kilbride* (arrived at the Nore on 15 June and placed in Category C reserve on 12 July. Returned to U.S. Navy in December 1946), [1943] *Kilchattan* (arrived at Sheerness on 17 June. Placed in reserve on 12 July 1945. Returned to U.S. Navy in December 1946); [1943] *Kilchrenan* and [1943] *Kildary* (both arrived at Sheerness on 22 June. Placed in reserve on 12 July 1945. Returned to U.S. Navy in December 1946); [1943] *Kildwick* (arrived at Sheerness on 10 June. Placed in reserve on 12 July 1945. Returned to U.S. Navy in December 1946); [1943] *Kilham* (arrived at Sheerness on 22 June. Placed in reserve on 12 July 1945. Returned to U.S. Navy in 1946); [1943] *Kilkenzie* (arrived at Sheerness on 22 June and placed in reserve in July 1945. Returned to U.S. Navy on 10 December 1946); [1943] *Kilhampton* (arrived at Sheerness on 17 June. Placed in reserve on 12 July 1945. Returned to U.S. Navy in 1946); [1943] *Kilmalcolm* (arrived at Sheerness on 18 June. Placed in reserve on 12 July 1945. Returned to U.S. Navy in December 1946); [1943] *Kilmarnock* (arrived at the Nore on 15 June and placed in Category C reserve on 12 July. Returned to U.S. Navy in December 1946); and the [1943] *Kilmartin,* [1943] *Kilmelford,* [1943] *Kilmington* and the [1943] *Kilmore* (all arrived at Sheerness on 18 June, placed in reserve on 12 July 1945 and returned to U.S. Navy in December 1946).

Minesweepers:

The 672-ton (ex-Canadian) *Bangor*-class sloops [1941] *Ingonish* (arrived at Sheerness on 14 June and placed in reserve on 5 July. Sold on 1 January 1948 and subsequently scrapped at Dunston, Gateshead,) and (ex-Canadian) [1941] *Lockeport* (arrived at Sheerness on 7 June and placed in reserve on 2 July. Sold on 1 January 1948 and subsequently scrapped at Dunston, Gateshead,).

At Chatham, all units in Category B reserve and all returned to U.S. Navy on 20 August 1945

Frigates:

The 1,085-ton *Captain*-class [1942] *Bazely* (arrived at Chatham on 14 June); [1943] *Drury* (arrived at the Nore on 17 June); [1943] *Garlies* (arrived at Chatham on 3 June); [1943] *Grindall* (arrived at Sheerness on 23 June; placed in reserve on 26 July); [1943] *Kempthorne* (at Belfast on 23 June and thence to Chatham and reserve on 25 July); and the [1943] *Pasley* (arrived at Sheerness on 14 June and placed in reserve on 13 July).

At London, all units in Category B reserve and constructive total losses

Frigates:

The 1,300-ton *Captain*-class [1943] *Duff* (mined off Ostend on 30 November 1944 and *hors de combat,* and in reserve at Sheerness after 22 December 1944. Returned to U.S. Navy on 1 November 1946); [1943] *Ekins* (mined off Ostend on 16 April 1945 and *hors de combat.* Nominally returned in June 1945 to U.S. Navy, but having arrived at London on 30 June was paid off on 5 July. Scrapped at Dordrecht in 1947); and [1943] *Halsted* (torpedoed on 11 June 1944 in English Channel; *hors de combat* and hulk written off and placed in reserve 18–19 June 1944. Nominally returned in 1946 to U.S. Navy. Sold on 1 November 1946 and scrapped in the Netherlands after 28 March 1947).

PORTSMOUTH AREA

At Portsmouth

Battleship:

The 30,600-ton *Queen Elizabeth*-class [1915] *Warspite* (paid off and placed in Category C reserve on 31 March 1945. Sold on 12 July 1946; wrecked en route to the breakers on 23 April 1947, scrapped *in situ*).

PLYMOUTH AREA

At Dartmouth

Light Cruiser:

The 4,850-ton *D*-class [1919] *Delhi* (damaged off Split on 12 February 1945 and deemed beyond economic repair in May 1945 at Chatham. Arrived at Dartmouth on

29 June and placed in Category C reserve on 6 July. Sold on 20 January 1948 and scrapped at Newport after March 1948).

Destroyers, all units scrapped in 1946:

The 1,360-ton *B*-class destroyers [1930] *Beagle* (paid off into Category C reserve on 24 May 1945 and arrived at Dartmouth on 2 June. Sold on 22 December 1945; arrived at Rosyth on 15 January 1946 and scrapped after June 1946); [1930] *Bulldog* (arrived at Dartmouth and placed in Category B reserve on 27 May 1945. Sold on 22 December 1945; arrived at Rosyth on 17 January 1946 and scrapped after March 1946); and the 1,475-ton F-class destroyer leader [1934] *Faulknor* (arrived at Dartmouth on 12 June placed in Category C reserve on 25 July 1945. Sold on 22 January 1946 and scrapped at Milford Haven after 4 April 1946).

Frigates, both units in Category B reserve:

The 1,370-ton *River*-class [1943] *Tavy* (arrived at Dartmouth and placed in reserve on 23 July. Scrapped at Newport after July 1953) and [1943] *Towy* (arrived at Dartmouth on 7 June and placed in reserve. Scrapped at Port Glasgow after June 1956).

At Falmouth, all units in Category C reserve

Anti-Aircraft Light Cruiser:

The 4,180-ton class-name [1916] *Caledon* (arrived at Falmouth on 26 April and laid up in reserve on 28 April 1945. Target ship after September 1946; returned to reserve on 7 August 1947. Placed on disposal list on 22 January 1948. Handed over to breakers on 11 March and scrapped at Dover after 1 April 1948).

Light Cruiser:

The 4,290-ton class-name [1919] *Capetown* (arrived at Plymouth on 21 September 1944. Placed in reserve and employed as accommodation ship at Falmouth after October 1944. Sold on 5 April 1946 and scrapped at Preston after 2 June 1946).

Destroyers:

The 905-ton *S*-class destroyers [1919] *Saladin* (arrived at Plymouth on 21 February 1945 and for disposal; paid off in June 1945. Sold on 26 June 1947 and scrapped at Llanelly after 3 July 1947); [1918] *Scimitar* (arrived at Plymouth on 19 February 1945 and placed in reserve: for disposal. Scrapped at Briton Ferry, in south Wales, after 30 June 1947); and the [1917] *Skate* (left Plymouth, under tow, for Milford Haven on 28 January 1945; to be placed in Category C reserve and for disposal. Placed on disposal list on 4 March 1947 and scrapped at Newport after 20 July 1947).

Frigate:

The 1,370-ton *River*-class [1943] *Teme* (torpedoed in southwest approaches on 29 March 1945; *hors de combat* and constructive total loss at Falmouth after 4 May. Sold on 8 December 1945 and subsequently scrapped at Llanelly).

Minelayer:

The 6,740-ton ex-cruiser-minelayer repair ship, [1924] *Adventure* (arrived at Falmouth on 23 June and placed in reserve on 25 July. Sold on 10 July 1947 and subsequently scrapped at Briton Ferry, south Wales).

Minesweepers:

The 710-ton *Hunt*-class sloop [1918] *Albury* (arrived at Cardiff on 24 January 1945; no further details. Sold on 13 March 1947); the 672-ton *Bangor*-class sloop [1942] *Mulgrave* (mined off Normandy on 8 October 1944 and towed to Le Havre. Arrived at Portsmouth on 2 November; *hors de combat* and constructive total loss, and placed in reserve on 20 December 1944. Sold on 15 May 1947 and scrapped at Llanelly after May 1947); the 710-ton *Hunt*-class sloops [1918] *Saltash* (arrived at Plymouth on 14 January 1945 and placed in reserve on 5 February. Sold on 13 March 1947); [1918] *Sutton* (arrived at Plymouth on 12 November 1944 and placed in reserve at Falmouth on 22 December 1944; laid up at Milford Haven after February 1945. Sold in July 1947 and subsequently scrapped at Liège, Belgium); and the 672-ton *Bangor*-class sloop [1941] *Vegreville* (arrived at Plymouth on 5 June and placed in reserve on 5 June. Scrapped at Hayle, Cornwall, after May 1947).

Repair Ship:

The 4,800-ton ex-Australian seaplane carrier [1928] *Albatross* (arrived at Falmouth on 1 August and placed in reserve on 3 August. Sold on 19 August 1946 into commercial service; scrapped at Hong Kong after 12 August 1954).

At Milford Haven, all units Category C

Destroyer:

The 1,190-ton *Town*-class destroyer ex-USS *Aulick* [1919] *Burnham* (laid up in reserve after 1 December 1944. Placed on disposal list on 4 March 1947 and scrapped at Pembroke Dock after 2 December 1948).

Frigate:

The 1,370-ton (Canadian) *River*-class [1943] *Chebogue* (foundered on 11 October 1944 after being torpedoed. Salved and constructive total loss; arrived at Pembroke Dock on 21 September 1945 and reduced to reserve status awaiting disposal on 25 September 1945. Scrapped at Milford Haven after February 1948).

Sloops:

The 1,105-ton *Shoreham*-class [1931] *Bideford* (arrived at Milford Haven on 8 June and placed in reserve in July 1945. Sold on 14 July 1949 and subsequently scrapped at Milford Haven); the 1,045-ton class-name [1928] *Bridgewater* (arrived at Milford Haven on 7 July; placed in reserve in the Clyde in July 1945 and laid up at Ardrossan in August 1945. Target ship in 1946–1947. Sold on 25 May 1947 and subsequently scrapped at Gelliswick, below Milford Haven); the 990-ton *Grimsby*-class [1935] *Deptford* (arrived at Milford Haven on 3 July and placed in reserve that same month. Sold on 8 March 1948 and scrapped at Milford Haven after 11 May 1948); the 1,045-ton *Hastings*-class [1930] *Folkestone* (arrived at Milford Haven on 25 September 1944 and placed in reserve on 15 January 1945; target ship prior to disposal. Sold on 25 May 1947 and subsequently scrapped at Milford Haven); the 990-ton *Grimsby*-class [1935] *Londonderry* (arrived at Milford Haven on 8 July and placed in reserve. Sold on 8 March 1948 and scrapped at Llanelly after 8 June 1948); [1934] *Lowestoft* (arrived at Cardiff on 12 July and placed in reserve. Sold on 4 October 1946 into commercial service); and the [1934] *Wellington* (arrived at Milford Haven on 6 August and placed in reserve on 19 August. Sold on 6 February 1947 and moored in the Thames as base ship).

Corvettes:

The 925-ton ex-French *Flower*-class [1940] *Alisma* (arrived at Milford Haven on 8 June and placed in reserve. Sold in either 1947 or 1948); ex-French Navy [1941] *Anchusa* (arrived at Milford Haven on 3 July and placed in reserve. Sold in 1946); (ex-Canadian) [1940] *Arrowhead* (arrived at Milford Haven on 14 June and placed in reserve on 27 June. Sold on 17 May 1947 and entered commercial service in 1948); [1940] *Azalea* (arrived at Milford Haven on 9 June and placed in reserve. Sold on 5 April 1946); ex-*Chelmer* [1942] *Balsam* (arrived at Cardiff on 21 March and docked on 24 March; placed in reserve on 25 June 1945. Scrapped at Newport after 20 April 1947); [1941] *Campion* (arrived at Milford Haven on 6 June and placed in reserve on 8 June 1945. Scrapped at Newport after 20 April 1947); ex-Dutch Navy *Frisio* [1940] *Carnation* (dates of arrival and passing into reserve not known; last recorded berth was at Greenock, from which it sailed on 6 June. Sold on 31 March 1948 into commercial service); [1940] *Clarkia* (arrived at Milford Haven on 9 June and subsequently placed in reserve. Employed as target ship and returned to reserve on 22 July 1947. Sold on 30 July 1947 and subsequently scrapped at Hayle, Cornwall); [1940] *Dahlia* (arrived at Milford Haven on 26 May. Scrapped at Gelliswick, below Milford Haven, after 20 October 1948); [1940] *Delphinium* (arrived at Milford Haven on 9 June. Sold in February 1949 and subsequently scrapped at Pembroke Dock); [1940] *Dianthus* (arrived at Milford Haven and placed in reserve on 10 June 1945. Sold in May 1949); (ex-Canadian) [1940] *Eyebright* (arrived at Milford Haven on 17 June. Sold on 17 May 1947); [1941] *Fritillary* (arrived at Milford Haven on 2 June and placed in reserve on 8 June 1945. Sold on 19 March 1946 and entered Panamanian commercial service in 1947); (ex-Canadian) [1940] *Hepatica* (arrived at Milford Haven on 16 June and placed in reserve. Scrapped at Llanelly after January 1948); [1940] *Honeysuckle* (arrived at Milford Haven on 1 June and placed in reserve on 8 June 1945. Scrapped at Grays, near Tilbury, after November 1950); ex-French [1940] *La Malouine* (arrived at Preston on 26 May and placed in Category B reserve on 8 June 1945. Scrapped at Gelliswick, below Milford Haven, after May 1947); [1941] *Narcissus* (arrived at Milford Haven and placed in reserve on 9 June 1945. Sold on 5 April 1946 into commercial service); [1940] *Rhododendron* (arrived at Milford Haven on 1 June and placed in reserve on 8 June. For disposal on 8 March 1946 and sold on 17 May 1947 into commercial service); [1941] *Snowdrop* (arrived at Milford Haven on 8 June and placed in reserve. Sold on 17 May 1947 and scrapped on Tyneside in 1949), [1941] *Stonecrop* (arrived at Milford Haven on 13 August and placed in reserve on 25 June 1945. Sold on 17 May 1947); and the (ex-Canadian) [1940] *Trillium* (arrived at Milford Haven and placed in reserve on 16 June. Sold on 17 May 1947 into commercial service).

Minesweepers:

The 710-ton *Hunt*-class sloop [1918] *Lydd* (arrived at Milford Haven and placed in reserve on 20 April 1945. Sold on 13 March 1947 and subsequently scrapped at Liège, Belgium); [1918] *Pangbourne* (arrived at Milford Haven on 20 February 1945 and placed in reserve two days later. Sold 13 March 1947); [1919] *Ross* (sailed from Swansea on 15 February and placed in reserve on 18 February 1945. Sold on 13 March 1947); and the [1918] *Selkirk* (paid off at Cardiff in February 1945; towed to Milford Haven on 19 April and placed in reserve next day. Sold on 17 May 1947 and subsequently scrapped at Liège, Belgium).

Miscellaneous Unit:

The 710-ton *Hunt*-class sloop [1918] *Alresford* (at Milford Haven and either passed or to pass into reserve; no dates. Sold on 13 March 1947 and subsequently scrapped at Liège, Belgium).

Aircraft Training Ships:

The 1,190-ton *Town*-class escort destroyer ex-USS *Laub* [1919] *Burwell* (arrived at

Milford Haven on 29 January 1945 and laid up in reserve in March 1945. Placed on disposal list on 4 March 1947 and subsequently scrapped at Milford Haven) and the 1,175-ton *Flower*-class escort sloop [1915] *Rosemary* (arrived at Milford Haven on 5 July and placed in reserve. Sold on 17 December 1947 and subsequently scrapped at Milford Haven).

Training Ship:
The 610-ton PC-class patrol sloop ex-*Chatsgrove* [1918] P.C. 74 (scrapped at Pembroke Dock in 1948).

At Barrow, all units in Category C reserve
Aircraft Target Ship:
The 1,060-ton *Town*-class destroyer ex-USS *Robinson* [1918] *Newmarket* (laid up after July 1943 as unfit for service. Arrived at Barrow on 1 July 1945 and placed in reserve on 4 July: for disposal. Arrived at Swansea on 20 September. Sold in November 1945 and subsequently scrapped at Llanelly).

Destroyers:
The 1,400-ton *D*-class destroyer leader [1932] *Duncan* (arrived at Barrow on 9 June and placed in reserve on 19 June; approved for sale on 8 July. Sold in September 1945 and subsequently scrapped at Barrow); the 1,480-ton *Shakespeare*-class [1920] *Keppel* (arrived at Barrow on 21 June placed in reserve on 24 June: for disposal. Sold on 25 July 1945 and subsequently scrapped at Barrow); and the 905-ton S-class destroyer [1919] *Shikari* (withdrawn from service in September 1944. Arrived at Barrow on 4 July and placed in reserve. Sold on 13 September 1945 and scrapped at Newport after 4 November 1945).

Escort Destroyers:
The 1,100-ton W-class [1917] *Walker* (arrived at Barrow on 1 June and placed in reserve on 2 June: for disposal. Approved for scrapping and sold, date unknown. Scrapped at Troon after 15 March 1946); [1918] *Westcott* (arrived at Barrow on 24 June and placed in reserve on 26 June 1945. Sold on 8 January 1946 and subsequently scrapped at Troon); the 1,120-ton W-class [1919] *Whitehall* (arrived at Barrow on 2 June and placed in reserve on 5 June 1945. For disposal on 25 July and sold on 25 August. Scrapped at Barrow after 27 October 1945); and the [1919] *Wolverine* (arrived at Barrow on 17 June and placed in reserve; sold on 28 January 1946 and scrapped at Troon after September 1946).

At Preston
Training Ship:
The 905-ton S-class destroyer [1919] *Sardonyx* (withdrawn from operational service in October 1944; arrived at Preston and placed in Category C reserve on 23 June 1945. Scrapped at Inverkeithing after September 1945).

REDUCING TO RESERVE
Capital Ship:
The 32,000-ton *Repulse*-class battlecruiser [1916] *Renown* (arrived at Plymouth on 10 July and in service as depot ship. Placed in Category B reserve at Devonport in March 1946. Approved for scrapping on 1 January 1948 and programme agreed on 19 March 1948. Placed in Category C reserve on 30 June 1948 and then paid off 3 August 1948. Scrapped at Faslane after 8 August 1948).

Heavy Cruiser:

The 9,800-ton Improved *Birmingham*-class [1917] *Hawkins* (at Gareloch and to berth at Falmouth in Category C reserve. Sold on 26 August 1947 and scrapped at Dalmuir after December 1947).

Aircraft Target Ship:

The 1,190-ton *Town*-class destroyer ex-USS *Abel P. Upshur* [1920] *Clare* (arrived and berthed at Barrow on 14 August and placed in Category C reserve two days later. Sold on 25 August 1945 and scrapped at Troon after 18 February 1947).

Destroyers, all units reduced to Category B unless otherwise stated:

The 1,870-ton *Tribal*-class [1937] *Ashanti* (on the Tyne after June 1944 and under repair; to complete April 1946. Work halted on 19 August and placed in Category C reserve at Rosyth. Target ship in 1947. Scrapped at Troon after 12 April 1948); the 1,370-ton *I*-class [1937] *Impulsive* (arrived and berthed at Harwich on 17 June and thereafter placed in reserve. Sold on 22 January 1946 and scrapped at Sunderland after 4 March 1946); the 1,690-ton *K*-class [1939] *Kelvin* (arrived and berthing at Dartmouth on 8 July. Sold on 6 April 1949 and subsequently scrapped at Troon); and the 1,540-ton *P*-class [1939] *Pathfinder* (constructive total loss at Plymouth and berthed at Falmouth after 16 May. Placed in Category C reserve on 30 November 1945. Trials ship in 1947 and scrapped at Milford Haven after November 1948).

Escort Destroyer:

The 1,087-ton Type III *Hunt*-class [1941] *Derwent* (*hors de combat* as result of air attack at Tripoli on 19 March 1943; at Devonport yard, Plymouth, after 11 August 1944. To berth at Falmouth and be placed in Category C reserve in August 1945. Sold on 8 November 1946 and scrapped at Penryn, Cornwall, after 21 February 1947).

Cutter:

The 1,546-ton U.S. Coast Guard *Banff*-class ex-*Cayuga* escort sloop [1931] *Totland* (arrived at Hartlepool on 3 August and passed into Category B reserve on 28 September; to berth at Falmouth. Returned to American ownership on 2 May 1946).

River Gunboat:

The 585-ton *Dragonfly*-class [1939] *Locust* (arrived and berthed at Harwich on 20 June, and placed in Category B reserve. Subsequently drill ship for reserve; sold on 24 May 1968 and subsequently scrapped at Newport).

Frigates, all units in Category B reserve unless otherwise stated:

The 1,300-ton *Captain*-class [1943] *Affleck* (torpedoed off Normandy on 26 December 1944; constructive total loss at Portsmouth and to berth at Barrow. Sailed from Portsmouth on 20 August 1945. Nominally returned to U.S. Navy on 1 September 1945 and hulk sold on 4 October 1947); the 1,318-ton *Colony*-class [1943] *Barbados* (arrived at Londonderry on 28 June. Returned to U.S. Navy on 15 April 1946); the 1,085-ton *Captain*-class [1942] *Bayntun* (arrived at Harwich on 16 July. Returned to U.S. Navy on 22 August 1945); the 1,318-ton *Colony*-class [1943] *Cayman* (arrived and berthed at Londonderry on 24 June. Paid off on 26 July and placed in Category B reserve on 20 August. Returned to U.S. Navy on 22 April 1946); the 1,085-ton *Captain*-class [1943] *Foley* (arrived and berthed at Harwich on 9 July. Returned to U.S. Navy on 22 August 1945); [1943] *Goodson* (torpedoed off Cherbourg on 25 June 1944 and constructive total loss at Portland. Arrived at Belfast on 6 July 1944; in care and maintenance after 18 July 1944. Nominally returned to

U.S. Navy on 21 October 1944. Sold on 9 January 1947 and scrapped at Whitchurch, Cork, Irish Free State, after October 1948); [1943] *Kingsmill* (arrived at Harwich on 18 May and placed in Category C reserve on 29 May. Returned to U.S. Navy on 22 August 1945); [1943] *Manners* (torpedoed and lost stern in the Irish Sea on 29 January 1945; initially in February 1945 to be cannibalized as constructive total loss but placed in Category B reserve at Barrow on 27 August. Nominally returned to U.S. Navy on 8 November 1945. Sold to Greek breaker on 3 December 1946); the 1,318-ton *Colony*-class [1943] *Papua* (berthed at Londonderry. Returned to U.S. Navy on 13 May 1946), [1943] *Pitcairn* (arrived at Londonderry on 23 May and placed in reserve. Returned to U.S. Navy on 11 June 1946), [1943] *St. Helena* (arrived in the Clyde on 2 June; to berth in reserve at Londonderry. On 23 April 1946 at Norfolk, Virginia, paid off and returned to U.S. Navy); [1943] *Sarawak* (arrived at Londonderry on 24 May and placed in Category B reserve on 29 August. Returned to U.S. Navy in May 1946), [1943] *Seychelles* (arrived at Londonderry on 28 June and placed in Category B reserve on 18 August. Returned to U.S. Navy in June 1946), the 1,370-ton *River*-class [1941] *Spey* (arrived at Dartmouth on 9 July and placed in Category B reserve. Transferred to Egyptian Navy in 1948; scrapped in 1990); [1943] *Tees* (arrived at Dartmouth and placed in Category C reserve on 24 June. Scrapped at Newport after 16 July 1955); the 1,318-ton *Colony*-class [1943] *Tobago* (at Londonderry in Category B reserve after 17 June. Returned to U.S. Navy on 13 May 1946); [1943] *Tortola* (arrived at Londonderry on 14 July and placed in Category B reserve on 30 August. Returned to U.S. Navy on 22 May 1946); the 1,300-ton *Captain*-class [1943] *Trollope* (written off after being torpedoed off Normandy on 6 July 1944. Nominally returned to U.S. Navy on 10 October 1944 but constructive total loss at Belfast and unallocated, in Category C reserve, after 28 November 1944. Sold by U.S. Navy on 10 January 1947 and ceased to be a British responsibility on 13 January 1947; apparently scrapped at Troon after July 1951); [1943] *Whitaker* (torpedoed on 1 November 1944 and towed to Belfast, arriving on 13 November. Deemed constructive total loss and placed in Category C reserve at Belfast after March 1945. Nominally returned to U.S. Navy on 3 December 1945; sold on 9 January 1947 and subsequently scrapped at Whitchurch, Cork, Irish Free State); the 1,370-ton *River*-class [1943] *Wye* (arrived at Dartmouth on 19 July and placed in Category C reserve. Scrapped at Troon after February 1955); and the 1,318-ton *Colony*-class [1943] *Zanzibar* (arrived and berthed at Londonderry on 18 June. Returned to U.S. Navy on 21 May 1946).

Corvettes, all units in Category B reserve:

The 925-ton *Flower*-class [1940] *Amaranthus* (arrived at Harwich on 3 August and either passed or to pass into reserve. Sold in 1946 into commercial service); [1941] *Bellwort* (arrived and berthing at Dartmouth on 9 July. Sold to Irish Free State in 1946; commissioned in February 1947. Scrapped after January 1971); [1941] *Bryony* (arrived at Dartmouth on 20 July and placed in reserve on 26 July. Expected sale to Greece not realized; accepted as weather ship on 11 December 1946. Reduced to reserve on 24 September 1947[?] and sold to Norway, date unknown. Renamed the *Polarfront II* on 6 May 1948); [1940] *Geranium* (arrived at Dartmouth on 2 July and placed in Category B reserve on 20 August; transferred to Danish Navy on 8 October); [1940] *Hydrangea* (arrived at Dartmouth on 23 July and placed in reserve on 20 August. Sold on 16 November 1946 and entered commercial service in 1948), [1940] *Nasturtium* (arrived and berthed at Dartmouth on 6 July; placed in reserve on 31 August. Sold on 28 November 1946 into Greek commercial service); [1941] *Pentstemon* (arrived at Dartmouth on 26 July and to be reduced to reserve after 24 September. Sold in 1946 into commercial service); [1940] *Primula* (arrived at Harwich and placed in Category B reserve on 24 June; placed in Category C reserve on 28 February. Sold on 22 July 1946 into commercial service); [1941] *Saxifrage* (arrived at Portsmouth on 6 July and placed in reserve on 5 October; to berth at Dartmouth. Transferred to Norwegian Navy in August 1947); the 980-ton Modified *Flower*-class [1943] *Willowherb* (arrived at Harwich on 3 July and placed in reserve on 18 August. Returned to U.S. Navy on 11 June 1946); and the 925-ton *Flower*-class [1941] *Woodruff* (arrived at Dartmouth on 3 July and placed in Category C reserve. Sold in 1947 into commercial service).

Minesweeper:

The 850-ton *Algerine*-class sloop [1942] *Fantome* (mined off Tunisia on 20 May 1943 and afforded temporary repairs at Bizerte. Returned to Britain under tow: declared constructive total loss at Plymouth and berthing at Milford Haven in Category C reserve. Sold in January 1947 and scrapped at Milford Haven after 22 May 1947).

Destroyer Depot Ships:

The 9,770-ton Improved *Birmingham*-class heavy cruiser ex-*Cavendish* [1917] *Vindictive* (paid off at Sheerness in June 1945. Sold in February 1946 and subsequently scrapped at Blyth) and the 8,100-ton requisitioned [1915] *Greenwich* (arrived and berthed at Portsmouth on 22 July, having been placed in Category B reserve on 4 July. Approval for scrapping on 13 March 1946 and placed in Category C reserve on 27 May. Sold on 11 July 1946 and after refit and conversion in Belfast entered into commercial service in 1948).

OTHER UNITS TO BE PAID OFF INTO RESERVE

Light Cruisers:

The 4,190-ton *Ceres*-class [1917] *Cardiff* (training ship after October 1940. Arrived at Portsmouth on 7 July; to berth in the Gareloch in Category C reserve, and did so on 15 October 1945. Sold on 26 January 1946 and scrapped at Dalmuir after 18 March 1946) and the 4,290-ton *Capetown*-class [1918] *Carlisle* (badly damaged in the Aegean by German aircraft on 9 October 1943. Constructive total loss and used as accommodation ship at Alexandria: in Category C reserve. Scrapped locally in 1949).

Sloops:

The 990-ton *Grimsby*-class [1936] *Fleetwood* (arrived and berthed at Hartlepool on 4 August and placed in Category B reserve. Fisheries and training ship between 1946 and 1959. Scrapped at Dunston, Gateshead, after 10 October 1959) and the 1,105-ton *Shoreham* class [1930] *Fowey* (arrived in Loch Ryan on 27 May. Guardship at Larne and Stranraer until December 1945; to pass to Category C reserve, unallocated. Sold in October 1946 into commercial service).

Frigates:

The 1,085-ton *Captain*-class [1943] *Burges* (arrived at Greenock on 6 June and to berth in Category C reserve at Harwich. Returned to U.S. Navy on 7 February 1946) and the 1,370-ton *River*-class [1942] *Cuckmere* (torpedoed in western Mediterranean on 11 December 1943: *hors de combat* and undergoing repair at Taranto. Scheduled to return to Britain and to pass into Category B reserve status. Returned to U.S. Navy in November 1946).

Corvettes:

The 925-ton *Flower*-class [1941] *Bergamot* (arrived at Gibraltar on 18 July. Berth unallocated but to pass into Category C reserve. Sold in May 1946 into commercial service),

[1941] *Cowslip* (arrived and berthed at Chatham on 2 August and subsequently placed in Category C reserve. Sold in July 1948 and scrapped at Troon after April 1949); the 980-ton Modified *Flower*-class [1942] *Dittany* (arrived and berthed at Sheerness on 13 August; subsequently placed in Category C reserve. Returned to U.S. Navy on 20 June 1946); [1941] *Genista* (arrived and berthed at Sheerness on 4 August; placed in Category C reserve at Chatham on 13 September 1945. Transferred to Air Ministry as weather ship in 1947 and scrapped at Antwerp after October 1961); the 980-ton Modified *Flower*-class [1942] *Linaria* (arrived at Portsmouth on 15 August; to reduce to Category C reserve at Dartmouth. Returned to U.S. Navy on 27 July 1946), the 925-ton *Flower*-class [1940] *Marguerite* (arrived at Sheerness on 4 August and placed in Category B reserve on 15 September. Transferred to Air Ministry as weather ship in 1947 and scrapped at Ghent, Belgium, after 8 September 1961); and the [1940] *Verbena* (arrived at Plymouth on 28 July; berthed at Pembroke Dock in Category C reserve on 5 September. Sold on 17 May 1947 but never entered Swedish commercial service; scrapped at Blyth after 1 October 1951).

Escort:

The 672-ton *Bangor*-class sloop [1940] *Peterhead* (having been sunk by a mine off Brest on 8 June 1944, salved and constructive total loss at Cardiff, where it arrived on 4 August; arrived at Milford Haven on 23 August and placed in Category C reserve the next day. Sold in 1947 and scrapped at Pembroke Dock after May 1948).

MISCELLANEOUS UNITS

The *Castle*-class corvette *Hadleigh Castle* (deployed to Gibraltar as relief for the *Lancaster Castle*. Placed in Category B reserve at Portsmouth on 31 January 1946. Sold in 1958 and scrapped after January 1959).

The 545-ton submarine [1940] *Upright* (sailed from Halifax, Nova Scotia, on 11 September. Sold on 19 December 1945 and scrapped at Troon after March 1946).

The 545-ton submarine [1941] *United* (sailed for home waters via Bermuda on 9 September. Placed in reserve at Londonderry on 14 October: for disposal. Scrapped at Troon after 8 February 1946).

The 545-ton submarine [1941] *Unruffled* (on the Bermuda station until 9 September. Placed in reserve at Londonderry in October: for disposal. Scrapped at Troon after 21 January 1946).

The 545-ton submarine [1942] *Unseen* (scrapped at Hayle, in Cornwall, after September 1949).

The 545-ton submarine [1943] (Norwegian) ex-*Varne*, *Ula* (remained in Norwegian service; scrapped at Hamburg in 1965).

A FINAL COMMENT

It is perhaps worth noting a number of episodes and facts that could could be classified as unusual but that could not be included because of the needs and demands of standardization. But

- on 7 February 1946 the *Algerine*-class minesweeper *Liberty* arrived at Sasebo.
- whereas most lend-lease ships were returned to the U.S. Navy either in British

or (more usually) American east coast ports, in February 1946 the *Captain*-class frigate *Spragge* was returned to the U.S. Navy in Subic Bay, the Philippines.

- on 10 December 1945 the *Captain*-class frigate *Narbrough* was at Libau, Latvia, which was part of the Soviet Union, on 19 January 1946 was at St. John's, Newfoundland, which was British and not part of Canada at this time, and six days later was at Boston, Massachusetts, which always has been in a world of its own, and
- on 8 September 1945 the *Captain*-class frigate *Bligh* stopped a yacht in the Irish Sea. The yacht had been stolen and was manned by escaping German prisoners of war who were attempting to return to Germany.

Why any German prisoners should seek to escape from British custody in September 1945, and specifically to return to a Germany in ruins, is not altogether obvious, but if this was indeed a case that the Germans, having lost one world war, were attempting to escape in order to return home and to start another, then this little known episode may well constitute the British Navy's greatest achievement of, but after, the Second World War.

As it was, a fate worse than war awaited the prisoners: they were taken to and put ashore, under arrest, at Liverpool. How much the better would their situation and treatment have been had they had been put ashore at Everton.

Sources: The Pink List of 15 August 1945; *The Red List*, part 2: *Minor War Vessels Abroad* of 2 September 1945; *The Green List: Landing Ships, Landing Craft and Landing Barges* of 3 September 1945; B.R. 1316, *Signal Letter Index and Confidential Number and Speeds of Merchant Ships, August 1944*; B.R. 619(2)(1944), *Distinguishing Pennants and Signal Letters; Lloyd's Registers of Shipping* for 1944–1945, 1945–1946, and 1946–1947; Francis E. McMurtie, ed., *Jane's Fighting Ships: 1944–1945 Edition* (London: David & Charles, 1978); H. T. Lenton and J. J. Colledge, *Warships of World War II* (London: Ian Allan, n.d.); J. J. Colledge, rev. Ben Warlow, *Ships of the Royal Navy: The Complete Record of All Fighting Ships of the Royal Navy* (London: Greenhill, 2003); *Dictionary of American Naval Fighting Ships*, 8 vols. (Washington D.C.: Department of the Navy, 1959–1981; http://www.naval-history.net/; http://www.uboat.net/allies/merchants/; and http://uboat.net/allies/ warships/ship/7282.html.

APPENDIX 15.2.

TABULAR REPRESENTATION OF THE BRITISH, IMPERIAL, AND COMMONWEALTH NAVAL STRENGTH IN THE INDIAN OCEAN, 15 AUGUST 1945

	a	b	c	d	e	f	g	Total
Battleships	2	-	-	-	-	-	-	2
Fleet carriers	-	-	-	-	-	-	-	-
Light carriers	-	-	-	-	-	-	-	-
Escort carriers	14	-	-	-	-	2	-	16
Heavy cruisers	3	-	-	-	-	1	-	4
Light cruisers	5	-	-	-	-	3	-	8
Anti-aircraft cruisers	-	-	-	-	-	-	-	-
Destroyers	16	1	-	-	-	13	-	30
Fighter-direction ships	1	-	-	-	-	3	-	4
Submarines	13	-	-	-	-	-	-	-
Frigates	-	22	-	-	-	14	6	42
Sloops	-	7	-	1	-	1	-	9
Corvettes	-	14	-	1	-	2	-	17
Escort destroyers	5	-	-	-	-	1	15	21
Cutters	-	4	1	-	-	1	-	6
Escorts	-	2	-	2	-	-	-	4
Patrol vessels	-	-	-	36	-	-	-	36
Monitors	-	-	-	-	-	2	-	2
Gunboats	-	-	-	-	-	3	-	3
Minelayers	-	-	3	-	-	-	-	3
Minesweepers	-	31	-	18	-	9	-	58
Auxiliary minesweepers	-	-	-	11	-	-	-	11
Danlayers	-	3	1	-	-	1	-	5
Named landing ships	-	-	-	-	20	-	-	20
Other landing ships	-	-	-	-	66	-	-	66
Survey ships	-	-	4	1	-	-	-	5
Salvage vessels	-	-	2	-	-	1	-	3
Tugs	-	-	10	11	-	-	-	21

	a	b	c	d	e	f	g	Total
Base and depot ships	2	-	5	6	-	-	-	13
Base and fleet tenders	2	-	3	-	-	1	-	6
Boom and gate vessels	-	-	30	1	-	1	-	32
Netlayer	-	-	-	-	-	1	-	1
Deperming ships	-	-	2	1	-	-	-	3
Repair ships	-	-	1	1	-	1	-	3
Maintenance ships	-	-	4	-	-	-	-	4
Training ships	-	-	-	6	-	-	-	6
Target ships	-	-	1	-	-	-	-	1
Accommodation ships	1	-	4	-	-	-	-	5
Hospital ships	-	-	4	-	-	-	-	4
Large/fast tankers	-	-	-	-	-	-	-	-
Small tankers	-	-	-	-	-	-	-	-
Water carriers	-	-	-	1	-	-	-	1
Colliers	-	-	-	-	-	-	-	-
Issuing ships	-	-	-	-	-	-	-	-
Stores ships	-	-	-	-	-	-	-	-
Floating docks	-	-	-	-	-	-	-	-
Others	-	-	-	-	-	-	-	-
Others	-	-	-	17	-	-	-	17
Totals	64	84	75	114	86	61	21	505

Key:

a. Units with the East Indies Fleet
b. Units with escort formations
c. Units with the Fleet Train and base and depot ships
d. Units of the Royal Indian Navy
e. Units with Force W
f. Other units assigned to the East Indies Fleet but non-operational, not on station, or on passage
g. Other units nominated as reinforcements for the East Indies Fleet

APPENDIX 15.3.

TABULAR REPRESENTATION OF BRITISH AND DOMINION NAVAL STRENGTH IN THE PACIFIC, 15 AUGUST 1945

	a	b	c	d	e	f	g	h	Total	i
Battleships	1	1	1	-	-	-	1	-	4	-
Fleet carriers	4	1	-	-	-	-	1	-	6	-
Light carriers	-	3	-	-	-	1	-	-	4	-
Escort carriers	-	-	-	5	2	2	-	-	9	-
Heavy cruisers	-	-	-	-	-	-	-	-	-	1
Light cruisers	6	2	-	-	-	2	1	-	11	1
Anti-aircraft cruisers	-	1	-	-	-	-	-	-	1	-
Destroyers	23	6	2	-	-	5	13	3	52	4
Fighter-direction ships	-	-	-	-	-	-	-	5	5	-
Submarines	-	-	23	-	-	4	2	-	29	-

	a	b	c	d	e	f	g	h	Total	i
Frigates	-	-	-	7	-	4	2	40	53	9
Sloops	-	-	-	19	2	10	-	7	38	8
Corvettes	-	-	-	-	-	-	-	-	-	6
Escort destroyers	-	-	-	-	-	7	-	5	12	-
Cutters	-	-	-	-	-	-	-	-	-	-
Escorts	-	-	-	-	-	-	-	-	-	-
Patrol vessels	-	-	-	-	-	-	-	-	-	5
Monitors	-	-	-	-	-	-	-	-	-	-
Gunboats	-	-	-	-	-	-	-	-	-	-
Minelayers	-	-	2	-	-	1	-	-	3	1
Minesweepers	-	-	-	-	-	-	10	-	10	35
Auxiliary minesweepers	-	-	-	-	-	-	-	-	-	37
Danlayers	-	-	-	-	-	-	-	2	2	3
Headquarters ships	-	-	-	1	-	2	-	-	3	-
Named landing ships	-	-	-	-	-	-	-	-	-	4
Other landing ships	-	-	-	-	-	-	-	-	-	-
Transport	-	-	-	1	-	-	-	-	1	-
Survey ships	-	-	-	-	-	-	-	-	-	8
Salvage vessels	-	-	-	2	-	1	-	-	3	-
Tugs	-	-	-	3	-	1	-	-	4	8
Training ships	-	-	-	-	-	-	-	-	-	-
Target ships	-	-	1	-	-	1	-	-	2	-
Base and depot ships	-	-	3	1	-	-	-	-	4	9
Base and fleet tenders	-	-	-	-	-	-	-	-	-	2
Boom and gate ships	-	-	2	1	-	4	-	-	7	18
Netlayers	-	-	-	-	1	-	-	1	2	-
Deperming ships	-	-	-	1	-	-	-	-	1	1
Repair ships	-	-	-	4	1	2	-	8	15	1
Maintenance ships	-	-	-	3	-	1	-	5	9	-
Accommodation ships	-	-	1	2	-	-	-	1	4	-
Hospital ships	-	-	-	3	2	1	-	-	6	-
Large/fast tankers	-	-	-	13	1	-	1	13	28	-
Small tankers	-	-	-	9	-	-	-	10	19	-
Water carriers	-	-	-	-	2	-	-	1	3	2
Colliers	-	-	-	1	1	-	-	1	3	-
Issuing ships	-	-	-	16	9	1	1	7	34	2
Stores ships	-	-	-	2	5	-	-	5	12	3
Floating docks	-	-	-	2	-	-	-	-	2	-
Others	-	-	-	-	-	-	1	1	2	8
Totals	34	14	35	96	27	49	33	115	403	176

Key:

a. Task Force 37/Task Force 113
b. Task Group 111.2
Technically this second carrier formation did not exist until 20 August, but its units sailed from Sydney for Manus on 15 August, and therefore the formation is included in these lists.
c. Other units on station
d. Task Force 112: units of the fleet train at sea, Manus, or advanced bases in the Pacific
e. Other Fleet Train units on station
f. Units *en route* for the Pacific, 15 August 1945
g. Other units assigned to the British Pacific Fleet and the Fleet Train but non-operational or not on station or not on passage
h. Units nominated to serve as reinforcements for the British Pacific Fleet or in the Fleet Train
i. Units of the Royal Australian, Canadian, and New Zealand Navies on station in the Pacific but not under Admiralty orders and not with the British Pacific Fleet

Notes:

The totals in this and the previous appendixes do not include numbered minesweeping launches and craft, landing craft, miscellaneous launches, and unclassified auxiliaries. In addition, certain units known to be in the Indian Ocean at this time—such as the heavy cruisers *Berwick* and *Devonshire* and light cruiser *Enterprise*, which were employed as troopships to Australia—have not been counted in this list because they were not assigned to formations herein.

Moreover, the various units gathered for Operation Zipper have not been included in appendix 15.2. The landing ships are listed as the units with Force W, but it seems that in addition to the listed landing ships, there were no fewer than 311 landing craft of all descriptions plus 112 merchantmen: see the author's *Grave of a Dozen Schemes*, pp. 210–217.

Likewise, various merchantmen and auxiliaries were assigned but cannot be identified other than their being listed in the *Signal Letter Index* as merchantmen: these units include such units as the 7,160-ton *Buffalo Park*, which was the original name of the *Empire Charlotte*, which was scheduled to go to the Pacific but was at Vancouver; the 10,902-ton *City of Paris*; the 5,428-ton [1919] *Gurna*; the 233-ton tugs *Rockcliffe* and *Rockmount*, which were scheduled to enter service in 1945 but apparently did not do so before the end of the war; the 7,176-ton *Samson*; the 2,742-ton *Talune*; and the 8,602-ton *Empire Silver*, which was a tanker. The 7,100-ton *Fort Kilmar* was also assigned, and on the strength of the operational orders issued for Zipper it can be identified as a victualling store issuing ship, if only for this one operation, but how it should be listed is quite another matter.

NOTES

1. INTRODUCTION

1. There were numerous Japanese bombings of cities in 1937 and 1938, but premeditated and systemic effort, in the form of three deliberate strategic bombing campaigns, took the form of Operation 100, conducted between 3 and 4 May and 7 October 1939, and Operation 101, conducted between 18 May and 4 September 1940. There was a third effort, Operation 102, which was staged between 27 July and 31 August 1941, but with the decision to prepare for a war in the Pacific this effort was curtailed.

2. One would suggest the two British institutions that were the representative of the democratic cause were Parliament and the BBC; in terms of the former, its triumph, its finest moment, was in July 1945 with the defeat of the Churchill government.

2. WASHINGTON AND LONDON

1. The "second to none" proposal was made in a report by the General Board of the U.S. Navy in a report to the secretary of the navy, and was to the effect that the service "should ultimately be equal to the most powerful maintained by any other nation in the world." Roskill, *Naval Policy between the Wars*, vol. 1: *The Period of Anglo-American Antagonism*, p. 20.

2. The figure has been based on the costs of the *Nelson* (£7,504,055) and *Rodney* (£7,617,799) and a conversion rate of $4.60 to the pound. The cost of the *Hood* was £6,025,000. The tripling of price is based upon the cost of the battlecruiser *Lion*, which, entering service in October 1912, was the first warship to cost the British taxpayer more than £2,000,000. Parkes, *British Battleships*, pp. 531, 644, and 654.

3. This sum included £269,964,650 with reference to interest payments on the national debt (eleven times more than the corresponding 1913–1914 figure) but what is perhaps surprising was the provision of £58,279,235—more than one quarter of state spending and more than the spending of all state departments excluding the armed services in 1913–1914—as "miscellaneous credits" set against departmental spending, the armed forces excluded.

4. Japan was the only non-white, non-European founding and council member of the League of Nations, the deputy secretary general of which was Dr. Nitobe Inazo.

These matters were evidence of achievement and justification for pride, an evidence of national standing and worth. "Internationalism" was extremely popular within Japan, especially within the Japanese elite and even with many army officers, in the twenties. See Nish, *Japan's Struggle with Internationalism,* and Tohmatsu and Willmott, *A Gathering Darkness*, pp. 1–11.

5. Boyer, *The Enduring Vision,* vol. 2: *From 1865,* p. xxxi. http://en.wikipedia.org/wiki/U.S._presidential_election,_1920. *United States Presidential Election, 1920.* Harding's result remains the largest winning margin (26.17%) in the history of U.S. presidential elections.

http://www.uselectionatlas.org/WIKI/index.php/1920_U.S._General_Election. *1920 U. S. General Election.* In the 96-member Senate, with 32 members standing, the Republicans gained ten seats to turn a 49–47 majority into 59–37 majority, and in the House, where the Republicans polled 69.4% to the Democrats' 30.1%, the 240–192 majority was transformed into an overwhelming 302–131 majority.

6. The nine powers were the original five—Britain, France, Italy, Japan, and the United States—plus Belgium, China, the Netherlands, and Portugal. The British delegation included single representatives of Australia, Canada, and New Zealand but not Newfoundland, South Africa, or India.

7. The total of forty capital ships does not include the *Australia* and *New Zealand.* The latter was stricken on 12 April 1921, i.e., before Washington, but not sold until 19 December 1921, and was scrapped in 1923; the former was stricken on 12 December 1921 and was scuttled off Sydney on 12 April 1924.

8. The *Colossus* was decommissioned and entered service as a hulk in 1923; it not scrapped until 1928.

9. Not included in this summary of the fate of British capital ships are two units included in the total of forty, the battleships *Erin* and *Canada,* which at the outbreak of war in 1914 had been under construction in British yards for Turkey and Chile respectively. The *Canada,* having been purchased by the British in 1914, was resold to Chile in April 1920 and entered Chilean service on 1 August of that year. The last survivor of Jutland, it was finally decommissioned in 1958 and was towed to Japan and scrapped in 1959. The *Erin* was placed in reserve in 1919 and was scrapped in 1922.

10. Ian Neary, ed., *Leaders and Leadership in Japan,* pp. 147–154 (Ian Nish, chapter 12, *The Leadership of Admiral Kato Tomosaburo*).

11. Breyer, *Battleships and Battle Cruisers,* p. 433. Greger, *Battleships of the World,* p. 76. M. J. Whitley, *Battleships of World War II: An International Encyclopedia* (London: Arms and Armour, 1998), p. 46.

12. Hamaguchi was one of the toughest of the inter-war cabinet and prime ministers, with a reputation for not standing for any nonsense on the part of the military and keeping the latter firmly under control. He was also fiscally very correct, and disastrously so for a Japan, at this time industrially on a par with Italy, that was severely affected by the onset of the Depression. Hamaguchi was shot in the Tokyo railway station at almost the same spot as Prime Minister Takashi Hara had been assassinated nine years before; after a period of recuperation, and victory in the general election of February, he returned to power in March but was obliged to resign in April 1931 and died on 26 August.

Hamaguchi and Herbert Hoover seem very similar in that both had to contend with economic, financial, and industrial problems that they did not understand, which overwhelmed them personally and discredited their administrations. There is also a curious similarity between Hoover and Jimmy Carter in this matter, and also on account of their both being engineers and their record of good works after leaving the White House.

13. Britain laid down the five units of the *King George V* class and the lead ship of the *Lion* class of battlecruisers, which was the *Téméraire* and not the *Lion*. The U.S. laid down the *North Carolina* and *Washington* and the *South Dakota* and *Massachusetts*. Greger, *Battleships of the World*, pp. 132, 171, and 238. Ian Sturton, ed., *All the World's Battleships: 1906 to the Present* (London: Conway Maritime Press, pp. 93–98, 129, and 179–181. Whitley, *Battleships of World War II*, pp. 137–151, 206, and 289–297.

14. Whitley, *Battleships of World War II*, pp. 45–53 and 169.

15. Alternatively, the point may be made by the assertion that the surest means of making the eyes of a British naval officer light up is to shine a beam of light into one of his ears.

3. ETHIOPIA AND SPAIN

1. See, for example, Janos and Slottman, *Revolution in Perspective*, and Szilassy, *Revolutionary Hungary*.

2. Barclay, *The Rise and Fall of the New Roman Empire*, pp. 133–137.

3. The Bulgarian-Greek border clashes compounded problems within Macedonia that were exacerbated by Bulgaria. There were four Balkan conferences that addressed Macedonian and border questions, but these basically foundered upon Bulgarian obduracy. In the end, on 9 February 1934, the Balkan Entente, consisting of Greece, Romania, Turkey, and Yugoslavia, agreed to recognize and accept existing borders and to support one another in the event of dispute, i.e., to check Bulgaria, though it should be noted that one year later, in March 1934, Austria, Hungary, and Italy likewise formed a pact that represented a balance of power in areas outside Macedonia where problems of borders, claim, and counter-claim, might emerge.

4. See, for example, http://www.en.wikipedia.org/wiki.Albania_between_wars, *History of Albania (1919–1939)*, and www.warwickac.uk/~lysic/1920salbania.htm, *Albania*.

5. The list is by no means complete, most obviously with reference to the frontiers of Germany and Poland (and not just with one another) and Hungary's borders with Austria, Czechoslovakia, and Yugoslavia. There was also the problem of repatriation of minorities, most obviously Turks and (an estimated 1,500,000) Greeks as part of the 1922–1923 settlement and of Bulgarians in the Petrich area of Macedonia, where Bulgarian, Greek, and Yugoslav claims vied for supremacy. It is perhaps worth noting that Greece and Turkey did attempt to sort out their differences with the treaties of October 1930 and December 1933. These and other episodes are but little noted in contemporary histories: http://www.encyclopedia.com/doc/1G1-17162649.html, *The League of Nations' predicament in Southeastern Europe (Woodrow Wilson and the League of Nations, Part 2)*, provides an introduction to these episodes.

6. Barnett, *The Collapse of British Power*, pp. 352–353 and 356.

7. Padfield, *The Battleship Era*, p. 260.

8. *Keesing's Contemporary Archives*, vol. 2: 1934–1937 (Keynsham, Bristol: Keesing's Publications, n.d.), p. 1805; meeting of 23 September between Mussolini and the British ambassador, Sir Eric Drummond, that was the subject of the press statement of 25 September 1935.

9. Coffey, *Lion by the Tail*, p. 141. It would seem that on 20 September, when this information was given to the Italians, the British had six capital ships, five heavy and six light cruisers, and two aircraft carriers in the Mediterranean, and even with destroyers and submarines the total of 144 warships on station would seem a little high. If, however, the total included all minelayers, minesweepers, sloops, coastal craft, and auxiliaries, the British units in the Mediterranean might number a gross, but the total does seem a little overstated.

10. Mercer, *Twentieth Century Day by Day,* p. 458: press reports reference Hoare's speech in the House of Commons of 22 October 1935.

11. The election came a month after George Lansbury (1859–1940), perhaps the most beloved leader in the history of the Labour Party, was caught between a Christian pacifist conscience and the demand for economic sanctions and with it the prospect of collective security requirements; defeated at the annual conference, he resigned. But the Labour Party was then caught in a second dilemma, whether to resist increased defense spending or to endorse such increases and trust the Conservative government.

12. Mercer, *Twentieth Century Day by Day,* p. 466. Italian forces entered Addis Ababa on 2 May, and Mussolini proclaimed the end of the war on week later in Rome.

13. Barclay, *The Rise and Fall of the New Roman Empire,* p. 154. Barclay gives the date of the Italian entry into Addis Ababa as 5 May.

14. A slightly amended version of the piece in the infamous radio broadcast of 27 September 1938 by Prime Minister Neville Chamberlain (1869–1940) that was the prelude to the abandonment of Czechoslovakia at Munich over the next three days.

15. To summarize, the overall numbers in the Mediterranean theater on 30 September 1935, and excluding all units en route to the theater, were as follows: in the western Mediterranean, two British and French battlecruisers, six heavy and two light cruisers, and one seaplane carrier; in the central Mediterranean, two Italian battleships, seven heavy and six light cruisers, and one seaplane carrier; in the eastern Mediterranean, four British battleships, five heavy and five light cruisers, and two aircraft carriers. In addition, at or en route to Aden were three British heavy and three light cruisers.

16. The *Queen Elizabeth* arrived at Gibraltar the next day, 1 October, and sailed in a matter of hours to Malta, arriving 3 October. It sailed on 7 October and arrived at Alexandria on the 10th. It became fleet flagship on 12 October and sailed two days later in formation with the *Resolution, Revenge,* and *Valiant,* and was at Haifa on the last day of the month. Entirely *en passant,* the Italian liner *Ausonia* caught fire in Alexandria on 18 October and burned for five days, becoming a total wreck; at the time the British rumor industry held deliberate sabotage in an attempt to wreck the anchorage and/or British warships. But for this last piece of useless information, source was ADM 53.98660: October 1935 log of the *Queen Elizabeth.*

17. Physically on the China station at this time were the *Berwick* and *Cornwall,* the light cruiser *Adventure,* and the *Darling, Decoy, Defender,* and *Diamond* of the 8th Destroyer Flotilla, the depot ship *Medway* of the 4th Submarine Flotilla, and the sloops *Falmouth, Folkestone, Grimsby, Lowestoft,* and *Sandwich; The Pink List,* 1 October 1935, gives no submarine on station: it also states that the destroyer leader *Bruce* was on station with the submarine formation.

18. Details of the movements of the *Sussex* have been taken from its logs for September and October 1935 (99668 and 99669 respectively). The first gave its position on 1 September as 19°05'South 147°09'East, on 6 September 07°22'South 155°57'East, and on 30 September 07°50'North 74°44'East. Tulagi is in 09°05'South 160°09'East. With no replenishment or port of call, it steamed at 20 knots for two weeks.

It should be noted that while it and the *Berwick* sailed to the eastern Mediterranean via Aden, the *Norfolk* did not. As noted in the text, it arrived at Aden on 11 September but remained there at least until 31 October, and it did not join the other two cruisers; moreover it was not in Aden when the *Sussex* arrived. ADM 53.98424: The log of the *Norfolk* for October 1935.

19. At which point one must note, in the interest of balance, what would undoubtedly have been an Italian acceleration of the working-up programs for the three light cruisers not in full service.

20. *Keesing's Contemporary Archives*, vol. 2: 1934–1937, p. 2103.
21. *Keesing's Contemporary Archives*, vol. 2: 1934–1937, p. 2191.
22. Thomas, *The Spanish Civil War*, p. 135 sets out both arguments, with which it is very difficult to disagree.
23. Sevilla is in 37°24'North 05°59'West; Córdoba in 37°10'North 04°46'West; Granada in 37°10'North 03°35'West; Pamplona in 42°49'North 01°39'West; Burgos in 42°21'North 03°41'West; Valladolid in 41°39'North 04°45'West; Salamanca in 40°58'North 05°40'West; and Oviedo in 43°21'North 05°50'West. Saragossa, present rendition Zaragoza, is in 41°39'North 00°54'West. Cádiz is in 36°32'North 06°18'West. La Coruña, alternatively Corunna, is in 43°22'North 08°24'West. Vigo is in 42°15'North 08°44'West; El Ferrol is in 43°29'North 08°14'West.
24. The Republican enclave was progressively eroded with Bilbao (43°15'North 02°56'West) finally surrendering after an eighty-day siege on 18 June 1937 and the Nationalist capture of Santander (43°28'North 03°48'West) on 25 August; the fall of Gijón on 21 October marked the end of Republican resistance in the north coast provinces. Irún is in 43°20'North 01°48'West.
25. Palma is in 39°35'North 02°39'East. Ibiza is in 38°54'North 01°26'East. (The fascist coup at Mahón/Port Mahon on Menorca was defeated, the officers involved being shot out of hand. Thomas, *The Spanish Civil War*, p. 162.) Barcelona is in 41°25'North 02°10'East. Valencia is in 39°29'North 00°24'West. Cartagena is in 37°36'North 00°59'West. Málaga is in 36°43'North 04°25'West.
26. There seems to be confusion about the *Barletta*—an Italian ship according to John F. Coverdale, *Italian Intervention in the Spanish Civil War*, p. 303; a cruiser according to Hugh Thomas, *The Spanish Civil War*, p. 439; an Italian warship according to Gabriel Jackson, *A Concise History of the Spanish Civil War* (New York: John Day, 1974), p. 146; and (of all things) a battleship according to Antony Beevor, *The Battle for Spain*, p. 323, for differing renditions—but this ship was a merchantman that was built in 1931 and that was requisitioned and entered service as an auxiliary cruiser in 1936. After being bombed it was repaired and returned to merchant service but was requisitioned a second time in 1940 and served as a minelayer until sunk in Bari harbor on 3 December 1943 by German aircraft. It was salved in 1948 and after reconstruction was returned to merchant service in 1949. This information was forwarded to the author by the head of the Italian Navy's historical office, Captain Francesco Loriga, in his letter of 30 July 2008.
27. Beevor, *The Spanish Civil War*, p. 99.
28. http://www.palgrave.com/pdfs/0333495608.pdf, pp. 4–5.
29. Thomas, *The Spanish Civil War*, pp. 144 and 153.
30. Thomas, *The Spanish Civil War*, p. 153, citing Luis María de Lojendio, *Operaciones Militares de la Guerra de España*, 1936–1939, p. 40.
31. Cherchell is in 36°36'North 02°11'East.
32. Beevor, *The Spanish Civil War*, p. 220. Thomas, *The Spanish Civil War*, p. 518. As is too often the case, accounts of this action differ considerably in terms of numbers, with the number of Republican destroyers varying between three (which seems to have been the number that made the attack that accounted for the *Baleares*) via five to nine, the latter figure being that used by Beevor and repeated in his *The Battle for Spain: The Spanish Civil War 1936–1939*, p. 360.
33. The sinking of the Nationalist gunboat *Edualdo Dato* off Algeciras (in 36°08'North 05°27'West) on 11 August 1936 by the *Jaime Primero* was perhaps the last real success of the Republican warships in the area of the strait.
34. There are different, and often fragmented, accounts of what happened to the *Jaime Primero*, but the account given here has been taken from Breyer, *Battleships and Battle*

Cruisers, 1905–1970, p. 324; Greger, *Battleships of the World*, p. 251; and Sturton, *All the World's Battleships*, p. 144.

35. With reference to the latter, perhaps the most (in)famous episode was the torpedoing of the *Miguel de Cervantes* outside Cartagena on 22 November 1936 by the submarine *Torricelli*, the Republican light cruiser surviving primarily because it was towed into the port before it could sink.

36. Sagunto is in 39°40'North 00°17'West.

37. Gijón is in 43°32'North 05°40'West.

4. JAPAN AND ITS "SPECIAL UNDECLARED WAR"

1. Canton, present-day Guangzhou, is in 23°08'North 113°20'East: Hainan Island is in 19°North 109°30'East.

2. Novosibirsk is in 55°04'North 83°05'East.

3. Between 13 December 1931 and August 1945 there were no fewer than fourteen administrations in Japan, with one premier, Konoye, heading three administrations. Only four prime ministers were civilians—perhaps surprisingly four admirals served as premiers—and of the 165 cabinet ministers who served in Showa governments prior to the surrender in 1945, no fewer than 62 were military officers. The average period of office for the twenty administrations between 29 September 1918 and 17 October 1941 was just thirteen months and 25 days. Jansen, *The Making of Modern Japan*, pp. 590–591. Tohmatsu and Willmott, *A Gathering Darkness*, pp. 70–71.

4. The Diet bill that provided for the state's assumption of powers regarding the direction of the economy and the full mobilization of the country was not passed until 26 March 1938, but in real terms such powers were held, and something approaching extensive mobilization of reserves was in place, in the last three or four months of 1937. The various measures resulted in the divisional strength of the Imperial Army doubling from seventeen to thirty-four formations by summer 1938.

5. The British treaty port of Tientsin was not subjected to blockade until 14 June 1939, when Japan, taking advantage of Britain's distraction, imposed a blockade that effectively closed the port, and the fact was that the Japanese were not in a position to blockade many small ports and bays in southern China, at least not before 1940–1941. Tsingtao, alternatively Qingdao, is in 36°04'North 120°22'East; Hong Kong is in 22°15'North 114°10'East; Macao is in 22°10'North 113°33'East.

6. The significance of the Pakhoi and Nanning moves was that these two places, with Nanning the rail link to French Indo-China, handled about half of all Chinese exports and imports in 1939.

The initial landing at Pakhoi seems to have been somewhat improvised, with two regiments from the Guards Infantry Division, one infantry regiment from the 38th Infantry Division, and two more infantry regiments from the 48th Infantry Division drawn from the garrison on Formosa. Source: e-mail of Hasegawa Rei of 9 April 2008.

Pakhoi, also given as Peihei and present-day Beihai, is in 21°29'North 109°10'East; Nanning is in 22°50'North 108°19'East; Hangchow Bay, alternatively Hangzhou Wan, is in 30°27'North 121°40'East; Foochow, alternatively Fuzhou, is in 26°09'North 119°17'East.

7. This episode saw the initial employment of seaplanes from the seaplane tender *Notoro*. The *Kaga* joined operations the following day and the *Hosho* on 1 February, and with the two carriers the Japanese were able to commit some seventy aircraft to a series of operations but the fact that it was not until 22 February that Japanese aircraft recorded their first kill was indicative that this episode was little more than a protracted skirmish and of minimal instructive value. The Japanese nonetheless did con-

duct a series of operations directed against the Soochow and Hangchow airfields, and in attacking the latter on 26 February aircraft from the *Hosho* shot down three Chinese aircraft. Peattie, *Sunburst: The Rise of Japanese Naval Air Power 1909–1941*, pp. 50–51. Mikesh, *The Rise of Japanese Naval Air Power* in *Warship* magazine, 1991, p. 102.

8. Peattie, *Sunburst*, pp. 105–109.

9. Such as the A2N1 Type 90 and A4N Type 95 then in service with the Kaigun air arm. Both short-ranged biplanes, however impressive they were when first built, were at best obsolescent by the mid-thirties.

10. Eden, *The Encyclopedia of Aircraft of World War II*, pp. 368–369. Peattie, *Sunburst*, pp. 88–89, 110–111.

11. Peattie, *Sunburst*, pp. 111–112.

12. Ibid., pp. 96.

13. Eden, *Encyclopedia of Aircraft*, pp. 374–375. Peattie, *Sunburst*, pp. 96.

14. Willmott, *Zero A6M* (Englewood Cliffs, N.J.: Prentice-Hall, 1983), p. 26.

15. Harries and Harries, *Soldiers of the Sun*, pp. 279–280.

16. And the fact that there were many operations involving as many as fifty aircraft does suggest that even more must have been conducted by formations that barely reached double figures.

17. Tohmatsu and Willmott, *A Gathering Darkness*, pp. xvii–xviii, 58, 66, 79–80, 100.

18. Drea, *In the Service of the Emperor: Essays on the Imperial Japanese Army* (Lincoln: University of Nebraska Press, 1998), p. 16.

19. It should be noted, however, that in addition to its amphibious and air commitments plus the movement of military formations and supplies to northern and central China, the Imperial Navy was involved in two other efforts in the course of the initial stages of the China war: a series of very minor coastal operations involving local bombardments and landings by small parties—invariably represented by Chinese authorities as defeats—and also riverine operations. Perhaps the most important of the latter saw the employment of destroyers, gunboats, and small landing groups on the middle Yangtse in 1938 in support of army formations advancing on the Wuhan cities. See, for example, Hsiung and Levine, *China's Bitter Victory*, p. 144, with reference to such operations in June 1938.

20. Chüankungtung and Fupukow seem not to be marked in atlases that were consulted, but the former is a few miles east of Pinghu (30°44'North 121°02'East) on Hangchow Bay (see note 5), while the latter is to the north of Changshu (31°39'North 120°45'East).

21. Tsingpu, present-day Qingpu, is in 31°10'North 121°06'East, and Paihokang is a few miles to the north. Soochow, present-day Suzhou, is in 31°21'North 120°40'East, and is some forty miles west of Shanghai, which is in 31°06'North 120°22'East.

22. Tachien is a few miles to the east of Wuhsing, alternatively given as Wuxing, and present-day Huzhou, is in 30°56'North 120°04'East; Changhing is in 31°03'North 119°54'East; Tangtu, present-day Dangtu, is in 31°34'North 118°31'East; Nanking, present-day Nanjing, is in 32°03'North 118°47'East.

23. Kinmen Island, alternatively known as Quemoy, is in 24°44'North 118°33'East. Source: e-mail of Hasegawa Rei of 8 April 2008.

24. Tsinan, present-day Jinan, is in 31°41'North 117°00'East, and Weihsien, present-day Wei Xiang, is in 36°46'North 119°14'East (this line is about 220 miles south of Peking).

25. Brice, *The Royal Navy and the Sino-Japanese Incident*, pp. 66–67.

26. Hsiung, *China's Bitter Victory*, p. 139. The Japanese forces involved in this operation were the 5th Infantry Division from the 2nd Army and formations and units from the 4th Fleet that included the carrier *Ryujo*, the heavy cruiser *Ashigara*, the light cruiser

Kuma, and the destroyers (arranged by classes and alphabetically and not in formations) *Fuji*, *Hishi*, *Susuki*, *Tade*, *Tsuta*, and *Yomogi*, the *Sagiri* and *Sazanami*, and the *Akatsuki*, *Hibiki*, *Ikazuchi*, and *Inazuma*. Source: e-mails of Hasegawa Rei of 8 and 9 April 2008.

27. The small scale of the Amoy operation can be gauged by the fact that the 2nd Landing Force used in the assault was drawn from base formations drawn from Kure, Sasebo, and Yokosuka, and not properly constituted Rikugun divisions.

28. The light cruisers (arranged by classes and alphabetically and not in formations) were the *Tatsuta* and *Tenryu*, the *Kiso* and *Tama*, the *Nagara* and *Yura*, and the *Jintsu* and *Naka*. Source: e-mail from Hasegawa Rei of 9 April 2008.

29. Brice, *The Royal Navy and the Sino-Japanese Incident*, pp. 92.

30. *Journal of the Royal United Services Institute*, vol. 84: *February to November 1939: Sino-Japanese War on Land: The Canton Front*, pp. 181–182.

31. Bias Bay, present-day Daya Wan, is in 22°37'North 114°45'East. One would note that the landing at Anzio in January 1944 could be represented in similar terms, and while it was one landing that commanded initial success because there were no German formations in the immediate area, the formations put ashore were then subjected to major attacks that were defeated primarily by virtue of the scale of naval gunfire and close air support available to the defense.

32. In making this statement one is only too aware that somewhere, at some time, there was such an operation, and one suspects that the *Glorious* and the Palestinian Uprising, 1935–1939, may emerge from the shadows to dispute what is written here, but a great deal does depend on definitions, specifically of "peace-keeping operations."
This was the original endnote, and, of course, once committed to paper evidence of the wrongness of the view was found—though whether the operations can be defined under the "peace-keeping" label is questionable.

The two operations that involved the use of a British carrier were those conducted in March and August 1927 against pirates in southern Chinese waters. There had been a number of small-scale operations between October 1923 and April 1925, but on 22 March 1927 there was an operation in the Bias Bay area involving the light carrier *Hermes*, heavy cruiser *Frobisher*, light cruiser *Delhi*, sloop *Foxglove*, and minesweeper *Marazion*. On 29 August 1927 there was a second operation which again involved the *Hermes* and *Foxglove*, this time with the light cruiser *Danae* and the destroyer *Sirdar*. On this occasion the light carrier *Argus*, en route to Shanghai, provided manpower for landing parties that were put ashore to destroy the homes and boats of the pirates, but the *Argus* did not operate either independently or in support of its older and larger companion.

There was a third operation, outside Bias Bay on 20 October 1927, but apparently this one involve only the submarine L. 4 which torpedoed and sank a merchantman that had been seized by pirates. No carrier was involved in this operation.
Sources: Three entries from the *Journal of the Royal United Services Institute*: "*A Punitive Expedition against Pirates*," vol. 72, February to November 1927, p. 421. Lecture "*The work of the British Navy in the Far East*" given by Captain L.D.I. Mackinon on 5 December 1928, vol. 74, February to November 1929, pp. 95–109. Commander W.G.A. Robson, "*Combined Operations with the Chinese against Pirates West River, 1923–25*," vol. 84, February to November 1939, pp. 101–104.

33. The places have been listed from west to east along the coast: Hoppo is in 21°37'North 109°11'East; Luichow, present-day Hoihon, is in 20°54'North 110°05'East; Shuitung, in German Schui-tung and apparently present-day Wuchwan, is in 21°29'North 110°46'East; Tinpak is in 21°30'North 111°06'East; Yeungkong is in 21°52'North 111°52'East; Towshan is in 22°04'North 112°53'East.

34. Swabue is in 22°48'North 115°22'East.

35. The places have been listed from north to south along the coast: Chinghai, present-day Chinhai, is in 29°57'North 121°42'East; Ninpo, inland from Chinghai, is in 29°54'North 121°33'East; Shipu, alternatively Shihpu, is in 29°13'North 121°57'East; Haimen is in 28°40'North 121°27'East; Wenchow is in 28°02'North 120°40'East.

36. The Japanese occupation of Foochow was conducted by the 48th Infantry Division and four battalions from the 18th Infantry Division, the latter then being used for the subsequent landing in Chaikiao Bay. The Foochow operation saw the employment of the seaplane carrier *Chiyoda*, heavy cruiser *Chokai*, and (arranged by classes and alphabetically and not in formations) the destroyers *Asakaze, Harukaze, Hatakaze,* and *Matsukaze* and the *Hatsuharu, Hatsushimo, Nenohi,* and *Wakaba* of the 2nd Fleet.

The Japanese possession of Foochow proved short-lived: the port was abandoned on 3 September, but was to be reoccupied in 1944, when it seemed, as the only major port not in Japanese hands, to be the most obvious point of landing in China for any American move to and beyond Formosa.

Source: e-mail of Hasegawa Rei of 8 April 2008.

37. Sungmen, present-day Sanmen Wan, is in 29°04'North 121°56'East; Chaikiao, alternatively Taichow Wan, present-day Taizhou Wan, is in 28°41'North 121°38'East.

38. Kiatze, present-day Kitchioh, is in 22°50'North 115°48'East.

39. See, for example, Dick Wilson, *When Tigers Fight: The Story of the Sino-Japanese War 1937–1945* (London: Penguin Books, 1984), p. 163.

40. Wuchi, present day Wuming, is in 23°12'North 108°11'East; Chien-chiang, present-day Qianjiang, is in 23°36'North 108°44'East.

41. Tohmatsu and Willmott, *A Gathering Darkness*, pp. 98–100.

42. By way of comparison, the most notable British carrier operations to date had never involved more than single carriers, though as planned the Taranto strike (November 1940) was to have involved two carriers, the *Eagle* and *Illustrious*. In the event this operation was conducted by two groups of Swordfish biplanes, one of twelve and the other of nine. Off Matapan (March 1941) the strike that crippled the Italian heavy cruiser *Pola* was the third such mission of the day, and was conducted by just nine torpedo-bombers from the *Formidable*: this was the largest of the three strikes, the first having been mounted by six and the second by five torpedo-bombers. In the *Bismarck* chase (May 1941) aircraft from two carriers operating independently of one another attacked the German battleship: the first attack was conducted by nine Swordfish biplanes from the *Victorious*, the second by fifteen Swordfish from the *Ark Royal*. The contrast with the Japanese operation of 7 December 1941—which involved a double strike, the first by 89 B5N2 Kates, 51 D3A1 Vals and 43 A6M2 Zeros, and the second by 54 Kates, 78 Vals, and 35 Zeros, for totals of 183 and 167 aircraft—speaks for itself.

Perhaps what should be mentioned are two seldom-noted facts: that there was a British operation involving two carriers—the *Argus* and the *Ark Royal*—in November 1940 that resulted in the flying of aircraft into Malta and that in the *Bismarck* chase there was a third carrier. The *Eagle*, deployed at Freetown with the battleship *Nelson*, was ordered to join the hunt for the German warship, but the action was over before it could come on the scene. Rohwer and Hummelchen, *Chronology of the War at Sea*, pp. 40–41, 56 and 63–64. Roskill, *The War at Sea*, vol. 1: *The Defensive*, pp. 300–301, 401–418, and 427–430.

43. Evans and Peattie, *Kaigun*, pp. 347–352.

44. On 7 December the Kaigun mustered 10 capital ships, 10 fleet and light carriers, 18 heavy and 20 light cruisers, and 112 destroyers. Willmott, *Empires in the Balance*, p. 116. At the Philippine Sea, Task Force 58 had four carrier groups, three with two fleet and two light carriers each and the fourth with one fewer light carrier, and one battle

group with seven battleships. In sum, these groups numbered 7 battleships, 8 fleet and 7 light carriers, 8 heavy and 13 light cruisers, and 97 destroyers, and 902 aircraft; the latter total compares to the 350 aircraft that were involved in the attacks on the U.S. Pacific Fleet and airfields at Pearl Harbor on 7 December 1941. H. P. Willmott, *June 1944* (Blandford: Blandford, 1984), pp. 202–203. H. P. Willmott with Tohmatsu Haruo and W. Spencer Johnson, *Pearl Harbor* (London: Cassell, 2001), pp. 190–191.

45. It is perhaps worth noting that at the battle off Midway Islands the four Japanese carriers embarked air groups that were smaller than those of their three American counterparts. The *Akagi, Hiryu,* and *Soryu* each embarked air groups with three eighteen-strong squadrons of A6M2 Zero fighters, B5N2 Kate torpedo-bombers, and D3A1 Val dive-bombers, the *Kaga* having an extra nine Kates. In addition the *Akagi* and *Kaga* carried single and the *Soryu* two reconnaissance aircraft. Thus the Japanese carriers embarked 229 aircraft, to which total have to be added a total of 21 aircraft that were to be flown to Midway after the atoll had been captured. The *Enterprise* embarked 79 aircraft, of which 27 were F4F-4 Wildcat fighters, the figures for the *Hornet* being 69 and 27, and for the *Yorktown* 75 and 25. Willmott, *The Barrier and the Javelin,* pp. 106–107. Morison, *History of United States Naval Operations in World War II,* vol. 4: *Coral Sea, Midway and Submarine Actions May 1942–August 1942,* pp. 90–91. Polmar, *Aircraft Carriers,* pp. 212.

46. Morison, *History of United States Naval Operations in World War II,* vol. 4, p. 19, and vol. 14: *Victory in the Pacific 1945,* pp. 21 and 382–385. Polmar, *Aircraft Carriers,* pp. 420–427 and 732–733.

A certain care needs be exercised with reference to the latter figures on account of one of the task groups having carriers detailed for night-fighting duties; these had smaller air groups than the other carriers, though their groups were nonetheless more or less at the 1941–1942 level of establishment; by war's end one carrier had an all-fighter group and numbered 110 aircraft.

5. NAVIES, SEA POWER, AND TWO OR MORE WARS

1. Roskill, *The War at Sea,* vol. 3, part 1, appendix C, "Italian Naval Losses. 10th June, 1940–8th September, 1943," pp. 379–381.

2. I must confess that when I first wrote this, it read that Italy was the only such country: I had totally forgotten France, which, I admit, does take some doing. My thanks to Anthony Clayton for this correction on 31 October 2007, which was the date when I telephoned Heathrow airport to warn aircraft coming into land that night lest they collide with my mother-in-law on her broomstick.

3. The lists of carriers and capital ships lost during the war are given in appendixes 2 and 3 respectively.

4. Potter, *Nimitz,* p. 451.

5. Willmott, *Pearl Harbor,* p. 175.

6. Keegan, *The Times Atlas of the Second World War,* pp. 98–99.

7. The fastest construction was by the Permanente Metals Corporation No. 2 Yard in Richmond, California (again a Kaiser yard), which was responsible for the laying down of the *Robert E. Peary* at one minute past midnight on 8 November 1942: it was launched at 1530 on 12 November, was completed on 18 November, and sailed on its first mission on four days later. See www.usmm.org/peary.html. The average time for laying down to completion for a Liberty Ship was forty-two days, and by 1944 was less than forty days.

8. Lane, *Ships for Victory,* pp. 30–40. It should be noted that in addition to the five there were the specialist naval yards at New London, Connecticut, and Bath, Maine, which concentrated on submarine and destroyer construction respectively.

The seven "additional" companies and yards were Seattle-Tacoma Shipbuilding Corporation at Tacoma, Washington; Western Pipe and Steel Company at San Francisco; Moore Dry Dock Company of Oakland; Consolidated Steel Corporation at Long Beach, California; Pennsylvania Shipyards Incorporated at Beaumont, Texas; Ingalls Shipbuilding Corporation at Pascagoula, Mississippi; and Tampa Shipbuilding and Engineering Company at Tampa, Florida.

A certain care needs be noted on one count: "companies" and "yards" were not synonymous. For example, Bethlehem had three major steel mills and also three, not one, yard in the northeast, at Quincy, Staten Island, and Sparrows Point (outside Baltimore), and it had repair yards at East Boston, Brooklyn, Hoboken (New Jersey), and Baltimore, and also at San Francisco and San Pedro: in 1940 it was building ships at four of its yards.

Lane, p. 36, cites an additional dozen companies in existence in 1940 and gives the total number of berths that were homes to ocean-going merchantmen under construction as fifty-three on 1 January 1941: on p. 38 he states that on 1 June 1940 just six private yards worked on navy orders, and by February 1941 this total had risen to sixty-eight.

9. Lane, *Ships for Victory*, p. 72.

10. And it needs be noted that British problems on this score were compounded by the fact that the British fleets were basically short-haul and the support shipping was likewise, whereas the needs of the Pacific theater were very different—and the only ships that could be requisitioned in order to provide for a fleet in the Pacific were ships from an already inadequate pool of shipping dealing with import needs.

11. The ultimate British objective was the raising of a fleet of four fleet, seven light, and eighteen escort carriers, four battleships, twelve cruisers, sixty destroyers, one hundred escorts, twenty-four submarines, nine hundred carrier- and three hundred land-based aircraft, and the provision of an amphibious lift for two divisions.

12. See, with reference to the previous two footnotes and this one, Willmott, *Grave of a Dozen Schemes*, various pages but most obviously pp. 75–77.

13. Calculations have been based on "shared" contributions being divided equally between parties.

14. Hancock and Gowing, *British War Economy*, p. 130. It is perhaps worth noting that at this time, in the winter of 1939–1940, there was a massive reduction in the size of British newspapers.

6. BRITAIN AND THE DEFEAT OF THE U-BOAT *GUERRE DE COURSE*

1. T. D. Manning, *The British Destroyer*, p. 23.

2. William Glover, "Manning and Training the Allied Navies," ch. 10 in Howarth and Law, *The Battle of the Atlantic* 1939–1945, p. 191.

3. Winton, *Convoy*, pp. 115–122.

4. Roskill, *The War at Sea*, vol. 3: *The Offensive*, part 1, *1st June 1943–31st May 1944*, appendix K, table II, *British, Allied and Neutral Merchant Shipping Losses from Enemy Action, according to Theatres 1st June, 1943–31st May, 1944*, p. 389.

5. Virtually all anti-submarine establishments were moved to Scotland in the wake of the fall of France, from Portland in Dorset, on the south coast, to Dunoon and Fairlie on the Firth of Clyde and to Campbeltown on the Mull of Kintyre, with the training of escorts undertaken at the shore establishment *Western Isles*, i.e. Tobermory on Mull, after July 1940. Roskill, *The War at Sea*, vol. 1, p. 359.

6. To these totals may be added 346,000 tons of explosives, 3,786,000 tires and 1,803 radars, 4,338 radios and 2,000 telephone sets, which would have been useful: these latter totals seem almost sweet, quaint, when set alongside today's numbers.

7. The balance, some 6.47% of tonnage, was shipped through the Black Sea ports in 1945.

8. The balance consists of ships that for a number of reasons were obliged to turn back: for example, of the 36 merchantmen originally with PQ.17, three were obliged to return to Reykjavik with damage caused either by running aground or by ice.

9. Gannon, *Operation Drumbeat*, p. xvii.

10. A total of twenty-one boats were sunk in the first six months of 1942, but seven of these were sunk in the Mediterranean, and one was sunk off Novaya Zemlya in the Arctic.

11. By the summer of 1942 there were five support groups, with carrier groups really appearing in numbers and effectiveness in summer 1943.

12. Roskill, *The War at Sea*, vol. 2, pp. 367–368.

13. Roskill, ibid., states that in the last eleven days of March 1943 ten merchantmen were lost in the North Atlantic compared to the 67 sunk in the first twenty days, but in the table of losses by theater (p. 486) gives a total of 95 merchantmen sunk in the North Atlantic in this month, presumably the balance being stragglers and ships sailing independently.

14. The total number of U-boats sunk between March and June 1943 was 89 and between July and October 1943 was 98. In terms of percentage shares, in the first four months warships accounted for 34.27% and land-based aircraft 49.44% of U-boat losses, and in the second four months the respective figures are 17.35% and 55.10% There is little doubt that inter-service considerations were instrumental in what would seem to be a deliberate demeaning of the contribution of land-based aircraft to the May 1943 success in naval accounts of proceedings. For example, in Roskill, *The War at Sea*, vol. 2, p. 377, there is a note in which the U-boat losses of April and May are given together, though why April should have been included is not obvious, but the figures are given in such a way that the land-based aircraft total (twenty-five and another four shared) is partially obscured by presentation under five separate headings, and warships thus head the list with sixteen kills (and with another six listed as shared).

15. In the first six months of 1942 land-based aircraft accounted for just seven U-boats, but in July land-based aircraft sank four U-boats and shared in the destruction of the fifth; in August the toll was four and two; in September four; and in October ten and one. With sixteen boats lost in this last month, at this time obvious problems relating to Allied aircraft and submarine armament presented themselves at this time.

16. Rössler, *The U-boat*, p. 188. Boats serving in the Arctic and Mediterranean were allowed to keep their main gun, and in summer 1944 a number of Type VIIC boats serving in the Baltic were refitted with their 88-mm guns.

17. The best study of the Royal Canadian Navy and the Second World War is undoubtedly Marc Milner's *North Atlantic Run: The Royal Canadian Navy and the Battle for the Convoys* (originally published, Annapolis, Md.: Naval Institute Press, 1985).

18. For an examination of the Walter boat's development, see Rössler, *The U-boat*, pp. 168–187. With reference to U. 792, see p. 266.

19. Möller and Brack, *The Encyclopedia of U-boats*, p. 156. Roskill, *The War at Sea*, vol. 3, part 1, p. 17, states that the 250 boats already under construction were to be completed, and originally 288 Type XXI submarines were to be completed by February 1945 and 140 Type XXIII submarines by the previous October. Rössler, *The U-boat*, p. 212, states that the 6 July 1943 program provided for the building of 72 Type XXII Walter boats, 108 Type XVII Walter boats, and 102 Type XXI boats.

20. Rössler, *The U-boat*, pp. 210–214.

21. Ibid., p. 265.

22. And for good measure two days later the Dutch submarine, having disposed of a

submarine that belonged to an enemy that occupied most of the Dutch homeland, sank a Japanese minelayer in the Java Sea, a warship that belonged to an enemy that occupied the Dutch East Indies.

23. And specifically with reference to how it was that, at a range of 8,400 yards, it inflicted such damage on the *Kirishima* in seven minutes, just after midnight 14–15 November 1942, that the Japanese battleship was abandoned and sank. One immediate counter to this argument would be the fact that the *South Dakota* survived this action, one in which range was down to about 5,000 yards. But in the action off North Cape the *Scharnhorst* survived what should have been a devastating opening salvo or two and returned fire before being hit by a single shell that reduced its speed to 22 knots and thus enabled the *Duke of York*, and perhaps more importantly, the British destroyers, to close and launch a series of torpedo attacks, which in turn ensured that the *Duke of York* and the cruisers would be able to close and administer the coup de grâce. Winton, *Death of the Scharnhorst*, pp. 114–144.

7. WITH FRIENDS LIKE THESE

1. Koh Chang, present-day Ko Chang and at the time given as Kohsichang, is an island in the Gulf of Thailand near the Thai-Cambodian border in 12°07'North 102°21'East.

2. To these one could add the ordeal of the armed merchant cruiser *Rawalpindi*, sunk by the German battleships *Scharnhorst* and *Gneisenau* on 23 November 1939 in the Iceland-Faeroes gap.

3. These were large destroyers; with full-load displacements between 2,950 and 4,018 tons, they were really small (and unarmored) light cruisers, the *Mogador* class, for example, having eight 5.5-in. guns and a top speed of 39 knots. Chesneau, *Conway's All the World's Fighting Ships, 1922–1946*, pp. 267–269.

4. Hankow (or Hankou), one of the three Wuhan cities, is some 600 miles upstream from Shanghai in 30°45'North 114°30'East.

5. Rohwer and Hummelchen, *Chronology of the War at Sea*, pp. 5–6, 9. Roskill, *The War at Sea, 1939–1945*, vol. 1: *The Defensive*, pp. 83–85, 114, 149. One of the French submarines, the *Doris*, was torpedoed and sunk by the U. 9 on 9 May.

6. Interestingly Roskill, *The War at Sea*, vol. 1, pp. 129 and 599, makes no reference to the *Valmy* in the sinking of U. 55, which is represented as the first sinking of a U-boat by air and naval units of the war. It should be noted that on 13 June 1940 the Italian submarine *Provana* was rammed and sunk by the French sloop *La Curieuse* off Oran, and this was two days before the French submarine *Morse* was mined and sunk off Sfax.

7. Roskill, *The War at Sea*, vol.1, appendix L, "Operation Dynamo—Summary of British and Allied Ships Employed, Troops Lifted, British Ships Lost or Damaged," p. 603, and vol. 3: *The Offensive*, part 2, appendix T, table 1, "Nominal List of British Commonwealth Major Warship Losses," p. 400.

8. These were on 21 May the *L'Adroit* sunk by aircraft off Dunkirk, on 23 May the *contre-torpilleur Jaguar* torpedoed by a motor torpedo boat off Dunkirk and the *Orage* sunk by aircraft off Boulogne, on 24 May the *contre-torpilleur Chacal* sunk by aircraft off Boulogne, on 30 May the *Bourrasque* sunk by a combination of mine and German artillery fire off Nieuwport, on 31 May the *Siroco* torpedoed by motor torpedo boats off Dunkirk, on 1 June the *Foudroyant* sunk by aircraft off Dunkirk.

9. And with one unforeseen (but in one sense inevitable) bonus: the battleship *Lorraine* and its four attendant cruisers re-entered service with the Allies in May 1943. It

should be noted that the French disarmed their own ships: the ships were not disarmed by the British.

10. Roskill, *The War at Sea*, vol. 1, p. 244, states that five destroyers cleared the harbor. http://www.tank-net.org/forums/lofiversion/index.php/t8027.html, citing James C. Bradford, ed., *The International Enclyclopedia of Military History*, and http://articles.gourt.com/en/Destruction%20of%20the%20French%20Fleet%20at%20Mers-el-Kebir both state that four destroyers escaped. Rohwer and Hummelchen, *Chronology of the War at Sea*, p. 27, states that three (named) destroyers arrived at Toulon.

11. Also damaged on 3 July was the *contre-torpilleur Mogador*: it lost its stern and was beached; it was repaired and sailed to Toulon where it was scuttled in November 1942.

12. At Dakar the French had the unfinished battleship *Richelieu*, two light cruisers, three *contre-torpilleurs*, seven destroyers, three submarines, and five auxiliary cruisers. Two of the submarines were sunk, and the *contre-torpilleur L'Audacieux* was beached after being badly damaged by the heavy cruiser *Australia*.

13. Clayton, *France, Soldiers and Africa*, pp. 132–136. Keegan, *The Times Atlas of the Second World War*, p. 79. Also the submarine *Caïman* was presented with the same choice, and was afforded safe conduct to Bizerte. It would appear that three *contre-torpilleurs* were afforded safe conduct and removed troops from Syria, but with such numbers it would seem that only metropolitan troops were withdrawn.
Djounieh, present-day Jôunie, is to the north of Beirut in 33°58'North 35°38'East.

14. Diégo Suarez, present-day Antseranana, is in 12°19'South 49°17'East.

15. It should be noted that in the whole tangled process whereby Operation Ironclad was conceived and authorized, the intention was to secure Diégo Suarez and not to become involved in operations across the whole of the island; moreover, there was very considerable opposition within the British high command to the operation. Gwyer and Butler, *Grand Strategy*, vol. 3: *June 1941–August 1942*, part 2, pp. 489–491.

16. Maromandia is in 14°10'South 48°06'East.

17. Kirby, *The War against Japan*, vol. 2: *India's Most Dangerous Hour*, pp. 142–144.

18. Majunga, present-day Mahajanga, is in 15°40'South 46°20'East. Tamatave, present-day Toamasina, is in 18°10'South 49°23'East. Tuléar, present-day Toliara, is in 23°20'South 43°41'East. Fort Dauphin, present-day Taolanaro, is in 25°01'South 47°00'East. Antsirabe is in 19°51'South 47°01'East. Ambositra is in 20°31'South 47°15'East. Alakamisy, present-day Fianarantsoa, is in 21°27'South 47°05'East. Ihosy is in 22°23'South 46°09'East.
The armistice was agreed on 5 November and concluded at 0001 on 6 November. One of the interesting features of this campaign was the use of British, South African, and King's African Rifles units in the operation, and it was the latter that conducted the advance from Majunga to Vatoavo, and ultimately moved down to the east coast at Manakara (in 22°09'South 48°00'East). H. Moyse-Bartlett, *The King's African Rifles: A Study of the Military History of East and Central Africa, 1890–1945* (Aldershot: Gale and Polden, 1956), pp. 579–609.

19. These were on 5 May the armed merchant cruiser *Bougainville* sunk by aircraft from the *Illustrious*, and the submarine *Bévéziers*, the only submarine at Diégo Suarez, was extensively damaged by carrier aircraft inside the port and, while not sunk, subsequently was deemed to be beyond economical repair and was stricken. The next day, 6 May, the gunboat *D'Entrecasteaux* was extensively damaged on by the destroyer *Laforey* and aircraft from the carrier *Indomitable*, and beached: it was subsequently written off. The submarine *Le Héroes* was sunk on 7 May 1942 by a corvette and Swordfish from the carrier *Illustrious*, and the submarine *Monge* was sunk on 8 May 1942 by the destroyers *Active* and *Panther*. Rohwer and Hummelchen, *Chronology of*

the War at Sea, p. 136. Le Masson, *Les Flottes de Combat*, 1947, p. 18. Wassilieff, *Un Pavillon Sans Tache*, p. 235. Roskill, *The War at Sea*, vol. 2: *The Period of Balance*, pp. 189–192, makes reference only to the sinking of *Le Héroes* by a carrier aircraft.

20. Three Japanese submarines were involved in this operation but only two, I. 16 and I. 20, were able to launch their single midget offspring, which were armed with two 17.7-in. torpedoes.

21. Roskill, *The War at Sea*, vol. 2, p. 192.

22. Obviously a certain care needs be exercised in making this point, and for a reason that is perhaps little appreciated: the submarine was in employment in more European navies in the inter-war period than is generally noted. In addition to Britain, France, Germany, Italy, and the Soviet Union, no fewer than thirteen European states, plus Turkey, possessed submarines between the wars. These were Denmark, Estonia, Finland, Greece, Latvia, the Netherlands, Norway, Poland, Portugal, Romania, Spain, Sweden, and Yugoslavia. Of all the European countries with coastlines only Albania, Belgium, Bulgaria, the Irish Free State, and Lithuania did not acquire submarines.
In South America Argentina, Brazil, Chile, and Peru possessed submarines.
But in terms of indigenous independent states in Africa and Asia, and excluding China and Japan from consideration, there were by 1941 but Liberia and South Africa on one continent and Iran and Thailand on the other. There were also Egypt and Iraq of somewhat uncertain status, and, lest they be forgotten, Afghanistan and Nepal: these last two possessed the world's most formidable defenses against naval forces.
The details were checked in various yearly editions of *Jane's Fighting Ships* and in Chesneau, *Conway's All the World's Fighting Ships*.

23. Eden, *The Encyclopedia of Aircraft of WWII*, p. 104.

24. Satahib, present-day Sattahip or Ban Sattahipp, is in 12°36'South 100°56'East.

25. http://en.wikipedia.org/wiki/Battle_of_Koh_Chang Battle of Kohn Chang. Guiglini, "A Resumé of the Battle of Koh Chang." Romé, *Les oubliés du bout du monde*.

26. http://www.avalanchepress.com/SiameseFleet.php (Mike Bennighof, *The Siamese Fleet*) and http://en.wikipedia.org/wiki/History_of_Thailand_(1932–1973). The country was known as Siam until 1939, when it was renamed Prathet Thai, or Thailand. It reverted to Siam in 1945 after the end of the war, but was renamed Thailand again in 1949.

27. Also in company was the escort carrier *Chenango*, but it was employed as a transport and was carrying 76 army fighters for future employment at Casablanca: Jenkins, *A History of the French Navy*, p. 330. Morison, *History of United States Naval Operations in World War II*, vol. 2: *Operations in North African Waters October 1942–June 1943*, p. 37

28. Roskill. *The War at Sea*, vol. 2, table 25, "Operation Torch: Maritime Forces Engaged," p. 319

29. In the Philippine Sea the Americans deployed formations that mustered 8 fleet and 7 light carriers, 7 battleships, 14 heavy and 18 light cruisers, and 67 destroyers: at Leyte 9 fleet, 8 light, and 29 escort carriers, 12 battleships, 5 heavy and 20 light cruisers, and 162 destroyers. Willmott, *The Second World War in the Far East*, p. 211.

30. Slightly amended from the author's *When Men Lost Faith in Reason: Reflections on War and Society in the Twentieth Century* (Westport, Conn.: Praeger, 2002), p. 80.

31. Expressed another way, after December 1941 the failure in front of Moscow indicated that the German military was not infallible and invincible, and the simultaneous entry of the United States into the war seemed to promise a widening of the war and Germany's ultimate defeat; certainly 1942 was the first year of significant advance of the Resistance and the Gaullist cause within both occupied and unoccupied France. Such calculations may explain the lack of serious and sustained resistance on Madagascar in and after May 1942, but there was also another factor at work. The gar-

rison of Madagascar consisted of *La Coloniale* and native units, and most definitely the former were much more inclined to the Gaullist cause than their metropolitan and *L'Armée d'Afrique* counterparts.

32. Anthony Clayton, *Three Marshals of France: Leadership after Trauma* (London: Brassey's, 1992), p. 73, but more generally pp. 70–77.

33. Garzke and Dulin, *British, Soviet, French and Dutch Battleships of World War II*, pp. 107–119.

34. For example, Jenkins, *A History of the French Navy*, p. 336, sets out the view that the the 77 ships scuttled at Toulon would have been a valuable addition to the Allied cause, given the scale of subsequent Anglo-American naval operations in Europe. While not denying that in war every single contribution to the whole is important and not to be demeaned, the author stands by the argument expressed in the text on three main grounds: first, that in real terms the French ships, with their needs for radars, improved armaments, and general overhaul, would have represented a commitment that U.S. yards could have handled, but all but certainly at disproportionate cost; second, by November 1942 the American building program that was to be the bedrock of naval victory was in place, and the French numbers were nickel-and-dime status in comparison; and third, French numbers might have been very useful, but prior to and during November 1942, not thereafter.

35. The first such unit was the U.S.-built British escort carrier *Biter*, which entered French service as the *Dixmude*: in August 1946 the British transferred the light carrier *Colossus* to the French Navy, and it remained in service as the *Arromanches* until 1974.

36. And, it must be said, ever since that time?

37. Originally part of an argument used in the author's *When Men Lost Faith in Reason*, pp. 147–150.

38. It should be noted, moreover, that de Laborde, generally known as *Comte Jean*, was an aristocrat with very definite views about such individuals as Darlan placed in authority over him. He hated the British, but even more he hated communism: for de Laborde the assault on the Soviet Union placed the Germans on the side of the angels, which, given German behavior on the Eastern Front, takes a stretch of the imagination.

39. http://en.wikipedia.org/wiki/Jean_de_Laborde: Jean de Laborde.

40. On 22 November the remaining Vichy air formations were ordered to abandon their bases and withdraw to the north preparatory to being disbanded, and German squadrons occupied the airfield at Istres (which is in 43°30'North 04°59'East some thirty miles northwest of Marseilles). http://bobhenneman.info/bhst.htm: *The Scuttle of the French Fleet at Touon* [*sic*], *November 27, 1942*.

41. And probably nearer the 12th than the 16th, E. & O. E. It would seem that the general view over the years has been that the French fleet could have sailed on or before 12 November with virtual impunity, but, of course, to have done so would have meant orders and arrangements being put in hand on the 8th or 9th, and that, given the divisions within the Vichy regime and de Laborde's attitude, was impossible.

42. To these should be added at least three other warships and nine submarines, and the fact that they were captured intact at Bizerte on 8 December does seem somewhat perverse, given what happened at Toulon. The torpedo-boats *Bombarde*, *L'Iphigénie*, and *La Pomone* and the submarines *Calypso* and *Circé*, the *Dauphin*, *Espadon*, *Phoque*, and *Requin*, and the *Nautilus*, *Saphir*, and *Turquoise* were captured on 8 December at Bizerte, and quite obviously their capture does raise any number of very difficult questions.

43. It would seem not deliberately: apparently the submarine was interned after being unable to sail within the stipulated time allowed it in the port.

44. Jeremiah 31:15, with apologies for the alteration.
45. The file is Cab 119.156b: see Willmott, *Grave of a Dozen Schemes*, pp. 60 and 246.
46. Garzke, *Battleships of World War II*, pp. 99–100.

8. ITALY AND THE WAR IN THE MEDITERRANEAN THEATER OF OPERATIONS

1. Valletta, on Malta, is in 35°54'North 14°32'East.
2. The Jabal Akhdar is the upland area inland from Benghazi and Derna in Cyrenaica.
3. Tripoli, present-day Tarabulus, is in 32°54'North 13°11'East. Benghazi, present-day Banghazi, is in 32°07'North 20°04'East. Derna, present-day Darnah, is in 32°46'North 22°39'East. Tobruk, present-day Tubruq, is in 32°05'North 23°59'East. Bardia, present-day Al Bardi or Al Burdi, is in 31°46'North 25°05'East.
4. Perim island is in 12°40'North 43°25'East at the southern entrance to the Red Sea.
5. Aden is in 12°47'North 45°03'East.
6. Berbera is in 10°28'North 45°02'East. Mogadishu, present-day Muqdisho, is in 02°02'North 45°21'East.
7. Keren is in 15°46'North 39°30'East. Massawa, present-day Mits'iwa, is in 15°37'North 39°28'East.
8. The One and a Half Degree Channel, through the southern Maldives, is in 01°30'North 73°30'East. Kobe is in 34°40'North 135°12'East. Timor is in 09°South 125°East.
9. Port Sudan is in 19°38'North 37°07'East.
10. The Dalac (present-day Dahlak) archipelago is in 16°North 40°East. Assab, present-day Aseb, is in 13°01'North 42°47'East. Addis Ababa, present-day Adis Abeba, is in 09°03'North 38°42'East.
11. Amba Alagi is in 12°59'North 39°33'East. Gondar, present-day Gonder, is in 12°39'North 37°29'East.
12. Keegan, *The Times Atlas of the Second World War*, pp. 50–51. Italian Navy in the Second World War: www.naval-history.net/WW2CampaignsItalianNavy.htm. Regina Marina: http://en.wikipedia.org/wiki/Regina.Marina. The campaign in East Africa after May 1941: http://en.wikipedia.org/wiki/Italian_guerrilla_war_in_Ethiopia.
13. Willmott, *The Great Crusade*, pp. 244–247.
14. http://www.ww2incolor.com/forum/showthread.php?p:88203. This source gives the 18 and 132 figures, but also states that Italy had 172 submarines, of which 128 were lost. It would seem that the 172 total includes various *Flutto*-class units that were destroyed on their slips and the 98-ton CC, 90-ton CM, 44-ton CB, and 13- and 14-ton CA classes.
15. Punto Stila is in 38°28'North 16°35'East. On the British side were the *Warspite*, *Malaya*, and *Royal Sovereign* and the *Eagle*, and on the Italian side the *Conte di Cavour* and *Giulio Cesare*, plus cruiser and destroyers.
16. The Taranto attack (11–12 November 1940) is sometimes represented as resulting in the sinking of three Italian battleships. In reality only one was sunk, the *Conte di Cavour*, and it was raised and salved. A second battleship, the *Caio Duilio*, was hit by a single torpedo but remained afloat, and a third battleship, the *Littorio*, was hit by no fewer than three torpedoes and its bow grounded, but it was not sunk. The British lost two Swordfish biplanes in this attack.
17. This action was fought in the general area of 35°North 21°East, some sixty miles southwest of Cape Matapan. In this action (28 March 1941) the Italians lost three heavy cruisers and two destroyers, and were perhaps a little fortunate not to have suffered

greater losses, with the battleship *Vittorio Veneto* hit by two torpedoes. Undoubtedly after this action, coming on the back of the Taranto episode, there was a certain Italian hesitation about the use of major units in the face of British carrier air superiority.

18. Overy, *The Air War, 1939–1945*, pp. 192–193.

19. In the interest of balance it needs be noted that only two of the Italian battleships, the *Littorio* and *Vittorio Veneto*, were modern, having been completed in the two months before Italy's entry into the war: the remaining four, the *Conte di Cavour* and *Giulio Cesare* and the *Andrea Doria* and *Caio Duilio*, had been reconstructed, 1933–1937 and 1937–1940 respectively, but only "made up the numbers."

20. The total of two light cruisers and eleven destroyers sunk in April and May 1941 must go alongside the total of the fleet carrier *Formidable*, the battleships *Barham* and *Warspite*, the light cruisers *Naiad*, *Orion*, and *Perth*, and four destroyers that were "severely damaged." In addition, four transports were sunk and a fifth, again, "severely damaged." Roskill, *The War at Sea*, vol. 1, p. 436.

21. In this period the British also lost the submarine *Perseus*, the (Australian) sloop *Parramatta*, and the corvette *Salvia* in, and the submarine H. 31 and (Canadian) corvette *Windflower* outside, the Mediterranean. Therefore, overall losses in this period were five capital ships, one fleet carrier, one escort carrier, four light cruisers, three destroyers, plus the submarines and escorts, and only the *Queen Elizabeth* and *Valiant* could be (and were) salved and returned to service.

22. In terms of numbers of carriers, Operation Pedestal was the largest British carrier operation prior to Operation Meridian, the attack on the refineries and airfields at Palembang in southern Sumatra, in January 1945. The carriers involved in Pedestal were the *Eagle*, *Furious*, *Indomitable*, and *Victorious*; coincidentally, the last two were also involved in Meridian.

23. Roskill, *The War at Sea*, vol. 2, pp. 337–338. Rohwer and Hummelchen, *Chronology of the War at Sea*, p. 179.

24. The Italians abandoned the sailing of convoys to Tripoli in the fourth week of January 1943, and on 23 January German and Italian forces abandoned the city; five Italian freighters (collectively of 24,781 tons), unable to leave the harbor, were scuttled on 20 January.

25. Roskill, *The War at Sea*, vol. 2, pp. 440–441.

26. The German occupation of peninsular Italy went alongside the evacuation of Sardinia on 10 September, some 25,000 troops, vehicles, and supplies being ferried across the Bonifacio Strait to Corsica, which in turn was abandoned between mid-September and 3 October. The greater part of German forces evacuated from Corsica were moved by air. One of the curious features of these evacuations was that there was very little in the way of Allied operations, by warships and submarines and by air, against the 15 steamers and 120 barges that the Germans employed to evacuate forces and supplies, primarily to either Livorno/Leghorn or Elba, and it was not until 21 September that bombers attacked shipping at Bastia in northern Corsica. The Germans ultimately lost some 18 vessels of 16,943 tons in the course of their double evacuation. Roskill, *The War at Sea*, vol. 3, part 1, p. 187.

27. Innsbruck is in 47°17'North 11°25'East; Klagenfurt is in 46°38'North 14°20'East; Graz is in 47°05'North 15°22'East; Ljubljana, historically Laibach, is in 46°04'North 14°30'East; Zagreb, historically Agram, is in 45°48'North 15°58'East.

28. Roskill, *H.M.S. Warspite*, p. 17.

29. Eden, *The Encyclopedia of Aircraft of World War II*, pp. 134–135: this source states that the bombs were the FX 1400 (as does Roskill, *The War at Sea*, vol. 3, part 1, p. 168).

Breyer, *Battleships and Battle Cruisers, 1905–1970*, p. 383, states that the *Roma* was hit by a single Type SD 1400-X bomb. Rohwer and Hummelchen, *Chronology of the War at Sea*, p. 231, states that the *Roma* was hit by a single FX 1200 bomb.
The Italian formation that sailed from La Spezia consisted of the battleships *Italia* (the *Littorio* renamed on 30 June 1943), *Roma*, and *Vittorio Veneto*, the light cruisers *Emanuele Filiberto Duca D'Aosta*, *Eugenio Di Savoia*, and *Raimondo Montecuccoli*, and eight destroyers, and it effected a rendezvous with a formation from Genoa that consisted of the light cruisers *Attilio Regolo*, *Giuseppe Garibaldi*, and *Luigi Di Savoia Duca Degli Abruzzi* and the torpedo-boat *Libra*.

30. There are conflicting summaries of the first two destroyer losses, with the *Antonio Da Noli* and *Ugolini Vivaldi* both damaged by German shore batteries, the former then being mined (9 September) and the latter being sunk by German aircraft next day. Chesneau, *Conway's All the World's Fighting Ships, 1922–1946*, p. 299.

31. The two boats sunk were the TA-24 and TA-29, which had been the *Arturo* and *Eridano* respectively: the vessel that escaped was the TA-32, which, interestingly, had been the Italian destroyer *Premuda* and previously the Yugoslavian destroyer *Dubrovnik*. The three vessels had been involved in a mine-laying operation.
By way of a footnote and to balance the British operations, two former Italian destroyer escorts, the TA-25 (ex-*Intrepido*) and TA-26 (ex-*Ardito*) were sunk by U.S. PT boats, which, one would admit, one never thinks of having served in the Mediterranean.

32. The *Euro* was sunk on 1 October 1943, seemingly at Leros; the *Axum* was lost on 28 December 1943; and the *Settembrini* was sunk on 15 November 1944, allegedly by the *Frament*, but in the ship's record in *Dictionary of American Fighting Ships*, vol. 2, p. 439, there is no reference to any incident on this or indeed any other day when it served in the North Atlantic and Mediterranian.

33. Sabang is an island off the northern tip of Sumatra in 05°53'North 95°17'East. The base was subjected to the Allied raid of 19 April 1944 (Operation Cockpit) by two formations, one consisting of the carriers *Illustrious* and *Saratoga*, the battlecruiser *Renown*, the heavy cruiser *London*, and three British and three American destroyers, and the other the British battleships *Valiant* and *Queen Elizabeth* and the French battleship *Richelieu*, the British light cruisers *Ceylon*, *Newcastle*, and *Nigeria*, the Dutch light cruiser *Tromp*, the New Zealand light cruiser *Gambia*, and one Dutch, four Australian, and four British destroyers; one British submarine was assigned rescue duties. With six navies contributing warships, this was perhaps one of the most cosmopolitan operations of the war (see Willmott, *Grave of a Dozen Schemes*, pp. 23, 64, and 161. George Town, in 05°25'North 100°19'East on Penang Island (present-day Pinang), provided the naval base where the U-boats were stationed.

34. There seems to be a confusion, most certainly on Internet discussion boards, about this episode, real or alleged, because it seems to read that the I. 504 shot down the American aircraft on 30 August 1945. This would seem to be a case of mistranslation or erroneous punctuation, and if it did shoot down a Mitchell bomber then it had to be some time before 15 August, but it would seem that this episode is fabrication and it never took place. It is a mark of the confusion surrounding these two boats that a number of accounts state that they were surrendered to the Americans on 30 August 1945, though other dates given include 28 August and (as per *Conway's All the World's Fighting Ships*, p. 306) 2 September 1945, even though the Americans were not at Kobe on these dates.

35. Information supplied by Hasegawa Rei in e-mail of 31 January 2008.

36. Information supplied by Hasegawa Rei in e-mail of 26 January 2008.

9. THE LESSER ALLIED NAVIES AND MERCHANT MARINES IN THE SECOND WORLD WAR

1. Such as the 660-ton fisheries protection vessel *Heimdal*, which reached Lerwick in the Shetland Islands on 14 June and on 30 June became the headquarters and depot ship for Norwegian forces at Rosyth.

2. The figures for these four countries were as follows: Denmark 311,101 of 760,000 GRT; Norway 588,767 of 2,100,000 tons; the Netherlands 405,164 of 2,616,000 tons; and Belgium 90,840 of 295,000 tons, together some 1,395,872 tons of an aggregate of 5,266,000 tons, or 26.51%.

3. Interestingly, and perhaps rather surprisingly, the amount of British shipping in French North African ports in June–July 1940 was about the same as the amount of French shipping that made its way to Britain in the last days before the armistice. As a result, the seizures by Britain and France of each other's ships roughly balanced one another, somewhere between the 250,000 and 300,000 tons markers.

4. One point of interest, and little known, is the fact that in 1940 Sweden undertook to provide Britain with three-fifths of its dry-cargo merchantmen outside the Baltic, something in the region of 340,000 GRT, and did so before the end of the year. In fact this amount of shipping, while small, was considerably more than three-fifths of Swedish resources, but for Britain it was a case of "every little bit helps."

5. In the period 1927–1929 average annual imports totaled 18,976,000 tons of food, drink, and tobacco and 37,277,000 tons of "other commodities," the latter including a whole range of raw materials, timber, petroleum, paper, textiles, and other items but not, under a separate and distinctive heading, manufactured or semi-manufactured goods. Of these totals London handled 6,112,000 tons/32.21% of the former and 9,245,000 tons/24.80% of the latter, overall some 15,357,000 tons/27.30% of all national imports that totaled 56,253,000 tons.

But what is interesting about the figures for this period is that while the second largest port was defined as "Chester to the Mull of Galloway" (i.e., identified primarily as Liverpool but in reality Birkenhead, Everton, and Manchester) with 5,202,000 tons of food, etc., and 6,798,000 tons of "other commodities," i.e., 27.41 and 18.24% and overall 21.33% of national totals, the third and fourth largest ports were Hull (2,385,000 tons/12.57% and 7,753,000 tons/20.80% and 10,138,000 tons/18.02%) and Bristol (1,827,000 tons/9.63% and 6,250,000 tons/16.77% and 8,077,000 tons/14.36%). In terms of "other commodities" Hull was larger than Liverpool: Glasgow was fifth on the list.

6. Most of the information in this last section dealing with the foreign merchant marines was gathered from Berhrens, *History of the Second World War,* pp. 91–109, being chapter 5, "The Calm Before the Storm (i) The Ships of the Conquered Nations and (ii) The Shape of Things to Come."

10. THE WAR ACROSS THE PACIFIC

1. Technically two heavy cruisers, the *Myoko* and *Takao*, survived, but both had been so heavily damaged—the *Takao* in the action off Samar in October 1944 and the *Myoko* in the South China Sea in December—that they were taken to Singapore but never repaired; the *Takao* was subjected to further attack by charioteers on 31 July 1945. After the surrender, the two ships were scuttled in the Strait of Malacca, the *Myoko* on 8 July and the *Takao* on 29 October 1946.

The total of forty-three cruisers includes two light cruisers requisitioned from the Manchurian Navy in 1943 and not included in previous totals.

2. The fleet carrier *Junyo* and escort carrier *Shimane Maru* were not sunk but incurred such damage that their only subsequent movement was to the breakers.

3. Because of peculiarity of use and means of destruction, submarines have not been included in this summary. In this period (24 November 1943 to 24 October 1944) the U.S. Navy lost the submarines *Capelin*, missing in the Indies in November-December 1943; the *Grayback*, sunk by Japanese aircraft in the East China Sea on 26 February 1944, and the *Trout*, sunk by Japanese warships off Okinawa three days later; the *Scorpion*, missing in either the East China Sea or the Yellow Sea in February; the *Tullibee*, sunk by its own torpedo off Palau on 26 March; the *Gudgeon*, missing off the Marianas in April; the *Herring*, sunk by shore-based artillery off the Kuriles on 1 June; the *Golet*, sunk by Japanese warships off northern Honshu on 14 June; the *Rabalo*, possibly mined in the Philippines on 26 July; the *Flier*, mined in the Balabac Strait on 13 August; the *Harder*, sunk by a Siamese destroyer on 24 August; the *Seawolf*, sunk in error by U.S. destroyer escort off the Philippines on 3 October; the *Escolar*, missing in the Yellow Sea in October; and the *Darter*, scuttled after running aground off Palawan, the *Shark*, sunk by Japanese warships in the Luzon Strait, and the *Tang*, sunk by its own torpedo off Formosa, all on 24 October. In addition, the S. 28 was lost during a training exercise off Pearl Harbor on 4 July. That constitutes a total of sixteen (plus one) units lost in this period, and, of course, there were losses incurred by other warships that were not properly fleet units per se (e.g., minelayers/sweepers and destroyer escorts, etc.).

4. Morton, *The United States Army in World War Two: Strategy and Command* (Washington, D.C.: Department of the Army: 1962), p. 125.

5. And these losses were to all causes and theaters; with reference to the latter, this means in both the European and Pacific conflicts. The total of five destroyers lost in October 1943 immediately provides reason to pause; the *Bristol* and *Buck* were sunk separately in the Mediterranean, the *Chevalier, Henley*, and *Porter* in the southwest Pacific.

6. See appendix 10.1 for the fleet, light, and escort carriers in U.S. service in the Second World War.

7. See appendix 10.2 for the American-built escort carriers in service with the British Navy in the Second World War.

8. Willmott, "The Second World War: The War against Japan," ch. 8 in *The American Military Tradition from Colonial Times to the Present*, ed. Carroll and Baxter (Lanham, Md.: Rowman and Littlefield, 2007), p. 201.

9. See appendix 10.3 for detail of U.S. wartime construction.

10. There is the problem of definitions. For example, the battleship *North Carolina*, with T.G. 58.4 in February 1945, was commissioned on 9 April 1941 and completed shake-down cruise before the attack on Pearl Harbor, but it did not enter the Pacific until 10 June 1942 and undertook its first operation in July–August. Its sister-ship, the *Washington*, was commissioned on 15 May 1941, was in dockyard between 3 November and 1 December 1941 for its third set of propellers, and on 13 December became a flagship; it sailed on its first operation, in the North Atlantic, in March 1942. Whether either or both of these two ships should be added to the other four is arguable.

11. THE JAPANESE SITUATION—AND A JAPANESE DIMENSION

1. Lu, "The New China Policy: Divide and Collaborate," in *Japan's Road to the Pacific War*, ed. Morley, pp. 318–24.

2. Cohen, *Japan's Economy in War and Reconstruction*, p. 3.

3. Nakamura, "Depression, Recovery and War, 1920–1945," in Hall et al., *The Cambridge History of Japan*, p. 453.

4. Cohen, *Japan's Economy in War and Reconstruction*, pp. 2–3.

5. Jones, *Manchuria since 1931*, pp. 104, 106–12, 116–17.

6. Ibid., pp. 151, 155–57, 162.

7. Naval Staff History, *The Second World War*, vol. 5: *The Blockade of Japan*, p. 65.

8. Examples of this inferiority include Japan's needing 1,012 and 272 man-hours to produce a ton of single-base smokeless powder and TNT respectively, compared to the 5.5 and 10 man-hours of the United States, and 11 hours for the TNT operating cycle compared to the 40 minutes in American factories. See Cohen, *Japan's Economy in War and Reconstruction*, p. 181.

9. Barnhart, *Japan Prepares for Total War*, pp. 46–49, 74–76, 160–161.

10. Cohen, *Japan's Economy in War and Reconstruction*, p. 134. Ike, *Japan's Decision for War: Records of the 1941 Policy Conferences*, pp. 7, 11.

11. Cohen, *Japan's Economy in War and Reconstruction*, p. 2.

12. Barnhart, *Japan Prepares for Total War*, pp. 95–96.

13. Cohen, *Japan's Economy in War and Reconstruction*, p. 6.

14. Nakamura, *Raw Materials Problems of Japanese War Economy*, p. 18, and *Depression, Recovery and War, 1920–1945*, p. 483.

15. Nakamura, *Raw Materials Problems of Japanese War Economy*, p. 4.

16. Jones, *Manchuria since 1931*, p. 136.

17. Pauer, "Lots of Friendship but Few Orders," in *International Studies 1986/3*, ed. Nish, pp. 10–37.

18. Naval Staff History, *The Second World War*, vol. 5: *The Blockade of Japan*, p. 4. Willmott, *The Great Crusade*, p. 331.

19. Cohen, *Japan's Economy in War and Reconstruction*, p. 251.

20. John Marshall, *The Guinness Book of Rail Facts and Feats* (Enfield, Middlesex: Guiness Superlatives, 1975), p. 97 (1940 figure).

21. Naval Staff History, *The Second World War*, vol. 5: *The Blockade of Japan*, p. 11.

22. Cohen, *Japan's Economy in War and Reconstruction*, p. 264, n. 112.

23. Very few of these ships displaced 500 tons, and the vast majority were less than 100 tons: the average displacement was 63 tons.

24. An average displacement of 388 tons. Some of these ships were of wooden construction.

25. Lengerer and Rehm-Takahara, "The Japanese Aircraft Carriers *Junyo* and *Hiyo*, part 1," p. 13, states that very little of this increase took place between 1921 and 1936, an assertion substantiated by Cohen

26. Parillo, *The Japanese Merchant Marine in World War II*, p. 52. In making this observation one would note that with 500 slips, of which one-third were over 500 feet and with a theoretical capacity of 900,000 tons per year, the output of Japanese yards was never more than 497,742 tons in any year between 1931 and 1941. One assumes that the specialist demands of warship construction were instrumental in the depression of output from its theoretical maximum.

27. Cohen, *Japan's Economy in War and Reconstruction*, p. 253. The major yards committed to building were Kure, Sasebo, Maizuru and Yokosuka.

28. Naval Staff History, *The Second World War*, vol. 5: *The Blockade of Japan*, p. 61.

29. A caveat must be entered, however, to balance the assertion that Japanese shipyards were unable to meet merchant and naval demands simultaneously. The limitations of the shipyards were in part the result of the low priority afforded merchantman construction in terms of finished steel consumption. Cohen, *Japan's Economy in War*

and Reconstruction, p. 130, cites percentage allocations as shown in the accompanying table, which indicates that by 1941 Japan had reached the situation whereby direct steel consumption by the armed forces was greater than that of the whole of industry.

	Merchant Shipbuilding	Army	Navy	Air Forces	Industry
1937	6	4	11	3	76
1938	7	10	11	5	67
1939	6	11	11	5	67
1940	5	14	16	7	58
1941	7	19	21	9	44

It can be seen from these figures, however, that merchant shipbuilding allocations declined by over a quarter between 1938 and 1940, while the impact of the China Incident led to almost a four-fold expansion of the Rikugun's demand for steel between 1937 and 1941. Total Japanese finished steel output, according to Cohen, *Japan's Economy in War and Reconstruction*, p. 128, was 5,630,000 tons in 1937, of which 5,147,000 tons was home-produced, and 5,565,000 tons in 1941, of which 5,120,000 tons was produced in the home islands.

Nevertheless, the overall point—that Japanese shipyard resources could not stretch to cover both mercantile and naval construction—is well made, and evidence to this effect is provided by the fact that the laying down of so important a fleet unit as the fleet carrier *Hiryu* was delayed a year because of shipyard congestion. See Japanese Monograph #145, Military History Section, Headquarters U.S. Army Forces Far East, *Outline of Naval Armament and Preparations for War*, part 1, p. 18.

30. Japanese Monograph #169, Military History Section, Headquarters U.S. Army Forces Far East, *Outline of Naval Armament and Preparations for War*, part 4, p. 59.

31. Cohen, *Japan's Economy in War and Reconstruction*, p. 252.

32. Willmott, *The Great Crusade*, p. 331. The figure compares to British totals of 9.46%, 9.00% and 9.35% for September 1941, December 1941, and March 1942 respectively for dry-cargo ships of 1,600 GRT and over, repairing, damaged, or not in service. See Behrens, *Merchant Shipping and the Demands of War*, pp. 69, 152.

33. Behrens, *Merchant Shipping and the Demands of War*, p. 23.

34. Returns for January 1943 indicate a total of 135 foreign ships of about 386,252 tons were in Japanese service, of which 23 ships of 108,405 tons were under charter. France (46,078 tons), Germany (23,974 tons), Italy (16,862 tons), and Norway (8,818 tons) each had five ships in Japanese service, while Sweden (two ships of 7,623 tons) and Greece (one 5,050-ton ship) provided the balance of charters.

A comparison with British returns makes obvious the inadequacy of such resources. On the basis of quarterly returns of ships of 1,600 GRT and over, Britain and its Empire went to war with 2,965 ships, of which 445 were tankers. The greatest number of ships under British control at any time in the war was 3,757 on 30 September 1940, of which foreign charters accounted for 178 tankers and 526 non-tankers. The peak of charters in British service was 231 tankers on 30 September 1941 and 619 non-tankers on 31 March 1942 (see Central Statistical Office, *History of the Second World War: Statistical Digest of the War*, p. 173).

35. Peattie, "Akiyama Sanyuki and the Emergence of Modern Japanese Naval Doctrine," *U.S. Naval Institute Proceedings*, 103, #1, pp. 60–69. Pelz, *Race to Pearl Harbor*, pp. 29–35, 39. Willmott, *The Barrier and the Javelin*, pp. 19–31.

36. Cohen, *Japan's Economy in War and Reconstruction*, pp. 50, 254.

37. Naval Staff History, *The Second World War: The Defeat of the Enemy Attack on*

Shipping, 1939–1945, vol. 1: *A Study of Policy and Operations, Text and Appendices*, pp. 2–4.

38. Parillo, *The Japanese Merchant Marine in World War II*, p. 89.

39. Command [Paper] 3758, Treaty Series No. 1 (1931), International Treaty for the Limitation and Reduction of Naval Armament, April 22, 1930, pp. 12–13. No restrictions were placed upon the number of ships of less than 600 tons and of ships between 600 and 2,000 tons, provided that the latter carried no guns over 155-mm, no more than four guns over 76-mm, and no torpedo tubes and could not make over 20 knots. The first provision, under Article 8(a), gave rise to the *Tomozuru* class. The second provision, under Article 8(b), saw the United States build the *Charleston* and *Erie*. Lenton, *American Gunboats and Minesweepers*, pp. 3–4. Silverstone, *U.S. Warships of World War II*, p. 238.

40. Perhaps predictably, not one of these four was employed in a commerce protection role at the outbreak of war.

41. Originally sixteen *Otori*-class units were to have been built, but orders for the last eight were cancelled as part of cost-cutting measures in order to provide funds for the construction of the *Yamato* and *Musashi*. See Japanese Monograph #145, *Outline of Naval Armament and Preparations for War*, part 1, p. 59. Ian Sturton, *All the World's Battleships, 1906 to the Present* (London: Conway Maritime Press, 1997), p. 197. It is stated that nine chasers were built in the place of the cancelled *Otoris*. This may have been the case, but these nine were ordered independently in the 1937 program.

42. Under the same program another eight-strong class was ordered, the *Ukuru* and its sisters being laid down between 9 October 1943 and 24 May 1944 and completed between 27 July 1944 and 8 April 1945.

43. At the outbreak of war the Kaigun deployed sixteen divisions of auxiliary submarine-chasers, one with four units and the others with three. The division with four units had four chasers under command and the others two chasers and one, much larger, netlayer. Japanese List, *The Imperial Navy in World War II*, pp. 108–10.

44. Campbell, *Naval Weapons of World War II*, pp. 89–93, 212.

45. Hackmann, *Seek and Strike*, pp. 433–34.

46. Naval Staff History, *The Second World War: The Defeat of the Enemy Attack on Shipping, 1939–1945*, vol. 1B: *A Study of Policy and Operations, Plans and Tables*, Plan 9.

47. This was a *Mikura*-class escort. Lengerer and Rehm-Takahara, "Japanese *Kaibokan* Escorts," part 2, pp. 173–74.

48. Friedman, *Naval Radars*, pp. 192, 196.

49. Brown, *Aircraft Carriers*, p. 23, states, on the basis of U.S. Bombing Survey reports, that the *Shokaku* was the first Japanese carrier to be fitted with radar, in September 1941, and that it was later fitted with the Type 21. Lengerer and Rehm-Takahara, "The Japanese Aircraft Carriers *Junyo* and *Hiyo*," part 3, p. 193, states that the *Hiyo* and *Junyo* were fitted with the Type 21 radar in July 1942. According to Norman Friedman, *Naval Radars*, p. 207, however, the Type 21 was a shore-based 3-m radar.

50. Preston, *U-boats*, p. 119, and *History of the Royal Navy*, p. 156.

51. Japanese Monograph #118, Military History Section, Headquarters U.S. Army Forces Far East, *Operational History of Japanese Naval Communications, December 1941–August 1945*, p. 203.

52. Ibid., pp. 219–21.

53. Naval Staff History, *The Second World War*, vol. 5: *The Blockade of Japan*, p. 7. Cohen, *Japan's Economy in War and Reconstruction*, p. 105. Lest the services' demands be considered excessive, it should be noted that in reality these allocations were not particularly generous. On the basis of calculations that provided shipping on the scale

of five tons per man in the tropics and three tons elsewhere, approximately 120,000 tons of shipping were needed to move a complete division by sea (Parillo, *The Japanese Merchant Marine in World War II*, pp. 1, 12–13, 77). Maintaining a division in action was an additional matter, but on the basis of the returns of European armies can be assumed to have been in the order of 250/300 tons per day. For first-phase operations in southeast Asia and the central Pacific the Rikugun employed eleven divisions, all but two of which were moved by sea. Given the continuing commitments of the Rikugun in Manchoutikuo and China, the scale of military allocation, which allowed approximately 1,300,000 tons of shipping for the assault forces bound for southeast Asia and about 1,000,000 tons of shipping for all purposes thereafter, could not have been anything other than marginal to requirements.

54. Central Statistical Office, *Statistical Digest of the War*, p. 295. This is an estimated figure for 3 October 1942.

55. Lengerer and Rehm-Takahara, "The Japanese Aircraft Carriers *Junyo* and *Hiyo*, part 1," p. 17. According to the much earlier Japanese Monograph #160, Military History Section, Headquarters U.S. Army Forces Far East, *Outline of Naval Armament and Preparations for War*, part 3, pp. 35–36, the *Kaigun* between November 1940 and December 1941 requisitioned about 750 ships of some 1,650,000 tons, of which 522 ships of about 1,150,000 tons had been converted before the start of the Pacific war. With some 200,000 tons of shipping not in need of such attention, 221 ships of about 460,000 tons were either undergoing or awaiting conversion in December 1941. These figures, being estimated, do not fully accord with one another and, of course, cannot be reconciled with Lengerer.

56. To give but one example, albeit slightly outside the "end of 1943" terms of reference: in April and May 1944, and as a direct response to the Truk and Koror losses and in anticipation of American moves against the Marianas and western Carolines, some 180,000 tons of shipping were requisitioned in order to move troops and material into the threatened areas (Naval Staff History, *The Second World War*, vol. 5: *The Blockade of Japan*, p. 90).

In April Japanese service and merchant shipping losses totaled 48 ships of 143,983 tons, in May 61 ships of 252,248 ton: Army requisitioning therefore (on a rough rule of thumb) increased shipping "losses" by almost half in these two months.

57. Two units were converted to serve as fleet carriers—the *Hiyo* and *Junyo*—and four as escort carriers—the *Chuyo, Kaiyo, Taiyo,* and *Unyo*. The other four were used as transports and sunk before taken in hand by the dockyards.

58. Lengerer and Rehm-Takahara, "The Japanese Aircraft Carriers *Junyo* and *Hiyo*: Part 1," pp. 13–14. The state subsidy provisions underwent considerable and subtle change during the thirties. The Law of 1932, which permitted a 20% greater subsidy for a ship of 19 knots compared to one of 13.5 knots, provided for quality at the expense of quantity by subsidizing a build-down on a two-for-one basis; the Law of 1935 provided subsidies on a straight new-for-old basis; and the Law of 1936 was a straight subsidy of new construction with no scrapping proviso and was limited to construction of ships of a minimum 6,000 tons displacement and a speed of 19 knots. When it is noted that at this same time the Navy Ministry chartered oilers at rates 38% above current market prices, the extent of state support is as obvious as the military implications of these laws, the Kaigun demanding that new oilers be equipped for underway refueling and high-speed pumping. The qualitative aspect of the oiler fleet thus begins to come into perspective, though somewhat quixotically the Kaigun also demanded that new oilers should be designed in order to mount 11-in. guns. See Parillo, *The Japanese Merchant Marine in World War II*, pp. 47–51.

59. Cohen, *Japan's Economy in War and Reconstruction*, p. 371.
60. Willmott, *Empires in the Balance*, p. 88.
61. Nakamura, *Raw Materials Problems of Japanese War Economy*, p. 15.
62. Ike, *Japan's Decision for War*, p. 216. Nakamura, *Raw Materials Problems of Japanese War Economy*, p. 13.
63. Ike, *Japan's Decision for War*, p. 217.
64. Naval Staff History, *The Second World War*, vol. 5: *The Blockade of Japan*, p. 7. Cohen, *Japan's Economy in War and Reconstruction*, p. 105.
65. Naval Staff History, *The Second World War*, vol. 5: *The Blockade of Japan*, p. 8. Two comments need to be made. First, in some measure the problem was without solution for Japan because of the triangular nature of its commitments. Ships could not necessarily avoid sailing in ballast on lines from the combat zones; sailings between Japan and the Southern Resources Area were another matter. Second, it was Britain's ability in large measure to avoid this problem that makes comparison between its and the Japanese position so difficult. Of the 8,600,000 tons of shipping requisitioned by Britain, an estimated 3,000,000 tons was taken by the armed forces and lost "permanently or semi-permanently" to trade. The largest single amount of shipping, 3,600,000 tons, was committed to military needs in the Indian Ocean, but was not employed solely in meeting military requirements. See Central Statistical Office, *Statistical Digest of the War*, p. 295.
66. Parillo, *The Japanese Merchant Marine in World War II*, pp. 97–98.
67. Central Statistical Office, *Statistical Digest of the War*, p. 23.
68. Ike, *Japan's Decision for War*, pp. 215–16. (In the 1939 review of industrial development the Cabinet Planning Board assessed the shipbuilding industry as "generally sufficient" for national needs, one of the very few sectors of the economy so described. See Parillo, *The Japanese Merchant Marine in World War II*, p. 52.)
69. The British total includes all units in service and launched prior to 31 December 1939 and is calculated on the basis of H. T. Lenton and J. J. Colledge, *Warships of World War II*. The American figures are provided by Silverstone, *U.S. Warships of World War II*, p. 100ff.
70. The British position is particularly difficult to assess because of the complications presented by the help Britain gave to and received from its Empire and the variety of escort types in service. Britain went to war with 38 escort sloops, 47 minesweeper sloops, and 11 patrol sloops, but in 1940 and 1941 launched 4 escort sloops, 139 minesweeper sloops which were mainly used as escorts, 31 destroyer escorts, and 209 corvettes. Britain also requisitioned escorts being built for Brazil and Turkey in British yards as well and acquired 50 WWI-vintage destroyers from the United States. Without infringing upon the Japanese story, it may be noted that between December 1941 and February 1943 the Kaigun commissioned one patrol boat, 17 submarine-chasers, and 3 minesweepers.

12. THE JAPANESE SITUATION—AND AN AMERICAN DIMENSION

1. The comparisons and ratios in the tables in terms of overall total number of engines and weight of airframe have been calculated on the basis of only those years when figures are available for both countries, i.e., 1941 to 1945.
2. For example, textile cloth and cotton imports fell by 65.46% and 67.98% respectively between 1936 and 1941, and wool imports by 60.45% between 1937 and 1940; compared to a 1937 index, in 1941 domestic rice and food production stood at 83 and 78.1 respectively and textile consumption at 60.4. It has been suggested that Japan as a nation in 1941 stood some 6% above malnutrition levels.

3. See appendix 12.1, "Raw Materials and Food Entering Japanese Ports between 1940 and 1945."

4. The heaviest losses to date had been incurred in March 1942, when a total of seven ships of 57,821 tons had been lost in the Southern Resources Area; the next heaviest losses had been in the previous month, i.e., in October 1942, when eleven ships of 48,899 tons had been sunk in Japanese home waters.

5. Note the statement of losses refers only to the Pacific and does not include Japanese losses, whether to carrier aircraft or submarines, in the Indian Ocean.

13. THE JAPANESE SITUATION—AND A SECOND JAPANESE DIMENSION

1. The 1st Surface Escort Division, based at Takao on Formosa, was formerly under the command of the 5th Fleet.

2. In March 1944 eight frigates joined the two divisions, four apiece, but in April 1944, in which month the 3rd S.E.D was established at Yokosuka and the 4th S.E.D. at Sasebo, fourteen frigates joined the 1st S.E.D. at Formosa. Two more joined the 2nd S.E.D., which had been transferred to Saipan: the formation was formally dissolved on 18 July 1944, i.e., a month after the American landings on the island.

3. Willmott, *The Battle of Leyte Gulf*, p. 57.

4. The month of February 1944, and with it Truk and overall losses of 33 merchantmen of 114,654 tons, being excluded from consideration: with that exception, Japanese merchant shipping losses in any single month did not exceed 100,000 tons until August 1944, when Japanese merchant shipping losses numbered 41 ships of 172,251 tons.

5. On 1 January 1944 there were some 861,000 tons of oilers "afloat," and in the year 824,000 tons of oilers were sunk; new construction and conversions plus one salvage added 812,000 tons and therefore more or less balanced the losses.

6. The situation was that conversions from merchantmen to oilers in 1942 amounted to 36,000 tons, in 1943 to 100,000 tons, and in 1944 to 182,000 tons; in 1945 the conversions from oilers to dry cargo merchantmen amounted to 318,000 tons. These figures, and those in the previous footnote, are given in the Naval Staff History, *The Second World War*, vol. 5: *The Blockade of Japan*, p. 97, but a certain caution needs be exercised for a reason that may not be immediately obvious: these totals balance exactly. The same source indicates (p. 98) that by tonnage more than two-thirds of the oilers nominally available were not in service on 15 August 1945.

7. A barrel of oil is 42 U.S. gallons, which is given as equivalent to 35 Imperial gallons, or 159 litres. On the basis of one gallon equaling eight pounds (which would be the density of water, not oil) 6.67 barrels would be the equivalent of one ton of 2,240 lbs., and therefore the 1941 reserve would constitute 2,998,500 tons and the March 1945 figure just 29,985 tons.

8. It is perhaps worth noting that the American submarine command, by virtue of signals intelligence, was given notice of the sailing of the *Hyuga* and *Ise*, and escorts, and apparently deployed eleven submarines across the South China Sea, though it seems that fifteen were on station. None made contact with the Japanese formation, and it also seems that another twelve were deployed across the line of advance between the Formosa Strait and home waters, again without result: see Blair, *Silent Victory*, pp. 848–849.

9. Naval Staff History, *The Second World War*, vol. 5: *The Blockade of Japan*, p. 97.

10. Blair, *Silent Victory*, p. 409.

11. In fact 23: one boat, the *Harder*, was sunk by a Siamese warship in August 1944.

12. For a full list of American submarine losses, see appendix 10.4, "U.S. Naval Losses in the Second World War."

13. Blair, *Silent Victory*, pp. 361–362.

14. Meigs, *Slide Rules and Submarine*, p. 156.

15. Theodore Roscoe, *United States Submarine Operations in World War II* (Annapolis, Md.: Naval Institute Press, 1949), p. 56.

16. The Mark XVIII torpedo (20' 5" in length, 3,154 lbs. weight, 575-lb. warhead, range 4,000 yards at 29 knots) was not wholly satisfactory, though it was more economical to make than the Mark XIV. Ironically, in 1950 it was replaced in service by the Mark XIV, which, in part at least, it had been designed to supersede. Blair, *Silent Victory*, pp. 281, 511–513. Campbell, *Naval Weapons of World War II*, p. 160. Roscoe, *Submarine Operations*, pp. 261–263, 298.

17. The U.S. Pacific Fleet deployed seventeen boats in May to meet the Japanese offensive in the central Pacific. Another nine boats that had left on patrol in either April or early May also joined the various patrol lines en route for Pearl Harbor. Roscoe, *Submarine Operations*, pp. 124–125. Willmott, *The Barrier and the Javelin*, pp. 307–309.

18. Blair, *Silent Victory*, pp. 857–865.

19. Naval Staff History, *The Second World War*, vol. 5: *The Blockade of Japan*, p. 125. Potter, *Nimitz*, p. 447. And, of course, this intention was put into effect, with the result that the sortie on the part of the battleship *Yamato* and escorts had to be made via the Bungo Channel and was detected and reported by the submarines *Hackleback* and *Threadfin;* the formation was caught by U.S. carrier forces the next day, 7 April, and the battleship, one light cruiser, and four destroyers were sunk, the remaining four destroyers being damaged to varying degrees.

20. Friedman, *U.S. Naval Weapons*, p. 112.

21. Naval Staff History, *The Second World War*, vol. 5: *The Blockade of Japan*, p. 35.

22. Ibid., p. 36, fn. states that whereas 9 warships and 54 merchantmen had been sunk by mines in the outer zone, during Operation Starvation the totals were 13 and 224 merchantmen (of 500 tons or more). My calculations are rather different—for example 42 and 152 merchantmen—but another 21 merchantmen, lost in Japanese home waters but to causes not known, were very likely sunk by mines, and the lists should be amended appropriately. As always with these tables, lies, damned lies, and statistics, but the various differences in matters of detail do not affect the basic point.

23. Ibid., p. 33. One would query the use of English herein: it is hard to see why the indefinite article was used.

Perhaps more pertinently, S. E. Morison's *History of United States Naval Operations in World War II*, vol. 14: *Victory in the Pacific, 1945*, does not mention Operation Starvation and any aspect of the mining effort—so perhaps the campaign was not important after all.

24. Willmott, *The Second World War in the Far East*, p. 198.

25. Naval Staff History, *The Second World War*, vol. 5: *The Blockade of Japan*, p. 40.

26. Ibid., p. 57.

27. Ibid., p. 6

28. Carter and Mueller, *U.S. Army Air Forces in World War II. Combat Chronology 1941–1945* (Washington, D.C.: Center for Air Force History, 1991), p. 610. Williams, *United States Army in World War II: Chronology 1941–1945* (Washington, D.C.: Office of the Chief of Military History, Dept. of the Army, 1960), p. 458. Naval Staff History, *The Second World War*, vol. 5: *The Blockade of Japan*, pp. 123, 126. The Privateer was the naval version of the Liberator heavy bomber.

29. Naval Staff History, *The Second World War*, vol. 5: *The Blockade of Japan*, p. 128

and pp. 156–157, being appendix N, "Merchant Shipping Passing through Shimonoseki Strait, Mines Laid and Ships Sunk."

30. The collapse of imports in such commodities as leather and sugar—the last cargo of the latter to arrive in a Japanese port did so in March 1945 and amounted to just 160 tons—was exceptionally severe, but in reality the volume of virtually all commodities was in decline in these last months; see chapter 2 and appendix 12.1.

14. THE JAPANESE SITUATION—AND ANOTHER, AND FINAL, DIMENSION

1. The total is perhaps somewhat surprising, but the actions were Java Sea (27–28 February 1942), Coral Sea (7 May 1942), Midway (4–7 June 1942), Savo Island (9 August 1942), Eastern Solomons (23–25 August 1942), Cape Esperance (11–12 October 1942), Santa Cruz (25–27 October 1942), first Guadalcanal (12–13 November 1942), second Guadalcanal (14–15 November 1942), Tassafaronga (30 November–1 December 1942), Kula Gulf (5–6 July 1943), Kolombangara (12–13 July 1943), Vella Gulf (6–7 August 1943), Vella Lavella (6–7 October 1943), Empress Augusta Bay (1–2 November 1943), Cape St. George (25–26 November 1943), Philippine Sea (19–20 June 1944), and Leyte Gulf (23–27 October 1944).

2. Willmott, *The Battle of Leyte Gulf*, pp. 3–4.

3. At least in terms of numbers of ships: in March 1945 service tonnage losses were greater than those incurred by the merchant marine.

4. In percentage terms the tonnage lost in Japanese home waters represented 14.86% of all losses in January 1944 and thereafter, by month, 7.12%, 8.76%, 17.94% (April), 15.46%, 17.46%, 23.80%, 8.26% (August), 9.32%, 7.20%, 22.59%, 4.06%, 8.50% (January 1945), 24.50%, 13.64%, 50.87% (April), 90.30%, 83.00%, 99.05%, and 98.51% in August 1945.

5. Potter, *Nimitz*, p. 1.

6. Potter, *Bull Halsey*, p. 171.

7. Willmott, *The Battle of Leyte Gulf*, pp. 249.

8. Halsey and Bryan, *Admiral Halsey's Story* (New York: McGraw Hill, 1947), pp. 220–221.

9. Potter, *Bull Halsey*, p. 335.

10. Willmott, *The Battle of Leyte Gulf*, pp. 196–197.

11. Morison, *History of United States Naval Operations in World War Two*, vol. 3: *The Rising Sun in the Pacific, 1931–April 1942*, p. 125.

12. As an entirely irrelevant aside, in Britain the Conservative Party's leadership, policies, and conduct in the 2005 general election were so bad as to ensure a third successive defeat, and it was suggested at the time that its election manifesto was no more than a *kamikaze* effort and should have been entitled *Tory! Tory! Tory!*

13. Genda Minoru, *Shinjuwan sakusen kaikoroku/Recollections of the Pearl Harbor Operation* (Tokyo: Yomiuri Shimbunsha, 1967), pp. 300–301.

14. Willmott, *Pearl Harbor*, pp. 145–154.

15. Exchange of e-mails involving the author, Edward S. Miller, and Keith E. Allen, 30 September–8 October 2000: Oil Storage at Pearl.

15. *FINIS*

1. The 2,144-ton (Polish) *Grom*-class destroyer [1936] *Blyskawica* perhaps deserves special mention. It and its sister ship were the fastest destroyers in the world when

built, and they made their way to Britain before the start of war in September 1939. On 15 August 1945 the *Blyskawica* was at Tobermory working up and in 1947 was returned to (communist) Poland where it remained the navy's flagship into the late sixties. After passing from active service, it was sticken and thereafter preserved in 1976.

2. For purposes of comparison it should be noted that with submarines and minesweepers not included in the lists, the British had four light cruisers and nine destroyers in the Mediterranean, with another light cruiser and three destroyers non-operational.

The 15th Cruiser Squadron consisted of the light cruisers *Orion* at Alexandria, the *Ajax* at St. Tropez, the *Arethusa* at Famagusta, and the *Sirius* at Trieste, with the *Aurora* undergoing refit at Malta. The 3rd Destroyer Flotilla consisted of the destroyer leader *Milne* and the destroyers *Lookout, Marne, Matchless, Meteor,* and *Musketeer,* and the 14th Destroyer Flotilla the destroyer leader *Jervis* and the destroyers *Chevron* and *Javelin.* In addition the destroyer *Active* was at Gibraltar in the capacity as depot ship, not with any formation, there were three non-operational destroyers in the Mediterranean, and there was a third destroyer formation in the Mediterranean but with three operational and one non-operational escort destroyers.

3. And one might add a rider. According to Samuel Eliot Morison, *History of United States Naval Operations in World War II,* vol. 11: *The Invasion of France and Germany* 1944–1945, p. 329, on 6 June 1945 the last U.S. naval formation left European waters, and on 16 June 1945 no U.S. naval vessel, whether warship, auxiliary, or landing ship or craft, remained in British waters. This claim is not fully convincing, because a fair number of warships which passed to the British under lend-lease provisions and which had incurred damage that was beyond economical repair had been returned pending disposal, and there is no getting away from the fact that the light cruiser *Memphis* was at Marseilles on 12 August and at Naples on 27 October, but there is no doubting the general correctness of Morison's statement.

4. See, for example, the author's *Grave of a Dozen Schemes, 1943–1945.*

5. The remaining eight ships were those that had been lost. Six British and one Dutch ships were lost in action, and one was expended as blockship at St. Nazaire in 1942. Of the forty that had stepped down from operational proceedings, eight had been scrapped prior to the end of the European war, and one of the destroyers transferred to the Soviet Union was sunk by a German submarine in the Arctic in January 1945.

6. As per Jeffrey G. Barlow's masterly *Revolt of the Admirals: The Fight for Naval Aviation, 1945–1950* (Washington, D.C.: Department of the Navy, 1994).

SELECTED BIBLIOGRAPHY

THE INTER-WAR PERIOD

Allen, Frederick Lewis. *Only Yesterday and Since Yesterday: A Popular History of the 20's and 30's*. New York: Bonanza Books, 1986.

Barclay, Glen St. J. *The Rise and Fall of the New Roman Empire: Italy's Bid for World Power, 1890–1943*. London: Sidgwick and Jackson, 1973.

Beevor, Antony. *The Battle for Spain: The Spanish Civil War, 1936-1939*. New York : Penguin Books, 2006.

——. *The Spanish Civil War*. London: Orbis, 1982.

Berend, Ivan T. *Decades of Crisis: Central and Eastern Europe before World War II*. Berkeley and Los Angeles: University of California Press, 1998.

Brendon, Piers. *The Dark Valley: A Panorama of the 1930s*. New York: Alfred A. Knopf, 2000.

Chambers, Frank P. *This Age of Conflict: The Western World—1914 to the Present*. New York: Harcourt, Brace, and World 1962.

Clubb, O. Edmund. *Twentieth Century China*. New York: Columbia University Press, 1964.

Coffey, Thomas M. *Lion by the Tail: The Story of the Italian-Ethiopian War*. London: Hamish Hamilton, 1974.

Command [Paper] 3758. Treaty Series No. 1. (1931). *International Treaty for the Limitation and Reduction of Naval Armament. April 22, 1930*. London: His Majesty's Stationery Office, 1931.

Coverdale, John F. *Italian Intervention in the Spanish Civil War*. Princeton, N.J.: Princeton University Press, 1975.

Edwards, Jill. *The British Government and the Spanish Civil War, 1936–1939*. London: Macmillan, 1979.

Jackson, Gabriel. *A Concise History of the Spanish Civil War*. London: Thames and Hudson, 1974.

Janos, Andrew C., and William Slottman, eds. *Revolution in Perspective: Essays on the Hungarian Soviet Republic of 1919*. Berkeley and Los Angeles: University of California Press, 1971.

Journal of the Royal United Services Institute. Vol. 84: February to November 1939. London: Royal United Services Institute, 1940.

Lee, Stephen E. *European Dictatorships, 1918–1945*. London: Routledge, 1987.

Marder, Arthur J. *Old Friends New Enemies: The Royal Navy and the Imperial Japanese Navy*. Vol. 1: *Strategic Illusions 1936–1941*. Oxford: Clarendon Press, 1981.

Nish, Ian, ed. *International Studies 1986/3: German-Japanese Relations in the 1930s*. London: London School of Economics and Political Science/Suntory Toyota International Centre for Economics and Related Disciplines, 1986.

——. *Japan's Struggle with Internationalism*. Basingstoke: Kegan Paul International, 1993.

Pauer, Erich. "Lots of Friendship but Few Orders: German-Japanese Commercial Relations in the late 1930s." In *International Studies 1986/3: German-Japanese Relations in the 1930s*, ed. Ian Nish. London: London School of Economics and Political Science/Suntory Toyota International Centre for Economics and Related Disciplines, 1986.

Roskill, S. W. *Naval Policy between the Wars*. Vol. 1: *The Period of Anglo-American Antagonism*. London: Collins, 1968. Vol. 2: *The Period of Reluctant Rearmament, 1930–1939*. London: Collins, 1976.

Szilassy, Sándor. *Revolutionary Hungary, 1918–1921*. Astor Park, Fla.: Danubian Press, 1971.

Thomas, Hugh. *The Spanish Civil War*. London: Eyre and Spottiswoode, 1961.

THE WAR IN THE FAR EAST

Allen, Thomas B., and Norman Polmar. *Code-Name Downfall: The Secret Plan to Invade Japan—and Why Truman Dropped the Bomb*. New York: Simon and Schuster, 1995.

Barnhart, Michael A. *Japan Prepares for Total War: The Search for Economic Security, 1919–1941*. Ithaca, N.Y.: Cornell University Press, 1987.

Blair, Clay, Jr. *Silent Victory: The U. S. Submarine War against Japan*. Philadelphia, Pa.: J. B. Lippincott, 1975.

Boyle, John Hunter. *China and Japan at War, 1937–1945: The Politics of Collaboration*. Stanford, Calif.: Stanford University Press, 1972.

Brendon, Piers. *The Dark Valley: A Panorama of the 1930s*. New York: Alfred A. Knopf, 2000.

Brice, Martin H. *The Royal Navy and the Sino-Japanese Incident*. London: Ian Allan, 1973.

Calvocoressi, Peter, Guy Wint, and John Pritchard. *Total War: The Causes and Courses of the Second World War*. Vol. 2: *The Greater East Asia and Pacific Conflict*. New York: Pantheon Books, 1989.

Carter, Worrall Reed. *Beans, Bullets and Black Oil: The Story of Fleet Logistics Afloat in the Pacific during World War II*. Washington, D.C.: U.S. Government Printing Office, 1953.

Chang, Iris. *The Rape of Nanking: The Forgotten Holocaust of World War II*. London: Penguin, 1998.

Cohen, Jerome B. *Japan's Economy in War and Reconstruction*. Westport, Conn.: Greenwood Press, 1949.

Crowley, James B. *Japan's Quest for Autonomy: National Security and Foreign Policy, 1930–1938*. Princeton, N.J.: Princeton University Press, 1966.

Cutler, Thomas J. *The Battle of Leyte Gulf 23–26 October 1944: The Dramatic Full Story, Based on the Latest Research, of the Greatest Naval Battle in History*. New York: HarperCollins, 1994.

Dower, John W. *War without Mercy: Race and Power in the Pacific War.* New York: Pantheon, 1986.

Drea, Edward J. *MacArthur's Ultra: Codebreaking and the War against Japan, 1942–1945.* Lawrence: University Press of Kansas, 1992.

Elphick, Peter. *Far Eastern File: The Intelligence War in the Far East 1930–1945.* London: Hodder and Stoughton, 1997.

——. *Singapore: The Pregnable Fortress: A Study in Deception, Discord and Desertion.* London: Hodder and Stoughton, 1995.

Evans, David C., and Mark R. Peattie. *Kaigun: Strategy, Tactics, and Technology in the Imperial Japanese Navy 1887–1941.* Annapolis, Md.: Naval Institute Press, 1997.

Feifer, George. *The Battle of Okinawa: The Blood and the Bomb.* Guilford, Conn.: First Lyons Press, 2001.

Frank, Richard B. *Downfall: The End of the Imperial Japanese Empire.* New York: Random House, 1999.

——. *Guadalcanal: The Definitive Account of the Landmark Battle.* New York: Random House, 1990.

Fukudome, Shigeru, with Mitsuo Fuchida et al., with introduction by Raymond O'Conner. *The Japanese Navy in World War 2: An Anthology of Articles by Former Officers of the Imperial Japanese Navy and Air Defence Force, Originally Published in the U. S. Naval Institute PROCEEDINGS.* Annapolis, Md.: Naval Institute Press, 1969.

Guiglini, J. "A Resumé of the Battle of Koh Chang." Trans. K. Macpherson. *Warship International,* no. 2 (1990).

Harries, Meirion, and Susie Harries. *Soldiers of the Sun: The Rise and Fall of the Imperial Japanese Army.* New York: Random House, 1991.

Holmes, W. J. *Double-Edged Secrets: U. S. Naval Intelligence Operations in the Pacific during World War II.* Annapolis, Md.: Naval Institute Press, 1979.

Howarth, Stephen. *Morning Glory: A History of the Imperial Japanese Navy.* London: Hamish Hamilton, 1983.

Hsiung, James C., and Stephen I. Levine. *China's Bitter Victory: The War with Japan, 1937–1935.* Armonk, N.Y.: East Gate, 1992.

Ienaga, Saburo. *The Pacific War: World War II and the Japanese, 1931–1945.* New York: Pantheon, 1978.

Ike, Nobutaka, trans. and ed. *Japan's Decision for War: Records of the 1941 Policy Conferences.* Stanford, Calif.: Stanford University Press, 1967.

Iriye, Akira. *Power and Culture: The Japanese-American War, 1941–1945.* Cambridge, Mass.: Harvard University Press, 1981.

James, D. Clayton. "American and Japanese Strategies in the Pacific War." In *Makers of Modern Strategy: From Machiavelli to the Nuclear Age,* ed. Peter Paret, with the collaboration of Gordon A. Craig and Felix Gilbert. Princeton, N.J.: Princeton University Press, 1986.

Japanese List. *The Imperial Navy in World War II: A Graphic Presentation of the Japanese Naval Organization and List of Combatant and Non-Combatant Vessels Lost or Damaged in the War.* Tokyo: Military History Section, Headquarters U.S. Army Forces Far East, 1952.

Japanese Monograph #118. Military History Section, Headquarters U.S. Army Forces Far East. *Operational History of Japanese Naval Communications. December 1941–August 1945.* Distribution by Office of the Chief of Military History, Department of the Army, Washington, D.C., 1952. Laguna Hills, Calif.: Aegean Park Press, 1985.

Japanese Monograph #145. Military History Section, Headquarters U.S. Army Forces

Far East. *Outline of Naval Armament and Preparations for War. Part 1.* Distribution by Office of the Chief of Military History, Department of the Army, Washington, D.C., n.d. Tucson, Ariz.: Tucson Books, n.d.

Japanese Monograph #149. Military History Section, Headquarters U.S. Army Forces Far East. *Outline of Naval Armament and Preparations for War. Part 2.* Distribution by Office of the Chief of Military History, Department of the Army, Washington, D.C., n.d. Tucson, Ariz.: Tucson Books, n.d.

Japanese Monograph #160. Military History Section, Headquarters U.S. Army Forces Far East. *Outline of Naval Armament and Preparations for War. Part 3.* Distribution by Office of the Chief of Military History, Department of the Army, Washington, D.C., n.d. Tucson, Ariz.: Tucson Books, n.d.

Japanese Monograph #169. Military History Section, Headquarters U.S. Army Forces Far East. *Outline of Naval Armament and Preparations for War. Part 4.* Distribution by Office of the Chief of Military History, Department of the Army, Washington, D.C., 1952. Tucson, Ariz.: Tucson Books, n.d.

Japanese Monograph #172. Military History Section, Headquarters U.S. Army Forces Far East. *Outline of Naval Armament and Preparations for War. Part 5.* Distribution by Office of the Chief of Military History, Department of the Army, Washington, D.C., 1952. Tucson, Ariz.: Tucson Books, n.d.

Jones, F. C. *Manchuria since 1931.* London: Oxford University Press, 1949.

Journal of the Royal United Services Institute. Vol. 74: February to November 1929. London: Royal United Services Institute, 1930.

Journal of the Royal United Services Institute. Vol. 84: *February to November 1939.* London: Royal United Services Institution, 1940.

Kirby, S. Woodburn, et al. *History of the Second World War: The War against Japan.* Vol. 1: *The Loss of Singapore.* London: Her Majesty's Stationery Office, 1957.

——. *The War against Japan.* Vol. 2: *India's Most Dangerous Hour.* London: Her Majesty's Stationery Office, 1958.

——. *History of the Second World War: The War against Japan.* Vol. 4: *The Reconquest of Burma.* London: Her Majesty's Stationery Office, 1965.

Lengerer, Hans. "Japanese *Kaibokan* Escorts: Part I1" *Warship* 30 (April 1984).

Lengerer, Hans, and Tomoko Rehm-Takahara. "Japanese *Kaibokan* Escorts: Part 2." *Warship* 31 (July 1984).

——. "Japanese *Kaibokan* Escorts: Part 3." *Warship* 32 (October 1984).

——. "The Japanese Aircraft Carriers *Junyo* and *Hiyo*: Part 1." *Warship* 33 (January 1985).

——. "The Japanese Aircraft Carriers *Junyo* and *Hiyo*: Part 3." *Warship* 35 (July 1985).

Lott, Arnold S. *Most Dangerous Sea: A History of Mine Warfare, and an Account of U.S. Mine Warfare Operations in World War II and Korea.* Annapolis, Md.: Naval Institute Press, 1959.

Lu, David. "The New China Policy: Divide and Collaborate." In *Japan's Road to the Pacific War: The China Quagmire: Japan's Expansion on the Asian Continent, 1933–1941. Selected Translations from Taiheiyo Senso e No Michi: Kaisen Gaiko Shi*, ed. James William Morley. New York: Columbia University Press, 1983.

Lundstrom, John B. *The First Team: Pacific Naval Air Combat from Pearl Harbor to Midway.* Annapolis, Md.: Naval Institute Press, 1984.

——. *The First Team and the Guadalcanal Campaign: Naval Fighter Combat from August to November 1942.* Annapolis, Md.: Naval Institute Press, 1994.

Mackinnon, Stephen R., Diana Lary, and Ezra E. Vogel. *China at War: Regions of China, 1937–1945.* Stanford, Calif.: Stanford University Press, 2007.

Marder, Arthur J., Mark Jacobsen, and John Horsfield. *Old Friends New Enemies: The Royal Navy and the Imperial Japanese Navy.* Vol. 2: *The Pacific War 1942–1945.* Oxford: Oxford University Press, 1990.

Miller, Edward S. *War Plan Orange: The U. S. Strategy to Defeat Japan, 1897–1945.* Annapolis, Md.: Naval Institute Press, 1991.

Morison, Samuel Eliot. *History of United States Naval Operations in World War II.* Vol. 3: *The Rising Sun in the Pacific, 1931–April 1942.* Boston, Mass.: Little, Brown, 1948.

——. *History of United States Naval Operations in World War II.* Vol. 4: *Coral Sea, Midway and Submarine Actions May 1942–August 1942.* Boston, Mass.: Little, Brown, 1949.

——. *History of United States Naval Operations in World War II.* Vol. 14: *Victory in the Pacific 1945.* Boston, Mass.: Little, Brown, 1960.

Morley, James William, ed. *Japan's Road to the Pacific War: The China Quagmire: Japan's Expansion on the Asian Continent, 1933–1941. Selected Translations from Taiheiyo Senso No Michi: Kaisen Gaiko Shi.* New York: Columbia University Press, 1983.

Nakamura, Takafusa. "Raw Materials Problems of Japanese War Economy: A Survey. 1937–1945." Brussels: Comité International d'Histoire de la Deuxième Guerre Mondaile: n.d.

——. "Depression, Recovery and War, 1920–1945." In *The Cambridge History of Japan,* ed. John W. Hall et al. Vol. 6: *The Twentieth Century.* Cambridge: Cambridge University Press, 1988.

Naval Staff History. *The Second World War: The War with Japan.* Vol. 4: *The South-East Asia Operations and Central Pacific Advance..* London: Admiralty Historical Section, 1957.

——. *The Second World War: The War with Japan.* Vol. 5: *The Blockade of Japan.* London: Admiralty Historical Section, 1957.

Pacific War Research Society. *Japan's Longest Day.* Tokyo: Kodansha, 1980.

Parillo, Mark P. *The Japanese Merchant Marine in World War II.* Annapolis, Md.: Naval Institute Press, 1993.

Parshall, Jonathan, and Anthony Tully. *Shattered Sword: The Untold Story of the Battle of Midway.* Washington, D.C.: Potomac Books, 2005.

Peattie, Mark R. "Akiyama Sanyuki and the Emergence of Modern Japanese Naval Doctrine." *U.S. Naval Institute Proceedings* 103, no. 1 (January 1977).

——. *Sunburst: The Rise of Japanese Naval Air Power 1909–1941.* Annapolis, Md.: Naval Institute Press, 2001.

Pelz, Stephen E. *Race to Pearl Harbor: The Failure of the Second London Naval Conference and the Onset of World War II.* Cambridge, Mass.: Harvard University Press, 1974.

Prados, John. *Combined Fleet Decoded: The Secret History of American Intelligence and the Japanese Navy in World War II.* New York: Random House, 1995.

Reynolds, Clark G. *The Fast Carriers: The Forging of an Air Navy.* Annapolis, Md.: Naval Institute Press, 1992.

Romé, Paul. *Les oubliés du bout du monde: Journal d'un marin d'Indochine de 1939–1941.* Dinard, France: Danclau, 1998.

Skates, John Ray. *The Invasion of Japan: Alternative to the Bomb.* Columbia: University of South Carolina Press, 1994.

Stripp, Alan. *Codebreaker in the Far East.* London: Frank Cass, 1989.

Thorne, Christopher. *The Issue of War: States, Societies and the Far Eastern Conflict of 1941–1945.* London: Hamish Hamilton, 1985.

Tohmatsu, Haruo, and H. P. Willmott. A *Gathering Darkness: The Coming of War to the Far East and the Pacific, 1921–1942*. Lanham, Md.: Scholarly Resources, 2004.

Ugaki, Matome. *Fading Victory: The Diary of Admiral Matome Ugaki, 1941–1945*. Trans. Masataka Chihaya and ed. Donald M. Goldstein and Katherine V. Dillon. Pittsburgh, Pa.: University of Pittsburgh Press, 1991.

Willmott, H. P. *Empires in the Balance: Japanese and Allied Pacific Strategies to April 1942*. Annapolis, Md.: Naval Institute Press, 1982.

———. *The Barrier and the Javelin: Japanese and Allied Pacific Strategies, February to June 1942*. Annapolis, Md.: U.S. Naval Institute Press, 1983.

———. *Grave of a Dozen Schemes: British Naval Planning and the War against Japan, 1943–1945*. Annapolis, Md.: Naval Institute Press, 1996.

———. *The War with Japan: The Period of Balance May 1942–October 1943*. Wilmington, Del.: Scholarly Resources, 2002.

———. *The Battle of Leyte Gulf: The Last Fleet Action*. Bloomington: Indiana University Press, 2005.

Y'Blood, William T. *Red Sun Setting: The Battle of the Philippine Sea*. Annapolis, Md.: Naval Institute Press, 1981.

Yoshuimura, Akira. *Battleship Musashi: The Making and Sinking of the World's Biggest Battleship*. Trans. Vincent Murphy. Tokyo: Kodansha, 1999.

Zeiler, Thomas W. *Unconditional Defeat: Japan, America and the End of World War II*. Wilmington, Del.: Scholarly Resources, 2004.

THE EUROPEAN WAR

Antier, Jean Jacques. *La Sabordage de la flotte française à Toulon*. Brest, France: Editions de la Cité, 1986.

Bekker, Cajus. *Hitler's Naval War*. Trans. and ed. Frank Ziegler. London: Macdonald and Jane's, 1974.

Blair, Clay. *Hitler's U-boat War: The Hunted 1942–1945*. London: Weidenfeld and Nicolson, 1999.

———. *Hitler's U-boat War: The Hunters 1939–1942*. London: Weidenfeld and Nicolson, 1997.

Calvocoressi, Peter, Guy Wint, and John Pritchard. *Total War: The Causes and Courses of the Second World War*. Vol. 1: *The Western Hemisphere*. New York: Pantheon Books, 1989.

D'Este, Carlo. *Fatal Decision: Anzio and the Battle for Rome*. London: HarperCollins, 1991.

Ellis, John. *One Day in a Very Long War: Wednesday 25th October 1944*. London: Jonathan Cape, 1998

Gannon, Michael. *Black May: The Epic Story of the Allies' Defeat of the German U-boats in May 1943*. London: Aurum Press, 1998.

———. *Operation Drumbeat: The Dramatic True Story of Germany's First U-boat Attacks along the American Coast in World War II*. New York: Harper and Row, 1990.

Glanz, David, and Jonathan House. *When Titans Clashed: How the Red Army Stopped Hitler*. Lawrence: University Press of Kansas, 1995.

Hinsley, F. H., and Alan Stripp, eds. *Codebreakers: The Inside Story of Bletchley Park*. Oxford: Oxford University Press, 1993.

Howard, Michael. *The Mediterranean Strategy in the Second World War*. New York: Praeger, 1968.

Howarth, Stephen, and Derek Law, eds. *The Battle of the Atlantic 1939–1945: The 50th Anniversary International Naval Conference*. London: Greenhill, 1994.
Kahn, David. *The Codebreakers: The Story of Secret Writing*. New York: Macmillan, 1967.
Kemp, Peter. *Decision at Sea: The Convoy Escorts*. New York: Elsevier-Dutton, 1978.
Kowark, Hannsjörg. *Hitler et la flotte française: Toulon 1940–1944*. Nantes, France: Marines Éditions, 1998.
Macintyre, Donald. *The Battle for the Mediterranean*. London: B. T. Batsford, 1964.
——. *The Naval War against Hitler*. London: B. T. Batsford, 1971.
Milner, Marc. *North Atlantic Run: The Royal Canadian Navy and the Battle for the Convoys*. Annapolis, Md.: Naval Institute Press, 1985.
Morison, Samuel Eliot. *History of United States Naval Operations in World War II*. Vol. 11: *The Invasion of France and Germany, 1944–1945*. Boston, Mass.: Little, Brown, 1957.
Naval Staff History. *The Second World War: The Defeat of the Enemy Attack on Shipping, 1939–1945*. Vol. 1: *A Study of Policy and Operations: Text and Appendices*. London: Admiralty Historical Section, 1957.
——. *The Second World War: The Defeat of the Enemy Attack on Shipping, 1939–1945: A Study of Policy and Operations*. Vol. 1A: *A Study of Policy and Operations*. London: Admiralty Historical Section, 1957.
——. *The Second World War: The Defeat of the Enemy Attack on Shipping, 1939–1945: A Study of Policy and Operations*. Vol. 1B: *Plans and Tables*. London: Admiralty Historical Section, 1957.
Overy, R. J. *The Air War, 1939–1945*. New York: Stein and Day, 1981.
——. *Why the Allies Won*. New York: Norton, 1996.
Rohwer, Jürgen. *The Critical Convoy Battles of March 1943: The Battle for HX.229/SC 122*. London: Ian All, 1977.
Showell, Jak P. Mallmann. *The German Navy in World War II: A Reference Guide to the Kriegsmarine, 1935–1945*. Annapolis, Md.: Naval Institute Press, 1979.
Syrett, David, ed. *The Battle of the Atlantic and Signals Intelligence: U-boat Situations and Trends 1941–1945*. Aldershot, Britain: Ashgate/Navy Records Society, 1998.
Tarrant, V. E. *The Last Year of the Kriegsmarine*. London: Arms and Armour Press, 1994.
Winton, John. *Death of the Scharnhorst*. London: Cassell, 1983.

GENERAL REFERENCE

Bartlett, Merrill L. *Assault from the Sea: Essays on the History of Amphibious Warfare*. Annapolis, Md.: Naval Institute Press, 1983.
Bradford, James C., ed. *The International Encyclopedia of Military History*. London: Routledge, 2005.
Dupuy, R. Ernest and Trevor N. Dupuy. *The Encyclopedia of Military History from 3500 B.C. to the Present*. New York: Harper and Row, 1986.
Earle, Edward Meade, ed. *Makers of Modern Strategy. Military Thought from Machiavelli to Hitler*. Princeton, N.J.: Princeton University Press, 1971.
Eden, Paul, general ed. *The Encyclopedia of Aircraft of World War II*. London: Amber, 2004.
Grenville. J. A. S. *A History of the World in the Twentieth Century*. Cambridge, Mass.: Harvard University Press, 1994.
Haack, H. *Steilers Hand-Atlas 1930–31*. Gotha: Justus-Perthes, n.d.
Hattendorf, John B., and Robert S. Jordan. *Maritime Strategy and the Balance of*

Power: Britain and America in the Twentieth Century. Basingstoke: Macmillan, 1989.

Jordan, Gerald, ed. *Naval Warfare in the Twentieth Century 1900–1945: Essays in Honour of Arthur Marder*. London: Croom Helm, 1977.

Keegan, John, ed. *The Times Atlas of the Second World War*. London: Times Books, 1989.

Kennedy, Paul. *The Rise and Fall of the Great Powers: Economic Change and Military Conflict from 1500 to 2000*. New York: Random House, 1987.

Marshall, John. *The Guinness Book of Rail Facts and Feats*. London: Guinness Superlatives, 1979.

Meigs, Montgomery C. *Slide Rules and Submarines: American Scientists and Subsurface Warfare in World War II*. Washington, D.C.: National Defense University, 1990.

Mercer, Derrik, editor-in-chief. *Twentieth Century Day by Day*. London: Dorling Kindersley, 2000.

Mills, Geoffrey T., and Hugh Ruckoff, eds. *The Sinews of War: Essays on the Economic History of World War II*. Ames: Iowa State University Press, 1993.

Milward, Alan S. *War, Economy and Society 1939–1945*. Berkeley and Los Angeles: University of California Press, 1979.

Paret, Peter, ed., with Gordon A. Craig and Felix Gilbert. *Makers of Modern Strategy from Machiavelli to the Nuclear Age*. Princeton, N.J.: Princeton University Press, 1986.

Reynolds, Clark G. *Command of the Sea: The History and Strategy of Maritime Empires*. New York: William Morrow, 1974.

Roberts, J. M. *Twentieth Century: The History of the World, 1901–2000*. New York: Viking, 1999

Rohwer, J., and G. Hummelchen. *Chronology of the War at Sea, 1939–1945: The Naval History of World War II*. Annapolis, Md.: Naval Institute Press, 1992.

Sandler, Stanley, ed. *Ground Warfare: An International Encyclopedia*. Vol. 1: *A–G*. Vol. 2: *H–Q*. Vol. 3: *R–Z*. Santa Barbara, Calif.: ABC Clio, 2002.

Stokesbury, James L. *A Short History of World War II*. New York: Perennial, 1980

Tucker, Spencer C., ed. *An Encyclopedia of American Military History*. Vol. 1: *A–G*. Vol. 2: *H–O*. Vol. 3: *P–Z*. New York: Fact on File, 2003.

———. *Naval Warfare: An International Encyclopedia*. Vol. 1: *A–F*. Vol. 2: *G–P*. Vol. 3: *Q–Z*. Santa Barbara, Calif.: ABC Clio: 2002.

Willmott, H. P. *The Great Crusade: A Complete New History of the Second World War*. London: Michael Joseph, 1989.

Winton, John. *Convoy: The Defence of Sea Trade 1890–1990*. London: Michael Joseph, 1983.

BRITAIN AND EMPIRE

Barnett, Correlli. *The Collapse of British Power*. London: Alan Sutton, 1984.

Behrens, C. B. A. *Merchant Shipping and the Demands of War*. London: Her Majesty's Stationery Office, 1955.

Central Statistical Office. *History of the Second World War: Statistical Digest of the War*. London: His Majesty's Stationery Office, 1951.

Clayton, Anthony. *The British Empire as a Superpower*. London: Macmillan, 1986.

German, Tony. *The Sea Is at Our Gates: The History of the Canadian Navy*. Toronto: McClelland and Stewart, 1990.

Gordon, G. A. H. *British Seapower and Procurement between the Wars: A Reappraisal of Rearmament*. Basingstoke, Britain: Macmillan, 1988.

Gwyer, J. M. A., and J. R. M. Butler. *Grand Strategy*. Vol. 3: *June 1941–August 1942*. Part 2. London: Her Majesty's Stationery Office, 1964.

Hackmann, Willem. *Seek and Strike: Sonar, Anti-submarine Warfare and the Royal Navy, 1914–54*. London: Her Majesty's Stationery Office, 1984.
Hancock, W. K., ed. *History of the Second World War: United Kingdom Civil Series: Statistical Digest of the War*. London: His Majesty's Stationery Office, 1951.
Hancock, W. K., and M. M. Gowing. *British War Economy*. London: His Majesty's Stationery Office, 1949.
Hope, Ronald. *A New History of British Shipping*. London: John Murray, 1990.
Humble, Richard. *The Rise and Fall of the British Navy*. London: Macdonald, 1986.
Kennedy, Paul M. *The Rise and Fall of British Naval Mastery*. London: Ashfield, 1976.
Postan, M. M. *History of the Second World War: United Kingdom Civil Series: British War Production*. London: Her Majesty's Stationary Office, 1952.
Preston, Antony. *History of the Royal Navy*. London: Hamlyn, 1983.
Roskill, S. W. *The War at Sea*. Vol. 1: *The Defensive*. London: Her Majesty's Stationery Office, 1954.
——. *The War at Sea*. Vol. 2: *The Period of Balance*. London: Her Majesty's Stationery Office, 1956.
——. *The War at Sea*. Vol. 3: *The Offensive*. Part 1: *1st June 1943–31st May 1944*. London: Her Majesty's Stationery Office, 1960.
——. *The War at Sea*. Vol. 3: *The Offensive*. Part 2: *1st June 1944–15th August 1945*. London: Her Majesty's Stationery Office, 1961.

THE UNITED STATES

Borg, Dorothy. *The United States and the Far Eastern Crisis of 1933–1938: From the Manchurian Incident through the Initial Stages of the Undeclared Sino-Japanese War*. Cambridge, Mass.: Harvard University Press, 1964.
Boyer, Paul S., et al. *The Enduring Vision: A History of the American People*. Vol. 2: *From 1865*. Lexington, Mass.: D. C. Heath, 1990.
Buckley, Thomas H. *The United States and the Washington Conference, 1921–1922*. Knoxville: University of Tennessee Press, 1970.
Craven, Wesley Frank, and James Lea Cate, eds. *The Army Air Forces in World War II*. Vol. 6: *Men and Planes*. Chicago: University of Chicago Press, 1955.
Cressman, Robert J. *The Official Chronology of the U.S. Navy in World War II*. Annapolis, Md.: Naval Institute Press, 2000.
Davidson, Joel R. *The Unsinkable Fleet: The Politics of U.S. Navy Expansion in World War II*. Annapolis, Md.: Naval Institute Press, 1996.
Esposito, Vincent J., ed. *The West Point Atlas of American Wars*. Vol. 1: *1689–1900*. Vol. 2: *1900–1953*. New York: Praeger, 1959.
Hagan, Kenneth J. *In Peace and War: Interpretations of American Naval History, 1775–1978*. Westport, Conn.: Greenwood, 1978.
——. *This People's Navy: The Making of American Sea Power*. New York: Free Press, 1991.
Hayes, Grace Person. *The History of the Joint Chiefs of Staff in World War II: The War against Japan*. Annapolis, Md.: Naval Institute Press, 1982.
Howarth, Stephen. *To Shining Sea: A History of the United States Navy, 1776–1991*. New York: Random House, 1991.
Lane, Frederic C., with Blanche D. Coll, Gerald J. Fischer, and David B. Tyler. *Ships for Victory: A History of Shipbuilding under the U.S. Maritime Commission in World War II*. Baltimore, Md.: Johns Hopkins Press, 1951.
Larabee, Eric. *Commander in Chief: Franklin D. Roosevelt, His Lieutenants, and Their War*. London: André Deutsch, 1987.
Potter, E. B. *Nimitz*. Annapolis, Md.: Naval Institute Press, 1977.

Stragan, Jerry E. *Andrew Jackson Higgins and the Boats That Won World War II.* Baton Rouge: University of Louisiana Press, 1994.

Tuchman, Barbara. *Stilwell and the American Experience in China.* New York: Macmillan, 1971.

Weir, Gary E. *Forged in War: The Naval-Industrial Complex and American Submarine Construction, 1940–1961.* Washington, D.C.: Department of the Navy, 1993.

JAPAN

Hall, John W., et al. *The Cambridge History of Japan. Vol. 6: The Twentieth Century.* Cambridge: Cambridge University Press, 1988.

Iriye, Akira. *After Imperialism: The Search for a New Order in the Far East, 1921–1931.* Cambridge, Mass.: Harvard University Press, 1965.

Jansen, Marius B. *The Making of Modern Japan.* Cambridge, Mass.: Belknap Press, 2000.

FRANCE

Clayton, Anthony. *France, Soldiers and Africa.* London: Brassey's Defence Publishers, 1988.

Jenkins, E. H. *A History of the French Navy: From Its Beginnings to the Present Day.* London: Macdonald and Jane's, 1973.

WARSHIPS

Belote, James H., and William M. Belote. *Titans of the Seas: The Development and Operations of Japanese and American Carrier Task Forces during World War II.* New York: Harper and Row, 1975.

Breyer, Siegfried. *Battleships and Battle Cruisers, 1905–1970.* Trans. Alfred Kurti. London: Macdonald and Jane's, 1973.

Brown, J. D. *Aircraft Carriers.* London: Macdonald and Jane's, 1977.

Campbell, John. *Naval Weapons of World War II.* London: Conway Maritime Press, 1985.

Carter, Worrall Reed, and Elmer Ellsworth Duvall. *Ships, Salvage and Sinews of War: The Story of Fleet Logistics Afloat in Atlantic and Mediterranean Waters during World War II.* Washington, D.C.: U.S. Government Printing Office, 1954.

Chesneau, Roger, ed. *Conway's All the World's Fighting Ships, 1922–1946.* London: Conway Maritime Press, 1980.

Compton-Hall, Richard. *Submarine Boats: The Beginnings of Underwater Warfare.* Leicester: Windward, 1983.

Friedman, Norman. *Naval Radars.* London: Conway Maritime Press, 1981.

——. *U.S. Aircraft Carriers: An Illustrated Design History.* London: Arms and Armour Press, 1983.

Garzke, William H., Jr., and Robert O. Dulin Jr. *British, Soviet, French and Dutch Battleships of World War II.* Annapolis, Md.: Naval Institute Press, 1980.

George, James L. *History of Warships: From Ancient Times to the Twenty-first Century.* Annapolis, Md.: Naval Institute Press, 1998.

Greger, René. *Battleships of the World.* Trans. Geoffrey Brooks. London: Greenhill, 1997.

Gröner, Erich. *German Warships 1815–1945.* Vol. 1: *Major Surface Vessels.* Rev. and expanded by Dieter Jung and Martin Mass. Annapolis, Md.: Naval Institute Press, n.d.

———. *German Warships 1815–1945*. Vol. 2: *U-boats and Mine Warfare*. Rev. and expanded by Dieter Jung and Martin Mass. Annapolis, Md.: Naval Institute Press, n.d.

Hansen, Hans Jürgen. *The Ships of the German Fleets, 1848–1945*. London: Hamlyn, 1973

Harris, Brayton. *The Navy Times Book of Submarines: A Political, Social and Military History*. Ed. Walter J. Boyne. New York: Berkley Books, 1997.

Hezlet, Arthur. *The Aircraft and Sea Power*. London: Peter Davies, 1970.

———. *The Submarine and Sea Power*. London: Peter Davies, 1967.

Hutchinson, Robert. *Submarines: War beneath the Waves from 1776 to the Present Day*. London: HarperCollins, 2001.

Jentschura, Hansgeorg, Dieter Jung, and Peter Mickel. *Warships of the Imperial Japanese Navy, 1868–1945*. Trans. Antony Preston and J. D. Brown. London: Arms and Armour Press, 1977.

Kemp, Paul. *U-boats Destroyed: German Submarine Losses in the World Wars*. London: Arms and Armour, 1997.

Lecalve, Franck, and Jean-Michel Roche. *Liste des Bâtiments de la flotte de guerre française de 1700 à nos jours*. Lorient, France: Société Française d'histoire Maritime, 2001.

Le Masson, Henri, general ed. *Les Flottes de Combat, 1947*. Paris: Société D'Éditions Géographiques, Maritimes et Coloniales, 1946.

Lenton, H. T. *American Gunboats and Minesweepers*. London: Macdonald and Jane's, 1974.

Lenton, H. T., and J. J. Colledge. *Warships of World War II*. London: Ian Allan, n.d.

Manning, T. D. *The British Destroyer*. London: Putnam, 1961.

Möller, Eberhard, and Werner Brack. *The Encyclopedia of U-boats: From 1904 to the Present*. London: Greenhill, 2004.

Musicant, Ivan. *Battleship at War: The Epic Story of the U.S.S. Washington*. San Diego, Calif.: Harcourt Brace Jovanovich, 1986.

Naval Historical Division. *Dictionary of American Fighting Ships*. Vol. 1: *A–B*. Vol. 2: *C–F*. Vol. 3: *G–K*. Vol. 4: *L through M*. Vol. 5: *N through Q*. Vol. 6: *R through S*. Vol. 7: *T through V*. Vol. 8: *W through Z*. Washington, D.C.: U.S. Government Printing Office, 1959, 1963, 1968, 1969, 1970, 1976, 1981, and 1981 respectively.

Padfield, Peter. *The Battleship Era*. London: Pan Books, 1972.

———. *War beneath the Sea: Submarine Conflict 1939–1945*. London: John Murray, 1995.

Parkes, Oscar. *British Battleships: Warrior to Vanguard, 1860–1950: A History of Design, Construction and Armament*. London: Seeley Service, 1966.

Parrish, Thomas. *The Submarine: A History*. London: Viking Penguin, 2004.

Polmar, Norman, with Minoru Genda, Eric M. Brown, and Robert M. Langdon. *Aircraft Carriers: A Graphic History of Carrier Aviation and Its Influence on World Events*. London: Macdonald, 1969.

Polmar, Norman. *The American Submarine*. Cambridge: Patrick Stephens, 1981.

Preston, Antony. *"V" and "W" Class Destroyers*. London: Macdonald, 1971.

———. *U-boats*. London: Excalibur, 1978.

Roskill, S. W. *H.M.S. Warspite: The Story of a Famous Battleship*. Annapolis, Md.: Naval Institute Press, 1997.

Rössler, Eberhard. *The U-boat: The Evolution and Technical History of German Submarines*. London: Cassell, 2001.

Silverstone, Paul H. *U.S. Warships of World War II*. London: Ian Allan, 1968.

Watts, A. J., and B. G. Gordon. *The Imperial Japanese Navy*. London: Macdonald, 1971.

GENERAL INDEX

INDEX OF WARSHIPS, SUBMARINES, AUXILIARIES, AND MERCHANTMEN

U.S. UNITS

CANADIAN UNITS

FRENCH UNITS

GERMAN UNITS

GREEK UNITS

ITALIAN UNITS:

JAPANESE UNITS:

DUTCH UNITS

POLISH UNITS

SPANISH UNITS

THAI UNITS

YUGOSLAV UNIT

INDEX OF AMERICAN WARSHIPS

The compiling of a table of American fleet units built during the period of the American involvement as a belligerent in the Second World War—between 7 December 1941 and 15 August 1945—is fraught with difficulty, and on any number of counts. Ships were laid down, launched, and commissioned, but whether under construction or in service, names and type could be changed, and with respect to names more than once, and there is a certain ambiguity of status with reference to merchantmen, whether in service or under construction, that were requisitioned and converted to service use: what dates are given for construction necessarily are questionable.

As a basic rule, warships are listed with their last service name, and this despite self-evident inconsistencies: for example, the fleet carrier *Leyte* is given as laid down in February 1944--before the battle after which it was named was fought--but to give its original name—the *Crown Point*—is likely to confuse rather than enlighten, though this means that the *Crown Point* necessarily gets no mention. Moreover, warships are listed only by final type (for example, light cruisers that were converted and served as light carriers are cited only as light carriers complete with name) and destroyers and destroyer escorts that were converted in order to serve in some other capacity (such as minelayers or transports) are not given dates of launch and/or commissioning after change.

The pages given here are those of the warship being laid down, launched, and commissioned. Dates of being laid down and/or launched before 7 December 1941 and after 15 August 1945 are not given. Warships canceled while under construction are not cited per se.

As always in such matters: E. & O. E: there are certain to be errors, of both commission and omission, in this list.

CHANGES OF NAME

The fleet carriers were the *Franklin D. Roosevelt* (CV-42), the ex-*Coral Sea;* the *Hancock* (CV-19), the ex-*Ticonderoga;* the *Hornet* (CV-12), the ex-*Kearsarge;* the *Lexington* (CV-16), the ex-*Cabo;:* the *Leyte* (CV-32), the ex-*Crown Point;* the *Philippine Sea* (CV-47), the ex-Wright; the *Princeton* (CV-37), the ex-*Valley Forge;* the *Ticonderoga* (CV-14), the ex-*Hancock;* the *Wasp* (CV-18), the ex-*Oriskany;* the *Yorktown* (CV-10), the ex-*Bon Homme Richard.*

The light fleet carriers, originally laid down and named as light cruisers, were the *Bataan* (CVL-29), the ex-*Buffalo;* the *Belleau Wood* (CVL-24), the ex-*New Haven;* the *Cabot* (CVL-28), the ex-*Wilmington;* the *Cowpens* (CVL-25), the ex-*Huntington;* the *Independence* (CVL-22), the ex-*Amsterdam;* the *Langley* (CVL-27), original name the *Fargo* and laid down as the *Crown Point;* the *Monterey* (CVL-26), the ex-*Dayton;* the *Princeton* (CVL-23), the ex-*Tallahassee;* the *San Jacinto* (CVL-30), originally the *Newark,* laid down as the *Reprisal.*

The escort carriers were the *Admiralty Islands* (CVE-99), the ex-*Chapin Bay;* the *Anzio* (CVE-57), originally the *Alikula Bay,* launched as the *Coral Sea* and renamed when in service; the *Attu* (CVE-102), the ex-*Elbour Bay;* the *Badoeng Strait* (CVE-116), the ex-*San Alberto Bay;* the *Bairoko* (CVE-115), the ex-*Portage Bay;* the *Block Island* (CVE-106), the ex-*Sunset Bay;* the *Bougainville* (CVE-100), the ex-*Didrickson Bay;* the *Cape Esperance* (CVE-88), the ex-*Tananek Bay;* the *Cape Gloucester* (CVE-109), the ex-*Willapa Bay;* the *Casablanca* (CVE-55), the ex-*Alazon Bay;* the *Commencement Bay* (CVE-105), the ex-*St. Joseph Bay;* the *Corregidor* (CVE-58), the ex-*Anguilla Bay;* the *Gilbert Islands* (CVE-107), the ex-*St. Andrews Bay;* the *Guadalcanal* (CVE-60), the ex-*Astrolabe Bay;* the *Hollandia* (CVE-97), the ex-*Astrolabe Bay;* the *Kula Gulf* (CVE-108), the ex-*Vermillion Bay;* the *Kwajalein* (CVE-98), the ex-*Bucareli Bay;* the *Lunga Point* (CVE-94), the ex-*Alazon Bay;* the *Makassar Strait* (CVE-91), the ex-*Ulitaka Bay;* the *Makin Island* (CVE-93), the ex-*Woodcliffe Bay;* the *Manila Bay* (CVE-61), the ex-*Bucareli Bay;* the *Mantanikau* (CVE-101), the ex-*Dolomi Bay;* the *Marcus Island* (CVE-77), the ex-*Kanalku Bay;* the *Munda* (CVE-104), the ex-*Tonowek Bay;* the *Point Cruz* (CVE-119), the ex-*Trocadero Bay;* the *Puget Sound* (CVE-113), the ex-*Hobart Bay;* the *Rendova* (CVE-114), the ex-*Mosser Bay;* the *Roi* (CVE-103), the ex-*Alava Bay:* the *Saidor* (CVE-117), the ex-*Saltery Bay;* the *St. Lo* (CVE-63), originally the *Chapin Bay,* launched as the *Midway* and renamed when in service; the *Salamaua* (CVE-96), the ex-*Anguilla Bay;* the *Salerno Bay* (CVE-110), the ex-*Winjah Bay;* the *Savo Island* (CVE-78), the ex-*Kaita Bay;* the *Siboney* (CVE-112), the ex-*Frosty Bay;* the *Sicily* (CVE-118), the ex-*Sandy Bay;* the *Solomons* (CVE-67), the ex-*Nassuk Bay;* the *Tripoli* (CVE-64), the ex-*Didrickson Bay;* the *Tulagi* (CVE-72), laid down as the *Fortezela Bay* and (correctly) renamed the *Forteleza Bay,* launched as the *Tulagi;* the *Vella Gulf* (CVE-111), the ex-*Totem Bay;* the *Wake Island* (CVE-65), the ex-*Dolomi Bay;* the *White Plains* (CVE-66), the ex-*Elbour Bay.*

The heavy cruisers were the *Canberra* (CA-70), the ex-*Pittsburgh;* the *Helena* (CA-75), the ex-*Des Moines;* the *Pittsburgh* (CA-72), the ex-*Albany;* the *Quincy* (CA-71), the ex-*St. Paul;* the *St. Paul* (CA-73), the ex-*Rochester.*

The light cruisers were the *Astoria* (CL-90), the ex-*Wilkes Barre;* the *Flint* (CL-97), the ex-*Spokane;* the *Houston* (CL-81), the ex-*Vicksburg;* the *Vicksburg* (CL-86), the ex-*Cheyenne;* the *Vincennes* (CL-64), the ex-*Flint.*

INDEX OF U.S. LEND-LEASE PRODUCTION OF ESCORT CARRIERS, FRIGATES, AND SLOOPS THAT SAW SERVICE IN THE BRITISH NAVY

ABOUT THE AUTHOR

H. P. Willmott was educated at the Universities of Liverpool and London and at the National Defense University and has been a lecturer at various universities in Britain and in the United States, including Temple University and the University of Memphis, and was a visiting lecturer at the Royal Norwegian Air Force Academy at Trondheim. In recent years he has been a visiting lecturer with De Montfort University, and he held the Mark W. Clark Chair in the Department of History at the Citadel, the Military College of South Carolina, and has been appointed a research associate with Greenwich Maritime Institute, University of Greenwich.

He has written extensively on warfare in general and the Second World War in particular, and among his publications with reference to the latter are *Empires in the Balance: Japanese and Allied Pacific Strategies to April 1942*; *The Barrier and the Javelin: Japanese and Allied Pacific Strategies, February to June 1942*; *The Great Crusade: A New Complete History of the Second World War*; *Grave of a Dozen Schemes; British Naval Planning and the War against Japan, 1943–1945*; *The Second World War in the Far East*; and *The War with Japan: The Period of Balance, May 1942–October 1943*. He was also the co-author, with Tohmatsu Haruo, of *A Gathering Darkness: The Coming of War to the Far East and the Pacific, 1921–1942*. He was awarded the Distinguished Book Award in the category of U.S. Military History by the Society for Military History in 2006 for the book *The Battle of Leyte Gulf: The Last Fleet Action* (Indiana University Press, 2005).